Educational Research

Planning, Conducting, and Evaluating Quantitative and Qualitative Research

John W. Creswell
University of Nebraska–Lincoln

Merrill
Prentice Hall

Upper Saddle River, New Jersey
Columbus, Ohio

Library of Congress Cataloging in Publication Data

Creswell, John W.
    Educational research: planning, conducting, and evaluating quantitative and qualitative
research / John Creswell.
       p. cm.
    Includes bibliographical references and indexes.
    ISBN 0-13-790502-5
    1. Education—Research—Methodology. I. Title.
LB1028 .C742 2002
370'.7'2—dc21

                                                      2001030644

Vice President and Publisher: Jeffery W. Johnston
Executive Editor: Kevin M. Davis
Development Editor: Julie Peters
Editorial Assistant: Amy Hamer
Production Editor: Mary Harlan
Design Coordinator: Diane C. Lorenzo
Cover Design: Thomas Borah
Cover Photo: SuperStock
Text Design: Carlisle Communications, Ltd.
Production Coordination: Elm Street Publishing Services, Inc.
Production Manager: Laura Messerly
Director of Marketing: Kevin Flanagan
Marketing Manager: Amy June
Marketing Coordinator: Barbara Koontz

This book was set in Berkeley by Carlisle Communications, Ltd. It was printed and bound by
Courier Kendallville, Inc. The cover was printed by Phoenix Color Corp.

Pearson Education Ltd., *London*
Pearson Education Australia Pty. Limited, *Sydney*
Pearson Education Singapore Pte. Ltd.
Pearson Education North Asia Ltd., *Hong Kong*
Pearson Education Canada, Ltd., *Toronto*
Pearson Education de Mexico, S.A. de C.V., *Mexico*
Pearson Education—Japan, *Tokyo*
Pearson Education Malaysia Pte. Ltd.
Pearson Education, *Upper Saddle River*, *New Jersey*

Merrill
Prentice Hall

10 9 8 7 6 5 4 3
ISBN: 0-13-790502-5

To Karen

Preface

The philosophy that guided the development of this text is twofold. First, research involves a process of activities rather than the application of isolated, unrelated concepts and ideas. Educators practice research following a general sequence of procedures—from the initial identification of a research problem to the final report of research. This means that understanding the sequence or flow of activities is central to inquiry. Thus, the text begins with specific chapters devoted to each step in the process of research and the inclusion of concepts and ideas within this process.

Second, the educational researcher today needs a large toolbox of approaches to study the complex educational issues in our society. No longer can we, as educators, use only experiments or surveys to address our research problems. Educators in this new century—whether conducting research or reading research to self-inform—need to know about both quantitative and qualitative approaches to inquiry and to have an in-depth understanding of the multiple research designs and procedures used in our studies today. Throughout the steps in the process of research, you will be introduced to both quantitative and qualitative approaches to examine each step and learn about their differences and similarities in application. The text will also introduce you to eight distinct quantitative and qualitative research designs or procedures that comprise the repertoire of the educational researcher today.

KEY FEATURES

This text is the first introduction to educational research to offer a truly balanced, inclusive, and integrated overview of the field as it currently stands. As you will see from the table of contents, the book's coverage is unique in its balanced presentation of quantitative, qualitative, and mixed method research. Moreover, it consistently examines foundational issues of research—for example, determining how to approach a project and understanding what constitutes data and how to analyze them—from both quantitative and qualitative perspectives. This approach helps students understand fundamental differences *and* similarities between and among these approaches. Three ideas are central to this text—it:

- ❿ Provides a balanced coverage of quantitative and qualitative research
- ❿ Helps students learn how to begin to do research
- ❿ Helps students learn how to read and evaluate research studies

Let's look at each of these in detail to see how they can help you achieve your course objectives.

Balances Coverage of Quantitative and Qualitative Research

This text provides a balanced coverage of all types of research designs. This provides readers with a complete picture of educational research as it is currently practiced. After an overview in Part I of the general nature of educational research and the specific quantitative and qualitative approaches to it, the book examines in depth the steps in the research process in Part II, Chapters 3–10:

1. identifying a research problem
2. reviewing the literature
3. specifying a purpose and research questions or hypotheses
4. collecting either quantitative or qualitative data
5. analyzing and interpreting either quantitative or qualitative data
6. reporting and evaluating the research

Looking at the process simultaneously from both quantitative and qualitative perspectives helps students understand what choices a researcher has available and what meaning exists for a particular choice.

After this discussion, in Part III students will learn the procedures for conducting specific types of quantitative, qualitative, and mixed method studies. Chapters 11–18 provide balanced coverage and examples of each of these types of educational research designs: experimental and quasi-experimental, correlational, survey, grounded theory, ethnography, narrative, mixed method, and action research.

Helps Students Learn How to Begin to Do Research

Both the research process and design chapters offer the researcher step-by-step guidance in the basic aspects of planning, conducting, and evaluating research. A number of features guide readers through the steps and procedures of research. For example, a fictional beginning researcher, Maria, who is also a high school teacher and new graduate student, is followed throughout Part II and Part III to illustrate one researcher's efforts and to provide students with a realistic perspective of the process of research and the selection of specific research designs. Other features include, but are not limited to:

▶ Tips on planning and conducting research in "Useful Information for Producers of Research"
▶ Checklists that summarize key points, such as evaluation criteria to use to assess the quality of a quantitative or qualitative study
▶ In-text examples of actual and hypothetical studies that illustrate the correct and incorrect ways of reporting research
▶ Follow-up activities in "Study Questions and Activities" to help students apply the concepts they've just learned
▶ The "Think Aloud" feature describes practices that the author has found useful

Helps Students Learn How to Read and Evaluate Research Studies

Direct guidance on reading research is offered throughout the text. To further help students become more skilled at interpreting and evaluating research, the text offers a number of features. Most important among these are the many articles included in the text and the "Useful Information for Consumers of Research" feature.

▶ The text provides annotated research articles in each of the design chapters in Part III. Two other articles—one qualitative, one quantitative—appear at the end of Chapter 1. All of these complete articles (there are numerous other, shorter article excerpts in the book) include highlighted marginal annotations that help students understand the structure of articles and the key issues with which a reader should be concerned when evaluating the quality and the applicable scope of each particular piece of research.

▶ The "Useful Information for Consumers of Research" feature appears at the end of every chapter and offers concrete guidance in interpreting and in evaluating research.

SUPPLEMENTARY MATERIALS

A number of ancillaries are available to complement the text. For students, a Study Guide and a Companion Website are available to reinforce and extend learning. Instructors may use the Instructor's Manual and Test Bank, a Computerized Test Bank, and customized PowerPoint slides and other materials on the Companion Website.

Study Guide   The Study Guide contains reprinted research articles accompanied by worksheets to help students apply what they have learned in the text. Exercises pertaining to Chapters 1–10 require students to analyze articles in terms of their components, the process of research, and differences in conducting quantitative and qualitative studies. Exercises for research design Chapters 11–18 ask students to evaluate reprinted quantitative and qualitative studies, thereby deepening their understanding of design distinctions. Also included are multiple-choice practice test items to assess understanding and prepare students for class exams.

Companion Website   You can find the Companion Website at www.prenhall.com/creswell. This free on-line learning site helps students master course content with interactive self-quizzes, challenging application problems, and Internet links to explore related topics. The site enables instructors to manage their course on-line with Syllabus Manager™ and provides access and print options for PowerPoint slides to enhance class lectures.

Instructor's Manual/Test Bank   An Instructor's Manual with Test Bank is available to accompany this text. For each chapter in the book, this manual provides strategies for teaching chapter content, lecture notes that summarize important concepts requiring review and reinforcement, and transparency masters for overhead use or as handouts to students. (Duplicates of these transparencies are provided electronically on the Companion Website in PowerPoint for instructors' use.) This manual also provides suggestions for when and how to use the supplements with the text.

The test bank portion of the book contains various types of items—multiple-choice, matching, short essay, and fill-in-the-blank—for each chapter. Questions ask students to identify and describe research processes and design characteristics they have learned, as well as classify and evaluate quantitative and qualitative studies and research situations.

Computerized Test Bank   A Computerized Test Bank, which is a replication of the printed test bank, is available on disk for Windows and Macintosh.

ACKNOWLEDGMENTS

Although this book was written during a four-year period, it was a culmination of 30 years of experience in conducting both quantitative and qualitative research in education and the social sciences. It could not have been written without the capable assistance of numerous individuals, such as graduate students, research assistants, and colleagues at the University of Nebraska–Lincoln. Dr. Dana Miller assisted in a timely and thorough review of many chapters. Vicki Plano Clark provided editorial assistance and a key conceptual eye for missing details. Dong Dong Zhang provided inspiration for many applied ideas and support at critical phases of the project. Other graduate students such as Michael Toland, Kathy Shapely, and many unnamed students in my graduate program area, Quantitative and Qualitative Methods of Education, and students in my classes on the foundations of educational research offered useful ideas. Dr. Bill Mickelson served as a statistics consultant and quantitative analysis reviewer.

I am also indebted to Kevin Davis at Merrill for initiating this book and providing the vision to launch it as the "next generation" research methods text in education. Julie Peters, my excellent development editor at Merrill, provided patience, support, and useful insights throughout the project. Martha Beyerlein, my production editor, served an invaluable role in the final days of book preparation.

Numerous reviewers nationally helped to shape this book as well. They include Sean Courtney, University of Nebraska–Lincoln; Kevin Crehan, University of Nevada–Las Vegas; Andrea Guillaume, California State University, Fullerton; Gretchen Guiton, University of Southern California; Rick Ittenbach, Johns Hopkins University; Tony Lam, University of Toronto–OISE; Robert R. Lange, University of Central Florida; Patti Lather, The Ohio State University; Jaekyung Lee, University of Maine; Geoff Mills, Southern Oregon University; Tamera Murdock, University of Missouri–Kansas City; LeAnn Putney, University of Nevada–Las Vegas; John Rausch, University of Oklahoma; Abbas Tashakkori, Florida International University; and Karen Westburg, University of Connecticut.

Brief Contents

Contents

An Overview of Educational Research

Learning how to conduct, evaluate, and use educational research requires understanding the process of research and its implementation using quantitative or qualitative approaches. In Part I, you will be introduced to the five steps in the process of research, and you will be able to distinguish between quantitative and qualitative approaches at each step in the process. Moreover, to help you apply the ideas presented, two complete journal articles follow Chapter 1. One article is quantitative and the other qualitative so that you can see the elements of both approaches within each step of the research process. For best results in understanding the ideas, first read Chapter 1 and examine the two articles before reading Chapter 2.

1

An Introduction to the Process of Research

Maria is an English teacher with 10 years of experience in a mid-sized metropolitan high school. Lately there have been a number of incidents in the area involving school violence and weapon possession.

▶ Jimmy, a 10th grader, was hiding a knife in his locker. A teacher saw it as she walked by the open locker during 3rd period.

▶ A 12th grade student, Sally, threatened a boy, telling him "he wouldn't see the light of day" unless he stopped harassing her.

▶ At a nearby high school, Sam, a junior, pointed a handgun at another student outside the school.

These incidents alarm district officials, school administrators, and teachers. Administrators at Maria's high school are concerned about the increased violence and presence of weapons at school. In light of this problem, the principal decides that a committee made up of teachers and administrators should be formed to develop guidelines about how the school should respond to these types of situations. When a notice goes out asking for teachers for this committee, Maria volunteers immediately. The committee will meet monthly beginning in the fall of the new school year.

Also beginning in the fall, Maria plans to enroll in a graduate program at the local university. She has already been accepted into a master's program that requires students to complete a research study as a requirement for graduation. Maria sees the graduate program and her school committee assignment as an opportunity to research school violence and weapon possession among high school students. Where does she begin? This chapter will show you how Maria can get started by identifying the steps used in the process of conducting research.

Maria's situation of balancing the dual roles of professional and graduate student may be familiar to you. Let's assess her present research situation:

▶ Maria recognizes the need to closely examine an important issue—school violence and weapons at school—although she is new to research. On the other hand, she is not a stranger to looking up topics in libraries or to searching the Internet when she has a question about something. She has occasionally looked at a few research journals, such as the *High School Journal* and *Theory into Practice*, in her school library and has overheard other teachers talking about research studies on the subject of school violence. Although she has no research background, she views it as an important endeavor for assisting her school committee as well as for fulfilling her graduate program requirements.

▶ In order to plan and complete research for her graduate program, Maria must overcome her fears about planning and conducting a study. To do this, she can begin to see research as a series of small, manageable steps rather than as a large, formidable task. Knowing these smaller steps might help set her mind at ease.

▶ Maria realizes that the topic of school violence and weapon possession is a sensitive issue. Gaining the cooperation of students and staff in order to study the issues will be challenging. It will call on her to be respectful of individuals and student learning as she engages in ethical research.

By now you may have identified with Maria's situation as you begin your own journey of learning about educational research. You may wonder if research matters, or whether it can provide the answers to today's questions. Moreover, you may need to learn where to begin conducting research or how to be sensitive, at the outset, to the people and places you plan to study. These topics are part of the *process of research,* the major idea introduced in this chapter.

By the end of this chapter, you should be able to:

▶ Describe several reasons for the importance of research
▶ Identify several problems with research today
▶ Define educational research
▶ Name the steps typically undertaken by researchers in the process of research
▶ Identify ethical issues important when implementing the research process
▶ Reflect on the skills you bring to this process
▶ Apply the research process to the two journal articles introduced at the end of this chapter.

WHY IS RESEARCH IMPORTANT?

Not all educators come with an understanding and appreciation of research. For some, research may seem like something that is important only for faculty members in the ivory tower of colleges and universities. Although it is true that college and university faculty members do conduct research, personnel in other educational settings also read and use research, such as school psychologists, principals, school board members, adult educators, college administrators, and graduate students. Interest in reading research and applying it to study educational issues and practices is predicated on valuing it and understanding its potential contribution in four important areas: adding to our knowledge of educational issues; improving practice; informing policy debates; and, on a personal level, building student research skills.

Adding to Knowledge About Educational Issues

Educators strive for continual improvement. This requires addressing problems or issues and searching for potential solutions. **Adding to knowledge** means that educators undertake research in order to contribute to existing information about issues. We are all aware of pressing educational issues being debated today, such as:

▶ the integration of AIDS education into the school curriculum
▶ sexual misconduct by school employees
▶ the uses and abuses of testing children in schools

▶ the education of pregnant teenagers
▶ binge drinking on college campuses

Research plays a vital role in addressing these issues. Through research we develop results that help to answer questions, and as we accumulate these results, we gain a deeper and deeper understanding of the problems. In this way, researchers are much like bricklayers who build a wall brick by brick, continually adding to the wall and, in the process, creating a stronger structure.

Carrying this analogy one step further, the wall can fill in a gap in an existing structure; it can expand an existing border; it can reinforce an old, crumbling wall; or it can provide an entirely new look to a courtyard. In a similar way, research accomplishes these objectives as it contributes to past research. A research report may:

▶ **address gaps in knowledge** by investigating an area of research that fills a void in existing information
▶ **expand knowledge** by extending research to new ideas or practices
▶ **replicate knowledge** by testing old results with new participants or at new research sites
▶ **add voices of individuals to knowledge,** individuals whose perspectives have not been heard or whose views have been minimized in our society

These different contributions that research makes to knowledge can be illustrated by an example of elementary school children learning social skills through playground games. For example, research may fill a void (address a gap in knowledge) about what is known about the types of social skills children develop, especially if past research has not examined this topic. To extend our understanding to new practices (expand knowledge), a study may be done that examines how children play, not on the school ground but on the way home from school. Another research study may examine if African-American children on their way home from school play in the same way as Asian-American children (thus replicating findings from one ethnic group to another). Finally, researchers might study Native-American children on reservations and record their conversations on the way home from school to provide voices of individuals not typically heard in middle-class white society (adding the voices of individuals). In all of these ways, research contributes to the knowledge of educational problems or issues.

Improving Practice

Research is also important because it suggests improvements for practice. Armed with research results, teachers or other educators become more effective professionals and their effectiveness translates into better learning for kids. For instance, through research, personnel involved in teacher education programs in schools of education know much more about training teachers today than they did 20 years ago. Zeichner (1999) summarizes the impact of research on teacher training during this period (see Table 1.1). Teacher trainers today know about the academic capabilities of students, characteristics of good teacher-training programs, the recurring practices in teacher-training programs, the need to challenge student beliefs and worldviews, and the tensions teacher educators face within their institutions. But before these research results can impact teacher training or any other aspect of education, individuals in educational settings need to be aware of results from investigations, to know how to read research studies, to locate useful conclusions from them, and to apply the findings to their own unique situation. Educators using research may be teachers in schools, superintendents in school district offices, school psychologists working with children with behavioral problems, or adult educators who teach immigrants English as a second language. For these individuals, research may help them improve their practices on the job.

TABLE 1.1	
Zeichner's (1999) Summary of Major Research Results in Teacher Education	
Research Conducted	**What Researchers Have Learned**
Surveys about students in teacher education programs	• From academic, social class, racial, ethnic, and gender characteristics of both teacher educators and their students, the research has challenged the misconception that students who go into teaching are academically inferior to those who go into other fields. • Despite changing U.S. demographics, teacher education programs admit mostly students who are white, monolingual English speakers.
Specific case studies of individual teacher education programs	• Successful teacher education programs have a coherent vision of good teaching and close links to local schools. • Researchers need to spend time living in teacher education programs to understand them.
Conceptual and historical research on teacher education programs	• Teacher education programs differ in their approaches, such as the importance of disciplinary knowledge versus students learning versus critiquing societal inequalities in schooling practices. • Programs throughout the 20th century have emphasized recurring practices such as performance-based teacher education.
Studies of learning to teach in different settings	• It is difficult to change the tacit beliefs, understandings, and worldviews that students bring to teacher education programs. • The impact of a program on students can be increased through cohort groups, portfolio development, case studies, and narratives in which they examine their beliefs.
The nature and impact of teacher education activities and self-studies	• Despite the sometimes unfavorable structural conditions of teacher educators' work, their voices are being heard. • Teachers, in these self-studies, describe the tensions and contradictions involved in being a teacher educator.

Research offers practicing educators *new ideas* to consider as they go about their jobs. From reading research studies, educators can learn about new practices that have been tried in other settings or situations. For example, the adult educator working with immigrants may find that small-group interaction that focuses on using cultural objects from the various homelands may increase the rate at which immigrants learn the English language. Research also helps practitioners *evaluate approaches* that they hope will work with individuals in educational settings. This process involves sifting through research to determine which results will be most useful. This process is demonstrated in Figure 1.1, which focuses on three steps that a classroom teacher might use (Connelly, Dukacz, & Quinlan, 1980). As shown in the figure, a teacher first decides what needs to be implemented in the classroom, then examines alternative lines of research, and finally decides which line of research might help accomplish what needs to be done.

For example, a reading teacher decides to incorporate more information about cultural perspectives into the classroom. Research suggests that this may be done with classroom interactions by inviting speakers to the room (line A) or by having the children consider and think (cognitively) about difficult cultural perspectives by talking with individuals at a local cultural center (line B). It may also be accomplished by having the children inquire into

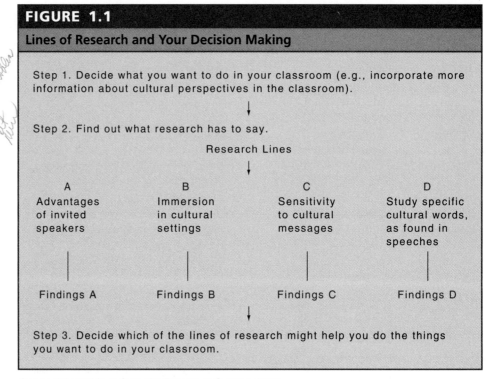

FIGURE 1.1

Lines of Research and Your Decision Making

Step 1. Decide what you want to do in your classroom (e.g., incorporate more information about cultural perspectives in the classroom).

Step 2. Find out what research has to say.

Research Lines

A	B	C	D
Advantages of invited speakers	Immersion in cultural settings	Sensitivity to cultural messages	Study specific cultural words, as found in speeches

| Findings A | Findings B | Findings C | Findings D |

Step 3. Decide which of the lines of research might help you do the things you want to do in your classroom.

Source: Adapted from Connelly, Dukacz, & Quinlan, 1980.

cultural messages imbedded within advertisements (line C), or identify the cultural subject matter of speeches of famous Americans (line D). A line of research is then chosen that helps the teacher to accomplish classroom goals. This teacher might be Maria, our teacher conducting research on weapon possession in schools and its potential for violence. Maria hopes to present options for dealing with this issue to her committee and needs to identify useful research lines and consider approaches taken by other schools.

At a broader level, research helps the practicing educator *build connections* with other educators who are trying out similar ideas in different locations. Special education teachers, for example, may establish connections at research conferences where individuals report on topics of mutual interest, such as using small-group strategies for discipline management in classrooms.

Informing Important Policy Issues

In addition to helping educators become better practitioners, research also creates conversations about important issues so educational concerns can be debated by policy makers. These individuals, who may range from federal government employees to state workers, to local school board members and administrators, discuss and take positions on educational issues important to constituencies. For these individuals, research offers results that can help them weigh various perspectives. When policy makers read and review research on issues, they are informed about current debates and stances taken by other public officials. To be useful, research needs to have clear results, be summarized in a concise fashion, and include data-based evidence. For example, research useful to policy makers might summarize the alternatives on:

- ▶ welfare and its effect on children's schooling among lower income families
- ▶ school choice and the arguments proposed by opponents and proponents
- ▶ state standards for student assessment at grades 4 and 8 in schools

Building Student Research Skills

On a personal level, the process of research helps individuals develop conceptual, writing, organizing, and presenting skills. For students in graduate programs, conducting research requires the use of conceptual skills in making sense of data, analyzing complex relationships among ideas, and synthesizing disparate ideas. To effectively read studies reported in the literature, individuals also need conceptual skills, which will assist them in analyzing material for relevant ideas. The dual concepts of synthesis and analysis also are involved when individuals conduct a review of the literature, identify dozens of studies, synthesize them for their connections, and combine them into a report. This literature review activity also helps to develop skills in organizing complex material.

When students develop a report of research, they expand on these organizational skills and they practice writing. For example, students practice writing when developing a concise, acceptable proposal for a master's thesis. By composing a research report and presenting it to an audience, students advance their skills in communicating ideas. For instance, when presenting a conference paper at a regional or national research conference, a student improves skills in organizing thoughts, using multimedia to present ideas, and answering audience questions.

SEVERAL PROBLEMS WITH RESEARCH TODAY

Despite the importance of research, we need to realistically evaluate its contributions. Sometimes these contributions are minimized because results, especially those from several studies, show contradictory or vague findings. An education aide for 27 years to the Education and Labor Committee of the U.S. House of Representatives expressed this confusion, "I read through every single evaluation . . . looking for a hard sentence—a declarative sentence—something that I could put into the legislation, and there were very few" (Viadero, 1999, p. 36). Not only are policy makers looking for a "declarative sentence," many readers of educational research search for some evidence that makes a direct statement about an educational issue. On balance, however, research accumulates slowly, and what may seem contradictory now may coalesce in time. Based on the information known, for example, it took more than four years to identify the most rudimentary variables about how chairpersons help faculty become better researchers (Creswell et al., 1990).

Compounding the situation is the issue of questionable data. The author of a particular research report may not have gathered information from people who are able to understand and address the problem. The number of participants may also be dismally low, which can cause problems in drawing appropriate statistical conclusions. The survey instrument used in a study may contain questions that are ambiguous and vague. At a technical level, the researcher may have chosen an inappropriate statistic for analyzing the data. Just because research is published in a well-known journal does not automatically make it "good" research.

To these issues we could add unclear statements about the intent of the study, the lack of full disclosure of data collection procedures, or inarticulate rendering of the research problem or issue that drives the inquiry in the first place. Research has limits, and you need to know how to decipher research studies because they may not be written as clearly and accurately as we would like. We cannot erase all "poor" research reported in the educational field; we can, however, as responsible inquirers, seek to reconcile different findings and employ sound procedures to collect and analyze data, and to provide clear direction for our own research.

UNDERSTANDING RESEARCH AS A PROCESS

We can now begin to establish a common understanding of what constitutes research in education. Educators can conduct research that focuses on individuals in educational settings, such as schools, colleges, agencies, homes, and social gatherings. Researchers should recognize that learning occurs in both formal and informal educational settings. What constitutes "research" is more difficult to pin down. Basically, it is:

▶ asking questions of some people
▶ gathering data
▶ reporting results from the data

On a more sophisticated level, researchers engage in distinct steps of inquiry, regardless of the approach to research (as discussed in Chapter 2 on "Quantitative and Qualitative Approaches") or the type of research design (as discussed in Chapters 11 through 18).

What are these steps? Years ago they were identified as the "scientific method" of inquiry (Kerlinger, 1972; Leedy & Ormrod, 2001). Using a "scientific method," researchers:

▶ identify a problem that defines the goal of research
▶ make a prediction that, if confirmed, resolves the problem
▶ gather data relevant to this prediction
▶ analyze and interpret the data to see if it supports the prediction and resolves the question that initiated the research

This approach to research is only partly true today—not all investigators or inquirers make predictions and gather data to support or contradict these predictions. We need to update this process to reflect the practices used today in educational research.

What Is Research?

Consistent with the "scientific method," research today is viewed as a *process*. All inquirers engage in certain steps as they conduct investigations. Although these steps do not need to be taken in the same order, they interrelate, and individuals cycle back and forth among the steps. This process is also *cyclical*. To present the process as deductive (top-down) or linear (one step always follows another) is too limited a perspective for today's educational approaches. Research also has a *beginning* and an *ending*. It typically begins with a problem or issue that needs to be studied and ends with a written report presented to someone who might ask for the information or use the information. A research problem is a typical place to begin a study, but not the only one. Finally, what are the actual *steps* in this process? Here the scientific method provides useful direction, especially for a beginning researcher. In a general sense, educators direct their research attention to problems, justify these problems within the ongoing conversation in a research area, specify questions they want answered, gather and analyze information, and make interpretations about what the information means. For our purposes, let's use the following working definition:

> **Research** is a cyclical process of steps that typically begins with identifying a research problem or issue of study. It then involves reviewing the literature, specifying a purpose for the study, collecting and analyzing data, and forming an interpretation of the information. This process culminates in a report, disseminated to audiences, that is evaluated and used in the educational community.

This process, shown in Figure 1.2, is visualized as a cyclical picture of interrelated steps. This figure will be our guide to the research process addressed in Part I of this text.

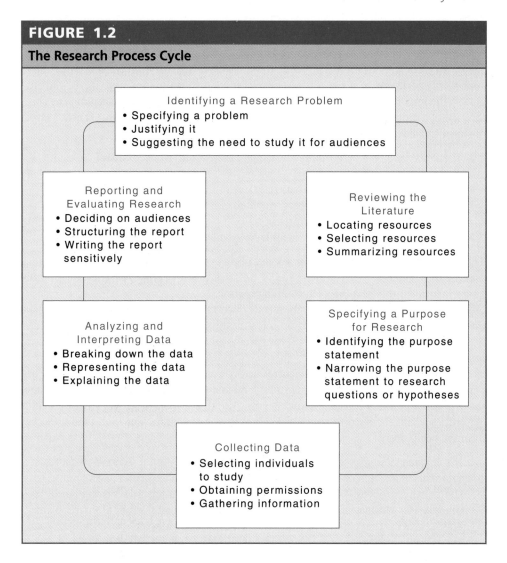

FIGURE 1.2

The Research Process Cycle

Identifying a Research Problem
- Specifying a problem
- Justifying it
- Suggesting the need to study it for audiences

Reporting and Evaluating Research
- Deciding on audiences
- Structuring the report
- Writing the report sensitively

Reviewing the Literature
- Locating resources
- Selecting resources
- Summarizing resources

Analyzing and Interpreting Data
- Breaking down the data
- Representing the data
- Explaining the data

Specifying a Purpose for Research
- Identifying the purpose statement
- Narrowing the purpose statement to research questions or hypotheses

Collecting Data
- Selecting individuals to study
- Obtaining permissions
- Gathering information

WHAT ARE THE STEPS IN THIS PROCESS?

As you read research or plan your own study, it is useful to know the basic structure of educational inquiry. This basic structure contains a limited number of key ideas central to every study, and learning them speeds the process of reading published research, identifying topics to include in a plan of study, and knowing how to organize results in a formal research report. This structure is contained in the **process of research,** a series of five steps used by researchers when they conduct a study. Each of these steps will be discussed in detail in Chapters 3 through 10, but they will be introduced here:

1. identifying a research problem
2. reviewing the literature
3. specifying a purpose for research
4. collecting data
5. analyzing and interpreting the data
6. reporting and evaluating research

Identifying a Research Problem

A research report begins with the investigator identifying a topic to study—typically an issue or problem in education that needs to be resolved. **Identifying a research problem** consists of specifying an issue to study, developing a justification for studying it, and suggesting the importance of the study for select audiences that will read the report. The specification of a problem delimits the subject matter and focuses attention on a specific aspect of study. Consider the following issues, each of which merits research:

▶ There needs to be a better understanding of the cognitive development of Asian-American children.
▶ Title I programs need to be evaluated.
▶ Studies on the use of parent-tutors for gifted children in the classroom need to be evaluated in light of their mixed results.
▶ There need to be better programs for teenage mothers in high schools.

These problems arise out of an educational need expressed by teachers, schools, policy makers, or researchers. We call these needs, or issues, *research problems.* They are typically found in introductory sections of a research report where researchers provide a rationale for their importance. In a formal sense, these introductory sections are called the "statement of the problem," and they include an issue, a justification for it based on past studies or practice, and the importance of studying it for specific audiences such as teachers, administrators, or researchers.

What particular markings of the introductory section will enable you to read and understand what authors are attempting to say? What components do researchers include in these research problem sections? How do you write this section to convey the importance of your issue and the need to study it? Let's take a look at Maria, our high school teacher from the beginning of the chapter, to see how she starts.

> Maria plans to study school violence and weapon possession in schools to gather information for her committee and as a requirement for her graduate program. She starts with a problem—escalating weapon possession among students in high schools. Her written research report will need a formal justification of the problem and statements that convey the importance of this issue for teachers, administrators, and school personnel in other high schools. To learn how to create and identify a research problem, Maria will follow steps such as those described in Chapter 3, "Identifying a Research Problem."

Reviewing the Literature

Many beginning researchers fear that they will plan and conduct a study that merely replicates prior research. On the other hand, faculty and advisors often fear that a student will plan a study that does not build on existing knowledge and does not add to the accumulation of findings on a topic. These fears emphasize the importance of reviewing the literature as an important step in the research process. **Reviewing the literature** means locating summaries, books, journals, and indexed publications on a topic, selectively choosing which literature is relevant, and then writing a report that summarizes that literature.

The skills needed for reviewing the literature develop over time and with practice. You can learn how to locate material in an academic library, access the CD-ROM databases available, choose and evaluate literature on your topic, and summarize it into a concise review. Library resources can be overwhelming, so having a strategy for searching the literature and writing the review is important. What resources will you first examine? How do you assess whether a resource is relevant? How do you organize the literature you have found? How do you compose a written summary that reviews the literature? Let's see what Maria does.

To inform her committee about the latest literature on school violence and to plan her own research, Maria needs to conduct a literature review. This process will involve becoming familiar with the university library holdings, spending time reviewing resources and making decisions about what literature to use, and writing a formal summary of the literature on school violence. She consults the library catalogue at her university and plans to search the computerized databases, such as ERIC. The types of procedures Maria will need to follow are described in Chapter 4, "Reviewing the Literature."

Specifying a Purpose for Research

The process of research begins when an individual selects a research problem and identifies relevant literature. The research problem then needs to be focused so that it can be studied. This focus comes from specifying an overall purpose or intent for research. This intent, found in the *purpose statement,* is the most important component of research because it introduces the entire study, signals the procedures to be used, and points toward the results to be found.

The **purpose for research** consists of identifying the major intent or objective for a study and narrowing it into specific research questions or hypotheses. The purpose statement contains the major focus of study (presented later in Chapter 5 as variables and a central phenomenon), the participants in the study, and the location or site of the inquiry. Then this purpose statement is narrowed into questions or predictions that guide data collection. How do you identify a purpose statement, research questions, and hypotheses in a research report? Where are they found? What elements are included in designing and writing them? Let's check again with our high school teacher, Maria.

> Maria now needs to write down the purpose of her study and formulate the questions she will ask of the individuals selected for her study. In draft after draft she sketches this purpose statement, recognizing that it will provide major direction for her study and help keep her focused on the primary aim of her study. From this broad purpose, Maria now needs to narrow her study to specific questions or statements that she would like her participants to answer. Chapter 5, "Specifying a Purpose and Research Questions or Hypotheses," provides information about the importance and design of these statements and questions.

Collecting Data *–599 c (pilot 570 c)*

Evidence helps provide answers to our research questions and hypotheses. To get these answers, researchers engage in the step of collecting or gathering data. **Collecting data** means identifying and selecting individuals for a study; obtaining their permission to be studied; and gathering information by administering instruments, through asking people questions or observing their behaviors. Of paramount concern in this process is the need to obtain good data from individuals and places. Once these individuals and places are identified, researchers write *method* or *procedure* sections into their research studies. These sections offer detailed, technical discussions about the mechanics and administration of data collection. Many decisions, however, go into creating a good data collection procedure. For example, how are the individuals selected for the study? How many are needed? What challenges exist in obtaining their cooperation? What are the actual mechanics of gathering information from them? Let's see how Maria handles this.

> At this point in the research process Maria needs to think about where she will conduct her study of school violence and weapon possession, who will participate in the study, what permissions she will need to obtain, what data she will collect, and

how she will proceed to gather the data. She needs to decide whether she will administer a survey to high school students in the district or engage in face-to-face interviewing with a few students. Whichever course she chooses, she will need the permission of high school students who are minors and permission from their parents. Chapter 6, "Collecting Quantitative Data," and Chapter 7, "Collecting Qualitative Data," describe the types of procedures Maria will need to follow in her study.

Analyzing and Interpreting the Data

Either during or immediately after data collection, you need to evaluate the information supplied by individuals in the study. Analysis consists of "taking the data apart" to determine individual responses and then "putting it together" to summarize it. **Analyzing and interpreting the data** indicates that researchers analyze the data; represent it in tables, figures, and pictures; and explain it for answers to research questions and statements asked in the study. It is found in the sections of a study usually titled *Results, Findings,* or *Discussions.*

How do researchers prepare and organize their data for analysis? Are computer programs useful in this process? What steps are involved in the actual process of analysis? How are scores for individuals reported in tables? How do researchers analyze the words obtained during interviews? How is an interpretation made of either scores or words from individuals in the study? These are questions that Maria also needs to ask herself.

If Maria collects information on surveys from students across the school district, she will need to enter the data into a computer program, choose a statistical procedure, conduct analyses, report the results in tables, and make an interpretation about whether the data confirm or disconfirm her expected trends or predictions. If she pursues face-to-face interviewing, she will collect audiotapes of students talking about weapon possession at school and transcribe these tapes to obtain a written record. With her transcriptions, she will engage in making sense of student comments through selecting specific sentences and paragraphs and by identifying themes. From these themes, she will interpret the meaning of student comments in light of her own personal stance and the suggestions found in past studies. For help in the data analysis and interpretation phase of her study, Maria will need to understand the research procedures described in Chapter 8, "Analyzing and Interpreting Quantitative Data," and in Chapter 9, "Analyzing and Interpreting Qualitative Data."

Reporting and Evaluating Research

After conducting her study, Maria writes a report and distributes it to fellow teachers, administrators in her school district, parents, students, and her graduate faculty committee. **Reporting research** involves deciding on audiences, structuring the report in a format acceptable to these audiences, and then writing the report in a manner that is sensitive to all readers. The audiences for research will vary from academic researchers who contribute and read journal articles, to faculty advisors and committees that review masters' theses and dissertations, to personnel in educational agencies and school districts who look for reports of research on timely topics. The structure will vary for each audience, from a formal reporting format for theses and dissertations to a more informal document for in-house school reports. In all types of reports, however, researchers need to be compassionate to individuals and avoid language that discriminates on the basis of gender, sexual orientation, race, or ethnic group.

The audience for a report will have its own standards for judging the quality and utility of the research. **Evaluating research** involves an assessment of the quality of a study using standards advanced by individuals in education. Unfortunately, there are no iron-clad standards for evaluating educational research, either inside the academic research committee on college and university campuses or outside in school districts or in local, state, or federal agencies. Still, we need some means for determining the quality of studies, especially published research or reports presented to practitioner audiences. What should these standards be? What audiences typically read educational research? What format or structure do these reports require? Let's look at how Maria handles these issues.

> Maria needs to think about how she will organize her final report to her school committee as well as to her university graduate committee. Her graduate committee likely has a structure in mind for her graduate research study, and she needs to visit with faculty about the format that students typically use. Her school report will likely be different than her research report. The school report will be informative, concise, and recommendation-oriented, and will include minimal discussions about methods and procedures. Whatever the audience and structure for her report, it must be respectful of the audience and be devoid of discriminatory language. Chapter 10, "Reporting and Evaluating Research," focuses on strategies that Maria might find helpful as she writes her final reports.

HOW IS THIS PROCESS IMPLEMENTED ETHICALLY BY RESEARCHERS?

The idea of respecting individuals provides an introduction to the importance of conducting research ethically. In all steps of the research process, you need to engage in ethical practices. You will be introduced to these issues in this text as they arise in the steps in the process (Part II) as well as in the specific research designs (Part III). In order to help you learn to consider these issues during every phase of research, they are briefly introduced here. At this stage in our discussion, ethical issues in research relate to respecting the rights of participants, honoring research sites that you visit, and reporting research fully and honestly.

Respecting the Rights of Participants

Ethical standards to use in research are available from professional associations. Examples of professional associations that offer helpful guidelines include the American Educational Research Association (AERA) (Ethical Standards of the American Educational Research Association, 1992); the American Psychological Association (APA) (Ethical Principles of Psychologists and Code of Conduct, 1992, Publication Manual, 1994); and the American Anthropological Association (AAA) (Fleuhr-Lobban, 1991).

According to these guidelines, individuals who participate in a study have certain rights, including the right to be briefed about the study. Before participating in research, individuals need to know the purpose, the aims, the use of results, and the likely social consequences the study will have on their lives. They also have the right to refuse to participate in a study, and can withdraw at any time. When they participate and provide information, their anonymity is protected and guaranteed by the researcher. Individuals are not to be offered excessive financial inducements to participate in a project. Participants also have the right to gain something from a study. Researchers need to actively look for ways to "give back" (or reciprocate) to participants in a study because the participants have freely provided their time. For example, in one study involving individuals with HIV, the author shared book royalties with the participants in the study. In another study, a researcher volunteered to help supervise lunchroom activities in exchange for information from students in the school.

Honoring Research Sites

It is important to respect the site where the research takes place. This respect should be shown by gaining permission before entering a site, by disturbing the site as little as possible during a study, and by viewing oneself as a "guest" at the place of study. For example, in a study in one high school classroom, the researcher sought permission from several individuals, including the school board responsible for ensuring that the rights of human subjects were protected, the research official in the school district, the principal of the school, the teacher in a government class, and the actual students who participated in the study and their parents.

Reporting Research Fully and Honestly

Respect should also be shown to audiences who read and use information from studies. Data should be reported honestly without changing or altering the findings to satisfy certain predictions or interest groups. In addition, studies completed by others should not be plagiarized, and credit should be given for material quoted from other studies. This credit involves citing the authors and the date of the publication, and listing the publication in the reference section of the study. In addition, research should be free of jargon and be understandable to those being studied. As ethical educators, we need to make every effort to communicate the practical significance of our research to the community of researchers and practitioners so inquiry will be encouraged and used.

 ## Think-Aloud About the Skills You Bring to This Process

At this point you may be considering whether you have the ability to read, evaluate, and actually conduct research. Knowing the process of research, you may say, does not guarantee an adequate research study. Certainly Maria, who is new to research, has these concerns.

   Let me set your mind at ease. You have already learned the skills of a researcher through your life experiences. From your personal, life experiences you bring to research important skills needed for the task. These skills include solving puzzles, employing a long attention span, using a library, and, of course, writing out your thoughts.

Solving Puzzles

Researchers look at problems as puzzles to solve. The steps in the research process are viewed as a series of puzzle pieces that the inquirer assembles. You already have skills in solving puzzles. You fit together the debits and credits to balance your checkbook. As a parent, you engage in multiple roles during the day that require juggling different tasks. These are puzzles that we work out by breaking them down into manageable parts ("What will be the demands on my time today?"), setting obtainable objectives ("I will have a busy day at work, so I will focus on my job today"), and possibly writing them down ("I need to make a list of what I need to accomplish today"). As you examine research studies or engage in the process of inquiry, assembling these parts of the puzzle—such as first working on a research problem and then specifying a purpose for a study—will require that all of the pieces fit together, like the many puzzles that we solve in daily living.

Lengthening Your Attention Span

Although we generally make time to complete the tasks we love, our attention span certainly varies from task to task. The process of research involves six steps that may span a period of six months or more. To read through a journal article and identify each of these steps, for example, requires patience as well as knowledge about what to look for. We all bring attention spans of varying lengths to the process of research. But if we consider the tasks we love and the amount of time we devote to them, we can see that we have already developed an attention span long enough to spend considerable time at research. Although research may lengthen your attention span, you already have a start in focusing in on topics of interest.

Using Libraries

The step in the research process requiring you to review the literature means spending some time in an academic library. For most of us, going to the library probably began in grade school with trips to the school library. Engaging in research requires spending time with library resources, a process that is facilitated by home computers and Internet connections to library catalogues. But the process of research requires that you use skills in locating studies, summarizing them, and writing a review of the literature. These skills are developed during research, if you do not already have them. They develop from our comfort level with a library and with experiences that began early in our schooling and continue on today.

Writing, Editing, and More Writing

If researchers were not writing reports of their studies, they would probably be out trying to write the "great American novel." Researchers cannot escape the ever-present aspect of writing as a key facet of research. As writers, we work through numerous drafts, receive reactions from others, and develop new drafts. Those individuals who write a 10-volume "History of the World," for example, either enjoy writing immensely or have spent their life on the task. This is nothing but hard, grind-it-out work. Research, in the end, involves writing the study for an audience. Do you enjoy writing and communicating your thoughts? Do you like to write in a journal or a diary? Do you like to write letters? You have probably written several essays in college already or worked on a research report with other students or a faculty member. In short, you have experience in writing. As you know, writing is more than recording ideas on paper or in a computer file. It is also organizing ideas, preparing interview questions, jotting down notes during an observation, and writing for permissions to use someone else's questions or articles. Writing exists in all phases of the creative process of planning and in conducting research.

APPLYING THE RESEARCH PROCESS TO ACTUAL STUDIES

In this book, especially in Chapters 2 through 10, we will refer to two journal articles that provide specific application of the steps in the research process. The two articles are:

Vooijs, M. W., & van der Voort, T. H. A. (1993). Learning about television violence: The impact of a critical viewing curriculum on children's attitudinal judgments of crime series. *Journal of Research and Development in Education, 26(3),* 133–142; and Asmussen, K. J. & Creswell, J. W. (1995). Campus response to a student gunman. *Journal of Higher Education, 66,* 575–591. Read these journal articles, on pages 18–41, *before* beginning Chapter 2, "Quantitative and Qualitative Approaches."

To assist in the process of reading these articles, you will note that marginal annotations are assigned to the sections in the articles that parallel the steps of the research process covered in this chapter. Also, the annotations signal the major characteristics of both *quantitative* and *qualitative* research to be discussed in Chapter 2. In Chapter 2 we will reflect back on these two articles frequently to demonstrate the authors' use of those characteristics.

As you read the articles, here are a few tips that you might use to help you understand the major ideas of both studies.

What cues can you use to understand the article? Look at the major headings. Also look for the major parts of the research process: problem, literature, purpose, data collection, data analysis, and overall structure of the report. The abstract is often incomplete and is therefore not a good place to look. How can you understand the statistics and other complex data analysis procedures? Look for the research question being raised and then ask yourself how the researchers addressed or answered it. What is the most important statement in an article? Look for the purpose statement, which typically begins with words such as, "The purpose of this study is," "The intent of the study is," or "The objective of this study is." Is the title useful in helping to understand the article? Not always. Titles are often short and may not contain all of the information you need to understand the direction of the study. Instead, look at the purpose statement, research questions, or hypotheses for this information.

KEY IDEAS IN THE CHAPTER

Why is research important? Research helps educators understand problems or issues through the accumulation of knowledge. It can assist educators in improving practice, and it focuses attention on important policy issues being discussed and debated by decision makers. Also, engaging in research provides valuable conceptual, writing, and presenting skills for students. Despite these strengths, however, *some* research today provides poor answers to our questions. Data can be both contradictory and inadequate in published studies. What constitutes "research" is also open for discussion today because of the many approaches found in education.

These problems necessitate a need for a basic definition and a process that can help the educational researcher when planning, conducting, and evaluating studies. Educational research is a cyclical process of steps that typically begins with identifying a research problem or issue of study. It then consists of reviewing the literature, advancing direction through research questions and statements, and then collecting, analyzing, and interpreting the data. This process culminates in a presented report that is evaluated and potentially used within the larger educational community. Overall, research is a systematic process of identifying a problem, gathering and analyzing data, and making an interpretation of the information to help address the problem.

It is helpful to see these aspects as a process consisting of six steps: (1) A "problem" or issue to study is identified. (2) The literature is reviewed to determine if others have studied the topic and existing literature is summarized. (3) A direction or focus for the study is created through a purpose statement and research questions or hypotheses. (4) Individuals to study and gather data from are identified. (5) The collected data are analyzed, synthesized, and interpreted. (6) A research report is written for audiences who, in turn, evaluate it for quality and use.

Researchers should engage in this process using good ethical practices. They should respect the rights of participants and research sites, as well as audiences who read the reports. Conducting research requires skills that are found in everyday experiences such as solving puzzles, focusing attention on topics, using the library, and writing.

USEFUL INFORMATION FOR PRODUCERS OF RESEARCH

▶ As you plan and conduct a study, keep in mind that research needs to be valuable to educators. Include comments in your study that convey the value to specific educational audiences.

▶ Use the general framework of the six steps for thinking about your plans and the conduct of research. These six steps make research manageable, help ensure that you conduct thorough inquiries, and provide a useful strategy for the design and writing of the research.

▶ Be ethical in conducting research. Respect the rights of participants, research sites, and individuals who will be readers of your study.

▶ Consider the skills that you need to develop to be a researcher. You may already have developed the skills of reading and writing, using library resources, solving puzzles, and focusing in on a topic of interest.

USEFUL INFORMATION FOR CONSUMERS OF RESEARCH

▶ As you examine a study, recognize that authors emphasize different reasons for undertaking their study. Look for suggestions by the author for practical applications of a study.

▶ Recognize that researchers proceed through a process of research and then construct sections of a study that reflect different steps in this process. For the research problem, examine the "introduction" to a study; for the literature review, explore the "literature review" section. For the data collection discussion, visit the "method" or "procedure" section, and for the data analysis and interpretation, see the "results" or "findings" as well as the "discussion" sections.

▶ Look for statements in the study where the researcher discusses respect for participants and sites.

STUDY QUESTIONS AND ACTIVITIES

1. Choose a published journal article from your college or university library that is of interest to you. Can you find the research problem, the literature review, the research questions, the data collection, the data analysis, and the interpretation in the study? Photocopy the article and label the six key components of the research process in the margins of the article.

2. Using the same article as you used to answer question 1, locate the statements by the author, in his or her own words, of the value of research. See how many reasons you can find and identify each reason.

3. Looking again at the article, do the authors demonstrate sensitivity to ethical issues? Identify passages in the study in which the author does or does not convey the rights of participants, a respect for the study site, or a concern for readers in the dissemination of the study.

4. Write an autobiographical essay on your present skills as a researcher. Comment on your abilities to solve puzzles, use your long attention span, visit the library, and write. Also comment on any other special talents you bring to research.

 Now go to our Companion Website to assess your understanding of chapter content with Multiple-Choice Questions, apply comprehension in Projects & Essays, and broaden your knowledge with links to related research topics on the Web.

Learning About Television Violence: The Impact of a Critical Viewing Curriculum on Children's Attitudinal Judgments of Crime Series

Marcel W. Vooijs
Tom H.A. van der Voort
Leiden University

Steps in the Research Process

This study explored the impact of an in-school curriculum designed to teach children 10–12 years of age to become more discriminate consumers of violent crime series. The results of the curriculum should be that children take the violent actions of the good guys less lightly, take a more critical stand towards the justification of these actions, and become more aware of the salient differences between violence in crime series and in real life. Using a quasi-experimental pretest-posttest control group design, the effects of the curriculum were assessed both immediately after the intervention and 2 years later. The results measured immediately after the intervention showed that children perceived the good guys' violent actions more critically. Furthermore, the curriculum resulted in an increased factual knowledge of differences between violence on television and in real life, and a decreased perceived television reality. The latter two effects were still demonstrable 2 years later.

Quantitative Characteristics

(01)   Over the last 30 years, most research on the impact of television violence has focused on the effects of violent fare upon children's aggressive behavior. Although there are a few critics who disagree (e.g., Freedman, 1984), most reviews of the research conclude that the depiction of violence in television programs increases the chance that children in the audience will act aggressively themselves (Andison, 1977; Hearold, 1979; Friedrich-Cofer & Huston, 1986). Since the mid-70s, researchers have broadened their attention from behavioral effects to affective and cognitive effects of violence viewing. Substantial evidence has been accumulated that exposure to violent programs may affect children's feelings and thoughts. In the long term, affective and cognitive effects may not only result in increased aggressive behavior, but may also be exhibited in more subtle forms of behavior than aggression (Pearl, 1982).

Identifying a research problem

A quantitative research problem requires description or explanation.

(02)   Research has shown that exposure to violent fare may decrease normal sensitivity to aggression (Dorr, 1982; Zillman, 1982). Children who were high viewers of televised violence or were experimentally exposed to violent films were less responsive in subsequent exposure to televised violence than were natural or experimentally-produced low viewers (Cline, Croft, & Courrier, 1973; Geen, 1981; Thomas, Horton, Lippencott, & Drabman, 1977). This effect is called habituation: Initially strong excitatory reactions grow weaker or vanish entirely with repeated exposure to stimuli of a certain kind (Zillman, 1982). If people become inured to violence from seeing much of it, they may react less sensitively to real-life aggression by, for example, not helping a victim.

Reviewing the literature

(03)   In addition, exposure to TV violence can strengthen the belief that aggression is desirable or acceptable to solve conflicts. Several studies have shown that greater viewing of violence is positively associated with attitudes favorable to the use of violence (Dominick & Greenberg, 1972; Greenberg, 1975). According to some experimental studies, the willing-

The quantitative literature plays a major role.

A brief version of this paper was presented at the XXIV International Congress of Psychology, Sydney, Australia, 1988, and was published in the Proceedings of the Congress (Volume 6). The research reported was supported by a grant from the Netherlands Foundation for Educational Research, The Hague.

Reprinted with permission from the *Journal of Research and Development in Education.*

ness to accept aggressive behavior in others increased by even brief exposure to violent programs. Such an effect has been reported by Leifer and Roberts (1972) and Drabman and Thomas (1974). The relation between violence viewing and aggressive attitudes may be due to the fact that dramatized violence in movies is conveyed without negative consequences. Neither perpetrators nor victims suffer much, and the perpetrator is often rewarded for antisocial actions (Potter & Ware, 1987).

(04)   Finally, there is evidence that television violence contributes to viewers' conceptions of social reality (Hawkins & Pingree, 1982). For example, people who are heavy viewers of television are more apt to think the world is violent and a "mean and scary" place than are light viewers. Unfortunately, the research evidence is not always consistent and the process of influencing seems very complex (Hawkins & Pingree, 1982). Among other things it is assumed that children's perceptions of social reality are particularly affected by television if children perceive television programs as real and if they have no pre-existing knowledge on the aspect of social reality in question. However, the role of television in shaping children's conceptions of social reality is generally regarded as significant (Pearl, 1982).

(05)   Until now, a few previous attempts have been made to mitigate the effects of television violence by in-school interventions (Vooijs & van der Voort, 1990). These curricula are based on the assumption that one can enable viewers to resist the undesirable consequences of viewing television violence and to benefit from television more fully. Only three curricula on television violence, all conducted in the United States, have been subjected to evaluation. In accordance with the majority of research studies on the impact of TV violence, these curricula mainly were concerned with children's learning of aggressive behavior from television. The interventions focused on reducing the aggressiveness-heightening effect of TV violence by decreasing children's perceived reality of television.

(06)   An intervention strategy employed by Doolittle (1975) emphasized the fictional and trick nature of violent drama, whereas Huesmann, Eron, Klein, Brice, and Fischer (1983) asked children to discuss the realism of violent television programs shown. However, neither type of intervention produced the intended reduction in children's reality perception of television, and the instruction did not result in a reduction of children's aggressiveness either. A third intervention study was more successful (Huesmann et al., 1983). Besides altering children's perceived reality of television, the intervention was designed to teach children directly that watching television violence is not desirable. The intervention again did not significantly alter children's judgment of the realism of violent television drama, but children's aggressiveness was reduced. Besides these specific school interventions, several curricula were developed to teach children about the general nature of television (Vooijs & van der Voort, 1990). A number of these curricula devoted attention to TV violence and aggression too. However, most curricula were not investigated for the extent to which they achieved their objectives.

(07)   The present study explored the effect of an in-school curriculum designed to modify the impact of television violence on children. In contrast to the American curricula on television violence, the curriculum was not primarily intended to reduce child aggression, but to alter the cognitive and affective effects of violence viewing on children. The curriculum was based on the belief that children's cognitive and affective learning from television violence is in itself an important issue that needs attention in education. In particular, the curriculum was aimed to counteract effects of violence viewing on children's beliefs and feelings about violence and on their images of social reality by encouraging children to form a more critical judgment of the value of violent scenes. If children are able to process

Specifying a purpose and research questions or hypotheses

The quantitative purpose statement, research questions or hypotheses seek measurable, observable data on variables.

televised information more critically they might be less influenced by what they see (Anderson, 1983, Corder-Bolz, 1982).

Changing Children's Attitudinal Judgments of TV Violence

(08)   The curriculum was meant for children 10–12 years of age. Three specific objectives were formulated. In order to resist the habituation effect of violence viewing, the first goal of the curriculum was that children take violent actions in television films more seriously (increased readiness to see violence). The curriculum was particularly aimed at having children take the violent actions of the good guys less lightly, as children already took the violent actions of the "bad guys" seriously of their own accord (van der Voort, 1986).

(09)   The curriculum's second objective was directed at counteracting aggressive attitudes that children might learn from television. Children should learn to go along less unquestioningly with the violent actions they see on television (reduced approval of violent actions). This objective was also concentrated on the violence used by the "hero." As was found in a preliminary study, most children spontaneously rejected the violence of the bad guys, whereas in the eyes of many children the good guys could do no wrong (van der Voort, 1986).

(10)   To enable children to resist undesirable effects of violence viewing on their conceptions of social reality, the third objective was to make children more aware of the unrealistic nature of dramatized violence, and of salient differences between violence on television and violence in real life (reduced perceived reality). A preliminary study suggested that no attention needed to be devoted to the unrealistic character of fantasy-type violent films such as violent cartoons and programs of The Incredible Hulk type. In the age-span from 9-12, these fantastic programs were seen increasingly as less realistic, and at the age of 12, children looked at the reality of these programs much the same way as adults did (van der Voort, 1986). Therefore, the curriculum was mainly concerned with crime series (police and detective films), film types which in the eyes of most children did give a picture that is more or less true to reality, and which did not forfeit any of their perceived reality within the age span studied (van der Voort, 1986).

(11)   The theoretical framework of the intervention strategy was derived from theory on attitude change. It was assumed that attitudinal judgments are learned predispositions that can be changed by new information (Fishbein & Ajzen, 1975; Zimbardo & Ebbesen, 1970; Zimbardo, Ebbesen, & Maslach, 1977). According to this assumption, the curriculum attempted to bring about the desired changes in attitudinal judgments of television violence by offering new information which was not compatible with the already existing ideas and which would function as an eye-opener for the children. In order to be effective, the new information should be illustrated clearly, explicitly stated, repeated, and presented by a credible source (Zimbardo et al., 1977). In accordance with these guidelines, the arguments were explicitly stated in a textbook and clearly illustrated by video-extracts from violent movies. In addition, much of the information was conveyed by experts who were interviewed on television, and who would be considered as credible sources.

(12)   The curriculum attempted to convince children of the seriousness of violence by confronting them, by means of television interviews, with (a) police officers who had actually shot suspects, and who related how deep an impression this event made on them; (b) victims of violence who told about the physical—and above all—the mental consequences which they had suffered, and (c) a doctor who explained the medical consequences of various types of violent acts. The unrealistic character of many

The quantitative literature justifies the research problem and provides direction for the study.

violent films became clear from, among other things, the commentary on excerpts from crime films given by real police officers and private detectives in which the differences between film and reality were pointed out. The questionable legitimacy of a large part of the violent actions of good guys in the films was made clear by explaining, among other things, that in reality police officers and private detectives were allowed to use violence only under extremely exceptional circumstances.

(13)   However, the presentation of novel information by credible sources may not suffice to change perceptions of TV violence. Children should learn to use this information during viewing and to process the televised information critically. In order to teach children to look at the violent films with literally new eyes, they were given so-called decentration assignments (Leyens, Herman, & Dunand, 1982). As understood by Leyens et al., decentration is a process whereby the viewer takes a distance from the immediate content of the film—the content usually centred upon—and concentrates explicitly on aspects usually not regarded immediately. The induction of decentration gives the viewer another frame of reference from which to evaluate what one sees. During and at the end of a lesson, decentration was induced by having children look at a new film extract with the task of watching out especially for the aspect which had just been dealt with. For example, the task could be to pay special attention to the reaction of a police officer in the film after shooting somebody, or to watch for the signs of physical damage shown by a victim of violence in the films.

(14)   The curriculum was developed in three stages, each of which resulted in a new version of the curriculum based on one or more empirical try-outs. The final version of the curriculum consisted of nine lessons of 45 minutes each. Each lesson highlighted a specific topic and included written information, video clips from current crime series, television interviews with experts and viewing exercises.

Research Questions

Specifying a purpose and research questions or hypotheses

(15)   The study on the effects of the curriculum was aimed at answering four questions. The first question was whether the curriculum produces the desired effects in the short term. Three criteria for testing the curriculum's effectiveness directly followed from the instructional objectives (a higher readiness to see violence, less approval of violence, and a lowered perceived reality of television). The factual information that children acquire from the lessons was interpreted as a fourth criteria.

The quantitative purpose statement, research questions, or hypotheses are specific and narrow.

(16)   The second question referred to the strength of the induced change. On the assumption that adults with a reasonable education must be considered sufficiently capable of assessing the true value of images of violence, the way in which students of a teachers' training college perceive television violence was employed as the norm. The extent to which the curriculum bridged the gap between children's perception of violent programs and those of adults was assessed by comparing children's criterion scores with the mean criterion scores of the adult norm group.

(17)   A third question was which types of children profit most from the lessons. This information is useful in order to establish what the intervention does to children who need it most. Eight child variables which are connected to children's perceptions of television (van der Voort, 1986) were involved in the study: five background variables (gender, SES, grade attended, school achievement, and aggressiveness), and three viewing variables (frequency with which television is watched, preferences for violent films, and the level of identification with television figures).

(18)   Finally, in a follow-up study the effects after 2 years were investigated. Testing for effects extended in time is of particular importance for television

curricula, because it is quite possible that the initially assessed curricula effects will be undone again by maturation, partly as a result of their growing experience with television, and partly as a result of their cognitive growth (Greenfield, 1984).

Method

Subjects

(19)   The effects of the lessons were tested in an experimental field study. The study was carried out in six schools, two schools attended by children with low socioeconomic status (SES), two medium-SES schools, and two high-SES schools. At each socio-economic level, one of the schools was assigned randomly to the experimental condition (lessons), and the other to the control condition (no lessons). In each school the fourth, fifth and sixth grades participated in the study. Therefore, both the experimental group ($N = 221$) and the control group ($N = 216$) consisted of nine classes. Sample attrition was less than 10%.

Collecting data

Design and Procedure

(20)   The study used a pretest/posttest/retest control group design. The experimental classes were given the teaching program over a period of 5 weeks, taught by trained project staff. In the week preceding the delivery of the first lesson in the experimental classes, the child variables school achievement, aggressiveness, viewing frequency, preference for violent films, and identification with television figures were assessed. To determine the immediate effects of the curriculum the subjects were pre and posttested on three criterion measures: (a) readiness to see violence; (b) approval of violent actions; and (c) perceived reality of violent films. A fourth criterion variable, the factual knowledge gained from the lessons, was measured only afterwards, to preclude testing effects and interaction effects between pretest and treatment (Campbell & Stanley, 1963).

(21)   To avoid social desirability effects, the posttests were administered by researchers whom the children had not seen before. To verify whether social desirability really was eliminated, the enjoyment of violence in television programs was included in the test battery as a control variable, and assessed both before and after the treatment. It was reasoned that if children would try to please the researchers by pretending to be more critical than they actually were at the end of the lessons, they would also pretend to enjoy violence in television programs less than prior to the lessons (an effect we were not aiming for). However, if the enjoyment of violence in television programs is not reduced, while the four intended curriculum effects do appear, there is reason to assume that social desirability has not played a significant role in the posttest.

(22)   In order to collect norm scores, the four measuring instruments for the criterion variables were also submitted to a sample of students from two teachers colleges ($N = 110$). The average score for each criterion variable was employed as the norm.

Quantitative data collection involves studying a large number of individuals.

(23)   Finally, the delayed curriculum effects were determined by administering the four criterion tests again 2 years later. This part of the study involved only those children who were in the fourth grade during the test of the curriculum's immediate effects (now sixth graders). Of the 127 fourth graders who had participated in the original study, 111 participated in the follow-up study.

Measuring Instruments

(24)   With the exception of the knowledge test, the measuring instruments for the criterion variables were adjusted versions of instruments which had al-

ready been developed for earlier research (van der Voort, 1986). For the purpose of the present study, the adjusted versions were tested again, and their psychometric qualities examined. We shall suffice here with a brief characterization of the content and the properties of the criterion tests.

(25)   *Readiness to see violence.* During this test children were confronted with 25 violent actions performed by the good guy which were shown on video. Using a 5-point scale running from "really dreadful" to "not so bad," each action was evaluated on its perceived seriousness. Cronbach's alpha was .93.

(26)   *Approval of violence.* The children were asked to evaluate the same 25 acts of violence with respect to the morality of the violent behavior. A 5-point scale was used, running from "entirely correct" to "entirely wrong." Cronbach's alpha was .91.

(27)   *Perceived reality of violent films.* The instrument contained short descriptions of 32 nonrealistic events and situations which are often seen in violent films. Children were asked to indicate on a 5-point scale whether they believed these events possible in real life. For example: "In police programs, villains are almost always caught. Does that happen in real life too?" Cronbach's alpha was .88.

(28)   *Knowledge.* The factual knowledge acquired from the curriculum was assessed by means of 38 multiple-choice questions. Cronbach's alpha was .88.

(29)   *Remaining variables.* Insofar as they were not already given in the study's design (gender, grade attended, and SES), the child variables were measured by means of instruments which had already been developed in an earlier study (van der Voort, 1986). These instruments were adopted without any alterations. The same was true of the control variable "enjoyment of violence in television programs."

Quantitative data collection is based on using instruments identified prior to the study.

Results

Short-term Effects

(30)   For each of the criterion variables, the mean pretest difference between the experimental and the control group was small and nonsignificant (see Table 1). In principle, therefore, when determining the short-term effects of the curriculum the pretest scores could be ignored. Nevertheless, the pretest measurements of the criterion variables were included as covariates in the analyses of covariance, because this can lead to a more precise result (Anderson et al., 1980). As a first step, the short-term effect of the curriculum was analyzed by means of a multivariate analysis of covariance (MANCOVA). Apart from the treatment factor, the background variables gender, grade attended, and socioeconomic status were included as factors in this analysis. After having ascertained from this multivariate analysis of covariance that the teaching program had a significant main effect on all the dependent measures together, $F(4, 395) = 205.89$, $p = .001$, it was determined by means of univariate analyses of covariance, for each dependent variable separately, whether it contributed to the multivariate program effect found. These analyses showed that the curriculum led to a higher "readiness to see violence," $F(1, 398) = 53.46$, $p = .00)$ and a decreased approval of the violent actions of the good guys, $F(1, 398) = 46.65$, $p = .00$. In addition, the curriculum produced a decreased "perceived reality," $F(1, 398) = 310.53$, $p = .00$, and an increased factual knowledge of differences between film and reality, $F(1, 398) = 652.19$, $p = .00$. The effect of the treatment on the control variable "enjoyment of violence in television programs" was not significant, nor was it meant to be. This finding suggested that social desirability played no significant role in the posttest measures.

Analyzing the data

Quantitative data collection involves gathering numeric data.

Quantitative data analysis consists of statistical analysis.

TABLE 1
Means and Standard Deviations for the Pretest and Posttest Measures of the Dependent Variables, Including the Norm Scores from Teachers' College Students

Dependent Measure	Time of Measurement	Control Group		Experimental Group		Norm Scores	
		M	**SD**	**M**	**SD**	**M**	**SD**
Readiness to see violence[a]	Pretest	1.94	0.58	1.97	0.58	—	—
	Posttest	1.97	0.64	2.39	0.73	2.69	0.78
Approval of violence[a]	Pretest	3.80	0.70	3.81	0.62	—	—
	Posttest	3.72	0.80	3.31	0.78	2.80	0.75
Perceived TV reality[a]	Pretest	2.75	0.49	2.83	0.50	—	—
	Posttest	2.57	0.50	1.85	0.57	2.12	0.38
Knowledge[b]	Pretest	—	—	—	—	—	—
	Posttest	0.50	0.12	0.77	0.15	0.82	0.08
Enjoyment of violence[a]	Pretest	1.59	0.30	1.65	0.30	—	—
	Posttest	1.59	0.31	1.65	0.29	—	—

Note. [a]Minimum score = 1, maximum score = 5. [b]The values represent proportions of correctly answered questions.

(31)   To examine whether the strength of the curriculum-induced changes in children's attitudinal judgments of television violence was related to children's factual knowledge, partial correlations were computed between the experimental subjects' knowledge scores and their posttest scores on each of the three attitudinal measures, controlling for the pretest scores on the attitudinal measure. Children with high knowledge scores showed a relatively strong increase in readiness to see violence, partial $r(221) = .24$, $p < .001$, and a relatively strong decrease in both approval of violent television actions, partial $r(221) = -.28$, $p < .001$, and perceived television realism, partial $r(221) = -.31$, $p < .001$.

Quantitative researchers take an objective and unbiased approach.

(32)   The extent to which the curriculum bridged the gap between children's perceptions of violent films and those of adults was assessed by comparing children's posttest scores with the norm scores obtained from the teachers college students (see Table 1). In this analysis, the pretest scores were left aside. This did not obstruct the interpretation of the differences between the mean posttest scores, because as mentioned earlier, the pre-experimental differences between the experimental and control group were negligible. Using one-way analyses of variance, significant differences were found to occur among the mean posttest scores of the control group, experimental group, and the adult norm group for each of the four criterion variables (readiness to see violence: $F(2, 544) = 41.82$, $p = .00$; approval of violence $F(2, 544) = 51.99$, $p = .00$; perceived TV reality: $F(2, 544) = 107,88$, $p = .00$, knowledge: $F(2, 544) = 341.03$, $p = .00$). When Duncan's Multiple Range Test (Kirk, 1968) was applied, each of the three contrasts between the three group means for each of the four criterion variables was significant at the 1% level.

Quantitative data analysis consists of describing trends, comparing groups, or relating variables.

(33)   From Table 1 it is clear that the curriculum was not equally effective in all respects. Though the lessons ensured that children had a greater readiness to see violence in the acts of the good guys and were slower to approve of them, for these criteria the differences between the vision of "untreated" children and adults were only narrowed by half. The effect on factual knowledge was more powerful; after the end of the lessons children knew almost as much about the conduct of (private) detectives as the norm group of adults. The teaching program had its biggest influence on the perceived reality of violent films. After the lessons the children even perceived violent films as being less realistic than did the teachers-to-be.

(34)   Possible interactions of child variables with the observed curriculum effects were determined for the child variables of gender, grade attended, and socioeconomic status in the MANCOVA discussed above (in which these variables were included as factors). For each of the other child variables separate multivariate analyses of covariance were carried out after first having dichotomized or trichotomized the scores on the child variable in question. In these MANCOVAs the treatment and the child variable in question were included as factors and the four criterion variables as dependent variables. A significant multivariate interaction only occurred for the child variables socioeconomic status, $F(14, 780) = 2.12, p = .01$, and grade attended, $F(14, 780) = 1.75, p = .04$. Subsequent univariate analyses of covariance showed that the interaction of socioeconomic status with the program effect only applied to the criterion variable "knowledge," $F(2, 395) = 3.17, p = .04$, but the variance explained was very small. The increase in knowledge appeared to be somewhat stronger for children from a high and low socioeconomic status than for medium-SES children. The interaction of grade attended with the program effect was found to apply only to the variables "readiness to see violence," $F(2, 395) = 3.79, p = .02$, and "approval of violence," $F(2, 395) = 4.46, p = .01$. On these variables only fifth and sixth graders showed a learning profit; fourth graders' perceptions of the violent actions of the good guys were not significantly altered by the curriculum, perhaps because this age group—as appeared from the pretest—was initially already more critical of the violent actions of the good guy.

Effects after 2 Years

(35)   This last finding had consequences for the follow-up study, carried out on those children who were in the fourth grade when they entered the study. Because if the curriculum has no demonstrable effect on the immediate posttests for the criteria "readiness to see violence," and "approval of violence," then unless there is a sort of sleeper-effect, no effect on the delayed posttest measurements will be encountered.

(36)   In a first step, the curriculum's effect after 2 years was analyzed with a multivariate analysis of covariance in which measurements made immediately after the end of the lessons (time 1) and the measurements made 2 years later (time 2) were concurrently involved (see Table 2). In the model of analysis employed, the measurement time was included as a within-factor; treatment, gender, and socioeconomic status were between-factors. In this analysis, the occurrence of a significant interaction between measurement time and treatment indicates that there has been a change in the curriculum effects over the 2-year period. According to the multivariate analysis of covariance there was indeed a significant multivariate treatment x measurement time interaction, $F(4, 96) = 31.95, p = .00$. Subsequent univariate analyses of covariance showed that this interaction held for each of the four criterion variables (readiness to see violence: $F(1, 99) = 9.43, p = .00$; approval of violence, $F(1, 99) = 4.75, p = .03$; perceived TV reality, $F(1, 99) = 33.85, p = .00$; knowledge, $F(1, 99) = 99.04, p = .00$).

(37)   For the criterion variables readiness to see violence and approval of the violent actions of the good guy, the interactions between measurement time and treatment had a similar character. In both cases the slight "advantage," which the experimental group still had over the control group at the time of the immediate posttest measurement turned into a slight "disadvantage" 2 years later. However, these interactions were not very meaningful. After all, they only had a bearing on the youngest age group, for whom, unlike the older children, no significant effect on these two variables could be detected on the immediate posttests. Moreover, the mean

TABLE 2
**Means and Standard Deviations for the Immediate (Time 1) and Delayed Posttest
Measures (Time 2) of the Criterion Variables**

Criterion Measure	Measurement Time	Control Group		Experimental Group	
		M	*SD*	*M*	*SD*
Readiness to see Violence	Time 1	1.97	0.64	2.34	0.73
	Time 2	2.01	0.56	1.91	0.50
Approval of Violence	Time 1	3.72	0.80	3.31	0.78
	Time 2	2.52	0.66	2.39	0.60
Perceived TV Reality	Time 1	2.57	0.50	1.85	0.57
	Time 2	2.52	0.37	2.26	0.58
Knowledge	Time 1	0.50	0.12	0.77	0.15
	Time 2	0.60	0.12	0.67	0.15

delayed posttest differences between the treated and the control group were not significant for either of the two variables (readiness to see violence: $F(1, 96) = 3.01$, $p = .09$; approval of violence: $F(1, 96) = 2.68$, $p = .11$).

(38)   It is more relevant to determine what has happened 2 years later to the immediate curriculum effects on knowledge and perceived reality, because on these criteria there was a significant and indeed large difference between the mean immediate posttest scores of both groups. These two short-term effects appeared to still exist 2 years later. At that time, the experimental group still showed a greater factual knowledge than the control group, $F(1, 96) = 8.35$, $p = .01$, and also, the experimental group still perceived violent films as less realistic, $F(1, 96) = 6.26$, $p = .01$.

(39)   However, the latter two curriculum effects have certainly been weakened. This reduction of the lesson effects was the result of two contrary movements which reinforced each other. On the one hand, the effect of the teaching program on the experimental group was diminished after 2 years, and on the other hand the control group made up for its initial disadvantage through maturation.

(40)   In order to investigate whether this weakening of the curriculum effects depended on the child variables being studied, multivariate analyses of covariance were carried out for each variable, with the treatment, measurement time, and the relevant child variable as factors. In these analyses the four criterion variables were once again treated simultaneously as dependent variables, and the pretest measures were incorporated as covariates. Because no significant interaction between measurement time, treatment, and the relevant child variable was found in any of these analyses, it was concluded that the observed weakening of the curriculum effects applied about equally to the various subgroups of children.

Discussion

(41)   In contrast to the American curricula on television violence (Doolittle, 1975; Huesmann et al., 1983), the present curriculum was not intended to reduce child aggression, but merely intended to encourage children to form a more critical judgment of the value of violent scenes, in particular those shown in crime series. The study shows that children can, in as short a time as nine lessons, acquire a more critical attitude toward television violence. The curriculum increased children's readiness to see violence, and violent actions of the good guys were less readily approved of. In addition,

Interpreting the data

the curriculum reduced children's perceived reality of violent television programs, an effect that was still demonstrable 2 years later.

(42)   The study did not investigate whether the curriculum modified children's attitudes toward real-life violence. However, because the lessons not only dealt with violence as depicted on television but also with violence as found in reality, the curriculum may have changed children's attitudes towards real-life violence as well. In addition, as the curriculum enables children to evaluate violent television contents more critically, children hopefully will be less susceptible to the influence of violent programs on children's attitudes toward real-life violence in the future (Anderson, 1983; Corder-Bolz, 1982).

(43)   Whereas earlier initiatives aimed at reducing children's perceived reality of television were not always effective, this is precisely the strength of the present teaching program. After the lessons, children considered the violent films to be less realistic than did the norm group of young adults, and the curriculum effect still held, though weakened, 2 years later. The curriculum's effectiveness in altering children's reality judgment of television may be partly due to the perspective from which the reality content of violent films was considered in the lessons. In the intervention strategy employed by Doolittle (1975) the fictional nature of television drama was emphasized; the fact that films are acted and that special effects are created by trickery. This approach probably is less suited for altering the reality perception of older elementary school pupils, because at that age they are of their own accord already sufficiently aware of the fictional nature of films (Morison, Kelly, & Gardner, 1981). In the present lessons, the fictional and trick nature of television drama were taken for granted. Instead, the plausibility of the events in the film was discussed; the points where films give a non-realistic view of reality were emphasized. Possibly, the didactic approach employed in the curriculum also contributed to the successful reduction of the perceived television reality. Earlier curricula (Huesmann et al., 1983) often used a discussion method, whereas in the present curriculum children are confronted directly with the differences between film and reality and are trained to watch out for these differences through concrete viewing assignments.

(44)   The curriculum was least successful in changing children's attitudinal judgments of the violent acts of the "good guys." The change in perception brought about was relatively small, and was limited to the older children in the study. However, according to the pretest the older children were initially least critical of the good guys' violent actions, and therefore needed the instruction the most.

(45)   The intervention strategy used in the curriculum is based on the assumption that children's attitudes toward television violence are learned predispositions that can be changed by offering children new information that is incompatible with the already existing ideas (Fishbein & Ajzen, 1975; Zimbardo, Ebbesen, & Maslack, 1977). The study shows that the curriculum resulted in a considerable increase in knowledge, an effect that was still observable 2 years later. The strongest curriculum effects on children's attitudes toward television violence were found among children who had a relatively high knowledge. This finding lends support to the assumption that the new knowledge imparted by the curriculum led to the changes found in children's attitudes toward television violence.

Quantitative interpretations compare results with predictions.

(46)   Earlier evaluative studies of television curricula established the relative effectiveness of a curriculum by comparing the results found for children who were subjected to the lessons to those found for children who had no lessons (Vooijs & van der Voort, 1990). By employing norm scores obtained from well-educated adults, the present study was able to establish

not only the relative effectiveness of the curriculum but also the extent to which the curriculum bridged the gap between children's judgments of violent programs and those of adults. The use of adult norm scores is to be recommended in further research because they enable the researcher to establish the strength of the curriculum effects.

(47)   Earlier evaluative studies of television curricula usually did not establish whether the curriculum effects depended on child characteristics (Vooijs & van der Voort, 1990). Because a great number of child variables were included in the present study, it was possible to establish which types of children benefited most from the lessons. Hardly any interactions between child variables and curriculum effects were found. Therefore, all children benefited from the lessons, irrespective of children's viewing frequency, preference for violent television programs, and other child characteristics that may increase children's susceptibility to the effects of television violence (van der Voort, 1986).

(48)   Testing for effects extended in time is of particular importance for television curricula because there is a serious risk that the effects initially found evaporate in the course of time or are being annulled through maturation (Greenfield, 1984). It is remarkable that the curriculum effects on knowledge and perceived television realism were still observable 2 years after the curriculum was delivered. However, in 2 years the effects have been considerably weakened. If we really want to turn children into critical consumers of television, a one-off initiative is not sufficient. In order to make the effects of the lessons deeper and more permanent, the lessons should be included in a longer, more broadly conceived curriculum.

Reporting the research

Quantitative research reports use standard, fixed structures and evaluation criteria.

References

Anderson, J. A. (1983). Television literacy and the critical viewer. In J. Bryant & D. Anderson (Eds.), *Children's understanding of television: Research on attention and comprehension* (pp. 297–330). New York: Academic Press.

Anderson, S., Auquier, A., Hauck, W. W., Oakes, D., Vandaele, W., & Weisberg, H. I. (1980). *Statistical methods for comparitive studies.* New York: Wiley & Sons.

Andison, F. S. (1977). TV violence and viewer aggression: A cumulation of study results, 1954–1976. *Public Opinion Quarterly, 41,* 314–331.

Campbell, D. T., & Stanley, J. C. (1963). Experimental and quasi-experimental designs for research on teaching. In N. L. Gage (Ed.), *Handbook of research on teaching* (pp. 171–247). Chicago: Rand McNally.

Cline, V. B., Croft, R. G., & Courrier, S. (1973). Desensitization of children to television violence. *Journal of Personality and Social Psychology, 27,* 360–365.

Corder-Bolz, C. R. (1982). Television literacy and critical television viewing skills. In D. Pearl, L. Bouthilet, & J. Lazar (Eds.), *Television and behavior: Ten years of scientific progress and implications for the eighties; Vol. 2: Technical Reviews* (pp. 91–101). Washington, DC: U.S. Government Printing Office.

Dominick, J. R., & Greenberg, B. S. (1972). Attitudes toward violence: The interaction of television exposure, family attitudes, and social class. In G. A. Comstock & E. A. Rubinstein (Eds.), *Television and social behavior; Vol. 3: Television and adolescent aggressiveness.* Washington, DC: U.S. Government Printing Office.

Doolittle, J. C. (1975). *Immunizing children against the possible antisocial effects of viewing television: A curricular intervention.* Doctoral dissertation, University of Wisconsin-Madison (University Microfilms No. 76-8582).

Dorr, A. (1982). Television and affective development and functioning. In D. Pearl, L. Bouthilet, & J. Lazar (Eds.), *Television and behavior: Ten years of scientific progress and implications for the eighties; Vol. 2: Technical Reviews* (pp. 68–77). Washington, DC: U.S. Government Printing Office.

Drabman, R., & Thomas, M. (1974). Does media violence increase children's toleration of real-life aggression? *Developmental Psychology, 10,* 419–421.

Fishbein, M., & Ajzen, I. (1975). *Belief, attitude, intention, and behavior: An introduction to theory and research.* Reading, MA: Addison-Wesley.

Freedman, J. L. (1984). Effect of television violence on aggressiveness. *Psychological Bulletin, 96,* 227–246.

Friedrich-Cofer, L., & Huston, A. C. (1986). Television violence and aggression: The debate continues. *Psychological Bulletin, 100,* 364–371.

Geen, R. (1981). Behavioral and physiological reactions to observed violence: Effects of prior exposure to aggressive stimuli. *Journal of Personality and Social Psychology, 40,* 868–875.

Greenberg, B. S. (1975). British children and television violence. *Public Opinion Quarterly, 39,* 521–547.

Greenfield, P. M. (1984). *Mind and media: The effects of television, computers, and video games.* Cambridge, MA: Harvard University Press.

Hawkins, R. P., & Pingree, S. (1982). Television's influence on social reality. In D. Pearl, L. Bouthilet, & J. Lazar (Eds.), *Television and behavior: Ten years of scientific progress and implications for the eighties; Vol. 2: Technical Reviews* (pp. 53–67). Washington, DC: U.S. Government Printing Office.

Hearold, S. L. (1979). *Meta-analysis of the effects of television on social behavior.* Unpublished doctoral dissertation, University of Colorado.

Huesmann, L. R., Eron, L. D., Klein, R., Brice, P., & Fischer, P. (1983). Mitigating the imitation of aggressive behavior by changing children's attitudes about media violence. *Journal of Personality and Social Psychology, 44,* 899–910.

Kirk, R. E. C. (1968). *Experimental design.* Belmont, CA: Brooks/Cole.

Leifer, A., & Roberts, D. (1972). Children's response to television violence. In J. Murray, E. Rubinstein, & G. Comstock (Eds.), *Television and social behavior (Vol. 2).* Washington, DC: U.S. Government Printing Office.

Leyens, J. P., Herman, G., & Dunand, M. (1982). The influence of an audience upon the reactions to filmed violence. *European Journal of Social Psychology, 12,* 131–142.

Morison, P., Kelly, H., & Gardner, H. (1981). Reasoning about the realities on television: A developmental study. *Journal of Broadcasting, 26,* 229–242.

Pearl, D. (1982). *Television and behavior: Ten years of scientific progress and implications for the eighties; Vol. 1: Summary Report,* Washington, DC: U.S. Government Printing Office.

Potter, W. J., & Ware, W. (1987). An analysis of the context of antisocial acts on prime-time television. *Communication Research, 14,* 664–686.

Thomas, M. H., Horton, R. W., Lippincott, E. C., & Drabman, R. S. (1977). Desensitization to portrayals of real-life aggression as a function of exposure to television violence. *Journal of Personality and Social Psychology, 35,* 450–458.

van der Voort, T. H. A. (1986). *Television violence: A child's-eye view.* Amsterdam: North Holland.

Vooijs, M. W., & van der Voort, T. H. A. (1990). Teaching television: The effects of critical television viewing curricula. *International Journal of Educational Research, 14,* 543–552.

Zillman, D. (1982). Television viewing and arousal. In D. Pearl, L. Bouthilet, & J. Lazar (Eds.), *Television and behavior: Ten years of scientific progress and implications for the eighties; Vol. 2: Technical Reviews* (pp. 53–67). Washington, DC: U.S. Government Printing Office.

Zimbardo, P., & Ebbesen, E. B. (1970). *Influencing attitudes and changing behavior.* Reading, MA: Addison-Wesley.

Zimbardo, P., Ebbesen, E. B., & Maslack, C. (1977). *Influencing attitudes and changing behavior.* Reading, MA: Addison-Wesley.

Campus Response to a Student Gunman

Steps in the Research Process

Kelly J. Asmussen
John W. Creswell

Qualitative Characteristics

(01)

Identifying a research problem

With increasingly frequent incidents of campus violence, a small, growing scholarly literature about the subject is emerging. For instance, authors have reported on racial [12], courtship and sexually coercive [3, 7, 8], and hazing violence [24]. For the American College Personnel Association, Roark [24] and Roark and Roark [25] reviewed the forms of physical, sexual, and psychological violence on college campuses and suggested guidelines for prevention strategies. Roark [23] has also suggested criteria that high-school students might use to assess the level of violence on college campuses they seek to attend. At the national level, President Bush, in November 1989, signed into law the "Student Right-to-Know and Campus Security Act" (P.L. 101-542), which requires colleges and universities to make available to students, employees, and applicants an annual report on security policies and campus crime statistics [13].

A qualitative problem requires exploration and understanding.

Reviewing the literature

The qualitative literature plays a minor role.

(02)

One form of escalating campus violence that has received little attention is student gun violence. Recent campus reports indicate that violent crimes from thefts and burglaries to assaults and homicides are on the rise at colleges and universities [13]. College campuses have been shocked by killings such as those at The University of Iowa [16], The University of Florida [13], Concordia University in Montreal, and the University of Montreal—Ecole Polytechnique [22]. Incidents such as these raise critical concerns, such as psychological trauma, campus safety, and disruption of campus life. Aside from an occasional newspaper report, the postsecondary literature is silent on campus reactions to these tragedies; to understand them one must turn to studies about gun violence in the public school literature. This literature addresses strategies for school intervention [21, 23], provides case studies of incidents in individual schools [6, 14, 15,], and discusses the problem of students who carry weapons to school [1] and the psychological trauma that results from homicides [32].

The qualitative literature justifies the research problem.

(03)

Specifying a purpose and research questions

A need exists to study campus reactions to violence in order to build conceptual models for future study as well as to identify campus strategies and protocols for reaction. We need to understand better the psychological dimensions and organizational issues of constituents involved in and affected by these incidents. An in-depth qualitative case study exploring the context of an incident can illuminate such conceptual and pragmatic understandings. The study presented in this article is a qualitative case analysis [31] that describes and interprets a campus response to a gun incident. We asked the following exploratory research questions: What happened? Who was involved in response to the incident? What themes of response emerged during the eight-month period that followed this incident? What theoretical constructs helped us understand the campus response, and what constructs were unique to this case?

The qualitative purpose statement and research questions are broad and general.

The qualitative purpose statement and research questions seek participants' experiences.

The Incident and Response

(04)

Analyzing the data

The incident occurred on the campus of a large public university in a Midwestern city. A decade ago, this city had been designated an "all-Amer-

Kelly J. Asmussen is assistant professor of criminal justice at Peru State College, and John W. Creswell is professor of educational psychology at the University of Nebraska-Lincoln.

ican city," but more recently, its normally tranquil environment has been disturbed by an increasing number of assaults and homicides. Some of these violent incidents have involved students at the university.

(05)   The incident that provoked this study occurred on a Monday in October. A forty-three-year-old graduate student, enrolled in a senior-level actuarial science class, arrived a few minutes before class, armed with a vintage Korean War military semiautomatic rifle loaded with a thirty-round clip of thirty caliber ammunition. He carried another thirty-round clip in his pocket. Twenty of the thirty-four students in the class had already gathered for class, and most of them were quietly reading the student newspaper. The instructor was en route to class.

(06)   The gunman pointed the rifle at the students, swept it across the room, and pulled the trigger. The gun jammed. Trying to unlock the rifle, he hit the butt of it on the instructor's desk and quickly tried firing it again. Again it did not fire. By this time, most students realized what was happening and dropped to the floor, overturned their desks, and tried to hide behind them. After about twenty seconds, one of the students shoved a desk into the gunman, and students ran past him out into the hall and out of the building. The gunman hastily departed the room and went out of the building to his parked car, which he had left running. He was captured by police within the hour in a nearby small town, where he lived. Although he remains incarcerated at this time, awaiting trial, the motivations for his actions are unknown.

(07)   Campus police and campus administrators were the first to react to the incident. Campus police arrived within three minutes after they had received a telephone call for help. They spent several anxious minutes outside the building interviewing students to obtain an accurate description of the gunman. Campus administrators responded by calling a news conference for 4:00 P.M. the same day, approximately four hours after the incident. The police chief as well as the vice-chancellor of Student Affairs and two students described the incident at the news conference. That same afternoon, the Student Affairs office contacted Student Health and Employee Assistance Program (EAP) counselors and instructed them to be available for any student or staff requesting assistance. The Student Affairs office also arranged for a new location, where this class could meet for the rest of the semester. The Office of Judicial Affairs suspended the gunman from the university. The next day, the incident was discussed by campus administrators at a regularly scheduled campuswide cabinet meeting. Throughout the week, Student Affairs received several calls from students and from a faculty member about "disturbed" students or unsettling student relations. A counselor of the Employee Assistance Program consulted a psychologist with a specialty in dealing with trauma and responding to educational crises. Only one student immediately set up an appointment with the student health counselors. The campus and local newspapers continued to carry stories about the incident.

(08)   When the actuarial science class met for regularly scheduled classes two and four days later, the students and the instructor were visited by two county attorneys, the police chief, and two student mental health counselors who conducted "debriefing" sessions. These sessions focused on keeping students fully informed about the judicial process and having the students and the instructor, one by one, talk about their experiences and explore their feelings about the incident. By one week after the incident, the students in the class had returned to their standard class format. During this time, a few students, women who were concerned about violence in general, saw Student Health Center counselors. These counselors also fielded questions from several dozen parents who inquired about the counseling services and the level of safety on campus. Some parents also called the campus administration to ask about safety procedures.

Qualitative data analysis consists of describing information and developing themes.

(09)   In the weeks following the incident, the faculty and staff campus newsletter carried articles about post-trauma fears and psychological trauma. The campus administration wrote a letter that provided facts about the incident to the board of the university. The administration also mailed campus staff and students information about crime prevention. At least one college dean sent out a memo to staff about "aberrant student behavior," and one academic department chair requested and held an educational group session with counselors and staff on identifying and dealing with "aberrant behavior" of students.

(10)   Three distinctly different staff groups sought counseling services at the Employee Assistant Program, a program for faculty and staff, during the next several weeks. The first group had had some direct involvement with the assailant, either by seeing him the day of the gun incident or because they had known him personally. This group was concerned about securing professional help, either for the students or for those in the group who were personally experiencing effects of the trauma. The second group consisted of the "silent connection," individuals who were indirectly involved and yet emotionally traumatized. This group recognized that their fears were a result of the gunman incident, and they wanted to deal with these fears before they escalated. The third group consisted of staff who had previously experienced a trauma, and this incident had retriggered their fears. Several employees were seen by the EAP throughout the next month, but no new groups or delayed stress cases were reported. The EAP counselors stated that each group's reactions were normal responses. Within a month, although public discussion of the incident had subsided, the EAP and Student Health counselors began expressing the need for a coordinated campus plan to deal with the current as well as any future violent incident.

The Research Study

Collecting data

(11)   We began our study two days after the incident. Our first step was to draft a research protocol for approval by the university administration and the Institutional Review Board. We made explicit that we would not become involved in the investigation of the gunman or in the therapy to students or staff who had sought assistance from counselors. We also limited our study to the reactions of groups on campus rather than expand it to include off-campus groups (for example, television and newspaper coverage). This bounding of the study was consistent with an exploratory qualitative case study design [31], which was chosen because models and variables were not available for assessing a campus reaction to a gun incident in higher education. In the constructionist tradition, this study incorporated the paradigm assumptions of an emerging design, a context-dependent inquiry, and an inductive data analysis [10]. We also bounded the study by time (eight months) and by a single case (the campus community). Consistent with case study design [17, 31], we identified campus administrators and student newspaper reporters as multiple sources of information for initial interviews. Later we expanded interviews to include a wide array of campus informants, using a semistructured interview protocol that consisted of five questions: What has been your role in the incident? What has happened since the event that you have been involved in? What has been the impact of this incident on the university community? What larger ramifications, if any, exist from the incident? To whom should we talk to find out more about the campus reaction to the incident? We also gathered observational data, documents, and visual materials (see table 1 for types of information and sources).

(12)   The narrative structure was a "realist" tale [28], describing details, incorporating edited quotes from informants, and stating our interpretations of events, especially an interpretation within the framework of organizational

Qualitative researchers take a reflexive and biased approach.

Qualitative data collection involves studying a small number of individuals or sites.

Qualitative data collection is based on using protocols developed during the study.

Qualitative data analysis consists of text analysis.

TABLE 1
Data Collection Matrix—Type of Information by Source

Information/Information Source	Interviews	Observations	Documents	Audio-Visual Materials
Students involved	Yes		Yes	
Students at large	Yes			
Central administration	Yes		Yes	
Campus police	Yes	Yes		
Faculty	Yes	Yes	Yes	
Staff	Yes			
Physical plant		Yes	Yes	
News reporters/papers/T.V.	Yes		Yes	Yes
Student health counselors	Yes			
Employee Assistance Program counselors	Yes			
Trauma expert	Yes		Yes	Yes
Campus businesses			Yes	
Board members			Yes	

Qualitative data collection involves gathering text or image data.

and psychological issues. We verified the description and interpretation by taking a preliminary draft of the case to select informants for feedback and later incorporating their comments into the final study [17, 18]. We gathered this feedback in a group interview where we asked: Is our description of the incident and the reaction accurate? Are the themes and constructs we have identified consistent with your experiences? Are there some themes and constructs we have missed? Is a campus plan needed? If so, what form should it take?

Analyzing the data

Themes

Denial

(13)   Several weeks later we returned to the classroom where the incident occurred. Instead of finding the desks overturned, we found them to be neatly in order; the room was ready for a lecture or discussion class. The hallway outside the room was narrow, and we visualized how students, on that Monday in October, had quickly left the building, unaware that the gunman, too, was exiting through this same passageway. Many of the students in the hallway during the incident had seemed unaware of what was going on until they saw or heard that there was a gunman in the building. Ironically though, the students had seemed to ignore or deny their dangerous situation. After exiting the building, instead of seeking a hiding place that would be safe, they had huddled together just outside the building. None of the students had barricaded themselves in classrooms or offices or had exited at a safe distance from the scene in anticipation that the gunman might return. "People wanted to stand their ground and stick around," claimed a campus police officer. Failing to respond to the potential danger, the class members had huddled together outside the building, talking nervously. A few had been openly emotional and crying. When asked about their mood, one of the students had said, "Most of us were kidding about it." Their conversations had led one to believe that they were dismissing the incident as though it were trivial and as though no one had actually been in danger. An investigating campus police officer was not surprised by the students' behavior:

> It is not unusual to see people standing around after one of these types of incidents. The American people want to see excitement and have a morbid curiosity. That is why you see spectators hanging around bad accidents. They do not

Qualitative data analysis consists of describing information and developing themes.

seem to understand the potential danger they are in and do not want to leave until they are injured.

(14)   This description corroborates the response reported by mental health counselors: an initial surrealistic first reaction. In the debriefing by counselors, one female student had commented, "I thought the gunman would shoot out a little flag that would say 'bang.' " For her, the event had been like a dream. In this atmosphere no one from the targeted class had called the campus mental health center in the first twenty-four hours following the incident, although they knew that services were available. Instead, students described how they had visited with friends or had gone to bars; the severity of the situation had dawned on them later. One student commented that he had felt fearful and angry only after he had seen the television newscast with pictures of the classroom the evening of the incident.

(15)   Though some parents had expressed concern by phoning counselors, the students' denial may have been reinforced by parent comments. One student reported that his parents had made comments like, "I am not surprised you were involved in this. You are always getting yourself into things like this!" or "You did not get hurt. What is the big deal? Just let it drop!" One student expressed how much more traumatized he had been as a result of his mother's dismissal of the event. He had wanted to have someone whom he trusted willing to sit down and listen to him.

Fear

(16)   Our visit to the classroom suggested a second theme: the response of fear. Still posted on the door several weeks after the incident, we saw the sign announcing that the class was being moved to another undisclosed building and that students were to check with a secretary in an adjoining room about the new location. It was in this undisclosed classroom, two days after the incident, that two student mental health counselors, the campus police chief, and two county attorneys had met with students in the class to discuss fears, reactions, and thoughts. Reactions of fear had begun to surface in this first "debriefing" session and continued to emerge in a second session.

(17)   The immediate fear for most students centered around the thought that the alleged assailant would be able to make bail. Students felt that the assailant might have harbored resentment toward certain students and that he would seek retribution if he made bail. "I think I am going to be afraid when I go back to class. They can change the rooms, but there is nothing stopping him from finding out where we are!" said one student. At the first debriefing session the campus police chief was able to dispel some of this fear by announcing that during the initial hearing the judge had denied bail. This announcement helped to reassure some students about their safety. The campus police chief thought it necessary to keep the students informed of the gunman's status, because several students had called his office to say that they feared for their safety if the gunman were released.

(18)   During the second debriefing session, another fear surfaced: the possibility that a different assailant could attack the class. One student reacted so severely to this potential threat that, according to one counselor, since the October incident, "he had caught himself walking into class and sitting at a desk with a clear shot to the door. He was beginning to see each classroom as a 'battlefield.' " In this second session students had sounded angry, they expressed feeling violated, and finally began to admit that they felt unsafe. Yet only one female student immediately accessed the available mental health services, even though an announcement had been made that any student could obtain free counseling.

(19)   The fear students expressed during the "debriefing" sessions mirrored a more general concern on campus about increasingly frequent violent acts

in the metropolitan area. Prior to this gun incident, three young females and a male had been kidnapped and had later been found dead in a nearby city. A university football player who experienced a psychotic episode had severely beaten a woman. He had later suffered a relapse and was shot by police in a scuffle. Just three weeks prior to the October gun incident, a female university student had been abducted and brutally murdered, and several other homicides had occurred in the city. As a student news reporter commented, "This whole semester has been a violent one."

Safety

(20)   The violence in the city that involved university students and the subsequent gun incident that occurred in a campus classroom shocked the typically tranquil campus. A counselor aptly summed up the feelings of many: "When the students walked out of that classroom, their world had become very chaotic; it had become very random, something had happened that robbed them of their sense of safety." Concern for safety became a central reaction for many informants.

(21)   When the chief student affairs officer described the administration's reaction to the incident, he listed the safety of students in the classroom as his primary goal, followed by the needs of the news media for details about the case, helping all students with psychological stress, and providing public information on safety. As he talked about the safety issue and the presence of guns on campus, he mentioned that a policy was under consideration for the storage of guns used by students for hunting. Within four hours after the incident, a press conference was called during which the press was briefed not only on the details of the incident, but also on the need to ensure the safety of the campus. Soon thereafter the university administration initiated an informational campaign on campus safety. A letter, describing the incident, was sent to the university board members. (One board member asked, "How could such an incident happen at this university?") The Student Affairs Office sent a letter to all students in which it advised them of the various dimensions of the campus security office and of the types of services it provided. The Counseling and Psychological Services of the Student Health Center promoted their services in a colorful brochure, which was mailed to students in the following week. It emphasized that services were "confidential, accessible, and professional." The Student Judiciary Office advised academic departments on various methods of dealing with students who exhibited abnormal behavior in class. The weekly faculty newsletter stressed that staff needed to respond quickly to any post-trauma fears associated with this incident. The campus newspaper quoted a professor as saying, "I'm totally shocked that in this environment, something like this would happen." Responding to the concerns about disruptive students or employees, the campus police department sent plainclothes officers to sit outside offices whenever faculty and staff indicated concerns.

(22)   An emergency phone system, Code Blue, was installed on campus only ten days after the incident. These thirty-six ten-foot-tall emergency phones, with bright blue flashing lights, had previously been approved, and specific spots had already been identified from an earlier study. "The phones will be quite an attention getter," the director of the Telecommunications Center commented. "We hope they will also be a big detractor [to crime]." Soon afterwards, in response to calls from concerned students, trees and shrubbery in poorly lit areas of campus were trimmed.

(23)   Students and parents also responded to these safety concerns. At least twenty-five parents called the Student Health Center, the university police, and the Student Affairs Office during the first week after the incident to in-

quire what kind of services were available for their students. Many parents had been traumatized by the news of the event and immediately demanded answers from the university. They wanted assurances that this type of incident would not happen again and that their child was safe on the campus. Undoubtedly, many parents also called their children during the weeks immediately following the incident. The students on campus responded to these safety concerns by forming groups of volunteers who would escort anyone on campus, male or female, during the evening hours.

(24)   Local businesses profited by exploiting the commercial aspects of the safety needs created by this incident. Various advertisements for self-defense classes and protection devices inundated the newspapers for several weeks. Campus and local clubs who offered self-defense classes filled quickly, and new classes were formed in response to numerous additional requests. The campus bookstore's supply of pocket mace and whistles was quickly depleted. The campus police received several inquiries by students who wanted to purchase handguns to carry for protection. None were approved, but one wonders whether some guns were not purchased by students anyway. The purchase of cellular telephones from local vendors increased sharply. Most of these purchases were made by females; however, some males also sought out these items for their safety and protection. Not unexpectedly, the price of some products was raised as much as 40 percent to capitalize on the newly created demand. Student conversations centered around the purchase of these safety products: how much they cost, how to use them correctly, how accessible they would be if students should need to use them, and whether they were really necessary.

Retriggering

(25)   In our original protocol, which we designed to seek approval from the campus administration and the Institutional Review Board, we had outlined a study that would last only three months—a reasonable time, we thought, for this incident to run its course. But during early interviews with counselors, we were referred to a psychologist who specialized in dealing with "trauma" in educational settings. It was this psychologist who mentioned the theme of "retriggering." Now, eight months later, we begin to understand how, through "retriggering," that October incident could have a long-term affect on this campus.

(26)   This psychologist explained retriggering as a process by which new incidents of violence would cause individuals to relive the feelings of fear, denial, and threats to personal safety that they had experienced in connection with the original event. The counseling staffs and violence expert also stated that one should expect to see such feelings retriggered at a later point in time, for example, on the anniversary date of the attack or whenever newspapers or television broadcasts mentioned the incident again. They added that a drawn-out judicial process, during which a case were "kept alive" through legal maneuvering, could cause a long period of retriggering and thereby greatly thwart the healing process. The fairness of the judgment of the court as seen by each victim, we were told, would also influence the amount of healing and resolution of feelings that could occur.

(27)   As of this writing, it is difficult to detect specific evidence of retriggering from the October incident, but we discovered the potential consequences of this process firsthand by observing the effects of a nearly identical violent gun incident that had happened some eighteen years earlier. A graduate student carrying a rifle had entered a campus building with the intention of shooting the department chairman. The student was seeking revenge, because several years earlier he had flunked a course taught by

(28)

this professor. This attempted attack followed several years of legal maneuvers to arrest, prosecute, and incarcerate this student, who, on more than one occasion, had tried to carry out his plan but each time had been thwarted by quick-thinking staff members who would not reveal the professor's whereabouts. Fortunately, no shots were ever fired, and the student was finally apprehended and arrested.

The professor who was the target of these threats on his life was seriously traumatized not only during the period of these repeated incidents, but his trauma continued even after the attacker's arrest. The complex processes of the criminal justice system, which, he believed, did not work as it should have, resulted in his feeling further victimized. To this day, the feelings aroused by the original trauma are retriggered each time a gun incident is reported in the news. He was not offered professional help from the university at any time; the counseling services he did receive were secured through his own initiative. Eighteen years later his entire department is still affected in that unwritten rules for dealing with disgruntled students and for protecting this particular professor's schedule have been established.

Campus Planning

(29)

The question of campus preparedness surfaced during discussions with the psychologist about the process of "debriefing" individuals who had been involved in the October incident [19]. Considering how many diverse groups and individuals had been affected by this incident, a final theme that emerged from our data was the need for a campuswide plan. A counselor remarked, "We would have been inundated had there been twenty-five to thirty deaths. We need a mobilized plan of communication. It would be a wonderful addition to the campus considering the nature of today's violent world." It became apparent during our interviews that better communication could have occurred among the constituents who responded to this incident. Of course, one campus police officer noted, "We can't have an officer in every building all day long!" But the theme of being prepared across the whole campus was mentioned by several individuals.

(30)

The lack of a formal plan to deal with such gun incidents was surprising, given the existence of formal written plans on campus that addressed various other emergencies: bomb threats, chemical spills, fires, earthquakes, explosions, electrical storms, radiation accidents, tornadoes, hazardous material spills, snow storms, and numerous medical emergencies. Moreover, we found that specific campus units had their own protocols that had actually been used during the October gun incident. For example, the police had a procedure and used that procedure for dealing with the gunman and the students at the scene; the EAP counselors debriefed staff and faculty; the Student Health counselors used a "debriefing process" when they visited the students twice in the classroom following the incident. The question that concerned us was, what would a campuswide plan consist of, and how would it be developed and evaluated?

(31)

As shown in table 2, using evidence gathered in our case, we assembled the basic questions to be addressed in a plan and cross-referenced these questions to the literature about post-trauma stress, campus violence and the disaster literature (for a similar list drawn from the public school literature, see Poland and Pitcher [21]). Basic elements of a campus plan to enhance communication across units should include determining what the rationale for the plan is; who should be involved in its development; how it should be coordinated; how it should be staffed; and what specific procedures should be followed. These procedures might include responding to an immediate crisis, making the campus safe, dealing with external groups, and providing for the psychological welfare of victims.

TABLE 2
Evidence from the Case, Questions for a Campus Plan, and References

Evidence from the Case	Question for the Plan	References Useful
Need expressed by counselors	Why should a plan be developed?	Walker (1990); Bird et al. (1991)
Multiple constituents reacting to incident	Who should be involved in developing the plan?	Roark & Roark (1987); Walker (1990)
Leadership found in units with their own protocols	Should the leadership for coordinating be identified within one office?	Roark & Roark (1987)
Several unit protocols being used in incident	Should campus units be allowed their own protocols?	Roark & Roark (1987)
Questions raised by students reacting to case	What types of violence should be covered in the plan?	Roark (1987); Jones (1990)
Groups/individuals surfaced during our interviews	How are those likely to be affected by the incident to be identified?	Walker (1990); Bromet (1990)
Comments from campus police, central administration	What provisions are made for the immediate safety of those in the incident?	
Campus environment changed after incident	How should the physical environment be made safer?	Roark & Roark (1987)
Comments from central administration	How will the external publics (e.g., press, businesses) be appraised of the incident?	Poland & Pitcher (1990)
Issue raised by counselors and trauma specialist	What are the likely sequelae of psychological events for victims?	Bromet (1990); Mitchell (1983)
Issue raised by trauma specialist	What long-term impact will the incident have on victims?	Zelikoff (1987)
Procedure used by Student Health counselors	How will the victims be debriefed?	Mitchell (1983); Walker (1990)

Discussion

(32)   The themes of denial, fear, safety, retriggering, and developing a campuswide plan might further be grouped into two categories, an organizational and a psychological or social-psychological response of the campus community to the gunman incident. Organizationally, the campus units responding to the crisis exhibited both a loose coupling [30] and an interdependent communication. Issues such as leadership, communication, and authority emerged during the case analysis. Also, an environmental response developed, because the campus was transformed into a safer place for students and staff. The need for centralized planning, while allowing for autonomous operation of units in response to a crisis, called for organizational change that would require cooperation and coordination among units.

(33)   Sherrill [27] provides models of response to campus violence that reinforce as well as depart from the evidence in our case. As mentioned by Sherrill, the disciplinary action taken against a perpetrator, the group counseling of victims, and the use of safety education for the campus community were all factors apparent in our case. However, Sherrill raises issues about responses that were not discussed by our informants, such as developing procedures for individuals who are first to arrive on the scene, dealing with non-students who might be perpetrators or victims, keeping records and documents about incidents, varying responses based on the size and nature of the institution, and relating incidents to substance abuse such as drugs and alcohol.

Qualitative interpretations situate findings within larger meanings.

(34)

Interpreting the data

Also, some of the issues that we had expected after reading the literature about organizational response did not emerge. Aside from occasional newspaper reports (focused mainly on the gunman), there was little campus administrative response to the incident, which was contrary to what we had expected from Roark and Roark [25], for example. No mention was made of establishing a campus unit to manage future incidents—for example, a campus violence resource center—reporting of violent incidents [25], or conducting annual safety audits [20]. Aside from the campus police mentioning that the State Health Department would have been prepared to send a team of trained trauma experts to help emergency personnel cope with the tragedy, no discussion was reported about formal linkages with community agencies that might assist in the event of a tragedy [3]. We also did not hear directly about establishing a "command center" [14] or a crisis coordinator [21], two actions recommended by specialists on crisis situations.

(35)

On a psychological and social-psychological level, the campus response was to react to the psychological needs of the students who had been directly involved in the incident as well as to students and staff who had been indirectly affected by the incident. Not only did signs of psychological issues, such as denial, fear, and retriggering, emerge, as expected [15], gender and cultural group issues were also mentioned, though they were not discussed enough to be considered basic themes in our analysis. Contrary to assertions in the literature that violent behavior is often accepted in our culture, we found informants in our study to voice concern and fear about escalating violence on campus and in the community.

(36)

Faculty on campus were conspicuously silent on the incident, including the faculty senate, though we had expected this governing body to take up the issue of aberrant student or faculty behavior in their classrooms [25]. Some informants speculated that the faculty might have been passive about this issue because they were unconcerned, but another explanation might be that they were passive because they were unsure of what to do or whom to ask for assistance. From the students we failed to hear that they responded to their post-traumatic stress with "coping" strategies, such as relaxation, physical activity, and the establishment of normal routines [29]. Although the issues of gender and race surfaced in early conversations with informants, we did not find a direct discussion of these issues. As Bromet [5] comments, the sociocultural needs of populations with different mores must be considered when individuals assess reactions to trauma. In regard to the issue of gender, we did hear that females were the first students to seek out counseling at the Student Health Center. Perhaps our "near-miss" case was unique. We do not know what the reaction of the campus might have been, had a death (or multiple deaths) occurred; although, according to the trauma psychologist, "the trauma of no deaths is as great as if deaths had occurred." Moreover, as with any exploratory case analysis, this case has limited generalizability [17], although thematic generalizability is certainly a possibility. The fact that our information was self- reported and that we were unable to interview all students who had been directly affected by the incident so as to not intervene in student therapy or the investigation also poses a problem.

(37)

Despite these limitations, our research provides a detailed account of a campus reaction to a violent incident with the potential for making a contribution to the literature. Events emerged during the process of reaction that could be "critical incidents" in future studies, such as the victim response, media reporting, the debriefing process, campus changes, and the evolution of a campus plan. With the scarcity of literature on campus violence related to gun incidents, this study breaks new ground by identifying themes and conceptual frameworks that could be examined in future cases. On a practical level, it can benefit campus administrators who are looking for a plan to respond to campus violence, and it focuses attention on questions that need to be addressed in such a plan. The large number of different groups of people who were affected by this particular gunman incident shows the complexity of responding to a campus crisis and should alert college personnel to the need for preparedness.

Epilogue

(38)

As we conducted this study, we asked ourselves whether we would have had access to informants if someone had been killed. This "near miss" incident provided a unique research opportunity, which could, however, only approximate an event in which a fatality had actually occurred. Our involvement in this study was serendipitous, for one of us had been employed by a correctional facility and therefore had direct experience with gunmen such as the individual in our case; the other was a University of Iowa graduate and thus familiar with the setting and circumstances surrounding another violent incident there in 1992. These experiences obviously affected our assessment of this case by drawing our attention to the campus response in the first plan and to psychological reactions like fear and denial. At the time of this writing, campus discussions have been held about adapting the in-place campus emergency preparedness plan to a critical incident management team concept. Counselors have met to discuss coordinating the activities of different units in the event of another incident, and the police are working with faculty members and department staff to help identify potentially violence-prone students. We have the impression that, as a result of this case study, campus personnel see the interrelatedness and the large number of units that may be involved in a single incident. The anniversary date passed without incident or acknowledgment in the campus newspaper. As for the gunman, he is still incarcerated awaiting trial, and we wonder, as do some of the students he threatened, if he will seek retribution against us for writing up this case if he is released. The campus response to the October incident continues.

Reporting the research

Qualitative researchers take a reflexive and biased approach.

Qualitative research reports use flexible and emerging structures and evaluation criteria.

References

1. Asmussen, K. J. "Weapon Possession in Public High Schools." *School Safety* (Fall 1992), 28–30.
2. Bird, G. W., S. M. Stith, and J. Schladale. "Psychological Resources, Coping Strategies, and Negotiation Styles as Discriminators of Violence in Dating Relationships." *Family Relations,* 40 (1991), 45–50.
3. Bogal-Allbritten, R., and W. Allbritten. "Courtship Violence on Campus: A Nationwide Survey of Student Affairs Professionals." *NASPA Journal,* 28 (1991), 312–18.
4. Boothe, J. W., T. M. Flick, S. P. Kirk, L. H. Bradley, and K. E. Keough. "The Violence at Your Door," *Executive Educator* (February 1993), 16–22.
5. Bromet, E. J. "Methodological Issues in the Assessment of Traumatic Events." *Journal of Applied Social Psychology,* 20 (1990), 1719–24.
6. Bushweller, K. "Guards with Guns." *The American School Board Journal* (January 1993), 34–36.
7. Copenhaver, S., and E. Grauerholz. "Sexual Victimization among Sorority Women." *Sex Roles: A Journal of Research,* 24 (1991), 31–41.
8. Follingstad, D., S. Wright, S. Lloyd, and J. Sebastian. "Sex Differences in Motivations and Effects in Dating Violence." *Family Relations,* 40 (1991), 51–57.
9. Gordon, M. T., and S. Riger. *The Female Fear,* Urbana and Chicago: University of Illinois Press, 1991.
10. Guba, E., and Y. Lincoln. "Do Inquiry Paradigms Imply Inquiry Methodologies?" In *Qualitative Approaches to Evaluation in Education,* edited by D. M. Fetterman. New York: Praeger, 1988.

11. Johnson, K. "The Tip of the Iceberg." *School Safety* (Fall 1992), 24–26.

12. Jones, D. J. "The College Campus as a Microcosm of U.S. Society: The Issue of Racially Motivated Violence." *The Urban League Review,* 13 (1990), 129–39.

13. Legislative Update. "Campuses Must Tell Crime Rates." *School Safety* (Winter 1991), 31.

14. Long, N. J. "Managing a Shooting Incident." *Journal of Emotional and Behavioral Problems,* 1 (1992), 23–26.

15. Lowe, J. A. "What We Learned: Some Generalizations in Dealing with a Traumatic Event at Cokeville." Paper presented at the Annual Meeting of the National School Boards Association, San Francisco, Calif., April 4–7, 1987.

16. Mann, J. *Los Angeles Times Magazine,* 2 June 1992, pp. 26–27, 32, 46–47.

17. Merriam, S. B. *Case Study Research in Education: A Qualitative Approach.* San Francisco: Jossey-Bass, 1988.

18. Miles, M. B., and A. M. Huberman. *Qualitative Data Analysis: A Sourcebook of New Methods.* Beverly Hills, Calif.: Sage Publications, 1984.

19. Mitchell, J. "When Disaster Strikes." *Journal of Emergency Medical Services* (January 1983), 36–39.

20. NSSC Report on School Safety. "Preparing Schools for Terroristic Attacks." *School Safety* (Winter 1991), 18–19.

21. Poland, S., and G. Pitcher. *Crisis Intervention in the Schools.* New York: Guilford Press, 1992.

22. Quimet, M. "The Polytechnique Incident and Imitative Violence against Women," *SSR,* 76 (1992), 45–47.

23. Roark, M. L. "Helping High School Students Assess Campus Safety." *The School Counselor,* 39 (1992), 251–56.

24. ———. "Preventing Violence on College Campuses." *Journal of Counseling and Development,* 65 (1987), 367–70.

25. Roark, M. L., and E. W. Roark. "Administrative Responses to Campus Violence." Paper presented at the Annual Meeting of the American College Personnel Association/National Association of Student Personnel Administrators. Chicago, 15–18 March 1987.

26. "School Crisis: Under Control" (1991). (1/2″ VHS cassette tape) National School Safety Center, A partnership of Pepperdine University and the United States Departments of Justice and Education.

27. Sherill, J. M., and D. G. Seigel (eds.). *Responding to Violence on Campus.* New Directions for Student Services, No. 47. San Francisco: Jossey-Bass, Fall 1989.

28. Van Maanen, J. *Tales of the Field.* Chicago and London: The University of Chicago Press, 1988.

29. Walker, G. "Crisis-Care in Critical Incident Debriefing." *Death Studies,* 14 (1990), 121–33.

30. Weick, K. E. "Educational Organizations as Loosely Coupled Systems." *Administrative Science Quarterly,* 21 (1976), 1–19.

31. Yin, R. K. *Case Study Research, Design and Methods,* Newbury Park, Calif.: Sage Publications, 1989.

32. Zelikoff, W. L., and I. A. Hyman. "Psychological Trauma in the Schools: A Retrospective Study." Paper presented at the Annual Meeting of the National Association of School Psychologists, New Orleans, La., 4–8 March 1987.

2

Quantitative and **Qualitative Approaches**

Maria, our high school teacher enrolled in a graduate program, wonders what approach she should take for her research project at the university. She hears about a new approach called "qualitative research" and learns that several new faculty members are strong proponents of the approach. However, she also realizes that several faculty members in her program have strong beliefs about the importance of collecting "hard" quantitative data instead of "soft" qualitative data. Maria thinks, "How do I choose between quantitative and qualitative research?"

Maria will need to look at several factors before making her decision. In order to make an informed choice, she needs to learn how quantitative and qualitative research differ. Moreover, since she will engage in research, she must apply the approach chosen to the steps in the research process. The way she will implement the steps differs depending on whether the study approach is quantitative or qualitative. For example, the selection of an approach will determine the wording of questions, the types of data collected, the procedures of analysis, and the format of the written report. Knowing these distinctions helps researchers design studies that meet the accepted criteria of each approach, resulting in a more credible study. In addition, recognizing the major characteristics of each approach assists readers in understanding and interpreting a published study.

This chapter focuses on 14 characteristics that differentiate quantitative research from qualitative research. Each characteristic will be applied within the context of the steps of the research process. To provide this framework we will begin with an introduction based on the two articles you have been assigned, the quantitative television violence study (Vooijs & van der Voort, 1993) and the qualitative gunman incident study (Asmussen & Creswell, 1995). We will also briefly sketch the historical development of quantitative and qualitative research and end the chapter with reasons you might choose one approach over the other.

By the end of this chapter, you should be able to:

▶ Identify major events in the historical development of quantitative and qualitative research.
▶ List the characteristics of both quantitative and qualitative research.
▶ Describe procedures for implementing the two approaches at each step of the research process.

▶ Describe the types of research designs typically associated with quantitative and qualitative research.

▶ Identify three criteria useful in choosing either the quantitative or qualitative approach for research.

ANALYZING THE INTENT OF THE TELEVISION VIOLENCE AND THE GUNMAN INCIDENT STUDIES

At the end of Chapter 1 you were asked to read two published journal articles. The journal articles address the potential of violence in the lives of children or young people. Beyond this common theme, they also illustrate several differences between quantitative and qualitative research. The articles are chosen to represent two different approaches to educational research. In the television violence study (Vooijs & van der Voort, 1993) we see a *quantitative approach* to research; in the gunman incident study (Asmussen & Creswell, 1995), we see a *qualitative approach* to inquiry.

Let's first summarize the overall intent of the television violence study (Vooijs & van der Voort, 1993). The authors of this *quantitative* study are concerned about the use of violence on television and how children react to it. They present a study to see if a special in-school curriculum for fourth-, fifth-, and sixth-grade children positively impacts the attitudes of children toward violence on television (see Paragraph 07). To examine this impact, the authors assign students to two groups (a control and experimental group), measure their attitudes toward television violence, and then provide the experimental group with a nine-lesson curriculum. The curriculum's intent is to instruct the children to take the violent actions in television films more seriously, to question violent actions, and to make the children more aware of the unrealistic nature of dramatized violence (Paragraphs 08–10). After concluding this curriculum, the researchers again assess the children's attitudes toward television violence and find that in as few as nine lessons, the children acquire a more critical attitude toward television violence (Paragraph 41).

Let's turn to a different type of study. The impact of potential violence on a college campus is the focus of the *qualitative* study (Asmussen & Creswell, 1995). This study explores a campus reaction to a gunman incident in which a student attempts to fire a gun at his classmates in a university classroom. Fortunately, the gun jams and the gunman panics and leaves the classroom. The gunman is later caught by police in a small town 12 miles south of the university community. This study traces how the campus reacts to this event over an eight-month period and it explores the diverse perspectives of students, faculty, psychologists, health center personnel, media, and administrators. From this data, the authors report five themes about the campus response to the incident.

In summarizing the major features of the two studies, we have focused attention on the *subject matter* of the studies. As you prepare to be an educational researcher, set aside for a moment the actual information in each study and reflect on the *research process* at work in each article.

In the television violence *quantitative* study, the researchers:	In the gunman incident, a *qualitative* research study, the researchers:
▶ obtain data consisting of numbers (i.e., scores from children on instruments)	▶ collect data consisting of words (i.e., text from participants during interviews)

- analyze these numbers using mathematical procedures (i.e., statistics)
- ask specific, narrow questions
- predict that the curriculum would impact student attitudes toward television
- remain invisible in the written report (i.e., do not mention themselves)

- analyze these words by describing events and deriving themes
- ask broad, general questions
- make no prediction about the campus response, but rely on participants to shape what they report
- remain visible and present in the written report (i.e., mention themselves)

Perhaps the differences between the two studies are easy to see. Are you beginning to recognize the ways in which the authors of these two studies differed in their research approaches to their subject matter? Before examining additional differences, we will briefly discuss the evolution of both approaches to research so that their meaning will become more evident.

A BRIEF HISTORY OF EDUCATIONAL RESEARCH

The 20th century began with one major approach to educational research and ended with two major approaches. This change unfolded slowly during the first half of the century but manifested itself dramatically during the last half of the century. The development of the two approaches—quantitative and qualitative research—is not a case of one approach replacing the other; instead, it reflects the addition of qualitative inquiry to the traditional quantitative approach. Today, both approaches have legitimacy as modes of educational research.

Whether we have *only* two approaches is subject to debate. Some authors feel that there are three major approaches (quantitative, qualitative, and critical, as suggested by Denzin & Lincoln, 1994). Others advance four possibilities (radical humanist, radical structuralist, interpretivist, and functionalist, as discussed by Burrell & Morgan, 1979). Undoubtedly, educators and social scientists will continue to debate the number and types of inquiry available to researchers. But, regardless of perspective, we cannot deny the widespread use and popularity of two dominant approaches: quantitative and qualitative.

One dilemma in this debate has been whether research is "purely" quantitative or "purely" qualitative, and as such is guided by one of two opposite and dichotomous approaches (see Firestone, 1987, and Smith, 1983), or whether research lies somewhere on a continuum (Reichardt & Cook, 1979). For example, in a study conducted about teenage smoking in high schools, researchers can:

- collect quantitative numbers to indicate the frequency of adolescent smoking
- gather interview data that includes words (or text) of students as they describe their tobacco use experiences

This example illustrates how a study can consist of both quantitative and qualitative elements, although in this case the emphasis of the study may be more heavily weighted toward one end of the continuum if the researchers stress the frequency of teenage smoking.

Figure 2.1 shows three possible configurations of weight. In research study A, the inquiry contains more qualitative than quantitative characteristics, while in study B the emphasis is reversed. In study C, the emphasis is tipped more heavily toward qualitative research. As you read about the two approaches in this and other chapters, remember to keep in mind that actual research is not based on a dichotomy, but on a *tendency* to be either quantitative or qualitative. Rarely is it a "pure" case of one or the other.

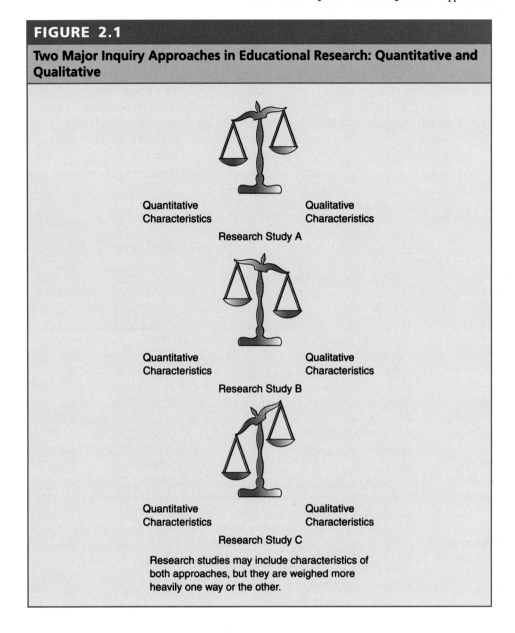

FIGURE 2.1

Two Major Inquiry Approaches in Educational Research: Quantitative and Qualitative

Quantitative   Qualitative
Characteristics   Characteristics

Research Study A

Quantitative   Qualitative
Characteristics   Characteristics

Research Study B

Quantitative   Qualitative
Characteristics   Characteristics

Research Study C

Research studies may include characteristics of
both approaches, but they are weighed more
heavily one way or the other.

The Development of Quantitative Research

To fully understand how the two approaches differ, we need to take a brief excursion into history (see De Landsheere, 1988, and Travers, 1992, for an expanded discussion). It is remarkable how similar quantitative research is today with its beginnings during the late 19th and early 20th centuries.

The initial ideas about educational research borrow heavily from the physical sciences, such as physics and chemistry. Just as atoms and molecules are subject to predictable laws and axioms, so also are patterns of children's behaviors in schools. Following this line of logic, early quantitative researchers begin identifying educational patterns by assessing or measuring individual abilities, collecting scores (or numbers) from individuals, and employing procedures of psychological experiments and large-scale surveys. In the history of the development of quantitative research, three historical trends are present: statistical procedures, test and measurement practices, and research designs. A chronology of these trends is shown in Table 2.1.

In statistics, quantitative research has emerged from 19th-century ideas of correlating and relating two or more ideas. Soon examining related ideas expanded into examining groups, and in the early 20th century researchers were comparing the average scores of groups of individuals in educational settings. These two initial ideas—relating ideas and

TABLE 2.1

Select Historical Developments in Quantitative Research

Statistical Procedures	Tests and Measurement Practices	Research Designs
• 1980s—challenging traditional approaches to statistical testing by examining the magnitude of relationships among variables, called effect size estimates	• 1980s—using standardized testing cutoff scores for children in schools	• 1990s—focusing on the sensitivity and power of experiments (Lipsey, 1990)
• 1970s—developing techniques for pooling data across several studies, called meta-analysis	• 1970s—developing standards for psychological and educational testing	• 1970s—elaborating the types of validity by Cook and Campbell (1979)
• 1970s—identifying models that examine causal relations among variables, called structural equation modeling	• 1960s—developing a theory that explains how items on an instrument differ in difficulty and discrimination, called item response theory	• 1960s—identifying types of quantitative research designs by Kerlinger (1964)
• 1970s—specifying models for studying the relationship among variables that are categorical, called log-linear models	• 1950s—inventing machinery for scoring tests	• 1960s—specifying the types of experiments available to researchers by Campbell and Stanley (1963)
• 1920s—using procedures for drawing conclusions about a population from a sample, called inferential statistics	• 1940s—using tests for selecting personnel during WWII	• 1930s—conducting a study over time by the Progressive Education Association
• 1900s—using comparisons of differences between group means, called *t*-tests	• 1930s—developing first achievement tests	• 1930s—identifying procedures for conducting experiments (Fisher, 1935)
• 1900s—applying procedures for reducing a large number of variables to a smaller set, called factor analysis	• 1930s—founding of the Buros Institute for Mental Measurement	• 1910s—using special designs for experiments, such as Thorndike's Latin Square designs
• 1890s—identifying the ability to predict scores using information from correlations, called a regression line	• 1920s—administrating the first Scholastic Aptitude Test (SAT)	• 1900s—surveying school dropouts by Thorndike
• 1880s—being able to associate or correlate two variables, called correlation analysis	• 1910s—using tests by the Army during WWI	• 1900s—comparing groups in experiments by Schuyten
	• 1890s—developing the first mental tests	• 1880s—studying children by G. Stanley Hall

Source: Abelson, 1995; De Landsheere, 1998; Vogt, 1999

comparing groups—are the origin of common statistics used today. Over time, these elementary statistical ideas have grown into complex models that interrelate numerous variables and test cause-and-effect or stimulus-response relationships. For example, does time on task cause better grades? How does depression relate to tobacco use among students?

In measurement, the concept of testing the mental ability of individuals originated in the late 19th century. With the advent of both World Wars, researchers with knowledge of testing and measurement were sought because of the military's need to select individuals and determine their readiness for combat. Also during the early 20th century, the idea of measuring an individual's performance or achievement developed. Standardized tests, such as the Scholastic Achievement Test (SAT), enabled college admissions personnel to predict an individual's future academic performance. By mid-century, measurement specialists were testing and using scoring machinery to facilitate scoring exams. Today, assessment extends to public school debates about standardized performance assessments for children in subjects such as math and science. For example, results of these assessments are often used to allow children to advance to the next grade or to permit inclusion in a gifted education program.

When compared with research designs today, the early approaches were simple and uncomplicated. Surveys of educational issues in the community began in the late 19th century. By the early 20th century, researchers were conducting educational experiments, drawing on the lessons learned from psychology. The idea of comparing the attitudes or performance of two groups, the basic concept behind experimental research, also took hold in the early 20th century. These early models of design were soon developed into more complicated designs involving multiple groups and multiple tests made by the investigators. By 1935, Fischer advanced the various forms of experimental designs, and from this point on through the 20th century, the designs became more sophisticated (e.g., following single individuals over time or alternating researcher interventions for one group). By 1963, Campbell and Stanley not only identified the various forms of experimental and quasi-experimental designs, but they also specified the strengths and weaknesses of each design. Also around this time, Kerlinger (1964) authored a book advancing the types of quantitative research designs used today, such as the experiment, the correlational study, and the descriptive survey.

These developments contributed to a major presence of quantitative research in education. Today, its stature is assessed by noting the numerous quantitative projects that are funded by federal agencies, such as the Department of Education and the National Institute of Health. Similarly, state agencies and private foundations support many quantitative projects. For example, the Spencer Foundation announced several quantitative studies in progress in their 1999 *Annual Report* (The Spencer Foundation, 1999), such as: Robert C. Calfee, "Design Experiments on Efficient and Effective Decoding—Spelling Instruction in the Primary Grades." Graduate School of Education, University of California, Irvine (p. 18).

The substantive presence of quantitative research is also seen in the numerous educational journals devoted to publishing and disseminating this form of research. For example, quantitative studies are published in the *Journal of Experimental Education,* the *Journal of Applied Measurement,* and the *Journal of Learning Disabilities.*

The Development of Qualitative Research

Today, qualitative research presents an alternative to the traditional form of quantitative research. However, its historical use in education is more recent than quantitative research. The ideas for qualitative research developed in the late 1800s and early 1900s outside of education. For example, qualitative studies of the poor in Great Britain and Europe, anthropological reports about indigenous cultures, and field work of sociologists in inner-city Chicago and with immigrants all appear in social science research up through the 1930s and 1940s (Bogdan & Biklen, 1998). However, the actual use of qualitative research in education is most apparent during the last 30 years, and a chronology of events in this brief history appears in Table 2.2. As seen in this table, three themes shape its history in education: philosophical ideas, procedural developments, and participatory and advocacy practices. Current studies today typically exhibit one or more of these themes.

By the late 1960s philosophers of education called for an alternative to the traditional quantitative approach (e.g., Guba & Lincoln, 1988). The traditional approach, they felt, re-

TABLE 2.2

Select Recent Historical Developments in Qualitative Research

Philosophical Ideas	Procedural Developments	Participatory and Advocacy Practices
• 2000s—clarifying the controversies, contradictions, and confluences among paradigms or worldviews (Denzin & Lincoln, 2000) • 1980s—identifying differences between naturalistic and traditional research (Lincoln & Guba, 1985) • 1980s—distinguishing between two philosophical approaches of idealism and realism (Smith, 1983) • 1970s—advocating an alternative approach, the naturalistic paradigm, to traditional research (Guba, 1978)	• 1990s—advancing a framework for conducting narrative research (Clandinin & Connelly, 2000) • 1990s—distinguishing among five different procedures of qualitative inquiry (Creswell, 1998) • 1990s—advancing alternative inquiry approaches (Denzin & Lincoln, 1994) • 1990s—presenting approaches to designing qualitative studies (Maxwell, 1996) • 1990s—advancing procedures for conducting grounded theory qualitative research (Strauss & Corbin, 1990) • 1990s—introducing a basic overview of qualitative research (Glesne & Peshkin, 1992) • 1990s—advancing ideas about ethnographic research (LeCompte, Millroy, & Preissle, 1992; Wolcott, 1994) • 1980s—introducing the design of qualitative research (Marshall & Rossman, 1989) • 1980s—presenting detailed procedures for qualitative data analysis (Miles & Huberman, 1984) • 1980s—introducing all aspects of designing a study (Bogdan & Biklen, 1982)	• 2000s—using collaborative, participatory approaches to research (Kemmis & McTaggart, 2000) • 1990—exploring issues about racial and cultural identity (Delgado & Stefancic, 1997) • 1990—examining a sensitivity to gay issues (Tierney, 1997) • 1990—advancing perspectives about inequality and marginalization (Carspecken, 1996) • 1990—advocating for a need to better understand racial identity (Sleeter, 1996) • 1990—examining feminist perspectives about qualitative research (Lather, 1991)

lied too much on the researcher's view of education and less on the research participant's view. Traditional investigations created a contrived situation where the research participant was "taken out" of context and placed within an experimental situation far removed from his or her personal experiences. To counter these traditional approaches, philosophers of education suggested an alternative form of research, called *naturalistic inquiry* or *constructivism,* to remedy these deficiencies (Lincoln & Guba, 1985). The central perspective of these new approaches is that educational research should consider the participant's view, describe it within a setting or context (e.g., a classroom), and explore the meaning people personally hold for educational issues. This thinking positions qualitative research as an alternative—at times adversarial—perspective to traditional research.

Another theme developed in qualitative research during the 1980s and early 1990s that softened this perspective. Several writers focused on the procedures of conducting qualitative research rather than on challenging quantitative research. Procedures such as writing qualitative research questions, conducting interviews and observations, and analyzing data for themes occupied writers' attention (Creswell, 1994, 1998; Tesch, 1990). Procedural discussions spanned from introductory steps in the qualitative research process (e.g., Glesne & Peshkin, 1992) to more complicated data analysis matrices (Miles & Huberman, 1994). Specific books constructed templates for planning qualitative dissertation and masters' theses (Creswell, 1994; Marshall & Rossman, 1995). Along with these efforts arose a discussion about "types" of qualitative research designs, such as case studies, grounded theory research, and narrative inquiry (e.g., Creswell, 1998; Strauss & Corbin, 1990; Stake, 1995) and the emergence of qualitative computer software programs for data analysis (e.g., Weitzman & Miles, 1995).

In the last decade we have seen an emergence of a third theme in educational qualitative research: participatory and advocacy practices. It developed from an impassioned concern for the inequity and needs of individuals in lower social classes, of women, and of members of certain racial groups, such as African-Americans and Hispanics (e.g., Carspecken, 1996). This theme has advocates in Denzin and Lincoln (2000) who take stock of qualitative inquiry today and report that:

- The qualitative researcher is not an objective, authoritative, politically neutral observer standing outside and above the text.
- The qualitative researcher is "historically positioned and locally situated (as) an all-too-human (observer) of the human condition." (Bruner, 1993, p. 1)
- Meaning is "radically plural, always open, and . . . there is politics in every account." (Bruner, 1993, p. 1)
- Qualitative inquiry is properly conceptualized as a civic, participatory, collaborative project. This joins the researcher and the researched in an ongoing moral dialogue. (p. 1049)

Ideas such as these challenge traditional research that holds firm to a neutral and objective stance. It also calls for the inquirers to report actively in their studies their own personal biases, values, and assumptions. It casts research into politics in which the rights of women, gays, lesbians, racial groups, and different classes in our society need to be considered, and different viewpoints emerge from both writing and reading qualitative reports. It also speaks to qualitative data collection procedures in which inquirers are sensitive to participants, actively collaborate with them (rather than *studying* them), and respect the dignity of each individual who offers data for research.

One interesting facet of these three themes is how they coalesce to shape qualitative research today. Also, proponents of all three themes form a sizable contingent of educational researchers. This diverse group presents many conference presentations at professional association meetings such as the American Educational Research Association (AERA) and at conferences specifically devoted to qualitative research. Major handbooks are available now, creating the broad landscape of qualitative research in education and in the social sciences (e.g., Denzin & Lincoln, 2000). With increasing frequency, funding agencies at the federal, state, and private levels support qualitative research projects. For example, the Spencer Foundation announced several qualitative studies in progress in their 1999 *Annual Report* (The Spencer Foundation, 1999), such as Anna Neumann, "Professors' Learning and Scholarly Identity Development in the Early Post-Tenure Career," Michigan State University (p. 39).

Major journals today also address qualitative research. Although many social science and education journals are open to publishing qualitative studies, several scholarly journals publish qualitative research, such as the *International Journal of Qualitative Studies in Education, Qualitative Inquiry, Anthropological and Education Quarterly, Qualitative Research Elementary School Journal,* and the *Journal of Counseling and Development.*

DISTINGUISHING BETWEEN QUANTITATIVE AND QUALITATIVE RESEARCH

With different historic origins, we begin to see several fundamental differences between quantitative and qualitative research. To learn more about these differences, we will continue the discussion begun in Chapter 1 about the steps in the research process. We will identify key characteristics of both quantitative and qualitative research and position these characteristics *within* the research process as shown in Figure 2.2. In this way, you will identify the differences between the two approaches in a meaningful way rather than simply learning the characteristics in an abstract sense. Understanding the characteristics within the process of research should enable you to make decisions about how to proceed (e.g., will you write research questions or hypotheses?) and how to design research within accepted practices if you plan and conduct a study. If you plan to read research, evaluate it, and use it, knowing the characteristics of each step of the process will enable you to recognize whether a published study is quantitative or qualitative. This knowledge will help you identify useful results and evaluate the quality of the study.

Let's begin with a framework that may assist you as you learn about characteristics of the two approaches within the process of research. We see in Figure 2.3 that each step in the process is implemented using either a quantitative or qualitative approach. Understanding the differences at each step, then, is important. Further, for the steps involving data collection, analysis, and report writing, more advanced procedures come into play, called "research designs." In this chapter you will be briefly introduced to each design, and they will be developed further in Part III of this text.

Identifying a Research Problem

Quantitative research is used to study research problems requiring:

▶ a description of trends or an explanation of the relationship among variables

Qualitative research is used to study research problems requiring:

▶ an exploration and understanding of a central phenomenon

In *quantitative research,* the investigator studies problems in which trends need to be described or explanations need to be developed for relationships among variables. Describing a trend means that the research problem can best be answered by a study in which the researcher seeks to establish the overall tendency of responses from individuals and to note how this tendency varies among people. For example, an investigator may seek to learn how voters describe their attitude toward a bond issue. Results from this study can

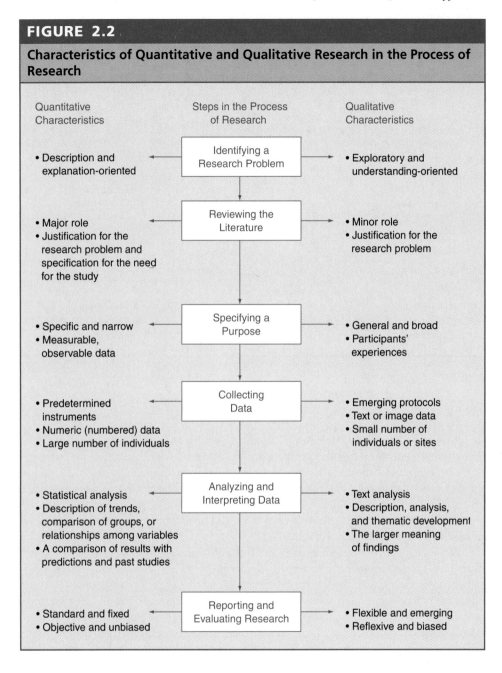

FIGURE 2.2

Characteristics of Quantitative and Qualitative Research in the Process of Research

Quantitative Characteristics	Steps in the Process of Research	Qualitative Characteristics
• Description and explanation-oriented	Identifying a Research Problem	• Exploratory and understanding-oriented
• Major role • Justification for the research problem and specification for the need for the study	Reviewing the Literature	• Minor role • Justification for the research problem
• Specific and narrow • Measurable, observable data	Specifying a Purpose	• General and broad • Participants' experiences
• Predetermined instruments • Numeric (numbered) data • Large number of individuals	Collecting Data	• Emerging protocols • Text or image data • Small number of individuals or sites
• Statistical analysis • Description of trends, comparison of groups, or relationships among variables • A comparison of results with predictions and past studies	Analyzing and Interpreting Data	• Text analysis • Description, analysis, and thematic development • The larger meaning of findings
• Standard and fixed • Objective and unbiased	Reporting and Evaluating Research	• Flexible and emerging • Reflexive and biased

inform the researcher about how a large population views an issue and how diverse their views are about the issue.

On the other hand, some quantitative research problems require that the investigator explain the extent to which two variables are related. Explaining a relationship among variables means that the researcher is interested in determining whether one or more variables might influence another variable. A detailed discussion about variables will follow in Chapter 5 (in "Describing the Family of Variables"), but for now, you need to know that a variable is an attribute (e.g., attitude toward the school bond issue) or characteristic of individuals (e.g., gender) that researchers study. For example, quantitative researchers may seek to know why certain voters register a vote against the school bond issue. The variables, gender and attitude toward the quality of the schools, may influence individual votes on the bond issue.

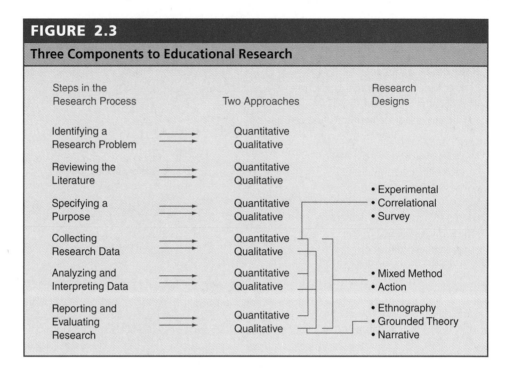

FIGURE 2.3

Three Components to Educational Research

The authors in the television violence study (Vooijs & van der Voort, 1993) describe trends on test scores and examine the relationship among variables. They record the children's test scores on several instruments, such as "readiness to see violence," and they describe average scores (means) and the variation of scores (standard deviations) in Table 1 of the article (see Paragraph 32). They also study whether one variable, the special curriculum on crime, influences the children's views toward violence on television. To examine this relationship, they investigate, for instance, whether the curriculum impacts student "approval of violence" (also see Table 1, Paragraph 32).

While quantitative research focuses on description and explanation, *qualitative research* examines a research problem in which the inquirer explores and seeks to understand a central phenomenon. An exploration means that little is known in the literature about the phenomenon of study and the researcher needs to learn more from participants. For example, we may not know much about the ways in which deaf children think when they use sign language, and qualitative research can explore this phenomenon from the perspective of the children. An understanding, on the other hand, suggests that the researcher needs to learn about the complexity of the phenomenon. The process of thinking when using sign language is a complex idea and all of the facets of it need to be studied qualitatively. A central phenomenon addressed in Chapter 5 ("Identifying the Central Phenomenon"), relates to the key idea of a qualitative study, typically expressed as a process or concept. Thus, the research problem of learning how best to teach children who are deaf requires both an exploration and an understanding of qualitative research about how the children think.

Both exploration and understanding are central features in the gunman case study (Asmussen & Creswell, 1995). In this qualitative research study, the authors are not interested in explaining the incident; rather, they seek to explore and gain a deeper understanding of how those on campus reacted to the incident (see Paragraph 03). They map the process in all of its complexity as it unfolds during an eight-month period of time following the incident.

Reviewing the Literature

In *quantitative research*, the literature:

▶ plays a major role
▶ justifies the research problem and creates a need for the direction (purpose statement and research questions or hypotheses) of the study

In *qualitative research*, the literature:

▶ plays a minor role
▶ justifies the research problem

A hallmark of *quantitative research* is a substantial literature review in a separate section at the beginning of the study. The literature plays a major role in two ways: justifying the need for the research problem and identifying the direction of the study. Justifying the research problem means that the researcher uses the literature to document the importance of the issue examined in the study. To accomplish this, a researcher searches the literature, locates studies that identify the problem as important to examine, and then cites this literature in the opening sections of a research report.

The literature also creates a need for the study, as expressed specifically in the purpose statement and the research questions or hypotheses. Identifying the direction of the study means that, based on the literature, the researcher identifies key variables worthy of study and potential relationships or trends that need to be examined. A literature review on college students, for example, may show that we know little about the problem of "binge drinking." Existing literature, however, may identify the importance of peer groups and styles of interacting among student peer groups. Thus, important research questions might address how peer groups and interaction styles influence binge drinking on college campuses. In this way, the literature in a quantitative study both documents the need to study the problem and provides direction for the research questions.

In the quantitative television violence study (Vooijs & van der Voort, 1993), extensive literature is cited at the beginning of the article (Paragraphs 01–06). In the opening passage, this literature is used to establish the importance of studying children's sensitivity to violence. The article then identifies a framework on attitude change (see Paragraph 11), and from studies of this framework, creates a need to study several variables, including the ways in which children critically process information about television violence (see Paragraph 13). In effect, the substantial literature review at the beginning of this article both justifies the importance of examining television violence and creates a need to examine a curriculum that might change children's viewing attitudes.

In *qualitative research*, the literature review plays a less substantial role at the beginning of the study. Although the inquirer may review the literature to justify the need to study the research problem, the literature does not provide major direction for the research questions. Instead, the research questions emerge during a study based on information supplied by the participants. To use the literature to foreshadow or specify the direction for the study is inconsistent with the qualitative approach of learning from participants. For example, one qualitative researcher who studied bullying in the schools cites several studies at the beginning of the research to provide evidence for the problem, but does not use the literature to specify the research questions. Instead, this researcher attempts to answer in the research the most general, open question possible, "What is bullying?", to learn how students construct their view of this experience.

The literature plays a minor role in the qualitative gunman incident study (Asmussen & Creswell, 1995). The article opens with references to support the importance of the problem of campus violence (see Paragraph 01). But in the next section of the study (Paragraph 04), the authors describe the incident, and the literature does not reappear until the final passages in the study in which the authors describe the need for campus planning. From reading this article, you can see much less literature "up front." The literature justifies the research problem and does not lead to the questions asked in the study. This means that in a qualitative study, the literature is of secondary importance while the views of the participants are of primary importance.

Specifying a Purpose for Research

In *quantitative research,* the purpose statement, research questions, or hypotheses:

▶ are specific and narrow
▶ seek measurable, observable data on variables

In *qualitative research,* the purpose statement, research questions, or hypotheses:

▶ are general and broad
▶ seek to understand the participants' experiences

In *quantitative research,* investigators ask specific, narrow questions to obtain measurable and observable data on variables. The major statements and questions of direction in a study—the purpose statement, the research questions, and the hypotheses—are specific and narrow because the researcher isolates a few variables to study. From a study of these variables, the investigator obtains data that can be measured or assessed on an instrument or observed on a scale. For example, in a study of adolescent career choices, the variable, the role of the school counselor, narrows the study to a specific variable of interest. To examine the impact of the school counselor on adolescent career choices requires obtaining data from students.

In the quantitative television violence study (Vooijs & van der Voort, 1993), the authors select (and narrow) their interest to a few variables. They wonder why children have a "readiness to see violence" or why they "approve of violence" (Paragraphs 25 and 26). They state specific questions they want answered, such as the types of children who profit most from the lessons on the crime series (see Paragraph 17). To learn this information, they obtain data from the children by collecting personal information on each child, such as gender, social economic status, grade attended, school achievement, and aggressiveness.

In *qualitative research* the purpose is much more open-ended than in quantitative research. Inquirers ask general, broad questions so that they can best learn from participants. This general direction is expressed in the purpose statement in which researchers identify a single phenomenon of interest. A qualitative study that examines the "professionalism" of teachers, for example, asks high school teachers, "What does it mean to be a professional?" This question focuses on understanding a single idea—being a professional—and the responses to it will yield qualitative data for research.

In the qualitative gunman case study (Asmussen & Creswell, 1995), the authors start with broad, open-ended questions to obtain participants' views about the incident (Paragraph 03). This questioning focuses on understanding the process of the campus reaction to the gunman incident. The researchers' intent is to allow the participants to talk openly about their experiences. For example, examine the authors' first general, broad question: "What happened?" (Paragraph 03).

Collecting Data

In *quantitative research,* the data collection consists of:

▶ collecting data on instruments identified prior to the study
▶ gathering numeric (numbered) data

▶ collecting information from a large number of individuals

In *qualitative research,* the data collection consists of:

▶ collecting data on protocols developed during the study
▶ gathering text (words) or image (picture) data

▶ collecting information from a small number of individuals or sites

In *quantitative research,* the investigator uses an instrument to measure the variables in the study. The instrument, located or developed prior to the study, is administered to participants, and the researcher collects numeric (or numbered) data. The intent of this process is to make claims or to generalize information from a small number of people to a large number. The larger the number of individuals studied, the stronger the claims. For example, on a survey to be sent to 500 parents in a school district, the researcher seeks information about parents' attitudes toward the educational needs of pregnant teenagers in the schools. The researcher selects an instrument, "Attitudes toward Education of Pregnant Teenagers," found through a search of library resources. The 500 parents who will receive this instrument represent a cross-section of people from all socioeconomic levels in the school district. After collecting and analyzing this data, the investigator will draw conclusions about all parents in this school district based on the representative sample studied.

Data collection is also an integral part of the quantitative television violence study (Vooijs & van der Voort, 1993). The authors study a large number of children (221 in the experimental group and 216 in the control group) in six different schools (Paragraph 19). They examine these large numbers of children so that they can obtain a good cross-section of the students in the six schools. In addition, the authors identify instruments for assessing the children's views toward television violence before the study begins. One instrument, for example, is the "Readiness to See Violence," a test consisting of 25 violent actions (Paragraph 25). On this instrument, the children rate their reactions to television violence, yielding numeric scores in the study.

In *qualitative research,* the inquirer does not begin data collection with a set instrument to measure distinct variables. Instead, the researcher seeks to learn from the participants in the study, and develops forms (in Chapter 7, we will call them "protocols") for recording data as the study proceeds. Examples of these forms include an "interview protocol," which consists of four or five questions, and an "observational protocol," in which the researcher records notes about the behavior of participants. Moreover, the inquirer seeks to gather text (word) or image (picture) data. From audio-recordings, transcriptions of text are typed to form a word database. Observing participants in their work or family setting, the researcher takes notes that will become a qualitative database. When young children are asked to write their thoughts in a diary, these diary entries become a text database. With each form of data, the qualitative inquirer gathers as much information as possible to collect detailed accounts for a final research report.

In the qualitative gunman case study (Asmussen & Creswell, 1995), the authors collect data from a few individuals on campus representing different constituents (e.g., administrators, counselors, "experts") (Paragraph 11). They do not use instruments constructed by other researchers; instead, they develop their own forms for recording information—an interview protocol (as discussed in Chapter 7, in "Using Protocols")—during the project (see Paragraph 11). They also take observational notes about the classroom in which the incident occurred and collect campus newspaper reactions to the crisis.

Analyzing and Interpreting Data

In *quantitative research,* the:

- data analysis consists of statistical analysis
- data analysis involves describing trends, comparing group differences, or relating variables
- interpretation compares results with prior predictions and past research

In *qualitative research,* the:

- data analysis consists of text analysis
- data analysis involves describing the information and developing themes
- interpretation situates the findings within the larger, more abstract meanings

In *quantitative research,* investigators analyze the data gathered on forms or instruments from participants using mathematical processes, called statistical procedures. This analysis consists of breaking down the data into parts to answer the research questions. Statistical procedures, such as comparing groups or relating scores for individuals, provide information to address the research questions or hypotheses. Quantitative researchers then interpret the results of this analysis in light of initial predictions or prior studies. This interpretation is an explanation as to why the results turned out the way they did, and often researchers explain how the results either support or refute the expected predictions in the study.

For example, in the quantitative television violence study (Vooijs & van der Voort, 1993), the researchers collect responses from the children and assign numbers to each child's score. They then mathematically examine the numerical differences between the group that experiences the curriculum and the group that does not, in terms of the children's views toward television violence. They examine this difference using statistical procedures, such as analysis of covariance (see Paragraph 30). For example, one statistical analysis shows that those children who experience the curriculum have a higher readiness to see violence and a decrease in their approval of violent actions of the "good guys" (Paragraph 30). The authors conclude the article with a discussion that interprets their results in comparison with the findings from other studies. In Paragraph 43, they suggest that their positive results may be partly due to the "reality content" of their lessons—an improved feature of their lessons that other authors did not consider.

In *qualitative research,* because the data consists of words or pictures, a different approach exists for data analysis. Typically, the researcher has gathered a text database, so the analysis of text consists of dividing it into groups of sentences (called text segments in Chapter 9 on "Coding Data") and determining the meaning of each segment. Rather than using statistics, the inquirer analyzes the words or pictures to describe the central phenomenon under study. This description typically includes contextual information about the people or idea being studied, such as the setting, the time, the individuals involved, and the circumstances in which the people experience the phenomenon. In some qualitative studies, the entire report is mostly a long description. In other projects, the inquirer proceeds to analyze the words or pictures to develop themes or broad categories of the participants' meaning. In using these two approaches, qualitative researchers generate a complex picture of their central phenomenon. From this complex picture, the inquirer makes an interpretation of the meaning of the data by reflecting on how the findings relate to existing research and by stating a personal reflection about the significance of the lessons learned during the study.

The authors of the qualitative gunman case study use these analysis and interpretation procedures (Asmussen & Creswell, 1995). They review their text data consisting of transcripts from interviews, written notes from observations, and documents, including newspaper accounts. They also have a videotape of a news conference filmed immediately after the incident (see Paragraph 11 for data sources). From this data (both words and images), the authors first describe chronologically the events for two weeks following the incident (Paragraphs 04–10). They then identify themes or patterns such as "Denial" (Paragraph 13) as a centerpiece of the study. Other themes portray the campus response as one of a need for safety and a need for campus planning, among others. Finally, in the discussion at the end of the article, the authors interpret the broader meaning of their description and themes (Paragraph 35), mentioning that the theme fits into larger psychological and social-psychological social science perspectives. In the Epilogue (Paragraph 38), they comment about the personal meaning of the incident.

Reporting and Evaluating Research

In *quantitative research,* the:

- research reports use standard, fixed structures and evaluative criteria

- researchers take an objective and unbiased approach

In *qualitative research,* the:

- research reports use flexible, emerging structures and evaluative criteria

- researchers take a reflexive and biased approach

In *quantitative research,* the overall format for a study follows a predictable pattern: introduction, review of the literature, methods, results, and discussion. This form creates a standardized structure for most quantitative studies. In addition, it also leads to specific criteria that researchers use to judge the quality of a quantitative research report. They are concerned about including an extensive literature review; creating testable research questions and hypotheses; using rigorous, impartial data collection procedures; selecting appropriate statistical tests; and forming interpretations that naturally flow from the data.

In addition, quantitative researchers engage in procedures to ensure that their own personal biases and values do not influence the results: They use instruments that have objective standards (such as "reliability" and "validity" as discussed in Chapter 6 on "Strategies for Locating and Selecting an Instrument"); they design studies to control for all variables that might introduce bias into a study; and they report research without referring to themselves or their personal reaction.

In the quantitative television violence study (Vooijs & van der Voort, 1993), the authors subdivide the research into standard sections typically found in quantitative studies. The headings reflect this division—research questions, method, results, and discussion (see Paragraph 15). The entire study conveys an impersonal, objective tone, and they do not bring either their biases or their personal opinions into the study. They use instruments to measure variables (Paragraphs 24–29) and employ complex statistical procedures (see Paragraph 30) to build objectivity into the study.

In *qualitative research,* on the other hand, researchers employ a wide range of formats to report their studies. Although the overall general form follows the standard steps in the process of research, the sequence of these "parts" of research tends to vary from one qualitative report to another. A study may begin with a long, personal narrative told in story form or a more objective, scientific report that resembles quantitative research. With such a variable structure, it is not surprising that the standards for evaluating qualitative research also are flexible. Qualitative reports, however, need to be realistic and persuasive in order to convince the reader that the study is an accurate and credible account. Qualitative reports typically also contain extensive data collection to convey the complexity of the phenomenon or process. The data analysis reflects description and thematic development as well as the interrelation of themes. In addition, qualitative inquirers reflexively discuss their role or their position in a research study (**reflexivity** means that the researchers reflect on their own biases, values, and assumptions and actively write them into their research). This may involve reflecting on their own experiences and discussing how they collaborated with participants in many phases of the project. They also discuss their past experiences and cultural backgrounds (e.g., Asian-American perspectives) that will affect the interpretations and conclusions drawn in their study.

In the case of the gunman incident (Asmussen & Creswell, 1995), the authors use a more scientific than storytelling structure. However, the scientific "parts" are not ordered in the sequence typically found in quantitative inquiry. The authors introduce "findings" early in the study when they chronicle the events following the incident (Paragraphs 04–10), rather than report them late in the study. They also end with an "epilogue" consisting of personal views by both authors about their experiences with violence and guns (Paragraph 38). In addition, throughout the study the authors use personal pronouns referring to themselves frequently (e.g., "we"). The extensive use of quotes from individuals also accentuates the personal approach in this study.

Summarizing the Characteristics of Both Types of Research

You have once again proceeded through the process of research, but this time with a perspective of identifying the major characteristics of both quantitative and qualitative research. Contrary to commonly held assumptions, the difference between quantitative and qualitative research is more than numbers versus words, or instruments versus interviews—the distinctions appear at all phases of the research process. As you proceed through Chapters 3 through 10, keep these distinctions and characteristics in mind. They will help you understand the two primary forms of educational research and identify whether a published study is quantitative or qualitative (or more precisely, more of one approach than the other).

To further summarize your understanding of both approaches, examine the two following definitions:

Quantitative research is an inquiry approach useful for describing trends and explaining the relationship among variables found in the literature. To conduct this inquiry, the investigator specifies narrow questions, locates or develops instruments to gather data to answer the questions, and analyzes numbers from the instruments using statistics. From results of these analyses, the researcher interprets the data using prior predictions and research studies. The final report, presented in a standard format, displays researcher objectivity and lack of bias.

Qualitative research is an inquiry approach useful for exploring and understanding a central phenomenon. To learn about this phenomenon, the inquirer asks participants broad, general questions, collects the detailed views of participants in the form of words or images, and analyzes the information for description and themes. From this data, the researcher interprets the meaning of the information, drawing on personal reflections and past research. The final structure of the final report is flexible, and it displays the researcher's biases and thoughts.

RESEARCH DESIGNS

In certain steps of the research process (see Figure 2.2 again), there are specific procedures typically used in quantitative and qualitative research. The procedures for collecting, analyzing, and reporting research in quantitative and qualitative research are called **research designs.** Although many types of designs are available for your use, the major ones are shown in Figure 2.4. As you can see, the research designs can be classified under quantitative and qualitative research and under combined forms of inquiry. As a brief introduction to each research design, Figure 2.4 also shows their primary use. This use and a synopsis of each of the eight designs provides an overview. Occasionally, in Part II on the steps of the research process, examples will be drawn from these designs to illustrate ideas. Later, in Part III, specific chapters will detail the procedures and use of each design. The eight major types

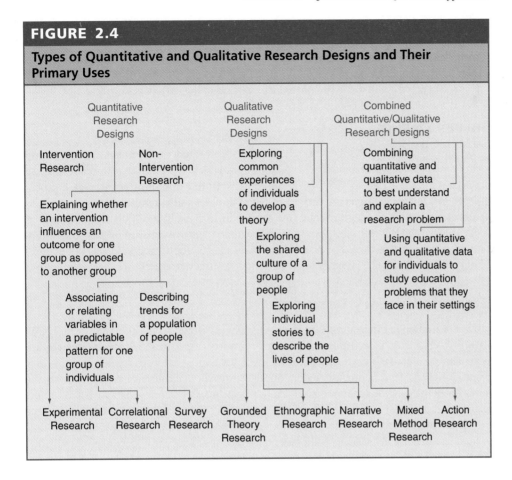

FIGURE 2.4

Types of Quantitative and Qualitative Research Designs and Their Primary Uses

of research procedures discussed in Part III are: experimental and quasi-experimental designs, correlational designs, survey designs, grounded theory designs, ethnographic designs, narrative research designs, mixed method designs, and action research designs.

Experimental and Quasi-experimental Designs

Some quantitative researchers seek to test whether an educational practice or idea makes a difference for individuals. *Experimental research* procedures are ideally suited for this study. **Experimental or quasi-experimental designs** (also called "intervention studies" or "group comparison studies") are procedures in quantitative research in which the investigator determines the impact of an intervention on an outcome for participants in a study. Investigators assess this impact by giving an experimental group an intervention and withholding the intervention from a control group. The intervention consists of activities or materials that are likely to cause a change in an outcome. In Chapter 11 you will learn more about the nature of interventions and the procedures of conducting an experiment of this type.

Correlational Designs

In some studies the researcher is unable to provide an intervention or to assign individuals to groups. Moreover, the focus is more on examining the association or relationship of one or more variables than in testing an intervention. **Correlational designs** are procedures in quantitative research in which investigators use a correlational statistical technique to describe and measure the degree of association (or relationship) between or among variables or sets of data. Researchers determine if variables occur together and whether they can predict outcomes. To accomplish this, investigators study a single group of individuals, rather than two or more groups as in an experiment, and assess the association among variables using the correlational statistic. Chapter 12 will detail the procedures in conducting correlational research.

Survey Designs

In another form of quantitative research, the investigator may not be able to intervene and form groups or may not be interested in relating variables. Instead, the researcher seeks to describe trends in a large population of individuals. In this case, a survey is a good procedure to use. **Survey designs** are procedures in quantitative research in which investigators administer a survey or questionnaire to a sample or to the entire population of people in order to describe the attitudes, opinions, behaviors, or characteristics of the population. From results of this survey, the researcher makes claims about trends in the population. Chapter 13 discusses the purpose and the design of survey research.

Grounded Theory Designs

Instead of studying a single group, an inquirer might want to examine a number of individuals who have all experienced an action, interaction, or process. **Grounded theory designs** are systematic, qualitative procedures that researchers use to generate a theory that explains, at a broad conceptual level, a process, action, or interaction about a substantive topic. The procedures for developing this theory include collecting primarily interview data, developing and relating categories (or themes) of information, and composing a figure or visual that portrays the theory. In this way, the theory is "grounded" in the data from participants. From this theory the researcher constructs hypotheses and predictions about the experiences of individuals. Chapter 14 discusses how to design and conduct grounded theory research.

Ethnographic Designs

Turning to qualitative research, an inquirer may be interested in studying one group of individuals, in the setting where they live and work, and in developing a portrait of how they interact. An *ethnographic study* is well suited for this purpose. **Ethnographic designs** are qualitative procedures for describing, analyzing, and interpreting a cultural group's shared patterns of behavior, beliefs, and language that develop over time. In an ethnography, the researcher provides a detailed picture of the culture-sharing group, drawing on various sources of information. The ethnographer also situates the group within its setting, explores themes or issues that develop over time as the group interacts, and details a portrait of the group. Chapter 15 identifies the procedures involved in conducting an ethnographic research design.

Narrative Research Designs

A researcher may not be interested in describing and interpreting group behavior or ideas or in developing a theory of collective experiences. **Narrative research designs** are qualitative procedures in which researchers describe the lives of individuals, collect and tell stories about these individuals' lives, and write narratives about their experiences. In education, these stories often relate to school classroom experiences or activities in schools. The researcher retells stories reported by individuals by focusing on a specific event or activities and analyzing them for categories of themes. The procedures involved in conducting a narrative study will be addressed in Chapter 16.

Mixed Method Designs

Data collection sometimes consists of a mix of both quantitative data (i.e., numbers) as well as qualitative data (i.e., text or images). In mixed method research, the researcher combines both forms of data to best explain and explore a research problem. **Mixed method designs** are procedures for collecting both quantitative and qualitative data in a single study, and for analyzing and reporting this data based on a priority, sequence, and level of integration of information. Conducting this type of study requires deciding on the priority or weight of each form of data (and approach) as well as the sequence of data collection (i.e., either quantitative first and qualitative second or vice versa). It also means determining how quantitative and qualitative data will be mixed at the stages of data collection, analysis, and interpretation. In Chapter 17 we introduce this recently conceptualized, emerging design in education.

Action Research Designs

Like mixed method research, *action research* often utilizes both quantitative and qualitative data, but the focus is much more applied in action research. The purpose of action research is to improve the practice of education by individuals conducting research on their own problems or issues in schools or educational settings. **Action research designs** are systematic procedures used by teachers (or other individuals in an educational setting) to gather quantitative and/or qualitative data about—and subsequently improve—the ways their particular setting operates, how they teach, and how well their students learn. In some action research studies, the purpose is to solve local, practical problems, such as a discipline classroom issue for a teacher. In other studies, the objective is to empower, transform, and emancipate individuals in educational settings. In Chapter 18, the procedures used in conducting action research will be identified.

CHOOSING A QUANTITATIVE OR QUALITATIVE APPROACH

Given two approaches to research and their accompanying research designs, on what basis do you select the best approach for designing or conducting your research? If you read a research study, how do you know whether the writer chose the best approach to use? **Choosing a quantitative or qualitative approach** means selecting either quantitative or qualitative research and employing it as a framework for planning, conducting, and evaluating a project. As you have probably already determined, making that choice at the outset of the study is necessary because many decisions hinge on whether the study is quantitative or qualitative. Given the importance of this decision, what factors should you consider? Three will be discussed here: the audience for a study, the experiences and training you bring to the research, and perhaps most importantly, the type of research problem that you need to address.

Fitting the Approach to an Audience

Researchers choose quantitative or qualitative research based on the audiences for their study. Educators write for several audiences, such as policy makers, faculty and graduate committees, editors and review boards, evaluators of grant proposals, and individuals in schools or educational settings who will read and possibly use the findings from a study. It is important that the audience or audiences be familiar with the approach used in a study.

Quantitative research may be more familiar to educators today who are trained in experimental research, survey designs, and statistical procedures. However, qualitative research now draws a substantial following, and through books, articles, conferences, and workshops, educators can obtain a much firmer grasp of qualitative inquiry than they could a few years ago. When students choose to use qualitative research, they may need to educate readers about the basic characteristics of a qualitative study. If such education is needed, it can occur through lengthy method discussions in the study (or in a presentation to the audience), or through the use of references to key qualitative readings in the research report. However, the need to do this is occurring less frequently.

Relating Your Experiences to an Approach

Researchers also choose an approach based on their personal experiences and training. Conducting research in either quantitative or qualitative research requires skills in conceptualizing research, conducting research, and writing the study. A quantitative researcher typically has taken some courses or training in measurement, statistics, and quantitative data collection approaches, such as experimental, correlational, or survey techniques. Qualitative researchers need experience in field studies where they practice gathering information in a setting and learn the skills of observing or interviewing individuals. Coursework or experience in analyzing text data is also helpful. Thus, the choice of approach must relate to the personal skills, training, and experiences of the researcher.

Matching the Problem and Approach

More will be said about the types of research problems best suited for quantitative and for qualitative research in the next chapter (see the section in Chapter 3 titled "Selecting a Quantitative or Qualitative Approach for Your Research Problem"), but for the moment, matching the problem to an approach is of primary importance. As introduced earlier in this chapter, the researcher chooses *quantitative research* when addressing a problem in which the issue requires that trends be described or that variable relationships be explained. For example, these trends often apply to a large number of people, such as the turnover for all teachers in a school district, reading scores of all elementary children in four schools, or career aspirations of all students in a higher education institution consisting primarily of minority students. In other studies, researchers may be interested in explaining the relationship among variables, such as why students choose to participate in athletic programs in colleges or universities, or gender or race differences in computerized adaptive testing in schools. In the television violence study, Vooijs and van der Voort (1993) are not only interested in modifying children's attitudes toward television violence, they also examine the impact of a specific school curriculum (a variable), from among many possible factors that might predict the children's attitudes (another variable).

Alternatively, *qualitative research* is generally used when the inquirer is interested in exploring and understanding a central phenomenon, such as a process or an event, phenomenon, or concept. This exploration is needed because little existing research exists on the topic or because the issue is complex and its complexity needs to be better understood. In the qualitative gunman case study (Asmussen & Creswell, 1995), the focus is on the process of how campus personnel respond to the incident—immediately after the incident, two months after the incident, and six months after the incident. Qualitative research is the approach of choice because it helps the authors explore a process that has not been examined before and that displays many complexities.

KEY IDEAS IN THE CHAPTER

Educators use either quantitative, qualitative, or some combination of approaches during each phase of the research process. Depending on the approach used, your research will be conducted differently. The two approaches may not exhaust all possibilities, but they are the most popular frameworks used in educational research. Consider them ends of a continuum rather than opposites, or dichotomies. Sometimes researchers combine them, but for the beginning student, it is easiest to separate them and learn about each approach independently.

Quantitative research began with the development of statistical procedures in the late 19th century. Many developments have been added since then, not only in statistics but also in measurement and testing and in the types of research designs. Qualitative research also has its antecedents in late 19th-century and early 20th-century history. However, it has only been in the last 30 years or so that qualitative research has been used in education. During this time, three discernible trends developed: the philosophical movement prior to the 1980s, the push toward procedures and rigor that began in the middle 1980s, and the more recent emphasis in the 1990s on advocacy and participatory research to address the needs of individuals in our society.

To examine the differences between the quantitative and qualitative approaches, turn to the research process. The types of problems studied, as well as how the literature is used, differ within each approach. The purpose and research questions also vary in scope, and the data collection is clearly distinguishable, with numbers and statistical analysis used in quantitative research and words and images in qualitative research. Because of the different types of data used, data analysis is also different. Different structures and approaches are also used when writing the research report. Definitions for quantitative and qualitative research, included in this chapter, highlight the characteristics of both forms of inquiry.

Researchers employ specific procedures for data collection, analysis, and report writing within the quantitative and qualitative approaches. Eight are emphasized in this text: experimental and quasi-experimental, correlational, survey, grounded theory, ethnographic, narrative, mixed method, and action research designs.

A researcher's choice of using either quantitative or qualitative approaches depends on several factors. The audience needs to be carefully considered. Also important are the personal experiences and training that the researcher brings to inquiry. Finally, and most importantly, the type of research problem, such as one in which variables need to be explained or related versus one that requires exploration or understanding, will shape whether the quantitative or qualitative approach is most appropriate.

USEFUL INFORMATION FOR PRODUCERS OF RESEARCH

▶ As you plan and conduct a study, discuss specifically the characteristics of the approach you are using. Refer to Figure 2.2 for words to describe your approach. By including these characteristics, you will demonstrate your knowledge of the research and help establish the credibility of your inquiry.

▶ Recognize that research is not either all quantitative or all qualitative, but tends toward one or the other (on a continuum).

▶ Use of qualitative research is a recent phenomenon in education. This means that individuals reviewing your qualitative plan for research may not be as familiar with qualitative characteristics. You will need to inform readers by sharing with them the characteristics described in this chapter.

▶ At each step in the research process, the arguments, words, and points you make will differ depending on whether you are conducting a quantitative or qualitative study.

USEFUL INFORMATION FOR CONSUMERS OF RESEARCH

▶ Examine the characteristics of Figure 2.2 to determine if a study is quantitative or qualitative.

▶ Because qualitative research came on to the research scene more recently than quantitative research, it may be harder to evaluate. The structure used in the report, as seen in headings, will be more flexible or varied.

▶ Expect that a quantitative study and a qualitative study will not look the same, since they differ in many steps of the research process.

STUDY QUESTIONS AND ACTIVITIES

Now go to our Companion Website to assess your understanding of chapter content with Multiple-Choice Questions, apply comprehension in Projects & Essays, and broaden your knowledge with links to related research topics on the Web.

1. Take the two definitions of quantitative and qualitative research used in this chapter and apply them to studies, pointing out specifically how the particular aspects of the definitions were used by the authors of the studies.

2. Find an article about either quantitative or qualitative research and identify the era in the historical development of research into which the study falls. Refer to Tables 2.1 and 2.2 for help.

3. Go through a study (either quantitative or qualitative) and place marginal notations on the article relating to the characteristics of the approach (refer to Figure 2.3). Examine the marginal notations for characteristics used in the quantitative television violence article (Vooijs & van der Voort, 1993) and in the qualitative gunman case article (Asmussen & Creswell, 1995).

II

The Steps in the Process of Research

With an introduction in Part I to the process of research and its implementation within quantitative and qualitative approaches, we can now explore in more detail the actual process of research in each step. Although this process is not as sequential as implied here, the steps do occur in both quantitative and qualitative educational research. By building an understanding of these steps, you can better plan and design your own study and read, evaluate, and apply findings from existing studies.

The chapters are:

▶ Chapter 3 Identifying a Research Problem
▶ Chapter 4 Reviewing the Literature
▶ Chapter 5 Specifying a Purpose and Research Questions or Hypotheses
▶ Chapter 6 Collecting Quantitative Data
▶ Chapter 7 Collecting Qualitative Data
▶ Chapter 8 Analyzing and Interpreting Quantitative Data
▶ Chapter 9 Analyzing and Interpreting Qualitative Data
▶ Chapter 10 Reporting and Evaluating Research

Identifying a Research Problem

Maria needs to begin the research required for the graduate program she attends. Where does she start? She has an interest in studying violence in schools because of her committee assignment at her own school. Unquestionably, this topic is an important issue to study, and the examination of it will aid her school committee. Maria needs to design her research, or have a plan in mind for her study. To do this, she needs access to individuals to study and she recognizes that the study will take time and resources. Assuming that she has the time and resources, she can begin designing her research. To do this she needs to move beyond the topic and identify a specific research problem or issue and then justify the importance of this problem in her written report. This chapter will describe the ways in which Maria can introduce her research and design and write about the research problem.

Educators start research projects with the idea of examining an important issue and learning how people feel or react to the issue. Research consists of identifying a research problem or issue, holding it up for close inspection to determine if it *can* be studied, and, if it can, then writing a description of it. In this chapter you will discover the importance of research problems, identify what constitutes good problems to study, distinguish between research problems best suited for quantitative and those best suited for qualitative research, and study the process involved in composing a written statement about the research problem. For those of you interested more in reading and evaluating research than in conducting a study, knowing how researchers construct a research problem statement and justify it for their study will help you better assess whether the study addresses a significant problem of practical use to you.

By the end of this chapter you should be able to:

▶ Identify the importance of a research problem.
▶ Distinguish between a research problem and the other elements of research.
▶ Identify criteria used to evaluate whether a research problem should and can be studied.
▶ Describe the five elements that comprise a "Statement of the Problem" section in a research study.
▶ Identify strategies useful in writing a "Statement of the Problem" section.

RESEARCH PROBLEMS EXPLORED IN THE TELEVISION VIOLENCE AND GUNMAN INCIDENT STUDIES

Let's revisit the quantitative television violence study (Vooijs & van der Voort, 1993). In the opening passages, the authors convey the research problem, or the issue or concern leading to the study. They identify several harmful effects of television violence in the first four paragraphs:

> . . . most reviews of the research conclude that the depiction of violence in television programs increases the chance that children in the audience will act aggressively. (Paragraph 01)

> If people become inured to violence from seeing much of it, they may react less sensitively to real-life aggression by, for example, not helping a victim. (Paragraph 02)

> In addition, exposure to TV violence can strengthen the belief that aggression is desirable or acceptable to solve conflicts. (Paragraph 03)

> Finally, there is evidence that television violence contributes to viewers' conceptions of social reality. . . . For example, people who are heavy viewers of television are more apt to think the world is violent and a "mean and scary" place than are light viewers. (Paragraph 04)

> Until now, a few previous attempts have been made to mitigate the effects of television violence by in-school interventions. . . . (Paragraph 05)

These passages indicate an educational problem: the potential negative effects of television violence on children. After seeing television violence, children may form their view of reality from the violence and act aggressively themselves. The authors feel that this is a pressing concern for our children and that our schools could possibly provide intervention to curb these negative conceptions of reality. In other words, we need to change or modify children's attitudes toward seeing violence on television. The authors establish a typical *quantitative* research problem—to *explain* whether the use of a school curriculum can change children's viewing attitudes. With these passages, the authors introduce the study and state the problem to be examined in their research.

The qualitative gunman case study (Asmussen & Creswell, 1995) also begins with the authors introducing the research problem: the escalating violence on college and university campuses.

> With increasingly frequent incidents of campus violence, a small, growing scholarly literature about the subject is emerging. (Paragraph 01)

> Recent campus reports indicate that violent crimes from thefts and burglaries to assaults and homicides are on the rise at colleges and universities. (Paragraph 02)

Like the television violence study, the authors state the educational problem in the opening paragraphs, and then devote the first two paragraphs to justifying the importance of this problem and the need to study it. Examine the tone and language of these opening passages. They do not attempt to *explain* or *predict* campus violence as in quantitative research; instead, they suggest that a problem exists that needs to be *explored*. The authors are less interested in explaining why campus violence occurs and more focused on exploring the campus reaction to a specific event.

As you can see, the authors present the research problem differently in quantitative and qualitative research. Before considering these differences in more depth, we need to first consider the importance of a "research problem": Why is it significant to single out the research problem from other steps in the research process; and *should* and *can* all problems in education be researched?

WHY IS A RESEARCH PROBLEM IMPORTANT?

Have you ever wondered why you continue reading a research study after looking at the title and the opening paragraphs? The author of the study more than likely has created a rationale for the study and has convinced you, in the opening passages, that the study is worth reading. This is an extremely important step in research. If you cannot design your study to create interest in your topic, you will not have many people reading and learning from your inquiry. Creating a need for your study and justifying it is a significant element in planning and writing good research.

The concept we are talking about is the research problem. **Research problems** are the educational issues or concerns studied by researchers. In education, a problem is a concern to educators that exists in our educational settings. Many issues or problems need to be addressed in educational research. Some important issues today are:

- the disruptions by at-risk students in classrooms
- the increase of teenage smoking
- the increase in violence on college campuses
- the lack of parental involvement in school issues for students with challenging behaviors
- the abuse of testing in the schools
- the lack of AIDS education at the elementary and middle school level in rural areas
- the mixed results of studies about how students learn science in elementary school

Issues such as these are active concerns for personnel in schools, on college campuses, and in other educational settings. As such, these concerns need to be studied so that policy makers can make better decisions, teachers and school officials have better practical solutions for problems, and researchers can add or extend knowledge. What are some other educational issues of which you are aware, either from media reports or personal experiences?

Although these issues can be easily identified, authors do not always clearly convey these issues in research reports. Researchers may not know how to introduce them or they may be unclear about the central issue that *does* drive their studies. For authors experienced with research, the research problems or issues are typically found in one of the opening paragraphs of the studies. Their precise form may be single sentences or several sentences that convey pressing concerns in education. To locate the research problem in a study, ask yourself questions such as:

- What was the issue or problem that the researcher wanted to address?
- What was the concern being addressed "behind" this study?
- Why was the study undertaken in the first place?
- Why is this study important?

Sometimes authors clearly state their research problem. For example, an author might say, "The problem addressed in this study is. . . ." In many cases, we are not so fortunate, and we are left as readers to determine the research problem being examined in the study. The above questions can help you in your search for the author's intent about the research problem in the study.

Distinguishing the Research Problem From Other Steps in Research

The author of a study should clearly separate the *research problem* from other steps in the process of research. It can be differentiated from the *topic* of the study (to be addressed later in this chapter), the *purpose* or intent of the study (to be considered in Chapter 5 on "Purpose Statement"), and specific *research questions* (also discussed in Chapter 5 in "Research Questions"). By discussing the research problem in a separate chapter in this text, we are emphasizing its importance in a research study. Part of this emphasis, then, is to recognize it as a distinct step in the process of research.

In the brief definitions that follow, consider the differences among these parts of research:

- A *research problem* is an educational issue or problem in a study.
- A *research topic* is the broad subject matter being addressed in a study.
- A *purpose* is the major intent or objective of the study.
- *Research questions* are questions that the researcher would like answered or addressed in the study.

The major differentiating factor is that these parts of research vary from a general presentation of ideas to the more specific. Let's examine a concrete illustration, as shown in Figure 3.1, to make this point. In this example, a researcher begins with a broad topic—distance learning. The inquirer then seeks to learn about a problem related to this topic: the lack of students in distance education classes. To study this problem, our educator then reformulates the problem into a statement of intent (the purpose statement): to study why students do not attend distance education classes at one community college. Examining this statement requires that our investigator narrow the intent to specific questions, one of which is: Does the use of Website technology in the classroom deter students from enrolling in distance education classes? The process involves narrowing a broad topic to specific questions. In this process, the "research problem" becomes a distinct step that needs to be identified to encourage readers to clearly see the issue.

Let's look at additional examples of purpose statements and research questions being reformulated into research problems. This will help you understand the differences between these steps in the process of research. For example, assume that a researcher advances

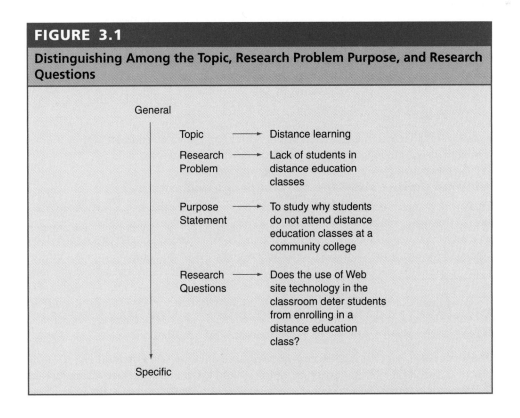

FIGURE 3.1

Distinguishing Among the Topic, Research Problem Purpose, and Research Questions

General

| Topic | → | Distance learning |

| Research Problem | → | Lack of students in distance education classes |

| Purpose Statement | → | To study why students do not attend distance education classes at a community college |

| Research Questions | → | Does the use of Web site technology in the classroom deter students from enrolling in a distance education class? |

Specific

a purpose statement, but intends for it to be a research problem. The first statement below is a statement about the intent or focus of a study while the second is a statement about an issue or concern in Third-World countries. Examine in the following illustration how a purpose statement might be restated as a research problem:

> ▌ *A purpose statement:* The purpose of this study is to examine the education of women in Third-World countries.
> ▌ A revision of it as a *research problem:* Women in Third-World countries are restricted from attending universities and colleges because of the culturally oriented, patriarchal norms of their societies.

In another example, assume that an individual presents a research question but intends for it to be a research problem. The first statement shows a question that needs to be answered in the study, while the second statement presents an issue or concern on college campuses that helps create a need for the study. Here is how a research question might be changed into a research problem:

> ▌ A *research question:* The research problem in this study is: What factors influence homesickness in college students?
> ▌ An improved version as a *research problem:* Homesickness is a major issue on college campuses today. When students get homesick, they leave school or start missing classes, leading to student attrition or poor achievement in classes during their first semester of college.

As you read ahead in this chapter as well as in the chapter about the "purpose" and the "research questions," consider how you can create a distinct conversation with your reader about the underlying issue or concern that leads to a need for your study. As you examine published studies, look for ways the authors include research problems, purpose statements, and research questions in their discussion.

Can and Should Problems Be Researched?

Just because a problem exists and an author can clearly identify the issue does not mean that the researcher *should* or *can* investigate it. Deciding whether a problem *should* be researched means determining that the study will contribute to educational knowledge by advancing research or adding to the effectiveness of practice. Whether an issue *can* be researched is dependent on having resources to study the issue and obtaining access to participants and research sites. When planning and conducting research, answering the following three questions can help you decide if the problem is researchable.

Will Your Study Contribute to Knowledge and Practice?

This question raises the *should* issue: Should you study the problem at all? A positive answer to this question lies in whether your study will contribute to knowledge and practice. One important reason for engaging in research, as we addressed briefly in Chapter 1 on "Why Is Research Important?", is to add to existing information and to inform our educational practices. Thinking more specifically now about the research problem, how will your study of the research problem contribute to knowledge and practice and in what ways? Knowing this information helps you create a strong rationale for your proposed study in the introduction and creates a justification for your study to readers. There are five ways to assess how a study of your research problem makes this contribution.

1. *A study of the problem contributes to knowledge if it fills a void or extends existing research.* A study can fill a void by covering topics not addressed in the published literature. It can also extend or build upon research conducted previously by studying new

participants or new sites, or by adding to existing ideas. For example, assume that a researcher examines the literature on the ethical climate on college campuses and finds that past research has examined the perceptions of students, but not of faculty. Conducting a study about faculty perceptions of the ethical climate would extend the research to examine another perspective on the issue.

2. *A study of the problem contributes to knowledge if it replicates a study with new participants or at new sites.* Replication means that a researcher duplicates a previous study with new participants and at new sites. The importance of this is that the findings can apply to many people and situations rather than be of value to only one setting where the initial research occurred. This type of study is especially important in quantitative experiments. In a quantitative study of ethical climate, for example, past research that was conducted in a liberal arts college can be tested (or replicated) at other sites, such as a community college or major research university.

3. *A study of the problem contributes to knowledge if the problem has not been studied or is understudied.* A problem may need to be explored because participants have not been previously studied, broad explanations (later to be called "theories") have not been tested with specific groups, or certain concepts to study participants are unknown. These reasons to study a problem are often cited by qualitative researchers. For example, in our illustration on ethical climate, research may be missing that considers ethical dilemmas experienced by students while they take exams. This problem could be an area for further study.

4. *A study of the problem contributes to knowledge if it gives voice to people not heard, silenced, or rejected in society.* Found in both quantitative and qualitative studies, this research adds to knowledge by presenting the ideas and the words of marginalized individuals. For example, although past studies on ethical climate have addressed students on predominantly white campuses, the voices of Native Americans have not been heard. A study of this type would add to educational knowledge.

5. *A study of the problem contributes to knowledge if it informs practice.* By examining the problem, research may lead to the identification of new techniques or technologies, the recognition of the value of historical or current practice, or the necessity to change current teaching practice. Individuals who profit from practical knowledge may be policy makers, teachers, or learners. For example, a study of ethical issues in a college setting may lead to a new honor code, new policies about cheating on exams, or new approaches to administering tests.

Do You Have Access to People and Sites?

Once you have determined that your educational issue *should* be researched, you need to determine if it *can* be researched. In order to research a problem, investigators need to gain permission to enter a site and to involve people at the location of the study (e.g., gaining access to an elementary school to study children who are minors). This access often requires multiple levels of approval from schools, such as district administrators, principals, teachers, parents, and students. Also, projects conducted under the auspices of educational agencies receiving federal funding (most colleges and universities) need to have institutional review approval to ensure that researchers protect the rights of their subjects. Your ability to gain access to people and sites can help determine if the issue can be researched. These factors will be explored in more depth in Chapter 6 on "Obtaining Permissions."

Do You Have the Time, Resources, and Skills to Study the Research Problem?

Even if you can gain access to the people and sites needed for your study, your ability to research the problem also depends on time, resources, and your research skills.

Time   When planning a study, investigators should predetermine the time required for data collection and data analysis. Qualitative studies typically take more time than quantitative studies because of the need to collect extensive data and analyze text data. Regardless of the approach used, the amount of time for data collection can be estimated by examining similar studies and gauging the amount of time they required. Developing a timeline for a study helps a researcher assess whether the study can be reasonably completed within the time available to the researcher.

Resources   Investigators need resources, such as funds for equipment, for participants, and for individuals to transcribe interviews. Researchers need to create a budget and obtain advice from other, experienced researchers about whether the anticipated expenses are realistic. Other resources may be needed as well, such as mailing labels, postage, statistical programs, or audio-visual equipment. Dependent upon these resource requirements, investigators may need to limit the scope of a project, explore funding available to support the project, or research the project in stages as funds are available.

Skills   The skills of the researcher also affect the overall assessment of whether the study of a problem is realistic. Investigators need to have acquired certain research skills to effectively study a problem—skills gained through courses, training, and prior research experiences. For those engaging in a quantitative study these skills may be in using computers, employing statistical programs, or creating tables for presenting information. The skills needed for qualitative researchers are the ability to write descriptive passages, to synthesize information into broad themes, and to use computer programs for entering and analyzing words from participants in the study.

SELECTING A QUANTITATIVE OR QUALITATIVE APPROACH FOR YOUR RESEARCH PROBLEM

Once you have determined that your research problem can and should be researched, you need to decide what approach to use in the study: quantitative or qualitative. There should be a match between your problem and the approach you use. (A combination of both approaches is introduced later in Chapter 17 on "Mixed Method Designs" and in Chapter 18 on "Action Research Designs.") What factors are important in determining this match? What type of research problem is best suited for quantitative research and what type for qualitative research?

We introduced information earlier in this chapter that will help you answer these questions. Let's look once again at the television violence study (Vooijs & van der Voort, 1993) and the gunman incident case study (Asmussen & Creswell, 1995). We can see that each study addresses a different type of problem. In the quantitative television violence study the authors were interested in violence on television; however, the actual problem was *explaining* the impact television violence has on young children. Explaining or predicting relationships among variables is an important characteristic of *quantitative* research, as we learned in Chapter 2 on "Identifying a Research Problem." Alternatively, in the qualitative gunman incident case study, the authors sought to *explore* campus reaction without preconceived ideas about what they would find. In Chapter 2 on "Identifying a Research Problem" we learned that exploring a problem is a characteristic of *qualitative* research.

These two factors—explanation and exploration—provide a standard you can use to determine whether your research problem is best suited for a quantitative or qualitative study. In Chapter 2, additional characteristics of both quantitative and qualitative research were discussed, and from these other characteristics we can identify helpful information to direct our approach to research. Here are some additional factors to consider:

Use *quantitative research* if your research problem requires you to:	Use *qualitative research* if a study of your research problem requires you to:
❭ measure variables	❭ learn about the views of individuals you plan to study
❭ assess the impact of these variables on an outcome	❭ assess a process over time
❭ test theories or broad explanations	❭ generate theories based on participant perspectives
❭ apply results to a large number of people	❭ obtain detailed information about a few people or research sites

DESIGNING AND WRITING THE "STATEMENT OF THE PROBLEM"

Educational researchers identify a research problem, evaluate whether it can and should be researched, and select either a quantitative or qualitative approach to study it. Now let's assess how the research problem is written into an actual research study.

The research problem is one component in the section of a study called the "Statement of the Problem." In formal reports such as theses and dissertations, investigators use the phrase "Statement of the Problem," but in published journal articles, authors typically call it the "Introduction." For convenience, we will call it the **"Statement of the Problem"** section and define it as an introductory passage in a research report that includes these five elements:

❭ the educational topic for the study
❭ the research problem within this topic
❭ a justification for the problem based on past research and practice
❭ deficiencies or shortcomings of past research or practical knowledge
❭ the importance of addressing the problem for diverse audiences

By identifying these five elements you can easily understand introductions to research study and write a good introduction to your own research report.

Introducing the Educational Topic

It is important to carefully consider the opening sentences of a "Statement of the Problem" section. The opening sentences affect whether readers will continue to examine the study; generate interest in the study; and provide an initial frame of reference for understanding the entire research topic. Given these factors, it makes sense to start with a broad topic that readers can easily understand. This way they can be brought into a study slowly and will be encouraged to continue reading.

Studies typically begin with the identification of a clear educational topic. An **educational topic** is the broad subject matter that a researcher wishes to address in a study. This topic, of course, will vary from study to study, and a reflection on topics reported in educational journals shows the vast enterprise of educational research today. As shown in Figure 3.2, the topic is stated in the title and introduced in the first sentences. It is important to note that the authors ease into the study with general ideas that most readers can understand (standardized tests, the education of American Indians, the problem-solving mode

FIGURE 3.2

Select Topics and First Sentences of Research Studies Reported in Educational Journals

The Impact of Mandated Standardized Testing on Minority Students

Richard G. Lomax, Mary Maxwell West, Maryellen C. Harmon, Katherine A. Viator, & George F. Madaus, 1995

One of the original reasons for the introduction of mandated standardized tests was to reduce the effects of patronage and thereby open educational opportunities and a range of occupations to a wider population of students (Madaus, 1991). However,...

Living and Working in Two Worlds
Case Studies of Five
American Indian
Women Teachers

BRENDA HILL, COURTNEY VAUGHN, AND SHARON BROOKS HARRISON, 1995

The Euro-American education of American Indians began under the auspices of missionaries and a few lay educators, with the ongoing purpose of remaking American Indians into the Euro-American image. In...

Inhibitors to Implementing a Problem-Solving Approach to Teaching Elementary Science: Case Study of a Teacher in Change

Mary Lee Martens, 1992

The problem-solving mode of teaching elementary science now recommended in many states implies change for many groups of professionals including teachers, administrators, and other individuals charged with implementing educational policy. Teachers, however,...

of teaching elementary science). For example, assume that an author begins the topic discussion with comments about plagiarism on college campuses. This approach may unnecessarily narrow the topic too soon and lose readers who have not studied or read about plagiarism. Instead, writers might begin with the broader topic of dishonesty on campus and the need to explore the values students learn during their college years.

The first sentence needs to create reader interest in the topic. Called the **narrative hook,** it serves the important function of drawing the reader into a study. Good narrative hooks fulfill these possible functions:

▶ They cause the reader to pay attention.
▶ They elicit a response, one that may be emotional or attitudinal, from the reader.
▶ They encourage the reader to continue to read on.

The form of the narrative hook varies from study to study, but one popular approach is to include statistical data in the opening sentence such as: More than 50 percent of the adult population experiences depression today. Another approach is to start with a provocative question: Why are school policies that ban smoking in high schools not being enforced? Studies that approach the narrative hook from a research standpoint might begin: School suspension is drawing increased attention among scholars in teacher education. In some studies, authors begin with a clear purpose of the study: The intent of this study is to examine how clients construe the therapist-client relationship. Although all of these are possibilities for educational researchers, the central idea is that a study begins with an introduction to a topic that the reader can easily understand and with a first sentence that creates reader interest.

Stating the Research Problem

After stating the topic in the opening discussion, the researcher then narrows it to an educational problem that needs to be examined. Recall that a **research problem** is an educational issue or concern being investigated by the researcher. As illustrated earlier, authors may present it as a single sentence or as a couple of short sentences (e.g., see Asmussen & Creswell, 1995). They may also pose several related aspects of a single research problem, such as in the television violence study. There, the authors provided four different harmful effects of television violence on children (they will act aggressively, they will not respond appropriately to reality, and so forth) (Vooijs & van der Voort, 1993).

To learn how to locate and write research problems, educators can examine introductory paragraphs of research articles. The questions to ask are: "What is the issue or concern being addressed by the author?" "Is there only one issue or are there several issues being presented?" A close inspection of the types of research problems advanced in published studies shows them to be of two general types. **Practical research problems** are those that arise from the setting and activities of educators. **Study-based research problems** emanate from a need to extend knowledge or resolve conflicting views in published studies. In some studies, authors advance both types. For the purpose of understanding each form, the following examples illustrate how research problems are reported in educational journal articles.

Here is an example of a *practical research problem* where Chinese boys are valued more than girls because of single-child policies:

> Since the late 1970s a single-child policy has been implemented by the Chinese government to control the largest population in the world. Selective abortion to choose a boy could inevitably skew the Chinese gender distribution, and is clearly prohibited by the government. As a result, although boys were valued higher than girls in traditional Chinese culture, many parents eventually have a girl as their single child. (Wang & Staver, 1997, p. 252)

Here is an example of a *study-based research problem* advancing the need for additional research that connects developmentally appropriate reading practices and teachers' approaches:

> Although both teacher beliefs about developmentally appropriate practices with young children and teacher theoretical orientation to early reading instruction have been previously studied, there is a lack of research that connects the two areas. (Ketner, Smith, & Parnell, 1997, p. 212)

In both cases, the investigator presents an issue or concern that needs to be addressed, but one anchors the research problem in practice and the other in research. Perhaps an ideal situation is to include both *practical* and *study-based* research problems in your introduction, as the following sentence illustrates: There is a need to better explain reading progress (the practical approach) as well as make up for a lack of research about developmentally appropriate practices and teacher orientation (the study-based approach).

Justifying the Research Problem

Whether the research problem is based on practice or on past studies, researchers need to justify studying it. **Justifying a research problem** means presenting reasons for the importance

of studying the issue or concern. This justification occurs in several paragraphs in an introduction where the author draws in evidence to document the need to study the problem. As
shown in Figure 3.3, researchers base this justification on:

⬧ suggestions from other researchers
⬧ personal work experiences (something witnessed in the workplace or experienced
  personally)

These justifications draw from different sources, are used in different types of approaches
(i.e., quantitative or qualitative), and typically find expression in select research designs
such as experiments, action research, or narrative research (to be addressed more specifically in the research design chapters in Part III).

Justification Based on Suggestions From Other Researchers

We will begin with the most "scholarly" justification—suggestions from other researchers
based on their studies. Researchers often justify the importance of their research problem
based on suggestions made by other authors in published studies. These justifications are
found in both quantitative and qualitative studies and they are usually located in the final
sections of journal articles in which authors comment about future research needs. For example, note the suggestions for future research in the concluding paragraph in the gunman
incident case study (Asmussen & Creswell, 1995):

> Events emerged during the process of reaction that could be 'critical incidents' in future studies,
> such as the victim response, media reporting, the debriefing process, campus changes, and the
> evolution of a campus plan. (Paragraph 37)

A researcher might cite Asmussen and Creswell (1995) and use this information as justification for the need to explore "campus plans."

Besides suggestions found in published studies, justification for a research problem can
be found in conference papers, research syntheses, or encyclopedias that report the latest
research, such as the *Encyclopedia of Educational Research* (Alkin, 1992). Detailed steps for

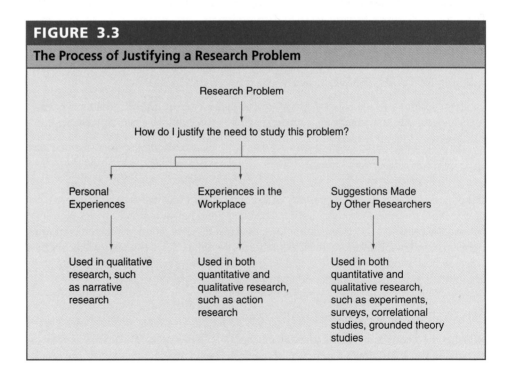

FIGURE 3.3

The Process of Justifying a Research Problem

locating these syntheses, encyclopedias, and journal articles will be discussed in Chapter 4 on "Locating Literature."

Justification may also be based on comments by authorities or experts who have researched educational issues. These experts have studied topics for years, and they understand future research needs that will contribute to knowledge. The experts can be identified and located through a search of library references, contacted at professional conferences, or found through Internet or Website addresses. Individuals who have spent entire careers becoming authorities on research problems generally welcome student questions or requests. It is important when approaching these individuals to consider questions you might ask them. Here is a short list of possibilities:

- What are you working on at present?
- Is my proposed topic and research problem worthy of study?
- Who else should I contact who has recently studied this topic and problem?

Although you may be hesitant to contact experts, such conversations yield useful leads for finding references. Established educators welcome such conversations.

Another authority on a particular research problem may be a student's faculty advisor or committee members. She or he may have a long-term research agenda examining an educational issue, an agenda based on a series of studies being conducted. By participating in the faculty member's research, students can learn about other studies and locate useful research to use as justification for their own research problems.

Justification Based on Personal Experiences

Evidence from past studies is frequently cited as a need for studying a research problem. However, evidence also can be obtained from practical work experience in educational settings. In some approaches to research, these personal experiences weigh heavily in justifying a research problem. They may arise from the personal experiences of the researcher or from experiences the researcher has seen or heard about in the workplace. The experiences of the researcher are often used as justifications in those studies with a practical orientation, such as solving a particular classroom dilemma in an action research study (see Chapter 18). They are also apparent in studies in which the researcher is the object of study, such as in narrative research (see Chapter 16). Consider the following two examples of researchers introducing their own experiences as justification for studying a research problem:

One researcher justifies the need to study students in a multiage middle school by referring to her own experiences in school. The study begins:

> In the spring of 1992, the opportunity to conduct classroom action research was offered to Madison, Wisconsin teachers. Though my daily schedule was already full, I was drawn to this opportunity because of its emphasis on practical, classroom-based research. . . . For me, multicultural curricula, cooperative learning, computer technology, and thematic education were exciting developments in classroom teaching. (Kester, 1994, p. 63)

Another researcher justifies the need for studying the ostracism of African-American students in schools by tracing personal family experiences. The study starts:

> When I was growing up, there was never a thought in my mind about whether or not I would go to school. It was given that I was going to go to school every day as long as my parents were alive and the Lord woke me up in good health. (Jeffries, 1993, p. 427)

Identifying Deficiencies in the Evidence

Following the justification of the research problem, the author next needs to suggest that the evidence is deficient or insufficient. A **deficiency in the evidence** means that the past literature or practical experiences of the researchers do not adequately address the research problem. In the "Statement of the Problem" the researcher summarizes the ways the literature or experiences are deficient. For example, deficiencies in the research may require a need to extend the research, replicate a study, explore a topic, or lift voices of marginalized people. A deficiency in practice means that good and workable solutions have not yet been identified for schools or other educational settings. As the researcher summarizes these deficiencies, good practice would be to identify two or three reasons why existing research and practice have been deficient in addressing the research problem, stating these reasons toward the end of the introduction to the study. In the following example, a researcher indicates weaknesses in past research and also reflects on personal experiences:

> The past research does not address the cultural differences of children in preschools. It also does not consider the multiple factors that explain teacher interactions with these students. From observing preschools, the need further exists to better understand how teachers interact with preschool children from different cultures.

Relating the Discussion to Audiences

Finally, the researcher identifies audiences—groups, individuals, and settings—that will profit if the deficiencies in existing knowledge and practice related to the research problem are addressed. **Audience** consists of individuals who will read and potentially use information provided in a research study. These audiences will vary depending on the nature of the study, but several often considered by educators include researchers, practitioners, policy makers, and individuals participating in the studies. One author, for example, in ending an introduction section, might comment about the importance of the study for school administrators:

> By exploring the need for athletic trainers in high schools, school administrators can identify potential issues that arise when trainers are not present, and coaches can better understand the circumstances in which trainers are most needed at athletic events.

As this example illustrates, authors often enumerate multiple audiences. Passages such as these are typically found in the concluding passage in the introduction or the "Statement of the Problem" section and explain the importance of addressing the problem for each audience. Like the narrative hook, this information continues to draw the reader into the study and it personalizes the research so that readers can see that the study will potentially provide meaningful information. When researchers include comments about the importance of the study for audiences, they remind themselves about the need to clearly identify useful results.

The Flow of Ideas in a "Statement of the Problem"

Let's assemble all five of the elements of a "Statement of the Problem" together to see how the ideas can flow when applied to an educational topic and research problem. First we will begin with several writing techniques that can assist you in designing this section of a study and in identifying the elements in a published study. Next we will view a template for the flow of ideas using an example about ethical issues in colleges. After that the discussion will include a "think aloud" about the processes of writing a "Statement of the Problem" section.

Writing Strategies

One strategy you can use as you write your "Statement of the Problem" section is to visualize this section as five paragraphs, with each paragraph addressing one of the five aspects of the section. Take these sections in order beginning with the topic, the research problem, the justification, the deficiencies, and the problem as it relates to audiences. Another writing strategy is to frequently use citations to the literature throughout this introductory passage. Multiple references add a scholarly tone to your writing and provide evidence from others, rather than from your own personal opinion. The use of citations in your study will build credibility for your work. A third strategy is to provide references from statistical trends to support the importance of studying the research problem. How many teenagers smoke? How many individuals are HIV positive? This form of evidence is especially popular in quantitative studies. Another writing strategy is to use quotes from participants in a study or from notes obtained from observing participants to begin your "Statement of the Problem" introduction. This approach is popular and frequently used in qualitative studies. Finally, be cautious about using quotes from the literature to begin a study, especially in the first sentence. Readers may not extract the same meaning from a quote as does the researcher. The quotes are often too narrow to be appropriate for an introductory section in which you seek to establish a research problem and provide justification for it. To use quotes effectively, readers often need to be led "into" as well as "out of" the quote. We will discuss specific writing strategies in more depth as we survey the entire research report in Chapter 10.

A Template for the Flow of Ideas

With these writing strategies in mind, we can now consider how to organize all five elements of a "Statement of the Problem" section. Examine the flow of ideas and a specific example shown in Figure 3.4. The specific illustration here is research about ethical issues on college campuses. Figure 3.4 shows the five elements in this section, a brief definition for each element, and an example to illustrate the topics a researcher might write about each element.

The researcher begins with the topic of ethical issues in colleges and narrows it to a specific problem: potential ethical violations among college football recruiters. Since this is

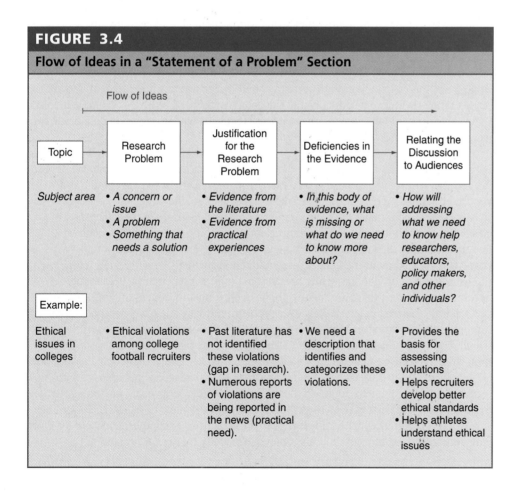

FIGURE 3.4

Flow of Ideas in a "Statement of a Problem" Section

a sensitive topic and could be difficult to study (is it researchable, then?), an investigation is merited. Also, from practical experiences on campuses, the researcher claims that violations are being reported in the news, but not openly to campus officials. The evidence, therefore, is deficient in describing these potential violations, and a study of this problem can help determine if violations occur, assist recruiters who seek to engage in ethical behavior, and aid athletes who need to be aware of ethical behavior on college campuses.

 ## Think Aloud About Writing a "Statement of the Problem"

The process of writing the "Statement of the Problem" can be modeled to provide additional details about the practice of research. I apply the five-step model regardless of whether the study is quantitative or qualitative. My introductions look similar for both quantitative and qualitative studies; however, close inspection of the research problem will indicate a different emphasis in the two studies. In quantitative studies, an emphasis is on the need for an explanation of outcomes while in qualitative studies, the researcher explores a *process, event, or phenomena.*

My introduction begins with a general discussion about the topic of the research. I try to present the first sentence as a good "narrative hook" so that readers will see this as an important educational topic worthy of study. The writing of this first sentence is difficult, and I may develop numerous revisions before I am satisfied that it will be general, timely, and understandable. I think about the wide range of students in my class who have varied backgrounds and majors, and whether they would understand and relate to my first sentence. I find it helpful to think about my audiences as a diverse group when I write the opening sentence of this passage.

As I've said, the opening paragraph needs to gently lead the reader into the study. My analogy for this is lowering a bucket into a well to get water. I hope to gently lower the bucket rather than drop it suddenly into the depths of the well. With this example in mind, I introduce the study in a paragraph or two and focus the reader's attention on a single subject area and its general importance in education.

With any given topic, several issues may present themselves. Some may be suggested by my experiences in a school or from a review of the past research on a topic. While reading about my topic in research articles (typically in journal articles), I am open to issues that need to be studied, and am most interested in specific issues that other authors suggest need to be studied. These issues are located in future research sections at the conclusion of articles. I often make a list of these suggestions for research on a piece of paper and try to follow up on one of them. When reviewing these studies, I try to become familiar with authors who are leaders in the field. These are often individuals who are cited frequently in published studies or who frequently present on a topic at conferences. Because of their expertise, I may contact these authors by phone or by e-mail to discuss my proposed study.

Once I have an understanding of a problem and can adequately justify studying it through evidence from the literature, I begin the process of writing the first section of a research report, the "Statement of the Problem." I follow my five elements for writing this section, write the section, and check it for all five elements. My goal is to present a solid rationale for why my study is needed, and I support this need with several arguments using multiple forms of evidence. I am apt to go overboard in citing evidence by using numerous citations in the introductory passage of my study (e.g., Jones, 1994; Smith, 1998; Davis, 2000). To ensure that the importance of the study is clear to the audience, I end the "Statement of the Problem" section with comments about the utility of the study for several audiences.

An example of one of my "Statement of the Problem" sections is shown in Figure 3.5. This is from a study about teenage smoking in high schools. I introduce the topic and research problem in the first paragraph. This shows how the topic and the research problem can sometimes blend together. I then cite evidence for this problem in the second paragraph. Note that I am not discussing any study in detail here in the introduction; in many

---

FIGURE 3.5

Sample "Statement of the Problem" Section

Statement of the Problem Elements	**Exploring the Conceptions and Misconceptions of Teen Smoking in High Schools: A Multiple Case Analysis**
The Topic The Research Problem Evidence Justifying the Research Problem	Tobacco use is a leading cause of cancer in American society (McGinnis & Foefe, 1993). Although smoking among adults has declined in recent years, it has actually increased for adolescents. The Center for Disease Control and Prevention reported that smoking among high school students had risen from 27.5 percent in 1991 to 34.8 percent in 1995 (USDHHS, 1996). Unless this trend is dramatically reversed, an estimated 5 million of our nation's children will ultimately die a premature death (Center for Disease Control, 1996). Previous research on adolescent tobacco use has focused on four primary topics. Several studies have examined the question of the initiation of smoking by young people, noting that tobacco use initiation begins as early as junior high school (e.g., Heishman, et al., 1997). Other studies have focused on the prevention of smoking and tobacco use in schools. This research has led to numerous school-based prevention programs and interventions (e.g., Sussman, Dent, Burton, Stacy, & Flay, 1995). Fewer studies have examined "quit attempts" or cessation of smoking behaviors among adolescents, a distinct contrast to the extensive investigations into adult cessation attempts (Heishman, et al., 1997). Of interest as well to researchers studying adolescent tobacco use has been the social context and social influence of smoking (Fearnow, Chassin, & Presson, 1998). For example, adolescent smoking may occur in work-related situations, at home where one or more parents or caretakers smoke, at teen social events, or at areas designated as "safe" smoking places near high schools (McVea, et al., in press).
Deficiencies in Evidence	Minimal research attention has been directed toward the social context of high schools as a site for examining adolescent tobacco use. During high school students form peer groups which may contribute to adolescent smoking. Often peers become a strong social influence for behavior in general, and belonging to an athletic team, a music group, or the "grunge" crowd can impact thinking about smoking (McVea, et al., in press). Schools are also places where adolescents spend most of their day (Fibkins, 1993) and are available research subjects. Schools provide a setting for teachers and administrators to be role models for abstaining from tobacco use and enforcing policies about tobacco use (O'Hara, et al., 1999). Existing studies of adolescent tobacco use are primarily quantitative with a focus on outcomes and transtheoretical models (Pallonen, 1998). Qualitative investigations, on the other hand, provide detailed views of students in their own words, complex analyses of multiple perspectives, and specific school contexts of different high schools that shape student experiences with tobacco (Creswell, in press). Moreover, qualitative inquiry offers the opportunity to involve high school students as co-researchers, a data collection procedure that can enhance the validity of student views uncontaminated by adult perspectives.
The Audience	By examining these multiple school contexts, using qualitative approaches and involving students as co-researchers, we can better understand the conceptions and misconceptions adolescents hold about tobacco use in high schools. With this understanding, researchers can better isolate variables and develop models about smoking behavior. Administrators and teachers can plan interventions to prevent or change attitudes toward smoking, and school officials can assist with smoking cessation or intervention programs.

of my studies, specific reference to individual studies will appear later in the literature review section. Following the evidence for the problem, I mention in the fourth paragraph the "deficiencies" in past studies and the need for extending past research. In the final paragraph, I appeal to various audiences (i.e., researchers, administrators, and teachers) to read and use this study.

EXAMPLES OF "STATEMENT OF THE PROBLEM" SECTIONS

You can learn much from reading introductions to studies, looking for the five elements, and noting sentences that capture the research problem. Examine the following two examples to see how a *qualitative* author and a *quantitative* author wrote their introductory sections of their studies. Following each example, we will relate the passages to each of the five elements of a "Statement of the Problem" section. The first example is a qualitative study by Brown (1998) on distance learning in higher education, and this passage presents the entire introduction to her study.

> Distance learning is an increasingly important aspect of higher education because it meets the needs of an expanding pool of nontraditional students who find education necessary for jobs in today's information age. Distance learning provides a flexible manageable alternative for this developing segment of society. However, students in distance classes work at computers miles apart at varying times of the day and night. This feeling of being alone is overcome when students join together in a community of learners who support one another (Eastmond, 1995). The process of forming a community of learners is an important issue in distance learning because it can affect student satisfaction, retention, and learning (Gabelnick, MacGregor, Matthews & Smith, 1990c; Kember, 1989; Kowch & Schwier, 1997; Powers & Mitchell, 1997). It may even affect faculty evaluations, which tend to be lower in distance education courses (Cordover, 1996).
>
> In reviewing the literature on distance learning for adults and nontraditional students in higher education, I found a decided lack of research about community-building within the class and within the institution. However, other research has paved the way for the exploration of this topic. Studies discussed the need for institutional support (Dillon, Gunawardena & Parker, 1989) and for student/student and student/faculty interaction (Hiltz, 1986; 1996; Powers & Mitchell, 1997) which appear to be steps in building a community of distance learners. (Brown, 1998, p. 2)

In this example, Brown opens with a comment about distance learning and its importance today (the topic). She then argues that there are several problems facing distance education: students feel alone (evidence from practice) and faculty evaluations are low (evidence from past research). Next she assesses a shortcoming in past research: the need to examine community-building (a deficiency in past research). Brown does not end the passage with implications for a specific audience, although she might have discussed the importance of addressing community building in distance learning for the student, teacher, or college personnel. Overall, Brown's statement of the problem section contains four of the five elements.

Next you will read the complete "Statement of the Problem" introducing a quantitative study by Davis et al. (1997) that was reported in a journal article. The study deals with the topic of tobacco use among high school students.

> Adolescent use of all tobacco products is increasing (3–6). By age 18 years, approximately two-thirds of United States teenagers have tried smoking and approximately one-fourth have smoked in the last 30 days (3). In addition, more than 20 percent of white adolescent males use smokeless tobacco products (4). Adolescent tobacco use has been reported by race/ethnicity, gender,

and grade level (5); however, the relationship between sports intensity, race, and tobacco use has not been studied to the best of our knowledge. (Davis et al., 1997, pp. 97–98)

This example models the elements of the "Statement of the Problem" section. Contained within two opening paragraphs in a journal article, it begins with a discussion about the prevalence of smoking in high school (the topic). The authors then advance the issue of a high rate of smokeless tobacco among athletes (the research problem) and provide evidence for this issue drawing on past studies and statistical trends (evidence from past research documenting this as a problem). Following this, the authors indicate that sports intensity (defined later in the study), race, and tobacco use have not been studied (a deficiency). Although no comments are made about an audience that might profit from a study addressing this issue, the intended audience is likely students, teachers, schools, coaches, and researchers who study high school students and adolescent tobacco use.

KEY IDEAS IN THE CHAPTER

A research problem is an educational issue or concern that the investigator presents and justifies in a research study. In a research report, the investigator introduces this problem in the opening paragraphs of a study. It may consist of a single sentence or several sentences. It is distinct from the topic of a study, the purpose, or the research questions. Before designing and writing about the problem, researchers need to consider whether it should and can be studied. It needs to contribute to knowledge and practice in order for it to be examined. The researcher must also have access to people and sites and possess the time, resources, and skills to study the problem. There also needs to be a match between the research problem and the approach—quantitative or qualitative—chosen for the study. Research problems best studied using the quantitative approach are those where the issue needs to be explained; the qualitative approach best fits a problem that needs to be explored.

The actual research problem is included in a section called the "Statement of the Problem," or introduction to a study. There are five elements that go into this section: the educational topic; the research problem; a justification for the problem based on past research and practice; deficiencies or shortcomings of past research or practice; and the importance of addressing the problem for diverse audiences. Several writing strategies assist in this process of designing and writing a "Statement of the Problem" section. These strategies include writing the elements of this section in order, using ample citations to the literature, and including references to statistical information in quantitative studies and quotes in qualitative studies.

USEFUL INFORMATION FOR PRODUCERS OF RESEARCH

▶ Assess whether a problem can and should be researched. Apply three criteria: Will a study of the issue contribute to knowledge and practice? Can the participants and sites be studied? Can the problem be researched given the researcher's time, resources, and skills?

▶ Identify and write a distinct research problem. Make it separate from the topic, the purpose of the study, and the research questions.

▶ Position the research problem in the "Statement of the Problem" section, and present it as the opening passage of a study.

▶ When writing the "Statement of the Problem," introduce the reader to the topic, convey the research problem, justify the need to study the research problem, identify deficiencies in the evidence, and target audiences who will profit from the study.

▶ Consider writing the "Statement of the Problem" section in five distinct paragraphs to ensure inclusion of all elements. Use extensive references, cite statistics for a quantitative study, and include quotes from participants for a qualitative study.

USEFUL INFORMATION FOR CONSUMERS OF RESEARCH

▶ The actual "problem" in a study may be hidden in the opening paragraphs. Look for the issue or concern leading to the study. Ask yourself what educational "problem" is being addressed that needs to be solved.

▶ Recognize that not all research problems should and can be researched. A problem *should* be researched if the investigator can claim that studying it will add to knowledge or practice. A problem *can* be researched if the inquirer has access to people and sites and if the investigator has the time, resources, and skills to adequately study the problem.

▶ Look for five elements in the introduction to a study: the general topic, the problem or issue, the evidence for this problem, the deficiencies in this evidence, and the importance of the study for audiences. This structure can help you understand the opening passages of a study and what the author is attempting to accomplish.

STUDY QUESTIONS AND ACTIVITIES

1. Read an educational research study and locate the sentence or sentences that the author uses to convey the research problem.

2. In the same research study you used to answer the previous question, identify the five elements of the "Statement of the Problem." Mark the passages where the author identified a topic, stated the issue, provided evidence, commented about deficiencies, and explained the importance of addressing these deficiencies for specific audiences. Also, discuss any elements that are left out.

3. Again using the same study, evaluate the research problem and discuss whether the author *should have* or *could have* studied the problem. Use the three criteria mentioned in this chapter for assessing whether a problem is researchable.

4. Look at the "Statement of the Problem" section in a study. Evaluate each of the following: where it is located in the study; the number of paragraphs and length of it; whether it introduces you to the study in a friendly way; and whether it conveys a scholarly emphasis of the need to address the research problem within the existing literature.

5. Present a topic and a research problem and state whether a quantitative or qualitative approach should be used. List three reasons explaining why you chose that approach.

6. Write a narrative hook for a proposed study on a topic of your choice. Share it with someone else and have that person critique it using the criteria for determining a good narrative hook presented in this chapter.

Now go to our Companion Website to assess your understanding of chapter content with Multiple-Choice Questions, apply comprehension in Projects & Essays, and broaden your knowledge with links to related research topics on the Web.

4

Reviewing the Literature

Our high school teacher Maria knows that she needs to review the literature for her school committee and to summarize the literature for the research project she is doing for her graduate program. Because she has not spent much time in the university library, she compiles a list of questions for her advisor:

1. Where do I start in reviewing the literature?
2. How do I locate the best materials to include in my summary?
3. Can I use the Internet to search for literature?
4. Does the library have many of the materials I need?
5. Are there any shortcuts for locating a large number of journal articles on the topic?
6. Should I gather and summarize both quantitative and qualitative studies?
7. Do you have an example of a literature review that I might examine?

As you begin to think about reviewing the literature for a research study, you may have questions similar to Maria's. You may even wonder why a literature review is important in the first place.

When planning and conducting research, reviewing the literature can help determine how your topic fits into the existing literature. Knowing this information will help avoid duplicating research that already exists. A literature review will also demonstrate to readers that you can read research, extract key elements from it, and summarize the existing knowledge. But most importantly, the literature review provides a justification for your study. This justification may be based on extending past research, filling a gap overlooked by others, or addressing a population or group that has not been studied.

Perhaps your reasons for reading research are to learn new ideas, share the latest findings with others (like Maria and her school committee), or locate practices that might improve learning in your classroom. If this is the case, knowing how researchers conduct a literature review will help you locate useful literature in library resources, read a journal article, and identify useful information in the "literature review" sections of studies. You may also need to know how to conduct a search of the many information databases available today. Knowing how researchers conduct research also provides criteria to assess the relevance of the materials on your topic.

A **literature review** is a written summary of articles, books, and other documents that describes the past and current state of knowledge about a topic. Researchers conduct a literature review as one element in the research process. This review documents the importance of the research problem in a study, cites useful explanations or theories to be tested, foreshadows the major questions in a study, and provides explanations for results or findings. This chapter will address these varied roles of the literature review and provide a five-step process that researchers typically use in conducting the review. This process involves: identifying terms to use in your literature search; locating literature; reading and checking the relevance of the literature; organizing the literature you have selected; and writing a literature review.

By the end of this chapter, you should be able to:

 ⟩ Distinguish between the use of literature in quantitative and qualitative research.
 ⟩ Identify key terms to use in a literature search.
 ⟩ Describe types of resources, especially databases, useful in research.
 ⟩ List criteria for assessing the relevance of literature for a review.
 ⟩ Design a visual picture—called a "literature map"—of the literature on your topic.
 ⟩ Describe how to write a summary of the literature.

EXAMINING LITERATURE CITED IN THE TELEVISION VIOLENCE AND THE GUNMAN INCIDENT STUDIES

In both the quantitative television violence study (Vooijs & van der Voort, 1993) and the qualitative gunman incident study (Asmussen & Creswell, 1995), the authors begin their articles by citing literature from other studies. You can identify this literature by noting when the researchers cite an author and a year, such as the reference to "Freedman, 1984" (Paragraph 01) in the television violence study or an author and a number indicating a reference at the end of the article, such as "Roark [24] and Roark and Roark [25]" in the gunman case study (Paragraph 01). Let's take a closer look at the two studies and examine the use of literature in quantitative and qualitative research.

Literature Review in a Quantitative Study

In the *quantitative* television violence study (Vooijs and van der Voort, 1993), the citations to the literature cluster around the beginning and the end of the article. First, the authors introduce literature in the opening paragraphs of the study (Paragraphs 01–06). A substantial number of citations (17 in Paragraphs 01 to 03) document the harmful effects of television violence on children. The use of literature here establishes the importance of the research problem (i.e., harmful effects). Second, immediately following this opening passage, the authors discuss the curriculum they used as the intervention in the experiment. They again cite the literature extensively to document a theory or explanation as to why children's attitudes might change by viewing this curriculum—the theory that predicts that attitudes change when individuals are presented with new information not compatible with existing ideas (see Paragraph 11). In this case, the use of literature documents predicted outcomes for the study. On a broader level, the entire discussion about the effects of the curriculum foreshadows the research questions (Paragraphs 15–18) on the impact of the curriculum on the children. Third, the literature is cited in the final section, the "Discussion." At this point it is used to explain the positive results of the curriculum (Paragraph 43) and to lend support that the theory was predictive of attitude change (Paragraph 45).

In summary, the literature in the television violence study:

▶ documents the importance of the research problem at the beginning of the study
▶ supports the theory or explanation used in the study
▶ foreshadows the research questions
▶ provides an explanation for the results at the end of the study by citing other studies and by returning to the theoretical predictions

Literature Review in a Qualitative Study

Now let's turn to a qualitative study to see what purpose the literature might play there. In the *qualitative* gunman case study (Asmussen and Creswell, 1995), the literature serves some of the same purposes and some different purposes than did the literature in the quantitative study. Like the television violence study, the authors also begin their article by citing literature to document the research problem of campus violence. They use the literature sparingly, however, citing only 10 references in the first two paragraphs (see Paragraphs 01 and 02). This use of literature in qualitative research is much less than its use in quantitative research. Their research questions at the end of the introduction (Paragraph 03), did not follow from this literature. Rather, the questions are general and open-ended so the researchers can learn from the participants in the study. Then, literature is cited again in the "Discussion" section at the end of the article (see Paragraphs 32–36). At this point, the authors use literature to discuss how their themes both reinforce and depart from findings in past research (Paragraph 33).

In summary, the literature in the qualitative gunman case study:

▶ documents the importance of the research problem at the beginning of the study
▶ does not foreshadow the research questions (which are broad in scope to encourage participants to provide their views)
▶ is used to compare and contrast with other studies at the end of the study

Comparing the Purpose of Literature in Quantitative and Qualitative Research

These two research studies illustrate the use of literature in both quantitative and qualitative studies. They also highlight several fundamental differences between the two approaches as summarized in Table 4.1. Table 4.1 illustrates three primary differences: the amount of literature cited at the beginning of the study, the use it serves at the beginning, and its use at the end of a study.

In a quantitative study, researchers discuss the literature extensively at the beginning of a study (see Vooijs & van der Voort, 1993). This serves two major purposes: It justifies the importance of the research problem and it provides a rationale for (and foreshadows) the purpose of the study and research questions or hypotheses. (Purpose statements, research questions, and hypotheses will be addressed in Chapter 5.) In many quantitative studies, the authors include the literature in a separate section titled "Review of the Literature" in order to highlight the important role it plays. The authors also incorporate the literature into the end of the study where the results are compared with prior predictions or expectations made at the beginning of the study.

TABLE 4.1
Differences in Extent and Use of Literature in Quantitative and Qualitative Research

Differences	Quantitative Research	Qualitative Research
Amount of literature cited at the beginning of the study	Substantial	Minimal
Use of literature at the beginning of the study	Justifies or documents the need for the study	Justifies or documents the need for the study
	Provides a rationale for the direction of the study (i.e., purpose statement and research questions or hypotheses)	
Use of literature at the end of the study	Confirms or disconfirms prior predictions from the literature	Supports or modifies existing findings in the literature

In a qualitative study, researchers typically use the literature to serve different purposes. Similar to quantitative research, the authors mention the literature at the beginning of the study to document or justify the importance of the research problem (e.g., Asmussen & Creswell, 1995). However, authors do not discuss the literature extensively at the beginning of a study. This allows the views of the participants to emerge without being constrained by the views of others from the literature. In some qualitative studies, researchers use the literature to support the findings (or the "themes," to be discussed in Chapter 9 on "Thematic Development"). Nevertheless, in many qualitative projects, the literature is often cited again at the end of the study to serve as a contrast or comparison with the major findings in the study. This contrast and comparison is not the same as prediction in quantitative research. In qualitative inquiry, researchers do not make predictions about findings. They are more interested in whether the findings of a study support or modify existing ideas and practices advanced in the literature, as shown in the gunman incident qualitative study (Asmussen & Creswell, 1995).

DESIGNING AND CONDUCTING A LITERATURE REVIEW

Regardless of whether the study is quantitative or qualitative there are common steps researchers use in conducting a literature review. As you read research, knowing these steps will help you understand the process researchers typically use in composing literature review passages in their studies. As you conduct research, understanding this process will give you tools for beginning a search of the literature and offer logical steps for writing a scholarly summary of it.

Although conducting a literature review follows no prescribed path, researchers who plan and conduct a study typically go through five interrelated steps. For individuals not conducting a study but looking for literature on a topic, only the first four steps apply. However, learning all five steps will provide a sense of how researchers proceed in reviewing the literature.

1. *Identify key terms* to use in your search for literature.
2. *Locate literature* about a topic by consulting several types of materials and databases, including those available at an academic library and on the Internet at Web sites.
3. *Read the literature and check its relevance* to your topic.
4. *Organize the literature* you have selected into a "literature map" of studies and documents on your topic.
5. If you plan to conduct research, *write a review* by developing summaries of the literature.

Identifying Key Terms

Identifying a few key terms (one or two words or short phrases) that adequately describe your topic will help in your search for literature. You should choose these carefully because they are important for initially locating literature in a library or Internet search. To identify these terms, you can use several strategies, outlined below:

▶ Write a preliminary "working title" for a project and select two to three key words in the title that capture the essence of your study. Although some researchers write the title last, a working title keeps you focused on the key ideas of the study. This working title can be revised at regular intervals during the research, if necessary (Glesne & Peshkin, 1992).

▶ Pose a short, general research question that you would like answered in the study. Select the two or three words in this question that best summarize the primary direction of the study.

▶ Look in a thesaurus of terms to find words that match your topic. Visit a college or university library that contains the Educational Resources Information Center (1991) database (hereafter referred to as ERIC or the ERIC database). One resource in the ERIC database is *A Thesaurus of ERIC Descriptors* (Educational Resources Information Center, 1967–) that includes a dictionary of terms (called *descriptors*). Examine the *Thesaurus* for terms that closely relate to your topic. An online ERIC *Thesaurus*, available at the ERIC Web site, http://searcheric.org, can be accessed by using a home computer and a search engine like AltaVista or Yahoo!.

▶ Go to the stacks in a college or university library and scan the table of contents of education journals from the last 7 to 10 years and look for key terms in titles to the articles.

You may recall that our high school teacher, Maria, needs to locate literature on weapon possession by high school students. After thinking about how she might get started, she writes down a working title, "Weapon Possession by High School Students." However, she wonders if the words, "weapon possession," will be useful in searching the literature. One way to determine this is to see if this term is in the ERIC *Thesaurus*. Using her home computer and the Yahoo! search engine, Maria locates the ERIC Web site: http://www.searcheric.org. After entering "weapon possession" in the *Thesaurus* search, she learns that it is not a term in the ERIC vocabulary and finds out that she should use the term "weapons" instead. She next determines that two additional terms, "high schools" and "students," are also in the ERIC vocabulary. To continue her search of the ERIC data to locate materials for her review (either in the library or online), Maria now has three terms that will likely yield literature: "weapons," "high schools," and "students."

Locating Literature

Having identified key terms, you can begin the search for relevant literature. You might be tempted to begin your search from a home computer by accessing Web sites and exploring the electronic literature available on a topic. Although this process may be convenient, not all literature posted on the Internet is dependable because, typically, it has not been reviewed and screened for quality. With increasing frequency, however, full-text documents are becoming available on the Internet and the quality will undoubtedly improve.

You might also begin your search by asking faculty or students to recommend good articles and studies to review. This approach may be helpful, but it lacks the systematic process found in searching library resources.

Using Academic Libraries

A sound approach is to begin your search in an academic library available on college and university campuses. By physically searching the stacks, reviewing microfiche, and accessing the computerized databases, you will save time because you will find comprehensive holdings not available through other sources. Although a town or city library may yield some useful literature, an academic library typically offers the largest collection of materials, especially research studies.

Academic library resources have changed considerably in recent years as they have moved toward more "online" texts for easy computer access, more CD-ROM databases, and more digital forms of information (Ferguson & Bunge, 1997). Two challenges face the beginning researcher. First, the researcher needs to locate material—a task often made difficult because of the large and complex holdings in a library, such as journals or periodicals (recent and bound), government documents, the microfiche collection, and indexes. To help locate material, you might use the services of a reference librarian or search through library holdings using a computer.

A second challenge is overcoming the frustration that arises when other library users have checked out materials you need, making them unavailable for use. When this occurs, researchers can use the library service of interlibrary loan as a means of obtaining the literature; however, this process takes time and requires patience.

Differentiating Between Primary and Secondary Sources

Because literature reviews summarize the current state of research, you should focus on locating original research reports. Being able to differentiate between primary (or original) sources and secondary sources is therefore important. A **primary source** consists of literature reported by the individual(s) who actually conducted the research or who originated the ideas. Research articles published by educational journals are an example of this type of source. A **secondary source,** on the other hand, is literature that summarizes primary sources. It does not represent material published by the original researcher or the creator of the idea. Examples of secondary sources are handbooks, encyclopedias, and select journals that summarize research, such as the *Review of the Educational Research.* Typically, you will locate both primary and secondary sources, but it is best to rely on primary sources. They present the literature in the original state and have not been subjected to the viewpoint of the author of the secondary source. Primary sources also provide the details of original research better than do secondary sources.

A meta-analysis study illustrates one type of secondary source material. **Meta-analysis** is a type of research report in which the author integrates the findings of many (primary source) research studies. This is done by evaluating the results of individual studies and deriving an overall index of the magnitude of results. The intent of this research is to determine the overall impact of variables on outcomes when studied by many researchers over numerous groups of people.

As both a type of study and a procedure for integrating findings, meta-analysis, created during the 1970s, developed because of concerns about the imprecise characterization of findings during a review of the literature (Cooper & Lindsay, 1998). Since its development, researchers have conducted and reported numerous meta-analysis studies, such as the classic study of the effectiveness of psychotherapy and the summary of results from 833 tests of treatments (Smith & Glass, 1977).

The process for conducting a meta-analysis follows systematic steps. The researcher locates studies on a single topic and notes the statistical results reported in the studies (such as correlations among variables or differences among group means, as discussed later in Chapter 8 on "Choosing a Statistical Test"). To compare all of the results across the studies, the investigator calculates the *effect size* for each study (effect size will be further described in Chapter 8, "Conducting Hypothesis Testing"). This effect size reports the magnitude of results for a study (e.g., how large the differences in improvement might be between clients who receive behavioral and ecological therapy). The researcher then averages the effect sizes for all studies (or all similar items) to derive an overall index. In this process, the investigator synthesizes the literature, providing a secondary source of primary research reports.

An illustration of a meta-analysis study as well as the difference between a primary and secondary source of information can be seen in Figure 4.1. In the top section we see the first page of a *primary source* research report, an investigation by Smetana and Asquith (1994). They examine the conceptions of parental authority and ratings of adolescent-parent conflict for 68 sixth, eighth, and tenth graders and their parents.

In the bottom section of Figure 4.1, we see that the original research by Smetana and Asquith (1994) is included as one of 27 studies reported in a *secondary source,* a meta-analysis published by Laursen, Coy, and Collins (1998). The 27 studies (shown in the table) integrated research examining parent-child conflict changes during early, mid- and late adolescence. Overall, the authors conclude from the meta-analysis that little support exists for the commonly held view that parent-child conflict rises and then falls across adolescence. Indeed, the primary source research report by Smetana and Asquith (1994) shows only a small positive change in parent-child conflict during early and mid-adolescent (an effect size of 0.09).

Historically, the division into primary and secondary sources has been a useful classification for literature in law and history (Barzun & Graff, 1985). However, it is not an adequate classification with the new forms of literature available to the researcher, such as articles and commentaries posted to Web sites.

As you consider the types of literature available and how to get started in your literature search, the classification in Figure 4.2 can be helpful in identifying types of library and Web site materials. Modified from a classification originally developed by Libutti and Blandy (1995), the figure is a guide to resources as well as a framework for getting started in a literature search.

Using this framework, you might begin your search at the bottom of the triangle by consulting summaries of research that synthesize numerous studies on a topic. From these broad summaries, you can work your way up to "early stage" literature found at the top. For many beginning researchers, starting with summaries is a good idea because they give an overview of topics at an entry-level discussion. Summaries also have a longer "life" from the initial idea stage and have undergone reviews for quality.

Summaries

Summaries provide overviews of the literature and research on timely issues in education. A compendium of available summaries is shown in Table 4.2. These sources include encyclopedias, dictionaries and glossaries of terms, handbooks, statistical indexes, and reviews and syntheses. These summaries introduce a beginning researcher to a problem area and help you locate key references and identify current issues. These entries are written by leading specialists in the field of education.

FIGURE 4.1

Example of a Primary Source (Journal article) and a Secondary Source (Meta-analysis)

Adolescents' and Parents' Conceptions of Parental Authority and Personal Autonomy

Judith G. Smetana and Pamela Asquith
University of Rochester

SMETANA, JUDITH G., and ASQUITH, PAMELA. *Adolescents' and Parents' Conceptions of Parental Authority and Personal Autonomy*. CHILD DEVELOPMENT, 1994, 65, 1147–1162. Conceptions of parental authority and ratings of adolescent-parent conflict were assessed in 68 sixth, eighth, and tenth graders and their parents. Boundaries of adolescent personal jurisdiction and conflict over these boundaries were examined. Participants judged the legitimacy of parental authority and rated the frequency and intensity of conflict regarding 24 hypothetical moral, conventional, personal, multifaceted (e.g., containing conventional and personal components), prudential, and friendship issues. Adolescents and parents agreed that parents should retain authority regarding moral and conventional issues. Parents treated multifaceted, friendship, prudential, and personal issues as more contingent on parental authority than did adolescents, based on conventional, prudential, and psychological reasons, whereas adolescents treated these issues as under personal jurisdiction, based on personal concerns. Personal reasoning and judgments increased with age. Multifaceted issues were discussed more than all other issues, but moral and conventional conflicts were more intense than all other conflicts. The findings are discussed in terms of previous research on parental authority and adolescent-parent conflict during adolescence.

◄ The original article as a primary source of information (Smetana & Asquith, 1994)

Youniss and Smollar (1985) serted that, during adolescence, pa relations shift from unilateral to r thority. Using a domain model cognitive development (Smetana, riel, 1983; Turiel & Davidson, 198 research has indicated, however, lescents' and parents' conceptions tal authority are differentiated; sh rental authority are found in som but not in others. Adolescents an were found to be unilateral in t ments of moral issues (defined a:

A meta-analysis as a secondary source of information (Laursen, Coy, & Collins, 1998)

Table 2   Parent-Adolescent Conflict Effect Size Estimates for Samples Included in Age Meta-Analyses

| | Effect Size Estimates | | | | | | | | | | | |
| | Early and Mid-adolescence | | | | Mid- and Late Adolescence | | | | Early and Late Adolescence | | | |
Study	n	Total r	Rate r	Affect r	n	Total r	Rate r	Affect r	n	Total r	Rate r	Affect r
Blase (1989)	63	.05	.00	.10	77	.08	.00	.15	52	-.02	.00	-.04
Block (1937)	352	-.56	-.56		440	.33	.33		264	-.82	-.82	
Carlton-Ford & Collins (1988)	40	-.08	-.08		40	.08	.08		40	-.08	-.08	
Connor et al. (1954)					119	.31	.31					
Flannery et al. (1991)	85	.22		.22								
Furman & Buhrmester (1992)	250	-.01	-.01		337	.14	.14		355	-.15	-.15	
Galambos & Almeida (1992)	66	-.09		-.09								
Greene & Grimsley (1990)	72	.13		.13								
Hagan et al. (1992)[a]	138	-.08	-.14	.09								
Inoff-Germain et al. (1988)	60	.00	-.04	.04								
Johnstone (1975)					1,317	-.01	-.01					
Kahlbaugh (1992)	20	.07	.04	.11								
Kahlbaugh et al. (1994)	41	.04	.11	-.04								
Khatri et al. (1993)	171	.29	.29									
Laursen (1993)					685	.00	.00	.00				
Lempers & Clark-Lempers (1992)	799	-.16	-.16		760	.06	.06		619	-.23	-.23	
Noack (1993)					38	.06	.06					
Papini et al. (1989)	193	.00		.00	201	.07		.07	164	-.08		-.08
Rajalu (1991)					365	-.05	-.05					
Schoenleber (1988)	44	-.22	-.22		44	.00	.00		44	-.22	-.22	
Sidhu & Singh (1987)					64	.03	.03					
Smetana (1989)	52	-.16	-.16		50	.19	.19		50	-.32	-.32	
Smetana (1991)	180	.07	.00	.15	158	.16	.16	.16	172	-.08	-.15	.00
Smetana & Asquith (1994)	68	.09	.12	.00								
Smetana et al. (1991)	28	.00	.00	.00								
Wierson et al. (1990)	122	.00	.00	.00								
Wierson & Forehand (1992)	184	.14		.14								

Note: n = participants included in effect size estimates. r = effect size estimate. Positive r values in contrasts of early adolescence and mid-adolescence, and in contrasts of mid-adolescence and late adolescence indicate greater conflict during mid-adolescence. Positive r values in contrasts of early adolescence and late adolescence indicate greater conflict during late adolescence.
[a] The number of participants reported for conflict rate and conflict affect differed; values reported here are averages.

Source: From Reconsidering changes in parent-child conflict across adolescence: A meta-analysis, by B. Laursen, K. C. Coy, & W. A. Collins, 1998, *Child Development,* (69), p. 823. Reprinted with permission of S.R.C.D.

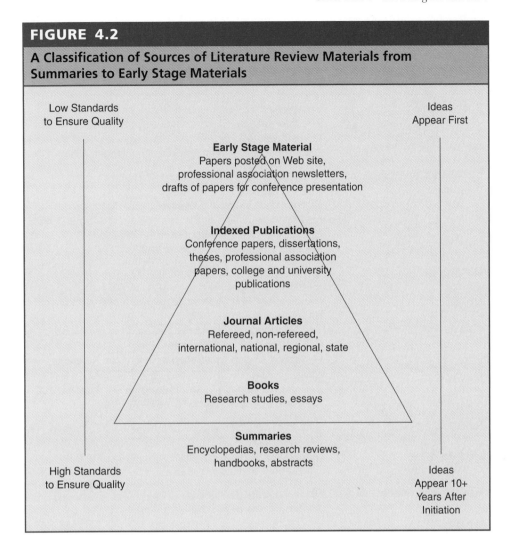

FIGURE 4.2

A Classification of Sources of Literature Review Materials from Summaries to Early Stage Materials

Low Standards to Ensure Quality

Ideas Appear First

Early Stage Material
Papers posted on Web site, professional association newsletters, drafts of papers for conference presentation

Indexed Publications
Conference papers, dissertations, theses, professional association papers, college and university publications

Journal Articles
Refereed, non-refereed, international, national, regional, state

Books
Research studies, essays

Summaries
Encyclopedias, research reviews, handbooks, abstracts

High Standards to Ensure Quality

Ideas Appear 10+ Years After Initiation

Encyclopedias   A good place to start when you know little about a topic is an *encyclopedia,* such as the *Encyclopedia of Educational Research* (Alkin, 1992). Sponsored by the American Educational Research Association (AERA), this encyclopedia provides the latest research under 16 broad topics, including the curriculum of elementary and secondary education, education of exceptional persons, and the organizational structure and governance of education. The appendix on "Doing Library Research in Education" is especially useful (Alkin, 1992, p. 1543).

Dictionaries and Glossaries of Terms   Another useful tool in the literature review and overall research process is a *dictionary* of research terms. These dictionaries contain most of the recent educational terms. For example, the *Dictionary of Statistics and Methodology: A Nontechnical Guide for the Social Sciences* (2nd edition, Vogt, 1999) defines statistical and methodological terms used in the social and behavioral sciences, which are often problematic for beginning researchers. *Qualitative Inquiry: A Dictionary of Terms* (Schwandt, 1997) is a reference book of qualitative terms where multiple and often contested points of view about their definitions are suggested. *Post-Modernism and the Social Sciences* (Rosenau, 1992) provides a glossary of postmodern terms related to studying issues of inequality and oppression in our society.

TABLE 4.2	
Types of Summaries Available in Academic Libraries	
Types of Summaries	**Sample Library Resources**
Encyclopedias	*Encyclopedia of Educational Research* (Alkin, 1992) *The International Encyclopedia of Education* (Husen & Postlethwaithe,1994) *Encyclopedia of American Education* (Unger, 1996)
Dictionaries and glossaries of terms	*Qualitative Inquiry: A Dictionary of Terms* (Schwandt, 1997) *Dictionary of Terms in Statistics and Methodology: A Nontechnical Guide for the Social Sciences* (Vogt, 1999) Glossary of post-modern terms, in *Post-Modernism and the Social Sciences* (Rosenau, 1992)
Handbooks	*Handbook of Research on Multicultural Education* (Banks & Banks, 1995) *Handbook of Research on Teacher Education* (Houston, Haberman, & Sikula, 1990) *The Handbook of Qualitative Research in Education* (LeCompte, Millroy, & Preissle, 1992) *Handbook of Qualitative Research* (Denzin & Lincoln, 2000) *Educational Research, Methodology and Measurement: An International Handbook* (Keeves, 1988)
Statistical indexes	*American Statistics Index* (Congressional Information Service, 1973–) *Digest of Educational Statistics* (National Center for Educational Statistics, 1997)
Reviews and syntheses	*Review of Educational Research* (1931–) *Annual Review of Psychology* (1950–)

Handbooks   There are numerous *handbooks* that provide chapters on content topics such as teaching, reading, curriculum, social studies, educational administration, multicultural education, and teacher education. Several handbooks are available on educational research topics. A handbook that addresses methods of research inquiry, the utilization of knowledge, measurement, and statistics, is *Educational Research, Methodology, and Measurement: An International Handbook* (Keeves, 1988). Two recent handbooks are also available on topics in qualitative research, *The Handbook of Qualitative Research in Education* (LeCompte, Millroy, & Priessle, 1992) and the *Handbook of Qualitative Research* (Denzin & Lincoln, 2000). In quantitative research, handbooks are available as well, such as the *Handbook of Applied Social Research Methods* (Bickman & Rog, 2000). For research that combines both the quantitative and qualitative research approach, you might want to refer to the *Handbook of Mixed Methods in the Social and Behavioral Sciences* (Tashakkori & Teddlie, in press).

Statistical Indexes   *Statistical indexes,* such as the annual *Digest of Educational Statistics* (National Center for Education Statistics, 1997), report educational trends useful in writing problem statements or literature reviews. The *Digest,* issued since 1933 by the U.S. government, compiles statistical information covering the broad field of American education from kindergarten through graduate school. It also reports information from many sources, including the surveys and activities carried out by the National Center for Educational Statistics (NCES).

Reviews and Syntheses   A final summary source consists of timely *reviews and syntheses* on topics in education, psychology, and the social sciences. For example, the *Review of Educational Research* (1931–) is a quarterly journal of the American Educational Research Association (AERA) that publishes lengthy articles synthesizing educational research on various topics.

Books

Academic libraries have extensive collections of books on a broad range of educational topics. Typically, an academic library offers a computerized system to search for books. This system permits searching by author, by title, or by subject area through the library book holdings. Also, through library computerized services, the book (and journal) holdings of many academic libraries in the United States can be searched online and ordered through interlibrary loan.

The books most useful in reviewing the literature will be those that summarize research studies or report conceptual discussions on educational topics. Textbooks used in classes are less useful because they typically do not contain reports of single research studies. They may, however, contain important references to the literature. The *Subject Guide to Books in Print* (1957–) or the *Core List of Books and Journals in Education* (O'Brien & Fabiano, 1990) are guides that might also be helpful in your literature search.

Journals, Indexed Publications, and Electronic Sources

Journal (or periodical) articles and conference papers that report research are prime sources for a literature review. As shown in Table 4.3, there are numerous journals that publish research in education. For those looking for journals in which to report research, Table 4.3 lists them based on their emphasis on the quantitative approach, the qualitative approach, or both. This classification is a rough guide, since journal preferences shift over time and with appointments of new editors. However, a classification such as this highlights the numerous publication outlets for both quantitative and qualitative research in education.

To locate articles in journals, consider searching an abstract series, indexes to journals, or the diverse databases in education and the social sciences. These resources are discussed in further detail below.

Abstract Series   Abstract series, which allow for a broad search of journal articles by subject area, are available in many fields. In educational administration, for example, you might examine the *Educational Administration Abstracts* (University Council for Educational Administration, 1966–) or in early childhood development, look at the *Child Development Abstracts and Bibliography* (Society for Research in Child Development, 1945–). You can usually find these abstracts by accessing the online library catalogue and using keywords, such as "abstracts," and the subject field or topic to determine if the library contains a specific abstract series. As shown in Figure 4.3 and 4.4, the words, "child development" entered into the subject search of an online academic library (see Figure 4.3) resulted in 12 entries, one of which was "child development abstracts" (see Figure 4.4).

Indexes   Another place to search for journal publications is in the *Education Index* (Wilson, 1929/32–), an index devoted primarily to periodicals and organized into subject areas and fields.

TABLE 4.3

Select Education and Social Sciences Journals that Emphasize Quantitative and Qualitative Research

Journals Emphasizing Quantitative Research	Journals Emphasizing Qualitative Research	Journals Emphasizing Both Quantitative and Qualitative Research
Educational and Psychological Measurement (Educational and Psychological Measurement)	*Anthropology and Education Quarterly* (Council on Anthropology and Education)	*Harvard Educational Review* (Harvard University)
Journal of Educational Research (American Educational Research Association)	*International Journal of Qualitative Studies in Education* (Falmer Press)	*American Educational Research Journal* (American Educational Research Association)
Journal of Educational Measurement (National Council on Measurement in Education)	*Journal of Contemporary Ethnography* (Sage)	*The Elementary School Journal* (University of Chicago Press)
Journal of Educational Psychology (American Psychological Association)	*Journal of Narrative and Life History* (Lawrence Erlbaum Associates)	*Educational Administration Quarterly* (University Council on Educational Administration)
Journal of Experimental Education (HELDREF Publications)	*Qualitative Family Research* (National Council on Family Relations)	*Reading Research Quarterly* (International Reading Association)
Journal of Psychology (Journal Press)	*Qualitative Health Research* (Sage)	*Research in the Teaching of English* (National Council of Teachers of English)
Journal of School Psychology (Behavioral Publications)	*Qualitative Sociology* (Human Sciences Press)	*Theory and Research in Social Education* (National Council for Social Studies)
Journal of Social Psychology (Journal Press)	*Qualitative Inquiry* (Sage)	*Theory into Practice* (Ohio State University)
Psychological Bulletin (American Psychological Association)	*Studies in Qualitative Methodology* (JAI Press)	*Journal of Adolescent Research* (Sage)
Psychological Review (American Psychological Association)	*Symbolic Interaction* (Society for the Study of Symbolic Interaction with JAI Press)	*Journal of Counseling and Development* (Counseling Association)
Research Quarterly for Exercise and Sport (American Alliance for Health, Physical Education and Recreation)	*Qualitative Research* (Sage)	*Journal of Research in Mathematics Education* (National Council of Teachers of Mathematics)
Research in Higher Education (Human Sciences Press)		*Journal of Research in Music Education* (Music Educators National Conference)
Applied Measurement in Education (National Council for Measurement in Education)		*Journal of Research in Science Teaching* (John Wiley and Sons)
		Review of Higher Education (Johns Hopkins Press)

Sources: Adapted from Fraenkel & Wallen (2000) and Preissle (1996).

FIGURE 4.3

**Online Subject Search in a University Academic Library
(http://iris.unl.edu/screens/iris.html)**

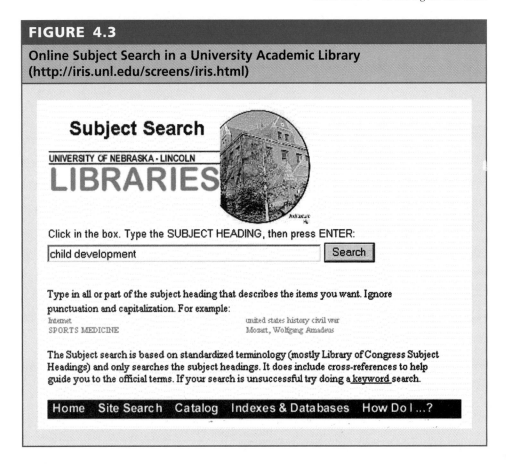

Databases

The most likely place to find journal articles is in databases that index journal articles both in print form and on CD-ROMs. By examining these databases, researchers can easily access hundreds of journal articles on educational topics. Computerized databases also facilitate searching the literature for conference papers and miscellaneous publications, such as papers from professional associations or education agencies. You might start a computerized search of the databases with the education data, followed by the psychological and sociological sources of information. Five important databases; outlined below, offer easy retrieval of journal articles and other documents related to education.

1. The print version of ERIC (Educational Resources Information Center, 1991), the CD-ROM version, *ERIC* (Educational Resources Information Center, 1986), and the Web site, http://www.accesseric.org, all offer access to the ERIC database. The Educational Resources Information Center, a national system of information in education, was established in 1966 by the U.S. Department of Education and the National Library of Education (NLE). Because of this public support, you can search the ERIC database free of charge.

    The ERIC database is the world's largest source of education information with nearly 1 million abstracts of documents and journal articles on education research and practice. You can search this extensive database in the following three ways:

    • on the Internet at http://www.accesseric.org (The "Think-Aloud" on page 103 will take Maria through an online ERIC search process to locate literature on weapon possession among high school students.)

FIGURE 4.4

**Online Subject Search Results in a University Academic Library
(http://iris.unl.edu/search/d?SEARCH=child+development)**

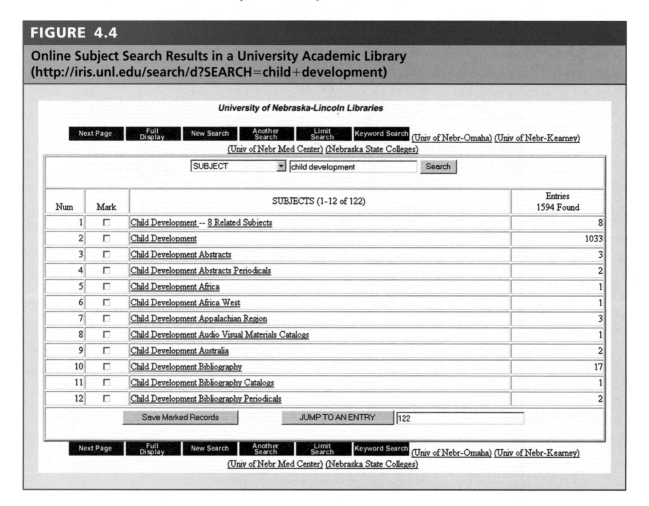

- on CD-ROMs available at many academic libraries, usually installed on library computers for your use (Educational Resources Information, Center, 1986)
- in print copy available in the stacks of academic libraries (Educational Resources Information Center, 1991)

Education information becomes included in the ERIC database through a review system by individuals at 16 sub-content clearinghouses (e.g., Adult, Career, and Vocational Education, Assessment and Evaluation), associated adjunct clearinghouses, and support components. Individuals at these clearinghouses examine the educational material, write abstracts, and assign terms or "descriptors" from the ERIC vocabulary to identify each source of information.

The ERIC database consists of two parts: journals, located in the *Current Index to Journals in Education* (CIJE)(Educational Resources Information Center, 1969–), and documents, found in *Resources in Education* (RIE)(Educational Resources Information Center, 1966–). *CIJE* is a monthly and cumulative index to information located in approximately 980 major educational and education-related journals. It provides a subject index, an author index, and abstracts of specific studies.

When you locate a journal article (CIJE) citation in ERIC, you will find a summary (or resume) of the article displaying major features of the study. A sample summary of a resume for a journal article in ERIC is shown in Figure 4.5. You can locate this sample at http://www.accesseric.org. This summary displays the letters

FIGURE 4.5

Sample ERIC Journal Article Resume (http://www.accesseric.org/searchdb/resumejou.html)

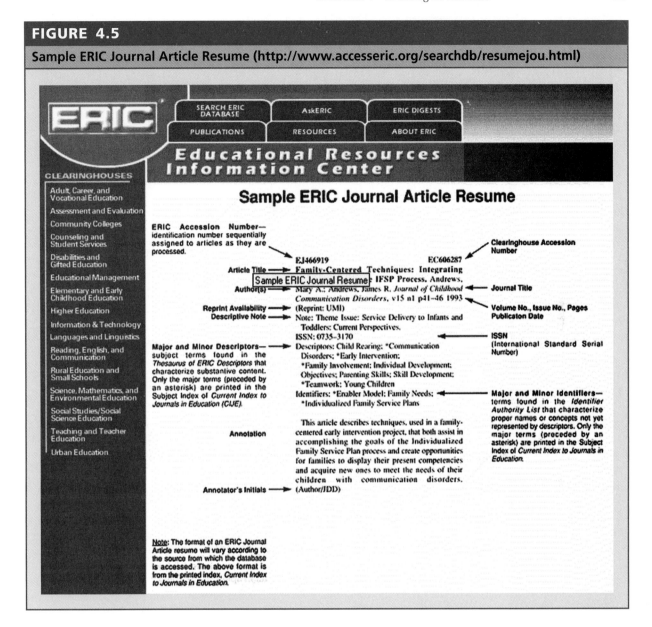

"EJ" assigned as the ERIC Accession Number to designate the item as an ERIC journal article. It also displays the author, the title, the major and minor "descriptors" assigned to the article, and a brief annotation describing the article.

RIE is a monthly and cumulative index to current research findings, project and technical reports, speeches, unpublished manuscripts, and books. It indexes education information by subject, personal author, institution, and publication type. A sample summary of a document in *RIE* is shown in Figure 4.6. This sample illustrates the use of letters "ED" to designate it as an ERIC document. Additional information includes the author and title, the "descriptors" assigned to the article by reviewers, and an abstract of the information.

2. *Psychological Abstracts* (American Psychological Association, 1927–) and the CD-ROM versions, *PsycLit* (SilverPlatter Information, Inc., 1986) and PsycINFO (see

FIGURE 4.6

Sample ERIC Document Resume (http://www.accesseric.org/searchdb/resumedoc.html)

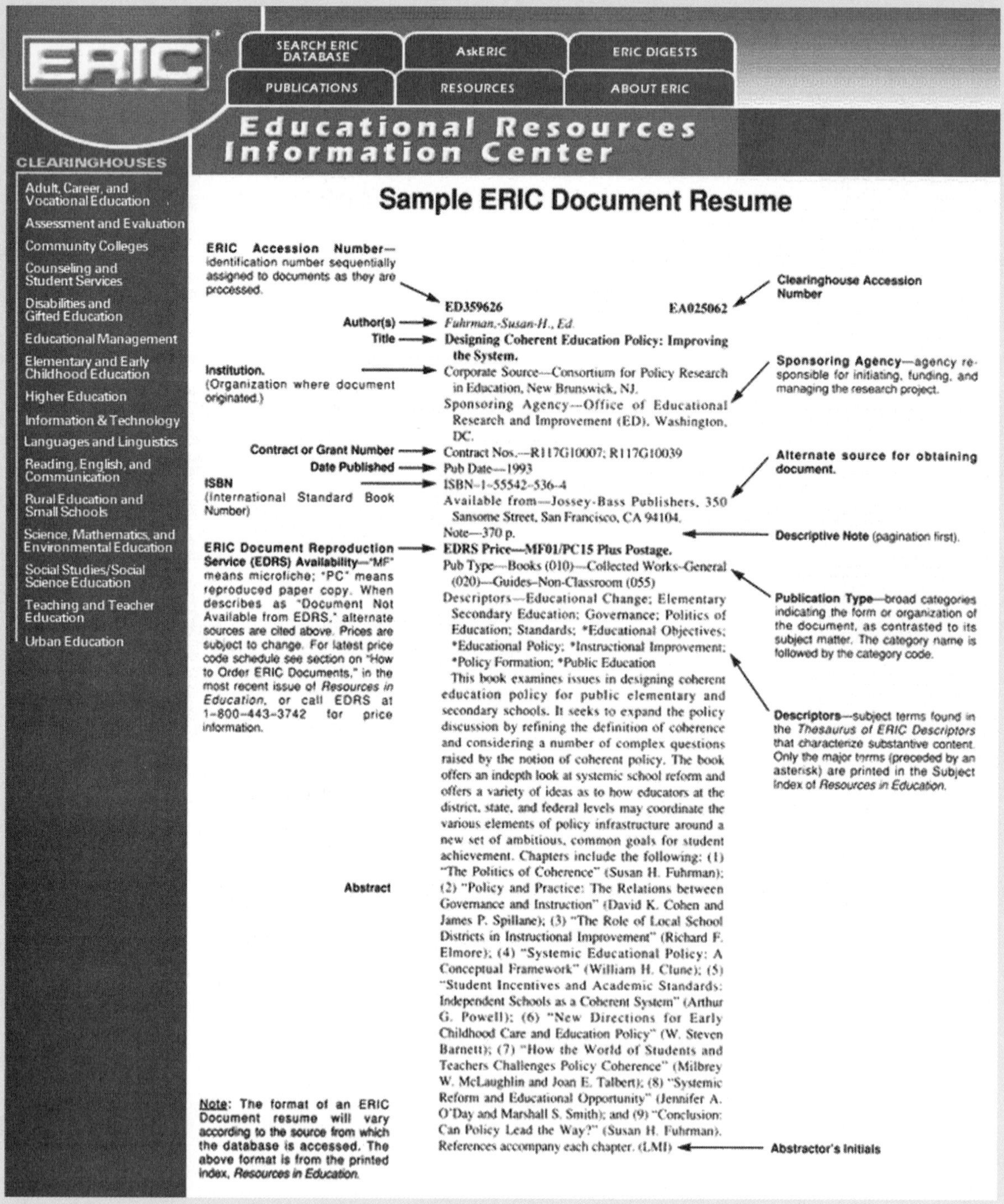

Sample ERIC Document Resume

http://www.apa.org) are important sources for locating research articles on topics broadly related to psychology. In October, 2000, PsycLit and PsycINFO consolidated into one database to provide a comprehensive source of psychological literature from 1887 to the present. This database is available in a printed version, on CD-ROM, and on the Web site. These databases are available in libraries or through online Web versions leased by the libraries and networked through campus computers.

These databases index more than 850 journals in 16 categories. They provide bibliographic citations, abstracts for psychological journal articles, dissertations, technical reports, books, and book chapters published worldwide. The print version has a 3-year cumulative index. An example of a journal record from PsycINFO printed from http://www.apa.org/psyinfo/about/ is shown in Figure 4.7. Similar to an ERIC record, this summary from PsycINFO includes key phrase "identifiers," as well as the author, title, the source, and a brief abstract of the article.

3. *Sociological Abstracts* (Sociological Abstracts, Inc., 1953–) is available in a printed version, on CD-ROM (*Sociofile,* SilverPlatter Information, Inc., 1974/86–), and in a library-leased Web version available to computers networked to the library. Information about this database can be located at http://infoshare1.princeton.edu:2003/databases/about/tips/html/sociofile.html. Available from Cambridge Scientific Abstracts, this database provides access to the world's literature in sociology and related disciplines. The database contains abstracts of journal articles selected from over 2,500 journals, abstracts of conference papers presented at sociological association meetings, dissertations, and books and book reviews from 1963 to the present.

4. The *Social Science Citation Index* (Institute for Scientific Information, 1969–) and the CD-ROM version, *Social Science Citation Index* (Institute for Scientific Information, 1989–), provide a database of cited references to journal articles. The citation index allows you to look up a reference to a work to find journal articles that have cited the work. *SSCI* fully covers 5,700 journals, representing virtually every discipline in the social sciences.

5. *Dissertation Abstracts* (University Micofilms International, 1938–1965/66) and the CD-ROM version *Dissertation Abstracts Ondisc (Computer File)* (University Microfilms International, 1987–) provide guides to doctoral dissertations submitted by nearly 500 participating institutions throughout the world. It is published in three sections: Section A: The Humanities and Social Sciences; Section B: The Sciences and Engineering; and Section C: Worldwide. Examining these sections, a researcher finds abstracts, (350-word summaries), of dissertations. A comprehensive index permits easy access to titles, authors, and subject areas.

Early Stage Literature

As the final major category of literature to review (see Figure 4.2 again), you might consult materials at an early stage of development that reviewers (e.g., journal editors or book publishers) have not screened for quality. This consists of newsletters, studies posted to Web sites, professional association newsletters, and drafts of studies available from authors. For example, electronic journals and research studies posted to Web sites and available on the Internet represent a growing source of research information. Some of the advantages and disadvantages of using these materials from the Internet appear in Table 4.4. Unquestionably, the easy ability to access and capture this material makes it attractive; however, because reviewers have not evaluated the quality of this information, you need to be cautious about whether it represents rigorous, thoughtful, and systematic research for use in a literature review.

FIGURE 4.7

Sample Journal Record from PsycINFO Database
(http://www.apa.org/psycinfo/about/sample.html)

Sample Records from PsycINFO Databases

The values in each field below vary from record to record. For a complete list of possible values for each field, plus a description of each field, please visit our Database Field Guide.

View a Journal Record
View a Book Record
View a Book Chapter Record

SAMPLE JOURNAL RECORD

Accession Number
1999-15929-001

Author
Kitzmann, Katherine M.

Affiliation
U Memphis, Dept of Psychology, Memphis, TN, US

Title
Effects of marital conflict on subsequent triadic family interactions and parenting.

Source
Developmental Psychology. 2000 Jan Vol 36(1) 3-13

ISSN/ISBN
0012-1649

Language
English

Abstract
(from the journal abstract) This study examined marital conflict's indirect effects on children through disruptions in family alliances and parenting. Forty married couples were observed interacting with their 6-8-year-old sons after pleasant and conflictual discussions. After conflictual discussion, fathers showed lower support/engagement toward sons, and coparenting styles were less democratic. Couple negativity was correlated with family negativity, regardless of the topic of discussion, which suggests continuity in the affective quality of the two family subsystems. Mothers' marital satisfaction moderated families' responses to the experimental manipulation. The results provide stronger evidence than previously available of a causal link between conflict and disrupted parenting. Further research is needed to identify which conflict-related disruptions in parenting influence the development of children's problems. ((c) 2000 APA/PsycINFO, all rights reserved)

Key Phrase Identifiers
marital conflict, subsequent disruptions in family alliances & parenting, married couples & their 6-8 yr old sons

Keywords (Thesaurus Terms)
Family Relations; Marital Conflict; Marital Relations; Parent Child Relations; Parental Characteristics; Marital Satisfaction; Sons; Spouses

Classification Codes
2950 Marriage & Family

Population
10 Human; 30 Male; 40 Female; 100 Childhood (birth-12 yrs); 180 School Age (6-12 yrs); 300 Adulthood (18 yrs & older)

Source: PsycINFO Database Record © 2000 APA, all rights reserved.

TABLE 4.4

Advantages and Disadvantages of Using the Internet as a Resource for a Literature Review

Advantages	Disadvantages
• There is easy access to material since the researcher can search any time of the day.	• Research posted to Web sites is not reviewed for quality by "experts."
• Web sites have a breadth of information on most topics.	• The research found on Web sites may have been plagiarized without the searcher's knowledge.
• Web sites provide a network that researchers can contact about their topic and research problem.	• Research studies may be difficult to find and time consuming to locate.
• Research posted to Web sites is typically current information.	• Web site literature may not be organized or summarized in a way that is useful.
• Web sites can be searched easily using a search engine and key words.	• Full-text electronic journals available on the Web are new and few in number.
• Select research studies can be printed immediately from Web sites.	

 Think-Aloud About Searching ERIC

Let's return again to our high school teacher, Maria, who wants to search the literature for information about the possession of weapons by high school students. I will walk through the steps Maria might follow to conduct an online computerized search of the literature and to use the ERIC database to access relevant literature. In the steps to follow, you will be introduced to ERIC Web site displays on the computer in order to follow Maria's progress. As you examine these Web site screens, realize that they are changed or updated from time to time, and the exact screen you may see when you run a search may differ form that presented here.

Step 1. Conducting an Online Web Search

I would recommend that Maria start with the ERIC database because she plans to search literature in the field of education and ERIC is the most comprehensive database for educational literature. Furthermore, let's assume Maria has a home computer and can access Web sites using a search engine like Yahoo! or AltaVista. She can run an ERIC search conveniently from her home computer, but she needs to plan and carefully use the search capabilities of the ERIC Web site.

Step 2. Using Two to Three Terms to Search

Maria narrows her search down to three words by writing out a tentative title to her study (see "Identifying Key Terms" in this chapter). She could choose "weapons," "high schools," and "students" as key words to use in the computerized search.

Step 3. Logging On to the Main Page of the ERIC Web Site

Her first step, then, would be to log on to the ERIC Web site available from The National Library of Education at http://www.accesseric.org. This Web site home page, shown in Figure 4.8, provides an introductory screen to options explaining the features of ERIC as well as linking into the "search ERIC Database" feature.

FIGURE 4.8

Home Page for the Educational Resources Information Center (ERIC) (http://www.accesseric.org)

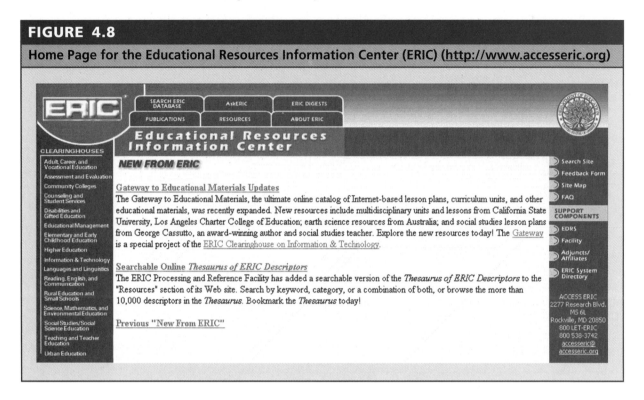

Step 4. Linking to the Search Page of ERIC

Maria should click on the link "Search ERIC Database," where she will be taken to the search page as shown in Figure 4.9. On this page she can learn about the ERIC database, see a sample journal article (i.e., EJ's) and document (i.e., ED's) resumes or abstracts with information she can receive (these samples were shown earlier as Figures 4.5 and 4.6), and search her topic using the online ERIC *Thesaurus*.

At the top of the Figure 4.9 screen, Maria will see the link "SEARCH ERIC DATABASE." She can click on this link to open the page for stating the descriptors she will use in her search and setting further specifications for her search.

Step 5. Entering Key Terms on the Search Page

As shown in Figure 4.10, Maria can now enter her terms to locate material on weapons and high school students. There are several important features to note on this page. First, she can enter up to three terms in the boxes on the left, such as:

Example 1. Entering terms separately

Term 1   weapons

Term 2   high schools

Term 3   students

Alternatively, she can enter the three terms as follows:

Example 2. Entering terms as one statement

Term 1   weapons and high school and students

This means that she will obtain only articles where all three terms are found as keywords in the abstract of the article. A keyword is a word found anywhere in the abstract or resume

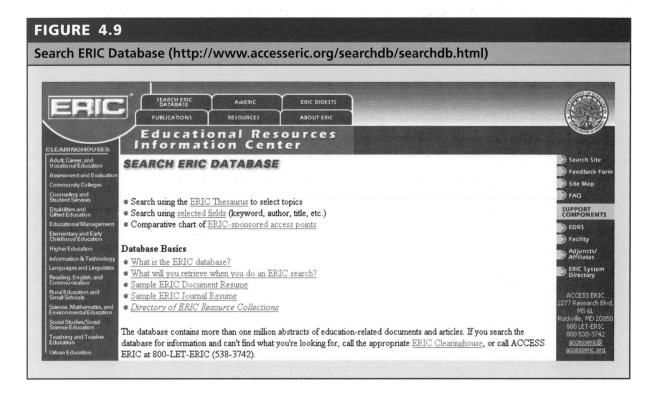

FIGURE 4.9

Search ERIC Database (http://www.accesseric.org/searchdb/searchdb.html)

of the article. I had Maria enter all three terms in one statement because it wanted her to place special information in the Term 2 and Term 3 boxes.

Step 6. Narrowing the Search to Journal Articles and Research Studies

As you saw in Figure 4.5 and 4.6, an abstract for a study contains different types of information, called fields. Maria can see these fields by using the pull-down menu under "keyword." For example, the fields, such as keyword, title, author, descriptor, and others appear. In total, there are 19 fields for each article (you can find the meaning of these fields at the bottom of the screen, under "searching assistance").

One field is of special note. The field "Publication Type" allows Maria to be selective about the articles she will obtain in her search. Placing the code "080" in Term 2 narrows the articles to journal articles, EJ information. This is helpful to Maria because journal articles are easily accessible in her academic library and they represent high-quality information that has been reviewed for quality. She can duplicate the articles and develop a file of the literature to share with her school as well as with her faculty committee at the university. In Term 3, I would have Maria place the code "143" to designate "research/technical" reports. In this way, Maria can locate studies that report the latest research on her topic.

Step 7. Identifying the Years To Be Searched

Finally, Maria can also narrow her search to specific years. In many searches, reviewing material for the last 10 years will suffice for school- or university-based research reports. Maria should indicate the search years from 1990 through 2000 for her search.

Step 8. Reviewing the Search Request

With this information, Maria can now run her ERIC search. She should click on the "submit" button and the computer will respond by summarizing her search request in a form it uses, shown in Figure 4.11. Maria should review this search request to determine if it

FIGURE 4.10

Search Request for the ERIC Database

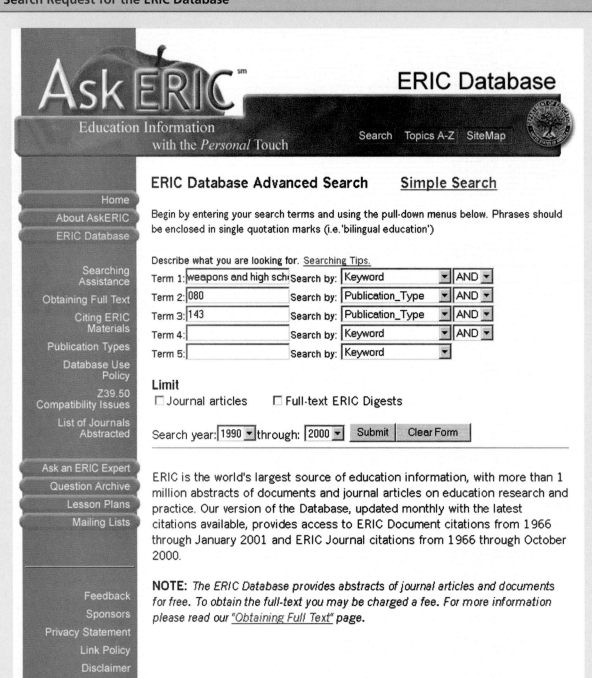

FIGURE 4.11

The Query Search Request in ERIC Language

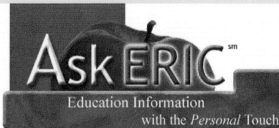 **ERIC Database**

Education Information
with the *Personal* Touch

Search   Topics A-Z   SiteMap

Home
About AskERIC
ERIC Database

Searching
Assistance
Obtaining Full Text
Citing ERIC
Materials
Publication Types
Database Use
Policy
Z39.50
Compatibility Issues
List of Journals
Abstracted

Ask an ERIC Expert
Question Archive
Lesson Plans
Mailing Lists

Your query is

((weapons and high school and students) AND
(080) :Publication_Type AND (143) :Publication_Type)
(AND (1990 OR 1991 OR 1992 OR 1993 OR 1994 OR
1995 OR 1996 OR 1997 OR 1998 OR 1999 OR
2000) :Publication_Date)

Please hit Submit if this is correct, otherwise, use your browser's back
arrow and update your selections.

Submit

AskERIC Survey: What do you think of our website?

Home	About AskERIC	ERIC Database	Ask an ERIC Expert	Question Archive
Lesson Plans	Mailing Lists	Searching Assistance	Obtaining Full Text
Citing ERIC Materials	Publication Types	Database Use Policy
Z39.50 Compatibility Issues	List of Journals Abstracted
Search	Topics A-Z	Sitemap

Feedback
Sponsors
Privacy Statement
Link Policy
Disclaimer

FIGURE 4.12

The Journal Articles Identified in the ERIC Search

[Return to search screen] [Previous] [Next]

7 documents found (7 returned) for query : *((weapons and high school and students) AND (080) :Publication_Type AND (143) :Publication_Type) (AND (1990 OR 1991 OR 1992 OR 1993 OR 1994 OR 1995 OR 1996 OR 1997 OR 1998 OR 1999 OR 2000) :Publication_Date)*

Score	Document Title
193	EJ576863. Kingery, Paul M.; Coggeshall, Mark B.; Alford, Aaron A.. Violence at School: Recent Evidence from Four National Surveys. Psychology in the Schools; v35 n3 p247-58 Jul 1998. 1998
192	EJ596254. Hill, Susan C.; Drolet, Judy C.. School-Related Violence among High School Students in the United States, 1993-1995. Journal of School Health; v69 n7 p264-72 Sep 1999. 1999
192	EJ558989. Valois, Robert F.; McKewon, Robert E.. Frequency and Correlates of Fighting and Carrying Weapons Among Public School Adolescents. American Journal of Health Behavior; v22 n1 p8-17 Jan-Feb 1998. 1998
191	EJ500854. Sheley, Joseph F.. Drugs and Guns among Inner-City High School Students. Journal of Drug Education; v24 n4 p303-21 1994. 1994
188	EJ525368. Martin, Sandra L.; And Others. Response of African-American Adolescents in North Carolina to Gun Carrying by School Mates. Journal of School Health; v66 n1 p23-26 Jan 1996. 1996
187	EJ476839. . Violence-Related Attitudes and Behaviors of High School Students--New York City, 1992. Journal of School Health; v63 n10 p438-40 Dec 1993. 1993
183	EJ500473. Coker, Ann L.; And Others. Correlates and Consequences of Early Initiation of Sexual Intercourse. Journal of School Health; v64 n9 p372-77 Nov 1994. 1994

[Return to search screen] [Previous] [Next]

Home	About AskERIC	ERIC Database	Ask an ERIC Expert	Question Archive	Lesson Plans	Mailing Lists
Searching Assistance	Obtaining Full Text	Citing ERIC Materials	Publication Types
Database Use Policy	Z39.50 Compatibility Issues	List of Journals Abstracted

contains the correct terms, such as "weapons," "high schools," and "students." This statement indicates the combining of terms, the narrowing to journal articles and research reports, and the delimiting of the search to the last 10 years. If the information is correct, clicking on the "submit" button actually runs the search.

Step 9. Reviewing a Report of the Articles and Documents Found

As shown in Figure 4.12, Maria's search locates seven articles and lists brief information about each article. Note that references are journal articles designated with the letters "EJ." The search request is printed at the top, and each article is given a score of relevance based on a content analysis of records to assess breadth of match, frequency, and density of the documents. Let's look at Figure 4.13. The first article by Kingery, Coggeshall, and Alford would be a good article for Maria to examine first because it addresses the topic she plans to study. She should click on the link to this article.

Step 10. Examining the Summary or Abstract of a Specific Study

Maria will be able to see from reading the reference to the article by Kingery, Coggeshall, and Alford that she has discovered a good citation about high school student weapon possession. This article is recent, it addresses the use of a survey like Maria plans to use, and it is published in a respectable journal, *Psychology in the Schools*. Moreover, Maria can examine the "descriptors" identified for this article and run additional ERIC searches using different terms to find additional literature. But for now, she should locate the article, make a copy of it, and summarize the major findings of the article for her school committee and graduate research project. She can then turn to references at the end of the article for additional relevant cita-

FIGURE 4.13

A Sample Abstract from the ERIC Search

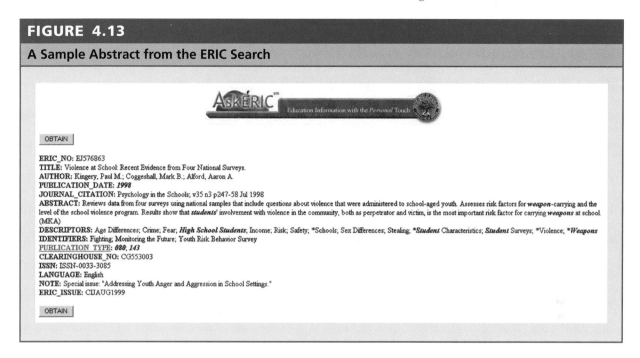

tions. Also, she may want to search through other databases, such as PsycINFO or Sociofile, for additional studies. Later, in a more comprehensive search, she can remove the limitation of journal articles and research reports to see all materials on her topic.

Reading the Literature and Checking It for Relevance

Let's return to the major steps in conducting a literature review. The process began with identifying key words and locating resources. Once resources are found, a major challenge is deciding what information to seek and use in a literature review (Alkin, 1992). Refer to Figure 4.2 to help you remember the levels for selecting articles: summaries, books, journal articles, indexed publications, and early stage material. The classification of types of literature already mentioned provides a priority for selecting resources.

Based on this classification, educators read through their literature, noting the titles of articles, the contents of abstracts at the beginning of the material (if they are present), and major headings in the study. This review helps determine if the information is relevant to use in a review. "Relevance" has several dimensions and you might consider the following criteria when selecting literature for a review:

> **Topic relevance:** Does the literature focus on the same topic as your proposed study?
>
> **Individual and site relevance:** Does the literature examine the same individuals or sites that you want to study?
>
> **Problem relevance:** Does the literature examine the same research problem that you propose to study?
>
> **Accessibility relevance:** Is the literature available in your library or can it be downloaded from a Web site? Can you obtain it easily from the library or a Web site?

If you answer "yes" to these questions, then the literature is relevant for your literature review.

Organizing the Literature

Once you have located the literature and checked it for relevance, the next step is to organize it for a literature review. This process involves copying and filing the literature. At this time you might scan it again to determine how it fits into the overall literature (later, in "Abstracting Studies," you can learn about reading it more carefully and noting elements to write the written summary of the literature). It also means constructing a visual picture of the literature—a "literature map"—to organize it, position your study within the literature, and use as a framework for presenting research to audiences about your topic.

Copying and Filing

After locating books, journal articles, and miscellaneous documents (such as the education documents in ERIC available on microfiche) in a library, you should make copies of the articles and studies and develop some system to easily retrieve the information. Copyright laws permit the duplication of only one complete article without the permission of the author. Placing the articles in file folders alphabetized by authors may be the most convenient way to organize the materials. Alternatively, you might organize the literature by sources, topic, or key words. However, using an author index may be the most convenient method because topics and key words you use in your literature review may shift as you work through drafts of the review.

Constructing a Literature Map

Reviewing and organizing the literature does more than put it in physical order. It helps to establish a conceptual picture of the information. Having a conceptual picture allows you to organize the literature in your mind, identify where the study fits into this literature, and convince others of the importance of your study.

This conceptual picture emerges through the construction of a literature map. A **literature map** is a figure or drawing that displays the research literature (e.g., studies, essays, books, chapters, and summaries) on a topic. This visual rendering helps you see overlaps in information or major topics in the literature and can help you determine how a proposed study adds or extends the existing literature rather than duplicates past studies. It is also a useful communication device that can help you convey to others, such as faculty committee members or an audience at a conference, the current picture of the literature on a topic.

The actual design of this map can take several forms. Figure 4.14 shows a chart which the researcher used to organize the literature hierarchically. Organized in top-down fashion, this chart portrays the literature that Hovater (2000) found on the topic of preservice training for teachers on multicultural topics. The topic is listed at the top: the need for teacher education programs to train culturally responsive teachers. Next the various program options that institutions of higher education have applied to meet this need are displayed. Hovater maps the literature into two broad areas: study abroad programs and U.S. programs. Within each of these areas, he documents further literature about attitudes of students, personal insights of teachers, and possible improvements in training. At the lower left-center of the map, Hovater advances his propsed study: to extend the literature addressing the question, "Do short-term study abroad programs in non-English speaking cultures help create cultural responsiveness in preservice teachers?"

Hovater's literature map includes several useful design features that you can include in a literature map. Here are some guidelines to follow when constructing your own literature map:

> ▶ Identify the key terms for your topic and place them at the top of the map. As discussed earlier, these key terms are found in draft titles, questions, or ERIC resources.

FIGURE 4.14

A Literature Map, Hierarchical Design

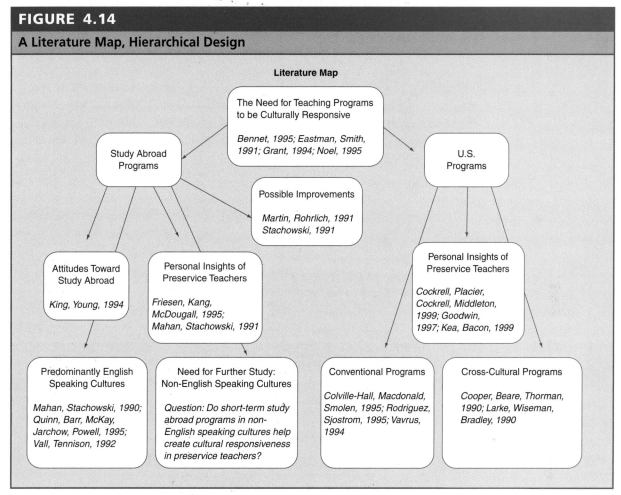

Source: Used by permission of Scott Hovater, 2000.

▶ Take the information you have located and sort it into groups of related topical areas or "families of studies." Think in terms of three or four groupings because these groups will likely be major sections in a written literature review.

▶ Provide a label for each box (later this label is useful as a heading in your literature review). Also, in each box, provide specific citations (e.g., Bennet) to studies that illustrate the contents of the box.

▶ Develop the literature map on as many levels as possible. Some branches in the drawing will be developed in more detail than others because of the extent of the literature. In some cases, one branch may be developed in greater detail because it is the primary area of focus of your research topic.

▶ Draw a box toward the bottom of the figure that says "my proposed study," "a proposed study," or "my study." Draw lines *connecting* the proposed study to other branches of the literature, indicating graphically how the proposed study adds or extends existing information. In this box you could state a proposed title, a research question, or the problem to be studied.

The map in Figure 4.14 shows a hierarchical design. Other designs—such as a circular design of interconnecting circles or a sequential design to show the literature narrowing and focusing into a proposed study—can also be used. We can see a circular design by shifting and changing Hovater's (2000) hierarchically designed map into a circular map, as shown in Figure 4.15.

Writing a Literature Review

Now that you have scanned the literature to determine its relevance and organized it into a literature map, it's time to read each source more carefully and construct the actual written summary of the literature. For the most part, this literature consists of journal articles and research reports found in library resources. Researchers use procedures for summarizing each study, providing a clear reference to it, and writing the literature review. This writing requires pulling together all aspects of the review to this point, such as:

- ▶ identifying and summarizing each study in an "abstract" that highlights important elements
- ▶ writing out complete citations for these summaries and developing headings using appropriate style manual formats
- ▶ using specific writing strategies related to the extent of the review, the type of review, and the concluding statements in a review

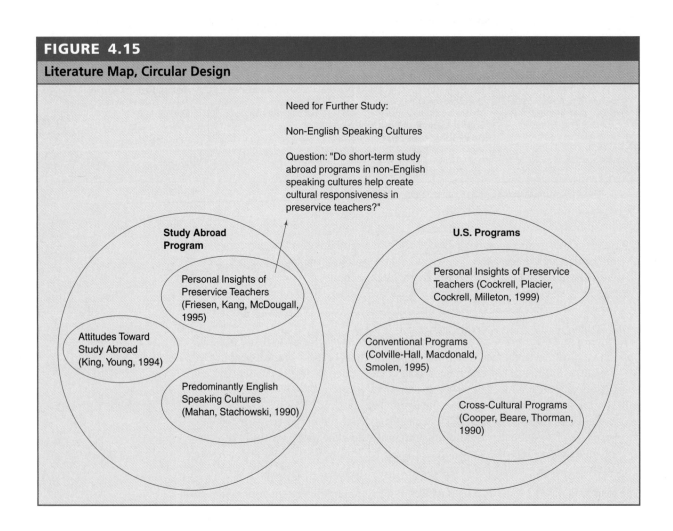

FIGURE 4.15

Literature Map, Circular Design

Need for Further Study:

Non-English Speaking Cultures

Question: "Do short-term study abroad programs in non-English speaking cultures help create cultural responsiveness in preservice teachers?"

Study Abroad Program

Personal Insights of Preservice Teachers (Friesen, Kang, McDougall, 1995)

Attitudes Toward Study Abroad (King, Young, 1994)

Predominantly English Speaking Cultures (Mahan, Stachowski, 1990)

U.S. Programs

Personal Insights of Preservice Teachers (Cockrell, Placier, Cockrell, Milleton, 1999)

Conventional Programs (Colville-Hall, Macdonald, Smolen, 1995)

Cross-Cultural Programs (Cooper, Beare, Thorman, 1990)

Abstracting Studies

During the process of reading the literature, researchers take notes on the information so that a summary of the literature is available for a written review. This notetaking is often an informal procedure in which the researcher identifies important ideas about the article or material and writes out rough notes on each source of information. Instead of this informal approach, a preferred strategy is to systematically record information about each source so that when readers see it in a literature review, they have a complete understanding of the material. This process also yields useful information for you to remember about the details of studies so that you can weigh their relevance for the review.

A systematic approach for summarizing each source of information is to develop an abstract for each one. An **abstract** is a summary of the major aspects of a study or article, conveyed in a concise way (for this purpose, often no more than 350 words), and inclusive of specific components that describe the information. You could simply use the abstracts often available at the beginning of journal articles, but this word-for-word use constitutes plagiarism. Moreover, these abstracts may be too brief because of word or space restrictions by journals or they may inadequately cover major elements of a study. Instead, you need to write your own abstracts of articles and materials. This calls for identifying the elements that go into a good abstract and learning how to write a brief summary.

The information you abstract will be either a research study or an essay, depending on whether the literature is a book, journal article, conference paper, or dissertation. Researchers typically give preference to research studies when summarizing the literature, but essays may provide important information as well, especially when little research exists on a topic.

Recall from Chapter 1 (in "What Is Research?") that a "research study" consists of asking questions of some people, gathering data, and reporting results to the questions. An **essay,** on the other hand, is a discussion about a topic where the author develops a thought and elaborates on it through points or themes. The abstracting process, described here, involves different elements for a research study than an essay. Further, there will be some slight variations—mostly in the headings for the elements—depending on whether the study is quantitative or qualitative.

Let's illustrate sample abstracts for both quantitative and qualitative research studies as well as an essay. To abstract elements for a *quantitative* research study, such as a journal article, conference paper, or dissertation or thesis, you might identify the:

- research problem
- hypotheses or research questions
- data collection procedure
- results of the study

A complete abstract reporting these four elements for a quantitative survey study by Metzner (1989) is shown in Figure 4.16. Notice in this abstract that the summaries of each element are kept short and that a complete reference to the work is listed at the top so that each abstract is fully documented. (Reference format will be addressed next in this chapter.)

For a *qualitative* research study, the topics are the same as those used in a quantitative study, but the headings reflect terms commonly used in qualitative research. Instead of hypotheses and questions, qualitative researchers state questions only because they do not use hypotheses (i.e., predictions) as you will see in Chapter 5 on "Qualitative Research." Instead of results, "findings" is a more acceptable qualitative term.

When abstracting a qualitative research study you might identify the:

- research problem
- research questions

FIGURE 4.16

Sample Abstract for a Quantitative Research Study

Metzner, B. (1989). Perceived quality of academic advising: The effect on freshman attrition. *American Educational Research Journal, 26*(3), 422–442.*

Research Problem:

Colleges and universities place emphasis on student retention, and academic advising positively intervenes to reduce dropout. However, surveys show extensive dissatisfaction with advisement. Empirical investigations of this relationship have provided equivocal results. Some studies show a positive relationship between retention and quality of advising; others have failed to discover an association.

Research Questions or Hypotheses:

No specific research questions or hypotheses were raised, but this reader can deduce them from the purpose statement. The general question was: Does the quality of advisement influence student attrition? The specific questions are: Is better advising associated with lower attrition than poor advising? Do changes in quality of advising (from good, poor, or no advising) affect retention differently?

Data Collection Procedure:

Freshmen at a public university were asked about the quality of advising they received, their intent to leave the institution, and their general satisfaction with the college experience. One thousand and thirty-three students completed questionnaires in their English Composition courses late in the fall semester of 1982.

Results:

In response to the question, "Is better advising associated with lower attrition than poor advising?", the results (of regression analysis) showed that good advising reduced dropout while poor advising failed to have any effect. Thus, levels of advising quality did impact freshman attrition differently. In response to the next question: "Do changes in the quality of advising (good, poor, none) affect retention differently?", the results showed that yes, the impact was different. Good advising helped to lower dropout more than no advising, and poor advising lowered dropout more than no advising. The implications of these results is that the best strategy for improving retention is to offer good advising to students who receive no advising.

*Abstracted with the assistance of Beth Caughlin, Bob Mann, Chad Abresch, Qian Geng, and Ling-Mean Heng from Education 800, University of Nebraska, Lincoln, Fall, 1998.

▶ data collection procedures
▶ findings

These elements were used to abstract a qualitative study by Creswell and Brown (1992), shown in Figure 4.17. This study explores the role of academic chairpersons in enhancing faculty research. Again there is a brief summary of each element and a complete reference to the article at the top of the abstract.

The elements abstracted in both the quantitative and qualitative examples illustrate typical information extracted from research studies. In other forms of abstracting, you may include additional information that critiques or assesses the strengths and weaknesses of the research.

FIGURE 4.17

Sample Abstract for a Qualitative Research Study

Creswell, J. W., & Brown, M. L. (1992). How chairpersons enhance faculty research: A grounded theory study. *The Review of Higher Education, 16*(1), 41–62.

Research Problem:

The authors mention that past research has addressed the correlates of scientific achievement and the research performance of faculty. However, an unexplored correlate is the role of the chairperson in influencing faculty scholarly performance. Since chairs are in a position to enhance and facilitate faculty scholarship, the role of the chair needs clarification.

Research Questions:

The central research question is implied in the title to the study: "How do chairpersons enhance faculty research?" More specifically, the authors asked chairs to discuss an issue involved in assisting faculty members in the department in his or her professional development. They were also asked to specify actions or roles in performing this assistance, identify reasons for assistance, note signs that the individual needed assistance, and indicate the outcomes of assistance for the individual.

Data Collection Procedure:

The authors collected semi-structured interview data from 33 chairpersons located in a variety of disciplines and types of institutions of higher education. Chief academic officers and faculty development personnel on the campuses nominated these chairs for the study. The authors used the procedures of grounded theory.

Findings:

The authors identified from the interviews seven major categories of roles engaged in by the chairpersons: provider, enabler, advocate, mentor, encourager, collaborator, and challenger. Further analysis then led to understanding how these roles played out for faculty at different stages of their careers. Four levels of faculty were used to illustrate their chair roles: beginning faculty, pre-tenured faculty, post-tenured faculty, and senior faculty. From these profiles, the authors identified a theoretical model of the chair's role and advanced propositions (or hypotheses) for future testing. These propositions related to the type of issue the faculty member experienced, the career stage issue of the faculty member, and the strategies employed by the chairperson.

For an essay, such as book or article material advancing opinions, conceptual frameworks, or issues, the elements to abstract are different from those used for a research study. They are more flexible in order to capture the major ideas in the material, such as the author's:

- questions or concerns
- arguments, points, or themes
- implications or importance of the information

Using a Style Manual

We have already seen how abstracts include a complete reference (or citation) to the information in the literature. Standard styles should be used for references when reporting the literature in research reports. Standard styles should also be used for headings, tables, figures, and the overall format of an acceptable research study. These standards can be found in **style manuals** available from professional organizations and publishers. When you use a style manual, the research (and the literature review) will have a consistent format for readers and other researchers, and this format will facilitate their understanding of the study.

The *Publication Manual of the American Psychological Association,* 4th edition (American Psychological Association, 1994) style manual (hereafter called the APA style) is the most popular style guide in educational research. Other guides available are *The Chicago Manual of Style,* 14th edition (University of Chicago Press, 1993), *A Manual for Writers of Term Papers, Theses, and Dissertation,* 4th edition (Turabian, 1973), and *Form and Style: Theses, Reports, and Term Papers,* 5th edition (Campbell & Ballou, 1977). These style manuals provide a consistent format for writing a research report. Three of the most frequently used approaches found in the *Publication Manual of the American Psychological Association* (4th ed.) (American Psychological Association 1994) will be emphasized here:

- end-of-text references
- within-text references
- headings

End-of-Text References   **End-of-text references** are the references listed at the end of a research report. In APA form, they are double-spaced and listed alphabetically by author. Only those references mentioned in the body of the paper are included in the end-of-text references. The APA manual provides examples of end-of-text references for 76 different types of documents. Below are illustrations of three common types of references in appropriate APA form.

An example of a *journal article* end-of-text reference in APA form is:

> Elam, S. M. (1989). The second Phi Delta Kappa poll of teachers' attitudes toward public schools. *Phi Delta Kappan, 70*(3), 785–798.

An example of a *book* reference in end-of-text APA form is:

> Shertzer, B., & Stone, S. C. (1981). *Fundamental of guidance* (4th ed.). Boston: Houghton Mifflin.

An example of a *conference paper* reference in end-of-text APA form is:

> Zedexk, S., & Baker, H. T. (1971, May). *Evaluation of behavioral expectation scales.* Paper presented at the meeting of the Midwestern Psychological Association, Detroit, MI.

As these examples show, the first line in an end-of-text reference is always indented and the remaining lines aligned with the margin. Also, observe the use of all lowercase letters (non-capitals) in the titles of the articles. In the journal article example, the authors capitalize all words in journal titles. In the book example, only the first word in the title of the book is capitalized (except when a colon is used in the title and where the first word following the colon is capitalized or when proper nouns are used).

Within-Text References   **Within-text references** are references cited in a brief format within the body of the text to provide credit to authors. In APA style, there are several conventions for indicating these in-text references. The following examples illustrate the appropriate use of APA style when you cite both single and multiple authors.

An example of a within-text reference in APA style in which the author refers to a single reference is:

> Rogers (1994) compared reaction times for athletes and nonathletes in middle schools . . .

As this reference shows, APA style requires that you provide last names of authors for within-text citation (a practice that varies from one style manual to another). This reference also includes information about the author(s) and the year of the publication. These references may also appear anywhere in the sentence.

An example of a within-text reference in APA style in which the author refers to multiple references is:

> Past studies of reaction times (Gogel, 1984; Rogers, 1994; Smith, 1989) showed
> . . . . Entire groups of studies have addressed the difficulty of test taking and reaction times (Gogel, 1984; Happenstance, 1995; Lucky, 1994; Smith, 1989).

As illustrated by this example, semicolons separate the different studies. Also, the authors are listed in alphabetical order, as in end-of-text references, rather than in chronological order based on the date of publication.

An example of a multiple author reference for two or more authors when first mentioned in the research is:

> The difficulty of test taking and reaction times has been examined by Smith, Paralli, John, and Langor (1994).

An example of a multiple author reference for two or more authors when the reference is mentioned a second and consecutive times in the research is:

> The study of test taking and reaction times (Smith et al., 1994)

In the above two examples, writers mention all of the authors the first time the reference appears in the research. In subsequent references to the *same* multiple authors, only the first author followed by "et al." is used.

Finally, authors reference all within-text references to original sources rather than citing a book or article that contains the reference. For example, an inadequate model would be:

> Smith (1994), as reported in Theobald (1997), said that . . .

An improved model would be:

> Smith (1994) said that . . .

Levels of Headings   As you write a literature review, consider the number of topics or subdivisions. **Levels of headings** in a scholarly study and literature review provide logical subdivisions of the text. Headings provide important clues for readers which help them understand a study. They also divide the material in the same way as do topics in an outline.

In APA style, the maximum number of levels of headings is five. As shown in Figure 4.18, these five headings differ in their use of upper- and lowercase letters, whether words are centered, left-aligned, or indented, and what text is underlined. Most educational studies include either two- or three-level headings. Authors infrequently use four- or five-level headings because their research is short and lacks the detail needed for that many subdivisions. Researchers use a five-level heading when they prepare long research reports (e.g., books), but typically two- to four-level headings will suffice for most educational research.

The choice of levels of headings in a literature review depends on the number of subdivisions of topics you use. Regardless of subdivisions, APA style requires that you use certain types of headings for a two-, three-, and four-level heading format. The following examples illustrate these three popular forms.

An example of a *two-level heading* in APA form that uses first and third levels is:

Review of the Literature (first level)

<u>Introduction</u> (third level)

<u>Social Support Research</u> (third level)

FIGURE 4.18

Heading in APA Style

CENTERED AND UPPERCASE HEADING   **(Level 5)**

Centered Uppercase and Lowercase Heading   **(Level 1)**

Centered, Underlined, Uppercase and Lowercase Heading   **(Level 2)**

Flush Left, Underlined, Uppercase, and Lowercase Side Heading   **(Level 3)**

Indented, underlined, lowercase heading ending with a   **(Level 4)**
period and sentence to follow. Here is the sentence to follow. . . .

Researchers typically use two

levels (**level 1** and **level 3**) or

three levels (**level 1, level 3,** and **level 4**).

Source: Adapted from American Psychological Association, 1994, p. 91.

An example of a *three-level heading* in APA form that uses first, third, and fourth levels is:

Review of the Literature (first level)

Introduction (third level)

Social support. (fourth level)

An example of a *four-level heading* in APA form that uses first through fourth levels is:

Review of the Literature (first level)

Social Support Research (second level)

Workplace Correlates (third level)

Interpersonal communication. "This form of communication involves two or . . . " (fourth level)

In addition to the challenge of formatting a heading, a common misconception among researchers is that headings are easy to describe. In fact, headings are difficult to develop and need to be short—two or three words—and state exactly and succinctly the content of the passage that follows.

Writing Strategies

As you write a literature review, several additional elements will need your attention: the extent of the review, the type of review, and the concluding statement of the review.

Extent of the Review   One question you often have to ask yourself is "How long should my literature review be?" There is no easy answer to this question, but you can begin by considering the type of research report you are writing (see Chapter 10 on "Types of Research Reports and Proposals" for more detail about the forms of reports). For dissertations and theses, you need an extensive review of the literature. It often comprehensively includes all sources of information identified in the classification of resources in Figure 4.2. Students comprehensively review the literature to document that their study does not duplicate past research, to demonstrate to faculty committees a knowledge of literature resources, and to show a command of selecting, abstracting, and summarizing scholarly literature.

For research plans or proposals, a less than comprehensive literature review may suffice. The literature review in proposals establishes the framework for a study and documents the importance of studying the research problem. Typically, the literature reviews for proposals run from 10 to 30 pages in length, although this can vary. A proposal literature review summarizes the citations obtained from searching databases, such as ERIC, PsycINFO, and Sociofile. For a journal article, the extent of the literature review varies, depending on its use and role in the study (as noted earlier). It is typically found in the introductory sections of an article.

Also related to the *extent* of the literature review is the question, "How far back in the literature do my references need to go?" When completing a dissertation or thesis, the search covers most published literature and the author examines sources back to the inception of the research topic. For research proposals and journal articles (and preliminary reviews), as a rough guide, the search mostly covers the last 10 years, focusing on the more recent studies. An exception to this procedure is when an earlier, classical study must be cited because it influences subsequent literature published in the last decade.

Type of Reviews   At this point you will need to determine how to present the summaries or notes taken on the articles and studies in the literature. The actual organization of the summaries varies depending on the type of research report being written and the traditions used on different campuses and in different journals. When writing a literature review for a dissertation or thesis, you might visit with an advisor to determine the appropriate format to use. However, the two models presented here—the thematic review and the study-by-study review—will serve you well. (See Cooper, 1984, for additional models.)

In a **thematic review of the literature,** the researcher identifies a theme and briefly cites literature to document this theme. No single study is discussed in detail. Instead, only the major ideas or results that support a theme are discussed. This approach is used frequently in journal articles, but students also use it for dissertations and theses in graduate programs. You can identify this form by locating a theme and noting the references (typically multiple references) to the literature used to support the theme.

For example, in a study by Brown, Parham, and Yonker (1996), the authors reviewed the literature about racial identity development of white counselors-in-training in a course on racial identity attitudes of white women and men. This passage, appearing in an early section in the study, illustrates a thematic approach:

> Among other things, racial identity is a sense of group belonging based on the perception of a shared racial heritage with a specific group and, as such, it has an impact on personal feelings and attitudes concerning distinguishable racial groups (Helms, 1990; 1994; Mitchell & Dell, 1992). Researchers agree that White Americans generally are not challenged to ask themselves, "What does it mean to be White?" (Pope-Davis & Ottavi, 1994) . . . (p. 511)

In this case, the authors review the literature about the theme "racial identity" and briefly mention references to support the theme. The authors do not discuss each reference separately and in detail.

In contrast to a thematic review, the **study-by-study review of the literature** provides a detailed summary of each study grouped under a broad theme. This detailed summary includes the elements of an abstract shown in Figure 4.16 and 4.17. This form of review typically appears in journal articles that summarize the literature and in dissertations and theses. When presenting a study-by-study review, authors link summaries (or abstracts) with transitional sentences and organize the summaries under subheadings that reflect themes and major divisions. Using the literature map concept discussed earlier in this chapter, these themes are the topics identified in boxes in the map.

The following review of the literature about cross-cultural competency and multicultural education in the journal *Review of Educational Research* by McAllister and Irvine (2000) illustrates a study-by-study review. Here, the authors discuss the research studies on Helms's racial identity model.

> Brown, Parham, and Yonker (1996) employed the White Racial Identity Scale to measure change in the white racial identity of thirty-five white graduate students who participated in a sixteen-week multicultural course. Eighty percent of the participants had previous multicultural training and most of them had had experiences with people from at least two different racial backgrounds, though the nature of these experiences is not defined. The authors designed the course based on three areas—acquisition of self knowledge, cultural knowledge, and cross-cultural skills—and they used a variety of teaching methods such as lectures, talks by guest speakers, and simulations. Results indicated that at the end of the course women endorsed more items than men did in the pseudo-independence stage on the White Racial Identity Scale, and men endorsed more items than women did in the autonomy stage. The authors draw a causal relationship between the course and those changes found in the group.
>
> Neville, Heppner, Louie, and Thompson (1996) also examined the change in White racial identity as well . . . (p. 8)

In this example, the authors describe only one study at a time. They provide detail about the research problem (whether the scale measures change) and imply the question in the study (whether men and women differ on the scale). They also identify data collection (i.e., 35 participate in the study) and summarize the results (men and women endorse items differently depending on their stage of development). After reviewing the first study, the authors move on to the next study for a similar detailed analysis, demonstrating a study-by-study review of the literature.

The Concluding Statement of the Review   The concluding statement of a literature review serves several purposes. It summarizes the major themes found in the literature and it provides a rationale for the need for your study or the importance of the research problem.

First, summarize the major themes. Ask yourself, "What are the major results and findings from all of the studies I have reviewed?" Your answer to this question will result in the identification of three or four themes that summarize the literature. Then, briefly summarize each theme. The summaries should emphasize the major ideas under each major heading in the literature review and highlight what the reader needs to remember from the summary of the review.

Besides stating the major themes in a review, you also need to suggest reasons why the current literature is deficient and why additional research on your topic is needed. These reasons address ways the proposed study will add to knowledge and they justify the importance of the research problem. Typically writers mention three or four reasons, which play a significant role in research because they often lead into the purpose statement, research questions, and hypotheses (to be addressed in Chapter 5).

The example below illustrates both the summary of themes and the author's justification of the need for additional research.

> The factors influencing faculty to be productive researchers found in the literature suggest three themes: early productivity (Did faculty begin publishing early in their careers?); mentoring (Did faculty apprentice under a distinguished researcher?); and support systems (Did faculty have adequate funding for their research?). These factors, although important, do not address the time faculty need to conduct

research. When faculty have allotted time for scientific investigations and inquiries, it helps to focus their attention, offers sustained momentum for research, and removes distracting activities that may draw their attention away from research.

In this example, three themes are stated and, from these themes, an area for future research—faculty time—is identified. Then, three reasons are given for why a study of faculty time is important.

KEY IDEAS IN THE CHAPTER

A literature review is a written summary of articles, books, and other documents that describes the past and current state of knowledge about a topic. This review serves the purpose of providing a need for a study and demonstrating that other studies have not addressed the same topic in exactly the same way. It also indicates to audiences that the researcher is knowledgeable about studies related to a topic.

Literature reviews are different for quantitative and qualitative research in three ways: the amount of literature cited at the beginning of a study, the purpose the literature serves at the beginning of a study, and its use at the end of a study. In quantitative research, investigators provide a detailed review of the literature to justify the major purpose and research questions of a study. In qualitative research, the inquirers use a limited amount of literature in the beginning of the study to allow participant views, rather than perspectives from the literature, to play a major role in the study. The literature is cited again at the end of studies in both quantitative and qualitative research, but its use is again different. In quantitative research, the literature at the end compares results with prior predication made at the beginning of the research. In qualitative research, researchers use the literature at the end to compare and contrast findings in the study with past literature.

Designing and conducting a literature review involves five interrelated steps. First, researchers identify key terms to use in their search of the literature. They look for these terms in titles, research questions, or the ERIC *Thesaurus.*

Next, researchers locate literature in library resources, such as summaries, books, journal publications and electronic sources, and early stage literature (e.g., information posted to Web sites).

After locating the literature, the researcher then reads the material and makes a determination of its relevance for use. Criteria to use are the relevance of the topic, the individuals or sites, the problem, and the accessibility of the information.

Researchers next locate and obtain the literature and organize it into a visual rendering of the literature, called a literature map. This map helps to organize past literature as well as portray how a proposed study fits into the overall literature.

The final step is writing the literature review. The investigator thoroughly reads the materials and creates a summary or abstract of each source of information. It is helpful at this point to use appropriate style manual formats and to consider the appropriate use of headings for the written literature review. Writing strategies are also used in this final step. Researchers need to consider the extent or length of the review for different types of research reports. The type of review will also vary, depending on the type of report. For journal articles, dissertations, and theses, a thematic literature review summarizes the literature by themes. For reviews of literature on topics for some journals and for dissertations and theses, a study-by-study approach presents each study in detail, highlighting the major elements of each one. Finally, researchers conclude a literature review by summarizing major themes and presenting reasons for a proposed study or the importance of studying a research problem. These reasons lead to a rationale for a study that is later specified in the purpose statement and research questions or hypotheses.

USEFUL INFORMATION FOR PRODUCERS OF RESEARCH

▶ Use the five-step process explained in this chapter for designing and conducting a literature review.

▶ Consider the different strategies for selecting key terms: choosing words from the project's title, selecting words from a brief question asked in the study, and using the ERIC *Thesaurus.*

▶ Begin a search of the literature with the most easily accessible material, such as published research studies reported in journals. Use the CD-ROMs in the library or the ERIC system Web site, http://www.accesseric.org, to search for literature.

▶ Begin with the ERIC database before using other databases to locate useful educational literature.

▶ Develop some means for organizing the literature you find, such as a filing system or a graphic rendering of the literature into groupings on a literature map.

▶ Realize that every source you locate may not provide relevant information for your literature review. To determine which to use, remember these four criteria: the relevance of the topic, the individuals or sites, the problem, and the accessibility of the information.

▶ Abstract studies before you begin to write the literature review. These abstracts provide a useful summary of studies and can be included in your review. Be sure to include all of the elements that go into a good abstract. (Refer back to Figures 4.16 and 4.17 for models.)

▶ Use an accepted style manual, such as the APA *Publication Manual,* for the end-of-text and within-text references as well as for the headings in your literature review. For most educational research reports, a two- or three-level heading format will suffice.

▶ Keep your literature review succinct and short. Decide whether a thematic or a study-by-study review is appropriate for your research report. Consider the type of review typically used by audiences for your report.

▶ Conclude your literature review with a summary of the major themes. Also discuss how the literature is deficient and how your study adds to the literature.

USEFUL INFORMATION FOR CONSUMERS OF RESEARCH

▶ Recognize that a literature review in a research report will contain many types of literature. Literature syntheses provide a broad summary of research. Books are less valuable as research guides, but they may report useful research. The most popular sources for literature reviews are journal articles. Other research literature is available in publications from conferences. Of less value is research posted to Web sites because it has typically not been reviewed for quality.

▶ Do not assume that all literature cited by an author in a report contains good and valid information. Researchers need to choose the literature to include in a review selectively. Apply the evaluation criteria for relevance found in this chapter to determine whether an author used relevant literature.

▶ As you evaluate a study, consider whether the author has made a good case that the study adds to existing knowledge. The study should explicitly specify how and in what way it adds to knowledge. A visual literature map of sources of information helps to convey the author's case.

▶ A research study should employ a consistent form for reporting references to the literature, both in the text as well as at the end of the report. In addition, the headings should be easy to identify and be descriptive of the passage that follows.

STUDY QUESTIONS AND ACTIVITIES

1. Run an ERIC search using the CD-ROM system of an academic library or using the ERIC Web site. Limit the search to journal articles, to research reports, and to the last 10 years of publications.

2. Abstract one of the research studies from a journal that you have found in the search. Locate major elements of the research, and summarize each element in a short, 350-word abstract. Use either a quantitative or a qualitative research study, but employ the headings that are consistent with the type of approach you choose.

3. Identify errors in references in published journal articles. Locate a published research study in an educational journal. Examine the end-of-text references. Go over each one and locate errors in APA style made by the authors. Alternately, select a book or a conference paper and examine it for errors.

4. Choose a topic and search ERIC, PsychINFO, Sociofile, and Dissertation Abstracts for sources of information on the topic. Also search references at the end of articles. Look for 20 good references to your topic.

5. Using Maria's topic on weapon possession among high school students, conduct a literature search in your library. Use the following sources and see what results you get: *Encyclopedia of Educational Research* (Alken, 1992); *Digest of Educational Statistics* (National Center for Educational Statistics, 1997); *Review of Educational Research;* the ERIC database; and Psychological Abstracts (or PsychLit or PsycINFO).

 Now go to our Companion Website to assess your understanding of chapter content with Multiple-Choice Questions, apply comprehension in Projects & Essays, and broaden your knowledge with links to related research topics on the Web.

Specifying a Purpose and Research Questions or Hypotheses

As you'll recall from Chapter 4, Maria selected the topic of school violence for her graduate research study and read the literature. She also narrowed her topic to the problem of increased weapon possession by high school students. Now she needs to identify a specific direction for her study and to formulate a purpose statement and research questions. If she approaches her study from a quantitative approach, she would write a question such as "What factors relate to attitudes toward weapon possession by students in high schools?" Approaching it from a qualitative approach, she might state, "What are students' experiences with weapons in high school?" These questions reflect different elements, and Maria can learn to write a focused purpose statement and well-developed questions or hypotheses by learning more about these different elements.

Researchers like Maria establish the direction for studies by writing specific purpose statements, research questions, or hypotheses. As the most important statements in a research report, they need to be clearly and carefully stated. On the basis of these statements, researchers identify the major intent of a study and the questions they would like participants to answer. For readers, these statements form the thesis statement of research; as such, they provide direction for the research goals, as well as for the results the reader should anticipate finding in the report. This chapter explores how to conceptualize and write purpose statements, research questions, and hypotheses in both quantitative and qualitative research.

By the end of this chapter, you should be able to:

- Distinguish among a purpose statement, hypotheses, and research questions.
- Identify types of variables in quantitative research.
- Describe the use of variables in theories.
- Explain whether variable relationships "prove" cause and effect.
- Write a quantitative purpose statement, hypothesis, and research question.
- Define a central phenomena in qualitative research.
- Describe the emerging design process in qualitative research.
- Write a qualitative purpose statement, a central research question, and sub-questions.

REEXAMINING THE TELEVISION VIOLENCE AND THE GUNMAN INCIDENT STUDIES

In both the television violence and the gunman incident studies (reprinted at the end of Chapter 1), the authors use purpose statements and research questions to provide the focus and central direction for the studies. In the quantitative television violence study, Vooijs and van der Voort (1993) end the introduction with a paragraph (Paragraph 07) identifying the purpose of the study and narrowing this purpose into four research questions (Paragraphs 15–18):

> "The present study explored the effect of an in-school curriculum designed to modify the impact of television violence on children." (Paragraph 07)

> "The first question was whether the curriculum produces the desired effects in the short term." (Paragraph 15)

> "The second question referred to the strength of the induced change." (Paragraph 16)

> "The third question was which types of children profit most from the lessons." (Paragraph 17)

> "Finally, in a follow-up study, the effects after 2 years were investigated." (Paragraph 18) (pp. 134–136)

Although the authors did not mention the site of the research, the purpose statement clearly conveys the intent of the study. The research questions are easy to identify because they are stated in a separate section titled "Research Questions." Readers can also follow these questions because of the identification of their order (e.g., "the first question," "the second question").

The qualitative gunman case study (Asmussen & Creswell, 1995) also includes both a purpose statement and research questions. At the end of the opening section, the authors mention the purpose statement in one sentence and then introduce five questions they seek to answer in the research:

> The study presented in this article is a qualitative case analysis [3] that describes and interprets a campus response to a gun incident. (Paragraph 03) We asked the following questions: What happened? Who was involved in response to the incident? What themes of response emerged during the eight-month period that followed this incident? What theoretical constructs helped us understand the campus response, and what constructs were unique to this case? (Paragraph 03) (p. 576)

As in the television violence study, the gunman study also needs to include in the purpose statement the site for the research. However, most of the elements we would expect to find are in place in the purpose statement. The open-ended, exploratory research questions seem to invite the campus personnel to tell their stories.

DISTINGUISHING AMONG PURPOSE STATEMENTS, RESEARCH QUESTIONS, AND HYPOTHESES

When you read reports such as these two studies, it is important to be able to identify the statements and questions providing major direction for the research. Researchers derive

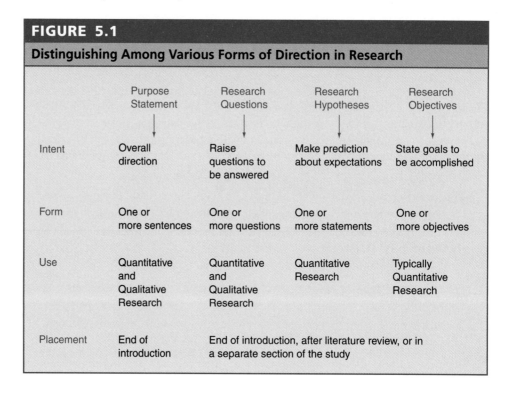

FIGURE 5.1

Distinguishing Among Various Forms of Direction in Research

	Purpose Statement	Research Questions	Research Hypotheses	Research Objectives
Intent	Overall direction	Raise questions to be answered	Make prediction about expectations	State goals to be accomplished
Form	One or more sentences	One or more questions	One or more statements	One or more objectives
Use	Quantitative and Qualitative Research	Quantitative and Qualitative Research	Quantitative Research	Typically Quantitative Research
Placement	End of introduction	End of introduction, after literature review, or in a separate section of the study		

them from searching the literature, building on past studies, and raising questions that need to be examined in practice. Four forms convey direction for research:

▶ purpose statements
▶ research questions
▶ research hypotheses
▶ research objectives

These forms differ in intent (their role in research), form (their appearance in studies), use (their application in quantitative and qualitative approaches), and placement (their location) in research reports. Knowing these differences can help you design, write, and evaluate them. An overview of these differences is shown in Figure 5.1.

Purpose Statement

We begin with the most important statement in research—the purpose statement. It describes succinctly the overall intent of the research, and it sets the direction for data collection and reporting results. Because of its significance, it demands your careful attention.

The **purpose statement** is a declarative statement that advances the overall direction or focus for the study. Researchers describe the purpose in one or more succinctly formed sentences. It is used both in quantitative and qualitative research and is typically found in the introduction or beginning section of research (or "Statement of the Problem" as discussed in Chapter 3). A good place to look for this statement is the last sentence of an introduction; it may be identified with words such as, "The purpose of this study is. . . ." A *quantitative* version of this purpose statement addressing teacher-parent communications and student achievement follows:

The purpose of this study is to examine the relationship between use of Internet communication between teachers and parents in a midwestern school district and student achievement on tests in high school social studies.

A *qualitative* version might be:

The purpose of this study is to explore parent stories regarding Internet communications with teachers about their students in one midwestern school district.

Research Questions

Research investigators narrow the purpose statement to specific research questions. **Research questions** are interrogative statements that narrow the purpose statement to specific questions that researchers seek to answer in their studies. Inquirers typically include multiple research questions to fully explore a topic and research problem. Although these questions are found in both quantitative and qualitative research, they assume different forms in the two types. In quantitative research, the questions relate variables, while in qualitative research, the questions include a central phenomenon to be explored. (Both variables and the central phenomenon will be discussed later in this chapter.) In some studies, both research questions and purpose statements appear—a good presentation style to clarify both the general and specific direction of a study. Research questions are typically found at the end of the introduction of the "Statement of the Problem" section or immediately following the review of the literature. To locate research questions, you might look for sections labeled "research questions" (e.g., Vooijs & van der Voort, 1993) or identify sentences in which the inquirer mentions a question that he or she would like answered. A quantitative research question takes this form:

Do parent-teacher Internet communications affect student performance in the classroom?

A qualitative research question is more open-ended, with this form:

What types of Internet experiences do parents have with teachers about the performance of the parents' children?

Hypotheses

In traditional educational research such as experiments, investigators often use hypotheses to narrow the purpose statement to specific predictions. **Hypotheses** are declarative statements in quantitative research in which the investigator makes a prediction or a conjecture about the outcome of a relationship. These predictions or conjectures are not simply an "educated guess"; rather, they are typically based on past research where investigators gathered evidence to advance a hypothesized relationship between variables (e.g., more leisurely reading improves college student achievement). Often researchers state multiple hypotheses to subdivide a major prediction into subparts. These hypotheses are stated at the beginning of a study, typically at the end of the introduction. Investigators also place them immediately after the review of the literature or in a separate section and identify them as "Hypotheses." To locate hypotheses, look for statements where the investigator relates one or more variables or makes predictions about the relationship of variables. An illustration of a predictive hypothesis is:

Students in high schools in the school district in which parents and teachers communicate through the Internet will have higher grades than students whose parents and teachers do not communicate through the Internet.

Research Objectives

Less popular as a form for stating direction is the research objective. A **research objective** is a statement of intent that specifies goals that the investigator plans to achieve in a study. Like hypotheses and research questions, one objective can be sub-divided into minor objectives for presentation in a study. Research objectives are used more often in quantitative research than in qualitative research. They are also frequently used in surveys in which investigators have clearly identified objectives to be conducted in the study (e.g., "The first objective will be to describe the incidence of depression." "The second objective will be to relate . . ."). Like hypotheses and research questions, objectives are found after the end of the introduction or the "Statement of the Problem," after the literature review, or in a separate section of the study. You can identify objectives by looking for words such as, "The objectives in this study are . . ." For instance, the following represent objectives for a study:

1. To describe the frequency of Internet communication between parents and teachers regarding the parents' children in high school social studies classes;
2. To describe the types (or categories) of Internet communication between parents and teachers;
3. To relate (a) frequency and (b) types of communication to student achievement in the class as measured by performance on tests.

Because of the limited use of research objectives in educational research today, our focus in this chapter will be on hypotheses and research questions as a means of narrowing and focusing purpose statements.

QUANTITATIVE RESEARCH

Before writing a purpose statement, research questions, or hypotheses, you need to thoroughly understand the nature and important role of variables. This section of the chapter addresses:

- variables—their definition, their types, their relationships within a theory, and their ability to predict cause and effect
- purpose statements—guidelines for their construction and practice scripts to guide you as you design and write them
- research questions—guidelines for their construction, descriptive, relationship, and comparison questions, and practice scripts to guide you as you design and write them
- research hypotheses—guidelines for their construction, null and alternative hypotheses, and practice scripts to guide you as you design and write them

Defining and Using Variables

Consider the following examples of variables typically studied in educational research:

- leadership style (by administrators)
- achievement in science (by students)
- interpersonal communication skills (of counselors)
- attitudes toward school choice (by school board members)
- teaching style (by college teachers)

These variables are key ideas that researchers seek to address in their studies. A **variable** is a characteristic or attribute of an individual or an organization that (1) can be measured or observed by the researcher and (2) varies among individuals or organizations studied (see Figure 5.2).

These two properties are necessary for an attribute or characteristic to be a variable. Some attributes, such as "socialization," cannot be measured, because they are too abstract. Some characteristics, such as "whether the children engage in thinking in the classroom," do not vary among people. Certainly all children think; what varies is how they think differently, such as when they engage in the activity of writing.

When we speak of a variable as a characteristic we mean personal aspects about individuals, such as their grade level in high school, their age, or their income level. An attribute, on the other hand, represents how an individual or individuals in an organization feel, behave, or think. When we talk about individuals having self-esteem, engaging in smoking, or displaying certain leadership behaviors, we are mentioning their attributes.

Researchers measure these attributes or characteristics. **Measurement** means that the researcher records information from individuals by:

▶ asking them to answer questions on an instrument (e.g., a student completes questions on a survey asking about self-esteem) or
▶ observing an individual and recording scores on an instrument (e.g., a researcher watches a student playing basketball and records scores on dribbling techniques)

In either case, student scores will probably vary (hence the name "variable"). That variables **vary** means that scores will assume different values depending on the type of variable being measured. For example,

▶ Gender varies by two possible scores: female = 2 and male = 1.
▶ High school grade level varies by four possible scores: senior = 4, junior = 3, sophomore = 2, and freshman = 1.
▶ Self-esteem varies by three possible scores: positive = 3, neither positive nor negative = 2, and negative = 1.

In the quantitative study on television violence (Vooijs & van der Voort, 1993), the authors measure the variable, "readiness to see violence" (Paragraph 25) by having the children rate 25 violent actions performed by the "good guy" on a video. The children record their scores on a 5-point scale from "really dreadful" to "not so bad" with their scores varying both at the beginning and the end of the experiment.

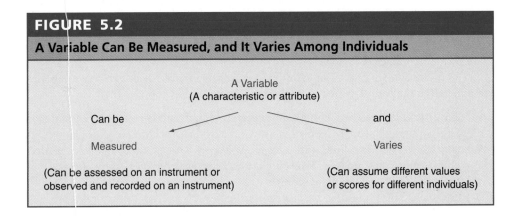

FIGURE 5.2

A Variable Can Be Measured, and It Varies Among Individuals

A Variable
(A characteristic or attribute)

Can be   and

Measured   Varies

(Can be assessed on an instrument or   (Can assume different values
observed and recorded on an instrument)   or scores for different individuals)

Differentiating Variables from Constructs

You may find that authors, especially in psychology and some fields of education, use the term "construct" instead of "variables" in their research studies. They both have the same meaning, but they differ in terms of level of abstraction. A **construct** is an attribute or characteristic expressed in an abstract, general way; a variable is an attribute or characteristic stated in a specific, applied way. The trend in educational research is to use variables rather than constructs in purpose statements, research questions, and hypotheses. But you should know the difference because they may be used interchangeably by authors. In the two examples below, you will see how an abstract term, the construct, can be restated in a specific applied way as a variable.

| Construct | $\longrightarrow$ | student achievement |
| Variable | $\longrightarrow$ | grade point average |

| Construct | $\longrightarrow$ | school leadership |
| Variable | $\longrightarrow$ | consensus-building style of leaders |

Distinguishing Between Categorical and Continuous Scores

When participants in a study complete a question, the researcher assigns a score to their response (e.g., "5" for strongly agree). This score is a value for the variable being measured, and investigators classify these scores into continuous and categorical scores. Knowing this classification will help you understand the different types of variables and how they are stated in purpose statements, research questions, and hypotheses.

Researchers score variables by grouping them into a limited number of categories or by using them to represent a value of some degree on a continuum, ranging from low to high levels (Gall, Borg, & Gall, 1996; Vogt, 1999). A **categorical score** is a value of a variable assigned by the researcher to a small number of groups or categories. This type of score is also called a "discrete" or "nominal" score, and may be illustrated by these examples:

▶ groups of students: males (1) and females (2), high ability (1) and low ability (2)
▶ types of instruction: groups of students who experience lectures (1), group of students who experience discussion (2), and groups of students who experience classroom activities (3)

A second type of score is based on assigning scores to values along a continuum. A **continuous score** is the value of a variable assigned by the researcher to a point along a continuum of scores, from low to high values. This type of score is also called an "interval," a "rating," or a "scaled" score. The most typical example of a continuous score would be age (e.g., from 25 years old to 65 years old) or height (e.g., from 5 feet to 6 feet tall). Often continuous scores indicate the extent to which individuals agree or disagree with an idea or rate the level of importance of an issue.

This information is helpful for identifying and using variables because these categories are reflected in purpose statements, research questions, and hypotheses that:

▶ relate a variable measured with a continuous score with another variable measured with a continuous score (e.g., math ability scores to math achievement scores)
▶ compare a variable measured with a categorical score with another variable measured with a continuous score (e.g., type of instruction, categorized into discussion and lecture, and math achievement scores)
▶ compare variables measured by a categorical score with another categorical score (e.g., type of instruction and the categories of high and low achievement scores)

As you read about the types of variables and their use in statements and research questions, you will see the use of categorical and continuous scoring of variables. Later, in Chapter 6, we will expand on these measures of variables in "Selecting Scales of Measurement."

Describing the Family of Variables

Many types of variables are used in designing purpose statements, research questions, and hypotheses. Understanding the "family of variables" requires learning the definition of each type of variable and understanding its role in providing direction for a study.

This "family" is shown in Figure 5.3. In this discussion you will learn about each type of variable in this figure, starting with the most important variables—the independent, intervening, and dependent. As shown in this figure, a useful way to think about organizing these variables is to consider them in a cause-and-effect relationship (Tuckman, 1999). Later in this chapter we will address how much confidence we can place in the "cause" actually influencing the "effect," and we will describe it as "probable cause." But for the moment, let's inspect the types of variables in this "family":

- ▶ independent variables: treatment and measured
- ▶ special types of independent variables: control and moderating
- ▶ intervening variables
- ▶ dependent variables
- ▶ confounding variables

Independent Variables

On the left in Figure 5.3 are the independent variables. An **independent variable** is an attribute or characteristic that influences or effects an outcome or dependent variable. In Figure 5.3, the arrows show how the independent variable influences the intervening variable

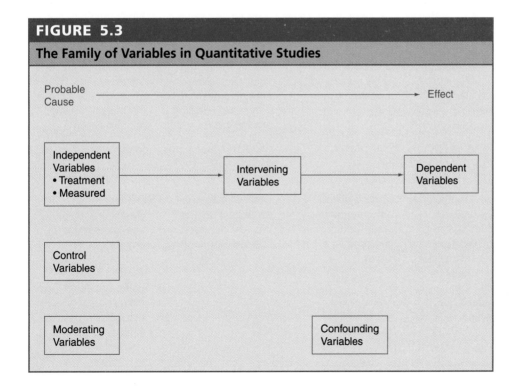

FIGURE 5.3

The Family of Variables in Quantitative Studies

and the dependent variable. In research studies and texts, the independent variable is known by different names, such as factor, treatment, predictor, determinant, measured, antecedent, or probable cause variable. Regardless of name, this type of variable is independent of the outcome, but it may influence the outcome.

Researchers study independent variables to see what effect or influence they have on the outcome. For instance, consider this research question:

Do students who spend more instructional time in class on math have higher math scores than students who spend less time?

Independent variable: Time on math instruction

Explanation: Time on math instruction influences the outcome, math scores.

Independent variables serve different purposes, and an overview of the types and their roles is shown in Table 5.1.

TABLE 5.1

Four Types of Independent Variables

	Treatment Variable	Measured Variable	Control Variable	Moderating Variable
Definition	An independent variable manipulated by the researcher	An independent variable that is measured in a study	A special type of independent variable that is of secondary interest and is neutralized through statistical or design procedures	A special type of independent variable that is of secondary interest and combines with another independent variable to influence the dependent variable
Type of Variable Measurement	A categorical variable actively manipulated by the researcher and composed of two or more groups	A categorical or continuous variable that is measured or observed in the study	A variable not directly measured but controlled through statistical or research design procedures	A categorical or continuous variable measured or observed as it interacts with other variables
Use in	Experiments	Experiments, surveys	Experiments, correlational studies	Experiments
Examples	Classroom learning: one group receives standard lecture and one group receives discussion; researcher assigns students to groups and thus manipulates group membership	Age of a child; performance on a test; attitudes assessed on a survey	Often demographic variables such as age, gender, race, socioeconomic level	Demographic variables such as age, gender, race, or socioeconomic level, a measured variable such as performance or attitude, or a manipulated variable such as classroom instruction

Treatment Variables   In educational experiments, researchers treat or manipulate at least one of the independent variables. A **treatment variable** is an independent variable that the researcher manipulates to determine the effect it will have on an outcome. It is always a categorically scored variable measuring two or more groups. These variables are sometimes referred to as "manipulated" variables or variables with "levels." For example, the researcher treats one group of participants to specific activities and withholds them from another group. Experimental researchers refer to these two groups as two "levels" (i.e., group 1, group 2) of this treatment variable.

In the following example, the treatment variable is the type of instruction used by the teacher in an elementary math classroom:

> In a study of student achievement outcomes in an elementary math classroom, the researcher gives one group small group discussion (level 1) and another traditional group lecture (level 2) to assess the independent variable, type of instruction.
>
> Independent treatment variable: Type of instruction is considered a treatment variable because the researcher intervenes with one group, level 1.

Measured Variables   In some experiments and other types of quantitative studies (e.g., surveys), the independent variable may not be a treatment variable manipulated by the researcher. Instead, it may be actively measured by the researcher. A **measured variable** is an independent variable that is measured or observed by the researcher and consists of a range of continuous or categorical scores for variables. For example, consider the research question,

> How does math ability influence achievement on the final quiz in the classroom?

The independent variable is a measured variable indicating math ability scores assessed by results on an ability test. Of course, a particular research study may contain both a treatment variable and a measured variable as in the following example:

> How does math ability and participation in small group discussion (level 1) influence achievement on the final quiz in the classroom?

In this example, the treatment variable is type of instruction (assuming that two groups are being compared—one that receives small group discussion and a second that receives a lecture). Math ability is a measured variable assessed by scores on an ability test.

Two Special Types of Independent Variables

Also shown in Figure 5.3 are two special types of independent variables found in quantitative research: control variables and moderating variables. They are aligned under the independent variables because they often cause or influence the intervening and dependent variables. But they differ in important ways from treatment and measured independent variables.

Control Variables   A control variable is typically not measured or manipulated in a study but is removed from the cause-and-effect relationship through use of statistical or research procedures. Since control variables play such a prominent role in experiments, they need to be introduced as an important member of the family of variables. A **control variable** is a variable that the researcher does not want to measure directly (Vogt, 1999) but that is important to consider and "neutralize" (Tuckman, 1999, p. 100) because it potentially influences the dependent variable. Typically control variables are personal, demographic attributes or characteristics (Tuckman, 1999), such as:

- gender
- socioeconomic status
- intelligence
- race

In quantitative studies these control variables are called *covariates* and they are statistically adjusted for their effects (see Chapter 8 on "Choosing a Statistical Test"). The investigator removes the control variable using statistical procedures so that the relationship between other independent variables and the outcome can be determined. Alternatively, experimental researchers use the procedure of assigning individuals to groups in special ways to control for their impact (see Chapter 11 on "Random Assignment").

For example, let's return to our example about math in the elementary school:

> In addition to the group intervention on type of instruction and the math ability scores, the researcher feels that gender may influence student performance on math quizzes. In effect, the researcher studies three independent variables:
> 1. type of instruction (categorical variable)
> 2. math ability scores (continuous variable)
> 3. gender (categorical variable for girls and boys)

The purpose statement for this study can be written as follows:

> This study addresses the impact of two types of instruction (small group and lecture group), math ability (measured on a test), and gender on math achievement in the elementary school math classroom.

This example illustrates a treatment independent variable (the groups), a measured independent variable (math ability scores), and a control variable (gender).

Moderating Variables   Moderating variables deserve our attention because they, too, are often used in educational experiments. Similar to control variables, these variables are of secondary interest in a study but they are measured because they impact the dependent variable. Unlike control variables, rather than being statistically or procedurally removed by the researcher, they are actually *studied* (Tuckman, 1999). A moderating variable is an attribute or characteristic that is measured, manipulated, or selected because it influences the dependent variable. In experiments, moderating variables exercise joint effects (called "interaction effects" in Chapter 11) on the dependent variable. For example, examine this hypothesis:

> Small group discussion for students with high prior test scores contributes to higher math quiz results than lecture discussion for students with low prior test scores.

The interaction of instruction with prior test scores (often stated as "type of instruction ✕ [times] prior test scores") in combination influences math quiz scores.

Locating Independent Variables   Independent variables are located in purpose statements, research questions, and hypotheses. To find them look for the variable that exercises influence or predicts an outcome. They may be described in categories or on a continuous scale of scores. They may also be of primary interest (treatment or measured variables) or of secondary interest (control or moderating variables).

Intervening Variables

In most educational situations, outcomes are seldom influenced by only one or more independent variables. Some variables exercise influence between the independent and dependent variables in the cause-and-effect sequence. An ***intervening variable*** is an attribute or characteristic that "stands between" the independent and dependent variables and exercises an influence on the dependent variable apart from the independent variable. Intervening variables transmit (or mediate) the effects of the independent variable on the dependent variable. Thus, they are also called "mediating" variables. In some quantitative studies, intervening variables are controlled using statistical procedures.

To demonstrate how intervening variables work, consider the logic of the sequence of variables shown in Figure 5.4. In this illustration, we first see that convenient office hours for students influences whether students will seek help from faculty (Step 1). However, this situation on most college campuses is too basic. Many factors besides office hours influence student visits with faculty. Convenient office hours convey an openness to students, and they show that faculty care about their students. They also encourage shy and reserved students who are unable to speak up in class to visit privately with faculty. Students are willing to take risks by visiting with faculty privately in their offices (Step 2). What began as a single factor explaining the help students seek from faculty has now become more complex. When faculty have convenient office hours, students become willing to take risks, and they seek help from faculty (Step 3). As an intervening variable, a willingness to take risks is influenced by convenient office hours and this, in turn, influences whether that student will seek help from a faculty member.

To locate mediating variables in purpose statements, research hypotheses, or questions:

▶ Ask yourself if any variables stand between the independent and dependent variables in a left-to-right sequence of events.

▶ In these statements or questions, look for the words "mediate" or "intervene." These words will provide a cue that the researcher intends to consider them as important influences on the dependent variable.

▶ Go into the results section and look at the statistical analysis of the data to determine if the researcher statistically controls for variables that may stand between the independent and dependent variables.

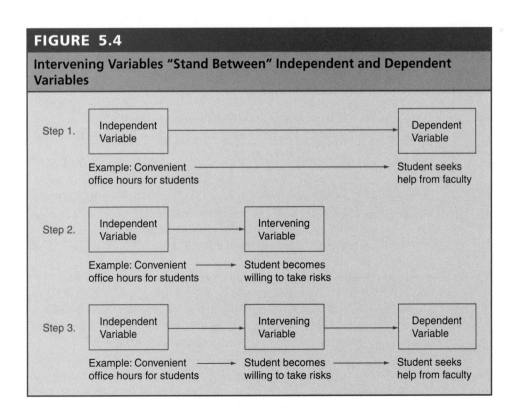

FIGURE 5.4

Intervening Variables "Stand Between" Independent and Dependent Variables

Dependent Variables

Look again at Figure 5.3. The arrows from the independent variable point toward the dependent variable. A **dependent variable** is an attribute or characteristic that is dependent on or influenced by the independent variable. They may be called the outcome, effect, criterion, or consequence variables. Researchers typically investigate multiple dependent variables in a single study, although in many studies, one of the dependent variables is typically of central interest.

Examples of dependent variables are achievement scores on a test, the organizational climate of a junior high school, the leadership skills of principals, or the cost-effectiveness of student affairs programs in colleges. To locate dependent variables in a study, examine purpose statements, research questions, and hypotheses for the outcome that the researcher wishes to predict or explain. Ask yourself, "What is the outcome in this study?"

Confounding Variables

One final variable in Figure 5.3 is the confounding variable. In this illustration, confounding variables are not directly in the probable cause-and-effect sequence. **Confounding variables** (sometimes called *spurious variables*) are attributes or characteristics that the researcher cannot directly measure because their effects cannot be easily separated from other variables, even though they may influence the relationship between the independent and the dependent variable. For example, for a high school student it may be impossible to separate an individual's race and prior discriminatory experiences as predictors of attitudes toward school. Thus, researchers measure the variables they can easily identify (e.g., race) and explain a limitation on their results (e.g., race was so interconnected with discriminatory experiences that it could not be easily separated as an independent measure).

 ## Think-Aloud About Identifying Variables

It is not always easy to identify variables in published studies, even with knowledge about the different types of variables and their roles. Here is a procedure I recommend to help you identify and organize variables to best understand a research report or plan your own study.

1. Take a piece of paper and write from left to right the words "independent," "intervening," and "dependent variables." Draw straight vertical lines between these words down the page.
2. Begin with the dependent variable. Examine a study (or consider your own project) and ask yourself: What are the outcomes the author seeks to explain in the study? Look at the title, the purpose statement, questions, or hypotheses for this variable. Place the dependent variable(s) under the column on the sheet.
3. Next identify the independent variable(s) in the study. What factors influence this outcome? Does more than one factor influence this outcome? If so, what types of factors are they? Is the independent variable assessed as two or more groups? Is it a variable where the author plans to intervene with one group and withhold an intervention with another group? Is some trait or characteristic of the participants being studied that influences the outcome? Does the author use language about controlling for a specific variable? List the independent variables on the sheet and write the type of independent variable in parenthesis after it (e.g., treatment, measured, or controlled).
4. Locate any intervening variables that may be used by the author. Are there any factors that mediate the influence between the independent and dependent variables in a cause-and-effect sequence? List these variables on your sheet.

With this process, you have compiled a list of major variables in the study. As a picture, this rendering will help reduce a complex study into a simple, understandable model of the research. It can help you identify and plan the variables for your own study, and it provides a useful visual for conveying the major direction of a research report to audiences such as faculty committees and conference attendees.

Variables in Theories

In Figure 5.3, the illustration shows arrows connecting and relating variables. What is the basis for researchers to claim that the variables are related? Often quantitative investigators turn to theories to locate variables and to identify appropriate relationships among variables.

A **theory** explains and predicts the relationship between independent and dependent variables. As shown in Figure 5.5, you might think about a theory as a bridge that connects the independent and dependent variables. Theories are no more than broad explanations for what we would expect to find when we relate variables. For example, we would expect peer groups to influence adolescent smoking because friends are important to young adults, and friends are in constant contact with students in social and school situations. A "theory about friendship" then becomes an explanation for why peers (independent variable) influence smoking behavior (dependent variable).

In quantitative research, investigators locate a theory in the literature, examine the predicted relationship among variables in the theory, and then test the relationships with new participants or at new sites. To test the theory, researchers write purpose statements, research questions, and hypotheses that advance the predicted relationships. For example, a theory of leadership might predict that when principals use consensus-building decision styles, their teachers feel more supported.

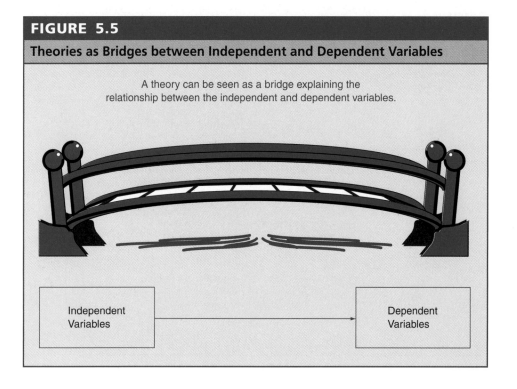

FIGURE 5.5

Theories as Bridges between Independent and Dependent Variables

A theory can be seen as a bridge explaining the relationship between the independent and dependent variables.

| Independent Variables | Dependent Variables |

Theories can be found in the research literature, and you may be familiar with some of them: a theory about how students learn; a theory about what motivates people; a theory about how adults learn; a theory about leadership styles; and a theory about personality.

The use of a theory provides a sophisticated approach to research. Unfortunately, educational researchers sometimes develop studies based on their own hunches and expectations rather than grounding their ideas in the research literature and existing theories. As shown in Figure 5.6, a researcher may identify different types of explanations for the relationship between the independent and dependent variables and base these explanations on different factors.

For example, assume that several researchers explore the relationship between teacher respect for cultural values (the independent variable) and student performance (the dependent variable) in elementary school. Researchers could proceed in several ways, but notice how each situation that follows involves an increasing number of tests of studies. This is one example of how explanations may be posed from a personal hunch to a sophisticated theory.

1. Some researchers have *hunches* or educated guesses as to why two variables might be related. For example, from personal experience, one researcher might feel that Hispanic children succeed in elementary school because the teacher is sensitive to cultural issues (e.g., the recognition and celebration of Hispanic holidays). No tests of this hunch have been made, and this approach represents less sophisticated research based on the experiences of the researcher.

2. At a more sophisticated level of research, educators can draw on a *theoretical rationale*—a logical statement for relating the variables—mentioned by authors in other studies. Assume that Jones, for example, found that Hispanic students learned best when teachers celebrated Hispanic holidays in class. With this theoretical rationale, we probably have more confidence in understanding the relationship between cultural sensitivity and performance in class (e.g., learning best).

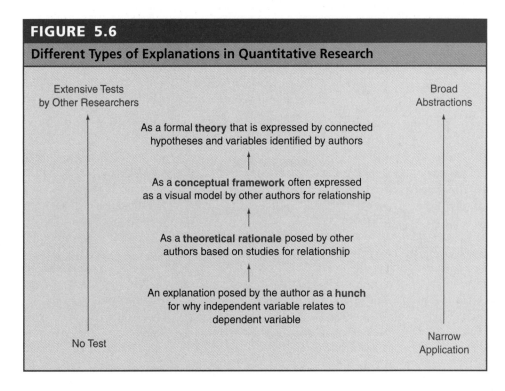

FIGURE 5.6

Different Types of Explanations in Quantitative Research

Extensive Tests by Other Researchers

Broad Abstractions

As a formal **theory** that is expressed by connected hypotheses and variables identified by authors

As a **conceptual framework** often expressed as a visual model by other authors for relationship

As a **theoretical rationale** posed by other authors based on studies for relationship

An explanation posed by the author as a **hunch** for why independent variable relates to dependent variable

No Test

Narrow Application

3. Moving to an even more sophisticated level, assume that five different authors have studied this relationship and found cultural sensitivity to be related to performance. Smith, for instance, developed a *conceptual framework* (e.g., see Figure 5.3) predicting this relationship to hold true. It was tested by Fox, Davis, Abel, and Sandoz. All found the relationship to hold true for different groups of Hispanic children. Now we have more confidence in the relationship because it has been tested multiple times with different Hispanic children.

4. Finally, assume that the relationship between cultural sensitivity and student performance is tested with many groups of *different* cultural orientations (e.g., Asian-Americans, Native Americans, African-Americans). In all of these situations, a positive relationship exists between teacher sensitivity and student performance. We are approaching a theory, a broad explanation of student performance based on cultural orientations. In short, a *theory* is an explanation for a prediction among variables that has been tested extensively.

Several options exist for researchers to state theories in their research. One approach is to state them using an "if . . . then" logic. *If* certain conditions are true, *then* the variables will be related. For example,

If achievement in math is gender-related, then because girls are socialized to be better at math, girls will perform better in math than boys.

Other theories are presented in research as discussions that predict the relationship between the variables. These sections are called a "theoretical rationale" or a "theory-base" for the study. Before advancing the research questions in the television violence study, Vooijs and van der Voort (1993) used a theoretical framework about attitude change (Paragraph 11).

Whether Variables Prove Cause and Effect

By now you may be wondering whether we can predict with any confidence the relationship between the independent and dependent variables. Can we say that the crime series curriculum actually causes children's attitudes toward violence on television to change?

Recall that in Figure 5.3 we discussed how the independent variable "probably" caused the effect. In this everyday world working with people, it is difficult to establish absolute cause and effect. Instead of proving cause and effect, we need to be cautious about our conclusions. **Probable causation** means that researchers attempt to establish a likely cause-and-effect relationship between variables, rather than *prove* the relationship. For example, one researcher decided to study whether autocratic leadership in a school caused teacher dissatisfaction. This is impossible to study because we cannot conclude with any confidence that an autocratic leader *caused* teacher dissatisfaction. If the research showed this to be the case, many factors other than leadership approach (e.g., years of service as a teacher, a teacher's personal dislike for the principal) likely influenced teacher dissatisfaction. Since we can never account for all the factors, the researcher can only say that "autocratic leadership *probably caused* teacher dissatisfaction."

To ensure that we can establish probable cause, we introduce control into our research procedures. **Control** means that the researcher attempts to study all factors that might help explain the relationship between an independent and dependent variable. In experiments, you may recall that we used control variables to statistically and procedurally exercise control. In addition, the use of variables can place some control into our studies. Stronger probable causality (or as it is often called, "causal inference") and more control are possible through four approaches, as shown in Figure 5.7.

FIGURE 5.7

Four Types of Probable Causality

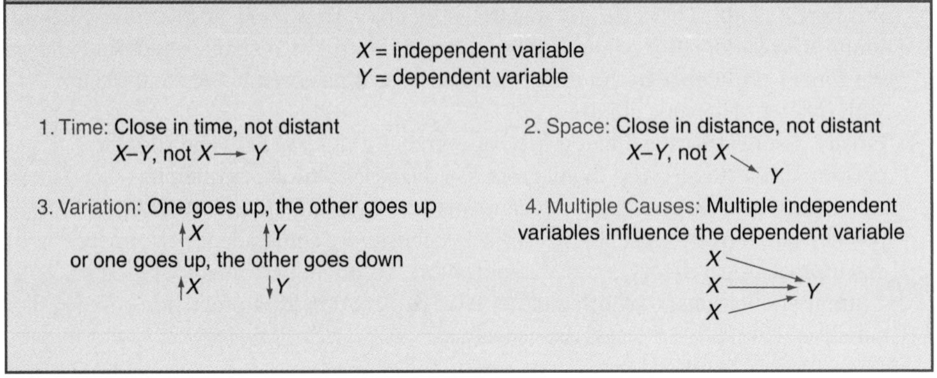

X = independent variable
Y = dependent variable

1. Time: **Close in time, not distant**
   $X–Y$, not $X \longrightarrow Y$

2. Space: **Close in distance, not distant**
   $X–Y$, not $X \searrow Y$

3. Variation: **One goes up, the other goes up**
   $\uparrow X$ $\uparrow Y$
   or one goes up, the other goes down
   $\uparrow X$ $\downarrow Y$

4. Multiple Causes: **Multiple independent variables influence the dependent variable**
   $X \longrightarrow Y$
   $X \longrightarrow Y$
   $X \longrightarrow Y$

1. Time—An independent variable probably causes the dependent variable if the time between the two variables is short rather than long. A special education teacher provides an immediate reward to students who perform well on spelling tests rather than waiting one or two days to provide the rewards.
2. Space—An independent variable probably causes the dependent variable if the geographical distance between the two variables is shorter rather than longer. A teacher in the special education classroom has a stronger impact on the children than does the principal of the school.
3. Variation—An independent variable probably causes the dependent variable if a change in one variable results in a change in the other. If the special education teacher provides rewards for good spelling performance, the children's performance becomes better in response to the rewards.
4. Multiple causes—The more independent variables that can be measured or observed, the more probable it is that causality can be explained for the dependent variable. The study of many factors that influence the performance of special education children in spelling provides a stronger case for probable causality than the study of only one factor.

Writing a Purpose Statement

With this background about variables, you are ready to design and write a quantitative purpose statement. A **quantitative purpose statement** identifies the variables, their relationship, and the participants and site for research. To write this statement, we will first specify the elements that go into a good purpose statement, display a script to help you design this statement, and indicate several examples to illustrate how to compose this statement using the script.

Guidelines

Several guidelines can help you prepare good purpose statements:

▶ Write the purpose statement in a single sentence.
▶ Begin the statement with key identifier words, such as "The purpose of this study," to clearly signal readers.
▶ If you plan to use a theory, introduce it in this statement by stating that you plan to "test a theory."

▶ Use the words "relate" or "compare" or "describe" to indicate whether variables will be related, groups will be compared, or variables will be described.

▶ If variables are related or groups compared, specify the independent and dependent variables and any control or intervening variables.

▶ State the independent variable (first position in the sentence) followed by the dependent variable (second position in the sentence). If control or mediating variables are used, state them last (in the third position in the sentence). The placement of these variables in this sentence is important because quantitative researchers often view variables as related from left to right.

▶ Identify the participants to be studied and the research site at which they will be studied.

Sample Scripts

To apply these guidelines, consider the following script that can be used to facilitate writing a purpose statement:

The purpose of this study is to test (the theory) by relating (the independent variable) to (the dependent variable) for (participants) at (the research site).

or

by comparing (group 1) with (group 2) in terms of (dependent variable) for (participants) at (the research site).

To apply this script, examine the following example for the case in which the researcher relates variables:

The purpose of this study is to test Fines' theory (1996) by relating leadership style (independent variable) to autonomy (dependent variable) for teachers (participants) in high schools in State X (research site).

The next example illustrates the use of the script in which the researcher compares two groups (as an independent variable) in terms of one dependent variable:

The purpose of this study is to test Smarts' theory (1999) by comparing autocratic leaders (group 1) with consensus-building leaders (group 2) in terms of the satisfaction of teachers (dependent variable) in colleges in State X (research site).

Both examples begin with the words, "the purpose of," to signal the reader. The independent variables precede the dependent variables in the statements. Also in both illustrations the authors found theories to test and they mentioned them in the beginning of the sentence. In other cases, a researcher may only have a hunch or a rationale and may not formally include a theory.

Maria, the high school teacher interested in studying weapon possession among high school students, might write the purpose statement with control variables in the third position:

The purpose of this study is to relate student misbehavior factors (i.e., fighting) (independent variable—*Position 1*) to attitudes toward weapon possession (dependent variable—*Position 2*) for students in the district's high schools (participants—site), controlling for gender, grade level, and race (*Position 3*).

Writing Research Questions

Research questions describe the participants' reaction to a single variable, compare groups on an outcome, or relate to variables. Research questions are found in all forms of quantitative research, such as in experiments, correlational studies, and surveys. Because they are less formal and phrased as questions, researchers today use them more than hypotheses. Questions also enable researchers to describe a single variable, a feature not available with hypotheses.

Guidelines

The basic steps in forming a research question are:

- Pose a question.
- Begin with "how," "what," or "why."
- Specify the independent, dependent, and mediating or control variables.
- Use the words "describe," "compare," or "relate" to indicate the action or connection among the variables.
- Indicate the participants and the research site for the study.

Three popular forms are available in quantitative research: descriptive questions, relationship questions, and comparison questions.

Descriptive Questions

Researchers use a **descriptive question** to identify participants' responses to a single variable or question. This single variable may be an independent, a dependent, or an intervening variable. The following is a script for writing a descriptive question:

How frequently do (participants) (variable) at (research site)?

An application of this script might be:

How frequently do African-Americans feel isolated on college campuses?

Relationship Questions

In most research studies, investigators seek to learn more than responses to single variables. They may examine the relationship between two or more variables. **Relationship questions** seek to answer the degree and magnitude of the relationship between two or more variables. These questions often relate different types of variables in a study, such as independent variables to dependent variables or dependent variables to control variables. The most common case is where the independent variable is related to the dependent variable. The following is a script for writing a relationship question:

How does (independent variable) relate to (dependent variable) for (participants) at (research site)?

As applied to the relationship between isolation and ethnic identity, the script suggests:

How do feelings of isolation relate to (or influence) the ethnic identity of African-Americans in the U.S.?

Comparison Questions

Researchers might ask a **comparison question** to find out how two or more groups differ in terms of one or more outcome variables. A comparison question is typically used in an experiment, and the researcher provides some intervention to one group and withholds it from the second group. A script for writing a comparison question would be:

How does (group 1) differ from (group 2) in terms of (dependent variable) for (participants) at (research site)?

When this script is applied in a comparison of African-Americans and Euro-Americans, we get:

How do African-Americans and Euro-Americans compare in their perceptions of ethnic identity?

Writing Hypotheses

Similar to research questions, hypotheses narrow the purpose statement in quantitative research. Researchers narrow the focus of the study to one or more hypotheses that provide a prediction about the outcome of the study. Hypotheses contain many of the elements of purpose statements, but they are written at a more specific level.

Guidelines

The basic steps in forming hypotheses are:

▶ State the independent, dependent, and control or intervening variables in first-, second-, and third-order positions.

▶ If groups are compared, explicitly state the groups; if variables are related, specify the relationship.

▶ Identify the participants and the site of the study.

▶ Make a prediction about changes (e.g., less, more favorable) or no changes (e.g., no difference). This is a statement tested by the researcher using statistical procedures (to be discussed in more detail in Chapter 8 on "Conducting Hypothesis Testing").

There are two types of hypotheses: the null and the alternative to the null. The basic characteristics of these two forms are shown in Table 5.2.

Null Hypotheses

The most traditional form of writing hypotheses is to state them as null hypotheses. **Null hypotheses** make predictions that in the general population there is no relationship between variables or no difference between groups on measured variables. A null hypothesis might begin with the words "There is no difference between" (the mean statistics of the groups selected from the population) or "There is no relationship between" (the relationship statistics of variables measured for individuals selected from the population).

An example of a null hypothesis script follows using the language, "no difference:"

TABLE 5.2

The Null and Alternative Hypotheses

Type of Hypothesis	Null Hypothesis	Alternative Hypothesis
Purpose	To test in the general population that there is no change, no relationship, no difference	The hypothesis that may be true if the null is rejected; it suggests a change, a relationship, or a difference
Specific Language Found in the Hypothesis	There is no difference, (or relationship) between. . .	Magnitude statements, such as higher, lower, more positive, more favorable
How Researchers Test the Hypothesis	A test of the hypothesis (see Chapter 8, "Hypothesis Testing")	A test of the hypothesis (see Chapter 8, "Hypothesis Testing")

There is no difference between (independent variable, group 1) and (independent variable, group 2) in terms of (dependent variable) for (participants) at (research site).

An example of the application of this script might be:

There is no difference between at-risk and non at-risk students and student achievement on math test scores for third-grade students in a midwest school district.

Independent variable: At-risk students (members and nonmembers)

Dependent variable: Student achievement test scores

Participants: Third-grade students

Site: X school district

Form and language: Null indicating no difference

Alternative Hypothesis

A popular form of hypothesis is to write an alternative hypothesis. In a **directional alternative hypothesis,** the researcher predicts the direction of a change, a difference, or a relationship for measured variables in a population. This prediction is typically based on prior research conducted by the investigator or reported by others in the literature (e.g., an explanation or theory reported in the literature). For scores measured for a sample from a population, this hypothesis predicts that the scores will be higher, better, or changed in some way. A typical form for writing hypotheses today, it is encountered in the literature more than any other type of hypothesis. A script for a directional alternative hypothesis is:

(group 1, independent variable) at (research site) will have (some difference, such as higher, lower, greater, lesser) on (dependent variable) than (group 2 of independent variable).

An example of this script is:

Students who participate in direct learning in four elementary schools will have higher achievement scores than students who participate in whole-language learning.

Independent variable: Learning (direct and whole language)

Dependent variable: Achievement test scores

Participants: Third grade students

Research Site: Four elementary schools

Key indicator: Directional, a prediction is implied

A variation on the directional hypothesis is the nondirectional hypothesis. In a **nondirectional alternative hypothesis** the researcher predicts a change, a difference, or a relationship for measured variables in a population but does not indicate the direction of this prediction (e.g., positive or negative). The nondirectional alternative is not as popular as the null hypothesis because it is not as precise or as testable as the null hypothesis. In common practice, however, researchers treat it as if it were a null and look for no difference. A script for a nondirectional alternative hypothesis is:

There is a difference between (group 1, independent variable) and (group 2, independent variable) in terms of (dependent variable)

An illustration of this script would be:

There is a difference between varsity athletes in high school who smoke and those who do not smoke in terms of athletic accomplishments.

In this example, the author does not state whether the difference will be positive or negative. Later, in Chapter 8 on "Conducting Hypothesis Testing," it will be viewed as a "two-tail" statistical test. An analysis of the variables in this statement shows:

Independent variable: Use of tobacco (smokers and nonsmokers)

Dependent variable: Athletic accomplishments

Participants: Varsity athletes

Sites: High schools

Key indicator: The words, "a difference," but the direction is not specified

QUALITATIVE RESEARCH

Turning to *qualitative* research, inquirers also use purpose statements and research questions to provide the major direction and intent for research. Unlike quantitative research, the qualitative researcher asks open-ended and broad questions that will enable the participants to share their views about the problem being studied (as discussed in Chapter 2 on "Specifying a Purpose for Research").

To extend this point, we can now be more specific about how quantitative and qualitative purpose statements and research questions differ. As shown in Figure 5.8, we have already discussed how *quantitative* research tends to be more closed because the researcher specifies in advance the variables of the study. Moreover, these variables may be identified in past research literature and expressed in broad theoretical explanations. Quantitative research seeks to learn about the relationship among variables, often expressed in amount of difference and whether an intervention, such as a treatment variable, influences a dependent variable. In short, these characteristics all contribute to a more closed approach to research before the study begins than does qualitative research.

In *qualitative* research the inquirer keeps the direction for a study open to best learn from participants. This means that participants are asked to describe the topic under study in their own words. Their interpretation becomes important as the researcher captures detailed stories and quotes from people being interviewed. It also suggests that events and

---

FIGURE 5.8

Basic Differences between Quantitative and Qualitative Purpose Statements and Research Questions

Quantitative—**more closed**	Qualitative—**more open-ended**
1. Probable cause and effect— Why did it happen?	1. Descriptive— What happened?
2. Use of theories— Why did it happen in view of an explanation or theory?	2. Interpretive— What was the meaning to people of what happened?
3. Assessing differences and magnitude— How much happened? How many times did it happen? What were the differences among groups in what happened?	3. Process-oriented— What happened over time?

activities unfold during the study and that qualitative researchers explore a topic that emerges during data collection.

This stance impacts how qualitative researchers locate and identify their research purpose statements and questions. They begin with a general topic and identify a research problem about this topic in the literature (as discussed in Chapter 3, "Introducing the Research Topic" and "Stating the Research Problem"). This research problem provides general direction for the purpose and the questions; it does not dictate a specific intent for their study or specific questions to address. The researcher then formulates a general direction, specifies an overarching question (later in this chapter called the "central question"), and identifies a small number of sub-questions. Although some qualitative researchers formulate their direction and questions directly from suggestions in the literature, a more open stance is to pose general questions that best provide wide latitude for participants to answer. In short, qualitative research questions emerge during a study and are not specifically set before the inquiry as in quantitative research. In this way, no predictions (and therefore hypotheses) are used in qualitative research; instead, the inquirer only poses research questions. In addition, both qualitative purpose statements and research questions start with a single idea that the inquirer wants to explore. This differs from exploring multiple ideas, such as independent and dependent variables as in quantitative research, that assume predetermined connections among ideas.

Our discussion about qualitative purpose statements and research questions will examine these topics in more detail. We will explore:

- the central phenomenon—its definition and use in qualitative purpose statements and research questions
- emerging processes—how the direction for qualitative research emerges during the process of inquiry
- purpose statements—guidelines for their construction and sample scripts for their design
- central questions—their importance in qualitative research, guidelines for their construction, and scripts for their design
- subquestions—their importance in qualitative research, guidelines for their construction, and scripts for their design
- differences between research questions and data collection questions

Identifying the Central Phenomenon

A central component of both the purpose statement and the research questions in qualitative research is the central phenomenon. The **central phenomenon** is an issue or a process explored in qualitative research. For example, as an issue, it could be:

- smoking among adolescents
- communication between a preservice teacher and a cooperating teacher
- the ethnic identity of Chinese-American immigrants

As a process it might address:

- the process by which academic department chairs help faculty members develop as teachers
- the process by which a community college curriculum committee develops a general education component
- the process of negotiation by a female superintendent

These examples illustrate the expression of the central phenomenon in a few words. They also show a focus on a single issue or process rather than relating two or more ideas as found in quantitative research (e.g., "How do alienation and isolation relate for the female super-intendent?") or comparing groups (e.g., "How do female principals and superintendents compare in their alienation?") This comment is not to suggest that comparisons or rela-tionships may not be explored in qualitative inquiry. Comparisons and relationships may emerge as the data analysis proceeds (e.g., as in grounded theory, the relating of categories of information to form propositions or hypotheses), but the qualitative inquirer *begins* with a single idea, focus, or concept to explore before gathering data.

A picture might best express the differences between explaining and predicting vari-ables in quantitative research and exploring a central phenomenon in qualitative research. As shown in Figure 5.9, one way to visualize this difference is by contrasting the explana-tion of an outcome (or dependent variable) by an independent variable (on the left of the figure) with the different image for a central phenomenon (on the right side of the figure). Rather than using cause-and-effect logic as in quantitative research, the qualitative re-searcher seeks to *explore* and *understand* one single phenomenon, and to do so requires con-sidering all of the multiple external forces that shape this phenomenon. At the beginning of a study, the qualitative researcher cannot predict the nature of external forces (i.e., Which ones will be important? How will they exercise influence?). Therefore the arrows about forces shaping the central phenomenon are multidirectional. If it is helpful for you to un-derstand the differences better from a *quantitative* perspective, consider the central phe-nomenon to be a single variable that needs to be explored.

Emerging Processes

Another central component about purpose statements and research questions in qualitative inquiry is that these statements and questions may change during the research process. Qualitative research is considered to be an emerging design. An **emerging process** indi-cates that the intent or purpose of a study and the questions asked by the researcher may change during the process of inquiry based on feedback or responses from participants. Questions and purposes may change because the qualitative inquirer allows the participant

---

FIGURE 5.9

How Researchers Explain or Predict Variables versus Exploring or Understanding a Central Phenomenon

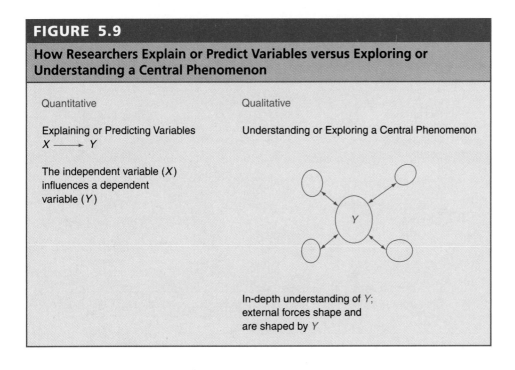

Quantitative

Explaining or Predicting Variables
$X \longrightarrow Y$

The independent variable (X)
influences a dependent
variable (Y)

Qualitative

Understanding or Exploring a Central Phenomenon

Y

In-depth understanding of Y;
external forces shape and
are shaped by Y

to set the direction and, in doing so, the researcher learns the participants' views rather than imposing his or her own view on the research situation.

An illustration of this process is shown in Figure 5.10. As you can see, the process of direction and question exploration is a dynamic one. Individuals may start with initial questions, shape them during initial data collection, and further change them as a result of multiple visits to the field to gather data. Revisions may continue throughout both data collection and analysis in a qualitative project. During this process, the overall direction of the study will change, and authors rewrite their purpose statement and research questions.

In the example illustrated by Figure 5.10, the researcher may begin with the general question about the experiences high school students have with smoking tobacco. During the initial interviews, the students may discuss locations where they often smoke, such as in front of the apartment complex across the street from the school or in the neighborhood park adjacent to the school. The researcher then focuses direction by asking more detailed questions about where students smoke. Then through more in-depth questioning, some students begin discussing their attempts to quit smoking and how these attempts either begin or are thwarted by friends in the neighborhood park near the school. Once again the questions change as the researcher delves deeper and deeper into the central phenomenon of high school students and smoking. Recall from Chapter 2 on "Analyzing and Interpreting Data" that the intent of qualitative research is to establish the detailed meaning of information rather than to generalize the results and standardize the responses from all participants in research.

Writing the Purpose Statement

Both the nature of an emerging process and the central phenomenon need to be articulated in qualitative purpose statements. Care needs to be given to writing a good purpose statement that reflects the direction of the study. A **purpose statement in qualitative research** indicates the need to explore or understand the central phenomenon with specific individ-

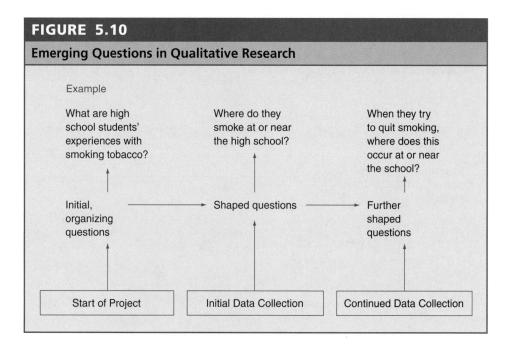

FIGURE 5.10

Emerging Questions in Qualitative Research

Example

What are high school students' experiences with smoking tobacco?

Where do they smoke at or near the high school?

When they try to quit smoking, where does this occur at or near the school?

Initial, organizing questions → Shaped questions → Further shaped questions

Start of Project   Initial Data Collection   Continued Data Collection

uals at a certain research site. As in quantitative research, inquirers write this purpose statement as a single sentence and typically include it in a study at the end of the introduction.

Guidelines

As you design this statement, be sure to:

- Use key identifier words to signal the reader, such as "The purpose of this study is."
- Consider mentioning that the study is "qualitative" since audiences may not be familiar with qualitative research.
- Become familiar with qualitative research designs (see Chapter 14 on "Grounded Theory Designs," Chapter 15 on "Ethnographic Designs," and Chapter 16 on "Narrative Research"), and indicate the type of research design you plan to use in your study.
- State the central phenomenon being explored.
- Use words that convey intent about the exploration of the central phenomenon, such as "explore," "discover," "understand," or "describe."
- Mention the participants in the study.
- Refer to the research site where the participants will be studied.

A Sample Script

These elements can be combined into a script for writing a qualitative purpose statement. A script for a qualitative purpose statement is:

> The purpose of this qualitative study will be to (explore? discover? understand? describe?) (the central phenomenon) for (participants) at (research site).

If we apply this script in the study of Internet classroom learning, we get:

> The purpose of this qualitative study is to describe classroom learning using the Internet for five high-schools student participating in a sign language class.

If we analyze this example, we find:

> The central phenomenon: Classroom learning using the Internet
>
> The participants: Five high-school students
>
> The research site: A class in sign language at X high school

Maria, our high school teacher studying weapon possession, might write this purpose statement:

> The purpose of this qualitative study is to explore the experiences with weapons of five high school students in the school district.

This example also follows our model for a qualitative purpose statement. It includes:

> The central phenomenon: Student experiences with weapons
>
> The participants: Five high school students
>
> The research site: The school district

Writing Research Questions

Research questions in qualitative research help narrow the purpose of a study into specific questions. **Qualitative research questions** are open-ended, general questions that the researcher would like answered during the study. The following general guidelines can help you design and write these questions (also, see Creswell, 1994; Creswell, 1998).

▶ Expect your qualitative questions to change and to emerge during a study to reflect the participants' views of the central phenomenon and your growing (and deeper) understanding of it.

▶ Use research questions instead of hypotheses to narrow your qualitative purpose statement. In qualitative research, variables are not used and they are not measured. Instead, the exploration of a central phenomenon and a detailed discussion about the phenomenon are the objects of the study.

▶ Ask only a few, general questions. Five to seven questions are enough to permit the participants to share information. A few questions place emphasis on learning information from participants, rather than learning what the researcher seeks to know.

▶ Ask questions that use neutral, exploratory language and refrain from conveying an expected direction (or nondirectional outcome if you are thinking like a quantitative researcher). For example, use action verbs such as "generate," "discover," "understand," "describe," or "explore" instead of words conveying cause-and-effect relationships, such as "affect," "relate," "compare," "determine," "cause," or "influence."

▶ Design and write two types of qualitative research questions: central questions and subquestions.

▶ Distinguish research questions from the questions that you will ask during your interview data collection or observation.

The Central Question

The **central question** is the overarching question being asked in a study. It is the attempt by the researcher to ask the most general question that can be addressed in a study. At the end of an introduction to a study, the author specifies the central question in a single, short, concise question. One way to develop this question is to ask yourself, "What is the most general question that could be asked in my study?" For those familiar with quantitative research, the central question might be viewed as a single, descriptive question where you seek to understand a single variable (such as a dependent variable).

When designing and writing this central question, several strategies may be helpful:

▶ Begin with the words, "how" or "what" rather than "why" so that you do not suggest probable causality (i.e., "why" something influences something) but instead connotate exploration.

▶ Specify the central phenomenon to be examined.

▶ Identify the participants in the study.

▶ Mention the research site for the study.

Since the participants may have already been mentioned in your purpose statement, you do not need to repeat this information for your central question when you include both a purpose statement and a central question in a study.

A script for a central research question that combines these elements is:

What is (the central phenomenon) for (participants) at (research site)?

The following example illustrates the application of this script to the study of creativity:

What is creativity for five students at Roosevelt High School?

Beginning word: "What"

Central phenomenon: Creativity

Participants: Five students

Research site: Roosevelt High School

Another example applies the script to the field of adult literacy:

What is self-esteem for adult literacy students in a community college?

Beginning word: "What"

Central phenomenon: Self-esteem

Participants: Adult literacy students

Research site: A community college

As these examples illustrate, central questions are short, concise, and focused on understanding a single phenomenon. Consistent with the qualitative research approach, these examples do not presume an outcome and they are neutral in language. They also do not compare groups or relate variables as in a quantitative study; instead, they explore a single idea.

Central questions may be challenging to write. Researchers may not be familiar with stating a broad, general question if they are trained in quantitative research to "narrow down" questions into specific variable relationships. Also, the challenge of writing central questions is to indicate a direction for the study but not to leave the direction wide open. When a central question is too open, readers and audiences for a study will not have enough information to understand the project. Alternatively, when the central question is too specific or too laden with assumptions, it does not offer enough latitude for participants to express themselves, and it can shape too dramatically the views of participants in one direction or another.

In Table 5.3, several specific examples illustrate central questions stated in terms that are too general, too focused, or too laden with assumptions. The examples are rewritten to illustrate improved versions of the questions. In the first example, the author states a central question so broadly that readers and audiences do not understand the central phenomenon under study. This situation often occurs when qualitative researchers take too literally the concept of open-ended questions to mean "anything goes."

In the second example, the author focuses the question too much. By asking about specific activities on a committee, the researcher may miss the larger process at work in the

TABLE 5.3		
Problems Typically Found in Central Questions in Qualitative Research		
Problems	**Poor Example of a Central Question**	**Better Example of a Central Question**
Too general	What is going on here?	What is the process being used by the general education committee at the liberal arts school?
Too focused	How did the committee make a curriculum decision about a course on the environment?	What is the process of the curriculum committee in making decisions about courses?
Too laden with assumptions	How did the curriculum committee address its alienation from the college administration?	What was the role of the college administration in the curriculum committee's deliberations?

committee and lose important information for the research report. In the final example, the researcher starts with the assumption that the committee is "alienated" from the college administration. Although this may be the case, the specification of a direction may limit too much what the inquirer can learn from a situation. To open the situation by asking about the "role of the college administration" includes the possibility that the role may be alienating, supportive, or may serve some in-between role.

Subquestions

In addition to a central question, qualitative researchers pose sub-questions. These **subquestions** refine the central question into subtopics or indicate the processes to be used in research. These subquestions contain the same elements as central questions (i.e., openended, emerging, neutral in language, and few in number), but they provide greater specificity to the questions in the study. Subquestions may be of two types: issue and procedural (Stake, 1995; Creswell, 1998), as shown in Table 5.4.

Issue Subquestions   **Issue subquestions** are questions that narrow the focus of the central question into specific topics the researcher seeks to learn from participants in a study. A script for an issue subquestion is:

> What is (the sub-question issue) for (participants—optional information) at (research site—optional information).

In a study, the subquestions would be stated immediately after the central question as follows:

> The central question addressed in this study will be: What is self-esteem for high school students? Subquestions to be addressed will be:

TABLE 5.4

Types of Subquestions in Qualitative Research

	Issue Subquestions	Procedural Subquestions
Intent	To subdivide the central question into detailed questions	To subdivide the central question into steps for data collection during the study
Example	*Central Question:*	*Central Question:*
	What does it mean to be a professional teacher?	What is the change process in the revision of a general education curriculum on a college campus?
	Issue Subquestions:	*Procedural Subquestions:*
	What do professional teachers do?	How did the process unfold?
	What is difficult/easy about being a professional educator?	Who were the people involved?
		What events occurred?
	When did the teacher first become aware of being a professional?	What was the outcome?

What is self-esteem as seen through friends?

What is self-esteem for the participant's family?

What is self-esteem as experienced in extracurricular activities in school?

As these examples illustrate, the central phenomenon, self-esteem, is divided into three topical areas that the researcher explores.

To identify issue subquestions for a study, consider how the central question can be divided into several topical areas. There is no firm guideline for engaging in this process, but consider the issues most likely to occur during a study so that you do not unduly limit the information you will obtain. Preliminary conversations or interviews with your participants can provide useful leads for these subquestions.

Procedural Subquestions   Procedural subquestions are the second form of subquestions in qualitative research. **Procedural subquestions** indicate the steps to be used in analyzing the data in the qualitative study. This form of writing subquestions is less frequently used than issue questions, because the procedures for a qualitative study will evolve and shift and cannot be identified early in a study. To write them, the researcher needs to know what these steps of analysis will be (a topic to be addressed in more detail in Chapter 9).

However, if the researcher knows the general steps to be taken later in analysis, procedural subquestions can be written. They provide those reviewing a study with a more precise understanding of the steps than do issue subquestions. A script for writing procedural subquestions is:

To study this central question, the following questions will be addressed in order in this study:

(What question will be answered first?)

(What question will be answered second?)

(What question will be answered third?)

To illustrate this script, assume for a moment that the steps in the process of data analysis will consist of first developing a description of events followed by the specification of themes and broad dimensions for understanding the phenomenon. Let's use the familiar example of the gunman incident case study (Asmussen & Creswell, 1995). Although the authors did not specify procedural subquestions in their study, they might have presented the central question and subquestions as follows:

The central question to be addressed in this study will be: What was the campus reaction to the gunman incident? The subquestions will be:

What were the events following the incident? (the chronology of activities in Paragraphs 04–10)

What were themes of individuals reacting to the incident? (the five themes, such as "Denial" in Paragraph 13)

What larger dimensions describe the overall campus reaction? (the sociological and psychological dimensions advanced in the "Discussion" section in Paragraph 35)

These three subquestions trace a procedure for analyzing the data, from describing the incident to specifying the themes to posing, at the conclusion of the study, a broad interpretation of responses to the incident. Although these subquestions do not provide specific material for interview or observation questions, they do help a reader visualize the steps to be taken later in data analysis.

TABLE 5.5

Differences Between Qualitative Research Questions and Interview Questions

Qualitative Research Questions	Qualitative Interview Questions*
• General questions • Focus and bound the study • Few in number, such as one central question and four to six subquestions	• Specific questions • Intended to gather data • Include questions to make the interviewee comfortable (i.e., ice-breakers) • Include probes for more detailed information • Include more questions than the central question and subquestions, as many as twelve, depending on length of the interview

*This also applies to questions when the researcher observes, gathers documents, or collects visual materials, such as videotapes.

Distinguishing Research Questions from Data Collection Questions

As we proceed into the phase of data collection, it is important to consider how the central and subquestions differ from the actual questions to be asked of participants in a study.

Individuals learning qualitative research often ask: "What is the relationship between the central question, the subquestions, and the types of questions that I will ask when I collect data?" To answer this question, examine the distinction between the research questions and the interview questions as outlined in Table 5.5.

While the research questions provide the general direction for the study, they are typically not directed to the participants in the study. For example, a research question might be: "How does a first-year college president describe his vision for the institution and how will he move people toward it?" A qualitative researcher would not presume to simply ask that, or even to narrow the discussion to the term "vision." During an interview, the researcher would use multiple questions to address this broader question, such as:

Where would you like to see the institution in five years?

How do you see the institution moving toward the goals you have described?

What is your role in the process?

What legacy would you like to leave as a result of your tenure here?

These questions asked during an interview address specific areas of inquiry; they are intended to gather data; they include probing questions for more detail; and they generally take the research question into more depth. Interview questions also need to set the interviewee at ease when the interview begins. For example, during an interview a qualitative researcher might ask the college president, "How long have you served at this institution?" In addition, a qualitative researcher sometimes ends an interview by asking for more information. A concluding questions, such as "Who else should I talk with to learn more about leadership on this campus?", can lead to useful data, the topic of Chapter 7.

KEY IDEAS IN THE CHAPTER

The primary reason for purpose statements, research hypotheses, and research questions is to signal the major direction or intent of a study. They are the most important statements in a study. A purpose statement is a sentence in an educational study that states the overall direction or objective of the study. Hypotheses are declarative statements that narrow the purpose statement into specific predictions about the relationship among variables. Research questions are interrogative statements that focus the purpose of the study into specific areas of inquiry.

Before designing and writing quantitative purpose statements and research questions and hypotheses, a firm understanding of the types of variables is needed. The three primary types of variables are independent, mediating, and dependent. Independent variables can be divided into treatment, measured, control, and moderating variables. Understanding the role of each type of variable and its subtypes is important. Further, variables are tested in quantitative studies using broad explanations, called theories. When relating variables, it is also important to consider how variables will be controlled so that the researcher can make claims of probable causality. With these understandings, quantitative researchers write purpose statements, hypotheses, and research questions using elements and guidelines to assist in this process.

In qualitative research, it is important to understand the role of a central phenomenon as well as the concept of an emerging process. With these two elements, qualitative inquirers write a purpose statement that identifies the central phenomenon, the participants, and the site for the study. This purpose statement is narrowed into two types of qualitative questions: a central question and subquestions. In the central question the researcher asks the most general question that can be asked in a study. This central question is then subdivided into subquestions called issue or procedural subquestions. These questions either subdivide the central question into topics or they indicate the steps used in analyzing and reporting the data.

USEFUL INFORMATION FOR PRODUCERS OF RESEARCH

- ▶ Write both a purpose statement and either hypotheses or research questions into your research study.
- ▶ For a quantitative study, know the differences among the types of variables. Be able to clearly identify the independent and dependent variables that you plan to study.
- ▶ Locate and identify a theory to test that will provide an explanation for the relationship among variables in your research questions and hypotheses.
- ▶ To draw strong causal inferences, use variables that are related close in time, in space, and in their variation with each other, and that are multiple.
- ▶ Write a purpose statement that includes the major elements advanced in this chapter.
- ▶ Write either hypotheses or research questions, but not both.
- ▶ If you write hypotheses, consider whether your statements are directional or nondirectional. Directional hypotheses are more popular today and reflect a prediction about the expected results of a study.
- ▶ If you write research questions, use the elements advanced in this chapter.
- ▶ Consider in your questions whether you are trying to describe a single variable, relate variables, or compare groups on a variable.
- ▶ For a qualitative study, know the significance of a central phenomenon and be able to identify the phenomenon in your study.
- ▶ Write one central question and subquestions using the elements advanced in this chapter.
- ▶ Clearly identify your subquestions as either issue or procedural subquestions and know the difference between the two types.

USEFUL INFORMATION FOR CONSUMERS OF RESEARCH

▶ Look for a purpose statement at the end of an introduction to a study. Words such as "the purpose of" should signal this statement. Alternative words might be "the objective of" or "the intent of."

▶ In a quantitative purpose statement (or hypotheses or questions), the independent variable should be stated in the first position, followed by the dependent variable in the second postion. Ask yourself: What outcome is being predicted in this study? What factors are advanced that might explain this outcome?

▶ Look for hypotheses or research questions at the end of the introductory section of a study.

▶ An explanation for how and why the variables are related in hypotheses or research questions will be called a "theory" or "a theoretical rationale." This passage should advance researchers' predictions about what they expect to find.

▶ In a qualitative study, look for the central phenomenon that provides a focus for the inquiry. This phenomenon should be stated in a few words and should represent the focus that the inquirer wants to understand.

▶ Qualitative researchers often pose one central question as the overriding general issue they wish to explore. Then they advance a small number of subquestions that either narrow the focus to specific topics or advance procedural steps to be used in their data analysis.

STUDY QUESTIONS AND ACTIVITIES

1. You have just learned how to identify independent and dependent variables in *quantitative* purpose statements, research questions, and hypotheses. For each of the examples below, specify the independent variable(s) ("i.v.") and the dependent variable(s) ("d.v.") by writing the initials above the words:

   a. What is the relationship between parental involvement in education and student reading performance?

   b. Our purpose in this study was to isolate the elements of accountability in a mastery learning program and determine if students' knowledge of accountability relates to changes in attitudes toward learning.

   c. Low degrees of mutuality, comprehensiveness, gender sensitivity, and congruence lead to functional mentoring relationships.

2. Show that you can identify the central phenomenon in *qualitative* purpose statements and research questions. In the following examples, place the initials "c.p." over the words indicating the central phenomenon.

   a. How are these conceptions of reading played out, or not played out, in the sixth grade classroom?

   b. In this article, I rely on critical views of culture and power to highlight aspects of sorority life that contribute to the marginalization and potential victimization of men.

   c. What are the major sources of academic change in a community college? What are the major processes through which change occurs?

3. Label each of the following hypotheses as "directional" or "nondirectional.
    a. Students are more likely to express willingness to seek help from the instructor in a supportive environment than a nonsupportive environment.
    b. Depending on your answer, change the statement in questions 3a. to the other type of hypothesis.

Now go to our Companion Website to assess your understanding of chapter content with Multiple-Choice Questions, apply comprehension in Projects & Essays, and broaden your knowledge with links to related research topics on the Web.

Collecting Quantitative Data

Let's assume that Maria, our high school teacher, decides to study her quantitative research question, "Why do students carry weapons in high school?" Maria is now ready to begin collecting data for her research. However, she is not sure how to locate a survey instrument to collect data. She wonders if she has the skills to design her own survey, and doesn't really know where to start. Moreover, she realizes that she needs to collect good, solid data to report to her school committee and to include in her graduate research. "How should I begin?" she asks herself.

This chapter will show you how Maria can get started by identifying and making decisions about the steps involved in quantitative data collection. Maria's basic interest is in collecting data that will help answer her research question. In order to do this, she needs reliable and accurate information. She also needs to obtain permission to study individuals, identify people to study, locate data and an instrument to gather information, and administer her procedures.

By the end of this chapter, you should be able to:

▶ Identify steps in the process of quantitative data collection.
▶ Describe the process of obtaining permissions to study individuals and research sites.
▶ Define different approaches used to sample participants for research.
▶ List different types of data often collected in quantitative research.
▶ Identify how to locate and select an instrument(s) for data collection.
▶ Describe procedures for recording and administering quantitative data collection.

REEXAMINING THE QUANTITATIVE TELEVISION VIOLENCE STUDY

Vooijs & van der Voort (1993) include data collection in the "Method" section. We can assume that the authors had permission to study the six schools. Although not explicitly stated, they probably obtained access and permissions from the school district, the principal, the teachers, and the students. Because they studied children under the age of 18, they also must have received both the parents' and childrens' consent to participate in the study.

The authors use a multiple-step procedure to identify students who will participate in the study. The first step involves selecting six schools in all, two each from low, medium, and high socioeconomic levels (see Paragraph 19). Then they randomly assign schools to the experimental and control groups, effectively removing socioeconomic levels (a control variable) as a predictor of student attitudes toward violence on television. Finally, within each school, they include in the study sample all students in the fourth through sixth grade, totalling 437 students. By including all students, they do not sample randomly using rigorous procedures.

After selecting these students, the authors collect scores on student attitudes using several instruments (see "Measuring instruments," Paragraphs 24–29). For example, they measure attitudes of the students toward violence (i.e., readiness to see violence, approval of violence, perceived reality of violent films). They also obtain information about student achievement (i.e., knowledge) as well as personal information about each individual (gender, grade attended, and social economic status).

As the television violence study illustrates, quantitative researchers use a process to collect data. This process contains several steps:

▶ *obtaining permissions*—identifying units of analysis, securing different types of permissions, and obtaining informed consent from participants
▶ *selecting participants*—specifying a population and sample, using probability or non-probability sampling, and choosing the size of the sample
▶ *identifying data options*—specifying variables, operationalizing variables, selecting scales of measurement, and choosing types of data and measures, observations, or documents
▶ *recording and administering data collection*—locating or developing an instrument, obtaining reliable and valid data, and administering procedures to collect data

OBTAINING PERMISSIONS

In quantitative data collection the aim is to gather information from individuals who can help you address the research questions or hypotheses. This means you must determine the individuals and sites to study. In order to respect individuals and sites, you need to obtain their permission before starting data collection. This will ensure that they cooperate in your study and provide data. Also, as an ethical researcher, you should not harm or injure any participants in your project. Federal legislation requires that you guarantee them certain rights and request their permission to be involved in your study.

At this point, you need to obtain permissions before you can proceed with your research. Ask yourself these questions: What individuals can best answer my research questions or hypotheses? Before I ask them to participate, who do I need to talk to to obtain consent for their participation? As a graduate student conducting research on a college or university campus, what procedures do I need to follow to receive institutional review board approval for my project?

Identifying Your Unit of Analysis

One of the first decisions you must make in data collection is determining who can best answer your research questions and hypotheses. For example, can the questions and hypotheses be best answered by collecting data from students, teachers, parents, adults, some combination of these individuals, or entire schools? The researcher must decide at what level (e.g., individual, family, school, school district) the data needs to be gathered. This is referred to as **unit of analysis.** In some studies, data are gathered from different levels (e.g., individuals and schools). Also, the data for measuring the independent variable may differ from the unit for assessing the dependent variable. For example, in the study of the impact of adolescent aggression on school climate, the independent variable, adolescent aggression, is measured by collecting data from individuals. The dependent variable, school climate, is measured by gathering measures of the entire school climate (e.g., whether students and teachers believe the school curriculum supports learning).

Securing Different Types of Permissions

In most educational studies, permissions are needed from several individuals and groups before you can gather data. Permissions may be required from:

▶ institutions or organizations (e.g., school district)
▶ specific sites (e.g., the secondary school)
▶ an individual participant or group of participants and their parents (e.g., 10th graders and their parents)
▶ your own campus (i.e., your university or college institutional review board)

Permission is often necessary before you can enter a site and collect data. This approval usually comes from leaders or persons of authority in organizations. Obtaining permissions from organizational personnel requires contacting them before the start of a study and obtaining their permission to enter and to study their setting.

The best way to seek permission from the necessary individuals or groups is to formally ask for it in a letter. Include the purpose of the study, the amount of time you will be at the site collecting data, the time required of participants, and how the data or results will be used. Also, state the specific activities to be conducted, the benefits to the organization or individual as a result of the study, and the provisions you have made to protect the anonymity of study participants. By providing this information, you will show a concern for the potential intrusion of the study into their workplaces and lives, and set the stage for realistic expectations on their part.

Obtaining Informed Consent

It is important to protect the privacy and confidentiality of individuals who participate in the study. In contrast to early research in education and the social sciences, investigators today are sensitive to the potential harm that participants may experience as a result of research.

Review Board Approval

In the last 30 years, colleges and universities have required that researchers guarantee minimal risk to participants and to seek their consent before collecting data. In the 1970s, federal legislation was created to monitor campus-based research because of human abuses in experiments (e.g., Nazi medical experiments, atomic bomb blast tests, and syphilis experiments on African Americans). Colleges and universities have established institutional review boards to oversee this review process. An **institutional review board** is a committee made up of faculty members who review and approve research so that the rights of the participants are protected. The creation of these boards is the one instance where research done on college and university campuses has been regulated (Howe & Dougherty, 1993).

The Process of Obtaining Approval from Review Boards

Institutional review boards implement guidelines developed by the Federal Drug Administration based on three ethical principles: respect for persons (their consent, their right to privacy, and anonymity); beneficence (weighing the benefits of research versus the risks to individuals); and justice (equity for participation in a study). By following the guidelines, researchers guarantee that participants retain their autonomy and judge for themselves what risks are worth taking for the purposes of research (Howe & Dougherty, 1993).

In practice, these guidelines, and the formation of institutional review boards that enforce them, means that researchers need to obtain approval for their research from the campus institutional review board before a study begins. To obtain approval, you are required to summarize the procedures in your research and supply evidence that participants will be offered certain protections.

The exact process of getting approval from the institutional review board varies from campus to campus. However, there are some basic steps that both student and faculty researchers should complete when seeking approval. Understanding this process will help you evaluate if a particular study has been conducted ethically, whether you are conducting research of your own or reading others' studies.

1. *Start by finding out about the review process used by the institutional review board on campus.* Identify individuals responsible for reviewing projects, locate the forms required for the review, and become familiar with the overall approval procedure. Campus review boards may have a brochure that describes this process.

2. *Determine what information the review board needs about your project.* The extent of the review and the concern of the institutional review board will be related to two factors [for example, see University of Nebraska at Lincoln (1997) guidelines]. The first is the level of risk that your participants will experience in the study (e.g., psychological, physical, emotional, legal, social, or economic). Is this risk less than minimal—no known risk? Is it minimal—risks encountered in daily life? Is it greater than minimal—risks beyond those ordinarily encountered in daily life? The higher the risk, the more detailed your project description needs to be, and the longer the review process will take.

   The second is if you are studying a special population considered to be of high risk. These populations include children under the age of 19 who need their own and their parents' consent to participate; mentally incompetent participants, victims, or persons with neurological impairments; pregnant women or fetuses; prisoners; and individuals with AIDS. Also included in this category are studies involving confidential records and/or pathological specimens and HIV testing.

   If your study involves the populations or information mentioned above, your project will be considered to have at least minimal or greater than minimal risk (as opposed to no known risk) and will subsequently be scrutinized closely by the institutional review board. Because many educational studies involve children under 19, these studies will require extensive review by the institutional review boards.

3. *Develop an informed consent form for participants to sign before they participate in the study.* Do this even if your project poses minimal risk to the participants. Consent is not needed in some cases because the participant's return of the instrument implies consent.

   An **informed consent form** is a statement that participants sign before they participate in research. This form should state that you will guarantee them certain rights, and that when they sign the form, they are agreeing to be involved in the study and acknowledge that their rights are protected.

   Figure 6.1 shows a consent form outlining the participants' rights, including their right to withdraw at any time from the study, their voluntary participation in the project, and their right to know the purpose of the study.

4. *Submit a description of your proposed study to the institutional review board.* This description includes the purpose of the study, the data collection process, the guarantees for protecting the participants, and a sample consent form.

FIGURE 6.1

An Example of an Informed Consent Form

Title: "Experiences in Learning Quantitative Research"   ◄——— Title

The following information is provided to help you decide whether you wish to   ◄——— Voluntary participation
participate in the present study. You should be aware that you are free to decide not
to participate or to withdraw at any time without affecting your relationship with this   ◄——— Right to withdraw
department, the instructor, or the University.

The purpose of this study is to relate past experiences with research to scores   ◄——— Purpose
on the quizzes in class.

Data will be collected using a brief survey at the beginning of the class. Then,   ◄——— Procedures
three quizzes will be given during the semester and your scores recorded. The
survey data and your quiz scores will be the only data collected in the study.

Do not hesitate to ask questions about the study before participating or during
the study. I would be happy to share the findings with you after the research is
completed. Your name will not be associated with the research findings in any way,
and only the researchers will know your identity.

Right to:
ask questions;
obtain results;
anonymity

There are no known risks and/or discomforts associated with this study. The   ◄——— No known risks
expected benefits associated with your participation are the information about the
experiences in learning research methods. If this study is later submitted for   ◄——— Benefits
publication, a by-line will indicate the participation of all students in the class.

Please sign this consent form. You are signing it with full knowledge of the nature
and purpose of the procedures. A copy of this form will be given to you to keep.

_____   _____   ◄——— Signature needed

Signature   Date

Jane W. Smith, Professor, City University (111-312-5432)   ◄——— Information about investigator

After you have completed the steps listed above, the review board will evaluate your project and determine whether the participants in your study are protected. If approved, you can proceed with the study. If denied, you will need to visit with the board representative to determine why the study was denied and what you need to change in your project description or procedures in order to get approval.

SELECTING PARTICIPANTS

Quantitative researchers generally agree that results from a study should apply widely to as many people as possible. To apply findings to a large group of individuals (called a population), you select a sample that is similar to the population, and study it. Because this sample is similar to the population, you can make claims about (or draw inferences to) the larger population. In this standard process in quantitative research, the more individuals in your sample, the better it will reflect the characteristics of the larger population, and the less likely you are to make errors in applying or generalizing findings from the sample to the population.

These issues are all important when selecting participants for your study. Answering the following questions will help you in the selection process: What group will you study? How will you select these individuals? How many participants will you need for your study?

Specifying the Population and Sample

In some educational situations, you will select individuals for your research based on who volunteers to participate or which individuals are available (e.g., a specific classroom of students). However, those individuals may not be similar (in personal characteristics or performance or attitudes) to all individuals that could be studied. Therefore, the best approach is to identify a population to study and then select individuals from within this population for your study. This way you can use your results to make generalizations about a large group of individuals, not just the people who volunteered or were available for the study.

We have already introduced several terms that may be new to you. At this point, it is important to distinguish among the "population," the "target population," and the "sample."

You will need to identify a population of individuals that can provide information to answer your research questions or hypotheses. A **population** is a group of individuals that comprise the same characteristics. For example, all teachers would make up the population of teachers, and all high school administrators in a school district would make up the population of administrators. As these examples illustrate, populations can be small or large. You need to decide to what group you would like to apply or generalize results.

In most research, names of individuals in the entire population (e.g., at-risk children) cannot be obtained. In some cases (e.g., all high school students), the population is too large to be studied in its entirety. In practice, quantitative researchers sample from a target population. A **target population** (sometimes called the "sampling frame") is a group of individuals with some common defining characteristic that the researcher can identify with a list of names.

With the target population clearly specified, researchers can identify a sample. A **sample** is a subgroup of the target population that the researcher plans to study for the purpose of making generalizations about the target population. In some cases, when the population is small, you can study the entire population. However, because of the small size, the statistics are of limited use in analyzing this group. Figure 6.2 shows some examples of target populations and samples.

In order to draw accurate conclusions about a target population, your sample needs to be representative of the population. Random sampling, to be discussed shortly, encourages this type of representation. However, a sample is only a sample; if you were to obtain another sample, the results may be slightly different. Thus, we say that a sample is only an *estimate* of the population and that the average scores from the sample only *approximate* the

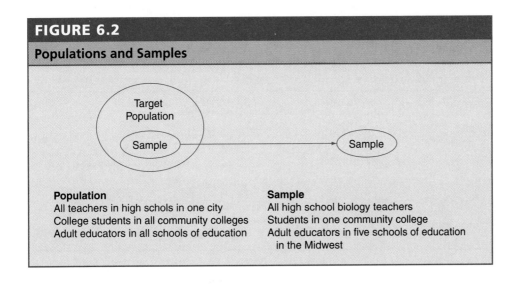

FIGURE 6.2

Populations and Samples

Population	Sample
All teachers in high schols in one city	All high school biology teachers
College students in all community colleges	Students in one community college
Adult educators in all schools of education	Adult educators in five schools of education in the Midwest

population values and are typically off by some percentage (say, $+/- 3\%$). This difference between the sample estimate and the true population score is called **sampling error.**

Let's illustrate how sampling error works. If we could obtain scores from sixth graders across the country about the importance of student-parent relationships, the average score might be a 30 on a 50-point scale. Of course, we cannot study *every* sixth grader, so instead we obtain a sample from one school district, and get an average score of 35 on the scale. The next time we might obtain a score of 33 and the next time a 36 because our sample will change from one school district to another. This means that our average score is five points, three points, and one point respectively away from the "true" population average. This difference between the sample estimate and the true population score is sampling error. Therefore, in all sampling procedures, since we cannot typically obtain the exact value of the population scores, we must rely on a sample that is an estimate of the population and that contains sampling error.

Probability and Non-Probability Sampling

As we just saw, the idea is to select a sample from a population in some systematic fashion. When this is not possible, a sample can still be chosen, but the claims about generalizing the results to a larger population will not be as strong. There are two popular approaches to sampling in educational research: probability sampling and non-probability sampling. In **probability sampling** the researcher selects individuals from the population that are representative of that population. This is the most rigorous form of sampling in quantitative research because the investigator can claim that the sample is representative of the population and, as such, can make generalizations to the population. A less rigorous form of sampling is called non-probability sampling. In **non-probability sampling,** the researcher selects individuals because they are available, convenient, and represent some characteristic the investigator seeks to study. As shown in Figure 6.3, there are several types of probability and non-probability sampling. Researchers decide which type of sampling to use in their study based on such factors as the amount of rigor they seek for their studies, the characteristics of the target population, and the availability of participants.

Probability Sampling

There are four basic types of probability sampling: simple random sampling, systematic sampling, stratified sampling, and multi-stage cluster sampling. We will discuss each of these in more detail below.

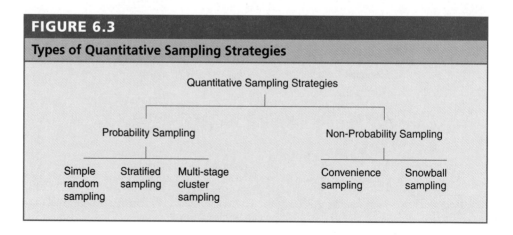

FIGURE 6.3

Types of Quantitative Sampling Strategies

Simple Random Sampling   The most popular and rigorous form of sampling from a population is simple random sampling. **Simple random sampling** means that the researcher selects participants (or units, such as schools) for the sample so that any sample of size N has an equal probability of being selected from the population. The intent of simple random sampling is to choose units to be sampled that will be representative of the population. Any bias in the population will be equally distributed among the units chosen. However, randomization is a fragile condition, as was seen during the Vietnam War when the drum used for selecting draftees was not turned sufficiently to result in random selection (Wilkinson and the Task Force on Statistical Inference, 1999).

The typical procedure used in simple random sampling is to assign a number to each individual (or site) in the population and then use a random numbers table, available in many statistics books, to select the individuals (or sites) for the sample. For this procedure, you need a list of members in the target population with a number assigned for each individual.

An example of a random numbers table is shown in Table 6.1. Researchers first assign numbers to all individuals in the population (say, a population of 100 individuals). Then, starting anywhere in the random numbers table, they match the numbers on their list to the numbers in the table. Using Table 6.1 as an example, let's start at the upper left of the table and go down the column. The first six individuals from the population of 100 having the numbers 52, 31, 44, 84, 71, and 42 would be chosen. This would continue down the column until the number needed for the sample is chosen. This procedure can be further illustrated with this example:

> Of the population of 600 Native-American students in a metropolitan school district, a random sample of 300 will be chosen using a random numbers table. The researcher assigns a number to each of the 600 Native-American students in the target population. The researcher then uses the random numbers table and randomly chooses a three-digit number (e.g., 037) in the table. Number 037 on the list of 600 is the first person chosen. Going on down the column in the random numbers table, the next number might be 151, and individual number 151 on the target population list is chosen. This procedure continues until all 300 individuals are selected.

TABLE 6.1											
Excerpt from a Random Numbers Table											
52	13	44	91	39	85	22	33	04	29	52	06
31	52	65	63	88	78	21	35	28	22	91	84
44	38	76	99	38	67	60	95	67	68	17	18
84	47	44	04	67	22	89	78	44	84	66	15
71	50	78	48	65	74	21	24	02	23	65	94
42	47	97	81	10	99	40	15	63	77	89	10
03	70	75	49	90	92	62	00	47	90	78	63
31	06	46	39	27	93	81	79	100	94	43	39

Source: Kerlinger, 1973, p. 714.

Systematic Sampling   A slight variation of the simple random sampling procedure is to use **systematic sampling.** This is done by choosing every "nth" individual or site in the population until the desired sample size is achieved. This procedure is not as precise and rigorous as using the random numbers table, but it may be more convenient because individuals do not have to be numbered and it does not require a random numbers table. To illustrate systematic sampling, assume a school district administrator wants to study parent satisfaction with the schools in the district. Using systematic sampling, the administrator would first identify a percentage of the parents to be studied (e.g., 20%). If there are 1000 parents in the school district, then 200 (or 20%) would be used for the study. The administrator uses an interval of five (200/1000, or 1 out of 5) to select parents from the mailing list (or target population list). Therefore, every fifth parent on the list will be sent a survey.

Stratified Sampling   Another type of probability sampling is stratified sampling. In **stratified sampling,** researchers stratify the population on some specific characteristic (e.g., gender) and then, using simple random sampling, sample from each stratum of the population. This allows for specific traits to be included in the sample.

One case where stratification is used is when the population reflects an imbalance of a trait to be included in the sample (e.g., gender—with women as well as men needed in the sample). For example, using simple random sampling to select a sample from a population with more women than men might result in no men being selected. In this situation, stratification ensures that the stratum desired (men) will be represented in the sample in proportion to which they exist in the population.

Another time that stratification is used is when a simple random sampling procedure would yield fewer participants in a specific category (e.g., men) than would be required or needed for data analysis. Having few men in a population, for example, would result in only a small number of men being selected during random sampling. This could possibly result in having numbers too small to statistically analyze.

The procedure for selecting a stratified random sample consists of (1) dividing the population by the stratum (e.g., men and women); and (2) sampling within each group in the stratum (e.g., women first and then men) so that the individuals selected are proportional to their representation in the total population.

Let's look at an example of how this procedure is applied. Looking at Figure 6.4, we can see that of the 9,000 Native-American children in the state, 3,000 are girls and

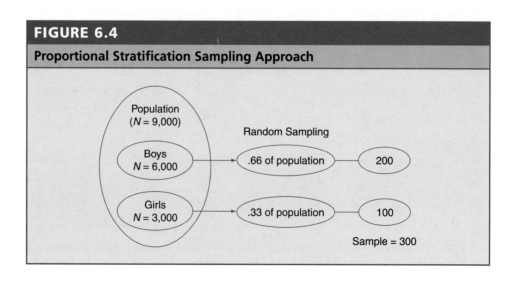

FIGURE 6.4

Proportional Stratification Sampling Approach

6,000 are boys. A researcher decides to choose a sample of 300 from this population of 9,000 children. A simple random sampling results in the selection of mostly boys because there are more boys than girls in the population. To make sure that boys are selected in proportion to which they are represented in the population, the researcher divides the list of 9,000 children into boys and girls. Then one-third (3000/9000) of the sample is chosen to be girls and two-thirds (6000/9000) boys. The stratification procedure consists of stratifying by gender—boys and girls—and selecting individuals in proportion to their representation in the total population.

Multi-Stage Cluster Sampling   A fourth form of probability sampling is multi-stage cluster sampling. In **multi-stage cluster sampling,** the researcher chooses a sample in two or more stages because either the populations cannot be easily identified or they are extremely large. If this is the case, it can be difficult to obtain a complete list of the members of the population. However, getting a complete list of groups or clusters in the population might be possible (Vogt, 1999). For example, the population of all at-risk students in the United States may be difficult to identify, but a researcher can obtain a list of the at-risk kids in select school districts. Using multi-stage cluster sampling, the researcher first randomly selects school districts in the United States. Second, the researcher obtains a list of the at-risk students in each of those school districts and randomly samples within each district. Breaking the process down like this makes it easier to identify groups and locate lists. However, with several stages to this design, it is complex and highly dependent on the characteristics of the population (Babbie, 1998).

Let's return to our Native-American example and consider how it might be done using multi-stage cluster sampling.

> The researcher realizes that the population of Native-American students in the United States will be difficult to identify. However, by clustering Native-American students into tribes, the researcher can easily locate the major tribes in the United States and randomly select students from individual tribes for the study.

Non-Probability Sampling

It is not always possible to use probability sampling in educational research. In some situations, you may need to involve participants who volunteer and agree to be studied. Further, you may not be interested in generalizing findings to a population, but only in describing a small group of participants in a study. Even when you do not select a sample from a population, however, you may be able to apply the results to a larger group. Replicating studies, a common practice in research where studies are repeated using many groups in different situations, provides some basis for generalizing findings broadly (Thompson, 1996).

Whether a study is replicated or not, non-probability sampling involves collecting data from available individuals or those willing to provide information. Two procedures that are frequently used in non-probability sampling are the convenience and snowball sampling approaches.

Convenience Sampling   One form of non-probability sampling is convenience sampling. In **convenience sampling** the researcher selects participants because they are willing and available to be studied. Because these participants have not been systematically selected, the researcher cannot say with confidence that they are representative of the population. However, the sample can provide useful information for answering questions and hypotheses.

Let's look at an example of convenience sampling.

> A researcher doing a study involving Native-American students finds that a large percentage of students in one school are Native Americans. The researcher decides to

study this group at this one school because they are available and because the researcher has the permission of the principal and can gain consent from the Native-American students to participate in the study. This is a convenience sample because the participants are convenient to the researcher and are available for the study.

Snowball Sampling   An alternative to convenience sampling is snowball sampling. In **snowball sampling,** the researcher asks participants to identify others to become members of the sample. For example, you might send surveys to a school superintendent and ask that copies be forwarded to the principals in that school district who will then be members of the sample. This form of sampling has the advantage of recruiting large numbers of participants for the study. By using this process, however, you give up control over who will be in the sample. It also eliminates the possibility of identifying individuals who did not return the survey, and those responding may not be representative of the population you seek to study. For example, participants who received the survey (e.g., principals who attended the Monday morning meeting with the superintendent) may not be representative of all individuals in the population (in this case, all principals in the school district).

Let's look at another example of snowball sampling.

A researcher asks the receptionist at a reservation health clinic to give out copies of a survey to all Native-American students who visit the clinic during the month. Students who receive the survey become participants in the study, thus ensuring an adequate number of participants. However, because they were a non-probability sample, the researcher cannot contact those who decide not to participate and cannot generalize from the sample to the population.

Sample Size

When selecting participants for a study, it is important to determine the size of the sample. There are bound to be differences between the results from a sample of people and results from the entire population, but if the sample is large enough, this difference is likely to be small and insignificant. The question is, how much is "large enough"?

As a general answer, select as large a sample as possible from the population or from the individuals available. A large sample means that you can use powerful statistics and generalize results from the sample to the population. The larger the sample, the more similar it will be to the population.

In some studies, you may only have a limited number of participants who are conveniently available to study. In other cases, factors such as access, funding, the overall size of the population, and the number of variables being studied will also influence the size of the samples.

Another way to determine the sample size is to select a sufficient number of participants for the statistical procedures you plan to use. This presumes that you have identified the statistic to use in analysis. As a rough estimate, an educational researcher needs:

- approximately 15 participants in each group in an experiment (see Chapter 11 on "Experimental and Quasi-Experimental Research")
- approximately 30 participants for a correlational study that relates variables (see Chapter 12 on "Correlational Research")
- approximately 350 individuals for a survey study, but this size will vary depending on several factors (see Chapter 13 on "Survey Research")

These numbers are estimates based on the size needed for statistical procedures, such as group comparisons, relating variables, and obtaining a large enough sample in a survey so that the sample is likely to be a good estimate of the characteristics of the population.

A more precise answer is to calculate the size of your sample using a sample size formula. **Sample size formulas** provide formulas based on several parameters that you can use to calculate the size of your sample. Using such a formula takes the guesswork out of determining the number of individuals to study. The formula also takes into consideration several factors important in determining size, such as confidence in the statistical test and sampling error. Further, the size of a sample is not dependent on your calculation of the formula—tables are available for you to look up the sample size with minimal information.

A sampling error formula is often used in survey study (see Fink & Kosekoff, 1985; Fowler, 1988) and a power analysis formula in an experiment (Cohen, 1977; Lipsey, 1990; Murphy & Myors, 1998). With the availability of sample size tables in which authors have already applied these formulas, you can identify the appropriate sample size for your experiment and survey study. Appendix A at the end of the text provides the parameters you need to consider, sample tables to locate the number of participants, and examples for using sampling error and power analysis formulas.

IDENTIFYING DATA OPTIONS

There are many types of quantitative data that can be collected in educational research. These include assessing individual performance (e.g., achievement tests, intelligence tests) and attitudes and opinions of individuals toward topics (e.g., adolescents' attitudes toward tobacco use in schools). It also includes observing behavior and recording it on a checklist (e.g., a list of motor skills used in playing basketball), and gathering information available in public records (e.g., the educational level of parents of elementary school children).

You need to choose which quantitative data to use to answer your research questions. This process starts by identifying variables and locating accepted definitions for them so that your research will add to educational knowledge and practice. Questions that will measure or observe the variables will come from these definitions. The questions must be appropriate for the type of data you wish to collect, and the scales need to match the questions so that you obtain good data. When choosing the types of quantitative data to use, select the type that provides information for your study while recognizing that some data measure performance and attitudes while other data reflects behaviors. This will help you select or develop a data collection instrument.

Look at Figure 6.5, which shows a flowchart of the activities done in collecting data. As you begin the process of data collection, ask yourself these questions: What are your variables? How are they defined? What questions with scales will best assess them? From the array of types of quantitative data, what types will best measure, observe, or document (based on scores) your variables?

Specifying Variables

As discussed in Chapter 5 in "The Family of Variables," research questions and hypotheses contain several variables. To determine what data need to be collected, you need to clearly identify the variables in your study. This will include variables that are described, variables that influence the outcome, the independent variables, and the outcome variables. Also identify any variables that need to be controlled. A useful strategy is to simply make a list of the variables so that you can determine what variables are operating in a study.

FIGURE 6.5

The Flow of Activities in Collecting Data

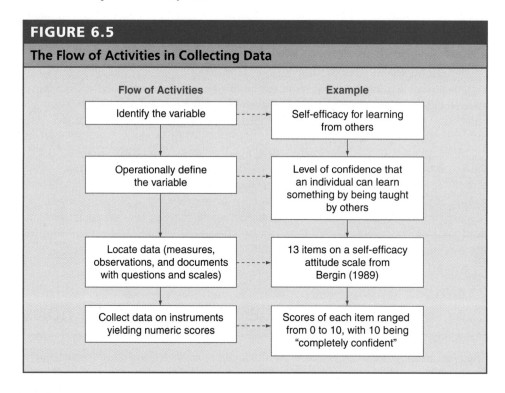

Operationally Defining Each Variable

In order to collect data on each variable, you next define how you want to measure, observe, or document the variable. Many definitions are possible, such as a dictionary definition, but researchers use an operational definition. An **operational definition** is the specification of how the variable will be defined and measured (or assessed) in a study. This definition is typically based on past definitions available in the literature. You might look in published research to find the latest, most-commonly used definition of a variable. Often this can be found in research reports in the section "definition of terms." Alternatively, you might examine research summaries, such as handbooks or encyclopedias, discussed in Chapter 4 on "Summaries" of the literature. In some situations, a clear, applied definition suitable for finding a measure is not available, and you need to construct your own. If this is the case, you should test it with other students or individuals knowledgeable about your topic and variable before you use it in your research. Using a dictionary to locate a definition may work as well, but remember that such a definition often reflects more common usage of a term rather than a research application.

Selecting Scales of Measurement

In addition to identifying your variables and defining how each is to be measured, you need to consider how to actually measure or assess the variables. This calls for locating questions with scales. For example, for a study of student attitudes toward the use of wireless laptops in a college classroom, a researcher might ask the *question,* "To what extent does the wireless laptop help you learn in the classroom?" The student might be given a response *scale* such as the following:

_____ To a great extent

_____ Somewhat

_____ To a less extent

TABLE 6.2

Types of Scales Used in Quantitative Research

Type of Scale	Examples of Questions Using the Scale:
Nominal scale (uses categories)	How much education have you completed? _____ No college _____ Some college _____ Bachelor degree _____ Graduate or professional work What is your class rank? _____ Freshman _____ Sophomore _____ Junior _____ Senior
Ordinal scale (uses implied or expressed rank order)	Has your advisor helped you select courses? _____ Not at all _____ To a small extent _____ To some extent _____ To a great extent _____ To a very great extent Rank your preference for type of graduate-level instruction from 1 to 4. _____ activity-based learning _____ lecture _____ small-group learning _____ discussion
Interval scale (uses equal intervals)	School is a place where I am thought of as a person who matters. _____ Strongly agree _____ Agree _____ Undecided _____ Disagree _____ Strongly disagree Colleges and universities should conduct research to solve economic problems of cities. _____ Strongly agree _____ Agree _____ Undecided _____ Disagree _____ Strongly disagree

As we learned in Chapter 5, on "Distinguishing Between Categorical and Continuous Scores," scores on scales to questions are classified into *categorical scores* (e.g., females and males, "to a great extent," or "to a less extent"), and *continuous scores* (e.g., age from 5 to 50). There are three major types of scales of measurement that can be grouped into categorical and continuous scores, as shown in Table 6.2. They are nominal scales or categorical scores; ordinal scales or categorical scores; and interval/ratio scales or continuous scores. **Scales of measurement** are therefore response options to questions that measure (or observe) variables in nominal, ordinal, or interval/ratio units. It is important to know scales of measurement for locating measures to assess your variables as well as for determining the appropriate statistics to use in data analysis (as will be discussed in Chapter 8 on "Choosing a Statistical Test").

Nominal Scales

Researchers use **nominal scales** (or **categorical scales**) to provide response options where participants check one or more categories that describe their traits, attributes, or characteristics. An example of a nominal scale would be gender, divided into the two categories of male and female. Another form of a nominal scale would be a checklist of "yes" or "no" responses. A semantic differential scale, popular in psychological research, is another type of nominal scale. This scale consists of bipolar adjectives that the participant uses to check his or her position. For example, in a psychological study of talented teenagers, researchers were interested in studying the teenagers' emotional response to their everyday activities

(Csikszentmihalyi, Rathunde, Walen, & Wong, 1993). The researchers used a semantical differential scale for teenagers to record their mood on several adjectives at certain times of the day. The researchers used a beeping device (p. 52) and the participants were asked to describe their mood as they were beeped, using the following scale:

	very	quite	some	neither	some	quite	very	
alert	0	0	·	—	·	0	0	drowsy

Although the researchers summed scores of teenagers across several questions such as this one, the response scale to each question was nominal or categorical.

Ordinal Scales

Researchers use **ordinal scales** (or **ranking scales**) to provide response options where participants rank from best or most important to worst or least important some trait, attribute, or characteristic. For example, individual performance in a race might be recorded for each runner from first to last place. Many attitudinal measures imply an ordinal scale as they ask participants to rank order the importance ("highly important" to "of no importance") or the extent ("to a great extent" to "a little extent") of topics. As this example illustrates, the information is categorical in a ranked order.

Interval and Ratio Scales

Another popular scale researchers use is an interval or rating scale. **Interval scales** (or **rating scales**) provide "continuous" response options to questions with assumed equal distances between options. These scales may have three, four, or more response options. The popular Likert scale ("strongly agree" to "strongly disagree") illustrates a scale with theoretically equal intervals among responses. Although an ordinal scale, such as "highly important" to "of no importance," may seem like an interval scale, we have no guarantee that the intervals are equal, as in the well-tested Likert scale.

Finally, a **ratio scale** (or **true zero scale**) is a response scale in which participants check a response option with a true zero and equal distances between units. Although this type of scale is seldom used in educational research, it is illustrated by the height of individuals (e.g., 50 inches, 60 inches) and income (from zero dollars to $50,000 in increments of $10,000).

Using a Combination of Scales

In educational research, quantitative investigators often use a combination of the three forms of scales. Of these, interval scales provide the most variation of responses and lend themselves to stronger statistical analysis. The best rule of thumb is, if you do not know in advance what statistical analysis you will use, create an interval scale. Interval scales can always be converted into ordinal or nominal scales (Tuckman, 1999), but not vice versa.

Let's illustrate how the three types of scales might be used in the television violence study (Vooijs & van der Voort, 1993). In this study, the children examined the 25 violent actions performed by the "good guy" on the video and rated each action on the variable, "approval of violence," using a 5-point scale from "entirely correct" to "not so bad." This scale does not have equal intervals: "entirely correct" and "correct" may not indicate the same degree of different as "uncorrect" and "not so bad." This is an *ordinal* scale.

Assume that the questions are changed slightly to ask each child if he or she agreed with the violence used in each action on the video. Further, assume the authors provide the response categories from "strongly agree" to "strongly disagree," a rating scale shown to exhibit equally distinct response options. This is an *interval* scale.

Let's change the scale one more time. Assume that the researchers ask the children to categorize the perception of the violence as either "high" or "low" in the video segments. This response option is categorical, or a *nominal* scale.

Choosing Types of Data and Measures

With operational definitions and scales in mind, you can look for instruments or checklists that provide a means for collecting data. An **instrument** is a tool for measuring, observing, or documenting quantitative data. Identified before the researchers collect data, the instrument may be a test, questionnaire, tally sheet, log, observational checklist, inventory, or assessment instrument. Instruments are used to measure achievement, assess individual ability, observe behavior, develop a psychological profile of an individual, or interview a person. There are four primary forms of instruments a quantitative researcher can use. They are:

- performance measures
- attitudinal measures
- behavioral observations
- factual information

These four types of quantitative data are summarized in Table 6.3. This table provides major forms of data, types of instruments or documents, definitions for the type of data, and a specific example of a source of information for collecting the data.

Performance Measures

You can use **performance measures** to assess an individual's ability to perform on an achievement test, intelligence test, aptitude test, interest inventory, or personality assessment inventory. Participants take tests that measure their achievement (e.g., the Iowa Test of Basic Skills), their intelligence (e.g., Wechsler), or their aptitude (e.g., Stanford-Binet). In addition, you could gather data that measures an individual's career interests or assesses personality traits. All of these measures can be obtained through instruments and tests readily available in the literature. Through past research, the tests are normed (tested with a number of individuals and average scores and variations in scores obtained) so that comparisons can be made between individual scores and typical scores for people who have taken the test. However, one drawback of performance data is that it does not address affective measures assessing individual attitudes, and they may be costly, time-consuming, and potentially biased toward specific cultural groups.

Attitudinal Measures

Alternatively, you can measure attitudes of individuals, a popular form of quantitative data for surveys as well as experiments. Researchers use **attitudinal measures** when they seek to assess affect or feelings toward educational topics (e.g., assessing positive or negative attitudes toward giving students a choice of school to attend). Although affective information can be gathered using these measures, the instruments need to be carefully designed so as not to bias responses and to encourage participants to answer questions honestly. Further, these measures do not yield information about specific behaviors.

An example of an attitudinal instrument measuring students' adaptation to college is the "Student Adaptation to College Questionnaire" available commercially from Western Psychological Services (Baker & Siryk, 1989). The first few questions from a total of 67 used on a two-page instrument are shown in Figure 6.6. This questionnaire begins with personal information questions (e.g., sex, date of birth, current academic standing, and ethnic background) and then asks students to indicate their attitude toward adapting to college on questions using a nine-point scale from "applies very closely to me" to "doesn't apply to me at all." Overall, the questions focus on the quality of the student's adjustment to the college environment (e.g., whether the student fits in well, feels tense, keeps up to date on academic work, makes friends, attends class, is satisfied with social life). These questions are summed (see added scores later in Chapter 8 on "Summed Scores"), to form four subscales: Academic Adjustment (24 questions), Social Adjustment (20 questions), Emotional Adjustment

TABLE 6.3

Types of Quantitative Data and Measures

Types of Data	Types of Tests, Instruments, or Documents to Collect Data	Definition of the Type of Test, Instrument, or Document	Example of the Specific Tests, Instruments, or Source of Information
Measures of Individual Performance	Achievement Test: Norm-referenced tests	A test where the individual's grade is a measure of how well he or she did in comparison with a large group of test takers (Vogt, 1999)	Iowa Test of Basic Skills
	Criterion-referenced tests	A test where the individual's grade is a measure of how well he or she did in comparison to a criterion or score	General Educational Development of GED Test Metropolitan Achievement Test Series on Reading
	Intelligence test	A test that measures an individual's intellectual ability	Wechsler Intelligence Scale for Children
	Aptitude test	A test to measure a person's ability to estimate how they will perform at some time in the future or in a different situation	Cognitive Ability: Binet-Simon Scale to identify a child's mental level General Ability: Stanford-Binet IQ Scale
	Interest Inventory	A test that provides information about an individual's interest and helps them make career choices	Strong Interest Inventory
	Personality Assessment	A test that helps a person identify and measure human characteristics that help predict or explain behavior over time and across situations (Thorndike, 1997)	Minnesota Multiphasic Personality Inventory
Measures of Individual Attitude	Affective Scale	An instrument that measures positive or negative affect for or against a topic	Attitudes toward Self-Esteem Scale Adaptive Behavior Scales
Observation of Individual Behavior	Behavioral Checklist	An instrument used to record observations about individual behavior	Flander's Interaction Analysis Behavioral Checklist in Reading Vineland Adaptive Behavior Scale
Factual Information	Public Documents or School Records	Information from public sources that provides data about a sample or population	Census data School grade reports School attendance reports

FIGURE 6.6

Example of an Instrument Measuring Attitudes

Student Adaptation to College Questionnaire (SACQ)
Robert W. Baker, Ph.D. and Bohdan Siryk, M.A.

Published by

WPS   WESTERN PSYCHOLOGICAL SERVICES
Publishers and Distributors
12031 Maple Boulevard
Los Angeles, California 50023

Name:_____   Date:_____

ID Number:_____   Sex: ☐F ☐M   Date of Birth:_____

Directions

Please provide the identifying information requested on the right.

The 67 items on the front and back of this form are statements that describe college experiences. Read each one and decide how well it applies to you at the present time (within the past few days). For each item, circle the asterisk at the point in the continuum that best represents how closely the statement applies to you. Circle only one asterisk for each item. To change an answer, draw an *X* through the incorrect response and circle the desired response. Be sure to use a hard-tipped pen or pencil and press very firmly. Do not erase.

Current Academic Standing: ☐Freshman ☐Sophomore ☐Junior ☐Senior

Semester: ☐1 ☐2 ☐Summer *or* Quarter: ☐1 ☐2 ☐3 ☐Summer

Ethnic Background (optional):   ☐Asian   ☐Black   ☐Hispanic
                                 ☐Native American ☐White ☐Other

In the example on the right, Item A applied very closely, and Item B was changed from "doesn't apply at all" to "applies somewhat."

Example

A. Ⓐ * * * * * * * *
B. * * * Ⓑ * * * ☒

Applies Very   Doesn't Apply
Closely to Me   to Me at All

1. I feel that I fit in well as part of the college environment.....................................
2. I have been feeling tense or nervous lately..
3. I have been keeping up to date on my academic work..
4. I am meeting as many people, and making as many friends as I would like in college............
5. I know why I'm in college and what I want out of it..
6. I am finding academic work at college difficult...
7. Lately I have been feeling blue and moody a lot...
8. I am very involved with social activities in college...
9. I am adjusting well to college..
10. I have not been functioning well during examinations...
11. I have felt tired much of the time lately...
12. Being on my own, taking responsibility for myself, has not been easy...........................
13. I am satisfied with the level at which I am performing academically............................
14. I have had informal, personal contacts with college professors.................................
15. I am pleased now about my decision to go to college...

Source: Partial sample from the *Student Adaptation to College Questionnaire* copyright © 1989 by Western Psychological Services. Reprinted by permission of the publisher, Western Psychological Services, 12031 Wilshire Boulevard, Los Angeles, California, 90025, U.S.A. Not to be reprinted in whole or in part for any additional purpose without the expressed, written permission of the publisher. All rights reserved.

(15 questions), and Goal Commitment—Institutional Attachment (15 questions). To read a review of this instrument and to learn how to interpret and use scores, see Dahmus, Bernardin, and Bernardin (1992).

Behavioral Observations

To collect data on specific behaviors, you can observe behavior and record scores on a checklist or scoring sheet. **Behavioral observations** consist of selecting an instrument to record a behavior, observing individuals for that behavior, and checking points on a scale that reflect the behavior (behavioral checklists). The advantage of this form of data is that the individual's actual behavior can be identified, rather than their views or perceptions. However, behaviors may be difficult to score, and gathering them is a time-consuming form of data collection. Further, if more than one observer gathers data for a study, they need to be trained in using consistent observational procedures. Also, with multiple observers, checks need to be made for consistency of scores among observers.

An example of a behavioral checklist is the "Measurement of Inappropriate and Disruptive Interactions" (MIDI) developed and used in the Saber-Tooth Project studying physical education curriculum changes in one middle school and two comparison schools

FIGURE 6.7

Example of an Observational Scoring Sheet with Fictitious Data

Social Skills Assessment

Teacher Alis Grade Level 08 Observer JC Date 2/3 Content Area Lacross School School A

	1	2	3	4	5	6	7	8	9	10	11	12	13	14	15	16	17	18	19	20	21	22	23	24	25
C	G	C	C	I	I	I	G	G	G	G	G	M	M	M	G										
B	I	O	V	I	I	I	I	I	I	T	T	I	I	I	T										
E	I	S	I	I	I	I	S	S	S	S	I	I	I	I	S										

	26	27	28	29	30	31	32	33	34	35	36	37	38	39	40	41	42	43	44	45	46	47	48	49	50
C																									
B																									
E																									

	51	52	53	54	55	56	57	58	59	60	61	62	63	64	65	66	67	68	69	70	71	72	73	74	75
C																									
B																									
E																									

	76	77	78	79	80	81	82	83	84	85	86	87	88	89	90	91	92	93	94	95	96	97	98	99	100
C																									
B																									
E																									

	101	102	103	104	105	106	107	108	109	110	111	112	113	114	115	116	117	118	119	120	121	122	123	124	125
C																									
B																									
E																									

	126	127	128	129	130	131	132	133	134	135	136	137	138	139	140	141	142	143	144	145	146	147	148	149	150
C																									
B																									
E																									

	151	152	153	154	155	156	157	158	159	160	161	162	163	164	165	166	167	168	169	170	171	172	173	174	175
C																									
B																									
E																									

C																									
B																									
E																									

C																									
B																									
E																									

Context Categories	Inappropriate Behaviors	Extent of Misbehavior:
Game:	Talking out/Noise:	Class: (15 or more students)
Practice:	Inactive:	Small Group: (4 or more students up to 15)
Cognitive:	Off-task:	Individual/s (less that 3 students)
Instruction:	Non-compliance:	
Management/Other:	Verbal offense:	

Source: Ward, P., Barrett, T. M., Evans, S. A., Doutis, P., Nguyen, P. T., & Johnson, M. K. (1999). Chapter 5: Curriculum effects in eighth-grade Lacrosse. *Journal of Teaching in Physical Education, 18,* 428–433. Reprinted with permission of the authors.

(Ward, 1999). This study examines teacher changes in the curriculum and student involvement in the changes. In one of the Saber-Tooth studies, the researchers observe activities in four classes where the teachers provide an instructional unit on lacrosse to eighth grade students (Ward, Barrett, Evans, Doutis, Nguyen, & Johnson, 1999). During this classroom unit, the researchers score inappropriate student behaviors and the extent of misbehavior using the MIDI scoring sheet in each class, as shown in Figure 6.7.

The legend, located at the bottom of the sheet, lists the codes that observers record in each cell above. These codes are the first letter of the appropriate word used to describe the context or focus on the lesson in which the behavior occurs (i.e., game, practice, cognitive, instruction, or management/other). The observers also record the type of inappropriate behavior during the primary event that involves the most students during the interval (i.e., talking out/noise, inactive, off-task, non-compliance, verbal offense). Finally, observers indicate who is engaged in the disruption to assess the extent of misbehavior in the class. Here, class behavior is described as involving 15 or more students; small group behavior is described as involving 4 or more students, up to 15; and individual behavior is described as involving less than 3 students. Data are collected on-site using this scoring sheet as the instrument, and three observers in the classes record their observations (identified by the column numbers) at an interval of 6-second observe and 6-second record format. The observers are cued by an audiotape recording that they listen to through earphones, and they mark their observations in the cells on the response sheet. For example, in the fictitious data shown in Figure 6.7 for observation 1, the observer records:

> Context = Game (G)
>
> Inappropriate Behavior = Inactive (I)
>
> Extent of Misbehavior = Individual/s (less than 3 students) (I)

From recording observations, the observer can then examine differences among students in their disruptive behaviors.

Factual Information

Quantitative, numeric data is also available in public educational records. **Factual information** or **personal documents** consist of numeric data in public records of individuals. This data may be grade reports, school attendance records, student demographic data, and census information. If these documents are in the public domain, they can often be easily obtained and can provide extensive information for educational studies. However, for some types of documents, access presents a problem, and permissions are needed. Just because data found in documents is readily available, it does not mean such information will provide good measures of variables.

Choosing One Type of Data and Measure over Another

Of the various types of data, several factors go into the decision to choose one form over another. When choosing which type to use, ask yourself the following questions.

- *What am I trying to learn about participants from my research questions and hypotheses?* If you are trying to learn about individual behaviors of parents at a student-parent conference meeting, then some form of behavioral checklist could be used to record your observations. If you are trying to measure the attitudes of teachers toward a bond issue, some form of attitudinal instrument is needed.
- *What information can realistically be collected?* Some types of data may not be collectible in a study because individuals are unwilling to supply it. For example, the study to assess whether students carry handguns to school would be difficult to determine because of the students' reluctance to share this information. On the other hand, information about the frequency of weapons or school documents reporting "suspensions" for weapon possession might be more easily obtained.

  For example, let's return to the quantitative research study underway by Maria, our high school teacher. Her general question, "Why do students carry weapons in high school?" may now be shaped into the following questions:
  a. "How frequently do students feel weapons are carried into high school?"
  b. "What general attitudes do high school students hold toward the possession of weapons in the schools?"
  c. "Does participation in extracurricular activities at school influence attitudes of students toward possession of weapons?"

d. "Are student suspensions for possession of weapons on the increase in high schools?"

To answer these questions, Maria needs to locate or develop a survey to send out to a sample of high school students ($N=350$) in the school district. This survey will measure student attitudes toward frequency of weapon possession (question a), assess student attitudes toward possession of weapons (question b), and gather data about the students (question c), such as age, level of education, race, gender, and extent of participation in extracurricular activities. With these three questions, she will focus primarily on collecting attitudinal data. To answer question (d), she will contact the school officials of several high schools and ask if she can obtain reports on student suspensions—school documents which report quantitative data.

▶ *How do the advantages of the data collection compare with its disadvantages?* For each type of data mentioned in Table 6.2, the advantages and disadvantages were discussed. While observing kids is the best way to learn about their behaviors, this data collection approach needs to be weighed against the issue of the labor-intensive effort it will require.

▶ *Who records the data?* Data may be self-reported where the participants provide the information, such as on achievement tests or on attitudinal questionnaires. Alternatively, the researcher may record the data on forms by observing, interviewing, or collecting documents. Having participants supply the data is less time-consuming for the researcher.

RECORDING AND ADMINISTERING DATA COLLECTION

Coupled with selecting the appropriate data is identifying an instrument that you can use to collect information. Searching for an instrument to use takes time; the process of developing an instrument takes even longer. Whichever procedure is used, you must have confidence that the scores obtained on the instrument will yield meaningful and useful data, and that the instrument will assess what you are trying to measure. In addition, inappropriate procedures of data collection will yield questionable data and lend to frustrating research experiences for yourself as well as for the people you are studying.

Several questions need to be addressed as you begin the process of recording and administering data collection:

▶ Will you develop your own instrument or locate one? What criteria will guide your decision?
▶ If you plan to use an existing instrument, how will you go about locating it? What criteria will determine whether it is a good instrument to use?
▶ Will the scores collected on the instrument you use provide reliable and valid data?
▶ What factors, such as standardization and ethics, are important during the actual collection of your data?

Let's look at these questions individually and see how researchers go about answering them.

Locating or Developing an Instrument

Three options exist for obtaining an instrument to use: you can develop one yourself, locate one and modify it, or locate one and use it in its entirety. Of these choices, locating one to use (either modifying it or using it in its original form) represents the easiest approach. It is more difficult to develop an instrument than to locate one and modify it for use in a study. **Modifying an instrument** means locating an existing instrument, obtaining permission to change it, and making changes in it to fit your participants. Typically authors of the original instrument require a copy of your modified version and the results from your study in exchange for your use of their instrument.

An instrument to measure the variables in your study may not be available in the literature or commercially. If this is the case, you will have to develop your own instrument, which is a long and arduous process. Developing an instrument consists of several phases, such as specifying the purpose of the instrument, reviewing the literature, writing the questions, and testing the questions. The steps recommended by Benson and Clark (1983), as shown in Figure 6.8, show the rigorous steps of planning, constructing, evaluating, and validating an instrument in four phases. In this process, reviewing the literature, developing items that measure what you want to learn, and creating simple scales, such as a rating scale ("strongly agree" to "strongly disagree") form the basic steps.

FIGURE 6.8

Steps in Developing or Constructing an Instrument

Phase I: Planning
- State purpose of test and target groups
- Identify and define domain of test
- Review literature on construct or variable of interest
- Give open-ended questions to target group
- Interpret open-ended comments
- Write objectives
- Select item format

Phase II: Construction
- Develop table of specifications
- Hire and train item writers
- Write pool items
- Validate content
- Have judges complete qualitative evaluation
- Develop new or revise items

Phase III: Quantitative Evaluation
- Prepare instrument for first pilot test
- Administer first pilot test
- Debrief subjects
- Calculate reliability
- Run item analysis
- Revise instrument
- Prepare for second pilot test

Phase IV: Validation
- Administer second pilot test
- Run item analysis
- Repeat steps of revision, pilot administration, and item analysis
- Begin validation
- Administer for validation data
- Continue validation

Source: Adapted from a flowchart provided by Benson & Clark, 1983.

Strategies for Locating and Selecting an Instrument

If you decide to use an existing instrument, you will typically be charged a fee by the publisher for use of the instrument. Locating an instrument in a form ready to be administered is not always easy. If this is the case, you can try the following strategies.

▶ *Look in published journal articles.* Often authors of journal articles will report instruments and provide a few sample items so that you can see the basic content included in the instrument. Examine references in published journal articles that cite specific instruments and contact the authors for inspection copies. Before you use the instrument, seek permission from the author. Also, look in appendices of published journal articles where sample items or complete instruments may be found. With limited space in journals, authors are including fewer examples of their items or copies of their instruments.

▶ *Run an ERIC search.* Use the term "instruments" and the topic of the study to search the ERIC system for instruments. Use the online search (http://www.accesseric.org) process of the ERIC database, discussed in Chapter 4, on "Databases." Use the same search procedure to locate abstracts to articles where the authors mention instruments that they have used in their studies.

▶ *Go to the ERIC Web site.* Click on the link to Evaluation and Assessment and use key words to locate instruments. Many of these instruments are researcher-developed scales (http://www.eericae.net/).

▶ *Examine guides to tests and instruments that are available commercially.* Examine the *Mental Measurements Yearbook* (MMY) (Impara & Plake, 1999) or the *Tests in Print* (TIP) (Murphy, Impara, & Plake, 1999), both of which are available from the Buros Institute for Mental Measurement. More than 400 commercial firms develop instruments that are available for sale to individuals and institutions. These Buros guides have been available since 1938 and contain extensive information about tests and measures available for educational research use. The MMY can be used to locate reviews and descriptions of English-language commercially published tests. The MMY is available on SilverPlatter in many academic libraries, and the Buros Web page is located at http://unl.edu/buros/.

Reliable and Valid Scores on Instruments

Any measure or observation taken on an instrument needs to provide an accurate assessment of the variable (i.e., be reliable) and enable the researcher to draw inferences to a sample or population (i.e., be valid). As you select or evaluate an instrument for a study, consider these two questions: Have scores from past uses of this instrument yielded accurate and reliable information? Have these scores enabled past researchers to draw justifiable inferences that are valid? Answering these questions requires a basic understanding of the concepts of reliability and validity in educational research.

Reliability   A goal of good research is to have measures or observations that are reliable. **Reliability** means that individual scores from an instrument should be nearly the same or stable on repeated administrations of the instrument, they should be free from sources of measurement error, and they should be consistent. Several factors can result in unreliable data, including when:

▶ questions on instruments are ambiguous and unclear
▶ procedures of test administration vary and are not standardized
▶ participants are fatigued, are nervous, misinterpret questions, or guess on tests (Rudner, 1993)

By using an instrument to measure a variable, researchers gather evidence to establish the stability and the consistency of scores. There are five basic procedures involved in establishing this evidence, as shown in Table 6.4. These procedures can be distinguished by the number of times the instrument is administered, the number of versions of the instrument that are administered, and the number of individuals who make an assessment of information. Given these features, the types of reliability are:

▶ test-retest reliability
▶ alternate forms reliability
▶ alternative forms and test-retest reliability
▶ inter-rater reliability
▶ internal consistency

The **test-retest reliability** examines the extent to which scores from one sample are stable over time from one test administration to another. To determine this form of reliability, the researcher administers the test at two different times at a sufficient time interval. If the scores are reliable, then they will relate (or will correlate) at a positive, reasonably high level, such as .6. This approach has the advantage of requiring only one form of the instrument; however, an individual's scores on the first administration of the instrument may influence the scores on the second administration. For example, a stable characteristic, such as creativity, is measured for sixth graders at the beginning of the year. Measured again at the end of the year, it is assumed that the scores will be stable during the sixth grade experience. If scores at the beginning and the end of the year relate, there is evidence for test-retest reliability.

Another approach is **alternative forms reliability.** This involves using two instruments, both measuring the same variables and relating (or correlating) the scores for the

TABLE 6.4

Types of Reliability

Form of Reliability	Number of Times Instrument Administered	Number of Different Versions of the Instrument	Number of Individuals Who Provide Information
Test-retest Reliability	Twice at different time intervals	One version of the instrument	Each participant in the study completes the instrument.
Alternate Forms Reliability	Each instrument administered once	Two different versions of the same concept or variable	Each participant in the study completes the instrument.
Alternate Forms and Test-retest Reliability	Twice at different time intervals	Two different versions of the same concept or variable	Each participant in the study completes the instrument.
Internal Consistency Reliability	Instrument administered once	One version of the instrument	Each participant in the study completes the instrument.
Inter-rater Reliability	Instrument administered once	One version of the instrument	More than one individual observes behavior of the participants.

same group of individuals to the two instruments. In practice, both instruments need to be similar, such as the same content, same level of difficulty, and same type of scales. Thus, the items for both instruments represent the same universe or population of items. The advantage of this approach is that it allows you to see if the scores from one instrument are equivalent to scores from another instrument that is intended to measure the same variables. The difficulty, of course, is whether the two instruments *are* equivalent in the first place. Assuming that they are, the researchers relate or correlate the items from the one instrument with its equivalent instrument. For example, an instrument with 45 vocabulary items yields scores from first graders that are compared with another instrument that also measures a similar set of 45 vocabulary items. It is assumed that both instruments contain items of equal difficulty. The fact that the items relate or correlate highly gives us confidence in the accuracy or reliability of the scores from the first instrument.

Alternate forms and test-retest reliability is simply a variance on the two previous types of reliability. In this approach, the researcher administers the test twice and also uses an alternate form of the test from the first administration to the second. This type of reliability has the advantages of both examining the stability of scores over time as well as having the equivalence of items from the potential universe of items. It also has all of the disadvantages of both test-retest and alternate forms of reliability. Scores may reflect differences in content or difficulty or in changes over time. For example, in the last example, the 45 vocabulary items are administered twice at two different time periods, and the actual tests are equivalent in content and level of difficulty. The researcher correlates or relates scores to both tests and finds that they correlate positively and highly. The scores to the initial instrument are reliable.

In **inter-rater reliability,** two or more individuals observe an individual's behavior and record scores, and then the scores of the observers are compared to determine whether they are similar. This method has the advantage of obtaining observational scores from two or more individuals, thus negating any bias that might be brought by one of the individuals. However, it has the disadvantage of requiring the observers to negotiate outcomes and reconcile differences in their observations, something that may not be easy to do.

For example, let's say two observers are viewing preschool children at play in their activity center. They observe the spatial skills of the children and record on a checklist the number of times each child builds something in the activity center. After the observation, the observers compare their checklists to determine how close their scores were during the observation. Assuming that their scores were close, they can average their scores and conclude that their assessment is accurate and reliable.

Scores from an instrument are reliable and accurate if they are **internally consistent** across the items on the instrument. If someone completes items at the beginning of the instrument one way (e.g., positive about negative affects of tobacco), then they should answer the questions later in the instrument in a similar way (e.g., positive about the health affects of tobacco). There are several ways to examine the consistency of responses. One way to determine this is to split the test in half and relate or correlate the items. This test is called the **Kuder-Richardson split half test** (KR20, KR21) and it is used when (a) the items on an instrument are scored as right or wrong as categorical scores; (b) the responses are not influenced by speed; and (c) the items measure a common factor. Since the split half test relies on information from only half of the instrument, a modification in this procedure is to use the **Spearman-Brown formula** that estimates full-length test reliability using all questions on an instrument. This is important because the reliability of an instrument increases as more items are added to the instrument. Finally, the **coefficient alpha** is used to test for internal consistency. If the items are scored as continuous variables (e.g., strongly agree to strongly disagree), the alpha provides a coefficient to estimate consistency of scores on an instrument. Calculations for the Kuder-Richardson split half, Spearman-Brown prophecy formula, and coefficient alpha are available in Thorndike (1997).

Validity   When examining an instrument, the first question you must ask yourself is if the scores are stable and consistently reliable. If so, the second question is then whether you can draw meaningful and useful inferences (or generalizations) from the scores—their validity. Seen in this way, reliability is an antecedent to validity: Scores cannot be valid unless they are first reliable. This perspective also characterizes validity as the larger, more encompassing term when you assess the choice of an instrument.

   Validity means that researchers can draw meaningful and justifiable inferences from scores about a sample or population. This definition is consistent with the *Standards for Educational and Psychological Testing* jointly formulated by the American Educational Research Association, the American Psychological Association, and the National Council on Measurement in Education (1999). Your ability to draw valid conclusions from data will be affected by several factors:

- poorly designed studies
- participant fatigue, stress, and misunderstanding of questions on the instrument
- inability to make useful predictions from scores
- poorly designed questions or measures of variables
- information that has little use and application

   To choose or evaluate a valid instrument for a study requires assessing whether scores from past uses of it are valid and useful for your purposes. There are several types of validity to consider, as shown in Table 6.5. When reviewing instruments for use in your study, consider whether the authors report validity for scores from its use and document this validity.

   The traditional perspective on validity is to discuss three forms: content, criterion-referenced, and construct validity. More recently, measurement specialists view validity as

TABLE 6.5

Types of Validity

Types of Validity	What Is Measured?	What Evidence Is Obtained to Substantiate it?
Content Validity	How well do the questions represent all of the possibilities of questions available?	Asking experts if the questions are representative of the area of interest
Criterion-related Concurrent	How well do the scores on the instrument relate to an outcome?	Selecting an outcome and correlating or relating the scores to it
Predictive	How well do the scores on the instrument predict a future outcome?	Selecting a future outcome and correlating the scores with it
Construct Validity	What do the scores on the instrument mean or signify?	Using statistical procedures, such as correlating scores with other scores; examining the correlation among questions on an instrument; or testing a theory against the scores
	What is the intended purpose or use for the scores from the instrument? Can we safely generalize from them?	Using non-statistical procedures, such as examining the values inherent in the interpretation of the scores; assessing the relevance of the scores for the purpose of the study; or considering the likely social consequences

a unitary concept (Thorndike, 1997) and advocate that scores are valid if they have use and result in positive social consequences (Hubley & Zumbo, 1996; Messick, 1980). Both the traditional and the more current conceptions are discussed in the following discussion about types of validity.

Content validity is the extent to which the questions on the instrument and the scores from these questions are representative of all the possible questions that could be asked about the content or skills. Researchers evaluate content validity by examining the plan and the procedures used in constructing the instrument. They examine the information about the objectives of the instrument, the content areas, and the level of difficulty of the questions. Typically researchers go to a panel of judges or experts and have them identify whether the questions are valid. This form of validity is useful when the possibilities of questions (e.g., achievement tests in science education) are well known and easily identifiable. It is less useful in assessing personality or aptitude scores (e.g., on the Stanford-Binet IQ test) when the universe of questions is less certain.

Instead of examining the specific questions on an instrument, another form of validity is to see if the scores predict an outcome they are expected to explain. **Criterion-related validity** is whether the scores from an instrument are a good predictor of some outcome (or criterion) they are expected to predict. For example, Graduate Record Examination (GRE) scores are expected to predict performance in graduate school. A portfolio assessment and a pencil and paper test should measure a student's ability to understand the content of an English methods class. In the first case, the scores "predict" an outcome; in the second, they estimate a person's scores on two measures. In both cases, a criterion is used to assess the outcome, and the scores are related or correlated by the researcher who seeks a high correlation (e.g., .60). This form of validity is especially useful for establishing that scores from an instrument can predict an outcome, but it requires that the outcome be clearly identified.

The most complicated form of validity is a third form—construct validity—because it can be evaluated in several statistical and non-statistical ways. **Construct validity** is a determination of the significance, meaning, purpose, and use of scores from an instrument. As discussed earlier in this chapter, variables are operationally measured. The question here is whether the measures (and their scores) adequately provide a good operational definition of the variable. Do the items on the instrument, for example, measure the underlying variable (or construct) that the researcher wants to measure? Are they useful in terms of the purposes of the instrument and the application of information from the scores to practice?

To establish evidence of construct validity, researchers employ both statistical and non-statistical procedures. Through statistical procedures you can:

- see if scores to items are related in a way that is expected (e.g., examine the relationship of a question on a "student depression instrument" to see if it relates to the overall scale measuring depression)
- test a theory and see if the scores, as expected, support the theory (e.g., test a theory of depression and see if the evidence or data supports the relationships in the theory)
- correlate the scores statistically with other variables or scales that should be similar (called *convergent validity*) or dissimilar (called *discriminant validity*) (Messick, 1980) (e.g., see if scores to question on one student depression instrument relate positively to items on another depression instrument or have little relation to items measuring anxiety)

You can also use non-statistical procedures to assess the interpretation (making sense of test scores) and use (application of test scores) (Humbley & Zumbo, 1996), such as:

- examining the consequences of interpreting test scores in terms of values (e.g., when student scores indicate "high depression," does this mean that depression is normal, abnormal, positive, negative, or realistic?)

FIGURE 6.9

Validity and Reliability Questions for Selecting/Evaluating a Test or Instrument

When selecting or evaluating an instrument, look for:

Reliability	Validity
1. Did the author check for it?	1. Did the author check for it?
2. If so, what form of reliability was reported?	2. If so, what type of validity was reported?
3. Was an appropriate type used?	3. Was more than one type reported?
4. Were the reliability values (coefficients) reported?	4. Were the values (coefficients) reported?
5. Were they positive, high coefficients?	5. Were they high positive, coefficients?

▶ examining the relevance and use of test scores (e.g., are the student scores on "depression" useful for screening? Are they useful for at-risk students more than normal achievers?)

▶ examining the consequences of using test scores (e.g., are the scores useful for policy decisions by the school? By teachers?)

Choosing a Reliable, Valid Instrument

In general, when examining instruments for possible inclusion in your study, you might consider several factors. First, is there information about the reliability and validity of scores from past uses of the instrument? Without this information you will know little about whether the scores you obtain on an instrument will be accurate (reliable) or useful in drawing inferences (valid) about your sample and population. Second, has the instrument been developed recently, or can you obtain the most recent version? With knowledge expanding in educational research, the use of an "old" instrument may now be outdated, inapplicable to your sample, or revised and improved by its author. Third, is the instrument widely cited by other authors? Frequent use by other researchers will provide some indication of its quality, and such applications will net scores for assessing reliability and validity. Fourth, are reviews available for the instrument? Look for published reviews about the instrument in the *Mental Measurements Yearbook* (MMY) or in journals, such as *Measurement and Evaluation in Counseling and Development*. Fifth, ask yourself the questions shown in Figure 6.9. This checklist requires that you consider the type of reliability and validity, whether the type was appropriate, and the values (or coefficients) obtained in past studies. Generally, coefficients in the range of .6 are acceptable (see Thorndike, 1997, for more information).

Think-Aloud About Locating a Reliable and Valid Instrument

Often I find beginning researchers developing their own instruments rather than taking the time to locate an existing instrument suitable for their study. Unquestionably, developing your own instrument requires knowledge about item or question construction, scale development, format, and length. Although some campuses may have courses that teach this information, most students develop instruments on their own with feedback (often not so pleasant) from advisors or consultants about how to change the instrument. I speak from personal experience, because in my doctoral dissertation I constructed my own instrument. After 11 versions and much feedback from exasperated faculty, I finally had a reasonable instrument to administer in my survey project.

I would encourage you to locate or modify an existing instrument rather than go through what I went through. Let me convey a specific experience. Earlier in the chapter I presented Figure 6.6, questions from the attitudinal instrument on student adaptation to college. How did I find this instrument?

I knew that I wanted to study how students adjusted to college and I began my search for an instrument to measure this variable. I first spent time with the ERIC database, using the descriptors of "students" and "college" and "adjustments" in my keyword online search. Although I found several good journal articles on the topic, none included a useful instrument. Examining the references in these articles still did not lead to a single instrument that I might use.

I turned to the Buros' instrument indices, the *Tests in Print* (TIP) and the *Mental Measurements Yearbook* (MMY) in our academic library. You may recall from earlier in this chapter that the TIP and MMY contain information about commercially available tests and instruments, including attitudinal instruments. Although our library contains hard copies of the TIP and MMY, I could have used the CD-ROM SilverPlatter version available in our library or visited the Buros Web site located at http://unl.edu/buros/ for more information about searching these resources.

Using the university library, I located the latest copy of the TIP, *Tests in Print V* (Murphy, Impara, & Plake, 1999) and looked under the alphabetized listing of tests, searching for any instruments that related to students, especially college students. After trying out several words, I found the "Student Adaptation to College Questionnaire" (SACQ). Reading through this brief description of the SACQ I learned basic information about the instrument, such as its purpose, the population for its use (i.e., college freshman), the publication date (1989) and its scales. This review also contained price information ($89.50 for 25 hand-scorable questionnaires and a manual), the time to administer it (20 minutes), authors, publishers, and a cross reference to a review of the instrument to be found in the MMY, 11th edition (Kramer & Conoley, 1992).

Next I was curious about whether scores reported on this instrument were both valid and reliable, so I looked up *The Eleventh Mental Measurements Yearbook* (Kramer & Conoley, 1992), and found a review of the instrument by E. Jack Asher, Jr., Professor Emeritus of Psychology, Western Michigan University, Kalamazoo, Michigan. I also searched the ERIC database and located the review article by Dahmus, et al. (1992) reported in the journal, *Measurement and Evaluation in Counseling and Development*.

Focusing mainly on the Asher review, I found that it addressed:

▶ the purpose of the questionnaire
▶ the sub scales on the questionnaire
▶ norms on the questionnaire obtained by the authors by administering it from 1980 through 1984
▶ evidence for validity of the scores from the instrument (i.e., criterion-related or predictive and construct validity)
▶ evidence for reliability of the scores based on coefficients of internal consistency
▶ the value of the manual, especially the inclusion of potential ethical issues in using the instrument
▶ the overall value of the instrument for college counselors and research applications
▶ the limitations of the instrument

After reviewing all of these topics about the questionnaire, Asher concluded by summarizing an overall positive impression of the instrument. Although somewhat dated (1989), the instrument has been widely used and positively reviewed. I decided it would be a good instrument to survey college students.

I next contacted the publisher, Western Psychological Services in Los Angeles, California, for permission to use the instrument and to obtain copies for my study. Using an instrument already developed by someone else, finding one with good validity and reliability scores, and locating a manual for using the instrument led to the early identification of means for collecting my data. You may not be as fortunate to locate an instrument as quickly as I did, but certainly this process is better than developing numerous versions of your own instrument that might have questionable validity and reliability.

Administering Procedures for Collecting Data

The actual process of collecting data differs depending on the data and the instruments or documents you use. However, two aspects deserve attention: the use of standard procedures and ethical practices.

Standardization

Instruments are typically used to assess performance and attitudinal measures. These instruments may consist of questionnaires that are mailed out to participants or handed out individually to people, or surveys that are administered over the telephone. Quantitative instruments are also used to conduct interviews face-to-face with individuals or in a focus group.

In all of these cases, it is important to use standard procedures. When procedures vary, bias is introduced into the study and the data may not be comparable for analysis. Written procedures help keep you, as well as other data collectors assisting in the process, on track. For interviewing, you apply the same procedures to each individual. Instructions provided on the interview form will help ensure that you follow a standard process. If others help in interviewing, they will need to be trained so that the procedures used by all interviewers are consistent. This training might involve a demonstration interview, followed by a trial interview and a critique of the trial so that all trainees follow the same procedures.

Observational data are collected by means of a researcher observing behavior and recording information on a tally sheet or an instrument for recording scores. In collecting observational data, training must occur first so that the researchers can collect data using standard procedures. A process similar to the one used in interviewing—demonstration, trial run, and a critique—might be used.

Researchers also collect public documents by obtaining permission to access this information and then taking notes or recording the information on a computer file. The compatibility of different databases is important if information is to be combined from several sources into one file for analysis (e.g., enrollment data and suspension data for students in high schools).

Ethical Issues

Data collection should be ethical and it should respect individuals and sites. Obtaining permission before starting to collect data is not only a part of the informed consent process but is also an ethical practice. Protecting the anonymity of individuals by assigning numbers to returned instruments and keeping the identity of individuals confidential offers privacy to participants. During data collection, the information is viewed as confidential and not shared with other participants or individuals outside of the project. Individuals who choose not to participate must be respected for their choice. Even when they provide assent to be involved, people may back out or not show up for an observation or interview. Attempts to reschedule may be futile and you might need to select another person for data collection rather than forcing an individual to participate.

In terms of the research site, you need to recognize that you will impact the site by your presence, however minimal it might be. Observing in a classroom, for example, may disrupt learning by distracting teachers and students, especially when you write down observations about their behavior on checklists. By obtaining permissions and clearly communicating the purpose of the study *before* you collect data, you can lessen the reservations some individuals may have about your presence in their educational setting.

KEY IDEAS IN THE CHAPTER

The process of data collection involves more than simply gathering information; it includes four interrelated steps. The first step is to obtain access to people by securing permissions to sites and participants in the study. Permissions may be needed from leaders of institutions or organizations, individuals at specific sites, participants (and their parents, for minor children), and a campus institutional review board.

The second step is to select participants for the study. This selection involves specifying the population and sample, determining how participants will be chosen, and deciding on an appropriate sample size.

The third step is to decide what type or types of data to collect. This decision is based on specifying the variables, defining these variables, and seeking measures and scales for them. Typical quantitative data consists of measures of performance and attitudes, observations of behavior, and records and documents.

The fourth step is to collect these types of data on instruments chosen prior to the study. Instruments are either developed by the researcher or selected from existing instruments and used in their original or modified form. One factor important in the choice of any instrument is whether it will yield scores that are both reliable and valid.

An important part of using instruments and collecting data is to administer the procedures in a standardized way and to employ ethical practices that respect the individuals and sites involved.

USEFUL INFORMATION FOR PRODUCERS OF RESEARCH

▶ When collecting data for a study, plan to engage in four steps: obtaining permissions, selecting participants, deciding on types of data to collect, and recording and administering data collection.

▶ Obtain permission to conduct a study. A research study often requires multiple levels of permission, ranging from campus institutional review boards to organizational and site leaders to individual participants. The process of seeking approval from a campus institutional review board may consist of several steps.

▶ Consider the provisions that need to be included in a consent form, such as shown in Figure 6.1.

▶ Identify the population and sample for a study. There are several types of probability and non-probability sampling. The most rigorous sampling will be simple random sampling. However, the research circumstances may dictate a form of non-probability sampling.

▶ Select as large a sample as possible. Use sampling formulas to be systematic in selecting the size of the sample.

▶ Consider how the research questions or hypotheses will be answered when deciding on what data type(s) to use. Then identify your variables, operationally define them, and select measures (e.g., performance and attitudes, observations of behavior, and factual and personal data) that fit the operational definitions.

▶ Consider the types of scales you plan to use on your instruments. These scales will affect the types of statistics to be used in analyzing the data. Make sure they relate to your questions.

▶ Decide whether to develop your own instrument or use or modify an existing instrument for your research. Locating instruments is easier, and several library references provide good access to them.

▶ Determine whether the administration procedure will provide self-reported data or researcher-reported data. This will depend on the type of data to be collected.

▶ Before deciding on an instrument to use, make sure that the scores from past uses of it are reliable and valid. There are several forms of reliability and of validity.

USEFUL INFORMATION FOR CONSUMERS OF RESEARCH

▶ In evaluating a study, determine if the researcher fully disclosed the data collection. Look in a "method" section for the four parts of data collection.

▶ Look for studies in which researchers use the most rigorous form of sampling—simple random, probabilistic sampling.

▶ A rigorous quantitative study often requires multiple types of quantitative data. A research study should provide detailed information about each and all forms of data collected during the investigation.

▶ If researchers use instruments in their data collection, they need to report whether the scores from the use of past instruments are both valid and reliable. Look for high, positive coefficients (e.g., .6 or above).

STUDY QUESTIONS AND ACTIVITIES

1. Identify the steps of data collection taken by an author in a published study. Locate a study and find the method or procedure discussion. Write next to the place in the article where the four steps in data collection are located.

2. Locate an instrument measuring individual performance that you might use in a quantitative study. First select a variable that you would like to measure in a study. Then go to the library and examine the sources for instruments by first running an ERIC search followed by examining the Buros SilverPlatter CD-ROM version of the *Tests in Print* (TIP) and *Mental Measurement Yearbook* (MMY). Identify one or two possible instruments for use in a study. Consider the procedures in the "Think-Aloud" in this chapter as a guide.

3. Locate a research instrument that measures individual attitudes. Consult journal articles, the TIP or MMY, or run an online ERIC database search. As an alternative, find a checklist used for an observational study using the same sources.

4. Select a quantitative study and evaluate whether the scores are valid. In your assessment, consider the types of validity reported by the authors and assess them. Use the question, "What is measured?" in Table 6.5 to identify the type(s) of validity.

5. Suppose you are assisting Maria with the design of her study. Apply the four steps of quantitative data collection and describe possible decisions that she could use to answer her research questions.

 Now go to our Companion Website to assess your understanding of chapter content with Multiple-Choice Questions, apply comprehension in Projects & Essays, and broaden your knowledge with links to related research topics on the Web.

7

Collecting Qualitative Data

Maria, our high school teacher, turns out to be a natural interviewer. As a secondary English teacher, she is comfortable interviewing and talking with students and teachers in high school. She is even comfortable asking them her qualitative question: "What meaning does weapon possession have for students in high schools?" The difficulty will be listening without injecting her own opinions, trying to take notes about what people have to say, and the lengthy transcribing of the interviews. This phase, she tells herself, will be a long process. But she likes talking with people and listening to their ideas. Maria enters qualitative data collection with mixed feelings.

For qualitative researchers like Maria, interviewing and talking with people comes naturally. She will proceed through qualitative steps in data collection that are remarkably like the process used in quantitative research: obtaining permissions, selecting participants, deciding on data to collect, administering the data collection, and recording the information. The differences will be in gaining access with assistance by specific individuals, collecting text or word data, and using researcher-developed protocols for recording information.

By the end of this chapter, you should be able to:

▶ Make decisions about obtaining permissions in qualitative research.
▶ Recognize alternative sampling strategies available for selecting participants in a qualitative study.
▶ Identify types of qualitative data and weigh the advantages and disadvantages of each form for use in research.
▶ Design an interview and an observational protocol.
▶ Identify the procedures and potential issues involved in gathering qualitative information.

REVISITING THE QUALITATIVE GUNMAN INCIDENT STUDY

Let's use the gunman case study to illustrate the steps used in the process of qualitative data collection (Asmussen & Creswell, 1995). In "The Research Study" section (Paragraph 11), the authors discuss the steps used to obtain permission to conduct the study from the university administration and the institutional review board. Unlike the television violence study, the authors collect information from a small number of sources and do not use instruments that measure variables. They gather information on campus reactions from a small number of people and develop their own interview guide to collect reactions. Posing only five questions during their interviews, the researchers allow room for participants to share their views. They record data to these interview responses on an "interview protocol," a data recording instrument the authors design (Paragraph 11). In short, their data collection procedures—gathering data from a few people, using broad questions, and recording data on their own protocols—reflect the steps in the qualitative data collection process. These steps are:

▶ obtaining permission to conduct the study
▶ selecting participants and sites purposefully to best understand the phenomenon
▶ identifying data from various sources such as observations, interviews, documents, and audio-visual materials
▶ administering and recording data using protocols, such as observational and interview protocols
▶ administering the data collection in a manner sensitive to individuals and sites

GAINING PERMISSION

Similar to quantitative research, gaining access to the site or individual(s) in qualitative inquiry involves obtaining permissions at different levels, such as the organization, the site, the individuals, and the campus institutional review boards. Of special importance is negotiating approval with campus review boards and locating individuals at a site that can facilitate the collection of data.

Seeking Institutional Review Board Approval

Researchers applying for permission to study individuals in a qualitative project must also go through the approval process of a campus institutional review board as outlined in Chapter 6. These steps include seeking permission from the board, developing a description of the project, designing an informed consent form, and having the project reviewed. Because data collection consists of lengthy periods of gathering information in the field and recording detailed personal views from individuals, qualitative researchers need to provide extensive documentation about procedures in their project description for the review boards. Moreover, the boards may not be familiar with the qualitative approach to educational research.

Several strategies might prove useful in negotiating qualitative research through the institutional review board process:

▶ Determine if individuals reviewing proposals on the review board are familiar with qualitative inquiry. Look for those individuals who have experience in conducting qualitative research. This requires a careful assessment of the membership of the review board.

‣ Develop detailed descriptions of the procedures so reviewers have a full disclosure of the potential risks to people and sites in the study.

‣ Detail ways you will protect the anonymity of participants. These might be by masking names of individuals, assigning pseudonyms to individuals and their organizations, or choosing to withhold descriptors that would lead to the identification of participants and sites.

‣ In your proposal to the board, discuss the need to respect the research site and to disturb or disrupt it as little as possible. When you gain permission to enter the site, you need to be respectful of property and refrain from introducing issues that may cause participants to question their group or organization. Doing this requires keeping a delicate balance between exploring a phenomenon in depth and respecting individuals and property at the research site.

‣ Detail how the study will provide opportunities to "give back" or reciprocate in some way to those individuals studied (e.g., you might donate services at the site, provide visibility for the needs of those studied, or share with them any monetary rewards you may receive from your study).

‣ Acknowledge that during your prolonged interaction with participants, you may adopt their beliefs and even become an advocate for their ideas.

‣ Specify potential power imbalances that may occur between yourself and the participants, and how your study will address these imbalances. For example, a power imbalance occurs when a researcher studies his or her own employer or employees in the workplace. If this is your situation, consider researching sites where you do not have a vested interest or collecting data in a way that minimizes a power inequality between yourself and participants (e.g., observing rather than interviewing).

‣ Detail how much time will be spent at the research site. This detail might include the anticipated number of days, the length of each visit, and the times when visits will take place.

‣ Provide additional detail about the nature of the interviews, and include in the project description a list of the interview questions so reviewers on the institutional board can determine how sensitive the questions may be. Typically, qualitative interview questions are open-ended and general in nature, lending support to a non-invasive stance by the researcher.

Gatekeepers

For qualitative research, permissions are needed at many levels to access a site. Because of the in-depth nature of extensive and multiple interviews with participants, it might be helpful for you to identify and make use of a gatekeeper. A **gatekeeper** is an individual who has an official or unofficial role at the site, provides entrance to a site, helps researchers locate people, and assists in the identification of places to study (Hammersley & Atkinson, 1995). For example, this individual may be a teacher, a principal, a group leader, or the informal leader of a special program, and usually has "insider" status at the site the researchers plan to study. Identifying a gatekeeper at a research site and winning his or her support and trust may take time. You might be required to submit written information about the project in order to proceed. Such information might include:

‣ why their site was chosen for study
‣ what will be accomplished at the site during the research study (i.e., time and resources required by participants and yourself)
‣ how much time you will spend at the site

▶ what potential there is for your presence to be disruptive
▶ how you will use and report the results
▶ what the individuals at the site will gain from the study (Bogdan and Biklen, 1998)

Let's look at an example of using a gatekeeper in a qualitative study.

While conducting a qualitative study exploring the behavior of informal student cliques that may display violent behavior, a researcher talks to many high-school personnel. Ultimately, the social studies coordinator emerges as a good gatekeeper. She suggests the researcher use the school cafeteria as an important site to see school cliques in action. She also points out specific student leaders of cliques (e.g., the punk group) that might help the researcher understand student behavior.

SELECTING PARTICIPANTS AND SITES

As in quantitative research, the dual processes of selecting participants and seeking permissions often require a coordinated procedure. However, the selection process in qualitative research differs substantially from its counterpart in quantitative research. In qualitative inquiry the intent is not to generalize to a population, but to develop an in-depth exploration of a central phenomenon (see Chapter 2, "Identifying a Research Problem"). Thus, to best understand this phenomenon, the qualitative researcher purposefully or intentionally selects individuals and sites. This distinction between quantitative "random sampling" and qualitative "purposeful sampling" is portrayed in Figure 7.1. In quantitative research, the focus is on random sampling, selecting representative individuals, and then generalizing from these individuals to a population. Often this process results in testing "theories" that explain the population. On the other hand, in qualitative research, you select people or sites that can

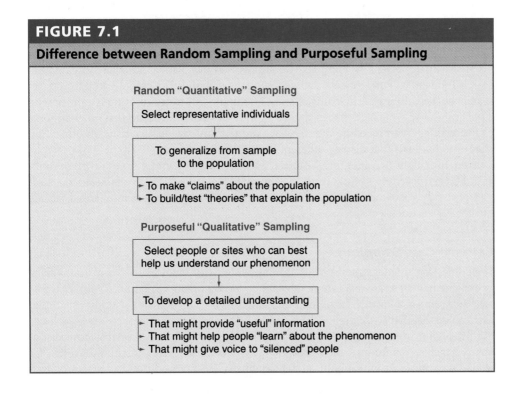

FIGURE 7.1

Difference between Random Sampling and Purposeful Sampling

Random "Quantitative" Sampling

Select representative individuals

To generalize from sample to the population

- To make "claims" about the population
- To build/test "theories" that explain the population

Purposeful "Qualitative" Sampling

Select people or sites who can best help us understand our phenomenon

To develop a detailed understanding

- That might provide "useful" information
- That might help people "learn" about the phenomenon
- That might give voice to "silenced" people

best help you understand the central phenomenon. This understanding emerges through a detailed understanding of the people or site. It can lead to information that allows individuals to "learn" about the phenomenon, or an understanding that provides voice to individuals who may not be heard.

Purposeful Sampling

The research term used for the qualitative sampling approach is called purposeful sampling. In **purposeful sampling,** researchers intentionally select individuals and sites to learn or understand the central phenomenon. The standard used in choosing individuals and sites is whether they are "information rich" (Patton, 1990, p. 169). Further, the words "individuals" and "sites" are carefully chosen. In any given qualitative study, you may decide to study a site (e.g., one college campus), several sites (three small liberal arts campuses), individuals or groups (freshman students), or some combination (purposefully sample two liberal arts campuses and several freshman students on those campuses). Purposeful sampling thus applies to both individuals and sites.

It is also important to understand the criteria that you use to purposefully sample sites or individuals and to be able, in a study, to advance the reasons for your sampling approach. Several discussions can be found in the literature about frequently used sampling strategies (see, for example, Miles & Huberman, 1994; Patton, 1990). As seen in Figure 7.2, there are nine frequently used purposeful sampling strategies that most educators use. These strategies are differentiated in terms of whether they are employed before data collection begins or after data collection has started. Further, each has a different intent, depending on the research problem and questions you would like answered in a study. All strategies apply to sampling a single time or multiple times during a study, and can be used when sampling from information-rich individuals, groups, or entire organizations and sites (see Patton, 1990, for further discussion on these types).

Maximal Variation Sampling

One characteristic of qualitative research is to present multiple perspectives of individuals in order to represent the complexity of our world (see Chapter 2, on "Identifying a Research Problem"). Thus, one sampling strategy is to build that complexity into the research when sampling participants or sites. **Maximal variation sampling** is a purposeful sampling strategy in which the researcher samples cases or individuals that differ on some characteristic. This procedure requires that you identify the characteristic and then find sites or individuals that display different dimensions of that characteristic. For example, a researcher might first identify the characteristic of racial composition of high schools, and then purposefully sample three high schools that differ on this characteristic, such as a primarily Hispanic high school, a predominantly white high school, and a racially diverse high school.

Extreme Case Sampling

Sometimes you are more interested in learning about a case that is particularly troublesome or enlightening, or a case that is noticeable for its success or failure (Patton, 1990). **Extreme case sampling** is a form of purposeful sampling in which the researcher studies an outlier case or one that displays extreme characteristics. Researchers identify these cases by locating persons or organizations that have been cited for achievements or that have distinguished themselves through their problems (e.g., certain elementary schools targeted for federal assistance). An autistic education program in elementary education that has received awards may be an outstanding case to purposefully sample.

FIGURE 7.2

Types of Purposeful Sampling

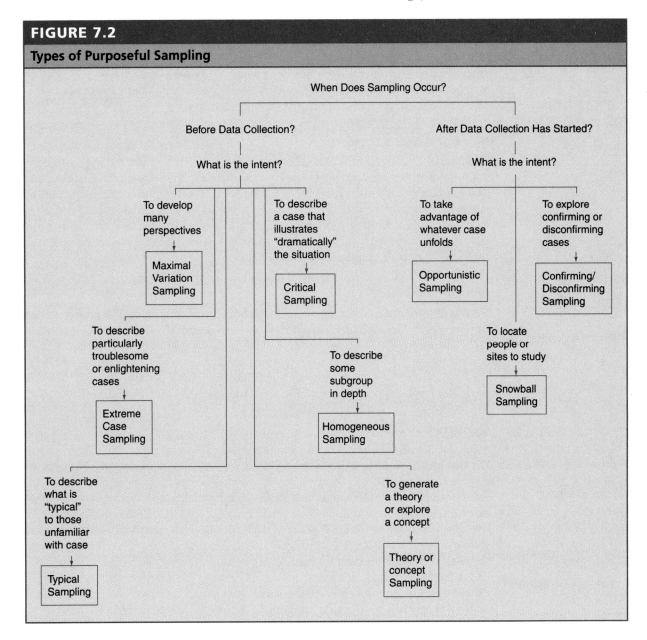

Typical Sampling

Some research questions address "What is normal?" or "What is typical?" **Typical sampling** is a form of purposeful sampling in which the researcher studies a person or site that is "typical" to those unfamiliar with the situation. What constitutes typical, of course, is open to interpretation. However, you might ask persons at a research site or even select a typical case by collecting demographic data or survey data about all cases. A researcher, for example, could study a typical faculty member at a small liberal arts college because that individual has worked at the institution for 20 years and embodies the cultural norms of the school.

Theory or Concept Sampling

Individuals or sites might also be sampled because they help the qualitative researcher understand a concept or a theory. **Theory or concept sampling** is a purposeful sampling strategy where individuals or sites are sampled because they can help the researcher generate or discover a theory or specific concepts within the theory. To use this method of sampling, the researcher needs a clear understanding of the concept or larger theory expected to emerge during the research. In a study of five sites that have experienced distance education, for example, the researcher studies these sites in order to generate a theory of student attitudes toward distance learning.

Homogeneous Sampling

Certain individuals may be sampled because they all possess a similar trait or characteristic. In **homogeneous sampling** the researcher purposefully samples individuals or sites based on membership in a subgroup that has defining characteristics. To use this procedure, you need to identify the characteristics and find individuals or sites that possess it. For example, in a rural community all parents who have children in school participate in a parent program. The researcher chooses members of this parent program to study because they belong to a common subgroup in the community.

Critical Sampling

Sometimes individuals or research sites represent the central phenomenon in dramatic terms (Patton, 1990). The sampling strategy here is to study a **critical sample** because it is an exceptional case and the researcher can learn much about the phenomenon. For example, a researcher studying teenage violence can study a high school where a student with a gun threatened a teacher. This situation represents a dramatic incident that portrays the extent to which some adolescents may embrace violent actions, and is therefore worthy of study.

Opportunistic Sampling

After data collection begins, you may find that new situations arise that need to be studied. **Opportunistic sampling** is purposeful sampling undertaken after the research begins in order to take advantage of unfolding events. In this process the sample emerges during the inquiry. Researchers need to be cautious about engaging in this form of sampling because it might divert attention away from the original aims of the research. On the other hand, it captures the developing or emerging nature of qualitative research nicely, and can lead to novel ideas and surprising findings. For example, a researcher might begin with maximal variation sampling of different pregnant teenagers in high schools. During this process the researcher finds a pregnant teenager who plans to bring her baby to school each day. Because a study of this teenager would provide new insights about balancing children and school, she is studied in depth throughout her pregnancy and during the months after the birth of her child.

Snowball Sampling

In certain research situations the researcher may not know the best people to study because of the unfamiliarity of the topic or the complexity of events. As in quantitative research, **snowball sampling** is a form of purposeful sampling that typically proceeds after a study begins and occurs when the researcher asks participants to recommend other individuals to study. This request, for example, may be posed as a question during an interview or through informal conversations with individuals at a research site. For example, in the gunman case study (Asmussen & Creswell, 1995), the authors asked interviewees if they could recommend other individuals to interview who might have a reaction to the incident. This procedure led to the purposeful sampling of individuals that was not anticipated when the project began. Interviewing the "expert" psychologist brought to the campus to help individuals through the crisis is an example of this.

Confirming and Disconfirming Sampling

A final form of purposeful sampling, also used after studies begin, is to sample individuals or sites in order to confirm or disconfirm preliminary findings. **Confirming and disconfirming sampling** is a purposeful strategy used during a study to follow up on specific cases in order to test out or explore further specific findings. Although this sampling serves to verify the accuracy of the findings throughout a study (see Chapter 9 on "Validating the Accuracy of Finding"), it also represents a sampling procedure used during a study. For example, a researcher finds out that academic department chairs support faculty in their development as teachers by serving as mentors to them. After initially interviewing chairs, this qualitative researcher confirms the mentoring role by sampling and studying chairs who have received praise from faculty as "good" mentors.

Sample or Research Site Size

The number of people and sites sampled vary from one study to the next. It is typical in qualitative research, however, to only study a few individuals or a few cases. This is because the overall ability of a researcher to provide an in-depth picture diminishes with the addition of each new individual or site. Although no set guide exists for how many participants or sites to use, typical guidelines are to:

▶ study one cultural-sharing group in an ethnography
▶ examine three to five cases in a case study
▶ interview 15 to 20 people during a grounded theory study
▶ explore the narrative stories of one individual in narrative research

Let's look at some specific examples to see how many individuals and sites were used. In a qualitative grounded theory study, the researcher examined 20 parents of children labeled as ADHD (Reid, Hertzog, & Snyder, 1996). More extensive data collection was used in a qualitative ethnographic study of the culture of fraternity life and the exploitation and victimization of women. Rhoads (1995) conducted 12 formal interviews and 18 informal interviews; made observations; and collected numerous documents. Studies may also address single individuals. For example, in the qualitative case study of Basil McGee, a second-year middle school science teacher, Brickhouse and Bodner (1992) explored his beliefs about science and science teaching and how his beliefs shaped classroom instruction.

IDENTIFYING DATA TO COLLECT

Another aspect of qualitative data collection is to identify the types of data that will address the research central question and subquestions. Based on the characteristics introduced in Chapter 2, you might remember that collecting qualitative data consists of obtaining the perspective of participants using data collection forms that are less structured and more open-ended than those used in quantitative research. Qualitative inquirers pose general, broad questions to participants, allowing them to share their views relatively unconstrained by the researcher's perspectives. In addition, qualitative researchers rely on multiple sources of information, and often add new forms of data collection to best understand the phenomenon being explored. Further, qualitative researchers engage in extensive data collection, spending a great deal of time with documents or in the field. Using this process, researchers gather detailed information in order to establish the complexity of their central phenomenon.

We can see the varied nature of qualitative forms of data when they are put into the following categories:

▶ observations
▶ interviews
▶ documents
▶ audio-visual materials

Specific examples of types of data in these four categories are shown in Figure 7.3. Variations on data collection in all four areas are emerging continuously. Most recently, videotapes, student classroom portfolios, and the use of e-mails as a source of visual materials are attracting increasing attention as forms of data. Table 7.1 shows each category of data collection listed above, the type of data it yields, and a definition for that type of data. Now let's take a closer look at each of the four categories and their strengths and weaknesses.

FIGURE 7.3

A Compendium of Data Collection Approaches in Qualitative Research

Observations

Gather fieldnotes by:
▶ conducting an observation as a participant
▶ conducting an observation as an observer
▶ spending more time as a participant than observer
▶ spending more time as an observer than a participant
▶ first observing as an "outsider," then participating in the setting and observing as an "insider"

Interviews

Conduct an unstructured, open-ended interview and take interview notes.
Conduct an unstructured, open-ended interview, audio-tape the interview, and transcribe the interview.
Conduct a semi-structured interview, audio-tape the interview, and transcribe the interview.
Conduct focus group interviews, audio-tape the interview, and transcribe the interview.

Documents

Keep a journal during the research study.
Have a participant keep a journal or diary during the research study.
Collect personal letters from participants.
Analyze public documents (e.g., official memos, minutes of meetings, records or archival material).
Analyze school documents (e.g., attendance reports, retention rates, dropout rates, or discipline referrals).
Examine autobiographies and biographies.
Take (or have participants take) photographs or videotapes (e.g., photo elicitation).
Collect or draw maps and seating charts.
Examine portfolios or less formal examples of students' work.

Audio-visual Materials

Examine physical trace evidence (e.g., footprints in the snow).
Videotape a social situation of an individual or group.
Examine photographs or videotapes.
Collect sounds (e.g., musical sounds, a child's laughter, or car horns honking).
Collect e-mail or electronic messages.
Examine possessions or ritual objects.

Source: Creswell, 1998; Mills, 2000.

TABLE 7.1		
Forms of Qualitative Data Collection		
Forms of Data Collection	**Type of Data**	**Definition of Type of Data**
Observations	Observational fieldnotes and drawings	Unstructured observational data consisting of observing and taking fieldnotes or constructing drawings about a setting
Interviews	Transcribed audio-tape or hand-recorded interview transcriptions	Unstructured interviews consisting of asking a few, open-ended questions and recording the views and meaning of participant interviewees
Documents	Documents that are optically scanned or used in their original state	Information that is available to the researcher in the form of both public or private sources
Audio-visual materials	Audio-visual materials that are transcribed or used in their original state	Audio-visual materials consisting of images or sounds of people or places recorded by the participant or by someone else

Observations

When educators think about qualitative research they often have in mind the process of collecting observational data in a specific school setting. Unquestionably, observations represent a frequently used form of data collection with the researcher able to assume different roles in the process (Spradley, 1980).

Observation is the process of gathering first-hand information by observing people and places at a research site. Unlike quantitative inquirers, qualitative inquirers do not use instruments developed by other researchers; rather, they design their own data-gathering observational forms. (Later we will discuss these forms as "observational protocols.") These forms are "unstructured" in that they do not rely on predetermined questions or scales, as do forms used in quantitative research. Using these unstructured forms, researchers record data such as the behaviors of individuals, chronological lists of the sequence of events, physical diagrams depicting the setting, and specific quotes of individuals.

As a form of data collection, observation has both advantages and disadvantages. Advantages include the opportunity to record information as it occurs in a setting, to study actual behavior, and to study individuals who have difficulty verbalizing their ideas (e.g., preschool children). Disadvantages include being limited to those sites and situations where researchers can gain access, and the difficulty in developing rapport with the necessary individuals at a site. This can occur if the individuals are unaccustomed to formal research (e.g., a non-university setting). Observing in a setting requires good listening skills and careful attention to visual detail. It also requires management of issues such as the potential deception by people being observed and the initial awkwardness of being an "outsider" without initial personal support in a setting (Hammersley & Atkinson, 1995).

Observational Roles

Despite these potential difficulties, observation continues to be a well-accepted form of qualitative data collection. Using it requires adopting a particular role as an observer. No one role is suited for all situations; observational roles vary depending on the researcher's comfort at the site, the rapport they have with participants, and how information can best be collected to understand the central phenomenon. Although many roles exist (see Spradley, 1980), three roles that are popular in educational research will be emphasized here.

Role of a Participant Observer   To truly learn about a situation, you can become involved in activities at the research site. This offers excellent opportunities to see experiences from the views of participants. A **participant observer** is an observational role adopted by researchers when they take part in activities in the setting they observe. As a participant, the researcher assumes the role of an "inside" observer who actually engages in activities at the site being studied. At the same time they are participating in activities, researchers record information. This role requires seeking permission to participate in activities and assuming a comfortable role as observer in the setting. It is difficult to take notes while participating, and some qualitative researchers wait to write down observations until after they have left the research site.

Role of a Non-Participant Observer   In some situations, you may not be familiar with the site and people to participate in the activities. A **non-participant observer** is an observer who visits a site and records notes without becoming involved in the activities of the participants. The non-participant observer is an "outsider" who sits on the periphery or some advantageous place to see the phenomenon under study (i.e., the back of the classroom), and watches and records the activities. This role requires less access than the participant role and gatekeepers and individuals at a research site may be more comfortable with it. However, by not actively participating, the researcher is partially removed from actual experiences, and the observations made may not be as concrete as if the inquirer had participated in the activities.

Changing Observational Roles   In many observational situations, it is advantageous to shift or change roles, making it difficult to classify your role as strictly participatory or nonparticipatory. A **changing observational role** is one where researchers adapt their role to the situation. For example, a researcher might first enter a site and observe as a non-participant, simply needing to "look around" in the early phases of research. Then the researcher might slowly become involved as a participant. Sometimes the reverse happens, and a participant becomes a non-participant. However, entering a site as a non-participant is a frequently used approach. After a short time, when rapport is developed, the researcher switches to a participant in the setting. Engaging in both roles permits the inquirer to be subjectively involved in the setting as well as to see the setting more objectively.

Here are two illustrations where researchers began as non-participants and changed into participants during the process of observing:

- One researcher studying the use of wireless laptop computers in a multicultural education methods class spent the first three visits to the class observing from the back row. He sought to learn about how the course was being conducted, the instructor's interaction with students, and the instructor's overall approach to teaching. Then, on his fourth visit, students began using the laptop computers and the observer became a participant by teaming with a student who used the laptop from her desk to interact with the instructor's Web site.

▶ A researcher decided to explore the disciplinary behavior of junior high students in a school cafeteria. New to the setting, the researcher began observing the students during lunch from a position just inside the cafeteria door. This observational post was used for the first month. After the students became used to seeing the researcher, she started eating lunch in the cafeteria and became a participant in the setting, observing student disciplinary behavior at the lunch tables.

The Process of Observing

As we just saw in the discussion of different observational roles, the qualitative inquirer engages in a process of observing, regardless of the role. This general process is outlined in the steps below.

1. *Select a site to be observed that can help you best understand the central phenomenon.* Obtain the required permissions needed to gain access to the site.
2. *Ease into the site slowly by looking around; getting a general sense of the site; and taking limited notes, at least initially.* Conduct brief observations at first, because you will likely be overwhelmed with all of the activities taking place. This slow entry helps to build rapport with individuals at the site and helps you assimilate the large amount of information.
3. *At the site, identify who or what to observe, when to observe, and how long to observe.* Gatekeepers can provide guidance as you make these decisions. You will also be limited by the practical requirements of the situation, such as the length of a class period or the duration of the activity.
4. *Determine, initially, your role as an observer.* Select from the roles of participant or non-participant during your first few observations. Consider whether it would be advantageous to change roles during the process in order to best learn about the individuals or site. Regardless of whether you change roles, consider what role will be used first and your reasons for it.
5. *Conduct multiple observations over time to obtain the best understanding of the site and the individuals.* Engage in broad observation at first, noting the general landscape of activities and events. As you become familiar with the setting, you can begin to narrow your observations to specific aspects (e.g., a small group of children interacting during reading time). A broad-to-narrow perspective is a useful strategy because it can keep you from becoming overwhelmed by information and it can help you locate insightful behavior or activities.
6. *Design some means for recording notes during an observation.* The data recorded during an observation are called fieldnotes. **Fieldnotes** are text (words) recorded by the researcher during an observation in a qualitative study. Later in this chapter we will learn about the actual recording form typically used, an "observational protocol." But for now, it is helpful to see how fieldnotes might be written in an actual observational session.

   Examine the sample fieldnotes shown in Figure 7.4. In this example, the student-observer engaged in participant observation when the instructor asked the class to spend 20 minutes observing an art object that had been brought into the classroom. This object was not familiar to the students in the class. It was from Indonesia and had a square, bamboo base and a horse-hair top. It was probably used for some religious activities. This was a good object to use for an observational activity because it could not be easily recognized or described. The students were asked to observe the object and record fieldnotes describing the object and reflecting on their insights, hunches, and themes that emerged during the observation.

FIGURE 7.4

Sample Fieldnotes from a Student's Observation of an Art Object

---

| Observational Fieldnotes | —Art Object in the Classroom |

Setting: Classroom 306
Observer: J
Role of Observer: Observer of object
Time: 4:30 p.m., March 9, 1999
Length of Observation: 20 minutes

Description of Object	*Reflective Notes* (insights, hunches, themes)
4:35 p.m <u>Touch</u> J tap on the base. Gritty wood, pieced together unevenly. The objects top feels like a cheap wig. The based was moved and the canning was tight. The wicker feels smooth.	—Many students touch the object—most walk up slowly, cautiously. —Several good analogies come to mind.
4:40 <u>Sight</u> The object stands on four pegs that holds a square base. The basic is decorated with scalloped carvings. The wood is a light, natural color and sanded smooth and finished. It is in the shape of a pyramid, cropped close at the bottom on the underside.	—This object is really hard to describe— perhaps J should use dimensions? But it has several parts.
4:50 <u>Sound</u> Students comment as they touched the object, "Oh, that's hair? Is it securely fastened?" A slight rustling is heard from brushing the bristles . . ."	—Pickup on good quotes from the students. —"Sounds" could definitely be one of my themes!
5:02 The object <u>smells</u> like roof-dry stale. It is odorless. But it has a musty, dusty scent to the top half, and no one wants to sniff it.	—This object seems to change smells the more J am around it—probably a dusty scent fits it best.

As we see in Figure 7.4, one student recorded the senses—touch, sight, sound, and smell—of the object, recording thoughts every five minutes or so. Notice that the student's fieldnotes show complete sentences and notations about quotes from other students. The notes in the right column indicate that this student is beginning to reflect on the larger ideas learned from the experiences and to note how other students in the class are reacting to the object. The heading at the top of the fieldnotes records essential information about the time, place, and activities being observed.

7. *Consider what information you will record during an observation.* For example, this information might include portraits of the participants, the physical setting,

particular events and activities, and personal reactions (Bogdan & Biklen, 1998). In observing a classroom, for example, you may record activities by the teacher, the students, the interactions between the students and teacher and the student-to-student conversations.

8. *Record descriptive and reflective fieldnotes.* **Descriptive fieldnotes** record a description of the events, activities, and people (e.g., what happened). **Reflective fieldnotes** record personal thoughts that researchers have that relate to their insights, hunches, or broad ideas or themes that emerge during the observation (e.g., what sense did you make of the site, people, and situation).

9. *Make yourself known, but remain unobtrusive.* During the observation, be introduced by someone if you are an "outsider" or new to the setting or people. Be passive, be friendly, and be respectful of the people and site.

10. *After observing, slowly withdraw from the site.* Thank the participants and inform them of the use of the data and the availability of a summary of results when you complete the study.

Figure 7.5 summarizes the 10 steps listed above. You might use the checklist in your own observational study or when evaluating the observations reported in a published study. The questions on this checklist are presented in roughly the order in which you might consider them before, during, and after the observation, but you can check off each question as you complete it.

Interviews

Equally popular to observation in qualitative research is interviewing. Conducting a qualitative **interview** is the process where researchers ask one or more participants in a study mostly general, open-ended questions and record their answers. This information is then transcribed or typed into a data file for analysis.

FIGURE 7.5

An Observational Checklist

_____ Did you gain permission to study the site?

_____ Do you know your role as an observer?

_____ Do you have a means for recording fieldnotes, such as an observational protocol?

_____ Do you know what you will observe first?

_____ Will you enter and leave the site slowly, so as to not disturb the setting?

_____ Will you make multiple observations over time?

_____ Will you develop rapport with individuals at the site?

_____ Will your observations change from broad to narrow?

_____ Will you take limited notes at first?

_____ Will you take both descriptive as well as reflective notes?

_____ Will you describe in complete sentences so that you have detailed fieldnotes?

_____ Did you thank your participants at the site?

Distinct from quantitative interviewing, the qualitative inquirer does not use an instrument with specific, predetermined scales. Instead, researchers ask a small number of open-ended questions that permit the participants to answer from their point of view. There are basically three types of interviews:

▶ structured interviews
▶ unstructured interviews
▶ semi-structured interviews

As shown in Figure 7.6, when interviewers collect data in *quantitative* research they use close-ended response options in structured interviews in which they obtain scores (or numerical values) to their questions. **Close-ended responses** are options to questions that specify the choices available to the participant. As discussed in Chapter 6, "Selecting Scales of Measurement," nominal, ordinal, and interval/ratio types of scales provide close-ended responses to questions. For example, assume a researcher asks this question in an interview:

Please mark your answer:
Student policies governing binge drinking on campus should be made more stringent.
_____ Strongly agree
_____ Agree
_____ Neither agree nor disagree (undecided)
_____ Disagree
_____ Strongly disagree

In this question, the participant is given five choices (an interval rating scale) from which to choose a response. The responses are "closed" in the sense that these five options, and only these five, may be used. During a **structured interview**, the researcher asks the participant questions with close-ended response options. This is the form of interviewing frequently used in quantitative research.

In *qualitative* research, open-ended questions are asked so that the participant can best voice their experiences unconstrained by any perspectives of the researcher or past research findings. An **open-ended response** to a question allows the participant to create the options for responding. For example, in a qualitative interview of athletes in high schools, a researcher might ask: How do you balance participation in athletics with your schoolwork? The athlete then creates a response to this question without being forced into response possibilities. The researcher often audio-tapes the conversation and transcribes the information

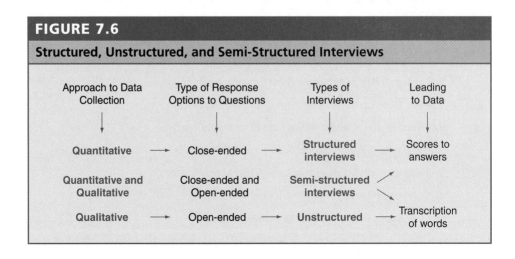

FIGURE 7.6

Structured, Unstructured, and Semi-Structured Interviews

Approach to Data Collection	Type of Response Options to Questions	Types of Interviews	Leading to Data
↓	↓	↓	↓
Quantitative →	Close-ended →	Structured interviews →	Scores to answers
Quantitative and Qualitative	Close-ended and Open-ended	Semi-structured interviews	
Qualitative →	Open-ended →	Unstructured →	Transcription of words

into words for analysis. This type of question is popular in qualitative research and is included in unstructured interviews. In an **unstructured interview,** the researcher asks open-ended questions that permit the participant to create response possibilities. This type of interview represents the most frequently used form of interviewing in qualitative research.

In addition to structured and unstructured interviews, semi-structured interviews are used in both quantitative and qualitative research. In **semi-structured interviews,** the researcher asks some questions that are close-ended and some questions that are open-ended. The advantage of this type of interviewing is that the predetermined close-ended responses can net useful information to support theories and concepts in the literature. The open-ended responses, on the other hand, can allow the participant to provide personal experiences that may be outside or beyond those identified in the close-ended options. For example, a researcher might ask a close-ended question followed by an open-ended question:

Please tell me the extent of your agreement or disagreement with this statement:
    Student policies governing binge drinking on campus should be made more stringent.
_____ Do you strongly agree?
_____ Do you agree?
_____ Are you undecided?
_____ Do you disagree?
_____ Do you strongly disagree?
Please explain your response in more detail.

_____

_____

_____

Semi-structured interviews are found in both qualitative and quantitative research, but they are more frequently used in quantitative research because they narrow the participants' responses and may restrict the multiple perspectives sought by qualitative inquirers.

In qualitative research, interviews are typically unstructured or, less frequently, semi-structured. These types of interviews have both advantages and disadvantages. Some advantages are that they provide useful information when participants cannot be directly observed and they permit participants to describe detailed personal information. As compared to observations, the interviewer also has better control over the types of information received since specific questions can be asked to elicit this information.

Some disadvantages are that interviews only provide information "filtered" through the views of the interviewers (i.e., the researcher summarizes the participants' views in the research report). Also, similar to observations, interview data may be deceptive and provide the perspective the interviewee wants the researcher to hear. Another disadvantage is that the presence of the researcher may affect how the interviewee responds. Interviewee responses also may not be articulate, perceptive, or clear. In addition, equipment issues may be a problem, and recording and transcribing equipment (if used) needs to be organized in advance of the interview. Also during the interview, researchers need to give some attention to the conversation with the participants. This attention may require saying little, handling emotional outbursts, and using ice-breakers to encourage individuals to talk. With all of these issues to balance, it is little wonder inexperienced researchers express surprise about the difficulty of conducting interviews.

Types of Interviews

Once you decide that the advantages of interviewing outweigh the disadvantages, you need to consider what form of interviewing will best help you understand the central phenomena and answer the questions in a study. There are a number of approaches to interviewing in qualitative research, including one-on-one interviews, focus group interviews, telephone interviews, and e-mail interviews. Which approach to use will ultimately depend on the accessibility of individuals to interview, the cost, and the amount of time available to interview.

One-on-One Interviews   The most time-consuming and costly approach is to conduct individual interviews. A popular approach in educational research, the **one-on-one interview** is the data collection process where the researcher asks questions to and records answers from only one participant in the study at a time. In a qualitative project, several one-on-one interviews may be used, such as asking administrators and student health counselors to provide their impressions of the gunman incident (see Asmussen & Creswell, 1995). One-on-one interviews are ideal for interviewing participants who are not hesitant to speak, are articulate, and who can share ideas comfortably.

Focus Group Interviews   Focus groups can be used to collect shared understanding from several individuals as well as to get views from specific people. A **focus group interview** is the process of collecting data through interviews with a group of people, typically four to six. The researcher asks a small number of general questions and elicits responses from all individuals in the group. Focus groups are advantageous when the interaction among interviewees will likely yield the best information and when interviewees are similar to and cooperative with each other. They are also useful when the time to collect information is limited and individuals are hesitant to provide information (although some individuals may be reluctant to provide information in any type of interview).

When conducting a focus group interview, care must be taken to encourage all participants to talk and encourage individuals to take their turn talking. This type of interview can pose challenges for the interviewer who lacks control over the interview discussion. Also, when focus groups are audio-taped, the transcriptionist may have difficulty discriminating among the voices of individuals in the group. Another problematic aspect of conducting focus group interviews is that the researcher often has difficulty taking notes because so much is occurring.

Let's consider an example of a focus group interview procedure:

> High school students, with the sponsorship of a university team of researchers, conducted focus group interviews with other students about the use of tobacco in several high schools (Plano Clark, Creswell, Miller, Harter, Mickelson, McEntarffer, & McVea, 2001). In several interviews, two student interviewers—one to ask questions and one to record responses—selected 6 students to interview in a focus group. These focus group interviews lasted one-half hour and the interviewers tape-recorded the interview and took notes during the interview. Because the groups were small, the transcriptionist did not have difficulty transcribing the interview and identifying individual voices. This process was enhanced by having each student, at the beginning of the interview, say his or her first name.

Telephone Interviews   It may not be possible for you to gather groups of individuals for an interview or visit one-on-one with single individuals. The participants in a study may be geographically dispersed and be unable to come to a central location for an interview. In this situation, a telephone interview is needed. Conducting a **telephone interview** is the process of gathering data using the telephone and asking a small number of general questions. A telephone interview requires that the researcher use a telephone adaptor that plugs into both the phone and a tape recorder for a clear recording of the interview. One drawback of this kind of interviewing is that the researcher does not have direct contact with the participant. This causes limited communication that may affect the researcher's ability to understand the interviewee's perceptions of the phenomenon. Also, the process may involve substantial costs for telephone time. Now let's look at an example of a telephone interview procedure:

> In a study of academic department chairpersons in colleges and universities, Creswell, Wheeler, Seagren, Egly, & Beyer (1990) conducted open-ended telephone interviews lasting 45 minutes each with 200 chairpersons located on campuses in the United States. They first obtained the permission of these chairpersons to participate in an interview through contacting them by letter. They also scheduled a time that would be convenient for the interviewee to participate in a telephone interview. Next, they purchased tape recorders and adaptors so that the interviews could be conducted from the office phones of the research team. They asked open-ended questions, such as "How did you prepare for your position?", "What type of support do you provide for faculty in your department?", and "What strategies are most effective?" The interviews yielded about 3000 transcript pages that were used in a report about the practices of chairpersons in enhancing the professional development of faculty in their departments.

E-Mail Interviews   A final form of interviewing that is useful in collecting qualitative data quickly from a geographically dispersed group of people is the e-mail interview. **E-mail interviews** consist of collecting open-ended data through interviews from individuals using computers and Web sites or the Internet. If you can obtain e-mail lists or addresses, this form of interviewing provides rapid access to large numbers of people and a detailed, rich text database for qualitative analysis. It can also promote a conversation between yourself as the researcher and the participants, so that through follow-up conversations you can extend your understanding of the topic or central phenomenon being studied. On the other hand, e-mail interviewing raises complex ethical issues, such as whether you have permission for individuals to participate in your interview, and whether you will protect the privacy of responses. In addition, it may be difficult, under some circumstances, to obtain good lists of e-mail addresses that are current or the names of individuals who will be well suited to answer your questions. For example, how do you locate e-mail addresses for children under the age of 10 who probably do not have an address? Despite these potential shortcomings, e-mail interviewing as a form of collecting data will probably increase due to the expanding possibilities of technology. Consider this example of an open-ended e-mail survey:

> Four researchers combined resources to develop an e-mail list of faculty who might be teaching courses in mixed method research (Creswell, Tashakkori, Jensen, & Shapely, in press). They began with an e-mail list of 31 faculty and sent an open-ended interview to these faculty inquiring about their teaching practices. They asked, for example, "Have you ever taught a course with a content of mixed methods research?", "Why do you think students enroll in a mixed method course?", and "What is your general assessment of mixed methods teaching?" After receiving the e-mail survey, the participants answered each question by writing about their experiences, and sent the survey back using the "reply" feature of their e-mail program. This procedure led to a qualitative text database of open-ended responses from a large number of individuals who have experienced mixed method research.

Conducting Interviews

In all of the various forms of interviewing, there are several general steps involved in conducting interviews:

1. *Identify the interviewees.* Use one of the purposeful sampling strategies discussed earlier in this chapter.

2. *Determine the type of interview you will use.* Choose the one that will allow you to best learn the participant's views and answer each research question. Consider a telephone interview, a focus group interview, a one-on-one interview, an e-mail interview, or some combination of these forms.

3. *During the interview, audio-tape the questions and responses.* This will give you an accurate record of the conversation. Use adequate recording procedures, such as lapel microphone equipment (small microphones that connect onto the shirt or collar) for one-on-one interviewing, and a suitable directional microphone (one that picks up sounds in all directions) for focus-group interviewing. Have an adequate tape recorder and telephone adapter for telephone interviews, and understand thoroughly mail programs for e-mail interviewing.

4. *Take brief notes during the interview.* Although it is sound practice to audio-tape the interview, take notes in the event the tape recorder malfunctions. These notes are recorded on a form called an "interview protocol," discussed later in this chapter. Recognize that notes taken during the interview may be incomplete because of the difficulty of asking questions and writing answers at the same time. An abbreviated form for writing notes (e.g., short phrases followed by a dash) may speed up the process.

5. *Locate a quiet, suitable place for conducting the interview.* If possible, interview at a location free from distractions and choose a physical setting that lends itself to audio-taping. This means, for example, that a busy teachers' or faculty lounge may not be the best place for interviewing because of the noise and the interruptions that may occur.

6. *Obtain consent from the interviewee to participate in the study.* Do this by having them complete an informed consent form when you first arrive. Before starting the interview, convey to the participant the purpose of the study, the time the interview will take to complete, the plans for using the results from the interview, and the availability of a summary of the study when the research is completed.

7. *Have a plan, but be flexible.* During the interview, stay to the questions, but be flexible enough to follow the conversation of the interviewee. Complete the questions within the time specified (if possible) to respect and be courteous of the participants. Recognize that a key to good interviewing is to be a good listener.

8. *Use probes to obtain additional information.* **Probes** are subquestions under each question that the researcher asks to elicit more information. Use them to clarify points or to have the interviewee expand on ideas. These probes vary from exploring the content in more depth (elaborating) to asking the interviewee to explain the answer in more detail (clarifying). As shown in Table 7.2, there are two types of probes: clarifying probes and elaborating probes. A specific illustration from the gunman case study is used in Table 7.2 to convey examples of both clarifying and elaborating probes.

9. *Be courteous and professional when the interview is over.* Complete the interview by thanking the participant, assuring him or her of the confidentiality of the responses, and asking if he or she would like a summary of the results of the study.

Let's return to our high school teacher, Maria, who needs to decide what data collection procedure to use. Since she has experience talking with students and fellow teachers, she decides interviewing would be best. She proceeds to conduct five interviews with students and five with teachers in her high school. After obtaining permission from the school district and the principal of her school, she must obtain permission from the students (and their parents or guardians) and the teachers. To select these individuals she will purposefully sample individuals who can speak from different perspectives (maximal variation sampling). She realizes there are different groups in the school, such as the "athletes," the

TABLE 7.2

Types of Probes Used in Qualitative Interviewing

	Examples	
	Clarifying Probes	**Elaborating Probes**
A question in the gunman case study asks, "What has happened since the event that you have been involved in?" Assume that the interviewee says, "not much" or simply does not answer.	Probe Areas *Comments to other students:* "Tell me about discussions you had with other students." *Role of parents:* "Did you talk with your parents?" *Role of news media:* "Did you talk with any media personnel?"	"Tell me more." "Could you explain your response more?" "I need more detail." "What does 'not much' mean?"

"singers," the "punkers," the "class officers," and the "cheerleaders." She identifies one student from each group, realizing that she will likely obtain diverse perspectives representing complex views on the topic of weapon possession. Next she selects five teachers, each representing different subject areas such as social studies, science, physical education, music, and drama. Next, she will need to develop five open-ended questions, such as "How do weapons come in to our school?" or "What type of weapons are in our school?" She needs to schedule interviews, conduct them, record information on audio-tapes, take notes, and respect the views and rights of the students and faculty participating in the interviews.

Documents

A valuable source of information in qualitative research can be documents. **Documents** consist of public and private records that qualitative researchers can obtain about a site or participants in a study and include newspapers, minutes of meetings, personal journals, and letters. These sources provide valuable information in helping researchers understand central phenomena in qualitative studies. They are categorized into public and private documents. Examples of public documents are minutes from meetings, official memos, records in the public domain, and archival material in libraries. Private documents consist of personal journals and diaries, letters, personal notes, and jottings individuals write to themselves. Other materials such as e-mail comments or Web site data can be considered both public and private, and they represent a growing data source for qualitative researchers.

Documents represent a good source for text (word) data for a qualitative study. They provide the advantage of being in the language and words of the participants, who have usually given thoughtful attention to them. They are also ready for analysis without the necessary transcription that is required with observational or interview data.

On the downside, documents are sometimes difficult to locate and obtain. Information can be protected from public use or located in distant archives, requiring the researcher to travel, which takes time and can be expensive. Further, the documents may be incomplete, inauthentic, or inaccurate. For example, not all minutes from school board meetings are accurate because they may not be reviewed for accuracy by the board members. Also, for personal documents such as diaries or letters, the handwriting may be hard to read, making it difficult to decipher the information.

Collecting Documents

With so much variation in the types of documents, no common procedure can be easily described. However, here are several useful guidelines for collecting documents in qualitative research:

1. Identify the types of documents that can provide useful information to answer the qualitative research questions.
2. Consider both public and private documents as sources of information for qualitative research.
3. Once the documents are located, seek permission to use them from the appropriate individuals.
4. If participants are asked to journal, provide specific instructions describing how they should go about it. These guidelines might include what topics and format to use, the length of journal entries, and the importance of writing their thoughts legibily.
5. Once permission to use documents is granted, examine the documents for accuracy, completeness, and usefulness in answering the research questions in your study.
6. Record information from the documents. This process can take several forms, including taking notes about the documents, or, if possible, optically scanning them so a text (or word) file is created for each document. Newspaper stories can easily be scanned to form a qualitative text database. For example, to obtain speeches on education given by the presidential candidates in the U.S. elections, a researcher could optically scan newspapers and develop a computer file (i.e., a text file) of presidential speeches.

Collecting personal documents can provide a researcher with a rich source of information. For example, consider a study that used women's journals.

> An important source for learning about women in superintendent positions is for them to keep a personal journal or diary of their experiences. A researcher asked three women superintendents to keep a diary for six months and record their reactions to being a woman in their capacity of conducting official meetings comprised primarily of men.

These journals were useful for learning about the working lives of women in educational settings.

Audio-Visual Materials

The final type of qualitative data to collect is visual images. **Audio-visual materials** consist of images or sounds that are collected to help the qualitative researcher understand the central phenomenon under study. Images or visual materials are being used more and more often in qualitative research. Photographs, videotapes, digital images, paintings and pictures, and physical traces of images (e.g., footsteps in the snow) are all sources of information for qualitative inquiry. One approach in using photography is the technique of photo elicitation. In this approach, participants are shown pictures (their own or those taken by the researcher) and asked to discuss the contents. These pictures might be personal photographs or albums of historical photographs (see Ziller, 1990).

The advantage of using visual materials is that people easily relate to images because they are so pervasive in our society. Images provide an opportunity for the participant to directly share their perceptions of reality. Images such as videotapes and films, for example, provide extensive data about real life as people visualize it. A potential disadvantage of using images is that they are difficult to analyze because of the rich information (e.g., how do you make sense of all of the aspects apparent in 50 drawings by practice teachers of what it is like to be a science teacher?). Also, researchers may influence the data collected. In selecting the photo album to examine or the type of drawing to be sketched, researchers may impose their meaning of the phenomenon upon participants, rather than obtain the participant's view. When videotaping, researchers face the issue of what to tape, where to place the camera, and the need to be sensitive to camera-shy individuals.

Collecting Audio-Visual Materials

Despite these potential problems, visual material is becoming more popular in qualitative research, especially with recent advances in technology. The steps involved in collecting visual material are similar to the steps involved in collecting documents:

1. Determine what visual material can provide information to answer research questions and how that material might augment existing forms of data, such as interviews and observations.
2. Identify the visual material available and obtain permission to use it. This permission might require asking all students in a classroom, for example, to sign informed consent forms (as well as have their parents sign them).
3. Check the accuracy and authenticity of the visual material if you do not record it yourself. One way to check for accuracy is to contact and interview the photographer or the individuals represented in the pictures.
4. Collect the data and organize it. The data may be optically scanned for easy storage and retrieval.

To illustrate the use of visual material, look at this example in which the researcher used cameras to obtain photographs:

> Polaroid cameras are given to 40 male and 40 female fourth graders in a science unit to record their meaning of the environment. The participants are asked to take pictures of images that represent attempts to preserve the environment in our society. As a result the researcher obtains 24 pictures from each child that can be used to understand how young people look at the environment. Understandably, photos of squirrels and pets outside are predominate among the pictures in this database.

ADMINISTERING AND RECORDING DATA

An essential process in qualitative research is recording data (Lofland & Lofland, 1995). This process involves recording information through research protocols and administering data collection while being sensitive to both field issues that may arise and ethical concerns that may affect the quality of the data.

Using Protocols

As already discussed, for documents and visual materials, the process of recording information may be informal (taking notes) or formal (optically scanning the material to develop a complete computer text file). For observations and interviews, qualitative inquirers use specially designed protocols. **Data recording protocols** are forms designed and used by qualitative researchers to record information during observations and interviews. We will now discuss the design and development of these protocols.

An Interview Protocol

During interviewing, it is important to have some means for structuring the interview and taking careful notes. As already mentioned, audio-taping interviews provides a detailed record of the interview. To augment the audio-tape, the interviewer takes notes during the interview. These notes, as well as the questions to be asked, are included in an interview protocol. An **interview protocol** is a form designed by the researcher that contains instructions for the process of the interview, the questions to be asked, and space to take notes on responses from the interviewee.

Development and Design of an Interview Protocol   To best understand the design and appearance of this form, examine the qualitative interview protocol used during the gunman case study (Asmussen & Creswell, 1995), shown in Figure 7.7. This figure is a reduced version of the actual protocol; in the original protocol, more space was provided between the questions to record answers. Figure 7.7 illustrates the components that might be designed into a typical interview protocol. These components are discussed below.

▶ It contains a header to record essential information about the interview, statements about the purpose of the study, a reminder that participants need to sign the consent form, and a suggestion to make preliminary tests of the audio-recording equipment. Other information you might include in the header would be the organization or work affiliation of the interviewees; their educational background and position; the number of years they have been in the position; and the date, time, and location of the interview.

▶ This header is followed by five brief open-ended questions that allow participants maximum flexibility in responding to the questions. The first question serves the purpose of an "ice-breaker" (sometimes called the "grand tour" question) to relax the interviewees and motivate them to talk. This question should be easy to understand and cause the participants to reflect on experiences that they can easily discuss, such as "Please describe your role in the incident." The final question on this particular instrument helps the researcher locate additional people to study.

▶ The core questions, two through four, are intended to address major research questions in the study. For those new to qualitative research, you might ask more than four questions to help elicit more discussion from interviewees and move through awkward moments when no one is talking. However, the more questions you ask, the more you are examining what you seek to learn rather than learning from the participant. There is often a fine line between your questions being too detailed or too general. A pilot test of them on a few participants can usually help you decide which ones to use.

▶ In addition to the five questions shown in Figure 7.7, the researchers might have used probes. For example, the words, "clarify" or "elaborate" might have been listed under each question. Some specific topics could also be used as probes, for example:

3. What has been the impact on the University community of this incident?
Probes: Clarify? Elaborate?
Probes: Incident being discussed? Concern reduced now? Students still afraid?
          Administrators taking action?

▶ Space is provided between the questions so that the researcher can take short notes about comments made by interviewees. These notes should be brief and can be stated in abbreviated form. The style for recording these notes varies from researcher to researcher.

▶ It is helpful for the interviewer to memorize the wording and the order of the questions in order to minimize losing eye contact. Provide appropriate verbal transitions from one question to the next. Recognize that individuals do not always respond directly to the questions being asked. For example, while asking question two, they may respond to question four.

FIGURE 7.7
Sample Interview Protocol

Interview Protocol
Project: University Reaction to a Gunman Incident Time of Interview: Date: Place: Interviewer: Interviewee: Position of Interviewee: [Describe here the project, telling the interviewee about the (a) purpose of the study, (b) individuals and sources of data being collected, (c) what will be done with the data to protect the confidentiality of the interviewee, and (d) how long the interview will take.] [Have the interviewee read and sign the consent form.] [Turn on the tape recorder and test it.] Questions: 1. Please describe your role in the incident. 2. What has happened since the event that you have been involved in? 3. What has been the impact on the University community of this incident? 4. What larger ramifications, if any, exist from the incident? 5. Who should we talk to to find out more about campus reaction to the incident?   (Thank the individuals for their cooperation and participation in this interview. Assure them of the confidentiality of the responses and the potential for future interviews.)

Source: Asmussen & Creswell, 1995.

◗ Closing comments remind the researcher to thank the participant and assure them of the confidentiality of the responses. This section may also include a note to ask the interviewee if they have any questions, and a reminder to discuss the use of the data and the dissemination of information from the study.

An Observational Protocol

A protocol is used to record information during an observation, just as it is in interviewing. This protocol is used for all of the observational roles mentioned earlier. An **observational protocol** is a form designed by the researcher before data collection that is used for taking fieldnotes during an observation. On this form, researchers record a chronology of events, a detailed portrait of an individual or individuals, a picture or map of the setting, or verbatim quotes of individuals. As with interview protocols, the design and development of observational protocols will ensure that the researcher has an organized means for recording and keeping observational fieldnotes.

Development and Design of an Observational Protocol   You have already seen a sample observational protocol in Figure 7.4 in which the student took notes about the art object in class. An observational protocol such as that one permits qualitative researchers to record information they see at the observational site. This information is both a description of what is observed and a reflection of personal ideas noted during the interview. For example, examine the sample observational protocol shown in Figure 7.8. This sample protocol illustrates the components typically found on a recording form in an observation. These components are discussed below.

▶ The protocol contains a header where the researcher records information about the time, place, setting, and observational role.

▶ Two columns follow the header. These columns divide the page for recording two types of data. (More than one page may be supplied for the protocol.)

▶ In the left column, the observer records descriptive notes, as mentioned earlier, which simply describe what is observed. The exact nature of this description may vary. In Figure 7.8, examples of possible descriptions to be written by the observer are listed. These may include a description of the chronological order of events. This description is especially useful if the observer is examining a process or event. Observers may also describe the individuals, physical setting, events, and activities (Bogdan & Biklin, 1998). The observer may also sketch a picture of the site to facilitate remembering details of the setting for the final written report.

▶ In the right column, the observer writes reflective notes. Reflective notes, you may recall, are comments by researchers about their experiences during an observation. These notes may record their experiences as observers, hunches about important results and insights, or emerging themes for later analysis.

FIGURE 7.8

A Sample Observational Protocol

Observation Protocol
Setting/Individual Observed:
Observer:
Role of Observer (Participant, non-participant, other _____):

Time:
Place:
Length of Observation:

| **Descriptive Notes** | **Reflective Notes** |
| (notes that describe what occurred at the site) | (notes about observer experiences, hunches, insights, themes) |

A description of what was observed
in chronological order:

[e.g., write about portraits of individuals,
the physical setting, events, and activities]

[possibly draw a sketch of the site]

Think-Aloud About Observing

I typically ask my graduate students to practice gathering qualitative data by observing a setting. One of my favorite settings is the campus recreational center where they can watch students learning how to climb the "wall." The "wall" is an artificial wall that is used by students to learn how to rock climb. At this site, we typically find students who are learning how to climb the wall and an instructor who is giving climbing lessons. The wall itself is about 50 feet high and has strategically located handholds to assist the climbers. Several colored banners are positioned in lines on the wall to provide routes for climbers to use to scale the wall. The objective is for a student to climb to the top of the wall and then rappel downward.

Before the observation, my students always ask what they should observe. Here are the instructions that I give them:

▶ Design an observational protocol using Figure 7.8 as a model.
▶ Go to the recreational center to the base of the wall. Find a comfortable place to sit on one the benches in front of the wall, and then observe for about 10 minutes without recording information. Take in all that is occurring and become acclimated to the setting.
▶ After these 10 minutes, start focusing on one activity at the site. It may be a student receiving instructions about how to put on the climbing gear, students actually scaling the wall, or other students waiting their turn to climb.
▶ Start recording descriptive fieldnotes. Consider a chronology of events, portraits of individuals, or a sketch of the site. (To provide a creative twist to this exercise, I might ask students to describe information about two of the following four senses: sight, sound, touch, or smell.)
▶ Record reflective fieldnotes during the observation.

After 30 minutes the observational period ends, and the students are asked to write a brief qualitative passage about what they observed, incorporating both their descriptive and their reflective fieldnotes. This final request takes the students from data collecting (observing) to data analysis (making sense of their notes) and to report writing (trying to compose a brief qualitative research narrative).

Field Issues in Administering Data Collection

Researchers who engage in qualitative studies typically face issues when collecting data that they need to resolve. Some common issues are the need to change or adjust the form of data collection once they enter the field. Beginning qualitative researchers often respond with surprise when asked about the amount of time needed to collect extensive data. To avoid this, limit data collection at the beginning of a study, such as to one or two interviews or observations, so that you can estimate the amount of time needed to collect data. Another concern is the amount of energy and focus required to establish a substantial database.

Prior to beginning a study, reflecting on potential issues that might arise during data collection can help anticipate potential problems. Figure 7.9 lists issues related to the type of data being collected. These issues include access to site problems, observations, interviews, document research, journals, and the use of video materials.

Issues related to locating and obtaining permission to use materials present a challenge to qualitative writers. The issues related to interviewing surface during ethnographic studies and include access concerns and sharing information with interviewees and participants in the cultural group. Case study writers, who gather extensive information, struggle with the time commitment and the details of interviewing.

FIGURE 7.9

Field Issues in Qualitative Research

Access

- gaining access to the site and individuals
- getting people to respond to requests for information

- deciding whether to collect information in the natural site
- determining whether one has sufficient "distance" to site

Observations

- determining whether fieldnotes are credible
- writing down "jottings"
- incorporating "quotes" into fieldnotes
- assuming an observer role and how to change roles

- learning how to best collect information from early field visits in case studies
- learning how to "funnel" from broad observations to narrow ones

Interviews

- saying little during interview
- having tapes that will work in the transcribing machine
- scheduling a time for all to participate in a group interview
- matching the level of questions to the ability of informants
- realizing the costliness and lengthy process of transcribing data
- using an appropriate level of questioning at the beginning of the interview
- interruptions during an interview
- difficulty scheduling an interview
- having confidence in interviewing skills
- having difficulty taking notes while interviewing
- conducting interviews with two or more individuals
- encouraging all participants to talk in a group interview

- asking appropriate questions
- learning to listen rather than talk in interviews
- handling emotional outbursts
- addressing participants who do not want to be audio-taped
- finding a transcriptionist and the right type of equipment in a case study and grounded theory project
- moving from ice-breakers to questions in the interview
- addressing when interviewees stray from the questions
- giving the interview questions to participants before the interview
- working with the logistics of the tape-recording equipment
- "bracketing" personal bias
- focusing the questions to ask in a group interview

Documents

- having difficulty locating materials
- having difficulty obtaining permission to use materials

- questioning the value of materials

Journals

- having people write complete journal entries
- having difficulty reading handwritten journals
- having informants express the difficulty of journaling

- having informants ask questions about how one might journal

Audio-video Materials

- having disturbing room sounds
- having problems videotaping in a small room

- having difficulties focusing and positioning the camera

Source: Adapted from Creswell, 1998.

Conducting interviews is taxing, especially for inexperienced researchers engaged in studies that require extensive interviewing, such as in grounded theory research. Equipment issues loom large as a problem in interviewing, and recording equipment as well as transcribing equipment need to be located and organized in advance of the interview. The process of questioning during an interview (e.g., saying little, handling emotional outbursts, and using ice-breakers) is sometimes awkward for interviewers. Many inexperienced researchers express surprise about the difficulty of conducting interviews and about the lengthy process involved in transcribing the audio-tapes from the interviews. In addition, asking appropriate questions and relying on informants to discuss the meaning of their experiences requires patience and skill on the part of the interviewer. In document research, the issues involve locating materials, often at sites far away, and obtaining permission to use the materials.

When the researcher asks participants in a study to keep a journal, additional field issues surface. Journaling is a popular data collection process in a case study. What instructions should be given to individuals prior to writing in their journals? Are all participants equally comfortable journaling? Is it appropriate for small children, who express themselves well verbally, but have limited writing skills? The researcher may also have difficulty reading the handwriting of participants who journal.

Recording video-tapes also raises issues for the qualitative researcher, such as keeping disturbing room sounds to a minimum, deciding on the best location for the camera, and determining whether to provide close-up shots or distance shots.

Ethical Issues in Data Collection

Qualitative researchers often spend considerable one-on-one time with participants and stay for long periods of time at a research site. Furthermore, interviewing to develop a deep understanding of an individual's experience may require probing, highly personal questions. These factors require that the qualitative researcher be especially concerned about ethical issues during data collection. This discussion offers some guidelines to consider and potential issues that may arise.

The criteria of the American Anthropological Association (see Glesne & Peshkin, 1992) reflect appropriate standards. For example, researchers need to protect the anonymity of the informants, such as assign numbers or aliases to them to use in the processes of analyzing and reporting data. In ethnographic studies of a group, qualitative researchers present composite pictures of the group rather than focus on any single individual.

Further, to gain support from participants, a qualitative researcher conveys to participants that they are participating in a study and informs them of the purpose of the study. A researcher must also not engage in deception about the nature of the study. What if the study is on a sensitive topic, and the participants would not want to be involved if they were aware of the topic? This issue, disclosure of the purpose of the research, is widely discussed in cultural anthropology and is handled by the researcher by presenting general, not specific, information about the study. Another issue likely to develop is when the participant shares information "off the record." While, in most instances, this information is deleted from analysis by the researcher, the issue becomes problematic when the information harms individuals. For example, when a researcher studied incarcerated Native Americans in prisons and learned about a potential "break-out" during one of the interviews, she concluded that it would be a breach of faith with the participant if she reported the matter, and she kept quiet. Fortunately, the break-out was not attempted.

Other ethical issues likely to arise are whether the researcher shares their experiences with informants in an interview setting, such as when a researcher admitted his own struggles with smoking during a study about adolescent smoking behavior with middle school children. Dealing with contradictory information may be problematic, as well. Hopefully, over time, repeated interviews or observations will provide insight about patterns and lead to findings that are less contradictory. Of course, reporting contradictory findings may reflect the situation as accurately as possible in some qualitative studies.

Issues likely to arise about the research site are whether the inquirer disrupts the individuals or groups at the site (e.g., causes a gym class to run overtime because of observations). The researchers may cause permanent changes by their presence unwelcomed by participants, such as taking "sides" during a focus group interview, or disclosing names during e-mail interviewing. Researchers may also act in an inappropriate way that reflects badly on all researchers (e.g., is rude to gatekeepers and fails to view the site as a "guest").

KEY IDEAS IN THE CHAPTER

The process of collecting qualitative data follows the same four steps as in quantitative research: gaining permission to conduct the study, selecting participants, deciding on the types of data to collect, and administering and recording the data. In gaining permission, qualitative researchers are sensitive to the potentially intrusive nature of their research, and are mindful of respect for individuals and sites, potential power imbalances, and "giving back," or reciprocating. They also seek out gatekeepers for access to information about who or what to study. The selection of participants is intentional and purposeful to best understand the central phenomenon under study.

With permission and the selection of participants and sites, the inquirer engages in data collection. Forms of qualitative data collection can be grouped into four basic categories: observations, interviews, documents, and audio-visual materials. In choosing the type of data to collect, researchers need to first answer the research questions and then weigh the advantages and disadvantages of each form of data. Once the decision is made to collect data, the inquirer develops means for recording information that might include informal notes or optical scanning of documents. Unstructured and semi-structured research protocols might also be used. For observations and interviews, protocols are developed before data collection to provide a structure for observing and interviewing and a means for recording information to use in data analysis. With the data collection procedures in place, the qualitative inquirer collects data. This collection is responsive to field issues likely to occur during data gathering and conducted ethically with respect for individuals and sites.

USEFUL INFORMATION FOR PRODUCERS OF RESEARCH

▶ Plan four phases when designing qualitative data collection: gaining permission, selecting participants, selecting and weighing different data types, and administering and recording data.

▶ Recognize that the campus institutional review board may need extra detail about your qualitative field procedures, such as protecting the anonymity of participants, respecting field sites, and providing reciprocity to participants.

▶ To obtain access to a field site, locate a gatekeeper on the "inside" who can provide needed permissions and access to people and places.

▶ Use a purposeful sampling strategy that matches your intent for the study. The intent will vary from one qualitative project to another. Consider using sampling at different levels (e.g., organization, site, individual, parent).

▶ It is better to select a few individuals or sites to study rather than many to provide an in-depth understanding of the phenomenon, as required in qualitative studies.

▶ Weigh the advantages and disadvantages of each major form of qualitative data and each subtype (i.e., observations, interviews, documents, and audio-visual material)

before selecting the type(s) to use in your study. Also consider what type of data will best address your research questions.
▶ Use the process steps for conducting an observation, interviewing, and collecting documents and visual material, as presented in this chapter.
▶ Consider how you will record information during data collection. Use interview and observational protocols to structure the data collection as well as to record information.

USEFUL INFORMATION FOR CONSUMERS OF RESEARCH

▶ In evaluating a qualitative data collection procedure in a research study, look for comments by the author about gaining permissions, selecting participants, selecting data types, and developing recording protocols.
▶ Examine the reasons why researchers select participants for a study. They should detail that the participants were intentionally selected with some goal or objective in mind.
▶ Look for extensive data collection in a qualitative study. It is not unusual for qualitative inquirers to collect different forms of data in a single study.
▶ Look for a systematic procedure for the recording of qualitative data. Researchers should discuss their use of protocols, such as interview and observational protocols. A sample protocol as an appendix to a study is helpful in understanding the questions asked.

STUDY QUESTIONS AND ACTIVITIES

1. Identify the steps of data collection taken by an author in a published study. Locate a study and find the method or procedure discussion. Write next to the place in the article where the four steps in data collection are located.
2. Gain experience in conducting an interview. First, develop an interview protocol for a problem you would like to study. Follow the guidelines for designing the protocol in this chapter. Next, find a participant for your study and conduct the interview using the recommended interviewing techniques.
3. Practice observing a research site. Select a site to observe and a central phenomenon you would like to study. Develop an observational protocol and record both descriptive and reflective fieldnotes during the observation.
4. Record notes about the potential issues that arose during your practice interview in question 2 or your practice observation in question 3. Share these notes with another student to see if they experienced the same concerns. Look at the field issues list provided in Figure 7.9 to identify which ones are relevant to your situation.

Now go to our Companion Website to assess your understanding of chapter content with Multiple-Choice Questions, apply comprehension in Projects & Essays, and broaden your knowledge with links to related research topics on the Web.

Analyzing and Interpreting Quantitative Data

One of the hardest parts of research for Maria, our high school teacher, is using statistics and analyzing the data. Through coursework at the university she has a basic knowledge of statistics, but she wonders if she can ever get through this phase of research. In preparation, she visits with her introductory statistics professor to learn how to proceed. He talks with her about how statistics is only one part of the process of data analysis and interpretation. In fact, he says, several decisions need to be made besides the actual statistical analysis. He focuses Maria's attention on these topics:

a. How will her analysis relate to her research questions?
b. What computer program will she use?
c. Will she input her data herself or find someone to help with this procedure?
d. What are the best choices for her statistics?
e. How will she present her results? In tables? In figures?
f. What does "interpreting" the data mean to her?

This phase of research consists of a series of important decision steps for researchers. Essentially Maria will engage in the process of taking the data apart (analysis), synthesizing it in terms of its more general meaning (interpretation), forming it into tables, figures, and discussion (representation), and anticipating future research studies (concluding the study).

The steps in this phase of research should help those planning or conducting research to determine the activities they need to conduct after collecting quantitative data. For those reading educational research reports, knowledge of these steps will help allay some fears that often pervade this component of the research process. It is all too easy to focus on statistics, their complexity, and the way they may thwart or even stop a reader from examining a study. As we will discuss in this chapter, our emphasis is not on statistics and their calculations, as important as they are, but on the *use* of statistics in the sequence of research activities. (Helpful books referenced at the end of the chapter will direct you to readings that identify statistical computations.) We will emphasize the entire process of data analysis and interpretation, including statistics and their procedures as one element of this process. This chapter will address specific tools you can use to organize and manage your numeric data, to explore and analyze the data, to develop visual and narrative renderings of your results, to make broad interpretations, and to adequately conclude a quantitative study.

By the end of this chapter, you should be able to:

▶ Describe the process of preparing and organizing your data for statistical analysis.
▶ Analyze data by exploring and describing it.
▶ Identify the steps in testing hypotheses (or research questions).
▶ Represent and report the results visually in tables, figures, and in a detailed presentation of the results.
▶ Write a conclusion for a study that summarizes and explains the results, and identifies future needs for research.

EXAMINING DATA ANALYSIS AND INTERPRETATION IN THE TELEVISION VIOLENCE STUDY

To obtain an overview of the process of data analysis and interpretation we can turn once again to the television violence study (Vooijs & van der Voort, 1993). With advanced statistics used by the authors, it is easy to focus on the statistical results and miss the overall picture of analysis and interpretation unfolding in this study. For example, the authors asked the children to score 25 violent actions, 25 acts of violence, and 32 non-realistic events and situations (see Paragraphs 25–27). The researchers then summed scores for each child to obtain an overall score for each variable, a necessary *preparation of the data for analysis*. We also see the authors reporting basic, descriptive statistics such as means and standard deviations (Tables 1 and 2, Paragraphs 32 and 40) to obtain a *general sense of trends* in the data. We see these general trends in *tables* provided to summarize the analysis.

A strength of this article is how the authors clearly identified the research questions (see Paragraphs 15–18). Although you may not be familiar with the statistical tests presented in this study (e.g., multivariate analysis of covariance in Paragraph 30 or partial correlation in Paragraph 31), you might focus on the questions asked and the responses provided to each question. For example, in Paragraph 15 we learn that the first question was, " . . . whether the curriculum produces the desired effects in the short term." Turning to the results, starting with Paragraph 30, we find that the authors simply present results of *hypothesis testing* to each question in the order in which they are introduced in Paragraphs 15 through 18. Thus, in Paragraph 30 we learn the results to this first question, " . . . the curriculum led to a higher 'readiness to see violence' . . . and a decreased approval of the violent actions of the good guys." Moving ahead through this "Results" section we see the authors responding to each research question in order.

Toward the end of the article, starting with the "Discussion" section of Paragraph 41, the researchers provide a broad *interpretation* of the meaning of these results. They summarize the key findings (see Paragraph 41), and explain why the results were successful (see Paragraph 43) and unsuccessful (see Paragraph 44). They *conclude* the article with aspects of their research they would recommend for future studies (see Paragraphs 46 and 47).

THE PROCESS OF ANALYSIS AND INTERPRETATION

We are ready now to expand on the key steps in the process of analyzing and interpreting data. These steps are presented in an order typically used by quantitative researchers, and embedded within each phase are specific concepts and tools of the quantitative researcher. Investigators:

▶ prepare and organize the data for analysis
▶ analyze the data to explore and describe it
▶ analyze the data to test hypotheses (or research questions)
▶ represent and summarize the data in tables, figures, and a detailed discussion of results
▶ conclude the research by summarizing key results, explaining the results, noting limitations, and advancing suggestions for future investigations

Preparing and Organizing the Data

Before analyzing the data, it needs to be organized in a manner suitable for analysis by a computer. **Preparing and organizing data for analysis** in quantitative research consists of assembling all data, transforming it into numeric scores, creating a data file for computer or hand tabulation, and selecting a computer program to use in performing statistical tests on the data.

Scoring Data

The first step for the quantitative researcher after collecting data on instruments is to score the data. **Scoring** means that the researcher assigns a numeric score (or value) to each response category for each question on the instruments used to collect data. For instance, assume that parents are sent a survey asking them to respond to questions about choice of school in the school district for their child. One question might be:

Please check the appropriate response to this statement:
"Students should be given an opportunity to select a school of their choice."
_____ Strongly agree
_____ Agree
_____ Undecided
_____ Disagree
_____ Strongly disagree

Assume that a parent checks "agree." What numeric score would be assigned to the response? Typically, after the responses come back to the researcher, numbers are assigned to response categories as follows: 5 = strongly agree; 4 = agree; 3 = undecided; 2 = disagree; and 1 = strongly disagree. Based on these assigned numbers, the parent who checks "agree" would receive a score of "4."

Several aspects about assigning numeric scores to responses are considered before analysis begins. All similar scales (the above example is an interval scale, as discussed in Chapter 6 on "Selecting Scales of Measurement") should have the same scoring. In our example, all response options for "strongly agree" to "strongly disagree" are assigned numbers from "5" to "1." Other scales may also be used on instruments, such as a nominal ordinal scale, shown below:

Please respond to the following question:
"What is the level at which you teach?"
_____high school _____ middle school _____elementary

The scoring for this categorical scale would be: 3 = high school, 2 = middle school, and 1 = elementary school. This type of scoring raises another consideration. The numbers assigned are arbitrary; high school could have been assigned a "1" and elementary school, a "3." In general, a good rule to follow is that the more positive responses and the higher or more advanced categories of information should be assigned higher numbers. For example, when two variables are correlated in data analysis, it is easier to have the higher values reflect the more positive or advanced categories of information.

Additional suggestions for scoring can help during this process. Researchers should double-check their scoring. Also, on some instruments, the score values are already on the questions, such as:

> Please respond to this question:
> "Fourth graders should be tested for math proficiency."
> _____(5) Strongly agree
> _____(4) Agree
> _____(3) Undecided
> _____(2) Disagree
> _____(1) Strongly disagree

Also notice in this example that the response categories are presented in order from positive to negative. This practice could lead to inflated positive scores, but the reverse could lead to augmented negative scores. Sometimes scoring is facilitated by the use of "bubble sheets" such as those often used in evaluating teachers in college classrooms. When students darken circles on these sheets, their responses can be optically scanned for analysis. For instruments available from commercial companies, scoring manuals are provided to facilitate the process of scoring responses.

Analyzing Different Types of Scores

Before conducting an analysis of scores, researchers consider what "types" of scores to use. This is important because the type of score will affect the information entered into the computer data file used in analysis. Consider Table 8.1 that presents three types of scores for six students: single-item scores, summed scores on a scale, and net or difference scores.

For a research study, you may wish to examine a single-item score. A **single-item score** is an individual score to each question for each participant in your study. These scores provide a detailed analysis of each person's response for checking for errors in responding or determining a response to a specific question. In one study, researchers asked individuals at a local school district meeting: Will you vote yes or no for the tax levy in the election next Tuesday? In scoring the data, the researcher would assign the value of "1" to a "no" response and a value of "2" to a "yes" response, and have a record of how each individual responded to each question. In Table 8.1, all six participants have individual scores to questions one, two, and three.

We need to be cautious about single-item responses because they may not reflect a consistent perspective from our participants. Participants may also misunderstand the question or the author may have worded the item so that it biases results. In short, responses to single questions may not be reliable and may not accurately reflect an individual's score (as discussed in Chapter 6 on "Reliability"). One solution to these problems is to form scales based on responses to single questions. **Summed scores** are scores of an individual added over several questions that measure the same variable. Researchers add the individual items to compute an overall score for a variable (or construct), such as adding together all of the values of the responses for questions 1–5, which measure self-perception, on a 40-item questionnaire. Scores may also be summed for an individual over all items on an instrument, such as combining all values for responses from a diagnostic instrument for self-efficacy.

TABLE 8.1

Types of Scores Used in Quantitative Analysis

	Single-Item Scores*		
	Question 1 Score	Question 2 Score	Question 3 Score
Jane	5	4	3
Jim	4	3	4
John	2	1	2
Jean	4	5	4
Julie	4	3	4
Johanna	5	4	5

	Summed Score or Scale*					
	Question 1	Question 2	Question 3	Question 4	Question 5	Summed Scores
Jane	5	4	3	4	4	20
Jim	4	3	4	4	3	18
John	2	1	2	2	3	10

	Net or Difference Scores		
	Pre-test Math Score	Post-test Math Score	Net-Difference Score
Jane	80	85	+5
Jim	76	77	+1
John	65	75	+10
Jean	95	97	+2
Julie	91	94	+3
Johanna	93	95	+2

*Question response scale is: 5 = strongly agree; 4 = agree; 3 = undecided; 2 = disagree; and 1 = strongly disagree.

When investigators form scales, they should check to see if they are reliable. Statistical procedures, such as the alpha coefficient (as introduced in Chapter 6 on "Reliability") provide a coefficient to determine the degree of relationship of questions on the scale. As shown in Table 8.1, the three participants—Jane, Jim, and John—have provided responses to five questions. The scores for each individual are summed to provide a single score representing all five questions.

Summed scores for individuals are used to develop an overall test score that can be compared from one time period to another. **Net** or **difference scores** are scores in a quantitative study that represent a difference or change for each individual. In experiments, for example, researchers often gather scores on instruments before the study begins (time 1) and after it ends (time 2). These scores are gathered on pre-tests and post-tests, which are measures collected during experimental research. (We will address this further in Chapter 11 on "Using Pre-tests.") Whenever researchers collect data at different points in time, net or difference scores can be calculated. As shown in Table 8.1, we see each of the six participants' pre-test math score, a summed score over all items on the test before a unit on math is taught. We also see their post-test math score, a summed score at the end of the unit that represents their overall score on a final test. The net score shows how their performance improved, in all six cases, between the pre- and post-test.

Selecting a Statistical Program

After scoring the data, researchers select a computer program to use to analyze their data. Academic researchers generally use statistical programs on the campus mainframe computer or programs available as microcomputer software. With the availability and low cost of software programs for microcomputers, data analysis can be conveniently conducted from a home computer. The hardest part is deciding which software package to use. Here are some guidelines to follow when selecting a statistical program. (See Leedy & Ormrod, 2001, for additional suggestions.)

▶ Find a program with thorough documentation for inputting data and for running and interpreting programs. Programs often have tutorials so that you can easily learn the key features and practice them using sample data sets. Free tutorials are often available from Web sites.

▶ User-friendliness is also important. Pull-down menus and easy data entry make a program easy to use.

▶ Look for a program with an extensive range of statistical tests. Descriptive and inferential statistics (parametric and non-parametric) should be included in the statistical test offerings of a computer program. (We will discuss these topics later in this chapter.)

▶ Examine the program for its capacity to handle a large amount of data. How many cases can be entered? What is the maximum number of variables it will allow? A program should adequately accommodate missing data and provide some provisions for handling the situation where some data are missing for a participant. Look for a program that has flexibility for data handling, can read data in many formats (e.g., numbers and letters), and can read files imported from spreadsheets or databases.

▶ Locate a program with the capability to output graphs and tables that can be used in your research reports.

▶ If you need to purchase the software program, weigh the costs of the various programs. Student versions of programs are available (although they may have limited statistical tests) at minimal cost.

▶ Consider whether the program you select accurately calculates the statistical test you wish to conduct. Use the Internet to check reviews of the software program and seek advice from others who may have used it. Although limited statistical procedures are available on spreadsheet programs, they are inadequate for conducting your statistical analysis.

▶ Select a program that is used on your campus so that you can find assistance to answer questions when they arise. Some programs may provide technical support to help answer questions, but it may be time consuming and costly.

With these criteria in mind, what are the most frequently used statistical programs available? Web sites contain detailed information about the various statistical analysis computer software programs and a listing of the statistical procedures available. Some of the more frequently used programs are:

▶ *Minitab13* (www.minitab.com). This is an interactive software statistical package available from Minitab Inc., 3081 Enterprise Drive, State College, PA 16801-3008.

▶ *StatView* (www.statview.com). This is another popular software program available from SAS Institute, Inc., SAS Campus Drive, Cary, NC 27513-2414.

▶ *SYSTAT* (www.spssscience.com). This is a comprehensive interactive statistical package available from SPSS Science, Inc., 233 S. Wacker Drive, 11th Floor, Chicago, IL 60606-6307.

▶ *SAS/STAT* (www.sas.com). This is a statistical program with tools as an integral component of the SAS system of products available from SAS Institute, Inc., SAS Campus Drive, Cary, NC 27513-2414.

▶ *SPSS Student Version 10.0 for Windows and Version 6.0 for Macintosh* (www.spss.com). This is an affordable, professional analysis program for students based on the professional version of the program, available from SPSS Science, Inc., 233 S. Wacker Drive, 11th Floor, Chicago, IL 60606-6307.

Inputting Data

When using a statistical analysis program, the first step is typically inputting the data into a grid. **Inputting the data** occurs when the researcher transfers the data from the responses on instruments to a computer file to be used for analysis. For those new to this process, this grid is similar to a spreadsheet table used in many popular software packages (e.g., Excel). Table 8.2 shows a small database for 50 high school students participating in a study on tobacco use in schools. A close inspection shows that the grid contains cells in rows and columns into which the researcher inputs data for analysis. Displayed in the first column is the number of each participant (called a "case") followed by an ID number assigned to each of the nine students. In the other columns are variables that the researcher is measuring (i.e., sex, grade, parents, and so forth). For each student a value or number has been assigned that reflects his or her score on the variable. At the bottom of the sheet is coding information that provides an association between the numbers and the response categories for participants collected on an instrument. The names for the variables are short and simple, but descriptive (no more than eight characters in SPSS, such as "gender," "smoke," or "chewer").

The actual process of inputting data into this grid (George and Mallery, 2001) to create an SPSS for Windows database is as follows:

▶ Enter the data from scores on the instruments in the cells of the grid by selecting a cell and by typing the appropriate value. Enter the data by rows for each individual and use the columns for the values of each variable.

▶ Assign an identification number to each participant and place this number in the first column or use the predetermined numbers assigned in column 1 by SPSS (i.e., 001, 002, 003, or 343, 344, 345). Although this information may repeat the assignment of each case (or individual) with information in the software program, your use of a number connects your data input grid to your database. Your own numbers may reflect the last three digits in the individual's social security number (e.g., 343, 344, 345), or some other identifying number.

▶ In SPSS, the column headers are presented as variables: var001, var002, var003, and so forth. Rather than use these headers, replace them with names of your variables (e.g., var001 could be replaced by "age").

▶ For each variable, assign the score that you determined for response options to questions (see "Scoring the Data," above). These scores to questions are called **values** in SPSS and quantitative data analysis. Similar to the procedure for variables, rather than numbers for the values, names (called "character strings") can be defined and used. For example, 1.00 = "Strongly disagree," 2.00 = "Disagree," and so forth. When tables are printed, having names rather than values (or variable numbers) make the tables easier to understand.

Exploring and Descriptively Analyzing the Data

After preparing and organizing the data, the investigator engages in data analysis. This process consists of making decisions with certain ends in mind, and using procedures on which to base these decisions. As shown in Figure 8.1, this process consists of two general steps: (1) exploring and describing the data, and (2) conducting statistical tests with the data.

TABLE 8.2

Sample Data Grid for Inputting Information

	id	gender	grade	parents	smoke	chewer	ability	peers	depress
1	1.00	1.00	10.00	1.00	1.00	2.00	1.00	2.00	70.00
2	2.00	1.00	11.00	1.00	1.00	2.00	3.00	1.00	75.00
3	3.00	2.00	12.00	2.00	2.00	1.00	2.00	3.00	80.00
4	4.00	1.00	11.00	3.00	2.00	1.00	4.00	2.00	75.00
5	5.00	2.00	10.00	3.00	1.00	1.00	3.00	4.00	60.00
6	6.00	2.00	12.00	2.00	1.00	1.00	2.00	4.00	70.00
7	7.00	2.00	12.00	1.00	1.00	1.00	1.00	3.00	75.00
8	8.00	1.00	11.00	2.00	2.00	1.00	4.00	2.00	78.00
9	9.00	2.00	11.00	2.00	2.00	2.00	3.00	1.00	81.00
10	10.00	2.00	10.00	3.00	1.00	1.00	3.00	2.00	60.00
11	11.00	1.00	11.00	3.00	2.00	1.00	4.00	3.00	75.00
12	12.00	2.00	12.00	2.00	1.00	1.00	2.00	1.00	76.00
13	13.00	1.00	10.00	1.00	2.00	1.00	4.00	4.00	81.00
14	14.00	2.00	10.00	3.00	1.00	1.00	3.00	4.00	76.00
15	15.00	1.00	12.00	2.00	2.00	2.00	3.00	3.00	84.00
16	16.00	2.00	12.00	1.00	1.00	1.00	3.00	3.00	78.00
17	17.00	2.00	11.00	2.00	2.00	1.00	2.00	2.00	80.00
18	18.00	1.00	11.00	3.00	1.00	1.00	1.00	2.00	70.00
19	19.00	2.00	10.00	1.00	2.00	1.00	2.00	1.00	82.00
20	20.00	2.00	11.00	1.00	1.00	1.00	3.00	1.00	70.00
21	21.00	1.00	12.00	1.00	2.00	1.00	4.00	4.00	85.00
22	22.00	1.00	10.00	2.00	2.00	2.00	3.00	2.00	70.00
23	23.00	2.00	11.00	2.00	2.00	1.00	2.00	3.00	75.00
24	24.00	1.00	12.00	1.00	2.00	2.00	3.00	1.00	80.00
25	25.00	2.00	10.00	2.00	2.00	2.00	1.00	2.00	76.00
26	26.00	1.00	11.00	1.00	2.00	1.00	2.00	3.00	82.00
27	27.00	2.00	11.00	2.00	2.00	1.00	4.00	1.00	79.00
28	28.00	1.00	12.00	1.00	2.00	1.00	2.00	2.00	81.00
29	29.00	2.00	12.00	2.00	2.00	1.00	3.00	3.00	75.00
30	30.00	1.00	10.00	2.00	1.00	1.00	3.00	1.00	68.00
31	31.00	2.00	10.00	1.00	1.00	1.00	3.00	2.00	60.00
32	32.00	1.00	12.00	2.00	1.00	2.00	1.00	4.00	61.00
33	33.00	2.00	11.00	1.00	1.00	1.00	1.00	3.00	76.00
34	34.00	1.00	12.00	2.00	1.00	1.00	2.00	2.00	88.00
35	35.00	2.00	12.00	1.00	1.00	1.00	4.00	1.00	70.00
36	36.00	2.00	12.00	2.00	1.00	1.00	4.00	3.00	71.00
37	37.00	2.00	10.00	1.00	1.00	1.00	4.00	4.00	78.00
38	38.00	1.00	10.00	2.00	1.00	1.00	3.00	1.00	69.00
39	39.00	1.00	10.00	1.00	2.00	1.00	3.00	4.00	82.00
40	40.00	1.00	10.00	2.00	2.00	1.00	3.00	4.00	84.00
41	41.00	2.00	12.00	1.00	1.00	1.00	2.00	3.00	75.00
42	42.00	1.00	12.00	3.00	2.00	2.00	2.00	2.00	79.00
43	43.00	2.00	11.00	3.00	1.00	2.00	1.00	1.00	68.00
44	4.00	1.00	12.00	1.00	2.00	2.00	2.00	4.00	88.00
45	45.00	2.00	11.00	2.00	2.00	1.00	3.00	3.00	81.00
46	46.00	1.00	12.00	2.00	2.00	1.00	4.00	2.00	82.00
47	47.00	2.00	11.00	1.00	1.00	1.00	2.00	1.00	70.00
48	48.00	1.00	12.00	1.00	1.00	1.00	4.00	4.00	70.00
49	49.00	2.00	10.00	1.00	1.00	1.00	3.00	3.00	65.00
50	50.00	1.00	11.00	1.00	1.00	1.00	1.00	2.00	57.00

Gender: 1 = male; 2 = female
Grade: 10 = 10th grade; 11 = 11th grade; 12 = 12th grade
Parents: Parent status 1 = married; 2 = divorced; 3 = separated
Smoke: Do you smoke cigarettes?: 1 = no; 2 = yes
Chewer: Do you chew tobacco?: 1 = no; 2 = yes
Ability (academic, based on grade point average in last semester): 1 = below 2.0; 2 = 2.1–2.9; 3 = 3.0–3.5; 4 = 3.6–4.0
Peers (peer group student most closely identifies with at school): 1 = athletes; 2 = singers; 3 = punkers; 4 = other
Depress = total score on an instrument measuring depression (scores from 20 to 100)

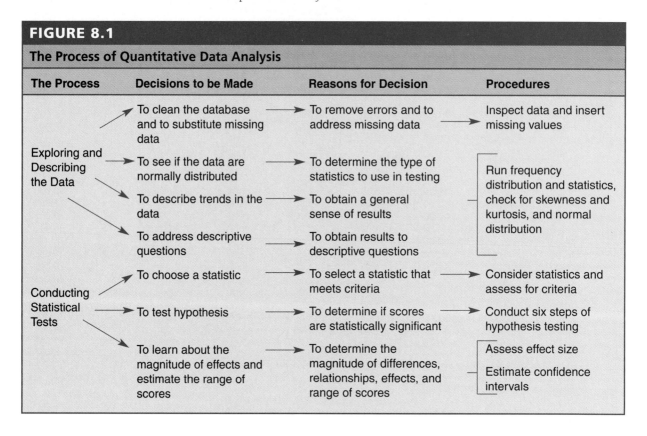

FIGURE 8.1

The Process of Quantitative Data Analysis

The Process	Decisions to be Made	Reasons for Decision	Procedures
Exploring and Describing the Data	To clean the database and to substitute missing data	To remove errors and to address missing data	Inspect data and insert missing values
	To see if the data are normally distributed	To determine the type of statistics to use in testing	Run frequency distribution and statistics, check for skewness and kurtosis, and normal distribution
	To describe trends in the data	To obtain a general sense of results	
	To address descriptive questions	To obtain results to descriptive questions	
Conducting Statistical Tests	To choose a statistic	To select a statistic that meets criteria	Consider statistics and assess for criteria
	To test hypothesis	To determine if scores are statistically significant	Conduct six steps of hypothesis testing
	To learn about the magnitude of effects and estimate the range of scores	To determine the magnitude of differences, relationships, effects, and range of scores	Assess effect size / Estimate confidence intervals

In exploring the data, the researcher inspects and examines it for errors and for missing data so that decisions can be made about substituting information for missing data. This phase also includes determining the shape of the distribution of scores in the data, which will aid in selecting the appropriate statistics to use. (We will discuss this later in this chapter.) It further involves describing trends in the data to obtain a general sense of the information, and to obtain specific results for descriptive research questions posed in the research study. Two procedures are central to this phase: (1) cleaning and accounting for missing data; and (2) calculating descriptive statistics to see if the data are normally distributed, to note trends in the data, and to answer research questions.

Cleaning and Accounting for Missing Data

Once the data have been organized into a computer file for analysis, the next step is to conduct a statistical analysis to explore the contours of the data. Before this can be done, however, attention needs to be given to the quality of the database. For instance, individuals may provide scores outside the range for variables, delete entire questions, or fail to show up during the collection of observational data. The researcher sometimes types a wrong number when inputting the data into the data grid, or sometimes misplaces a test when instruments are turned in to the test administrator. Because these problems may occur, the researcher needs to clean the data and decide how to treat missing data.

Cleaning the Data   Researchers clean the data because of errors in scoring that the participant makes or that the researcher makes when inputting the data. **Cleaning the data** is the process of visually inspecting the data for scores (or values) that are outside the accepted range. One way to accomplish this is by examining the data grid. For large databases, a frequency distribution (discussed shortly) will provide the range of scores to detect responses outside of acceptable ranges. For example, participants may provide a "6" for a strongly agree to strongly disagree scale when there are only five response options. Alternatively, the researcher might type a score for a participant as "3" for gender, when the only legitimate values are "1" for females and "2" for males.

Another procedure is to use SPSS for Windows 10.0 and have the program "sort cases" in ascending order for each variable. This process arranges the values of a variable from the smallest number to the largest, enabling you to easily spot out-of-range or misnumbered cases. A crosstable of two variables (i.e., using the "crosstabs" feature in SPSS for Windows 10.0) enables you to examine your data for illogical possibilities when comparing two variables. Whatever the procedure, a visual inspection of data helps to clean the data and free it from visible errors before you begin the data analysis.

Assessing Scores for Missing Data   Sometimes data are missing to individual questions or items on instruments. **Missing data** is information that is not supplied by participants to specific questions or items. This information may be lost, or individuals may skip questions, may be absent when observational data is collected, or may actually refuse to complete a sensitive question. These issues all lead to missing data in a database, and the researcher needs to incorporate them for statistical analysis and for ethical reasons. Because statistical tests require certain numbers of participants for their use, missing data will reduce the statistical options available for your statistical analysis (recall the sample size issues introduced in Chapter 6 on "Sample Size"). It also causes problems when two scores are needed for analysis of each variable or question using certain statistical procedures (such as in correlational analysis, to be discussed later and in Chapter 12). Missing values are part of the practice of research. For ethical reasons, investigators need to report how these values were handled so that readers can interpret the results (George & Mallery, 2001).

How should you handle missing data? The most obvious approach is to avoid having missing data by providing questions that participants are willing to answer and are capable of answering. In some research situations, you can contact individuals to determine why they did not respond (see Chapter 13 on "Response Rates"). When individuals do not respond, something is wrong with your data collection, which may indicate faulty planning in your design.

Assuming, however, that the database contains missing data, you will need to do something about it. There are several technical procedures that can help you. One procedure is to eliminate participants with missing scores from the data analysis, including only those participants for which complete data exists. This practice, in effect, may severely reduce the number of overall participants for data analysis. Instead, some researchers recommend substituting values for the missing cases. When the variable is categorical, this means substituting a value, such as "−9," for all missing values in the data grid. When the variable is continuous (i.e., is based on an interval scale), the process is more complex. Using SPSS for Windows (George & Mallory, 2001), the researcher can have the computer program substitute a value for each missing score, such as the group mean value for a variable for each missing data. (However, this practice means that you make certain assumptions about the normality of your data.) George and Mallory (2001) recommend that up to 15% of the missing data can be substituted with mean scores without altering the overall statistical findings. The discussion about handling missing values in the SPSS for Windows program (see George & Mallory, 2001) provides procedures to perform this substitution.

As an alternative, some researchers also recommend running a regression analysis (to be discussed later in this chapter) with the missing variable as the dependent variable (Gall, Borg, & Gall, 1996). The regression equation provides a predicted value that then can be typed into the data grid for missing values. Perhaps an easier solution is to use a non-parametric statistical test (to be discussed later) that has fewer assumptions than parametric tests.

Calculating Descriptive Statistics

The exploration and description of data helps to identify the distribution of scores so that an appropriate statistic can be chosen. It also aids researchers in assessing the general trends in the data and, more specifically, in answering descriptive research questions in their studies. These objectives can be accomplished by running a frequency distribution and its statistics, and checking the distribution of scores for a variable to determine if they are normally distributed.

To conduct this frequency analysis using a computer program requires knowledge about several concepts. Statistics will be reported for scores from participants who complete instruments or are observed by the researcher. These **statistics** are the numbers derived from formulas to measure aspects of a set of data. Many helpful books provide details about different statistics, their computation, and central arguments (e.g., see Abelson, 1995; Wright, 1997; and Gravetter & Wallnau, 2000). Here we will briefly introduce the family of statistics available to educators, define commonly used statistics, and review the use of statistics in calculating frequency distributions and in exploring and describing the data.

As shown in Figure 8.2, the family of statistics consists of two basic types: descriptive and inferential.

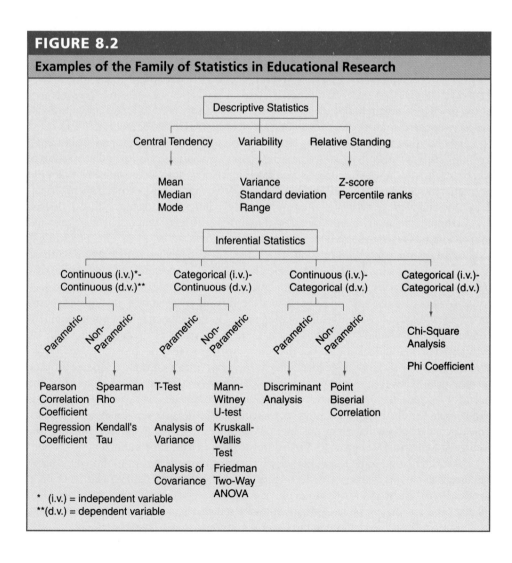

FIGURE 8.2

Examples of the Family of Statistics in Educational Research

Descriptive statistics present information that helps a researcher describe responses to each question in a database and determine both overall trends and the distribution of the data. Below are some important terms to know when dealing with descriptive statistics.

▶ **Measures of central tendency** are summary numbers that represent a single value in a distribution of scores (Vogt, 1999). They are expressed as an average score (the mean), the middle of a set of scores (the median), or the most frequently occurring score (the mode).

▶ **Measures of variability** indicate the spread of the scores in a distribution. Variance, standard deviation, and range all indicate the amount of variability in a distribution of scores. This information helps us see how dispersed the responses are to items on an instrument. Variability also plays an important role in many advanced statistical calculations.

▶ **Measures of relative standing** are statistics that describe one score relative to a group of scores. Two frequently used statistics are the z-score and the percentile rank.

The other basic type of statistics are inferential statistics. **Inferential statistics** enable a researcher to draw conclusions, inferences, or generalizations from a sample to a population of participants. Our focus for the moment will be on descriptive statistics because they will be used to explore and describe the data in the initial phases of data analysis. (Inferential statistics will be discussed later.)

As shown in Figure 8.2, descriptive statistics can be categorized into three basic types: central tendency, variability, and relative standing. Specific definitions of each statistic are presented in Table 8.3, but what is of importance is how each statistic is used in determining if the data are normally distributed, determining the trends in the data, and generating descriptive results to address research questions.

Determining the Distribution of Scores   In defining these terms, we see that information is needed to calculate these descriptive statistics based on our understanding of the distribution of scores. A typical or normal distribution of scores by participants can be represented by a graph that approximates a bell-shaped curve, called a **normal distribution** or **normal probability curve.** Scores can be normally distributed in a form known as a bell-shaped curve, as shown in Figure 8.3. Given a large sample, the scores for a question or variable would reflect the normal curve distribution. The percentage of scores likely to fall within each standard deviation from the mean is shown. For example, 68% of the scores fall between $+1$ and -1 standard deviations from the mean. Percentile scores can also be associated with each standard deviation. For example, 2.28% of the scores fall two standard deviations below the mean and 97.72% fall above the mean in the distribution.

Unquestionably, not all distributions, especially those of a small sample size, reflect a bell-shaped curve. As shown in Figure 8.4, the actual shape of a frequency distribution of scores may be negatively skewed to the right, positively skewed to the left, concentrated around the mean (negative kurtosis) or resemble a flat picture (positive kurtosis). In a **skewed distribution,** the scores tend to pile up toward one end of the scale and they taper off slowly at the other end (Gravetter & Wallnau, 2000). In a **kurtosis distribution,** the scores pile up at the middle or spread out to the sides. In computer programs that produce values for these frequency distributions, a 0.0 indicates a normal distribution, and a plus $(+)$ or minus $(-)$ score indicates a departure from the normal curve distribution. Technically, most distributions, then, are not normal and will exhibit some skewness or kurtosis. We often use a standard such as $+1$ or -1 to determine how far the distributions depart from normalcy. Other data certainly relate to making this decision and informing your choice of statistical test, such as the size of the sample, the equality of variance when groups are being compared, and the assumptions of statistical tests. At a minimum, it is helpful to

TABLE 8.3

Descriptive Statistics

Measures of Central Tendency

▶ The mean is the most popular statistic to analyze responses of all participants to items on an instrument. A **mean** is the arithmetic average of all of the scores. The researcher determines this measurement by summing all of the scores and then dividing the sum by the number of scores. In calculating other types of scores for other statistics, the mean plays an important role.

▶ The median is used less frequently in educational research. The **median** is the score that divides rank-ordered scores into halves. In short, 50% of the scores lie above the median and 50% lie below the median. To calculate this score, the researcher arrays all scores in rank order and then determines what score, the median, is halfway between all of the scores. It can also be calculated using percentiles.

▶ The mode is more frequently used than the median, but not as popular as the mean. The **mode** is the score that appears most frequently in a list of scores. It is used when researchers want to know the most common score in an array of scores on a variable.

Measures of Variability

▶ The standard deviation is a measure of the dispersion of scores. The **standard deviation** is the average of all scores as they differ from the mean score. To calculate this, the researcher finds how each score differs from the group mean, squares this difference, and then takes the average of all of the differences and the square root of that value. The standard deviation also plays an important role in calculating many statistics. The square of the standard deviation is the **variance,** another measure useful in calculating other statistics.

▶ The range of scores can also be analyzed. The **range of scores** is the difference between the highest and the lowest scores to items on an instrument. If scores are widely dispersed around the mean, there is higher variability of scores than if they are narrowly dispersed around the mean. These scores can be plotted out on a graph using a procedure in a computer program.

Measures of Relative Standing

▶ A measure of relative standing is the standard score. A **standard score** is a calculated score that enables a researcher to compare scores from different scales. It involves the transformation of a raw score into a score with relative meaning. A **z-score** is a popular form of the standard score, and it has a mean of 0 and a standard deviation of 1. The procedure is to take a score, subtract it from the mean of all scores, and divide it by the standard deviation. This yields a z-score or a standard score that can be compared to other scores from other scales. Using standardized scores is also central to calculating many statistics.

▶ Another measure of relative standing is the percentile rank. A **percentile rank** of a particular score is defined as the percentage of participants in the distribution with scores at or below a particular score. It is used to determine where in a distribution of scores an individual's score lies in comparison with other scores.

Source: Definitions adapted from Vogt (1999) and Gravetter & Wallnau (2000).

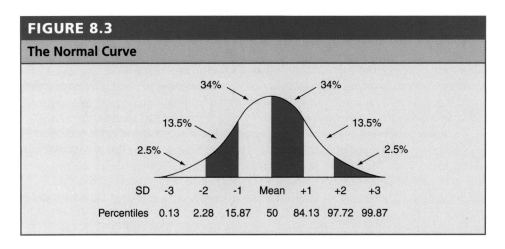

FIGURE 8.3

The Normal Curve

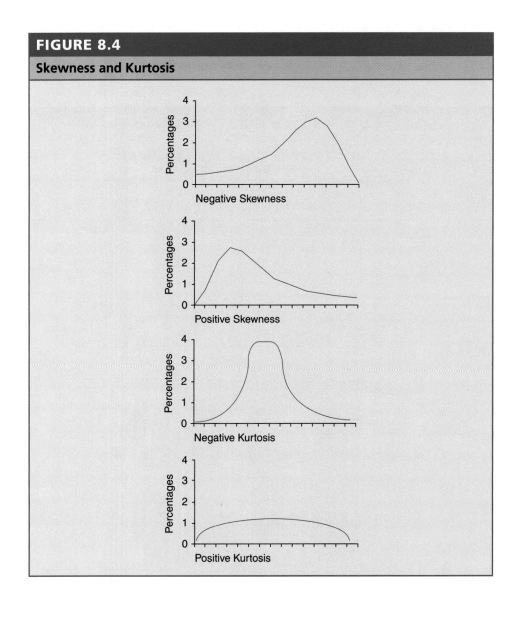

FIGURE 8.4

Skewness and Kurtosis

see the shape of the frequency distribution of your scores, rather than to use it as definitive evidence of normalcy or non-normalcy of data.

Identifying Trends and Addressing Research Questions   Using SPSS Version 10.0 for Windows, we can run frequency distributions for data to show the trends in a categorical variable and to determine whether the data are normally distributed for a continuous variable. We will use the sample data grid in Table 8.2 for data for this analysis.

You may recall that one variable addressed the peer group affiliation of each student (i.e., athletes, singers, punkers, and others). Thus, we have a categorical or nominal variable of four groups. Examine Table 8.4, which shows descriptive statistics for this one question or variable. Using the FREQUENCIES subprogram of SPSS Version 10.0 for Windows we can generate a table indicating the number (frequency) of the total of 50 individuals in each group. This subprogram also results in the percentage of the total in each group. (Valid percent takes into account missing data; we do not have any cases of that in this example.) Finally, we have the cumulative percent in each group that is not valuable information (except to indicate how many individuals were in the "other" category) since we do not have a continuous scale but have measured this variable in categories (or nominal data). Table 8.4 also shows a bar chart for each group where we can inspect frequencies for each stu-

---

TABLE 8.4

Descriptive Statistics for the Categorical Variable, "Peer Group Affiliation"

		Peer Group Affiliation			
		Frequency	Percent	Valid Percent	Cumulative Percent
Valid	athletes	12	24.0	24.0	24.0
	singers	14	28.0	28.0	52.0
	punkers	13	26.0	26.0	78.0
	other	11	22.0	22.0	100.0
	Total	50	100.0	100.0	

Peer Group Affiliation

dent peer group affiliation. This chart shows that the "singers" were the largest group (i.e., the mode) followed by the "punkers," thus noting trends in the data.

Let's look at a second example to see how we can identify trends and information about the distribution of scores from a continuous variable. Look back again at Table 8.2 on page 227. There is a variable measuring the student's total score on a depression instrument; ranging from 45 to 99. As shown in Table 8.5, we can use the FREQUENCIES program for SPSS Version 10.0 for Windows to provide a histogram with a normal curve superimposed to help decide if the data are normally distributed for this one variable. We can also calculate descriptive statistics (range, mean, standard deviation, and variance) for this variable and calculate the descriptive statistics of skewness and kurtosis. Kurtosis and skewness values between $+1$ and -1 are considered to be excellent, but a value between $+2$ and -2 is considered acceptable. Although the histogram does not display perfect normalcy, we do know that the statistics for kurtosis and skewness were less than $+1$ and -1 ($-.387$, $-.410$), indicating only minor kurtosis and skewness. We also know that the students scored an average of 78.46 on the depression instrument, but that there was considerable variation in scores (s.d. = 6.89, variance = 47.47). The scores ranged over 28 points for the students.

Not only can the descriptive statistics and graphs provide valuable information about the distribution of scores and the general trend in scores, they can also be used to address descriptive research questions. As mentioned in Chapter 5 on "descriptive research questions," these questions describe responses for the entire set of participants for select variables. The researcher may describe responses to either the independent or dependent variable or both. The intent is to describe responses to single questions or to single variables using statistical procedures of central tendency and variation.

For example, the following poses a descriptive question and types of descriptive statistics—central tendency and variation—typically found in a study:

Descriptive Question: To what extent were the high school students depressed?
Response Options: The students completed an instrument measuring their overall depression as indicated on a single score.
Results as shown in Table 8.5:
The average for the students was 74.58, displaying a moderately high level of depression. With an average of 74.58 and a standard deviation of 6.89, the scores varied considerably. They ranged from a low of 60 to 88.

The results to this question reported descriptive statistics of central tendency and variability (mean, standard deviation, and range).

Analyzing Data for Hypothesis Testing

Although some research questions are answered in the preliminary analysis, more complex questions often need to be addressed by making inferences from a sample to a population. To accomplish this requires three interrelated activities:

- choosing a statistical test to use
- using hypothesis testing to determine if the null will be rejected or fail to be rejected
- if the null is rejected, assessing how large and the range of differences among group means or between variables, using the additional indicators of effect size and confidence intervals

Choosing a Statistical Test

For many quantitative researchers, the use of descriptive statistics is only the beginning of their data analysis. Typically, researchers are interested in comparing responses of groups or relating two or more variables from a sample drawn from a population. Since the scores

TABLE 8.5

Descriptive Statistics for the Continuous Variable, "Depression"

Statistics		
Depression Score		
N	Valid	50
	Missing	0
Mean		74.5800
Median		75.0000
Mode		70.00
Std. Deviation		6.8901
Variance		47.4731
Skewness		−.410
Std. Error of Skewness		.337
Kurtosis		−.387
Std. Error of Kurtosis		.662
Range		28.00
Minimum		60.00
Maximum		88.00

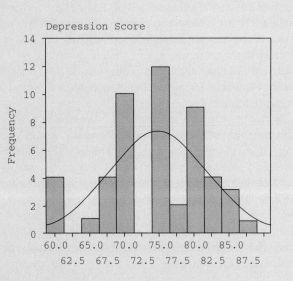

		Depression Score			
		Frequency	Percent	Valid Percent	Cumulative Percent
Valid	60.00	3	6.0	6.0	6.0
	61.00	1	2.0	2.0	8.0
	65.00	1	2.0	2.0	10.0
	67.00	1	2.0	2.0	12.0
	68.00	3	6.0	6.0	18.0
	69.00	1	2.0	2.0	20.0
	70.00	8	16.0	16.0	36.0
	71.00	1	2.0	2.0	38.0
	75.00	7	14.0	14.0	52.0
	76.00	5	10.0	10.0	62.0
	78.00	2	4.0	4.0	66.0
	79.00	2	4.0	4.0	70.0
	80.00	3	6.0	6.0	76.0
	81.00	4	8.0	8.0	84.0
	82.00	4	8.0	8.0	92.0
	84.00	2	4.0	4.0	96.0
	85.00	1	2.0	2.0	98.0
	88.00	1	2.0	2.0	100.0
	Total	50	100.0	100.0	

from studying a sample are only an estimate of a larger population, researchers conduct hypothesis testing. **Hypothesis testing** is a procedure for making decisions about results by comparing an observed value with a population value to determine if no difference or relationship exists between the values.

You may recall from Chapter 5 on "Hypotheses" that hypotheses are predictions about expected results that are made by comparing groups or relating variables from a sample. Conducting this test requires understanding both the statistics typically used to make inferences from a sample to a population and the procedural steps in actually testing a hypothesis.

Because the intent of much quantitative research is to draw inferences or conclusions about a population from a sample, inferential statistics are used. To understand inferential statistics you need to learn about the decisions that go into their selection as an appropriate statistical test.

Return to Figure 8.2 once again. On the right side is the branch of the statistics family relating to inferential statistics. Inferential statistics are divided into two basic types: parametric statistics and non-parametric statistics. **Parametric statistics** are statistical tests based on the premise that the population from which samples are obtained follows a normal distribution and the parameters of interest to the researcher are the population mean and standard deviation. These statistics apply to hypothesis testing (to be discussed later) because researchers seek to estimate population characteristics from a sample. If a large number of individuals participate in a study, certain assumptions about their scores typically hold true. These assumptions need to be met to use parametric statistics; violating them means that inappropriate inferences are drawn from scores. These assumptions are listed below.

1. The variables are measured in interval scales.
2. Scores from any two individuals in a study are independent of each other—one person's score is not dependent on another person's score.
3. The distribution of population scores is normally distributed (see Figure 8.3).
4. When the research involves two or more groups of subjects, each representing different populations, the variables that distinguish each population are similarly distributed (i.e., equal variances) among each population (Hittleman & Simon, 1997).

When researchers use non-parametric statistics, their tests require fewer assumptions. In the list of four assumptions above, only the second assumption, the independent observations of scores, is required for a non-parametric test. **Non-parametric** (or **distribution free**) **statistics** are statistical tests that only make the assumption of the independent observations of scores for each individual in the study. In these tests, the data are typically measured in categorical scores (e.g. females and males) on either the independent or dependent variable. Non-parametric tests are typically not as sensitive as parametric tests. You should probably use a non-parametric test whenever possible, recognizing that in many research situations, the assumptions of normalcy are difficult to meet.

We are now at a point to realistically consider the most frequently used statistical tests in educational research. Look at Table 8.6. The first column presents the statistical test and the remaining columns show criteria you might use in choosing the statistical test for your analysis. A **statistical test** is the procedure for calculating the actual statistic (e.g., *t*-statistic, *F*-statistic).

The criteria for choosing a statistic in Table 8.6 provides a means for selecting a statistical test for your data analysis. As shown in this table, seven factors go into this decision (also see Rudestam & Newton, 1992, for similar criteria).

1. *Determine the type of quantitative research question or hypothesis you would like to analyze.* As mentioned in Chapter 5, most quantitative questions and hypotheses either compare groups in terms of an outcome or relate one or more variables.

TABLE 8.6

Statistical Tests and Statistics Frequently Used in Educational Research and Criteria for Choosing the Statistic for Hypothesis Testing

Statistical Test/Test Statistic	Type of Hypothesis /Question	Number of Independent Variables	Number of Dependent Variables	Number of Covariates	Continuous or Categorical Independent Variable	Continuous or Categorical Dependent Variable	Type of Distribution of Scores
T-test (independent samples)	Group comparison	1	1	0	Categorical	Continuous	Normal distribution
Analysis of variance	Group comparison	1 or more	1	0	Categorical	Continuous	Normal distribution
Analysis of covariance	Group comparison	1 or more	1	1	Categorical	Continuous	Normal distribution
Multiple analysis of variance	Group comparison	1 or more	2 or more	0	Categorical	Continuous	Normal distribution
Mann-Whitney U test	Group comparison	1	1	0	Categorical	Continuous	Non-normal distribution
Kruskall-Wallis test	Group comparison	1 or more	1 or more	0	Categorical	Continuous	Non-normal distribution
Friedman's Chi-square test	Group comparison	2 or more	2 or more	0	Categorical	Continuous	Non-normal distribution
Chi-square	Category within group comparison	1	1	0	Categorical	Categorical	Non-normal distribution
Pearson product moment correlation	Relate variables	1	1	0	Continuous	Continuous	Normal distribution
Multiple regression	Relate variables	2 or more	1	0	Continuous	Continuous	Normal distribution
Spearman rank-order correlation	Relate variables	1	1 or more	0	Categorical	Categorical	Non-normal distribution
Point-Biserial correlation	Relate variables	1	1	0	Categorical	Continuous	Non-normal distribution
Phi-coefficient	Relate variables	1	1	0	Categorical	Categorical	Non-normal distribution

2. *For the research question or hypothesis, identify in it the number of independent variables.* In some experiments, more than one variable is analyzed, such as when groups are compared (variable 1) and a variable is controlled statistically (variable 2). In the experimental design chapter (Chapter 11 on "Experimental and Quasi-Experimental Research), experiments with this configuration of independent variables will be discussed. Also, in correlation studies (see Chapter 12 on "Correlational Research"), more than one independent variable is used as a predictor of an outcome. These are situations where you will find more than one independent variable in a research question or hypothesis.

3. *Identify the number of dependent variables in your research question or hypothesis.* Typically researchers use only one dependent variable or, if multiple dependent variables are of interest, each variable is analyzed one by one. There are times, however, when researchers use multiple dependent variables in the analysis; if this is the case, statistical procedures are available to permit such an analysis.

4. *Identify whether covariates are used in the research question or hypotheses, and, if they are, identify how many are used.* Covariates, as you may recall from Chapter 5 on "The Family of Variables," are variables that confound the analysis and need to be statistically controlled. Covariates often appear in experiments, as will be discussed later in Chapter 11 on "Experimental and Quasi-Experimental Designs."

5. *Consider the scale of measurement for your independent variable(s) in the research question or hypotheses.* A basic division of scales into categorical or continuous captures the possibilities of nominal and ordinal (categorical) and interval/ratio scales (continuous) and is much easier to use than trying to determine whether you have categories, ranked data, or equal intervals of data.

6. *Identify the scale of measurement for your dependent variables.* Identify whether you used continuous or categorical scales of measurement.

7. *Determine if your scores on the variables in your research questions or hypotheses are normally distributed or whether they are skewed.* This criterion was introduced earlier. Certain statistics have been designed to work best with normally distributed data and others with non-normally distributed data.

Let's illustrate how you might use these seven criteria. Assume that you want to compare adult learners who have experienced three types of instruction: lecture, lecture plus discussion, and small group activities. This comparison will be made in a community college classroom using their attitudes toward creative writing and their scores on a creative writing test. Assume that you seek to study the following quantitative research question:

> How do community college students who participate in lecture, lecture plus discussion, and small group activities compare in terms of attitudes toward creative writing and a final grade of a writing test?

Applying the seven criteria, we can conclude the following:

▶ This research question is a "group comparison" question where three groups (i.e., learners experiencing lecture, lecture plus discussion, and learners participating in small group activities) are compared in terms of (a) attitudes toward creative writing and (b) scores on a writing test.

▶ The number of independent variables in this study consists of one—type of instruction—but this variable consists of three groups.

▶ There is analysis of one dependent variable at a time. The number of dependent variables is two (i.e., attitudes and test scores), but let's decide to analyze each separately (which is often done) so that we can see how the group differences impact each dependent variable.

▶ There are no covariates being controlled or introduced in this research question.

▶ The scale of measurement for the independent variable would be categorical (i.e., three groups).

▶ The scale of measurement for the dependent variable would be continuous for both variables. Attitudes toward creative writing are represented by scores from 60 to 100 on a 100-point continuous scale and writing test scores are continuous from, say, 10 to 50 on a 50-point scale.

▶ There is a normal distribution of scores. The final criterion—whether the data is normally distributed—needs to be determined from a descriptive analysis (as mentioned earlier), the plotting of scores on a graph, and an examination of the skewness and kurtosis. Let's assume that the data seem to be normally distributed.

▶ From a consideration of all of these criteria, we would conclude that the appropriate statistical test would be analysis of variance.

Let's return to the example of Maria, our high school teacher. Maria needs to identify the most appropriate statistic to use in her data analysis. She can turn to her statistics professor at the university for help, but this individual is often busy, and he might expect Maria to be able to identify her own statistical procedures. Maria could also turn to her fellow graduate students for help, especially those that seem to excel in statistics class. She might also ask her advisor for help. In the end, she decides to use the criteria found in this chapter on "Choosing a Statistic" to help her out. Then she will go to her advisor to confirm her choices.

Maria asks herself the following questions about the data she has collected on her instruments and her research questions:

1. Am I trying to compare groups or relate variables?
2. For each hypothesis and research question, how many independent variables do I plan to analyze? Dependent variables? Covariates?
3. For each independent variable, what is my scale of measurement? (categorical or continuous)
4. For each dependent variable, what is my scale of measurement? (categorical or continuous)
5. Can I make the assumption that my scores are normally distributed in the population of all possible scores?
6. What statistical test and test statistic should I then use?

Conducting Hypothesis Testing

Inferential statistics allow you to make inferences from a sample to a population. Since we can seldom study an entire population because of size, expense, and ease of identification, we need to study samples and draw inferences to the population. Of course, sample data can only estimate the population, and any given sample may be in error because its characteristics do not reflect the population characteristics or parameters, assuming that the sample is randomly chosen. Hypothesis testing allows us to test whether the sample data differ from the population values. For example, in an experiment (discussed in Chapter 11), we are often interested in whether there is a difference between sample means of the control and experimental groups. In a correlational study (presented in Chapter 12), we may be interested in whether there is a relationship between the scores of two variables for individuals. In Chapter 13, on survey research, we might ask whether there is an association between participation in one category (e.g., types of peer group affiliations in a high school) and behaviors in another category (e.g., smoking or not smoking).

Hypothesis testing allows us to test these differences or relationships. The procedures to be used are documented in statistics books (e.g., Gravetter & Wallnau, 2000), so the presentation here will be to inform you about six general steps and to define important terms. In this section, we will also provide a specific example from the high school smoking database (see Table 8.2) to illustrate the steps.

There are six steps in hypothesis testing:

1. Establish a null and alternative hypothesis.
2. Set the level of significance or alpha level for rejecting the null hypothesis.
3. Collect data.
4. Compute the sample statistic, typically using a computer program.
5. Make a decision about rejecting or failing to reject the null hypothesis.
6. Determine the magnitude of differences if a statistically significant difference or relationship is found.

Establishing a Null and Alternative Hypothesis   When you use inferential statistics, you are testing a hypothesis. As you may recall from Chapter 5 on "Writing Hypotheses," the null hypothesis is a prediction about the population and is typically stated using the language of "no difference" (or "no relationship" or "no association"). The alternative hypothesis, on the other hand, indicates a difference (or relationship or association), and the direction of this difference may be positive or negative (alternative directional hypotheses) or *either* positive or negative (alternative non-directional hypotheses). The prediction included in the hypotheses, you may recall, is based on expectations related from past studies of the topic.

Keep in mind that you may actually write a research question instead of a hypothesis (e.g., Are there differences between smokers and non-smokers and their scores on the depression scale?). Although the language of research questions differs from hypotheses, for purposes of making inferences from a sample to a population, research questions are analyzed using the same steps as hypothesis testing.

Let's examine again the sample database presented in Table 8.2 on high school smoking. In this illustration, we will use two examples of null and alternative hypotheses. Recall that this database consists of personal data (e.g., whether students smoke or not), group data (e.g., peer affiliation—athletes, singers, punkers, and other), and individual attitudinal data (e.g., scores on a depression scale). The two null and alternative hypotheses can be stated as follows:

> *Null Hypothesis #1:*
> There is no difference between smokers and non-smokers on depression scores.
> *Alternative Hypothesis #1 (non-directional and directional):*
> There is a difference between smokers and non-smokers on depression scores.
> (*Or, written another way*):
> Smokers are more depressed than non-smokers.
> *Null Hypothesis #2:*
> There is no difference between smokers and non-smokers and peer group affiliation.
> *Alternative Hypothesis #2 (non-directional and directional):*
> There is a difference between smokers and non-smokers and peer group affiliation.
> *Or:* Smokers belong to the punkers peer group more than non-smokers.

In both sets of hypotheses, the researcher seeks an answer and will test whether differences in observed scores are real, or due to chance or error. This calls for establishing a decision standard to use.

Setting the Level of Significance or Alpha Level   We need to determine what kind of data would be expected if there is "no difference." (We will use "no difference" instead of "no relationship" in our example because it frequently appears in educational experiments.)

Now you need to think in terms of a population, such as the population of all sample means differences between smokers and non-smokers on the depression scale for all high school students. If we were to collect a large number of these means, and if the null hypothesis is true ("no difference"), the distribution would be a normal curve, as illustrated earlier in Figure 8.3.

Let's redraw this picture now and indicate some areas on both ends of this normal curve, where we would expect to obtain scores of extreme, low-probability values. As shown in Figure 8.5, we see a normal curve illustrating the distribution of sample means of all possible outcomes if the null hypothesis is true. We would expect most of our sample means to fall in the center of the curve if the hypothesis is true, but a small number would fall at the extremes. In other words, we would expect to find that for our sample of smokers and non-smokers that their depression scores are similar, but in a small percentage of cases, they might actually be different, if the means of the two groups were really identical in the population. What standard should we use to determine that they are "different"?

We need to set a standard—a level of significance as a boundary for making this decision—and mark this boundary precisely on the graph. A **significance level** (or **alpha level**) is a probability level that reflects the maximum risk you are willing to take that any observed differences are due to chance. It is typically set at .01 (1 out of 100 times the sample statistic will be due to chance) or .05 (5 out of 100 times it will be due to chance). This means that 1 out of 100 times (or 5 out of 100 times) an extremely low probability value will actually be observed if the null hypothesis is true. The area on the normal curve for low probability values if the null hypothesis is true is called the **critical region.** If sample data (i.e., the difference between smokers and non-smokers on depression) falls into the critical region, the null hypothesis is rejected. This means that instead of "there is no difference" as stated in the null hypothesis, we find the alternative to exist: "there is a difference."

See in Figure 8.5 how this critical region occurs at *both* ends of the normal curve. In a null hypothesis, we do not know whether the observed value will be greater or less than we would expect (that the mean scores are similar for smokers and non-smokers). When the

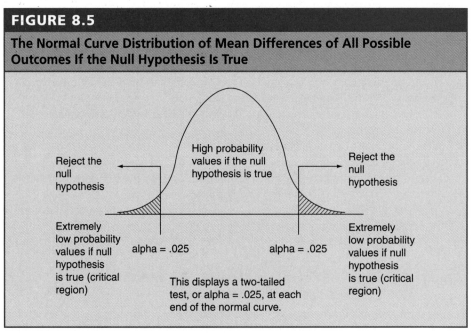

FIGURE 8.5

The Normal Curve Distribution of Mean Differences of All Possible Outcomes If the Null Hypothesis Is True

Source: Adapted from Gravetter & Wallnau, 2000.

critical region for rejection of the null hypothesis is divided into two areas at the tails of the sampling distribution, we have a **two-tailed test of significance** (Vogt, 1999). On the other hand, if we place the region only at one end for rejection of the null hypothesis, we have a **one-tailed test of significance.** One-tailed tests are only used when previous research indicates a probable direction (e.g., a directional, alternative hypothesis). On the other hand, a two-tailed test of significance is more conservative or demanding, because the area of rejection at either end of the curve is less than a one-tailed test. We say that a one-tailed test has more power, which means that we are more likely to reject the null hypothesis.

In addition, the one- or two-tailed test of significance relates to our hypotheses. If we say that there is no difference between smokers and non-smokers on depression scores, then we open up the possibilities for the difference to be greater or lesser—a *two-tailed* test. On the other hand, if we use the alternative hypothesis and say that the smokers are more depressed than non-smokers, then we have a *one-tailed* test. Thus, the more conservative posture is to use a two-tailed test and to locate the critical region at both ends of the sampling distribution.

One further point also requires clarification at this time. Although the alpha level of significance is useful for setting the critical region for rejection of the null hypothesis, it also establishes the potential error that may occur by deciding to reject the null hypothesis based on the observed value.

Let's consider four possible outcomes that could occur during hypothesis testing. These possibilities are outlined in Table 8.7. The columns in this table represent the actual state of affairs in the population: There is no difference between smokers and non-smokers on depression scores (said another way, smokers and non-smokers are equally depressed), or there really is a difference between smokers and non-smokers on depression scores.) The information in the rows shows the two decisions that researchers make based on actual data they receive: to reject the null hypothesis or to fail to reject the null. Given these factors, we have four possible outcomes—two possible errors that may occur and two possible positive outcomes in hypothesis testing:

1. The researcher can reject the null hypothesis (i.e., there is a difference) when the population values are truly that there is no effect. A **Type I error** occurs when the

TABLE 8.7

Possible Outcomes in Hypothesis Testing

Decision Made by the Researchers Based on the Statistical Test Value	State of Affairs in the Population	
	No Effect: Null True	Effect Exists: Null False
Reject the null hypothesis	**Type I error** (false positive) (probability = alpha)	Correctly rejected: no error (probability = power)
Fail to reject the null hypothesis	Correctly not rejected: no error	**Type II error** (false negative) (probability = beta)

Source: Adapted from Tuckman, 1999; Wright, 1999.

null hypothesis is rejected by the researcher when it is actually true. The probability of this error rate is alpha.

2. The researcher can commit an error by failing to reject the null hypothesis. A **Type II error** occurs when the researcher fails to reject the null hypothesis when an effect actually occurs in the population. The probability of this error rate is called "beta." In practical terms, a Type II error is typically considered less of a problem than a Type I error, because failing to reject (finding no difference) is less misleading than rejecting (finding a difference). In educational research, we need to be cautious about saying "there is a difference" when one actually does not exist.

3. The researcher can reject the hypothesis when it should be rejected because an effect exists.

4. The researcher can fail to reject the null hypothesis when it should not be rejected because there was no effect. This is a correct decision and, therefore, no error is committed. The **power** in quantitative hypothesis testing is the probability of correctly rejecting a false null hypothesis.

Let's summarize our points about setting the alpha level:

▶ We need to establish a criterion for determining what is an acceptable difference.
▶ Thinking in terms of a population of values, we can use a normal curve to indicate all possible values.
▶ We can identify a point where we say that if the null hypothesis is true, an extremely low probability value will occur.
▶ We can identify this boundary exactly by marking the critical region (or alpha level) of significance.
▶ This region can be marked at both ends of the curve or only at one end. A more conservative approach is to mark it at both ends.
▶ The critical region (or alpha level) of significance serves several purposes. It marks the region of rejection of the null hypothesis, and it indicates the probability of a Type I error—when the researcher rejects the null hypothesis (i.e., there is a difference) when, in fact, no effect was present.

Applying these ideas to our high school smoking study, we can now make an important decision: We set the alpha = .05. Being cautious researchers, we set the alpha level at both ends or have critical regions at .025 at each end of the normal curve. This means that 5 times out of 100 we will say that (the means of) smokers are different than non-smokers on their depression scores when, in fact, they are similar. Stated in hypothesis form, five-hundredths of the time we will reject the null hypothesis when it should have been retained. Looking up this .25 value on a distribution of normal scores, we find a *z*-value of 1.96 (or a *t*-value of 2.01 for 50 participants in our smoking study) at each end of the curve. Finally, it is important to establish this expected value *before* we collect data so that we have a decision point in mind and do not arbitrarily set this point *after* we collect data.

Collecting Data   As discussed in Chapter 6, quantitative researchers collect numeric data in the forms of scores. These scores are reported on instruments by participants or they are recorded on instruments (e.g., observational score sheets) by researchers. Scoring the data as well as inputting it into a computer file for analysis represents the first step in analyzing it. After cleaning the data, examining it for trends, and exploring the distribution of scores (in continuous data), the researcher is ready to continue with the next step in hypothesis testing.

In our high school smoking study, we completed this first step by collecting data from 50 students on personal variables and on the depression scale (shown in Table 8.2).

Computing the Sample Statistic   Now we need to use the inferential statistics summarized in Table 8.2 and calculate the statistic. This means that we need to decide what statistics to use in our analysis. Based on the five criteria set forth above in "Choosing a Statistical Test," we select a statistic and use a computer program (such as SPSS for Windows, Version 10.0) to run the analysis. We obtain a statistical test value and a probability (*p*-value) for the value. A ***p*-value** is the probability (*p*) that a result could have been produced by chance if the null hypothesis were really true.

Let's reconsider our null hypotheses in our high school smoking study.

Null Hypothesis #1:
There is no difference between smokers and non-smokers on depression scores.
Statistical test of choice, using Table 8.6:
Type of hypothesis: group comparison
Number of independent variables: one
Number of dependent variables: one
Number of covariates: none
Scale for independent variable: nominal or categories (smokers, non-smokers)
Scale for dependent variable: interval or continuous (depression scores)
Type of distribution: assumed to be normal
Statistical test: *t*-test (*t*)

Null Hypothesis #2:
There is no difference between smokers and non-smokers and peer group affiliation.
Type of hypothesis: categories of two variables
Number of independent variables: one
Number of dependent variables: one
Number of covariates: none
Scale for independent variable: nominal or categories (smokers, non-smokers)
Scale for dependent variable: nominal or categories (four peer group categories)
Type of distribution: assumed to be normal
Statistical test: chi-square statistic (X^2)

We next run the statistical analysis using SPSS for Windows, Version 10.0 using the two programs for a *t*-test and for a chi-square analysis: *T*-TEST and CROSSTABULATIONS. The output for these two statistical tests is shown in Table 8.8 and Table 8.9.

Making a Decision About Rejecting or Failing to Reject   As shown in Table 8.8 and Table 8.9, we are testing two hypotheses: (1) There is no difference between non-smokers and smokers and depression scores and (2) There is no difference (or association) between non-smokers and smokers and peer group affiliation. We have determined that the statistical tests of choice for these two hypotheses are a *t*-test for independent samples and a chi-square analysis.

In Table 8.8, this independent-samples *t*-test analysis indicates that the 26 non-smokers have a mean of 69.77 on the depression scale, while the 24 smokers have a mean of 79.79, a difference of −10.02 points between the two groups. The two-tailed significance test indicates a $t = -7.49$ with 48 degrees of freedom, resulting in a two-tailed significance value of .00. This $p = .00$ is statistically significant because it is less than $p < .05$. Leverne's test for equality of variance shows no significant difference between the two groups ($p = .27$ which is greater than $p < .05$), so we can assume that they are equally variable. Our overall conclusion is that there *is* a difference between non-smokers and smokers and their depression, and we reject the null hypothesis (there is no difference) and accept the alternative (there is a difference).

TABLE 8.8

T-test for Independent Samples for Smoking (Not a smoker, Smoker) on Depression

Variable	Number of Cases	Mean	Standard Deviation	SE of Mean
Depression score				
Non-smoker	26	69.77	5.33	1.05
Smoker	24	79.79	3.97	.81

Mean difference = −10.02
Leverne's Test for Equality of Variance: F = 1.26, Significance = 0.27 ← Test if the variances are equal for the two groups

Variances	t-value	DF	2-Tail Signifiance	SE of Difference	95% Confidence Interval	Effect Size
Equal	−7.49	48	.00	1.34	Lower:−12.71 Upper:−7.33	2.154

↑ *t*-test statistic   ↑ Observed *p*-value

In making this statement, we follow this procedure:

1. Look at the value of the statistical test and its associated *p*-value. This can be done by examining your computer printout.
2. Determine if the observed *p*-value is less than or greater than the value obtained from a distribution of scores for the statistic (with certain degrees of freedom and with either a one- or two-tailed test at a significance level). You can determine this table *p*-value by hand by comparing the value of the test statistic with the value in a distribution table for the statistic. For example, the *t*-test, the *F*-statistic, Pearson correlation, and the chi-square all have distributions available in many statistics books (e.g., Gravetter & Wallnau, 2000). Alternatively, you can let the computer program identify the observed *p*-value and you can interpret whether it is greater or less than your alpha value.
3. Decide to reject or fail to reject the null hypothesis. We need to next decide if our *p*-value is statistically significant to reject or fail to reject the null hypothesis.

Statistical significance is when the observed values (e.g., before and after a treatment in an experiment, the difference between mean scores for two or more groups or the relationship between two variables) provides a statistical value (*p*-value) that exceeds the predetermined alpha level set by the researcher. A *p*-value is the probability (*p*) that the test statistic could have been produced by chance if the null hypothesis were really true. With computer programs, such as SPSS Version 10.0 for Windows, the use of this table is not necessary because the program calculates the critical value and indicates whether or not the observed value of the statistic is significant.

This decision is based on a set of rules, such as those advanced by Johnson and Christensen (2000) and available in many statistics books:

TABLE 8.9

Chi-Square Analysis, Smoking by Peer Group Affiliation

Smoke Cigarettes?* Peer Group Affiliation Crosstabulation

			athletes	singers	punkers	other	Total
			peer group affiliation				
Smoke Cigarettes?	No	Count	8	6	6	6	26
		Expected Count	6.2	7.3	6.8	5.7	26.0
		Residual	1.8	−1.3	−.8	0.3	
	Yes	Count	4	8	7	5	24
		Expected Count	5.8	6.7	6.2	5.3	24.0
		Residual	−1.8	1.3	0.8	−3	
Total		Count	12	14	13	11	50
		Expected Count	12.0	14.0	13.0	11.0	50.0

Chi-square test statistic

	Value	df	Asymptotic Sig. (2-sided)	
Pearson Chi-Square	1.710[a]	3	.635	←Observed *p*-value
Likelihood Ratio	1.734	3	.629	
Linear-by-Linear	.258	1	.611	
N of Valid Cases	50			

a. 0 cells (.0%) have expected count less than 5. The minimum expected count is 5.28.

Symmetric Measures

		Value	Approx. Sig.
Nominal by	Phi	.185	.635
Nominal	Cramer's V	.185	.635
N of Valid Cases		50	

a. Not assuming the null hypothesis.
b. Using the asymptotic standard error assuming the null hypothesis.

Rule 1   If the probability value is less than or equal to the significance level, then reject the null hypothesis, and conclude that the research finding is statistically significant. For example:

▶ if probability value is less than or equal to .05
▶ then reject the hypothesis
▶ and conclude that the finding is statistically significant (e.g., the two groups have statistically different means)

Rule 2   If the probability value is greater than the significance level, then fail to reject the null hypothesis, and conclude that the research finding is not statistically significant. For example:

- if probability value is greater than 0.05
- then fail to reject the null hypothesis
- and conclude that the finding is not statistically significant (e.g., the two groups are similar, they do not have statistically different means)

We can also make a decision about the observed values reported in our second hypothesis—whether non-smokers and smokers are different in terms of their peer group affiliation. As shown in Table 8.9, in the chi-square statistical test we are examining the association between categories of data (i.e., about smoking and peer group affiliation) for our 50 high school students. The top table shows cells containing information about the observed count in each cell and an expected count. For example, for athletes, we expected 6.2 individuals to be non-smokers, and instead found 8. These expected counts are determined by using information from the rows and columns and the overall total. In the next table in Table 8.9, we see the actual statistical test. The Pearson chi-square test=1.71, with $df=3$, resulted in a *p*-value (or significance level) of .635. At p < .05, .635 is not statistically significant, and our conclusion is to fail to reject the null hypothesis and conclude that there is no detectable difference between smokers and non-smokers and peer group affiliation. Although we might have anticipated that the "punkers" group had more smokers than non-smokers, or that the "athletes" group had more non-smokers than smokers, our statistical test did not find these results to be present.

Interpreting the Results in Terms of Statistical and Practical Significance   Thus, in Tables 8.8 and 8.9, we have two inferential statistical tests with one rejecting the null hypothesis and the other failing to reject the null hypothesis. Although the decision to reject or fail to reject provides useful information, it does not indicate the magnitude of differences in mean scores, especially in the case when the null hypothesis is rejected (as in our *t*-test example). Thus, we turn to two additional types of information to help us decide how large the difference actually might be and to estimate the range of values: effect size and confidence intervals.

Effect size is a statistical procedure that developed from studies comparing results from many studies in meta-analysis (introduced in Chapter 5 on "Primary and Secondary Sources"). It is important to not only know whether the statistical test was significant (through *p*-values), but also to quantify the strength of a conclusion from a significance test. How strong was the difference? Effect size provides one indicator of this strength. **Effect size** is a means for identifying the strength of the conclusions about group differences or about the relationship among variables in a quantitative study. The calculation of this coefficient differs for statistical tests (e.g., R^2, eta^2, $omega^2$, Phi, or Cohen's D) (American Psychological Association, 1994).

In addition to effect size, confidence intervals provide additional information to hypothesis testing. Therefore, researchers should consider reporting *p*-values and statistical significance, effect size, and confidence intervals. A **confidence interval** or **interval estimate** is the range of upper and lower statistical values that are consistent with observed data and are likely to contain the actual population mean. Since means are only estimates of population value, they can never be precise, and sample means indicate a *point estimate* of the population mean. It is helpful, then, to consider a range of values around the sample mean that it could take given the multiple collection of samples. Researchers set a confidence interval around this mean value of the sample to illustrate the potential range of scores that are likely to occur. Moreover, this occurrence is framed as a percent, such as 95% of the time (95 out of 100), the population values will be within the range of the interval. Moreover, this interval can be identified by upper and lower limits, the values that define the range of the interval.

We can examine effect size to gauge the magnitude of differences between groups in our high school smoking example. A researcher, for example, could examine the means in Table 8.8 and see that the mean scores were 10.02 points apart, a sizable difference on a 100-point scale. Effect sizes are calculated in terms of standard deviation units. For the *t*-test statistic, the effect size can be calculated with the equation:

$$ES = Mean_{smokers} - Mean_{non\text{-}smokers} / Standard\ Deviation_{weighted}$$

Where the standard deviation$_{weighted}$ can be obtained by averaging the standard deviations for the smokers and non-smokers, taking into account the size of the groups.

Using this equation, we see in Table 8.8 an effect size of 2.154. This means that the average smoker would be over two standard deviations higher than a non-smoker in terms of depression.

Turning to our second illustration, as shown in the chi-square analysis of Table 8.9, we see the Phi coefficient with a value of .185 and an approximate significance of .635. The Phi coefficient is a measure of the strength of the association between two categorical variables (two nominal variables). A value of .185 is a weak association and we need additional evidence that smokers and non-smokers do not differ in terms of their peer group affiliation. The report of effect size along with *p*-values and statistical significance is a practice recommended for quantitative researchers (Wilkinson and the Task Force on Statistical Inference, 1999).

Another practice used today in interpreting the magnitude of difference is to report confidence intervals. Turning to the high school smoking example again, as illustrated in Table 8.8, the computer program reports a confidence interval for the differences between the means of the two groups. If a large number of samples were drawn from the population, 95% of the mean differences would fall between the lower and the upper values reported in the statistics for a *t*-test. Confidence interval information at a level of 95% is shown in Table 8.8. This conveys that if we could collect a large number of samples of high school students, we might estimate that 95% of the scores for depression would fall between −12.71 and −7.33, around the difference of −10.02 between non-smokers and smokers. To know this range provides a more accurate estimate of the population values, and it provides additional information about results to hypothesis testing and effect size calculations.

Representing and Reporting Results

When researchers conclude the statistical testing, they next turn to representing the results in tables and figures and reporting results in a discussion. You might include these results in a section labeled "Results." Several points might aid in your construction of this section and help you understand the contents of a published results section.

This section should address or respond to each research question or hypothesis. A typical approach is to respond to each question or hypothesis one by one in the order in which they are introduced earlier in the study (e.g., in a "Research Question" section, such as found in Vooijs & van der Voort, 1993). In reporting the results, the researcher also stays closely to the statistical findings without drawing broader implications or meaning from them. The implications are identified in the concluding section of a research study. Further, this section includes summaries of the data rather than the raw data (e.g., the actual scores for individuals). A results section includes:

▶ tables that summarize statistical information
▶ figures (charts, pictures, drawings) that portray variables and their relationships
▶ detailed explanations about the statistical results

Tables

Researchers display data in tables that summarize statistical results to research questions or hypotheses. A **table** is a summary of quantitative data organized into rows and columns. Typically, tables for reporting results contain quantitative information, but they might contain text information such as summaries of key studies found in the literature (and incorporated earlier in a study, before the results). One advantage of using tables is that they can summarize a large amount of data in a small amount of space. Below are some guidelines for creating tables.

▶ Although multiple statistical tests can be presented in one table, a general guideline is to present one table for each statistical test. Sometimes, however, data from different statistical analyses can be combined into a single table. For example, all descriptive data to questions (mean, standard deviation, and range) can be combined into a single table. However, each inferential test should be presented in an individual table.
▶ Readers should be able to easily grasp the meaning of a table. Tables should organize data into rows and columns with simple and clear row and column headings. Also, the title for the table should accurately represent the information contained in the table and be as complete a description as possible.
▶ It is important to know the level of statistical detail for descriptive and inferential statistics to report in tables. An examination of tables in scholarly journals typically provides models to use for the level of detail required for each type of statistical test. In addition, the *Publication Manual of the American Psychological Association* (American Psychological Association, 1994) provides examples of the detailed information to be reported in a descriptive table (e.g., mean, standard deviation, and N, or number of participants) and inferential tables (e.g., correlation, analysis of variance, and regression). As an additional aid, you might view the typical output for statistics using SPSS for Windows (e.g., George & Mallery, 2001) and the optional output statistics available for each statistical test.
▶ Authors typically report notes that qualify, explain, or provide additional information in the tables, which can be helpful to readers. Often these notes include information about the size of the sample reported in the study, the probability values used in hypothesis testing, and the actual significance levels of the statistical test.

Figures

Discerning the difference between tables and figures is not all that clear. A table includes a summary of quantitative data while a figure presents information in graphs or in visual pictures (American Psychological Association, 1994). Thus, a **figure** is summary of quantitative information presented as a chart, graph, or picture that shows relations among scores or variables. Tables are preferred to figures (American Psychological Association, 1994) because tables convey more information in a simple form.

Figures are suitable for visually presenting information in graphs and pictures in results sections of studies. The *Publication Manual of the American Psychological Association* (American Psychological Association, 1994) suggests several standards for designing a good figure. A good figure:

▶ augments, rather than duplicates, the text
▶ conveys only essential facts
▶ omits visually distracting detail
▶ is easy to read and understand
▶ is consistent with and is prepared in the same style as similar figures in the same article
▶ is carefully planned and prepared (p. 142)

Various types of figures are found in educational research studies:

▶ **bar charts** and **line graphs,** which depict trends and distributions of data (see the figure in Table 8.4)
▶ **scatterplots,** which illustrate the comparison of two different scores and how the scores regress or differ from the mean (see Figure 12.1)
▶ **line graphs,** which display the interaction between two variables in an experiment (see Figure 11.6)
▶ **charts,** which portray the complex relationship among variables in correlational research designs (see Figure 12.5)

The *Publication Manual of the American Psychological Association* (American Psychological Association, 1994) provides illustrations of a line graph, a bar graph, a scatterplot, and a correlational path model. In all of these examples, the figure title is placed at the bottom of the figure. This is different from table titles, which are placed at the top of the table.

Detailed Presentation of Results

Although tables and figures summarize information from statistical tests, the researcher needs to describe in detail the results of the statistical tests. In a **presentation of results,** the researcher presents detailed information about the specific results of the descriptive and inferential statistical analyses. This process requires explaining the central results of each statistical test and presenting this information using language acceptable to quantitative researchers.

For the results to each statistical test, the investigator summarizes the findings in one or two sentences. These sentences should include sufficient statistics in order to provide a complete picture of the results. They should also include information necessary for reporting results to each statistical test. What represents "sufficient" information depends on the specific type of test. At a minimum:

▶ report whether the hypothesis test was significant or not
▶ provide important information about the statistical test, given the statistics
▶ include language typically used in reporting statistical results

The information about the statistical test, for example, might include a report on degrees of freedom and sample size for the chi-square statistic, and means and standard deviations for descriptive statistics (American Psychological Association, 1994).

Figure 8.6 shows examples of results statements for both descriptive and inferential statistics. For descriptive statistics, the means, standard deviations, and the range of scores show useful information about results. For inferential statistics, information such as the alpha level used, the actual *p*-value, the critical region of rejection, the test statistic results, the degrees of freedom, and effect size should be reported. Interval estimates reported as confidence intervals might also be mentioned. One guideline for statistical results recommends that when reporting a *p*-value, effect size estimates should always be reported (Wilkinson and the Task Force on Statistical Inference, 1999).

FIGURE 8.6

Examples of Results Statements Using an Analysis of Variance Test

Descriptive Statistics

The students who received questions averaged $M = 4.5$ with a $S.D. = .98$ on math scores.

Inferential Statistics

Standard Statement

The means and standard deviations for each treatment group are presented in Table 2. The analysis of variance revealed a statistically significant difference between the groups, $F(3,8) = 8.98$, $p = 0.0001$.

Effect Size Added

The means and standard deviations for each treatment group are presented in Table 2. The analysis of variance revealed a significant difference among the groups, $F(3,8) = 8.98$, $p < .05$, effect size $= .93$ SD.

Alpha and Actual P-Value Indicated

The means and standard deviations for each treatment group are presented in Table 2. At an alpha of .05, the analysis of variance revealed a significant difference among the groups, $F(3,8) = 8.98$, $p = .034$.

Ideal Model

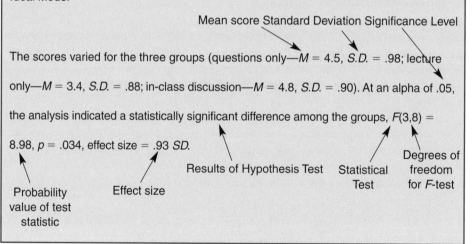

Concluding the Research

After reporting and explaining the detailed results, researchers conclude a study by summarizing key findings, developing explanations for results, suggesting limitations in the research, and making recommendations for future inquiries.

Summarizing Results

In the process of interpreting results, researchers first summarize the major findings and present the broader implications of the research for distinct audiences. A **summary** is a statement that reviews the major conclusions to each of the research questions or hypotheses. This summary is different than the results: It represents general, rather than specific, conclusions. Specific conclusions in the results would include detail about statistical tests, significance levels, and effect sizes. General conclusions state overall whether the hypothesis was rejected or whether the research question was supported or not supported. The research ends with statements by researchers about positive implications of the study. **Implications** are those suggestions for the importance of the study for different audiences. They elaborate on the significance for audiences presented initially in the statement of the problem section (see Chapter 3 on "Relating the Discussion to Audiences"). In effect, now that the study has been completed, the researcher is in a position to reflect (and remark) on the importance of the study.

Developing Explanations

After this summary, researchers explain why their results turned out the way they did. Often this explanation is based on returning to predictions made from a theory or conceptual framework that guided the development of research questions or hypotheses. In addition, these explanations may include a discussion about the existing literature and how the results either confirmed or disconfirmed prior studies. Thus, readers frequently find past research studies being presented by authors in this passage. A model of contrasting and comparing results with theories, bodies of literature, or current conventional wisdom typifies the explanations developed at the conclusion of a study.

Advancing Limitations

Researchers also advance limitations or weaknesses of their study that may have affected the results. **Limitations** are potential weaknesses or problems with the study that are identified by the researcher. These weaknesses are enumerated one by one, and they often relate to inadequate measures of variables, loss or lack of participants, small sample sizes, errors in measurement, and other factors typically related to data collection and analysis. These limitations are useful to other potential researchers who may choose to conduct a similar or replication study. Advancing these limitations provides a useful bridge into making suggestions for future studies that are needed to address these weaknesses. Limitations also help readers judge to what extent the findings can or cannot be generalized to other people and situations.

Suggesting Future Research

Researchers next advance future research directions based on the results of the present study. **Future research directions** are suggestions made by the researcher about additional studies that need to be conducted based on the results of the present research. These suggestions are a natural link to the limitations of a study, and they provide useful direction for new researchers and readers who are interested in exploring needed areas of inquiry or applying results to educational practice. Noting these future research directions provides useful information for educators beginning their research. These educators often need an "angle" to pursue to add to the existing knowledge, and future research suggestions, typically found at the conclusion of a research study, provide useful direction. For those reading a study, future research directions highlight areas that are unknown and provide boundaries for using information from a specific study.

KEY IDEAS IN THE CHAPTER

After collecting numeric scores on instruments or through observations, quantitative researchers need to prepare and organize their data for statistical analysis. This process consists of assigning numeric scores to each response option on instruments (if the instrument does not already include this information), determining whether single-item, net, or summed scores will be used in the analysis, and selecting a computer software program to analyze the data. Next, the investigator enters the data into a computer file by building a data set grid with variables and values. With the data set built, the researcher begins the process of initial analysis: exploring and describing the data, and conducting descriptive statistical analysis.

This exploration involves cleaning the data and accounting for missing data and then running descriptive statistics that address several aspects of research. These aspects are to note whether the data are normally distributed to help decide what inferential test to conduct, to identify general trends in the data, and to answer descriptive research questions.

Many research studies test hypotheses or compare groups and relate variables in research questions. In effect, the researcher uses hypothesis testing procedures to determine whether the null hypothesis should be rejected or should fail to be rejected. This process involves choosing a statistical test to use and applying the steps of hypothesis testing. These steps are to establish the null and alternative hypotheses and to set a decision boundary for rejecting the null, called an alpha or significance level. Then the procedure calls for collecting data, computing the sample statistic using a statistical test, making a decision to reject or to fail to reject, and then examining the magnitude of differences or a relationship, if such outcomes have been found. Magnitude of differences or relationships is determined by calculating effect sizes and confidence intervals to form complete interpretations of results. Results are then reported in summary form through tables, figures, and detailed explanations. These explanations require providing essential information about the statistical test (this information will vary by statistic), and using language acceptable to quantitative researchers.

Finally, investigators conclude their research by summarizing the detailed results in general statements. They also provide explanations for their findings based on prior predictions made in the literature or in theories, and they will typically contrast their results with past research. It is also important in concluding a study to advance limitations to the research, noting potential weaknesses that might have affected the results. These limitations build directly into suggestions for future research that will improve the weaknesses and further contribute to the literature on a topic.

USEFUL INFORMATION FOR PRODUCERS OF RESEARCH

▶ As you design or plan quantitative research, consider the broad processes of analyzing and interpreting the data as discussed in this chapter, such as preparing and organizing your data, analyzing it descriptively and inferentially, summarizing the results visually and in a discussion, and concluding a study by summarizing and explaining the results. These topics could be headings in your plan for a study or in the final report.

▶ In quantitative research, score your data and then input it into a computer program using a grid.

▶ Choose a computer program that offers a large number of statistical procedures.

▶ Run a descriptive analysis to clean the data and answer descriptive questions.

▶ Choose your statistical analysis based on the type of question asked, the variables, the scale of measurement, and the distribution of scores.

▶ If hypotheses are being tested, examine the data for statistical significance and effect size.

▶ Represent data in tables and figures using the APA style manual.

USEFUL INFORMATION FOR CONSUMERS OF RESEARCH

▶ To best understand the statistics presented in a research report, ask yourself what the research questions were that the investigator sought to answer and look for a discussion of results that match these research questions.

▶ Understand that the selection of statistics by a researcher needs to be based on specific criteria. Examine the data collected to determine if the right decision was made based on the seven factors identified in Table 8.6.

▶ When researchers compare groups (as in an experiment), look not only for a report of the statistical test but also information about confidence intervals and effect sizes for interpreting the magnitude of group differences.

STUDY QUESTIONS AND ACTIVITIES

1. Use Table 8.6 and write a brief quantitative research question and then select the most appropriate statistic to analyze it. Assume that your scores are normally distributed.

2. Locate a small database (e.g., a sample size of 10 to 20 individuals) and, using a microcomputer and the SPSS Version 10.0 for Windows or Version 6.0 for the Macintosh, enter the database into the grid.

3. Calculate basic statistics for this small quantitative database. For the database created in question 2, conduct a statistical analysis to find measures of central tendency and variability.

4. Design a statistical table to report results. For the results obtained in question 3, develop a table following the style manual guidelines in this chapter from the American Psychological Association (1994).

 Now go to our Companion Website to assess your understanding of chapter content with Multiple-Choice Questions, apply comprehension in Projects & Essays, and broaden your knowledge with links to related research topics on the Web.

Analyzing and Interpreting Qualitative Data

Now that Maria, our high school teacher, has completed several qualitative interviews, she is curious about how to make sense out of the information. This data is not like numbers, she tells herself as she examines a 20-page transcript of one interview that she typed from the audiotape. As she casually reads through her open-ended interview questions and the student's responses, she begins to see how the student characterizes weapon possession at his school. Taking a long time just to read through this one transcript, she feels like she has collected an overwhelming amount of information. "How will I make sense of it?" she asks. "And when I interpret this information," she continues, "my own meaning may not be right!"

You may share some of Maria's concerns because of the text (and possibly image) data that need to be analyzed. The procedures used in qualitative research are different than those you learned in Chapter 8 on quantitative data analysis. Qualitative analysis takes time and involves a close reading of each form of information, such as Maria's interview. Next it requires assembling a broad understanding of the information, such as drawing a picture to represent the major ideas. This is a fluid form of representation; much more so than the tables and figures that you learned about in quantitative data analysis. Interpretation of the data is also different, because it involves personal views held by the researcher, without the use of prior predictions or literature on which to base this interpretation. It is little wonder that Maria is concerned about her personal interpretation of the data.

In this chapter you will learn about the processes of the initial management of your qualitative data, its analysis through preliminary reading and reflecting, the development of descriptions and themes, representing the information in pictures, and making broad interpretations of the information.

By the end of this chapter, you should be able to:

- ▶ Describe how to organize and transcribe qualitative data.
- ▶ Decide whether to hand- or computer-analyze your data.
- ▶ Read through and form initial impressions of text data.
- ▶ Conduct coding of a transcript or text file.
- ▶ Develop a detailed qualitative description.

▶ Generate a qualitative theme.
▶ Represent qualitative data in visual images and diagrams.
▶ Make a qualitative interpretation from your data.

REEXAMINING QUALITATIVE DATA ANALYSIS IN THE GUNMAN CASE STUDY

In the gunman qualitative study (Asmussen & Creswell, 1995), the authors briefly discuss data analysis procedures in Paragraph 12. They tell about describing details, incorporating quotes, and making an interpretation of events. In addition, there are both a description and thematic development of their findings. They chronicle the events for 2 weeks following the incident, providing a detailed description of those events (Paragraphs 04–10). They also analyze the data to generate themes, such as the five they present in Paragraphs 13–31.

They include one table (Paragraph 11) to represent a matrix of data collection, but the article consists mostly of discussion. In the final section of the article, they interpret the larger meaning of the study by considering two broad perspectives—the psychological and the social-psychological—to explain the significance of the study (see Paragraph 35). Finally, they briefly discuss their approach to validating the accuracy and credibility of their account. They do this by taking the case study back to select participants for feedback and by incorporating participants' comments into the final report (see Paragraph 12).

GENERAL CONSIDERATIONS IN QUALITATIVE DATA ANALYSIS AND INTERPRETATION

The steps qualitative researchers use to analyze and interpret their data are similar to those used by quantitative analysts. Qualitative researchers engage in this process:

▶ preparing and organizing the data for analysis
▶ exploring the data
▶ describing and developing themes from the data
▶ representing and reporting the findings
▶ interpreting the findings
▶ validating the accuracy and credibility of the findings

Because of the detailed steps that go into this process, it is helpful to begin with a general overview and to describe some essential features of it.

Figure 9.1 outlines this general process. As shown in the figure, qualitative researchers first collect data and then prepare it for data analysis. This analysis initially consists of developing a general sense of the data, and then coding description and themes about the central phenomenon. Let's look at some of the features of this process in more detail.

As this process shows, it is primarily inductive in form, going from the particular—the detailed data (e.g., transcriptions or typed notes from interviews)—to the general—codes and themes. Keeping this in mind helps you understand how qualitative researchers produce broad themes or categories from diverse detailed databases. Although the initial analysis consists of subdividing the data (later we will discuss "coding" the data), the final goal is to generate a larger, consolidated picture (Tesch, 1990).

A useful conceptualization is to think about the process as including both simultaneous and iterative (cycling back and forth) phases. In qualitative research, the data collection and

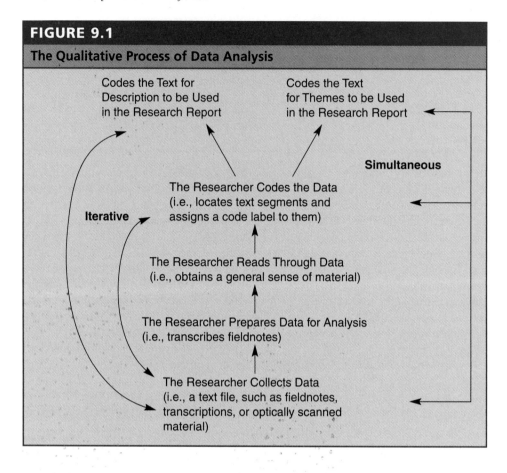

FIGURE 9.1

The Qualitative Process of Data Analysis

analysis (and perhaps the report writing) are simultaneous activities. While the grounded theorist collects data, for example, he or she is also analyzing other information previously collected, looking for major ideas. The process of data collection and analysis, typically conducted in two sequential steps in *quantitative* research, does not apply in *qualitative* inquiry. Here, you need to collect and analyze data to determine what questions to ask in an emerging design.

The phases are also iterative, where you will cycle back and forth between data collection and analysis. In narrative studies, you will need to collect individual stories from individuals; as your analysis of their stories proceed, however, you may need to return for more information to fill in gaps in their stories.

Qualitative researchers analyze their data by reading through it several times and conducting an analysis each time. For example, later we will discuss how to scan your information (first time through), code (or categorize) it (second time through), and generate themes (third time through). This process of cycling through a database several times is a common practice in qualitative research.

Unquestionably, there is not one single way to analyze qualitative data—it is an eclectic process in which you try to make sense of the information. Although several guidelines exist for this process (see Dey, 1993; Miles & Huberman, 1994), other writers will minimize the importance of this phase of research (e.g., Wolcott, 1994). Thus, the approaches to data analysis espoused by qualitative writers will vary considerably.

When you read about the research designs in Part III of this text, you will find data analysis procedures that differ for grounded theory, ethnography, and narrative research.

These analysis procedures will relate to the outcomes intended in each of these qualitative research designs. For example, the creation of a narrative report requires that you analyze an individual's story for a chronology of events. For a description of the ethnographic cultural scene, however, you will analyze observational fieldnotes.

In the analysis and interpretation of qualitative data, the researcher makes sense of the data. In making this interpretation, it is important for writers to recognize that their views and perspectives, rooted in personal cultural and historical factors, ultimately shape their interpretations. The interpretation that you make of a transcript, for example, will differ from the interpretation that someone else makes. This does not mean that your interpretation is better or more accurate, it simply means that you bring to your interpretation your own perspective. Although all research has this aspect to it, qualitative inquirers both acknowledge and openly discuss their interpretive stances. This stance will become more evident later, when we consider how to write qualitative research in Chapter 10.

Preparing and Organizing the Data for Analysis

Initial preparation of the data for analysis requires organizing the vast amount of information, transferring it from spoken or written words to text, and making decisions about whether to analyze the data by hand or by computer.

Organizing Data

At an early stage in qualitative analysis, researchers organize their data into file folders, index cards, or computer files. Organization of data is critical in qualitative research because of the large amount of information gathered during a study. New researchers are surprised by the extensive data that an interview can yield. For example, a one-half hour interview will often result in about 20 pages of single-spaced transcription. With this sizable amount of data, transcribing and organizing information requires a system of organization. This organization could take several forms, such as:

- developing a matrix or a table of sources that can be used to help organize the material (see the table in the gunman incident qualitative study, Asmussen & Creswell, 1995)
- organizing the materials by type: all interviews, all observations, all documents, and all photographs or other visual materials; as an alternative, you might consider organizing the materials by participant, site, location or some combination of these approaches
- keeping duplicate copies of all forms of data

Transcribing Data

You might remember from Chapter 7 on "Observing" and "Interviewing" that you often obtain words to be analyzed by interviewing participants or when recording fieldnotes during observations. These words need to be converted to a form for data analysis. At other times you will only listen to tapes or simply read through fieldnotes to begin the process of analysis. When time is short or funds are scarce, qualitative inquirers may have only a few interviews or a few observational notes transcribed. The most complete procedure, however, is to have all interviews and all observational notes transcribed. As a general rule of thumb, it takes approximately 4 hours to transcribe 1 hour of tape (Dana Miller, personal communication, April 11, 2000). As you can see, the process of transcription is labor-intensive and you will need to allow adequate time for it.

Transcription is the process of converting audiotape recordings or fieldnotes into text data. Figure 9.2 lists suggestions for conducting a taped interview from the transcriptionist's point of view. You may use a transcriptionist to type your text files or you can transcribe

FIGURE 9.2

Hints for Transcribing Audiotaped Interviews

Hints for Taped Interviews: The Transcriptionist's View
Donald Callen Freed
Word Processing Center at
Teachers College, University of Nebraska at Lincoln

The following suggestions are a result of several years of experience transcribing research interview tapes. They are offered for your consideration in order that your transcription may be easier and less time consuming. These suggestions were originally developed for persons who have their tapes professionally transcribed, although many are applicable to those who transcribe their own tapes.

1. Please use an external microphone. This places voices closer to the microphone, and away from the noise of the tape recorder itself. If you must use a machine with an internal microphone, place it as close to *both* interviewer and interviewee as possible. High quality tape recorders also ensure better results and reduce background noise, especially if an external microphone is not available. (Most electronic supply shops have external microphones, which are very inexpensive.)

2. For telephone interviews, please use a telephone pick-up device.

3. Please keep the microphone and/or tape recorder away from possible loud-noise interference—electronic devices, the telephone on a desk, coffee cups or glasses that might be set on the same table as the microphone, etc. An important word or phrase can be lost with the interference of one loud noise.

4. Interviewers: Try to induce slower, more distinct speech by speaking calmly yourself. Try asking questions slowly and distinctly, so that the interviewee will respond in a like manner. Practice keeping your voice up all the way to the end of the sentence, using clear diction. Important questions or probes are sometimes lost because the interviewer trails off or speaks less distinctly at the end of the sentence.

5. Use *new, high quality* tapes and good, well-maintained recording equipment. If you must rely on previously used tapes, make sure they have been used only once or twice. Older tapes often have bleed-over from previous recordings, and are more likely to jam in a machine. In general, transcription equipment works best with 60-minute tapes. Standard-size cassette tapes work much better than micro- or mini-cassettes, and are more easily turned over in an interview.

6. Think clearly about the format you want for your printed transcription. Consider the margin size and the amount of space you want left for comments, double or triple spacing, large margins for coding purposes, etc.

Following these steps can ensure better quality for your research transcriptions, making research easier and your results more accurate. A transcriptionist can only type what he or she can hear. A small amount of forethought and attention to detail on the interviewer's part can result in a better interview tape and transcription.

Source: Condensed from the January 1990 "Words" newsletter, Teachers College Word Processing Center, University of Nebraska–Lincoln, Marlene Starr and Donald C. Freed, editors.

the information yourself. In either case, for interview data, transcriptionists need special equipment to help create the transcript. This equipment consists of a machine that enables the transcriber to start and stop tape recordings or to play them at a speed so that they can be easily interpreted. Here are a few more transcription guidelines to follow to ensure that the data from tapes or fieldnotes can be easily analyzed:

- Create 2-inch margins on each side of the text document so you can jot down notes in the margins during data analysis.
- Leave extra space on the page between the interviewer's comments and the interviewee's comments. This enables the reader of a transcript to clearly distinguish between speakers during data analysis.

▶ Highlight or mark in some way the questions asked by the interviewer. These questions will not be analyzed, and identifying them clearly can allow the analyst to skip over them.

▶ Use complete, detailed headers that contain information about the interview or observational session. The headers in the interview and observational protocols in Chapter 7 show the type of content to be included in a transcription.

▶ Transcribe all words, and type the word [pause] to indicate when individuals being interviewed take a lengthy break in their comments. These pauses may provide useful information about times when interviewees cannot or will not respond to a question. Other actions occurring during an interview can also be noted. For example, type [laughter] when the interviewee laughs; [telephone rings] to indicate a phone call that interrupts the interview; or [inaudible] to mark when the transcriptionist cannot determine what is being said. As a general approach, transcribing all words will provide data that captures the details of an interview.

Analysis by Hand or Computer?

With the popularity of computers, researchers have a choice about whether to hand-analyze data or to use a computer. As you prepare to analyze your data, you need to decide if you are going to hand- or computer-analyze your data. The **hand-analysis of qualitative data** means that researchers read the data, mark it by hand, and divide it into parts. Traditionally, analyzing text data involves using color-coding to mark parts of the text or by cutting and pasting text sentences onto cards. A **computer-analysis of qualitative data** means that researchers use a qualitative computer program to facilitate the process of storing, analyzing, and making sense of the data. These computer programs provide a data organizing, managing, and searching tool for your research; they do not perform the analysis—you need to provide directions and make decisions when using the programs.

With the development of these types of computer programs, you have a choice as to whether to use hand-coding or a computer analysis. You might base your decision on several factors. Use a computer program when you:

▶ are analyzing a large database (e.g., more than 500 pages of transcripts or fieldnotes) and need to organize and keep track of extensive information

▶ are adequately trained in using the program and are comfortable using computers

▶ have resources to purchase a program or can locate one to use

▶ need a close inspection of every word and sentence to capture specific quotes or meanings of passages

A hand analysis, however, may be preferred when you:

▶ are analyzing a small database (e.g., less than 500 pages of transcripts or fieldnotes) and can easily keep track of files and locate text passages

▶ are not comfortable using computers or have not learned a qualitative computer software program

▶ want to be close to the data and have a hands-on feel for it without the intrusion of a machine

▶ when you have time to commit to a hand-analysis, since it is a labor-intensive activity to manually sort, organize, and locate words in a text database

Qualitative Computer Programs

Several computer programs are available that allow a researcher to store text files and identify text for data analysis (see Weitzman & Miles, 1995, for a review of 30 such programs). Figure 9.3 presents a brief review of six popular programs found at http://www.sagepub.com. A **qualitative computer program** is a program that stores and organizes qualitative data

FIGURE 9.3

Qualitative Analysis Microcomputer Software (found at www.sagepub.com link to software listing)

ATLAS.ti

ATLAS.ti is a powerful software workbench for the qualitative analysis of large bodies of textual, graphical, audio, and video data. It offers a variety of tools for accomplishing the tasks associated with any systematic approach to "soft" data.

Features:
- It uses an object-oriented graphical user interface.
- ATLAS can process textual, graphical, audio, and video data.
- It uses intuitive and easy on-screen coding (drag and drop).
- It allows for flexible definition of data segments.
- ATLAS has simultaneous displays of data segments in context, codes, and memos.
- A virtually unlimited number of documents, segments, codes, and memos are available.
- It has "mind mapping" and graphical network editing.
- It assigns annotations to all type of units, data segments, codes, memos, etc.
- It allows theory building and reuse: You can create and transfer knowledge networks between projects.
- ATLAS can generate PROLOG code for building knowledge-based systems.
- It can link data segments with Hypertext capabilities.
- ATLAS is a powerful retrieval tool with Boolean, semantic, and proximity-based operators.
- It has super codes, which capture hypotheses.
- It gives you easy, document-based handling.
- It uses Object Explorer, a hierarchical browser for navigating inside the project.
- It has a time-based backup mechanism, which means no frustration even after power failures.
- ATLAS can export and import XML data.
- It uses generation of HTML format for publication of research on the World Wide Web.

QSR N5 (NUD*IST 5.0)

New from QSR, N5 is the latest version of the NUD*IST software used for code-based qualitative analysis. It combines efficient management of Non-numerical Unstructured Data with powerful processes of Indexing, Searching, and Theorizing.

Features:
- Offers a complete toolkit for rapid coding, thorough exploration, and rigorous management and analysis.
- With a full command language for automating coding and searching, N5 powerfully supports a wide range of methods.
- Its command files and import procedures make project setup very rapid, and link qualitative and quantitative data.
- Tolerant of large data sets, it ships with QSR Merge, which seamlessly merges two or more projects (N4 or N5) for teams or multi-site research.
- Documents are imported singly or in batches, in plain text with automatic formatting to the chosen unit of text.
- Coding on-screen, with new immediate access to the code system, allows the researcher to monitor and manage the emergence of ideas.
- Coded material is displayed for reflection, revision of coding, and coding-on to new categories.
- With searches of coding or text accessed by new, visual displays, the researcher can test hypotheses, locate patterns, or pursue a line of inquiry to a confident conclusion.
- N5 is on the PC platform, has low system requirements, and comes with new detailed online help, new tutorials, and user guides.
- N5 users can use N4 (PC) projects without conversion and can upgrade projects to NVivo, if desired.

FIGURE 9.3 (CONTINUED)

Qualitative Data Analysis Microcomputer Software

NVivo

QSR NUD*IST Vivo (NVivo) opens a new generation of qualitative programs, supporting rich, editable text and multimedia capabilities with finely focused searching, hyperlinking, modeling, and code-based theorizing.

Features:
- All documentation is handled as editable rich text, enabling "visual coding" by highlighting, font changing, etc.
- A "Node System" provides structured and unstructured ways of representing project topics: any person, place, thing, process, idea, document feature or theme in the project.
- Documents and nodes can be inter-linked by hyperlink-style jumps to provide cross-referencing networks. In this way commentary "memo" documents can be made for nodes and other documents; and nodes can be constructed to act as "extract" references for topics mentioned in documents.
- Documents are fully editable, and the editing does not upset or invalidate existing coding and linking.
- Documents and nodes (and what they represent) can be given any number of "attributes" (properties) to describe and characterize them.
- Documents and nodes can be grouped into any number of "sets" for whatever purpose the user desires.

Ethnograph

The Ethnograph v5.0 for Windows™ PCs is a versatile computer program designed to make the analysis of data collected during qualitative research easier, more efficient, and more effective.

Features:
- You can import your text-based qualitative data, typed up in any word processor, straight into the program.
- The Ethnograph helps you search and note segments of interest within your data, mark them with code words, and run analyses which can be retrieved for inclusion in reports or for further analysis.
- The Ethnograph will handle your project data files and documents whether your data comes in the form of interview transcripts, fieldnotes, open-ended survey responses, or other text-based documents.

WinMAX

WinMAX is a powerful tool for text analysis that can be used for grounded theory oriented "code and retrieve" analysis as well as for more sophisticated text analysis, enabling both qualitative and quantitative procedures to be combined. The program has a simple and easy-to-use interface of four main windows showing the texts already imported, the list of codes, the list of coded segments, and the text itself.

Features:
- A unique feature is that codes can be weighted to give a measure of the significance of a piece of coding, making it possible to retrieve only the most important segments given a particular coding.
- Codes can easily be copied, merged, split or deleted, as your requirements become clearer while you explore the text.
- WinMAX allows you to attach memos to codes or to lines of text to record your emerging thoughts as you work with the text, and the memo manager keeps track of your memos and helps you to select from them according to a range of criteria: the activated texts or codes, the author, the date written, or any character string they contain.
- WinMAX also allows you to define case variables in parallel with your text in order to record and analyze, for instance, the age or gender of speakers.
- Data matrices can be imported and exported between SPSS, SAS, or other statistical packages, although winMAX will perform basic quantitative analysis of your coding, including an analysis of coding frequency and any weighting you have applied.
- The software has powerful retrieval functions, allowing Boolean, proximity and semantic retrieval.

FIGURE 9.3 (CONTINUED)

Qualitative Data Analysis Microcomputer Software

- Coding can also be performed automatically and functions are provided for the analysis of open-ended questions in surveys and for teamwork.
- There is visualization of basic functions like codes and memos.
- It allows for complex and flexible coding and retrieval functions (Boolean, proximity and semantic retrieval).
- It has lexical search and automatic coding capabilities.
- This program lets you merge qualitative and quantitative data.
- It allows you to import and export data matrices.
- WinMAX contains complex and powerful theory building tools.
- The software does unique functions like weight variables and teamwork procedures.
- Special procedures for the analysis of open-ended questions are included.

HyperResearch

HyperRESEARCH is a powerful qualitative analysis program which guides you through a research project from the initial stages of coding and retrieval to the final phases of theory building and hypothesis testing. The functional simplicity and reliability of the software, combined with its powerful advanced features, make HyperRESEARCH an excellent tool for qualitative researchers at any level.

Features:
- HyperRESEARCH v2.0 enables you to code and retrieve, build theories, and conduct analyses of your data.
- It allows you to work with text, graphics, audio and video sources—making it an invaluable research analysis tool.
- It has tools for a variety of analyses, including expert systems capabilities for testing hypotheses.
- It has the ability to work with multiple data types, such as text, graphics, audio, and video sources, and provides the flexibility to integrate all of the data necessary to conduct your research.
- Specifically designed for ease of use, this program has a menu-driven "point and click" interface that allows you to focus your time on the project, not on running the program.
- HyperRESEARCH eliminates the need for costly workshops and further software instruction. It provides a turnkey solution by employing a built-in help system and several tutorials with step-by-step instructions.

Source: Adapted from software listing found at www.sagepub.com.

(i.e., text, such as transcribed interviews or typed fieldnotes) and facilitates the process of analyzing data. A popular program, for example, is NUD*IST (Non-numerical Unstructured Data Indexing, Systematizing, and Theorizing) from Sage Publications. This program is available on either the Macintosh or PC platform, is inexpensive, and contains typical features of many qualitative computer programs. These features are the ability to store text (or image) files, to retrieve segments (or sentences) of text using key words, and to search for and locate segments of text to document themes or categorize ideas. It also presents visual images (i.e., branch diagrams) of the themes and their relationships, and produces printouts of segments of text for evidence for themes.

To use a typical qualitative computer program, follow these steps:

1. Convert a word processing file into a text file. The word processing file will be a transcribed interview, a set of fieldnotes, or other text, such as a scanned document.
2. Select a computer program to use. This program should perform the functions mentioned above, and be suitable for your microcomputer.
3. Enter a file into the program and give it a name.
4. Go through the file and mark sentences or paragraphs of ideas that pertain to what the participant is saying in the text.

5. Provide a code label for the blocked text. Continue this process of marking text and providing code labels for the entire text file.
6. After blocking and assigning labels to text, search for all text matching each code, and print out a file of these text passages.
7. Collapse these code labels into a few broad themes, or categories, and include evidence for each category.
8. Again print out these results and use the different ways participants talk about the theme in the written qualitative narrative.

Exploring the Data

After your data have been organized and transcribed and the decision to hand- or computer analyze it has been made, it is time to begin data analysis. The first step in data analysis is to explore the data by reading through all of your information to obtain a general sense of the information. A **preliminary exploratory analysis** in qualitative research consists of obtaining a general sense of the data, memoing ideas, thinking about the organization of the data, and considering whether more data are needed. For example, Agar (1980) suggests you ". . . read the transcripts in their entirety several times. Immerse yourself in the details, trying to get a sense of the interview as a whole before breaking it into parts." (p. 103). Writing memos in the margins of fieldnotes, transcripts, or under photographs helps in this initial process of exploring the data. These memos are short phrases, ideas, concepts, or hunches that occur to you. These steps help form an initial analysis of the data.

In the qualitative gunman incident study, Asmussen & Creswell (1995) collected many forms of data as displayed in their Table 1 matrix of data collection types and sources (see Paragraph 11). To begin making sense of this diverse information, they spent time reviewing all of the documents and transcriptions. Although they might have specifically reported this process (e.g., in Paragraph 12), they looked over fieldnotes from observations, interview data, newspapers, and videotapes of the television coverage to obtain an initial reading of the campus reaction to the incident.

Describing and Developing Themes from the Data

Beyond having a general understanding of your data, you also need to answer your research questions. This process involves examining the data in detail to describe what you learned and developing themes or broad categories of ideas from the data. **Describing and developing themes from the data** consists of answering the major research questions and forming an in-depth understanding of the central phenomenon. Not all qualitative projects include both description and theme development. Description, as you will learn in Chapter 15 on "Ethnographic Research," is a central feature of reporting what you learn about a cultural group and the setting in which it lives and interacts. On the other hand, thematic development plays a central role in grounded theory (described in Chapter 14), where you generate themes or categories of information from your data. A narrative study, discussed in Chapter 16, typically includes both—a description of the events in an individual's story and the themes that emerge from that story.

What is most important at this time is how you proceed from a database to generating a description, a theme, or both for a qualitative study. Several procedures are used in this process:

▶ coding text (or image) data
▶ developing a description from the data
▶ defining themes from the data
▶ connecting and interrelating themes

Coding Data

The process of analyzing text (or images) in qualitative research begins when the inquirer codes the data. **Coding** is the process of segmenting and labeling text to form descriptions and broad themes in the data. Although there are no set guidelines for coding data, some general procedures exist (see Creswell, 1994; Tesch, 1990).

Using a visual model like the one in Figure 9.4 will help you learn this procedure. The object of the **coding process** is to make sense out of text data, divide it into text or image segments, label the segments, examine codes for overlap and redundancy, and collapse these codes into themes. Thus, this is an inductive process of narrowing data into a few themes (J. David Creswell, personal communication, January 1, 2001). Several steps are involved in coding data. Although there is no definite procedure, Tesch (1990) and Creswell (1994) recommend the following steps:

1. Get a sense of the whole. Read through all of the transcriptions carefully. Jot down in the margins some ideas as they come to mind.
2. Pick one document (e.g., one interview, one fieldnote). Choose the most interesting, the shortest, or the one on the top of the pile. Go through it, asking the question, "What is this about?" Consider the underlying meaning and write it down in the margin in two or three words, drawing a box around it.
3. Begin the process of coding the document. This process involves identifying text segments, placing a bracket around them, and assigning a code word or phrase that accurately describes the meaning of the text segment. Sentences or paragraphs that all relate to a single code are called a **text segment. Codes** are labels used to describe a segment of text or an image. Codes can address many different topics, such as those listed below. (See also see Bogdan & Biklen, 1992.)
   ◗ setting and context (e.g., classroom)
   ◗ perspectives held by participants (poor learners)
   ◗ participants' way of thinking about people and objects (problem children)
   ◗ processes (disruptions during the class)
   ◗ activities (student sitting quietly)
   ◗ strategies (teacher giving time-out)
   ◗ relationship and social structure (students talking to each other)
   As seen in these examples, codes can be stated in the participant's actual words (i.e., a student's perspective about other students, such as "poor learners") which are

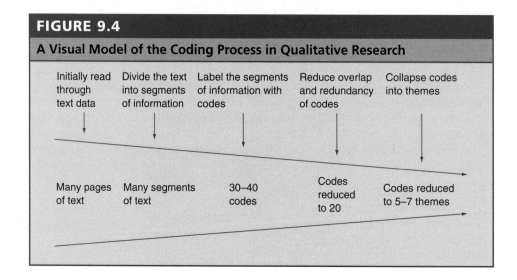

FIGURE 9.4

A Visual Model of the Coding Process in Qualitative Research

Initially read through text data	Divide the text into segments of information	Label the segments of information with codes	Reduce overlap and redundancy of codes	Collapse codes into themes
Many pages of text	Many segments of text	30–40 codes	Codes reduced to 20	Codes reduced to 5–7 themes

called *in vivo codes*. They can also be phrased in standard educational terms (a researcher referring to "a classroom"), or expressed in the language of the observer (a researcher's statement about "students talking to each other").

4. After coding an entire text, make a list of all code words. Cluster together similar codes and look for redundant codes. Your objective is to reduce a long list of codes to a smaller, more manageable number, such as 25 to 30. It is best not to over-code the data because, in the end, you will need to reduce the codes to a small number of themes.

5. Take this list and go back to the data. Try out this preliminary organizing scheme to see whether new codes emerge. Circle specific quotes from participants that support the codes.

6. Reduce the list of codes to get 5 to 7 themes or descriptions of the setting or participants. **Themes** are similar codes aggregated together to form a major idea in the database. In the literature you might find that themes are also called categories (e.g., in grounded theory research), dimensions, issues, or perspectives. Regardless of the name, identify the 5–7 themes by examining codes that are most frequently discussed by participants, are unique or surprising, have the most evidence to support them, or those that might be expected from studying the phenomenon. The reason for the small number of themes is that it is best to write a qualitative report providing detailed information about a few themes rather than general information about many themes. A **description** is a detailed rendering of people, places, or events in a setting in qualitative research. Codes, such as "seating arrangements," "teaching approach," or "physical layout of the room," might all be used to describe a classroom where instruction takes place.

7. From the coding and the themes, construct a narrative description and possibly a visual display of the findings for your research report.

 ## Think-Aloud About Coding a Transcript for Themes

In this Think-Aloud I will illustrate not only coding a transcript but also developing multiple codes and themes. I will also illustrate the preliminary data analysis process of jotting notes in the margin in a first reading of the data.

Figure 9.5 shows a sample transcript from an interview and the codes, themes, and ideas that I recorded in the margins. This transcript resulted from an interview from a project exploring the changes in the curriculum in a rural high school (Jones, 1999). Overall, the interviewee talks about changes in the high school from a traditional curriculum to a school based on service-learning in the community. Jones asks questions in the interview and "LU," the interviewee, provides responses. Look over the codes on the left and the themes and other ideas recorded in the margins in this figure. I will take you through my thinking as I coded this transcript.

▶ Notice that the margins on the left and right are extra wide so I could jot down my ideas there.

▶ On the left side I inserted codes; on the right side, ideas and emerging themes. These features could have been reversed (e.g., codes on the right), but I prefer this organization.

▶ For codes, I used two or three words as labels. These were the actual words used by the participant, "LU." Sometimes I listed codes as possible alternatives.

▶ I placed boxes around key words that I wanted to use as codes or possibly themes.

▶ By bracketing (drawing a bracket around sentences in the left margin) I identified sentences that seem to "fit together" to describe one idea, my text segments. Notice that not all sentences were bracketed. I did not use all of the data because I needed

FIGURE 9.5

Coding a Page from a Sample Interview Transcript

The Process of Reconstructing Curriculum in a Rural High School Setting

Codes Here		Themes (And other Ideas) Here
	JJ: One thing, Lucy, that I've heard talked about was the fact that schools reflect the strengths of communities. What do you perceive as strengths of Greenfield as a community and how that relates to schools?	
Close-knit community	LU: Well, I think Greenfield is a fairly close-knit community. I think people are interested in what goes on. And because of that, they have a sense of ownership in the schools. We like to keep track of what our kids are doing and feel a connection to them because of that. The downside of that perhaps is that kids can feel that we are looking TOO close. But most of the time, that is the nurturing environment that we do provide an atmosphere of concern and care.	Potential theme: The community
Health of community or community values	To back up, you said the health of the community itself is reflected in schools. A lot of times communities look at schools and say they are not doing this or they aren't doing that, or we're missing something in our schools. I think perhaps we look at the school and see, this is probably a pretty conservative community overall, and look to make sure that what is being talked about in the schools really carries out the community's values. There is a little bit of an idealization I think, perhaps in terms of what we thought of "basic education." [And I think there might be a tendency to hold back a little bit too much because of that idealization of "you know, we learned the basics, the reading, the	Idea: getting a good sense here for the community and its values
Change is threatening	writing and the arithmetic."] So you know, any change is threatening. And I think that goes for the community as well as what we see reflected at the school. Sometimes that can get in the way of trying to do different things. I think, again, idealization, older members of the community forget, some of the immaturity that they experienced when they were in school and forgetting that kids are kids. So there is a little bit too much of that mental attitude. But for the most part, I think there is a sense of we're all in this together, and concern for the kids.	A good quote
	JJ: In terms of looking at leadership strengths in the community, where does Greenfield set in a continuum there with planning process, understanding the need to plan, forward-thinking, visionary people. You talked about that a little bit before.	Potential theme: Leaders
Visionary skills of talented People	LU: I think there are people that have wonderful visionary skills. I would say that the community as a whole would be . . . would not reflect that. I think there are people who are driving the process, but the rest of the community may be lagging behind a little bit. I think we have some incredibly talented people who become frustrated when they try to implement what they see as their . . .	Idea: returns to description of community again

Source: Reprinted with permission of Jean Jones, Ph.D.

to reduce it to 5 to 7 themes for my final research report. I asked myself, "What are they talking about here?", drew a bracket around key sentences that related to a code, and assigned a code label.

▶ On the right, I listed potential themes in the transcript. Also on the right you will see my early jottings (e.g., "getting a good sense here for the community and its values") and I highlighted a good quote that I might use in my final research report.

The process now, beyond this single page, will be to continue my coding and theme development so that I can construct a description of the community and write about themes relating to this curriculum change in a rural high school setting.

Using Codes to Build Description

Now that you know the general process and have examined an actual example of coding a transcript, we need to explore how to use codes to build description and themes in qualitative research. Beginning with description, we can explore what it attempts to accomplish, how you might use it, and how it appears in a narrative or research report.

Since description is a detailed rendering of people, places, or events in a setting in qualitative research, it is easiest to start the analysis after the initial reading and coding of the data. In some forms of qualitative research design, such as in ethnography or in case studies, the researcher provides considerable description of the setting. Developing detail is important, and the researcher analyzes data from all sources (e.g., interviews, observations, documents) to build a portrait of individuals or events. To describe an event, the analyst might ask, "What occurred in this setting?" as in the gunman case study (Asmussen & Creswell, 1995). Alternatively, the researcher might describe an individual by asking, "What is this person like?" For describing a place, the question might be, "What is this place like?"

Description needs to be detailed so that the reader is transported to a research site or can visualize a person. It takes experience and practice to describe the detail in a setting. For example, examine these two illustrations and see the differences in level of detail.

▶ **Poor example:** The education building that was being built consisted of three floors.
▶ **Better example:** As the education building developed, it was held together with iron beams that crossed and connected. These were lifted in place by a giant crane with a line secured around each beam as it was placed on the proper floor of the structure. A worker underneath the beam fastened it in place. As we watched the beam being lifted, it tipped back and forth, leading us to wonder if the crane operator securely fastened it. One slip and disaster would follow, but the beam landed securely in place.

Another good example is the following passage from a short story by Budnitz (2000). The author was writing about the common process of preparing pancakes.

> He was mixing stuff up in a bowl; flour slopped over the edges and sprinkled on the counter and the floor. I'll have to clean that up, I thought. . . . There was butter bubbling and crackling in the frying pan. . . . He poured in the batter, it was thick and pale yellow; and the hissing butter shut up for a while. . . . There were two large lumpy mounds there, side by side, bubbling inside as if they were alive, turning brown on the edges. He turned them over and I saw the crispy undersides with patterns on them like the moon; and then he pressed them down with the spatula, pressed them flat and the butter sputtered and hissed. (pp. 91–92)

By reading vivid short stories or examining qualitative studies, you can find illustrations where writers used detail to take an ordinary experience (like pancake making) and transport you to the setting so that you can almost feel (or taste) the situation.

Let's take an illustration that you have already read—the descriptive passage in the gunman case study (Asmussen & Creswell, 1995). Figure 9.6 reports the events that happened

FIGURE 9.6

Elements of Description in a Narrative Passage

The Incident and Response

Description builds from broad to narrow

Situate the reader in the place or context

Provide details

The incident occurred on the campus of a large public university in a Midwestern city. A decade ago, this city had been designated an "all-American city," but more recent, its normally tranquil environment has been disturbed by an increasing number of assaults and homicides. Some of these violent incidents have involved students at the university.

The incident that provoked this study occurred on a Monday in October. A forty-three-year-old graduate student, enrolled in a senior-level actuarial science class, arrived a few minutes before class, armed with a vintage Korean War military semiautomatic rifle loaded with a thirty-round clip of thirty caliber ammunition. He carried another thirty-round clip in his pocket. Twenty of the thirty-four students in the class had already gathered for class, and most of them were quietly reading the student newspaper. The instructor was en route to class.

Detail to create a sense of "being there"

Use of action verbs and vivid modifiers and adjectives

The gunman pointed the rifle at the students, swept it across the room, and pulled the trigger. The gun jammed. Trying to unlock the rifle, he hit the butt of it on the instructor's desk and quickly tried firing it again. Again it did not fire. By this time, most students realized what was happening and dropped to the floor, overturned their desks, and tried to hide behind them. After about twenty seconds, one of the students <u>shoved</u> a desk into the gunman, and students ran past him out into the hall and out of the building. The gunman <u>hastily departed</u> the room and went out of the building to his parked car, which he had left running. He was captured by police within the hour in a nearby small town, where he lived. Although he remains incarcerated at this time, awaiting trial, the motivations for his actions are unknown.

Just describe the "facts," not interpret situation

Use of quotes or italics to emphasize ideas or "reflective" comments

Campus police and campus administrators were the first to react to the incident. Campus police arrived within three minutes after they had received a telephone call for help. They spent several <u>anxious</u> minutes outside the building interviewing students to obtain an accurate description of the gunman. Campus administrators responded by calling a news conference for 4:00 P.M. the same day, approximately four hours after the incident. The police chief as well as the vice-chancellor of Student Affairs and two students described the incident at the news conference. That same afternoon, the Student Affairs office contacted Student Health and Employee Assistance Program (EAP) counselors and instructed them to be available for any student or staff requesting assistance. The Student Affairs office also arranged for a new location, where this class could meet for the rest of the semester. The Office of Judicial Affairs suspended the gunman from the university. The next day, the incident was discussed by campus administrators at a regularly scheduled campuswide cabinet meeting. Throughout the week, Student Affairs received several calls from students and from a faculty member about "disturbed" students or unsettling student relations. A counselor of the Employee Assistance Program consulted a psychologist with a specialty in dealing with trauma and responding to educational crises. Only one student immediately set up an appointment with the student health counselors. The campus and local newspapers continued to carry stories about the incident.

Source: Asmussen & Creswell, 1995, pp. 576–577.

2 weeks following the gunman incident on campus. The discussion of these events illustrates several features of description that you might include in your own qualitative description or note in a published research report. The labels indicate that:

- The passage starts broadly with the midwestern city and narrows to the campus, then the classroom, and finally the incident. This broad-to-narrow description is intended to help the reader understand the context or place of the incident and provide a sense of a "real" place where this near-tragedy occurred.
- The authors attempt to use vivid details to create the description. We know, for example, that the rifle was a "Korean War military semiautomatic" and exactly how many "clips" of rounds could be loaded into this weapon.

▶ The action comes alive in this description through the use of action verbs and movement-oriented modifiers and adjectives. The gunman did not walk out of the building, but "hastily departed."

▶ The authors do not make an interpretation or evaluate the situation—they simply report the "facts" as they heard about them from data sources. Times (e.g., 4:00 P.M.) illustrate detail about the specific occurrence of events.

▶ The passage includes quotes to provide emphasis and realism in the account. These quotes are short, even one word (e.g., "disturbed"). They may be longer, such as a short phrase or a sentence, but in a brief journal article, writers need to be concerned about space available for the narrative, and generally keep the quotes as short as possible.

Using Codes to Develop Themes

In addition to description, the use of themes is another way to analyze qualitative data. Because themes are similar codes aggregated together to form a major idea in the database, they form a core element in qualitative data analysis. Like codes, themes have labels that typically consist of no more than two to four words (e.g., "denial," "campus planning").

Through initial data analyses, you may find 30–50 codes. In subsequent analyses, these codes are reduced to 5–7 major themes through the process of eliminating redundancies and codes that cannot be conveniently categorized. There are several types of themes, and authors typically identify them as:

▶ *ordinary themes:* themes that a researcher might expect to find (e.g., "exposure to tobacco at school")

▶ *unexpected themes:* themes that are surprises and not expected to surface during a study (e.g., "unenforced school tobacco use policies")

▶ *hard-to-classify themes:* themes that contain ideas that do not easily fit into one theme or that overlap with several themes (e.g., "students gather in the park")

▶ *major and minor themes:* themes that represent the major ideas, or minor, secondary ideas in a database

For example, a major theme might be: attempts to quit smoking. Minor themes might be: physical reaction, peer pressure to continue smoking, or starts and stops.

It might be helpful to examine a narrative passage in a qualitative research report. Figure 9.7 is a portion of the discussion of the "safety" theme found in the gunman incident study (Asmussen & Creswell, 1995). The marginal annotations mark elements that are included in the theme.

"Safety" is considered an "ordinary" theme because it is one that we might expect participants to discuss on the campus where the incident occurred. Several participants mention this theme, so the authors select it and use the exact wording of participants. The authors analyze their data for multiple perspectives on this theme of "safety." **Multiple perspectives** means that evidence for a theme is based on several viewpoints from different individuals and sources of data. Multiple perspectives, as you may recall from Chapter 2, are important when conveying the complexity of the phenomenon. In this passage, for example, the authors report the perspectives of:

▶ the chief student affairs officer

▶ university board members

▶ campus security officers

▶ the counseling and psychological services office

▶ a professor on campus

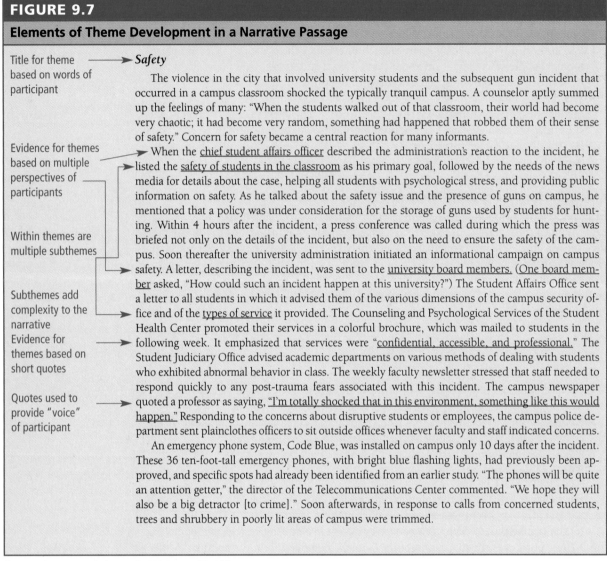

FIGURE 9.7

Elements of Theme Development in a Narrative Passage

Title for theme based on words of participant → *Safety*

The violence in the city that involved university students and the subsequent gun incident that occurred in a campus classroom shocked the typically tranquil campus. A counselor aptly summed up the feelings of many: "When the students walked out of that classroom, their world had become very chaotic; it had become very random, something had happened that robbed them of their sense of safety." Concern for safety became a central reaction for many informants.

Evidence for themes based on multiple perspectives of participants → When the <u>chief student affairs officer</u> described the administration's reaction to the incident, he listed the <u>safety of students in the classroom</u> as his primary goal, followed by the needs of the news media for details about the case, helping all students with psychological stress, and providing public information on safety. As he talked about the safety issue and the presence of guns on campus, he mentioned that a policy was under consideration for the storage of guns used by students for hunting. Within 4 hours after the incident, a press conference was called during which the press was briefed not only on the details of the incident, but also on the need to ensure the safety of the campus. Soon thereafter the university administration initiated an informational campaign on campus

Within themes are multiple subthemes → safety. A letter, describing the incident, was sent to the <u>university board members. (One board member</u> asked, "How could such an incident happen at this university?") The Student Affairs Office sent a letter to all students in which it advised them of the various dimensions of the campus security of-

Subthemes add complexity to the narrative → fice and of the <u>types of service</u> it provided. The Counseling and Psychological Services of the Student Health Center promoted their services in a colorful brochure, which was mailed to students in the

Evidence for themes based on short quotes → following week. It emphasized that services were "<u>confidential, accessible, and professional.</u>" The Student Judiciary Office advised academic departments on various methods of dealing with students who exhibited abnormal behavior in class. The weekly faculty newsletter stressed that staff needed to respond quickly to any post-trauma fears associated with this incident. The campus newspaper

Quotes used to provide "voice" of participant → quoted a professor as saying, "<u>I'm totally shocked that in this environment, something like this would happen.</u>" Responding to the concerns about disruptive students or employees, the campus police department sent plainclothes officers to sit outside offices whenever faculty and staff indicated concerns.

An emergency phone system, Code Blue, was installed on campus only 10 days after the incident. These 36 ten-foot-tall emergency phones, with bright blue flashing lights, had previously been approved, and specific spots had already been identified from an earlier study. "The phones will be quite an attention getter," the director of the Telecommunications Center commented. "We hope they will also be a big detractor [to crime]." Soon afterwards, in response to calls from concerned students, trees and shrubbery in poorly lit areas of campus were trimmed.

Source: Asmussen & Creswell, 1995, pp. 582–583.

It is also useful to see that the authors have one major theme and several minor themes subsumed under the major theme. Diagrammed, this thematic development would be:

Major theme: safety

Minor themes (or subthemes): safety of students in the classroom; types of services

Finally, to add realism to this passage, the authors include short quotes from their interviews and newspaper accounts.

One more aspect of theme development is not represented in this passage. A realistic presentation of information does not present only one side or the other. In an attempt to capture the complexity of situations, qualitative researchers actively analyze data for contrary evidence. **Contrary evidence** is information that does not support or confirm the themes and provides contradictory information about a theme. Had the authors of the gunman case study searched for this evidence, for example, they might have found that some students actually felt "safe" because the gunman left quickly or because they could out-number the gunman.

One final point to note about developing themes is that you will reach a point where a theme is fully developed and new evidence will not provide additional insight. **Saturation** is the point where a theme is developed and detailed and no new information can add to its specification. Unquestionably the point at which you achieve saturation is a judgment call, but most qualitative researchers realize when this point occurs. In the development of the theme of "quit attempts in smoking," the researchers drew on their extensive interviews with high school students. The found evidence through specific examples and quotes to illustrate the theme, and when they returned to the interview transcriptions, no new information surfaced during their reading and re-reading of the transcripts. They concluded that they had reached saturation on this theme. A check with participants (see "Validating the Accuracy of Findings" later in this chapter) confirmed that they had adequately specified this theme.

Connecting and Interrelating Themes

Many qualitative studies include only description and themes for analysis. However, by adding the layering of themes or interconnecting them, you can build sophistication and complexity into your research. Thus, qualitative data analysts represent this complexity by layering and interconnecting themes.

Layering themes builds on the idea of major and minor themes, but organizes the themes into layers from basic elementary themes to more sophisticated ones. **Layering the analysis** (also called first and second order abstractions) means representing the data using interconnected levels of themes. Minor themes are subsumed within major themes and major themes lead to broader themes. The entire analysis becomes more complex as the researcher works *upward* toward broader and broader levels of abstraction. The number of layers may vary from two to four or five, and recognizing these layers will help you read more complex qualitative studies.

Some layering occurred, for example, in the gunman incident study (Asmussen & Creswell, 1995), although the authors did not specifically refer to this analysis procedure. Examine Figure 9.8. This figure shows that the authors used four layers, including the database as one layer. The authors collected data from several sources (layer 1) and analyzed it to develop a description of events (layer 2). From this description they then formed five themes (layer 3) and combined these themes into two broad perspectives (layer 4). Knowing how layering works will help you see how the authors began with the details and worked their way up to the more general themes in their analysis.

A second thematic analysis approach interconnects the themes. **Interconnecting themes** means that the researcher connects the themes to display a chronology or sequence of events, such as when qualitative researchers generate a theoretical and conceptual model (see Chapter 14 on grounded theory research) or report stories of individuals (see Chapter 16 on narrative research). Often qualitative researchers draw a visual diagram or figure to portray the interconnection of themes. For example, look at Figure 9.9. Here we see a sample chart used in a qualitative grounded theory study (Creswell & Brown, 1992). The researchers examine the practices used by 33 academic department chairs to enhance the research of faculty in their college or university units. As shown in the figure, the authors identify numerous themes within each box in the diagram. But in addition, arrows show that the boxes are connected in a sequence. In this sequence, the process of enhancing faculty research performance relates to the type of faculty issue (e.g., getting started with research), signs that this issue is important (e.g., as identified by the chair), the context of stages of the faculty member's career (e.g., beginning), and the larger institutional context (e.g., good for the department). It also includes the specific strategies employed by the chair (e.g., the chair as a provider), and the outcomes of using that strategy (e.g., too early to tell).

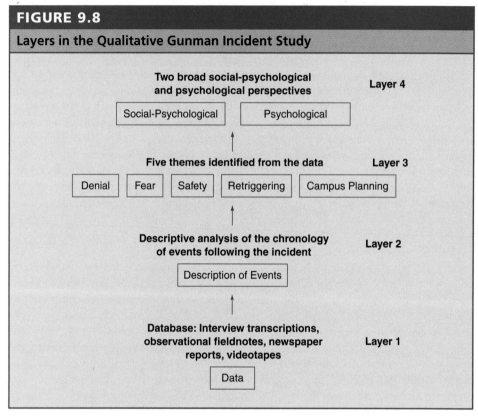

FIGURE 9.8

Layers in the Qualitative Gunman Incident Study

Source: Asmussen & Creswell, 1995.

In short, this process displays an interconnected set of events or activities in the process of chairs' enhancing faculty members' performances. In Chapter 14 we will discuss these linkages in more detail, but, from this example, you can see how qualitative researchers connect themes to build a complex picture of a phenomenon and a process.

Reporting and Representing Findings

After you code the data, analyze it for description and themes, and layer and interconnect themes, you report findings to your research questions. This calls for constructing a narrative to explain what you have found and displaying findings in tables and figures.

Constructing a Narrative

The primary form for representing and reporting findings in qualitative research is a narrative discussion. A **narrative discussion** is a written passage in a qualitative study in which authors summarize, in detail, the findings from their data analysis. There is no set form for this narrative, which can vary widely from one study to another. However, it is helpful to identify some frequently used forms, shown in Table 9.1. Several of these forms have already been discussed, such as developing description, theme, or interconnecting themes. Others are important, too, especially in advocacy and participatory forms of qualitative inquiry such as raising questions, challenging assumptions based on evidence supplied by participants, or reflecting on how participants change (e.g., become empowered, become advocates, become involved) during the research. Your decision about which form or forms to use depends on the purpose of your research and the type of data you have analyzed for your findings.

FIGURE 9.9

Interconnecting Themes or Categories in a Qualitative Study

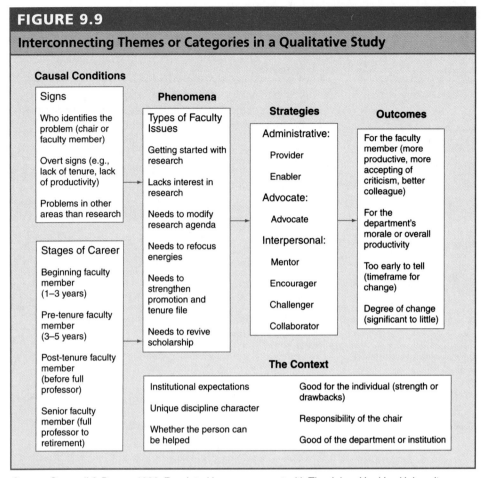

Source: Creswell & Brown, 1992. Reprinted by arrangement with The Johns Hopkins University Press.

A related topic is the procedure you use during data analysis to help construct the narrative discussion. As you make multiple passes through your database looking for description and themes, there are some other things to look for that will be useful for the narrative:

▶ *Identify dialogue that provides support for themes.* For example, in a study about reading disabilities of four middle school students, Kos (1991) provides this dialogue about the theme "reading-related stress" for a student named Karen. (Kos' comments are labelled "R," while Karen's comments are labelled "K.")

K: I feel that it's very difficult for me.
R: Mm hmm.
K: And sometimes I can read a book and some books are kind of difficult. And um, my mom said that you have to read or . . . or you won't get nowhere.
R: What do you think about that?
K: Um, I think, I think it's sad. And um, like Mom says, that you, you might be having a night job picking up trash and sweeping.
R: Mm hmm.
K: And you wouldn't have a regular job like my mom and make some money.
R: Mm. But somebody has to pick up the trash.
K: Yeah, *somebody*. But *I* don't know who! (pp. 885–886)

TABLE 9.1

Forms of a Narrative Discussion in Qualitative Research

Forms of Narrative Discussion	Examples
A discussion that presents a chronology	The chronology of a teacher's experiences with her special education coordinator leading to her resignation from the school
A discussion that describes events and setting (context)	A description of adolescents reading "teen" magazines
A discussion of themes	A discussion about the theme of the "in-classroom" landscape of a teacher
A discussion of a figure	A figure presenting a model of the process of art therapy with clients
A discussion about layering or interconnecting themes	A discussion about the levels of complexity in a campus response to a gunman incident
A discussion incorporating past literature and research studies	A discussion incorporating past literature of efforts to develop campus plans for potential violence
A discussion raising further questions that need to be addressed	A discussion that raises questions about the equality and fair treatment of women
A discussion using participants' views to challenge accepted or hidden assumptions	A discussion that probes practices of discrimination in our schools
A discussion about how participants are empowered or change	A discussion about how a teacher, by sharing her story, felt empowered

▶ *Look for dialogue in the participants' native language or in the regional or ethnic dialect.* A study that examines the life histories of African-American women by Nelson (1990) includes examples of "code-switching," African-American dialect, to convey the novel metaphors of casual kitchen-table discourse:

> I'm trying to communicate a shoe box full when you only give them (the words) a matchbox. I'm trying to relate the spiritual meaning. (p. 151)

▶ *Use metaphors and analogies in a narrative discussion.* In reporting on the competition and concerns surfacing during the implementation of distance education in the state of Maine, Epper (1997) writes metaphorically about how student and citizen support is a "political football" game:

> As the bickering went on, many students stood by watching their education dreams tossed around like a political football. Some were not content to sit on the sidelines. From the islands, valleys, backwoods, and far reaches of the state came letters to the faculty senates, legislators, and newspapers. (p. 566)

▶ *Collect quotes from interview data or during observations of individuals.* These quotes can capture feelings, emotions, and ways people talk about their experiences.

▶ *Locate multiple perspectives and contrary evidence.* Identify these perspectives based on different individuals, sources of information, or multiple views held by one person.

▶ *Look for vivid detail.* Find good descriptions of an individual, event, or activity.

▶ *Identify tensions and contradictions in individual experiences.* For example, Huber and Whelan (1999) report the personal stories of a female teacher who experiences a lack of support about a special education student in the classroom. They discuss the tension this teacher feels between being in control in her classroom and the out-of-class pressure that she experiences from her school coordinator.

Providing Visual Data Displays

Qualitative researchers often display their findings visually (Miles & Huberman, 1994) by using figures or pictures that augment the discussion. Different ways to display data are listed below.

- Create a visual image of the information in the form of a comparison table (see Spradley, 1980) or a matrix, a table that compares groups on one of the themes or categories in a study (see Miles & Huberman, 1994 for additional examples). In a qualitative study of the meaning of "professionalism," a researcher collected statements from both women and men teachers in a school. Statements from these teachers, shown in Table 9.2, are included in a comparison table to show that females and males can differ in their approaches to professionalism.
- Develop a hierarchical tree diagram that visually represents themes and their interconnections (Figure 9.8 for the gunman incident case study, Asmussen and Creswell, 1995).
- Present figures with boxes to show the connection among themes (see Figure 9.9 from the grounded theory study by Creswell and Brown, 1992).
- Depict the physical layout of the setting. As shown in Figure 9.10, Miller, Creswell, and Olander (1998) display the physical setting of a soup kitchen in their study. This was provided so that the reader could visualize where different activities happened.
- Describe personal or demographic information for each person or site in the research. In a study of the types of technology used by instructors in college classrooms, the researcher described each instructor and his or her primary delivery style in a demographic table, shown in Table 9.3. The six individuals studied in this qualitative study displayed different personal characteristics as well as diverse approaches to using technology. This table provides the reader with various demographic information for each instructor, such as number of years teaching, gender, class level of instruction, instructional approach used in the class, and his or her primary form of technology use.

Interpreting Findings

Interpretation involves making sense of the data, or the "lessons learned," as described by Lincoln and Guba (1985). **Interpretation** means that the researcher steps back and forms some larger meaning about the phenomenon based on personal views and/or comparisons

TABLE 9.2

A Sample Comparison Table Used to Represent Information in a Qualitative Study

Female Statements about "Professionalism"	Male Statements about "Professionalism"
• Helping fellow teachers is part of my day. • When another teacher asks for advice, I am generally a good listener. • It is important, once I achieve a certain level of experience, that I become a mentor to other teachers, especially new ones. • Caring about how other teachers employ high standards in their classroom is a sign of my own professionalism.	• Being concerned about following the coordinator's advice about curriculum shows a high level of professionalism. • It is important to be in charge in the classroom and to be aware of student off-task behavior. • I set standards for myself, and try to achieve these goals each year. • It is necessary that each teacher "pull" their weight in this school—a sure sign of professionalism.

FIGURE 9.10

Sample Diagram of the Physical Layout in a Qualitative Study

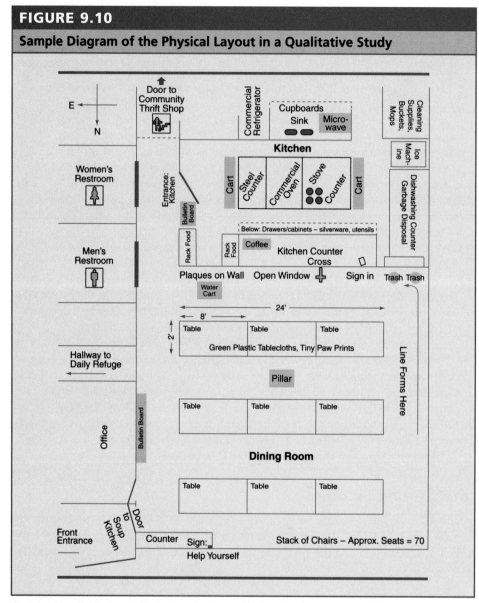

Source: Miller, D. M., Creswell, J. W., & Olander, L. *Qualitative Inquiry, 4*, 469–491, copyright © 1998 by Sage Publications. Reprinted by permission of Sage Publications.

with past studies. It is often difficult to discern where reporting findings end and making interpretations begins. A qualitative stance is that all findings and all interpretations are subjective assessments by the researchers, and that individuals can never be "neutral" or remove themselves from the study to report "objectively." Thus, when you examine the final passages in a qualitative study, look for personal interpretations by the researcher. This interpretation often comes in the final section of a study under "Conclusions," "Interpretations," or "Implications," and it contains:

- personal reflections of the researcher about the meaning of the data
- personal views compared or contrasted with the literature
- limitations of the study
- suggestions for future research

TABLE 9.3

A Sample Demographic Table in a Qualitative Study

Name	Years Teaching	Gender	Class Level of Instruction	Instructional Approach in the Classroom	Primary Form of Technology in the Classroom
Deb	25	Female	12	Discussion	Internet
Harry	20	Male	11	Critique	Not used
Joan	18	Female	11	Discussion	Web site and Internet
Ray	20	Male	12	Interactive	Web site, Internet, wireless laptops
Scott	15	Male	11	Discussion	Not used
Owen	36	Male	10	Lecture	Internet

Conveying Personal Reflections

Because qualitative researchers believe that personal views can never be kept separate from interpretations, personal reflections about the meaning of the data are included in the research study. These personal interpretations may be based on hunches, insights, and intuition. Often it is the researcher who has been to the field and visited personally at great length with individuals. Therefore, the researcher is in a good position to reflect and remark on the larger meaning of the data. The two examples that follow illustrate the diversity in interpretation found in qualitative studies.

In the classic ethnography of the "sneaky kid," Wolcott (1983) reflects about the meaning of learning for Brad:

> Learning—in the broad enculturative sense of coming to understand what one needs to know to be competent in the roles one may expect to fulfill in society, rather than in the narrow sense of learning-done-at-school—is an ongoing process in which each human engages throughout a lifetime. (p 24)

The next example shows how researchers can offer interpretative commentary about new questions that need to be answered. In the discussion by Tierney (1993), who spoke with a 40-year-old African American who had AIDS on a university campus, the researcher left the interview with unanswered questions:

> How do we create understandings across differences so that we are able to acknowledge and honor one another, rather than bring into question one another's legitimacy? It is incumbent on me as the author, then, to present these voices as fully and carefully as possible; at the same time, it is necessary for the reader or methodologist or administrator who does not understand these realities to try to come to terms with them. (p. 27)

Making Comparisons with the Literature

Interpretation may also contain references to the literature and past studies. Similar to what a quantitative researcher does, the qualitative inquirer interprets the data in view of this past research, showing how the findings both support and contradict prior studies. This interpretation may compare qualitative findings with reported views of a social science concept found in the literature, or it may combine personal views with an educational or social science term or idea. In a qualitative study of sibling interaction between a young man with Down's syndrome and his three brothers, Harry, Day, and Quist (1998) conclude their study with interpretive comments about the inclusion of "Raul" in situations outside of the family setting. They relate their own views to those in the literature:

> We strongly believe, as does much literature on the topic (Hurley-Geffner, 1995; Schnorr, 1990), that the first requirement must be an inclusive and continuous school structure that keeps students with disabilities with their community and family peers from elementary school right through high school. (p. 297)

Limitations and Future Research

Also similar to the quantitative researcher, the qualitative researcher suggests possible limitations or weaknesses of the study and makes recommendations for future research. These limitations may address problems in data collection, unanswered questions by participants, or better selection of purposeful sampling of individuals or sites for the study. Implications for future research may include the use of the findings for practice (e.g., classrooms, schools, or with certain people, such as adults or teenagers), or the need for further research (e.g., by gathering more extensive data or by asking additional questions of participants). Implications for decisions might also be stated, such as planning for new practices (e.g., better campus planning about how to handle violent incidents).

Validating the Accuracy of Findings

Often examined throughout a study, and especially at the end, is the qualitative practice of validating the findings. **Validating findings** means that the researcher determines the accuracy or credibility of the findings through strategies such as member checking or triangulation. Several qualitative researchers have addressed this idea (e.g., Creswell & Miller, 2000; Lincoln & Guba, 1985). The terms used to describe it vary (e.g., see authenticity and trustworthiness in Lincoln and Guba, 1985) and the types vary in number (see eight forms in Creswell and Miller, 2000). Our attention here will be on three primary forms typically used by qualitative researchers: triangulation, member checking, and auditing.

Qualitative inquirers triangulate among different data sources to enhance the accuracy of a study. **Triangulation** is the process of corroborating evidence from different individuals (e.g., a principal and a student), types of data (e.g., observational fieldnotes and interviews), or methods of data collection (e.g., documents and interviews) in descriptions and themes in qualitative research. The inquirer examines each information source and finds evidence to support a theme. This ensures that the study will be accurate because the information is not drawn from a single source, individual, or process of data collection. In this way, it encourages the researcher to develop a report that is both accurate and credible.

Researchers also check their findings with participants in the study to determine if their findings are accurate. **Member checking** is a process where the researcher asks one or more participants in the study to check the accuracy of the account. This check involves taking a study back to participants and asking them (in writing or in an interview) about the accuracy of the report. Participants are asked about many aspects of the study, such as whether the description is complete and realistic, if the themes are accurate to include, and if the interpretations are fair and representative of those that can be made.

Researchers may also ask a person *outside* the project to conduct a thorough review of the study and report back, in writing, the strengths and weaknesses of the project. This is the process of conducting an **external audit,** where a researcher hires or obtains the services of an individual outside the study to review different aspects of the research. The auditor reviews the project and writes or communicates an evaluation of the study. This audit may occur both during and at the conclusion of a study, and auditors typically ask questions such as those mentioned by Schwandt and Halpern (1988):

▶ Are the findings grounded in the data?
▶ Are inferences logical?
▶ Are the themes appropriate?
▶ Can inquiry decisions and methodological shifts be justified?
▶ What is the degree of researcher bias?
▶ What strategies are used for increasing credibility?

Let's return to Maria, our high school English teacher who reflects on whether her own interpretation is "right." You may recall that Maria realizes that the interpretation of her findings includes her own perspectives drawn from personal experiences. As a Latino, she realizes the same marginalization that some of the kids she interviews about weapon possession feel. She realizes, as well, that family support or lack of support plays a prominent role in Hispanic families, and that her interpretation of themes (e.g., "student alienation," or "right to protect myself") will reflect her own concerns about these issues. How can Maria separate herself from her findings? Of course, the qualitative answer is that any interpretation *must* include the researcher's personal stance. The larger question is whether Maria's report is both accurate and credible to those she studies. Maria can validate her report by convening a small group of students and teachers she interviewed and having them read the narrative of her themes. In this process, the group will openly discuss whether the themes reflect their experiences, and then Maria can make additions or changes to her thematic discussion to report accurately and credibly on student and teacher experiences.

KEY IDEAS IN THE CHAPTER

In a qualitative study, initial data management consists of organizing the data, transcribing interviews and typing fieldnotes, and making the decision to analyze the data by hand or by computer. Qualitative researchers conduct a preliminary analysis of the data by reading through it to obtain a general sense of the data. Major analysis of qualitative data consists of coding the data and forming descriptions of people, places, or events. The process of coding is one of reducing a text or image database to themes (or categories) and descriptions. It also involves using the codes to develop themes about the central phenomenon being studied. In addition, qualitative researchers layer their analysis and interconnect themes to present the complexity of the phenomenon.

Findings in a qualitative study are reported in a narrative discussion comprising many formats, such as a chronology, questions, or commentary about any changes that the participants experience. In addition, findings may be presented in figures or visual displays of information. From this reporting and representing of findings, qualitative researchers make an interpretation of the meaning of the research. This interpretation consists of advancing personal views, making comparisons between the findings and the literature, and suggesting limitations and future research. To check the accuracy of their research, qualitative inquirers often employ validation procedures such as member-checking, triangulation, and/or auditing.

USEFUL INFORMATION FOR PRODUCERS OF RESEARCH

▶ Keep in mind as you analyze and interpret data that the picture you assemble will be inductive—organizing and reporting findings beginning with the details and working up to a general picture.

▶ Realize the extensive time that transcribing takes. If you plan to transcribe your interviews or fieldnotes yourself, use the guidelines recommended in this chapter.

▶ Consider using a computer program if you are analyzing a large database consisting of more than 500 pages of text. A computer analysis of your data has both advantages and disadvantages.

▶ If you decide to use a computer program, weigh the features of the program you plan to purchase. Try out the tutorials and explore the features of programs available from the Web site http://www.sagepub.com before you purchase a program.

▶ Take the time to read through all of your data to obtain a general sense of it before you conduct a detailed analysis.

▶ When you code your text data, use the steps in the process identified in this chapter. Try not to over-code the material, and remember that the final report will typically include only 5–7 themes.

▶ Use the coding model shown in Figure 9.5 in this chapter for procedures on how to segment text, assign labels, identify themes, and jot down useful ideas on a transcript.

▶ If you code for description, look for vivid detail that will transport a reader into the setting and events in your narrative.

▶ Consider the different types of themes you can identify during coding. Unexpected themes offer surprising findings that spark reader interest, but ordinary, hard-to-classify, and major and minor themes also add complexity to a study.

▶ Design a qualitative study with thematic complexity. Use layering and interconnecting themes, as well as a combination of description and themes.

▶ Many possibilities exist for constructing a narrative about the findings. Consider the recommended strategies in this chapter such as using dialogue, metaphors, analogies, tensions, and contradictions.

▶ To augment your narrative discussion about findings, consider visual displays such as comparison tables, charts with boxes, and descriptive tables.

▶ Include your own views in your interpretation of findings because you can never completely remove yourself from interpretation and personal experiences.

▶ Consider using at least two validation strategies when you conduct qualitative research. The most frequently used strategies are member checking and triangulation.

USEFUL INFORMATION FOR CONSUMERS OF RESEARCH

▶ As you read a qualitative study, remember that the researcher will be presenting information inductively from the narrower themes to the broader themes. Throughout the study the narrative will likely build from the specific (e.g., database) to the general (e.g., broad themes).

▶ Look to see if an author mentions all of the steps in the data analysis process that were discussed in this chapter (e.g., a preliminary reading, the coding, description, thematic development, and interpretation). In well-developed qualitative studies, most of these aspects will be included.

▶ As you look for findings in a study, first examine the research to determine if the authors describe an event or the setting and then search for the themes in their study, which are often identified by headings in the article.

▶ To see the complexity and make sense of themes, identify multiple perspectives mentioned by different individuals or cited from different sources.

▶ Because qualitative researchers report findings in the form of a narrative discussion, examine qualitative research for these discussions and realize that discussions may take many forms.

▶ Data displays are intended to augment the narrative discussion. They should be easy to understand and clearly related to themes or description.

▶ Realize that the "conclusions," "interpretations," or "implications" sections of qualitative research typically include the researcher's personal views. This inclusion acknowledges that all research is biased.

▶ Check that validation strategies were discussed by the author when evaluating qualitative research.

STUDY QUESTIONS AND ACTIVITIES

1. Find one page of a transcript of an interview. Using Figure 9.5, code the page by writing code words and brackets around sentences in the left margin. In the right margin list two or three potential themes emerging from the data.

2. Log on to a qualitative computer software program Web site and download the tutorial. Complete the tutorial to learn about the major features of the software program.

3. Locate a qualitative journal article in which the author provides a description of an event, activity, or process. Use the headings to help you locate this description. Then, using the marginal annotations provided in Figure 9.6, identify descriptive features such as (a) the context, (b) broad to narrow description, (c) use of action verbs and vivid modifiers, and (d) quotes.

4. Examine a theme in a published journal article. Use the marginal annotations provided in Figure 9.7 to identify (a) the name of the theme, (b) evidence for multiple perspectives on the theme, (c) subthemes, and (d) quotes.

Now go to our Companion Website to assess your understanding of chapter content with Multiple-Choice Questions, apply comprehension in Projects & Essays, and broaden your knowledge with links to related research topics on the Web.

10

Reporting and Evaluating Research

Maria, our high school teacher, plans on presenting her completed research to both her school committee and her faculty advisor in her graduate program. She thinks about how to write these reports, recognizing that the structure for each will be different. She realizes that the school committee will be interested in key results and practical implications with only minor interest in the research methods or procedures used. On the other hand, her faculty advisor will require Maria to present her study in an appropriate thesis form that has traditionally been used in the graduate program. Maria needs to consider how to report her research to different audiences so that they will each evaluate it in as positive a way as possible.

Researchers like Maria write their reports to make them accessible to different audiences. Dissertations and theses, journal articles, and conference papers all vary in format. Shaping reports as either quantitative or qualitative research also alters the physical structure of a study. Writing them in a scholarly way, sensitive to individuals and standards of research, helps audiences understand and appreciate them. In addition, these individuals and audiences will be evaluating the quality of the research and its usefulness. Maria needs to produce a research report that is targeted for her audiences and that meets their expectations.

In this chapter we will first examine the multiple audiences for research reports, the different types of research reports, and the commonly used physical structures (e.g., format, headings, topic sequence) for these reports. Then, we will consider the scholarly aspects of writing, such as including non-discriminatory language and encoding reports with research terms. We will also discuss the importance of other writing strategies, such as conveying a point of view consistent with quantitative or qualitative research, balancing content and research ideas, and interconnecting sections of the report so that it will be consistent and easy to read. We end with a discussion of various criteria useful in evaluating both quantitative and qualitative research reports.

After reading this chapter, you should be able to:

▶ Identify factors important in writing for audiences
▶ Distinguish among the different types of research reports and proposals: dissertations or theses, journal articles, and conference papers.

▶ Describe the physical structure of quantitative and qualitative research reports.

▶ Explain the characteristics of a plan or proposal for a dissertation, thesis, or conference paper.

▶ Use scholarly writing strategies in order to be sensitive to individuals and helpful to readers in understanding the research.

▶ List criteria for evaluating research reports and proposals.

THE REPORT WRITING STRATEGIES USED IN REEXAMINING BOTH THE TELEVISION VIOLENCE AND GUNMAN INCIDENT STUDIES

Let's examine one final time the television violence study (Vooijs & van der Voort, 1993) and the gunman incident case study (Asmussen & Creswell, 1995). Both of these studies are actual reports of research found in journal articles. This means that as "research" studies, they address problems or issues, raise questions, and portray the collection of data to answer the questions (see Chapter 1 on "What Is Research?"). Further, as is apparent to you now as a knowledgeable researcher or evaluator of research, they both reflect the six-step research process introduced in this text. They include a research problem, the use of literature, the collection and analysis of data, interpretation of the meaning of the data, and a format for writing the report (see Figure 1.2 in Chapter 1).

This process constitutes a "structure" (or organization) for each study, and each element of this process is illustrated with specific examples, as shown in Tables 10.1 and 10.2. These tables present elements of the research process (in the two left columns) and the content addressed in the study (in the right column). This structure provides a roadmap to the article and helps you to read, understand, and potentially use the findings.

In addition to having an underlying structure for these two research reports, the authors use specific writing strategies typically found in scholarly publications. One such strategy is to be respectful of the participants in the study. For example, in the television violence study, the authors do not associate names of children with their scores (see Paragraph 30, in which they report group results). In the gunman case study, the authors discuss how they respect the rights of the gunman and the students undergoing counseling (see Paragraph 11).

Another strategy, seen in both studies, is to write using a point of view consistent with a quantitative approach (e.g., impersonal, with the researchers in the background) and a qualitative approach (e.g., personal). The television violence study is presented with the researchers in the background and the use of the impersonal point of view (Paragraph 31). The researchers "report" results in an objective way. On the other hand, in the gunman case study, the authors refer to themselves occasionally, including an epilogue which conveys their personal experiences (Paragraph 38).

A third strategy is to use literary devices such as a detailed description of the events, which can be seen in the gunman incident on campus (Paragraphs 04–10). Finally, a strategy used by the authors in each study is to balance discussing their *procedures* with conveying *content* about what they learned. In the end, readers such as school committees, faculty advisors, and other educators will read these studies, form an impression of them, and potentially use the findings.

TABLE 10.1

Structure of a Quantitative Article

	The Research Process	The Subject Matter of the Study
The Research Problem	The issue	Issue of the effects of violence on children's behavior
	Past studies	Research studies that support this issue
		Attempts to address this issue through interventions and curricula
	Deficiencies in past research	Attempts not successful
	Purpose statement	Effects of curriculum on children's ability to be critical of TV violence
	Value of study	Need for such a study
	Experimental intervention	The curriculum objectives:
		a. take good guy more seriously
		b. question hero's violence
		c. distinguish between TV and real-life violence
		d. nine lessons for 45 minutes each
The Research Question	Explanation/prediction	Theory on attitude change
		Assumptions of this theory
		Application of theory to specific study
	Research questions	Four research questions:
		a. short-term effects of curriculum (higher readiness to see violence, less approval of violence, lowered perceived reality of TV, factual information obtained)
		b. Strength of change (adults compared with children)
		c. Type of children who profit most (eight variables)
		d. long-term effects of curriculum after two years
Data Collection	Participants and schools in the study	Fourth through sixth graders ($N = 437$)
		Six schools (different SES)
	Experimental procedures	Assignments to control and experimental
		Pretest/posttest/retest design
	Instruments used	Instruments, their psychometric properties (video, descriptions, scales, reliabilities)
Data Analysis	Answer or results to question 1 (short-term effect)	Students experiencing the curriculum acquired a more critical attitude toward violence
	Answer or results to question 2 (strengths of change)	Students changed more than adults: perceived violence to be less realistic
	Answer or results to question 3 (type of children)	Children who were of high or low SES increased knowledge more than medium SES students
		Fifth and sixth graders changed more than fourth graders
	Answer or results to question 4 (long-term effect)	Some long-term effects on knowledge and perception of reality
		Weakened curriculum effects after 2 years (for all types of children)
Interpretation	Summary of major results	Return to intent of study and major findings about changes in children after curriculum
	Explanation for results	Reasons why these results occurred
		Reasons why insignificant results occurred
	Confirmation of prediction/theory	Return to theory and support for assumptions of theory

TABLE 10.1 (CONTINUED)

Structure of a Quantitative Article

The Research Process		The Subject Matter of the Study
	Future research needs	Need for adult/children comparisons Need to study all types of children Need for longer lessons
Report Writing	Standard format	Typical quantitative sections such as research questions, method, results, and discussion
	Objective, unbiased reporting	Authors do not mention themselves, report objectively the results

Source: Vooijs and van der Voort, 1993.

TABLE 10.2

Structure of a Qualitative Article

The Research Process		The Subject Matter of the Study
The Research Problem	The issue	Growing campus violence (the research and examples)
	The research literature Purpose statement Research questions	Need for more study to identify strategies for reaction In-depth case study Five exploratory research questions
Data Collection	A rationale for qualitative research and type of design	Institutional review board review Reasons for a qualitative study Case study design
	Detailed data collection procedures	Data collection matrix of sources Interview questions
Data Analysis and Findings	Description of the case	Description of the incident: general to specific Reaction 2 weeks after the incident
	Themes	Five themes of denial, fear, safety, retriggering, planning Use of quotes to provide evidence for themes Use of multiple perspectives to provide evidence for themes
Interpretation	Summary of major conclusions Return to past literature	Broader themes of organizational and social-psychological response How past literature supports themes How literature does not support themes How faculty and students were silent on themes
	Limitations of study	Limitations: need to consider cultural groups more and gender; limited generalizability; self-reported
	Significance of study Accuracy of the report	Importance of study for themes; benefits for campuses Verification approaches of member-checking and triangulating data
Report Writing	Flexible structure—scientific qualitative format	Realist narrative structure
	Reflexive position of authors	Use of personal pronouns, authors bring themselves into the Epilogue of the study

Source: Asmussen and Creswell, 1995.

AUDIENCE

For groups and individuals to understand and potentially use findings from research, the written report needs to be presented in a way that is acceptable to the intended audiences. Thus, a cardinal rule for writing is to "write for the audience." Unquestionably, different audiences employ varied standards, as shown in Table 10.3.

Rules and procedures in place at colleges and universities govern the criteria used by faculty advisors and committees. Journal reviewers and journal editors employ criteria presented once a year (typically) in their journals. These criteria set forth, at least in general terms, the standards they use in reviewing a study submitted for publication, the types of research they seek to publish, and guidelines for authors to follow when submitting manuscripts. Policy makers and practicing educators in schools and other educational settings evaluate studies in terms of their clarity, simplicity, and utility for practice. Conference paper reviewers often use specific guidelines for reviewing proposals submitted for presenta-

TABLE 10.3
Audiences for Research

Audiences	Standards
Faculty (advisor/committees)	• Standards used in the past in program area • Standards traditionally used by each individual faculty member • Standards used at the college or university
Journal Reviewers	• Use of published standards printed typically once for each volume • Separate standards may be published for quantitative and qualitative • Editor must reconcile differing opinions among reviewers
Policy Makers	• Ease of understanding results • Immediate application of results • Clarity and brevity of ideas
Practicing Educators in the Field	• Relevance of problem or issue being studied • Ease of identifying results • Practical suggestions from a research study
Conference Paper Reviewer	• Whether the researcher has submitted the proper materials • Whether the proposal fits the conference theme or the priorities for the conference • Whether the project summary is clearly written, organized, and addresses the guidelines for a summary
The Researcher	• Standards of the outlet for the study (e.g., faculty, journal, practitioners, conferences) • Standards related to the five elements and the seven phases in the process of research • Standards related to quantitative and qualitative criteria

---

FIGURE 10.1

Maria's Notes about Audiences for Her Report

Notes to myself:

1. *What will be the interests of the people of my school committee?*
   Owen (school administrator and chair) wants data and needs to know how we will use findings
   Ray (finance director) wants "numbers"
   Dana (English teacher) wants "rich" stories
   Deb (social studies teacher) wants good "visuals"
   Carolbel (music teacher) wants it to "sing out" to the public
   Isabel (parent) wants to know what this means for her 5 kids in school

2. *What will my advisor and faculty at the University want for my graduate research paper?*
   Harry (chair) wants high "scholarly" standards and insightful questions and findings
   Joan (member of committee) wants to see that I know the literature
   Howard (member of committee) wants to know if people in the "field" can use results

3. *What do I need to do now?*
   a. ask for past reports from school to see how reports have been written
   b. obtain from Harry past research studies to study their format
   c. learn from Harry about timetable for submitting and receiving approval of my research

---

tion. In short, researchers need to consider the audience for the study and use both general standards available in the literature and specific standards for quantitative and qualitative research.

Maria needs to consider how she will write her research reports for both her school committee and for her graduate advisor. Look at Maria's notes, shown in Figure 10.1. She considers the interests of each member of the school committee so that she can include some practical implications for each. As for her graduate advisor, she recognizes that he has high standards, has supervised many theses before, and probably has a format in mind for her final thesis report. She also creates a "to do" list to remind herself to get the information she needs before she proceeds with this phase of the process. We can see that Maria has an understanding of the important issues in reporting and evaluating research: the type of report, the physical structure of it, the writing of it, and how it will be evaluated.

TYPES OF RESEARCH REPORTS AND PROPOSALS

As you can see, researchers need to compose different types of reports. You may already be familiar with these forms, but reviewing their basic characteristics reminds us of the diversity of reports issued by researchers. A **research report** is a completed study that reports an investigation or exploration of a problem, identifies questions to be addressed, and includes data collected, analyzed, and interpreted by the researcher. It is composed for audiences, varies in length and format, and differs for quantitative and qualitative research.

The six types of research reports and proposals are:

- dissertations and theses
- dissertation and thesis proposals
- journal articles

▶ conference papers
▶ conference paper proposals

Students prepare dissertations and theses as a requirement for their doctoral and masters' programs. After completing the dissertation or thesis, researchers often condense it into a journal article for submission to an educational journal. Alternatively, they may present an abbreviated version of the dissertation or thesis at a national, regional, or state conference and receive comments from attendees about it. After making revisions based on these comments, they might submit it to a journal for possible publication. Thus, all three types of reports may be interconnected in the process of research.

Dissertations and Theses

Dissertations and theses are the doctoral and masters' research reports prepared for faculty and graduate committees. The length of a dissertation or thesis can vary and is often determined by tradition. Faculty advisors and committees may prefer one approach over another, which could affect which form is used. The doctoral dissertation might range from the shorter dissertation of 100 pages to more than 400 pages. These dissertations, conducted by more advanced graduate students, are usually longer than masters' theses. Masters' theses may run from 50 to 100 pages. In general, qualitative studies are much longer than quantitative studies. This is because the qualitative researcher needs to explain and justify the qualitative approach, and because the lengthy findings include quotes and present multiple perspectives.

The process of preparing a dissertation or thesis involves planning the study (i.e., writing the proposal) and presenting it to an advisor and a faculty committee (see Appendix B for strategies for defending a research proposal). After receiving approval to conduct the study, the student completes the study and defends it before a faculty committee.

Dissertation and Thesis Proposals

A **dissertation or thesis proposal** is a plan for a research report, initiated and developed before the research actually begins. We will not discuss proposals for external funding here because they are adequately covered elsewhere [see Locke, Spirduso, & Silverman (1999)]. Before discussing research proposals, however, it is helpful to distinguish them from research reports so the differences can clearly be seen.

One essential difference between proposals and reports is the timing involved. In a proposal, the researcher writes about what *will* take place; in the final study, the investigator writes about what *has* taken place. This means that a proposal will likely be written using a future verb tense (i.e., will) to describe the action. In a final study, the past verb tense (i.e., was) describes what has already occurred. However, one exception to this is when the researcher conducts a pilot project before carrying out the main study. The proposal often includes this pilot study, and a researcher describes it as action that has already occurred.

Another distinction between a proposal and the final study is in the report of results and future research. In a proposal, the results have not been compiled, nor has the researcher developed insight into future research needs. The proposal stops with the methods or procedure. A completed study, however, incorporates results and future research directions because data has already been collected and analyzed.

To develop a dissertation or thesis, students create a proposal, which is a formal description of a plan to investigate a research problem. This process begins by considering what topics to include in a plan so that readers can fully understand the project. The next step is to organize and format the plan to be consistent with quantitative or qualitative research. This initial planning process ends with a student presentation of the proposal to a committee.

The Importance of Proposals

Proposing research is a major step in conducting research for a graduate program. The skills used in writing a proposal are the same skills needed for seeking external funding from public and private funding sources and for writing a plan for conducting a small-scale research study in school districts or other educational settings. Whether educators conduct their own research or evaluate someone else's plan, knowing the importance of a proposal and the elements that go into it are important.

The **purpose of a proposal** is to help an investigator think through all aspects of the study and anticipate problems. A research proposal also provides a written document that faculty and advisors on the graduate committee can read, evaluate, and critique in order to improve a study. The research plan or proposal becomes a document to *sell* the study—a written narrative that must convince the faculty of the need, importance, and value of the proposed study. A well-defined proposal can facilitate the process of obtaining permissions to study a site or educational setting. A proposal provides information to gatekeepers and those in authority so that they can determine the likely impact of a study at their site. Finally, a proposal provides criteria used by those evaluating and reviewing a study to assess the quality of a project. Knowing the proper elements of a good proposal permits evaluators to examine projects for these elements, and to determine, once a project is completed, whether it fulfilled its goals.

Quantitative and Qualitative Dissertation and Thesis Proposals

Typical quantitative and qualitative proposal formats for both dissertation and thesis reports are shown in Figure 10.2. The topics in both formats address the major ideas faculty often seek to know about a project. As can be seen in the format for a quantitative proposal, most of the plan is included in three major sections: the Introduction, the Review of the Literature, and the Methods.

FIGURE 10.2

Format for a Quantitative and a Qualitative Proposal

Quantitative Format	Qualitative Format
Title Page	Title Page
Abstract	Abstract
Introduction	Introduction
Statement of the Problem	Statement of the Problem
Purpose and Research Questions or Hypotheses	The Purpose and Research Question
Theoretical Perspective	Delimitations and Limitations
Definition of Terms	Procedure
Delimitations and Limitations of the Study	Qualitative Methodology and Design
Review of the Literature	Research Site and Purposeful Sampling
Methods	Data Analysis Procedures
Study Design	Researcher's Role and Potential Ethical Issues
Procedures, Instruments, Reliability, Validity	Methods of Validation
Data Analysis	Preliminary Findings
Preliminary Results	Anticipated Outcomes of the Study and Tentative
Potential Ethical Issues	Literature Review (Optional)
Timeline, Budget, and Preliminary Chapter Outline	Timeline, Budget, Preliminary Chapter Outline
References	References
Appendices	Appendices

A qualitative proposal is less standardized than a quantitative proposal. By allowing the study to emerge and to be based on the views of participants, qualitative researchers support a flexible and open format for a proposal. Still, it is important for researchers to convey enough information to the readers to convince them of the merits of the study. Recognizing the need for flexibility, recent authors have advanced several formats for a qualitative proposal (e.g., Creswell, 1994; Marshall & Rossman, 1999) to provide guidance for students. Their recommendations, however, are flexible enough to allow a study to emerge and to evolve based on what the researcher learns from participants in the field.

As seen in Figure 10.2, the overall format for a qualitative proposal contains only two major sections—the introduction and the procedure. You will notice that the qualitative proposal format does not contain a separate section on literature review; instead it is combined with a discussion on the anticipated outcomes of the study, positioned near the end of the proposal, and characterized as optional. As mentioned in Chapter 2, "Reviewing the Literature," in qualitative research the literature documents the need to study the problem, but it does not lead to the research questions, as it does in quantitative research. This literature use allows for the inclusion of broad research questions and room for the participants to share their views. In defending this position to faculty unfamiliar with qualitative research, you would provide this rationale for not including a separate literature review section in your proposal. However, if faculty request that you include in a proposal a complete literature review, it is wise to comply with the request. Still, at the end of the review, you might state that the review is tentative and it will be developed or completed later, after learning about the participants' views. This stance would be consistent with good qualitative research.

Turning again to Figure 10.2, the qualitative proposal concludes with a "Procedure" section where the student presents the major characteristics of qualitative research and design, and information about sampling and data analysis. The final section presents a preliminary investigation of your topic, if you have completed such a study. This preliminary study might include interviews with a couple of individuals or field observations of short duration. The chief advantage of such an approach is to test whether you can collect and analyze data from participants and see if your overall design is workable in the field before receiving approval from your faculty committee.

Journal Articles

A journal article is prepared for readers of scholarly publications as well as for the editor and individuals who review the study. A **journal article** is a polished, shorter research report that has been sent to an editor of a journal, accepted for inclusion, and published in a volume of the journal. Two to three reviewers provide comments about the study. The editor then makes a decision that typically falls into one of three categories: accept, revise and resubmit, and reject. Typically, the reviewers accept the manuscript provisionally based on successful revisions by the author.

A journal article is much shorter than a thesis or dissertation because of page limitations imposed by publishers and editors of journals. Still, qualitative journal articles are much longer than quantitative articles because of the extensive quotes and the discussions of descriptions and themes that cannot be conveniently condensed into tables, as in quantitative research. The format of quantitative and qualitative journal articles varies from one journal to another.

Conference Papers and Proposals

A norm of research is that individuals publicly share their research reports so that information is accessible to the general education community. One way to do this is by presenting a paper at a professional association conference.

Conference Papers

A **conference paper** is a research report presented to an audience at a state, regional, national, or international conference typically sponsored by professional associations (e.g., American Educational Research Association, American Association of Teacher Educators). Developing and presenting a conference paper from a research study helps to publicize the study, provides a research entry for a resume, and helps to advance the work of the author within the educational research community. The conferences may be organized for researchers, practitioners, or policy makers. Researchers prepare conference papers for audiences who attend the conference as well as for individuals who review and accept the papers for presentation. Typically the length of a conference paper is about the same as a journal article—about 25 pages plus tables, figures, and appendices.

Conference Proposals

A **conference proposal** is a short summary of a study, typically about three pages long, that reviewers use to determine whether a research study should be presented at a conference. The format of a conference proposal needs to conform to the guidelines provided by the conference association.

During or after the completion of a study, the process of presenting a conference paper begins. A researcher sends a proposal to the conference organizers, who issue a "Call for Proposals" months in advance of the conference. This call is intended to invite proposals for paper presentations at the conference. In response to this call, authors develop a short proposal about the study and submit it for review. If the proposal is accepted, the author is obligated to attend the conference and present the paper based on the proposal. Following acceptance, the author develops a completed paper, presents it at the conference, and distributes it to conference participants. At the conference, typically three or four research papers are organized into a single session and each author has about 15 to 20 minutes to present his or her study. Alternatively, a session may be organized into a "symposium" composed of several papers addressing the same theme from different individuals who have collaborated together during the research.

Sample Guidelines for Proposals

To illustrate the process of developing a proposal for a conference paper, we will examine the American Educational Research Association (AERA) "Call for Proposals" reprinted each year in their journal, the *Educational Researcher*. The format of paper presentations at AERA has changed in recent years to allow for more innovative forms of presentations, such as interactive paper sessions, performances, and town meetings. The most common form of presenting a single research study, called a paper session, requires that an author submit six sets of materials by a set deadline. The guidelines for submitting a proposal are outlined below.

▶ Attach a cover sheet with information about the author, the title, and the type of format used.
▶ Include a 2,000 word summary (about three pages, excluding references) in 12-point type on 8 1/2 by 11 paper, single spaced. This summary needs to address: (a) objectives or purposes; (b) perspectives(s) or theoretical framework; (c) methods, techniques, or modes of inquiry; (d) data sources or evidence; (e) results and/or conclusions/point of view; and (f) educational or scientific importance of the study.
▶ Include two 3 × 5 index cards with the author's name and address and the presentation title.
▶ Include four self-addressed, business-size, stamped envelopes (American Educational Research Association, 1999, p. 33).

The researcher sends this material to a program coordinator of one of the topic divisions in AERA or to a program coordinator of one of the numerous special interest groups

(SIGs). To decide what division to send your material to, you might contact the AERA central office. (They can be contacted through their Web site at www.aera.net.) The proposal is reviewed by two to three reviewers who do not know the identity of the author. The review process may take 2 to 3 months, at which time the author is informed of whether the proposal has been accepted or rejected.

THE PHYSICAL STRUCTURE OF A REPORT

We have already addressed the broader aspect of identifying your audience and considered the types of research reports advanced by educators. Now, we can turn to several details about actually writing the report.

A nationally known author on the subject of writing, Natalie Goldberg, has stressed the importance of understanding the "physical structure" of a writing project (Goldberg, 2000). **Physical structure of a study** is the underlying organization of topics that form a structure for a research report. A good structure makes a study easy to construct, read, and understand. Think about a journal article that you have recently read. Was it difficult or easy to understand? Were you able to read it quickly, or did you labor? A study with a clear structure is easy to understand and is read quickly, in spite of the complexity of the subject matter.

Identifying the Physical Structure

Being able to identify the underlying structure of a research report will help you write a study, as well as understand one. This is not always easy, but four following techniques can help:

1. The easiest approach is to examine the different levels of headings used in a study. These headings are road signs used by an author to convey major points in a study. Although some headings are better descriptors of content than others, examining them helps you identify the structure of a study.
2. Look for the six steps in the research process that were introduced in Chapter 1 and developed further in Chapters 3 through 10. All reports, whether quantitative or qualitative, should contain a research problem, literature, a purpose statement and questions or hypotheses, data collection, data analysis and interpretation, and a reporting format.
3. Look for the research questions (or hypotheses) and the answers researchers develop to these questions (or hypotheses). For every question asked, researchers should pose an answer. These are not always easily found, but examining the "Introduction" to a study (for the questions) and the "Results" or "Findings" (for the answers) is a good place to start.
4. Finally, become familiar with the structures of different types of reports, especially approaches using quantitative and qualitative research.

The Structure of a Quantitative Report

The structure of a quantitative report is shown in Figure 10.3. The topics in this figure should be familiar because they reflect the ideas advanced in Chapters 3 through 10 of this book.

The body of the paper comprises five major sections. These are the same five sections typically found in published quantitative reports. Knowing this structure will help you read studies and understand where to look for information. For journal articles, the front mat-

FIGURE 10.3

The Front, Body, and Back Matter of a Quantitative Study

Front Matter

Title page
Abstract of the study (optional)

Body of the Paper

Introduction
    Statement of the problem
    Purpose statement
    Research questions or hypotheses
    Theoretical or conceptual explanation

Review of the Literature
    Review of the previous research
    Summary of major themes
    How present study will extend literature

Methods
    Sample and site
    Access and permissions
    Instruments and their reliability and validity
    Interventions (if used)
    Procedures of data collection
    Analysis of the data

Results
    Descriptive analysis of all data
    Inferential analysis to address questions/hypotheses
    Tables and figures to display the data

Discussion
    Summary of major results
    Relationship of results to existing studies
    Limitations of the study
    Implications for future research
    Overall significance of the study

Back Matter

References
Appendices (e.g., instruments, key questions)

ter and the back matter sections are limited because of space limitations. For a dissertation or thesis, the researcher includes more front matter to help the reader understand the organization of the study, and the sections are labeled as chapters. One front matter section, the abstract, is optional in reports, but, if written completely (e.g., to include the elements of an abstract as mentioned in Chapter 4), it helps the reader identify the major parts of a study.

Another part of the body of the paper is the "Method" discussion. This section is likely to vary from one research report to another because of the different procedures authors use for their research designs. (See Chapters 11 through 13 for the quantitative research designs of experimental and quasi-experimental, correlational, and surveys.)

The Structure of A Qualitative Report

For a qualitative dissertation, thesis, and journal article, the structure varies considerably. The standard five-section structure seen in Figure 10.3 may not be appropriate for a qualitative study. For a qualitative report, such as a dissertation or thesis, it is not uncommon to have six to eight chapters. For example, Miller (1992) conducted a qualitative ethnography case study of the experiences of a first-year president. She included the following 11 chapters:

Chapter 1	Introduction to the Study
Chapter 2	Path to the Presidency
Chapter 3	Early Surprises and Challenges
Chapter 4	Building Relationships
Chapter 5	Presidential Roles
Chapter 6	Providing Vision and Leadership
Chapter 7	Initiating Change
Chapter 8	External Constituents
Chapter 9	Struggles and Difficulties
Chapter 10	The Spouse's Role
Chapter 11	Summary, Conclusions, and Implications

The 11-chapter structure places emphasis on themes that emerged during the study. It does not include a separate chapter on the literature review or the specific procedures of the study.

The flexible structure found in Miller's dissertation is also seen in journal articles and conference papers reporting qualitative research. Just as there are multiple perspectives from participants in a study, there are also many variations in how researchers interpret and report their findings. Some forms of qualitative reports will emphasize description, while others will focus on themes or personal interpretations of findings by the author. This flexible format for reporting undoubtedly makes reading qualitative research difficult for those new to the approach. Although the structures for reporting continue to emerge, knowing several prominent variations will help you begin to see the focus of authors as they report their research.

Variation in the structure of a qualitative study can be seen in several models for writing qualitative research:

▶ A *scientific model* is similar to a quantitative study where all or most of the five sections (introduction, review of the literature, methods, results, and discussion) are present.

▶ A *storytelling model* can have varied structure. The author uses literary devices (e.g., metaphors, analogies, plot, climax) and persuasive, creative writing to present the study.

▶ A *thematic model* is when the author presents and discusses major themes that arise in a database. Often this model uses extensive quotes and rich details to support the themes.

▶ A *descriptive model* is when the author relies on detailed description of people and places to carry the narrative. A study in this mode might convey "a typical day in the life" of an individual.

▶ A *theoretical model* is when the author either starts with a theory (e.g., a theoretically oriented case study), ends with a theory (e.g., grounded theory), or modifies an existing theory based on views of participants.

▶ *An experimental, alternative, or performance model* can also be used for presenting research. For example, researchers can write a poem, a fictional story, a drama, or a highly personalized account, called an auto-ethnography. (See Denzin, 1997 or Richardson, 2000 for extensive discussion about these new forms of reporting.) For example, rather than writing a research report, the qualitative inquirer develops a play which captures better the "unruly, multi-sited, and emotionally laden" subject matter better than standard writing (Richardson, 2000, p. 934).

Although the varieties of qualitative reports vary from the traditional theory-scientific approach to the more experimental, it is helpful to see two broad genres of structures—the scientific and storytelling—which many qualitative research reports include. The scientific and storytelling qualitative structures are illustrated in Figure 10.4 and Figure 10.5. As you can see, the formats differ in the basic topics included and the headings used to convey the topics. Both differ, as well, from the quantitative structure.

FIGURE 10.4

The Front, Body, and Back Matter of a Scientific Qualitative Structure

Front Matter

Title page
Preface and Acknowledgements (optional)
Table of contents (optional)
List of tables (optional)
List of figures (optional)
Abstract of the study (optional)

Body of the Paper

Introduction
    Statement of the Problem
    Purpose Statement
    Research Questions

Procedures
    Rationale for qualitative approach
    Sample and site
    Access and permissions
    Data gathering strategies
    Data analysis approach

Findings
    Description of site or individuals
    Analysis of themes

Discussion
    Major findings
    Comparison of findings with existing studies
    Limitations
    Implications for future research
    Overall significance of the study

Back Matter

References
Appendices (e.g., figures, interview or observational protocols)

> ## FIGURE 10.5
>
> ### Front, Body, and Back Matter of a Qualitative Storytelling Structure
>
> Front Matter
>
> Title page
> Preface and Acknowledgments (optional)
> Table of contents (optional)
> List of tables (optional)
> List of figures (optional)
> Abstract of the study (optional)
>
> Body of the Paper
> Specific Description of Individual of Interest in the Study
> Author's Relation or Connection to the Participant
> The Data Collected During the Study
> A Specific Incident to Understand the Individual's Life
> The Meaning of the Incident
> Larger Understanding of the Group of People to Which the Individual Belongs
> A Comparison of the Meaning with Published Studies
> Return to Author's Personal Meaning of the Individual and Events
>
> Back Matter
>
> References

In a **qualitative scientific structure** the researcher includes detailed procedures of inquiry and follows a traditional form for reporting research that includes the introduction, the procedures, the findings, and a discussion. However, as distinct from a quantitative report, a scientific qualitative report still differs from a standard quantitative format. In the qualitative "scientific" approach, inquirers refer to *procedures* instead of methods, and *findings* instead of results. In addition, Figure 10.4 shows that the format includes a rationale for qualitative research, a description of the site or individuals, and an analysis of themes. This format is found in specific qualitative designs such as case studies and in grounded theory studies.

Figure 10.5 displays a less recognizable format—the storytelling structure. A **qualitative storytelling structure** is a flexible approach to writing a qualitative report. The meaning of the study unfolds through descriptions, the author's reflection on the meaning of the data, a larger understanding of the phenomenon, and a return to the author's stance on the topic. Figure 10.5 begins with a description or vignette of an individual and brings the *procedures* into the study at the midpoint. It ends with the meaning of the phenomenon, and presents this meaning in terms of the larger understandings, a comparison with published studies, and the author's own experiences. This format is found in qualitative research designs such as ethnographies and narrative research.

Comparing Quantitative and Qualitative Reports to a Novel

An alternative to viewing the structure of both quantitative and qualitative research is to examine the narrative action of the study. Barth (1999) discusses the curve of dramatic action to visually portray fiction. This curve is useful for comparing the novel with forms of educational research. The **curve of dramatic action** shows that the action in a story rises to a climatic peak, or turning point, and then falls to resolution, or denouement.

Examine Figure 10.6. Here we see the curve of dramatic action in four types of reports: a novel, a quantitative study, a qualitative scientific article, and a qualitative storytelling ar-

FIGURE 10.6

The Curve of Dramatic Action for Novels, Quantitative, and Qualitative Research

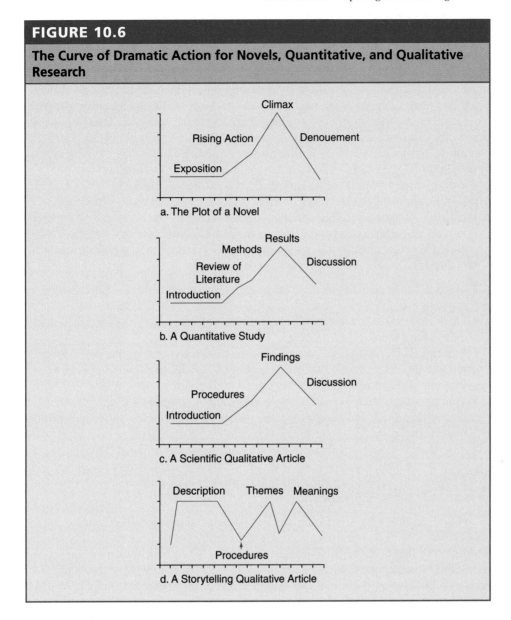

a. The Plot of a Novel

b. A Quantitative Study

c. A Scientific Qualitative Article

d. A Storytelling Qualitative Article

ticle. Notice that the lines are similar for the plot of a novel, a quantitative article, and a scientific qualitative article. For a storytelling article the line is different—several peaks appear in the study, giving emphasis to dramatic action for several facets of the study, such as description of individuals or sites, themes, and overall meanings. A storytelling article builds action in several ways, and the relative emphasis on each action phase may vary from one study to another.

Think-Aloud About the Structure of a Study

Having discussed the structure of various forms of research reports, I want to return now to an approach to examining the structure of research regardless of these forms. Reexamine Tables 10.1 and 10.2 that display the structure of the television violence study (Vooijs & van der Voort, 1993) and the gunman incident case study (Asmussen & Creswell, 1995).

Notice that the research process steps and the subject matter are presented in separate columns.

I think of a study as two parallel railroad tracks. The researcher proceeds ahead on both tracks at the same time. One of the tracks (the right column in Tables 10.1 and 10.2) represents the *subject matter* of the study. In every study, the writer addresses a topic and a research problem. From the study researchers learn about possible resolutions to the problem, such as whether children's attitudes about watching television change (i.e., the television violence study) or unrelated reactions of different participants on campus to a violent incident that necessitates a need for better campus planning (i.e., the gunman case study). In short, as a reader, we learn about the subject matter of the study.

But the second track is the *research* track (the column on the left in Tables 10.1 and 10.2). In addition to the subject matter, we also have the research track consisting of steps in the process of research and the specific procedures within each step.

Readers and writers of research need to see both the subject matter and the research process tracks to understand and evaluate a study. How did I "see" these two tracks? And what value does "seeing" the two tracks provide?

▶ I used the analogy of two railroad tracks going the same direction to help visualize a study.

▶ I looked at the study and examined the headings closely. They were good road signs to help me understand each article.

▶ Realizing that all educational studies are composed with six steps, I searched for a research problem, a question, data collection, data analysis and interpretation, and the writing structure.

▶ When reading a study I could give emphasis to both, to learn about the results or findings in a study as well as to "see" the research procedures so that I could critically evaluate the study.

▶ As a researcher, knowing that the research exists as well as the subject matter enables me to understand the underlying research process of a published study, determine what findings I should identify, and to evaluate whether the research is rigorous enough to use in my own study.

Not all studies are perfect examples of research. Editors of journals make choices about what to publish. Sometimes an article is published because the research problem is a timely issue that needs to be addressed, even if this issue is not studied using rigorous procedures. In other cases, the methods are strong, and they cause the editor to accept an article for publication. I am not discouraged if one of the six steps is missing or is addressed only minimally. But, as a developing researcher, you need to understand both the "research" and "subject matter" tracks to fully understand a research report.

SCHOLARLY WRITING

In addition to understanding and using the structure of a study, researchers think about the more micro-level writing that occurs in a research report. Our focus will be on writing to:

▶ be sensitive and not discriminate against individuals
▶ use appropriate research terms
▶ employ a point of view consistent with quantitative and qualitative approaches
▶ balance research and content
▶ interconnect parts of a study

Writing Sensitively

Writers should strive for studies that are respectful of people and places being examined. Studies submitted to dissertation or thesis committees, to journals, or to conferences will be rejected if authors are insensitive to individuals and cultural groups.

The American Psychological Association has compiled information and developed guidelines about the use of nondiscriminatory language for research (American Psychological Association, 1994). These guidelines state that using nondiscriminatory language means avoiding demeaning attitudes, including biased assumptions, and awkward constructions that suggest bias because of gender, sexual orientation, racial or ethnic group, disability, or age. One helpful suggestion, developed by Maggio (1991), is to test your written research report for discriminatory language by:

- substituting your own group for groups being discussed
- imagining that you are a member of the group
- revising your material if you feel excluded or offended

Another approach is to spend some time studying examples of discriminatory language constructions and how these constructions might be changed to be inclusive and sensitive in your writing. To find these examples, you might examine the three guidelines for reducing bias in language recommended by the American Psychological Association in the APA Style Manual (American Psychological Association, 1994).

1. Describe at an appropriate level of specificity. This means that the writer needs to use specific terms for persons that are accurate, clear, and free of bias. For example:

   - be specific
     Poor: man   **Preferred:** men and women
     Poor: over 62   **Preferred:** ages 63–70

2. Be sensitive to labels. This means calling people what they prefer to be called and acknowledging that preferences for names change over a period of time. Writers should not use their own group as the standard against which to judge others. For example:

   - use adjectival forms
     Poor: the gays   **Preferred:** gay men

   - put "people" first followed by a descriptive phrase
     Poor: schizophrenics   **Preferred:** people diagnosed with schizophrenia

   - use parallel cultural standards, rather than labels
     Poor: husband and wife   **Preferred:** man and woman

3. Acknowledge participation of people in a study. Participants need to be specifically identified in a language they use. For example:

   - use impersonal terms
     Poor: subjects   **Preferred:** participants
     Poor: informants   **Preferred:** participants

   - use non-stereotypical bias and non-biased adjectives
     Poor: woman doctor   **Preferred:** doctor
     Poor: non-aggressive women   **Preferred:** non-aggressive participants

   - use specific cultural identity
     Poor: American Indians   **Preferred:** Cherokees

    ❱ put people first, not their disability
        Poor: mentally ill person   **Preferred:** person with mental illness

Encoding the Terms of Research

As these non-discriminatory guidelines suggest, certain terms are preferred over others for referring to participants in a study. Likewise, in the field of research, certain terms need to be included to convey your understanding of research. Your research will be partly judged on the basis of your appropriate use of standard terms in both quantitative and qualitative research. For example, to call the sampling "random" in qualitative research instead of "purposeful" shows your lack of understanding of the basic differences between the two. When you read a research report, you can see the level of the author's research sophistication because of the choice of words. The glossary at the end of this text and the use of emphasized words (words in bold type) throughout the chapters are meant to focus your attention on those words that are central to speaking and writing as a researcher.

    Below are some other ideas that might be helpful in building your vocabulary and using research words.

    ❱ As you write your study, consult the dictionaries of terms mentioned in Chapter 4, on "Summaries" in literature review, such as the quantitative dictionary of terms (Vogt, 1999) and the qualitative dictionary (Schwandt, 1997).

    ❱ When writing a research report, encode your writing with the language of research. In this case, **encoding** is the intentional use by an author of specific terms to convey ideas, such as using research terms. It will enhance the acceptability of your research to graduate committees, publishers, and conference attendees. For example, in Chapter 5 on "Research Questions," the terms "compare," "relate," and "explore" were intentionally used in constructing research questions. These are words that convey to readers your scholarly knowledge of research. This emphasis on encoding continues in the discussion of data collection and analysis. Include research words such as "statistical test," "thematic development," and a "numeric" file and "text" file.

    ❱ The degree to which language is established before the study begins differs depending on if the research is quantitative or qualitative. In quantitative research, researchers operationally define the variables *before* they are measured. In qualitative research, the definitions of the central phenomenon emerge *during* a study. In qualitative research, the language is less set. The researcher begins a study with a central phenomenon to be explored, but is open to how the participants might define this phenomenon and recognizes that participants will likely define it differently. The implication of this distinction is that researchers write extensive definitions into proposals or plans in quantitative research but seldom include them in qualitative research. In qualitative research, definitions included in the final report are often those generated by participants at research sites.

Using Point of View

The presence of the researcher in the study varies between quantitative and qualitative research. In quantitative research, the investigator is in the background narrating the study—an omniscient third person. For example, the researcher "reports" the results of the study and "explains" their importance. The first person pronoun, "I," is not used and instead the writer uses the impersonal point of view. This form of writing also includes the use of past tense to create distance between the report and the writer, and some passive constructions. For example, in a quantitative report you might find the following passive construction:

    The results were reported at a significance level of $p < .01$.

Also, a quantitative writer seldom mentions the first names of individuals in a study, and also emphasizes objectivity of the results.

In qualitative research, on the other hand, the researcher is typically present and in the foreground in the narrative report of the study. This presence occurs through the use of the first person pronoun, "I" (or the collective "we"), and the writer discusses personal experiences during the study (e.g., their difficulty in collecting data, their reflection on themes derived from the data). The author may present sidebars, such as paragraphs, interpreting the personal meaning of themes or personal statements about experiences, such as the Epilogue in the gunman case study (Asmussen & Creswell, 1995). The qualitative researcher also seeks to present a persuasive story and often writes in a lively manner using metaphors, contradictions, and ironies. The study may end with questions that remain unanswered, much like many novels or short stories. Further, qualitative inquirers mention first names of participants (typically using aliases to protect the identity of individuals), and the level of detail, especially in the description, brings the writer and the reader close together.

Balancing Research and Content

Some researchers feel that their report must demonstrate their knowledge of research more than the content or subject matter of their studies. Other researchers feel just the opposite. Regardless of emphasis, scholarly writing includes a balance between conveying knowledge about research *and* knowledge about the subject matter of the study. When researchers over-emphasize methods, they may feel a need to convince faculty, graduate committee members, or journal editors of their knowledge of research methods. An under-emphasis, on the other hand, may indicate that the person lacks skills or knowledge about research. A good research report contains a balance between a discussion about research and the actual content of the study (remember the two parallel railroad tracks?). This balance is in roughly a 50-50 proportion. For example, compare the following two models of a methods discussion about surveying department chairpersons.

Below is a poor model that overly emphasizes the research approach:

In this project, survey random sampling will be used so that each department chair has an equal probability of being selected. Moreover, it is important to use stratification procedures so individuals in the sample are selected in proportion to which they are represented in the population . . .

Now let's look at a better model that provides a balance between content and research:

In this project, 400 academic chairpersons were randomly sampled so that results could be generalized to the population of academic chairpersons in Research I institutions of higher education (N=2000 chairs). Moreover, the 400 chairpersons represented both men and women chairs in proportion to which they were represented in the total population (300 males; 100 females).

The good model includes comments by the researcher that not only convey an understanding of adequate survey research methods but also inform the reader about subject matter of the actual study—that chairpersons will be studied in research institutions.

Interconnecting Sections for Consistency

Another writing strategy used in research is to interconnect the sections of your research report so that you provide a consistent discussion to readers. One way to establish the interconnection of the parts of a research plan or study is to use key concepts as linking devices. **Linking devices** are words or phrases that tie together sections of a research report.

In a quantitative report, *stating the variables,* using their exact name each time, can help connect the parts. Consider the many times that researchers mention the variables in their studies. The title specifies the variables in a study; they are also included in the purpose statement and research questions. They are again reiterated in operational definitions in the method section. When researchers use the exact same terms each time the variables are mentioned, they provide a useful linkage among parts of a report.

Another linking device in a quantitative study is to *use the same research questions or hypotheses* wherever they appear in the research report. A slight change in wording can throw readers off and convey different meanings in your research. When you introduce research questions or hypotheses early in the study (as they often appear), include the *exact same words* when you return to them in the results of your study.

In a qualitative study, *state the same phenomenon* being explored each time it is introduced. You may introduce the phenomenon in the title, in the statement of the problem section, in the purpose statement, the research questions, and in your findings. For example, the phenomenon "campus response" appears several times throughout the gunman case study (Asmussen & Creswell, 1995), such as in the title, the purpose, and the conclusions.

In both quantitative and qualitative projects, *repeat the problem* throughout the study. This binds the entire proposal or report together. Researchers may present the research problem in the introductory part of a proposal and emphasize its importance during the discussion about research questions or hypotheses. It is discussed again during the data collection and analysis as the investigators provide results to address the problem. It may also appear in the future research section at the end of a study when researchers talk about the need for additional research.

EVALUATING RESEARCH

Both during the process of conducting a study as well as at its conclusion, the researcher needs to consider the quality of the project. The improvement of practice, the quality of policy debates, and the advancement of knowledge, as mentioned in Chapter 1, all call for high quality educational research. It becomes important, then, to consider the evaluation of research by asking: "What criteria should be used?"

Standards

Because quantitative and qualitative are different approaches to research, each merits its own criteria for evaluation. However, both approaches reflect the broader research process (i.e., the six steps in the research process), and some common elements should play into the evaluative criteria, as well. Also, the audiences for research, mentioned earlier in this chapter, will employ criteria such as:

▶ Does the research meet the standards for publication?
▶ Will the research be useful in our school?
▶ Will the research advance policy discussions in our region?
▶ Will the research add to our scholarly knowledge about a topic or research problem?
▶ Will the research help solve some pressing educational problem?

These are important questions, and the answers will shape how we evaluate a research report. Because of the various audiences involved, no single standard for research can be uniformly applied. One way to think about the standards for research are to answer the question, "Is this study good research?" and to apply standards based on research criteria to answer it.

When we turn to "research" standards for quantitative and qualitative research, we find that more consensus exists about what is considered "good" in quantitative research than in qualitative research. The specific use of qualitative research in education, as noted in Chapter 2, is much more recent than quantitative research. In addition, with flexible structures used in writing qualitative reports, different criteria can be applied.

To provide some guidance about research standards you might use, we will discuss one set of quantitative standards useful for judging a research report. We will also evaluate several standards available for judging qualitative research.

Quantitative Standards

In a study by Hall, Ward and Comer (1988), the authors had a panel of judges rate 128 educational *quantitative* articles. The specific shortcomings of these articles in order of their importance were:

- validity and reliability of data-gathering procedures
- weaknesses in the research designs
- limitations of the study were not stated
- research design not appropriate for the problem
- inappropriate sampling
- results of analysis not clearly reported
- inappropriate methods used to analyze data
- unclear writing
- assumptions not clearly stated
- data-gathering methods not clearly described

As you can see, quantitative evaluators were most concerned about aspects related to the data collection, analysis, and the reporting of results of a study—the research design phase of the projects.

Qualitative Standards

Turning to qualitative research, the criteria for a good research report vary depending on your emphasis as a researcher. In Chapter 2 on "The Development of Qualitative Research," we discussed the major ideas in three themes in educational research: philosophy, procedures, and participation/advocacy. When we examine current perspectives about judging qualitative research, ideas within each of the three themes combine to form our evaluation criteria. For example, as one interested in the philosophical ideas behind qualitative research, you might draw from perspectives about what constitutes knowledge (e.g., an evolving design) or reality (e.g, subjective experiences). As a procedural researcher, you might emphasize the importance of rigorous data collection (e.g., multiple forms of data) and analysis (e.g., multiple levels of analysis). As a participatory/advocacy writer, you might stress the importance of collaboration (e.g., researcher collaborates on equal terms with participants) and persuasive writing (e.g., does it seem "true to participants?").

Let's examine three sets of criteria for evaluating qualitative research developed by three authors within a 6-year timeframe. As seen in Table 10.4, the standards reflect both overlap and differences. They all speak to the importance of the participant in the research study, as well as standards set within research communities. Writing persuasively and with respect for participants is also paramount in all three standards. But writing from a point of self-awareness and being sensitive to reciprocity and the impact of the study on readers, such as its emotional and intellectual impact, differs. In combination, they all offer philosophical, procedural, and reflexive standards for you to use in evaluating qualitative inquiry.

Evaluation Using a Process Approach

Criteria are available for evaluating the details of a quantitative study [for example, see Tuckman's (1999, p. 431) list of 25 questions] or a qualitative study [Stake's (1995, p. 131) list of 20 questions for a qualitative case study]. This discussion of evaluation would not be

TABLE 10.4

Three Sets of Standards for Evaluating the Quality of Qualitative Research

Lincoln's (1995) Philosophical Criteria:	Creswell's (1998) Procedural Criteria	Richardson's (2000) Participatory and Advocacy Criteria
• Standards set in the inquiry community such as guidelines for publication. • Positionality: The "text" should display honesty or authenticity about its own stance and about the position of the author. • Community: All research takes place in, is addressed to, and serves the purposes of the community in which it was carried out. • Voice: Participants' voices must not be silenced, disengaged, or marginalized. • Critical subjectivity: Researchers need to have heightened self-awareness in the research process and create personal and social transformation. • Reciprocity: Reciprocity must exist between the researcher and those being researched. • Sacredness of relationships: The researcher respects the sacredness of the relationships and collaborates on equal terms with participants. • Sharing privileges: The researcher shares rewards with persons whose lives they portray.	• It employs rigorous data collection, which involves multiple forms of data, extensive data, and a long period in the field collecting data. • It is consistent with the philosophical assumptions and characteristics of a qualitative approach to research. These include an evolving design, the presentation of multiple perspectives, the researcher as an instrument of data collection, and the focus on participants' views. • It employs a tradition of inquiry, such as case study, ethnography, grounded theory, or narrative inquiry as a procedural guide for the study. • It starts with a single focus on a central phenomenon rather than a comparison or relationship (as in quantitative research). • It is written persuasively so that the reader experiences *being there.* • Analysis consists of multiple levels of analysis to portray the complexity of the central phenomena. • The narrative engages the reader because of unexpected ideas, and believable and realistic information. • It includes strategies to confirm the accuracy of the study.	• Substantive contribution: Does this piece contribute to our understanding of social life? • Aesthetic merit: Does this piece succeed aesthetically? Does the use of practices open up the text, invite interpretative responses? Is the text artistically shaped, satisfying, complex, and not boring? • Reflexivity: How did the author come to write this text? Is there adequate self-awareness and self-exposure for the reader to make judgments about the point of view? • Impact: Does this affect me? Emotionally? Intellectually? Move me to write? Move me to try new research practices? Move me to action? • Expression of a reality: Does this text embody a fleshed out sense of lived experiences? Does it seem "true"?

Source: Lincoln, 1995; Creswell, 1998; Richardson, 2000.

complete without relating evaluation to the steps of the *process of research* addressed in this book. The steps in this process are presented to illustrate complete, rigorous quantitative and qualitative research. Since evaluation will differ depending on whether the study is quantitative or qualitative, Figures 10.7 and 10.8 provide criteria specifically related to the six steps introduced in Chapter 1. Reviewing them after completing a study or examining them while assessing the quality of a published research report can provide a detailed evaluation needed in educational research.

FIGURE 10.7

Checklist for Evaluating the Process of a Quantitative Study

Title for the Study
_____ Does it reflect the major independent and dependent variables?
_____ Does it express either a comparison among groups or a relationship among variables?
_____ Does it convey the participants and site for the study?

Problem Statement
_____ Does it indicate an educational issue to study?
_____ Has the author provided evidence that this issue is important?
_____ Is there some indication that the author located this issue through a search of past literature or from personal experiences?
_____ Does the research problem fit a quantitative approach?
_____ Are the assumptions of the study consistent with an approach?

Review of the Literature
_____ Are the studies about the independent and dependent variables clearly reviewed?
_____ Does the review end with how the author will extend or expand the current body of literature?
_____ Does the study follow the American Psychological Association style?

Purpose, Hypotheses, and Research Questions
_____ Does the author specify a purpose statement?
_____ Is the purpose statement clear, and does it indicate the variables, their relationship, and the people and site to be studied?
_____ Are either hypotheses or research questions written?
_____ Do these hypotheses or questions indicate the major variables and the participants in a study?
_____ Does the purpose statement and hypotheses or research questions contain the major components that will help a reader understand the study?
_____ Has the author identified a theory or explanation for the hypotheses or questions?

Data Collection
_____ Does the author mention the steps taken to obtain access to people and sites?
_____ Is a rigorous probability sampling strategy used?
_____ Has the author identified good, valid, and reliable instruments to use to measure the variables?
_____ Are the instruments administered so that bias and error are not introduced into the study?

Data Analysis and Results
_____ Are the statistics chosen for analysis consistent with the research questions, hypotheses, variables, and scales of measurement?
_____ Is the unit of analysis appropriate to address the research problem?
_____ Are the data adequately represented in tables and figures?
_____ Do the results answer the research questions and address the research problem?
_____ Are the results substantiated by the evidence?
_____ Are generalizations from the results limited to the population of participants in the study?

Writing
_____ Is the structure of the overall study consistent with the topics addressed in a quantitative study?
_____ Are educational and social science terms carefully defined?
_____ Are variables labeled in a consistent way throughout the study?
_____ Is the study written using extensive references?
_____ Is the study written using an impersonal point of view?
_____ Is the study written appropriately for intended audience(s)?

FIGURE 10.8

Checklist for Evaluating the Process of a Qualitative Study

Title for the Study
_____ Does it reflect the central phenomena being studied?
_____ Does it reflect the people and site being studied?

Problem Statement
_____ Does it indicate an educational issue to study?
_____ Has the author provided evidence that this issue is important?
_____ Is there some indication that the author located this issue through a search of past literature or from personal experience?
_____ Does the research problem fit a qualitative approach?
_____ Are the assumptions of the study consistent with a qualitative approach?

Review of the Literature
_____ Has the author provided a literature review of the research problem under study?
_____ Has the author signaled that the literature review is preliminary or tentatively based on the findings in the study?
_____ Does the study follow the American Psychological Association style?

Purpose and Research Questions
_____ Does the author specify both a purpose statement and a central research question?
_____ Does the purpose statement and central question indicate the central phenomenon of study and the people and place where the study will occur?
_____ Are subquestions written to narrow the central question to topic areas or foreshadow the steps in data analysis?

Data Collection
_____ Has the author taken steps to obtain access to people and sites?
_____ Has the author chosen a specific purposeful sampling strategy for individuals or sites?
_____ Is the data collection clearly specified and is it extensive?
_____ Is there evidence that the author has used a protocol for recording data?

Data Analysis and Findings
_____ Were appropriate steps taken to analyze the text or visual data into themes, perspectives, or categories?
_____ Was sufficient evidence obtained (including quotes) to support each theme or category?
_____ Were multiple layer themes or categories derived?
_____ Did the findings answer the research questions?
_____ Were the findings realistic and accurate? Were steps taken to support this conclusion through verification?
_____ Were the findings represented in the themes or categories so that multiple perspectives can be easily seen?
_____ Were the findings represented in narrative discussions or in visuals?

Writing
_____ Was the account written persuasively and convincingly?
_____ Was the overall account consistent with one of the many forms for presenting qualitative research?
_____ Was the account written to include literacy approaches, such as the use of metaphor, surprises, detail, dialogue, and complexity?
_____ Was it written using a personal point of view?
_____ Was it written for audience(s)?

KEY IDEAS IN THE CHAPTER

Researchers write their reports with their audiences in mind. The audiences differ for five types of research reports. These reports are dissertations and theses, dissertation and thesis proposals, journal articles, conference papers, and conference paper proposals. Reports vary in purpose, length, and format. The structure of a report is how the topics are organized and how they are presented to a reader. A good structure facilitates the reading, understanding, and composing of a research study. The structure of a study can be determined by examining the headings and by looking for the process steps of research. Readers can also search for answers researchers provide to questions (or hypotheses) and become familiar with typical structures used in educational research studies. The structure of a quantitative report follows a standard format: introduction, review of the literature, methods, results, and discussion. Several models of presentation are available in qualitative research: scientific, storytelling, thematic, descriptive, theoretical, and experimental. The differences among types of qualitative research, quantitative research, and a novel can be seen in a study of their curve of dramatic action.

When writing a scholarly study or proposal, use non-discriminatory language. Language should avoid demeaning attitudes, biased assumptions, and awkward constructions that suggest bias because of gender, sexual orientation, racial or ethnic group, disability, or age. The language of research can be specific, sensitive to stereotyped labels, and acknowledge participation of people in a study. Studies need to be written using good research terms, such as those found in glossaries, encoded with appropriate language, and framed within either a quantitative or qualitative approach. The point of view of a study for a quantitative project tends to be the omniscient third-person style of writing. For qualitative research, the point of view may be expressed through first person or the collective standpoint. In a qualitative study, the writer tends to be more in the foreground than in a quantitative study. Writers need to balance content about their subject matter with good research discussions. The sections of a report need to interrelate so that a proposal or a final study is an integrated set of ideas. Linking devices, such as variables, hypotheses or research questions, key concepts or a phenomenon, and the problem of the study interconnect sections in a research report.

The criteria for evaluating the quality of a study differ depending on the evaluator. Evaluators may be faculty, journal editors and reviewers, policy makers and practicing educators, and conference paper reviewers. Evaluators look for different characteristics of a good quantitative or qualitative study. Although no set standards exist, several general guidelines are available that researchers might use to evaluate a study. Quantitative evaluators are most concerned about aspects related to data collection, analysis, and the reporting of results. Qualitative researchers are concerned about the data collection as well, but also the persuasiveness of the study and the self-awareness of the researcher.

USEFUL INFORMATION FOR PRODUCERS OF RESEARCH

▶ Write in a way that meets the needs of your audiences.
▶ Design and write your research report following the appropriate structure for the type of report advanced in this chapter.
▶ Write quantitative research to include an introduction, a review of the literature, a method, results, and discussion.
▶ Write qualitative research using either a scientific or storytelling structure. Also consider the other structural variations presented in this chapter.

▶ When you design a proposal for a doctoral dissertation or thesis, consider that the structure will vary depending on whether the proposal is for quantitative or qualitative research.

▶ If you plan a paper for a scholarly conference, follow the guidelines provided by the professional association sponsoring the conference.

▶ Write your report sensitively, following the three guidelines for reducing bias advanced by the American Psychological Association.

▶ To make your research scholarly and easy to read, write your report using research words, advancing a consistent standpoint, and employing consistent style for references and headings.

▶ Interrelate sections of a study. Consider how words can provide linking devices for all parts of a study.

USEFUL INFORMATION FOR CONSUMERS OF RESEARCH

▶ After writing your project, evaluate it using the standards advanced in this chapter for quantitative and qualitative research.

▶ To identify how a research report is structured, examine headings, look for the research process steps used in this book, search for results that answer the questions or hypotheses, and become familiar with the varied structures for dissertations, theses, journal articles, proposals, and conference papers.

▶ It is sometimes difficult to identify the structure of a qualitative study because of the variations that exist. Consider looking first for whether the study conforms to a scientific approach or a storytelling approach.

▶ To best understand the structure of an educational research report, compare it with a novel. The action of research and a novel is both parallel and different, depending on whether the study is qualitative or quantitative.

▶ Research reports should be free of language that presents demeaning attitudes, bias, and awkward constructions that suggest bias because of gender, sexual orientation, racial or ethnic group, disability, or age.

▶ This chapter offers a checklist for evaluating the quality of quantitative and qualitative research. Use these checklists to assess the overall quality of a study.

STUDY QUESTIONS AND ACTIVITIES

1. Find a journal article and develop an outline of the major elements. Use the four suggestions for identifying the structure advanced in this chapter as a guide.

2. Find a journal article and identify the point of view used by an author. Discuss whether the author uses the first person, the collective, or the omniscient point of view. Provide specific examples to document one or more voices in the study.

3. Change the point of view of the author in the journal article you read for question 2. Discuss specifically how the words will be altered to reflect an alternative point of view.

4. Identify the words in a journal article the author uses to convey a research sense of the study. Also discuss where the author uses these words and how they are either good quantitative or qualitative words.

5. Select either a quantitative or a qualitative study published in an educational journal and critique it. Using the checklist in this chapter, discuss the strengths and the weaknesses of the article.

Now go to our Companion Website to assess your understanding of chapter content with Multiple-Choice Questions, apply comprehension in Projects & Essays, and broaden your knowledge with links to related research topics on the Web.

PART III

Research Designs

Chapters 11 through 18 address eight different research designs frequently used in educational research. The first three are quantitative, the next three are qualitative, and the final three combine quantitative and qualitative approaches.

The intent is to provide more advanced information than was found in the discussions in Part I and II. Specifically, Part III will take you into the details of the procedures of both quantitative and qualitative and combined research. These procedures relate to ways researchers collect, analyze, and report data.

The chapters in this section are:

▶ Chapter 11: Experimental and Quasi-Experimental Designs
▶ Chapter 12: Correlational Designs
▶ Chapter 13: Survey Designs
▶ Chapter 14: Grounded Theory Designs
▶ Chapter 15: Ethnographic Designs
▶ Chapter 16: Narrative Research Designs
▶ Chapter 17: Mixed Method Designs
▶ Chapter 18: Action Research Designs

In each chapter, you will be introduced to a short history of the design, the major types or forms of the design, the key characteristics that describe each design, steps in conducting the design, and a checklist for evaluating the design.

In addition, each chapter contains a complete journal article that illustrates the design. Marginal notations within the article will help you understand where to locate the (a) quantitative or qualitative characteristics (or both) of research (as introduced in Chapter 2 on "Distinguishing Between Quantitative and Qualitative Research") and (b) key characteristics of the design (as stated in the design chapter). A discussion about "Applying What You Have Learned" will take you through the major research process steps (as you learned in

Chapters 3–10) in the article. In this way you will have a three-way picture of each article: (1) the steps in the research process; (2) quantitative or qualitative research characteristics (or both); and (3) the key characteristics of the specific research design as introduced in the design chapter.

We will begin each chapter with a short passage about Maria, our high school teacher, and illustrate how she would choose and use the research design illustrated in the chapter. In reading these brief scenarios about Maria, we need to recognize that she will select a design that is best suited for her research problem, her audiences, and her own personal style. All scenarios presented in Chapters 11 through 18 address the more general issues of school violence and weapon possession among high school students, but each of Maria's designs will take a slightly different orientation toward these issues.

11

Experimental and Quasi-Experimental Designs

Let's assume that Maria, our high school teacher, chooses a quantitative quasi-experimental design for her graduate school research project. Her research question might be: "Do students who receive in-class instruction about the dangers of weapon possession in high school differ in terms of attitudes toward weapons than students who do not receive instruction about the dangers of weapon possession?" In using an experimental design to answer this question, Maria would divide students into groups and manipulate (or intervene with) one group so that those students receive the special instruction about the dangers of weapon possession. To do this, Maria might ask a fellow teacher if students in the instructor's two health classes could participant in an experiment during the semester. Treating each class as a separate group, Maria would then ask the instructor to introduce to one group a series of discussions about the dangers of weapon possession in the schools. For the other class, the instructor would proceed with the standard health curriculum. At the beginning of the year, students in both classes would complete an instrument to measure their attitudes toward the dangers of weapons in schools. Then, during the semester, one class would receive the special discussions about weapon possession. At the end of the semester, the instructor could administer the instrument measuring attitudes toward weapons to both classes. Maria's expectation is that students who had the special discussions about weapons will have less positive attitudes about the possession of weapons in school than the class that did not have the discussions. If this occurs, she can conclude that the special discussions in class help to change students' attitudes toward weapon possession.

The steps Maria took, such as creating groups, administering an intervention, and assessing the outcome of the intervention, are procedures used in experimental research. Thus, the first design we will discuss here is experimental research, a respected, frequently used design in educational research. If you conduct an experiment, your objective is to assess the impact of an intervention (e.g., a new instructional approach) on an outcome (e.g., student learning). Because the procedures control for extraneous factors, experiments provide the best test of all educational designs of probable cause and effect (see Chapter 5 on "Whether Variables Prove Cause and Effect"). This cause-and-effect type of thinking can be seen in such educational experiments as:

▶ testing whether elementary students with learning disabilities achieve better if they monitor their own "on-task" behavior (Kellogg, 1997)

▶ examining whether a voice-mail linkage between classes in a school contribute to communications between teachers and parents (Cameron & Lee, 1997)

▶ studying the effects of collaborative test taking on retention of math among third-grade students (Billington, 1994)

In all of these examples, the investigator assesses the impact of an idea or practice on an outcome. This basic idea is central to experiments. **Experimental or quasi-experiment research designs** (also called "intervention" or "group comparison" designs) are procedures in quantitative research in which the investigator determines the impact of an intervention on an outcome for participants in a study. With some variations, all experiments fit into this procedural approach.

This chapter addresses experimental procedures and covers basic concepts you will need to know to understand, plan, and design experimental and quasi-experimental research. In this chapter, the term "experiment" will be used as a general term for all types of experiments, recognizing that the focus here will be on "true" experiments and "quasi-experiments," forms frequently found in educational research.

By the end of this chapter you should be able to:

▶ Identify major events in the historical development of experimental and quasi-experimental research.

▶ Describe key characteristics of this form of research.

▶ Distinguish between different types of experiments.

▶ Describe steps in conducting an experimental or quasi-experimental study.

▶ List criteria for evaluating an experimental study.

A BRIEF HISTORY OF EXPERIMENTAL DESIGNS

Experimental research began in the late 19th and early 20th centuries with psychological experiments. By 1903, Schuyler used experimental and controls groups, and his use became so commonplace that he felt no need to provide a rationale for them. Then in 1916, McCall designed the idea of randomly assigning individuals to groups (Campbell & Stanley, 1963). Authoring a major book in 1925 on *How to Conduct an Experiment,* McCall firmly established the procedure of comparing groups. In addition, by 1925 statistical procedures useful in experiments in psychology and agriculture were discussed in Fisher's (1936) *Statistical Methods for Research Workers.* In this book, Fisher advanced the concept of randomly assigning individuals to groups before starting an experiment. Other developments in statistical procedures at this time (e.g., Chi-square goodness of it and critical values), and the testing of significance of differences (e.g., Fisher's 1935 *The Design of Experiments*) enhanced experimental research in education. Between 1926 and 1963, five sets of textbooks on statistics had undergone multiple editions (Huberty, 1993).

A major advancement in understanding experiments and their types was identified by Campbell and Stanley in 1963. They specified 15 different types of experimental and quasi-experimental designs and evaluated each design in terms of potential threats to validity. These designs are still popular today. Then, in 1979, Cook and Campbell elaborated on quasi-experimental designs, expanded the discussion about validity threats (discussed later in this chapter) and isolated four types commonly discussed in current texts: internal, external, construct, and statistical conclusion validity. These two books—Campbell and Stanley and Cook and Campbell—established the basic designs, the notation, the visual representation, the potential threats to designs, and the statistical procedures of educational experiments.

Since the 1980s, the use of computers and improved statistical procedures have played substantial roles in the increasing sophistication and complexity of experiments. Researchers now employ multiple independent and dependent variables, compare more groups than simply a control and experiment, and study different types of units of analysis, such as entire organizations, groups, and individuals (Boruch, 1998; Newman, 2000). Procedural refinements represent the latest development in experiments, and a number of "how to" books (e.g., Bausell, 1994) are available for the educational researcher. Also, books that link statistical procedures with experimental design in terms of designing sensitive experiments and the use of power (e.g., Lipsey, 1990) represent new ideas about strengthening procedures in experimental studies.

Experimental researchers today study entire schools (e.g., intensive schoolwide campaigns to prevent childrens' use of tobacco, alcohol, and drugs) and classrooms (e.g., different teacher-based approaches that enhance student cognitive achievement). They examine teacher and student issues, such as the impact of small classes on students (Boruch, 1998). Also, different types of educational settings are sites for testing educational innovations, such as using preschools to study enrichment programs, magnet schools to assess reading achievement, high schools to explore dropout prevention programs, and colleges to identify high-risk students (Boruch, 1998).

KEY CHARACTERISTICS OF EXPERIMENTAL DESIGNS

Writers often refer to experiments as "group comparison studies" because researchers typically compare different groups in terms of one or more outcomes. Experiments are also called "intervention studies" because researchers intervene, or manipulate the experiences of participants in the research (e.g., giving stickers to some children and not to others). They can be called "treatment effectiveness" studies (Lipsey, 1990) because investigators examine the effects of an experimental treatment. Regardless of the name, when investigators design or conduct experiments, they seek to maximize the influence of the independent variable on the dependent variable and to minimize the influence of extraneous factors or procedures that will likely affect this relationship. There are five key characteristics of experimental research designs:

▶ Participants are selected and assigned to groups, such as control and experimental groups.
▶ An intervention is applied to one or more groups.
▶ Outcomes are measured at the end of the experiment.
▶ Procedures are designed that address potential threats to validity.
▶ Statistical comparisons of different groups are conducted.

In discussing these five characteristics and types of experimental designs, we will refer to a single experimental study so that you can apply the characteristics and see how different experimental procedures vary.

Suppose that a researcher is interested in encouraging adolescents to reduce their smoking. A high school has an in-house program to treat individuals caught smoking on school grounds. In this large metropolitan high school, many students smoke and the smoking infractions each year are numerous. Students who are caught are required to take a special civics class (all students are required to take civics anyway) in which the teacher introduces a special unit on the health hazards of smoking. In this unit, the teacher discusses health issues, uses images and pictures of the damaged lungs of smokers, and has students write about their experiences as smokers. Let's also assume that this instructor offers several civics classes during a semester, and we will refer to this experimental situation as the "civics-smoking experiment."

Selecting Participants and Assigning Them to Treatments

When conducting an experiment, you need to initially identify your experimental unit of analysis and randomly assign individuals to this unit (if possible). Then you need to employ procedures to control for variables that might influence the relationship between the treatment and the outcome.

Experimental Unit of Analysis

One of the first steps in conducting an experiment is to decide on your experimental unit. An **experimental unit of analysis** is the smallest unit treated by the researcher during an experiment. When we use the term "treated," it means the experimental treatment. An **experimental treatment** is when the researcher physically intervenes to alter the conditions experienced by the experimental unit. This treatment may be a:

- reward for good spelling performance
- special type of classroom instruction, such as small group discussion
- different type of assignments, such as homework instead of classroom work
- different type of program or activity, such as lessons on the hazards of smoking or drinking

Although data will be collected from individuals, the experimental unit actually treated differs from one experiment to another. The experimental unit receiving a treatment may be a single individual, several individuals, a group, several groups, or an entire organization. Table 11.1 lists these different types of experimental units. As you look at it, think about the experimental unit that might be involved in our civics-smoking experiment.

The Individual as the Experimental Unit   An experimental researcher may treat only one individual or several individuals. (These will later be referred to as "single-subject designs.") The procedure is to select individuals, monitor their behavior, administer a treatment for a

TABLE 11.1
Different Types of Experimental Units

Experimental Unit "Treated" by the Researcher	The Experimental Unit for Treatment in the "Civics-smoking" Experiment:
A single individual	The researcher "treats" one student smoker.
Several single individuals	The researcher "treats" more than one student smoker, but examines each student individually.
Single group	The researcher "treats" one entire class.
Two groups	The researcher "treats" one of two classes.
Three groups	The researcher "treats" two of three classes.
An organization	The researcher "treats" an entire school.

specified period of time, and then withdraw the treatment and see if the initial behavior changed. As applied to our civics-smoking experiment, student smokers assigned to the special civics class will be the experimental unit treated. For example, an individual student, Jim, may have the frequency of his smoking monitored for a month. Then Jim receives a treatment by the teacher consisting of a special reading assignment on the health hazards of smoking. After the assignment is completed, the researcher examines whether Jim's smoking is reduced as a result of the treatment. Although many variations on this experiment are possible, one is to study several individual smokers in the civics class, one by one.

A Group or Groups as the Experimental Unit   The most common experiment is for a researcher to compare *two groups* of participants. This experiment requires assigning individuals to the two groups. An **experimental group** is a group in an experiment that receives the treatment (e.g., the activity or procedure) that the researcher would like to test. The **control group** is the group in an experiment that does *not* receive the treatment. A *treatment,* then, is what researchers do to the experimental group and withhold from the control group.

In the civics-smoking experiment, assigning student-smokers to a control group may be unwise because they do not receive the benefit of the class sessions on the health hazards of smoking. Rather than restricting the treatment to the experimental group and depriving other students of the benefits of learning, researchers sometimes contrast the experimental group with a comparison group. A **comparison group** receives an alternative treatment (e.g., a variation of the new procedure or activity) rather than nothing at all so that they can benefit during an experiment. In our civics-smoking experiment, three classes of student smokers may be involved in the study. One class receives the discussion about the health hazards (experimental group #1); a second class receives information about damaged lungs of smokers (experimental group #2); and a comparison group receives the assignment to write about and discuss their experiences with smoking (a comparison group). In this situation, all three groups receive something that might help them reduce their smoking.

When more than two groups are compared, the experiment is called a **between-group** design. In this type of design, the researcher compares results between different groups in terms of outcome scores (e.g., frequency of smoking). In other experiments, rather than test multiple groups, the researcher may choose to study a *single group* and provide the new idea or approach to this single group at some point in time during the experiment. This form of experimental design, where one group receives a treatment, is a **within-group** design.

In a single group civics-smoking experiment, the researcher studies one entire special civics class composed of smokers. At different times during the semester, the teacher introduces a treatment, such as first the discussion, then the information about damaged lungs, and finally the exercise in writing about smoking experiences. After each treatment, the researcher measures the students' frequency of smoking in order to assess whether smoking habits changed as a result of each treatment.

The Organization as the Experimental Unit   Researchers may test an idea or practice by administering a treatment to an experimental unit larger than an individual or group, such as an *organization* (e.g., an entire school or school district). For example, three schools have implemented the special civics class for students caught smoking on school grounds. The control school uses the standard civics curriculum, whereas the two experimental schools use the special discussions about the health hazards of smoking. The researcher compares the three schools and notes whether the frequency of smoking decreases in the two experimental school classes.

Random Assignment

When schools or individuals are assigned to different treatments, the researcher must also assign individuals to different treatments. The most rigorous approach for this is to randomly assign individuals to the treatments. **Random assignment** is the process of assigning individuals at random to groups or to different conditions of a group in an experiment. (These conditions will be addressed shortly.) The random assignment of individuals to groups (or conditions within a group) distinguishes a rigorous, "true" experiment from an adequate, but less-than-rigorous, "quasi-experiment" (to be discussed later in the chapter).

Random assignment is used so that any bias in personal characteristics is equally distributed among the groups or conditions. By randomization, the investigator provides *control* for extraneous characteristics of the participants that might influence the outcome (e.g., student ability, attention span, motivation). The experimental term for this process is "equating" the groups. **Equating groups** means that the researcher randomly assigns individuals to groups and equally distributes any variability of individuals between or among the groups or conditions in the experiment. In practice, personal factors that participants bring to an experiment can never be totally controlled—some bias or error will always affect the outcome of a study. However, by systematically distributing this potential error among groups, the researcher theoretically distributes the bias randomly. In our civics-smoking experiment, the researcher can take the list of offender smokers in the school and randomly assign them to one of two special civics classes.

Random assignment should not be confused with **random selection.** Both are important in quantitative research, but they serve different purposes. As mentioned in Chapter 6 on "Probability Sampling," quantitative researchers randomly select a sample from a population. In this way, the sample is representative of the population and results obtained during the study can be generalized to the population. Experiments (as opposed to surveys, to be discussed later in Chapter 13 on "Survey Research Designs") often do not include random selection of participants for several reasons. Participants often are individuals who are available to take part in the experiment or who volunteer to participate. Although random selection is important in experiments, it may not be logistically possible. However, a cornerstone for a good experiment is to randomly *assign* individuals to groups whenever possible. In the civics-smoking experiment, the researcher may randomly select individuals from the population of offender smokers (especially if there are too many for the special civics classes). However, most likely all the offenders will be placed in the special civics classes, giving the researcher control over random assignment rather than random selection.

Other Procedures for Control Over Extraneous Factors

In randomly assigning individuals, we say that we are controlling for extraneous variables that might influence the relationship between the new practice (e.g., discussions on health hazards) and the outcome (e.g., frequency of smoking). **Extraneous factors** are any influences in the selection of participants, the procedures, the statistics, or the design likely to affect the outcome and provide an alternative explanation for our results than what we expected. In all experiments, there is always some random error (where the scores do not reflect the "true" scores of the population) that can never be controlled, but researchers try to control extraneous factors as much as possible. Random assignment is a decision made by the investigator *before* the experiment begins. Other control procedures that are used both before and during the experiment are using pretests, matching participants, blocking variables, and using covariates.

Using Pretests and Posttests   To "equate" the characteristics of the groups, experimental researchers may use a pretest. Assume that we are interested in whether the special civics class affects students' attitudes toward smoking. In this experiment, we could measure attitudes before the treatment (i.e., by having a discussion about health hazards) and after, to see if the discussion has an effect on student attitudes. In this experiment, we need a pretest to measure students' attitudes.

A **pretest** provides a measure on some attribute or characteristic that is assessed for participants in an experiment before they receive a treatment. After the treatment the researcher takes another reading on the attribute or characteristic. A **posttest** is a measure on some attribute or characteristic that is assessed for participants in an experiment after a treatment. In our example, this would be assessing students' attitudes toward smoking at the end of the semester after the experimental treatment. A pretest-posttest comparison of attitudes toward smoking would provide a clearer reading on actual smoking behavior than using the posttest measure alone.

Pretests have advantages as well as disadvantages. They take time and effort to administer (e.g., students have to fill out an instrument early in the semester). They can also raise the participants' expectations about the outcome (e.g., students might anticipate questions later about their smoking attitudes and inflate or deflate their responses later in the semester). The pretest may influence the experimental treatment (e.g., students may ask questions about the treatment because of the pretest on attitudes toward smoking). When attitudinal or achievement tests are used as pretests, the scores may also affect posttest scores because participants can anticipate the questions on the posttest based on their experiences with the pretest.

Using Covariates   Because pretests may affect other aspects of the experiment, they are often statistically controlled using the procedure of covariance rather than simply comparing them with posttest scores. **Covariates** are variables that the researcher controls for using statistics and that relate to the dependent variable, but do not relate to the independent variable. The researcher needs to control for these variables that have the potential to covary with the dependent variable. Often these variables are scores on a pretest, but they might be any variables correlated with the dependent variable. The statistical procedure of analysis of covariance adjusts the scores on the dependent variable to account for the covariance. This procedure becomes another means for equating the groups and controlling for potential influences that might affect the dependent variable.

An illustration related to our civics-smoking example shows how the researcher removes the variance between a covariate and a dependent variable in order to assess the variance between the independent and dependent variable. Examine Figure 11.1 that portrays two sets of circles. The top part shows two variables, an independent variable and a dependent variable, without a covariate. The variability in rates of smoking that has been explained by type of instruction is indicated by the darkened area; the unexplained variability (called error) is shown with a hatch mark. In the bottom part of Figure 11.1, we introduce a covariate: parents who smoke. Now we can see that the explained variance increases, and the total amount of unexplained variability (error) actually decreases because more variance is explained. By adding a covariate related to parents who smoke, the researcher increases the amount of explained variance in rates of smoking and decreases the unexplained variance. The statistical procedure of covariance (see Chapter 8, "Choosing a Statistical Test") removes the variance shared by the covariate and the dependent variable, so that the variance between the independent and dependent variable (plus error) is all that remains. This test allows the researcher to more accurately assess the relationship between the treatment and the outcome (i.e., rate of smoking) because the amount of error is reduced.

Matching Participants   Another procedure used for control in an experiment is to match participants on one or more personal characteristics. **Matching** is the process of identifying one or more personal characteristics that influence the outcome and assigning individuals with that characteristic equally to the experimental and control groups. Typically, experimental researchers match on one or two of the following characteristics: gender, pretest scores, or individual abilities.

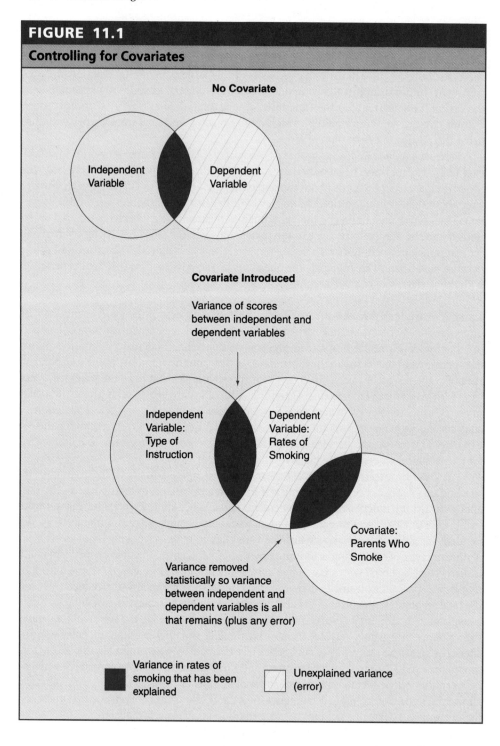

FIGURE 11.1

Controlling for Covariates

No Covariate

Independent Variable

Dependent Variable

Covariate Introduced

Variance of scores between independent and dependent variables

Independent Variable: Type of Instruction

Dependent Variable: Rates of Smoking

Covariate: Parents Who Smoke

Variance removed statistically so variance between independent and dependent variables is all that remains (plus any error)

Variance in rates of smoking that has been explained

Unexplained variance (error)

For example, examine Figure 11.2, which displays matching individuals (say, 10 girls and boys) on gender to the experimental and control groups. Returning to our high school civics-smoking experiment, we might assign the student smokers equally to two special civics classes (assuming that one class receives the treatment and the other does not) based on gender. In this way, our prior knowledge, for example, that boys may smoke more than girls, controls for the potential influence of gender on frequency of smoking. Procedurally,

FIGURE 11.2

The Marching Process Based on Gender

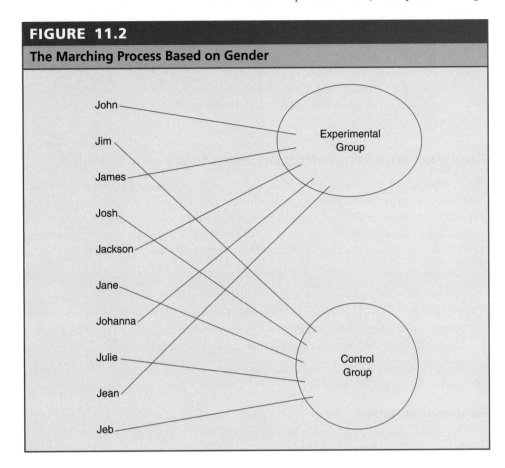

this matching process means assigning the first boy to the control group, the second to the experimental, the third to the control, and so forth. The researcher repeats this process for girls. By using this procedure, we control before the experiment begins for the potential extraneous factor of gender in the experiment.

Selecting Homogeneous Samples   Another approach used to make the groups comparable is to choose **homogeneous samples** by selecting people who vary little in their personal characteristics. For example, we might assume that the students in the two civics classes (one receives the lecture on "health hazards" and the second does not) are similar in terms of characteristics that students bring to the experiment, such as their academic grade point average, gender, racial group (e.g. Caucasian, African-Americans), or prior abilities in civics. When the experimenter assigns students to the two classes, the more similar they are in personal characteristics or attributes, the more these characteristics or attributes are controlled in the experiment. For example, if all of the smokers assigned to the two civics classes were juniors, then class level would be controlled in the experiment. Unfortunately, this situation is unlikely to occur in our civics-smoking study, and the researcher may need to use other procedures to control for individuals belonging to different grade levels.

Using Blocking Variables   One such procedure is to "block" for grade level before the experiment begins. A **blocking variable** is a variable the researcher controls before the experiment starts by dividing (or "blocking") the participants into subgroups (or categories) and analyzing the impact of each subgroup on the outcome. The variable (gender, for example), can be blocked into males and females; similarly, high school grade level can be blocked into four categories—freshmen, sophomores, juniors, and seniors. In this procedure, the researcher forms homogeneous subgroups by choosing a characteristic common to all participants in the study (e.g., gender or different age categories). Then the investigator randomly assigns individuals to the control and experimental groups using each category of the variable. For example, if the students who participate in the experiment are 15 and 16 years old, an equal number of 15- and 16-year-olds are randomly assigned to the control and experimental groups.

Applying an Intervention or Treatment

Once participants have been selected, they will be randomly assigned to either a treatment condition or the experimental group. Experimental researchers then intervene (or manipulate) one condition (or level) of a treatment variable. In our example, the researcher in the high school would manipulate one form of instruction in the special civics class—provide activities on the health hazards of smoking. Diagrammed, the procedure would be:

Identify a treatment variable → type of classroom instruction in the civics class

Identify the conditions (or levels) of the variable → classroom instruction can be (a) regular topics or (b) topics related to the health hazards of smoking

Manipulate the treatment conditions → provide special activities on health hazards of smoking to one class and withhold them from another class

This diagram introduces several new concepts that we will discuss using specific examples so that you can see how they work.

Treatment Variables

In experiments, you need to focus on the independent variable. Remember from Chapter 5 that these variables influence or affect the dependent variable in a quantitative study. Recall as well that the two major types of independent variables were "treatment" and "measured" variables. In experiments, treatment variables are independent variables that the researcher manipulates to determine their effect on the outcome, or dependent variable. Treatment variables are categorical variables measured using nominal scales (see Chapter 6 on "Selecting Scales of Measurement"). For example, treatment independent variables used in educational experiments might be:

- ▶ type of instruction (small group, large group)
- ▶ type of reading group (phonics readers, whole-language readers)

Conditions

In both of these examples, we have two categories within each treatment variable. In experiments, treatment variables need to have two or more categories, or levels. In an experiment, **levels** are categories of a treatment variable. For example, type of instruction might be divided into: (a) standard civics lecture, (b) standard civics lecture plus discussion about health hazards, and (c) standard civics lecture plus discussion about health hazards and slides of damaged lungs. In this example, we have a three-level treatment variable.

Manipulating the Treatment Conditions

The experimental researcher manipulates one or more of the treatment variable conditions. In other words, in an experiment, the researcher physically **intervenes** (or manipulates) with one or more condition so that individuals experience something different in the experimental conditions than those in the control condition. This means that to conduct an experiment, you need to be able to manipulate at least one condition of an independent

FIGURE 11.3
The Experimental Manipulation of a Treatment Condition

Independent Variables	*Dependent Variable*

1. Age (cannot manipulate)
2. Gender (cannot manipulate)
3. Types of instruction (can manipulate)
    a. Some receive lecture (control)
    b. Some receive lecture plus health-hazard discussion
       (comparison)
    c. Some receive lecture plus health-hazard discussion
       plus slides of damaged lungs from smoking (experimental)
	Frequency of Smoking

variable. It is easy to identify some situations in which you might measure an independent variable and obtain categorical data, but not be able to manipulate one of the conditions. As shown in Figure 11.3, the researcher measures three independent variables—age, gender, and type of instruction—but only type of instruction (and more specifically two conditions within it) is manipulated. The treatment variable—type of instruction—is a categorical variable with three conditions (or levels). Some students can receive a lecture—the traditional form of instruction in the class (the control group). Others receive something new, such as a lecture plus the health hazards discussion (a comparison group) or lecture plus the health hazards discussion plus slides of damaged lungs from smoking (another comparison group). In summary, experimental researchers manipulate or intervene with one or more conditions of a treatment variable.

Measuring Outcomes

In all experimental situations, researchers are interested in whether a treatment condition influences an outcome or dependent variable, such as a reduced rate of smoking or achievement on tests. In experiments, the **outcome** (or "response," "criterion," or "posttest") is the dependent variable that is the presumed effect of the treatment variable. It is also the effect predicted in a hypothesis in the cause-and-effect equation. Examples of dependent variables in experiments might be:

▶ achievement scores on a criterion-referenced test
▶ test scores on an aptitude test
▶ scores on an attitude scale
▶ performance of behaviors

Good outcome measures are sensitive to treatments in that they respond to the smallest amount of intervention. Outcome measures (as well as treatment variables) also need to be valid so that experimental researchers can draw valid inferences from them.

Addressing Potential Threats to Validity

Another major characteristic of experimental designs is that procedures are designed to address potential threats to validity. Although we introduced the concept of validity in Chapter 6, here we will discuss it within the context of statistical and design issues of an experiment, instead of an important element in evaluating an instrument for a quantitative study.

When conducting an experiment, you need to design a study to minimize certain "threats" that will compromise your ability to draw valid inferences from scores. A **threat to validity** means statistical and design issues may threaten the experiment so that the conclusions reached from data may provide a false reading about probable causality—the relationship between the treatment and the outcome. Four threats to validity, first introduced by Campbell and Stanley in 1963, were later refined and expanded by Bracht and Glass in 1968 and further developed by Cook and Campbell in 1979. Knowing them will help you weigh potential issues that may arise during an experiment. The four, presented in the order in which they typically appear in the literature, are summarized in Table 11.2.

TABLE 11.2

Threats to Validity in an Experiment

Threats to Statistical Conclusion Validity These are threats that arise in an experiment from the use of statistics.

- Low statistical power
- Violated statistical assumptions
- Recognition of chance in multiple comparisons
- Measures with low reliability
- Lack of standard procedures
- Uncontrolled environmental factors
- Selection of heterogeneous participants

Threats to Internal Validity These are threats that arise with participants or from procedures in an experiment.

Threats related to participants and their experiences:
- History
- Maturation
- Regression
- Selection
- Mortality
- Interaction between selection and maturation, history and instrumentation
- Treatments (diffusion, compensatory equalization, compensatory rivalry, and resentful demoralization)

Threats related to the procedures used in an experiment:
- Testing
- Instrumentation

Threats to Construct Validity These are threats that arise from the measures used for the variables.

- Inadequate definitions of measures
- Single measures of variables
- Ability of participant to guess results
- Presentation by participants of competence
- Expectancies by the experimenter

Threats to External Validity These are threats that reduce an experimental researcher's ability to generalize sample data to other persons, settings, and situations.

- Inability to generalize results to different groups
- Inability to generalize results from one setting to another
- Inability to generalize results to past or future situations

Statistical Conclusion Validity

In experimental research, the choice and use of statistics will affect whether proper conclusions are drawn from a study. **Threats to statistical conclusion validity** represent potential problems that threaten drawing correct inferences because of the statistical procedures. There are several potential threats in the use of statistics, as discussed by Cook and Campbell (1979). For example:

- low statistical power because the sample size is small (see Appendix A for a discussion about statistical power)
- violation of assumptions of the statistical tests, such as using parametric statistics when, in fact, the data are not normally distributed
- use of unreliable measures (see Chapter 6 on "Reliability")

Experimental researchers can plan studies so that these statistical issues are considered, such as the use of adequate sample size in our high school civic-smoking experiment.

Threats to Internal Validity

A number of threats to drawing appropriate inferences relate to the actual design and procedures used in an experiment. **Threats to internal validity** are problems that threaten drawing correct inferences that arise because of the experimental procedures or the experiences of participants. Of all of the threats to validity, these are the most severe because they can compromise an otherwise good experiment. The following threats to internal validity and recommended procedures to address them are widely discussed in the literature about experimental designs (see Cook & Campbell, 1979; Reichardt & Mark, 1998; Tuckman, 1999). To make each potential threat as realistic as possible, we will illustrate them using the hypothetical situation of the civics-smoking experiment.

The first category addresses threats *related to participants* in the study and their experiences:

- **History:** Time passes between the beginning of the experiment and the end, and events may occur (e.g., additional discussions about the hazards of smoking besides the treatment lecture) between the pretest and posttest that influence the outcome. In educational experiments, it is impossible to have a tightly controlled environment where all events are monitored. However, the researcher can have the control and experimental groups experience the same activities (except for the treatment) during the experiment.
- **Maturation:** Individuals develop or change during the experiment (i.e., become older, wiser, stronger, and more experienced), and these changes may affect their scores between the pretest and posttest. A careful selection of participants who mature or develop in a similar way (e.g., individuals at the same grade level) for both the control and experimental groups helps guard against this problem.
- **Regression:** When researchers select individuals for a group based on extreme scores, they will naturally do better (or worse) on the posttest than the pretest regardless of the treatment. Scores from individuals, over time, regress toward the mean. For example, the selection of heavy smokers for an experiment will probably contribute to lower rates of smoking after treatment because the teens selected started with higher rates at the beginning of the experiment. The selection of individuals who do not have extreme scores on entering characteristics (e.g., heavy smokers or extreme scores on pretests) may help solve this problem.
- **Selection:** "People factors" may introduce threats that influence the outcome, such as selecting individuals who are brighter, more receptive to a treatment, or more familiar with a treatment (e.g., teen smokers ready to quit) for the experimental group. Random selection may partly address this threat.

▸ **Mortality:** When individuals drop out during the experiment for any number of reasons (e.g., time, interest, money, friends, parents who do not want them participating in an experiment about smoking), drawing conclusions from scores may be difficult. Researchers need to choose a large sample and compare those who drop out with those who remain in the experiment on the outcome measure.

▸ **Interactions with selection:** Several of the threats mentioned thus far can interact (or relate) with the selection of participants to add additional threats to an experiment. Individuals selected may mature at different rates (e.g., 16-year-old boys and girls may mature at different rates during the study). Historical events may interact with selection because individuals in different groups come from different settings. For instance, vastly different social-economic backgrounds of students in the teen smoking experiment may introduce uncontrolled historical factors into the selection of student participants. The selection of participants may also influence the instrument scores, especially when different groups score at different mean positions on a test whose intervals are not equal. If the scale for measuring number of cigarettes is ambiguous (e.g., number of cigarettes per week or per day?) groups are likely to interpret the scale differently.

The next category addresses threats *related to treatments* used in the study:

▸ **Diffusion of treatments:** When the experimental and control groups can communicate with each other, the control group may learn from the experimental group information about the treatment and create a threat to internal validity. The diffusion of treatments (experimental and non-experimental) for the control and experimental groups needs to be different. As much as possible, experimental researchers need to keep the two groups separate in an experiment (e.g., have two different civic classes participate in the experiment). This may be difficult when, for example, two civic classes of students in the same grade in the same high school are involved in an experiment about teen smoking.

▸ **Compensatory equalization:** When only the experimental group receives a treatment, an inequality exists that may threaten the validity of the study. The benefits of the experimental treatment (i.e., the goods or services believed to be desirable) need to be equally distributed and equally compensated among the groups in the study. To counter this problem, researchers use comparison groups (e.g., one group receives the health hazard lecture, while the other receives a handout about the problems of teen smoking) so that all groups receive some benefits during an experiment.

▸ **Compensatory rivalry:** When assignments to the control and experimental group are publicly announced, compensatory rivalry may develop between the groups because the control group feels that it is the "underdog." Researchers can try to avoid this threat by attempting to reduce the awareness and expectations of the presumed benefits of the experimental treatment.

▸ **Resentful demoralization:** When a control group is used, individuals in this group may become resentful and demoralized because they perceive that they receive a less desirable treatment than other groups. One remedy to this threat is for experimental researchers to provide a treatment to this group after the experiment has concluded (e.g., after the experiment, all classes receive the lecture on the health hazards of smoking). Researchers may also provide services equally attractive to the experimental treatment but not directed toward the same outcome as the treatment (e.g., a class discussion about the hazards of teen driving with friends).

The following category addresses threats that typically occur during an experiment and *relate to the procedures* of the study:

▶ **Testing:** A potential threat to validity is that participants may become familiar with the outcome measures and remember responses for later testing. During some experiments, the outcome is measured more than one time, such as in pretests (e.g., repeated measures of number of cigarettes smoked). To remedy this situation, experimental researchers measure the outcome less frequently and use different items on the posttest than those used during earlier testing.

▶ **Instrumentation:** Between the administration of a pretest and a posttest, the instrument may change, introducing a potential threat to the internal validity of the experiment. For example, observers may become more experienced during the time between a pretest and the posttest and change their scoring procedures (e.g., observers change the location to observe teen smoking). Less frequently, the measuring instrument may change so that the scales used on a pretest and a posttest are dissimilar. To correct for this potential problem, procedures should be standardized so that the same observational scales or instrument is used throughout the experiment.

Threats to Construct Validity

Threats to construct validity are problems that threaten drawing correct inferences because of the measures used in the experiment for the treatment (independent variable) and the outcome (dependent variable). In order to reduce this threat, the researcher needs to find good definitions of the measures in the literature. Also, researchers can collect multiple measures (e.g., number of cigarettes smoked and whether smoking habits have changed, and how). They can also use multiple experimental treatments when possible (e.g., a civics lecture on the hazards of smoking and another treatment of a handout on the problems of smoking). The measures also need to be complex enough so that participants cannot guess what the experimenters hope to find. For example, a more complex measure than "number of cigarettes you smoke per day" is "Have you changed your smoking habits during the last week?" When measures are collected by researchers, the participants may respond because they want to present themselves as competent (e.g., responses to questions about smoking may be influenced by individual attitudes about smoking as a "cool" thing to do). Likewise, when researchers administer instruments, they may create expectancies that can bias the data (e.g., assume the researcher in the civics experiment is a smoker himself and has expectations about the difficulty of smoking cessation). Apprehensiveness by participants, if detected, needs to be controlled by clear instructions to participants and by the use of experimental researchers who have no expectations or personal agendas.

Threats to External Validity

By ruling out extraneous factors and assuming that the treatment influences an outcome, researchers make claims about the generalizability of the results. **Threats to external validity** are problems that threaten drawing correct inferences from the sample data to other persons, settings, and past and future situations. According to Cook and Campbell (1979), three threats may affect this generalizability:

▶ **Interaction of selection and treatment:** This threat to external validity involves the inability to generalize beyond the groups in the experiment, such as other racial, social, geographical, age, gender, or personality groups. One strategy researchers use to increase generalizability is to make participation in the experiment as convenient as possible for all individuals in a population.

▶ **Interaction of setting and treatment:** This threat to external validity arises from the inability to generalize from the setting where the experiment occurred to another setting. For example, private high schools may be different from public high schools, and the results from our civics experiment on smoking may not apply outside the public high school where the researcher conducts the experiment. This threat may also result from trying to generalize results from one level in an organization to another. For example, treatment effects obtained from studying entire school districts cannot be generalized to specific high schools. The practical solution to an interaction of setting and treatment is for the researcher to analyze the effect of a treatment for each type of setting.

▶ **Interaction of history and treatment:** This threat to external validity develops when the researcher tries to generalize findings to past and future situations. Experiments may take place at a special time (e.g., at the beginning of the school year) and may not produce similar results if conducted earlier (e.g., students attending school in the summer may be different than students attending school during the regular year) or later (e.g., during semester break). One solution is to replicate the study at a later time rather than trying to generalize results to other times.

In our experiment on civic-smoking, the researcher would need to be cautious about generalizing results to other high schools, other students in civic classes, and other situations where discussions about the hazards of smoking take place. The behavior of adolescents who smoke may change due to factors associated with the cost of cigarettes, parental disapproval, and advertising. Because of these factors, it is difficult to generalize the results from our civics experiment to other situations.

Comparing Groups Statistically

In an experiment, the investigator compares scores for different treatments on an outcome. A **group comparison** is when a researcher obtains scores for individuals or groups on the dependent variable and makes comparisons of their means and variance both within the group and between the groups. (See Keppel, 1991, for detailed statistical procedures for this process.)

To visualize this process, let's consider some actual data from an experiment by Gettinger (1993), who sought to determine the effects of an error correction procedure on the spelling of third graders. As shown in Figure 11.4, Gettinger's experiment is visualized in three ways. As one facet of her study, Gettinger examined whether the error correction procedure related positively to spelling accuracy (Phase #1). She then created three groups of students, Class A, Class B, and Class C. Class A (the control group) received regular spelling practice on 15 words consisting of workbook exercises, writing sentences containing each word, and studying words on their own. Class B (the comparison group) had the same experience except that they studied a reduced number of words on a list—three sets of five words each. Class C (the experimental group) used an error-and-correction practice procedure consisting of correcting their own tests, noting incorrect words, and writing both the incorrect and correct spelling for each word. As shown in Phase #2, all three groups received the same spelling practice for 6 weeks, then the experimental group received the error correction procedure for 6 weeks, and after a third 6 weeks, all three groups were tested. Phase #3 shows the statistical comparisons made among the three groups on each of the three tests. Class A improved slightly (from 10.3 on Test 1 to 11.1 on Test 3) while Class B's scores decreased over the three tests. Class C, the experimental group, improved considerably. F-test values showed that when all three groups were compared, the scores varied significantly on Test 2 and Test 3. These statistical comparisons took into consideration both the mean scores and the variation between and within each group to arrive at statistical significance at $p < .05$.

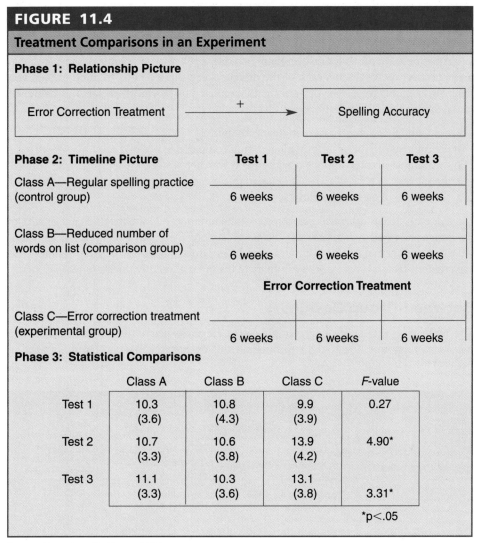

FIGURE 11.4

Treatment Comparisons in an Experiment

Phase 1: Relationship Picture

| Error Correction Treatment | + → | Spelling Accuracy |

Phase 2: Timeline Picture

	Test 1	Test 2	Test 3
Class A—Regular spelling practice (control group)	6 weeks	6 weeks	6 weeks
Class B—Reduced number of words on list (comparison group)	6 weeks	6 weeks	6 weeks

Error Correction Treatment

| Class C—Error correction treatment (experimental group) | 6 weeks | 6 weeks | 6 weeks |

Phase 3: Statistical Comparisons

	Class A	Class B	Class C	*F*-value
Test 1	10.3 (3.6)	10.8 (4.3)	9.9 (3.9)	0.27
Test 2	10.7 (3.3)	10.6 (3.8)	13.9 (4.2)	4.90*
Test 3	11.1 (3.3)	10.3 (3.6)	13.1 (3.8)	3.31*

*$p < .05$

Source: Based on Gettinger, 1993

TYPES OF EXPERIMENTAL DESIGNS

Although all experiments have common characteristics, their use and applications vary depending on the type of design used. The most common designs you will find in educational research are:

- **Between-Group Designs**
  - true experiments (pre- and posttest, posttest only)
  - quasi-experiments (pre- and posttest, posttest only)
  - factorial designs
- **Within-Group or Individual Designs**
  - time series experiments (interrupted, equivalent)
  - repeated measures experiments
  - single-subject experiments

Being able to identify these types of designs and their major characteristics will help you choose a suitable design for your study or permit a thoughtful evaluation of an experimental design used in a published study.

A basic set of criteria for differentiating among types of experimental designs is shown in Table 11.3. As we discuss each of the designs, keep these criteria in mind to help you distinguish among them. The designs are differentiated by several characteristics, as shown in the first column in Table 11.3:

 ▌ the random assignment of participants to groups
 ▌ the number of groups or individuals being compared
 ▌ the number of interventions used by the researcher
 ▌ the number of times the dependent variable is measured or observed
 ▌ the control of extraneous variables

For each design discussed below, you will be introduced to the major characteristics of the design and its advantages and disadvantages. Among the disadvantages will be its potential threats to internal validity—an idea already introduced—but now related specifically to each design. Table 11.4 presents a summary of the internal validity threats for each design.

Between-Group Designs

The most frequently used designs in education are those where the researcher compares two or more groups. Illustrations throughout this chapter underscore the importance of

TABLE 11.3

Types of Experimental Designs

	True Experiment	Quasi-Experiment	Factorial	Repeated Measures	Time Series	Single Subject
Random assignment?	Yes	No	May be used	No	No	No
Number of groups/individuals compared?	Two or more	Two or more	Two or more	One group	One group	One individual studied at a time
Number of interventions used?	One or more interventions	One or more interventions	Two or more interventions	Two or more interventions	One or more interventions	One or more interventions
Number of times the dependent variables measured/observed?	Once	Once	Once	After each intervention	After each intervention	Multiple points
Controls typically used?	Pretest, matching, blocking, covariates	Pretest, matching, blocking, covariates	Pretest matching blocking, covariates	Covariates	Group becomes its own control	Individuals become their own controls

TABLE 11.4

Threats to Internal Validity in Types of Experimental Designs

	True Experiment	Quasi-Experiment	Factorial	Time Series	Repeated Measures	Single Subject
To Participants:						
History	Controlled	Potential threat	Controlled, if random assignment	May be a threat if short intervals not used	May be a threat if short intervals not used	Potential threat
Maturation	Controlled	Potential threat	Controlled, random assignment	Can be controlled if pattern detected	Controlled	Controlled
Regression	Controlled	Potential threat	Controlled, random assignment	Can be controlled if unusual scores noted	Controlled	Controlled
Selection	Controlled	Potential threat	Controlled, if random assignment	Controlled	Controlled	Controlled
Mortality	Controlled	Potential threat	Controlled, if random assignment	Can be controlled if drop-outs noted	Controlled	Controlled
Interaction of selection and maturation, history, and instrumentation	Controlled	Potential threat	Controlled, if random assignment	Controlled	Controlled	Controlled
To Procedures:						
Testing	Potential threat if pre- and posttest used	Potential threat if pre- and posttest used	Potential threat if a pre- and posttest used	With repeated measures and observations before (interrupted design), likely to diminish over time	Potential threat if pre- and posttest used	Controlled
Instrumentation	Potential threat if instrument or observational procedures change	Potential threat if instrument or observational procedures change	Potential threat if instrument or observational procedures change	Can be controlled if procedures monitored	Can be controlled if procedures monitored	May be a threat if multiple inverventions used

these designs. We will begin with the most rigorous between-group design available to the educational researcher, the true experiment.

True Experiments

True experiments comprise the most rigorous and strong experimental designs because of equating the groups through random assignment. The procedure for conducting major forms of true- and quasi-experiments, viewing them in terms of activities from the beginning of the experiment to the end, is shown in Table 11.5. In **true experiments**, the researcher randomly assigns participants to different conditions of the experimental variable. Individuals in the experimental group receive the experimental treatment while those in the control group do not. After investigators administer the treatment, they compile average (or mean) scores on a posttest. One variation on this design is to obtain pretest as well as

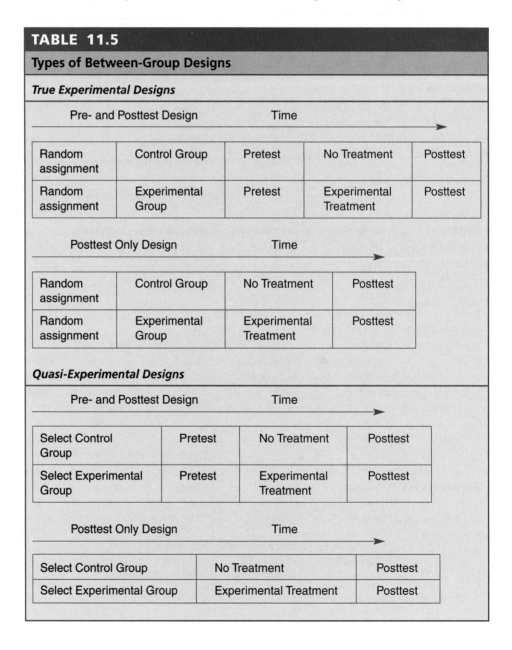

TABLE 11.5

Types of Between-Group Designs

True Experimental Designs

Pre- and Posttest Design   Time →

| Random assignment | Control Group | Pretest | No Treatment | Posttest |
| Random assignment | Experimental Group | Pretest | Experimental Treatment | Posttest |

Posttest Only Design   Time →

| Random assignment | Control Group | No Treatment | Posttest |
| Random assignment | Experimental Group | Experimental Treatment | Posttest |

Quasi-Experimental Designs

Pre- and Posttest Design   Time →

| Select Control Group | Pretest | No Treatment | Posttest |
| Select Experimental Group | Pretest | Experimental Treatment | Posttest |

Posttest Only Design   Time →

| Select Control Group | No Treatment | Posttest |
| Select Experimental Group | Experimental Treatment | Posttest |

posttest measures or observations. When experimenters collect pretest scores, they may compare net scores (the differences between the pre- and posttests). Alternatively, investigators may relate the pretest scores for the control and experimental groups to see if they are statistically similar, and then compare the two posttest group scores. In many experiments, the pretest is a covariate and statistically controlled by the researcher.

Because individuals are randomly assigned to the groups, most of the threats to internal validity do not arise. Randomization or equating the groups minimizes the possibility of history, maturation, selection, and the interactions between selection and other threats. Treatment threats, such as diffusion, rivalry, resentful demoralization, and compensatory equalization are all possibilities in a between-group design because two or more groups exist in the design. When true experiments include only a posttest, it reduces the threats of testing, instrumentation, and regression because a pretest is not being used. If a pretest is used, it introduces all of these factors as possible threats to validity. Instrumentation exists as a potential threat in most experiments, but if researchers use the same or similar instrument for the pre- and posttest or enact standard procedures during the study, instrumentation threats are held to a minimum.

Quasi-Experiments

In education, many experimental situations occur in which researchers need to use intact groups. This might happen because of the availability of the participants or because the setting prohibits forming artificial groups. **Quasi-experiments** include assignment, but not random assignment of participants to groups. This is because the experimenter cannot artificially create groups for the experiment. For example, studying a new math program may require using existing fourth-grade classes and designating one as the experimental group and one as the control group. Randomly assigning students to the two groups would disrupt classroom learning. Because educators often use intact groups (schools, colleges, or school districts) in experiments, quasi-experimental designs are frequently used.

Returning again to Table 11.5., we can apply the pre- and posttest design approach to a quasi-experimental design. The researcher assigns intact groups the experimental and control treatments, administers a pretest to both groups, conducts experimental treatment activities with the experimental group only, and then administers a posttest to assess the differences between the two groups. A variation on this approach, similar to the true experiment, uses only a posttest in the design.

The quasi-experimental approach introduces considerably more threats to internal validity than the true experiment. Since the investigator does not randomly assign participants to groups, the potential threats of maturation, selection, mortality, and the interaction of selection with other threats are possibilities. Individuals assigned to the two groups may have selection factors that go uncontrolled in the experiment. Because two groups are compared, the treatment threats may also be present. In addition, when the pretest-posttest design is used, additional threats of history, testing, instrumentation, and regression also may occur. While the quasi-experimental design has the advantage of utilizing existing groups in educational settings, it introduces many threats that need to be addressed in the design of the experiment.

Factorial Designs In some experimental situations, it is not enough to know the effect of a single treatment on an outcome—several treatments may, in fact, provide a better explanation for the outcome. **Factorial designs** represent a modification of the between-group design in which the researcher studies two or more categorical, independent variables, each examined at two or more levels (Vogt, 1999). The purpose of this design is to study the independent and simultaneous effects of two or more independent treatment variables on an outcome.

For example, in our civics-smoking experiment, the researcher may want to examine more than the effect of the type of instruction (i.e., lecture on health hazards of smoking versus standard lecture) on frequency of smoking. Assume that the experimenter wishes to examine the combined influence of type of instruction and level of depression in students (e.g., high, medium, and low scores on a depression scale) on rates of smoking (as the posttest). Assume further that the investigator has reason to believe that depression is an important factor in rates of teen smoking, but its "interaction" or combination with type of smoking is unknown. The study of this research problem requires a factorial design. Thus, "depression" is a blocking or moderating variable and the researcher makes random assignment of each "block" (high, medium, and low) to each treatment instructional group. This design has the advantage of a high level of control in the experiment. It allows the investigator to examine the combination or interaction of independent variables to better understand the results of the experiment. If only a posttest is used, internal validity threats of testing and instrumentation do not exist. If the researcher randomly assigns individuals to groups, the threats related to participants and their experiences (history, maturation, regression, selection, mortality, and interaction of selection and other factors) are minimized.

However, with multiple independent variables in a factorial design, the statistical procedures become more complex and the actual results become more difficult to understand. What does it mean, for example, that depression and type of instruction interact to influence smoking rates among teens? Which independent variable is more important, and why? As researchers manipulate additional independent variables, more participants are needed in each group for statistical tests and the interpretation of results becomes more complex. Because of this complexity, factorial designs typically include at the most three independent variables manipulated by the researcher.

Let's examine more closely the steps in the process of conducting a factorial design. The researcher identifies a research question that includes two independent variables and one dependent variable, such as "Do rates of smoking vary under different combinations of type of instruction and levels of depression?"

To answer this question, the experimenter identifies the levels of each factor or independent variable:

- **Factor 1**—Types of instruction
  - Level 1—a health-hazards lecture in civics class
  - Level 2—a standard lecture in civics class
- **Factor 2**—Levels of depression
  - Level 1—high
  - Level 2—medium
  - Level 3—low

Because two levels of instruction and three levels of depression are being measured, the design is called a "two by three" factorial design. It is written as "2 × 3" to indicate the levels involved in each independent variable. With three independent variables, the design might be a "2 × 3 × 4" design, with the third variable consisting of four levels.

In the 2 × 3 design, investigator then assigns participants to six groups so that all groups receive each level on one independent variable (e.g., type of instruction) and each level on the second independent variable (e.g., level of depression). Table 11.6 shows the formation of the six groups and the assignment of participants to each group based on the three levels (i.e., low, medium, and high) of "depression" and the two levels (i.e., health-hazards lecture, standard lecture) of instruction.

In this process, the researcher creates six groups and assigns student smokers to each group. All students first complete the instrument measuring their level of depression. The researcher scores the instrument and divides the students into low, medium, and high groups based on their depression scores. Further, remember that our study is being con-

TABLE 11.6

Factorial Design Groups Assigned to Two Treatments

	Extent of Depression	Type of Instruction	Dependent Variable
Group 1	Low depression scores	Receives health-hazards lecture	Posttest (Scores on instrument measuring smoking)
Group 2	Medium depression scores	Receives health-hazards lecture	Posttest (Scores on instrument measuring smoking)
Group 3	High depression scores	Receives health-hazards lecture	Posttest (Scores on instrument measuring smoking)
Group 4	Low depression scores	Receives standard lecture	Posttest (Scores on instrument measuring smoking)
Group 5	Medium depression scores	Receives standard lecture	Posttest (Scores on instrument measuring smoking)
Group 6	High depression scores	Receives standard lecture	Posttest (Scores on instrument measuring smoking)

ducted in two special civics classes—in one class, the students receive a lecture on the health hazards of smoking and in the second class, the teacher provides standard lectures on civics topics. Thus, in our factorial design, three groups will receive the health lecture in one civics class and the other three groups will receive the standard lectures in the other civics class. This procedure uses quasi-experimental research in which the investigator uses intact classes for the experiment (two high school civics classes).

At the conclusion of the experiment, the investigator asks all participants to complete a posttest. This posttest will measure the rate of smoking for individuals in the experiment. The means of posttest scores are organized into six cells to visually portray their differences, as shown in Figure 11.5. A *cell* represents each group in an experiment and it contains the mean scores for individuals in each group. Once the mean scores are computed, the researcher compares the scores to determine whether they are statistically different. The null hypothesis would be that the means are not different, while the alternative would be that they are different.

Let's add one more element into this statistical portrait of scores arrayed in cells as shown in Figure 11.5. Using the parametric statistic of analysis of variance (ANOVA), as discussed in Chapter 8 on "Choosing a Statistical Test," the researcher examines the effect of each independent variable separately and in combination on the dependent variable. Using a statistical software program, analysis of variance will produce statistical results for main effects and interaction effects. **Main effects** are the influence of each independent variable (e.g., type of instruction or extent of depression) on the outcome (e.g., the dependent variable, rate of smoking) in an experiment. **Interaction effects** exist when the influence on one independent variable depends on (or covaries with) the other independent variable in an experiment.

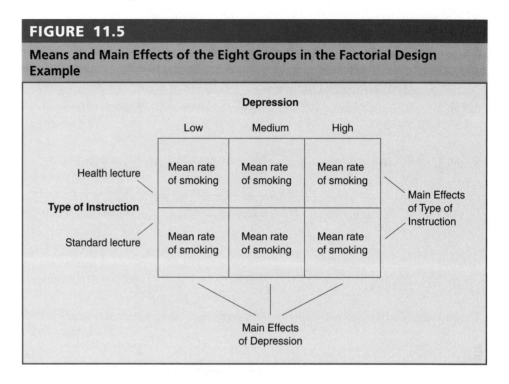

FIGURE 11.5

Means and Main Effects of the Eight Groups in the Factorial Design Example

Researchers often graph the main and the interaction effects to help readers visualize them. The graphs in Figure 11.6 portray possible main effects and interaction effects in our hypothetical civics-smoking experiment. Graph (a) displays the results of scores on the posttest (i.e., rate of smoking) and the three factors of depression. The researcher graphs scores for both the groups who receive the health-hazards lecture and the standard lecture in the civics class. As is seen in this graph, the level of depression for both groups increases with the extent of smoking. Because the lines are parallel and do not cross, an interaction effect is not present.

However, the results of the experiment could be different, as shown in graphs (b) and (c). In graph (b), the scores for the groups receiving the standard lecture increase as depression increase. Alternatively, scores for students who experience the health hazards lecture decrease as their depression scores decrease. When these scores are plotted, the lines crossed, showing an interaction effect. In graph (c), the lines again are not parallel, displaying an interaction effect. Typically, in factorial designs, the investigator graphs these trends and explains the meaning of the combination of independent variables.

Within-Group or Individual Designs

In any given experiment, the number of participants may be limited and it may not be possible to involve more than one group. In these cases, researchers study a single group using a **within-group experimental design.** Also, the experimenter might examine single individuals (**within individual design**). This type of design assumes several forms: time series, repeated measures, and single-subject designs.

Time Series

When an experimental researcher has access to only one group and can study them over a period, a time series design is a good experimental approach. A **time series** design consists of studying one group, over time, with multiple pretest and posttest measures or observa-

FIGURE 11.6

Graphs of Scores Showing Main Effects and the Interaction Effects

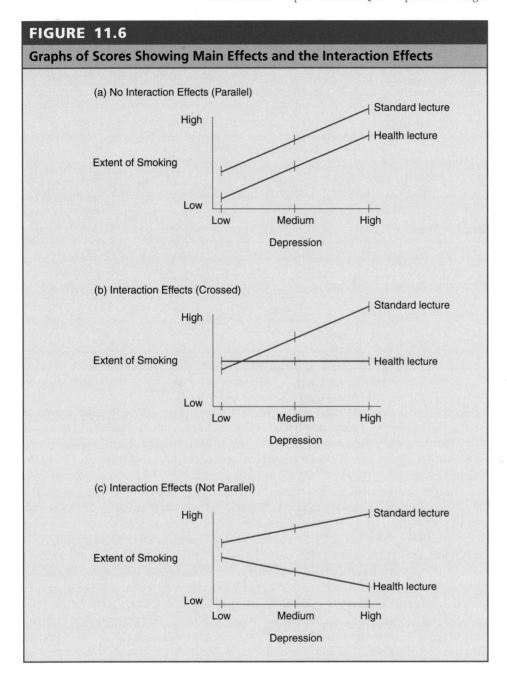

(a) No Interaction Effects (Parallel)

Standard lecture
Health lecture

High
Extent of Smoking
Low

Low   Medium   High

Depression

(b) Interaction Effects (Crossed)

Standard lecture
Health lecture

High
Extent of Smoking
Low

Low   Medium   High

Depression

(c) Interaction Effects (Not Parallel)

Standard lecture
Health lecture

High
Extent of Smoking
Low

Low   Medium   High

Depression

tions made by the researcher. This design does not require access to large numbers of participants and it requires only one group for the study. It is ideal for examining change in an entire system (e.g., a school district) where it would be difficult to find a control group or system willing to cooperate. On the other hand, this design is labor-intensive because the researcher needs to gather multiple measures.

These multiple measures are seen in two important variations of this design. As shown in Table 11.7, the first is the **interrupted time series** design. This procedure consists of studying one group, obtaining multiple pretest measures for a period of time, administering an intervention (or interrupting the activities), and then measuring outcomes (or posttests) several times. Data analysis in this example consists of examining difference

TABLE 11.7

Time Series Experimental Designs

Interruped Time Series Design

Time →

Select Participants for Group	Pretest Measure or Observation	Pretest Measure or Observation	Pretest Measure or Observation	Intervention	Posttest Measure or Observation	Posttest Measure or Observation	Posttest Measure or Observation

Equivalent Time Series Design

Time →

Select Participants for Group	Measure or Observation	Intervention	Measure or Observation	Intervention	Measure or Observation	Intervention	Measure or Observation

scores between the pretests and posttests or posttest only scores and using the pretests as covariates. A variation, also seen in Table 11.7, uses an **equivalent time series** design in which the investigator alternates a treatment with a posttest measure. The data analysis then consists of comparing posttest measures or plotting them in order to discern patterns in the data over time.

The time series design permits significant control over threats to internal validity. The effects of history are not always clear-cut. History effects are minimized by the short time intervals between measures or observations. However, threats to validity may occur because of the overall length of data collection in this design. The maturation of participants may be a problem, although the researcher can estimate changes in maturation by studying them and removing them statistically in the design. To control for statistical regression, researchers can also observe the scores on the pretests and control for unusually high or low scores. Since only one group is studied, the issues of selection and treatment are not relevant, although individuals can choose to drop out of the study. Testing may be a problem, but the repeated measures or observations over time may diminish the effects of testing. When researchers change the instrument during multiple testing, they may also introduce threats to validity.

In our hypothetical experiment in the high school civics class, our examples thus far consist of studying two civics classes (presumably taught by the same instructor). If only *one* class is available, we could use a time series design. It would involve collecting multiple measures of smoking behavior among smokers as pretests. Then the teacher would introduce the intervention, "health-hazards discussion," followed by multiple measures of smoking behavior on posttests. A plot of this pretest and posttest data would reveal whether the health lecture contributed to reduced smoking among the students in the class.

Repeated Measures

Another experimental design that has the advantage of employing only a single group is a repeated measures design. In a **repeated measures design,** all participants in a single group

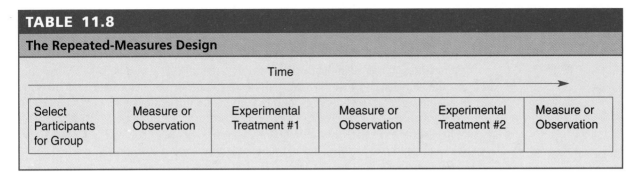

TABLE 11.8

The Repeated-Measures Design

Time					
Select Participants for Group	Measure or Observation	Experimental Treatment #1	Measure or Observation	Experimental Treatment #2	Measure or Observation

participate in all experimental treatments with each group becoming its own control. The researcher compares a group's performance under one experimental treatment with their performance under another experimental treatment. The experimenter decides on multiple treatments (as in factorial designs) but administers each separately to only one group. After each administration, the researcher obtains a measure or observation. The steps in this design are shown in Table 11.8.

After selecting participants, the researcher decides on different experimental treatments to determine the effect of each on one or more outcomes. An outcome measure or observation follows the first experimental treatment and then a second outcome measure or observation is taken following the second experimental treatment. Variation in outcome measures are then assessed for differences from treatment to treatment.

In terms of threats to internal validity, this design is not affected by threats related to comparing groups (i.e., selection, treatments, regression, mortality, maturation, or interactions with selection). Without use of a pretest, testing and instrumentation are not threats in this design. History is a potential problem in that events may occur during the experiment that raise the potential for extraneous influences to affect the outcome measure. One experimental treatment may influence the next treatment, and researchers need to make the treatments as distinct as possible.

Applying this design to our civics-smoking experiment, assume that the investigator only has access to one civics class and can employ several interventions: a lecture on health hazards; cartoons that depict "bad breath" between couples when one individual smokes; and a handout about the rising cost of a pack of cigarettes. Notice in this example that the three treatments all address teen smoking issues, but they are distinct concerns (i.e., health, relationships, and cost). During the semester, the researcher asks the teacher to introduce each intervention separately, and the investigator measures the rate of smoking after each intervention.

Single-Subject Designs

Often in experiments, it is more important to learn about the behavior of single individuals than group behavior or performance. **Single-subject research** (also called $N=1$ research, behavior analysis, or within-subjects research) involves the study of single individuals, their observation over a baseline period, and the administration of an intervention. This is followed by another observation after the intervention to determine if the treatment affects the outcome. Without random assignment, this design is a quasi-experimental rather than an experimental design. The researcher studies the behaviors of *single* individuals (one or more) rather than a group of subjects, with the subject becoming its own control in the experiment (see Cooper, Heron, & Heward, 1987; Neuman & McCormick, 1995).

The investigator seeks to determine if an intervention impacts the behavior of a participant by observing the individual over a prolonged period of time and recording the behavior before and after the intervention. The researcher assesses whether there is a relationship between the treatment and the target behavior or outcome. The key characteristics of a single-subject study are:

> ▶ Prior to administering the intervention, the researcher establishes a stable baseline of information about the individual's behavior. A *stable baseline* means that behavior for an individual varies little over several sessions or days. A behavior is stable if (a) variability over time is minimal, and (b) there is no upward or downward trend in performance over time (Poling & Grossett, 1986).
>
> ▶ The researcher repeatedly and frequently measures behavior (i.e., the outcome) throughout the experiment based on making observations and recording scores for each individual.
>
> ▶ After administering the intervention, the researcher notes the patterns of behavior and plots them on a graph. This pattern may be ascending, descending, flat, or variable. Data are typically analyzed by visually inspecting the data rather than by using statistical analysis. In particular, the researcher notes how the behavior of the individual has changed after the intervention, after withdrawing the intervention, or during multiple interventions.
>
> ▶ In a graphic analysis of the data, the single-subject researcher plots behaviors for specific individuals on a graph. On this graph, the vertical axis records percentages or counts of the behavior being studied. Alternatively, the horizontal axis displays the days or sessions in which the observations occur. The plot can show data for several individuals or multiple dependent variables for a single individual.

Single-subject research has the advantage of obtaining data on single individuals, such as the learning and behaviors of children with disabilities, where a person-by-person analysis is needed. It also controls for many threats to internal validity. Since only one individual is studied at a time, groups are not involved and the threats to selection, treatments, mortality, maturation, regression, and interactions with selection are not relevant. Assuming that observers use the same standard procedures, instrumentation may not be a problem. When multiple treatments are used, the learning from one intervention may affect the second intervention, and history may be an issue since the experiment takes place over time.

A/B Design   Because single-subject studies employ different research designs, the best way to understand them is to examine graphs that show the monitoring of behavior and the administration of an intervention. The simplest design is the A/B design. An **A/B design** consists of observing and measuring behavior during a trial period (A), administering an intervention, and observing and measuring the behavior after the intervention (B). This design is shown in Figure 11.7 for a study about elementary children and their achievement in solving math problems. In this study, the researcher observes baseline behavior and then employs an intervention of feedback to the students about their performance in math.

A variation on this design is an A/B/A, or a reversal design, where the researcher establishes a baseline behavior, administers an intervention, and then withdraws the intervention and determines if the behavior returned to the baseline level. Another variation is an A/B/A withdrawal design. In this design, researchers may implement one or more treatments. The disadvantage of this type of design is that in some studies the withdrawing of the intervention may have serious effects on the participants in the study, raising an ethical issue for the researcher. This design may also introduce negative irreversible effects and it requires numerous sessions or observational periods because of the use of multiple interventions.

Multiple Baseline Design   A frequently used single-subject design is the **multiple baseline design,** as shown in Figure 11.8. In this design, each participant receives an experimental treatment at a different time (hence, multiple baselines exist) so that treatment diffusion will not occur among participants. Researchers choose this design when the

FIGURE 11.7

A/B Single-Subject Design

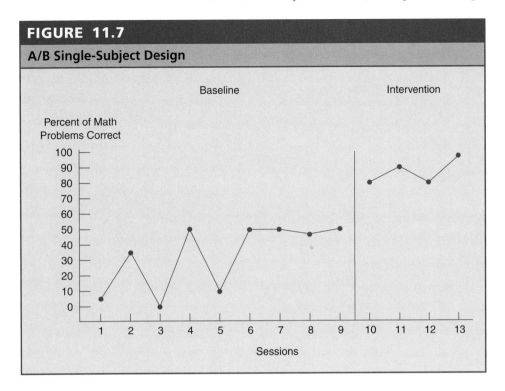

treatment (e.g., skill or strategy being taught) cannot be reversed and doing so would be unethical or injurious to participants. In the example shown in Figure 11.8, five individuals participate in the study and the behavior of each is plotted. Variations on this approach could involve different types of behaviors for the participants or behaviors for participants in different settings. The results of this design may be less convincing than the reversal design and it may introduce negative consequences if the treatment is withheld for an extended period.

Alternating Treatments   A final type of single-subject design is the alternating treatment. An **alternating treatment design** is a single-subject design in which the researcher examines the relative effects of two or more interventions and determines which intervention is the more effective treatment on the outcome. As shown in Figure 11.9, four elementary students participated in the experiment on solving math problems. In this study there were two treatment conditions: practice with feedback from the teacher and practice with a student "coach" in the class. After establishing a baseline of behavior, the researcher implemented the two different experimental treatments and plotted behavior after the treatments. In this type of design, potential problems with threats to internal validity from treatment diffusion may result, but the design permits a test of multiple treatments simultaneously to determine their effect on outcomes.

STEPS IN CONDUCTING EXPERIMENTAL RESEARCH

As we learn about the different types of experimental designs, we have also begun to understand some of the procedures involved in conducting an experiment. Although there is no set procedure for conducting an experiment, it is helpful to understand the general process before one begins.

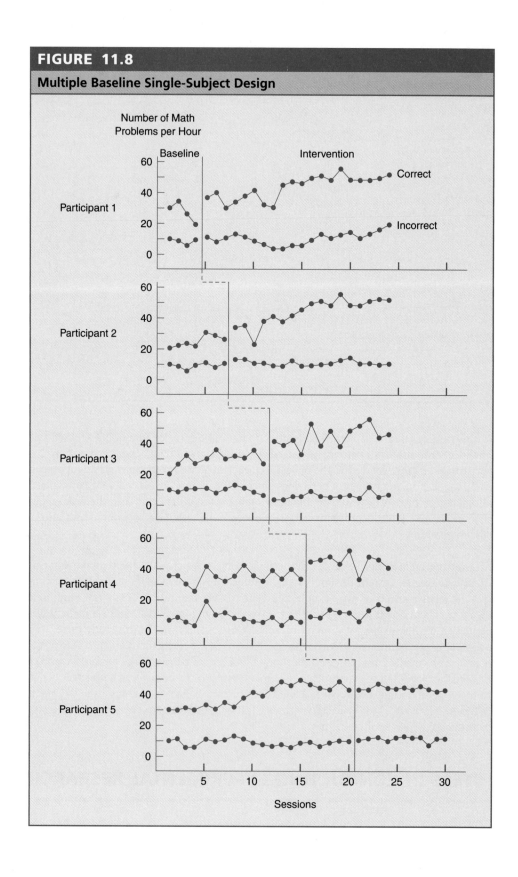

FIGURE 11.8

Multiple Baseline Single-Subject Design

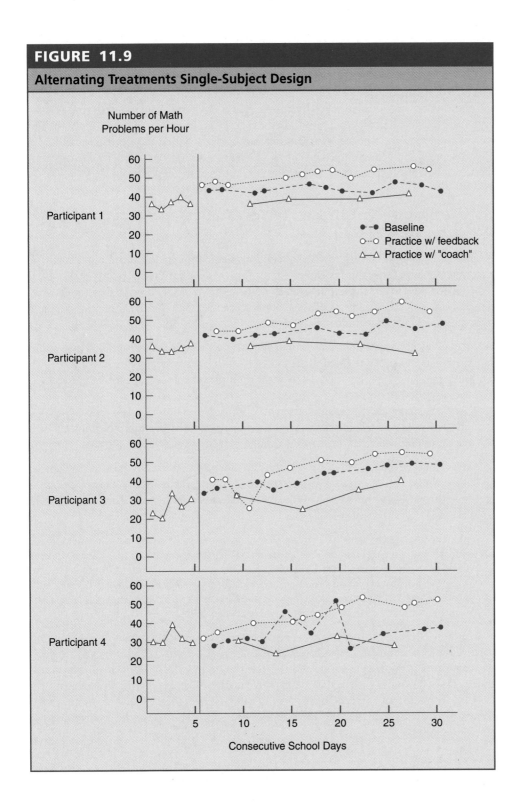

FIGURE 11.9

Alternating Treatments Single-Subject Design

Number of Math
Problems per Hour

Participant 1

Participant 2

Participant 3

Participant 4

●–● Baseline
○⋯○ Practice w/ feedback
△–△ Practice w/ "coach"

Consecutive School Days

Step 1. Decide If an Experiment Addresses the Research Problem

The type of issue studied by experimenters is the need to know whether a new practice influences an outcome. Of all designs in education, it is the best design to use to study cause-and-effect relationship. However, to study these issues, you must be able to control the setting of the experiment as well as manipulate one level of the independent variable. An experiment is not the best choice when the problem calls for generalizing results to a population or when you cannot manipulate the conditions of the experiment.

Step 2. Form Hypotheses to Test Cause-and-Effect Relationships

A hypothesis, you will recall from Chapter 5, advances a prediction about outcomes. The experimenter establishes this prediction (in the form of a null or alternative hypothesis) and then collects data to test the hypothesis. Hypotheses are typically used in experimental research more than are research questions, but both can be used. When stating experimental hypotheses, follow these guidelines:

▶ Independent variables should contain at least one variable with multiple levels, and the researcher needs to manipulate one of the levels. Dependent variables are outcomes, and experimenters often study multiple outcomes (e.g., student learning and attitudes).
▶ Variables are measured on an instrument or recorded as observations. They need to produce valid and reliable scores. You need to give special attention to choosing measures that will result in scores with high construct validity.

Hypotheses are often based on relationships found in studies by past researchers or contained within theories that are being tested and continually revised. An example of several hypotheses was included in a study about college students' willingness to seek help from faculty.

> (a) Students would be more likely to express willingness to seek help from the instructor in the supportive statement condition than in the neutral statement condition; (b) younger students would be less likely to express willingness to seek help from an instructor than would older students, independent of support condition; and (c) students would be more likely to express willingness to seek help from an instructor when the class size is small than when it is large, independent of support condition. (Perrine, Lisle, & Tucker, 1996, pp. 44–45)

In these hypotheses, the researchers establish predictions about what they will find in their study. They compared two groups, the experimental group, which received supportive statements from the professor, and the control group, which received no supportive statements. The students in both groups then rated the likelihood they would seek help from the instructor for six academic problems. The first hypothesis directly tests this group comparison. The second and third hypotheses control for the age of the student and the size of the class.

Step 3. Select an Experimental Treatment and Introduce It

The key to any experimental design is to set levels of treatment and apply one level to each group, such as one level to an experimental group and another level to a control group. Then the groups are compared on one or more outcomes. Interventions may consist of programs or activities organized by the researcher. In deciding what intervention to use, you might consider several factors:

▶ The experimental researcher should select an intervention of adequate "dosage" (Lipsey, 1998). This means that the intervention must last long enough and be strong enough to actually have an impact on the outcome.

▶ A good intervention is one that has been used by other researchers and it should predict a change in the outcome. The review of the literature and an assessment of past theories as predictions for relationship help researchers locate an intervention that should predict change.

▶ Experimental researchers should choose an intervention that can be implemented with as little intrusion in the setting and on the participants as possible. This means that the researcher needs to respect the school or non-school setting being studied, and gain the cooperation of sponsors at the site as well as the participants in the study.

▶ Choose an intervention based on a small pilot test. Select a group of participants in the population and provide the intervention to them. This approach may be a pre-experimental design with a single group (to facilitate ease of implementation) or an intervention of a short duration. It may involve as few as five or six subjects (Bausell, 1994). From this pilot, you can draw conclusions about the potential impact of the intervention for the final experiment.

Step 4. Identify Study Participants

When conducting an experimental study the researcher needs to answer several questions. Who will participate in the experiment? Participants in an experimental study are those individuals tested by the researcher to determine if the intervention made a difference in one or more outcomes. Investigators may choose participants because they volunteer to be studied or they agree to be paid a small stipend for their involvement in the experiment. Alternatively, the researcher may select participants who are available in well-defined, intact groups that are easily studied. For example, a study of third-grade reading may require that the researcher use existing classes of third-grade students. Regardless of the participants, investigators must be careful about the ethical issue of not disadvantaging some participants by withholding a beneficial treatment and advantaging others by giving them the treatment.

How many people will you study? In an ideal experiment, the researcher forms at least one control and one experimental group (Bausell, 1994). In many experiments, the size of the overall number of participants (and participants per group) is dictated by practical issues of the number of volunteers who enroll for the study or the individuals available to the researcher. The researcher also uses statistics to analyze the data, and these statistics call for minimum numbers of participants (see Chapter 6 on "Sample Size").

How should the participants be chosen? If possible, you should randomly select individuals for the experiment from the study population so that inferences can be made from the results to the population. This selection is accomplished through numbering the individuals in the population and randomly selecting participants using a random numbers table. In practice, this procedure may not always be possible because the population cannot be easily identified or you may not have access to all people in the population. However, since a basic premise of all quantitative research is that the findings will be generalized, random selection enables an investigator to make inferences about the population. When random selection cannot be done, then an alternative is to conduct multiple experiments with different participants of the population so that some inference of generalizability or external validity can be made.

How should the individuals be assigned to groups? An optimal situation is to randomly assign the individuals to groups, but this procedure may not always be feasible. Also, to provide added control over extraneous factors, matching, blocking, selecting homogeneous groups, and the use of covariates is recommended.

Step 5. Choose a Type of Experimental Design

One aspect of preparing for the experiment is choosing the design and providing a visual diagram of it. You need to make several decisions based on your experience with experiments, the availability of participants for the study, and your ability to practically control for extraneous influences in the project before choosing a design. The criteria in Table 11.3 will help lead to the selection of a design.

Step 6. Conduct the Experiment

Conducting the experiment involves procedural steps consistent with the design selected. It may involve:

▶ administering a pretest, if you plan to use one
▶ introducing the experimental treatment to the experimental group or relevant groups
▶ monitoring the process closely so that the threats to internal validity are minimized
▶ gathering posttest measures (the outcome or dependent variable measures)
▶ using ethical practices by debriefing the participants by informing them of the purpose and reasons for the experiment, such as asking them what they thought was occurring (Newman, 2000)

Step 7. Organize and Analyze the Data

Three major activities are required at the conclusion of the experiment: coding the data, analyzing the data, and writing the experimental report. Coding the data means that the researcher needs to take the information from the measures and set up a computer file for data analysis. This procedure begins with cleaning the data to make sure that unusual data are not entered in the computer file through keystroke errors or errant mistakes by those who complete the instruments. The database can be explored for these errors by running a descriptive analysis of it using a statistical analysis program and noting variables for which unusual data exists. This descriptive analysis can provide the first review of the outcomes of the study, and scanning the results can provide an understanding of the responses of all participants to the outcome measures. This step becomes the first phase of the data analysis.

After a descriptive analysis of all participants, the researcher begins the analysis of comparing groups in terms of the outcomes. This is the heart of an experimental analysis, and it provides useful information to answer the hypotheses or research questions in the study. The statistic of choice is a group comparison statistic, such as the *t*-test or the family of parametric analysis of variance statistics (e.g., analyis of variance, analysis of covariance).

Step 8. Develop an Experimental Research Report

The experimental report follows a standard format. In the methods or procedures for an experiment, the researcher typically includes information about:

▶ participants and their assignment
▶ the experimental design
▶ the intervention and materials
▶ control over extraneous variables
▶ dependent measures or observations

As in a quantitative study, this report is written using standard terms for research (e.g., intervention, control, experimental group, pre- and posttest) and an objective, impartial point of view.

CRITERIA FOR EVALUATING EXPERIMENTAL RESEARCH

The key characteristics and the procedures form a basis for evaluating an experimental study. The following list, adapted from Bausall (1994) present criteria useful in this evaluation:

- Does the experiment have a powerful intervention?
- Does it employ few treatment groups (e.g., only two)?
- Will participants profit from the intervention?
- Is there some systematic way the researcher derived the number of participants per group?
- Were an adequate number of participants used in the study?
- Were valid, reliable, and sensitive measures or observations used?
- Did the study control for extraneous factors?
- Did the researcher control for threats to internal validity?

APPLYING WHAT YOU HAVE LEARNED: AN EXPERIMENTAL STUDY

Read the experimental study on page 352 and apply some of the ideas discussed in this chapter. Note the marginal annotations that identify characteristics of experimental research *and* quantitative research.

> Schelske, M., & Deno, S. (1994). The effects of content-specific seminars on student teachers' effectiveness. *Action in Teacher Education, 16*(1), 20–28.

In response to the issue of miseducative and misguided field experiences for student teachers, Schelske and Deno (1994) examine the effect of content-specific seminars on student teaching behaviors in the classroom. This experimental study compares two approaches to training student teachers in seminars: using content-specific seminars that address coping and management topics, and using the traditional discussion approach that addresses student teachers' behaviors in the classroom and pupils' on-task behavior. This article listed above is chosen because it is a "true" experiment and because the authors clearly identify both the intervention and outcome measures.

As you review this article, look for elements of the research process:

- the research problem and use of quantitative research
- use of the literature
- the purpose statement and research hypotheses or questions
- types and procedures of data collection
- types and procedures of data analysis and interpretation
- the overall report structure

The Research Problem and Use of Quantitative Research

The research problem—see Paragraphs 03–04

Characteristics of quantitative research—see the annotations on the left side of the page

The authors introduce the research problem in the third paragraph where they mention that field experiences for student teachers can often be miseducative and misguided. Also, they infer that current training programs may not translate the research on effective teaching into lessons that student teachers can use in their teaching. This problem is based on a need derived from past research and it is related to understanding an outcome, student teacher effectiveness.

The article contains key characteristics of a quantitative study:

- predicting effective teaching behaviors for students who experience content-specific seminars (Paragraph 02)
- focusing on variables and their relationship (Paragraph 02)
- providing substantial literature at the beginning of the study to set the stage to examine factors that influence student teaching behavior (Paragraphs 03, 05)
- collecting information from a sizable number of individuals ($N=24$) (Paragraph 06)
- using existing instruments to collect data (Paragraphs 11–12)
- collecting numeric scores (e.g., Paragraph 11)
- statistically analyzing the data (e.g., Paragraph 14)
- analyzing group differences using the *t*-test (e.g., Paragraphs 14, 17)
- writing objectively (e.g., Paragraph 18)
- making interpretations based on comparing the results with initial predictions (Paragraph 23)
- using a report structure typically found in quantitative research (see headings, such as method, results, and discussion)

Use of the Literature

Literature used to justify the problem—Paragraph 03

Literature used to justify the intervention—Paragraph 05

Literature used to explain their results—Paragraph 23

In this experimental study, we find substantial literature, especially past studies, that document the importance of the intervention—the content seminars related to classroom management and personal coping skills. Although we do not see a separate literature review section, the literature at the beginning is used to justify the problem and to foreshadow the purpose of the study. At the end of the study, the authors return to the literature to discuss explanations for their results based on past studies.

The Purpose Statement and Research Questions

Purpose Statement—see Paragraphs 01 and 02

The authors introduce the intent of the study in the abstract and in Paragraph 02. Notice how the purpose statement in Paragraph 02 begins, "The purpose of the study . . ." This statement shows a comparison of the seminars and it indicates an outcome—"effective teaching behaviors." The authors do not advance hypotheses or research questions in this study. Their introduction might have helped a reader understand the specific questions that will be addressed in the research.

Types of Procedures of Data Collection

Participants—Paragraph 06

Instruments used—Paragraphs 11–13

Numeric data—Paragraph 11

The strength of this article lies in the identification of procedures. We learn about 26 students who participated in the study. The researchers randomly assign students to three groups, a sign of a true experiment. The intervention (independent variable—experimental treatments and control), the dependent measures, and the instruments are clearly discussed. The authors also report on validity and reliability, where possible (see Paragraphs 12 and 13). By discussing the scales of measurement on these instruments, the authors convey that numeric scores are collected on the instruments. Although not specifically mentioned, the randomization process helps to equate the groups and reduce threats to internal validity. Because faculty observers are trained in the use of the instruments, threats to instrument validity may have been reduced. However, moderating variables likely to influence the outcome (e.g., support provided to student teachers by their supervising teacher) are not controlled in this study.

Types and Procedures of Data Analysis and Interpretation

Data analysis procedures—Paragraphs 14–21

Interpretation—Paragraphs 22, 23

The authors report in Paragraph 14 that they use *t*-tests to compare the groups in the experiment. They refer to the small size of each group, but reflect on the power such a group would provide. The power, .64, is below accepted standards of .80 advocated by experimental researchers (e.g., see Lipsey, 1990). In this section we learn that the original three groups are collapsed into two groups, and the statistical comparisons are significant (at $p < .05$) on one dependent measure (classroom management ability) and not on the other (pupil off-task behavior).

Based on these findings, the researchers suggest explanations for the results in Paragraphs 22 and 23. Apparently their result about classroom management is supported in other studies, and the authors reference research that supports their conclusions.

The Overall Reporting Structure

Quantitative structure—Paragraphs 01–25

This report of research falls within standard guidelines for writing quantitative investigations. It begins with a problem and purpose, moves on toward methods and results, and ends with a discussion. This format is standard in a quantitative study. Also, consistent with quantitative research, the authors did not talk about themselves and their role in the study, but remained in the background reporting results.

KEY IDEAS IN THE CHAPTER

Experimental researchers test an idea (or practice) to determine its effect on an outcome. Researchers decide on an idea with which to "experiment," assign individuals to experience it (and have some individuals experience something different), and then determine whether those who experienced the idea or practice performed better on some outcome than those who did not experience it.

The ideas used in experiments today were mostly in place by the first few decades of the 20th century. The procedures of comparing groups, assigning individuals to treatments, and statistically analyzing group comparisons had developed by 1940. During the 1960s the types of experimental designs were identified and the strengths (e.g., control over potential threats) of these designs specified by 1980. Since 1980, computers, improved statistical procedures, and more complex designs have advanced experimental research.

Today, several key characteristics help us understand and read experimental research. Experimental researchers select and assign participants to groups or other units. They apply an intervention to one independent variable by giving an experimental treatment to one condition of the treatment variable and they control for extraneous factors through techniques such as matching, blocking, covariance, and selecting homogeneous participants. They measure one or more outcomes after the experimental treatment has been administered, they design experiments that monitor four types of threats to validity, and they make statistical comparisons of different treatment variable conditions.

Various aspects of these characteristics are included in types of experimental designs. There are several types of between-group designs. A "true" experiment involves random assignment of participants to groups or units. This form of an experiment is the most rigorous and controlled of all types. A quasi-experimental design involves the use of an intervention, but not random assignment of participants to groups. A factorial design also involves two or more groups, but the researcher tests for the interaction of two or more independent variables.

Another type of design involves a within-group or within-individual procedure where a single group or single individuals are studied. A time series design involves studying a single group and collecting typically more than one outcome measure. A repeated measures experiment also involves only one group, but the researcher tests more than one intervention with this group by alternating administrations of the experimental treatment. A single-subject design examines one individual at a time by establishing a baseline of behavior for the individual, administering the intervention, and determining the long-term impact of the intervention on behavior when it is withdrawn.

The steps in experimental research involve deciding if an experiment is the best design, forming hypotheses, and selecting an experimental treatment to administer. Then the researcher identifies participants and, if possible, randomly assigns them to groups or units, chooses a type of design, conducts the experiment, and analyzes and reports results. To evaluate the success of this process, the experimenter assesses the groups, intervention, measures or observations, and extraneous factors and control over threats to validity.

USEFUL INFORMATION FOR PRODUCERS OF RESEARCH

▶ When you design an experimental study, use the five characteristics as major features of your "Methods" discussion: selecting and assigning participants, applying an intervention, measuring outcomes, addressing potential threats to validity, and conducting statistical tests that compare different groups.

▶ Use random assignment of participants to groups whenever possible. This equating of groups removes many potential threats to validity in drawing inferences from scores.

▶ When designing and writing an experiment, distinguish between random selection and random assignment in your discussion—they serve two different purposes in research.

▶ Consider how you will control for extraneous factors in an experiment. Use pretests, statistically control for covariates, match participants, or select homogeneous samples to better control for characteristics of participants that might influence the relationship between the independent and dependent variables.

▶ In designing your study, distinguish in the "Methods" section the treatment variable, your intervention, and the actual treatment condition you manipulate.

▶ Also in designing your study, clarify your experimental outcome (the dependent variable) you seek to measure.

▶ Select a type of experimental design based on Table 11.3, and identify the potential threats to internal validity that typically relate to this design.

▶ In most experimental research, the statistical test of choice is a group comparison statistic, such as the *t*-test, analysis of variance, or analysis of covariance.

▶ In planning your experiment, it might be helpful to draw a visual picture of the flow of procedures in your experiment, such as is shown in Table 11.5.

▶ When designing and conducting your experiment, follow the eight-step process as a general guide for your procedures.

USEFUL INFORMATION FOR CONSUMERS OF RESEARCH

▶ In reviewing an experimental study, recognize that researchers study different experimental units, such as individuals, groups, or entire organizations.

▶ When you read an experiment, realize that the researcher may not have randomly assigned individuals to groups because of practical limitations in the experimental situation. These experiments, called quasi-experiments, are still valuable, but they do not have the same rigor as true experiments.

▶ Recognize that all types of experiments involve an intervention where the investigator manipulates a treatment variable. Ask yourself as you read an experimental study: What variable is being physically manipulated by the researcher?

▶ Researchers should identify the type of experimental design they use in a research report. If this is unclear, use Table 11.3 and the criteria differentiating the designs as a guide to determine the type they use.

▶ Also useful in determining the type of experimental design in a study is to recognize that there are two broad types: between-group (in which the researcher compares several groups) and within-group (in which the researcher compares only one group or its variation, a within-individual design).

ADDITIONAL RESOURCES YOU MIGHT EXAMINE

For additional detailed discussions about types of experiments and validity issues in experiments (internal, external, construct, statistical conclusion), see:

Campbell, D. T., & Stanley, J. C. (1963). Experimental and quasi-experimental designs for research. In N. L. Gage (Ed.) *Handbook on research in teaching* (pp. 1–80). Chicago: Rand-McNally.

Cook, T. D., & Campbell, D. T. (1979). *Quasi-experimentation: Design and analysis issues for field settings*. Boston: Houghton Mifflin Company.

Bracht, G. H., & Glass, G. V. (1968). The external validity of experiments. *American Educational Research Journal, 4,* 73–81.

For resources on experimental designs, see:

Bausell, R. B. (1994). *Conducting meaningful experiments*. Thousand Oaks, CA: Sage.

Boruch, R. F. (1998). Randomized controlled experiments for evaluation and planning. L. Bickman & D. J. Rog (Eds.), *Handbook of applied social research methods* (pp. 161–191). Thousand Oaks, CA: Sage.

Hinkelmann, K., & Kempthorne, O. (1994). *Design and analysis of experiments*. New York: Wiley.

Reichardt, C. S., & Mark, M. M. (1998). Quasi-experimentation. In L. Bickman & D. J. Rog (Eds.), *Handbook of applied social research methods* (pp. 193–228). Thousand Oaks, CA: Sage.

For designing sensitive experiments, power analysis, and statistical procedures, see:

Keppel, G. (1991). *Design and analysis: A researcher's handbook*. Englewood Cliffs, NJ: Prentice-Hall.

Lipsey, M. W. (1990). *Design sensitivity: Statistical power for experimental research*. Newbury Park, CA: Sage.

The Effects of Content-Specific Seminars on Student Teachers' Effectiveness

Experimental Research Characteristics

Quantitative Characteristics

Mark Schelske, *St. Olaf College*
Stanley Deno, *University of Minnesota*

Abstract

The quantitative (01) purpose statement, research questions, or hypotheses are specific and narrow.

This study compares the effects of two approaches to student teaching seminars: structured, content-specific training seminars and general education discussion seminars. The study was based on the premise that seminars during student teaching are potentially important avenues to assist prospective teachers in developing critical teacher behaviors. Student teachers were randomly assigned to one of three treatment groups: coping skills training classroom management training, or general education discussion. During the 10-week student teaching period, five 2-hour seminars were conducted for each group. Trained faculty observers collected observational data on the student teachers' classroom management abilities, their overall student teaching performance, and on the academic engagement of the student teachers' pupils. The results indicate that content specific training seminars positively affected the student teachers' classroom management skills, their overall classroom effectiveness, and the on-task behavior of their pupils.

(02)

The quantitative purpose statement, research questions, or hypotheses seek measurable, observable data on variables.

All research on teaching is intended to broaden our understanding of teaching, improve teaching, and develop effective ways to prepare individuals who wish to teach (Shulman, 1986). This study was based on the assumption that establishing a highly competent teacher work force requires intervention with teachers to assist them in developing their teaching potential early in their careers. One opportunity for early intervention that is common to educators is their student teaching experience. The purpose of this study was to determine if content-specific seminars operated in conjunction with a student teaching program would result in more effective teaching behaviors in students compared with discussion seminars based on educational issues less directly related to effective teaching. College faculty members determined student teacher effectiveness through direct classroom observations of the student teachers' classroom behaviors and the academic on task behavior of their pupils.

Enhancing Student Teaching

(03)

The quantitative literature justifies the research problem and provides direction for the study.

In this study we focused on student teaching as an essential preparatory experience common to all prospective teachers. However, it cannot be assumed that student teaching is always a direct path to future teaching success. Research has effectively demonstrated that field experiences can often be miseducative and misguiding to the student teachers (Lanier & Little, 1986; Lortie, 1975). The dominant ideas in training new teachers follow a linear, causal analysis of classroom phenomena (Lanier & Little, 1986). The key to establishing training mechanisms that enhance teacher effectiveness is to translate the research on effective teaching into lessons that teachers can incorporate into their teaching (Zumwalt, 1982).

(04)

A quantitative research problem requires description or explanation.

This study was based on the premise that training seminars for student teachers during their field experiences are potentially important avenues to assist prospective teachers in developing effective teaching behaviors. Although seminars are often a common part of a student teacher's experience, we could find no studies in the literature that measured the impact of student teaching seminars upon the pupils in the student teachers' classrooms. Additionally, the research about effective teaching focuses primarily on practicing teachers and tends to ignore student teachers.

Seminar Content

(05) Two factors—classroom management and personal coping skills—are consistently cited in the research literature as important characteristics of successful teachers. First, effective teachers exhibit classroom management and organization skills that facilitate more productive classroom environments for themselves and their pupils. In general, effective teachers establish productive expectations, set reasonable rules, organize their classrooms, and treat students enthusiastically and personably (Brophy & Good, 1986; Doyle, 1980, 1986; Emmer, Sanford, Evertson, Clements, & Martin, 1981; Emmer, Sanford, Clements, & Martin, 1982). Second, the literature also indicates that successful teachers utilize more effective personal coping skills (Forman, 1982; Sharp & Forman, 1985). Although no single profile of a prototypical effective teacher exists, there are clear differences between competent and incompetent teachers (Bridges, 1985; Lilley & Wilkenson, 1983; Parkay, 1980; Rosetti, 1985; Scheck & Rhodes, 1980; Shreeve, Rodebaugh, Norby, Stueckle, Goetter, Zyskowski, deMichele, & Midgley, 1986). A common source of teacher failure is the teacher's inability to cope with the stresses and rigors of teaching. Teachers who cannot cope with high degrees of stress are more hostile, less supportive, and more authoritarian and overcontrolling than their peers who possess effective coping skills (Belcastro, 1982; Cichon and Koff, 1980; Forman & Cecil, 1986; Kyricaou & Sutcliffe, 1978; Petrusich, 1966, 1967). For this study, then, contrasting student teaching seminars were developed around classroom management and organization, and around coping with stress in teaching.

Method

Participants and Placement

(06) The participants were 26 student teachers enrolled at a four year private residential liberal arts college. The 12 male and 14 female participants had an average cumulative GPA of 3.16. All were in the second semester of their senior year.

Experimental researchers select participants and assign them to groups.

Procedures

(07) Participants were randomly assigned to one of three seminar conditions—coping skills, classroom management, or educational discussion. The student teaching seminar was a common part of the field experience but the content of those seminars was typically determined ad hoc by the faculty members responsible for supervision. Student teachers in each of the three groups met with the experimenter five times during the semester. The first meeting occurred just prior to the beginning of their student teaching assignments. The other four sessions were scheduled during the 2nd, 4th, 6th, and 7th weeks of their 9 week student teaching experience. Meetings took place on campus for 2 hours at the end of the school day, for a total of 10 hours. Two training seminar series and one discussion series were conducted. The seminar topics are described in Figure 1 below.

Experimental researchers apply an intervention to the experimental group and not to the control group.

Coping Skills.

(08) The coping skills training program used in this study was Meichenbaum's (1985) *Stress Inoculation Training* program. The program was selected for the study because its prescriptive methodology would be useful in research and replication and because it was used in previous research (For-

---

The quantitative literature plays a major role.

Quantitative data collection involves studying a large number of individuals.

FIGURE 1
Seminar Topics

Activity	Coping	Management	Discussion
Seminar 1 (prior to teaching)	• potential stress • research on teacher stress	• role of management • effective rules • the first day	• importance of student teaching
Seminar 2 (week 2)	• stressors identified • impact of stress • need to cope	• transitions and seatwork • intensive monitoring	• human relations • diversity issues
Seminar 3 (week 4)	• relaxation • coping defenses—denial	• anticipating problems • decision making	• health issues • drugs and alcohol • AIDS in schools
Seminar 4 (week 6)	• problem solving • self-talk strategies	• recitation and presentations • misbehavior	• cooperating teachers • group support
Seminar 5 (week 7)	• reflections • diagnose coping problems	• management problems • review	• job hunting • interviewing

man, 1982; Guzicki, 1984; Sharp & Forman, 1985). The goals of the stress inoculation program are to assist participants in identifying internal and external sources of stress and trouble, reducing the impact and occurrence of problematic situations, and establishing cognitive structures that assist in the prevention of future coping problems.

Classroom Management.

(09)   The second training seminar series was organized around 5 key classroom management teaching activities identified in the research literature: rules and expectations, seatwork, transitions, presentations and recitations, and misbehavior and interventions (Brophy & Good, 1986; Doyle, 1986; Emmer et al., 1981, 1982). The key to effective management is the teacher's understanding of the complex events within his/her classroom, and his/her ability to monitor and direct the social and educational processes that comprise the complex events of schoolrooms. The goal of the classroom management series was to teach participants how to establish high levels of order in the classroom to facilitate a productive environment for students.

Discussion Group.

(10)   The third group was the educational discussion group. The educational discussion seminar treatment replicated the traditional student teaching seminar program that had been in place in previous semesters at the College. The topics chosen for this series of seminars were suggested by the education faculty and were some of the topics that have been discussed in previous years. The topics chosen included human relations, AIDS in the schools, and job hunting and interviewing. The themes discussed in the two training groups were not covered in the discussion group. The content was focused primarily on educational issues not directly related to classroom teaching behaviors.

Quantitative data collection is based on using instruments identified prior to the study.

Dependent Measures

(11) Three instruments were used to determine student teacher effectiveness. Two instruments were used to measure the student teachers' behaviors in the classroom and the third instrument was used to measure their pupils' on-task behavior. Data were collected twice, during the 4th and 8th weeks of student teaching. The Component Rating Scales (Emmer et al., 1981) is a 50-item. 5-point likert-type scale that was used to measure teachers' classroom management skills. The reliability coefficients of the scale ranged from .44 to .83 with a mean of .60 ($p < .05$ to $p < .001$). The other instrument used to rate the student teachers' behaviors was the Student Teacher Evaluation scale (1989). The scale consisted of 18 items rated on a 5-point likert-type and included items related to professional competencies, personal qualities, and coping skills. At the time of this study there was no empirical data on the reliability or criterion validity for the items of this scale. Items had been selected from the literature by members of the education faculty as indicators of successful student teaching experiences.

Researchers measure the outcomes for both groups at the end of the experiment.

Quantitative data collection involves gathering numeric data.

(12) A modified version of the Student Engagement Ratings (SER; Emmer et al., 1981) from the Classroom Management Improvement Study was used to measure pupil on-task percentages in this study. The reliability of the SER to measure "off-task" pupil behavior (of interest in this study) was .74 ($p < .001$). In order to design the procedures for observations, the experimenter and a faculty observer simultaneously observed a videotape of classroom scenes. Once 100% inter-rater agreement had been achieved while observing the video, they did simultaneous observations in a senior high classroom to establish the content validity of the instrument to differentiate between on and off-task pupil behavior.

(13) The observers who collected the data in this study were five faculty members from the education department at the College. Evidence exists that faculty ratings are useful measures of teacher skills (Evertson & Green, 1986; Nisbett & Wilson, 1977). Four of the faculty observers were blind raters who did not know to which treatment group their student teachers were assigned (the experimenter was the fifth). Each rater was provided training on how to use the instruments. A training video containing seven vignettes representing different classroom situations was developed by the experimenter to train the faculty how to calculate the pupil on-task behavior in the student teachers' classrooms. The scores of the faculty observers were compared to the experimenter's scores to establish the percentage of interrater agreement for this measure (from 86–100%). To check for rater bias after the field observations, a one way analysis of variance was conducted between the means of the ratings done by the five faculty. This analysis revealed no reliable differences between the raters ($p < .57$). Ratings of student teachers by their cooperating teachers, while very helpful, were not used in the analysis because comparability across the 26 cooperating teachers could not be established.

Experimental researchers design experiments to address potential threats to validity.

Measures

Quantitative data analysis consists of statistical analysis.

(14) Results were analyzed on the dependent measures using apriori orthogonal contrasts (*t*-tests). This procedure allows for the pooled error variance for the entire sample to be used (23 degrees of freedom) for each contrast instead of the error variance for each separate treatment group (only 8 degrees of freedom). Consequently, the relatively small sample size did not inhibit meaningful inferential analysis. In addition, a power test was conducted to determine whether using a sample size of twenty-six would provide adequate statistical power for this study. The power was calculated to be .64, which was acceptable for this analysis.

(15)   The same contrast was used in the analysis of each dependent measure. The contrast involved combining the data of both the coping and management groups compared to the discussion group's data. This provided the basis for analyzing the overall effects of the training programs.

Results

(16)   To determine if reliable differences existed between the groups dependent data were statistically analyzed using t-tests of apriori orthogonal contrasts. The data from the two training groups was combined and then contrasted with the discussion group.

(17)   The first analysis focused on the student teachers' classroom management skills. Data from faculty ratings of student teachers using the Component Rating Scales are reported in Table 1.

(18)   Inspection of the table reveals that the combined raw group means of both of the training groups were over 30 rating points higher than the means of the Discussion Group. The average score per inventory item on the 5-point scale was 3.7 for the two training groups and 3.1 for the discussion group (5 was the highest score). The apriori orthogonal contrast was conducted using t-tests on the combined training group mean compared to the discussion group mean. The means, standard deviations, t-value, and associated probability are reported in Table 1. The orthogonal contrast reported in Table 1 indicate reliable differences between the combined training group mean and the discussion group mean at the $p < .01$ level, $t(23) = 2.47$.

(19)   The second research question examined overall student teaching performance. The faculty observers rated their overall performance on the Student Teaching Evaluation. The results are presented in Table 2. The total possible score on the Student Teaching Evaluation was 90.

(20)   The scores for the management and coping training groups had a slightly higher range (50 to 88) than student teachers in the discussion group (52 to 80). Also, the mean of the training groups was higher ($M = 74.2$) than of the discussion group ($M = 65.6$). The t-test contrasting the combined means of the two training groups and the mean of the discussion group revealed a reliable difference ($p < .05$).

(21)   The third analysis was directed at pupil on-task behavior. To provide for a more straightforward analysis, the percentage of pupil "off-task" be-

TABLE 1
Comparisons of Faculty Ratings of Student Teachers' Classroom Management Ability

Group Contrasts	N	M	SD	T-value	P
Coping and Management	18	180.9	30.5	2.47	.01
Discussion	8	149.6	25.7		

TABLE 2
Comparisons of Faculty Ratings of Student Teachers' Overall Effectiveness

Group Contrasts	N	M	SD	T-value	P
Coping and Management	18	74.2	11.3	1.85	.03
Discussion	8	65.6	9.8		

havior on the modified Student Engagement Rating was computed instead of "on task" and "waiting on task" to estimate pupil behavior in the classroom. These data are reported in Table 3. An examination of the means in the table reveal that the management and coping training groups had a lower (more preferred) raw mean score (13.2%) than the discussion group (20.5%). The range of off-task percentages obtained was lower for the training groups (4-33%) compared to the discussion group (7-55%). The apriori orthogonal contrasts on the difference between the combined mean of the two training groups and the discussion group mean produced an associated $p = .06$, $t = 1.63$.

Discussion

(22) The first question investigated in the present study was whether coping skills training and classroom management training seminars resulted in more effective classroom management skills in student teachers than did discussion seminars not directly related to classroom experiences. The results from both of the faculty ratings provide a basis for concluding that content specific training seminars contribute more to the development of effective classroom management skills. At the same time, the discussion seminars may contribute to other aspects of professional development not addressed in this study. The superiority of the classroom management skills of the training groups compared to the discussion group may be attributed to several factors. The seminar content of the classroom management group focused on teaching trainees to master specific target behaviors essential to the development of superior classroom skills. Apparently the training sessions enhanced their management skills in a way that was observed by the faculty in their higher ratings. Of interest is the fact that the coping seminars also affected the management behaviors of the student teachers, as evidenced by the means scores of the coping group. Perhaps this occurred because the student teachers were more relaxed and resilient to classroom stressors. Their coping skills might have allowed them, while in class, to access previously learned classroom management information (from teacher education classes) and to implement effective management strategies. The findings that both personal coping skills and classroom management skills contributed to effective classroom management is consistent with the results of previous research by Sharp and Forman (1985) in which teachers trained in either management or coping skills demonstrated an increase in their approval of pupils' classroom behaviors. The results from both sets of faculty ratings of student teachers consistently viewed the participants in the training seminars as generally more effective student teachers than the participants in the discussion group.

(23) Of considerable interest to us were the findings with respect to the on-task behavior of pupils in the trainees' classrooms. Though the results were not statistically significant, the results provide some basis for concluding that both coping skills and management skills training seminars specifically designed to increase student teacher effectiveness in the classroom produce higher percentages of pupil on-task behavior than seminar

> Quantitative interpretations compare results with predictions.

TABLE 3
Comparisons of Percentage of Pupil Off Task Behavior

Group Contrasts	N	M	SD	T-value	P
Coping and Management	18	13.2	−7.9	1.63	0.06
Discussion	8	20.5	14.9		

content that discusses general educational issues. Several possible explanations exist for this finding. Student teachers trained in classroom management skills may provide a more organized, orderly, and well managed classroom, which influences their pupils' on-task behavior. A major component of the management treatment was teaching student teachers how to maintain high levels of pupil academic engagement. Previous research has demonstrated a direct relationship between a teacher's ability to effectively manage their classroom and pupil on-task behavior and achievement (Brophy & Good, 1986; Doyle, 1986; Emmer et al., 1981, 1982). The student teachers trained in coping skills may have produced higher pupil on-task behavior because during the seminars they developed personal solutions for dealing with classroom stressors. Learning how to cope with the stress and frustration of trying to keep pupils on task received a lot of time and attention during problem solving discussions in the training seminars. The student teachers, therefore, might have been less likely to allow teaching frustrations to interfere with their efforts to keep pupils on task. Coping skills provided them the patience, persistence, and stamina necessary to establish appropriate behavior in their pupils. A tempting conclusion providing a parsimonious explanation for the similar outcomes of the two training groups is that both groups felt more comfortable, relaxed, and in charge of their classrooms, enabling them to function more easily and freely in this new environment.

Future Research

(24) As suggested by Sharp and Forman (1985), it would be interesting to investigate the effectiveness of a combined coping and management treatment program. A combined program might be more powerful than the individual treatment programs. Another design consideration for future studies is to include a non-training seminar condition that discusses coping and management issues but is not instructional. This would address whether the content (coping/management) or the format (the role of the faculty) is more important in the student teachers' skill development. This would inform teacher education programs if structured training in coping and management skills is the most effective course, or if informal discussions on coping and management issues would be as effective.

Implications

(25) The findings of this study have direct implication for institutions of higher education with teacher education programs. By implementing a content-specific seminar training program in conjunction with their student teaching program, it is likely that student teachers and their pupils will both benefit. This implies that teacher education programs could improve the on-task behavior of their student teachers' pupils and develop more effective classroom managers and overall teachers if they implemented training seminar programs that focus on the development of personal coping skills and effective classroom management behaviors.

Quantitative research reports use standard, fixed structures and evaluation criteria.

References

Bridges, E. M. (1985). Managing the incompetent teacher—What can principals do? *National Association of Secondary School Principals Bulletin, 69*(479), 57–65.

Brophy, J., & Good, T. L. (1986). Teacher behavior and student achievement. In M. C. Wittrock (Ed.), *Handbook of research on teaching* (pp. 328–375). New York: American Educational Research Association.

Cichon, D. J., & Koff, R. H. (1980). Stress and teaching. *NASSP Bulletin, 64,* 432–436.

Doyle, W. (1980). *Classroom management.* West Lafayette, IN: Kappa Delta Pi.

Doyle, W. (1986). Classroom organization and management. In M. C. Wittrock (Ed.), *Handbook of research on teaching* (pp. 392–431). New York: American Educational Research Association.

Emmer, E. T., Sanford, J. P., Evertson, C. M., Clements, B. S., & Martin, J. (1981). *The Classroom Management Improvement Study: An experiment in elementary school classrooms.* Austin: University of Texas, R & D Center for Teacher Education. (ERIC Document Reproduction Service No. ED 178 460)

Emmer, E. T., Sanford, J. P., Clements, B. S., & Martin, J. (1982). *Improving classroom management and organization in junior high schools: An experimental investigation.* Washington, DC: National Institute of Education. (ERIC Document Reproduction Service No. ED 261 053)

Evertson, C. M., & Green, J. L. (1986). Observation as inquiry and method. In M. C. Wittrock (Ed.), *Handbook of research on teaching* (pp. 162–213). New York: American Educational Research Association.

Forman, S. G. (1982). Stress management for teachers: A cognitive-behavioral program. *Journal of School Psychology, 20*(3), 180–187.

Forman, S. G., & Cecil, M. A. (1986). Teacher Stress. In T. R. Kratochwill (Ed.), *Advances in school psychology: Vol. 5* (pp. 203–229). Hillsdale, New Jersey: Lawrence Eribaum Associates.

Guzicki, J. A. (1984). *The effects of cue-controlled relaxation and stress inoculation in reducing teacher anxiety.* Unpublished doctoral dissertation. University of San Francisco, California.

Kyriacou, C., & Sutcliffe, J. (1978). A model of teacher stress. *Educational Studies, 4*(1), 1–6.

Lanier, J. C., & Little, J. W. (1986). Research on teacher education. In M. C. Wittrock (Ed.), *Handbook of research on teaching* (pp. 527–569). New York: American Educational Research Association.

Lilley, A., & Wilkinson, W. J. (1983). Personal characteristics of teachers and their oral interactions in further education classrooms. *Research in Science and Technological Education, 1*(1), 53–63.

Lortie, D. (1975). *Schoolteacher.* Chicago: University of Chicago Press.

Meichenbaum, D. (1985). *Stress inoculation training.* New York: Pergamon Press.

Nisbett, R. E., & Wilson, T. D. (1977). Telling more than we can know: Verbal reports on mental processes. *Psychological Review, 84*(3), 231–359.

Parkay, F. W. (1980). Inner-city high school teachers. The relationship of personality traits and teaching style to environmental stress. *Urban Education, 14*(4), 449–470.

Petrusich, M. M. (1966). Some relationships between anxiety and the classroom behavior of student teachers. *Dissertation Abstracts International, 27,* 1691A. (University Microfilms No. 66–12, 038)

Petrusich, M. M. (1967). Separation anxiety as a factor in the student teaching experience. *Peabody Journal of Education, 44*(May), 353–356.

Rosetti, R. (1985). Teacher tolerance and its relationship to teacher traits and disciplinary effectiveness. (ERIC Document Reproduction Service No. ED 264 191).

Scheck, D. C., & Rhodes, G. A. (1980). The relationship between junior high school teachers' rated competence and locus of control. *Education, 100*(3), 243–248.

Sharp, J. J., & Forman S. G. (1985). A comparison of two approaches to anxiety management for teachers. *Behavior Therapy, 16*(4), 370–383.

Shreeve, W., Radebaugh, M., Norby, J. R., Stueckle, A. F., Goetter, W., Zyskowski, C., de Michele, B., & Midgley, T. K. (1986). Why teachers flunk: Evaluation and probation of teachers, counselors, and principals in Washington state. *The Clearing House, 59*(5), 207–210.

Shulman, L. S. (1986). Paradigms and research programs in the study of teaching. In M. C. Wittrock (Ed.), *Handbook of research on teaching* (pp. 3–36). New York: American Educational Research Association.

Student teaching evaluation. (1989). Northfield, MN: St. Olaf College, Department of Education.

Twentieth Century Fund. (1983). *Making the grade.* New York: Twentieth Century Fund, Inc.

Wilson, C. F. (1979). *Stress profile for teachers.* Rights reserved by the author.

Zumwalt, K. (1982). Research on teaching: Policy implications for teacher education. In A. Lieberman & M. W. McLaughlin (Eds.), *Policy making in education* (pp. 215–248). Chicago: University of Chicago Press.

Mark Schelske holds a Ph.D. in Educational Psychology from the University of Minnesota. Former public school special education teacher and administrator in alternative education settings. Specializes in teacher education, faculty development, and program development in alternative and inner-city schools. His research interests focus on the development of prospective teachers, and educational interventions with youth at risk. Has published articles in *The Teacher Educator* and *Equality.* This study was awarded the 1992 ATE Distinguished Dissertation Award.

Stanley Deno holds a Ph.D. in Educational Psychology from the University of Minnesota. Specializes in educating teachers to work with students who have mild disabilities. His research focuses on curriculum based measurement and instructional interventions. Major publications have appeared in: *Exceptional Children, American Education Research Journal, Journal of Special Education, Journal of Educational Psychology,* among others.

12 *Correlational Designs*

Let's go back to our high school teacher, Maria, and have her choose a quantitative correlational design for her graduate school research project. Her research question might then be: "Is there a relationship (or association) between the extent of student involvement in physical fights and use of alcohol at school, and number of suspensions for weapon possession?" By using a correlational design to answer this question, Maria seeks to determine if patterns exist between fighting, alcohol use, and weapon possession so that school officials might better predict which individuals might be inclined to carry weapons at school. The procedures Maria would use for her study consist of accessing school district reports about individuals cited for fighting, alcohol possession, and weapon possession. She would correlate the students' scores using a statistic (such as the Pearson correlation coefficient that relates the variables), determine if the association for each relationship is positive or negative, and then assess the strength of the relationship. With this information, school officials might be able to determine if fighting or alcohol use are good predictors of weapon possession by students.

In some educational situations, neither the treatment nor the ability to manipulate the conditions are conducive to an experiment. In these cases, educators might turn to a correlational design. This design permits testing whether two variables occur together in some predictable pattern, such as whether musical creativity and academic achievement correlate for elementary education students. This information could be helpful to teachers trying to encourage creativity among children (Auh, 1997). This design also allows individuals to predict an outcome from initial scores, such as the ability of college admission counselors to predict a student's success in college based on his or her high school ACT or SAT scores. In Maria's situation, if she can discern the factors that correlate positively with weapon possession, she can develop sound recommendations for her school committee and the school district.

Correlational designs provide an opportunity for you to predict scores and explain the relationship among variables. The published studies listed below illustrate several applications of correlational designs.

▶ What factors predict academic achievement for at-risk high school students? Anderson and Keith (1997) correlated a number of factors with academic achievement and found ability, quality of schooling, student motivation, and academic coursework to be positively related to student achievement.

▶ Do teachers who use whole-language orientations to reading also use developmentally appropriate practices in reading? In a correlational study to explore this question, Ketner, Smith, and Parnell (1997) found a positive relationship between teachers who endorsed developmentally appropriate practices and their use of the whole language approach to reading instruction.

▶ What factors help explain why faculty in schools of pharmacy become published researchers during their careers? Jungnickel (1993) found that the more faculty networked with off-campus colleagues, saw themselves primarily as researchers, spent time publishing, and received personnel support for their research, the more they published in refereed journals.

In these examples the researchers are interested in predicting an outcome (i.e., achievement for at-risk students), exploring the association between two variables (i.e., the endorsement and actual practice of teachers) and explaining a complex connection among many variables (i.e., all the multiple factors that contribute to faculty research performance). In **correlational research designs,** investigators use a correlation statistical technique to describe and measure the degree of association (or relationship) between two or more variables or sets of scores. In this design, the researchers do not attempt to control or manipulate the variables, and they relate, using the correlation statistic, two or more scores for each individual (e.g., a student motivation and a student achievement score for each individual).

To understand correlational designs, you need to understand several concepts introduced in this definition. In addition, you need to know how to apply these concepts if you plan to design a correlation study or to serve as a knowledgeable reader and evaluator of correlational studies. This chapter provides a fundamental understanding of the concepts and their applications.

By the end of this chapter you should be able to:

▶ Identify major events in the historical development of correlational research.
▶ Distinguish between explanatory and prediction designs.
▶ Describe six key characteristics of correlational designs.
▶ Identify steps in conducting a correlation study.
▶ List the criteria for evaluating a correlational research report.

A BRIEF HISTORY OF CORRELATIONAL DESIGNS

The history of correlational research draws on the themes of the origin and development of the correlation statistical test and the procedures for using and interpreting the statistical test. Statisticians first developed the procedures for calculating the correlation statistics in the late 19th century (Cowles, 1989). Although British biometricians articulated the basic ideas of "co-relation" during the last half of the 1800s, it was Karl Pearson who presented the familiar correlation formula we know today in a paper before the Royal Society in England in November, 1895 (Cowles, 1989). Interestingly, Pearson used illustrations from Darwin's theory of evolution and Sir Francis Galton's ideas on heredity and natural inheritance to advance his ideas about correlation. For example, one idea Pearson explored was to study Galton's idea of the relationship between the left cubit (the distance between the elbow of the bent left arm and the tip of the middle finger) and stature for adult males (Cowles, 1989).

In presenting ideas about correlations, Pearson not only articulated the formula for a correlation, he also presented concepts familiar to the quantitative researcher today, such as the importance of sample size, the value of precise measurement, and the use of unbiased samples. However, Pearson was only one of several British biometricians around the turn of the century who refined and extended ideas about correlations (De Landsheere, 1998). In 1897, Yule (Pearson's student) developed solutions for correlating two, three, and four variables. With Pearson, Yule also advanced the theory of regression and the ability to predict scores using information based on correlating correlation coefficients. By 1904, Spearman published ideas about a correlation matrix to display the coefficients, and he also advanced a formula (Spearman's rho) for data that did not fit a normal distribution.

After the turn of the 20th century, and for almost 50 years, refinements in educational research design centered on experimental procedures rather than correlational designs. However, during this time, Fisher (1935) pioneered significance testing and analysis of variance, an important concept in studying the difference between observed and predicted scores in correlational analysis. It was not until 1963 that Campbell and Stanley provided new impetus to correlational research with their classical treatise on experimental and quasi-experimental designs. In this discussion, they included correlational research as one of the designs, albeit a less rigorous and more invalid design than experiments. In using correlational research, they encouraged investigators to both recognize and specify the extensive threats to validity inherent in this form of research.

During the 1970s and 1980s, with the advent of computers, improved knowledge about measurement scales, and the need to study complex associations among many variables, quantitative researchers initiated correlational studies. Instead of the physical control available to experimental researchers through techniques such as randomization and matching, correlational researchers sought control through statistical procedures. With computers, they could statistically remove the effects of a large number of variables to examine the relationship among a small set of variables. They could explore the combination of variables (e.g., age, gender, and SAT scores) and an outcome (e.g., college grade point average). From simple regression—the analysis of the variability of a single dependent variable by a single independent variable—the technique of using multiple regression to analyze the collective and separate effects of two or more independent variables on a dependent variable emerged (Pedhazur, 1997). Taking regression to the next step by advancing a theoretical model, collecting data, and estimating the fit of the data to the model led researchers to advanced correlational techniques of path analysis (Kline, 1998). Today, with the use of multiple statistical procedures such as factor analysis, reliability estimates, and regression, we can test elaborate models of variables with highly reliable measures, a technique called structural equation modeling (Kline, 1998). Both path analysis and structural equation modeling are beyond the scope of this introductory text, but they will be briefly introduced in this chapter so that you can see how they build on and extend basic correlational procedures founded over a century ago.

DESIGNS FOR EXPLANATION AND PREDICTION

With these historical developments largely related to statistical procedures, it makes sense to consider correlational research more of a statistical procedure than a research design. (A design, you may recall, means procedures for data collection, analysis, interpretation, and reporting research, as discussed in Chapter 2 on "Research Designs.") However, years ago research method writers specified correlational research as one of the quantitative "designs" (e.g., see Campbell & Stanley, 1963). With the sophisticated applications and explicit procedures of correlations, such as regression, path analysis, and causal modeling, correlational research can rightfully take its place among our designs in quantitative research.

Examining correlational research as a design, then, we can say that there are two primary forms: explanation and prediction. Correlational research helps to explain the association between two or more variables or to predict an outcome.

The Explanatory Design

Classroom teachers may want to correlate two variables, such as the students' sense of humor and performance in drama, in order to determine whether content and exercises on forms of humor need to be included in the class content. College administrators may need to know whether possession of weapons in the dorms relates to campus violence so that they can develop appropriate policies on weapon possession. Campus officials may also seek to explain the complex factors contributing to binge drinking among students in order to establish regulations for alcohol use on college and university property. These examples illustrate the many applications for explaining the association between or among variables.

Various authors refer to explanatory correlational research as "relational" research (Cohen & Manion, 1994, p. 123), "accounting-for-variance studies" (Punch, 1998, p. 78), or "explanatory" research (Fraenkel & Wallen, 2000, p. 360). Since one basic objective of this form of correlational research is to explain the association between or among variables, we will use the term explanatory research in this discussion. An **explanatory research** design is a correlational design in which the researcher is interested in the extent to which two variables (or more) co-vary—where variance or changes in one variable is reflected in variance or changes in the other. Correlations may consist of a simple association between two variables (e.g., sense of humor and performance in drama) or more than two (e.g., pressure from friends or feelings of isolation that contribute to binge drinking). Explanatory studies are conducted at one point in time—the explanation is based not on future or past information, but on data collected at the present moment. Also, during data analysis correlational researchers treat all participants as if they are a single group as opposed to the multiple groups typically used in experiments.

When examining a study reported in the literature, how would you identify it as an explanatory correlational study? Look for the following characteristics, which are common in this type of study.

- *The investigators correlate two or more variables.* They will report the correlation statistical test and mention the use of multiple variables. Readers will find these variables specifically mentioned in the purpose statement, the research questions, or the tables reporting the statistical procedures.
- *The researchers collect data at one point in time.* Evidence for this procedure will be found in the administration of instruments "in one sitting" to students. In correlational research, the investigators are not interested in either past or future performance of participants.
- *The investigator analyzes all participants as a single group.* As compared to an experiment that involves multiple groups or treatment conditions, the researcher collects scores from only one group and does not divide the group into categories (or factors). Unlike experimental research, all levels of information from the group are used. Rather than divide scores on self-esteem into "high" and "low" categories of scores, as would be done in experimental research, a correlational researcher uses all scores on a continuum, such as from 10 to 90.
- *The researcher obtains at least two scores for each individual in the group—one for each variable.* In the method discussion, the correlational investigator will mention how

many scores were collected from each participant. For example, for each individual in a study of optimism and appropriate health behaviors, the researcher would collect two scores: an optimism score and a health behavior score.

▶ *The researcher reports the use of the correlation statistical test (or an extension of it) in the data analysis.* This is the basic feature of this type of research. In addition, the researcher includes reports about the strength and the direction of the correlational test in order to provide additional information.

▶ *Finally, the researcher makes interpretations or draws conclusions from the statistical test results.* It is important to note that the conclusions do not establish a probable cause-and-effect (or causal inference) relationship because the researcher can only use statistical control (e.g., control over variables using statistical procedures) rather than the more rigorous control of physically altering the conditions (i.e., such as in experiments). In correlational research, the investigator "takes the participants as they are" without experimental intervention. Thus, authors of a correlational study often use the phrase "degree of association between two variables" (Thorndike, 1994, p. 1107), a connotation that conveys a general co-occurrence between variables rather than "probable causality." (See Chapter 5 on "Whether Variables Prove Cause and Effect.") It also accounts for why correlational writers sometimes refrain from using the terms "independent variable" and "dependent variable" and instead refer to the correlation of two "variables," a meaning consistent with something less than the independent variable influencing the dependent variable. They also employ the phrase "relationship" about correlations among variables. As researchers increasingly incorporate statistical control over variables (such as in path analysis) and structural equation modeling, stronger claims exist for causal inference.

Let's turn to an explanatory correlational study by Anderson and Keith (1997) to illustrate this type of design. Despite gains in achievement test scores, African-American, Hispanic, and low-income students typically achieve below the levels of Caucasian, Asian, and high-income students. African-American and Hispanic students also drop out of school at higher rates than their Caucasian peers. To better understand the factors that explain academic success of these at-risk students, Anderson and Keith conducted a correlational study. They proposed a theoretical model composed of eight variables (family social economic status, ethnicity, gender, ability, quality of schooling, parental involvement, motivation, and academic coursework) and one outcome variable (academic achievement). They studied one group comprising sophomores in high school who indicated they were of non-Asian minority origin and whose SES composite scores fell within the bottom quartile of the SES range. The data collection involved gathering information during the base year (1980) and two years later (1982), but, for purposes of analysis, data from both years were analyzed together as if they were collected at one point in time. For each participant ($N = 7{,}355$), they collected measures on each variable, correlated all variables, and then determined (through a structural equation modeling) the fit of the data to the model. They found that each of the variables except parental involvement explained a significant amount of variance in academic achievement.

The Prediction Design

Instead of simply relating variables—two variables at a time or a complex set such as in our last example—in a prediction design researchers seek to anticipate outcomes by using certain variables as predictors. For example, superintendents and principals need to identify teachers who will be successful in their schools. To select teachers that have a good chance of success, the administrators can identify predictors of success using correlational research.

As another example, college administrators seek to admit students who will perform well in their colleges. By identifying factors that predict good success, such as a high grade point average during the senior year in high school, admissions committees develop a list of criteria for reviewing applicants to the school. In both of these illustrations, being able to predict an outcome was important. Prediction studies, therefore, are useful because they help anticipate or forecast future behavior.

The purpose of a **prediction research design** is to identify variables that will positively predict an outcome or criterion. In this form of research, the investigator identifies one or more predictor variables and a criterion (or outcome) variable. A **predictor variable** is the variable used to make a forecast about an outcome in correlational research. In the case of predicting teacher success in a school, the predictor may be "mentoring" during teacher training, or "years of experience teaching." In much prediction research, investigators often use more than one predictor variable.

The outcome being predicted in correlational research, on the other hand, is called the **criterion variable.** In our example, teacher success is the criterion variable. Although more than one outcome can be predicted, the typical educational study includes only one criterion variable.

To identify a prediction study, look for the following characteristics.

▶ *The authors typically include the word "prediction" in the title.* It might also be in the purpose statement or research questions.
▶ *The researchers typically measure the predictor variable(s) at one point in time and the criterion variable at a later point in time.* Therefore, you should examine a study to determine if a "time" dimension is built into the design. For example, the predictor of teacher success, "mentoring," is measured during a students' teacher training program, while "success" is measured later, after the students have performed as teachers.
▶ *The authors are interested in forecasting future performance.* This intent is usually articulated in the purpose statement or in the research questions. In the justification of the research problem, writers will also mention their intent to "predict" some outcome.

A prediction study will report correlations using the correlation statistical test, but it may include advanced statistical procedures. For example, the author may be interested in several predictors that help explain the criterion. While simple linear regression (explained later) addresses this interest, multiple regression (also addressed later) provides a more complex formula.

Let's view a prediction study to see the procedures the researchers used. Royal and Rossi (1999) were concerned about the problem of teacher isolation and sought to identify the factors that predict a better sense of community for high school teachers. Their study included several predictors and one overall criterion (sense of community). They collected data from three large high schools and gathered several measures. Sense of community was based on an 85-item measure that differentiated among a student-related measure of community, a co-worker measure, and a school-related measure. Predictors were time-related variables (e.g., tenure in the school), work arrangements (e.g., mentoring, teaching teams), and school organization variables (e.g., innovation in the school). In this configuration of variables, the researchers assumed that the predictor variables operated earlier in time than the criterion (e.g., innovations were initiated and then teachers developed a sense of community). The investigators correlated these predictors and the outcome variables and also conducted a multiple regression to find that the predictors had different effects on each criterion variable. Overall, school tenure, student interaction, and innovation were the best predictors of the measures of a sense of community in the schools.

KEY CHARACTERISTICS OF CORRELATIONAL DESIGNS

Within explanatory and prediction studies, researchers employ specific procedures related to the use, the presentation, the interpretation, and the application of correlational statistical procedures. These procedures include:

- ▶ graphing pairs of scores to identify the form of the association (or relationship) among variables, the direction of the association, and the degree of association
- ▶ calculating the correlation coefficient statistic, using it for several purposes, displaying it in a matrix, assessing the strength of the association, and employing it in hypothesis testing
- ▶ extending (in some cases) the analysis beyond the correlational statistical test to advanced statistics for addressing research questions or hypotheses

Graphing Pairs of Scores

In correlational designs, researchers calculate a correlation coefficient (identified by r) that measures and describes the association or relationship between two scores or sets of scores. However, before we discuss calculating this coefficient, we will explore how sets of scores can be plotted on a graph to yield useful information about:

1. the form of the association between sets of scores
2. the direction of the association between the scores
3. the magnitude of the association between the scores

Correlational researchers seek the association or relationship between two variables or sets of scores and develop this understand by exploring the form, direction, and magnitude of the association.

A Scatterplot Example

Researchers plot scores for two variables on a graph to provide a visual picture of the form of the scores. This allows researchers to identify the type of association among variables and locate extreme scores. Most importantly, this plot can provide useful information about the form of the association—whether the scores are linear (follow a straight line) or curvilinear (follow a U-shaped form). It also indicates the direction of the association (e.g., one score goes up and the other goes up, as well) and the degree of the association (whether the relationship is perfect, with a correlation of 1.0, or less than perfect).

A plot helps to assess this association between two scores for participants. A **scatterplot** (or **scatter diagram**) is a pictorial image displayed on a graph of two sets of scores for participants. These scores are typically identified as X and Y, with X values represented on the horizontal axis and Y values represented on the vertical axis. A single point indicates where the X and Y scores intersect.

Using scales on the horizontal (abscissa) axis and on the vertical (ordinate) axis, the investigator plots points on a graph for each participant. Examine the scatterplot of scores in Figure 12.1, which shows both a small data set for 10 students and a visual plot of their scores. Assume that the correlation researcher seeks to study whether the use of the Internet by high school students is related to their level of depression. (It is assumed that students who use the Internet excessively are also depressed individuals because they are trying to escape and not cope with present situations.) From past research, we would predict this situation to be the case. Scores on the use of the Internet are measured by asking the students how many hours per week they spend searching the Internet; individual depression scores are measured on an instrument with proven valid and reliable scores. Assume that there are 15 questions about depression on the instrument with a rating scale from 1 = strongly disagree to 5 = strongly agree. This means that the summed scores will range from 15 to 45.

As shown in Figure 12.1, hypothetical scores for 10 students are collected and plotted on the graph. Several aspects about this graph, listed below, will help you understand it.

▶ The hours of Internet use variable is plotted on the *X* axis, the horizontal axis.
▶ The depression variable is plotted on the *Y* axis, the vertical axis.
▶ Each student in the study has two scores: one for hours per week of Internet use and one for depression, which is based on a total score for all questions on the depression instrument.
▶ A mark (or point) on the graph indicates the score for each individual on depression and hours of Internet use each week. There are 10 scores (points) on the graph, one for each participant in the study.

The mean scores (M) on each variable are also plotted on the graph. The students used the Internet an average 9.7 hours per week and their average depression score was 29.3. Drawing vertical and horizontal lines on the graph that relate to the mean scores (M), we can divide the plot into four quadrants and assign a minus (−) to quadrants where scores are "negative" and a plus (+) to quadrants where the scores are "positive." In our example, to have a depression score below 29.3 (M) is positive because that suggests that the students with such a score have less depression. To score above 29.3 (M) indicates more severe depression, and this is "negative." Alternatively, to use the Internet less than 9.7 (M) hours per week is "positive" (i.e., because students can then spend more time on homework), while to spend more time than 9.7 hours is "negative" (i.e., overuse of Internet searching is at the expense of something else). To be both highly depressed (above 29.3

FIGURE 12.1

Example of a Scatterplot

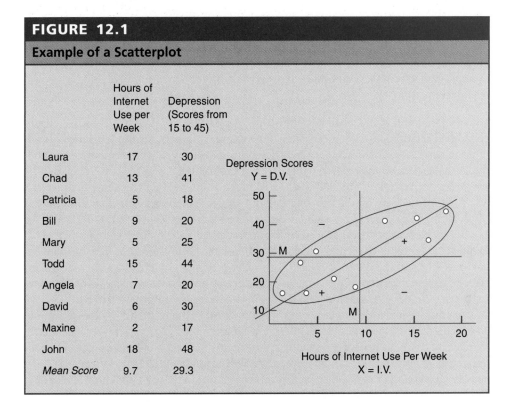

	Hours of Internet Use per Week	Depression (Scores from 15 to 45)
Laura	17	30
Chad	13	41
Patricia	5	18
Bill	9	20
Mary	5	25
Todd	15	44
Angela	7	20
David	6	30
Maxine	2	17
John	18	48
Mean Score	9.7	29.3

on depression) and to use the Internet frequently (above 9.7 on Internet use), is what we might have predicted based on past literature.

It's important to note three aspects about the scores on this plot. First, the direction of scores shows that when *X* increases, *Y* increases as well, indicating a positive association. Second, the points on the scatterplot tend to form a straight line. Third, the points are reasonably close to a straight line if we were to draw a line through all of them. These three ideas relate to direction, form of the association, and the degree of relationship that we can learn from studying this scatterplot.

Direction of the Association

When examining this graph, it is important to identify if the points (where in graph the scores intersect) move in the same or opposite directions. In a **positive correlation** (indicated by a "+" correlation coefficient) the points move in the same direction—when *X* increases, so also does *Y* increase or, alternatively, if *X* decreases, so also does *Y* decrease. In a **negative correlation** (indicated by a "−" correlation coefficient), the points move in the opposite direction—when *X* increases, *Y* decreases and when *X* decreases, *Y* increases. If scores on one variable do not relate in any pattern on the other variable, there is no linear association. But typically some association exists, and by placing "+" and "−" in the quadrants as in our example, you can determine the direction of the association among scores.

Form of the Association

Correlational researchers identify the form of the plotted scores as linear or non-linear. In the Internet and depression example, we found a positive, linear relationship. This type of relationship is only one of several possibilities that might result from actual data. In reality, the relationship might assume any one of the forms shown in Figure 12.2.

Linear Relationship   Part (a) of Figure 12.2 depicts a **positive linear relationship** of scores, where low (or high) scores on one variable relate to low (or high) scores on a second variable. In our example, low scores on depression are associated with low scores on number of hours using the Internet per week.

Part (b) of Figure 12.2 depicts a **negative linear relationship** result, where low scores on one variable relate to high scores on the other variable. Low scores on depression, for example, might be associated with high scores on use of the Internet, suggesting a negative relationship.

Uncorrelated and Non-linear Relationships   In part (c) of Figure 12.2, we see an **uncorrelated relationship** of scores. In this distribution the variables are independent of each other. A particular score on one variable does not predict or tell us any information about the possible score on the other variable. In our example, the scores for depression and the scores for Internet use are plotted irregularly on the graph without any particular pattern.

A **curvilinear or non-linear relationship** shows a U-shaped distribution in scores. This distribution in part (d) of Figure 12.2 shows an increase, plateau, and a decline in the *Y*-axis variable with increasing values of the *X*-axis variable. The distribution in part (e) of Figure 12.2 indicates a decrease, plateau, and an increase in the *Y*-axis variable with increasing values of the *X*-axis variable. For example, it is possible that as Internet use increases, so also does depression, up to a point where the Internet actually becomes a coping mechanism for stress and depression begins to decrease [as illustrated in part (d)].

Another example of this form of distribution would be the relationship between anxiety and points scored in a tennis match. With low anxiety initially, a tennis player might score many points, but this may decline as anxiety sets in. As the match progresses, however, anxiety actually helps keep the tennis player alert, and, as anxiety builds, performance actually goes up. In short, a plot of anxiety and points scores would show a curvilinear relationship [such as in part (e) of Figure 12.2].

FIGURE 12.2

Patterns of Association Between Two Variables

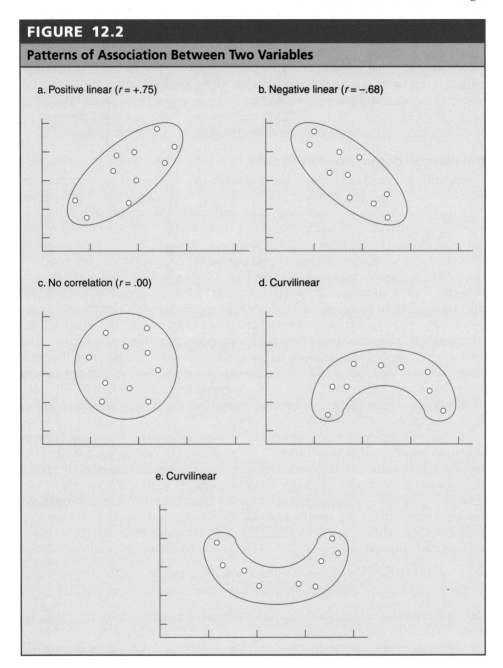

a. Positive linear ($r = +.75$)

b. Negative linear ($r = -.68$)

c. No correlation ($r = .00$)

d. Curvilinear

e. Curvilinear

Degree of Association

From the scatterplot, we can also learn how well the data points fit on a straight line. (Later we will discuss how to calculate and place this line.) A perfect correlation is one in which the points all fit exactly on the line. **Degree of association** means that the association between two variables or sets of scores is a correlation coefficient of -1.00 to a $+1.00$, with 0.00 indicating no linear association at all. This association between two sets of scores reflects whether there is a consistent, predictable association between the scores (Gravetter & Wallnau, 2000).

Calculating the Association Between Variables

Correlational researchers correlate two or more variables using the procedure of calculating the Pearson correlation statistic. Since researchers seek to describe the association or relationship between two or more than two variables, what procedures do they actually use? A basic understanding of the correlation statistic, in non-technical terms, is needed. Understanding the basic purpose of this coefficient and knowing when to use it and how to interpret it are useful when planning a study or understanding references to it in a published study.

The Pearson Correlation Coefficient

A **correlation** is defined as a statistical test to determine the tendency or pattern for two (or more) variables or two sets of data to vary consistently. In the case of only two variables, this means that two variables share common variance, or they co-vary together. To say that two variables co-vary has a somewhat complicated mathematical basis. **Co-vary** means that we can predict a score on one variable with knowledge about the individual's score on another variable. A simple example might illustrate this point. Assume that scores on a math quiz for fourth-grade students range from 30 to 90. We are interested in whether scores on an in-class exercise in math (one variable) can predict the student's math quiz scores (another variable). If the scores on the exercise do not explain the scores on the math quiz, then we cannot predict anyone's score except to say that it might range from 30 to 90. If the exercise could explain the variance in all of the math quiz scores, then we could predict the math scores perfectly. This situation is seldom achieved; instead, we might find that 40% of the variance in math quiz scores is explained by scores on the exercise. This narrows our prediction on math quiz scores from 30 to 90 to something less, such as 40 to 60. The idea is that as variance increases, we are better able to predict scores from the independent to the dependent variable (Gall, Borg, & Gall, 1996).

The statistic that expresses a correlation statistic as a linear relationship is the **Pearson product-moment correlation coefficient** (remember that Karl Pearson first published the formula). It is also called the bivariate correlation, the zero-order correlation, or simply the Pearson r, and it is indicated with an "r" for its notation. The statistic is calculated for two variables (r_{xy}) by multiplying the z scores on X and Y for each case and then dividing by the number of cases minus 1 (e.g., see the detailed steps in Vockell and Ashner, 1995). You may find the mathematical calculations illustrated in many introductory statistics books. In basic terms, Gravetter and Wallnau (2000, p. 531) conceptually show the computation to be:

$$r = \frac{\text{degree to which } X \text{ and } Y \text{ vary together}}{\text{degree to which } X \text{ and } Y \text{ vary separately}}$$

More important than understanding the mathematical calculation is knowing how to interpret and use the statistical coefficient.

By calculating this statistic, researchers obtain a coefficient that measures the degree of association between two variables (e.g., number of library books borrowed and extent of participation in school leadership activities). The statistic r is not a percentage, but a coefficient that ranges in value from $r = -1.00$ to $+1.00$. It requires continuous data (discussed in Chapter 8) for both variables being correlated. (Later you will learn about other statistics when nominal or ordinal scales are measured.) Thus, when using the Pearson correlation statistic, the researcher assumes that the data are normally distributed. Another assumption is that the range of scores are broad enough to distinguish among cases. In other words, the scores need to vary or be distributed along a continuum on both variables being correlated.

Use of the Pearson Correlation Coefficient   The correlation statistic has many applied uses in educational research. It is used to determine the magnitude of association between two variables and to detect the direction (the sign, "+" or "−") of a relationship. It is also used to examine the test-retest reliability between two sets of scores to demonstrate the stability of scores among observers or from one administration of a test to another. It has value for assessing the internal consistency of scores, another form of reliability, and it can establish construct validity—whether inferences can be drawn from scores because they interrelate to measuring some underlying trait or characteristic. The statistic is also used to test theories when researchers collect data to confirm or disconfirm hypotheses. Finally, the Pearson correlation statistic is the foundation for more sophisticated statistics, such as partial correlations and approaches that involve predictions, such as multiple regression.

Displaying the Coefficients in a Matrix   Correlation researchers typically display correlation coefficients in a matrix. A **correlation matrix** presents a visual display of the correlation coefficients for all variables in a study. In this display, all variables are listed on both a horizontal row and a vertical column in the table. Correlational researchers present correlation coefficients in a matrix in published research reports.

An example of this can be seen in Table 12.1, which reports coefficients for the correlation of six variables in a study of variables associated with school satisfaction among middle school students. Notice that all six variables are listed in both the horizontal rows and the vertical columns. To simplify the table, the authors assigned numbers to the variables and only included the numbers in the horizontal row. Further, coefficients ranging between −.33 and + .65 are reported in cells in the table. Only the lower half of the cells are filled because the half of the cells above the diagonal would simply repeat the same information. Finally, the asterisks indicate whether the coefficient statistics are statistically significantly correlated at the $p < .05$ and $p < .01$ levels.

Assessing the Strength of the Association   Correlational researchers interpret the magnitude and direction of the correlations. As already mentioned, the coefficient r takes on values ranging from +1.00 to −1.00. With numbers indicating strength and valence signs indicating direction, the statistic provides a measure of the magnitude of the relationship between two variables. Although the correlation measures the degree of relationship, many researchers prefer to square the correlation and use the resulting value to measure the strength of the relationship (Gravetter & Wallnau, 2000). In this procedure, researchers calculate the **coefficient of determination,** which assesses the proportion of variability in one variable that can be determined or explained by a second variable. For example, if you obtain a $r = + .70$ (or −.70), squaring this value leads to $r^2 = .49$ (or 49%). This means that almost half (49%) of the variability in Y can be

TABLE 12.1

Example of a Correlation Matrix

Variables	1	2	3	4	5	6
1. School satisfaction	—					
2. Extra-curricular activities	−.33**	—				
3. Friendships	24	−.03	—			
4. Self-esteem	−.17	.65**	.24*	—		
5. Pride in school	−.09	−.02	.49**	.16	—	
6. Self-awareness	.29**	−.10	.39**	.03	.22	—

*$p < .05$
**$p < .01$

determined or explained by *X*. For example, we might say that parents' education level explains 49% of students' satisfaction with school ($r^2 = .49$).

Other standards for interpreting the strength of the association also exist. General guidelines indicate whether the size of the coefficient provides meaningful information about the strength of association between two variables. One such guide is available in Cohen and Manion (1994). Consider the following interpretations given the following size of coefficients:

▶ **.20–.35:** When correlations range from .20 to .35, there is only a slight relationship; this relationship may be slightly statistically significant for 100 or more participants. This size of a coefficient may be valuable to explore the interconnection of variables, but of little value in prediction studies.

▶ **.35–.65:** When correlations are above .35, they are useful for limited prediction. They are the typical values used to identify variable membership in the statistical procedure of factor analysis (the intercorrelation of variables with a scale), and many correlation coefficients for bivariate relationships fall into this area.

▶ **.66–.85:** When correlations fall into this range, good prediction can result from one variable to the other. Coefficients in this range would be considered very good.

▶ **.86 and above:** Correlations in this range are typically achieved for studies of construct validity or test-retest reliability. In fact, researchers want their reliability and validity tests to be this high. When two or more variables are related, correlations this high are seldom achieved, and, if they result, then two variables actually measure the same underlying trait and should probably be combined in data analysis.

Correlations and Hypothesis Testing   Given a coefficient for the strength of the association between two variables, how do we know if the value is meaningful? One way to find out is to use significance testing. In hypothesis testing, we are selecting a sample and drawing inferences from the sample to the population. For correlational research, the null hypothesis would be that there is no association or relationship among the scores in the population. Testing this hypothesis involves setting a level of significance, calculating the test statistic, examining whether the correlation coefficient value falls into the region of rejection, and rejecting or failing to reject the null hypothesis (see Chapter 8 on "Conducting Hypothesis Testing"). In correlational research, the Pearson *r* squared expresses the magnitude of association between the two variables or sets of scores. As such, it represents the effect size (see Chapter 8 on "Interpret the Results in Terms of Statistical and Practical Significance")—another means of assessing the magnitude of the relationship regardless of hypothesis testing.

Using Correlation Coefficients for Prediction   Correlation researchers use the correlation statistic to predict future scores. Plotting the relationship of scores provides results about the direction of the relationship, but it does not provide specific information about predicting scores from one value to another. We need to turn to one more concept, the regression line, to understand prediction.

A **regression line** is a line of "best fit" for all of the points of scores on the graph. This line comes the closest to all of the points on the plot and it is calculated by drawing a line that minimizes the squared distance of the points from the line. Examine Figure 12.3, which is the same graph used in Figure 12.1, indicating the association between "hours of Internet use per week" and "depression scores" for middle school students. Figure 12.3 now contains additional information: more detail about the regression line. You can see how the line comes close to all of the points on the graph and is drawn at a diagonal consistent with the positive correlation between Internet use and depression scores.

FIGURE 12.3

Simple Regression Line

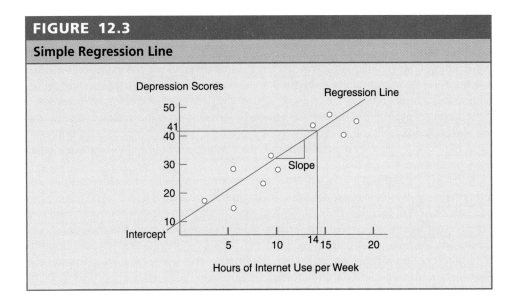

The calculation of this line holds value for predicting scores on the outcome (i.e., depression) with knowledge about the predictor (i.e., hours of Internet use per week). Based on a mathematical formula, a researcher can calculate an equation that expresses this line:

$$Y \text{ (predicted)} = b(X) + a$$

where
 Y = predicted score on depression
 X = actual score on number of hours of Internet use
 b = slope of the regression line (called the unstandardized regression coefficient)
 a = the intercept or a constant, the value of the predicted Y (depression) score when $X = 0$

An individual who uses the Internet 14 hours per week would expect to have a depression score of 41. This score can be estimated by drawing a vertical line from the score for the X-axis variable up to the regression line and over to the Y-axis variable. Alternatively, using the regression formula,

$$\text{If } a = 6, b = 2.5, \text{ and } X = 14$$

$$\text{Then } Y \text{ (predicted)} = 2.5(14) + 6 = 41$$

Other Measures of Association

The Pearson correlation coefficient is useful for describing and measuring the association between two variables *if the association is linear.* As shown in the patterns of association in Figure 12.2, the association may be curvilinear (or non-linear). If a Pearson r is used to estimate a curvilinear association, it would provide an underestimate of the correlation. Therefore, researchers use different statistics than the Pearson r to calculate the relationship between variables for a curvilinear distribution and for relating ranked data.

Instead of the Pearson r coefficient, researchers use the **Spearman rho** (r_s) correlation coefficient for non-linear data and for other types of data measured on ordinal scales (rank order scales). There are two situations that merit the use of the Spearman rho. The first is when you are measuring the association between variables when both variables are measured on an ordinal level (rank order) scale. (See Chapter 6 on "Selecting Scales of Measurement.") In many educational situations it is easier to rank the data (e.g., teachers ranking students' creative abilities) than using some other scale of measurement. The second situation is when the data show a consistent relationship, but not necessarily a linear relationship (i.e., with data points fitting a straight line). A consistent relationship means that when *X* increases, *Y* also increases. This relationship, although consistent, may not be linear and fit a straight line. A plot of the association would show, for example, a curvilinear association between the scores. Even if the scores are measured using interval scales (e.g., strongly agree to strongly disagree), and the plot of the scores reveals a non-linear relationship, the researcher can convert the interval scales to ranked scores (i.e., highest score = 1, the next highest = 2) and calculate the Spearman rho statistic.

When one variable is measured as an interval or ratio scale and the other has two different values (a dichotomous scale), the correlation statistic should not be the Pearson *r* but the **point-biserial correlation.** Assume that a researcher correlates continuous, interval scores on depression with males and females (a dichotomous variable). A point-biserial correlation statistic is used by converting the dichotomous variable (males, females) into numerical scores by assigning a males = 1 and a females = 2. Using these numbers and the Pearson formula for ordinal data, the researcher calculates the point-biserial correlation coefficient that measures the degree and direction of association between males and females on depression.

A variation of this theme of using different types of scales in assessing the association between two variables is the phi-coefficient. The **phi-coefficient** is used to determine the degree and direction of association when *both* variable measures are dichotomous. In our example, males and females might be correlated with drug usage (no and yes). In this situation, the researcher also converts both dichotomous variables to numeric values (males = 1, females = 2; no to drugs = 1, yes to drugs = 2) and then uses the Pearson formula for converted scores.

Using Advanced Statistical Procedures

Correlational researchers use advanced statistics to control for variables and to examine the combination of factors that affect outcomes. Up to this point, we have been considering primarily the linear association between only two variables. Using a Pearson *r* statistic, we can calculate the relationship between the two variables and express it in a coefficient that has a direction as well as a strength or magnitude. More advanced statistics are often used in educational research that build on the Pearson *r* with more than two variables. They are:

▶ partial correlation
▶ multiple correlation or regression
▶ path analysis and latent variable causal modeling (structural equation modeling)

Partial Correlations

In many situations in education, we cannot reduce our studies to only two variables. Often a third, fourth, or fifth variable requires study to determine its impact on an outcome or dependent variable. Let us begin with the situation of a third variable only. Recall from Chapter 5 the type of variable called a mediating or intervening variable. This variable, you may recall, "stands between" the independent and dependent variables and influences both of them. This variable is different than a control variable that influences the outcome in an experiment; the intervening variable is associated with *both* the independent and dependent variables. This statistical procedure uses **partial correlations.**

A picture of two variables followed by the inclusion of a third can help explain partial correlations. Examine Figure 12.4 that shows a bivariate (two-variable) correlation in the top half and a three variable (partial) correlation analysis in the bottom half. Assume that a

FIGURE 12.4

Common Variance Shared for Bivariate and Partial Correlations

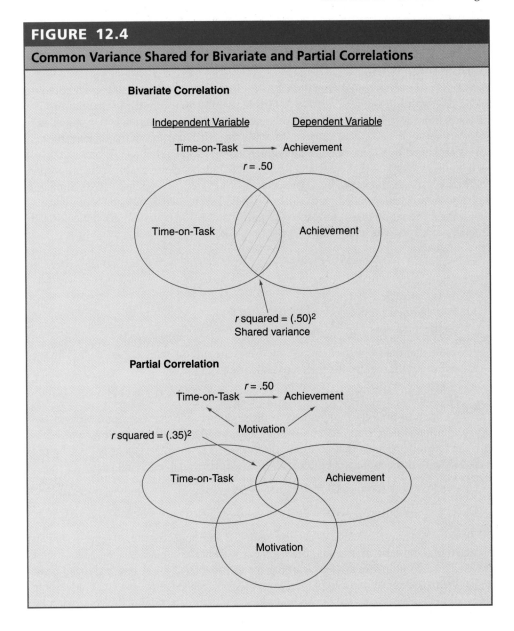

researcher conducts a study correlating time-on-task with achievement for middle school children. After gathering the scores, our investigator calculates a Pearson correlation coefficient with the results of $r = .50$. Figure 12.4 indicates this association as well as the r squared, or the proportion of common shared variance between the two variables. However, the situation is more complicated. Student motivation, a third variable, may also influence both the students' time-on-task as well as their achievement in class. The researcher identifies this third variable based on a literature review and a study of past theories that have shown factors likely to influence student achievement. In the design, motivation needs to be removed so that the relationship between time-on-task and achievement can be more clearly determined. A partial correlation statistical analysis can be used that removes the shared variance in both time-on-task and achievement by motivation. The mathematical calculations for this coefficient are reviewed in statistics books; however, it is based on the correlation coefficients among all three variables and their variances. The hatch-marked area indicates this shared variance left after removing the effects of motivation, and the $r_{12.3}$ = .35 is now lower than the original correlation of r = .50.

Multiple Regression

Consider a more complicated situation where multiple independent variables may combine to correlate with a dependent variable. **Multiple regression** (or **multiple correlation**) is a statistical procedure for examining the combined relationship of multiple independent variables with a single dependent variable. In regression, the variation in the dependent variable is explained by the variance of each independent variable (the relative importance of each predictor), as well as the combined effect of all independent variables (the proportion of criterion variance explained by all predictors), designated by R^2 (Kline, 1998). Similar to the regression equation mentioned earlier, predicted scores on an outcome can be generated using an equation that is similar to the simple regression equation, but it includes additional predictors. The equation is:

$$Y \text{ (predicted)} = b_1 (X1) + b_2 (X2) + a$$

Where
  Y = the predicted scores
  b_1 = a constant for the slope of $X1$ (b_2, for $X2$)
  a = the intercept

Assume that the slope for b_1 = .24 and b_2 = .19 and the intercept is 10.77. The prediction equation for the two independent variables would be:

$$Y \text{ (predicted)} = .24 (X1) + .19 (X2) + 10.77$$

If we want to predict an individual's score on a quiz, for example, from time-on-task ($X1$) and prior achievement ($X2$), we would substitute their scores on these two measures into the formula. Assume that time-on-task is 10 and prior achievement is 70. The predicted score of this combination of the two independent variables would be:

$$Y \text{ (predicted)} = .24 (10) + .19 (70) + 10.77$$

$$Y \text{ (predicted)} = 26.47 \text{ or rounded to 26 on the quiz}$$

Let's extend our example to illustrate a couple of additional features of regression. Suppose that time-on-task, motivation, prior achievement in the subject area, and peer friends are predicted to influence student learning (or achievement) for at-risk high school students. We may want to know how these variables *in combination* predict student learning. Knowing this information is probably more realistic than determining the correlation between time-on-task and achievement; it models the complex world in which high school students live. In short, a complicated situation exists, and we need to determine how each variable individually and in combination helps explain the variation in student learning. This information will help us isolate factors that can be changed in a high school or issues to be addressed with the students.

We can calculate regression coefficients for each variable, assess the combined influence of all variables, and provide a picture of the results. A **regression table** shows the overall amount of variance explained in a dependent variable by all independent variables, called R^2 (R squared). It also shows the regression weight—the amount of contribution of each variable controlling for the variance of all other variables, called beta—for each variable. Examine the regression table shown in Table 12.2. Here we see four predictor variables of student learning. The coefficients in the right column are the beta weights for each independent variable. A **beta weight** is a coefficient indicating the magnitude of prediction for a variable after removing the effects of all other predictors. A beta weight is reported in standardized form (recall from Chapter 8 on "Calculating Descriptive Statistics" that a

TABLE 12.2

Sample Regression Table: Student Learning (Outcome Variable)

Predictor Variables	Beta
Time-on-Task	.11
Motivation	.18
Prior Achievement	.20*
Peer Friend Influence	.05

$R = .38$

R squared $= .15$

*$p < .05$

$N = 90$

z-score standardizes the measures so that all variables can be compared), and is interpreted like a Pearson r, with a value from -1.00 to $+1.00$. It should be noted that regression tables often report a B-value (an unstandardized coefficient), but these values, while useful in a prediction formula, do not allow researchers to compare the relative strength of each independent variable as a predictor because the value may be scored in different units. For example, one variable may be scored on a 5-point scale and another one on a 3-point scale.

As seen in Table 12.2, the predictor "prior achievement" explains the most variance, followed by "motivation." Below the table we see the correlation of the combination of variables (the multiple correlation designated by R) of .38 and the proportion of variability explained in the dependent variables by all of the predictors (R^2) of .15. Recall that the value, R^2, called the coefficient of determination, represents the proportion of variability explained by the independent variables in the dependent variable. In reporting results, correlational researchers should indicate not only the statistical significance of the test but also the effect size variance, R^2.

Path Analysis and Structural Equation Modeling

We can also see the predictor variables operating to explain the association in the outcome in a visual model. As shown in the top half of Figure 12.5, three of the four predictors are positively correlated with learning: time-on-task, motivation, and prior achievement. The fourth variable, peer friend influence, has a negative association. A researcher could advance this model, indicate valences ($+$ or $-$) to indicate the direction of relationships, gather data, and test the relationships to determine whether predictions of direction (positive and negative) hold true.

When the data are organized and displayed in a time sequence (e.g., prior achievement precedes motivation), we are using path analysis. **Path analysis** is a statistical procedure for testing a theory about a causal sequence of three or more variables on an outcome variable. Now examine the lower half of Figure 12.5. Here we see the variables organized in a sequence—prior achievement followed by peer friend influence, motivation, time-on-task, and finally student learning. Beta weight values (from Table 12.2) are placed on the paths among the variables.

Assume that a theory exists in the literature about student learning among at-risk high school students. In this theory, researchers have identified factors that influence students' learning and have even hypothesized that high entering abilities (e.g., prior achievement) leads to high motivation. This, in turn, contributes to student learning (to take only one path in the model). Using multiple regression, we can determine the weight of each predictor variable with all other variables in the model held constant. In this way, an assessment is made

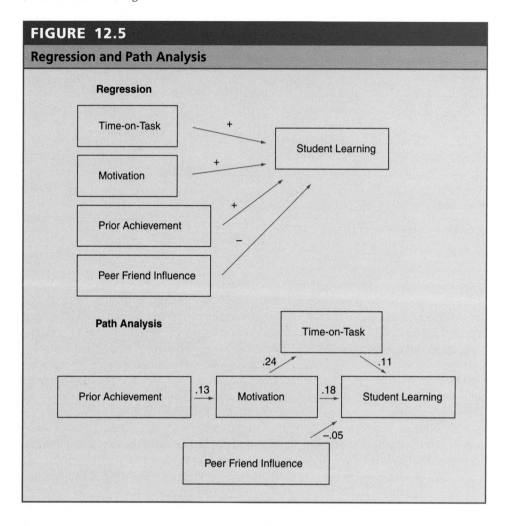

FIGURE 12.5

Regression and Path Analysis

about the combined contribution of each independent variable as well as its contribution, controlling for other variables in the path. For example, prior achievement may be correlated with student learning, $r = .43$, but its effect on student learning decreases because the variance of motivation (directly in the path) also exercises an influence. In this way, we can estimate the importance of each variable directly (Pearson's r) and indirectly (the weight of the partial variable).

The steps in path analysis are:

▶ identify a theory to test and draw a figure of the theory
▶ locate measures for variables in the theory
▶ correlate the variables in the theory
▶ determine if the correlations are consistent with the theory

One final extension of correlation analysis—and beyond the scope of this book, but useful to know because it is appearing more frequently in educational research—is causal modeling. In **latent variable causal modeling** (also called **structural equation modeling**) the researcher uses a procedure similar to path analysis but which yields more valid and reliable measures of the variables being analyzed. For each variable in the path (called latent variables), the researcher obtains multiple measures of the variables (called manifest variables). The manifest variables are the only ones actually measured by the researcher. The analysis of the manifest variables provides more valid and reliable measures for each variable specified in the model. For additional information on the procedures used in latent causal modeling, see Kline (1998).

STEPS IN CONDUCTING A CORRELATIONAL STUDY

From our discussion about the key characteristics of correlational research, we can begin to see steps emerge that you might use when planning or conducting a study. The following steps illustrate the process of conducting correlational research.

Step 1. Determine If a Correlational Study Best Addresses the Research Problem

A correlational study is used when a need exists to study a problem requiring the identification of the direction and degree of association between two sets of scores. It is useful for identifying the type of association, explaining complex relationships of multiple factors that explain an outcome, and predicting an outcome from one or more predictors. Correlational research does not "prove" a relationship; rather, it indicates an association between two or more variables.

Since groups are not being compared in a correlational study, researchers often use a research question rather than a hypothesis. Sample questions in a correlational study might be:

▶ Is creativity related to IQ test scores for elementary children? (associating two variables)
▶ What factors explain a student teacher's ethical behavior during the student-teaching experience? (exploring a complex relationship)
▶ Does high school class rank predict a college student's GPA in the first semester of college? (prediction)

Step 2. Identify Individuals to Study

Ideally, the researcher should randomly select the individuals so that the results might be generalized to a population. The group needs to be of adequate size for use of the correlational statistic, such as $N = 30$; larger sizes contribute to less error variance and better claims of representativeness. For instance, a researcher might study 100 high school athletes to correlate the extent of their participation in different sports and their use of tobacco. Permissions need to be obtained from school authorities and approval needs to be granted from the institutional review board.

Step 3. Identify Two or More Measures for Each Individual in the Study

Since the basic idea of correlational research is to compare participants in this single group on two or more characteristics, measures of variables in the research question need to be identified (e.g., literature search of past studies), and instruments that measure the variables need to be obtained. Ideally, these instruments should have been used in prior studies and the validity and reliability scores should be reviewed. Permissions, if needed, must be obtained from publishers or authors to use the instruments. Typically one variable is measured on each instrument, but a single instrument might contain both variables being correlated in the study.

Step 4. Collect Data and Monitor Potential Threats

The next step is to administer the instruments and collect at least two sets of data from each individual. The actual research design is quite simple as a visual presentation. Two data scores are collected for each individual until scores are obtained from each person in the study. This is illustrated with three individuals as follows:

Participants:	Measures or Observations:	
Individual 1	01	02
Individual 2	01	02
Individual 3	01	02

This situation holds for describing the association between two variables or for predicting a single outcome from a single predictor variable. To understand more complex relationships, researchers collect multiple independent variables.

A small sample database for 10 college students is shown in Table 12.3. The investigator seeks to explain the variability in first-year grade point averages for these 10 graduate students in education. Assume that our investigator has identified these four predictors in a review of the literature. In past studies, these predictors have positively correlated with achievement in college. The researcher can obtain information for the predictor variables from the college admissions office. The criterion, grade point average during the first year, is available from the registrar's office. In this regression study, the researcher seeks to identify which one factor or combination of factors best explains the variance in first-year graduate student GPAs. A review of this data shows that the scores varied on each variable, with more variation among GRE scores than among recommendation and fit-to-program scores. Also, it appears that higher college GPA and GRE scores are positively related to higher first semester GPA scores.

In this example, since the data were available from admissions offices, the researcher need not be overly concerned about procedures that threaten the validity of the scores. However, a potential for restricted range of scores—little variation in scores—certainly exists. Other factors that might affect the researcher's ability to draw valid inferences from the

TABLE 12.3

Example of Data Collected in a Regression Study

Student	College GPA	GRE Scores (Composite)	Strength of Recommendations (1–10 scale)	Fit to Program (1–10 scale)	First Semester GPA in Graduate School (4-point scale)
Lindsey	3.5	950	8	6	3.10
Palmira	3.6	1120	9	7	3.60
Anne	3.0	1000	9	8	3.10
Ren	3.8	1250	8	9	3.70
Lucy	3.2	1150	7	7	3.40
Kent	3.5	1000	8	8	3.10
Jason	3.2	900	6	6	3.00
Andrew	3.4	950	7	7	3.10
Dave	3.9	1200	9	9	3.80
Eric	3.7	1140	8	8	3.70

results are the lack of standard administration procedures, the conditions of the testing situation, and the expectations of participants.

Step 5. Analyze the Data and Represent the Results

The objective in correlational research is to describe the degree of association between two or more variables. The investigator looks for a pattern of responses and uses statistical procedures to determine the strength of the relationship as well as its direction. A statistically significant relationship, if found, does not imply causation (cause and effect) but merely an association between the variables. More rigorous procedures, such as those used in experiments, can provide better control than those used in a correlational study.

The analysis begins with coding the data and transferring it from the instruments into a computer file. Then the researcher needs to determine the appropriate statistic to use. An initial question is whether the data are linear- or curvilinear-related. A scatterplot of the scores (if a bivariate study) can help determine this question. Also, consider whether:

▶ Only one independent variable is being studied (Pearson's correlation coefficient).
▶ A mediating variable explains both the independent and dependent variables and needs to be controlled (partial correlation coefficient).
▶ More than one independent variable needs to be studied to explain the variability in a dependent variable (multiple regression coefficient).

Based on the most appropriate statistical test, the researcher next calculates whether the statistic is significant based on the scores. For example, a *p*-value is obtained in a bivariate study by:

▶ setting the alpha level
▶ using the critical values of an *r*-table, available in many statistics books
▶ using degrees of freedom of $N - 2$ with this table
▶ calculating the observed *r* coefficient and comparing it with the *r*-critical value
▶ rejecting or failing to reject the null hypothesis at a specific significance level, such as $p < 0.05$

In addition, it is useful to also report effect size (r^2) (as discussed in Chapter 8). In correlational analysis, the effect size is the Pearson's correlation coefficient squared. In representing the results, the correlational researcher will present a correlation matrix of all variables as well as a statistical table (for a regression study) reporting the R and R^2 values and the beta weights for each variable. In addition, for path analysis, a visual model is included in the discussion with values on paths to indicate the contribution of each variable to the outcome, controlling for the effects of all of the other variables in the model.

Step 6. Interpret the Results

The final step in conducting a correlational study is interpreting the meaning of the results. This requires discussing the magnitude and the direction of the results in a correlational study, considering the impact of intervening variables in a partial correlation study, interpreting the regression weights of variables in a regression analysis, and developing a predictive equation for use in a prediction study.

In all of these steps, an overall concern is whether the theory or the hypotheses or questions are supported. Further, the researcher considers whether the results confirm or disconfirm findings from other studies. Also, a reflection is made about whether some of the threats discussed above may have contributed to erroneous coefficients and the steps that might be taken by future researchers to address these concerns.

CRITERIA FOR EVALUATING CORRELATIONAL DESIGNS

To evaluate and assess the quality of a correlational study, you might use the following criteria:

▶ Is the size of the sample adequate for hypothesis testing? (sufficient power?)
▶ Does the researcher adequately display the results in matrixes or graphs?
▶ Is there an interpretation about the direction and magnitude of the association between two variables?
▶ Is there an assessment of the magnitude of the relationship based on the coefficient of determination, *p*-values, effect size, or the size of the coefficient?
▶ Is the researcher concerned about the form of the relationship so that an appropriate statistic is chosen for analysis?
▶ Has the researcher identified the predictor and the criterion variables?
▶ If a visual model of the relationships is advanced, does the researcher indicate the expected direction of the relationships among variables? Or the predicted direction based on observed data?
▶ Are the statistical procedures clearly identified?

APPLYING WHAT YOU HAVE LEARNED: A CORRELATIONAL STUDY

To apply ideas in this chapter, read through the correlational study on page 387, noting the marginal annotations that identify the characteristics of both correlational *and* quantitative research.

> Ting, S. R. (2000). Predicting Asian Americans' academic performance in the first year of college: An approach combining SAT scores and noncognitive variables. *Journal of College Student Development, 41*, 442–449.

Ting (2000) studied factors (SAT scores and noncognitive variables) that predict Asian-Americans' academic performance and retention in college. Asian-Americans are highly accomplished in college, but they face problems such as a discrepancy between education and income, insufficient mastery of English, racism, loneliness, isolation, and anxiety. Ninety-six Asian-American students in one public land-grant research university participated in the study. Predictors were assessed at the new student orientation at the beginning of the year. Students completed an instrument measuring psychosocial factors (e.g., positive self-concept and understanding and coping with racism), and they provided entering SAT scores. Two criterion variables, measured later at the end of the fall and spring semesters, were grade point average and retention. Although the author reported the correlation coefficients, of primary interest was the combination of predictors in explaining grade point average. Statistically significant predictors of both the fall and the spring grade point averages were SAT math scores and a realistic self-appraisal system.

This article was chosen because it presents a prediction study using data from Asian-Americans. It includes correlation analysis as well as the use of the advanced regression statistics. The predictors and the criterion variables were clearly identified in this study and it contained useful, straightforward tables to present the data.

As you review this article, look for elements of the research process listed below:

▶ the research problem and the use of quantitative research
▶ the use of the literature

▶ the purpose statement and research questions or hypotheses
▶ types and procedures of data collection
▶ types and procedures of data analysis and interpretation
▶ the overall reporting structure

The Research Problem and Use of Quantitative Research

The research problem—see Paragraph 03

Characteristics of quantitative research—see the marginal annotations on the left side of the page

In the third paragraph, the author introduces the research problem—that Asian-American college students continue to face problems such as racism, psychological and mental problems, loneliness, and isolation. This issue, plus the need for more studies about the psychosocial adjustment of Asian-Americans (paragraph 08), requires an examination of the predictors of academic success.

The article contains key characteristics of a quantitative study. It:

▶ addresses a research problem focused on a need to predict factors that explain academic success and retention (Paragraph 03)
▶ identifies predictors in the literature that influence success and retention (Paragraphs 04–08)
▶ focuses the purpose statement on relating variables, specifically SAT and psychosocial variables to student GPA and retention (Paragraph 08)
▶ collects numeric data (Paragraph 10) from a large number of students (Paragraph 09)
▶ relies on instruments, such as the NCQ, identified before the study began (Paragraph 10)
▶ conducts statistical analysis (Paragraph 14), using descriptive statistics (Paragraph 15), correlations (Paragraph 18), multiple regression (Paragraph 18) and discriminant analysis (Paragraph 17)
▶ analyzes the data by describing trends (Paragraph 15) and analyzing variables (Paragraph 18)
▶ is written objectively with the researcher in the background (e.g., Paragraph 15) and uses a standard approach to the structure (e.g., method, results, discussion) (see headings throughout)
▶ forms interpretations based on comparing results with predictions from past studies (e.g., Paragraphs 18–24)

Use of the Literature

Paragraphs 04–08

The literature at the beginning of the study helps to identify the predictors that potentially affect the academic success and retention of Asian-Americans. One by one the author introduces these predictors and draws on specific studies. The author also introduces an instrument, the Noncognitive Questionnaire (NCQ), that is used in the study.

The Purpose Statement and Research Questions

The purpose statement—Paragraph 08

Research questions—not stated

The author clearly identifies the purpose statement in Paragraph 08. This statement indicates that predictor variables will be examined in terms of two outcomes: GPA and retention. Research questions, however, are not stated, and perhaps the use of research questions is redundant with the purpose statement. Therefore, the author may feel that both questions and a statement are not needed.

Types of Procedures of Data Collection

Paragraph 12

The data collection consists of administering an instrument to students at the new student orientation. This instrument consists of the Noncognitive Questionnaire. In Paragraph 11 we learn about the validity and reliability of this instrument. The outcome measures related to GPA and retention are obtained later based on student consent (Paragraph 12), but we learn little about the process of accessing student records.

Types and Procedures of Data Analysis and Interpretation

Data analysis—Paragraph 14

Interpretation—Paragraphs 18–24

The author employs several data analysis procedures that are not discussed, such as descriptive statistics (Paragraph 14) and correlations (Paragraph 18). The discussion about data analysis consists of information about the multiple regression analysis using SPSS and the procedures involved in this analysis. However, the author did present a correlation matrix (Paragraph 18) and provide an interpretation of the direction of the scores (Paragraph 15). The investigator uses the advanced statistics of regression analysis that examine the combined influence of the predictors on fall and spring GPA (Paragraph 18). The regression formula enables the researcher to predict outcomes based on the combination of multiple factors.

In reporting the results, as well as the data analysis, the author does not check for the linear distribution of scores (although this procedure may have been done). In Paragraph 26, however, the author did mention the small sample size for multiple regression analysis, a factor that might have contributed to a non-normal distribution of scores.

The Overall Reporting Structure

Objectivity—Paragraph 15 (as an example)

Structure—the headings throughout the report

The tone of this report is consistent with a quantitative study—the objective researcher reporting the results (e.g., see Paragraph 15). Also, the overall structure supports a quantitative study with headings that reflect methods, results, and discussion.

KEY IDEAS IN THE CHAPTER

In some educational situations, neither the treatment nor the ability to manipulate the conditions are conducive to an experiment. In this case, educators turn to a correlational design. In correlational research, investigators use a correlation statistical technique to describe and measure the degree of association (or relationship) between two or more variables or sets of scores. In this design, the researchers do not attempt to control or manipulate the variables, and they relate, using the correlation statistic, two or more scores for each individual (e.g., a student motivation and a student achievement score for each individual).

The history of correlational research draws on the themes of the origin and development of the correlation statistical test and the procedures for using and interpreting the statistical test. Statisticians first identified the procedures for calculating the correlation statistics in the late 19th century. In the late 1800s, Karl Pearson developed the familiar correlation formula we use today. Today, with the use of multiple statistical procedures such as factor analysis, reliability estimates, and regression, researchers can test elaborate models of variables using correlational statistical procedures.

Although a correlation is a statistic, its use in research has contributed to a specific research design called correlational research. This research has taken two primary forms of research designs: explanation and prediction. A explanatory correlational design explains or clarifies the degree of association among two or more variables at one point in time. Researchers are interested in whether two variables co-vary, in which a change in one variable is reflected in changes in the other. An example is whether motivation is associated with academic performance. In the second form of design, a prediction design, the investigator identifies variables that will positively predict an outcome or criterion. In this form of research, the researcher uses one or more predictor variables and a criterion (or outcome) variable. A prediction permits forecasting future performance, such as whether a student's grade point average in college can be predicted from his or her high school performance.

Underlying both of these designs are key characteristics of correlational research. Researchers plot two scores measuring each variable on a graph for each participant. From this graph, the form of association among the two variables, the direction of the association, and the degree of association can be determined. When a linear relationship exists between the scores, the Pearson correlation coefficient statistic is used to assess this association. Often these correlations are displayed in a matrix and they have multiple uses (e.g., reliability, testing theories, and to serve as a foundation for more advanced statistics). Most importantly, the correlation statistic indicates the strength of relationship between two variables and ranges from $+1.00$ to -1.00. Hypothesis tests can determine if there is an association between the variables in the population. When the form of the association of two scores is non-normal and based on categorical rather than continuous scales, statistical tests other than the Pearson correlation are appropriate, such as the Spearman rho, the point-biserial correlation, and the phi-coefficient. As a foundation for advanced statistics, the correlation statistic contributes to procedures such as partial correlations, multiple regression, path analysis, and latent variable causal modeling.

Steps in conducting a correlational study are to use the design for associating variables or making prediction; identify individuals to study; specify two or more measures for each individual; collect data and monitor potential threats to the validity of the scores; analyze the data using the correlation statistic for either continuous or categorical data; and interpret the strength and the direction of the results.

USEFUL INFORMATION FOR PRODUCERS OF RESEARCH

▶ Identify whether you plan to examine the association between or among variables or use correlational research to make predictions about an outcome.

▶ Plot on a graph the association between your variables so that you can determine the direction, form, and strength of the association.

▶ Use appropriate correlational statistics in your design based on whether the data are continuous or categorical and whether the form of the data are linear or non-linear.

▶ Present a correlation matrix of the Pearson coefficients in your study.

▶ Use advanced statistics employing the correlation statistic for associating more than two variables and modeling complex relationships.

USEFUL INFORMATION FOR CONSUMERS OF RESEARCH

▶ Recognize that a correlation study is not as rigorous as an experiment because the researcher can only control statistically for variables rather than physically manipulate variables. Correlational studies do not "prove" relationships; rather, they indicate an association between or among variables or sets of scores.
▶ Correlation studies are research in which the investigator seeks to explain the association or relationship among variables or to predict outcomes.
▶ Realize that all correlational studies, no matter how advanced the statistics, all use a correlation coefficient as their base for analysis. Understanding the intent of this coefficient helps you determine the results in a correlational study.

ADDITIONAL RESOURCES YOU MIGHT EXAMINE

For additional detailed discussions about the correlation statistic and more advanced statistics, see:

Gravetter, F. J., & Wallnau, L. B. (2000). *Statistics for the behavioral sciences* (5th ed.). Belmont, CA: Wadsworth/Thomson Learning.

Williams, F. (1992). *Reasoning with statistics: How to read quantitative research* (4th ed.). Ft. Worth: Harcourt Brace Jovanovich College Publishers.

Salkind, N. J. (2000). *Statistics for people who (think they) hate statistics.* Thousand Oaks, CA: Sage.

For discussions about more advanced correlational procedures, especially regression analysis and structural equation modeling, see:

Kline, R. B. (1998). *Principles and practice of structural equation modeling.* New York: Guilford Press.

Pedhazur, E. J. (1997). *Multiple regression in behavioral research: Explanation and prediction* (3rd ed.) Ft. Worth, TX: Harcourt Brace College Publishers.

**Quantitative
Characteristics**

A quantitative research
problem requires
description or
explanation.

Predicting Asian-Americans' Academic Performance in the First Year of College: An Approach Combining SAT Scores and Noncognitive Variables

Siu-Man Raymond Ting

(01)   *Factors related to academic performance and student retention of Asian-American freshmen (N = 96) at a predominantly white university in the southeast were studied. In addition to SAT-mathematics score, three noncognitive variables were found to be significant predictors of GPA: realistic self-appraisal system, successful leadership experience, and demonstrated community service. Realistic self-appraisal and demonstrated community service were significant indicators of student retention. Implications for student affairs professionals and limitations of the study were discussed.*

(02)   Asian Americans are the fastest growing minority group in universities in the United States (American Council on Education, 1998). Between 1976 and 1996, the number of Asian American college students tripled from 2% to 6% of the total undergraduate student population (Snyder, 1999). The current estimated population of Asian-Americans is only 4% of the U.S. population (U.S. Census Bureau, 1999). These figures imply Asian Americans may be slightly overrepresented in universities. They also reflect an increase in recent Asian immigration to U.S. and an emphasis on education among Asian cultures. This trend is likely to continue: by the year 2050, Asian Americans will constitute 10% of the U.S. population, primarily because of immigration (Atkinson, Morten, & Sue, 1993). To match the needs of this increasing population, student affairs professionals and other educators must gain more information about Asian Americans, including factors affecting their academic performance and retention in universities.

(03)   Asian Americans are often portrayed as a model minority because of their hard work and educational achievements, and for earning family incomes close to White Americans (Kao, 1995; Okutsu, 1989; Taylor & Stern, 1997). Asian American students were found to spend significantly more time on homework and parents have higher educational expectations for their children than White Americans did (Mau, 1997). In spite of their accomplishments, Asian Americans continue to face problems such as a discrepancy between education and income (Atkinson et al., 1993), insufficient mastery of English (Sue & Sue, 1990), racism (Delucchi & Do, 1996; Leung, 1990; Tan, 1994), and psychosocial and mental problems such as loneliness, isolation, and anxiety (Solberg, Ritsma, Davis, Tata, & Jolly, 1994). Research studies show that, at colleges and universities, Asian Americans still face many challenges including inadequate services (Greene, 1987), challenge of affirmative action policy on admissions (Selingo, 1999), psychosocial problems when adjusting to universities (Abe & Zane, 1990), alcohol and substance abuse (Chi, Lubben, & Kitano, 1989), and less involvement than their White counterpart in student activities (Wang & Sedlacek, 1992). Many Asian Americans have expressed an interest in participating in student activities and also stated that they were not involved because of time constraints (Wang & Sedlacek, 1992). The resultant social isolation affects social well-being and student reten-

Reprinted with permission from *The Journal of College Student Development.*

Siu-Man Raymond Ting is Assistant Professor of Educational Research and Leadership and Counselor Education at North Carolina State University.

tion of ethnic minorities in universities (Loo & Rolison, 1986). Asian Americans were found to experience difficulties in social adjustment and dissatisfaction with the campus services (Abe & Zane, 1990; Bennet & Okinaka, 1989; Sue & Zane, 1985). Similar to other ethnic minorities, Asian Americans who were dissatisfied about the quality of campus life and felt socially alienated were more likely to drop out (Bennet & Okinaka, 1989; Sue & Zane 1985).

(04)

The quantitative literature plays a major role.

Owing to their minority status and cultural background, Asian American students face many challenges in universities. Nonetheless, little has been found explaining academic performance of Asian Americans. Traditional studies adopting standardized test scores and high school grade-point-average GPA to predict students' academic performance have produced low validity (Fuertes, Sedlacek, & Liu, 1994). In addition, more bias in the validity of using SAT scores and high school GPA to predict college first year GPA was found for ethnic minorities than in the majority group (Sedlacek, 1998; Stone, 1990). The U.S. Education Department also issued a guideline reminding universities not to use SAT scores as the sole admission criterion (Healy, 1999). Therefore, this guideline reflects the possibility that SAT does not accurately portray academic abilities of Asian Americans.

(05)

The quantitative literature justifies the research problem and provides direction for the study.

Recent studies have shifted the focus to noncognitive or nontraditional factors. Astin (1993) found that student involvement in college, including physical and psychological energy devoted to college experience affected learning and personal development. Tinto (1993) reported in his Student Departure Model that a student's decision to remain or leave a university campus is a function of the student's personal and academic background and how well she or he integrates into the academic and social life of the campus. Adopting attribution theory to explore student motivation for academic studies, Yan and Gaier (1994) found that all students attributed academic success first to their efforts, then to ability, strategies, and finally to luck. Gender differences were not found. They reported that Asian American students had less of a self-serving bias than White American students did. A self-serving bias refers to the tendency to take credit for success but denying responsibility for failure. Owing to cultural influences on Asian Americans attributed effort as equally important for success and failure or even more important for failure. Placing greater emphasis on individualism and autonomy, Yan and Gaier found that White Americans were significantly less likely than their Asian American colleagues to attribute failure to lack of effort. In summary, noncognitive factors were found to explain student academic performance and such factors may vary among different ethnic groups.

(06)

Employing eight psychosocial variables in the Noncognitive Questionnaire (NCQ), Tracey and Sedlacek (1984, 1985, 1987) better predicted academic performance and student retention of Black and White students than using SAT scores. The Noncognitive Questionnaire (Tracey & Sedlacek, 1984, 1989) was designed to assess psychosocial aspects that influence college success: personal goals, college expectation, academic self-concept, self-appraisal system, leadership experience and community service in high school, knowledge acquired in a field, ability to understand and cope with racism, and availability of a strong support person.

(07)

The NCQ was found to have effective predictability of academic performance and student retention for different student populations: Asian Americans (Fuertes et al., 1994), African Africans (Boyer & Sedlacek, 1988; Sedlacek & Adams-Gaston, 1992); Hispanics (Fuertes & Sedlacek, 1995), White Americans and African Americans (Ting & Robinson, 1998; Tracey & Sedlacek, 1984, 1985, 1987), specially admitted students (Ting, 1997; White & Sedlacek, 1986), and low-income and first-generation students (Ting, 1998). Correlations with college grades and retention were significantly higher than the SAT scores alone when the noncognitive variables were used in conjunction with standardized test scores and earlier grades. In Fuertes et al.'s study, community service, realistic self-appraisal, and positive self-concept were found to be equally effective compared with SAT-math and SAT-verbal scores in predicting Asian Americans' first year GPAs. No significant predictors were found for student retention in the first year. In addition to confirming the predictive validity of Tracey and Sedlacek's (1984) psychosocial variables, Ting and Robinson (1998) also found that parent education level and need for financial aid were related to students' academic performance in the first year of college.

In summary, compared with other ethnic minorities, professional literature shows that Asian Americans are able to attain their educational goals although they experience challenges in college, particularly in the area of psychosocial adjustment. However, comparatively fewer studies were found studying how psychosocial adjustment may affect Asian Americans' academic performance and retention. Sedlacek (1998) suggested that each university should study psychosocial factors affecting student academic success. Although Fuertes et al. (1994) reported psychosocial predictors of academic success of Asian Americans, their study was based on a campus where Asian Americans comprised 9% of the student population, which may not be representative of U.S. population. Therefore, generalization of this study is somewhat limited. The purpose of the current study was to use SAT scores and Tracey and Sedlacek's psychosocial variables to predict Asian American students' GPA and retention in the first year of college.

Method

Participants

At a Southeastern public land-grant research university, 96 first-year Asian American students participated in the study in Fall 1996 as a part of the survey of the Noncognitive Variables Research Committee. This sample represents over 90% of the new Asian American freshmen at the university. The participants' mean age was 18.19. Fifty-nine of the participants were men and 37 were women.

Measures

NCQ. The NCQ was designed to assess psychosocial aspects that affect student success in college. It contains 23 items: 18 Likert-type, 2 multiple choice, and 3 open-ended. The NCQ's eight scales are listed here (with the range of scores) are: (a) positive self-concept (7–27), (b) realistic self-appraisal system (4–14), (c) understanding and coping with racism (5–25), (d) preference of long-term goals (3–13), (e) a strong support person (3–15), (f) successful leadership experience (3–13), (g) demonstrated community service (2–8), and (h) acquired knowledge in a field (2–8). Tracey and Sedlacek (1984) reported a 2-week test-retest reliability of a range from .74 to .94, with a median of .85 for the NCQ scales. Interrater reliability on the three open-ended NCQ items ranged from .73 to 1.00. The NCQ appears to have promising content validity, and strong construct and predictive validity (Ting & Robinson, 1998).

Predictors. Students' scores on the NCQ and the combined SAT score (verbal and mathematics) were the predictors.

Criterion variables. One criterion was academic performance during the freshmen year. This was measured by term GPA for the Fall and Spring semesters. The second criterion was retention at the end of Fall and Spring indicated by registration records. The students were categorized as being enrolled (coded as 1) or as having dropped out (coded as 0).

The quantitative (08) purpose statement, research questions, or hypotheses are specific and narrow.

The quantitative purpose statement, research questions, or hypotheses seek measurable, observable data on variables.

(09)

Quantitative data collection involves studying a large number of individuals.

(10)

Quantitative data collection is based on using instruments identified prior to the study.

Quantitative data collection involves gathering numeric data.

(11)

(12)

Correlational researchers seek the association or relationship between two variables or sets of scores.

Correlation researchers use the correlation statistic to predict future scores.

Procedure

(13) *Data collection.* The data was collected as a part of the study of the all-university Noncognitive Variables Research Committee. At the new student orientation, each student received a packet that included the NCQ (Tracey & Sedlacek, 1984) and a demographic and personal background form. Over 90% of the new students attended the orientation where they met in small groups and were invited to participate voluntarily in the study completing the NCQ. Participants consented to access of their academic records. SAT scores and registration status in the first year were obtained from their university records.

Quantitative data analysis consists of statistical analysis.

(14) *Data analysis.* College performance is defined here as students' GPA and continued enrollment. The author employed step-wise multiple regression analysis with the SPSS for windows (version 8.0) for the analysis. The author attempted to explore the relationships to noncognitive variables first before combining with SAT scores and background variables. Therefore, all NCQ variables were entered first in a step-wise procedure, then SAT scores. Such procedure was adopted for comparing two different measures in previous similar studies (Tracey & Sedlacek, 1981; Fuertes et al., 1994). Discriminant analysis was conducted to predict student retention.

Results

(15) **Quantitative researchers take an objective and unbiased approach.**

Table 1 shows the means and standard deviations of the predictor and criterion variables. The noncognitive variable scores were similar to those in the Fuertes et al. (1994) study, except that the scores of preference for long-term goals and acquired knowledge in a field were smaller. Table 2 illustrates a correlation matrix between college first-year GPA and predictor variables. SAT-math score and realistic self-appraisal were positively related to students' GPA in Fall and Spring.

Correlational researchers correlate two or more variables using the procedure of calculating the correlation statistic.

Quantitative data analysis consists of describing trends, comparing groups, or relating variables.

TABLE 1
Means and Standard Deviations of
Predictors and Criterion Variables

Variable	All Students	
	M	**SD**
SAT-verbal	537.53	105.79
SAT-math	621.29	77.60
Positive self-concept	19.04	2.44
Realistic self-appraisal system	10.53	1.84
Coping with racism	18.60	2.36
Preference of long-term goals	8.40	1.70
Availability of a strong support person	13.51	1.44
Successful leadership experience	8.77	1.97
Demonstrated community service	5.21	1.44
Acquired knowledge in a field	3.63	1.12
Fall GPA	2.92	0.98
Spring GPA	2.88	.87

Note. Number of students in Fall = 93; Number of students in Spring = 80.

TABLE 2
Correlation Coefficients between First-Year GPA and Predictor Variables

Variable	Fall GPA	Spring GPA
SAT-verbal scores	.06	.02
SAT-Mathematics scores	.44[**]	.48[**]
Positive self-concept	.10	.15
Realistic self-appraisal system	.32[*]	.31[*]
Coping with racism	−.04	−.10
Preference of long-term goals	.01	−.09
Availability of a strong support person	.15	−.07
Successful leadership experience	−.18	.05
Demonstrated community service	.04	−.08
Acquired knowledge in a field	.08	.12

[*]$p < .01.$ [**]$p < .001.$

Correlational researchers present correlation coefficients in a matrix.

(16)   Table 3 shows the prediction for GPA in Fall and Spring semesters. The multiple regression model explained 26.2% of the variance of Fall GPA. Realistic self-appraisal, successful leadership experience, and SAT-math scores were significant predictors. In the Spring, the regression model accounted for 31.3% of the variance. Realistic self-appraisal, demonstrated community service, and SAT-math scores were significant indicators for Spring GPA.

(17)   Employing discriminant analysis with stepwise procedure, realistic self-appraisal and demonstrated community service were the effective indicators

Correlational researchers use advanced statistics to control for variables and to examine the combination of factors that affect outcomes.

TABLE 3
Multiple Regression Models Predicting Fall and Spring GPAs

Variable		R	R^2	Standardized Beta	t
Fall semester					
All students	Realistic self-appraisal system	.32	.10	.32	2.75[*]
	Successful leadership experience	.39	.15	−.23	3.85[***]
	SAT-math scores	.51	.26	.35	4.44[***]
Spring semester					
All students	Realistic self-appraisal system	.31	.10	.30	2.92[**]
	Demonstrated community service	.38	.15	−.24	−.21[*]
	SAT-math scores	.56	.31	.41	4.31[***]

[*]$p < .01.$ [**]$p < .005.$ [***]$p < .001.$

In the Fall semester, $F = 10.267$; $p < .002$ for the regression model with realistic self-appraisal system; $F = 8.04$, $p < .001$ for the regression model with realistic self-appraisal system and successful leadership experience; $F = 10.54$; $p < .0001$ for the regression model with realistic self-appraisal system, successful leadership experience, and SAT-mathematics score.

In the Spring semester, $F = 8.52$; $p < .005$ for the regression model with realistic self-appraisal system; $F = 6.65$, $p < .002$ for the regression model with realistic self-appraisal system and demonstrated community service; $F = 11.55$; $p < .0001$ for the regression model with realistic self-appraisal system, demonstrated community service, and SAT-math score.

for fall student retention (Wilks's Lambda $= .861$, $\chi^2 = 13.36$, $df = 2$, and $p < .001$). In Spring, no variables were found to explain student retention.

Discussion

Quantitative (18) interpretations compare results with predictions.

The current study revealed both cognitive and noncognitive variables for academic success of Asian American students in the first year of college. SAT-math score and NCQ variables as a group appear to be similarly important indicating the students' GPA. Regarding SAT-math score, previous studies show similar findings for Asian Americans (Fuertes et al., 1994: Sue & Abe, 1988). SAT-verbal score was not a predictor, probably because being a land-grant institution, the studied university was popular for science and technology disciplines. Also, Asian Americans have a tendency to value applied science versus arts and social studies (Sue & Sue, 1990). In addition to their cultural values, Sue and Sue (1990) suggested that other reasons for such a tendency include choosing to study in better-paid fields and struggle with English even after a few generations in the U.S; therefore most Asian American students studied in these majors.

(19)   The noncognitive predictors in the current study explained a higher percentage of variance for student success than did Fuertes et al. (1994). In addition, a major difference between the two studies should be mentioned here. At the institution where the current study was conducted, Asian Americans comprised 3% of the student population, a closer representation of the current U.S. population than the institution where the earlier study was conducted.

(20)   Realistic self-appraisal, successful leadership experience, and demonstrated community service were important predictors of the students' GPA. A realistic self-appraisal system was a consistent predictor for first-year GPA and retention. The need for self-understanding and proper self-evaluation is clear. In regard to a proper self-appraisal system, Asian American students need to understand their minority situation, recognize their level of academic performance and position and be able to cope with the social environment of the campus. They also need to be able to reward themselves appropriately for achievement as well as respond positively to failure or to obstacles such as racism. In Fuertes et al. (1994), a realistic self-appraisal system was also a factor related to first-year academic performance and continual enrollment beyond the sophomore year.

(21)   Successful leadership experience reflects the ability to communicate, engage in a social group, establish relationships in social situations, organize and complete a task in a team. Asian American students who had such experience would adjust better to a university campus than those who did not. In Fuertes et al.'s (1994) study, this factor was not found; however, a similar factor demonstrated community service was found to be an indicator for academic performance.

(22)   Noncognitive variables were related to student retention probably because they helped students cope with reported psychosocial stresses including loneliness, isolation, and anxiety (Abe & Zane, 1990; Solberg et al., 1994; Sue & Zane, 1985) and racism (Delucchi & Do, 1996; Leung, 1990; Tan, 1994). Specifically, minority students who have a realistic self-appraisal system understand their minority situation, recognize the social environment of the campus and understand ways to work through the existing system. Therefore, they are more likely to remain on the same campus.

(23)   Demonstrated community service was another indicator for student retention and academic performance. Community service reflects the ability for the Asian American students to have a sense of belonging and establish

a link to the community. Asian Americans were found to be the most distant group from other ethnic minorities (Abe & Zane, 1990). They experienced problems adjusting to college life such as loneliness, anxiety, and depression (Abe & Zane, 1990; Loo & Rolison, 1986). Being an ethnic minority, Asian Americans need to integrate with the majority and other ethnic minority groups and contribute to the community in order to ease their adjustment and accomplish their academic goals (Sue & Sue, 1990).

(24)   Professional literature reports academic support and student service programs that may enhance academic performance of Asian Americans (House & Wohlt, 1990; Mueller 1993; Tan, 1995). An ethnic minority student in a predominantly White American campus may experience isolation and loneliness (Loo & Rolison, 1986). In the process of integrating to the campus community, they particularly need a person who can help them when they have problems. Mueller (1993) reported a mentor program for Asian Americans and other ethnic minorities that enhanced students' academic and psychosocial development in the first year of college. Tan (1995) found that such mentors could enhance minority student satisfaction about university life and academic performance. This mentor or role model can be a faculty member, a student affairs professional or a peer. Therefore, Asian American students can benefit from student service by being both mentor or mentees. Tan (1995) also found that the Asian American and African American students did not feel their role models had to be from their own ethnic group.

(25)   A tutoring program helped improve Asian American freshmen's cumulative GPA after they had participated in it for a semester (House & Wohlt, 1990). Therefore, faculty and student affairs professionals, particularly those who teach first-year seminars should consider similar programs for Asian American students.

(26)   A few methodological limitations should be noted. First, the current study was based on only one institution and the sample size was relatively small for multiple analyses. Regarding the number and type of analyses, the small sample size increased the risk of Type I error. However, the alpha for all major analyses was comparatively small, below .05 level. Also, the results for the current study seem to be compatible with other studies mentioned in the Discussion and Introduction sections. However, further study with a larger sample is needed to examine the validity of the current findings. Second, this is a 1-year study. Indicators of success for years beyond the freshman year should be explored in future research.

(27)   In conclusion, the current results indicate that both SAT scores and selected noncognitive variables can predict academic performance of Asian American students. However, such information about variations among Asian American subgroups are still lacking. Student affairs professionals should continue to investigate this topic, including differences within Asian American populations. Other noncognitive variables unidentified in this study, yet related to Asian American's college academic performance over 4 years, included positive self-concept, preference of long-term goals, availability of a strong support person, acquired knowledge in a field, and coping with racism (Fuertes et al., 1994). In this regard, longitudinal studies are needed to provide additional information about which noncognitive variables are important for Asian Americans' long-term persistence and success in colleges and universities.

Quantitative research reports use standard, fixed structures and evaluation criteria.

Correspondence concerning this article should be addressed to Siu-Man Raymond Ting, Educational Research and Leadership and Counselor Education, North Carolina State University, 520 Poe Hall, Box 7801, Raleigh, NC 27695-7801: raymond_ting @ncsu.edu

References

Abe, J. S., & Zane, N. W. (1990). Psychological maladjustment among Asian and White American college students: Controlling for confounds. *Journal of Counseling Psychology, 37,* 437–444.

American Council on Education. (1998). *Minorities in higher education.* Washington, DC: Author.

Astin, A. W. (1993). *What matters in college? Four critical years revisited.* San Francisco: Jossey-Bass.

Atkinson, D. R., Morten, G., Sue, D. W. (Eds.). (1993). *Counseling American minorities: A cross-cultural perspective* (5th ed.). Dubuque, IA: W. C. Brown.

Bennet, C., & Okinaka, A. M. (1989, March). *Factors related to persistence among Asian, Black, Hispanic, and White undergraduates at a predominantly White university: Compared between first-and fourth-year cohorts.* Paper presented at the annual meeting of the American Educational Research Association, San Francisco, CA.

Boyer, S. P., & Sedlacek, W. E. (1988). Noncognitive predictors of academic success for international students: A longitudinal study. *Journal of College Student Development, 29,* 218–222.

Chi, I., Lubben, J. E., & Kitano, H. H. (1989). Differences in drinking behavior among three Asian-American groups. *Journal of Studies on Alcohol, 50,* 15–23.

Delucchi, M., & Do. H. D. (1996). The model minority myth and perceptions of Asian Americans as victims of racial harassment. *College Student Journal, 30,* 411–414.

Fuertes, J. N., & Sedlacek, W. E. (1995). Using noncognitive variables to predict the grades and retention of Hispanic students. *College Student Affairs Journal, 14* (2), 30–36.

Fuertes, J. N., Sedlacek, W. E., & Liu, W. M. (1994). Using the SAT and noncognitive variables to predict the grades and retention of Asian-American university students. *Measurement and Evaluation in Counseling and Development, 27,* 74–84.

Greene. (1987, November 18). Asian-Americans find U.S. college insensitive, form campus organizations to fight bias. *The Chronicle of Higher Education,* p. A38–A40.

Healy, P. (1999, December 15). Education Department releases new draft guide to use of tests in admissions. *The Chronicle of Higher Education.* [on-line]. Available: http://www.chronicle.com/daily/99/12/99121501n.htm.

House, J. D., & Wohlt, V. (1990). The effect of tutoring program participation on the performance of academically underprepared college freshmen. *Journal of College Student Development, 31,* 365–370.

Kao, G. (1995). Asian-Americans as model minorities? A look at their academic performance. *American Journal of Education, 103,* 121–159.

Leung, P. (1990). Asian-Americans and psychology: Unresolved issues. *Journal of Training and Practice in Professional Psychology, 4* (1), 3–13.

Loo, C. M., & Rolison, G. (1986). Alienation of ethnic minority students at a predominantly White university. *Journal of Higher Education, 57,* 58–77.

Mau, W. C. (1997). Parental influences on high school students' academic achievement: A comparison of Asian immigrants, Asian-Americans, and White Americans. *Psychology in Schools 34,* 267–277.

Mueller, M. K. (1993). *ALANA Intervention Program,* Port Huron. MI: Saint Clair County Community College. (ERIC Document Reproduction Service No. ED 361 043)

Okutsu, J. K. (1989). Pedagogic "hegemonicide" and the Asian-American student. *Amerasia Journal, 15,* 233–42.

Sedlacek, W. E. (1991). Using noncognitive variables in advising non-traditional students. *NACADA Journal, 11,* 75–82.

Sedlacek, W. E. (1998, Winter). Multiple choices for standardized tests. *Priorities, 10,* 1–15.

Sedlacek, W. E., & Adams-Gaston, J. (1992). Predicting the academic success of student-athletes using SAT and noncognitive variables. *Journal of Counseling and Development, 70* (6), 24–27.

Selingo, J. (1999, December 3). A quiet end to the use of race in college admissions in Florida. *The Chronicle of Higher Education,* p. A 31.

Snyder, T. (1999). *Digest of education statistics, 1998* [On-line]. Available: http://nces.ed.gov/pubsearch/pubsinfo.asp?pubid = 1999036.

Solberg, V. S., Ritsma, S., Davis, B. J., Tata, S. P., & Jolly, A. (1994). Asian-American students' severity of problems and willingness to seek help from university counseling centers: Role of previous counseling experience, gender, and ethnicity. *Journal of Counseling Psychology, 41,* 275–279.

Stone, B. (1990). Prediction of achievement by Asian-Americans and White children. *Journal of School Psychology, 30*(1), 91–99.

Sue, S., & Abe, J. (1988). *Predictors of academic achievement among Asian-American and White students.* (College Board Rep. No. 88–11). New York: College Entrance Examination Board.

Sue, S., & Zane, N. W. (1985). Academic achievement and socioemotional adjustment among Chinese university students. *Journal of Counseling Psychology, 32,* 570–579.

Sue, D. W., & Sue, D. (1990). *Counseling the culturally different: Theory and practice.* (2nd ed.). New York: Wiley.

Tan. D. L. (1994). Uniqueness of the Asian American experience in higher education. *College Student Journal, 28,* 412–421.

Tan, D. (1995). Perceived importance of role models and its relationship with minority student satisfaction and academic performance. *NACADA Journal, 15*(1), 48–51.

Taylor, C. R., & Stern, B. B. (1997). Asian-Americans: Television advertising and the "model minority" stereotype. *Journal of Advertising, 26,* 47–61.

Ting, S. R. (1997). The Excellence-Commitment-and-Effective-Learning (ExCEL) program: A group intervention for academically high-risk students. *NACADA Journal, 17,* 48–51.

Ting, S. R. (1998, Winter). Predicting first-year grades and retention of college students of first-generation and low-income families. *Journal of College Admission, 158,* 14–23.

Ting, S. R., & Robinson, T. L. (1998). First-year academic success: A prediction model combining cognitive and psychosocial variables for European- and African-Americans. *Journal of College Student Development, 39,* 599–610.

Tinto, V. (1993). *Leaving college: Rethinking the causes and cures of student attrition* (2nd ed.). Chicago: University of Chicago Press.

Tracey, T. J., & Sedlacek, W. E. (1981). Conducting student retention research. *National Association of Student Personnel Administrators Field Report, 5*(2), 5–6.

Tracey, T. J., & Sedlacek, W. E. (1984). Noncognitive variables in predicting academic success by race. *Measurement and Evaluation in Guidance, 16,* 171–178.

Tracey, T. J., & Sedlacek, W. E. (1985). The relationship of noncognitive variables to academic success: A longitudinal comparison by race. *Journal of College Student Personnel 26,* 410.

Tracey, T. J., & Sedlacek, W. E. (1987). Predicting college graduation using noncognitive variables by race. *Measurement and Evaluation in Counseling and Development, 19,* 177–184.

Tracey, T. J., & Sedlacek, W. E. (1989). Factor structure of the noncognitive questionnaire: Revised across samples of Black and White college students. *Educational and Psychological Measurement, 49,* 637–648.

U.S. Census Bureau. (1999). *Resident population estimates of the United States by sex, race, and Hispanic origin: April 1, 1990 to August 1, 1999* [on-line]. Available: http://www.census.gov/pubsearcg/pubsinfo.asp?pubid = 1999036.

Wang, Y. Y., & Sedlacek, W. E. (1992). Asian-Americans and student organizations: Attitudes and participation. *Journal of College Student Development, 33,* 214–221.

White, T. J., & Sedlacek, W. E. (1986). Noncognitive predictors: Grades and retention of specially admitted students. *Journal of College Admissions, 3,* 20–23.

Yan, W. & Gaier E. L. (1994). Causal attributions for college success and failure: An Asian-American comparison. *Journal of Cross-Cultural Psychology, 25,* 146–158.

13 Survey Designs

Let's say our high school teacher, Maria, chooses a quantitative survey design for her graduate school research project. Her research question might be: "What factors explain high school students' attitudes toward weapon possession in school?" By using a survey design to answer this question, Maria would seek to understand the attitudes of all high school students in the district in order to describe trends in students' thinking. A survey design can provide an economical and efficient means of gathering data from a large number of students. She would randomly select a sample of students, send them a mailed questionnaire, analyze the results, and generalize results from the sample to the population.

Most people, like Maria, are familiar with surveys. We often receive surveys to record opinions as voters, to register approval of consumer products, and to measure opinions about electoral candidates. To many people, survey research is simply a "survey" instrument, such as a questionnaire or interview. Although we "survey" people using an instrument in educational research, the instrument is only one aspect of a broader procedure of survey designs. Moreover, survey procedures have more uses than only measuring opinions about issues. For example, survey designs are frequently used to:

- describe trends, such as community interest in school bond issues or state or national trends about mandatory student uniform policies
- determine opinions about policy issues, such as whether students should be given a choice of schools to attend
- identify characteristics of a group, such as the years of experience and educational degrees of teachers in public and private schools
- understand important beliefs and attitudes, such as student feelings about AIDS education in middle schools, or college student beliefs about what constitutes abusive behaviors in dating relationships
- identify practices, such as the prevalence of students carrying weapons in middle schools and high schools
- evaluate programs, such as the success of a robotics program in science classes
- follow up on graduates from community colleges 5, 10, and 15 years later to learn about their employment.

With its many applications, survey research is a popular design in education. **Survey research designs** are procedures in quantitative research in which investigators administer a survey to a sample or to the entire population of people in order to describe the attitudes, opinions, behaviors, or characteristics of the population. In this procedure, survey researchers collect quantitative, numeric data using questionnaires (e.g., mailed questionnaires) or interviews (e.g., one-on-one interviews), and statistically analyze the data by describing trends about responses to questions and testing research questions or hypotheses. They also interpret the meaning of the data by relating results of the statistical test back to past research studies.

Survey designs differ from experimental research in that they do not involve a treatment given to participants by the researcher. Because survey researchers do not experimentally manipulate the conditions, they cannot explain as well as experimental researchers can the relationship between the independent and dependent variables. Thus, survey research is seen as less rigorous. Survey studies describe trends in the data rather than offer rigorous explanations. When compared with correlational designs, survey research has much in common. Survey researchers often correlate variables, but their focus is directed more toward learning about a population and less on relating variables or predicting outcomes as is the focus in correlational research.

By the end of this chapter you should be able to:

▶ Identify major events in the historical development of survey research.
▶ Describe the use of cross-sectional and longitudinal survey designs.
▶ Identify the key characteristics of survey designs.
▶ List the steps in conducting survey research.
▶ Identify criteria useful for evaluating survey research.

A BRIEF HISTORY OF SURVEY RESEARCH

Surveys have been widely used in education for many years. Early surveys date back to 1817 when Marc Antoine Jullien de Paris designed a 34-page international survey of national education systems (De Landsheere, 1988). In the 1890s, G. Stanley Hall surveyed children, and by 1907, the Pittsburgh Survey examined social problems including educational issues ranging from educational planning for school buildings to issues of slow-learning children in classrooms (Bogdan & Biklen, 1998).

During the period from World War I to World War II, the modern survey as we know it began to emerge. Factors that contributed to its development were improvements in sampling techniques and the development of different scales of measurement. Surveys found wide application in many social science fields, including marketing research, journalism, public opinion research, and organizations and charities (Neuman, 2000). By mid-century, efforts were underway to establish standardized questions through surveys being undertaken at the U.S. Department of Agriculture. Scales improved through the development of the Likert scale (e.g., strongly agree to strongly disagree). Also, guidelines were written for writing clear questions, standardizing interviewing questions, training interviewers, and checking for consistency among interviewers (Fowler, 1988).

During World War II, surveys examined issues central to the war effort such as the morale of soldiers, production capacity for weapons, and the effectiveness of bombing. Through these studies, survey researchers refined and developed their techniques of large-scale assessments, enabling the emergence of large social research organizations in American universities after the war. For example, social research centers were established at Berkeley (Survey Research Center), at the University of Chicago (National Opinion Research Center), and at the University of Michigan (Institute for Social Research). Also, opinion polling organizations, such as Gallup, Roper, and the Rand Corporation, furthered the understanding of large-scale data collection. The founding of polling and survey organizations, combined with the use of computers, the availability of data archives and storage, and funding from the federal government, helped to establish the popularity of surveys in education by the mid-century (Neuman, 2000).

In recent years, both federal and state governments have funded national and state surveys, such as the Youth Risk Behavior Survey developed by the U.S. Center for Disease Control and Prevention (Valois & McKewon, 1998). Electronic surveys, such as CATI (computer-assisted telephone interviewing), VR (voice recognition), TDE (touchtone data entry), and other approaches represent innovations in self-administered questionnaires that make use of the computer and telephones (Babbie, 1998). Web sites and the Internet are increasingly being used for surveys. Survey researchers can now generate an e-mail survey, place questionnaires on computer disks in word-processing formats, or create a hypertext and place surveys on Web sites (Nesbary, 2000). Electronic surveys and communications will probably revolutionize the use and applications of survey research in the future.

TYPES OF SURVEY DESIGNS

Despite the many applications of surveys today, there are two basic types of research surveys: cross-sectional and longitudinal. Figure 13.1 shows that each type serves a different purpose. Cross-sectional designs are used to collect data that reflect current attitudes, opinions, or beliefs. Longitudinal designs are used to study individuals over a period of time.

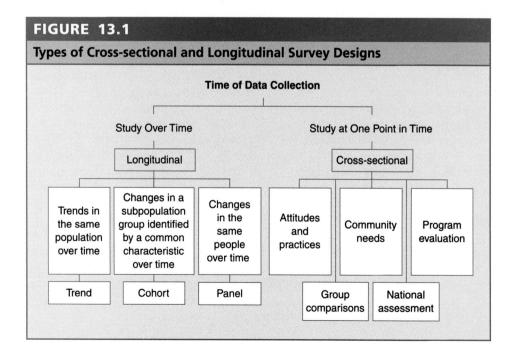

FIGURE 13.1

Types of Cross-sectional and Longitudinal Survey Designs

Cross-Sectional Survey Designs

The most popular form of survey design used in education is a cross-sectional survey design. In a **cross-sectional survey design,** the researcher collects data at one point in time. For example, when middle school children complete a survey about teasing, they are recording data about their present views. This design has the advantage of measuring current attitudes or practices. It also provides information in a short amount of time, such as the time required for administering the survey and collecting the information.

Cross-sectional designs are of several types. A cross-sectional study can *examine current attitudes, beliefs, opinions, or practices.* Attitudes, beliefs, and opinions are ways that individuals think about issues, whereas practices are their actual behaviors. For example, three authors conduct a survey of the practices of reading teachers in elementary schools (Morrison, Jacobs, & Swinyard, 1999). The purpose of the study was to relate the personal, recreational reading of elementary teachers to their literacy instructional practices. Using a list of elementary teachers nationwide (obtained from a professional mailing list company), the researchers mailed 3,600 questionnaires to a probability sample. Of this sample, 52.3% responded to the four-page questionnaire consisting of 21 questions and several items asking for demographic information such as gender, age, and years of teaching experience. Overall, the authors concluded that teachers who saw themselves as readers were more likely than teachers who did not see themselves as readers to use recommended literacy instructional practices (e.g., "read aloud a picture book to your class," p. 88).

Another cross-sectional design *compares two or more educational groups* in terms of attitudes, beliefs, opinions, or practices. These group comparisons may compare students with students, students with teachers, students with parents, or they may compare other groups within educational and school settings. For example, one study compared 98 rural and urban secondary school teachers from 11 school systems in Georgia and North Carolina in terms of their sources of stress and symptoms of burnout (Abel & Sewell, 1999). This group consisted of 52 rural teachers and 46 urban teachers (a non-probability sample), who volunteered to participate in the study. The researchers delivered packets that included two instruments, the Sources of Stress Questionnaire and the Maslach Burnout Inventory, to participating school districts. The teachers mailed the instruments back to the researchers. The statistical analysis of the data showed significantly greater self-reported stress for urban teachers than rural teachers because of poor working conditions and poor staff relations.

A cross-sectional design can *measure community needs* of educational services as they relate to programs, courses, school facilities projects, or involvement in the schools or in community planning. For example, community needs of Hispanic, Spanish-monolingual residents in Florida were studied by Batsche, Hernandez, and Montenegro (1999). The authors felt that survey researchers used methods for reaching Hispanic residents that were more appropriate for non-Hispanic residents. To correct this problem, they designed procedures for an assessment interview survey for identifying needs and priorities for human service programs in the Tampa Bay, Florida, area. For example, they used the name "Hispanic" because it was the accepted term used by the people being surveyed. The instrument allowed individuals to identify themselves both by race and ethnicity. In order to identify the population to study, clubs and organizations were contacted by mail and asked to provide lists of individuals known to be Spanish-monolingual. The researchers first translated the instrument into Spanish and had it reviewed by the local Hispanic community, who translated it back into English to identify discrepancies. The researchers also conducted public meetings to explain the purpose and importance of the needs assessment. Further, the times of the interviews were scheduled to avoid religious events and cultural holidays observed by the Hispanic residents.

Some cross-sectional designs *evaluate a program,* such as a survey that provides useful information to decision makers. In one study, students (and their parents) who had completed a suburban community college enrollment options program responded to surveys evaluating the program (Kiger & Johnson, 1997). This program provided opportunities for high school students to enroll in the community college. A 23-item survey asked the students and their parents their perceptions, such as whether the program helped "formulate long-term educational goals" (p. 691). An overall positive relationship resulted between student and parent perceptions, although their perceptions differed. Parents wanted the student to use the program as a "hands-on" career identification and planning tool, but students saw the program as an opportunity to "try out" the role of being a college student.

A final type of cross-sectional design is a large-scale assessment of students or teachers, such as a *statewide study or a national survey* involving thousands of participants. For example, the Higher Education Research Institute at the University of California at Los Angeles conducted a faculty survey in 1992–93 of all operating institutions of higher education, which totalled 2,582 colleges and universities. The four-page instrument assessed many factors about faculty members and resulted in a sample of 29,771 full-time college and university faculty. Dey and Hurtado (1996) analyzed this national data to examine attitudes toward institutional attempts to regulate forms of on-campus speech. They found that the majority of faculty supported the prohibition of "hate speech" on campus while being much less likely to support the right of administrators to ban extreme speakers.

Longitudinal Survey Designs

An alternative to using a cross-sectional design is to collect data over time using a longitudinal survey design. A **longitudinal survey design** involves the survey procedure of collecting data about trends with the same population, changes in a cohort group or subpopulation, or changes in a panel group of the same individuals over time. Thus, in longitudinal designs, the participants may be different people or the same people. An example of the study of the same people would be research about high school graduates and their current occupation (e.g., student, food service worker, insurance agent), 1 year, 2 years, and 5 years after graduation. Another example of a longitudinal design would be a follow-up with graduates from a program or school to learn their views about their educational experiences. Several types of longitudinal designs are available to the educational researcher, including trend, cohort, and panel designs (Babbie, 1998).

Trend Studies

In some surveys, researchers aim to study changes within some general population over a period of time (Babbie, 1998). This form of longitudinal research is called a trend study. **Trend studies** are longitudinal survey designs that involve identifying a population and examining changes within that population over time. A popular example of this design is the Gallup Poll, which is used during an election to monitor trends in the population of voters from the primary to the final election. Applied to education, this type of study might focus on high school seniors (a population) and study the trends of their attitudes toward dating during the years 2001, 2002, and 2003. In this study, different seniors are studied each year, but they all represent the same population (high school seniors). The researcher can use this data to assess how trends change over time.

Cohort Studies

Rather than studying changing trends in a population, the researcher may be interested in identifying a subgroup in the population, called a cohort, that possesses a common defining characteristic. A **cohort study** is a longitudinal survey design in which a researcher identifies a subpopulation based on some specific characteristic and then studies that subpopulation over time. All members of the cohort must have the common characteristic, such as being 18 years old in the year 2001. If age is that characteristic, the researcher studies the group *as the group ages.* For example, a cohort group of 18-year-olds is studied in the year 2001. Five years later (in 2006), a group of 23-year-olds is studied. (They may or may not be the same individuals studied in 2001.) Five years after that (in 2011), a group of 28-year-olds is studied. While the individuals studied each time might be different, they must have been 18 years old in the year 2001 in order to qualify as representatives of the cohort group.

Panel Studies

A third type of longitudinal survey design is the panel study design. Distinct from both the trend and the cohort study, a **panel study** is a longitudinal survey design in which the researcher examines the same people over time. The high school seniors studied in 1998 will be the same people studied in 2000, 1 year after graduation, and again in 2002, 2 years after graduation. One disadvantage of panel design is that individuals may be difficult to locate, especially 2 years after graduating from high school. The advantage to this type of study, however, is that the individuals studied will be the same each time, allowing the researcher to determine actual changes in specific individuals. Because of this, the panel study is the most rigorous of the three longitudinal designs.

Let's look at an actual study where two authors used a longitudinal panel design to examine how adolescents with learning disabilities made the transition from vocational-technical schools to work (Shapiro & Lentz, 1991). The authors surveyed two groups of high school seniors: one with learning disabilities and one without learning disabilities. They were surveyed at graduation and at 6-, 12-, and 24-month intervals after graduation to learn about their occupational and living experiences. The surveys were sent to seniors who graduated in 1986 and 1987. At graduation, both groups held remarkably similar future plans. Only 50% of the individuals with learning disabilities, however, indicated they had specific future plans at graduation. The group with learning disabilities also had lower rates of enrollment in education after high school than the other group. Further, only about half of all the students studied felt that their training in high school related to their work after graduation.

KEY CHARACTERISTICS OF SURVEY DESIGNS

Whether a survey design is longitudinal or cross-sectional, there are key characteristics of both that will help you design a survey or read and evaluate a published survey study. Survey researchers engage in the processes of:

- sampling from a population
- collecting data through questionnaires or interviews
- designing instruments for data collection
- obtaining a high response rate
- designing and using a mailed questionnaire
- conducting an interview survey

Sampling from a Population

Survey researchers typically select and study a sample from a population and generalize results from the sample to the population. Implied within this statement are several concepts that we first introduced in Chapter 6 on "Specifying the Population and Sample" and that need to be reviewed as they apply to survey research.

We will use the single-stage survey design (rather than the multi-stage, cluster design mentioned in Chapter 6), as a framework for our discussion. There are three terms that need to be defined here: the population, the target population or sampling frame, and the sample. Figure 13.2 shows the differences among these three terms. At the broadest level we have the *population,* in which a group of individuals possesses one characteristic that distinguishes them from other groups. For example, we might have a population made up of high school teachers, individuals who all teach in high schools, or school counselors, individuals who occupy counselor positions in all levels of educational schools. At a more specific level, researchers do not always study an entire population, either because individuals cannot be identified or because lists of names cannot be obtained. (Lists are used when mailing out a questionnaire.) In practical, operational terms, researchers study a *target population* (sometimes called the sampling frame). This is the list or record of individuals in a population that a researcher can actually obtain. For example, a researcher might obtain a list of all secondary high school teachers in one school district. This list constitutes the target population or sampling frame. It is the group of individuals from which the researcher chooses a sample and generalizes results. At the most specific level, researchers select a *sample* from the target population. These are the individuals who are actually studied.

We also learned in Chapter 6 that the target population can be stratified so that the sample consists of individuals with specific characteristics (e.g., an equal number of women and men). The most rigorous form of sampling is to use random sampling, employing a procedure such as using a random numbers table, and, in this process, to select a sample representative of the population so that claims or inferences can be drawn from the sample to the population.

In survey research, it is important to select as large a sample as possible so that the sample will exhibit similar characteristics to the target population. Also, in survey studies it is sometimes difficult to obtain a good list of the target population. For example, individuals who belong to high school gangs may not be easy to identify, nor would lists be readily at-

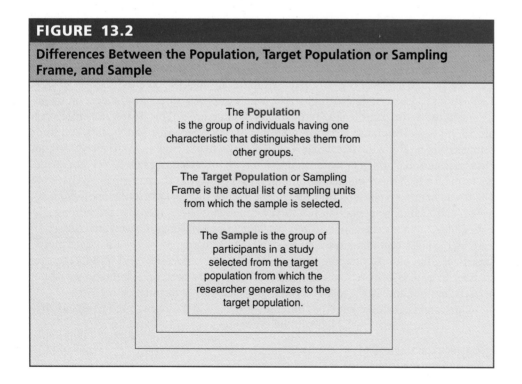

FIGURE 13.2

Differences Between the Population, Target Population or Sampling Frame, and Sample

The **Population**
is the group of individuals having one characteristic that distinguishes them from other groups.

The **Target Population** or Sampling Frame is the actual list of sampling units from which the sample is selected.

The **Sample** is the group of participants in a study selected from the target population from which the researcher generalizes to the target population.

tained for left-handed individuals working as tutors in college writing centers. In many cases, however, the target population can be identified for study, and, after several attempts, a good list of individuals for the target population can be compiled. It is also possible in survey research to study the entire population because it is small (e.g., members of literacy councils in a state) and can be easily identified. This type of survey study, sometimes called a *census study,* permits conclusions to be drawn about the entire population. Therefore, random sampling, hypothesis testing, and the use of inferential statistics are not necessary. For this type of study, survey researchers simply report descriptive statistics about the entire population.

When a sample is selected from a population, however, certain factors may limit a survey researcher's ability to draw valid inference from the sample to the population. Salant and Dillman (1994) identify several factors in good survey research that may compromise drawing these inferences:

▶ *To reduce coverage error,* have a good sampling frame list on which to select individuals. When researchers use a good, complete list, their coverage of the population is said to be adequate and not error-prone.

▶ *To reduce sampling error,* select as large a sample from the population as possible. The larger the sample, the more the participants will be representative of the entire population and reflect attitudes, beliefs, practices, and trends of the population. Recognize that all samples selected will only be estimates of population values. Recall from Chapter 6 that sampling errors occur in all surveys.

▶ *To reduce measurement error,* use a good instrument with clear, unambiguous questions and response options. Such instruments will encourage individuals to respond and answer correctly. Later in this chapter we will discuss how to construct a questionnaire to reduce the possiblity of this error.

▶ *To reduce non-response error,* use rigorous administration procedures to achieve as large a return rate as possible. Later in this chapter we will discuss these procedures.

Collecting Data Through Questionnaires and Interviews

One characteristic of survey research is that many different forms of surveys can be used. Survey researchers collect data using two basic forms: questionnaires and interviews. Researchers need to consider the forms and weigh the advantages and disadvantages of each. These forms can be distinguished based on who completes or records the data on the instrument: the participants (called respondents or interviewees) or the researcher (see Figure 13.3). A **questionnaire** is a form used in a survey design that participants in a study complete and return to the researcher. The participant marks choices to questions and supplies basic personal or demographic information. An **interview survey,** on the other hand, is a form on which the researcher records answers supplied by the participant in the study. The researcher asks a question from an interview guide, listens for answers or observes behavior, and records responses on the survey. The quantitative interview procedures, discussed here, are not to be confused with qualitative interviewing. In *quantitative survey interviews,* the investigator uses a structured or semi-structured interview consisting of mostly closed-ended questions, provides response options to interviewees, and records their responses. In *qualitative survey interviews,* an interviewer asks open-ended questions without response options and listens to and records the comments of the interviewee.

There are several different types of questionnaires and interviews used in quantitative survey research. Here we will highlight the major types used in education:

▶ mailed questionnaires
▶ electronic questionnaires

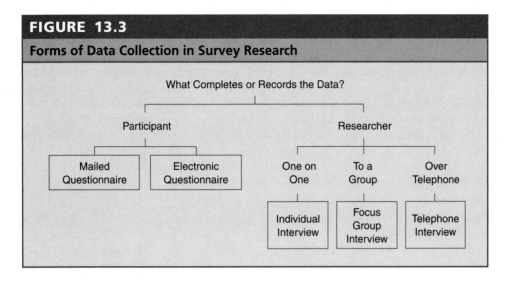

FIGURE 13.3

Forms of Data Collection in Survey Research

- one-on-one interviews
- focus group interviews
- telephone interviews

Mailed Questionnaires

A **mailed questionnaire** is a form of data collection in survey research in which the investigator mails a questionnaire to members of the sample. Researchers might develop their own questionnaire, modify an existing one, or use one that they have located in the literature. The process consists of locating or developing a questionnaire, sending it out to the sample of the population, using repeated contacts with the sample to obtain a high response rate, checking for potential bias in responses, and analyzing the data. (These procedures will be discussed later in this chapter.)

A mailed questionnaire is a convenient way to reach a geographically dispersed sample of a population. The mail facilitates collecting data quickly, often in as little time as 8 weeks from the first mailing to the conclusion of data collection. A mailed questionnaire is economical because it involves only duplication and mailing expenses. The disadvantage of mailed questionnaires is that the individual surveyed may not be personally invested in the study and may decide not to return the instrument. Also, because the researcher does not have a means for explaining questions, participants may misinterpret items on the survey.

Electronic Questionnaires

With increased use of Web sites and the Internet, electronic questionnaires are becoming popular. The **electronic questionnaire** is a survey instrument for collecting data that is available on the computer. Several variations exist, but a popular form is computer-assisted self-interviewing (Babbie, 1998). In this approach, the participant in a study logs onto a computer, uses the Internet or a Web site to locate and download a questionnaire, completes the questionnaire, and sends the completed questionnaire back to the researcher. Other approaches using electronic questionnaires include voice recognition using the telephone keypad and computerized self-administered questionnaires (Babbie, 1998). Electronic surveys provide an easy, quick form of data collection, although their actual use may be limited because not all participants have access to computers or are comfortable using Web sites and the Internet.

One-on-one Interviews

One-on-one interviews are a form of survey data collection. In **one-on-one interviewing in survey research,** investigators conduct an interview with an individual in the sample and record responses to closed-ended questions. The process involves developing or locating an instrument and training the interviewer(s) in good interview procedures. This training consists of learning how to provide instructions during the interview, maintaining confidentiality about the interview, asking the exact question on the interview guide, completing the interview within the time allocated, being courteous, and not interjecting personal opinions into the interview. When multiple interviewers are used, all individuals are trained to use the same procedure so that researcher bias and influence will not intrude into the study.

One-on-one interviews are useful for asking sensitive questions and enabling interviewees to ask questions or provide comments that go beyond the initial questions. Interviews lead to a high response rate because the interviews are scheduled in advance and sample participants typically feel obligated to complete the interview. However, one-on-one interviews do not protect the anonymity of the participant as questionnaires do. Researchers may also prejudice participant answers, either knowingly or unknowingly through comments or body language. Also, not all interviewees are comfortable disclosing information about themselves during the interview.

Focus Group Interviews

An alternative to a one-on-one interview is to administer a survey to a focus group. In quantitative **focus group interviews in survey research,** the researcher locates or develops a survey instrument, convenes a small group of people (typically a group of 4 to 6) who can answer the questions on the instrument, and records their comments to the instrument. For example, this group might consist of parents who are being asked to evaluate a new math or science curriculum in a school. It might also be a group of international students who are asked about their integration into an American university setting. During processes such as these, researchers ask the group questions on an instrument and record or take notes on the group conversation.

Focus groups provide for interaction among interviewees, collection of extensive data, and participation by all individuals in a group (Krueger, 1994). A disadvantage of focus group interviews is that they require the researcher to find consensus on questions so one score can be marked for all individuals in the group. In addition, some individuals may dominate the conversation, leading to responses that do not reflect the consensus of the group.

Telephone Interviews

In **telephone interview surveys,** the researcher records the participant's comments to questions on instruments over the telephone. The researcher develops or locates an instrument, obtains the telephone numbers of participants in the sample, conducts the telephone calls, and asks the participants to answer questions on the instrument. Telephone interviews allow the researcher easy access to interviewees who are geographically dispersed. However, the researcher cannot see any nonverbal communication on the part of the participant. Telephone interviews also involve considerable expense for the telephone calls, and people often dislike them because of their prior personal experiences with calls from survey firms asking for information.

Designing Instruments for Data Collection

When survey researchers design an instrument for data collection, they typically perform the following steps:

1. *They write different types of questions.* These include personal, attitudinal, and behavioral questions; sensitive questions; and closed- and open-ended questions.

2. *They use strategies for good question construction.* This includes using clear language, making sure the answer options do not overlap, and posing questions that are applicable to all participants.
3. *They perform a pilot test of the questions.* This consists of administering the instrument to a small number of individuals and making changes based on their feedback.

Personal, Attitudinal, and Behavioral Questions

It is useful to first consider the general forms of the types of *content* that questions might take on a survey instrument. There are three popular types. *Background questions* (or *demographic questions*) assess the personal characteristics of individuals in your sample. These questions can be easy to answer (i.e., gender) or difficult (i.e., level of income). Here are some examples of background questions:

What is your age? _____
How many years of teaching have you completed? (end of school year) _____

A second group of questions relates to obtaining individual *attitudes or opinions* from individuals in your sample. For example, you might ask:

How much do you agree or disagree with this statement:
Most days I am enthusiastic about being a student.
_____ Strongly agree
_____ Agree
_____ Neither agree or disagree
_____ Disagree
_____ Strongly disagree

A third group of questions can solicit information about the actual *behavior* of individuals in the sample. For example:

Did you take a semester off during any of your 4 years of college?
_____ Yes
_____ No

Sensitive Questions

Some surveys contain sensitive questions that must be developed and used with care. Sensitive question might have to do with:

- sexual behavior (e.g., use of condoms)
- drug and alcohol use (e.g., use of cocaine)
- mental health issues (e.g., paranoid behavior)
- illegal activities (e.g., evading taxes)
- controversial public issues (e.g., same-sex marriages)

Depending on your topic, you may decide to use sensitive questions. If the questions are not tactfully stated, individuals may either over- or underrepresent their views, leading to bias in responses. Several strategies might be used to provide good questions (Neuman, 2000). You might include a sensitive question late in the survey, after the individual has "warmed up" by answering neutral questions and has established some rapport with the researcher. Also, prefatory comments can lead the respondent into the question:

Instead of: Have you ever used marijuana?
You might ask: In past surveys, many men have reported that at some point in their lives they have used marijuana. This could have happened before adolescence, during adolescence, or as an adult. Have you ever smoked marijuana?

Open- and Closed-Ended Questions

You may recall from our discussion about interviewing in Chapter 7 that there are three types of question responses: closed-ended, open-ended, and semi-structured. Although all three are found in survey research, you will typically find closed-ended questions. In **closed-ended questions in surveys,** the researcher poses a question and provides pre-set response options for the participant. A closed-ended question might be:

> There are many reasons why adults wish to get more education. What is your most important reason for coming to adult basic education classes? (Check one.)
> _____ To be able to help my children with their school work
> _____ To get a better job
> _____ To improve myself
> _____ To get a high school equivalency diploma

Here, the author provides a question followed by a limited number of response options. These options need to be mutually exclusive, or distinct from each other, and include the typical responses an individual might provide.

Closed-ended questions such as the example above are practical because all individuals will answer the question using the response options provided. This enables a researcher to conveniently compare responses. They are useful for sensitive questions because participants might feel more comfortable knowing the parameters of response options. Closed-ended questions also provide a means for coding responses or assigning a numeric value and statistically analyzing the data.

There are times, however, when you want to probe a little deeper and explore the many possibilities that individuals might create for a question. In this case, open-ended questions are best. **Open-ended questions in a survey** are questions for which researchers do not provide the response options; the participants provide their own responses to questions. For example:

> Why are you attending adult education classes?
>
> _____
>
> _____

In an open-ended question, the participant supplies an answer. This question does not constrain individual responses, and it opens up the possibilities. It is ideal when the researcher does not know the response possibilities and wants to explore the options. Further, an open-ended question allows a participant to create a response within their cultural and social experiences instead of the researcher's experiences (Neuman, 2000).

On the other hand, open-ended questions have drawbacks of coding and analysis. The researcher needs to categorize the responses into themes, a process that may take considerable time. Open-ended responses cannot easily be statistically analyzed like closed-ended responses unless the researcher develops some system for coding the responses into numeric categories (e.g., "getting a better job" was mentioned 15 times).

One further option is the use of **semi-closed-ended questions in a survey.** This type of question has all the advantages of open- and closed-ended questions. The technique is to ask a closed-ended question and then ask for additional responses in an open-ended question. For example:

> There are many reasons why adults wish to further their education. What is your most important reason for coming to adult basic education classes? (Check one.)
> _____ To be able to help my children with their school work
> _____ To get a better job
> _____ To improve myself

_____ To get a high school equivalency diploma

_____ Other _____

_____

This question provides the typical response categories to the question, but it also allows respondents to write in answers that may not fit the response choices. While it also provides limited open-ended information to encourage responses, it does not overburden the researcher with information that needs to be coded.

Question Construction

As you select an instrument or develop one of your own, pay attention to the quality of the questions. Using good questions helps participants feel that they understand the question and can provide meaningful answers. Good questions are clear and unambiguous and will not confuse the participants. They also show respect for the participant by being sensitive to gender, class, and cultural needs of participants (see Chapter 10 on "Writing Sensitively"). For example, in the community needs survey mentioned earlier (Batsche, Hernandez, & Montenegro, 1999), the researchers used the term "Hispanic" out of respect for the term the Spanish-monolingual residents called themselves. By using good questions, you are encouraging the participant to complete the instrument.

When you construct questions for a survey questionnaire or interview, be sure the answers fit the questions, include major response options, and do not overlap. These strategies for constructing good questions are identified in Table 13.1. First, read the poor question. Next, determine the problem. Then, read the improved question. When you write questions (or review those provided by others), you might assess them in terms of whether you have written a clear question and a clear response, and whether you have asked questions that are within the participant's ability to answer. A review of these potential question construction problems and some solutions will provide guidance for survey development.

▶ *The question is unclear.* This usually occurs because words are vague or imprecise. Identify the unclear or vague words and replace them with words understood by participants in the study.

▶ *There are multiple questions.* Here, the question actually contains two or more questions, called a double- or triple-barreled question. Reduce the multiple questions to a single question.

▶ *The question is wordy.* When the question is too long, cut out unnecessary words to simplify and shorten the question. Look for excessive use of prepositions (e.g., more than three) or qualifying statements that lengthen the question.

▶ *The question is negatively worded.* If the question contains one or more negatives, such as "should not," the meaning becomes unclear. Restate the question in a positive way.

▶ *The question includes jargon.* Jargon may not be familiar to all participants in a study. Eliminate the jargon and use words familiar to all participants.

▶ *There are overlapping responses.* This may lead to confusion when answering a question. Make sure that the response options do not overlap by creating distinct options.

▶ *There are unbalanced response options.* In this case, the responses may be unbalanced in terms of naturally occurring intervals. Response options may start with an "importance" word (e.g., "very important") and end with an "extent" word (e.g., "to a little extent"), rather than a matching adjective (e.g., "not important"). Decide on a single response option and use it consistently for all response categories for a question.

▶ *There is a mismatch between the question and the answers.* The responses may not match the "action" word used in the question. Identify the verb or adjective in the question

TABLE 13.1

Common Problems in Item Construction in Survey Designs

Example of a Poor Question	Problem	Example of an Improved Question
Do you support gun control? _____ Yes _____ No _____ Don't know	Unclear question because of vague words	Do you believe that guns do not belong in schools? _____ Yes _____ No _____ Don't know
Do you believe that guns and knives do not belong in schools? _____ Yes _____ No _____ Don't know	Two or more questions	Do you believe that knives do not belong in schools? _____ Yes _____ No _____ Don't know
Whenever violence occurs in schools, weapons are typically found in school lockers. Do you believe that students should have guns in their lockers? _____ Yes _____ No _____ Don't know	Wordy or lengthy questions	Should students have guns in their lockers? _____ Yes _____ No _____ Don't know
Students should not carry weapons and not have them in their lockers. Do you agree? _____ Strongly agree _____ Agree _____ Undecided _____ Disagree _____ Strongly disagree	Question contains negatives	Should students have guns in their lockers? _____ Yes _____ No _____ Don't know
Should students pack a 45 at school? _____ Yes _____ No _____ Don't know	Question contains jargon	Should students carry a handgun at school? _____ Yes _____ No _____ Don't know
How many times have you seen a student carry a handgun? _____ 0 times _____ 1–2 times _____ 2–3 times _____ More than 3 times	Response categories overlap	How many times have you seen a student carry a handgun? _____ 0 times _____ 1–2 times _____ 3–4 times _____ More than 4 times
To what extent do you feel that handguns are a problem at your school? _____ A great extent _____ Some _____ Not very important _____ Not a problem	Unbalanced response options	To what extent do you feel that handguns are a problem at your school? _____ A great extent _____ Some extent _____ Little extent

TABLE 13.1

Common Problems in Item Construction in Survey Designs (continued)

Example of a Poor Question	Problem	Example of an Improved Question
To what extent do you feel that handguns are a problem at your school? _____ Very important _____ Important _____ Little importance	Mismatch between the question and the responses	To what extent do you feel that handguns are a problem at your school? _____ A great extent _____ Some extent _____ Little extent
How often have you seen students carry semi-automatic weapons at school? _____ None _____ 1 time _____ 2 times _____ 3 or more times	Respondent does not have understanding to answer question	How often have you seen students carry a rifle at school? _____ None _____ 1 time _____ 2 times _____ 3 or more times
How many students have you seen carrying guns at school? _____ 1 student _____ 2 students _____ 3 students _____ More than 3 students	Not all respondents can answer the question—branching needed	Have you seen students carrying guns at school? _____ Yes _____ No →If Yes, how many students? _____ 1 student _____ 2 students _____ 3 students _____ More than 3 students

that will be the basis for the response options and create options using this word. (For example, if the question says "to what extent," the answer will say "a great extent.")

- *The question includes overly technical language.* When this occurs, the respondent may not have the level of understanding needed to respond to the question. Simplify the question so that all individuals will know the meaning of the words and can respond to the question.
- *Not all questions are applicable to all participants.* If some participants cannot answer the question, include "branching" or "contingency questions." These questions follow the original question and provide options to include all participants.

Pilot Testing the Questions

After good questions have been developed using principles of question construction, a researcher pilot tests the questions. This helps determine that the individuals in the sample are capable of completing the survey and that they can understand the questions. A **pilot test** of a questionnaire or interview survey is a procedure in which a researcher makes changes in an instrument based on feedback from a small number of individuals who complete and evaluate the instrument. The participants in the pilot test provide written comments directly on the survey, and the researcher modifies or changes the survey to reflect those concerns. Since the pilot group provides feedback on the questionnaire, they are excluded from the final sample for the study.

For example, a survey of 100 middle school students' attitudes toward school might begin with a pilot test of an instrument with 50 questions. In this pilot test, the researcher selects 15 students to complete the instrument. The investigator then asks them to mark any problems on the survey, such as poorly worded questions, responses that do not make sense, or if it takes an excessive amount of time to complete the instrument. Based on student feedback, the researcher then revises the instrument before sending it out to the sample in the study.

Obtaining a High Response Rate

Survey researchers seek high response rates from participants in a study so that they can have confidence in generalizing the results to the population under study. When using interviews, the response rate is high because individuals interviewed typically consent to the interview in advance. However, when questionnaires are used, the number of responses returned (through mail or electronically) will vary. In either case, survey researchers place emphasis on obtaining a high response rate to their questionnaire or interview.

Response Rates for Mailed Questionnaires

As mentioned above, a high response rate creates a stronger claim in generalizing results from the sample to the population. A **response return rate** is the percentage of questionnaires that are returned from the participants to the researcher. In many survey studies reported in leading educational journals, the response rate for mailed questionnaires is often cited as 50% or better. However, this rate will fluctuate depending on proper notification, adequate follow-up procedures, respondent interest in the study, the quality of the instrument, and use of incentives.

Researchers use several strategies to encourage high return rates. One is to *prenotify participants* that they will receive a questionnaire. Individuals are sent an introductory letter telling them that a survey will be mailed in 2 weeks and asking for their permission to be studied. Another strategy is to *use good follow-up procedures*. Figure 13.4 shows a three-step procedure that might be used.

1. Mail out the original questionnaire.
2. Follow it 2 weeks later with a second questionnaire to the individuals who have not responded (called non-respondents).
3. After another 2 weeks, send a postcard to the non-respondents reminding them to complete the questionnaire.

Although additional steps might be taken, this three-step process should help you attain a good return rate. The time period for each notification will vary, of course, depending on

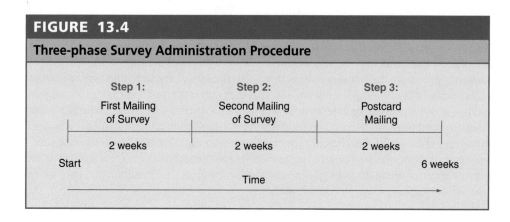

FIGURE 13.4

Three-phase Survey Administration Procedure

Step 1:	Step 2:	Step 3:
First Mailing of Survey	Second Mailing of Survey	Postcard Mailing
2 weeks	2 weeks	2 weeks

Start

6 weeks

Time

the study. For most questionnaires mailed within the United States, however, this format should allow the researcher to conclude data collection in 6 weeks.

Another way to encourage a high response rate is to *study a problem of interest* to the population under study. If individuals in the sample are interested in the issue, they will be more apt to complete the survey. Also, *using a brief instrument* usually encourages a high return rate. Typically, a three-page instrument will take less than 15 minutes to complete.

A final strategy is to *consider the use of incentives* to encourage individuals to return the instrument. Studies show mixed results on the impact of incentives, even small ones like giving enough money for a cup of coffee (Babbie, 1998). As a researcher, you need to weigh the costs of incentives against their potential help with returns. In many cases, survey researchers combine many of the strategies mentioned so far—prenotification, follow-up procedures, and clear instrument constructions—with modest incentives to encourage high returns.

Response Bias

With return rate, the key issue is not necessarily how many people returned an instrument, but whether those that *did* return it were biased in their responses. **Response bias** occurs in survey research when the responses do not accurately reflect the views of the sample and the population. For example, the individuals who return a questionnaire may be overly negative or positive. Thus, survey researchers monitor their returns to assess whether they display bias. This approach is called wave analysis. **Wave analysis** is a procedure to check for response bias in which investigators group returns by intervals (e.g., each week) and check to see if the answers to a few select questions change from the first week to the final week in a study, indicating response bias. Individuals responding in the final week of survey administration are as close to non-returns or non-respondents as possible. However, their responses should be similar (i.e., and not biased) to those returning instruments in the first week. If they differ, researchers report that the responses may be biased and not representative of the sample and the population.

Planning and Designing a Mailed Questionnaire

Because of the popularity of mailed questionnaires for student research projects, they deserve special attention. We will focus on three aspects of using mailed questionnaires:

- a cover letter to invite participants to complete the questionnaire
- the form and construction of the questionnaire
- statistical procedures typically used to analyze data from a mailed questionnaire

We will use a mailed questionnaire from VanHorn-Grassmeyer (1998) as a specific example. VanHorn-Grassmeyer (1998) studied 119 individuals new to the field of student affairs (e.g., student activity leaders) in colleges and universities in the central United States and Canada. Her purpose was to explore the perceptions, attitudes, and behaviors of professionals regarding their professional practices. As one aspect of her data collection, she mailed a self-designed questionnaire to the participants. This instrument consisted of five parts:

1. a cover letter
2. closed-ended questions asking participants about their background (i.e., demographic questions)
3. closed-ended questions addressing practices or behaviors (e.g., I claim responsibility when I've made a "bad call" professionally) and attitudes (e.g., I benefit from collaborative reflection with colleagues)
4. open-ended questions permitting respondents to add their perceptions (e.g., In your opinion, what defines a competent student affairs professional?)
5. closing instructions thanking the participant for taking part in the study

This cover letter and mailed questionnaire comprised a five-page packet, which can be seen in Figures 13.5 and 13.6 as they were originally reported in VanHorn-Grassmeyer's dissertation. Inspecting these examples can provide useful ideas for designing your own cover letter and questionnaire.

A Cover Letter

A major component of a mailed questionnaire consists of a cover letter inviting the participant to take part in the study and to complete the instrument. The same type of cover letter could be used, as well, for an interview. When we inspect the cover letter in Figure 13.5, we find these major elements:

> *Importance of participant:* To encourage individuals to complete the questionnaire, they need to know why they are being sent the instrument. The first few sentences indicate the importance of recipients and the value of their response. It is often helpful to begin a cover letter with this statement, as illustrated in this example.
>
> *Purpose of the study:* Include a statement indicating, succinctly, the intent or purpose of the study. This statement not only informs the participant about the nature of the study, it also fulfills an important "informed consent" (see Chapter 6 on "Obtain Informed Consent") provision of identifying the purpose of the study for participants.
>
> *Assurances of confidentiality:* Also, to comply with informed consent and to be ethical, the investigator assures the individual of confidentiality (i.e., not identifying individuals specifically).
>
> *Sponsorship:* The cover letter includes the advisor's name as well as the institution where VanHorn-Grassmeyer works. In addition, the letter might have been written on letterhead stationery to add additional sponsorship.
>
> *Completion time and returns:* Two procedural items also need to be addressed: the amount of time the survey will take to be completed and the process for returning the instrument to the author.

Questionnaire Construction

Examine Figure 13.6 to see a complete mailed questionnaire. This instrument contains features of good questionnaire construction. It is short and encourages a busy professional to return it. The instrument begins with demographic or personal questions that respondents can easily answer and, in the process of answering them, they become committed to completing the form. For variety, the author used different types of closed-ended questions, from checking the appropriate response (e.g., "years of employment") to a Likert scale ("strongly disagree" to "strongly agree"), to a frequency scale ("never" to "often"). The questionnaire also contains open-ended items to encourage participants to elaborate on their experiences and definitions (e.g., "What defines a competent student affairs professional?"). It also contains a pleasing layout with much "white space" between the questions and the use of one scale (e.g., "strongly disagree" to "strongly agree") for multiple questions so that responses do not have to be repeated and space can be conserved.

Data Analysis of a Research Questionnaire

When comparing groups or relating variables, the statistical analysis of questionnaire data extends beyond simple descriptive analysis. Examine the steps identified in Figure 13.7. These steps include survey analysis typically used for analyzing mailed questionnaire data. It includes reporting response rate and checking for bias in responses. The researcher also descriptively reports aggregate responses to each item on the questionnaire. This process helps to discern general patterns of responses and variation (variance and standard deviation) in results. Typically, researchers using mailed questionnaires also correlate all of the

FIGURE 13.5

Sample Cover Letter

Cover Letter Components	
	July 10, 1996
	Dear Colleague,
Importance of participant	As a relative newcomer to the profession of student affairs, you undoubtedly have ways in which you enhance your practice. Graduate preparation programs, associations, and seasoned professionals must be aware of the strategies that are most useful to you and other professionals in order to help promote professional development, competency, and commitment to the field. Your response to this survey can greatly enhance our understanding.
Purpose of the study	I am conducting this research to explore how professionals new to the field of student affairs enhance their practice. I want to measure the extent to which new professionals use individual and collaborative (that is, in interaction with other professionals) strategies including reflection, and opportunities for development. I will also measure how new professionals view their own skills and knowledge. My population is new professionals in the west-central part of the U.S. and Canada.
Assurances	Your participation in this research is, of course, voluntary. Your confidentiality and anonymity are assured. Return of the survey to me is your consent for your responses to be compiled with others. Although the survey is coded to allow for follow-up with non-respondents, you will not be individually identified with your questionnaire or responses. Please understand that use of this data will be limited to this research, as authorized by the University of Nebraska at Lincoln, although results may ultimately (and hopefully!) be presented in formats other than the dissertation, such as journal articles or conference presentations. You also have the right to express concerns to me at the number below, my major professor Dr. John
Sponsorship	Creswell at the UNL Department of Educational Psychology address shown above, or the UNL Institutional Review Board.
Completion time	I greatly appreciate your participation in this research. *The survey will take approximately 15–20 minutes to complete.* **Please return the survey within two**
Returns	**weeks (by July 25)** *in the enclosed, self-addressed, stamped envelope.* This will save a follow-up mailing to you.
	If you have been in the field for more than five years, please note as much on survey item #1 and return the entire instrument to me.
	Thank you for your interest and participation in this study. I genuinely appreciate your time.
	Sincerely,
Sponsorship	Kimberly VanHorn Grassmeyer Associate Director, Student Assistance Center University of Kansas, Lawrence KS 66045 913.864.4064; kgrassmeyer@ukans.edu

Source: Reprinted with permission from Kimberly VanHorn Grassmeyer, Ph.D.

FIGURE 13.6

ENHANCING PRACTICE:
NEW PROFESSIONALS IN STUDENT AFFAIRS

I. DEMOGRAPHICS:

1. Years of employment in Student Affairs:
   ___ a. current Graduate Student
   ___ b. 0 up to 2 years
   ___ c. more than 2, up to 5 years
   ___ d. more than 5 years
   If d, do not complete remainder of survey.
   Return in envelope provided. Thank you.

2. Graduate program practical experiences *(check any of the following that apply to your experience):*
   ___ a. assistantship in student services (paid training experience)
   ___ b. practica in student services (unpaid training experience)
   ___ c. mentoring relationship with a mid- or senior-level administrator
   ___ d. peer group interactions such as case studies, problem-solving
   ___ e. peer group interactions more social in nature
   ___ f. other out-of-class experience: _____

3. National professional associations in which you are a member *(rank 1-3 in order of importance to you):*
   ___ a. AAHE   ___ d. AERA   ___ g. NASPA
   ___ b. ACPA   ___ e. ASHE   ___ h. NAWE / NAWDAC
   ___ c. ACUHO   ___ f. NACA   ___ i. Other: _____

4. Gender: ___ a. female   ___ b. male

II. PROFESSIONAL PRACTICE:

1. Indicate the amount of institutional funding you received in the past academic year for participation in professional development conferences and workshops off-site:
   ___ a. none   ___ c. $101 to $250   ___ e. $501 to $1000
   ___ b. less than $100   ___ d. $251 to $500   ___ f. more than $1000

2. Indicate the amount of personal funds you spent in the past academic year for participation in professional development conferences and workshops off-site:
   ___ a. none   ___ c. $101 to $250   ___ e. $501 to $1000
   ___ b. less than $100   ___ d. $251 to $500   ___ f. more than $1000

3. What professional development costs *(full or partial)* does your institution absorb for you?
   (check any of the following that apply):
   ___ a. association membership dues for more than one association
   ___ b. association membership dues for only one association
   ___ c. on-site seminars and workshops
   ___ d. staff retreats
   ___ e. subscriptions to professional journals and newsletters
   ___ f. release time for participation in programmed activities
   ___ g. release time for personal reflection and renewal
   ___ h. release time for courses related to my work
   ___ i. tuition assistance for courses related to my work

4. To what extent do you feel your graduate program prepared you for your work in student affairs?
   ACADEMICALLY: ___ a. not at all   EXPERIENTIALLY: ___ a. not at all
       ___ b. a little bit   ___ b. a little bit
       ___ c. fairly well   ___ c. fairly well
       ___ d. very well   ___ d. very well

FIGURE 13.6

Sample Mailed Questionnaire (continued)

Enhancing Practice Survey, p.2

Using the following 1 - 5 scale, please indicate by circling the most correct response, the degree to which you agree with the statements listed below:

1	2	3	4	5
strongly disagree	disagree	neutral	agree	strongly agree

1 2 3 4 5   5. I have a strong personal commitment to my professional growth and development.

6. Regarding my professional practice, I value the opinions of my:
1 2 3 4 5   a. colleagues
1 2 3 4 5   b. mentor(s)
1 2 3 4 5   c. graduate program peers

1 2 3 4 5   7. When I reflect on my practice, I know more than I'm really able to describe.

1 2 3 4 5   8. I believe my instincts compare favorably with colleagues I respect.

1 2 3 4 5   9. I have a responsibility to contribute to the development of other student affairs professionals.

1 2 3 4 5   10. My institution expects continued professional development of its staff.

1 2 3 4 5   11. I know that I need to consciously enhance my professional practice.

1 2 3 4 5   12. I like to talk with other professionals about my decision-making and professional practice.

1 2 3 4 5   13. I know most of what I will need to guide my practice.

1 2 3 4 5   14. I feel a sense of connection to the field of Student Affairs.

1 2 3 4 5   15. I have a professional responsibility to continue to learn and develop in my daily work.

1 2 3 4 5   16. I benefit from collaborative reflection with colleagues.

1 2 3 4 5   17. I believe my institution should ensure that I grow as a professional.

1 2 3 4 5   18. I consider myself to be a strong student affairs administrator.

1 2 3 4 5   19. I expect to continue working in student affairs for at least ten years.

20. I receive encouragement for continuing professional growth and development from:
1 2 3 4 5   a. institutional colleagues
1 2 3 4 5   b. my senior student affairs offficer

1 2 3 4 5   21. I still have a lot to learn from experience and practice.

22. I continue to learn a great deal from my:
1 2 3 4 5   a. colleagues
1 2 3 4 5   b. mentor(s)
1 2 3 4 5   c. graduate program peers

1 2 3 4 5   23. I have a sense of self-efficacy and confidence in my work.

FIGURE 13.6

Sample Mailed Questionnaire (continued)

Enhancing Practice Survey, p.3

1	2	3	4	5
strongly disagree	disagree	neutral	agree	strongly agree

1 2 3 4 5   24. I maintain a strong network of or connection to:
1 2 3 4 5   a. professional colleagues
1 2 3 4 5   b. mentor(s)
1 2 3 4 5   c. graduate program peers

1 2 3 4 5   25. I believe my professional development is my responsibility.

1 2 3 4 5   26. I prefer close supervision over my activities at this point in my career.

1 2 3 4 5   27. I have learned about as much as I can of student development theory.

1 2 3 4 5   28. I am able to function autonomously in my professional role.

1 2 3 4 5   29. I have a professional responsibility to promote/advance the student affairs field.

Using the following 1 - 5 scale, please indicate by circling the most correct respose, how regularly you practice the activities listed below:

1	2	3	4	5
never	rarely	sometimes	regularly	often

1 2 3 4 5   30. At least one of my institutional job performance measures (e.g. annual review, annual goals) includes an expectation for professional growth and development.

1 2 3 4 5   31. I read professional journals and periodicals to keep current in the field.

1 2 3 4 5   32. I make time for collaborative (with other professionals) reflection.

1 2 3 4 5   33. I claim responsibility when I've made a "bad call" professionally.

1 2 3 4 5   34. I consciously think back to and apply theory as I go about decision-making and professional practice.

1 2 3 4 5   35. I attend conferences even when I'm expected to personally absorb the majority of the cost of attendance.

1 2 3 4 5   36. I utilize the expertise of others (listed in a-b-c) to enhance my professional practice:
1 2 3 4 5   a. colleagues
1 2 3 4 5   b. mentor(s)
1 2 3 4 5   c. graduate program peers

1 2 3 4 5   37. After taking action or employing a strategy, I reflect to determine whether it was appropriate, and how I might respond differently next time.

1 2 3 4 5   38. I second-guess my actions in professional situations.

1 2 3 4 5   39. I seek out opportunities to share my professional knowledge and learning with other professionals.
      Indicate how you have done so:
      ___ a. write for publication in professional journals, newsletters, etc.
      ___ b. present sessions at retreats, workshops and/or conferences
      ___ c. collaborate with others who seek advice and assistance
      ___ d. other methods: _____

FIGURE 13.6

Sample Mailed Questionnaire (continued)

Enhancing Practice Survey, p.4

1	2	3	4	5
never	rarely	sometimes	regularly	often

1 2 3 4 5   40. I serve on institution-wide committees, task forces, ad hoc groups, etc.

1 2 3 4 5   41. I seek out opportunities to enhance my professional knowledge and practice.

1 2 3 4 5   42. I attend professional association conferences (regional/state or national).
For this question only: 1=never, 2=rarely, 3=some years, 4=every year, 5=more than one each year

1 2 3 4 5   43. I feel confident when making particularly difficult professional decisions.

1 2 3 4 5   44. I record my thoughts about professional practice in a journal/diary.

1 2 3 4 5   45. I consciously think back to and apply personal experiences as I go about decision-making and professional practice.

1 2 3 4 5   46. I make time for individual professional reflection.

III. SHORT ANSWER QUESTIONS:
Please respond briefly to the following questions, *using an additional sheet if necessary:*

47. Think back on one of the most difficult professional decisions you've made in your current position, one that involved a situation with others (colleagues, students, supervisees). Please describe how you reached that decision, what factors you considered, who, if anyone, you consulted with beforehand, and whether & how you processed it afterward.

48. In your opinion, what defines a competent student affairs professional? Would you describe yourself in those terms? Why or why not?

THANK YOU FOR YOUR PARTICIPATION AND CANDID RESPONSES.
Please return your survey in the enclosed stamped envelope before July 22nd.

Source: Reprinted with permission from Kimberly VanHorn Grassmeyer, Ph.D.

FIGURE 13.7

Checklist for Analyzing Questionnaire Data

_____ Step 1. Identify response rate and response bias.

      _____ Develop table for percent of responses to the survey.

      _____ Develop table for the wave analysis response bias.

_____ Step 2. Descriptively analyze the data to identify general trends.

      _____ Calculate and present a table of descriptive statistics (mean, variance, and range) for each question on the instrument.

      _____ Analyze data to develop a demographic profile of the sample (analyze questions about personal factors).

      _____ Analyze data to provide answers to descriptive questions in the study (if any).

_____ Step 3. Write the report presenting the descriptive results or use advanced statistics.

      _____ Develop scales by combining questions on the instrument (i.e., correlate items using the statistical procedure of factor analysis).

      _____ Check for the reliability of the scores on the scales (i.e, use a coefficient of internal consistency).

      _____ Check for the validity of the scores on scales (or factors)(i.e., use factor analysis).

      _____ Analyze data using inferential statistics to address research questions or hypotheses (i.e., comparing groups, relating variables).

questions (see Chapter 12 on "Correlation Matrix") and attempt to build scales that reflect multiple questions. As with all instruments, scores need to be reliable and valid, and statistical procedures such as internal consistency checks (e.g., the alpha reliability statistic) and validity (e.g., factor analysis) represent means for making these assessments. Finally, the researcher tests hypotheses or research questions using inferential statistics.

Conducting an Interview Survey

Instead of a mailed survey, researchers might collect quantitative data using an interview survey instrument. In using this form of data collection, we need to know the stance of the interviewer, recognize the importance of training interviewers (if there is more than one), and know the general steps in administering this form of data collection. To understand this process, we will use a telephone interview as an example.

Stance of the Interviewer

Interview surveys are used less frequently than mailed questionnaires in educational research. Interview procedures often involve the need for the researcher to establish rapport with and gain the cooperation of the interviewee. This role is facilitated by initial requests for an interview consisting of information included in the cover letter. During an interview, the researcher should remain neutral and should not share opinions (e.g., "I think that budget cutting is a good idea, too.") It is also important to use a positive tone of questioning and to have a neutral appearance.

Training of Interviewers

If more than one interviewer is involved in a research project, training is needed for each person. This training might consist of a role-playing demonstration by an experienced researcher and a practice interview by the individual researchers who will be conducting the interviews. It is important during this training for interviewers to become familiar with the questions so that they will know if the responses match the questions. Training also covers potential interruptions during interviews or questions interviewees might have about the interview. Problems can arise during an interview, such as the interviewer:

- does not ask the questions in order (e.g., question 3 is asked before question 2)
- intentionally subverts the process because of disinterest in the topic (e.g., the interviewer does not take time to probe on questions)
- brings certain expectations to the interview about how the individuals will answer (e.g., the interviewer prefaces the question with "I think you already know the answer to this . . .")
- dresses or appears inappropriately for the interview (e.g., wears shorts when the interviewee is dressed in a suit)
- is disrespectful by not using names the interviewee wants to be called (e.g., referring to the individual as "Latino" instead of "Hispanic")

Steps in Interviewing

The steps in conducting an interview involve obtaining an interview survey to use and training individual interviewees (if more than one person will be conducting the interviews). Then the researcher gains access to the participant through a formal invitation, such as a cover letter, and establishes a time and place to conduct the interview. During the interview, the survey researcher asks questions, indicates the response options to questions, and records participant answers. The pace of the interview is set to be comfortable for the interviewee. If open-ended questions are asked, the interviewer writes down answers to the questions (or records them on tape). The interview ends with the researcher thanking the individual for the interview and telling the participant what the next step will be in the study. After the interview, the researcher may want to write down comments that help explain the data, such as the demeanor of the interviewee or specifics about the situation (e.g., "It was so noisy I could hardly hear at times."). The interviewer might also record any personal feelings about the interview (e.g., "I felt uneasy during this interview and perhaps did not probe as much as I could have.").

A Telephone Interview Guide

An example of a telephone interview guide is shown in Figure 13.8. This interview guide was for a telephone interview with 200 academic department chairpersons surveyed to understand how chairpersons assisted faculty in their units (Creswell, Wheeler, Seagren, Egly, & Beyer, 1990). Consisting of 25 questions, each interview lasted, on average, about 45 minutes and all interviews were audio-taped. Six interviewers assisted in the process of data collection and their training consisted of a demonstration and a practice interview. This guide was constructed to include:

- introductory remarks to help establish rapport and direction for the interview (e.g., the amount of time required)
- clearly marked boxes with instructions for each question in the interview so that each interviewer on the research team would ask the same question
- closed-ended response options for each question with space between questions permitting the interviewer to write in additional comments
- numbers in parentheses to indicate the column number for coding the response into a data grid of a computer file for statistical analysis (see Chapter 8 on "Inputting Data")

FIGURE 13.8

Sample Telephone Interview Guide

Structured Interview Schedule A

Interviewer's Code Sheet

Pre-Interview Information

    Interviewer's ID _____   (1–2)
    Institutional Code No. _____   (3–5)
    Date of Interview _____   (6–10)
    Discipline Code (Carnegie) for Interviewee _____   (11–12)
    Gender of Interviewee (1) Female _____ (2) Male _____   (13)

[Note to interviewer: Mark # on your tape counter for potentially interesting quotes.]

Interview Information

Interviewer's Introduction

> We appreciate your willingness to be interviewed today. As we indicated earlier, the purpose of our project is to interview department chairs (or their institutional equivalent) who are considered exceptional in assisting faculty on college and university campuses and to identify specific ways in which they enhance the professional growth and development of faculty in their units. This project is being sponsored by the Lilly Endowment and TIAA-CREF, and the information will be used in the preparation of a practical handbook.
>
> The interview should last from 30 to 40 minutes. In our earlier communication with you, we described the nature of our interview questions. Should we go over the question areas at this time? (Pause for response.)

4. How were you selected?   (25)
    (1) National search _____
    (2) Administrative appointment _____
    (3) Elected by faculty _____
    (4) Other _____

5. Please tell me some information about your appointment.

    Do you have a specific length of appointment in calendar years? (Probe: reappointed?)
    (1) Yes, # of years _____
    (2) No _____
    (3) Uncertain _____   (26–27)

    If yes, is this length typical on your campus?
    (1) Yes _____
    (2) No _____
    (3) Uncertain _____   (28)

    Do you serve at the pleasure of faculty in your unit or administrators?
    (1) Faculty _____
    (2) Administrators _____
    (3) Some combination _____   (29)

6. How long do you expect to stay in your current position?
    [Interviewer: Cite reasons where possible.]

    (1) Don't know _____
    (2) Certain number of years _____
    (3) Up to my dean _____
    (4) As long as I want _____
    (5) Up to the faculty _____

STEPS IN CONDUCTING SURVEY RESEARCH

The steps in the process of conducting survey research follow the general process of research identified in Chapters 2 through 10. Survey steps, however, address primarily the procedures for collecting data, analyzing data, and writing the final report.

Step 1. Decide If a Survey Is the Best Design to Use

A researcher needs to decide whether survey research is the best design to use in the study. Surveys help describe the trends in a population or describe the relationship among variables or compare groups. Instances where surveys are most suitable are to assess trends or characteristics of a population; learn about individual attitudes, opinions, beliefs, and practices; evaluate the success or effectiveness of a program; or identify the needs of a community.

There are several advantages to using surveys. They can be administered in a short period of time, they are economical as a means of data collection, and they can reach a *geographically* dispersed population. Further, the participants can be canvassed anonymously without being influenced by the researcher. However, survey data is self-reported information, reporting only what people think rather than what they do. Sometimes the response rates are low and researchers cannot make claims about the representativeness of the results to the population. As mentioned earlier, surveys do not control for many variables that might explain the relationship between the independent and dependent variables, and they do not provide participants flexibility in responding to questions (unless open-ended questions are included).

Step 2. Identify the Research Questions or Hypotheses

Both research questions and hypotheses can be addressed in a survey design. Surveys lend themselves to hypothesis testing because you will be studying a sample to draw inferences to a population. Forms of research questions or hypotheses are those that:

▶ describe the characteristics or trends of a population of people, such as the frequency of tobacco use among male high school students
▶ compare groups in terms of specific attributes, such as a comparison of teachers and administrators about attitudes toward "inservice" learning days
▶ relate two or more variables, such as a survey of teachers to relate "burnout" to number of years of teaching

Step 3. Identify the Population, the Sampling Frame, and the Sample

The process of survey research begins with identifying the population. This step requires defining the population, determining the number of people in it, assessing whether they can be reached, and obtaining a list of names (i.e., the sampling frame) for identifying a sample. Also, the population may need to be stratified before sampling so select characteristics of the population (e.g., males and females) are represented in the sample.

Once the target population has been identified and a list of its members is compiled, you can select the sample, preferably using random sampling procedures. You will need to identify an adequate sample size, using the sampling error formula in Appendix A or the other recommendations advanced in Chapter 6 on "Sample Size."

Step 4. Determine the Survey Design and Data Collection Procedures

The researcher must also determine if the survey study will be cross-sectional or longitudinal. The decision of using a longitudinal or cross-sectional design relates to the nature of the problem studied, access to participants, and the time available to the researchers for data collection. For example, learning about the longitudinal development of adolescent social skills in schools requires following adolescents over time and devoting extensive time to data collection. In contrast, examining parents' attitudes toward discipline in schools requires a cross-sectional study at one point in time where attitudes can be measured immediately and quickly.

Consider also whether data collection will be based on questionnaires (mailed or electronic) or interviews (individual, focus group, or telephone), and weigh the advantages and disadvantages of each form.

Step 5. Develop or Locate an Instrument

A researcher needs an instrument to collect or measure the variables in a study. Recall from Chapter 6 that it is easier to locate an instrument than to develop one. Standards of reliability and construct validity need to be applied to scores from existing instruments. If a study addresses only a few variables, researchers can design their own instruments. A check for the reliability and validity of scores from this instrument during data analysis is most important.

Step 6. Administer the Instrument

This step is perhaps the most time-consuming phase of survey research. It involves seeking and obtaining permission to conduct the survey and using procedures for data gathering, such as training interviewers or preparing questionnaires for mailing. It requires continually following up to obtain a high response rate, checking for response bias if questionnaires are used, and preparing the data for analysis by coding the information from the instruments into a computer file.

Step 7. Analyze the Data to Address the Research Questions or Hypotheses

The data analysis procedures will reflect the types of research questions or hypotheses the researcher plans to address in the study. Analysis consists of noting response rates, checking for response bias, conducting descriptive analysis of all items, and then answering descriptive questions. It might also involve testing hypotheses or research questions using inferential statistics.

Step 8. Write the Report

The survey study should be written using a standard quantitative structure that consists of an introduction, the review of the literature, the methods, the results, and the discussion. Specify in the "Methods" section of the study detailed information about the survey procedures. Include in the "Discussion" section comments about the generalizability of the results to the population.

CRITERIA FOR EVALUATING SURVEY RESEARCH

Whether the research consists of interviews or mailed questionnaires, survey studies need to meet high standards of quality. If you plan to conduct a survey, you need to design and write a methods section in your study that conveys the detailed survey research procedures. For educators who read and seek to use results from surveys, a checklist of elements to include in a survey design can provide basic information to look for in a published study. The following checklist, based on the key concepts introduced in this chapter and adapted from Fowler (1988) and Neuman (2000), provides one guide for educators to use.

- Was the target population or sampling frame clearly described and specified?
- Was the sampling procedure specified? If simple random sampling was not used, were modifications from it explained? (e.g., non-probability sampling, stratified sampling, and multi-stage cluster sampling)
- Was the sample clearly identified and the basis on which it was chosen specified? (e.g., size, use of random numbers table, or the sampling error for the sample)
- Did the type of survey (i.e., longitudinal or cross-sectional) match the questions or hypotheses advanced by the author?
- Was it clear whether a questionnaire or an interview survey comprised the form of data collection? And did the researcher identify the basis for selecting or developing the instrument?
- Was information reported on reliability and validity of scores from past use of the questionnaire or interview?
- Did the author mention the dates on which the questionnaire or interview was administered?
- Were the administration procedures clearly identified?
- If a questionnaire was used, were the procedures for obtaining responses identified? Were follow-up procedures used to ensure a high return rate?
- If an interview survey was used, were the field procedures for collection of this information specified? Were demographic characteristics, previous experience, training, and monitoring discussed for the interviewer(s)?
- Was a sample of the questionnaire items or the interview questions available to help determine if good item construction was used?
- Did the data analysis match the research questions or hypotheses to be answered in the study?
- Did the researcher check on the reliability and validity of scores from the data collection in the study?
- Was the study written scientifically and ethically? (i.e., followed a standard structure, indicated a sensitivity to bias, and was respectful of ethical issues)

APPLYING WHAT YOU HAVE LEARNED: A SURVEY STUDY

To apply the ideas in this chapter, read the survey study on page 428, noting the marginal annotations that identify characteristics of survey and quantitative research.

Gallik, J. D. (1999). Do they read for pleasure? Recreational reading habits of college students. *Journal of Adolescent & Adult Literacy, 42,* 480–488.

The Gallik (1999) study addresses recreational reading by college students and whether students who read recreationally obtain high grade point averages. As a survey study, this research examines students' practices measured cross-sectionally. The study is chosen because it demonstrates a high return rate (139 out of 151) based on an instrument given to students in classes, includes the actual survey instrument used, and presents detailed information about the use of the survey.

As you review this article, look for elements of the research process:

 ❱ the research problem and use of quantitative research
 ❱ use of the literature
 ❱ the purpose statement and research questions
 ❱ types and procedures of data collection
 ❱ types and procedures of data analysis and interpretation
 ❱ the overall writing structure

The Research Problem and Use of Quantitative Research

See Paragraph 02 and throughout the study

The author introduced the research problem in the second paragraph: the problem for students of not reading well and its importance as a cornerstone for success in school and life.

The study demonstrates a quantitative approach to research:

 ❱ a focus on a research problem of the need for students to read (Paragraph 02)
 ❱ a substantial literature review on reading skills at the beginning that foreshadows a need to examine the relationship between reading and achievement (Paragraphs 02–12)
 ❱ the relationship of variables related to reading, achievement, and group differences (Paragraphs 13–14)
 ❱ data collection based on an instrument developed by the researcher (Paragraph 17), that gathers numeric data (Paragraph 17), from 151 students (Paragraph 16)
 ❱ statistical data analysis (Paragraph 18), consisting of percentages, differences among groups (Chi-square statistic), and the relationship among variables (Pearson correlations) (Paragraph 18)
 ❱ the analysis of results to each research question (Paragraphs 19–40) and the interpretation of the meaning of the results (Paragraphs 44–45)
 ❱ a writing structure that begins with the problem, the methods, the results, and the discussion (see entire study), and reports "objective" results in terms of statistical findings with the research in the background

Use of the Literature

See Paragraphs 02–12

In these paragraphs you find past studies reviewed about reading and other academic skills. Paragraph 09 focuses the study toward the reading habits of college students, and Paragraph 11 relates reading to nonacademic reading. Paragraph 13 indicates the gap in past research: none of the studies addressed the relationship between pleasure reading and academic achievement. In this way, by reviewing the literature, the author sets the stage for the purpose and research questions.

The Purpose Statement and Research Questions

See Paragraphs 01 and 13

The author states the purpose of the study initially in Paragraph 01, and then introduces four research questions in Paragraph 13. These questions show several types of quantitative questions: numbers 1 and 4 are descriptive; number 2, a relationship; and number 3, a comparison.

Types of Procedures of Data Collection

See Paragraphs 15–17

The section on survey data collection was clearly specified by the author. Rather than a simple random sample, the researcher selected a convenience sample of students in composition and writing classes. This means that claims about generalizing the results to all students is suspect, despite author comments about selecting courses that would yield a good cross section of students. The questionnaires were handed out to students, a procedure that contributes to a high return rate (139 out of 151). The author developed an instrument, although there was no explanation for the source of the questions. A copy of the instrument helps a reader understand the types of information collected and evaluate the quality of the questions. As this instrument shows (Paragraph 17), different types of scales were used, from closed-ended nominal (male-female) and ordinal (rarely/never, sometimes, frequently), to open-ended, fill-in-the-blank questions.

Types and Procedures of Data Analysis and Interpretation

See Paragraphs 19–41 for data analysis results

See Paragraphs 44–45

The data analysis in this study addressed the survey questions asking for descriptive, group comparisons and relationship results. Percentages, Pearson product-moment correlations, and Chi-square statistics are used. Tables reporting percentages portray the descriptive data.

The larger interpretation of the meaning of the results is found in the concluding paragraphs of the study. Knowing that reading is related to grade point average helps make predictions about academic success (Paragraph 45), aides in our understanding of students with superior academic skills (Paragraph 45), and suggests that reading improves attention and concentration (Paragraph 45). This last interpretation (Paragraph 45), as well as the suggestion that reading needs to be developed during the elementary years (Paragraph 44), do not seem to logically follow from the data in this study.

The Overall Writing Structure

This study follows a standard quantitative structure and is logically developed from the problem statement to the interpretation of results at the end. The survey procedures are clearly delineated for the reader.

KEY IDEAS IN THE CHAPTER

This chapter provides an overview of survey research. Although broad in scope, survey research is a form of quantitative research where the investigator identifies either the sample or the population, collects data through questionnaires or interviews, and draws conclusions or makes inferences about the population. It is a useful design to use when researchers seek to collect data quickly and economically, study attitudes and opinions, and survey geographically dispersed individuals. Surveys are also useful for assessing information at one point in time (a cross-sectional study), or over time (a longitudinal study). Survey researchers emphasize sample selection, collect data using questionnaires and interviews, administer well-tested instruments with good questions, and seek a high response rate from participants.

The steps in conducting a survey consist of determining if a survey design is best, forming questions or hypotheses, and identifying a population and possibly a sample to study. Then the researcher identifies the type of survey to reach this sample or population, collects data to ensure a good rate of response and minimal response bias, and statistically analyzes the data to answer descriptive questions or to address relationship or comparison questions or hypotheses.

USEFUL INFORMATION FOR PRODUCERS OF RESEARCH

▶ Identify whether your study is cross-sectional or longitudinal. Longitudinal surveys take more time to complete because you are studying individuals over time.
▶ In your research, distinguish between the population, the target population, and your sample. Choose a random sample so that you can make claims or generalize to your population. Consider the sources of error that may affect your ability to generalize findings to the population.
▶ Specify the type of data collection instrument that you use, such as questionnaires or interviews.
▶ Conduct a pilot test of your questions, whatever your type of data collection instrument, so that it can provide useful information.
▶ Be aware of how you pose sensitive questions to participants. Realize that they may need some introductory comments before they are asked to respond to sensitive questions.
▶ A number of potential problems arise when you create your own questions. Study Table 13.1 for a list of problems you should consider when writing your own questions.
▶ A typical high response rate is above 50%, but check for response bias through wave analysis when you use a mailed questionnaire.
▶ Design a mailed questionnaire to include a cover letter, a clear layout of questions, and instructions to the participant. Your instrument should be kept as short as possible.
▶ If you conduct an interview, adopt a neutral stance and record responses accurately. Follow the procedures advanced in this chapter.

USEFUL INFORMATION FOR CONSUMERS OF RESEARCH

▶ Surveys are used for many purposes in research. When evaluating a study, consider the intent of the author to describe trends, determine attitudes or opinions, describe characteristics of a population, identify practices, evaluate programs, or follow up on individuals over time.
▶ Mailed questionnaires are a popular form of data collection in educational research. However, these instruments need to be carefully designed. Determine whether the researcher used attitudinal, behavioral, and demographic questions in the instrument.
▶ A questionnaire response rate of 50% is considered adequate for most surveys. Examine the response rate of a survey study published in the literature and determine if it reaches this percentage. Also consider whether survey researchers addressed the question of response bias and checked to determine if their responses were biased.

ADDITIONAL RESOURCES YOU MIGHT EXAMINE

Several books provide an excellent introduction to survey research. An introduction to survey research is found in the "toolkit" series on survey research by Arlene Fink (1995). This nine-volume series by Fink and associates comprehensively addresses all aspects of survey development from asking questions to writing reports. See:

Fink, A. (1995). *The survey handbook.* Thousand Oaks, CA: Sage.

An introductory book by Priscilla Salant and Don Dillman (1994) provides a nontechnical overview to survey research with a focus on survey instruments. Their information about errors common in surveys and the costs associated with survey administration offers useful guides for the beginning researcher. See:

Salant, P., & Dillman, D. A. (1994). *How to conduct your own survey.* New York: John Wiley & Sons.

Floyd Fowler (1988) has issued a short book on survey research that is popular in introductory survey research courses. He focuses on sampling and design issues, as well as highlighting ethical issues and errors in survey designs. See:

Fowler, F. J. (1988). *Survey research methods.* Newbury Park, CA: Sage.

In a more advanced treatment of survey research, Earl Babbie has authored several books that provide a detailed, technical understanding (Babbie, 1990; 1998). His books broadly assess social research, but they are applicable to education. See:

Babbie, E. (1990). *Survey research methods.* Belmont, CA: Wadsworth.

Babbie, E. (1998). *The practice of social research* (8th ed.). Belmont, CA: Wadsworth.

Quantitative Characteristics

Do they read for pleasure?: Recreational Reading Habits of College Students

Survey Research Characteristics

Jude D. Gallik

(01)

A quantitative research problem requires description or explanation.

Does a relationship exist between academic achievement and the time spent in recreational reading? A significant connection was found between achievement and the time these college students spent reading for pleasure during vacations.

When my colleagues and I interview prospective students, we always seem to ask about their reading habits. Do you read for pleasure? we ask, hoping for the "yes" that we think will reveal an interest in matters academic and thereby portend future collegial success. We ask this question, over and over, year after year, because we assume that there is a relationship between reading and academic success: We believe that better students read more than poorer ones. Our assumption, however, has yet to be supported with scientific or statistical evidence. The purpose of this study was to reveal some evidence to either dispute or support our assumption that a positive relationship exists between the amount of time spent in recreational reading and academic achievement.

(02)

The quantitative literature justifies the research problem and provides direction for the study.

Why do we think reading is so important? According to the Report of the Commission on Reading in the United States (Anderson, Hiebert, Scott, & Wilkinson, 1985), reading is a cornerstone for success, not just in school, but throughout life. The Commission noted, "Without the ability to read well, opportunities for personal fulfillment and job success will inevitably be lost" (p. 1). In their research with adult readers, Kirsch and Guthrie (1984) found that reading is a necessary aspect of job and career development, especially in responding to changes. They further reported that to the adults in their study, "reading is not an inconsequential aspect of life outside the classroom" (p. 230).

(03)

Reading skills are important throughout the lifespan, and recreational reading has been found to improve reading comprehension, writing style, vocabulary, spelling, and grammatical development (Krashen, 1993). The effect of recreational reading on vocabulary development was demonstrated by Sarangi, Nation, and Meister (cited in Krashen, 1993). In their study readers learned the meaning of 45 invented words contained in the novel *A Clockwork Orange* (Burgess, 1984) simply by reading the novel, with no special instructions to attend to new words. In addition to improving reading skills, pleasure reading has been found to be associated with improved writing skills.

(04)

The quantitative literature plays a major role.

One study (Krashen, 1984) compared the pleasure-reading habits of college freshmen who wrote essays that were rated either highly competent or of low competence. Those writing highly competent essays reported more pleasure reading at all ages, especially in high school. No poor essay writer reported "a lot" of pleasure reading during high school. Another study (Applebee, 1978) found that outstanding high school writers (National Council of Teachers of English award winners) reported reading an average of 14 books for pleasure over summer vacation alone, significantly more than the average of 11 books per year reported elsewhere (Gallo in Applebee, 1978).

Jude D. Gallik is the director of Learning Support Services for Schreiner College, 2100 Memorial Blvd., Kerrville, Texas 78028, USA.

Reprinted with permission from the *Journal of Adolescent & Adult Literacy.*

(05)   The relationship between reading and other academic skills becomes evident at the elementary level. Anderson, Wilson, and Fielding (1988) found that, for 5th graders, the amount of time spent reading books outside of school was the best predictor of reading comprehension, vocabulary, and speed. They also found that independent reading was associated with gains in reading achievement. Other studies found that one of the best predictors of leisure reading in 5th graders was reading achievement (Greaney, 1980; Greaney & Hegarty, 1987). Students in 4th, 8th, and 12th grade who reported more reading outside school were found to perform better on a test of reading comprehension (Foertsch, 1992). Taylor, Frye, and Maruyama (1990) found that reading as little as 15 minutes a day contributed significantly to gains in reading achievement for 5th and 6th graders.

(06)   The relationship between gender and time spent in recreational reading is well established; girls consistently read more than boys at every age studied (Blackwood, Flowers, Rogers, & Stalk, 1991; McCreath, 1975; Witty, 1961). Unfortunately, another consistent finding is that the amount of time spent in recreational reading declines in the middle school years (Clary, 1991; Greaney, 1980; McCoy, Larson, & Higginson, 1991).

(07)   Although some people suggest that television viewing may reduce time spent in pleasure reading, studies over the last 30 years have consistently refuted this assumption. Witty (1961) found that the amount of time spent watching TV actually declined as the student progressed through school, with 12th graders watching an average of 3 hours less television per week than 9th graders. Greaney and Hegarty (1987) found no relationship between amount of time spent watching television and amount of time spent reading books. Libsch and Breslow (1996) also reported a decline in the amount of time spent watching television between 1976 and 1992.

(08)   An overall decline in time spent reading may have occurred over the past few decades. In their study, Ross and Simone (1982) found that 10th, 11th, and 12th graders reported reading 1 hour or less outside of school, a slight decline from the 1.3 hours per day reported by Witty (1961) for the same grades. Declines in amount of time spent reading were also noted by Libsch and Breslow (1996) when they compared 1976–78 and 1992–94 data on high school seniors' recreational reading habits. During both periods, about half of all seniors reported reading one to five nonassigned books each year. Those reading six or more books decreased from 37% to 25%. Those reading no books increased from 14% to 22%. College-bound seniors in the study reported reading more than the noncollege bound, but the number of college bound who reported reading no books has doubled since 1976.

(09)   The reading habits of college students have not received as much attention in the literature as those of younger students. McCreath (1975) reported on the reading habits and interests of 89 primarily African American students enrolled in a reading improvement course at an urban community college. While most of the students surveyed reported positive attitudes toward reading, only 38% said that they regularly or often read for pleasure, while 58% reported that they only sometimes or never read. However, the majority did report reading a newspaper regularly or often. McCreath (1975) also investigated relationships among reading habits, reading interests, and reading improvement, but found no statistically or practically significant relationships.

(10)   Blackwood et al. (1991) studied the pleasure reading habits of 333 college seniors enrolled at a small, public, U.S. liberal arts university. In response to a survey, 88% reported reading for pleasure, primarily newspapers, and most reported spending more time reading during vacations

than when classes were in session. Both male and female students reported reading for pleasure about 2.5 hours each week while classes were in session, and slightly more during vacations. In this study, the researchers also considered the effect of parental encouragement, parental education, and parental occupation on the amount of reading reported by the students surveyed. None of these factors was found to be significantly related to amount of time spent reading.

(11)   In another study, Sheorey and Mokhtari (1994) examined the reading habits of 85 college students enrolled in an elective developmental reading course at a large university in the midwestern United States. They reported that students read an average of 4.75 hours per week. Students who scored higher on a test of reading comprehension reported spending slightly more time on nonacademic reading, 5.85 hours per week, than those with lower reading ability, who reported spending an average of 3.65 hours per week, but this difference was not statistically significant.

(12)   The study by Jeffries and Atkins (1996) focused primarily on reading interests of 261 college students enrolled in introductory media courses. They analyzed the responses by college major and found that humanities majors had the highest mean number of books read. Interestingly, the humanities majors did not differ from other majors in the average number of hours spent watching television, a finding consistent with those of Greaney and Witty mentioned previously.

Purpose of the Study

(13)   While the studies with college students often examined time spent in pleasure reading, the type of reading the students did, and levels of reading achievement, none specifically examined the relationship between overall academic achievement and amount of time spent in pleasure reading.

The quantitative (14)   The purpose of the present study was to find answers to the following
purpose statement,   questions:
research questions or   **1.** How much time do college students spend in pleasure reading?
hypotheses seek   **2.** Is there a relationship between academic achievement in college (as
measurable, observable   measured by cumulative grade-point average) and the amount of time
data on variables.   spent in pleasure reading?

The quantitative   **3.** Do significant differences exist between various groups (gender,
purpose statement,   age, student classification) in the amount of time spent pleasure reading?
research questions,   **4.** What type of reading material(s) do the students prefer?
or hypotheses are
specific and   (15)

Conducting the Survey

narrow.

(15)   The sample consisted of students enrolled in four sections of first-year   Survey researchers
composition and three upper level writing classes at a small, church-   select a sample from a
affiliated, private liberal arts college located in central Texas, USA. These   population.
courses were selected because of the likelihood that they would yield the
best cross-section of students, without being skewed toward any specific
major. The composition courses are required of all first-year students, regardless of major. Students in all majors are required to take one of two
upper level classes: Advanced Composition or Technical Writing. The
third upper level class, Creative Writing, typically attracts students from
a variety of majors. Both lower and upper level classes were included in
order to provide additional variables (age and student classification) to
consider when analyzing the data. Established classes were used to administer the surveys because it was likely to result in a much higher return than if the surveys were mailed to students.

(16)   A total of 151 surveys were administered in the English composition   Survey researchers seek
courses. In two of the courses, I administered them. In the remaining   high response rates.
courses, the surveys were administered by the course instructors. Twelve

Quantitative data collection involves studying a large number of individuals.

surveys were not included in the data analysis due to one of two conditions: One or more of the questions were not answered or more than one answer was given to any question. Of the 139 usable surveys, 77 were completed by women and 62 were completed by men. The breakdown by student classification was as follows: 74 freshmen, 17 sophomores, 31 juniors, and 17 seniors. In terms of age, the sample consisted of 79 students in the 17–20 bracket, 41 students in the 21–24 bracket, 7 students in the 25–29 bracket, and 12 students age 30 or older.

(17)

A survey entitled "Recreational Reading Habits of College Students" was developed for this study (see Figure). It consisted of four demographic questions (age, gender, student classification, cumulative grade-point average), two questions about participation in special programs (Honors program for high-achieving students or comprehensive support program for students with learning disabilities) and two questions about recreational reading (time spent on recreational reading when classes are in session, and time spent on recreational reading during vacations). In addition, the survey elicited information about reading interest, asking whether the student would read more if more time were available and how frequently different types of material were read (e.g., novels, newspaper, poetry). Students who indicated that they read novels or nonfiction were asked to specify favorite authors or categories. Due to a design flaw in the survey, the information on frequency for nonfiction is incomplete.

Survey researchers develop or use instruments to collect data.

Quantitative data collection is based on using instruments identified prior to the study.

Survey of Recreational Reading Habits

Quantitative data collection involves gathering numeric data.

1. Please indicate your gender: Male _____ Female _____

2. Please indicate your student status:
   Freshman _____ Sophomore _____ Junior _____ Senior _____ Other (specify) _____

3. Please indicate your age: 17–20 _____ 21–24 _____ 25–29 _____ 30 or older _____

4. Please indicate your cumulative GPA:
   Less than 1.5 _____ 1.6 to 2.0 _____ 2.1 to 2.5 _____ 2.6 to 3.0 _____ Over 3.0 _____

5. Are you a current or former Learning Support Services (LSS) student? Yes _____ No _____

6. Are you in the Honors Program? Yes _____ No _____

7. Please indicate the amount of time you spend each week on recreational reading (not required for classes) when school is in session.
   Less than 1 hour _____ 1–2 hours _____ 3–5 hours _____ 6–10 hours _____ Over 10 hours _____

8. Please indicate the amount of time you spend each week on recreational reading (not required for classes) during vacations.
   Less than 1 hour _____ 1–2 hours _____ 3–5 hours _____ 6–10 hours _____ Over 10 hours _____

9. If you had more free time, would you read more? Yes _____ No _____

10. Please indicate how often you read each of the following:

	Rarely/never	Sometimes	Frequently
Newspaper	_____	_____	_____
Magazines	_____	_____	_____
Comic books	_____	_____	_____
Poetry	_____	_____	_____
Letters/e-mail/chat rooms	_____	_____	_____
Internet	_____	_____	_____
Novels	_____	_____	_____

(Please specify preference: science fiction, mystery, etc., & favorite author)

Nonfiction books	_____	_____	_____

(Please specify preference: biography, self-help, religious, etc.)

Survey researchers use questionnaires or interviews to collect data.

(18)   The data regarding amount of time spent reading recreationally were summarized by category (e.g., less than 1 hour, 1 to 2 hours) and percentages of students for each category presented. Chi-square and Pearson product-moment correlations were used to determine whether significant differences existed between groups in the amount of time spent reading for pleasure. Data collected on types of reading materials preferred by students were summarized by category and the most and least preferred materials presented as percentages.

Time Spent Reading

(19)   Total responses for time spent in recreational reading each week while classes are in session are shown in Table 1. While classes are in session, 63% of the respondents report reading 2 hours or less each week. At the other end of the continuum, only 13% of students surveyed report 6 or more hours per week when classes are in session.

(20)   Total responses for recreational reading each week when classes are not in session are shown in Table 2. Forty-eight percent of students reported reading 2 hours or less each week while on vacation, significantly less than the 63% who reported reading less than 2 hours each week when classes are in session, indicating that amount of time spent reading increases when classes are not in session. During vacations, 25% of students reported reading more than 6 hours each week, an increase over the 13% who reported doing so when classes are in session.

Relationship Between Academic Achievement and Recreational Reading

(21)   Pearson product-moment correlations were performed to determine the relationship between reported cumulative grade-point average and amount of time spent reading for pleasure while classes were in session and during vacations. An insignificant correlation ($r = .08$) was found be-

TABLE 1
Time Spent Reading Recreationally: Classes in Session

Hours per Week	Number of Students	Percentage of Students
Less than 1 hour	40	29
1–2 hours	47	34
3–5 hours	33	24
6–10 hours	12	8
More than 10 hours	7	5

TABLE 2
Time Spent Reading Recreationally: During Vacation

Hours per Week	Number of Students	Percentage of Students
Less than 1 hour	29	21
1–2 hours	38	27
3–5 hours	38	27
6–10 hours	22	16
More than 10 hours	12	9

tween cumulative grade-point average and pleasure reading while classes were in session. However, a weak but statistically significant correlation ($r = .275$, $p = .01$) was found between cumulative grade-point average and time spent reading for pleasure during vacations.

Group Differences in Pleasure Reading

(22) The data were analyzed using chi-square calculations to determine whether any significant differences in time spent pleasure reading existed between any groups. Group differences were calculated in terms of student classification, gender, age, participation in the college's Honors program, and participation in the college's support program for students with diagnosed learning disabilities.

(23) No statistically significant differences were found due to student classification. No gender differences were found between males and females for time spent reading while classes were in session; however, a difference between males and females that approached significant levels ($p = .08$) was found when amount of time spent reading during vacations was examined.

(24) The chi-square calculation indicated a statistically significant difference when age was compared to amount of reading during vacations. However, since more than one fifth of the cells had a frequency of less than 5, the value may have been inflated, thereby making the significance suspect. A Pearson product-moment correlation was then conducted to compare the relationship between age and amount of reading during vacations, resulting in a weak but statistically significant difference ($r = .313$, $p = .01$).

(25) No statistically significant differences were found between students enrolled in the learning disabilities support program or students in the Honors program and the remaining students surveyed in the amount of time spent reading while classes were in session or during vacations.

Reading Interests

(26) Students were asked to indicate how frequently they engaged in eight different types of pleasure reading. Table 3 summarizes the responses. The survey instrument had spaces below the questions on novels and nonfiction reading where the students were asked to specify their preferences in those areas. Unfortunately, a number of the survey respondents misinterpreted the layout of the question about nonfiction books, and used the lines which were intended for indicating the frequency to indicate the type of reading they did. This design error resulted in only 84 of the students responding correctly to the question.

TABLE 3
Reading Interests

	Rarely/Never	Sometimes	Frequently
Newspaper	21	64	54
Magazines	6	58	75
Comic books	123	15	1
Poetry	57	65	17
Letters/e-mail/chat rooms	28	46	65
Internet	42	42	55
Novels	42	51	46
Nonfiction books*	35	29	20

*Notification total does not equal sample total of 139. Design flaw in survey caused some students to respond incorrectly to the question.

(27)   Magazines were the most popular type of reading material, reported to be read frequently by 75% of the respondents. Letters, e-mail, and chat rooms were the next most popular, with 65% of students indicating frequent reading. Comic books were clearly the least popular reading material, with 88% of students reporting that they rarely or never read comic books.

(28)   The survey provided a space for students to specify their preference for types of novels read. Only 49 of the students chose to indicate a preference in regard to novel reading. Of those responding, the most frequently mentioned categories were mysteries and horror, with Mary Higgins Clark, Stephen King, Dean Koontz, and John Grisham the most frequently mentioned authors. For nonfiction reading, 67 students reported preferences, with biographies, self-help, and religious/spiritual the most frequently listed.

(29)   The survey question, "If you had more free time, would you read more?" could be considered an overall indicator of interest in reading. Seventy-six percent of all respondents answered yes. No statistically significant differences were found between any of the groups in their responses to this question; however, 80% of women answered yes, compared to 72% of men, which may be indicative of a general tendency for women to read more than men.

How Much Do They Read?

(30)   The primary purposes for this study were to find out how much time students at this college spent reading for pleasure and to determine whether there was indeed a relationship between amount of recreational reading and academic achievement as indicated by cumulative grade-point average.

(31)   The finding that 63% of students reported spending less than 2 hours per week reading for pleasure while classes are in session was not unexpected, considering that most students have a significant amount of required reading and other work for their classes. The amount of time reported by students spent on recreational reading (both on vacation and when classes are in session) is consistent with the average of 2.5 hours per week reported by Blackwood et al. (1996).

(32)   However, both the present study and the Blackwood et al. study differ significantly from the findings of Sheorey and Mokhtari (1994) who reported an average of 4.75 hours per week of recreational reading. The fact that the Sheorey and Mokhtari study was conducted at a large university and the other two were at small colleges seems insufficient explanation for the difference. The reason for the disparate results in amount of time spent reading for pleasure most likely lies in the differences in the construction of the time categories from which students were to select and the way in which the data were analyzed. Sheorey and Mokhtari report that their subjects were provided with five categories of time frames: 0–4 hours, 5–9 hours, 10–14 hours, 15–19 hours, and 20 hours or more.

(33)   In contrast, the current study provided time frames of less than 1 hour, 1–2 hours, 3–5 hours, 6–10 hours, and over 10 hours, while Blackwood et al. provided time frames of less than 1 hour, 1–2 hours, 3–4 hours, and over 4 hours. The much larger time frame provided by Sheorey and Mokhtari at the lower end of the scale, 0–4 hours, could therefore account for their report of an average of 4.75 hours per week spent in pleasure reading. Students who did not read at all, and those who read as many as 4 hours per week were placed in the same category, whereas in the present study, this same group of students would have fallen into three different time frames. The use of this larger time frame could result in an inflated estimate of the amount of time spent on recreational reading, particularly when the data are presented as a mean.

(34)   Sheorey and Mokhtari reported that their calculation for the mean amount of time spent on recreational reading was based upon the numerical value assigned to each category (i.e., 0–4 hours was considered category 1, 5–9 hours was category 2). A mean of 1.5 was reported, which represented the mean of the assigned number of the category selected. This category mean was then converted to represent a specific number of hours, although it is unclear exactly how that conversion was accomplished. Calculating a mean in this fashion does not take into account the fact that all students selecting category 1 (0–4 hours) could have been reading only 2 hours or less each week or, conversely, all the students could have been reading for 4 hours each week. One would have to conclude that using a mean to report the number of hours of pleasure reading when such large time frame categories were used was inappropriate.

(35)   Although students generally read more while on vacation than when classes are in session, almost half (48%) read only 2 hours or less per week even during vacations. This finding is somewhat surprising given that 76% of students indicated that they would read more if they had more time. One possible explanation for this response is that, while one might assume that being on vacation from school would give students more time, the students do not in fact have more time to read during vacations. It could be that many students work during school vacations, leaving no more time for leisure reading than when classes are in session. This contention may be supported by the fact that 14 respondents who answered yes to the question about reading more also indicated that they spent fewer hours in pleasure reading during vacations than when classes are in session. The finding that such a high percentage (76%) of students expressed a positive attitude toward reading (as measured by their interest in reading more) is, to an educator, reassuring.

(36)   The statistically significant correlation between recreational reading during vacations and cumulative grade-point average ($r = .275$, $p = .01$) indicates that our favorite interview question, "Do you read for pleasure?" is a useful and relevant one. However, the answer should be weighed cautiously, since information about pleasure reading will only account for about 8% of the variation in cumulative grade-point average (the coefficient of determination is the square of the correlation coefficient). Pleasure reading in itself is not a strong predictor of achievement in college.

Who Reads the Most?

(37)   Findings regarding group differences in amount of time spent reading for pleasure must be interpreted with consideration for the small number of subjects in some of the grouping categories. The finding that there was no significant difference in the amount of pleasure reading by students in the learning disabilities support program, when compared with those not in the program, was unexpected. Because many of the students in the learning disabilities support program have below-average levels of reading achievement, they were expected to spend less time reading for pleasure than non-learning-disabled students—considering the strong relationship that has been found between reading achievement and amount of time spent reading for pleasure (Foertsch, 1992; Sheorey & Mokhtari, 1994). However, the sample of 139 included only 19 students who were currently or formerly enrolled in the learning disabilities support program. This small number may have been insufficient to reveal any significant differences.

(38)   Similarly, students enrolled in the Honors program were expected to report more time spent in recreational reading. Here, also, the small number (11) of students who reported participation in the Honors program may

have affected the results, which indicated that Honors students had reading habits no different than those of non-Honors students.

(39)   The small sample size of some of the age groups may be responsible for the finding of a statistically significant relationship between age and amount of time spent reading for pleasure. The results indicated that older students tended to read more. However, only 7 students were in the age 25–29 category, and 12 students were in the 30 or older category, so the findings would have to be considered suspect. Another confounding factor is the very specific nature of the sample. The older students in this study had chosen to enroll in a baccalaureate program at a nontraditional age. This fact makes them a very select group and limits the usefulness of the results.

(40)   No significant differences were found between students of different classifications: Seniors didn't spend more time reading for pleasure than first-year students. This finding may indicate that reading habits are already well established by the time a student enters college, so that the experience of being a college student does not influence how much more time will be spent on reading recreationally if the student is not already so inclined. The finding may also simply reflect the fact that all college students, regardless of classification, spend the vast majority of their reading time and energy on academic pursuits, rather than recreational ones.

What Do They Read?

(41)   In order to get a full and complete picture of reading interests, survey questions regarding the type of reading preferred by respondents would need to be much more detailed than the items included on the survey for this study. For example, the survey used by Blackwood et al. (1991) included 13 questions about which section of the newspapers were read, 10 questions about what type of magazines were read, and 14 categories about nonfiction books. Other studies of reading interest (Jeffries & Atkins, 1996; Ross & Simone, 1982) have included questions at a similar level of detail. Because determining areas of reading interest was not one of the primary purposes of this study, survey questions about the type of reading material and the frequency such material was read were of a more general nature. However, more specific information in this regard would provide a richer picture of the recreational reading habits of college students.

(42)   The results of the present study were consistent with the results of the studies mentioned here in finding newspapers and magazines to be among the most preferred. The present study was the only one that allowed respondents a choice of "letters/e-mail/chat rooms" as a type of recreational reading. This option is significant because it was the second most popular type of pleasure reading selected, with 47% of students indicating frequent reading in that category. Because reading interests were of secondary importance, there was no analysis to determine whether any significant differences existed between groups in their interests.

(43)   One limitation of this study has already been noted in regard to the limited number of survey questions about types of material read. Another limitation may lie in the use of the terms *academic achievement* and *recreational reading*. Consistent with the purposes of this study, these terms were defined rather broadly. Further research that defined these terms more narrowly could provide more detailed information about the relationship between recreational reading and academic achievement in college students.

Implications

(44)   The results from this and other studies suggest that recreational reading habits are acquired fairly early in an individual's school life, probably in el-

Quantitative
interpretations compare
results with predictions.

ementary school given that numerous studies show a decline in time spent reading that begins in middle school. If students are to have good reading skills and positive attitudes toward reading, these must be developed during the elementary years.

(45)

The positive relationship that this study found between cumulative grade-point average and time spent in recreational reading has several implications. First, knowing about students' recreational reading habits is helpful in making predictions about their future academic success. Second, this relationship could indicate that students who spend more time reading have, in general, superior academic skills, and these skills help them achieve academic success. Finally, spending time in recreational reading could indicate that an individual has the ability for sustained attention and concentration necessary for academic success.

(46)

Quantitative research
reports use standard,
fixed structures and
evaluation criteria.

One area for further study would be to compare reading achievement directly to cumulative grade-point average, so that achievement could be separated from time spent in recreational reading to determine its significance as a contributing factor in college success. Another area that warrants further attention is recreational reading habits over a lifetime. While we know that time spent reading declines during the middle school years, we do not know if the decline is permanent, or whether individuals may increase their time spent in pleasure reading at different times in their lives.

References

Anderson, R.C., Hiebert, E.H., Scott, J.A., & Wilkinson, I.A.G. (1985). *Becoming a nation of readers: The report of the commission on reading.* Washington, DC: The National Institute of Education.

Anderson, R., Wilson, P., & Fielding, L. (1988). Growth in reading and how children spend their time outside of school. *Reading Research Quarterly, 23,* 285–303.

Applebee, A. (1978). Teaching high achievement students: A survey of the winners of the 1977 NCTE achievement awards in writing. *Research in the Teaching of English, 1,* 41–53.

Blackwood, C., Flowers, S.S., Rogers, J.S., & Staik, I.M. (1991, November). *Pleasure reading by college students: Fact or fiction?* Paper presented at the annual meeting of the Mid-South Educational Research Association Conference, Lexington, KY.

Burgess, A. (1987). *A clockwork orange.* New York: W.W. Norton.

Clary, L.M. (1991). Getting adolescents to read. *Journal of Reading, 34,* 340–345.

Foertsch, M. (1992). *Reading in and out of school.* Washington, DC: U.S. Department of Education.

Greaney, V. (1980). Factors related to amount and type of leisure time reading. *Reading Research Quarterly, 15,* 337–357.

Greaney, V., & Hegarty, M. (1987). Correlates of leisure time reading. *Journal of Research in Reading, 10,* 3–20.

Jeffries, L, & Atkins, D.J. (1996). Dimensions of student interest in reading newspapers. *Journalism and Mass Communication Educator, 51,* 15–23.

Kirsch, I.S., & Guthrie, J.T. (1984). Adult reading practices for work and leisure. *Adult Education Quarterly, 34,* 213–232.

Krashen, S. (1984). *Writing: Research, theory and applications.* Torrence, CA: Laredo.

Krashen, S. (1993). *The power of reading: Insights from the research.* Englewood, CO: Libraries Unlimited.

Libsch, M.K., & Breslow, M. (1996). Trends in non-assigned reading by high school seniors. *NASSP Bulletin, 80,* 111–116.

McCoy, D., Larson, B., & Higginson, B. (1991, October), *Surveys of independent reading: Pinpointing the problems, seeking the solutions.* Paper presented at the annual meeting of the College Reading Association, Arlington, VA.

McCreath, E.E. (1975). An investigation of reading habits, reading interests, and their relationship to reading improvement of students at an urban open door junior college. In G. McNinch & W. Miller (Eds.), *Reading: Convention and inquiry* (pp. 100–106). Clemson, SC: National Reading Conference.

Ross, B., & Simone, N. (1982). *Reading interests of tenth, eleventh and twelfth grade students.* Unpublished master's thesis, Kean College of New Jersey, Union, NJ.

Sheorey, R., & Mokhtari, K. (1994). The reading habits of college students at different levels of reading proficiency. *Reading Improvement, 31,* 156–166.

Taylor, B., Frye, M., & Maruyama, K. (1990). Time spent reading and reading growth. *American Educational Research Journal, 27,* 351–362.

Witty, P. (1961). A study of pupil's interest, grades 9, 10, 11, 12. *Education, 82,* 100–110.

14

Grounded Theory Designs

Let's return to Maria, our high school teacher, to see how she would design a grounded theory study for her school committee and her graduate research project. Her research question might be: "What is the process by which students are apprehended for weapon possession in their high schools?" To study this question, she needs to identify a process to examine, such as the process of students' being apprehended for carrying weapons. She also needs several people to interview, such as students actually caught, and teachers and administrators involved in the process. From interviewing these individuals, Maria can identify a general process that typically occurs in many student situations. She develops a "theory" of the process of being apprehended, and specifies the elements of this theory, such as:

▶ why (or the causal factors) students are apprehended, such as early warning signs of intent they share with others, incidents of fighting with other students, and suspensions from school

▶ the context in which students are apprehended, such as at their lockers, after school hours on school property, or by themselves or in groups

▶ the student strategies that occur after being caught, such as rationalizing their actions, accepting responsibility, or projecting their problems onto friends

▶ the outcomes or consequences of these strategies, such as being suspended from school, being directed into counseling groups, or contacting parents.

From elements such as these, Maria develops a theory of the process of "being apprehended" for weapon possession in hope that this theory will provide an explanation that school officials might use to identify early warning signs for students who may be prone to possess weapons in high schools.

Many individuals' experiences in education, such as the process of being apprehended for weapons, need to be better understood. For instance, how do first-year teachers cope? How do students relate to the inclusion of cultural components into their classrooms? How do faculties develop into productive researchers? How does a school establish a curriculum that involves learning in the community? To answer each of these questions, we can identify a theory from the literature and test it. Alternatively, we might first collect data and *generate* a theory that explains the process. This second approach seems ideal because the theory is "grounded" in the data. It may provide a better explanation than a theory borrowed "off-the-shelf" because it fits the situation, actually works in practice, is sensitive to individuals in a setting, and may represent all of the complexities actually found in the process. Grounded theory is a procedure to help researchers generate a theory.

To see how this works in practice, let's examine three published grounded theory studies.

▶ In a study of the process of career development, Richie, Fassinger, Linn, and Johnson (1997) generated a theoretical model of career development of 18 high achieving African American-Black and white women. They explored critical influences in the careers of 18 prominent, highly achieving African American-Black and white women in eight occupational fields. From interview data, they developed a theoretical model that visually portrayed how sociocultural conditions, personal backgrounds, and current work influenced the women's strength and perseverance, internal standards, passion for work, and interconnectedness with others in their careers.

▶ A study in adult literacy focused on what adult basic education was like for an adult student (Courtney, Jha, & Babchuk, 1994). The authors interviewed 45 students who had enrolled in adult basic education courses at community colleges. Based on this data, the authors detailed the process the adult students experienced. Students first entered the class—initial impressions—(e.g., encountering the teacher, being there, using rules of engagement) and then experienced being in class—the routine—(e.g., signing in and sitting down, working with books, getting time, forming a friendship with the teacher). Two hypotheses emerged from understanding this process: that students experienced these two phases (i.e., initial impressions and the routine) and that they compared their adult basic education classroom experiences with earlier school experiences.

▶ In a study about learning to write in an interactive, televised writing class, Neff (1998) used grounded theory procedures. She conducted a study of her own classroom to learn how students developed as writers, to assess the role distance education played in this process, and to explore the influence distance education had on the subject of teaching composition using distance learning technology. Through an extensive array of data collection (e.g., her own journal, videotapes of classes, and interviews with students), she generated two theoretical models identifying the complex factors surrounding the themes of being a "student" and a "writer."

These three studies illustrate grounded theory practices. A **grounded theory design** is a systematic, qualitative procedure used to generate a theory that explains, at a broad conceptual level, a process, an action, or interaction about a substantive topic. A central element of this definition is the generation of a theory. In grounded theory research, this theory is a "process" theory—it explains an educational process of events, activities, actions, and interactions that occur over time. Also, grounded theorists proceed through systematic procedures of collecting data, identifying categories (used synonymously with themes as discussed in Chapter 9 on "Describing and Developing Themes from Data"), connecting these categories, and forming a theory that explains the process.

This chapter will introduce you to these procedures. As you read about grounded theory, consider the broader educational processes you have experienced and how grounded theory provides a qualitative procedure useful to better understand them.

By the end of this chapter you should be able to:

▶ Identify major events in the historical development of grounded theory research.
▶ Distinguish among three different designs available for conducting grounded theory research.

▶ Identify the strengths and weaknesses of grounded theory research.
▶ Describe six key characteristics of grounded theory designs.
▶ Identify steps in conducting a grounded theory study.
▶ List criteria useful for evaluating a grounded theory research report.

A BRIEF HISTORY OF GROUNDED THEORY DESIGNS

Two sociologists, Barney G. Glaser and the late Anselm L. Strauss developed grounded theory in the late 1960s. It evolved out of their work with terminally ill patients at the University of California San Francisco Medical Center. In studying these patients, Glaser and Strauss recorded and publicized their methods of research. This led to many individuals contacting Glaser and Strauss to learn more about their research methods. In response, Glaser and Strauss developed a pioneering book that expounded in detail on their grounded theory procedures, *The Discovery of Grounded Theory* (1967). This book laid the foundation for the major ideas of grounded theory used today, and it became a procedural guide for numerous dissertations and research reports. In *Discovery*, Glaser and Strauss took the position that the current theory in sociology overly stressed verifying and testing theories rather than discovering the concepts (variables) and hypotheses based on actual field data from participants. A theory discovered during data collection will "fit the situation being researched and will work when put into use" (Glaser & Strauss, 1967, p. 3) better than a theory identified before a study begins.

The ideas in *Discovery* reflected the background of both authors. Glaser trained in quantitative research at Columbia University with noted researchers who were interested in the inductive development of theory using quantitative and qualitative data. This inductive perspective led him to embrace the importance of generating theory from the perspective of participants in a study. Strauss, on the other hand, came to grounded theory from the University of Chicago with a strong history and tradition in qualitative field research. This background led Strauss to emphasize the importance of field research—going to individuals and listening closely to participants' ideas.

In the years since *Discovery*, both Glaser and Strauss have independently authored several books that refine and explain their early methods (Glaser, 1978; 1992; Strauss, 1987). In 1990 and again in 1998, Anselm Strauss teamed with a community nursing health researcher, Juliet Corbin, to take the techniques and procedures of grounded theory to new levels. They introduced a more prescriptive form of grounded theory with predetermined categories and with concerns about validity and reliability.

Their systematic approach, although embraced by new qualitative researchers (Charmaz, 2000), provoked a critical response from Glaser (1992) that he detailed in a book to "set researchers using grounded theory on a correct path." (p. 3) In the main, Glaser was concerned about how Strauss use preconceived categories and frameworks that did not allow theory to emerge during the process of research. He also took issue with what he saw as an emphasis on simply describing acts rather than actively conceptualizing patterns or connections in the data that would lead to theory.

"So who's got the real grounded theory?" asks Charmaz (2000). Her question was more than rhetorical; she answered it by advancing her own approach to grounded theory, the "constructivist" method (Charmaz, 2000). Charmaz felt that both Glaser and Strauss (and Strauss and Corbin) were much too systematic in their procedures. Grounded theorists needed to stress more flexible strategies, emphasize the meaning participants ascribe to situations, acknowledge the roles of the researcher and the individuals being researched, and expand philosophically beyond a quantitative orientation to research.

TYPES OF GROUNDED THEORY DESIGNS

From this historical sketch, we can see that perspectives about conducting grounded theory research have differed depending on the advocate for a particular approach. However, three dominant designs are discernible: the systematic procedure allied with Strauss and Corbin (1998), the emerging design, associated with Glaser (1992), and the constructivist approach espoused by Charmaz (1990, 2000).

The Systematic Design

The systematic design for grounded theory is widely used in educational research, and it is associated with the detailed, rigorous procedures that Strauss and Corbin identified in 1990 and elaborated in their second edition on techniques and procedures for developing grounded theory (1998). It is much more prescribed than the original conceptualization of grounded theory in 1967 (Glaser & Strauss, 1967). A **systematic design in grounded theory** emphasizes the use of data analysis steps of open, axial, and selective coding, and the development of a logic paradigm or a visual picture of the theory generated. In this definition three phases of coding exist.

In the first phase, **open coding,** the grounded theorist forms initial categories of information about the phenomenon being studied by segmenting information. These categories can be based on all data collected, such as interviews, observations, and researcher's memos or notes. Typically researchers identify categories and subcategories, such as seen in the grounded theory study by Knapp (1995). She examined the career development of 27 educational trainers in career development. In interviews with these trainers she learned about their adaptability and resilience. One page from her study, shown in Figure 14.1, portrays several categories that Knapp identified from her data, such as specialization, transferable skills, finding a focus, and learning on-the-job. In this coding presentation, we find that Knapp also indicates the sources of information that support the categories, such as interviews, focus groups, journals, memos, and observations.

To consider another example of open coding, see Figure 14.2 that displays the coding for a study of 33 academic chairpersons in colleges and universities and their roles in enhancing faculty research (Creswell & Brown, 1992). The authors organized their presentation of open coding differently than Knapp and included broad categories, categories, properties, and dimensionalized examples, and followed the systematic procedures of Strauss and Corbin (1998). The major features of this table are the seven categories of roles: provider, enabler, advocate, mentor, encourager, collaborator, and challenger. However, the authors introduce two new ideas into our understanding of open coding. **Properties** are subcategories in grounded theory of open codes that serve to provide more detail about each category. Each property, in turn, is dimensionalized in grounded theory. A **dimensionalized property** means that the researcher views the property on a continuum and locates, in the data, examples representing extremes on this continuum. For example, the chair, as a provider (category), engages in funding faculty (a property), that consists of possibilities on a continuum of extent of funds ranging from long-term start-up seed money to short-term travel money (dimensionalized property).

In the second phase, **axial coding,** the grounded theorist selects one open coding category, positions it at the center of the process being explored (as the core phenomenon), and then relates other categories to it. These other categories are the causal conditions (factors that influence the core phenomenon); strategies (actions taken in response to the core phenomenon); contextual and intervening conditions (specific and general situational factors that influence the strategies); and consequences (outcomes from using the strategies). This phase

FIGURE 14.1

An Example of Coding Categories in Grounded Theory

Categories	Coding Sources
Specialization	
definition	1, 2, 5, 6, 7, 10, 12, 13, 14, 15, 16, 17, 18, 19, 20, 21, 25, 26
generalist	1, 5, 7, 10, 12, 14, 15, 16, 19, 21, 23, 24
change agent	13, 17, J
Transferable skills	
previous job experience	CO2, 1, 3, 4, 5, 6, 8, 9, 11, 12, 13, 14, 15, 17, 19, 20, 22, 23, 24, 25, 26
cross training in another department	7, 8, 12, 17, 18, 19, 22, 23, 24, 25
Finding a focus	
entering field serendipitously	5, 6, 8, 9, 10, 11, 13, 15, 16, 19, 20, 22, 23, 24, J, M
occupational fit	2, 3, 4, 5, 6, 7, 8, 10, 11, 12, 13, 14, 15, 16, 17, 18, 19, 20, 21, 22, 23, 25, 26, J
turn down promotions	2, 12, 18, 23
understanding self	3, 6, 16, 17, 18, 19, 21, 22, 23, 24, 25
having a personal mission	3, 14, 16, 17, 18, 19
personally well grounded	2, 6, 13, 14, 19
other centered	CO2, 3, 8, 11, 13, 14, 15, 16, 17, 18, 19, 20, 21, 22, 24
Learning On-the-Job	
wandering around in the dark	CO2, 15, 22, M
trial and error	CO2, 2, 15, 16, 23, 24
gradual development	1, 4, 5, 6, 7, 8, 9, 17, 20, 22
facilitating training	1, 8, 11, 17, 20, 21, 24, 26
keeping current	CO2, 1, 2, 4, 5, 6, 8, 10, 11, 12, 15, 16, 17, 20, 21, 24, 26
learning environment	CO2, 18, 24, 26, F

	KEY
#	Interview
CO#	Pilot
F	Focus groups
J	Journal
M	Memo
O	Observation

Source: Reprinted with permission from Sharon Knapp, Ph.D.

FIGURE 14.2

An Example of Coding Categories in Grounded Theory with Properties and Dimensionalized Properties

Table 1
Open Coding of Chairperson's Role

Broad Categories*	Category	Properties	Dimensionalized Examples	
Administrative role	Provider	With funding	Start-up seed money	Short-term travel
		With nonfinancial aid	Laboratory equipment	Student personnel
	Enabler	With more money	Faculty committees	Long-term sabbatical
		With more visibility	Faculty committees	Administrative assignments
External role	Advocate	For resources	Short-term funds	Long-term facilities
		For interaction	With faculty	With students
		To assist politically	With dean	With faculty
Interpersonal role	Mentor	By role modeling	Time management	Working with others
		By sharing expertise	About research topics	About specific journals
		By reviewing and critiquing	Before manuscript submission	After manuscript submission
	Encourager	By hands off	No pressure	Choice belongs to professor
		By recognition and appreciation	Private communication	Public communication
		By general support	Personal friendship	Professional collegiality
		By task-specific encouragement	Supporting ideas	Encouraging specific book or article
	Collaborator	By jointly setting goals	Informal discussion	Formal performance reviews
		By working together on projects	Writing grant proposals	Writing journal articles
	Challenger	By prodding	Gentle reminder	Direct formal conversation
		By inspiring	Discussing general possibilities	Discussing specific examples
		By evaluating and monitoring	Bi-weekly conferences	Annual review

Source: Creswell & Brown, 1992.

*Strauss and Corbin define a category as "a classification of concepts." Concepts are conceptual labels placed on discrete happenings, events, and other phenomena, while properties are "attributes or characteristics pertaining to a category," and dimensions are "location of properties along a continuum" (1990, 61).

involves drawing a diagram, called a **coding paradigm,** which portrays the interrelationship of causal conditions, strategies, contextual and intervening conditions, and consequences.

To illustrate this process, first examine Figure 14.3. In this figure, we see the open coding categories on the left and the axial coding paradigm on the right. A grounded theory researcher identifies one of the open coding categories as the core category that is central to a theory (later we will review the criteria for selecting this core category). Then, this core category becomes the centerpoint of the axial coding paradigm. Examining this paradigm, you can see that there are six boxes (or categories) of information:

1. *Causal conditions*—categories of conditions that influence the core category
2. *Context*—the specific conditions that influence the strategies
3. *Intervening conditions*—the general contextual conditions that influence strategies
4. *Strategies*—the specific actions or interactions that result from the core phenomenon
5. *Consequences*—the outcomes of employing the strategies

In addition, viewing this coding paradigm from left-to-right, we see that the causal conditions influence the core phenomenon, the core phenomenon and the context and intervening conditions influence the strategies, and the strategies influence the consequences.

This third phase of coding consists of selection coding. In **selective coding** the grounded theorist writes a theory from the interrelationship of the categories in the axial coding model. At a basic level, this theory provides an abstract explanation for the process being studied in the research. It is the process of integrating and refining the theory (Strauss & Corbin, 1998) through such techniques as writing out the story line that interconnects the categories and sorting through personal memos about theoretical ideas (see memos later in the chapter). In a story line, a researcher might examine how certain factors influence the phenomenon leading to the use of specific strategies with certain outcomes.

Use of these three coding procedures means that grounded theorists use set procedures to develop their theory, rely on analyzing their data for specific types of categories in axial coding, and use diagrams to present their theories. A grounded theory study using this approach might end with hypotheses (called propositions by Strauss and Corbin, 1998) that make explicit the relationship among categories in the axial coding paradigm.

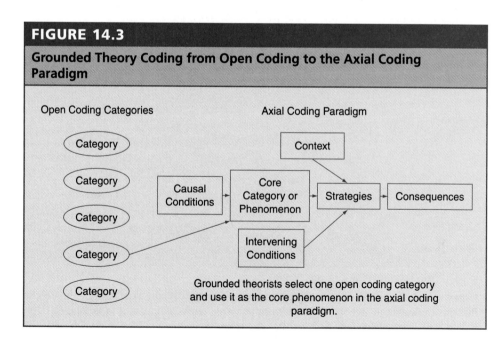

FIGURE 14.3

Grounded Theory Coding from Open Coding to the Axial Coding Paradigm

Open Coding Categories   Axial Coding Paradigm

Category

Category

Category

Category

Category

Context

Causal Conditions → Core Category or Phenomenon → Strategies → Consequences

Intervening Conditions

Grounded theorists select one open coding category and use it as the core phenomenon in the axial coding paradigm.

A study of the process of coping by eleven women who have survived childhood sexual abuse illustrates this systematic procedure (Morrow & Smith, 1995). In this study we learn that the women felt threatened, helpless, and powerless, but that they survived and coped by managing their feelings (e.g., avoiding or escaping feelings; not remembering experiences). They also address their feelings of hopelessness and powerlessness using strategies such as seeking control in other areas of their life, reframing abuse to give the illusion of control, or simply rejecting power issues. As an example of the systematic procedure associated with Strauss and Corbin (1990; 1998), the authors include the process of open coding, axial coding, and generating a theoretical model. They had clearly identified sections of the study for discussion about each component of axial coding (e.g., causes of feelings and helplessness, the strategies used, and the consequences). A diagram illustrates the "theoretical model" for surviving and coping, and they discuss this diagram as a sequence of steps in the process of coping behavior.

The Emerging Design

Although Glaser participated with Strauss in the initial book on grounded theory (Glaser & Strauss, 1967), Glaser has since written an extensive critique of the Strauss approach. In this critique, Glaser (1992) feels that Strauss and Corbin (1990) had overly emphasized rules and procedures, a preconceived framework for categories, and theory verification rather than theory generation. (See Babchuk, 1996, 1997, for a thorough review of how grounded theory has been used over the years and continues to be used.) Glaser, on the other hand, stresses the importance of letting a theory emerge from the data rather than using specific, pre-set categories (Glaser, 1992), such as we saw in the axial coding paradigm (e.g., causal conditions, content, intervening condition, strategies, and consequences). Moreover, for Glaser, the objective of a grounded theory study is for the author to explain a "basic social process." This explanation involves the constant comparative coding procedures of comparing incident to incident, and incident to category, as well as category to category. The focus is on connecting categories and emerging theory, not on simply describing categories. In the end, the researcher builds a theory and discusses the relationship among categories without reference to a diagram or picture.

The more flexible, less prescribed form of grounded theory research as advanced by Glaser (1992) can be distilled into several major ideas.

1. Grounded theory exists at the most abstract conceptual level rather than the least abstract level as found in visual data presentations such as a coding paradigm.
2. A theory is grounded in the data and it is not forced into categories.
3. A good grounded theory must meet four central criteria: fit, work, relevance, and modifiability. By carefully inducing the theory from a substantive area, it will fit the realities in the eyes of participants, practitioners, and researchers. If a grounded theory works, it will explain the variations in behavior of participants. If the theory fits and works, it has relevance. The theory should not be "written in stone" (Glaser, 1992, p. 15) and should be modified when new data are present.

Larson's (1997) study portrays a grounded theory study consistent with Glaser's approach. The goal for Larson (1997) was to write a "theory in-process" (p. 118) for high school social studies teachers' conception of discussion in their classrooms. This example of an emerging design takes the reader through six conceptions that emerged in the data: discussion as recitation; as a teacher-directed conversation; as an open-ended conversation; as posing challenging questions; as guided transfer of knowledge to the world outside the classroom; and as practice of verbal interaction. Larson also interrelated factors that influenced these conceptions, such as student diversity and lesson objectives.

In this emerging grounded theory approach, Larson's attention was on developing an explanation for discussion in high school social studies classrooms. His procedure was to generate categories by examining the data, refining the categories into fewer and fewer categories, comparing data with emerging categories, and writing a theory of several processes involved in classroom discussions. This article might be seen as theme development with the processes discussed within each theme. No diagram of the theory was presented.

The Constructivist Design

The constructivist approach has been articulated by Kathy Charmaz (see Charmaz, 1990; 2000) as a philosophical position between the more positivist (i.e., more quantitative) stance of Glaser and Strauss and Corbin and postmodern researchers (i.e., those that challenge the importance of methods). Overall, her focus is on the subjective meanings ascribed by participants in a study. She is more interested in the views, values, beliefs, feelings, assumptions, and ideologies of individuals than in gathering facts and describing acts. Charmaz suggests that any vestiges that obscure experiences, such as complex terms or jargon, diagrams, or conceptual maps, detract from grounded theory and represent an attempt to gain power in their use. Using active codes, such as "recasting life," best captures the experiences of individuals. Moreover, a grounded theory procedure does not minimize the role of the researcher in the process. The researcher makes decisions about the categories throughout the process (Charmaz, 1990). The researcher brings certain questions to the data, along with a "store of sociological concepts" (p. 1165) The researcher also brings values, experiences, and priorities. Any conclusions developed are suggestive, incomplete, and inconclusive.

In applying this approach, a grounded theorist explains the feelings of individuals as they experience a phenomenon or process. The constructivist study mentions the beliefs and values of the researcher and eschews predetermined categories, such as found in axial coding. The narrative is written to be more explanatory, more discursive, and more probing of the assumptions and meanings for individuals in the study.

One of Charmaz's own research studies illustrates the central elements of this approach to grounded theory. In a study of the processes involved in the experiences of 20 men with chronic illnesses (e.g., multiple sclerosis, renal failure, diabetes), Charmaz (1994) explores how and in what way their illnesses have precipitated a personal identity dilemma. She contends that chronic illness threatens men's "taken-for-granted" masculine identities. Her findings explored several dilemmas such as risking activity versus forced passivity, remaining independent versus becoming dependent, maintaining dominance versus becoming subordinate, and preserving a public persona versus acknowledging private feelings. These dilemmas clustered into several processes the men experienced—awakening to death, accommodating to uncertainty, defining illness and disability, and preserving self.

Using a constructivist approach to grounded theory, she clearly articulates that her purpose is to understand "what it means to have a disease" (Charmaz, 1994, p. 284). She reports the feelings of the men, using active code labels such as "awakening," "accommodating," "defining," and "preserving." These codes signal basic processes the men are experiencing. Charmaz interrelates their experiences, their conditions, and their consequences in a narrative discussion without the use of diagrams or figures to summarize these processes. She ends with thoughts more suggestive and questioning of the data [e.g., "What are the conditions that shape whether a man will reconstruct a positive identity or sink into depression?" (pp. 283–284)] than conclusive.

STRENGTHS AND WEAKNESSES OF GROUNDED THEORY

To reconcile the three approaches would be to diminish the importance of each. As you consider conducting a grounded theory study, you need to weigh how strongly you want to emphasize procedures, use predetermined categories in analysis, position yourself as a researcher, and decide how to end the study, whether it is with tentative questions or more specific hypotheses. Equally important is your assessment about the strengths—and the weaknesses—of using grounded theory.

Returning to the basic reason for the emergence of this design, grounded theory provides a means for developing theory in which theories are inadequate or non-existent. For instance, the study of certain educational populations (e.g., children with attention disorders), existing theories may have little applicability to special populations. Also, for the beginning researcher, grounded theory offers a step-by-step procedure for analyzing data. Having this procedure available may be helpful to students when they defend qualitative studies before faculty committees. As a systematic process, grounded theory exhibits the rigor quantitative researchers like to see in an educational study. In grounded theory research, the data collection process contains a self-correction nature. Based on analyzing one set of data, the researcher obtains direction from the analysis for the next set of data (Charmaz, 2000). Also, an emphasis on comparative methods enables one to build categories systematically from incident to incident and from incident to category. The researcher stays close to the data at all times in the analysis.

On the other hand, grounded theory has certain potential weaknesses. The procedures, at least those advanced by Strauss and Corbin (1998), may lead to a premature commitment to a set of analytic categories (Robrecht, 1995) and a lack of conceptual depth (Becker, 1993). Also, grounded theory has a distinct language that some educators may view as jargon and in need of careful definition (e.g., constant comparative, open coding, axial coding). One criticism is that these terms are not always clearly defined (Charmaz, 2000), although Strauss and Corbin (1998) provide numerous definitions at the beginning of each chapter of their book. Finally, with the varied approaches to this design and the continual emergence of new perspectives, readers may become confused and not know which procedures would best produce a well-developed theory.

KEY CHARACTERISTICS OF GROUNDED THEORY DESIGNS

Some of this confusion may be lifted, however, by discussing grounded theory characteristics from the perspective of all three types of designs. Grounded theory can incorporate a systematic approach, a flexible emerging design, and the use of active code to capture the experiences of participants. In the six characteristics that follow, you can find elements of the systematic, emerging, and constructivist approaches. Characteristics that grounded theory researchers use in their designs are:

- studying a process related to a substantive topic
- sampling theoretically involving the simultaneous and sequential collection and analysis of data
- constantly comparing data with an emerging theory

▶ selecting a core category as the central phenomenon for the theory
▶ generating a theory that explains a process about the topic

Studying a Process

Although grounded theorists might explore a single idea (e.g., leadership skills), they more frequently examine a process because the social world that we live in involves people interacting with other people. Grounded theorists generate an understanding of a process related to a substantive topic. A **process** in grounded theory research is a sequence of actions and interactions among people and events pertaining to a topic (Strauss & Corbin, 1998). The educational topic could be AIDS prevention, achievement assessment, or counseling between a school counselor and a student. In all of these topics, researchers can isolate and identify actions and interactions among people. Grounded theorists call these isolated aspects categories. **Categories** in grounded theory designs are themes of basic information identified in the data by the researcher and used to understand a process. A category for the process between a school counselor and student, for example, may be the student's understanding of "success" in the session.

As discussed in Chapter 9 on "Coding Data," there are several types of labels or titles that are used for themes or categories. In grounded theory research, a frequently used form is called in vivo codes. **In vivo codes** are labels for categories (or themes) that are phrased in the exact words of participants, rather than in the words of the researcher or in social science or educational terms. Researchers identify these words by examining passages of transcripts or observational fieldnotes to locate phrases mentioned by participants that capture the intent of a category. For example, rather than use the social science concept "upward mobility," a participant might call this idea "go'in up the ladder." Using in vivo coding, the researcher would use the phrase "go'in up the ladder" to describe the category. Because categories become major headings in research reports, this phrase would be used as the heading of the discussion about the open coding category "go'in up the ladder."

It is helpful to see how the two ideas of process and categories relate to activities that are typically applied by a grounded theorist. Examine the flow of activities as shown in Figure 14.4. A researcher begins with a research problem, such as the need to examine how academic chairpersons balance their work and personal lives. The central phenomenon, then, becomes a "balance of work and personal life." To study this central phenomenon, the grounded theorist frames it as a process, such as the "process by which chairs balance their work and personal lives" (alternatively, the process of "imbalance" might be explored). Whatever the process, it has a sequence of activities, actions by people, and interactions among people. The actions of the chair might include exercising early in the morning and visiting with faculty later in the morning about stressful situations in the department. Here we have several activities, organized into a sequence, exhibiting actions by people. As the grounded theorist studies chairs (e.g., through interviews or observations), an understanding of the process of balancing work and personal life slowly emerges. The researcher categorizes this information drawing on evidence to support each category. This phase is the open coding phase. Then the researcher starts organizing the categories into a model (axial coding), and interrelating the categories to form a theory that explains the process of balancing work and personal life. In this example, the process emerges from the problem and the need to explore the central phenomenon, and the categories develop from data collection.

As grounded theorists conduct a study, they often use a phrase for the process starting with a gerund word (i.e., "ing" words)(as recommended by Charmaz, 2000). This phrase appears in titles and purpose statements and will signal the action of the study. Below are

FIGURE 14.4

A Process and Categories within the Flow of Research in Grounded Theory

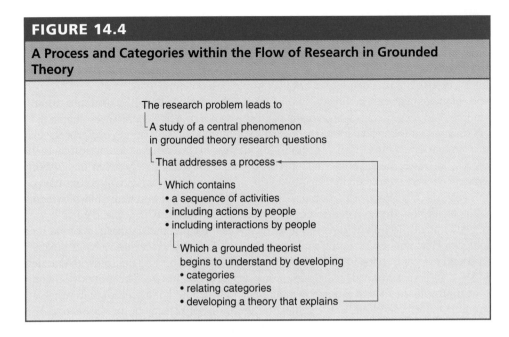

The research problem leads to

A study of a central phenomenon
in grounded theory research questions

That addresses a process

Which contains
• a sequence of activities
• including actions by people
• including interactions by people

Which a grounded theorist
begins to understand by developing
• categories
• relating categories
• developing a theory that explains

several titles for grounded theory studies where we can see the use of gerund words, a key category of interest, and the broader topic being explored:

▸ "Deciphering Chronic Pain" (Baszanger, 1997)—the process of deciphering; the category of chronic pain; the implied topic of patients
▸ "Educating every teacher, every year: The public schools and parents of children with ADHD" (Reid, Hertzog, & Snyder, 1996)—the process of educating teachers; the implied category of relations between parents and schools; the topic of children with ADHD
▸ "'Discovering' Chronic Illness: Using Grounded Theory" (Charmaz, 1990)—the process of patients discovering their illness; the category of chronic illness; the implied topic of disease
▸ "African-American Females: A Theory of Educational Aspiration" (Ponec, 1994)—the process of support systems; the category of educational aspiration; the topic of African-American female adolescents

Using Theoretical Sampling

The data collected by grounded theorists to establish these processes includes many forms of qualitative information (see Chapter 7 on "Identify Data to Collect"). Researchers can collect observations, conversations, interviews, public records, respondents' diaries and journals, and the researcher's own personal reflections (Charmaz, 2000). Many grounded theorists, however, rely heavily on interviewing, perhaps as a way to best capture the experiences of participants in their own words, which is an approach consistent with the constructivist position (Charmaz, 2000; Creswell, 1998).

In the purposeful sampling of individuals to interview or observe, grounded theory espouses a unique perspective that distinguishes it from other qualitative approaches to data collection. Grounded theorists sample theoretically using a procedure involving the simultaneous and sequential collection and analysis of data. **Theoretical sampling** in grounded theory means that the researcher chooses forms of data collection that will yield text and images useful in generating a theory. This means that the sampling is intentional and focused on the generation of a theory. For instance, when a grounded theorist decides to study children's choice of a school, students and their parents are good candidates for interviews because they are actively involved in the process of selecting a school and can speak from firsthand experience. On the other hand, school personnel (e.g., the principal) may have useful information to inform this process, but they would be less central than the students and parents, who are making the choices. In this project, the grounded theorist would begin with students and their parents who actually make the choice of schools.

Beyond sampling data for its theoretical value, grounded theorists also espouse the idea of using an emerging design. An **emerging design** in grounded theory research is the process in which the researcher collects data, analyzes it immediately rather than waiting until all data are collected, and then bases the decision about what data to collect next on this analysis. The image of a "zig-zag" helps understand this procedure, as shown in Figure 14.5. As illustrated in this figure, the grounded theorist engages in initial data collection (e.g., the first collection of interview data), analyzes it for preliminary categories, and then looks for clues about what additional data to collect. These clues may be categories that are underdeveloped, missing information in the sequence of the process being studied, or new individuals that can provide insight into some aspect of the process. The grounded theorist then returns to the field to gather this additional information. It is a procedure in which the inquirer refines, develops, and clarifies the meanings of categories for the theory. This process weaves back and forth between data collection and analysis, and it continues until the inquirer reaches saturation of a category. **Saturation** in grounded theory research is a state in which the researcher makes the subjective determination that new data will not provide any new information or insights for the developing categories.

Identifying this process in a published grounded theory study requires closely examining the data collection and analysis process and noting whether the researcher seems to be recycling between data collection and data analysis. For example, in a study of the processes of men experiencing chronic illness, Charmaz (1990) carefully documents how she interviewed more than once 7 of the 20 men in her study to refine her emerging categories.

Analyzing Through Constant Comparative Procedures

In grounded theory research, the inquirer engages in a process of gathering data, sorting it into categories, collecting additional information, and comparing the new information with emerging categories. This process of slowly developing categories of information is called the

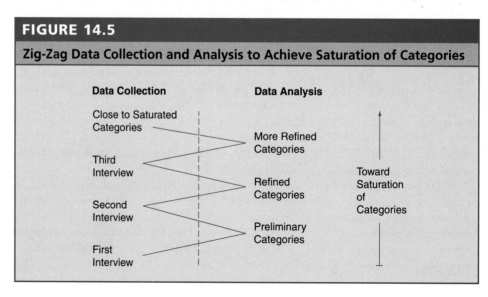

FIGURE 14.5

Zig-Zag Data Collection and Analysis to Achieve Saturation of Categories

constant comparative procedure. **Constant comparison** is an inductive (from specific to broad) data analysis procedure in grounded theory research of generating and connecting categories by comparing incidents in the data to other incidents, incidents to categories, and categories to other categories. The overall intent is to "ground" the categories in the data. As shown in Figure 14.6, raw data are formed into indicators (I)(Glaser, 1978)—small segments of information that come from different people, different sources, or the same people over time. These indicators are, in turn, grouped into several codes (e.g., Code A, Code B, Code C), and then formed into more abstract categories (e.g, Category I, Category II). Throughout this process, the researcher is constantly comparing indicators to indicators, codes to codes, and categories to categories. This is done to eliminate redundancy and to develop evidence for categories. In addition, the grounded theorist compares the emerging scheme with the raw data to ground the categories in the information collected during the study.

In this process the grounded theorist asks questions of the data. Glaser (1992), for example, suggests that the inquirer ask:

- What is the data a study of?
- What category or what property of what category does this incident indicate?
- What is actually happening in the data?
- What is the basic social psychological process or social structural process in the action scene? (p. 51)

In a grounded theory study of becoming an adult student in New Zealand, Cocklin (1996) collected observations, interviews, participant diary accounts, questionnaires, and documentary materials from teaching staff in one secondary school. In this study Cocklin described the process of refining his categories (called themes) by returning to his data over and over again as themes emerged. He commented:

> While doing this transcription and organization, and as an activity I undertook at weekends, statutory holidays, and term vacations, I also engaged in a continuous process of reflection and analysis which included placing interpretive comments alongside the transcribed data (see Figure 2). These comments, akin to the derivation of properties and hypotheses, I also subjected to ongoing analysis and development as the year progressed and data emerged. . . . (p. 97)

Selecting a Core Category

From among the major categories derived from the data, the grounded theorist selects a core category as the central phenomenon for the theory. After identifying several categories

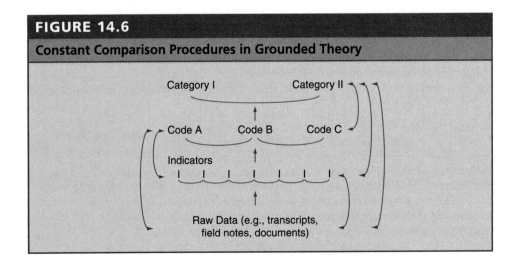

FIGURE 14.6

Constant Comparison Procedures in Grounded Theory

(e.g., say 8–10 depending on the size of the database), the researcher selects a **core category** as the basis for writing the theory. (See Figure 14.3 for a visual of this process.) This selection may be based on several factors, such as its relationship to other categories, its frequency of occurrence, its quick and easy saturation, and its clear implications for development of theory (Glaser, 1978). It is a category that can "process out", in other words, be developed as the center or main theme of the process (Glaser, 1978). Listed below are detailed criteria that Strauss and Corbin (1998) identify for choosing a central (or core) category.

1. It must be central; that is, all other major categories can be related to it.
2. It must appear frequently in the data. This means that within all or almost all cases, there are indicators pointing to that concept.
3. The explanation that evolves by relating the categories is logical and consistent. This is no forcing of data.
4. The name or phrase used to describe the central category should be sufficiently abstract.
5. As the concept is refined, the theory grows in depth and explanatory power.
6. When conditions vary, the explanation still holds, although the way in which a phenomenon is expressed might look somewhat different. (p. 147)

We can illustrate a core category by turning to an actual grounded theory study. As shown in Figure 14.7, Mastera (1996) developed a theoretical model of the "stages of forging a curriculum." In this study, she examined three undergraduate colleges from three states in the Midwest that were engaging in the process of changing their general education curricula. Semi-structured interviews with 34 faculty and administrators led to a theory about forging a curriculum. As shown in Figure 14.7, at the center of this theory was the phenomenon (or core category), "stages in forging a curriculum," consisting of several properties: calling for action, selecting the committee, norming the committee, setting the direction, designing the curriculum, approving the curriculum design, and approving the courses. Mastera's overall model showed how these stages were affected by changes, shaped by institutional context, led to strategies for leveraging the discourse on the committees, and contributed to specific consequences, such as revising the general education curriculum. In this process, Mastera identified early in open coding the importance of her phenomenon or core category, "stages," although "selecting labels that captured this staged process proved to be more elusive." (p. 59)

Generating a Theory

In identifying a core category and the process categories that explain it, grounded theorists have generated a middle-range theory. The entire procedure leads to generating a theory based on data collected by the researcher. This **theory** in grounded theory research is an abstract explanation or understanding of a process about a substantive topic grounded in the data. Because the theory is close to the data, it does not have wide applicability or scope, such as "grand" theories about human motivation that apply to many people and situations. Nor is it a "minor working hypothesis" (Glaser & Strauss, 1967, p. 33), such as an explanation for students in one school or classroom. Instead, the theory is "middle-range" (Charmaz, 2000), drawn from multiple individuals or data sources, that provides an explanation for a substantive topic.

It is useful to consider how grounded theorists actually present their theory in three possible ways: as a visual coding paradigm, as a series of propositions (or hypotheses) or as a story, written in narrative form.

Theory appears in studies as the visual coding model or coding paradigm discussed earlier in the systematic procedures of Strauss and Corbin (1998). We have viewed several

FIGURE 14.7

Example of a "Core Category" in a Theoretical Model of "Stages of Forging a Curriculum"

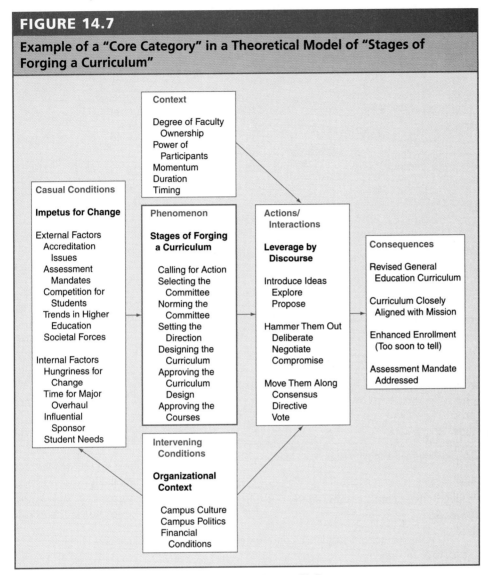

Source: Reprinted with permission from Georgianne Mastera, Ph.D.

of these coding paradigms already, but a slightly different version is seen in Brown's (1993) model of ethnic minority students' process of community building. As shown in Figure 14.8, Brown explored the process of community building among 23 Black and Hispanic freshmen during the first 6–10 weeks at a private, predominantly white university in the Midwest. In this study, an inductively developed process of campus community building was derived from the data. The theory or model of this process is shown in Figure 14.8. Based largely on the predetermined, systematic categories of intervening conditions, strategies, causal conditions, and phenomena, Brown developed a picture of the process as the key theoretical description of the process.

Brown's study also illustrates a visual model and the use of theoretical propositions (or hypotheses) for conveying a theory. **Theoretical propositions** in grounded theory research are statements indicating the relationship among categories, such as in the systematic approach to axial coding that include causal conditions, the core category or phenomenon, the context, intervening conditions, strategies, and consequences. After presenting her visual

FIGURE 14.8

Example of a Theory—A Model of Ethnic Minority Students' Process of Community Building

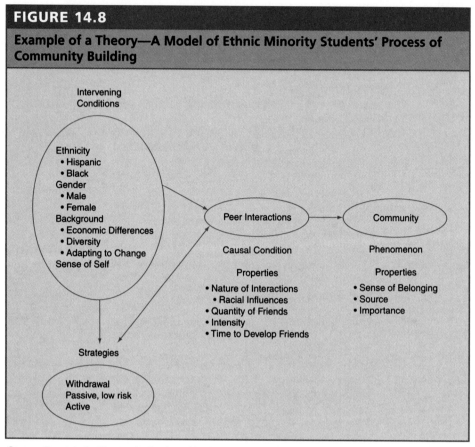

Source: Reprinted with permission from Martha L. Brown, Ph.D.

model, Brown identifies propositions and sub-propositions that interrelate her categories in the model:

> 1.0 Peer interactions influence community-building among Black and Hispanic college freshmen.
>
> 1.1 The more time students spend with peers, the greater their sense of community. The more their free time is spent alone, the greater the feelings of loneliness and alienation.
>
> 1.2 The more free time students spend on campus interacting with peers in the residence halls, the greater their sense of community.
>
> 1.3 Active involvement in small groups within the institutional setting (i.e., residence hall floors, freshmen seminar groups, intramural sports teams, clubs) will facilitate feelings of community.

Returning again to Figure 14.8, we can see that Brown is interrelating the causal conditions about interactions and friends in the proposition and sub-propositions. In additional propositions in her study, Brown continued to identify propositions that interrelated other aspects of her model.

Although the "theory" may be easy to identify in a grounded theory study when the author presents it as a visual coding paradigm or as a series of propositions, a discussion written in the form of a story (Strauss & Corbin, 1998), may be less obvious to a reader. In the process of integrating the categories, grounded theorists develop a sense of what the research is all about and start writing a descriptive story about the process. Strauss and Corbin (1998) recommend that the researcher:

> . . . sit down and write a few descriptive sentences about "what seems to be going on here." It make take two, three, or even more starts to be able to articulate one's thoughts concisely. Eventually, the story emerges. (p. 148)

After refinement and reworking, grounded theorists include these stories in their research reports as a means for describing their theory of the process. A good example of this type of passage is a descriptive story about teen drug use cited by Strauss and Corbin (1998):

> What keeps striking us about these interviews is that, although many teens use drugs, few go on to become hard-core users. It seems to be a kind of teenage experimentation, a developmental phase in their lives that marks the passage from child to teen and from teen to adult. They learn about drugs and also themselves, gain acceptance from their peers, and challenge adult authority through using drugs. It is a very specific behavior that sets them apart from family, but, at the same time, makes them one of the teen group. (p. 149)

In this passage the authors identify a causal condition (i.e., "developmental phase"). They also mention the outcomes (i.e., "marks the passage"), and establish context (e.g., "sets them apart from family"). Through this descriptive story, the authors interrelate several categories of axial coding to form a theoretical discussion about the process of teen drug use—a third form for writing theory into a grounded theory project.

Using Memos

Throughout the grounded theory procedure, grounded theorists memo to themselves. Memo writing is a tool in grounded theory research that provides for researchers an ongoing dialogue with themselves about the emerging theory (Charmaz, 1990). **Memos** are notes the researcher writes throughout the research process to elaborate on ideas about the data and the coded categories. In memos, the researcher explores hunches, ideas, and thoughts, and then takes them apart, always searching for the broader explanations at work in the process being examined. Memos help direct the inquirer toward new sources of data, shape which ideas to develop further, and prevent paralysis from mountains of data. However, grounded theory studies do not often use memoing or, if they do, they do not provide evidence of how it was used (Babchuck, 1997).

We can illustrate memoing in a study about the process of identity loss by individuals with Alzheimer's disease. Orona (1997) discussed memoing to:

1. free associate and help her write whatever thoughts she became aware of
2. unblock at times when she felt she could not quite describe in words what was occurring in the data
3. begin conceptualizing by tracking ideas from raw data to coding and on to categories

The memos can be short or long, more detailed and related to codes and categories, or broader and more abstract. Here is an illustration of a short, detailed memo written by Charmaz (1990) during her study of terminally ill patients and the "identifying moments" in the hospital when patients developed new insight into themselves.

> It became clear to me that how a particular chronically ill person was identified by others sometimes became revealed to them in the course of a moment's encounter or interaction. These moments gave the ill individual new reflections of self, often revealing that he (or she) is not the person he felt he was. . . . Negative identifying moments are those shrouded in embarrassment and devaluation. . . . One woman described a demeaning encounter with a social service agency when in the course of a moment, she saw herself as being defined as someone not worth helping. She

said, "All I can do is dissolve in tears—there is nothing I can do. I just get immobilized. . . ." (Charmaz, 1994, pp. 110–111)

This passage illustrates how a grounded theorist can write a memo, use it in a study, highlight her own reflexive thoughts in a way consistent with qualitative research, and use the memo to highlight categories of information (i.e., "negative identifying moments").

STEPS IN CONDUCTING A GROUNDED THEORY STUDY

Given the different types of grounded theory procedures—systematic, emerging, and constructivist—alternative steps might be taken by researchers when they engage in inquiry. The approach taken here will be the systematic form of inquiry because it consists of easily identifiable steps, is frequently used for grounded theory research, and provides a procedure that beginning researchers will find useful.

Step 1. Decide If a Grounded Theory Design Best Addresses the Research Problem

A grounded theory design is appropriate when you want to develop or modify a theory, explain a process, and develop a general abstraction of the interaction and action of people. As such, it offers a macro-picture of educational situations rather than a detailed microanalysis. Because of the generation of an abstract process, it seems suitable for sensitive topics, such as the coping process of women who have been sexually abused (Morrow & Smith, 1995) or any research problem situation in which individuals need their privacy protected. Grounded theory also seems applicable for those individuals who are trained in quantitative research but that want to explore a *qualitative* procedure that is rigorous and systematic. For example, in educational fields in which *qualitative* research has made slow inroads, such as counseling and school psychology, inquirers are turning to grounded theory as a useful procedure (e.g., see one of many examples, such as Frontman & Kunkel's 1994 grounded theory study about how counselors construe success with clients).

Step 2. Identify a Process to Study

Because the intent of grounded theory research is to explain a process, you need to identify early a tentative process to examine in your grounded theory study. This process may change and emerge during your study, but a preliminary idea of the process is identified at this step. This process should naturally follow from your research problem and research questions that you seek to answer. It needs to involve people who are acting or interacting with identifiable steps or sequence in their interactions. It is helpful to write down this process early in your plan for a study, such as "What is the process of coping for first year teachers?" or "What is the process by which faculty develop into productive researchers?"

Step 3. Seek Approval and Access

As with all research studies, you need to obtain approval from the institutional review board. You also need access to individuals who can provide insight into the process that you plan to study. Like other studies, this step involves seeking approval to collect data, appraising individuals of the purpose of your study, and guaranteeing protection of the site and participants as you conduct the inquiry.

If you plan to use the "zig-zag" approach to data collection and analysis, it is difficult to plan ahead and receive approval for collecting data. This approach relies on collecting data, analyzing it, and using this information to determine the next step in data collection. Thus, as you seek permission to conduct a grounded theory study, it is helpful to appraise reviewers of this process and the tentative nature of the data collection procedures at the beginning of the study.

Step 4. Conduct Theoretical Sampling

The key concept in grounded theory data collection is to gather information that can assist in your development of a theory (e.g., individuals who have experienced the process you are studying). Grounded theorists use many forms of data (such as those mentioned in Chapter 8 on "Identify Data to Collect"), but many researchers rely on interviews to best capture the experiences of individuals in their own words. A characteristic of grounded theory research, however, is that the inquirer collects data more than once, and keeps returning to data sources for more information throughout a study until the categories are saturated and the theory is fully developed. There is no precise timeline for this process and researchers need to make the decision as to when they have fully developed their categories and the theory. One rule of thumb in graduate student research and interviewing is to collect at least 20 to 30 interviews during data collection (Creswell, 1998). This general guideline, of course, may change if you collect multiple sources of data, such as observations, documents, and your own personal memos.

Step 5. Code the Data

The process of coding data occurs during data collection so that you can determine what data to collect next. It typically begins with the identification of open coding categories and using the constant comparative approach to compare data with incident and incident to category until the category is saturated. A reasonable number of 10 categories may suffice, although this number depends on the extent of your database and the complexity of the process you are exploring. McCaslin (1993), for example, conducted a grounded theory study of the complex question of leadership in rural communities. In exploring "What is leadership?", he identified 50 categories from observing and interviewing individuals participating in educational leadership development programs in six counties.

From open coding you will proceed to axial coding and the development of a coding paradigm. This involves the process identified in Figure 14.3 of selecting a core category from the open coding possibilities and positioning it at the center of the axial coding process as a core category. From here you will likely return to data collection or re-analyze your data to identify causal conditions, intervening and contextual categories, strategies, and consequences to develop the axial coding process. This information can be assembled in the form of a coding paradigm or visual picture of the process in which you indicate with arrows the direction of the process.

Step 6. Use Selective Coding and Develop the Theory

The final process of coding is selective coding, in which you begin to develop your theory. This involves interrelating the categories in the coding paradigm. It may involve refining the axial coding paradigm and presenting it as a model or theory of the process. It may include writing propositions that provide testable ideas to be further explored, although varied perspectives exist about whether the researcher or someone else might test the proposition or use them in practice. If you present your theory this way, it can be presented as a series of propositions or sub-propositions. This stage may also involve writing a story, or a narrative that describes the interrelationships among categories.

Step 7. Validate Your Theory

It is important to determine if your theoretical explanation makes sense to participants and is an accurate rendering of events and their sequence in the process. In grounded theory research, validation is an active part of the process of research (Creswell, 1998). For example, during the constant comparative procedure of open coding, the researcher triangulates data between the information and the emerging categories. The same process of checking data against categories occurs in the axial coding phase. The researcher poses questions that relate the categories, and then returns to the data and looks for evidence, incidents, and events—a process in grounded theory called **discriminant sampling.** After developing a theory, the grounded theorist validates the process by comparing it with existing processes found in the literature. Also, outside reviewers may substantiate the theory, such as participants in the project who judge the grounded theory using "canons" of good science, including as validity and credibility of the data (Strauss & Corbin, 1998).

Step 8. Write a Grounded Theory Research Report

The structure of your grounded theory report will vary from a flexible structure in the emerging and constructivist design to a more quantitatively oriented structure in the systematic design. As compared with other qualitative designs, such as ethnography and narrative research, grounded theory studies tend to be more scientifically structured to include a problem, methods, discussion, and results. In addition, the point of view of the writer in the systematic approach is sometimes third person and objective in tone. All grounded theory projects, however, end with the theory generated by the researcher reporting his or her abstraction of the process under examination.

CRITERIA FOR EVALUATING A GROUNDED THEORY DESIGN

Criteria for evaluating a grounded theory study rely on an assessment of the theory (Glaser 1978; 1992) as well as the overall procedure used in generating it (Strauss & Corbin, 1990; 1998).

When evaluating the study, ask about the theory:

▶ Is there an obvious connection or fit between the categories and the raw data?
▶ Is the theory useful as a conceptual explanation for the process being studied? In other words, does it work?
▶ Does the theory provide a relevant explanation of actual problems and a basic process?
▶ Can the theory be modified as conditions change or further data are gathered?

Next, ask about the process of research:

▶ Is a theoretical model developed or generated? Is the intent of this model to conceptualize a process, an action, or an interaction?
▶ Is there a central phenomenon (or core category) specified at the heart of this model?
▶ Does the model emerge through phases of coding? (e.g., from initial codes to more theoretically oriented codes, or from open coding, to axial coding, to selective coding)

▶ Does the researcher attempt to interrelate the categories? (e.g., propositions, discussion, a model or diagram)

▶ Does the researcher gather extensive data so as to develop a detailed conceptual theory well saturated in the data?

▶ Does the study show that the researcher validated the evolving theory by comparing it to data, examining how the theory supports or refutes existing theories in the literature, or checking the theory with participants?

APPLYING WHAT YOU HAVE LEARNED: A GROUNDED THEORY STUDY

To apply the ideas in this chapter, first read the grounded theory study on page 464, noting marginal annotations that identify the characteristics of grounded theory research and qualitative research.

> Feen-Calligan, H. (1999). Enlightenment in chemical dependency treatment programs: A grounded theory. In C. A. Malchiodi (Ed.), *Medical art therapy with adults,* 141–161. London: Jessica Kingsley Publishers.

The Feen-Calligan (1999) grounded theory study addresses the role that art therapy plays in individuals' recovery from chemical addiction. Based on interviews with therapists, psychiatrists, and patients, Feen-Calligan analyzed the information for open codes and identified the categories of spectrum disease, underlying turbulence, treatment program, arts as healing, waves of treatment, and health care changes. She then selected the core category or phenomenon of "enlightenment" as the centerpiece of her theory. A coding paradigm of this core category presented causes of it, strategies used by therapists, the context in which the strategies were used, and the consequences to the patients from using the strategies. At the end of the study we find theoretical propositions interrelating the categories of the coding paradigm. A useful list of art tasks mentioned by the therapists and the inclusion of art developed by patients adds value and interest to this study.

This study was chosen because it focuses on a process (becoming enlightened during the recovery). It also employs solid grounded theory procedures consistent with the approach of Strauss and Corbin (1998) and it "educates" the reader about grounded theory by keeping the reader posted about each step in the process as it is taken. The article further uses a table to clearly illustrate the initial categories and a diagram to show the interrelationship of categories. The study ends with propositions or hypotheses that make the connections among the categories and the emerging theory explicit. The author did not explicitly mention memoing, but she may have incorporated this procedure into her research activities.

As you review this article, look for elements of the research process:

▶ the research problem and the use of qualitative research
▶ use of the literature
▶ the purpose statement and research questions
▶ types and procedures of data collection
▶ types and procedures of data analysis and interpretation
▶ the overall writing structure

After you read the article and reflect on these elements, read the following analysis of the study.

The Research Problem and Use of Qualitative Research

The research problem—see Paragraphs 02–04

Use of qualitative research—see the marginal annotations on the left side of the page

After an introductory paragraph summarizing the major aspects of the study, Paragraph 02 introduces the problem addressed in this study: the public health issue in our society of chemical addiction. Among the treatment options, one approach is art therapy, and the author suggests that no theory exists to explain the role of art therapy in treating chemical addictions.

This article has many key markings of qualitative research:

- It explores the process of the role of art therapy to help a person become enlightened in response to chemical dependency. (Paragraph 04)
- The literature is used to focus the study on treatment for chemical dependency. (Paragraph 03)
- The author uses self-reflection by including one of her own studies. (Paragraph 03)
- The purpose of the study is identified in the first sentence of the article. (Paragraph 01)
- Data are collected from a few individuals ($N=19$). (Paragraphs 06, 08)
- There is a collection of words or text through interviews (Paragraphs 08–09) and there is the use of images (the pictures of the patients). (e.g., Figure 6.2 in Paragraph 27)
- The researcher uses her own forms rather than using existing instruments. (Paragraph 09)
- The analysis of text is done by coding. (Paragraphs 11–20)
- The author interprets the findings within the larger, more abstract value of art therapy and self-reflection and self-awareness. (Paragraph 56)
- A flexible writing structure is used to reflect topics addressed in a grounded theory study. (e.g., Paragraph 11 on open coding)

Use of the Literature

See Paragraph 02

With a couple of minor exceptions, the entire literature in this study is cited at the beginning where it is used to describe the importance of the problem (addiction and the need for treatment). Consistent with qualitative inquiry, the literature plays a minor role and does not influence the questions being addressed by the researcher.

The Purpose Statement and Research Questions

Purpose statement—see Paragraph 01

Central question—see Paragraph 05

Interview questions—see Paragraph 09

The author opens with a statement about the intent of the study: to explore the role of art therapy in individuals' recovery from chemical addiction. The exact process being studied might have been made more explicit, and one does not know whether the process being examined is the recovery or the use of art in therapy.

The central question in this study helps to clear up some of this mystery. The author asks, "What is the theory that explains the process of art therapy in addiction treatment?" Generating a theory that explains this process is further supported by the specific interview questions aimed at understanding the role of art therapy, its outcomes, and the facility's treatment philosophy.

Types of Procedures of Data Collection

See Paragraphs 06–10

Qualitative data were collected from a small number of individuals ($N=19$), but these were people intentionally sampled because they could provide information for the generation of the theory. They experienced art therapy in therapist-client situations. Inconsistent with the "zig-zag" approach, the author did not seem to make multiple passes to the field to collect data except for the second contact with therapists to obtain recommendations about patients who might participate in the study. The data collection consisted of interviewing and collecting pictures of art rather than using additional sources of information (e.g., personal journals by therapists and patients).

Types of Procedures of Data Analysis and Interpretation

Data analysis—see Paragraphs 11–20

Interpretation—see Paragraphs 56–57

The author reports that she engaged in three forms of coding the data: open coding to generate initial categories, axial coding to form connections among the categories, and selective coding to help her develop a story that connected the categories. Consistent with grounded theory procedures, she identified her core category (central phenomenon) after initial coding. Specifically, from among the six categories listed in Table 6.1, she selected "self-expression" and "self-awareness" as the main theme and, using the words of participants in the study, called this core category "enlightenment." She then "processed out" this category in terms of categories related to it and drew a diagram of this process (see Figure 6.1, axial coding). She explained each of the categories in this diagram and made the relationships explicit through six hypotheses or propositions. In addition, to help the reader understand this core category, she introduced it in the title of the study and included it in the introduction (Paragraph 01). Feen-Calligan's open coding table and axial coding diagram provide useful models for representing findings in a grounded theory study.

Interpretation of the findings comes in the final section of the study in which Feen-Calligan relates her finding about enlightenment to the value of art therapy in general, and the self-awareness and self-reflection that aids individuals in recovery.

The Overall Writing Structure

See the headings used in the study

By examining the headings, you can see that this article closely resembles a scientific study. It begins with the literature and the problem, then proceeds to data collection and findings. The systematic procedures of coding discussed here (open, axial, and selective) give a strong procedural flavor to the study and emphasize rigor. The use of a diagram and tables also underscore the more scientific approach to this report.

KEY IDEAS IN THE CHAPTER

A grounded theory design is a set of procedures used to systematically generate a theory that explains, at a broad conceptual level, a process about a substantive topic. This design was developed by sociologists Barney Glaser and Anselm Strauss at the University of California San Francisco in the late 1960s. Glaser and Strauss both collaborated on a book and also wrote independent books on the procedures of grounded theory. The original thrust behind grounded theory was to develop a theory "grounded" in the data rather than use one borrowed from the social sciences literature. The evolution of grounded theory has led to disagreements between Glaser and Strauss and with others, such as Charmaz. Charmaz has advanced her own approach to grounded theory research.

Grounded theory research consists of three types of designs. The systematic procedure of Strauss and Corbin (1998) involves using predetermined categories to interrelate the categories, visual diagrams, and specific propositions or hypotheses to make the connections explicit. The emergent design, consistent with Glaser (1992), relies on exploring a basic social process without pre-set categories. The constructivist approach of Charmaz (2000) focuses on subjective meanings by participants, explicit researcher values and beliefs, and suggestive or tentative conclusions.

Despite these differences, six aspects characterize grounded theory. Grounded theorists employ this design to explore a process around a substantive topic. They theoretically sample using a procedure of simultaneous data collection and analysis. Grounded theorists analyze their data for increasing levels of abstraction by using constant comparative procedures and asking questions about their data. During analysis of the data for categories, grounded theorists identify a core category (or central phenomenon) that will "process out" (Strauss, 1978) into a theory. Grounded theorists explore this process in order to develop a theory. Throughout the grounded theory procedure, grounded theorists memo to themselves.

On balance, grounded theory provides a means for generating a theory "grounded" in the participant's views rather than using an existing theory, it offers a step-by-step procedure for conducting the design, and it enables an inquirer to let the study emerge through analysis close to the data. Central to this process are the steps of open coding, axial coding, and selective coding in which a theory emerges that is presented and explained through strategies such as a visual picture, a series of propositions (or hypotheses), or a narrative description.

USEFUL INFORMATION FOR PRODUCERS OF RESEARCH

▶ When planning a grounded theory study, use the steps for conducting a study advanced in this chapter.
▶ Consider whether your grounded theory study will be systematic, emergent, or constructivist. Make this decision based on reviewing the arguments for each design type and determining whether you prefer a more flexible or prescribed approach to grounded theory research.
▶ The visuals presented in this chapter can be adapted and used to display several processes and to create tables and diagrams, such as the "zig-zag" data collection and the constant comparative approach.
▶ Creating a visual diagram of your theory helps to clearly identify the categories and see their interrelationships.
▶ Validate your theory by using constant comparative procedures, triangulating during the research, and by employing member-checking with participants in your study.

USEFUL INFORMATION FOR CONSUMERS OF RESEARCH

▶ Educators can use the criteria for evaluating a study and the six characteristics of a grounded research study to assess the quality of a published study.

▶ When examining a study to determine if it is a grounded theory project, you might look at the title to determine if the words "grounded theory" are included. Also, most grounded theory projects clearly include an exploration of a process, and the authors should identify this process in the purpose statement or research questions.

▶ A sign of grounded theory research is that the author employs multiple passes to the field to collect data. A well-refined theory (and categories) consists of saturation and zig-zagging back and forth between data collection and analysis to build the categories and theory.

▶ Look for a visual model of the theory. This model is the centerpiece of the grounded theory study and represents the author's attempt to visualize the process under study.

ADDITIONAL RESOURCES YOU MIGHT EXAMINE

Several major books are available to provide the procedures used in grounded theory research. Examine the books by Strauss:

Strauss, A. (1987). *Qualitative analysis for social scientists.* New York: Cambridge University Press.

Strauss, A., & Corbin, J. (1998). *Basics of qualitative research: Techniques and procedures for developing grounded theory,* (2nd ed.). Thousand Oaks, CA: Sage.

Examine the books by Glaser:

Glaser, B. G. (1992). *Basics of grounded theory analysis.* Mill Valley, CA: Sociology Press.

Glaser, B. G. (1978). *Theoretical sensitivity.* Mill Valley, CA: Sociology Press.

You might also consult the original book they developed together:

Glaser, B., & Strauss, A. (1967). *The discovery of grounded theory.* Chicago: Aldine.

For a recent perspective on grounded theory from a constructivist perspective, examine the book chapter by Charmaz (2000) and look at her journal articles for applications of her approach:

Charmaz, K. (1990). 'Discovering' chronic illness: Using grounded theory. *Social Science Medicine, 30,* 1161–1172.

Charmaz, K. (1994). Identity dilemmas of chronically ill men. *The Sociological Quarterly, 35,* 269–288.

Charmaz, K. (2000). Grounded theory: objectivist and constructivist methods. In N. K. Denzin and Y. S. Lincoln (Eds.), *Handbook of qualitative research,* (2nd ed., pp. 509–535). Thousand Oaks, CA: Sage.

Qualitative
Characteristics

Enlightenment in Chemical Dependency Treatment Programs: A Grounded Theory

Grounded Theory
Research
Characteristics

Holly Feen-Calligan

Introduction

The qualitative purpose
statement and research
questions are broad and
general.   (01)

This chapter describes a study which explores the role of art therapy in recovery from chemical addiction. This study is "grounded" in the interview data of eleven art therapists, four psychiatrists and five individuals in recovery. The grounded theory method used to analyze the data involves identifying a "central phenomenon" in the data. In this study, "enlightenment" emerged as the central phenomenon. It is hoped that the results will inform practice through contributing to the development of the theoretical basis of art therapy in recovery from addiction.

Grounded theorists
generate a theory.

Grounded theorists
study a process related
to a substantive topic.

The qualitative purpose
statement and research
questions seek
participants'
experiences.

Chemical Addiction

Grounded theorists
select a core category as
the central
phenomenon.

(02)

Considered to be the largest and most serious public health problem facing our society, the cost of chemical addiction in health care, unemployment, poverty, and violence is immense (Chopra 1997; Steele 1997). Various approaches to treating chemical addiction, including Alcoholics Anonymous (AA), outpatient psychotherapy and inpatient rehabilitation programs, have at best experienced mixed success (Miller 1995). Employees of hospital based rehabilitation programs are well aware of the high relapse rates among their patients. Among those who remain substance free, many fail to achieve recovery in the full sense of the word, leading dissatisfied or unfulfilled lives. Adding to the treatment dilemma are statistics showing an increasingly diverse patient population with more complicated medical problems (Craddock *et al.* 1997) and reductions in health care funding available to treat the problem (Van Leit 1995). Given this situation, alternative treatments need to be explored.

(03)

One such alternative or complementary treatment is art therapy. The use of art in chemical dependency treatment programs has been documented since the 1950s (Ulman 1953) and the benefits of art therapy have been addressed in the literature (Albert-Puleo and Osha 1976–77; Allen 1985; Devine 1970; Foulke and Keller 1976; Moore 1983). Generally, art therapy is believed to help circumvent verbal defensiveness, often thought to be typical of addicts. Art therapy contributes to addicts' ability to get in touch with feelings numbed by chemicals and contributes to increased personal awareness of motivation for chemical use. Such personal awareness can be empowering and help to provide the self-confidence and strength necessary to pursue a life of sobriety "one day at a time." The process of mastering art processes and interpretation of art works parallels mastery of painful feelings. There is a reflective or even spiritual experience inherent to the creative process (Burke 1985; Chickerneo 1990) that seems to help individuals to trust spiritual concepts espoused in recovery programs such as "Let go and let God" (Feen-Calligan 1995).

The qualitative literature
justifies the research
problem.

Qualitative researchers
take a reflexive and
biased approach.

(04)

Because many benefits of art therapy were observed when patients were admitted for longer periods of stay than is typical in treatment programs today, it is less clear just how art therapy has been adapted for shortened hospital stays. No *theory* currently exists about the role of art therapy in chemical addiction treatment programs. In order to determine practical uses of art therapy in treatment programs given today's health care realities, it is important to develop a theory of how art therapy can be used with this population.

A qualitative problem
requires exploration and
understanding.

(05)   The "grounded theory" tradition was selected as the method of data collection and analysis because of its potential to contribute to the development of theory. Grounded theory is a qualitative research method developed in the 1960s by two sociologists, Barney Glaser and Anselm Strauss (1967), that uses a systematic set of procedures to understand processes and interactions in order to develop theory about a particular phenomenon. The aim of this study is to generate theory about art therapy in recovery from addiction, 'grounded in,' or based upon the interviews of art therapists, psychiatrists, and individuals in recovery. The study sought to answer the following question: What is the theory that explains the process of art therapy in addiction treatment?

Data Collection and Analysis

> Qualitative data collection involves studying a small number of individuals or sites.

(06)   In the first phase of the study, eleven art therapists and four psychiatrists were interviewed about the process of using art with chemical dependency patients. A theoretical sampling procedure was used in which respondents were selected for what they could contribute to the evolving theory (Strauss and Corbin 1990). The art therapists were selected from a list of members of the Art Therapy/Addiction Counselor (AT/AC) Network, a peer-support group formed by members of the American Art Therapy Association. Among the art therapists, nine worked with adults, two with adolescents. Four art therapists worked in outpatient settings, in programs of one month to one year duration. Four worked in hospitals in psychiatric inpatient, outpatient and day treatment programs, in programs ranging from three days to three weeks. Others practiced in settings including a residential substance abuse program for women and children, a domestic violence program, and a residential adolescent substance abuse program, with a range in length of stay from three to six months. One art therapist was a supervisor of a county-wide substance abuse program. All art therapists lived and worked in the United States, in Michigan, Ohio, Illinois, Kentucky, Massachusetts, South Carolina and California.

> Grounded theorists theoretically sample to best develop the theory.

(07)   Psychiatrists were selected because of their work in addiction psychiatry, and all were associated with major medical centers and had outpatient practices. Consistent with grounded theory procedures (Conrad 1978), psychiatrists were interviewed as a comparison group to help evaluate the conditions under which the art therapy model would hold. Although the focus of this research is upon adult medical settings, interviewing professionals in related settings helps the researcher "to be theoretically sensitive to the range of conditions that might bear upon the phenomenon under study" (Strauss and Corbin 1990, p. 161). Furthermore, a formal theory must emerge from studying phenomena examined under many different types of situations.

> Qualitative data collection involves gathering text or image data.

(08)   In order to understand more about an individual's first-hand experience with art therapy, the views of recovering individuals were solicited. The art therapists interviewed in the first phase were contacted a second time for recommendations of patients who might complete a questionnaire or consent to be interviewed. In the second phase of the study, four questionnaires were completed by individuals who, at the time, were patients in treatment programs. One individual in longer term recovery was also interviewed. This individual had participated in an inpatient treatment program at the beginning of his recovery several years earlier, and had remained active in art. Although only one individual in longer-term recovery was interviewed, this person's experiences assist with relating conditions, actions/interactions and consequences to the phenomenon being studied (Strauss and Corbin 1990).

(09)   Interviews were conducted both face-to-face, and over the phone when necessary. All interviews were audio taped and transcribed, verbatim.

Qualitative data collection is based on using protocols developed during the study.

Interviews ranged from 30 to 90 minutes in length. Interviews of psychiatrists and art therapists were open-ended and began by asking respondents to describe their work with patients, their view of the role of art therapy in the patient's recovery, how progress or successful outcome is assessed and the facility's philosophy of treatment. Other questions covered descriptive information about their practices and any other information thought to be relevant. Individuals in recovery were asked to describe their experiences with art therapy or making art and the relationship between art making and recovery. They were asked whether a particular work of art created had special meaning for them, and what therapists should understand about someone in recovery.

(10)   The transcribed interviews were mailed to the respondents for verification purposes requesting clarification or additions when necessary. Additional verification was provided through triangulation. That is, the responses from the psychiatrists verified those of the art therapists with regard to the causal conditions of chemical addiction and strategies to address the problems. Rich description allows readers to make decisions about the transferability of the findings.

Open Coding

(11)   The procedures for data analysis in grounded theory involve three types of coding procedures: open coding, axial coding, and selective coding. Open coding consists of naming and categorizing data. As interview transcriptions are reviewed, concepts or themes with similar properties are grouped together. The categories are arranged and rearranged until 'saturated;' that is, until I was satisfied that the concepts were similar and should be grouped together. Six major categories emerged in the open coding process. These categories were named using 'in vivo codes,' terms drawn directly from the data. The in vivo codes (six major categories) were named: (1) spectrum disease, (2) underlying turbulence, (3) type of treatment program, (4) art as healing, (5) waves of treatment, and (6) health care changes. In open coding, not only are categories grouped together, but properties of the categories are also examined as well as dimensions or ranges of the properties. Considering the properties of categories helps the researcher to know that the categories are properly grouped together, or are saturated.

Qualitative data analysis consists of text analysis.

Grounded theorists use constant comparative analysis procedures for coding.

(12)   The first category, "spectrum disease," refers to the spectrum of problems an addicted person often has. There is a spectrum of severity and chronicity of problems experienced, and a range in ages of patients. Chemical addiction is a spectrum illness because it falls along a continuum of related disorders associated with it. Medical doctors often have great difficulty diagnosing the primary disorder, as substance abuse often is intertwined with a psychiatric disorder. Older chemically addicted patients also often have medical problems. Furthermore, there is a spectrum of treatment philosophies, ranging from addiction models (disease concept) to psychiatric models of treatment. Thus, one property of the spectrum disease is the diagnosis. The dimensions of diagnoses range from substance abuse as a primary disorder to a dual diagnosis coexisting with a psychiatric diagnosis. Table 6.1 lists the six categories, their properties and dimensions.

Qualitative data analysis consists of describing information and developing themes.

(13)   The second category, "underlying turbulence," reflects the addicts' motivation for use. Usually the motivation for use had to do with control. Controlling moods and feelings was commonplace, either to feel more high, or more low (in the case of bipolar, dually diagnosed individuals), or to numb out or fill an inner emptiness. Often there was a trauma, loss or stressor that precipitated use. This was true of individuals coming from families with or without histories of chemical dependence.

(14)

TABLE 6.1
Open Coding of Art Therapy in Chemical Dependency Treatment Programs

Category	Properties	Dimensionalized examples	
Spectrum disease	Diagnosis	Primary substance abuse	Dual diagnosis
	Problem manifested	Biological/medical problems	Psycho-social problems
	Treatment philosophy	Addiction model (disease concept)	Psychiatry model
	Age of patient	Adolescent	Older adult
Underlying turbulence	Control feelings	Feel less depressed	Feel less anxious
	Painkiller	Numb painful feelings	Fill inner emptiness
	Reason for use	Psychic pain	Physical pain
		Genetic predisposition	Coping or learned behavior
Treatment program	Type of facility	Inpatient	Outpatient
	Treatment Type	Free Standing	General hospital
		Pharmacology	Psychotherapy
		Behavioral	Uncovering
		Group therapy	Individual
Art as healing	Benefits	Self-expression	Self-awareness
	Stages in art process	Resistant	Reflective
	Approaches	Structured/didactic	Unstructured/open studio
	Themes	Absence of self	Self-portraits
	Media	Pencils	Paint
	Art products	Colorless	Colorful
Waves of treatment	Process	Assessment	Ongoing evaluation
	Evidence of progress	Rough sea	Calm sea
		Patient statements	Patient behaviors
Health care changes	Shortened time in hospital	Days	Months
	Service	Less specialized	Generalized
	Job changes	Fewer staff	Increased responsibilities

(15)   "Treatment programs" consisted of type of facility with which the respondents were affiliated—free standing or hospital based; inpatient or outpatient. This category includes type of treatment, other than art therapy, prescribed by the treatment program. Pharmacology, drug education, group or individual therapy and activity therapy are types of treatment mentioned in the data. The treatment program category also includes the approach to treatment, encompassing behavioral through uncovering/analytic approaches.

(16)   The category, "art as healing," represents the "benefits of art therapy," for example, art is beneficial to encouraging expression of feelings and increased self-awareness. Respondents were aware of stages experienced by the individual making art. Resistance to making art was common at first; however as art was created, individuals became willing participants and reflective about their art. The healing in art often becomes evident in color use—from less to more color used, and from lack of human figures to inclusion of the self. Different approaches to art therapy were used with dimensions ranking between assigning art tasks through using open studio approaches. Art tasks mentioned by the respondents are listed in Table 6.2.

(17)   The metaphor, "waves" was used by a psychiatrist to represent treatment progress, despite some temporary regression. In the course of treatment the waves become increasingly rough before they became calm again. Both professionals and individuals in recovery identified certain 'waves' in

the treatment process, the violent rush of feelings followed by calm, experienced with a certain rhythm or expected regularity as treatment progressed.

(18)   The last category, "health care changes," emphasized the increasingly shorter treatment periods and more generalized services offered by treatment programs.

Axial Coding

(19)   Once major themes are identified, a second level coding procedure called axial coding was conducted. Axial coding puts the data back together in new ways by making connections between categories. Axial coding involves identifying a single category as the central phenomenon and exploring its relationship to the other categories. The central phenomenon is identified as well as the conditions that give rise to it, the context in which it is embedded, the action or interactional strategies by which it is handled, and the consequences of those strategies. In axial coding a paradigm model is created which visually portrays the relationship among the categories (Strauss and Corbin 1990). Figure 6.1 represents the axial coding paradigm model.

Selective Coding

(20)   The third set of coding procedures is selective coding, where the theory is developed. In selective coding, researchers build a story that connects the categories. A discursive set of propositions is generated and validated against the story (Strauss and Corbin 1990).

The Experience of Enlightenment in Art Therapy

(21)   The following sections describe the experience of enlightenment through the narratives of art therapists, psychiatrists, and people in recovery from

(22)

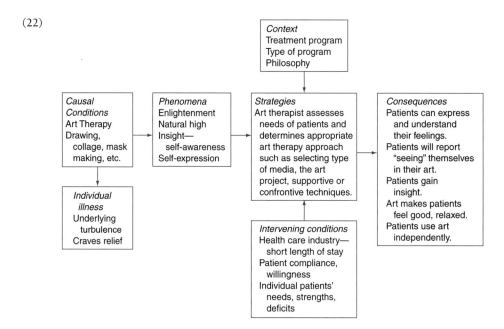

FIGURE 6.1

Axial Coding: Paradigm Model of Art Therapy in Chemical Addictions Treatment Programs

addictions. Enlightenment is defined as self-awareness or insight, self-expression and a natural high. Being enlightened is critical to recovery from addiction.

(23)   The individuals about whom this chapter is written have chosen the path of recovery. They crave relief from the insanity of addiction. Initially, in treatment programs, art therapy provides relief. According to one recovering individual, "I find myself doodling and looking at [the doodles], it relieves pressure and is relaxing." An art therapist agrees, "patients just want to do art so they don't have to think about all this other stuff . . ." Art provides a quiet refuge away from the chaos of life (Brezine, cited in Bailey 1993). The hypnotic sketching sound of the pencil, back and forth, takes one away temporarily, and is comforting and soothing. "Artwork provides the environment of calmness that acts as a hearing aid for the heart" (Bailey 1993, p. 39). A person who has been alienated from the true self may experience a new sense of being, in the quiet. According to one recovering person, "in a very simple and viable fashion the art therapy revealed the anxiety, frustration, pain, and hopelessness associated with my dependency in a gentle and fun process."

(24)   Not only can an art group be quiet and relaxing, but it can be playful and fun. "I looked forward to art therapy because it gave me the opportunity to be a kid again . . . it allowed me to have fun during this earth shaking life change . . ." says one recovering individual. Everyone has a need for elation . . . for the cessation of pain . . . and to have an ecstatic dimension to our lives (Jung, cited in Segaller 1989). Chickerneo (1990) connected the playful quality of art as facilitator of spirituality in recovering alcoholics. The sense of contented bliss in art and play mimics what is sought through drink. "The craving for alcohol was the equivalent on a low level of the spiritual thirst of our being for wholeness" (Jung, cited in Bauer 1982). The playful handling of art materials, the energy mobilized in the process, and the contemplative nature of art at once soothes, relaxes, energizes, and lifts one up to a "natural high." Someone experiencing a natural high feels "en-lightened," or relieved, as if a load had been taken off one's shoulders.

(25)   The enjoyment experienced through doing and working together with others in a room is reminiscent of a sewing circle or quilting bee. There is a feeling of belonging, of camaraderie, of pleasure, of fellowship. Says one recovering person, "It showed how well we can work with one another and how people see things different[ly] from others." The First Tradition of Alcoholics Anonymous states that most individuals cannot recover unless there is a group, and recovering individuals find that they cannot keep the gift of sobriety unless they give it away (Alcoholics Anonymous 1988). A psychiatrist believes:

(26)   If you provide a setting where the patient feels comfortable to begin their treatment, and start talking about their disorder, I think you've done 80 percent of the work . . . If the patient feels comfortable, if they feel less need to use resistance . . . because you're sort of getting [therapy] to them in a way that they're not aware that . . . through art they're starting to talk about their issues . . . it's a unique process of its own.

(27)   The benefits of play, quiet reflection and working together are directly experienced as individuals dabble with art media. Through direct experience, we learn, we gain insight, we become "enlightened." A psychiatrist explains, ". . . you can't learn how to swim by *talking* about swimming. The only way you learn how to swim is by walking into that pool with a swimming instructor, and beginning to swim." Considering the individuals who relapse because they didn't *do* their aftercare plans, makes *doing* seem ever so important. As Harms (1973) suggests, many addicts experience a lack

FIGURE 6.2
"This is my favorite because it is basically me. You go into a party and you want to be cool or want to look big or you want to be special and the only way you can do it is to do what the crowd says. It was me a couple of years ago."

of impulse for any activity. Therefore, to do *any* activity reduces the tendency toward lethargy and repeating old habits.

(28)   Self-expression is enlightening. One psychiatrist thought "patients have major needs to be able to express their view of their problems . . . many of them have limitations in their ability to identify problems." Self-expression implies the ability to find a voice for the feelings, and words to represent the problems. Words are important because:

> . . . whatever words [people] use are where their feelings lie. Not *my* words—just like notes on a page come from the composer, so those notes are important to the composer. If I were using my notes, they wouldn't help. . . . (psychiatrist)

(29)   Articulation of problems and feelings reduces their mystery and sense of being overwhelmed by them (Foulke and Keller 1976). Traumatic events can be mastered in the art work because the patient is now taking an active role. The process of expressing feelings on paper can be encouraged in a way that patients achieve some mastery over their feelings. According to one recovering individual, "my recovery felt much more real and at-

tainable as I pondered the picture I had created of what I thought my road to recovery would look like."

(30)   One of the ways art therapy helps foster self-expression is its tendency to reveal the unexpected, and to connect with the emotional self the cognitive self may be blocking. An individual in recovery recalls, "We had to draw ourselves on a rainy day. I drew just me—nothing or no one else around me and the raindrops were only around me. It made me aware of my self-centeredness." An art therapist had this to say:

> I had a woman in my office . . . and we went through an early recollection, and harvested the meaning out of it . . . we had not done the art work. She then took out a picture . . . she drew of the early recollection and it changed the meaning entirely. She started to cry when she was talking about it. She looked at the picture and said, "Oh, my gosh." The meaning had been about needing help from others, and she looked at the picture and . . . because her friend's arms were around her in this early recollection from childhood, and she was sturdy and strong and tall just like the friend, but the arms around her, she realized it was about intimacy—that it was important to her not so much because she needed the friend's help but because the friend was close and touching her. It was pretty powerful . . . we had come up with a script from the early recollection, and we changed the script, because of the art work.

(31)   The potential of art to reveal the unexplained and the unexpected, to bring to conscious awareness inner desires and feelings means uncovering what addicts wanted to cover up by use of substances. Yet, there must be some uncovering to allow healing from within. Because,

> . . . just as with a burn wound, when you have a scab at the top, everything looks just fine, as if it were healing. We all know that unless you peel off those scabs and uncover the wound it can't heal from underneath, and won't. (psychiatrist)

FIGURE 6.3
The Road to Recovery: "Although it is very simple, it represents a very big picture."

(32)   Recovering individuals may experience this sort of powerlessness over the symbolism that arises in their art work, yet ironically, they are empowered by the symbolism as well. Individuals learn to recognize their personal symbols, styles and colors and learn what significance they have. Self-awareness is improved as the uniqueness of the individual is revealed, and

patients become aware of personal strengths. "These classes brought a lot out of talent out of me I didn't even know I had," says one recovering individual. "It showed me the direction I need to stay focused on, the direction I need to go in."

(33)   The "image" as concrete and permanent is important to this process. "Words come cheap in some ways, and I think the symbols, the art work gives it greater meaning and a little more impact," according to one art therapist. For example:

> One client . . . in therapy for three weeks . . . she is very focused and very involved in AA. She's got a sponsor. She says,"I'm going to do this right, no matter what." And I said to her, "you know, you've never put yourself in any of your drawings—Where are you in this recovery?" "I'm a spectator," is what she said. (art therapist)

(34)   The art work can and does serve as concrete evidence of the individual's progress toward goals. Many programs used Step Books or workbooks wherein patients demonstrate through writing or drawing how they have made progress toward the Twelve Steps of AA.

> . . . [Clients] had to set five measurable goals . . . to accomplish within . . . two weeks, and then they came back to their counselor. So maybe someone would set a goal for their first step they would do an "inner-outer" [self] poster, for their second step they would do [a] "sanity-insanity" [drawing], so maybe they would take that back and show their counselor, and talk about what they learned from that. (art therapist)

Art Interventions

(35)   In the beginning of treatment, the combination of biological, psychological and social factors in the etiology and symptomology of the disease call for a thorough assessment on the part of the treatment program, necessary to understand all the factors in the individual's illness. "A part of any illness is pathology which is destructive behavior, and treatment involves altered behavior" (a psychiatrist). Recovery presumes abstinence, but recovery in the full sense of the word involves "understanding the stress that's resulted in the culmination of the addiction wherein there may have been predisposition, but without the stress may not have necessarily occurred" (a psychiatrist). Recovery involves understanding the alienation and emptiness that lead to use of substances in the first place.

(36)   Certain interventions are used by art therapists, depending upon the needs of the patient, the philosophy of the treatment facility, the length of time someone might be in treatment and other intervening conditions. Many art therapists design art experiences based on the theme or lecture presented in the treatment program. The art therapist may assign an art project responsive to patients' needs, and in conjunction with the treatment milieu. The art therapy approach often requires balancing addiction and psychiatric considerations simultaneously (Miller 1995). A therapist might balance a disease concept focus (e.g., "Just for today . . . I will not drink/use") with a more insight-oriented understanding of the self and feelings. Therapists may facilitate enlightenment in terms of "a power greater than ourselves" or facilitate enlightenment through insight and personal awareness.

(37)   Often, patients who first enter treatment, are resistant to treatment, and in denial. In these cases, a therapist may use humor and play to encourage comfort with art making and engagement in therapy.

> I draw this little stick figure, and I show them and ask, "Can you draw better than that?" They say, "No." And I say "good, because otherwise I'd feel kind of intimidated if you did." And then they laugh, and it's kind of an ice breaker, and

then we go from there. And I say, "The only thing I ask is that you put a little meat on that figure, because I'm not really into a lot of thin people, you know being full figured," and they kind of laugh, and so nine times out of ten, I get some wonderful things. (art therapist)

(38) The use of humor tends to deflect negative thinking that may prevent someone from participating in art. A therapist may assure patients "it is best not to be an artist to do art therapy," to help individuals become comfortable with their art expression.

> I say stuff like, "everybody has a visual language. You had a visual language when you were little that was primary before you had a verbal language. When you dream you dream in your visual language . . . I'd like you just to trust yourself. If your little perfectionist pops up . . . put him out in the hallway so that you can be allowed to honor this part of yourself. I'd like you to just back off and give yourself, and whatever comes to your mind, I'd like you not to judge it . . . I'd like you to just draw with your non-dominant hand" . . . And then I say, "I'd like you to just try this once . . . and don't decide what it means, don't even think about what it means. We'll get into that after you do it. We'll talk about it, and if you just give it an opportunity and see . . . what comes out of it, you might find that it's useful for you." (art therapist)

(39) Some individuals have such low self-concept, they are afraid to succeed (an art therapist). They may say, "I can't draw, I can't do that." It is important that art therapists remember not everyone is quick or willing to try to put their thoughts and feelings in the form of art (a recovering individual) . . . According to one recovering person, "I think it's the word art that scares us. Remember we don't believe we can do anything right."

(40) As treatment progresses, some patients experience a period of darkness and pain. There is a confusing mix of emotions. Patients at once feel warmth, pain, closeness and distance. There are waves of progress and regression, more progress, less regression.

> . . . the longer we go, the deeper and darker the [art] gets. And when they start really touching into those places that have been hidden and anesthetized for so long . . . all the things that are coming out . . . It's almost like something's been festering. (art therapist)

(41) When there is obvious pain, therapists may use empathy, acceptance, validation, listening, and supporting. They may use metaphor to distance the pain. More fluid media such as oil pastels and paints foster freedom of expression, and to help individuals come to terms with painful areas in their lives. Verbal description of the art process and images depends upon what is sensed about the patient's needs and readiness to talk. Therapists may ask individuals to speak about some aspect of the art process they are comfortable to speak about. They may interpret certain issues as expressed in the art product, however they may choose to wait to discuss them until the individual is able to face certain realities in their lives without being so overwhelmed they return to drinking and drugging. Artistic expression itself is one step toward objectifying subjective concerns, toward facing realities.

(42) A therapist may encourage continuing with art after discharge. Writing a journal may be used for increased self-exploration and to assist individuals in recognizing and drawing out triggers to relapse. Table 6.2 lists art tasks, or strategies mentioned by the respondents.

Intervening Conditions

(43) Intervening conditions are structural conditions that facilitate or constrain interventions offered (Strauss and Corbin 1990). Certain intervening conditions facilitate art therapy—psychiatrists who believe in it, and recovering individuals willing to give it a try. Yet, conditions existing within the

(44)

TABLE 6.2
Art Tasks Mentioned by the Respondents (Causal Conditions/Strategies)

Whole body outline drawn actual size, filled in with the effects of substances on the body

Round robin pass around drawings to create stress, and how the stress is dealt with

Draw what happens after you use substances

Group murals

Draw your addiction and what would it say?

Draw your feelings

Draw: Who I am/Who I was/Who I hope to be

Writing songs about addiction

Progressive relaxation/guided imagery

Find and illustrate a "power" symbol

Make a spiritual symbol: "What gives you faith?"

Inner and outer consequences of substance abuse

Mandalas

Family portraits

Draw your drinking history and where this leads

What does depression look like?

The Amusement Park Technique (Hrenko and Willis 1996)

Draw: Who are you blaming?

Draw triggers to substance use

Likes and dislikes

Create a door of opportunity and a door of challenge

Bridge drawing (Hays and Lyons 1981)

Draw yourself using/yourself sober

Create a group tree and leaves representing things you are thankful for and things you have lost

Masks

Media

Pastels, Collage, Colored pencils, Markers, Music, Creative writing, Paint, Charcoal, Crayons, Colored paper, Sandtray

broader health care industry are considered constraints. According to one psychiatrist, in recent years inpatient treatment has dramatically changed. There is less time to work with someone, and the focus is primarily detoxification and getting patients into a less intense level of care.

> In outpatient oriented treatment programs a lot of the things we used to do . . . are not being done or they're being done in a very superficial, limited kind of way. In lots of instances they're just down to sort of a consultation, an analysis of what somebody needs and trying to arrange to get that done on an outpatient basis . . . They're bumping everything down to the lowest level of cost . . . in a model that is very analogous to what the auto industry has gone through. If a robot can do it then you don't have to be doing it. If a human is necessary, but if you can train someone at five dollars an hour to do it versus somebody at nine dollars an hour to do it, then you're going to have the five dollars an hour person do it. I think that's the kind of shrinkage we're seeing in the entire system. (psychiatrist)

(45)   An art therapist notes her job title change from art therapist to mental health worker/rehab coordinator, along with a change in job description— less art therapy and more of other kinds of case management services:

> We've been bought out by a company . . . they own a hundred or so hospitals across the nation. They have this model hospital . . . and they're trying to base their other hospitals on this model. It's . . . a way to save money . . . by lowering staff. About nineteen people got laid off in September, and the nursing-to-patient ratio also decreased. I think it used to be 3 or 4 patients to one staff, now it's 5 to 1 . . . I think everyone across the board is feeling the stress of it. I guess we're supporting one another within our units . . . even though people get floated from unit to unit at times. We all talk about it and use humor a lot to get through it.

(46)   Other art therapists describe programs designed to be three weeks, that are now one week in duration. Patients who thought they were to be admitted for a certain length of time, were informed that day they were to be discharged, because the insurance wouldn't approve more time. One art therapist noticed that instead of one three-week stay, she might see someone for three one-week stays over the course of a year, losing a day of progress in each transition. Therapists who were accustomed to prescribing painting or other longer term projects, found the length of time a patient stayed in the hospital did not allow for such involved projects. A therapist may have to balance creating art work, which involves time, against the time a patient is likely to be on the unit. This decrease in treatment time seemed to represent the greatest concern for art therapists.

(47)   The issues and difficulties encountered by those attempting to treat clients or plan treatment strategies is complicated by the changing nature of drug treatment client populations. Clinicians in treatment programs have always struggled with patients not ready for recovery, who are in denial, have not "hit bottom," nor admitted powerlessness. Even patients who seem sincere in desiring recovery often relapse. Treatment programs today admit patients with multiple problems in addition to substance abuse that need to be addressed concurrently. "It is hard to deal with them in a chemical dependency model, when there were patients much more fragile" (an art therapist).

> Our age range will go from 19–86. When you get to that high end you get a lot of alcoholic dementia, and associated nutrition problems and neurological problems . . . And then within the group, with the dual disorders, it could be alcohol, heroin or crack, or depression or schizophrenia. (art therapist)

Consequences

(48)   In spite of these conditions, many reported positive outcomes of art therapy. One art therapist believes:

> art therapy *can* be used well in conjunction with "brief therapy" or at least shorter-term therapy because of the ability to cut through the initial, more superficial stages of the therapeutic process, and move to the deeper content and emotional impact of particular issues at a quicker pace. Also, art therapy assignments can be given over the evenings/weekends between therapy sessions that can build on what has already been processed in group. Art therapy lends itself to self-empowerment and awareness, and as a client begins to pick up on his/her own symbols, color use, style, etc., it becomes more self-motivating, which may ultimately impact long-term outcome measures. Journaling, dream work, etc. are very good on-going techniques.

(49)   When patients are progressively moving toward healthy awareness, there is increased insight: Something 'clicks.' Individuals begin sorting things out and taking responsibility for their recovery. '[In drawing] my

personal solar system I realized where I stood with my family and where things in my life were' (a recovering individual). '[I drew a] bridge, a strong one, high above the water, with strong supports, guardrails, reaching the midpoint and now facing the reality that I am addicted. It's becoming easier' (an individual in recovery).

(50)   One art therapist noticed a transition in the colors used:

> They would start moving away from the darker colors, the reds and the blacks. They would start to invest more in the art . . . and you would just see they would start using the projects to understand themselves, or they would use their journals . . . But the other thing . . . the symbol of the sun or a bright image in the center of something, usually in the beginning of treatment . . . would be enveloped with darkness . . . the patients would show their addiction of something like the light being blocked, like there'd be a dark black circle around. At the end of the treatment there would be this opening.

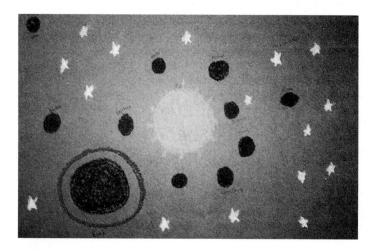

FIGURE 6.4
Mike's Galaxy: "With this I realized where I stood in my family and where things in my life were."

(51)   The individual in long term recovery interviewed paints all canvases in black first, then adds color on top:

> I never really know how to put really light colors together and match them really well. That's mainly why I always start with deep dark colors, and I put the light in as I go along. I got confused, I didn't know how to do it so I just painted all black and where these lines are, colors . . . Everyone has a light and a dark side but they never admit the personalities they have.

(52)   "The light bulb that clicks on," or "the light at the end of the tunnel," are common metaphors for enlightenment, for awareness or relief. In professional literature, Johnson (1990) discusses the transformation from darkness to light she found in adolescent and adult substance abuse patients' poetry and art work. She compares her findings with Whitfield's simplification of the Twelve Steps: 'struggle, confusion, surrender, seeing the light.' (Whitfield, cited in Johnson 1990, p. 301).

Propositions

(53)   Co-founder of Alcoholics Anonymous W. B. Bill (1987) describes his experiences with recovery:

FIGURE 6.5

"This is my recovery picture. The guy at the bottom is stuck inside the crack pipe, which is his addiction. He wants to get out, but he doesn't know how. He is chained to drugs. On top is my recovery machine. You go into it addicted on whatever chemical you choose to use and then you come out punching your addiction. At the bottom I have foot stomping alcoholism and drug addiction with an addict looking on who wants recovery."

> Suddenly the room lit up with a great white light. It seemed to me, in the mind's eye, that I was on a mountain and that a wind not of air but of spirit was blowing. And then it burst upon me that I was a free man. Slowly the ecstasy subsided. I lay on the bed, but now for a time I was in another world, a new world of consciousness. All about me and through me there was a wonderful feeling of Presence, and I thought to myself, "So this is the God of the preachers!" (p. 2)

(54)   Drawing from the story of enlightenment, the following propositions are offered.

1. The art experiences of recovering individuals in treatment programs contribute to a sense of enlightenment.

2. Individuals may experience one or more forms of enlightenment. Sometimes forms of enlightenment are experienced in succession, and sometimes simultaneously. Individuals may experience a natural high, a soothing, or playful sense of relief or a spiritual attunement. Self-expression is enlightening through sharing oneself and dividing problems. Last, self-awareness or insight is achieved through direct experiences with art.

3. Different interventions can be used by the therapist to encourage enlightenment, depending on the needs of patients, and the intervening conditions present. A therapist may foster enlightenment through recognizing the needs of the individual patients and responding to their needs through organizing the environment, the art materials, and the art directives and approach. Humor, education, and empathy are strategies employed. A therapist may match media with expressive needs—structured media may be used when individuals need support and containment. Fluid media may be used when individuals require assistance with uncovering and self-expression.

4. Certain conditions exist which impinge upon the success of an art therapy program: the decrease in the length or time, patients who are more ill, patients who do not want to participate, constrain the potential for enlightenment.

5. Art therapy works in conjunction with the two major philosophical approaches to chemical addiction—the disease concept and psychiatric models of treatment. Different forms of enlightenment promoted by art therapy parallel the two philosophies of treatment: The natural high/spiritual sense of enlightenment is akin to realizing a higher power that can restore sanity (Step 2)(AA 1988). Enlightenment experienced through insight or personal awareness augments the psychiatric model of treatment.

6. Art therapy offers benefits to short-term care: art assignments given over weekends or in the evenings help bring consistency to the treatment, and bridges the treatment program and the home environment. One reason why art therapy works, might be because it introduces how to work independently through journaling and doing art work on one's own. It requires doing, and changing behavior.

Conclusion

(55)   "Individuals who are relatively happy and who can live their lives without the use of drugs and alcohol," according to one psychiatrist, "is the desired outcome of chemical addiction treatment." However, as another psychiatrist noted, statistics show "a whole lot of people don't get better from getting an episode of treatment . . . [or] from multiple episodes of treatment, and part of that may not be the treatment, it may be the way that particular treatment is applied or utilized is less effective with that person . . ." Finding the most effective treatment for each person is a challenge. Art therapy deserves consideration for its potential to contribute to the treatment, the relative happiness of each individual living life without drugs and alcohol. The benefits of art therapy in chemical dependency treatment are many, yet art therapy, like health care in general, feels the constraints of cost containment. This study offers little in the way of solutions, yet, hopefully greater awareness of the issues can lead to problem solving.

(56)   This study supports the value of art therapy in addiction recovery. The major finding concerns the phenomenon of enlightenment experienced in art therapy. Enlightenment in art therapy helps individuals to understand important concepts in recovery such as "letting go and letting God." It emphasizes the value of quiet, reflective time or play time. Self-reflection is viewed as empowering. Greater self-awareness helps individuals to understand and resolve the stress which precipitated the substance use in the first place. Enlightenment can mean the difference between abstinence and recovery in the full sense of the word.

Qualitative interpretations situate findings within larger meanings.

(57)   Although the art therapists expressed concern over the decreasing length of time patients were admitted to treatment, treatment strategies remained relatively unchanged over time. They may be fewer, or performed in shorter duration, yet the types of art interventions described in art therapy literature in years past are quite similar to those used today. It could be that no one has a better idea! Or, it could be that the interventions, despite the constraints upon them, are working to some extent, that they're trustworthy and not affected by the passing of time or the amount of time a patient is in treatment.

(58)   Recommendations for further studies would be to continue to interview individuals who have had art therapy in treatment programs, both current patients or individuals in longer term recovery for whom art has been important. Exploring the role of art in recovering individuals who

were not in treatment programs would also provide important information about the potential uses or consequences of art. Artists who are addicts (and/or recovering addicts) and continue to make art would help the researcher be theoretically sensitive to the range of conditions that impact art and recovery.

(59)
Qualitative research reports use flexible and emerging structures and evaluation criteria.

It is my hope that this study helps to explain the theory of art therapy in recovery from chemical addiction. In the words of one psychiatrist, "Treatment is an art. Treatment is art therapy, that's what treatment is, if it's good treatment."

References

Albert-Puleo, N. and Osha, V. (1976–77) "Art therapy as an alcoholism treatment tool." *Alcohol Health and Research World,* Winter, 28–31.

Alcoholics Anonymous (1988) *Twelve Steps and Twelve Traditions* (37th printing). New York: AA.

Allen, P. B. (1985) "Integrating art therapy into an alcoholism treatment program." *American Journal of Art Therapy 24,* 10–12.

Bailey, J. (1993) "How art heals." *St. Anthony Messenger,* February, 36–41.

Bauer, J. (1982) *Alcoholism and Women.* Toronto: Inner City Books.

Bill, W. (1987) *As Bill Sees It.* New York: Alcoholics Anonymous World Services.

Burke, K. (1985) "When words aren't enough . . . a study of the use of art therapy in the treatment of chemically dependent adolescents with special focus upon the spiritual dimension." *Dissertation Abstracts International* 46, 08–A, p. 2166 (University Microfilms No. AAD85–23, 669).

Chickerneo, N. (1990) "New images, ancient paradigm: A study of the contribution of art to spirituality in addiction recovery." *Dissertation Abstracts International.* Order no. 9110801.

Chopra, D. (1997) *Overcoming Addictions.* New York: Harmony Books.

Conrad (1978) "A grounded theory of academic change." *Sociology of Education* 55, 101–112.

Craddock, S. G., Rounds-Bryant, J. L., Flynn, P. M. and Hubbard, R. L. (1997) "Characteristics and pretreatment behaviors of clients entering drug abuse treatment: 1969 to 1993." *American Journal of Drug and Alcohol Abuse 23,* 1, 43–59.

Devine, D. (1970) "A preliminary investigation of paintings by alcoholic men." *American Journal of Art Therapy 9,* 115–128.

Feen-Calligan, H. (1995) "The use of art therapy in treatment programs to promote spiritual recovery from addiction." *Art Therapy: Journal of the American Art Therapy Association 12,* 46–50.

Foulke, W. E. and Keller, T. W. (1976) "The art experience in addict rehabilitation." *American Journal of Art Therapy 15,* 75–80.

Glaser, B. and Strauss, A. (1967) *The Discovery of Grounded Theory.* Chicago: Aldine.

Harms, E. (1973) "Art therapy for the drug addict." *Art Psychotherapy 1,* 55–59.

Hays, R. E. and Lyons, S. J. (1981) "The bridge drawing: A projection technique for assessment in art therapy." *The Arts in Psychotherapy 8,* 207–217.

Hrenko, K. D. and Willis, R. (1996) "The amusement park technique in the treatment of dually diagnosed, psychiatric inpatients." *Art Therapy: Journal of the American Art Therapy Association 13,* 261–264.

Johnson, L. (1990) "Creative therapies in the treatment of addictions: The art of transforming shame." *The Arts in Psychotherapy 17,* 299–308.

Miller, N. (1995) *Addiction Psychiatry: Current Diagnosis and Treatment.* New York: Wiley-Liss, Inc.

Moore, R. (1983) "Art therapy with substance abusers: A review of the literature." *The Arts in Psychotherapy 10,* 251–260.

Segaller, S. (Producer/Director)(1989) *The Wisdom of the Dream, Vol. 1, 2, 3.* [Film]. USA: Border Television.

Steele, C. (1997) "On the front lines: Fighting drugs in Dayton." *Community 2,* 2, 2–7.

Strauss, A. and Corbin, J. (1990) *Basics of Qualitative Research: Grounded Theory Procedures and Techniques.* Newbury Park, CA: Sage Publications.

Ulman, E. (1953) "Art therapy in an outpatient clinic." *Psychiatry 16,* 55–64.

Van Leit, B. (1995) "Managed mental health care: Reflections in a time of turmoil." *American Journal of Occupational Therapy 50,* 428–434.

Whitfield, C. (1987) *Healing the Child Within.* Deerfield Beach, FL: Health Communications, Inc.

Further Reading

Clemmens, M. C. (1997) *Getting Beyond Sobriety: Clinical Approaches to Long-Term Recovery.* San Francisco: Jossey Bass.

15

Ethnographic Designs

Let's assume that Maria, our high school teacher, chooses to conduct a qualitative ethnography study for her graduate research project. Her project might address this question: "How does her school committee address the issue of weapon possession in their high school?" Assume that her teacher-administrator committee, composed of seven individuals (including herself), will be meeting monthly to discuss (1) the issue of weapons in the high school, and (2) the school's response to this weapon possession. She visits with Owen, the chair of the committee, who agrees to talk with members about whether Maria can use their monthly committee deliberations for her graduate school project. If Maria gets this approval, she will have the elements of a good ethnographic study. The group will meet frequently and develop shared perspectives about weapon possession. Maria, as a participant, will be able to closely observe the activities of the group and take notes so that she can describe the activities of the group and the themes they develop about student weapon possession. She may also have the opportunity to conduct informal interviews with members of the committee to gather additional data. By the end of the year she can write an ethnography about how her committee "works." By conducting this ethnographic study, Maria can identify how a school committee, composed of diverse representatives, can pool their expertise to identify strategies to curb weapon possession and violence in schools.

Maria will research her own committee, a group of people. In fact, the term "ethnography" literally means, "writing about groups of people" (LeCompte & Schensul, 1999, p. 21). Using this design, the researcher identifies a group of people to study, visits the setting of the group, notes how they behave, think, and talk, and develops a general portrait of the group. This design has utility because ethnographers can capture "rules" of behavior, such as the informal relationships among teachers who congregate at favorite places to socialize (Pajak & Blasé, 1984). It can provide a detailed day-to-day picture, such as the thoughts and activities of a search committee hiring a new principal (Wolcott, 1974, 1994). It can also explore how groups develop over time, such as the drinking game rituals of fraternity members that humiliate and marginalize women (Rhoads, 1995). Thus, ethnography is useful for learning about groups (e.g., teachers, students, or staff members), studying entire schools (e.g., successful, innovative, or violence-ridden), or examining processes, events, or activities (e.g., participating in a graduate program).

Listed below are some examples of studies that illustrate ethnographic research:

▶ In a study of a 12-year-old with Down's syndrome and his family, Harry, Day, and Quist (1998) conducted an ethnography to better understand the social relationship that occurs between a youth with significant disabilities and his family and peers without disabilities. They asked, "How can information on the process of inclusion among a group of firmly bonded siblings assist us in facilitating inclusive relationships outside the family?" (p. 291). Raul, a Spanish-speaking young man with Down's syndrome, could only utter four garbled words at a time. However, he interacted closely with his three brothers. Their attendance at a summer camp provided an opportunity for the researchers to gather data about how Raul related to his non-disabled siblings. Noting these interactions provided insight into patterns of behavior (e.g., "big brothering" and "reciprocal play") and enabled the researchers to draw conclusions about Raul's peer interactions in non-family settings.

▶ Four women who had reentered the university as full-time doctoral students became participants in a study by Padula and Miller (1999). In this case study, the authors wondered about the students' decision to return to school, how they described their reentry experiences, and how the graduate experience changed their lives. Through interviewing and observing these women, the researchers found several themes about beliefs that these women held. For example, the women believed that their graduate experiences did not meet their needs; they compared themselves with younger students; and they felt a general need to finish their programs as quickly as possible.

▶ Fraternity settings are a site where women are often exploited and victimized. Group rituals such as drinking games (Whale Tales), roughing up a person (Dog Piles), and chasing women when drunk (Beer Goggling) serve to marginalize women and make them passive participants in their own victimization. In a critical ethnography, Rhoads (1995) studied the culture of one fraternity and its practices that rendered women powerless and marginalized. The fraternity, Alpha Beta, frequently characterized women as "tools" or "whores," engaged in games where women could only observe from the sidelines, and enacted macho rituals that reinforced hostile conceptions of women.

As illustrated in these studies, **ethnographic designs** are qualitative research procedures for describing, analyzing, and interpreting a culture-sharing group's shared patterns of behavior, beliefs, and language that develop over time. Central to this definition is culture. A **culture** is "everything having to do with human behavior and belief." (LeCompte, Preissle, & Tesch, 1993, p. 5). It can include language, rituals, economic and political structures, life stages, interactions, and communication styles. To understand the patterns of a culture-sharing group, the ethnographer typically spends considerable time "in the field" interviewing, observing, and gathering documents about the group in order to understand their culture-sharing behaviors, beliefs, and language. As distinct from other qualitative designs, ethnography includes detailed descriptions of behavior, beliefs, and language rather than the generation of a theory, as found in grounded theory research. Also, ethnography examines groups, rather than individuals, as found in narrative designs.

By the end of this chapter you should be able to:

▶ Identify major events in the historical development of ethnographic research.
▶ Distinguish among three types of ethnographic designs.

▶ Describe the key characteristics of ethnography.
▶ Identify steps in conducting an ethnography study.
▶ List criteria useful for evaluating an ethnographic research report.

A BRIEF HISTORY OF ETHNOGRAPHIC RESEARCH

Ethnography as practiced in education has been shaped by cultural anthropology and by an emphasis on the issues of writing about culture and how ethnographic reports need to be read and understood today. This theme lies at the heart of understanding current practices in ethnography and it unfolds briefly here and in several other writings (e.g., see Bogdan & Biklen, 1998; Denzin, 1997; LeCompte, Preissle, & Tesch, 1993; and Wolcott, 1999).

The roots of educational ethnography lie in cultural anthropology. In the late 19th and early 20th centuries, anthropologists explored "primitive" cultures by visiting other countries and becoming immersed in their societies for extensive periods of time. They refrained from "going native" and identifying too closely with the people they were studying so that they could write an "objective" account of what they saw and heard. At times, these accounts compared distant cultures on other continents with the American way of life. For example, Margaret Mead, a well-known anthropologist, studied childrearing, adolescence, and the influence of culture on personality in Somoa (Mead, 1928).

Observations and interviews became standard procedures for collecting data "in the field." Also, under sociologists at the University of Chicago in the 1920s through the 1950s, research focused on the importance of studying a single case—whether that case was an individual, a group, a neighborhood, or a larger cultural unit. For example, Chicago sociologists conducted qualitative analyses of personal and public documents to construct a view of the life of Polish immigrants (Thomas & Znaniecki, 1927). With an emphasis on city life, they depicted ordinary life in United States' cities, such as the Jewish ghetto, the taxi-dance hall, the professional thief, the hobo, and the delinquent (Bogdan & Biklen, 1998). In highlighting the lives of these individuals, they provided "insider" perspectives by reporting detailed accounts of individuals that are often marginalized in our society.

The infant interdisciplinary area of educational anthropology began to crystallize during the 1950s and continued to develop through the 1980s (LeCompte, Preissle, & Tesch, 1993). Jules Henry depicted elementary school classrooms and high schools as tribes with rituals, culture, and social structure, while George and Louise Spindler examined educational decision-making, curriculum content, and teaching (LeCompte, Preissle, & Tesch, 1993). Educational anthropologists focused on subculture enclaves, such as:

▶ career and life histories or role analyses of individuals
▶ microethnographies of small work and leisure groups within classrooms or schools
▶ studies of single classrooms abstracted as small societies
▶ studies of school facilities or school districts that approach these units as discrete communities (LeCompte, Preissle, & Tesch, 1993, p. 14)

In studies such as these, educational ethnographers developed and refined their procedures borrowed from anthropology and sociology. From the 1980s to the present, anthropologists and educational anthropologists have identified techniques of focusing on a cultural scene, conducting observations, analyzing data, and writing up the research (e.g., Fetterman, 1998; Wolcott, 1992, 1994, 1999).

A watershed event in ethnography, according to Denzin (1997), was the publication of the book *Writing Culture* (Clifford & Marcus, 1986). Ethnographers have been "writing their way out" (Denzin, 1997, p. xvii) of this book ever since. Clifford and Marcus raised two issues that have commanded much attention in ethnography in general and within educational research. The first is the crisis of representation. This crisis consists of a reassessment of how ethnographers interpret the groups they are studying. Denzin (1997) argued that we can no longer view the researcher as an objective reporter who makes omnipresent pronouncements about the individuals being studied. Instead, the researcher is only one voice among many—individuals such as the reader, the participants, and the gatekeepers—who need to be heard. This has led to a second crisis: legitimacy. No longer do "canons" of validity, reliability, and objectivity of "normal science" represent the standards. Each ethnographic study needs to be evaluated in terms of flexible standards embedded within the participants, historical and cultural influences, and the interactive forces of race, gender, and class. Viewed this way, ethnographies need to include perspectives drawn from feminist thought, racial views, sexual perspectives, and critical theory, and they need to be sensitive to race, class, and gender. Ethnographies today are now "messy," and find presentation in many forms, such as a performance, poem, play, novel, or a personal narrative (Denzin, 1997).

TYPES OF ETHNOGRAPHIC DESIGNS

With this history, it is easy to see that an eclecticism pervades educational ethnographies today. See Table 15.1 for a sampling of the various forms. For a new researcher being introduced to ethnography, the long list is less important than a focus on primary forms being

---

TABLE 15.1

Types of Ethnographies

- Realist ethnography—an objective, scientifically written ethnography
- Confessional ethnography—a report of the ethnographer's fieldwork experiences
- Life history—a study of one individual situated within the cultural context of his or her life
- Autoethnography—a reflective, self-examination by an individual set within his or her cultural context
- Microethnography—a study focused on a specific aspect of a cultural group and setting
- Ethnographic case study—a case analysis of a person, event, activity, or process set within a cultural perspective
- Critical ethnography—a study of the shared patterns of a marginalized group with the aim of advocacy
- Feminist ethnography—a study of women and the cultural practices that serve to disempower and oppress them
- Postmodern ethnography—an ethnography written to challenge the problems in our society that have emerged from a modern emphasis on progress and marginalizing individuals
- Ethnographic novels—a fictional work focused on cultural aspects of a group

Sources: Van Maanen, 1988; Denzin, 1997; LeCompte, Preissle, & Tesch, 1993

published in educational reports. Unquestionably, an ethnography does not always fit cleanly into categories, but three forms seem to frequently emerge:

▶ the realist ethnography
▶ the case study
▶ the critical ethnography

Realist Ethnographies

A realist ethnography is a popular approach used by cultural anthropologists. Characterized by Van Maanen (1988), it reflects a particular stance taken by the researcher toward the individuals being studied. A **realist ethnography** is an objective account of the situation, typically written in the third-person point of view, reporting objectively on the information learned from participants at a field site. In this ethnographic design:

▶ The realist ethnographer narrates the study in a third-person dispassionate voice and reports on what is observed or heard from participants. The ethnographer does not offer personal reflections in the research report and remains in the background as an omniscient reporter of the "facts."
▶ The researcher reports objective data in a measured style uncontaminated by personal bias, political goals, and judgment. The researcher may provide mundane details of everyday life among the people studied. The ethnographer also uses standard categories for cultural description (e.g., family life, work life, social networks, and status systems).
▶ The ethnographer produces the participants' views through closely edited quotations, and has the final word on how the culture is to be interpreted and presented. (Van Maanen, 1988)

This type of ethnography has a long tradition in cultural anthropology and has been used in education, as well. For example, Wolcott (1974, 1994) used a realist approach to ethnography to study the activities of a committee appointed to select a principal. This study addressed the process a school selection committee experienced as they interviewed candidates for a principalship. Wolcott started with candidate number seven, and discussed the committee's deliberation for each candidate (except one) until the final individual was identified. Following this description of the interviewing process, Wolcott interpreted the committee's actions in terms of a lack of professional knowledge, their "variety reducing" behavior, and the reluctance of schools to change.

As a realist ethnography, Wolcott provided an account of committee deliberations as if he were looking in from the outside, reported the procedures objectively, and included participants' views. The interpretation at the end presented Wolcott's view of the patterns he saw in the selection committee cultural group.

Case Studies

Writers often use the term "case study" in conjunction with ethnography (e.g., see LeCompte & Schensul, 1999). A case study is an important type of ethnography, although it differs in several important ways. Case study researchers may focus on a program, event, or activity involving individuals rather than a group per se (Stake, 1995). Also, when case study writers research a group, they may be more interested in describing the activities of the group instead of identifying shared patterns of behavior exhibited by the group. The ethnographer searches for these shared patterns that develop as a group interacts over time. Finally, case study researchers are less likely to identify a cultural theme to examine at the beginning of a study, especially one from anthropology, and instead focus on an in-depth exploration of the actual "case."

Although some researchers identify "case" as an object of study (Stake, 1995), others consider it to be a procedure of inquiry (e.g., Merriam, 1998). A **case study** is an in-depth exploration of a bounded system (e.g., an activity, event, process, or individuals) based on extensive data collection (Creswell, 1998). "Bounded" means that the case is separated out for research in terms of time, place, or some physical boundaries.

It is useful to consider the types of cases that qualitative researchers often study:

▶ The "case" may be a single individual, several individuals separately or in a group, a program, events, or activities (e.g., a teacher, several teachers, or the implementation of a new math program).

▶ The "case" may represent a process consisting of a series of steps (e.g., a college curriculum process) that form a sequence of activities.

▶ As shown in Figure 15.1, a "case" may be selected for study because it is unusual and has merit in and of itself. When the case itself is of interest, it is called an **intrinsic case.** The study of a bilingual school illustrates this form of a case study (Stake, 2000). Alternatively, the focus of a qualitative study may be a specific issue, with a case (or cases) used to illustrate the issue. This type of case is called an **instrumental case,** because it serves the purpose of illuminating a particular issue. The gunman case study (Asmussen & Creswell, 1995) portrays an instrumental case of a campus to portray reactions to an incident. Case studies may also include multiple cases, called a **collective case study** (Stake, 1995), in which multiple cases are described and compared to provide insight into an issue. Several schools, for example, might be studied to illustrate alternative approaches to school choice for students.

FIGURE 15.1

Types of Qualitative Case Studies

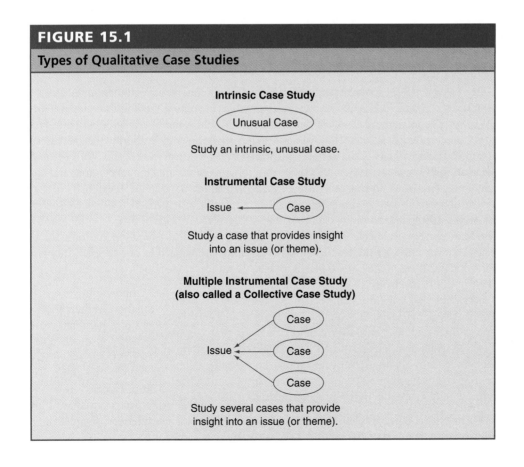

Intrinsic Case Study

(Unusual Case)

Study an intrinsic, unusual case.

Instrumental Case Study

Issue ◀— (Case)

Study a case that provides insight
into an issue (or theme).

**Multiple Instrumental Case Study
(also called a Collective Case Study)**

(Case)
Issue ◀— (Case)
(Case)

Study several cases that provide
insight into an issue (or theme).

▶ The researcher seeks to develop an in-depth understanding of the case through collecting multiple forms of data (e.g., pictures, scrapbooks, videotapes, and e-mails). Providing this in-depth understanding requires studying only a few cases, because for each case examined, the researcher has less time to devote to exploring the depths of any one case.

▶ The researcher also locates the "case" or "cases" within their larger context, such as geographical, political, social, or economic settings (e.g., the family constellation consisting of grandparents, siblings, and "adopted" family members).

An example of a case study is the study of four reading-disabled middle school students by Kos (1991). The study examined what factors contributed to the development of reading disabilities in adolescents. The author tutored the four students, observed their reading alone and reading in class, conducted interviews, and gathered school records on each student. All four students, who were between the ages of 13 and 15, were unable to read materials above the third-grade level. After describing each student, the author identified four themes that emerged about each student: reading behavior, negative and frustrating experiences with instruction, anxiety about reading, and histories about reading in kindergarten and first grade. From these individual case analyses, the author then compared the four individuals and found the students to be aware of their deficiencies, to display a connection between reading disability and stress, and to be unable to integrate various reading strategies.

This case study illustrates a study of four bounded systems—specific individuals—and an assessment of patterns of behavior for each individual and for all four students. The researcher focused on the issue of reading disabilities and conducted an in-depth examination of four cases to illustrate this issue. Multiple forms of data were collected, and the analysis consisted of both description and thematic development.

Critical Ethnographies

When Denzin (1997) spoke of the twin crises of representation and legitimation, he was responding to profound changes in our society, such as becoming more multinational, joining a world economy, and changing demographics to include more racial groups. These factors have created a system of power, prestige, privilege, and authority that serves to marginalize individuals of different classes, races, and gender in our society. With roots in German thinking of the 1920s, the historical problems of domination, alienation, and social struggle are now playing out within educational and social science research.

Ethnography now incorporates a "critical" approach (Carspecken, 1995; Carspecken & Apple, 1992; and Thomas, 1993) to include an advocacy perspective to ethnography. **Critical ethnographies** are a type of ethnographic research in which the author is interested in advocating for the emancipation of groups marginalized in our society (Thomas, 1993). Critical researchers are typically politically minded individuals who seek, through their research, to advocate against inequality and domination (Carspecken & Apple, 1992). For example, critical ethnographers might study schools that provide privileges to certain types of students, create inequitable situations among members of different social classes, and perpetuate boys "speaking up" and girls being silent participants in class.

The major components of a critical ethnography are summarized in Figure 15.2. These factors, such as a value-laden orientation, empowering people by giving them more authority, challenging the status quo, and a concern about power and control, play out in an ethnography in specific procedural characteristics, listed below:

▶ The critical ethnographer studies social issues of power, empowerment, inequality, inequity, dominance, repression, hegemony, and victimization.

FIGURE 15.2

Characteristics of Critical Ethnography

- Critical researchers are usually politically minded people.
- Critical ethnographers speak to an audience on behalf of their participants as a means of empowering participants by giving them more authority.
- Critical ethnographers seek to change society.
- Critical ethnographers identify and celebrate their biases in research. They recognize that all research is value-laden.
- Critical ethnographers challenge the status quo and ask why it is so.
- Critical researchers seek to connect the meaning of a situation to broader structures of social power and control.
- Critical researchers seek to create a literal dialogue with the participants they are studying.

Source: Adapted from Carspecken & Apple, 1992; Thomas, 1993.

▶ Researchers conduct critical ethnographies so that their studies do not further marginalize the individuals being studied. Thus, the inquirers collaborate, actively participate with participants, negotiate the final written report, use care in entering and leaving a site, and reciprocate by giving back to people being studied.

▶ The critical ethnographer is self-conscious about his or her interpretation, recognizing that interpretations reflect our own history and culture. Thus they can only be tentative and questioning, subject to how readers, as well as participants, will view the account.

▶ Critical researchers position themselves in the text to be reflexive and self-aware of their role, and to not remain in the background. This means identifying biases and values, acknowledging views, and distinguishing among textual representations by the author, the participants, and the reader. No longer is the ethnographer an "objective" observer, as in the realist approach.

▶ This non-neutral position for the critical researcher also means that he or she will be an advocate for change to help transform our society so that people are less oppressed and marginalized.

▶ In the end, the critical ethnographic report will be a "messy, multilevel, multimethod" approach to inquiry, full of contradictions, imponderables, and tensions (Denzin, 1997).

The critical ethnographic study of one principal in an "inclusive" elementary school (Keyes, Hanley-Maxwell, & Capper, 1999) illustrates many of these features. The overall purpose was to describe and define the role of administrative leadership in an inclusive school for students with a high incidence of disability classifications (e.g., cognitive, emotional, learning, speech, and language). With the objective of generating a new theory that would empower individuals in the school, the authors began with a framework for empowering leadership: support, facilitation, and possibility.

Based on extensive fieldwork consisting of shadowing the principal (Marta) observing classrooms, conducting individual and focus group interviews, and reviewing weekly announcements, the researchers compiled a picture of Marta's leadership that included a personal belief system of spirituality. Marta's spirituality valued personal struggle, espoused the dignity of individuals, merged the professional and the personal, believed that people were doing their best, and emphasized the importance of listening and of dreams. In the end, Keyes et al. provided a "vision for equity nourished by spiritual beliefs" (p. 233) and posed the concluding questions, "School reform for what? Empowering leadership for whom?" (p. 234)

As an ethnography of a school that embraces a critical perspective, the project focused on the issue of empowerment felt by marginalized students and teachers in the school. The principal sought active collaborative participation through a shared dialogue with teachers and students. The researchers advocated for a change and highlighted the tensions that opened up new questions rather than closing down the conversation. Although the authors' views were not made explicit in the text, their interest in change and a new vision for leadership in schools for individuals with disabilities were clear.

KEY CHARACTERISTICS OF AN ETHNOGRAPHIC DESIGN

With the diverse approaches to ethnography identified in a realist, a case study, and a critical approach, it is not easy to identify characteristics they have in common. However, for those learning about ethnographies, the following characteristics typically mark an ethnographic study:

> - an exploration of cultural themes drawn from cultural anthropology
> - the study of a culture-sharing group
> - an examination of shared patterns of behavior, belief, and language
> - a collection of data through fieldwork experiences
> - a description and analysis of themes about the culture-sharing group
> - a presentation of description, themes, and interpretation within the context or setting of the group
> - a reflexivity by the researcher about her or his impact on the research site and the cultural group

Examining Cultural Themes

Ethnographers typically study cultural themes drawn from cultural anthropology. Ethnographers do not venture into the field looking haphazardly for anything they might see. Instead, they are interested in adding to the knowledge about culture and studying specific cultural themes. A **cultural theme** in ethnography is a general position, declared or implied, that is openly approved or promoted in a society or group (see Spradley, 1980, for a discussion about cultural themes). As with all qualitative studies, this theme does not serve to narrow the study; instead, it becomes a broad lens that researchers use when they initially enter a field to study a group, and they look for manifestations of it. As Wolcott (1999) says, we can see "culture at work." (p. 125)

What are these cultural themes? They can be found in introductory texts in cultural anthropology. Wolcott (1999) mentions introductory texts that discuss themes in cultural anthropology, such as those by Kessing, Haviland, or Howard. They can also be found in dictionaries of concepts in cultural anthropology, such as Winthrop's (1991). Another approach is to locate the cultural theme being explored in ethnographic studies in education. Authors announce them in titles or at the beginning of the study. You can see them in purpose statements in ethnographies or in research questions as a "central phenomenon" (see Chapter 5 on "Identifying the Central Phenomenon"). For example, here are several cultural themes explored by authors:

> - *persistence* in distance education courses (Garland, 1993)
> - the "coming out" stages of gay *identity development* (Rhoads, 1997)

▶ development of students' *social skills* in Japan (LeTendre, 1999)
▶ *enculturation* in an early childhood program among the Maori in New Zealand (Bauermeister, 1998)

Learning About a Culture-Sharing Group

Ethnographers learn from studying a culture-sharing group at a single site. Less frequently authors examine single individuals (e.g., see Wolcott's 1974, 1994, single case study of a principal). In the study of a group, ethnographers identify a single site (e.g., an elementary classroom), locate a group within it (e.g., a reading group), and gather data about the group (e.g., observe a reading period). This distinguishes ethnography from other forms of qualitative research (e.g., narrative research) that focus on individuals rather than groups of people. A **culture-sharing group** in ethnography is two or more individuals that have shared behaviors, beliefs, and language. For example, groups were studied in these ethnographies:

▶ 47 students in a distance education course in resource management and environment-related subjects (Garland, 1993)
▶ 16 elementary student teachers (Goodman & Adler, 1985)
▶ 40 college students in an organization who had identified themselves as either gay or bisexual (Rhoads, 1997)

Groups such as these typically possess certain characteristics, which are listed in Table 15.2. A group may vary in size, but the individuals in the group need to be interacting for some time (e.g., more than a couple of weeks up to 4 months) to develop shared patterns of be-

TABLE 15.2

The Study of a Culture-Sharing Group in a Third-Grade Elementary Classroom

Characteristics of a Culture-Sharing Group	An Example
The group consists of two or more individuals, and it may be small or large.	A small group—Two readers in a classroom A larger group—Six to ten readers in a classroom
The group interacts on a regular basis.	For a period three times a week, the group meets to discuss a reading.
The group has interacted for some time.	Since the beginning of September, the reading group has met three times a week for three periods.
The group is representative of some larger group.	The small reading group is representative of third-grade readers.
The group has adopted some shared patterns of behaving, thinking, or talking.	The group has certain rituals they perform as they begin to read, such as sitting on the floor, opening their book to the assigned page, and waiting to speak until the teacher calls on them to answer a question.

having, thinking or talking. The group is often representative of a larger group, such as a reading group within a third-grade classroom.

Often ethnographers study groups unfamiliar to them in order to be able to look at them in a "fresh and different way, as if they were exceptional and unique" (LeCompte, Preissle, & Tesch, 1993, p. 3). Individuals sometimes mistake a cultural group with an ethnic group. Ethnic groups are self-identified individuals in a sociopolitical grouping that have recognized public identity, such as Hispanics, Asian Pacific Islanders, and Arab Americans (LeCompte & Schensul, 1999). Using these ethnic labels can cause problems in an ethnography because the labels may not be terms used by the individuals themselves.

Discerning Shared Patterns

Ethnographic researchers look for shared patterns of behavior, beliefs, and language that the culture-sharing group adopts over time. This characteristic has several elements to it. First, the culture-sharing group needs to have adopted shared patterns that the ethnographer can discern. A **shared pattern** in ethnography is a common social interaction that stabilizes as tacit rules and expectations of the group (Spindler & Spindler, 1992). Second, the group shares any one or a combination of behaviors, beliefs, and language.

▶ A **behavior** in an ethnography is an action taken by an individual in a cultural setting. For example, Wolcott (1974, 1994) studied how a principal's selection committee acted as they deliberated about selecting a candidate.

▶ A **belief** in an ethnography is how an individual thinks about or perceives things in a cultural setting. For example, Padula and Miller (1999) found that women doctoral students in psychology shared the concern that they were not able to invest much energy in their families.

▶ **Language** in an ethnography is how an individual talks to others in a cultural setting. In a study of life-history narratives of two African-American women, Nelson (1990) analyzed code-switching—switching from standard English to Black English vernacular. Sara, for example, used the repetitive, parallel clause structure found in Black church tradition when she said: "It is pain, suffering, determination, perseverance." (p. 147)

These shared patterns raise several practical questions that ethnographers need to address in a study. How long does the group need to stay together to "share"? This question cannot be answered in isolation from a specific study. Unquestionably, the longer the group is together the more the individuals will adopt shared behaviors and ways of thinking and the easier it will be for an ethnographer to discern patterns. However, assessment techniques are available for gathering data quickly from a group that may be shared for a short period of time (LeCompte & Schensul, 1999). Fraternity members may form shared beliefs with new pledges quickly or school boards may develop common understandings through "board retreats" that allow an ethnographer to quickly assess patterns.

Another issue is whether the patterns are ideal (what *should* occur), actual (what *did* occur), or projective (what *might have* occurred). As an ethnographer observes or interviews, examples of all three patterns may emerge from the data. An ethnographer visiting a third-grade classroom might observe the reading group to see what did occur, interview the teacher to identify what might have occurred, and consult with the curriculum coordinator as to what the school district hoped would have occurred.

Engaging in Fieldwork

Ethnographers collect data through spending time at participants' sites where they live, work, or play. To best understand patterns of a cultural group, an ethnographer spends considerable time with the group. The patterns cannot be easily discerned through questionnaires or brief encounters. Instead, the ethnographer goes "to the field," may live or frequently visit the people being studied, and slowly learns the cultural ways the group behaves or thinks. **Fieldwork** in ethnography means that the researcher gathers data in the setting where the participants are located and where their shared patterns can be studied.

This data collection involves:

▶ **Emic data** is information supplied by participants in a study. Emic often refers to first-order concepts, such as local language, concepts, and ways of expression used by members in a cultural-sharing group (Schwandt, 1997). In an ethnographic study of a soup kitchen for the homeless, Miller, Creswell, and Olander (1998) interviewed and recorded "stories" supplied by Michael, Dan, Sarah, and Robert and used quotes from these individuals to construct their perspectives.

▶ **Etic data** is information representing the ethnographer's interpretation of the participant's perspectives. Etic typically refers to second-order concepts, such as the language used by the social scientist or educator to refer to the same phenomena mentioned by the participants (Schwandt, 1997). In the soup kitchen study (Miller, Creswell, & Olander, 1998), the authors formed themes as their interpretation of participants' data that represented how the soup kitchen worked.

▶ **Negotiation data** consists of information which the participant and the researcher agree to use in a study. Negotiation occurs at different stages in research, such as agreeing to entry procedures for a research site, mutually respecting individuals at the site, and developing a plan for giving back or reciprocating with the individuals being studied. Again in the soup kitchen study (Miller, Creswell, & Olander, 1998), the authors sought out a gatekeeper to gain entry, helped advocate for the homeless with funding agencies, and participated in serving lunches on a regular basis.

During fieldwork, the ethnographer uses a variety of research techniques to gather data. Table 15.3, which is a composite list from LeCompte and Schensul (1999) and Wolcott (1999), displays mainly qualitative and a few quantitative forms of data collection. Of these possibilities, observation and unstructured interviewing are popular among ethnographers. To see the range of data collection that might be gathered in a single ethnography, examine the following forms used by Rhoads (1995) in his ethnographic study of fraternity life.

▶ 12 formal structured interviews which lasted from 1 to 2 hours
▶ 18 less formal interviews recorded in hand notes
▶ participation in both open fraternity parties and private rituals that were open to only a few outsiders
▶ ongoing discussions with several key participants who explained the significance of various fraternity practices
▶ a review of numerous documents, including the university Greek handbook, minutes from chapter meetings, class papers, and the fraternity liability policy

Describing, Analyzing for Themes, and Interpreting

Ethnographic researchers describe and analyze the culture-sharing group, and make an interpretation about the patterns seen and heard. During data collection the ethnographer begins to forge a study. This consists of analyzing the data for a description of both the individuals and sites of the culture-sharing group; analyzing patterns of behavior, beliefs, and language; and reaching some conclusions about the meaning learned from studying the people and the site (Wolcott, 1994).

A **description** in ethnography is a detailed rendering of individuals and scenes in order to depict what is going on in the culture-sharing group. This description needs to be detailed and thick, and needs to identify specifics. It serves to place the reader figuratively

TABLE 15.3

Popular Forms of Data Collected by Ethnographers

- Casual conversation
- Life history, life-cycle interview
- Key informant (participant) interview
- Semi-structured interview
- Structured interview
- Survey
- Household census, ethnogenealogy
- Questionnaire (written and/or oral)
- Projective techniques
- Observations (non-participant to participant)
- Tests
- Content analysis of secondary text or visual material
- Focus group interview
- Elicitation techniques (e.g., looking at a scrapbook and talking about memories)
- Audiovisual material (e.g., audio or visual record, such as camera recording)
- Spatial mapping (e.g., recording ways data varies across units, such as group and institution)
- Network analysis (e.g., describing networks in time and space)

Sources: LeCompte & Schensul, 1999; Wolcott, 1999.

in the setting, to transport the reader to the actual scene, to make it real. This involves awakening the reader's senses through the use of adjectives, nouns, and verbs that elicit sounds, sights, feelings, and smells. To do this requires singling out some detail to include while excluding others. It means describing events, activities, and places without veering too far from the actual scene of attention and the people whose shared patterns need to be discerned. Passages from ethnographies that "describe" are long and detailed. Sometimes, ethnographers or case study writers provide a description from a general picture to the specific setting in which an event or events take place. For example, examine Figure 15.3 that maps the descriptive passage in the gunman incident case study (Asmussen & Creswell, 1995). The researchers began with describing the town, then narrowing the description to the campus, and finally focusing on the classroom in which the incident occurred.

In another example, Wolcott (1994) describes a candidate for a principal's position who ended up "Mr. Fifth" in the competition:

> Committee members were cordial in their greetings and introductions when Mr. Fifth appeared for his interview. He was directed to choose one of the (few) comfortable chairs in the meeting room, prompting the personnel director to joke, "It won't be this comfortable again." After a folksy prelude, the director of elementary education asked, "What things have you been doing and how have you been involved?" (p. 129)

In this short descriptive passage, Wolcott conveys the feelings of propriety and anxiety, shares the appearance of the room, relates the language of the committee, and provides a sense of the feelings of the committee toward candidates.

The distinction between description and analysis is not always clear. Certainly analysis moves away from reporting the "facts" to making an interpretation of people and activ-

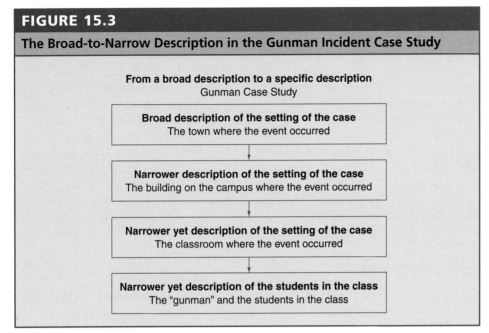

FIGURE 15.3

The Broad-to-Narrow Description in the Gunman Incident Case Study

From a broad description to a specific description
Gunman Case Study

Broad description of the setting of the case
The town where the event occurred

Narrower description of the setting of the case
The building on the campus where the event occurred

Narrower yet description of the setting of the case
The classroom where the event occurred

Narrower yet description of the students in the class
The "gunman" and the students in the class

Source: Asmussen & Creswell, 1995.

ities. As part of making sense of the information, **data analysis** in ethnography consists of distilling how things work and naming the essential features in themes in the cultural setting. Consistent with the process identified in Chapter 9 on "Describing and Developing Themes from Data," the ethnographer segments the text (or images), codes them, and formulates a small set of non-overlapping themes. In an ethnography, however, these themes map the shared patterns of behavior, thinking, or talking. The difficulty is in reducing the themes down to a small set and providing adequate evidence for each. The themes are evident in the ethnographies described below.

▶ In an ethnographic study of conflict resolution between "typically developing" children and children with disabilities in an integrated preschool, Malloy and McMurray (1996) found several conflicts related to goals, oppositions, strategies, outcomes, and the teacher's role.

▶ A case study examined student teachers' perspectives toward social studies in elementary-level schools (Goodman & Adler, 1985). Student teachers viewed social studies as: a nonsubject; human relations; citizenship indoctrination; school knowledge; an integrative core of the elementary curriculum; and education for social action.

After description and analysis comes interpretation. In **interpretation,** the ethnographer draws inferences and forms conclusions about what was learned. This phase of analysis is the most subjective. The researcher relates both the description and the themes back to a larger portrait of what was learned. It often reflects some combination of the researcher making a personal assessment, returning to the literature on the cultural theme being explored, and raising further questions based on the data. It might also include addressing problems that arose during the fieldwork that render the account tentative and hypothetical, at best. In the ethnography of Raul, the 12-year-old with disabilities and his brothers, family, and friends (Harry, Day, & Quist, 1998), interpretation consisted of the authors reflecting on the differences between exclusion in a nonfamily setting and unconditional acceptance in a family.

Understanding a Context

Ethnographers present the description, themes, and interpretation within the context or setting of the culture-sharing group. The **context** for an ethnography is the setting, situation, or environment that surrounds the cultural-group being studied. It is multilayered and interrelated, consisting of such factors as history, religion, politics, economy, and the environment (Fetterman, 1998). This context may be a physical location such as a description of the school, the state of the building, the color of the classroom walls, or the sounds coming down the hall. It may also be the historical context of individuals in the group, whether they have experienced suppression, domination, or are an emerging people who have arrived excited about their new land. It may be the social condition of the individuals, their long-time reunions to build kinship, their status as a profession, or their earnings and geographic mobility. The economic conditions may also be presented to include their income levels, their working-class or blue-collar background, or the systems of finance that keeps them below the poverty level.

Being Reflexive

Ethnographic researchers make interpretations and write their report reflexively. **Reflexivity** in ethnography means that the researcher is aware of and openly discusses his or her role in the study in a way that honors and respects the site and people being studied. Because ethnographic research involves a prolonged stay at a site, researchers are concerned about their impact on the site and the people. They negotiate entry with key individuals and plan to leave the site as undisturbed as they found it. As individuals who have a history and a cultural background themselves, they realize that their interpretation is only one that can be made and that their report does not have any privileged authority over other interpretations that readers, participants, and other researchers may have. It is important, therefore, for ethnographers to position themselves within their report and identify their standpoint or point of view (Denzin, 1997). They do this by talking about themselves, sharing their experiences, and mentioning how their interpretations shape their discussions about the sites and culture-sharing groups. One researcher who studied identity development of adolescent females through reading teen magazines (Finders, 1996), documented her role as follows:

> I did not want to be viewed as a teacher or someone in authority. (p. 73)
> I gained their trust slowly and negotiated a relationship that did not fit their established patterns with significant adults. (p. 73)
> On several occasions, a girl would not allow me to see a note that she deemed "too obscene." I did not report such incidents as writing on a restroom wall or faking illness to avoid an exam. (p. 74)

Being reflexive also means that authors' conclusions are often tentative or inconclusive, leading to new questions that need to be answered and pondered. The study might end with questions that beg for answers or multiple perspectives or viewpoints for the reader to consider.

STEPS IN CONDUCTING AN ETHNOGRAPHY

There are probably as many procedures for conducting an ethnography as there are ethnographers. From the early days in cultural anthropology when researchers were "sent" without guidance to remote islands or countries to conduct their ethnography, today we have procedures, albeit general procedures, to guide your conduct of an ethnography. A highly structured approach can be found in Spradley (1980), who has advanced a 12-stage "Developmental Research Sequence" for conducting an ethnography. As shown in Figure 15.4, this sequence begins with the researcher locating an informant (today we would call this person a "participant"—see Chapter 10 on "Writing Sensitively"). Then the ethnographer cycles between collecting data and making analyses of various types, such as a taxonomy or a comparison table to explore relationships among ideas (see Spradley's componential analysis). Other authors besides Spradley have also suggested guidelines, such as Fetterman (1998), LeCompte and Schensul (1999), and Wolcott, (1999).

Instead of Spradley's highly structured approach, we will consider a series of steps that represent a general template rather than a definitive procedure for conducting an ethnography. Moreover, the considerations of ethnographers and case study writers differ procedurally, and we will consider both similarities and differences among our three forms of ethnography: realist, case study, and critical. An overview of the steps used in each type of design is shown in Table 15.4.

FIGURE 15.4

Spradley's Developmental Research Sequence

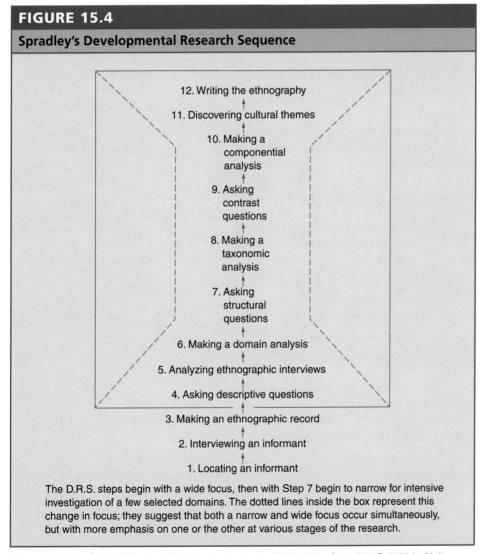

12. Writing the ethnography
11. Discovering cultural themes
10. Making a componential analysis
9. Asking contrast questions
8. Making a taxonomic analysis
7. Asking structural questions
6. Making a domain analysis
5. Analyzing ethnographic interviews
4. Asking descriptive questions
3. Making an ethnographic record
2. Interviewing an informant
1. Locating an informant

The D.R.S. steps begin with a wide focus, then with Step 7 begin to narrow for intensive investigation of a few selected domains. The dotted lines inside the box represent this change in focus; they suggest that both a narrow and wide focus occur simultaneously, but with more emphasis on one or the other at various stages of the research.

Source: Table from *The Ethnographic Interview* by James P. Spradley. Copyright © 1979 by Holt, Rinehart, and Winston, reproduced by permission of the publisher. This material may not be reproduced in any form or by any means without the prior written permission of the publisher.

TABLE 15.4

Procedures for Conducting a Realist Ethnography, a Case Study, and a Critical Ethnography

Procedures	Realist Ethnography	Case Study	Critical Ethnography
Identify your intent, the appropriate design, and how intent relates to your research problem.	The problem relates to a culture-sharing group and how it works. The problem requires detailed description of the daily lives of people. The problem relates to understanding a cultural theme. Identify your cultural theme.	The problem relates to developing an in-depth understanding of a "case" or bounded system. The problem relates to understanding an event, activity, process, or one or more individuals. Identify the type of "case," such as intrinsic, instrumental, or collective.	The problem relates to a need to address inequities in our society or schools. The problem calls for action and advocacy. Identify the "critical" issue (e.g., inequality) that you wish to explore.
Discuss how you plan to receive approval and gain access to study sites and participants.	Receive approval from institutional review board. Locate a research site using purposeful sampling procedures. Identify a gatekeeper to provide access. Guarantee provisions for respecting the site.	Receive approval from institutional review board. Locate a research site using purposeful sampling procedures. Identify how many cases you plan to study. Identify a gatekeeper to provide access. Guarantee provisions for respecting the site.	Receive approval from institutional review board. Locate a research site using purposeful sampling procedures. Identify a gatekeeper to provide access. Guarantee provisions for respecting the site.
Collect appropriate data emphasizing time in the field, multiple sources of information, and collaboration.	Spend extensive time at the site and with the culture-sharing group. Enter the site slowly and build rapport. Plan to reciprocate for data provided. Emphasize observations and record fieldnotes.	Collect extensive data using multiple forms of data collection (observations, interviews, documents, audio-visual materials).	Collaborate with participants by actively involving them in data collection. Collect multiple forms of data that individuals are willing to provide.

Step 1. Identify Intent and the Type of Design, and Relate Intent to Your Research Problem

The first and most important step in conducting research is to identify why you are undertaking a study, which form of design you plan to use, and how your intent relates to your research problem. These factors need to be identified in all three forms of ethnographies and case studies. The intent of your research and the type of problem you seek to study will differ significantly depending on if you plan to conduct a realist, case study, or critical ethnography.

For a realist ethnography, the focus is on understanding a culture-sharing group and using the group to develop a deeper understanding of a cultural theme. The culture-sharing group may be an entire school or a single classroom. The themes may include such topics as

TABLE 15.4

Procedures for Conducting a Realist Ethnography, a Case Study, and a Critical Ethnography *(continued)*

Procedures	Realist Ethnography	Case Study	Critical Ethnography
Analyze and interpret your data within a design.	Read through data to develop an overall understanding of it. Develop a detailed description of the cultural setting to establish a context for the group being studied. Develop themes about the culture-sharing group. Make interpretations in view of the cultural theme you are studying.	Read through data to develop an overall understanding of it. Describe the case(s) in detail and establish a context for it. Develop issues or themes about the case(s). If more than one case is studied, consider a within-case analysis followed by a cross-case analysis.	Read through data to develop an overall understanding of it. Develop a detailed description of the cultural setting to establish a context for the group being studied. Develop themes that relate to the "critical" issues that are being explored in the ethnography. Identify changes that need to occur, advocate for specific changes, and advance a plan for change.
Write and report your research consistent with your design.	Report it as an objective study. As a researcher, remain in the background in the written report. Keep your biases out. Identify how your exploration of the cultural theme advances knowledge.	Report it based primarily on description of the case, or weigh description, analysis, and interpretation differently or equally. Choose to be objective or subjective in your reporting. Include your biases. Generalize to other cases.	Report it as a call to action to address that "critical" issue that you are studying. Include a specific plan of action for change based on your findings. Discuss how you, as well as those you studied, changed (be reflexive).

enculturation, acculturation, socialization, institutionalized education, learning and cognition, and child and adult development (LeCompte, Preissle, & Tesch, 1993).

For a case study, the focus is on developing an in-depth understanding of a case, such as an event, activity, or process. In education, this often includes the study of an individual or several individuals, such as students or teachers. The important consideration is how you will use the case, such as whether it has intrinsic merit, is instrumental in understanding an issue, or whether it provides information about several cases that can collectively be compared.

In a critical ethnography, the intent changes dramatically from those used in a realist or case study project. A critical ethnographer seeks to address an inequity in society or schools, plans to use the research to advocate and call for changes, and typically identifies a specific issue (e.g., inequality, dominance, oppression, or empowerment) to study.

Step 2. Discuss Approval and Access Considerations

In this step all three types of designs follow a similar procedure. You need to receive approval from the institutional review board (see the steps in Chapter 6 on "The Process of Obtaining Approval"). You also need to identify the type of purposeful sampling that is available and that best answers your research questions. In this process, locate a site for your research and then identify a gatekeeper that can provide access to the site and participants for study. In all research, you need to guarantee provisions for respecting the site and actively design in the study how to reciprocate to the individuals at the site. This means that you will guarantee to disturb the site as little as possible and to follow good ethical practices such as guaranteeing privacy and anonymity, not deceiving individuals, and informing all participants of the purposes of your research.

Step 3. Use Appropriate Data Collection Procedures

We can see from Table 15.4 that the three designs have several common features with an emphasis on extensive data collection, using multiple procedures for gathering data, and the active involvement of participants in the process.

In a realist ethnography, because you will likely spend considerable time with individuals in the field (e.g., up to 4 months or more), you need to enter the site slowly and as unobtrusively as possible. Building rapport with gatekeepers and key participants is essential for your long-term contacts. In many realist accounts, an emphasis is placed on taking field-notes and observing the "cultural scene." Interviews and artifacts such as drawings, relics, and symbols are also important forms of data. Any data that can help you develop an in-depth understanding of the shared patterns of the cultural group would be useful.

For a case study, the intent is to develop an in-depth understanding of a case or an issue, and researchers collect as many types of data to develop this understanding as possible. For example, in the gunman incident (Asmussen & Creswell, 1995) as discussed in Chapter 1, the authors provided a table in Paragraph 11 that showed 13 sources of information including interviews, observations, documents and audio-visual materials. The provision of a table specifically focused on data collection sources emphasized the extent of data collection.

In a critical ethnography, the data collection is less focused on time in the field or on the extent of data and more on the active collaboration between the researcher and the participants during the study. Because the intent of a critical ethnography is to help bring about change that affects the lives of participants, the participants need to be involved in learning about themselves and what steps need to be taken to improve their equity, to provide empowerment, or to lessen their oppression. This collaboration may involve participants in the design of the study, the formulation of research questions, the collection of data, or the analysis of the data collected. It may also include having participants actively write the final research report with you.

Step 4. Analyze and Interpret Data within a Design

In all ethnographic designs, you will engage in the general process of developing a description, analyzing your data for themes, and providing an interpretation of the meaning of your information. These are typical data analysis and interpretation procedures found in all qualitative studies. However, the different types of ethnographic designs vary in their approach to these procedures.

In a critical ethnography, you need to consider a balance among description, analysis, and interpretation so that each becomes an important element of your analysis. Moreover, you can discuss in your interpretation how you learned about the cultural theme, actively reflect back on what information existed in the literature, and advance how your study added to the understanding of the cultural theme. In a case study, again the analysis follows description, analysis, and interpretation, but the analysis procedures will vary depending on whether you are studying a single case or multiple cases. A typical case study procedure for multiple cases is to first analyze each case separately, and then to conduct a cross-case analysis (see Stake, 1995) to identify common and different themes among all of the cases.

In a critical ethnography, the description, analysis, and interpretation are shaped to focus in on the "critical" issue being explored in your study. Specifically, you need to interpret your findings in view of the changes that need to occur and to advocate for improvements in the lives of your participants. Often critical ethnographers will advance a plan for change with specific steps that need to occur. For example, in a study about improving the conditions for women's ice hockey teams in Canada, Theberge (1997) ends her study with an appeal for action. She calls for "a more fully transformative vision of hockey that would offer empowerment in a setting that rejects violence and the normalization of injury in favor of an ethic of care." (p. 85)

Step 5. Write the Report Consistent with Your Design

A realist ethnography is written as an objective report of information about the culture-sharing group. Your personal views and biases will be kept in the background, and a discussion at the end of the study should indicate how the research contributes to knowledge about the cultural theme based on understanding the shared patterns of behavior, thinking, or language of the culture-sharing group. On the other hand, a case study may emphasize the detailed description of the case. Entire case studies are written with a description in mind rather than a thematic development, such as Stake's (1995) descriptive case study of "Harper School." Other case studies will balance description with themes, such as the gunman incident case study by Asmussen and Creswell (1995). One additional factor that sets case studies apart from other ethnographic designs is that the author may discuss generalizing the findings to other cases, especially if researchers examine multiple case studies. Although qualitative researchers are reluctant to generalize their findings, the use of multiple case studies provides some ability to identify findings using cross-case analysis that are common to all cases. When this occurs, case study writers may suggest that their findings are generalizable, but they only make modest claims in this direction.

In a critical ethnography, the researchers conclude their reports with the "critical" issue that initiated the study, and discuss how they as well as the participants have changed or benefited from the research. Included within a "call for action" by the critical ethnographer may be a reflection about changes they and the participants have experienced. Undoubtedly, in all forms of research, the investigators change, but critical ethnographers, as self- conscious researchers, highlight these changes for themselves and their participants.

CRITERIA FOR EVALUATING AN ETHNOGRAPHIC DESIGN

The criteria for evaluating an ethnography first begins with applying the standards used in qualitative research mentioned in Chapter 10. Then, specific factors need to be considered within ethnography proper. Consider these questions as you read an ethnography or review a study you have conducted:

- Is the culture-sharing group or the case clearly identified and specified?
- Are patterns identified for the group or case?

▶ Is the group or the case described in detail?

▶ Do you learn about the context surrounding the group or the case?

▶ Does the author reflect on his or her role in the study?

▶ Is there a broader interpretation made of the meaning of the patterns or the case?

▶ Does the interpretation naturally flow from the description and the themes?

▶ From reading the ethnography, does the reader have a sense about how the culture works from the participant's or researcher's viewpoint?

▶ Has the author checked the accuracy of the study by using procedures such as triangulating among data sources or taking the study back to participants for review?

APPLYING WHAT YOU HAVE LEARNED: AN ETHNOGRAPHIC STUDY

To apply the ideas in this chapter, first read the ethnographic study on page 505, noting the marginal annotations that identify the key characteristics of an ethnography as addressed in this chapter and the characteristics of qualitative research (see Chapter 2 on "Distinguishing Between Quantitative and Qualitative Research.")

> Finders, M. J. (1996). Queens and teen zines: Early adolescent females reading their way toward adulthood. *Anthropology and Education Quarterly, 27,* 71–89.

Finders' (1996) study addresses how teen magazines shape the identity of adolescent females. As an ethnography, the study considers a small group of four seventh-grade girls who were considered "social queens" and the impact of teen magazine reading on their constructs of social roles and relationships. Data gathering consisted of observations, interviewing the girls, and written artifacts. From this data, the author identified themes of "rite of passage," "negotiating a presentation of self," and "you don't have to think about it." The article ends with the author advocating for literacy learning a "pedagogy that cracks the veneer of this 'light reading'" (p. 84) and challenges the way that teen magazines represent social roles.

The study was chosen because it follows sound ethnographic procedures (e.g., clearly defined group, understanding patterns of behavior, and observational data collection) and illustrates an example of critical ethnography with a focus on studying a gender issue and advocating for specific changes in our language arts classrooms.

As you review this article, look for elements of the research process:

▶ the research problem and use of qualitative research

▶ use of the literature

▶ the purpose statement and research questions

▶ types and procedures of data collection

▶ types and procedures of data analysis and interpretation

▶ the overall writing structure

The Research Problem and Use of Qualitative Research

See Paragraphs 02–03

The research problem or issue in this study is announced in Paragraph 02 when the author refers to the narrow topics and limited range of roles for females presented in teen magazines. Added to this is the problem that young female adolescents construct their sense of self through reading these magazines.

This study displays many key markings of a qualitative study:

▶ an exploration of a problem about how young female teens construct a sense of self (Paragraph 02)
▶ the minimal use of the literature and its application to discuss the problem at the beginning of the study (Paragraph 03)
▶ open-ended and broad questions about adolescent females reading teen magazines (Paragraph 03)
▶ the collection of data from a small number of participants—four early adolescent girls (Paragraph 04)
▶ the collection of words (text) from the adolescents and the use of the researcher's own forms of data collecting (Paragraph 06)
▶ the analysis of text by reporting words of the adolescents (e.g., see Paragraph 10)
▶ the description and analysis of themes about developmental issues, the Queens reading "Zines," and reading "fluff" (Paragraphs 10–41)
▶ the interpretation of the findings within the larger meaning of teaching subliterature (Paragraphs 42–50)

Moreover, the study also displays characteristics of a critical ethnography:

▶ It examined the theoretical concept of social roles (Paragraph 03) and the issue of vulnerability of the adolescent readers (Paragraph 47).
▶ The researcher discussed her trust and negotiated a relationship with the teens that would not further marginalize them. In this way, the researcher openly discussed her position (Paragraph 07).
▶ The researcher was sensitive to the role of women in the social, political, and developmental context of schools and reading (e.g., see Paragraph 03).
▶ The researcher also became an advocate for the needs of teens by recommending changes for teaching subliterature (see Paragraphs 42–50).
▶ The author left the study with additional questions, such as what would happen to one of the teens, Cleo, because "there was no place for her" (Paragraph 50).

Use of the Literature

See Paragraph 03

As in most qualitative studies, the literature in this article played a minor role. It documented the reading of the literature by young girls and it set the "conversation" (Paragraph 03) to which this study was to add.

The Purpose Statement and Research Questions

See Paragraph 03

At the end of this paragraph we find a general purpose statement by the author that the study will add to the ongoing conversation about perspectives of adolescent females reading teen magazines and address how literacy shapes (and constrains) social roles. The author asks the question, "How do early adolescent females read literature that falls outside the realm of fiction?" (Paragraph 03).

Types of Procedures of Data Collection

See Paragraphs 04, 06–08

Participant observation, interviews, and collecting written artifacts became the major forms of data collected. This process involved 1 year of data collection and consisted of participant observation, interviewing, and collecting written artifacts from the participants both in and out of school.

Types of Procedures of Data Analysis and Interpretation

Data Analysis—see Paragraphs 10–41

Interpretation—see Paragraphs 42–50

The author interwove both description and thematic development. This can be seen in Paragraph 16, for example, where the author first described the shared patterns of behavior by the adolescents, documenting a detailed description of the reading of the girls within the theme of "Crossing Developmental Boundaries: Zine Reading as a Rite of Passage." In this theme, we hear about the inclusion and exclusion of members from the "queens" and how the girls sought answers to their questions from the magazines. We meet Lauren, Angie, Tiffany, and Cleo.

An interpretation ends the study with the author reflecting on the larger meaning of teen magazines in teaching reading. The author believes these magazines need to come into the classroom and be examined as social scripts that shape the lives of teenage girls.

The Overall Writing Structure

In many ways, this study is traditionally structured to emphasize a problem, the data collection, the data analysis, and the interpretation and recommendations. What makes it unusual is the cultural concept—social roles—highlighted at the beginning of the study and the advocacy by the researcher for change emphasized at the end. These elements are clearly part of a critical approach to ethnography.

KEY IDEAS IN THE CHAPTER

An ethnography is a useful design for studying groups in education, their behaviors, beliefs, and language, and how they develop shared patterns of interacting over time. Ethnographic research is a qualitative design for describing, analyzing, and interpreting the patterns of a culture-sharing group. Culture is a broad term to encompass all human behavior and beliefs. Typically, it includes a study of language, rituals, structures, life stages, interactions, and communication. Ethnographers visit the "field," collect extensive data through such procedures as observation and interviewing, and write up a cultural portrait of the group within its setting. Thus, an ethnographer stresses cultural concepts and they study a group of individuals at a single site. The researcher examines shared patterns of behaviors, beliefs, and language that have developed over time by engaging in fieldwork such as observing and interviewing people where they live and work. The analysis begins with describing and analyzing the culture-sharing group and interpreting their patterns within the context of culture-at-work. Overall, the ethnographer employs a reflexive inquiry style of being self-conscious about the research and the writing, and being respectful of participants.

The origins of this approach are found in anthropology, sociology, the application of anthropological methods to education, and postmodern, reflexive concerns about interpreting data and writing reports. These historical factors have led to three types of ethnographies: realist, case studies, and critical studies. The steps in conducting these ethnographies involve starting with an interest in studying a cultural theme, identifying a bounded site and examining shared patterns for a group. The researcher poses general research questions to identify shared patterns of behavior, beliefs, or language, and collects extensive fieldwork data. From this data a general portrait of how the culture-sharing group works is developed though description, analysis, and interpretation. The interpretation and writing is sensitive to reflexivity of the researcher, and varied forms of writing structures are used.

Conducting an ethnography involves clarifying the intent of the study, selecting an appropriate design, and relating the design to the research problem in the study. Then the researcher needs to seek approval to conduct the study and obtain access to study sites and participants. Once this is accomplished, the ethnographer collects data using multiple sources of information and spending considerable time in the field. After gathering information, the analysis of data consists of describing, analyzing, and interpreting. Some researchers, when conducting a critical ethnography, will identify changes that need to occur and will actively advocate and plan for them. When writing the final research report, ethnographers and case study writers employ practices consistent with their designs, such as being objective, generalizing findings, and discussing how they and the participants changed during the research process.

USEFUL INFORMATION FOR PRODUCERS OF RESEARCH

▶ Clarify the intent you have for your ethnographic research. Consider whether you plan to develop patterns and a portrait of a culture-sharing group, provide an in-depth description and analysis of a "case," or advocate for an issue based on studying a culture-sharing group.

▶ Recognize that many ethnographies today are written using a critical perspective. Read about these forms of ethnographies by consulting books such as Thomas (1993), Carspecken (1995), or Denzin (1997).

▶ If you conduct a case study, determine whether the issue (instrumental) or the case itself (intrinsic) is of primary interest for addressing your research problem.

▶ When conducting a realist ethnography, identify a cultural theme that you wish to explore. This cultural theme is the central phenomenon of your study.

▶ As you collect data in the field for a realist ethnography, look for shared patterns of behavior, beliefs, or language that develop over time.

▶ Engaging in fieldwork and collecting data involves negotiating relationships with participants and key gatekeepers at research sites. Be respectful of sites and individuals as you conduct your study.

▶ Consider in your ethnography how you will balance description of the culture-sharing group or case, analysis of themes about the group or case, and interpretation of the meaning of the description and analysis. Ideally, you should give them equal weight, but this would depend on the purposes and the research questions you plan to address in your study.

▶ Context is important in ethnographies and case studies. Include it in your description as well as in your themes.

▶ Much has been written about how we interpret the "text," or written report, in ethnographic research. Recognize and discuss in your report your own position that affects your interpretation, and acknowledge that multiple interpretations exist in any report, such as those of readers and participants in the study.

▶ Consider the steps in the process of conducting an ethnography and make adjustments in them to reflect the type of design you use. See Table 15.4 as a guide.

USEFUL INFORMATION FOR CONSUMERS OF RESEARCH

▶ To identify the cultural theme in a realist ethnography, look at the purpose statement and the research question for the central phenomenon being examined.

▶ Recognize that the final ethnographic report or case study will vary in structure because of the differences among a realist ethnography, a case study, and a critical ethnography.

▶ Among several factors to use in evaluating an ethnography or case report, especially consider whether the author collects multiple forms of data and spends considerable time in the field gathering information.

▶ The information researchers may report in an ethnography or case study may be insights from examining a portrait of a culture-sharing group, contributions to understanding cultural themes, an in-depth exploration of a case that has not been examined before, or a plan for action to change or remedy inequities in education and in our society.

ADDITIONAL RESOURCES YOU MIGHT EXAMINE

A number of books, listed below, are available to expand your understanding of educational ethnographic research.

Harry Wolcott (1992, 1994, 1995, and 1999) has authored four recent books which, taken as a series, introduce you to all facets of understanding and conducting ethnographic research. His conversational style illustrates good writing and serves as an accessible means for understanding ethnography. His 1999 book is perhaps the best overview of ethnographic practices and ideas available today. Examine Wolcott's books:

Wolcott, H. F. (1992). *Writing up qualitative research.* Newbury Park, CA: Sage.

Wolcott, H. F. (1994). *Transforming qualitative data: Description, analysis, and interpretation.* Thousand Oaks, CA: Sage.

Wolcott, H. F. (1995). *The art of fieldwork.* Walnut Creek, CA: AltaMira.

Wolcott, H. F. (1999). *Ethnography: A way of seeing.* Walnut Creek, CA: AltaMira.

Margaret LeCompte and Jean Schensul (1999) have authored a "toolkit" of seven short books that provide an excellent introduction to ethnography. See their introductory book as a guide to their "toolkit":

LeCompte, M. D., & Schensul, J. J. (1999). *Designing and conducting ethnographic research,* Ethnographer's Toolkit, Number 1. Walnut Creek, CA: AltaMira.

Another introductory text, now in its third edition, is the book on ethnography for educators by Robert Bogdan and Sari Biklen (1998). This book is a good introductory text to all facets of educational ethnography. See:

Bogdan, R. C., & Biklen, S. K. (1998). *Qualitative research for education: An introduction to theory and methods* (3rd ed.). Boston, MA: Allyn & Bacon.

Practical step-by-step approaches to educational ethnography can be found in two books. David Fetterman's (1998) book, now in its second edition, is like a travelogue, identifying and discussing the major landmarks every ethnographer encounters. For steps and examples in writing fieldnotes in an ethnography, examine the book by Robert Emerson, Rachel Fretz, and Linda Shaw (Emerson, Fretz, & Shaw, 1995). See:

Fetterman, D. M. (1998). *Ethnography: Step by step.* (2nd Ed.). Thousand Oaks, CA: Sage.

Emerson, R. M., Fretz, R. I., & Shaw, L. L. (1995). *Writing ethnographic fieldnotes.* Chicago: University of Chicago Press.

Finally, two books to consult on case study research are Bob Stake's (1995) book on the art of case study research and Sharon Merriam's (1998) introduction to case studies. See:

Stake, R. E. (1995). *The art of case study research.* Thousand Oaks, CA: Sage.

Merriam, S. B. (1998). *Qualitative research and case study applications in education.* San Francisco: Jossey-Bass.

Qualitative
Characteristics

Queens and Teen Zines: Early Adolescent Females Reading Their Way toward Adulthood

Ethnography
Research
Characteristics

Margaret J. Finders
Purdue University

(01)   *This article documents the reading of teen magazines by middle-class Euro-American seventh-grade girls. Examining the reading of teen zines as a literacy event provides an opportunity to explore how the girls perceive and construct their social roles and relationships as they enter a new cultural scene, the junior high school. Documenting this particular reading practice provides a window onto the complex social negotiations in operation as early adolescent females use literacy to shape emerging social roles. This study holds implications for literacy pedagogy that considers how textual representations serve to define and constrain social roles.*

(02)   Against a backdrop of feminist scholarship that emphasizes the social, political, and historical construction of gender (Biklen and Pollard 1993; Britzman 1993; Fine and Macpherson 1993; Griffin 1985; hooks 1990), a growing body of research has begun to examine the contents of teen zines, magazines marketed for adolescent consumption, magazines marketed to serve adolescent females, in the words of the managing editor of *Seventeen,* "to inform, entertain and give teenage girls all the information they need to make sound choices in their lives" (Peirce 1990:496–497). While teen zines that target the adolescent female claim a focus on personal growth and self-improvement, scholars critique them, citing a narrowness of topics presented and a limited range of available roles for females. According to recent research, magazines such as *Sassy, Seventeen,* and *YM* constrain choices for the adolescent female to a traditional model of finding an adult place in society largely through men and commodities (Evans et al. 1991; Peirce 1990; Stretch 1991). Yet, as you will see, the adolescent females in this study demonstrated little ability to render such an ideology visible. One 12-year-old girl, for example, described her reason for reading teen zines in this way: "They tell you about woman stuff."

(03)   Such "woman stuff" has been the focus of research studies that examine the social, political, and developmental nature of reading. Both school structure and popular adolescent literature have been criticized because they seem to constrict the roles available to young women and serve to reinscribe them into patriarchy (Apple 1986; Gilligan 1988; Stretch 1991). Furthermore, Christian-Smith argues that "through literacy, young women construct and reconstruct their desires and gender subjectivities, as well as their awareness of social differences and power relations" (1993:1–2). In a study of women romance readers, Radway (1984) argues that reading was constructed as a "declaration of their independence." Following Radway's 1984 study, Willinsky and Hunniford conducted a parallel study of avid young adult romance readers. They report:

> The experience may be vicarious but not the pleasure. . . . With the young readers in this study, whom we found as given to these pleasures as Radway's adults, reading the romance this seriously, they appear on the verge of a total surrender on a number of fronts; they are, in effect, taking more from the books than the adults, more than many of us in education would want to ask. [1993:93]

A qualitative problem requires exploration and understanding.

Ethnographers start with cultural themes.

The qualitative literature justifies the research problem.

Anthropology & Education Quarterly 27(1):71–89. Copyright © 1996. American Anthropological Association.

Reprinted with permission of *Anthropology & Education Quarterly.*

Willinsky and Hunniford argue that while Radway's readers cited a private pleasure and an escape from their daily responsibilities, the young romance readers' selection was based on a consistent concern with appearances, a new awareness of physical development, a desire to have a romance just like the heroine's, and a belief that they would live this way (1993:93). In another study of young adult readers, Cherland maintains that girls used reading "in order to exercise agency within approved social domains" (1994:173). She argues that such reading may serve as "combative" (as an escape from being good) and "compensatory" (as a way to feel more powerful). These studies examine fiction reading as it intertwines with an evolving sense of self. As scholars critique the limited subject positions available to adolescent females, the purpose of this article is to add to the ongoing conversation by including the perspective of the adolescent female reading teen magazines. How do early adolescent females read literature that falls outside the realm of fiction? Documenting the lived experiences of early adolescent females fills a gap in our understanding of adolescence by adding to our growing understanding of complex social negotiations in operation as early adolescent females use literacy to shape their social roles,[1] and in turn, how literate practices serve to define and constrain their social roles.

The Study

(04)   To more fully understand the perspective of the adolescent female, I undertook a yearlong ethnographic study at one midwestern junior high school during the 1992–93 school year (Finders, in press). This article is a slice of a much larger ethnographic study in which I followed four early adolescent girls (two sets of self-proclaimed best friends and their larger circle of friends) from May of their sixth-grade year through the completion of seventh grade. I focused on seventh graders because seventh grade marked the beginning of the secondary school experience within the district; within the larger culture, secondary school serves as a marker of entry into adolescence. Thus by virtue of enrollment in a junior high school, focal students were at the threshold of adolescence, at a critical juncture in their academic as well as their social development. In September, they faced an unfamiliar cultural scene, the junior high school. They were just beginning to negotiate their way into this new adolescent arena, learning the social codes as they carved out a sense of shared identity within new groups. Through literate practices, I explore the rules and rituals that accompany entry into adolescence, documenting how adolescent girls perceive and negotiate their social roles and relationships.

(05)   Based upon a sociocultural theoretic framework,[2] emphasis was placed on documenting naturally occurring key incidents, specifically literacy events (Heath 1982).[3] Literacy events serve as a lens to bring into focus the competing expectations and assumptions that the early adolescent female must negotiate among in order to participate fully in each context. The goal of the larger project was to document how each event was framed from the point of view of key participants. By documenting who is present, where and when and for whom such events occurred, I attempt to make visible the tacit rules and demands that shape such events and ultimately shape available social roles within particular social networks. An examination of a group's literacy events will lead to a richer understanding of the dynamics of social networks. Such a focus demands an ethnographic approach (Erickson 1986; Spradley 1980).

(06)   Data were obtained by participant-observation (Spradley 1979, 1980) as well as interviewing and collecting written artifacts from participants. I spent 1 year documenting literate practices both in and out of school, tagging along to athletic events and the mall, listening in on phone conversa-

---

Left margin notes:

The qualitative literature plays a minor role.

The qualitative purpose statement and research questions are broad and general.

The qualitative purpose statement and research questions seek participants' experiences.

Qualitative data collection involves studying a small number of individuals or sites.

Qualitative data collection is based on using protocols developed during the study.

Qualitative data collection involves gathering text or image data.

Right margin notes:

Ethnographers typically study a group of people.

Enthographers look for shared patterns of behaviors, beliefs, and language.

Ethnographers spend extensive time in fieldwork.

tions, hanging out at slumber parties, and observing language arts classrooms.

(07)   I was initially introduced to students in the language arts classrooms as someone from the university who was interested in learning about seventh graders' reading and writing practices. My presence in each classroom was for the most part nonparticipatory. I did not want to be viewed as a teacher or someone in authority; so I did not take on any of the teaching duties and tried not to interact with students during this time. Students gradually became aware that there were particular students that were the focus of my attention. Comments from students such as, "Oh, she's writing a book about girls," seemed to appease curious students. By meeting with focal students informally outside the school context, I gained their trust slowly and negotiated a relationship that did not fit their established patterns with significant adults. In October, for example, I overheard one focal student announcing, "That's not a teacher; that's Peg." I consciously chose dress to distinguish myself from school personnel, most often wearing jeans and tennis shoes.

> **Qualitative researchers take in a reflexive and biased approach.**

(08)   As seventh graders, the focal students had limited access to social outings outside the school context, and I occasionally drove them to a pizza parlor or to the mall. This allowed me the opportunity not only to observe them in induced natural contexts but to negotiate a relationship with them that did not position me as an authority figure. Early, there were moments in which I was tested by focal students. On several occasions, a girl would not allow me to see a note that she deemed "too obscene." I did not report such incidents as writing on a restroom wall or faking illness to avoid an exam. I avoided conveying any negative judgment, and as the study progressed, I slowly gained their trust and was permitted to receive literacies still deemed "too gross" for parents or teachers. As the year progressed, focal students began to see their roles as my teacher and wanted me to understand what being a teenager was really like. In order to, as they said, "get it right," I was soon being invited to their slumber parties and dances.

(09)   As the study unfolded, teen zines became a central focus because, as will become clear, one group of girls used the zine as a marker, a yardstick to measure how one was progressing into womanhood, possession serving as a sign of one crossing the boundary from childhood into adolescence. As noted earlier, two distinct groups of girls were the centerpiece of the larger study. Teachers, administrators, and the girls themselves identified separate and clearly bounded friendship groups. Individual members carefully patrolled the borders between friendship groups. One group, those called tough cookies by one parent, did not report reading teen zines, and I never observed them carrying zines at school or home. For the other group of friends, those referred to as social queens by parents, reading and carrying a teen zine served, it seems, as a visible rite of passage, as a cultural practice to mark oneself as separate from children, as unlike those other "little kids" and ready to handle "woman stuff." It became increasingly clear that teen zines were used by this group, the social queens, to patrol the borders around their friendship network. Teen zines served as signs to make visible the boundaries between adolescents and children.

> **Qualitative data analysis consists of describing information and developing themes.**

Crossing Developmental Boundaries: Zine Reading as Rite of Passage

(10)
> **Qualitative data analysis consists of text analysis.**

Lauren:[4]	What do they [the "tough cookies"] read? They probably just read books. They have nothing better to do?
Angie:	They probably don't even read these [*holds up a copy of Sassy*].

Tiffany:	Did you guys see this? God, I'm gonna get some of these [*holds open a page from* YM *and points to a pair of pants*]. Isn't this so cool?
Angie:	Way cool. My mom's gonna let me get some. Do you think I kinda look like her? [*Points to a model in* Sassy]
Lauren:	Oh, yeah, right. Give me that. It's my copy. Give me that, you dork.
Angie:	Give it to me. Who's the dork? Let me have it. Let me read you something.
Tiffany:	Know what? I'm gonna get *YM*. My dad said he'd loan me the money. He'll forget, and I won't have to pay him back.
Angie:	Did you take this best friend quiz?
Lauren:	Did you see that article about who's in and who's out? I think he is so cool. He's a total babe. I mean B-A-B-E.

(11)   After one year of documenting the reading and writing practices of early adolescent females, I regularly came to expect scenes like this one, played out like a well-rehearsed script, girls turning to the pages of teen zines, seeking answers to questions about their place in an adolescent world. The girls in this group turned to the models for advice on their appearance and action. They denied adult presence and most often consumed these magazines hidden behind closed doors, far outside the judgmental gaze of significant adults. Teen zines were most often read in private places such as bedrooms and school restrooms, places that might be considered safe havens from adults and boys.

> Ethnographers describe the culture-sharing group.

> Ethnographers describe the context of the culture-sharing group.

(12)   While, of course, adults produce these magazines, the girls perceived zines as exclusively their own, as out-of-bounds for adults and beyond the reach of children. The girls never acknowledged any adult presence behind the youthful images, and most often considered the models to be the authors. When pushed by me to unpack the "they" that the early adolescents so often referred to in their talk about the magazines ("They tell you about boys and stuff," "They show you cool stuff," "They know what it's like to be a teenager today"), each focal student pointed to photographs of models within the magazines, and each denied adult presence behind the text.

(13)   Looking to the models as older, more knowledgeable peers, the early adolescents sought their advice on hair care, fashion, friendships, entertainment, and sexual encounters. Regarding such topics as "woman stuff," the social queens were in a sense claiming for themselves adult positions. Yet at the same time they rejected this position. Searching for answers to questions about womanhood, the girls hid their concerns from adult women, arguing, "They don't understand." From their perspective, the models, in contrast to their mothers or teachers, "know what's it's like to be a teenager today."

(14)   Their emerging sexuality, while clearly the central focus of such "woman stuff," was hidden from significant adults. From the queens' perspective, romance and sexuality were clearly aligned with appropriate adult behavior, yet regarded as taboo in the presence of adults. Conversations that surrounded the reading of teen zines were often labeled "too gross" for parents or teachers. The mature content was the stuff of an emerging sexual self. Caught between competing social roles, the queens negotiated topics that were deemed too obscene for an adult audience in the company of their peers.

(15)   Distinguishing between adults and teens, girls in this social group reported with pride that their teachers and parents did not approve of such reading practices, making such comments as, "She [my mother] wants me to read books, but I read *Sassy*," "I put one [teen zine] in my notebook and

read it during class, and Mr. T doesn't even know it," "My mom doesn't like them. I hide them in my science folder." Those who carried zines were in a sense using literacy to make visible their entry into adolescence. Literacy served as an act of self-presentation. Not only were the queens documenting interest in what they considered mature content, but perhaps what is more important, they were demonstrating their defiance of adult authority by breaking the perceived rules of what constituted appropriate reading materials.

(16)   The presence of zines was used to document one's passage into adolescence, and zine absence was noted as well. I, like many middle-class Euro-American adults, assumed that teen zines were the rave of all seventh-grade girls. Before I continue with a more detailed description of the reading practices of these seventh-grade girls, it must be noted that while the introductory scene is typical, it depicts only one part of the school population. It marks a boundary around one particular group of girls. The only girls who carried zines at school were the social queens, the group of friends who were active in extracurricular school activities and social events. While the queens regularly reported reading and buying zines, the other group denied reading them. Likewise, I saw no magazines in their homes.

(17)   Lauren, a member of the social queens and one of the peer-reported "most popular" girls in the school, regularly referred to her friends as "normal teenagers" and as "regular teens" and often cited *Sassy* as a source of proof for appropriate teen dress and conduct. "See, this is cool," she reported, matching a magazine photograph of a pair of shorts with her own. Using teen zines as a way of borrowing authority, Lauren assessed her appearance and dress against the standards present in the magazine. On another occasion, after describing *YM* to me, Lauren asked, "What do the other girls [referring to Cleo and her friends, those girls who were considered by the queens to be "dogs" and "little kids"] read? They probably just read books. They don't have anything better to do." Notice Lauren's distinction between friendship groups. From her perspective, zines were markers for adolescents who were no longer "girls" but now were defining themselves as teens. In contrast to appropriate girls' behavior to just "read books" because "they don't have anything better to do," teenagers, according to Lauren, were compelled by their newly acquired roles as adolescents to concern themselves with physical appearance and meeting zine standards of "cool." Queens used the teen zine as a way to document a rejection of the position of child.

(18)   Angie, another of the social queens, wondered of Cleo's group, "Don't they care what they look like? They look like little kids. God, they wouldn't even know what to do with stuff like this," pointing to fashions in a current zine. The queens referred to those who did not read zines or adhere to their standards as "little kids" rather than "normal teenagers." Borrowing authority from the pages of the zines, the social queens measured status by the closeness of their match to zine fashions and used the zines to mark particular groups of early adolescent females as insiders.

(19)   In contrast to Lauren's and Angie's embrace of zines, Cleo, one of the focal students who was a resident of a trailer park on the extreme eastern edge of town, was keenly aware that zines were not for her. Early in the year, one seventh-grade language arts teacher suggested that *Seventeen* magazine might be a possible publication source for some of her students' recent poems. Cleo told me privately, "That's not for me." Although her tone may have been intended to convey that she was far above this type of material, Cleo, at age 12, was already keenly aware of her place in the peer dynamic, her place in terms of socioeconomic status. Cleo's perception of zines as "not for me" matched the facts that she

did not have the economic resources necessary to participate in the social events surrounding the reading of zines, and zines were, in fact, used against her to mark her as deficient.

(20)   Zine readings serve these adolescents at a very literal level. They created visible boundaries. On the social-sexual journey toward adulthood, they provided signposts to document progress. Zine readings serve adolescents to unite particular groups of peers and exclude others, serving as a powerful tool to mark insiders and outsiders.

(21)   When one examines zines as literacy event, it becomes quite apparent why Cleo would not be interested in them, why she could so matter of factly report that these magazines were "not for me," and why Lauren would turn to teen zines. Zines were marketed for one particular type of reader, the social queen, the middle-class female.

(22)   So this becomes the story of the queens and the zines.

Queens Reading Zines: Negotiating a Presentation of Self

Ethnographers analyze the culture-sharing group for themes.

(23)
Angie:	Hey, did you guys know that . . . [*and she begins to read from* Sassy, *one of the most popular teen zines.*]
Lauren:	Let me have that. [*She pulls the magazine from Angie's grasp. Angie attempts to continue reading by shoving up against Lauren's shoulder.*]
Tiffany:	That really pisses me off. Mine never comes first. [*She rips the magazine out of her friend's hand. The girls laugh and wrestle over possession.*]
Angie:	Do you know what it's got? [*Leaning across the library table, she grabs the magazine back, flips through the pages, searching for one article.*] It's got this really gross article about sleeping with *your* step-dad.
Lauren:	God, that is gross. I wouldn't sleep with my step-dad. Can you even imagine you and Larry?
Tiffany:	Gross.
Lauren:	Gross.

(24)   This brief exchange between seventh-grade girls typifies conversations that surround the reading of teen zines. After careful analysis of repeated occurrences of zine reading, three themes emerged from my data: (1) reading was an exclusive social event, (2) reading was used to ascribe special status, and (3) experiences reported in the magazines were appropriated by the girls as their own.

Reading as an Exclusive Social Event

(25)   First, reading of these magazines was rarely a solitary act. While a socio-cultural perspective focuses on literacy as socially based and culturally specific (Langer 1991), beyond learning meaning in culturally appropriate ways, the girls in this study quite literally read in groups. Zine reading was fiercely social. Groups of girls crowded together on a bed, in a large recliner, or in the corner of the school library to devour the cherished possession and negotiate a unified front as to their collective opinion of each article and advertisement. Often times, the arrival in the mail of a teen zine necessitated a "sleep over" to "hang together and look at our magazines." Social queens made arrangement to gather with the expressed purpose of "just hanging out and looking at magazines." These seventh-grade girls often bagged up back issues to cart to a Friday-night slumber party.

(26)   I spent five hours at one such event. When I arrived at Angie's, her mother let me in and said, "Just follow the noise. They're already upstairs." I walked into Angie's bedroom, hairspray mist creating a perfumed fog, music and giggles vibrating the glossy teen photographs and celebrated

designer labels that had been carefully removed from clothing or torn from the pages of teen zines and taped to the walls. Once I settled in on a corner of the bed, the girls quit screaming and resumed their activities. Angie returned to her position, curling and spraying Tiffany's long auburn locks in front of a full-length mirror that was framed with images of adolescent beauty, snapshots of friends juxtaposed with the latest models trimmed from the pages of *Sassy* and *Seventeen*. Beside me, Lauren continued to flip through the pages of a zine, making a series of statements, "This is cool," "He is so cute," "This dress is so totally awesome." Such statements were regularly interrupted with a question, "Do you think he is cute?" "Do you think that's cool?" "God, she's pretty?" After each question, usually delivered with a tone that conveyed an assumed answer, Tiffany and Angie would turn from the mirror to glance momentarily at the picture in question and then together would answer "Yeah" or "Not."

(27)   It was almost always a mutual agreement. The girls rarely disagreed, and when they did, they argued until a consensus was reached. Someone would have to give up on her opinion. Someone always did. No page was turned until the girls all agreed about fashion or face, beauty or body.

(28)   These girls, it seems, were performing as members of what Goffman (1959) calls "performance teams," defined as "any set of individuals who co-operate in staging a single routine" (Goffman 1959:79). According to Goffman, individuals on a team work together backstage in order to present a unified front when they are on center stage. Scenes like this one, played out in the girls' bedrooms and in the school restrooms, match what Goffman described as backstage rehearsals for their more public performances. Goffman describes such private arenas as backstage regions defined in the following manner:

> Here costumes and other parts of personal front may be adjusted and scrutinized for flaws. Here the team can run through its performance, checking for offending expressions when no audience is present to be affronted by them; here poor members of the team, who are expressively inept, can be schooled or dropped from the performance. [Goffman 1959:112]

On this particular Friday night, these early adolescents were practicing their emerging adolescent roles, rehearsing their opinions with the help of a carefully constructed script, the teen zine. Allocated to backstage regions, the queens used zines to check and test ways of being adolescent. Those who were deemed in need of remediation were schooled by the others with the zine serving as an authoritative textbook. Queens made such remarks as, "Duh, you are so stupid. Look at this" (pointing to a page in *Sassy*), and "Geez, you should wear your hair like this" (pointing to a page in *YM*).

(29)   At this developmental period, while much may have appeared unstable, zines provided solid guidelines. The girls often reported, "See, it shows you what's cool." At a time when all rules and rituals appear to be in flux, when even her body forsakes her, the early adolescent can turn to the pages of a teen zine for firm control. This illusion of stability provides a sense of power and control in a world that is often perceived as out of control. In entering the new social arena of adolescence, zines served as a handbook.

Reading as a Tool to Ascribe Special Status

(30)   Second, the girls used teen zines to assign special status. At a literal level, there appeared to be two dimensions of status building: being first to possess the latest issue of a zine, and what is more important, ownership of that copy. Note Tiffany's comment, "That really pisses me off. Mine never comes first." For these girls, it was very important to be first; copies borrowed from

a friend or from the library carry much less clout. When a magazine was borrowed, one could not control the circulation as readily, and one could not control distribution of individual pages. The girl who arrived at school or at a slumber party first with the latest issue of a teen zine tucked under her arm wielded more power and prestige, controlling circulation of the latest important information about fashion, beauty, and entertainment.

(31)   When a magazine arrived, the girls whom I talked to rushed to obtain that coveted position of being first by calling a best friend before the cover of the magazine has even been opened. As the phone was ringing, one hurried to find an article worthy of reading into the receiver in order to prove that one was indeed first. Being first merited clout because one's name became attached to the latest information. Comments such as "Lauren says that there is this awesome fingernail polish in *YM*," and "Lauren says that the Mall of America is bigger than a bunch of football fields" circulated around the junior high.

(32)   On another level, status was achieved by possessing the closest match to the teens in the text. Although Angie had been the envy of two of her best friends since she began subscribing to *Sassy* in the middle of her sixth-grade year, she did not hold the powerful position of director. It is hardly surprising that that role was assigned to Lauren, who was claimed by all as "the prettiest" with "the best bod," and "she's the one with the most boyfriends." In other words, Lauren's physical features represented the closest match to those present on the pages of any zine. As director, Lauren regularly orchestrated the actions and opinions of the other girls. So whenever the girls got together to negotiate their collective opinions, Lauren most often held the magazine and held the final word.

Appropriating Reading Experiences

(33)   A strong sense of community bridged from those present in the text to those present in the immediate context. The queens talked about the articles as if each carried an implicit command that one must follow in order to achieve high status. Their talk implied a powerful connectedness to the teens in the magazines. Following is one such incident in which the conversation weaves in and out from text to immediate bedroom scene, lacing them together in the present:

Angie: So what did Ronnie say about me?
Lauren: He said that you are fine. He goes, "She's a babe."
Tiffany: Come on, Lauren.
Angie: You know what? I just broke out in zits majorly.
Tiffany: Me too. It must be zit week or something.
Lauren: I know, I look in the mirror and, God. Did you take this kissing quiz [reference to a quiz in one of the teen zines]?
Tiffany: I was giving Sara the quiz on the phone. Do you have any sweats?
Angie: I don't have any sweats. I got some stretch pants you can wear.
Tiffany: Dang, this curling iron doesn't even work.
Lauren: Maybe I should get some of these [reference to jeans in advertisement]. When I get older, I'm gonna get braces so my teeth will look like this. [*Points to model in teen zine.*]
Angie: I want to try on those colored pocket pants of yours. Can I?
Lauren: Do it. Ouch! *Watch* where you sit.
Tiffany: Okay, here's this thing. [*She begins reading from a zine.*] "As my boyfriend and I are leaving my house to go to the game, my little sister had to come along [*inaudible, breaks into laughter*], and, and she asks me why I had put so many tissues in my bra."

Girls appropriated the experiences reported in the articles as their own. Just as Angie said, "sleeping with *your* step-dad," Lauren and Tiffany, regularly used the pronouns "you" and "your" and directly made claims that the young women in the advertisements and articles were "just like me." In interviews, they said such things as "It [*Sassy*] tells the most embarrassing things of *your* life," and "I read it [*Sassy*] because I want to know about AIDS and stuff, and I want to know what happens to girls *just like me.*" In some ways the teens in the zines were just like them. A content analysis of the three top-selling teen magazines revealed those zines were populated in the following manner: Euro-American females, 65.2 percent; Euro-American males, 24.5 percent; non-Euro-American females, 7.7 percent; and non-Euro-American males, 2.6 percent; with adults of any color rare and limited to the even rarer educational career article (Evans et. al 1991:109).

(34)   The invisibility of adults and the strong sense of sameness may have fostered a sense of seamless connection between their friends and experiences with those in the zines. Zines were often held up almost like a mirror and used, it seems, to reinforce cultural standards of adolescent beauty. Just as books provide mirrors for early adolescents (Willinsky and Hunniford 1993), the teen zine was held up as looking glass to assess one's physical appearance. Social queens often pointed to teen zines and asked, "Do you think I look like her?" "Do you think my hair looks like this?" "Do you think these jeans would look good on me?"

(35)   Lacking a critical distance that fiction creates, zines were received as truth: "They tell you about woman stuff" and "I want to know what happens to girls just like me." Similar to Bakhtin's (1981) suggestion that words come out of other people's mouths, the girls often quite literally lifted phrases directly from the pages to become part of the language of the social queens. When I asked the social queens to describe their best friends, their descriptions contained not only the rhythms and constructions but often times the exact words that fill the texts of the teen zines. According to Shuman, one may "appropriate another's voice as a means of borrowing authority" (1993:136). The girls in this study, it seems, borrowed authority from zine models. Here are some descriptions of their best friends: "She has her thick, dark, luxurious hair that you could die for and beautiful sky-blue eyes," "She has a perfect creamy complexion and a perfect posture," "Yeah, Angie is pretty. She has a perfect face, but her hips are too wide." In separate interviews, when asked to describe a best friend, the word "perfect" emerged in seven out of eight interviews and was repeated at least twice in three. As one listens in, one is struck by the emphasis upon perfection, on the singular standard that is so well established that a 13-year-old is marked because her hips are already "too wide" by an agreed upon standard that celebrates slimness. Certainly, this emphasis on physical perfection cannot be attributed solely to the reading of teen zines. Yet one cannot deny the power of the repeated occurrence of these girls' reading zines and asking, "Am I fatter than her?" "Do I kinda look like her?" One cannot deny the power of the representation of the singular model available to adolescent females in these magazines.

Reading Fluff: "You Don't Have to Think about It"

(36)   In December of their seventh-grade year, Tiffany reported that she was "finally allowed to spend my own Christmas money to get *Sassy.* " She had succeeded, in her own words, "by ragging my mom for about a year." Their disagreements over teen magazines became clear during my first visit to their home. Following is a bit of transcription from that evening.

M.F.:   What else do you read? Do you read any magazines?
Tiffany: *YM. [She giggles and looks at her mother out of the corner of her eye.]*

M.F.:   Do you get that at home?

Tiffany: I don't get them, but I get them at the library. [*She turns to plead for her mother to buy the magazine for her.*] But, Mom, get them. That's what I read.

Mother: [*Laughs and reaches over to the magazine rack to pick up a copy of* YM.] I'm not really comfortable with these teen magazines.

Tiffany: Mom!

Mother: She likes to read trash.

Tiffany: Yep!

Mother: Well, the advertisements are just too sensual.

Tiffany: [*Taking the copy from her mother, she slowly turns the pages, scrutinizing each one.*] What advertisements?

Mother: Maybe when she gets older she can get those magazines. I can't think that that reading experience will *broaden* your horizons. [*Her sarcastic tone and glance are directed toward Tiffany. She turns back to me.*] But she is reading.

One can sense the tensions in this parent. On the one hand she did not want her daughter to be exposed to such "sensual" materials, but on the other hand she acknowledged that such contents motivated her daughter's reading. She explained further about her daughter's time spent reading *YM*. "I know it's not wasted. It's still reading, but it's like fluff." Later in the conversation, this parent admitted that she, like her daughter, often enjoyed what she called "reading fluff." She said, "I do a lot of studying now, and I think I've got to find something that's just that [fluff]. When I pick something up, a *McCalls* or a newsstand-type magazine and read those things, you don't have to think about it. I suppose that's very similar to what you do, Tiff."

(37)   Clearly, Tiffany's reading was very similar to her mother's account of reading as "fluff." What was missed in this discussion of "fluff reading" was Tiffany's misreading of the advertisements. In magazines that according to Evans et. al 1991 give 46 percent of their total space over to advertisements, it might seem remarkable that Tiffany was blind to it. On the following day at school, I asked Tiffany to explain about the advertisement in the magazines. She insisted, "There aren't any ads." And she proceeded to prove it to me. Pulling the latest issue of *Sassy* from her notebook, turning from ads to articles through full- and half-page ads, she argued, "This tells you about fingernail polish. This shows you about makeup. This is about zits and stuff. *See?*"

(38)   Tiffany's emphasis on "See?" illustrates her use of these magazines as a kind of proof. She trusted the editors to do exactly what those at *Seventeen* had promised, "to provide her with all of the information she needed to make sound choices" (Peirce 1990:496–497). The seduction of these magazines is powerful. While it may appear that Tiffany was just extremely naive, the layout of teen zines is, in fact, quite seductive. Articles and advertisements look remarkably alike. Articles often times are presented as whole-page photos with a column on the left that details the dress complete with designer names and suggested retail prices.

(39)   The social queens in this study used the articles and advertisements alike as criteria for establishing their own social roles and for judging those of others. They pointed to the models in the pages to ask, "Am I fatter than her?" "Would that look good on me?" "Do you think that's cool?" "Do I look like her?" rehearsing their values and opinions with the assistance of these magazines marketed specifically for them. They measured their friends and foes alike by the singular standard that permeates the pages of *YM*, *Sassy*, *Teen*, and *Seventeen*. Queens called other girls "woof-woofs" and literally barked at those who they deemed did not measure up to standards of physical beauty.

(40)   While some parents may label teen zines "fluff," they are neither benign nor neutral. They transport a powerful economic ideology into the lives of these early adolescents who are bathed in a set of societal norms for women. Teen zines echo the larger societal influences that constrict and enable particular gendered roles. Just as Tiffany's mother described this type of reading as reading in which "you don't have to think," the girls demonstrate little ability to render such an ideology conscious. The comment "What advertisements?" illustrates dramatically how these teens are lulled into accepting such a constrictive economic package. When one observes how readily these girls appropriate the words, experiences, and images as their own, one can hardly deny the impact of these texts upon the social construction of self. These teens accepted such images as a ruler by which adolescent girls measure their own successes as they try on more adult roles. Such messages, while quite overt to critical scholars, remain invisible to these early adolescents. These girls were left to their own devices to interpret, integrate, and mediate the images and text. These messages read over and over become scripts for the girls and will be impossible to revise unless they are made visible.

(41)   Teen zines were generally consumed hidden behind closed doors, far outside the judgmental gaze of significant adults. Even within the pages themselves, there is a notable lack of adult images (Evans et. al 1991). By concealing any adult presence, teen zines were embraced by early adolescent females as their own; yet the layout and content are orchestrated by adults to make these early adolescents into a particular kind of female.

Teaching Subliterature: Implications for Pedagogy

(42)   These magazines, like their teen-romance-novel companions, are most often shunned by parents and teachers and cast into the category of subliterature. Considered lacking in literary qualities, these texts find no home in school curricula. I am not suggesting, however, that zines should be disregarded as trash reading or be censored. On the contrary, I wonder what might happen if some of the arguments made by feminists and researchers began to circulate in language arts classrooms? The consequence of allocating zines to the realms of subliterature is leaving the social scripts tacit and unexamined.

Qualitative interpretations situate findings within larger meanings.

(43)   Teachers that I talked with characterized magazines as "light reading, something they can do on their own," and they required novels read during reading time at school. One reported, "I want them to read novels. They can choose whatever they want, but it has to have a sustained story. That stuff [reference to magazines] they can read on their own time." Tiffany's mother explained that this kind of reading material was the kind of reading in which "you don't have to think." Teachers, as well, considered magazines to be "light reading," implying a lack of necessity for critical thinking.

(44)   I advocate a pedagogy that cracks the veneer of this "light reading." I advocate a pedagogy that situates reading not simply as an aesthetic experience but a political act as well. Moss (1995) challenges existing assumptions about the relationships between texts and readers. She argues that the assumptions that texts are potentially powerful in their effect rest upon a notion of vulnerable readers. Moss argues further:

Ethnographers interpret and write from a reflexive position.

> For what matters about texts is not the content alone, but the way that content can be mobilized and used by readers. And feminists would expect differences here to be governed, not by randomly individual choice, but by social and collective histories. In other words, we would expect there to be conflicting readings, which could not be settled by reference to the text alone. Rather than attempting to close things down by fixing once and for all what the text means,

feminism would fore-ground the social strategies readers bring to the text. [1995:162]

(45)   Moss advocates a pedagogical approach that calls for an ethnography of reading which would replace a personal response to reading and "stress the role diverse social and cultural practices play in shaping how texts get read" (1995:163). I strongly agree. In order to examine the seemingly homogeneous model that is presented to teens in such a slick package, the cultural assumptions beneath the images must be brought to the surface. What if the slim white models who populate the pages of teen zines found their way into an ethnography of reading? Provided with an arena for critical discussion, students might open up the possibilities for multiple perspectives.

(46)   This, of course, is complicated by the very nature of the marketing of teen zines, perceived by the girls to be just outside the boundaries. The very facts that mothers and teachers grimaced and refused to buy or buy into them lead some teens straight to these sources. So by appropriating teen zines into a curriculum, by changing the perceived boundaries, any critique will lose some of its power by the very fact that placement within the context of the classroom has lessened the appeal and stolen exclusive ownership. What makes them so appealing is that they are "just for me," and they are perceived of as outside the control of adults. Like the girls in Cherland's (1994) study, this reading served as "combative" (as an escape from being good) and "compensatory" (as a way to feel more powerful). Rather than embrace the literacies that the school promotes, these teens were looking for unsanctioned literacies in order to stake their own claim, to mark their separation from the established authority. Such renegade reading served as a powerful tool to gain status and group solidarity. Like the Smithton women reading romances (Radway 1984), the social queens used zine reading as a "declaration of their independence." In order to move into adulthood, these early adolescents sought unsanctioned literacies to demonstrate independence. For them, the content of the curriculum constructed clear boundaries, dividing sanctioned from unsanctioned literacies. Using teen zines as curricular content devalues the keen sense of exclusive rights and diminishes the power of possession as a visible marker of adolescent control. Furthermore, classroom-based critiques of the zines will, of course, be social interactions in which the participants stand to gain and lose status among peers. How powerful can a pedagogy be if it counters critique by its very willingness to examine it? There are no simple answers.

(47)   Yet how can one expect a critical stance when there is no suggestion of any alternative readings? The social queens were becoming exactly what marketers have trained them to be, consumers and competitors for men's desires. At age 12 and 13, they had few resources or experiences to resist such powerful images. They were, indeed, vulnerable readers. And a pedagogy must provide them with the tools to become critical readers and thinkers.

(48)   I advocate a more explicit examination of the complexities that shape literacy learning, an unmasking of the ways in which textual representations construct social roles. I advocate a pedagogy that explicitly acknowledges the political motivations that serve to define and limit available social roles. For example, examining the social, historical, and cultural motivations of particular roles available—in texts, classrooms, and the larger culture—will lead students to more critical awareness and thus, it is hoped, to the ability to revise those roles. A teacher might contrast *Sassy* with *Teen Voices* (an alternative magazine, published by Women's Express, Inc., that does not accept advertising), inviting students to ponder over the implications of advertising, pushing students toward more fully understanding how economics enable and constrain texts. Clearly, the girls' re-

jection of adult influence may blunt the power of any school-based critique of these popular texts. But if students learn to ask questions about the construction of social roles available in all texts and are taught to analyze the race, class, and gender relations as they are represented in texts, especially in other canonical works, students will learn to be critical consumers and producers of texts. Asking political questions about the social roles available in fiction, nonfiction, and the larger culture, teachers may begin to assist these early adolescents in adopting a critical stance. It becomes clearer in examining how these teens read zines that what is missing is the necessary addition of layers of critical reflection, an exploration of the ways in which particular texts situate individuals. Bringing a sociocultural pedagogy into the classroom is a necessary step. In addition to learning to ask about the aesthetic of any text, students need to learn to ask about its politics. Who is being privileged? Why are these stories being told at this particular historic moment? How might the woman's role be represented differently at a different historic period? Whose interests are being served? Teaching early adolescents to ask questions about the sociocultural construction of roles will lead students to a deeper understanding of how textual representations reflect and define the roles available in the larger culture.

(49)   In looking for solid answers, in seeking stability in this new social arena, the queens turned to texts as authoritative. Just as Tiffany reported, "This tells you about fingernail polish. This shows you about makeup. This is about zits and stuff," zines served as a kind of proof. "See, they show you what's cool," Angie explained. For Angie and her friends, there was no awareness of how these texts served to constrain their lived experiences. For these teens, these texts were embraced with little sense of answering back, no critical doubt, no disruption, no tension. To these early adolescents, the zine was authoritative and monovocal. There appeared to be no sense of a text as dialogic (Bakhtin 1981). While according to Bakhtin (1981) there is a constant struggle between the authoritative and internally persuasive functions of discourse, no such struggle was evident in the reading of teen zines. How can one expect a critical stance when there is no awareness of the motivations that hide behind texts, where there has been no sense of negotiating, no answering back? I am suggesting that we open up classroom discussions to how texts situate us.

(50)   As educators we might create a tiny tear in the seamless packaging of these zines. Rather than deny the power of such texts by allocating them to the realm of subliterature, I might suggest that we investigate, as Miller (1994) argues, how texts serve to define and limit lived experiences. If we deny our power as educators, we deny our students the opportunity to rewrite cultural and social scripts. We must teach skills in examining text as socially constructed for particular purposes. Unaware of alternative roles, the queens turned solely to teen zines to guide and measure their growth into womanhood. The other group, who for the most part were missing from this discussion, might appear to have resisted the singular role construction for the adolescent female, yet they hardly fared better. With neither the economic resources nor the political clout to speak out, they remained silent as the queens wielded their borrowed power over them. While Lauren, Angie, and Tiffany rehearsed their roles to secure their place in society through romance and commodities, Cleo was reminded again and again that there was no place for her.

Qualitative research reports use flexible and emerging structures and evaluation criteria.

Margaret J. Finders is an assistant professor of English education at Purdue University, and author of *"Just Girls": The Literate Life and Underlife of Early Adolescent Girls,* in press.

Notes

Acknowledgments. I appreciate the helpful commentary on earlier drafts of this article made by Julie Cheville, Carolyn Colvin, and Cynthia Lewis.

1. Social roles, as used here, are defined as performances assigned to a given status in a given context, as the enactment of rights and duties attached to a given status. Drawing extensively on Erving Goffman (1959, 1961), I use the term *social role* to suggest that one's role shifts depending on who is present and what the established expectations are of those present. In this manner, I argue that roles are not static but represent multiple and shifting selves.

2. This sociocultural framework is based on the theory that all utterances take place within a social situation; there is no such thing as an isolated speaker or text (Vygotsky 1962, 1978). Thought is mediated through language, which is a product of social interrelationships, a dialectic between self and community. Extending the theories of Vygotsky, Wertsch (1991) draws on Bakhtin (1981) to develop a more comprehensive understanding of voice as dialogic that emphasizes the dynamism of every text and the situatedness of the speaker within cultural, historical, and institutional settings.

3. Throughout this study, I maintained a focus on literacy events as defined by Heath as "a conceptual tool useful in examining within particular communities of modern society the actual forms and functions of oral and literate traditions and co-existing relationships between spoken and written language. A literacy event is any occasion in which a piece of writing is integral to the nature of participants' interactions and their interpretive processes" (1982:93).

4. All names used in this article are pseudonyms, required by the human-subjects protocol.

References Cited

Apple, Michael
1986 Teachers and Texts: A Political Economy of Class and Gender Relations in Education. New York: Routledge.

Bakhtin, Mikhail M.
1981 The Dialogic Imagination. Austin: University of Texas Press.

Biklen, Sari, and Diane Pollard
1993 Gender and Education: Ninety-Second Yearbook of the National Society for the Study of Education. Chicago: University of Chicago Press.

Britzman, Debra
1993 Beyond Rolling Models: Gender and Multicultural Education. *In* Gender and Education: Ninety-Second Yearbook of the National Society for the Study of Education. Sari Biklen and Diane Pollard, eds. pp. 25–42. Chicago: University of Chicago Press.

Cherland, Meredith
1994 Private Practices: Girls Reading Fiction and Constructing Identity. London: Taylor and Francis.

Christian-Smith, Linda
1993 Constituting and Reconstituting Desire: Fiction, Fantasy and Feminity. *In* Texts of Desire: Essays on Fiction, Feminity and Schooling. Linda Christian-Smith, ed. Pp. 1–8. London: Falmer Press.

Erickson, Frederick
1986 Qualitative Methods in Research on Teaching. *In* Handbook of Research on Teaching, 3rd edition. M. C. Wittrock, ed. Pp. 119–161. New York: Macmillan.

Evans, Ellis, Judith Rutberg, Carmela Sather, and Charli Turner
1991 Content Analysis of Contemporary Teen Magazines for Adolescent Females. Youth and Society 23(1):99–120.

Fine, Michelle, and Pat Macpherson
1993 Over Dinner: Feminism and Adolescent Female Bodies. *In* Gender and Education: Ninety-Second Yearbook of the National Society for the Study of Education. Sari Biklen and Diane Pollard, eds. Pp. 126–154. Chicago: University of Chicago Press.

Finders, Margaret
In press "Just Girls": The Literate Life and Underlife of Early Adolescent Girls. New York: Teachers College Press.

Griffin, Christine
1985 Typical Girls: Young Women from School to the Job Market. New York: Routledge and Kegan Paul Methuen.

Gilligan, Carol
1988 Moral Voices: Adolescent Development and Secondary Education. Cambridge, MA: Harvard University Graduate School of Education.

Goffman, Erving
1959 The Presentation of Self in Everyday Life. New York: Doubleday & Company.
1961 Asylums: Essays on the Social Situation of Mental Patients and Other Inmates. Chicago: Aldine Publishing.

Heath, Shirley Brice
1982 Protean Shapes in Literacy Events: Evershifting Oral and Literate Traditions. *In* Spoken and Written Language: Exploring Orality and Literacy. Deborah Tannen, ed. Advances in Discourse Processes, 9. Pp. 91–117. Norwood, NJ: Ablex.

hooks, bell
1990 Yearning: Race, Gender and Cultural Politics. Boston: South End Press.

Langer, Judith
1991 Literacy and Schooling: A Sociocognitive Perspective. *In* Literacy for a
    Diverse Society. Elfrieda Hiebert, ed. Pp. 9–27. New York: Teachers
    College Press.
Miller, Richard
1994 Fault Lines in the Contact Zone. College English 56(4):389–408.
Moss, Gemma
1995 Rewriting Reading. *In* Debates and Issues in Feminist Research and
    Pedagogy. Janet Holland and Maud Blair, eds. Pp. 157–168.
    Clevedon: Open University.
Peirce, Kate
1990 A Feminist Theoretical Perspective on the Socialization of Teenage
    Girls through Seventeen Magazine. Sex Roles 23(9/10):491–500.
Radway, Janice
1984 Reading the Romance: Women, Patriarchy and Popular Fiction.
    Chapel Hill: University of North Carolina Press.
Shuman, Amy
1993 "Get Outa My Face": Entitlement and Authoritative Discourse. *In*
    Responsibility and Evidence in Oral Discourse. S. Hill and J. Irvine,
    eds. Pp. 135–160. New York: Cambridge University Press.

Spradley, James
1979 The Ethnographic Interview. Fort Worth: Holt, Rinehart and Winston.
1980 Participant Observation. New York: Holt, Rinehart and Winston.
Stretch, Cynthia
1991 From Self-Awareness to Self-Mastery: Literacy and the Discourse of
    Body Consciousness in Teen Magazines. Unpublished manuscript.
Vygotsky, Lev
1962 Thought and Language. Cambridge, MA: Harvard University Press.
1978 Mind in Society. Cambridge, MA: Harvard University Press.
Wertsch, James
1991 Voices of the Mind: A Sociocultural Approach to Mediated Action.
    Cambridge, MA: Harvard University Press.
Willinsky, John, and R. Mark Hunniford
1993 Reading the Romance Younger: The Mirrors and Fears of a
    Preparatory Literature. *In* Texts of Desire; Essays on Fiction, Feminity
    and Schooling. Linda Christian-Smith, ed. Pp. 87–105. London:
    Falmer Press.

Narrative Research Designs

L et's say our high school teacher, Maria, chooses a narrative design for her research project studying the possession of weapons by high school students. Assume that Maria's teacher friend, Millie, encountered a student in the high school who was hiding a weapon in his locker. To study this situation, Maria's research question might be: "What were Millie's experiences in confronting and addressing a student who had a weapon at school?" To study this question, Maria will need to interview Millie and listen to her stories about her experiences with the student, with other teachers, and with the school principal. After listening to Millie's stories, Maria will organize them into a chronology that retells Millie's experiences. Perhaps Maria will identify themes in Millie's experiences and even bring in her own knowledge about other teachers who have experienced similar incidents. In order to retell the experiences of a teacher, Maria may share the retelling with Millie and have her help shape the final research report. This research becomes a teacher's story of actual experiences in a high school.

People like Millie live storied lives. They tell stories to share their lives with others and to provide their personal accounts about classrooms, schools, educational issues, and the setting in which they work. When people tell stories to researchers, they feel listened to, and their information brings researchers closer to the actual practice of education. Thus, stories enrich the lives of both the researcher and the participant. For example, consider the stories in the following narratives either collected by teachers or told by teachers.

▶ Ms. Meyer had two children in her fifth- and sixth-grade class write stories about their personal lives. Anthony, a 9-year-old who considered himself an inventor and writer, kept a scientific journal of his discoveries and wrote an expressive piece about his grandmother. Anita, an 11-year-old, wrote about the good times she had in a swimming pool, learning to play kickball, and being able to succeed at something (McCarthey, 1994).

▶ Christie talked about her first-year teaching experiences when she taught reading, math, poetry, and social studies. She shared her hopes and dreams as a new teacher (Rust, 1999).

▶ Leo told stories about his professional development as a primary school teacher in Belgium. He discussed his "career breakdown" where he taught third grade for 8 years without any commitment or enthusiasm. During this time he coped by doing things outside of school, such as training as a librarian and engaging in freelance journalism (Kelchtermans, 1993).

These examples illustrate narrative research in which individuals tell their personal, firsthand accounts to researchers. The term "narrative" comes from the verb "to narrate," or "to tell (as a story) in detail" (Ehrlich, Flexner, Carruth, & Hawkins, 1980, p. 442). In **narrative research,** inquirers describe the lives of individuals, collect and tell stories about people's lives, and write narratives of individual experiences (Connelly & Clandinin, 1990). As a distinct form of qualitative research, a narrative typically focuses on studying a single person, gathering data through the collection of stories, reporting individual experiences, and discussing the meaning of those experiences for the individual. The specific procedure of retelling or restorying the participant's story—to be described later in this chapter—is a unique qualitative analytic procedure used only in narrative research.

These factors distinguish narrative from other forms of qualitative inquiry. With a focus on an individual and personal (and social) experiences, narrative is typically more micro-analytic than the broader system and group perspective found in ethnographic research. Also, with the objective of learning about one individual, the intent is *not* on developing a theory that applies to many people, such as found in grounded theory.

Narrative designs are frequently used as a form of research in education. National research conferences have devoted sessions and papers to it and educational journals have increasingly published stories reported by teachers, students, and other educators. New books are now available from publishers that provide essential information about the process of conducting this form of qualitative inquiry. For individuals searching for a research design that reports the personal stories of educators, narrative research may be ideal. For educators looking for personal experiences in actual school settings, narrative research studies offer practical, specific insights.

By the end of this chapter you should be able to:

- Identify major events in the historical development of narrative research.
- Describe the major types of narrative studies.
- Identify the key characteristics of narrative research.
- Explain the strengths and weaknesses of narrative research designs.
- Describe the steps used in conducting a narrative study.
- List criteria for evaluating a narrative study.

A BRIEF HISTORY OF NARRATIVE RESEARCH

Despite substantial interest in narrative research, its methods or procedures in qualitative inquiry are still being developed and are infrequently discussed in the literature (Errante, 2000). It is all too common to hear a narrative study presented at a research conference or to read a published study in a leading educational journal and then not learn about the actual procedures used in conducting the study.

Two factors have contributed to a need for procedural guidelines. First, because narrative research has roots in diverse disciplines, little agreement exists about its form. The "narrative turn," as Riessman (1993) calls it, embraces all of the human sciences, so that this form of research is not the providence of any specific field of study. Writers in literature, history, anthropology, sociology, socio-linguistics, and education all lay claim to narrative and have developed discipline-specific procedures. Like the art and science of portraiture discussed recently in the social sciences, this design involves drawing portraits of individuals and documenting their voices and their visions within a social and cultural context (Lawrence-Lightfoot & Davis, 1997).

Secondly, a comprehensive overview of this design of research in education did not emerge until recently. In 1990, educators D. Jean Clandinin and Michael Connelly provided the first overview of narrative research for the field of education. In their informative, classic article, "Stories of Experience and Narrative Inquiry" published in the *Educational Researcher* (Connelly & Clandinin, 1990), they cite many social sciences applications of narrative, elaborate on the process of collecting narrative fieldnotes, and discuss the writing and structure of a narrative study. This article expands their earlier discussion about narrative within the context of teaching and learning in classrooms (Connelly & Clandinin, 1988). More recently, these two authors expanded their ideas in a book titled *Narrative Inquiry* (1999), which openly espouses "what narrative researchers do" (p. 48).

Within the field of education, several trends have influenced the development of narrative research. Cortazzi (1993) suggests three factors. First, there is currently an increased emphasis on teacher reflection. Second, more emphasis is being placed on teachers' knowledge—what they know, how they think, how they develop professionally, and how they make decisions in the classroom. And third, educators seek to bring teachers' voices to the forefront by empowering teachers to talk about their experiences. For example, "Our Own Stories," reported by Richard Meyer (1996), is a collection of stories about teachers sharing their experiences, whether they are sitting in the teachers' lounge at noon or after school. Additional collections of stories about educators as teachers and curriculum developers can be found in McEwan and Egan (1995). For women in general, as well as for women teachers, their stories to children, to adolescent girls, and to their own female associates often take on a feminine repertoire to serve their female audiences (Degh, 1995). Hearing these stories have encouraged educational studies using the narrative approach. In fact, within education recently, a special interest group in the American Educational Research Association has been formed to create an ongoing discussion about narrative research.

A growing list of interdisciplinary social scientists outside education have offered procedural guidance for narrative reports as a form of qualitative research (e.g., see the psychologists Lieblich, Tuval-Mashiach, and Zilber, 1998; the sociologist, Cortazzi, 1993, and Riessman, 1993). Interdisciplinary efforts at narrative research have also been encouraged by the *Narrative Study of Lives* annual series that began in 1993 (e.g., Josselson & Lieblich, 1993).

QUESTIONS USEFUL FOR DETERMINING TYPES OF NARRATIVE DESIGNS

Narrative research can assume multiple forms. Today, narrative inquirers need to consider what *type* of narrative study to conduct. Narrative may be considered an overarching category for a variety of research practices (see Casey, 1995, 1996), as shown in Figure 16.1. For individuals planning a narrative study, a decision is needed about the type of narrative practice to use. Each type of narrative provides a structure for conducting the study and ready references for how to conduct the project that faculty, journal reviewers, and book publishers will recognize. For those reading narrative studies, it is less important to know

---

FIGURE 16.1

Examples of Types of Narrative Research Forms

- Autobiographies
- Biographies
- Life Writing
- Personal Accounts
- Personal Narratives
- Narrative Interviews
- Personal Documents
- Documents of Life
- Life Stories and Life Histories
- Oral Histories
- Ethnohistories
- Ethnobiographies
- Autoethnographies
- Ethnopsychologies
- Person-centered Ethnographies
- Popular Memories
- Latin-American *testimonios*
- Polish memoirs

Source: Adapted from Casey, 1995, 1996.

---

what *type* of narrative is being used and more important to recognize the essential *characteristics* of the type being used. To this end, the following four questions can help determine the type of narrative being proposed or used in a study.

Who Writes or Records the Story?

Determining who will write and record the individual's story is a basic distinction in narrative research. A **biography** is a form of narrative study in which the researcher writes and records the experiences of another person's life. Typically, biographies are constructed from records and archives (Angrosino, 1989), although researchers may use other sources of information, such as interviews and photographs, as well. In an **autobiography**, the narrative account is written and recorded by the individual who is the subject of the study. Autobiographies are less frequently found in educational research, although accounts of teachers as professionals have recently been reported (Connelly & Clandinin, 1990).

How Much of a Life Is Recorded and Presented?

This question introduces a second distinction among narrative studies. In anthropology, numerous examples exist of stories of an individual's entire life. A **life history** is a narrative story of an individual's entire life experiences. Anthropologists, for example, engage in life history research to learn about the individual's life within the context of a culture-sharing group. Often the focus includes turning points or significant events in the life of an individual (Angrosino, 1989). However, in education, narrative studies typically do not involve the account of an entire life but instead focus on an episode or single event in the individual's life. A **personal experience story** is a narrative study of an individual's personal experience found in single or multiple episodes, private situations, or communal folklore (Denzin, 1989). Clandinin and Connelly (2000) broaden the personal experience story to be both personal and social, and have conveyed this stance as the essence of the experiences reported about teachers and teaching in schools.

Who Provides the Story?

A third approach for identifying the type of narrative is to examine closely who provides the story. This factor is especially relevant in education, where types of educators or learners have been the focus of many narrative studies. For example, **teachers' stories** are personal accounts by teachers of their own personal classroom experiences. A popular form of narrative in education, teachers' stories have been extensively reported to capture the lives of teachers as professionals and to examine learning in classrooms (e.g., see Connelly & Clandinin, 1988). Other narrative studies focus on students in the classroom. In children's stories, the children in classrooms are asked to present orally or in writing their own stories about their learning experiences (e.g., see Ollerenshaw, 1998). Many different individuals in educational settings can provide stories, such as administrators, school board members, custodians, food service workers, and other educational personnel.

Is a Theoretical Lens Being Used?

Another question that shapes the character of a narrative is whether and to what extent the researcher uses a theoretical lens in developing the narrative. A **theoretical lens** in narrative research is a guiding perspective or ideology that provides structure for advocating for groups or individuals and writing the report. This lens may be to advocate for Latin-Americans using *testimonios,* reporting the stories of women using a feminist lens (e.g., Personal Narratives Group, 1989), or collecting the stories of marginalized individuals. In all of these examples, the narrative researcher provides a "voice" for individuals whose voices may not be heard adequately in education.

Can Narrative Forms Be Combined?

In a narrative, it is possible to have the different elements listed above combined in the study. For example, a narrative study may be biographical because it is written and reported by the researcher about a participant in a study. This same study may focus on a personal study of a teacher. It may also address an event in the life of a teacher, such as a dismissal from a school (Huber & Whelan, 1999), resulting in a partial life story, or a personal narrative. In addition, because this individual is a woman, a theoretical lens may be used to examine power and control issues in the school. This leads to a feminist narrative. The final resulting narrative is thus a combination of different elements: a biography, a personal story, a teacher's story, and a feminist perspective.

KEY CHARACTERISTICS OF NARRATIVE DESIGNS

Despite the many forms of narrative inquiry, they share several common characteristics. Before reviewing the key characteristics, we will discuss them in general terms and relate them to the qualitative characteristics of research as developed in Chapter 2.

As shown in Table 16.1, narrative researchers explore an educational research problem by understanding the experiences of an individual. As in most qualitative research, the lit-

TABLE 16.1

The Research Process, Qualitative Characteristics, and Narrative Research Characteristics

The Research Process	Qualitative Characteristics (see Chapter 2)	Narrative Research Characteristics
Identify a research problem	• A qualitative problem requires exploration and understanding.	• Seeks to understand and represent experiences through the stories individual(s) live and tell.
Review the literature	• The qualitative literature plays a minor role. • The qualitative literature justifies the research problem.	• Seeks to minimize the use of literature and focus on the experiences of the individual(s).
Develop a purpose statement and research questions	• The qualitative purpose statement and research questions are broad and general. • The qualitative purpose statement and research questions seek participants' experiences.	• Seeks to explore the meaning of the individual's experiences as told through a story or stories.
Collect qualitative data	• Qualitative data collection is based on using protocols developed during the study. • Qualitative data collection involves gathering text or image data. • Qualitative data collection involves studying a small number of individuals or sites.	• Seeks to collect field texts that document the individual's story in his or her own words.
Analyze and interpret qualitative data	• Qualitative data analysis consists of text analysis. • Qualitative data analysis consists of describing information and developing themes. • Qualitative interpretations situate findings within larger meanings.	• Seeks to analyze the stories by retelling the individual's story. • Seeks to analyze the stories by identifying themes or categories of information. • Seeks to situate the story within its place or setting. • Seeks to analyze the story for chronological information about the individual's past, present, and future.
Write and evaluate a study	• Qualitative research reports use flexible and emerging structures and evaluation criteria. • Qualitative researchers take a reflexive and biased approach.	• Seeks to collaborate with the participant when writing the research study. • Seeks to write the study in a flexible storytelling mode. • Seeks to evaluate the study based on the depth, accuracy, persuasiveness, and realism of the account.

erature review plays a minor role, especially in directing the research questions, and the inquirer emphasizes the importance of learning from participants in a setting. This learning occurs through stories told by individuals, such as teachers or students. The stories constitute the data and the researcher typically gathers it through interview or informal conversations. These stories, called field texts (Clandinin & Connelly, 2000), provide the raw data for researchers to analyze as they "retell" the story based on narrative elements such as the problem, characters, setting, actions, and resolution Ollerenshaw & Creswell, 2000). In this process, researchers narrate the story and often identify themes or categories that emerge. Thus, the qualitative data analysis may be both a description of the story and themes that emerge from it, as discussed in Chapter 9 on "Describing and Developing Themes from Data." In addition, the researcher often writes into the reconstituted story a chronology of events describing the individual's past, present, and future experiences lodged within specific settings or contexts. Throughout this process of collecting and analyzing data, the researcher collaborates with the participant by checking the story and negotiating the meaning of the database. The story of the researcher may also be interwoven into the final research report as he or she gains personal insight.

This brief overview of the process highlights specific characteristics of research often found in narrative reports. As shown in Figure 16.2, there are seven major characteristics that you might use to identify narrative research as you read or to conduct your own study. These are:

- focusing on individual experiences
- reporting a chronology of the experiences
- collecting the individual stories told to the researcher or gathered through field texts
- restorying the individual stories
- coding the stories for themes
- describing the context or setting of the individual stories
- collaborating throughout the process of research with the individuals whose stories are being reported

Focusing on Individual Experiences

In narrative research, the inquirer often studies a single individual. Narrative researchers focus on the experiences of one or more individuals. In a study conducted about Stephanie, a primary school teacher, the researchers (Connelly & Clandinin, 1988) collected stories about her day-by-day planning of teaching and the planning done "on the fly." Although less frequent, examples can also be found of narrative studies of more than one individual

---

FIGURE 16.2

Major Characteristics of Narrative Research

- **Experiences of an individual**—social and personal interactions
- **Chronology of experiences**—past, present, and future experiences
- **Life stories**—first-person, oral accounts of actions obtained through field texts (data)
- **Restorying** (or retelling or developing a metastory) from the field texts
- Coding the field texts for **themes or categories**
- Incorporating the **context or place** into the story or themes
- **Collaboration** between the researcher and the participants in the study, such as negotiating field texts

Source: Adapted from Clandinin & Connelly, 2000; Lieblich, Tuval-Mashiach, & Zilber, 1998; and Riessman, 1993.

(see the stories of Anthony and Anita writing about personal experiences that introduced this chapter, McCarthey, 1994).

In addition to the *study* of an individual, the researcher is most interested in *exploring the experiences* of that individual. For Clandinin and Connelly (2000) these **experiences** in narrative inquiry are both personal—what the individual experiences—as well as social— the individual interacting with others. This focus on experience draws on the philosophical thoughts of John Dewey, who saw that an individual's experience was a central lens for understanding a person. One aspect of Dewey's thinking was to view experience as continuous (Clandinin & Connelly, 2000), where one experience led to another experience. Thus, narrative researchers focus on understanding an individual's history or past experiences and how they contribute to present and future experiences.

Reporting a Chronology of Individual Experiences

Understanding the individual's past as well as the present and future is another key element in narrative research. Narrative researchers analyze and report a chronology of an individual's experiences. When researchers focus on understanding an individual's experiences, they elicit information about a participant's past, present, and future. **Chronology** in narrative designs means that the researcher analyzes and writes about the individual's life using a time sequence or chronology of events. Cortazzi (1993) suggests that it is the chronology of narrative research with an emphasis on sequence that sets narrative apart from other genres of research. For example, in a study about a teacher's use of computer technology in a high school classroom, the inquirer would include information about the teacher's introduction to computers, current computer use, and future goals and aspirations. The story reported by the researcher would include a discussion about the sequence of events for this teacher.

Collecting Stories

To develop this chronological perspective of individual experiences, the narrative researcher asks the participant to tell a story (or stories) about his or her experiences. Narrative researchers place emphasis on collecting the stories told to them by individuals or gathered from a wide variety of field texts. These accounts might arise during informal group conversations (Huber & Whelan, 1999) or from one-on-one interviews. A **story** in narrative research is a first-person oral telling or retelling of an individual. Often these stories have a beginning, a middle, and an end. Similar to basic elements found in good novels, these aspects involve a predicament, conflict, or struggle; a protagonist or character; and a sequence with implied causality (a plot) during which the predicament is resolved in some fashion (Carter, 1993). In a more general sense, the story might include the elements typically found in novels, such as time, place, plot, and scene (Connelly & Clandinin, 1990). For those relating to narrative from a literary perspective, the sequence might be the development of the plot as it unfolds, the emergence of a crisis or turning point, and the conclusion or denouement. Narrative researchers hope to capture this story line as they listen to individuals tell their stories.

Stories can be collected using many forms, which speaks to the collection of field texts gathered by narrative researchers. **Field texts** represent information from different sources collected by researchers in a narrative design. Up to this point, our examples have illustrated collecting stories by using discussions, conversations, or interviews between a researcher and one individual. However, the stories might be autobiographical, with the researcher reflecting on his or her own story and interweaving that story with those of others. For example, in the sample study at the end of this chapter, Huber and Whelan (1999) discuss how their own stories interrelated with the stories of Naomi, a rural, junior/senior high teacher, as she told about her decision to leave her position in the school district. Often the researcher's role in the inquiry process may be central, in which they find themselves in a "nested set of stories" (Connelly & Clandinin, 2000, p. 63). Journals are another form used for collecting stories, as well as field notes written by either the researcher or the participant. Letters may also be used to make meaning of experiences. These letters may be written back and forth between participants, research collaborators, or between the researchers and participants (Connelly & Clandinin, 2000). Family stories, photographs, and memory boxes—collections of items that trigger our memories—are other forms used for collecting stories in narrative research.

Restorying the Stories

After individuals tell a story about their experiences, narrative researchers retell the story in their own words. Narrative researchers retell (or restory or remap) the story reported by the participant in the study in order to provide order and sequence to it. **Restorying** is the process in which the researcher gathers stories, analyzes them for key elements of the story (e.g., time, place, plot, and scene), and then rewrites the story to place it in a chronological sequence. When individuals tell a story, this sequence is often missing or not logically developed. By restorying, the researcher provides a causal link among ideas. There are several ways to restory the narrative.

Examine the transcript from a narrative project addressing adolescent smoking behavior (Ollerenshaw & Creswell, 2000), shown in Table 16.2. This table displays the process of restorying interview data for a high school student who is attempting to quit smoking. The process involves three stages:

1. The researcher conducts the interview and transcribes the conversation from an audiotape. This transcription is shown in the first column as "raw data."
2. Next the narrative researcher retranscribes the raw data by identifying the key elements of the story. This is shown in the second column. The key at the bottom of the table indicates the codes used by the researcher to identify the setting [s], characters [c], actions [a], problem [p], and resolution [r] in the student's transcript.
3. Finally, the narrative researcher restories the student's account by organizing the key codes into a sequence. The sequence presented in this passage is setting, characters, actions, problem, and resolution, although another order might have as easily been used to restory the account. This restorying begins with the place (McDonald's), the characters ("I," the student), and then the events (behaviors such as "shaky" and "hyper"). The researcher reworks the transcription to identify the elements of the story and reforms (or restories) the elements into a logical sequence of activities.

At stage 2, to clearly identify these elements, the researcher might organize them into a table like the one illustrated in Table 16.3. This table describes five elements used in restorying (Ollerenshaw, 1998). The setting is the specific situation of the story, and it can be illustrated by such factors as time, locale, or year. The characters in a story may be discussed as archetypes or portrayed through their personalities, behaviors, styles or patterns. The actions are the movements of the individuals in the story, such as the specific thinking or behaving that occurs during the story. The problem represents the questions or concerns that arise during the story or the phenomena that needs to be described or explained. The resolution is the outcome of addressing the problem—the answer to a question or the conclusion reached in the story. It may involve an explanation about what caused the character to change in the story.

These elements—setting, characters, actions, problem, and resolution—illustrate only one example of the elements that narrative researchers look for as they restory an individual's experiences. They might also use the elements of the Three-Dimensional Space Narrative Structure advanced by Clandinin and Connelly (2000). As shown in Table 16.4, the

TABLE 16.2

Retranscribing and Restorying a Transcript

Transcription of Audiotape (Raw Data)	Retranscription by the Researcher*	Restory by the Researcher
Well, I know it wasn't the first time but I remember this one most vividly. Almost . . . about a year ago, I had been trying to quit and I hadn't smoked for about, I'd say about a month or more. I think I just didn't want to do it anymore. There was this guy that I liked at McDonald's, but he didn't like me, he liked my best friend. We all worked at McDonald's after school until close. Oh, wow, I had nicotine fits a lot. Sometimes you get shaky. You get really high, you know, just like you need to go get some fresh air. You need to get a cigarette, just like, you know, you just get really hyper and start bouncing off the walls. I calmed down after a little bit, but . . . I was tempted to start again during the month I quit. Uhm, well my friends would be smoking outside by the tree, so it was like you know, you look at it and you're just like, it kind of looks like a cupcake or something good, you know. Just like you want, but then they ask you, "Hey, do you want to drive or something? Just say, "No." So I'm trying to quit but I can't do it. They understand but then it's just like, "Okay, I gotta go home now" and I get to go to bed. Sometimes I just go back inside the school cause you can't smoke inside there, so . . . I might have slipped maybe one or two but I mean, I was upset, tense. This guy I liked started going out with my best friend and so then I got really upset and started just smoking again just like, you know. That's the one that I really remember . . . me and her were best friends no more.	about a year ago, [s] I [c] had been trying to quit and I hadn't smoked for about, I just didn't want to do it anymore. [p] was this guy [c] that I liked [a] at McDonald's [s], but he didn't like me, he liked my best friend [c]. I had nicotine fits [a] a lot. You get shaky [a]. You get really high [a]. You need to go get some fresh air. You need to get a cigarette[a]. You just get really hyper and start bouncing off the walls [a]. I calmed down after a little bit [a], friends [c] would be smoking outside by the tree [s]. It looks like a cupcake or something-good [a]. Hey, do you want to drive or something?[a] "No. I'm trying to quit [a]." I'd go to bed [a]. Sometimes I just go back inside the school [s] cause you can't smoke inside there, [a] I slipped maybe one or two but [a], I was upset, tense [a]. This guy I liked started going out with my best friend [a] I got really upset and started just smoking again [a]. That's the one that I really remember . . . me and her were best friends no more [r].	• A year ago, I worked at McDonald's and I didn't buy cigarettes for about a month. • I had nicotine fits. • I got shaky. • I got high. • I got hyper. • I started bouncing off the walls. • I needed air. • I went outside. • Friends were smoking by the tree. • I wanted a cigarette because they looked good. • I wanted to drive. • I went inside the school. • I went home to bed. • I calmed down. • The guy I liked from McDonald's started dating my friend. • I got upset and tense. • I slipped one or two cigarettes. • I started smoking again. • We're not friends any more.

*Key to codes in the retranscription: setting [s], characters [c], actions [a], problem [p], and resolution [r]

Source: Adapted from Riessman, 1993.

TABLE 16.3

Organizing the Story Elements Into the Problem-Solution Narrative Structure

Setting	Characters	Actions	Problem	Resolution
Context, environment conditions place, time, locale, year, and era	Individuals in the story described as archetypes, personalities, their behaviors, style, and patterns	Movements of individuals through the story illustrating the character's thinking or behaviors	Questions to be answered or phenomena to be described or explained	Answers to question and explanations about what caused the character to change.

Source: Adapted from Ollerenshaw, 1998.

TABLE 16.4

The Three-Dimensional Space Narrative Structure

Interaction		Continuity			Situation
Personal	Social	Past	Present	Future	Place
Look inward to internal conditions, feelings, hopes, aesthetic reactions, moral dispositions	Look outward to existential conditions in the environment with other people and their intentions, purposes, assumptions, and points of view	Look backward to remembered stories and experiences from earlier times	Look at current stories and experiences relating to actions of an event	Look forward to implied and possible experiences and plot lines	Look at context, time, and place situated in a physical landscape or in a setting bounded by characters' intentions, purposes, and different points of view

Source: Adapted from Clandinin & Connelly, 2000.

three dimensions of interaction, continuity, and situation create a "metaphorical" (p. 50) inquiry space that defines a narrative study. As researchers construct their story (either their own or someone else's), they would include information about:

▶ **interaction**—the personal interaction based on an individual's feelings, hopes, reactions, and dispositions as well as the social interaction to include other people and their intentions, purposes, assumptions, and points of view

▶ **continuity**—a consideration of the past that is remembered, the present relating to experiences of an event, and the future, looking forward to possible experiences

▶ **situation**—information about the context, time, and place within a physical setting with boundaries and character's intentions, purposes, and different points of view

Coding for Themes

As with all qualitative inquiry, the data can be segmented into themes (see Chapter 9 on "Describing and Developing Themes from Data"). Narrative researchers may code the data of the stories into themes or categories. The identification of themes provides the complexity of a story and adds depth to the insight about understanding an individual's experiences. As with all qualitative research, a small set of themes, such as five to seven, are identified by the researcher. These themes may be incorporated into the passage that retells the individual's experiences or included as a separate section in a study. These themes, which are typically major ideas that result from the story, may be presented after the retelling of the story.

Describing the Setting or Context

Narrative researchers describe in detail the setting or context in which the individual experiences the central phenomenon. In the restorying of the participant's story and the telling of the themes, the narrative researcher includes rich detail about the setting or context of the participant's experiences. The **setting** in narrative research may be friends, family, workplace, home, social organization, or school—the place where a story physically occurs. In some narrative studies, the restoried accounts of an educator may actually begin with a description of the setting or context before the events or actions of the story are conveyed. In other cases, information about the setting is woven throughout the story.

Collaborating with Participants

Throughout the process of research, narrative researchers collaborate with the individual being studied. **Collaboration** in narrative research means that the inquirer actively involves the participant in the inquiry as it unfolds. This collaboration may include many steps in the research process, from formulating the central phenomena to be examined, to deciding which types of field texts will yield helpful information, to writing the final "restoried" rendition of the individual's experiences. Collaboration involves negotiating relationships between the researcher and the participant to lessen the potential gap between the narrative told and the narrative reported (Clandinin & Connelly, 2000). It may also include explaining the purpose of the inquiry to the participant, negotiating transitions from gathering data to writing the story, and arranging ways to intermingle with participants in a study (Clandinin & Connelly, 2000). Collaboration often calls for a good working relationship between teachers and researchers, an idealized situation that takes time to develop and time to come to a mutually illuminating story between the researcher and the teacher (Elbaz-Luwisch, 1997).

STRENGTHS AND WEAKNESSES OF NARRATIVE DESIGNS

Emphasizing the importance of collaboration can be a strength as well as a weakness of this form of inquiry. Unquestionably, when researchers seek out and collect the stories of educators about their personal and social experiences in schools or other educational settings, they establish a close bond with the participants. This may help reduce a commonly held perception by educators that research is distinct from practice and has little practical application. For the educators actually being studied, sharing their stories may make them feel that their stories are important and that they are being heard. Narrators give "voice" and identity to educators in this form of research. Moreover, telling a story helps individuals understand topics that they may need to process and understand (McEwan & Egan, 1995). Finally, telling stories is a natural part of life, and individuals all have stories about their experiences to tell others. In this way, narrative research captures an everyday, normal form of data that is familiar to individuals.

That stories might arise in normal conversation also raises potential problems that narrative researchers need to consider. This relates to the telling of the story by the participant to the researcher and the researcher telling the story in a narrative report, a process that is labor-intensive.

When assessing the story told by the participant, researchers need to consider whether the story is authentic. The participant may "fake the data" (Connelly & Clandinin, 1990, p. 10), providing a Pollyanna story or a story with a typical Hollywood ending, where the good guy or girl always wins. This distortion of the data may occur in any research study, and it especially presents an issue for narrative researchers who rely heavily on self-reported information from participants. The collection of multiple field texts, the triangulation of data, and member-checking (as discussed in Chapter 9 on "Validating the Accuracy of Findings") can help ensure that good data are collected. Also, participants may not be able to tell the "real" story. This inability may arise when experiences are simply too horrific to report or too raw to recall (e.g., Holocaust victims, disaster victims). It may also occur when individuals fear sanctions against them if they report their story, such as in sexual harassment cases. The real story may also not emerge because individuals simply cannot recall it—the story is buried too deeply in the subconscious. It may also occur because the stories are based on events that happened years ago, leading to early memories that may distort events and provide inventions of past actions (Lieblich, Tuval-Mashiach, & Zilber, 1998). Although distortion, fear of reprisal, and inability to tell may plague storytellers, narrative researchers remind us that stories are "truths of our experiences" (Riessman, 1993, p. 22) and that any story told has an element of truth in it.

The telling of the story by the participant also raises the issue of who "owns" the story. In reporting stories of individuals marginalized in our society, narrative researchers run the risk of reporting stories that they do not have permission to tell. At the minimum, narrative inquirers can obtain permission to report stories, and inform individuals of the purposes and use of the stories at the beginning of the project. Still, a contested issue in narrative research is who ultimately "owns" the story told by the participant.

Along with the potential problem of ownership is also the issue about whether the participant's voice is somehow lost in the final narrative report. For example, when restorying exists, it is possible for the report to reflect the researcher's story, and not the participant's story. Using extensive participant quotes and the precise language of the participants, along with carefully constructing the time and place for the story, may help to ameliorate this problem. A related issue is whether the researcher gains in the study at the expense of the participant. Careful attention to reciprocity or giving back to participants, such as serving as a volunteer in a classroom or providing an award for participating in the study, will maintain "gains" for both the researcher and the participant.

STEPS IN CONDUCTING NARRATIVE RESEARCH

During the conduct of a study, the potential weaknesses discussed above need to be considered and addressed. Regardless of the type or form of narrative research, educators who conduct a narrative study proceed through similar steps, as shown in Figure 16.3. Seven major steps comprise the process typically undertaken during a narrative study. A visualization of the process as a circle shows that all steps are interconnected and not necessarily linear. The use of arrows to show the direction of steps is meant only to be suggestive and not proscriptive of a process that you might use.

FIGURE 16.3

Steps in Conducting Narrative Research

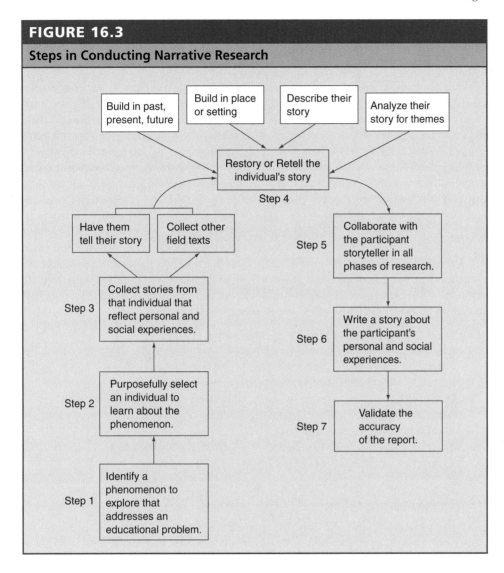

Step 1. Identify a Phenomenon to Explore That Addresses an Educational Problem

As with all research projects, the process begins by focusing on a research problem to study and identifying, in qualitative research, a central phenomenon to explore. Although the phenomenon of interest in narrative is the "story" (Connelly & Clandinin, 1990), the story must be about some issue or concern that needs to be addressed. For example, the issue for Huber (1999), in a narrative study of children in a classroom, consisted of stories about the difficulties that she and her student teacher, Shaun, had meeting the diverse needs of students. This included children excluding other children, using hurtful words with each other, and persistently using anger and aggression to "solve" problems. When exploring issues such as these, the researcher seeks to understand the experiences—either personal or social—of an individual or individuals in an educational setting.

Step 2. Purposefully Select an Individual to Learn about the Phenomenon

The researcher next finds an individual or individuals who can provide an understanding of the phenomenon. The participant may be someone who is typical or someone who is critical to study because he or she has experienced a specific issue or situation. The study of Naomi was a critical case about the issue of teacher conflict between a special education junior/senior high teacher and a supervising teacher over the placement of a special needs student (Huber & Whelan, 1999). Other options for sampling, as introduced in Chapter 7 on "Purposeful Sampling," are also available. While many narrative studies examine only a single individual, several individuals may be studied in a project, each with a different story that may conflict or be supportive of each other.

Step 3. Collect the Story from That Individual

The intent of the researcher is to collect field texts that will provide the "story" of an individual's experiences. Perhaps the best way to gather the story is to have the individual tell about his or her experiences, either through personal conversations or interviews. But other field texts such as those listed below, can also be gathered.

- Have the individual record their story in a journal or diary.
- Observe the individual and record field notes.
- Collect letters sent by the individual.
- Assemble stories about the individual from family members.
- Gather documents such as memos or official correspondence about the individual.
- Obtain photographs, memory boxes (a collection of items that trigger memories), and other personal/family/social artifacts.
- Record the individual's life experiences (e.g., dance, theater, music, film, art, and literature). (Clandinin & Connelly, 2000)

Step 4. Restory or Retell the Individual's Story

Next the researcher reviews the data that contains the story and retells it. This process includes examining the raw data, identifying elements of a story in it, sequencing or organizing the story elements, and then presenting a retold story that conveys the individual's experiences. This process is based on the assumption that the story told by the participant will be better understood by the listener and the reader if it is resequenced into a logical order.

What elements does the researcher locate in the raw data? In what order are these elements arranged? Narrative researchers differ about the elements to select, although in general the narrative elements found in a literary analysis of a novel are most frequently mentioned. For example, time, place, plot, and scene are major elements located in stories by researchers (Connelly & Clandinin, 1990). Focusing on the plot, the researcher might identify an abstract of the events or actions, orient the listener, convey the complicating action, evaluate its meaning, and resolve the action (Cortazzi, 1993). Another inquirer might examine the story for setting, characters, actions, problem, and resolution (Ollerenshaw & Creswell, 2000). Although several analytic strategies exist for locating and sequencing a story, all procedures order the story for the reader and listener using literary elements.

Step 5. Collaborate with the Participant Storyteller

This step is one that interacts with all the other steps in the process. The researcher collaborates with the participant during the research process. This collaboration can assume several forms, such as negotiating entry to the site and the participant, working closely with the participant to obtain field texts to capture the individual experiences, and writing and telling the individual's story in the researcher's words.

Step 6. Write a Story about the Participant's Experiences

The major step in the process of research is for the author to write and present the story of the individual's experiences. Although there is no single way to write the narrative report, it is helpful to include several features of narrative. The restory by the researcher certainly claims a central place in the narrative report. In addition, some narrative researchers include an analysis to highlight specific themes that emerged during the story.

Typically a specific literature section is not included and the literature and research studies about the problem are incorporated into the final sections of the study. Since readers are often not familiar with narrative, researchers write a section about the importance of narrative research and the procedures involved in it so that readers can be informed of the process of research. As with all qualitative research, the inquirer is present in the narrative report and is referenced using the first-person pronoun.

Step 7. Validate the Accuracy of the Report

Researchers often validate the accuracy of their narrative accounts. When collaboration exists with participants, this validation may occur throughout the project. Several validation practices addressed in Chapter 9 on "Validating the Accuracy of the Findings," such as number-checking, triangulating among data sources, and searching for disconfirming evidence, are useful to determine the accuracy and credibility of a narrative account.

CRITERIA FOR EVALUATING NARRATIVE RESEARCH

As a form of qualitative research, narrative needs to be consistent with the qualitative criteria identified in Chapter 10 on "Qualitative Standards." In addition, there are specific "narrative" aspects that those reading and evaluating a study might consider. Use the following list of questions to evaluate your own or someone else's narrative report.

- Does the researcher focus on individual experiences?
- Is there a focus on a single individual or a few individuals?
- Did the researcher collect the story of an individual's experience?
- Was there a restorying by the researcher of the participant's story?
- In the restorying, was the participant's voice as well as the researcher's voice heard?
- Did the researcher identify themes that emerged from the story?
- Did the story include information about place or setting of the individual?
- Did the story have a temporal, chronological sequence including the past, present, and future?
- Is there evidence that the researcher collaborated with the participant?
- Does the story adequately address the purpose and questions of the researcher?

APPLYING WHAT YOU HAVE LEARNED: A NARRATIVE RESEARCH STUDY

To apply the ideas in this chapter, read the narrative study on page 541, noting the marginal annotations that identify characteristics of qualitative research. (See Chapter 2 "Distinguishing between Quantitative and Qualitative Research." See also characteristics of narrative designs in the section "Key Characteristics of Narrative Designs.")

> Huber, J., & Whelan, K. (1999). A marginal story as a place of possibility: Negotiating self on the professional knowledge landscape. *Teaching and Teacher Education, 16,* 381–396.

The Huber and Whelan (1999) study addresses the experiences of a single teacher, Naomi, a rural junior/senior high teacher. In conversation with the researchers, Naomi shares her story of her struggle to understand and resist the response she receives from Brian, an individual in the school responsible for placing special needs students. Alicia is a special needs student in Naomi's class. The first tension develops with Brian over whether Naomi can dialogue with Alicia's parents about Alicia's special needs program. Brian apparently disapproves. Then the question arises over who would be responsible for determining and assigning Alicia's grade in Naomi's classroom. Although Naomi is not involved in determining Alicia's grade, her name is recorded beside the assigned grade on the report card. When Naomi questions this practice, Brian deflects his responsibility onto others and is critical of Naomi's ability to understand how to mark students with special needs. In response to other confrontations, Brian recommends that the school administrators fire Laura, Naomi's program aide. Meanwhile, the principal of the school responds to Naomi by consistently dismissing her concerns. In the end, Naomi resigns her position with the district, feeling that she has no choice but to leave.

After the authors tell Naomi's story, they next identify the themes in the story. They reflect on how the story provides insight into Naomi's in-classroom and the out-of-classroom experiences. The authors also see Naomi negotiate at the "borders" of power, confrontation, silence, and arrogance by individuals at the school. Although the authors initially believe that Naomi's story is one of hopelessness and miseducation, in the end they conclude that it has deeper meaning. It reflects a resistance, a power that Naomi had given to herself. She has, in effect, authored her own stories that run counter to those being scripted for her in the school.

You can see that this article has interesting layers of meaning and useful insights for educators as we consider our own issues in the educational workplace. As a narrative design, the clearly told story of Naomi with people, contexts, a flow of events, and a denouement marks the article as useful reading for those learning narrative research. As a qualitative study filled with issues of power, marginalization, and boundary crossing, this study embraces an emancipatory and participatory perspective (see Chapter 2 on "The Development of Qualitative Research") in which questions of agency, advocacy, powerlessness, and marginalization play a central role.

As you examine the study, locate the following parts of the research process:

 ▶ the research problem and use of qualitative research.
 ▶ the use of the literature
 ▶ the purpose statement and research questions
 ▶ the types and procedures of data collection
 ▶ the types and procedures of data analysis and interpretation
 ▶ the writing structure

After you have read through this article and noted the location and quality of each part (using the paragraph numbers), then turn to the analysis in the following sections and compare your analysis with mine.

The Research Problem and Use of Qualitative Research

See Paragraphs (03) and throughout the article

In Paragraph 03 the author identifies the possibility of miseducation occurring in our schools when individuals struggle to understand and resist situations within their school context. Naomi experienced contradictions, gaps, and silences in her work in the school.

This article displays the characteristics of a qualitative research study listed below.

- the exploration and understanding of the complexity of one individual's experiences in the school (Paragraphs 08–17)
- a minimal use of literature and, when literature is mentioned, it reflects on the school landscape for professional teachers (e.g., Paragraph 02) or the research approach of narrative inquiry (Paragraph 04)
- a broad and general purpose of the study—to make sense of a teacher's story (Paragraph 03)
- a focus on the participant's experiences by exploring a "storyteller/teacher who lived this experience" (Paragraph 03)
- collecting data (i.e., words) using procedures that involved conversations between a group of five teachers during an 18-month period of time (Paragraph 04)
- studying only one single individual (Paragraph 10)
- analyzing the conversations and stories of Naomi by decribing or retelling her story (Paragraphs 10–17)
- interpreting the meaning of Naomi's story in a general sense about her power of resistance (Paragraphs 52–56)
- using a flexible reporting structure that advances Naomi's story (Paragraphs 10–17) followed by classroom- and borders-related themes (Paragraphs 20–51)
- reporting in a personal, reflexive style in which the authors identify how their own views changed as a result of listening to and reflecting on Naomi's story (Paragraphs 55–56)

The Use of the Literature

See Paragraphs 06, 52, and 53

As in most qualitative studies, the literature plays a minor role. In this study there is little literature, and when it appears, it documents the stories told on the "professional knowledge landscape" (Paragraph 05) or approaches to narrative research (Paragraph 04). Much of the literature used is "methodological literature"—that is, it informs or educates readers about the research design of narrative research rather than focusing on the content or topic of teachers in schools. This literature provides references, concepts, and language of narrative research. Also, there is no theory to test from the literature, an approach typically taken by authors in qualitative studies. By keeping the literature to a minimum, the researchers learn from and take direction from Naomi's experiences.

The Purpose Statement and Research Questions

See Paragraph 03

The authors indicate the purpose or intent of the study early, in Paragraph 03. They discuss making sense out of a teacher's story. This paragraph actually summarizes the entire study and indicates the central phenomenon of miseducation that is the focus of the study. No research questions are mentioned to provide specific direction for the study.

Types of Procedures of Data Collection

See Paragraph 04

As a qualitative study, this article reports text data—the words of Naomi, the teacher. However, the authors provide only minimal evidence about their data collection. We do learn that five teachers engaged in conversations over 18 months. These conversations were audiotaped and transcribed and represent the text data used in the study. The authors do not explicitly identify their purposeful sampling technique, but we assume that it is purposeful. Three of the five women are authors and their advisor in this study, and the authors refer frequently to their own stories as well as Naomi's story. Although all five individuals participated in a conversation about their lives as teachers (Paragraph 08), this particular study focused on only one person, Naomi, who is seen as a co-researcher in the study.

Types and Procedures of Data Analysis and Interpretation

> See Paragraphs 08–17 for the "restory"
>
> See Paragraphs 18–51 for themes
>
> See Paragraphs 52–56 for interpretations

In the passage on "reconstructing Naomi's experiences," we find the first-level analysis of Naomi's story. This is the restorying of Naomi's story by the researchers. It includes contextual information (rural junior/senior high school landscape), characters (Brian, Alicia, and Laura), specific events (tension in the relationship, intolerance, and silence), and the resolution or denouement (leaving the school). Following this restorying, the authors identify themes about the teacher landscape (in-classroom and out-of-classroom) and the borders (ownership, negotiations, homeplaces, positional power, sameness, confrontation, arrogance, judgment, and silence). The analysis thus consists of a description of Naomi's situation (the "restorying") and the identification of themes (classroom experiences and borders).

The authors develop the larger interpretation of Naomi's story in the final passage of the study. We learn about Naomi's caring for others (Paragraph 53), and the researchers' sense of the hopelessness of Naomi's story (Paragraph 54). On further reflection (and interpretation), the authors' rereading of Naomi's story uncovered strong images of her. Her resistance was seen by the researchers as a source of strength that she could use to help her live with the isolation she felt in her school (Paragraph 56).

The Overall Writing Structure

We see in this article a flexible, qualitative writing structure without a distinct review of the literature and a well-formed method discussion. As in a qualitative study, it is a storytelling narrative structure with Naomi's story and the themes that emerge from it as a major narrative approach. In addition, the author's use of references and comments about narrative research, throughout the article, add research interest to the study. For example, they emphasize early the importance of story for individuals to make meaning of their lives. They focus on the individual experiences of a single individual, and they include collaboration between the researcher and the participant. Throughout the story, they highlight the context of Naomi's workplace and use a temporal sequence, illustrated by the chronological presentation of her story. The authors' inclusion of strong method and research design content adds to the sophistication of this study. Although Naomi's voice might have been heard through more direct quotes, this study has many layers of meaning and insight for narrative researchers and those understanding the experiences of teachers in schools.

KEY IDEAS IN THE CHAPTER

Narrative research has emerged as a popular form of qualitative research. It has become a viable way to study teachers, students, and educators in educational settings. All of these individuals have stories to tell about their experiences. Narrative inquirers describe the lives of individuals, collect and tell stories about people's lives, and write narratives of individual experiences. These qualitative studies focus on identifying the experiences of a single individual or several individuals and understanding their past, present, and future experiences.

Narrative researchers collect stories from individuals and retell or restory the participants' stories into a framework, such as a chronology of the characters, the setting, the problem, the actions, and a resolution of those actions. In addition, the inquirer may gather field texts and form them into themes or categories and describe, in detail, the setting or context in which the stories are told. Throughout the research process, the researcher emphasizes collaboration between the researcher and the participant.

The steps in conducting a narrative study are to identify a problem suited for narrative research and to select one or more participants to study. Researchers then collect stories from the participant about his or her life experiences and retell the story to form a chronology of events that may include the characters, setting, problem, actions and a resolution. Throughout this process collaboration occurs with the participant, and the story composed by the researcher tells of the participant's life experiences.

USEFUL INFORMATION FOR PRODUCERS OF RESEARCH

▶ Individuals planning or conducting a narrative study can employ the steps in the process identified in this chapter.
▶ Consider the type of narrative design you plan to use. Ask yourself the following four questions: Who writes or records the story? How much of a life is recorded and presented? Who provides the story? Is a theoretical lens being used?
▶ The three steps used in restorying provide a structure for processing a transcript and developing a retelling of the participant's story.
▶ As you listen to a participant's story, consider some of the potential issues that may arise, such as whether the story is authentic, whether data are distorted, whether individuals can tell the story, and who "owns" the story.

USEFUL INFORMATION FOR CONSUMERS OF RESEARCH

▶ Consumers can review the steps in the research process in this chapter to determine how narrative inquirers conduct a study.
▶ The evaluation criteria discussed in this chapter can be used to assess the quality of a narrative study.
▶ When narrative researchers conduct an inquiry, they need to report that they have checked the accuracy of their findings. Look for reports about triangulating data, member-checking, or providing disconfirming evidence for themes.
▶ The narrative journal article reported in this study provides one example of narrative research. It can be used to identify the major characteristics of a narrative study and to model the composition of a narrative study.

ADDITIONAL RESOURCES YOU MIGHT EXAMINE

A major book to consult is the text on narrative inquiry by Clandinin and Connelly (2000). This text captures all aspects of narrative designs from learning to think narratively, to constructing a story using the three-dimensional model, to the types of field texts that narrative researchers collect. It also includes information about composing a narrative text and using the forms available in dissertations and books. See:

Clandinin, D. J., & Connelly, F. M. (2000). *Narrative inquiry: Experience and story in qualitative research.* San Francisco: Jossey-Bass.

Another useful book in education and teacher education is the book edited by McEwan and Egan (1995) on *Narrative in Teaching, Learning, and Research.* This volume provides helpful examples of specific narrative studies in education. Examine:

McEwan, H. & Egan, K. (1995). *Narrative in Teaching, Learning, and Research.* New York: Teachers College Press, Columbia University.

Several journals have published excellent overviews of narrative research as applied to the field of education. One article often cited is the Connelly and Clandinin (1990) discussion on "Stories of Experience and Narrative Inquiry" in the *Educational Researcher.* This article is especially good at identifying the procedures used in conducting a narrative study. Another article in the *Educational Researcher* is by Kathy Carter (1993) on "The Place of Story in the Study of Teaching and Teacher Education." This article presents the pros and cons of studying the stories of teachers, such as the political context of story and the issues of gender, power, ownership, and voice. A third article by Kathleen Casey (1995, 1996), titled "The New Narrative Research in Education," is found in the *Review of Research in Education.* This article addresses the history of narrative research and surveys many topics in narrative research, such as various types (e.g., autobiographical reflections), issues (e.g., plastic identities), and methodological concerns (e.g., nuanced discussions of emotions). See:

Connelly, F. M., & D. J. Clandinin (1990). Stories of experience and narrative inquiry. *Educational Researcher, 19*(5), 2–14.

Carter, K. (1993). The place of a story in the study of teaching and teacher education. *Educational Researcher, 22*(1), 5–12, 18.

Casey, K. (1995/1996). The new narrative research in education. *Review of Research in Education, 21,* 211–253.

One entire issue of the journal *Teaching and Teacher Education* (Gudmundsdottir, 1997) addresses "Narrative Perspectives on Research on Teaching and Teacher Education." Including major international writers on narrative research, this volume provides examples of specific narrative studies as well as thoughtful discussions about topics that critique as well as support narrative designs. See:

Gudmundsdottir, S. (1997). Introduction to the theme issue of "narrative perspectives on teaching and teacher education." *Teaching and Teacher Education, 13*(1), 1–3.

Outside the field of education in the social sciences are several books useful to understanding narrative designs. Riessman (1993) provides thoughtful procedures for analyzing and reporting narratives; Josselson and Lieblich (1993) provide a six-volume series on the study of narrative lives; and Cortazzi (1993) also includes systematic approaches to narrative analysis. Examine:

Riessman, C. K. (1993). *Narrative analysis.* Newbury Park, CA: Sage.

Josselson, R., & Lieblich, A. (Eds.). (1993). *The narrative study of lives* (Vol. 1). Thousand Oaks, CA: Sage.

Cortazzi, M. (1993). *Narrative analysis.* London: The Falmer Press.

Qualitative Characteristics

A Marginal Story as a Place of Possibility: Negotiating Self on the Professional Knowledge Landscape

Narrative Research Characteristics

Janice Huber, Karen Whelan*
The Centre for Research for Teacher Education and Development, Faculty of Education, University of Alberta, Edmonton, Alberta, Canada

Abstract

(01)   Drawing on a two-year study focusing on teacher identity and marginalization within diverse school landscapes, we explore the educative and miseducative qualities of responses as told through one teacher's story. By reconstructing and making meaning of this story through the conceptual framework of the "professional knowledge landscape" [Clandinin, D. J., & Connelly, F. M. (1995). *Teacher's professional knowledge landscapes,* New York: Teachers College Press], we consider how this teacher's identity—which we understand narratively as "story to live by"—shapes, and is shaped, within the in- and out-of-classroom places on her school landscape. Through a final retelling of this narrative, we pay close attention to the response which emerged from each of these fundamentally different places and we examine this teacher's negotiation of her story to live by in relation to a school story of inclusion. This focus enables us to name borders of power, judgment and silence, and "bordercrossings" [Anzaldúa, G. (Ed.). (1990). *Making face, making soul = Haciendo caras: Creative and critical perspectives of feminists of color.* San Francisco: Aunt Lute Books], which are shaped within "public homeplaces" [Belenky, M., Bond, L., & Weinstock, J. (1997). *A tradition that has no name: Nurturing the development of people, families, and communities.* New York: BasicBooks]. We believe that this story is a place of possibility—possibility for understanding the central role that presence to our narrative histories plays in enabling us to live and to sustain stories that run counter to those being scripted for us on school landscapes. © 1999 Elsevier Science Ltd. All rights reserved.

(02)   Storytellers are influenced by the telling of their own stories. Active construction and telling of a story is educative: The storyteller learns through the act of storytelling . . . [and] in their telling in relationship . . . It is an education that goes beyond writing for the self because it has a responsive audience, which makes possible both an imagined response and an actual response. These possibilities, the imagining of response and the response, are important for the storyteller. The possibilities are important in an educative way because the meaning of the story is reshaped and so, too, is the meaning of the world to which the story refers. (Clandinin & Connelly, 1995, p. 155/56)

(03)   This paper is about the storytelling to which Clandinin and Connelly refer. It is about telling stories to our selves and to others with whom we are in relationship. It is about how this telling, active construction, living out, and reconstruction of our stories, influences our selves and those around us. Response and imagining of possibilities live at the centre of what this paper is about. The teacher's story we make sense of within this

A qualitative problem requires exploration and understanding.

Narrative researchers focus on the experiences of a single individual.

---

*Corresponding author. Tel.: +403-492-7770; fax: +403-492-0113.

Reprinted from Huber, J., & Whelan K. (1999). A marginal story as a place of possibility: Negotiating self on the professional knowledge landscape. *Teaching and Teacher Education, 15,* 381–396 with permission from Elsevier Science.

The qualitative purpose statement and research questions are broad and general.

The qualitative purpose statement and research questions seek participants' experiences.

(04)
The qualitative literature plays a minor role.

Qualitative researchers take a reflexive biased approach.

(05)

paper is a story of "miseducative" (Dewey, 1938) qualities, a story in which impossible contradictions, gaps, and silences are named. This story is situated within one school context in which the storyteller/teacher who lived this experience uncovers her struggle to understand and to resist the response she received through negotiating her self within her professional surroundings. Located within a western Canadian province, in a large junior/senior high school, this story centres around issues of integrating students with special needs into "regular" programs. A context is described in which students with special needs are identified for individualized programming within a segregated setting in the school. Students who were labelled as "special needs" were selectively integrated into what is traditionally defined as "non-academic" courses, and were assigned classroom aides to assist with individualized programming.

This story was shared within the context of a narrative inquiry (Carr, 1986; Clandinin & Connelly, 1994; Connelly & Clandinin 1988, 1990) including eighteen months of taped and transcribed research conversations between a group of five teacher co-researchers who felt the need to construct a community away from our school landscapes, where our most vulnerable stories could be explored. The telling of this story was important for this particular teacher and for all of us as co-researchers-storytellers, storylisteners, and storyresponders in relationship with one another. The storytelling context, shaped by a responsive audience, was profoundly educative in that through the sharing of this story, the meaning of it was reshaped from beginning images of hopelessness to those of possibility.

Our paper begins by situating this inquiry within a narrative conceptualization of teacher identity and the professional contexts in which teachers live and work. Our restructuring of the first meeting with the teacher co-researchers with whom we are in conversation provides an introduction to the methodological grounding which shapes our study. The introduction also provides an overview of the story we worked to understand in conversation within our teacher inquiry group and throughout this paper. Unpacking this story through the framework and narrative language developed by Clandinin and Connelly (1995) in their conceptualization of a "professional knowledge landscape" revealed the storied qualities of this school context and the central role response played within this storying. We conclude this paper by focusing on the ways in which response was continuously negotiated and lived out on this school landscape. Our purpose in this final exploration is to uncover the borders shaped out of response, as well as the possibilities for "bordercrossings" (Anzaldúa, 1987)—those hopeful meeting places where the retelling of our stories creates possibilities for imagining our selves in relation with others in new ways.

1. Understanding Identity as "Story to Live By"

(06)

The qualitative literature justifies the research problem.

Our understanding of teacher identity is grounded within Connelly and Clandinin's (in press) narrative conceptualization of identity as "story to live by". In their research into teacher knowledge and school contexts, they reveal how we tell storied compositions of our lives to "define who we are, what we do, and why . . ." (Connelly & Clandinin, 1999). A sense of fluidity shapes our story to live by as it is composed over time, recognizing the multiplicity of situations and experiences we embody. These multiple storylines interweave and interconnect, bearing upon one another and on how we come to understand our selves (Clandinin, 1997). We live, tell, retell, and relive our life stories (Clandinin & Connelly, 1998) as we negotiate our selves within and across various contexts. For example, within the context of our own lives, we may draw upon our understanding of our selves as women to make meaning of a particular experience. Although this knowing will also be present as we make sense of our selves in other situations, it may dwell in the background while our self understanding of being elementary teachers may come more to the foreground as we make sense of another situation. As teachers, our story to live by is "both personal—reflecting a person's life history—and social—reflecting the milieu, the contexts in which teachers live" (Connelly & Clandinin, 1999).

Qualitative data collection involves studying a small number of individuals or sites.

(07) Understanding teacher identity as story to live by calls for a relational understanding between teachers and the contexts in which they work. In this way, teachers both shape and are shaped by their particular school landscapes. Considering schools as professional knowledge landscapes creates openings for exploring the storied nature of teacher identity while also challenging us to think about each school context from multiple vantage points. In the next section of this paper, we reconstruct a teacher's story, following the shifting nature of her story to live by as she composes her teaching life both inside and outside of her classroom context on the professional knowledge landscape of her school.

2. Reconstructing Naomi's[1] Experiences

Qualitative data collection is based on using protocols developed during the study.

Narrative researchers collaborate with participants.

Narrative researchers collect studies form individuals.

(08) It is our first time coming together with our group of teacher co-researchers. We are nervous and somewhat uncertain of how the evening will unfold, yet in the same moment, our sense of excitement and anticipation draws us to this conversation. We are a group of both strangers and acquaintances, gathering from various school landscapes. In the privacy of Janice's living room, we sit together, surrounded by candlelight, food, and wine. A common storyline joins us together—our lives as teachers.

Qualitative data collection involves gathering text or image data.

Narrative researchers retell the story.

Narrative researchers report a chronology of individual experiences.

(09) This common experience enables us, with ease, to pick up on the threads of our lives, connecting stories of where we last saw one another. After a few moments, the room becomes quiet, a sign that it is time to begin this new research conversation between us. Feeling a need to tell of our selves, as researchers positioned at the university, we [including our advisor, Jean Clandinin) each share stories of what has brought us to this exploration of a narrative understanding of teacher knowledge and identity. Our stories, centering around research themes of margins (Anzaldúa 1987, 1990) and positionings (Miller, 1994), create an opening for our co-researchers who are positioned as teachers on the landscape, to begin to share their stories. The circle of storytelling broadens as we go around the living room, listening to each teacher-coresearcher share of her life. When our storytelling has passed nearly full circle, there is one last pause, an invitation for Naomi, who has not yet spoken, to share her story.

Qualitative data analysis consists of describing information and developing themes.

Qualitative data analysis consists of text analysis.

(10) Naomi begins to tell the story of herself by situating her narrative within a rural junior/senior high school landscape. She describes her teaching assignment as very specialized, being the only teacher in this position within her school and school district over an eight-year period. Naomi's description speaks, to a certain degree, of the loneliness and isolation which surrounded her as she composed her teaching life, a context she describes in her own words when she states, "I really didn't have anyone that I could plan with." Having noted how this particular positioning shaped her life as a teacher on this school landscape, Naomi quickly emphasizes that her sense of marginalization was far more profound than her

[1]Because of the vulnerable nature of this story, pseudonyms have been assigned to the characters in order to protect their identities.

visible positioning on the landscape as the only teacher of a specialized program. She begins to describe this deeper sense of marginalization when she says, "Certainly when I started teaching there, I don't think I was on the margin at all. As time went on, though, I very much became an outsider." Naomi unpacks her knowledge of becoming an outsider by recounting how she came to recognize that she was not following the "status quo" story of her school. The magnitude of choosing to position herself in this way was expressed when she reflected, "I guess personally I made that choice but as a result of it, I quit my job because I couldn't be there anymore and agree." Naomi explained that in order for her to make sense of her experience and to continue to exist on this school landscape, she consciously chose to position herself outside the "school story"—a story shaped by a mandate of inclusion for students with special needs (Clandinin & Connelly, 1995, 1996). She reflected her deepening awareness of this story by saying, "I think I initially started to go there [outside the school story], maybe not consciously, but I think soon it was a conscious decision and I was not prepared to be there in any other way . . . , I think it was the only way that I could make sense. It was the only way that I could exist."

(11)   Naomi's sharing in this first conversation speaks to us of her internal struggle, of her need to live in a space where she could "make sense" of her experiences in an "educative" (Dewey, 1938) way, constructively shaping her ongoing practice. In our second conversation as a research community, Naomi moves deeper into this story. She does this by unpacking experiences which led her to resign from her teaching position, leaving the school and her teaching community.

(12)   Naomi began to speak of these experiences by introducing herself and "the special needs teacher" (who we named Brian) as two central characters in the story. In her first few words, Naomi positioned herself as living within her classroom on her school landscape. Through Naomi's eyes, Brian was positioned as someone who had influence in her program, yet lived distantly from the physical space of her classroom. At the outset, we learned from Naomi that Brian, alone, determined the placement of each special needs student. We also discovered that when a student with special needs (who we named Alicia) was placed in Naomi's room, a program aide (who we named Laura) was assigned to work with Alicia. Outlining the constraints of her timetable and teaching assignment, Naomi emphasized her struggle to negotiate a meaningful program for Alicia so that she would experience success.

(13)   The tension in the relationship between Naomi and Brian became apparent at the first reporting period, and was heightened at each successive reporting period. At the centre of this tension was the confusion over who would be responsible for determining and assigning Alicia's grade. In the first reporting period Naomi both determined and assigned Alicia's grade. However, she was troubled by being prevented, by a school directive, from indicating to Alicia's parents that she was working on a program which had been modified to meet her particular learning needs. Through Naomi's telling, we learned that her desire for authentic dialogue with parents was in conflict with Brian who lived a story of keeping parents happy at all costs.

(14)   In the second reporting period, another special needs aide, with whom Naomi had little interaction, informed her that Brian would " do the mark" for Alicia. Naomi was not involved in determining Alicia's grade, yet she discovered that her name was recorded beside the assigned

grade on the report card which was sent home. In this situation, and in those following, Naomi attempted to understand this practice through conversation with Laura, the special needs program aide who was working in her classroom; the special needs teacher, Brian; her principal; her vice principal; and her colleagues on staff. As the plotline in this story developed, Naomi continued to question Brian's practice in "marking" the student's work. In Naomi's telling of the story, it appeared to her as though Brian deflected his responsibility onto others and eventually storied her as a teacher who simply did not understand how to mark students with special needs.

(15) As the story continued, a border began to appear between Naomi and Brian. Her intolerance over the absence of communication and understanding which was shaping their relationship led Naomi to request a meeting between Brian, Laura, and herself. Having Laura present at the meeting was responded to with resistance from Brian. However, Naomi insisted that Laura's voice be present because of her intimate understanding of Alicia and the classroom program. Following the meeting, Naomi learned that Brian storied the event as an upsetting exchange, as he felt Laura's questions had embarrassed him in front of Naomi. In response to their meeting, he requested that the school administrators "fire" Laura. Naomi countered his telling of this event to the administration with her own version of what happened, and Laura's position was maintained.

(16) Naomi described the aura of silence she experienced as the story continued to unfold into the second school year. At the edges of this silence, Naomi recalled witnessing "horrendous things" continuing to take place. Conversation in relation to the growing dilemma surrounding this school story begins to occur only in secrecy, when "nobody was in the vicinity." For Naomi, her school landscape became a place where there was an intolerance for tension. Because her story to live by necessitated exploring tension in relationship with others, her understanding of the complexities of her school landscape was pushed further to the margins.

(17) Naomi countered this push, continuing to resist the school story by challenging Brian's living out of it. Her principal responded to Naomi by consistently dismissing her concerns, eventually telling her that she must either support Brian or say nothing at all. Naomi's story closed with a profound sense of loss in the relationship she had lived with her principal. Her deeply felt sense of marginalization, shaped by the conflicting nature of the stories being lived and told on her school landscape, ultimately led her to leave her school community and to resign her position with the district. Finding no place for her story to "exist" on this school landscape, Naomi felt she was left with no choice but to leave.

3. Retelling Naomi's Story in Terms of the Professional Knowledge Landscape

Narrative researchers develop themes.

(18) While Naomi's recounting of her experience as a marginalized member of this school community was painful and troubling, her story holds educative promise for understanding school contexts and teachers' stories to live by. This promise led us to reconsider Naomi's story by focusing on the shaping nature of Naomi's school context on her story to live by as a teacher.

Narrative researchers describe the setting or context.

(19)   We begin this exploration by drawing on Clandinin and Connelly's (1995) conceptual framework of the "professional knowledge landscape"[2] which enabled us to make meaning of Naomi's story through a focus on her story to live by and on her experience in "two fundamentally different places" on her school landscape—"the one behind the classroom door with students, and the other in professional places with others" (p. 5). When we discuss the physical space *inside* Naomi's classroom, we draw upon Clandinin and Connelly's (1995) metaphor by referring to this place on her school landscape as her "in-classroom" space. When we discuss Naomi's experience *outside* her classroom on this school landscape, we refer to these spaces as "out-of-classroom" places. Inquiring into Naomi's experience within each of these places, her in-classroom and her out-of-classroom places on this school landscape, allowed us to examine the unique qualities of these places and the differing ways in which Naomi authored her life within each.

4. Naomi's In-classroom Place on the Professional Knowledge Landscape

(20)   The conceptual framework of the professional knowledge landscape views teachers as actively engaged practitioners who are attempting to author meaningful lives, telling and retelling themselves through their classroom practice (Clandinin and Connelly, 1995) as they respond to the shifting policy expectations and social issues which surround their work, and to the specific needs of their students. From this vantage point, teachers are not viewed as empty vessels waiting to be filled by the ideas of others, but are understood as "holders and makers of knowledge" (Clandinin, 1997, p. 1).

(21)   Within the in-classroom place on the professional knowledge landscape of schools, the moral authority for a teacher's understanding of her story to live by (Connelly & Clandinin, 1999) is self-authored, shaped by each

---

[2]An in-depth understanding of the term "professional knowledge landscape" is developed by Clandinin and Connelly (1995) in *Teachers' professional knowledge landscapes*. Our work in this paper draws upon Clandinin and Connelly's following description:

> A landscape metaphor . . . allows us to talk about space, place, and time. Furthermore, it has a sense of expansiveness and the possibility of being filled with diverse people, things, and events in different relationships. Understanding professional knowledge as comprising a landscape calls for a notion of professional knowledge as composed of a wide variety of components and influenced by a wide variety of people, places, and things. Because we see the professional knowledge landscape as composed of relationships among peoples, places, and things, we see it as both an intellectual and a moral landscape. (p. 4/5)

A central focus in this paper is toward understanding the relationship between one teacher's story of marginalization on her school landscape and her identity. Clandinin and Connelly's metaphor helped us uncover the multi-dimensional qualities of this teacher's context. Viewing her professional landscape from multiple vantage points provided insight into her knowledge context while also engaging us in questions of relationship—between this teacher and the shifting people, places, and things on her school landscape. Understanding this teacher's story from a place perspective, we were able to explore her differing experience in two very different places on her school landscape, her "in-classroom place" and the "out-of-classroom" places. The temporal qualities of this teacher's narrative created openings for us to inquire deeply into the ways the story of inclusive education was shaping her school landscape. By focusing on the personal history the teacher embodied as she negotiated her professional landscape, her knowing of her self in relation to a variety of diverse people, places, things, and events, became visible.

teacher's particular narrative history and negotiated in relation with students. Because teachers position themselves within their classrooms around the story they embody of themselves as teachers, the in-classroom place on the professional knowledge landscape of schools is often characterized by a sense of safety and secrecy. While Clandinin and Connelly (1995) caution that this secrecy should not be glorified, they also note that it plays an important role in shaping the epistemological nature of the in-classroom place on the professional knowledge landscape as a space in which teachers feel "free from scrutiny . . . [and are able] to live stories of practice" (p. 13) which honour their embodied knowing. It is in this way that the in-classroom place on the professional knowledge landscape is epistemologically and morally grounded in narrative knowledge. This narrative grounding enables the in-classroom place to be educative for teachers, as their stories to live by can be negotiated without judgment framed by the "theoretical knowledge and the abstract rhetoric of conclusions found in the professional knowledge landscape outside the classroom" (p. 12).

(22) As we listened to Naomi tell stories of her in-classroom place on her school landscape, she shared telling images of how she viewed this space. Early in her storytelling, Naomi described her in-classroom place as "*my* space,"—an important image which awakened us to her strong sense of agency within this space. Beginning to describe her concerns about Brian's placement of Alicia into her classroom, Naomi explained, "Because he was special needs . . . he was involved in everybody else's program. And so you couldn't really just sort of say, "Well as long as you stay out of *my* space, I'll deal with this . . . because he was a part of your space." Naomi's description of her in-classroom place helped us to see that this was a space of belonging for Naomi, a secure place for her "self authorship" of her story to live by as teacher—one she felt determined to protect and uphold (Carr, 1986).

(23) We were also drawn to Naomi's images of herself as a teacher within her classroom space through her stories of experience with students. Naomi's understanding of her in-classroom place, and her ability to shape it, were evident when she discussed her struggle with the constraints of her teaching time-table. Recognizing the limitations this time-table placed upon her students and, in this particular story, upon Alicia, Naomi said,

> After I got to know my grade seven classes then [Alicia] was in one too where we met. Generally I had my students for a 40 minute class and an 80 minute class. Well, 40 minutes for all of my students was too short, for [Alicia] it was *really*, I mean she would just barely get her stuff out and get started and now it's time to finish . . . that class just really wasn't the type of setting that she should have been in. But my other two grade seven classes were a lot better, so finally after many discussions I got her moved into a different grade seven class that only had 80 minute blocks and so I'd see her twice one week and only once the next week, so that wasn't the best, but it was better than that 40 minute class and it was a much better environment. Plus she was in the biggest grade seven class and then afterwards she was in the smallest one.

(24) Naomi placed significance in this event and, as she told this story, we began to see that one of the threads woven into the story she was composing was that of working in close relationship with students. Naomi's focus on what was best for this particular student led her to the out-of-classroom place on her school landscape and into "many discussions" with colleagues. Within her recounting of this experience, there was a sense that the negotiation of Alicia's timetable on the out-of-classroom place may have been difficult. However, Naomi appeared to view the negotiation as morally necessary because, as she described, Alicia's first class placement "just . . . wasn't the type of setting that she should have been in." We were also left with the sense that, regardless of the difficulties Naomi experienced through this

out-of-classroom negotiation, she eventually felt that she was able to successfully negotiate a better situation for Alicia. In this way and in this particular instance, we felt as though the story she was authoring as teacher was honored, both within her in-classroom place and on the out-of-classroom places on the professional knowledge landscape of her school.

(25)   Other qualities of Naomi's ability to negotiate her identity within her classroom were shared as she storied her relationship with Laura. We learned of the relationship which developed between Naomi and Laura when Naomi said, "I did have an aide and she was absolutely wonderful and she basically taught me how to modify and that type of thing, you know, meet that little girl's needs." By storying Laura as a co-teacher, Naomi made visible the deep sense of respect and validation she felt towards this woman. She described how their relationship enabled them to modify a program which made sense for Alicia. Through Naomi's telling of their relationship, we saw her recognition of Laura as a person who mattered in her life. Her words spoke to us of a relationship in which mutuality created openings for educative conversation, risk taking, and the imagining of possibilities for a student who had been defined as "special needs." It was being in relation which enabled them to work together in the best interests of Alicia.

(26)   Naomi's story of Laura created an image of negotiation which occurred with authenticity. We wonder if the relationship they shared may have led Naomi to become more trusting of the out-of-classroom place on her school landscape with the intent of also engaging there "in conversations where stories can be told, reflected back, heard in different ways, retold, and relived in new ways" (Clandinin & Connelly, 1995, p. 13). Being in relationship was an overlapping thread in Naomi's story of both her students and Laura. This led us to believe that relational understanding of experience was the central plotline in Naomi's story to live by. These two stories of Naomi's in-classroom place on her school landscape also revealed that, within this space, Naomi was deeply engaged in living and retelling this story of herself in negotiation with those who shared the in-classroom space—the students and Laura.

(27)   This was not the plotline which Naomi's telling took on as she continued to unpack more of her experience on this school landscape surrounding her work with Alicia and other students with special needs. Increasingly, Naomi's crossing of borders between the in- and out-of-classroom places on her school landscape created tensions for her. As Clandinin and Connelly's (1995) work highlights, "when teachers leave their classrooms and move into another place on the professional knowledge landscape, they leave the safe secrecy of the classroom and enter a public place on the landscape" (p. 14). These out-of-classroom places on the professional knowledge landscape are "dramatically different epistemological and moral place[s]" (p. 14). In the next section of this paper we explore numerous qualities of the out-of-classroom place on Naomi's school landscape and the ways they shaped her story to live by.

5. Naomi's Out-of-Classroom Place on the Professional Knowledge Landscape

(28)   In contrast to the safety and self-authorship which shape the in-classroom place on the professional knowledge landscape, the out-of-classroom place is one largely defined by a sacred story of theory over practice (Clandinin & Connelly, 1995). In this out-of-classroom place, policies and prescriptions, holding "theoretical knowledge claims", are delivered from above via the conduit—the dominant communication pipeline which links teachers' lives to their school boards, governing agencies, and associations. This theoretical knowledge arrives into the

lives of teachers in the form of new curriculum material, textbooks, and policy mandates. They are scripted into teachers' lives, often with no substantive place for conversation about what is being "funneled down." Teachers are often left to make sense of these materials behind their classroom doors in secrecy and silence, negotiating these theories in relation to their story to live by.

(29)   The sacred theory-practice story enters the school landscape with a "moral push," leaving teachers caught in what Clandinin and Connelly (1995) describe as a "split existence." Teachers begin to struggle with their own knowing—knowing that is grounded in their narrative histories and is embedded within their in-classroom practice—and their negotiation of a sacred knowing, a prescriptive "you should" kind of knowing which shares the out-of-classroom place on the professional knowledge landscape. It is this tension which causes teachers to experience the out-of-classroom place as abstract, a place that "floats untethered" with "policy prescriptions [that] . . . are torn out of their historical, narrative contexts" (Clandinin & Connelly, 1995, p. 11). On the out-of-classroom place, the self-authorship, which can be felt within the in-classroom place, becomes defined by an abstract "other", and the moral quality of the landscape becomes pre-scripted from outside. In this way, the out-of-classroom place can become a "de-personalized" and disconnected place for teachers to live their storied lives.

(30)   In Naomi's story we are presented with an explicit example of the dilemmas and sense of split existence which become shaped by a teacher's movement between these two profoundly different places of knowing, defined by dramatically different moral qualities. The sacred story which arrived onto Naomi's landscape from some abstract place along the conduit, appeared to be one of inclusion; a story loaded with moral implications for teachers. Naomi first faced this new school story when a student with special needs was placed in her classroom and, in her telling of the story, we sensed there was little discussion surrounding the placement—it was simply an expectation. Describing her understanding of this situation, Naomi said, "[Brian] picked which teacher they'd go in with." As Naomi recounted how the story of inclusion began to take hold on the professional knowledge landscape of her school, we began to see her story coming into conflict with the larger school story, and with those positioned distantly, outside of her classroom context: office support staff, other program aides, Brian, and the school administrators.

(31)   Naomi faced her first moral dilemma on the out-of-classroom place when she was met with a prescriptive message from the office staff regarding the reporting process for students with special needs, such as Alicia. Naomi's intention was to communicate openly and honestly with the parents about Alicia's program. However, when she attempted to enter a conversation with the office staff about this process, offering her knowing and understanding of Alicia as she had lived it in her classroom, she came into direct conflict with the conduit and was told, "No, we want her [Alicia] to do the same as everybody else . . . . We're not going to do a different style of report card." Feeling strongly about this issue, Naomi countered this response with, "That's fine. I'll just type up a letter and tell her mom, explaining to her what we've been working on." She was met with, "No, you can't do that either." On the out-of-classroom place, as Clandinin and Connelly (1995) point out, "teachers are not, by and large, expected to personalize conduit materials by considering how materials fit their personality and teaching styles, classrooms, students, and so forth" (p. 11). Naomi was disturbed by the depersonalized message she received in this situation and the way in which she was forced to send home a mark in the report card which she felt "wasn't the truth." It was in this critical moment of

"self-sacrifice" that we saw Naomi's determination to live by what she knew. There was a sense of future possibility as she discussed her intention not to be constrained by the story of inclusion shaping the school landscape outside her classroom during the next reporting period.

(32)   The impact of the out-of-classroom place on Naomi's story was felt again when she told of receiving another prescriptive massage regarding the marking process, this time sent from Brian via his program aide. Naomi recalled the aide saying, "You're not supposed to do a mark for [Alicia], [Brian] is going to do all the marks for all the kids." The distance with which this message was delivered led us to wonder about the pervasive story which was shaping Naomi's school landscape—one in which spaces for authentic conversation were diminishing. By introducing a new character into the story, a "messenger" to deliver information, Brian re-shaped the relational space between himself and Naomi, creating distance and separation. Naomi's response to this widening gap in their relational space was to seek out further conversation and connection so that she might better understand the marking process being implemented by Brian. As she recounted her story of this incident, Naomi recalled thinking to herself, "I'm sure he's going to come and have a meeting with me because he's never been in this classroom. He doesn't have any idea what [Alicia] is doing, so how could he possibly make a mark for her?" However, as Naomi remembered the unfolding events within this story, she shared that Brian did not come to speak with her and in the growing absence of conversation between them, a mark was entered into Alicia's report card, with Naomi's name placed beside it. The story, centering around inclusive practice, once again took on an abstract quality (Clandinin & Connelly, 1995) as the characters in this story lived out their practice in a distant, depersonalized, and disconnected manner.

(33)   The embeddedness of this story within her school landscape became apparent as Naomi struggled to create openings for conversation with Brian. However, as she told the story, we came to see that these attempts ended in disappointment, creating further dilemmas for her. Clandinin and Connelly (1995) describe that in the absence of places for conversation on policies funneled down the conduit onto the school landscape, "discussion . . . is removed from matters of substance to matters of personality and power" (p. 11). Listening to Naomi's story, we heard how she experienced this shift from conversation to personality and power, as she described Brian's reaction to a meeting she had arranged between him, Laura, and herself. "I requested that [Laura] be there because, you know, she too works with [Alicia] so she should contribute to this. I mean she probably knows the most out of all of us how [Alicia] feels during all of those activities." Naomi was troubled when Brian responded to her request with resistance. Naomi said, "He didn't want [Laura] there and I just said, 'Well she, in my class, she works with [Alicia] in my classroom so, she's coming'." Brian's apparent devaluing of Laura's position on the school landscape came into direct conflict with the relational story Naomi lived by within her classroom, placing stress on the intended conversation which she had imagined would shape their meeting.

(34)   Following this meeting, Naomi recalled how she felt Brian's final response was played out through personality, position, and power, "He wanted [Laura] fired because she asked him questions that embarrassed him in front of me." This dramatic and alarming response to what Naomi had imagined as a conversation to bridge their understanding between the in- and out-of-classroom places on the school landscape only served to create further distance between Naomi and Brian and their stories of one another.

(35)   Personality and power become even more embedded in discussions outside Naomi's classroom context as the story Naomi was authoring even-

tually came into direct conflict with Brian's story. When Naomi questioned Brian about his positioning within the school story, she described him defining it as a "power-over" (Josselson, 1994) positioning in which he would "monitor" and "supervise" her practice, and the practice of others within the school. Naomi recalled,

> One day I got really angry at [Brian] and I said, 'Tell me what your job is here?' I said, 'You know, you just live off the sweat and tears of the other teachers here.' He told me that he had to be hired in our school to monitor the teachers because we weren't caring enough individuals and we were just cruel to the kids and he was there to save them.

(36)   Unpacking how troubled she was by Brian's description of himself as being hired to monitor her because she was cruel to Alicia within her classroom, Naomi said, "He told me that one day, that he was hired to monitor me as well as the others and I said to him, 'So . . . do you view yourself as being my supervisor?' He responded by saying. 'Yeah' and I said, 'Well, that would be the day, and if you're ever in that position, it will certainly be the day that I cease to work here.' In Naomi's telling of this angry exchange between them, we sensed her struggle with this story. Caught between the borders of personalities and positions of power, shaped by the larger school story, we recognized her hopelessness in being able to enter into an educative conversation surrounding students with special needs in places outside her classroom on the landscape of her school.

(37)   This critical absence of a space for conversation for Naomi reached its final, dramatic conclusion when she discovered that her principal, whom she respected, cared for, and trusted, attempted to silence her knowing in the face of the dominant school story. Describing two stories of the distance she began to experience between herself and her principal, Naomi recounted being "called down" to her principal's office after school to address the increasing tension between Brian and herself. As she told this story over the discussion of their confrontational exchange which had taken place between herself and Brian regarding his position in the school story in relation to her own, she said:

> As a result . . . my principal call[ed] me down and sa[id],'Did you have a talk with [Brian] today?' 'Yup.' 'Well what happened?' Did it get, you know, a little out of hand?' And I said, 'I don't know, I don't think it got out of hand, it was just very truthful.' 'Well did you tell him that you didn't think he did much at our school?' And I said, 'Yes, I told him exactly that. That's exactly how I feel and I would tell him that again because I haven't changed my opinion at all since.'

(38)   The determination and conviction with which Naomi spoke about this exchange gave us insight into the strength of her story and her recurring need for "truthful" conversation. Naomi's sense of connection with Alicia and Laura created a moral space in which their knowing of one another shaped a relationship where care was central. In her telling of the story, we saw that Naomi was unwilling to compromise her "self positioning" as a teacher who cared about her students and Laura. However, we learned that, in her first meeting with her principal regarding this tension, the message Naomi received was, "You can't tell people stuff like that . . . ." In a second meeting with her principal, behind the closed doors of his office, Naomi's story to live by bumped up against the school story once again, and in this meeting as well, Naomi received a silencing response. "He said things like well, 'We do all kinds of things in our school, Naomi, graduation and volleyball teams and na, na, na and we have special needs here.' And I'm kind of going, 'Oh yeah. How does a [special needs] program fit into extra curricular, you know?'. Her principal replied by saying, "We have to support those things and if we can't support them, then the least

we can do is say nothing at all." It was at this moment in Naomi's story-telling that we were most profoundly struck by the shaping nature of the out-of-classroom place on Naomi's story to live by. Temporally casting her relationship with her principal in a past sense, Naomi shared, "I *did* really like my principal." We imagine Naomi's embodied knowing of this man may have been at least partially shaped by her recognition of his response, which seemed to honor her agency during the tension surrounding Laura's dismissal, resulting in her position being maintained. Naomi expressed her painful awakening to a different understanding of her principal as she began to realize that the person, with whom she had always found a space for authentic conversation outside her classroom, was also no longer able to hear her words. In one silencing instance Naomi was told to "say nothing at all," and, in another, she recalled her principal saying, "Look, I don't want to get involved with special needs. I know nothing about it, as long as everybody's quiet and happy . . ."

(39)   Reinforcing this message, we discovered that Naomi's vice principal would only enter into conversation with her in the hidden corridors of the school when, ". . . nobody was in the vicinity." In the face of the powerful school structures and prescriptive conduit story which was shaping the professional knowledge landscape of her school, Naomi's story was pushed aside, to a place of silence. As she continued to resist the "accepted school story," her story to live by became marginalized, moving further and further to the edges of what was defined as acceptable on her school landscape. Naomi described her outside positioning in our first conversation when she said, "I guess I went to the margins [of the "status quo" story of the school] because I wasn't willing to participate in some of the things that I saw happening [t]here . . . You do live in that isolation . . ." Ultimately the dilemmas which arose out of the abrasion between these two dramatically different moral spaces on the landscape—Naomi's in-classroom and out-of-classroom places—became too overwhelming for Naomi. It was at this point that she decided that she must leave the school.

6. Response on the Out-of-Classroom Place on Naomi's School Landscape

(40)   By carefully following Naomi's story as it wove its way through both the in- and out-of-classroom places on the professional knowledge landscape of her school, we were struck by the essence of response as it developed in Naomi's story, both how it was given and the ways in which it was received. In this particular story, our challenge to more fully understand response was intensified as we learned of a school community, at least through the eyes of one teacher, where her story to live by came to live at the margins of the school story, surrounded by a profound sense of silence and isolation. The tensions which emerged between Naomi's story and the school story brought forward the significant gap formed as imagined and actual response came into conflict on the school landscape. The presence of this tension caused us to wonder about response—both how it is shaped by the school story and, in turn, how it shaped Naomi's story to live by. As we listened to, read, and re-read Naomi's story, we began to look more closely at response. Living with this story over time enabled us to see some of the ways that response shaped, and was shaped by, Naomi's story to live by, her relationships with her colleagues, and the larger school story of inclusion.

(41)   Interweaving our previous unpacking of Naomi's story, through our focus on the in- and out-of-classroom places on her landscape, we continue this inquiry by exploring how the story of school, shaped through response, impacted Naomi's story to live by. Making meaning of Naomi's story, as lived out on a professional knowledge landscape, enabled us to il-

lustrate that the teacher story Naomi was authoring was deeply grounded within her narrative knowing of herself as living in relationship with others. Such a view of Naomi's story revealed that as she crossed the border between her in- and out-of-classroom places on her school landscape, she consistently attempted to negotiate her relational story through conversation with various other characters with whom she interacted. It was both the actual and imagined response received by Naomi, as well as the response she gave in return, that uncovered the ways in which the borders on Naomi's school landscape were constructed and lived out.

(42)   The dilemmas Naomi faced as she crossed these borders eventually drew forth her counterstory of resistance and insubordination (Nelson, 1995)—her story to live by which became a counterstory within her particular school landscape. Naomi named her "counterstory to live by" in our initial research conversation when she said, "I went to the margins . . . because I wasn't willing to participate in some of the things I saw happening there and as a result of that, I wasn't following the status quo of my school." Naomi's reconstruction of herself within her spoken text highlighted her determination to live her story in a way which she felt was educative. Even though this determination to stay with her story eventually led her to resign, there was a hopeful edge to her telling in that she came to see her resignation as an educative alternative to negotiating her story on a school landscape which she increasingly experienced as miseducative. In the final section of this paper, we return to Naomi's storytelling of her professional knowledge context, looking closely at the borders and bordercrossings shaped out of the response on both the in- and out-of-classroom places on this school landscape. As we take a closer look at response by naming these borders and bordercrossings, we hope to gain further insight into the story Naomi authored as it was negotiated within and between borders shaped by the school story of inclusion.

Qualitative data analysis consists of describing information and developing themes.

7. Borders and Bordercrossings on the Professional Knowledge Landscape

7.1 Borders of Ownership

(43)   The first border made present to us through the telling of this story, one of ownership, spoke to us of the significance of the in-classroom place in Naomi's life as a teacher. It is not surprising to us that this place, described with such passion by Naomi as "*my* space," was one she held sacred and was determined to protect. Looking carefully at this protective stance provided us insight into the nature of Naomi's response, where it came from, and the border that was shaped as a result. Naomi's classroom was a visible space on the landscape in which we were able to see her living her story in a meaningful and educative manner as highlighted through her telling of the relational story she composed alongside the students and Laura. We saw a shift in the safety of Naomi's classroom place, however, when the story of inclusion began to break through the protective border she had constructed around herself and her classroom. We believe the construction of this border was grounded within Naomi's narrative history with previous school stories imposed upon her, and was shaped along with her present response to a school story of inclusion she had little understanding of, and even less authority to negotiate as a member of this school landscape. Faced with the threat this school story presented in relationship to her story, she struggled to protect the one place on the landscape she intimately understood, a place which made moral sense to her as she worked in relation with her students.

7.2 Negotiating Bordercrossings

(44)   Naomi's understanding of the restrictive structures imposed from the out-of-classroom place on the school landscape was evident through her discussion of negotiating the school timetable to meet the needs of her students. In this context, the school timetable became symbolic of a "sacred story" (Crites, 1971) in the out-of-classroom place. These kinds of stories can confine students' and teachers' lives within predetermined frameworks and can become "internalized" and "absorbed" into a "taken-for-grantedness" (Greene, 1993, 1995) of experience. Naomi's knowledge of this sacredness made the crossing of this border even more significant. Her response, reflected through her re-negotiation of the school timetable, indicated her courage and conviction to stand up to this story of school even when this task seemed a challenge. Her success in addressing this challenge was a critical moment in Naomi's story. The response she received was a hopeful sign of possibility within the larger school landscape as it affirmed her knowing while also helping her to recognize that the story she was authoring could be honoured in places beyond the boundaries of her classroom. In this event, we saw a shift in Naomi's internal border of ownership. This shift enabled her to recognize the importance of her story to live by and the place it had in reshaping the borders constructed between her classroom and those outside her classroom.

7.2.1. Bordercrossings, within Public Homeplaces

(45)   The response given and received in the relational space between Naomi and Laura was not evident within the telling of this story, yet this does not diminish its importance in Naomi's experience of living on this school landscape. Through Naomi's telling of the value of Laura to this program, a much different story of ownership and borders emerged, quite different from how Naomi storied the borders between herself and Brian. Naomi was open to the presence of Laura in her classroom and together they shaped a relational space, through response, which we imagine enabled both of them to live a story that made sense. As we read and reread Naomi's telling description of Laura, we were left with the image of "seamless" (Clandinin & Connelly, 1997), although continuously negotiated, border-crossings in which the "self" was never placed in jeopardy, but rather, was enriched by seeing and being present to the other. In Buber's (1965) sense of "making present," Naomi was able to recognize herself through her relation to this other self, her program aide, Laura. The fluidity of distance and relation negotiated between them was ever-present. As Friedman (1965), referring to Buber, highlights:

> Making the other present means 'to imagine the real' to imagine quite concretely what another . . . is wishing, feeling, perceiving, and thinking . . . a bold swinging into the other which demands the intensest action of one's being . . . One can only do this as a partner, standing in a common situation with the other. (p. 29)

Naomi's deeply felt sense of Laura as a woman who embodied knowing of Alicia, made visible Naomi's "bold swinging" into the story she perceived Laura was living. The "public homeplace" shaped between Naomi and Laura was the classroom, a safe place in which they could authentically enter into one another's presence (Belenky, Bond, & Weinstock, 1997).

7.3 Borders of Positional Power

(46)   The borders of positional power emerged for Naomi when she recognized that the larger school story of inclusion being played out on her school landscape came to define Brian as someone who had direct power

and influence within her in-classroom place. Naomi's tension with Brian centered around his positioning which allowed him to solely select the teachers with whom the students with special needs would be placed. Her understanding of the role Brian played within the school context drew forth an immediate border for Naomi, between herself and Brian. Naomi saw herself positioned on one side, with no voice in decision making, while Brian was positioned on the other side, with a powerful decision making voice. This border of power manifested itself in multiple ways through the response exchanged on the school landscape.

7.3.1 Sameness

(47)   In the discussion surrounding the report card which took place at the school office, the border was shaped by response which dictated a message of unity in which, "We all must be the same"—a message common on school landscapes and one shaped by forces of power and control in out-of-classroom places. Naomi's challenging of this response was seen as a threat to the unified story of school. Unlike the response she received regarding the school timetable, this response restricted her story to live by and forced her into conflict with the school story of inclusion. In this social context, personal relation in favour of the elements of pure collectivity" (Friedman, 1965, p. 25) and Naomi's story to live by, with its central plotline of human relatedness, was placed at great risk.

7.3.2 Distance

(48)   A border of distance became present in the story through the manner in which the second reporting period was addressed. The face-to-face conflict which emerged through the response to "sameness" sent from the school office was reshaped to a more distant and evasive form of response as messages were delivered indirectly from those in positions of power on the school landscape. Naomi's telling of her expectation that Brian would come and meet with her regarding the marks he placed on Alicia's report card, awakened us to a widening gap forming between the imagined and actual response which took place in this story, and how profoundly this response was being shaped by the larger school story. When Brian's actual response of not coming to engage in conversation with Naomi did not meet with her expectation, her tension over this distance between her imagined and his actual response was intensified and the space between solidified. As Friedman (in Buber, 1965) writes, "When [we] fail to enter into relation . . . the distance thickens and solidifies; instead of making room for relation it obstructs it" (p. 22). It became apparent to us that as the school story of inclusion thickened and reified itself on the school landscape, so too, did the relational story being lived out between Naomi and Brian. For Naomi, this distancing response came in conflict with her embodied knowing of living in relationship with others, pushing the story she was attempting to author into a vulnerable and isolating place on this school landscape.

7.3.3 Confrontation

(49)   Naomi's need to confront the multiple borders, forming both within herself and between herself and others on the exterior landscape of her school, caused her story to live by to enter an even more fragile state as her experience and understanding of the story of inclusion became even more marginalized. Naomi's recognition of her more vulnerable place on this school landscape did not prevent her from attempting to create an opening through conversation with Brian regarding the report cards, however, in the process, she inadvertently strengthened the existing borders between them, shaping additional ones as well. The relational story Naomi

was determined to negotiate was "rapidly redefined on the landscape as [a] conflicting story" (Clandinin & Connelly, 1995).

7.3.4 Arrogance

(50)   One of these additional borders appeared to be that of arrogance as Brian responded to Naomi's search for understanding by consciously separating himself from both Naomi and Laura, redefining his positioning to Naomi in terms of power over as her "supervisor" and "monitor." This new event in the space between brought forth an emotional response in Naomi which caused a shift in her image of Brian as well as her image of self (Josselson, 1992). This new border or arrogance hastened the solidification process of the school story and caused Naomi to rage against it as her story to live by struggled to survive. It was becoming, "more and more difficult to penetrate the increasingly tough layer which [had] settled down on . . . [her] being" (Buber, 1965, p. 78).

7.4 *Borders of Judgment and Silence*

(51)   Naomi's conscious decision to live her story—one which ran counter to the school story—positioned her in a place of extreme vulnerability. This was powerfully illuminated through the silencing response she received from her school administrators regarding Brian and the school story of inclusion. The message of support and acceptance of the school story at any cost was uncovered for us in Buber's (1965) description of social contexts in which, "the life between person and person seems to retreat more and more before the advance of the collective" (p. 73). The response from both her principal and vice-principal created a border of secrecy and silence, pushing Naomi's story to live by to the far "ragged edges" (Greene, 1994) of the advancing school story. Living on that edge equated to living in isolation as the space for relatedness became more scarce on Naomi's school landscape. For Naomi, who understood her world through deep and connected relationship with others, this edge became too fragile a place on which to stand. Without the embeddedness of her relational story within this social context, Naomi had no "place" to "exist." Hope came through an ultimate act of resistance for Naomi—leaving her school. Like bell hooks (1997), who so knowingly describes this critical moment of self recovery, "standing on the edge of the cliff about to fall into the abyss, I remember who I am" (p. 182), we imagine that Naomi may have experienced a similar awakening. We have no way of knowing what Naomi's response of resistance may have done to reshape the school story of inclusion. However, we do know that Naomi's leaving moved her to an educative place in which she could be true to herself—one best described through her own words:

> I think that's very difficult to stand on the outside of things and say, 'Yes, I will fight for this.' I think that it's only really when you come into those places of 'there is an end to this' that you can make that choice . . . I made the decision that if things weren't going to change there, then I was going to leave. . . . I made that decision, now I'm free to say what I want.

Qualitative interpretations situate findings within larger meanings.

8. Imagining Possibilities

> Those who have been excluded by the mainstream, or who have chosen to live and/or learn apart from it, may be the very people to help us find particularly effective ways to learn in community—ways less skewed by conformity, less dominated by institutional aspirations; ways perhaps truer to the basic human needs we all . . . share—to first and foremost feel that we matter to those around us (Heller, 1997, p. 160)

(52)   There is no doubt that Naomi was profoundly influenced by telling and living her story of herself on this school landscape. Had she a choice in living

her story, she may not have eventually resigned from her position at this school. However, as Clandinin and Connelly (195) have highlighted, "teachers must, of necessity, tell stories . . . because . . . [storytelling] is . . . the most basic way, that humans make meaning of their experience" (p. 154). Naomi's need to mediate her story to live by as she negotiated the school landscape, shifted her experience of this professional context from educative to miseducative. This may not have occurred if she had continued to tell her story only within the confines of her in-classroom place on the school landscape. Unlike so many of the teachers with whom Clandinin and Connelly worked, who told "cover stories" of themselves as a way to manage their tensions between the in- and out-of-classroom places on the professional knowledge landscape, Naomi did not, even though doing so was at her own peril, pushing her to a marginalized and isolated place on her school landscape (p. 157). So what was it that drew Naomi to keep trying to tell her story on the out-of-classroom place on her school landscape even after she was told to be silent?

(53)　We believe that Naomi's resistance to telling a cover story was grounded within her story to live by of "one-caring" for others (Noddings, 1984). It was this that enabled her to remain ever present to her embodied knowledge of herself. Because Naomi's embodied knowing of herself as a teacher was immersed in an "ethic of care," she could not take her gaze off her responsibility as the lived in caring relation with her students. It was this thread within Naomi's story that made it necessary for her to cross over the border between her in- and out-of-classroom places. However, radically different from the response she had experienced within her in-classroom place, the response on the out-of-classroom place was not grounded in relation but, instead, shifted to negotiating her story to live by through a conduit-delivered mandate on inclusive education. In the beginning fragments of her story, we sensed her hopefulness about this negotiation but as her story continued it seemed to become evident to Naomi that little, if anything, was negotiated on the out-of-classroom place. Although this moral dilemma caused tension for Naomi, she refused to deny her knowing or to fall into the plotline inscribed for her through the school story.

(54)　Early on in our work, as Naomi shared her story of marginalization and again as we pulled it forward from the transcript, we felt a deep sense of hopelessness about the way in which we read her story as profoundly and miseducatively shaping her story to live by. We kept focusing on the conclusion of this story and Naomi's decision to leave her school landscape. What we could not see at such a distance from her telling were the possibilities which her story offered. Only as we began to explore the intricacies of Naomi's story did we begin to awaken to the educative ways in which the meaning of this story was reshaped. It was Naomi's resistance, lived out in this story, that became educative for each of the teacher co-researchers engaged in this inquiry.

(55)　Our first awakening occurred as we tried to make sense of what drew Naomi to keep trying to tell her story on the out-of-classroom place on her school landscape even after she was told to be silent. We were drawn back to Naomi's introduction to her story where she described her sense of living outside the status quo story of her school. What could we learn from her story of choosing to position herself in such a marginal place on her school landscape? Returning to the literature where other writers had shared their experiences of such positionings, we began to reread Naomi's story in new ways.

(56)　Were these marginal positionings not more hopeful than those positionings which shaped the living and telling of cover stories? Anzaldúa (1990) helped us to think harder about what can happen to our sense of self as these masking roles exact a toll—"After years of wearing masks we may become just a series of roles, the constellated self limping along with its broken limbs" (p. xv). Naomi's story certainly did not present such an empty and debilitating image of herself. On the contrary, our continual rereading of Naomi's story led us to uncover stronger images of her personhood. Naomi's story was not one of internalized oppression imposed upon her from a distance. Instead, we saw Naomi as a woman who was intent on acquiring her own agency, of authoring her own story to live by. Unlike the school story which seemed disembodied, Naomi's story to live by was grounded in a narrative history which seemed to offer her the strength to sustain her isolated positioning in places on her school landscape outside her classroom. Drawing on Hurtado's (1996) notion of how we acquire and use "subjugated knowledge," we wondered if Naomi's deep sense of presence to her embodied knowing of self had enabled her to temporarily suspend or repress the "knowledge" pouring onto her school landscape through a sacred story of inclusive education. Was her alternative understanding of this story what enabled her to "resist structures of oppression and create interstices of rebellion and potential revolution" (p. 386)? Had it been her presence to her own knowing which had enabled her to dwell within an in-between positioning, gaining the courage to name the lack of spaces for differing ways of knowing to exist on her school landscape? We believe so. And, in this believing, we came to recognize Naomi's story as a place of possibility—possibility for understanding the central role that presence to our narrative histories plays in enabling us to live and to sustain stories that run counter to those being scripted for us on school landscapes.

Acknowledgements

We wish to express our gratitude to D. Jean Clandinin and F. Michael Connelly for their ongoing contributions to our work, and would also like to acknowledge the support of their grant through the Social Sciences and Humanities Research Council of Canada.

It is necessary for us to recognize the relational context in which this paper was written. Our knowing is a relational knowing that can never be reduced by a hierarchical ordering of names.

> Qualitative research reports use flexible and emerging structures and evaluation criteria.

References

Anzaidúa, G (Ed.). (1990). *Making faces, making soul = Haciendo caras: Creative and critical perspectives by feminists of color.* San Francisco: Aunt Lute Books.

Anzaidúa, G. (1987). *Borderlands: The new mestica = La frontera.* San Francisco: Aunt Lute Book Company.

Belenky, M., Bond, L., & Weinstock, J. (1997). *A tradition that has no name: Nurturing the development of people, families, and communities.* New York: BasicBooks.

Buber, M. (1965). *The knowledge of man.* (M. Friedman, & R. G. Smith, Trans.). London: George Allen and Unwin Ltd.

Carr, D. (1986). *Time, narrative, and history.* Bloomington, IN: Indiana University Press.

Clandinin, D. J. (1997). Authoring lives: stories to live by on the professional knowledge landscape. AERA address, April, 1997.

Clandinin, D. J., & Connelly, F. M. (1998). Asking questions about telling stories. In C. Kridel (Ed.), *Writing educational biography: Explorations in qualitative research* (pp. 202–209). New York: Garland.

Clandinin, D. J., & Connelly, F. M. (1994). Personal experience methods. In N. K. Denzin and Y. S. Lincoln (Eds.), *Handbook of qualitative research* (pp. 413—427). London: Sage Publications.

Clandinin, D. J., & Connelly, F. M. (1995). *Teachers' professional knowledge landscapes.* New York: Teachers College Press.

Clandinin, D. J. & Connelly, F. M. (1996). Teachers' professional knowledge landscapes: Teacher stories—stories of teachers—school stories—stories of schools. *Educational Researcher, 25*(3), 24–30.

Connelly, F. M., & Clandinin, D. J. (1988). *Teachers as curriculum planners: Narratives of experience.* Toronto, ON: The Ontario Institute for Studies in Education.

Connelly, F. M., & Clandinin, D. J. (1990). Stories of experience and narrative inquiry. *Educational Researcher, 19*(5), 2–14.

Connelly, F. M., & Clandinin, D. J. (1999). *Storied identities: Storied landscapes.* New York: Teachers College Press, in press.

Crites, S. (1971). The narrative quality of experience. *Journal of the American academy of religion, 39*(3), 291–311.

Dewey, J. (1938). *Experiences and education.* New York: Collier Books.

Greene, M. (1995). *Releasing the imagination: Essays on education, the arts, and social change.* San Francisco: Jossey-Bass Inc.

Greene, M. (1994). Multiculturalism, community, and the arts. In A. Dyson, & C. Genishi (Eds.), *The need for story: Cultural diversity in classroom and community* (pp. 11–27). New York: Teachers College Press.

Greene, M. (1993). Diversity and inclusion: toward a curriculum for human beings, *Teachers College Record, 95*(2), 211–211.

Heller, C. (1997). *Until we are strong together: Women writers in the Tenderloin.* New York: Teachers College Press.

hooks, b. (1996). *Bone black: Memories of girlhood.* New York: Henry Holt and Company.

Hurtado, A. (1996). Strategic suspensions: feminists of color theorize the production of knowledge. In N. Goldberger, J. Tarule, B. Clinchy, & M. Belenky (Eds.), *Knowledge, difference, and power: Essays inspired by Women's Ways of Knowing* (pp. 372–388). New York: BasicBooks.

Josselson, R. (1992). *The space between us: Exploring the dimensions of human relationships.* San Francisco: Jossey-Bass Publishers.

Miller, J. (1994). "The surprise of a recognizable person" as troubling presence in educational research and writing, *Curriculum Inquiry, 24*(4), 503–512.

Nelson, N. (1995). Resistance and insubordination, *Hypatia, 10*(2), 23–40.

Noddings, N. (1984). *Caring: A feminine approach to ethics and moral education.* Los Angeles: University of California Press.

Mixed Method Designs

Let's assume that Maria, our high school teacher, chooses to collect both quantitative and qualitative data. She might decide to conduct a survey and also engage in follow-up interviews with a few students to explain the importance of weapon possession in high schools. She would be interested in both explaining the factors associated with weapon possession and exploring the meaning of weapons to students in more detail. Her research question in the initial (quantitative) phase of the study would be: What factors relate to attitudes toward weapon possession? In the follow-up (qualitative) phase, her question would be: What are students' experiences with weapons in high schools?

To conduct this study, Maria would need time for collecting and analyzing both quantitative and qualitative data. Maria would also need to prepare an organized project so that she knows when the quantitative and qualitative phases will occur in her study. Designing a picture of her procedures, deciding what quantitative results will lead to her qualitative interviews, and interpreting, overall, results from both phases, will be challenging tasks for Maria as she undertakes a rigorous, mixed method design in educational research.

To engage in a mixed method design, such as Maria's project, you conduct a research study in which you collect, analyze, and report both quantitative (i.e., numbers) and qualitative (i.e., words and images) data. Consider the advantages of collecting *both* forms of information. Quantitative data, such as scores on instruments, yield specific numbers that can be statistically analyzed and can produce results to assess the frequency and magnitude of trends. It also offers useful information describing a large number of people. On the other hand, qualitative data, such as open-ended interviews that provide actual words of people in the study, offer many different perspectives on the study topic and provide a complex picture of the situation. When quantitative and qualitative data are combined, "we have a very powerful mix" (Miles & Huberman, 1994, p. 42).

Educators such as policy makers appreciate the "numbers" of broad trends as well as the "words" of specific individuals. Teachers seek out the "words" of children to support the latest "numbers" in trends about the educational needs of kids. With qualitative research being recognized and appreciated by more and more educators, and with quantitative research long-established as an approach, mixed method research has become popular as a "legitimate inquiry approach" (Brewer &

Hunter, 1989, p. 28). If you have access to both quantitative and qualitative data, and seek to take advantage of the strengths of each, a mixed method project is a rigorous, suitable procedure for a study. If you are reading a research study in which the authors collect both forms of data, they are using a mixed method design, although they may not label it as such.

By perusing educational journals, you can find good illustrations of mixed method studies. For example, consider the following research projects.

▶ In a study about science attitudes and achievements of seventh- and eighth-grade students, Houtz (1995) first collected quantitative data and then gathered qualitative data to help explain the quantitative results. She collected quantitative, demographic data and scores on three attitude and achievement tests. Not satisfied that she could explain the quantitative results from this data, she then turned to qualitative, open-ended interviews with teachers, the school principal, and a university consultant. With this information, she explored the reasons why attitudes toward science improved while differences appeared in achievement for seventh-grade students.

▶ Nath, Ross, and Smith (1995/1996) took a different approach to data collection. They conducted a study about the implementation process of a cooperative learning model—where students actively helped each other learn—in one elementary school. The investigators collected classroom observations, individual and focus group interviews (qualitative data) and also questionnaires (quantitative data) from the principal and teachers in the school. They analyzed both sets of data simultaneously to understand the process of implementing the model and concluded that teachers became proficient in using the model but needed considerable planning and monitoring to ensure its success.

▶ Two researchers (Klassen & Burnaby, 1993) used both quantitative and qualitative approaches to explore the topic of adult immigrants to Canada who spoke little English and who had little literacy experience. Available census statistics and survey data first provided quantitative information about the immigrants. Then the researchers turned to qualitative data "for a richer understanding" (p. 377). They collected qualitative interviews from nine Latin American adults and learned that literacy needs exist in both Spanish and English for immigrants to Canada.

In all three of the above studies, the authors collected both quantitative and qualitative data. In two of them, they collected the data sequentially and in the other, concurrently or simultaneously. Although not apparent in these three examples, the authors may have given different weight to the quantitative and qualitative data collection.

A **mixed method research design** is a procedure for collecting both quantitative and qualitative data in a single study, and analyzing and reporting this data based on a priority and sequence of information.

By the end of this chapter you should be able to:

▶ Identify major events in the historical development of mixed method research.
▶ Distinguish among three types of mixed method designs.
▶ Weigh strengths and weaknesses of mixed method research.
▶ Describe six key characteristics of this form of research.
▶ Describe steps in conducting a mixed method study.
▶ List criteria useful in evaluating a mixed method design.

A BRIEF HISTORY OF MIXED METHOD DESIGNS

To best understand the underlying characteristics of mixed method research, it is helpful to examine briefly the origin of this design. Its historical development has been sketched elsewhere (e.g., Datta, 1994; Tashakkori & Teddlie, 1998) and this review builds on these earlier discussions. This history is best displayed through several phases:

- the initial interest in mixing forms of quantitative data collection (late 1950s)
- the expansion of forms to include both quantitative and qualitative data (1970s to present)
- the question of mixing worldviews and methods (mid 1980s to present)
- the rise of interest in procedures (late 1980s to present)
- the advocacy for a distinct mixed method design (1990s to present)

Mixing Forms of Quantitative Data

Since the 1930s, educational and social science investigators have combined research methods of data collection in their studies (Sieber, 1973). However, it was the multitrait, multimethod approach advanced by Campbell and Fiske (1959) that stimulated interest in employing multiple methods in a single study. Campbell and Fiske's interest was not in mixed method research; rather, they sought to develop valid psychological traits. To develop these traits, they suggested a process whereby researchers would collect multiple measures of multiple traits, and assess each measure by at least two methods. When scores were correlated and placed into a matrix—a multimethod, multitrait matrix resulted. An investigator could determine if the trait was valid by examining this matrix and assessing whether the measures of the trait correlated higher with each other than they did with measures of different traits involving separate methods. Evidence from these correlations provided useful information about different forms of validity. But at a broader level, the use of multiple methods to measure a trait encouraged other researchers to collect more than one type of data, even if this data was only quantitative, such as peer judgement scores and word association tests.

Expanding Use of Combined Quantitative and Qualitative Data

Soon others were collecting both quantitative and qualitative data. By 1973, Sieber suggested the combination of in-depth case studies with surveys, creating a "new style of research" and the "integration" of research techniques within a single study (Sieber, 1973, p. 1337). A few years later, Jick (1979) used the combination of surveys, semi-structured interviews, observations, and archival materials to provide a "rich and comprehensive picture" (p. 606) of anxiety and job insecurity during organizational mergers.

Jick's (1979) study was more than an examination of mergers; his article used the merger study to illustrate the procedure of triangulating data. Triangulation, a term drawn from naval military science, is the process where sailors use multiple reference points to locate an object's exact position at sea (Jick, 1979). Applied to research, it meant that investigators could improve their inquiries by collecting and converging (or integrating) different kinds of data bearing on the same phenomenon. This improvement would come from blending the strengths of one type of method and neutralizing the weaknesses of the other. For example, in a study of middle school principal leadership, a researcher can augment qualitative observations of behavior with a quantitative survey that provides greater confidence in the generalizability of results. On the other hand, qualitative observations can provide the context in which this leadership is enacted, and help clarify quantitative statistical relationships and numeric findings. To triangulate or converge data in a single study continues to be an attractive approach to mixed method research today.

Questioning the Integration of Worldviews and Methods

Further developments on procedures, however, had to wait for several years. The paradigm debate developed that would question the legitimacy of mixed method research (Reichardt & Cook, 1979). This debate was more than tension between those who embraced traditional quantitative research and those advocating for qualitative inquiry. Basically, the issue was whether a researcher who used certain methods also needed to use a specific worldview— the "compatibility" (Tashakkori & Teddlie, 1998) between worldviews and methods. Worldviews are the broad philosophical assumptions researchers use when they conduct studies. Although some researchers may not recognize it, they make assumptions about knowledge (e.g., math scores exist for seventh graders) and how it can be obtained (e.g., we can measure math ability using standardized achievement tests). Those who argued for "incompatibility" said that quantitative methods (e.g., student scores on an instrument) belonged to the quantitative worldview (e.g., an attempt to measure, objectively, student achievement). Further qualitative methods (e.g., an observation of students) should be undertaken only within a qualitative worldview (e.g., the researcher assesses reality subjectively through his or her lens). The logic of this argument led to the conclusion that mixed method research was untenable because a single worldview did not exist for the inquiry.

The worldview-method argument played out for several years, during the late 1980s and early 1990s, especially at national conferences such as the American Evaluation Association annual meetings (Reichardt & Rallis, 1994). But it has largely diminished because of several factors. Some said that those who argued for the incompatibility of worldviews and methods created a false dichotomy (Reichardt & Cook, 1979) that does not hold under close inspection. For example, there is an "objective" reality (e.g., the classroom), but there is also a "subjective" reality (e.g., we see different things as we look at a classroom). Certainly some methods are more closely associated with one worldview than the other, but to categorize them as "belonging" to one method more than another creates an unrealistic situation.

Others contended that mixed method research has its own philosophical worldview. The pragmatists, for example, believe philosophically in "what works" for a particular research problem under study and that all methods should be used in understanding a research problem (e.g., see discussion by Tashakkori & Teddlie, 1998). Closely related to the pragmatist position is the "unity thesis," which asserts that the idea of worldviews is mistaken and incoherent (Walker & Evers, 1988; Creswell, Goodchild, & Turner, 1996), thus opening the possibility for using mixed methods without substantial concern for its philosophical underpinnings. In addition, the "dialectical" position, embraced by Greene and Caracelli (1997), recommends that researchers report the worldviews they hold—thus honoring worldviews as important—as well as collect both quantitative and qualitative data.

Developing Procedures for Mixed Method Studies

Another factor that quieted the debate was the increased interest in the procedural aspects of mixed method research. Authors explored the "purposes" of mixed method research, identified alternative designs that might be used, and specified a notation system and visual models for these designs.

The idea of triangulation had already introduced one purpose for mixing methods— to integrate multiple databases to best understand a phenomenon and research problem (Rossman & Wilson, 1985). Other reasons soon emerged. Quantitative and qualitative data could be collected separately in two phases so that data from one source could enhance, elaborate, or complement data from the other source (Rossman & Wilson, 1985; Greene, Caracelli, & Graham, 1989). In more complicated designs, the data collection could extend from two to three phases (e.g., see Miles & Huberman, 1994) or be collected from multiple levels in an organization, such as the district, school, teacher, and student (e.g., see Tashakkori & Teddlie, 1998). It could also be nested, with one form of data becoming "less dominant" in a "dominant" design based on the other form of data (Creswell, 1994).

Central to this thinking about different models or designs has been the visualization of procedures and the use of a notation system designed by Morse (1991). This system, shown in Figure 17.1, is a way to portray the procedures in mixed method designs.

▶ Arrows indicate the sequential collection of data (e.g., qualitative collected first followed by quantitative).
▶ A "+" shows the simultaneous collection of both quantitative and qualitative data.
▶ Uppercase letters indicate a priority given to one form of data over the other.
▶ Lowercase letters show a lower priority for one form of data over the other.
▶ Shorthand labels for quantitative (quan) and qualitative (qual) simplify the terms.

Figure 17.1 also portrays two sample designs. As shown in Study #1, a researcher places an emphasis on both quantitative and qualitative data and integrates or combines the data in the study. In Study #2, the investigator emphasizes quantitative data in the first phase of a study followed by a minor emphasis on qualitative data in the second phase of the study. Later in this chapter we will consider names for these designs and explore several variations of them.

Advocating for a Distinct Design

With emerging procedures, a notation system, and specific designs, the discussion recently has turned to viewing mixed method research as a separate and distinct design. To experiments, surveys, grounded theory, and others, we now add mixed method research. Advocates for this design have written entire chapters and books about mixed method designs

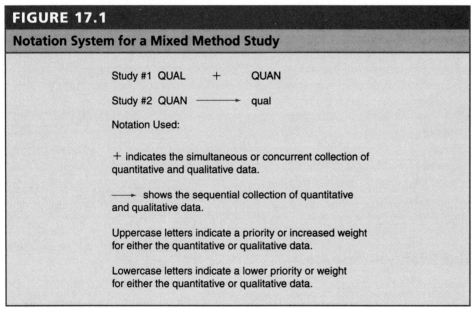

FIGURE 17.1

Notation System for a Mixed Method Study

Study #1 QUAL   +   QUAN

Study #2 QUAN ⟶ qual

Notation Used:

+ indicates the simultaneous or concurrent collection of quantitative and qualitative data.

⟶ shows the sequential collection of quantitative and qualitative data.

Uppercase letters indicate a priority or increased weight for either the quantitative or qualitative data.

Lowercase letters indicate a lower priority or weight for either the quantitative or qualitative data.

Source: Morse, 1991.

(Greene & Caracelli, 1997; Reichardt & Rallis, 1994; Tashakkori & Teddlie, 1998). In addition, refinements continue in the process of integrating quantitative and qualitative data analysis (Caracelli & Greene, 1993), the use of computer programs for merging quantitative statistical programs with text analysis programs (Bazeley, 2000), and the identification and discussion of numerous mixed method studies reported in the scholarly literature (e.g., Greene, Caracelli, & Graham, 1992; Datta, 1994; Creswell, Goodchild, & Turner, 1996).

TYPES OF MIXED METHOD DESIGNS

Although work has begun on identifying types of mixed method designs, many models and approaches have been advanced in the literature (to review the possibilities, see the helpful discussions by Greene, Caracelli, & Graham, 1989; Morgan, 1998; Steckler, et al., 1992; and Tashakkori & Teddlie, 1998). The strategy authors have taken is to review published studies and classify them by type of design (e.g., see Greene, Caracelli, & Graham, 1989).

Before examining the types of designs, it might be helpful to reflect on useful strategies for identifying a mixed method study reported in the published literature. One strategy is to ask the following questions to help you identify a study as mixed method research:

▶ *Is there evidence in the title?* Look at the title to determine if it includes words such as "quantitative and qualitative," "mixed method," or other related terms to signify the collection of both quantitative and qualitative data. Related terms might be "integrated," "combined," "triangulation," "multimethod," "mixed model," or "mixed methodology." (See Reichardt & Rallis, 1994; Tashakkori & Teddlie, 1998.)
▶ *Is there evidence in the data collection section?* Examine the "methods" or "procedure" section where the author addresses data collection. Are the forms of quantitative data (i.e., numbers reported) and qualitative data (i.e., words or images) discussed as part of the data collection procedure?
▶ *Is there evidence in the purpose statement or the research questions?* Examine the abstract or the introduction of the study to identify the purpose or research questions. Do these statements indicate that the researcher intends to collect both quantitative and qualitative data during the study?

Having identified the study as mixed method, next determine the type of mixed method design the author is using. You might ask the following questions:

▶ *What priority or weight does the researcher give to the quantitative and qualitative data collection?* Often one form of data is given more attention or emphasis; however, they are sometimes treated equally.
▶ *What is the sequence of collecting the quantitative and qualitative data?* Determine what comes first and then second in the data collection.
▶ *How does the researcher actually analyze the data?* Determine if the data are combined in one analysis or kept separate.

Using these three questions, you can locate and identify most mixed method designs commonly used in educational research. Figure 17.2 illustrates three of these designs: the triangulation design, the explanatory design, and the exploratory design.

The Triangulation Design

From the historical sketch you have already gained a familiarity with the triangulation design (Jick, 1979). The purpose of a **triangulation mixed method design** is to simultaneously collect both quantitative and qualitative data, merge the data, and use the results to

FIGURE 17.2

Types of Mixed Method Designs

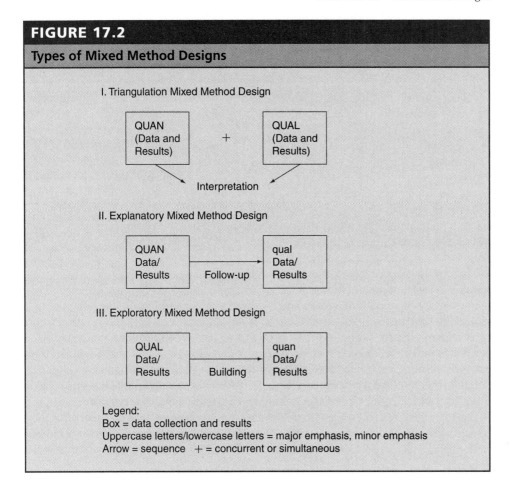

I. Triangulation Mixed Method Design

QUAN (Data and Results)   +   QUAL (Data and Results)

Interpretation

II. Explanatory Mixed Method Design

QUAN Data/Results   Follow-up   qual Data/Results

III. Exploratory Mixed Method Design

QUAL Data/Results   Building   quan Data/Results

Legend:
Box = data collection and results
Uppercase letters/lowercase letters = major emphasis, minor emphasis
Arrow = sequence   + = concurrent or simultaneous

best understand a research problem. A basic rationale for this design is that one data collection form supplies strengths to offset the weaknesses of the other form. For example, quantitative scores on an instrument provide strengths to offset the weaknesses of qualitative documents. Alternatively, qualitative, in-depth observation offers strength to quantitative data that does not adequately provide information about the setting.

How does the process of a triangulation study work? The researcher gathers both quantitative and qualitative data, compares results from the analysis of both data, and makes an interpretation as to whether the results from both data support or contradict each other. The direct comparison of the two data sets provides a "triangulation" of data sources. As shown in Figure 17.2, in this design:

▶ *The mixed method researcher gives equal priority to both quantitative and qualitative data (see QUAN and QUAL).* The researcher values both quantitative and qualitative data and sees them as approximately equal sources of information in the study. For example, interview data is as important as the scores gathered on an instrument.

▶ *The mixed method researcher collects both the quantitative and qualitative data simultaneously during the study.* Documents about what the students learn in preschool are reviewed, for example, at the same time that the researcher collects observations on student behavior using a checklist.

▶ *The mixed method researcher compares the results from quantitative and qualitative analysis to determine if the two databases yield similar or dissimilar results.* For instance, qualitative themes identified during interviews are "quantified" and given a score as to their frequency. These scores are then compared with scores from instruments measuring variables that address the same ideas as the themes.

The strength of this design is that it combines the advantages of each form of data; that is, quantitative data provides for generalizability while qualitative data offers information about the context or setting. This design enables a researcher to gather information that uses the best features of both quantitative and qualitative data collection. One difficulty with this design is the need to translate one form of data into the other form so that the databases can be integrated and compared. Moreover, even if integration is possible, inconsistent results may emerge, making it necessary to collect additional data to reconcile the differences.

In a triangulation mixed method study, Russek and Weinberg (1993) collected both quantitative and qualitative data at the same time and used results from both forms to understand the implementation of technology in an elementary school. They sought to examine how 16 elementary school teachers implemented two sets of supplementary mathematics lessons, one utilizing the calculator and one utilizing the computer. To study this process, they conducted qualitative interviews with teachers and administrators, made informal classroom observations, examined school documents, and obtained teacher responses to open-ended questions on questionnaires. Quantitatively, they gathered classroom observation checklists, Lesson and Workshop Evaluation Forms, and collected two self-reported measures of teacher feelings, attitudes, and concerns (i.e., the Self-Evaluation Questionnaire and the Stages of Concern Questionnaire). Their purpose in mixing methods was to provide a complete picture of the implementation process. They discussed how triangulated data could show convergence, inconsistency, and complementary results. For example, they compared results from teacher questionnaires with interview themes about using both the calculator and computers in the classroom. Finding inconsistencies in the results, they attributed this difference to the teachers' reluctance to put on paper what they revealed freely in their oral remarks. They also felt that the questionnaire was less valid because the teachers might have felt that the questionnaires would be placed into their files as part of their permanent personnel record.

The Explanatory Design

Instead of collecting data at the same time, a mixed method researcher might collect quantitative and qualitative information sequentially or in two phases. This design, also shown in Figure 17.2, is an explanatory mixed method design, perhaps the most popular form of mixed method designs in educational research. An **explanatory mixed method design** (also called a two-phase model, Creswell, 1994) consists of first collecting quantitative data and then collecting qualitative data to help explain or elaborate on the quantitative results. The rationale for this approach is that the quantitative data and results provide a general picture of the research problem; more analysis, specifically through qualitative data collection, is needed to refine, extend, or explain the general picture. Referring back to Figure 17.2, you can see that in this design,

▶ *The mixed method researcher places a priority on quantitative data (QUAN) collection and analysis.* This is done by introducing it first in the study and having it represent a major aspect of data collection. A small qualitative (qual) component follows in the second phase of the research.
▶ *The mixed method researcher collects quantitative data first in the sequence.* This is followed by the secondary qualitative data collection. Researchers often present these studies in two phases, with each phase clearly identified in headings in the report.
▶ *The mixed method researcher uses the qualitative data to refine the results from the quantitative data.* This refinement results in exploring a few typical cases, probing a key result in more detail, or following up with outlier or extreme cases.

This design has the advantage of clearly identified quantitative and qualitative parts, an advantage for readers as well as for those designing and conducting the study. Unlike the triangulation design, the researcher does not have to converge or integrate two different forms of data. This design also captures the best of both quantitative and qualitative data— to obtain quantitative results from a population in the first phase, and then refine or elaborate these findings through an in-depth qualitative exploration in the second phase. The difficulty in using this design, however, is that the researcher needs to determine what aspect of the quantitative results to use in the follow-up (e.g., a rejected hypothesis or a hypothesis that failed to be rejected?). Also, this design is labor-intensive, and it requires both expertise and time to collect both quantitative and qualitative data.

A two-phase project by Blustein et al. (1997) is a good example of an explanatory design. Their research examined the school-to-work transition for 45 work-bound adults (ages 18–29) who had been out of high school for less than 10 years and who were neither college graduates nor current college students. The authors described their data collection and analysis strategy as follows: to "employ two initial quantitative methods to help focus and circumscribe our qualitative explorations" (p. 373). They gathered information from the 45 adults using a single interview protocol that contained closed- and open-ended questions. To this end, they first correlated two indexes to adaptive transition obtained from the closed-ended questions (i.e., job satisfaction and congruence). Isolating 14 variables for further analysis, they began the second phase, where they identified participants with either notably high or low scores on each measure and examined passages in their interview transcription to learn more about their transition experiences.

The Exploratory Design

Rather than first analyzing or collecting *quantitative data* as is done in the explanatory design, the mixed method researcher might begin with *qualitative data* and then collect quantitative information. The purpose of an **exploratory mixed method design** is the procedure of first gathering qualitative data to explore a phenomenon, and then collecting quantitative data to explain relationships found in the qualitative data. A popular application of this design is to explore a phenomenon, identify themes, design an instrument, and subsequently test it. Researchers use this design when existing instruments, variables, and measures may not be known or available for the population under study. Again refer to Figure 17.2. In this design,

▶ *The mixed method researcher emphasizes the qualitative data (QUAL) more than the quantitative data (quan).* This emphasis may occur through presenting the overarching question as an open-ended question or discussing the qualitative results in more detail than the quantitative results.

▶ *The mixed method researcher has a sequence to data collection that involves first collecting qualitative data followed by quantitative data.* Typically in these designs, the researcher presents the study in two phases with the first phase involving qualitative data collection (e.g., interviews, observations) with a small number of individuals followed by quantitative data collection (e.g., a survey) with a large, randomly selected number of participants.

▶ *The mixed method researcher plans on the quantitative data to build on or explain the initial qualitative findings.* The intent of the researcher is for the quantitative data results to refine and extend the qualitative findings. The initial qualitative exploration leads to detailed, generalizable results through the second quantitative phase.

One advantage of this approach is that it allows the researcher to identify measures actually grounded in the data obtained from study participants. The researcher can initially explore views by listening to participants rather than approach a topic with a predetermined set of variables. However, it has the disadvantage of requiring extensive data collection as well as the time required for this process. The testing of an instrument adds considerably to the length of time this design requires to be implemented. It also requires researchers to make decisions about the most appropriate themes to measure in the follow-up quantitative phase of the study.

In the exploratory mixed method design by Holland, Chait, and Taylor (1989), the researchers used qualitative data to develop and test a quantitative instrument. They examined the effectiveness of boards of trustees in liberal arts and comprehensive colleges. The authors state that "the qualitative approach to this topic provided the basis for the development of a grounded theoretical framework that could subsequently be subjected to more rigorous quantitative specification and empirical testing" (p. 439). The qualitative first phase of the study consisted of interviews with 46 trustees at 10 colleges. From this data, the researchers identified six board competencies (e.g., understand institutional context, builds capacity for learning). In the second phase of the study, the researchers identified 12 new sites, developed the competencies into a questionnaire, and gathered self-reported data from trustees. They also collected interviews and obtained institutional performance measures. A third phase was to test the instrument more broadly with 357 trustees at the 12 sites used in the second phase.

STRENGTHS AND WEAKNESSES OF MIXED METHOD RESEARCH

Before learning the actual steps researchers use to conduct a mixed method study, you might consider first whether this design is an appropriate one to use. Designing and conducting a mixed study requires both quantitative and qualitative data. But the availability of this data is not reason enough to engage in this form of inquiry. Making a decision as to the appropriateness of this form of design requires weighing the strengths and weaknesses.

Mixed method research is a good design to use if you seek to build on the strengths of both quantitative and qualitative data. It may help provide a complete picture of a research problem. For example, to assess both outcomes of a study (i.e., quantitative) as well as the process (i.e., qualitative) helps us develop "a complex" picture of social phenomenon (Greene & Caracelli, 1997, p. 7). Mixed method research also may be a means for incorporating a qualitative component into an otherwise quantitative study. Certain student program areas are less accepting of qualitative research than others. In these program areas, a mixed method study enables a student to negotiate a project that contains a qualitative component.

These advantages, however, must be weighed against the disadvantages of mixed method studies. This design requires training in both quantitative and qualitative research. Further, this design may be difficult to "sell" to reviewers not familiar with the design. They may need background information such as what is presented in this chapter. In addition, mixed method studies require extensive data collection (Bryman, 1988), more than the amount required to conduct a study that is either quantitative or qualitative. The costs and amount of time needed may be prohibitive for a single researcher. Indeed, an examination of published mixed method studies often shows that many are conducted by multiple, team researchers with external funds to support the extensive data collection procedures (e.g., Way et al., 1994). Finally, those who wish to conduct mixed method research need to assess the potential audiences for their studies. Have other researchers presented mixed method studies to your faculty committee? to a conference where you hope to present? to journals where you plan to publish your study?

KEY CHARACTERISTICS OF MIXED METHOD DESIGNS

All three types of mixed method designs include basic characteristics that distinguish this design from others. In reviewing the following six characteristics, consider incorporating them into your plan for a study if you intend to conduct a mixed method study. Also look for them in a mixed method study you might be reviewing or reading. They are:

- a justification by the researcher about why both quantitative and qualitative data are being collected
- the collection of both quantitative and qualitative forms of data
- information about the priority being given to quantitative or qualitative data
- information about the sequencing of the quantitative and qualitative data collection
- an analysis of the data shaped by the particular mixed method design
- a visual or figure that portrays the procedures of the design

Justifying Mixed Method Research

Readers and those that review mixed method studies need to know why you are mixing methods. Mixed method researchers include a justification or rationale for their use of both quantitative and qualitative data. For example, you may suggest that collecting quantitative data in a second phase is important to empirically test the themes from the qualitative first phase of the study (i.e., exploratory design). Alternatively, you may suggest that the "best" understanding of a problem emerges from using both quantitative (i.e., generalizable) as well as qualitative (i.e., in-depth, contextual) data (i.e., triangulation design). Whatever the rationale, an important component of any mixed method study is the reason for mixing or collecting quantitative and qualitative data. This rationale can typically be mentioned early in the study, such as in the introduction.

Collecting Quantitative and Qualitative Data

In any mixed method study, there should be a clear indication that you are collecting both quantitative and qualitative data. Methods of data collection are typically associated with either numbers or numeric data and words or text and image data. Mixed method researchers collect both quantitative and qualitative data.

A broader picture of data forms, introduced earlier in Chapters 6 and 7, is shown in Table 17.1. In this table, the columns show both methods and data. In practice, mixed method researchers use different methods to collect different forms of data. In a mixed method study, researchers include specific forms of both quantitative and qualitative data and incorporate this discussion into the methods or procedure section of the study.

Giving Priority to Quantitative or Qualitative Data

Mixed method researchers advance the weight or priority to the collection of quantitative and qualitative data. Three options are available to the researcher for prioritizing data:

- Quantitative and qualitative data are of equal weight.
- Quantitative data is of greater weight than qualitative data.
- Qualitative data is of greater weight than quantitative data.

Weight or **priority** means that the researcher in a mixed method design places more emphasis on one type of data than the other in the research and the written report. This

TABLE 17.1

Quantitative and Qualitative Methods of Data Collection and Types of Data

Quantitative Research		Qualitative Research	
Methods of Data Collection	**Data**	**Methods of Data Collection**	**Data**
Instruments (e.g., questionnaire, closed-ended interview; closed-ended observation)	Numeric scores	Open-ended interviews	Text data from transcribed interviews
Documents (e.g., census, attendance records)	Numeric scores	Open-ended questions on questionnaires	Text data transcribed from questionnaires
		Open-ended observations	Fieldnotes (text) from researcher's notes
		Documents (e.g., private or public)	Text data optically scanned from diaries, journals, letters, or official documents
		Visual materials	Image data from pictures, photography, or audiotapes

emphasis may result from personal experience with data collection, the need to understand one form of data before proceeding to the next, or the audience to which the research is directed. Whatever the reason, in examining a mixed method study for the author's priority, ask the following questions.

- What is emphasized more in the purpose statement—exploration or prediction of outcomes?
- Which data collection process—quantitative or qualitative—is given the most attention in the methods and results sections (e.g., number of pages in a report)?
- Which data collection process is examined in the most depth (e.g., detailed statistical analysis or multiple layered thematic analysis)?

Sequencing Quantitative and Qualitative Data

Mixed method researchers advance the **sequence** of data collection using concurrent or sequential approaches. Again, several options exist for the sequencing of data collection:

- The researcher collects both quantitative and qualitative data at the same time.
- Quantitative data is collected first, followed by qualitative data.
- Qualitative data is collected first, followed by quantitative data.

    If the purpose of the study is to explain quantitative results further with qualitative data (i.e., explanatory design) or to develop an instrument from qualitative data (i.e., exploratory design), the procedures should clearly indicate this sequence. The data collection procedures are independent of each other and typically presented as phases. If the intent of the study is to converge or triangulate the findings (i.e., triangulation design), then the data are collected at the same time and the researcher is explicit about this process. This process involves two data collection efforts that proceed simultaneously and are related to each other.

Analyzing Data Within Designs

One of the most difficult challenges for the mixed method researcher is how to analyze data collected from qualitative and quantitative research. This is more than simply being able to link or intersect data and numbers, although this connection does present some challenges. Several authors have begun the discussion about data analysis in mixed method research (Caracelli & Greene, 1993; Tashakkori & Teddlie, 1998). To examine options for data analysis, reflect back on the type of design and the options for analysis within each design. An overview of these options is presented in Table 17.2. This list is not meant to be comprehensive and to limit the creative potential of a mixed method researcher; it is largely to focus the discussion and present typical analytic procedures discussed by writers and illustrated in mixed method studies.

Analysis in a Triangulation Design

Of all of the designs, this analysis is perhaps the most difficult and controversial. The standard approach seems to be to converge or compare in some way both quantitative data (e.g., scores) with qualitative data (e.g., text). One way is to provide a discussion about the themes emerging from the data and how they support or refute the statistical analysis. In a study conducted about controversial art on college campuses (e.g., a painting or novel), the researcher might collect questionnaires from campus constituents as well as interview data from administrators, faculty, and students. The two sources of data might then be compared to determine if the interviews supported the questionnaire results.

    Another approach is to combine the qualitative and quantitative data to arrive at new variables or new themes for further testing or exploration. In the controversial art case, the interview data and questionnaires' scores could be combined to produce a new variable, such as the sensitivity of campus constituents to some forms of art. This variable becomes information for further exploration.

    Some mixed method researchers quantify qualitative data so that they can be directly compared with statistical results. The information from the interviews with campus personnel could be reduced to themes, and counts could be made of the number of times the themes were reported. The frequency of these themes could then be compared directly with the descriptive statistics about information from scales. Alternatively, the researcher might analyze the questionnaires, develop themes (or scales) that reflect issues surrounding campus art, and compare the themes to those generated by campus personnel during the qualitative interviews.

Analysis in an Explanatory Design

Because the data are collected in distinct phases, the analysis of an explanatory design is easier to see and conduct than in a triangulation design. A popular approach is to collect quantitative data and look for extreme cases to follow up in a qualitative phase. In a mixed method study about the transition of adults from school to work, Blustein et al. (1997) first conducted a quantitative correlational analysis of transition measures (i.e., job satisfaction and congruence) and then employed the results to provide an "in-depth and focused approach to analyze the corresponding qualitative narratives" (p. 373). Specifically,

TABLE 17.2

Type of Mixed Method Design and Data Analysis/Interpretation Procedures

Type of Mixed Method Design	Examples of Analytic and Interpretive Procedures
Triangulation (QUAN and QUAL data collected simultaneously)	• *Quantifying qualitative data:* Qualitative data are coded, codes are assigned numbers, and the number of times codes appear are recorded as numeric data. Quantitative data are descriptively analyzed for frequency of occurrence. The two data sets are compared. • *Qualifying quantitative data:* Quantitative data from questionnaires are factor analyzed. These factors then become themes that are compared with themes analyzed from qualitative data. • *Comparing results:* The results from qualitative data collection are directly compared with results from quantitative data collection. Statistical trends are supported by qualitative themes or vice versa. • *Consolidating data:* Qualitative data and quantitative data are combined to form new variables. Original quantitative variables are compared with qualitative themes to form new quantitative variables. (Caracelli & Greene, 1993)
Explanatory (QUAN followed by qual)	• *Following up on outliers or extreme cases:* Gather quantitative data and identify outlier or residual cases. Collect qualitative data to explore the characteristics of these cases. (Caracelli & Greene, 1993) • *Explaining results:* Conduct a quantitative survey to identify how two or more groups compare on a variable. Follow up with qualitative interviews to explore the reasons why these differences were found. • *Using a typology:* Conduct a quantitative survey and develop factors though a factor analysis. Use these factors as a typology to identify themes in qualitative data, such as observations or interviews. (Caracelli & Greene, 1993) • *Examining multi-levels:* Conduct a survey at the student level. Gather qualitative data through interviews at the class level. Survey the entire school at the school level. Collect qualitative data at the district level. Information from each level builds to the next level. (Tashakkori & Teddlie, 1998)
Exploratory (QUAL followed by quan)	• *Locating an instrument:* Collect qualitative data and identify themes. Use these themes as a basis for locating instruments that use parallel concepts to the qualitative themes. • *Developing an instrument:* Obtain themes and specific statements from individuals that support the themes. In the next phase, use these themes and statements to create scales and items as a questionnaire. Alternatively, look for existing instruments that can be modified to fit the themes and statements found in the qualitative exploratory phase of the study. After developing the instrument, test it out with a sample of a population. • *Forming categorical data:* Site-level characteristics (e.g., different ethnic groups) gathered in an ethnography in the first phase of a study becomes a categorical variable in a second phase correlational or regression study. (Caracelli & Greene, 1993) • *Using extreme qualitative cases:* Qualitative data cases that are extreme in a comparative analysis are followed in a second phase by quantitative surveys. (Caracelli & Greene, 1993)

they identified individuals with high and low scores (i.e., extreme cases) on the dependent measures and then conducted a qualitative, thematic analysis using interviews with these individuals.

Alternatively, within an explanatory design, the researcher might seek to explain the results in more depth in a qualitative phase of the study. This was the approach taken by Houtz (1995) in her study of attitudes and achievement of seventh- and eighth-grade science students. She first gathered survey data and found that her data on achievement and attitude were contradictory. Accordingly, in a follow-up qualitative phase, she interviewed science teachers, the school principal, and the university consultant.

Less frequently seen within the explanatory design is the use of a typology generated through quantitative data collection and the use of this typology as a framework for identifying themes in a qualitative database. If Houtz (1995) had actually looked for themes based on her statistical results, she would have used this approach. Another procedure is to conduct a multilevel study, much like the quantitative procedures in multilevel modeling. The application of this approach would have been to study children's attitudes, teachers' attitudes, and organizational characteristics that support views toward science in a school. In this project, the survey of children might be followed by teacher interviews, and then by census or document data from organizational school records.

Analysis in an Exploratory Design

In this design, the substantial qualitative data collection becomes a means for developing or locating quantitative instruments, forming categorical information for later quantitative data collection, or developing generalizations from a few, initial qualitative cases. Perhaps the most popular use is to generate an instrument well grounded in the qualitative data from participants in a study. In the case of a researcher who studied first-year teachers in reservation-based, Native-American elementary schools, the existing instruments were not sensitive enough to identify the cultural factors that affected this first-year experience. Thus, interviews were initially conducted with first-year teachers, themes and supporting statements were identified, and an instrument was generated to measure broadly the experiences of first-year teachers. As an alternative to this approach, the researcher might have identified the themes and located an instrument using the library resources mentioned in Chapter 4.

In addition, an exploratory qualitative data collection might be used to identify categories of information to be combined with continuous data in a statistical analysis. In the above example, the experiences of the first-year teachers gathered through interviews could be categorized into their stages of development, such as "initiation," "apprentice," and "recruit," and be categorized and used in a correlational or regression analysis. Individuals in these categories, as well, might be identified as an unusual or extreme case and serve as the basis for extensive analysis across a population. For instance, Native-American first-year teachers who saw themselves as in the "initiation" phase might be surveyed across several reservations.

Visualizing the Procedures

Mixed method researchers often provide a **visualization** or figure of their design depicting the procedures. A visualization is a figure like the examples of Figure 17.2 that indicates the process of data collection. It consists of labeling the quantitative and qualitative data, indicating the sequence of activities (using arrows or plus signs), and emphasizing the priority (using lowercase or uppercase letters). By including this visualization, the researcher helps readers identify the sequence of data collection, an important aid when collecting multiple forms of data. The notation system by Morse (1991), described in Figure 17.1, can be useful in developing this visualization.

STEPS IN CONDUCTING A MIXED METHOD STUDY

Now that you have a basic understanding of mixed method research, you can turn to specific steps typically undertaken by researchers when they use this design. These steps are not meant as a lock-step procedure, only as a general guide to help you get started. See Figure 17.3 for an overview of this process.

Step 1. Determine If a Mixed Method Study Is Feasible

The first step in the process is to assess the feasibility of using this design. You need skills in gathering both quantitative and qualitative data, time to collect extensive information, and a working knowledge of the different types of designs. Also important is whether audiences such as graduate committees, publishers, other researchers, and practitioners in educational settings will appreciate the complexity of your mixed method study.

Step 2. Identify a Rationale for Mixing Methods

Assuming that a study is feasible, you need to consider why you are collecting both quantitative and qualitative data. The rationale for the three designs should provide a good starting point. Be explicit in this rationale, and include it early in your research plan or report.

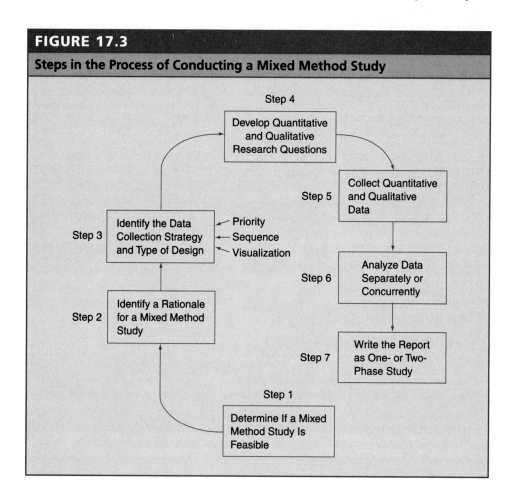

FIGURE 17.3

Steps in the Process of Conducting a Mixed Method Study

Step 3. Identify a Data Collection Strategy

Identifying your rationale for the study will lead to planning your procedures for collecting data. You need to know:

▶ the priority you will give to quantitative and qualitative data
▶ the sequence of your data collection, if you do not plan to collect the data concurrently
▶ the specific forms of quantitative data (e.g., attendance records) and qualitative data (e.g., pictures) you will collect

Once these decisions have been made, create a visual picture of the procedures. Use the notation system in Figure 17.1 and the models shown in Figure 17.2 of three types of designs to help you.

Step 4. Develop Both Quantitative and Qualitative Questions

With the specific design in mind, next develop your research questions. Depending on the type of design, these questions can be identified prior to a study or they may emerge during the study. For instance, in a two-phase design, the questions for the second phase cannot be realistically identified early in the study—they will emerge as the study progresses. Alternatively, for a triangulation design, the questions can be presented before data collection and be specified in detail.

If both quantitative and qualitative questions can be identified, pose both sets of questions. Typically, researchers present both exploratory questions and analytic-variable questions in a mixed-method study. As mentioned in Chapter 5, quantitative questions specify the relationship among independent and dependent variables. They may be written in the null form, but are typically written to convey an alternative directional form (e.g., the more mentoring, the greater the publications of faculty). Qualitative questions are open-ended and non-directional in nature, and seek a description of the phenomenon being addressed.

Step 5. Collect Both Quantitative and Qualitative Data

Collecting data in a mixed method study follows the procedures for data collection identified in Chapters 6 and 7. For a mixed method study, the sequence in which you collect the data will depend on the type of design. However, in all designs, this phase of the research will be lengthy and require good record keeping of the information. Statistical programs and text analysis programs, as discussed in Chapter 8 and 9, can provide useful systems for storing, managing, and recording the data.

Step 6. Analyze Data Separately or Concurrently

The data analysis will also relate to the specific type of mixed method design you are using. Quantitative data analysis may be analyzed separately (as in the explanatory and exploratory designs) or integrated (as in the triangulation design). Specific techniques have emerged for data analysis, as discussed in Table 17.2.

Step 7. Write the Report as a One- or Two-Phase Study

The final step in a mixed method study is to write a scholarly report of the project. There are some variations in the writing structure of mixed method studies, as outlined below.

▶ *The report is written in two phases.* The report contains one phase to specify the problem and the literature. Then, for the phases of data collection, analysis, and interpretation, two sections—one quantitative and one qualitative—are used for each phase.

▶ *The report integrates the quantitative and qualitative phases of the study in each section.* The problem statement, for example, contains a need to explore (qualitative) and to predict or explain outcomes (quantitative). The research questions are posed as both quantitative and qualitative questions, and the data collection is in one section displaying an integration of quantitative and qualitative forms. The data analysis is an attempt to converge the two databases, and the results and interpretation are formed into information that shed light on the research problem. This structure is typically found in a triangulation design.

CRITERIA FOR EVALUATING A MIXED METHOD STUDY

An understanding of the basics of mixed method research and a review of the steps in the process of conducting a study provide indicators for criteria that readers and study planners might use to evaluate a mixed method study. Consider these questions as you design or review a study:

▶ Does the study employ at least one method associated with quantitative research and one method associated with qualitative research?
▶ Is it called a mixed method (or a similar term) study?
▶ Is there a rationale for why the author intends to mix methods in a single study and what will be gained in this process?
▶ Does the author indicate the type of mixed method study being presented? Alternatively, can you identify the type from reading the rationale or from a visual figure depicting the flow of data collection activities?
▶ Does the author mention the priority given to the quantitative and qualitative data and the sequence of their use in the study?
▶ Is the study feasible, given the amount of data to be collected and the monies, time, and expertise required?
▶ Have research questions been written for both the quantitative and the qualitative methods in the study?
▶ Have the quantitative and qualitative data collection procedures been clearly identified?
▶ Is the procedure for data analysis consistent with the type of mixed method study being presented?
▶ Is the written structure of the study consistent with the type of mixed method study being proposed?

APPLYING WHAT YOU HAVE LEARNED: A MIXED METHOD STUDY

To apply the ideas in this chapter, first read the mixed method research study on page 582, noting the marginal annotations that identify quantitative and qualitative characteristics as well as the five characteristics of a mixed method study.

Way, N., Stauber, H., Nakkula, M. J., & London, P. (1994). Depression and substance use in two divergent high school cultures: A qualitative and quantitative analysis. *Journal of Youth and Adolescence, 23*(3), 331–357.

The Way et al. (1994) article addresses the relationship of adolescent depression and substance abuse in a suburban and an inner-city high school. The study begins with a substantial quantitative orientation (i.e., priority) in phase one and then includes a minor qualitative study in phase two. Thus, the project is sequential, in which the results from the quantitative study were used to select participants, generate questions, and provide a context for the qualitative analysis. The actual integration of quantitative and qualitative data occurred in the interpretation and discussion phase of the study. We see here an explanatory mixed method design.

In the first-phase quantitative study, 164 high school students from a suburban school and 242 students from an inner-city high school completed questionnaire instruments during one class period at school. From data about depression and substance use (i.e., cigarettes, alcohol, marijuana, and harder drugs), the researchers compared student responses across schools, between females and males, among the different categories of substance use, and among grade levels. The most important quantitative finding was that a distinction existed between the two schools in patterns of substance use as predictors of depression. Therefore, the investigators followed up on this finding using qualitative research. In the second phase of the study, 19 students were interviewed who were in the top 10% of the sample in terms of depression scores in the two high schools. The interview questions focused on substance use, and from this data, the researchers identified qualitative themes about the meaning of substance use and the interpersonal and peer pressure to abuse substances. From the qualitative data, the researchers learned that the relationships among depression and substance use may be related to the varied meanings of depression and substance use, and that these meanings were informed by cultural contexts of the schools.

This article was chosen because it includes the collection of both quantitative and qualitative data; provides an example of an explanatory design, a popular design in educational research; and has clearly identified quantitative and qualitative sections.

As you review this article, look for elements of the research process:

- the research problem and the type of design
- the use of the literature
- the purpose statement and research questions
- the types and procedures of data collection
- the types and procedures of data analysis and interpretation
- the writing structure

The Research Problem

Paragraphs 01–04

The authors introduce the research problem early in the study, in the opening paragraph. This problem is a need to understand the relationship between depression and substance use, and how gender, ethnicity, social class, and environment affect this relationship (see Paragraph 02). The authors base their evidence on past research studies. Further evidence might have been drawn from practice. For example, is substance use on the rise? Or is depression a major problem for adolescents?

This research problem passage also indicates a strong quantitative focus on the need to predict factors that explain the relationship between depression and substance abuse. Since the problem is stated as an examination of the relationship among variables (e.g., gender, ethnicity, social class, depression, and substance use) the authors are foreshadowing a quantitative framework (QUAN) for this study.

The Literature Review Paragraphs

Paragraphs 01–04

As seen in this article, the literature review is combined with the introduction/statement of the problem rather than as a distinct section in the study. From substantial references to the literature, the inclusion of variables, and a discussion of their relationships and differences, the literature indicates a strong quantitative orientation to the study.

The Purpose Statement and Rationale for Mixed Method Research

Paragraphs 05–06, 27

The purpose statement ("In the present study . . .") continues to emphasize a strong quantitative component to this study: the examination of a "relationship," the specification of variables, and the differences among schools. This statement also introduces the concept that both quantitative and qualitative methods will be used, indicating a mixed method study. In addition, looking back at the title, we now see that it announces this study as a mixed method design by indicating the inclusion of both quantitative and qualitative analysis.

In Paragraph 06, the authors introduce their reason for mixing methods. It is reintroduced in Paragraphs 27–28. We learn that the quantitative data provides a "context" for the qualitative data and that the qualitative data explores "possible explanations" for the quantitative findings about distinctions between the two schools in substance use. Specifically, we learn that depression by students who abused substances differed between the two high schools. Consequently, although not explicitly identified by name, the authors used an explanatory design with an initial quantitative first phase followed by a qualitative phase to explore the results about student depression in more detail. A visualization of the explanatory mixed method design, such as the model shown in Figure 17.2, would have been most useful to help readers conceptualize the process of quantitative and qualitative data collection.

Collection of Quantitative and Qualitative Data

Quantitative Data Collection—Paragraphs 07–16

Qualitative Data Collection—Paragraphs 27–33

The quantitative data collection is introduced first in this explanatory design. It consists of a large sample ($N = 164$), collection of scores or numeric data, a focus on instruments (i.e., Children's Depression Inventory and Substance Use), permissions, and data collection procedures. Since the intent of this design was to conduct qualitative research to explain the quantitative results, the qualitative data collection followed the quantitative data collection. In the qualitative phase, the researchers examined their "most noteworthy" quantitative finding about depression among the students in both schools. They collected data from 19 students who were in the top 10% of depression scores from both the suburban and urban schools. They conducted interviews with these students, yielding text data for analysis.

The clear separation of the quantitative and qualitative data collection indicates a two-phase design with the quantitative data collection preceding the qualitative data collection.

Analyzing and Interpreting Quantitative and Qualitative Data

Quantitative Results—Paragraphs 17–26

Qualitative Results—Paragraphs 34–47

Interpretation of Quantitative and Qualitative Results—Paragraphs 48–63

The authors report quantitative results using statistical analysis. This analysis was first based on descriptive statistics about the two schools, and then included inferential statistics that correlated and tested hypotheses (i.e., regressions) about the relationship among variables. In addition, gender differences and grade differences were also analyzed in terms of descriptive and inferential statistics about depression and substance use. This section displayed an increasingly detailed analysis from general trends and hypotheses to a more specific focus on gender and grade level.

The qualitative results reported three themes as indicated by headings: "Substance Use: Escape from Problems or Cause of Problems?", "Interpersonal Relationships and Substance Use," and "Peer Pressure and Substance Use." It also included multiple perspectives from students (e.g., Millie, Mara, Glen, and others), the frequent use of quotes to capture the voice of the participants, and the meaning that depressed youth ascribed to substance use.

The interpretation of the meaning of the results is explained in the "Summary and Discussion" section. Here we find a summary of the quantitative findings followed by a comparison of these findings with past literature and predictions from that literature (Paragraphs 48–58). Then the interpretation turns to the qualitative results, focusing on depressed students from both schools, and reviewing the themes (Paragraphs 59–63).

The Overall Writing Structure

The clear separation of the quantitative phase from the qualitative phase makes this study easy to read and identify as a sequential, two-phase study. The explanation for mixing methods might have been identified more clearly, but the intent was to build on and extend a significant quantitative result about depression. The markings throughout this study—the title, the purpose statement, the separate data collection analysis, the integration of results into an interpretation at the end of the project, the traditional quantitative structure, and the use of themes in the qualitative results—displayed many good elements of a mixed method study.

KEY IDEAS IN THE CHAPTER

With a better understanding of qualitative research and the advantages of collecting both quantitative and qualitative data, mixed method research designs are becoming popular in education. From initial multimethod quantitative studies have emerged designs that incorporate quantitative data (e.g., scores from instruments, scores from observations, and census data) and qualitative data (e.g., open-ended interviews, observations, documents, and visual materials). Today, writers talk about a separate design in education—the mixed method design—where investigators collect and analyze at least one quantitative method of data and one qualitative method of data with attention to sequence and priority.

Three major types of mixed method designs are found in educational research. The triangulation design is based on the collection of both quantitative and qualitative data simultaneously with the purpose of converging or integrating the data. The explanatory design begins with quantitative data collection and analysis followed by qualitative data collection and analysis. In this way, the researcher follows up on quantitative findings with qualitative explorations. In the exploratory design, the data collection is reversed from the explanatory design. The mixed method researcher first gathers qualitative data and then builds on the analysis of it using quantitative data.

A major characteristic of this design is a need to justify or provide a rationale for mixing methods. Researchers also collect both quantitative and qualitative data, and provide a priority or weight and often a sequence to collecting both forms of data. Data analysis needs to relate to the type of design being used, and this analysis may involve transforming data, following up or explaining outlier or extreme bases, or using qualitative themes to develop a quantitative instrument.

The steps in conducting a mixed method design involve assessing the feasibility of the study and presenting a rationale for mixing methods. It also involves making decisions about the priority and sequence of the analysis and developing research questions that are needed for the study. Researchers then collect both quantitative and qualitative data and analyze them together or separately, depending on the design being used. The final research report may present the study as one phase or as two phases, based on the research design chosen for the project.

USEFUL INFORMATION FOR PRODUCERS OF RESEARCH

▶ When presenting your mixed method research to others, discuss your design as a distinct design in educational research with procedures that have now been recently documented in the literature.

▶ In the design of a mixed method study, identify the advantages that will accrue from collecting both quantitative and qualitative data. Let these advantages point you toward the most appropriate design (e.g., triangulation, explanatory, exploratory) to study your research problem. In this chapter, the advantages of each design are specified.

▶ Of the three designs, recognize that it is easier to conduct a sequential explanatory or exploratory design than a triangulation design. With a triangulation design, you need to converge both quantitative and qualitative databases (e.g., numbers and text) and possibly collect additional data if the two databases are in conflict.

▶ Recognize that in selecting a mixed method design you have taken on a challenging project. Mixed method research involves extensive data collection and data analysis. Weigh the tradeoff between drawbacks of time and resources and the advantages of collecting both quantitative and qualitative data to understand your research problem.

▶ Use the two factors, priority and sequence, to help you decide what mixed method research design is appropriate for your study.

▶ To best present the procedures in your mixed method design, create a visual or figure that portrays the steps in the process. Use the guidelines about notation, introduced in this chapter, to help you design this visual.

USEFUL INFORMATION FOR CONSUMERS OF RESEARCH

▶ Because mixed method designs have been only recently identified as a specific design in educational research, authors of studies may not label their research as mixed method. You might identify a mixed method study by determining whether the researcher collects both quantitative and qualitative data to examine a research problem.

> ▶ When reading a mixed method study, look for a visual or figure of the procedures to help you understand the flow of activities in the mixed method research. If such a visual is not present, you may want to sketch out the sequence of activities, including when the quantitative and qualitative data were collected, how they were analyzed, and the intent for using both forms of data.
>
> ▶ Because mixed method designs have only recently been discussed as a distinct design, there are not evaluative criteria to judge this type of study. But since both quantitative and qualitative data are being collected, you might judge a mixed method study on the basis of the quantitative and qualitative criteria introduced in Chapter 10 on "Evaluating Research." Also in this chapter are several standards that you might apply to help assess the quality of a mixed method study.
>
> ▶ To locate useful information from mixed method studies, look for the detailed picture that emerges from qualitative research and the generalizable results that emerge from quantitative research. This combined impact—the detail and the general—can help you best understand a research problem in education.

ADDITIONAL RESOURCES YOU MIGHT EXAMINE

The most recent book available on mixed method research is the overview provided by Tashakkori and Teddlie (1998). This book presents a history of mixed method research, the various types of research designs, details about collecting both quantitative and qualitative data, and various data analysis strategies for integrating text and numeric data. See:

Tashakkori, A., & Teddlie, C. (1998). *Mixed methodology: Combining qualitative and quantitative approaches.* Thousand Oaks, CA: Sage.

Another recent book is the Jossey-Bass sourcebook on evaluation by Greene and Caracelli (1997). Although aimed at the field of evaluation, this book provides a good overview of the types of mixed method designs and illustrates the process of mixed method research with numerous examples. Examine:

Greene, J. C., & Caracelli, V. J. (Eds.). (1997). *Advances in mixed-method evaluation: The challenges and benefits of integrating diverse paradigms.* New Directions for Evaluation, no. 74. San Francisco, CA: Jossey-Bass.

A recent book on mixed method research is the Jossey-Bass sourcebook on evaluation by Reichardt and Rallis (1994). This book discusses many topical issues related to mixed method research and presents a good conceptual overview of the paradigm debate between quantitative and qualitative researchers. See:

Reichardt, C. S. & Rallis, S. E. (1994). *The qualitative-quantitative debate: New perspectives* (pp. 5–11). New Directions for Program Evaluation, Number 61. San Francisco: Jossey-Bass Publishers.

Three journal articles are especially good at introducing you to mixed method research. The article by Morgan (1998) provides the best example of decision areas, such as priority and sequencing, that go into determining the most appropriate mixed method research design for you to use. A second article by Morse (1991) pioneered the notation system we now use in mixed method research, and Creswell (1999) also offers an overview of the history, the types of designs, and steps in the process of conducting a mixed method study. Explore:

Morgan, D. L. (1998). Practical strategies for combining qualitative and quantitative methods: Applications to health research. *Qualitative Health Research, 3,* 362–376.

Morse, J. M. (1991). Approaches to qualitative-quantitative methodological triangulation. *Nursing Research, 40,* 120–123.

Creswell, J. W. (1999). Mixed-method research: Introduction and application. In G. J. Cizek (Ed.), *Handbook of educational policy* (pp. 455–472). San Diego, CA: Academic Press.

Depression and Substance Use in Two Divergent High School Cultures: A Quantitative and Qualitative Analysis

Niobe Way,[1] Helena Y. Stauber,[2] Michael J. Nakkula,[3] and Perry London[4]

Research has generally concluded that adolescent depression and substance use are strongly interrelated, but has rarely considered how this relationship may vary across diverse populations. In this study, we used quantitative and qualitative methods to explore the relationships among depression and cigarette, alcohol, marijuana, and harder drug use across two culturally disparate environments: a suburban and an inner-city high school. Our sample included 164 suburban and 242 inner-city high school students. The students completed Kovacs' Children's Depression Inventory of 1985 and substance use measures derived from various sources. In-depth semistructured interviews were conducted with subjects who scored in the top 10% of the CDI (N = 19) from both schools. Our quantitative findings indicated a positive association between depression and cigarette, marijuana, and harder drug use among the suburban students, and no association between depression and the use of any substances for the urban students. There were no significant differences in levels of reported depression across samples. However, with the exception of marijuana use, suburban students reported greater involvement in substance use than urban students. Our qualitative analyses suggest that across-school differences in the relationships among depression and substance use may be related to the varied meanings of depression and substance use that are informed by cultural context.

Way, N., Stauber, H. Y., Nakkula, M. J., & London, P. (1994). Depression and substance use in two divergent high school cultures: A quantitative and qualitative analysis. *Journal of Youth and Adolescence, 23*(3), 331–357. Reprinted with permission of the author.

The research was funded by the National Institute of Drug Abuse (NIDA), Grant No. 1 R01 DA-06844, Perry London, principal investigator. The views, opinions, and findings contained in their article are not to be construed as NIDA's position or policy.

[1]Post-Doctoral Fellow, Psychology Department, Yale University. B.A. from University of California, Berkeley, and Ed.D. from the Graduate School of Education, Harvard University. Research interests include the phenomenology of high-risk behavior and social development among urban adolescents. To whom reprint requests should be addressed at Department of Psychology, Yale University, Box 208205, New Haven, Connecticut 06520.

[2]Doctoral student in Counseling and Consulting Psychology, Graduate School of Education, Harvard University. B.A. from Mount Holyoke College and Ed.M. from the Graduate School of Education, Harvard University. Research interests include the relationships among high-risk behavior, personality variables, and cultural context.

[3]Instructor in Human Development and Psychology, Graduate School of Education, Harvard University. B.A. from Michigan State University, M.A. from University of Minnesota—Duluth, and Ed.D. from Harvard Graduate School of Education. Research interests include integrating quantitative and qualitative methods in social science research and the phenomenology of high-risk behavior.

[4]Formerly Dean of the Graduate School of Applied and Professional Psychology, Rutgers University, and Professor of Education, Graduate School of Education, Harvard University. B.A. Yeshiva University, M.A. and Ph.D. Teachers College, Columbia University. Research interests included adolescent high-risk behavior and ethnic and religious identity development. Deceased June 1992.

Introduction

(01)

A quantitative research problem requires description or explanation.

Over the past 30 years an abundance of research on adolescents and young adults has investigated the relationships among depression and substance use. The results of these studies suggest that adolescents or young adults who are heavy cigarette, drug, or alcohol users are more likely to show signs of depression than light or nonusers (Aneshensel and Huba, 1983; Braucht *et al.,* 1973; Kaminer, 1991; Kaplan *et al.,* 1980; Kaplan *et al.,* 1984; Kennedy *et al.,* 1987; Paton *et al.,* 1977; Reinherz *et al.,* 1991; Robins and Przybeck, 1985; Shiffman and Wills, 1985; Simons *et al.,* 1991). Researchers and practitioners have typically concluded that there is a strong association between depression and substance use among adolescents (Blau *et al.,* 1988; Kaplan *et al.,* 1984; Reinherz *et al.,* 1991; Simons *et al.,* 1988).

(02)

The quantitative literature plays a major role.

There has been little research, however, that has explored the effects of gender, ethnicity, social class, or environment (e.g., urban vs. suburban) on the relationships among depression and substance use. The few studies that have examined such sociodemographic differences have concluded that this type of investigation is critical (Dembo *et al.,* 1979; Paton and Kandel, 1978; Prendergast, 1974; Siegel and Ehrlich, 1989). Paton and Kandel (1978) report widely disparate relationships between depression and substance use among different ethnic groups, and between males and females within selected ethnic groups. They found no relationship between depression and drug use among either black or Puerto Rican adolescents; however, this relationship was highly significant for white adolescents, with higher levels of depression associated with higher levels of drug use. Furthermore, the relationship between depression and drug use was significantly stronger for the white girls in the sample than for the white boys.

(03)

The quantitative literature justifies the research problem and provides direction for the study.

Siegel and Ehrlich (1989) report socioeconomic status (SES) differences in levels of depression among adolescent substance abusers. The high SES, white adolescent substance abusers scored significantly higher on the depression scale (The Children's Depression Inventory) than the low SES, white adolescent substance abusers. Their findings suggest that the relationships among depression and substance use may vary across social class. Siegel and Ehrlich (1989) state that the low success rates among treatment programs for drug-abusing adolescents may be related to a failure to "take into account the possibility that adolescents from different ethnic or socioeconomic backgrounds may take drugs (and alcohol) for different reasons" (p. 925). Drug and alcohol use may not be related to depression for lower SES adolescents as it is for higher SES adolescents.

(04)

While researchers have examined gender, ethnic, social class, or environmental (e.g., rural vs. urban) differences in levels of drug use (Kaplan *et al.,* 1984; Kaplan *et al.,* 1980; Siegel and Ehrlich, 1989), type of drug use (Hager *et al.,* 1971; Harris, 1971; Siegel and Ehrlich, 1989; Smart and Fejer, 1969), and levels of depression (Baron and Perron, 1986; Doerfler *et al.,* 1988; Kaplan *et al.,* 1980; Siegel and Ehrlich, 1989), they rarely have looked for such sociodemographic differences in the *relationships* among depression and substance use.

(05)

The quantitative purpose statement, research questions, or hypotheses are specific and narrow.

In the present study we used both quantitative and qualitative methods to explore the relationships among depression and cigarette, alcohol, marijuana, and harder drug use in two culturally divergent school environments: an inner-city public high school and a suburban public high school. The inner-city school and the suburban school are characterized by differences in racial and ethnic composition, social class, geographic location, and educational and community resources. We assume that differences we may find between the two schools reflect a complex combination

Mixed method researchers collect both quantitative and qualitative data.

of these social class, racial, ethnic, and environmental factors. Rather than attempting to tease out the differential effects of such factors, as was done in the previously cited studies (e.g., Paton and Kandel, 1978), our analyses are conducted at a more macro level where individual contributions coalesce to form the distinct community of the school culture.

(06)   We conducted an integrative analysis of quantitative and qualitative data in which quantitative results were used to select participants, generate questions, and provide a context for the qualitative analysis. Therefore, the paper is divided into two methods and results sections, one for the quantitative analysis and one for the contingent qualitative analysis. The two sets of findings are synthesized through a single discussion section.

Mixed method researchers justify their use of mixing methods.

Mixed method researchers can provide a visual picture of procedures.

Quantitative Analysis

Method

Subjects

Mixed method researchers sequence the quantitative and qualitative data collection.

(07)   The sample included 164 students from a suburban high school (grades nine [$N = 44$], ten [$N = 36$], eleven [$N = 35$], and twelve [$N = 49$], 75 boys, 89 girls) and 242 students from an inner-city high school (grades nine [$N = 45$], ten [$N = 33$], eleven [$N = 68$], and twelve [$N = 96$], 108 boys and 134 girls). Both schools were located in the Greater Boston area. The students from the suburban high school primarily described themselves as Irish-American (26%), Italian-American (11%), Irish and Italian-American (5%), or white with no ethnicity specified (45%). The students from the inner-city high school primarily described themselves as African-American (35%), Puerto Rican or Dominican (31%), Haitian (12%), white (7%), or American Indian (4%).

Quantitative data collection involves studying a large number of individuals.

(08)   The suburban students came from predominantly middle- or working-class families, while the urban students came from predominantly working-class or poor families. These variations in social class were inferred from the parents' educational backgrounds, their current occupations, the families' housing situations, and the percentage of students who receive subsidized lunches (see Table I).

Quantitative researchers take an objective and unbiased approach.

(09)   In addition to social class differences, the schools had substantially different dropout rates: It is projected that 32% of the freshman students in the urban school vs. 4% in the suburban school will not graduate. Due to this important distinction, our study does not attempt a broad description of the comparative experiences of inner-city and suburban youth. However, while the elevated dropout rate in the urban school restricts the generalizability of our findings, our inclusion of students from the four high school grade levels makes it possible to capture the experiences of numerous inner-city students who are potential dropouts. As such, while this study does not reflect the behavioral and emotional characteristics of students who have dropped out, neither does it provide a uniform picture of inner-city students who have fully circumvented risk for dropping out.

(10)   In both schools, students were recruited for the study through presentations made to their classrooms by members of our research team. In the suburban school where tracking exists, equal numbers of required courses were targeted for presentation within each academic track, allowing us to reach a sample of students that was representative of the whole school population. In the urban school there is no tracking, but large numbers of students receive special education services. As such, we targeted proportional numbers of mainstream vs. special education classrooms for our presentations. Across all of the classrooms from which we recruited in both schools, 80–90% of the students agreed to participate. Of those students who agreed to participate, 98% in both schools agreed to *both* the

TABLE I
Student Reports of Parent Job-Type, Parent Education Levels, Family Housing, and School-Reported Percentages of Subsidized Lunches

| | Parents' Jobs | | | |
| | Suburban School | | Urban School | |
	Mothers	Fathers	Mothers	Fathers
"Professional"	21%	40%	4%	4%
"Semiprofessional"	16	10	9	6
Business person	6	9	8	8
Own business	1	8	5	6
Blue-collar job	12	19	25	39
Office-clerical	22	3	4	0
Other	5	4	5	5
Unemployed	16	4	39	20
Don't know	0	1	4	13

| | Parents' Education | | | |
| | Suburban School | | Urban School | |
	Mothers	Fathers	Mothers	Fathers
Graduate school	11%	16%	2%	2%
College grads	23	35	7	7
Some college	18	14	9	9
High school grads	25	12	21	16
Trade school	14	13	7	7
Less than twelfth grade	5	5	33	23
Don't know	4	5	23	35

| | Housing | |
	Suburban School	Urban School
Project housing	0%	19%
Two- or three-family homes	12	36
Apartments	4	28
Single-family homes	84	15
Rent home	12	71
Own home	82	27

| | Students eligible for subsidized lunches | |
	Suburban School	Urban School
	3%	80%

questionnaire and the interview. Participants were paid five dollars for completing the questionnaire measures and five dollars to participate in a follow-up interview.

Questionnaires

(11)   *Children's Depression Inventory (CDI).* All students completed the CDI (Kovacs, 1985), a 27-item questionnaire designed to assess the severity of de-

Quantitative data collection is based on using instruments identified prior to the study.

Quantitative data collection involves gathering numeric data.

pressive symptoms from mid-childhood through late adolescence. The scale, based on the BDI for adults, measures symptoms such as disturbances in mood, eating behaviors, self-esteem, and interpersonal behavior. For each item, students are asked to check one of three descriptions that best applies to them during the last 2 weeks (e.g., "I am sad all the time," "I am sad many times," "I am sad once in a while"). Responses to each item are scored on a 0–2 scale (from *least depressed* to *most depressed*). A total score of 19 or above, out of a maximum of 54 points, is considered a strong indicator of depression (Kovacs, 1982). According to Kovacs (1983), the CDI's "readability" is at the first grade level, thus increasing its accessibility to students in a high school population at various levels of literacy. The CDI has been used with urban and suburban samples and has typically indicated minor or no significant differences by grade, sex or race (Doerfler *et al.,* 1988; Finch *et al.,* 1985; Kovacs, 1980–1981). The CDI has shown high internal consistency ranging from .71 to .86, and test–retest reliability ranging from .38 to .87, depending on the length of time between tests and the population studied (Kovacs, 1983; Saylor *et al.,* 1984). It has also been reported to be strongly related to other self-report measures of constructs associated with depression (e.g., self-concept, hopelessness, and anxiety; Doerfler *et al.,* 1988; Kovacs, 1982; Way *et al.,* 1990). In the present study, inter-item reliability, using Chronbach's α, was .80 for the urban school and .88 for the suburban school.

(12)   *Substance Use Scales.* Our substance use scales were derived from the Institute of Behavioral Science's Health Questionnaire (Donovan *et al.,* 1985) and the California Substance Use Survey (Skager and Firth, 1988). Additional questions were developed in consultation with students from each school who advised us on the use of appropriate and accessible language for their age group and cultures.[5] Separate measures for cigarettes, alcohol, marijuana, and harder drugs (e.g., cocaine and LSD) employed Likert-type scales to assess the age at which the student started using the particular substance, the frequency of use, the amount of use at any one time, and when, where, and with whom the use typically occurs. Total scores for each measure included age of initiation, frequency, amount, and patterns of use.

(13)   The alcohol use measure, for example, was comprised of 9 equally weighted questions: 1 for age of initiation ("How old were you when you had your first drink?"), 2 for frequency of use (e.g., "How often do you drink alcohol?"), 2 for amount of use at any one time (e.g., "When you drink, how many whole drinks do you usually have at a time?"), and 4 for patterns of use (i.e., "When do you usually drink alcohol?" "What kind of alcohol do you drink most often?" "Have you ever gotten drunk during school?" "In the past year, have you ever been too drunk or hung over to stay at school?"). An overall alcohol score, is the summed total of the individual responses to each of these nine equally weighted questions. Rather than simply assessing frequency of use, the alcohol scale taps into other factors that contribute to the severity of alcohol-use problems. As a case in point, a student who reports drinking on average three beers at a time every week during the weekends, and has occasionally gotten drunk during school would receive a higher score on the alcohol measure than a peer who reports drinking a six pack of beer at a time about once a month during the weekends, and has never gotten drunk during school. However, if this latter student has occasionally gotten drunk during school,

---

[5]These consultations with students, some with reading disabilities, allowed us to create measures that are accessible to students with diverse reading skills.

then he or she would receive the same score as the former student. Scaling and scoring procedures were similar for each of the substance use measures.[6]

(14)   For the urban school, inter-item reliability for cigarettes was .82, for alcohol .86, for marijuana .78, and for harder drugs .73. For the suburban school, inter-item reliability for cigarettes was .86, for alcohol .84, for marijuana .82, and for harder drugs .92.

Procedure

(15)   Parental consent forms were distributed and collected prior to questionnaire administration. Consent forms provided a brief description of the study and emphasized the confidentiality of student responses. In addition, prior to completing the questionnaires, all students were verbally assured of full confidentiality. Questionnaires were identified by number codes rather than student names. The researchers maintained a list with participants' names and corresponding code numbers for the purpose of identifying students for follow-up interviews.

(16)   All 406 participants completed the questionnaires during one class period. To maximize the comfort of participants and the likelihood of honest responses, teachers were asked to leave the classroom during questionnaire administration. At least two research team members were present throughout the administrations to distribute and collect questionnaires, monitor student contact, and respond to students' questions and concerns. The use of simple language made the questionnaires accessible to most students. However, in a small number of cases ($N = 8$) where reading deficiencies were profound, a team member read the questions aloud to students in a private setting.

Results

Comparisons Across Schools

Quantitative data analysis consists of statistical analysis.

(17)   *Means Analysis.* The mean scores and standard deviations for depression and substance use, and a comparison of means across schools are shown in Table II. Levels of reported depression did not differ significantly across schools. The mean depression score (9.2) and the range of scores (0–31) in the suburban school were very similar to the mean depression score (9.4) and range (0–29) in the urban school. There were significant differences between schools, however, in reported prevalence of students' drug and alcohol use. Suburban students reported using significantly more cigarettes, alcohol, and harder drugs than the urban students.[7] The average score for marijuana use was similar across schools (see Table II).

Mixed method researchers analyze data based on their design type.

Quantitative data analysis consists of describing trends, comparing groups, or relating variables.

(18)   *Correlation and Multiple Regression Analyses.* The results of analyses of correlation among depression and different substances are shown in Table III. In both schools, all forms of substance use were highly intercorrelated. Depression scores among the students in the suburban sample were positively correlated with cigarette use ($r = .33, p < .0001$), with marijuana use ($r = .24, p < .0021$), and with harder drug use ($r = .22, p < .0037$).

---

[6]Throughout this paper, the phrases "levels of substance use" or "levels of cigarette, alcohol, marijuana use or harder drug" are intended to describe patterns of use inclusive of but not limited to frequency of use.

[7]For the urban students, relatively little harder drug use was reported, resulting in a non-normal distribution for this variable. However, harder drug use was normally distributed in the suburban sample. This discrepancy should be kept in mind when examining the results regarding harder drug use.

TABLE II
Mean Scores, Standard Deviations, and Comparisons of Means Across Schools[a]

	Suburban school	Urban school	p Value
Depression	9.2 (7.1)	9.4 (5.9)	NS
Cigarette smoking	5.5 (5.9)	3.7 (4.9)	.001
Alcohol use	16.8 (10.1)	11.7 (8.4)	.0001
Marijuana use	6.8 (6.7)	6.4 (5.9)	NS
Harder drug use	24.0 (6.0)	22.2 (1.1)	.001

[a]Standard deviations are in parentheses.

TABLE III
Correlations Among Depression and Substance Use

Suburban School	Depression	Cigarette smoking	Alcohol use	Marijuana use	Harder drug use
Depression	—	.33[a]	.14	.24[b]	.22[b]
Cigarette smoking		—	.58[a]	.65[a]	.41[a]
Alcohol use			—	.57[a]	.39[a]
Marijuana use				—	.72[a]
Harder drug use					.

Urban school	Depression	Cigarette smoking	Alcohol use	Marijuana use	Harder drug use
Depression	—	.06	−.04	−.06	.07
Cigarette smoking		—	.53[a]	.42[a]	.22[a]
Alcohol use			—	.54[a]	.23[a]
Marijuana use				—	.26[a]
Harder drug use					—

[a]$p < .0001$.
[b]$p < .01$.

Depression and alcohol use was not significantly correlated ($r = .14$, $p < .074$); however, the nonsignificant correlation went in the same direction as the other significant correlations. A multiple regression analysis showed that substance use (the combined effect of cigarettes, alcohol, marijuana, and harder drugs) explained 16% of the variability ($p < .001$) in depression for the suburban sample. Depression, however, was not significantly correlated with *any* of these substances in the urban sample.

Comparisons Within Schools

Gender Differences

(19)   *Means Analyses.* Means and standard deviations for depression and each substance, for boys and girls across both schools, are shown in Table IV. In the urban sample, males and females did not have significantly different depression scores, yet the girls were overrepresented in the top 10% of the

sample, with 19 of the 24 highest depression scores.[8] The findings were similar for our suburban sample: males and females did not have significantly different depression scores, but again, the girls were overrepresented in the top 10% of the sample with 11 of the 16 highest depression scores.

(20)   Females in the suburban sample used significantly less alcohol, marijuana, and harder drugs than males (see Table IV). There was no gender difference for cigarette use. Urban girls' scores on cigarettes, alcohol, marijuana, and harder drugs were not significantly different from boys' scores. However, when we looked at differences between girls and boys within the dominant ethnic groups in the urban school (African-American, Puerto Rican, and Haitian), we found that African-American girls, on average, scored significantly lower on the marijuana scale than African-American boys (means = 6.6 and 10.3, respectively, $p < .03$). No other statistically significant gender differences in substance use were found within or across ethnic groups.

(21)   *Correlation and Multiple Regression Analyses.* The results of the correlation analyses for the depression and substance use scores for girls and boys can be seen in Table V. Similar to the findings for the entire urban sample,

TABLE IV
Means and Standard Deviations Across Gender Within Each School[a]

	Suburban school			Urban school		
	Girls	Boys	p Value	Girls	Boys	p Value
Depression	9.8 (7.7)	8.5 (6.4)	NS	10.1 (6.1)	8.6 (5.5)	NS
Cigarette smoking[b]	5.2 (6.0)	5.8 (5.8)	NS	4.2 (5.2)	3.1 (4.5)	NS
Alcohol use	14.5 (9.6)	19.4 (10.1)	.002	11.0 (8.2)	12.5 (8.8)	NS
Marijuana use	5.3 (4.6)	8.6 (8.3)	.004	5.9 (5.2)	7.1 (6.6)	NS
Harder drug use	22.8 (3.3)	25.4 (9.2)	.03	22.1 (1.1)	22.2 (1.2)	NS

[a]Standard deviations are in parentheses.
[b]Standard deviations are high relative to the means for cigarette smoking because the analyses include nonsmokers, which lowers the means. This results in a wide range of variation above each mean for smokers.

TABLE V
Pearson Correlations Between Depression and Substance Use Across Gender Within Each School

	Urban		Suburban	
	Females	Males	Females	Males
	Depression	Depression	Depression	Depression
Cigarette smoking	.07	.07	.40[a]	.24[b]
Alcohol use	.01	−.10	.21[b]	.10
Marijuana use	−.04	−.05	.35[a]	.23[b]
Harder drug use	.07	.08	.36[a]	.26[b]

[a]$p < .001$.
[b]$p < .05$.

[8]Six of these 19 were Haitian girls, revealing that a highly disproportionate percentage of very depressed girls were Haitian (only 12% of our sample were Haitian). The mean depression score for Haitian girls was 14.8, by far the highest mean in our sample.

data from urban girls alone and from urban boys alone revealed no significant correlation between depression and substance use of any kind.

(22)   For the girls in the suburban sample, depression was correlated with the use of cigarettes ($r = .40$, $p < .0001$), alcohol ($r = .21$, $p < .05$), marijuana ($r = .36$, $p < .0006$) and harder drugs ($r = .36$, $p < .0006$). For the boys in the suburban sample, there were significant correlations between depression and the use of cigarettes ($r = .24$, $p < .03$), marijuana ($r = .22$, $p < .05$), and harder drugs ($r = .25$, $p < .03$), but not between depression and alcohol use.

(23)   These correlational findings suggest that the relationship between depression and substance use may be stronger for girls than for boys in the suburban sample. To test this possibility, multiple regression models were created using interaction effects of gender and each of the substances (separately) in the prediction of depression. These multiple regression models revealed that gender interacted significantly with marijuana and with harder drugs in the prediction of depression. Marijuana alone accounted for 5% of the variance in depression in the suburban school ($p < .002$). Although the main effect of gender ($p < .07$) did not significantly enhance the prediction of depression ($R^2 = .07$), the addition of the interaction variable for marijuana and gender ($p < .03$) to the model containing both main effects did significantly enhance the explained variance in depression ($R^2 = .10$). The picture was similar for harder drug use and gender. Harder drug use alone accounted for 5% of the variance in depression in the suburban school ($p < .003$). The addition of gender ($p < .09$) to the model was not significant ($R^2 = .06$); however, the addition of the interaction variable for harder drug use and gender ($p < .007$) to the model significantly enhanced the explained variance in depression ($R^2 = .11$). Gender did not interact significantly with alcohol or cigarettes in the prediction of depression.

(24)   These multiple regression findings indicate that, as suggested by the correlational findings, there are significant gender differences in the relationship between depression and marijuana use, and between depression and harder drug use within the suburban sample. However, there are no significant gender differences in the relationship between depression and alcohol use or depression and cigarette use.

Grade Differences

(25)   *Analysis of Variance.* The grade differences in reported levels of depression and cigarette, alcohol, marijuana, and harder drug use within the two schools are shown in Table VI. Within the suburban school, there were significant differences between grades in levels of cigarette ($p < .0005$), alcohol ($p < .0001$), and marijuana use ($p < .0001$). Students in the eleventh and twelfth grades reported greater alcohol use than did the ninth- and tenth-grade students, and greater cigarette use than the tenth-grade students. The twelfth graders also reported heavier patterns of marijuana use than the ninth and tenth graders, while the eleventh graders reported a heavier pattern of marijuana use than did the ninth graders. Within the urban school, grade differences were found only for alcohol use ($p < .01$). Eleventh graders reported greater alcohol use than did twelfth graders. No other grade differences were found in patterns of substance use in the urban school (see Table VI.)

(26)   *Multiple Regression Analyses.* Interactions between grade level and substance use were examined to determine whether they predicted depression. No significant interaction effects were found in either school. For each grade, the relationships between depression and substance use of

TABLE VI
Mean Differences Across Grade for Depression and Substance Use

	Suburban school						
	Grades					Scheffé	
	9	**10**	**11**	**12**	**F Value**	**Contrasts**	**N**
Depression	9.9	7.5	9.2	9.8	.93	NS	163
Cigarette smoking	4.6	2.7	7.6	7.2	6.26[a]	10 < 11 and 12	160
Alcohol use	10.8	13.5	20.4	21.8	14.80[a]	9 and 10 < 11 and 12	162
Marijuana use	4.1	4.5	8.7	9.5	8.05[a]	9 and 10 < 12, 9 < 11	160
Hard drug use	22.4	22.2	25.2	25.9	3.29	NS	157

	Urban school						
	Grades					Scheffé	
	9	**10**	**11**	**12**	**F Value**	**Contrasts**	**N**
Depression	7.8	8.8	8.9	10.8	3.08	NS	231
Cigarette smoking	4.6	4.0	4.4	3.1	1.41	NS	230
Alcohol use	11.4	14.5	13.6	9.6	4.02[b]	12 < 11	224
Marijuana use	5.8	8.4	6.9	5.8	1.74	NS	225
Hard drug use	22.0	22.0	22.3	22.3	.87	NS	222

[a] $p < .001$.
[b] $p < .01$.

each type were similar to the overall relations (i.e., across all grades) between these variables in each school.

Qualitative Analysis

Method

(27)   Perhaps our most noteworthy quantitative finding was the distinction between the two schools in patterns of substance use as predictors of depression. Depression was significantly correlated with cigarette, marijuana, and harder drug use in the suburban school, whereas in the urban school, depression was not significantly correlated with any type of substance use. As an initial step in exploring possible explanations for this finding, we analyzed interviews from the most depressed students (according to the CDI) in both schools.

A qualitative problem requires exploration and understanding.

(28)   Our analyses focused on the following questions: (a) How might students with similarly high depression levels across the two schools differ in their perspectives on substance use? (b) How might these possible differences in perspectives begin to explain why depression and substance use are differentially related across the schools?

The qualitative purpose statement and research questions seek participants' experiences.

Subjects

(29)   Our qualitative analyses were conducted on interview data from the 19 students across both schools who scored in the top 10% of our sample on the CDI, with depression scores ranging from 19 to 30. This range is consistent with the top 10% of scores reported by Kovacs (1985) in her large

Qualitative data collection involves studying a small number of individuals or sites. (30)

Qualitative data collection is based on using protocols developed during the study. (31)

Qualitative data collection involves gathering text or image data.

normative sample for the CDI. The 19 students comprise all of the subjects in the top 10% of the CDI scores who were interviewed.[9]

The suburban sample included 10 students: four boys (1 ninth grader, 1 tenth grader, 1 eleventh grader, and 1 twelfth grader) and 6 girls (3 ninth graders, 1 tenth grader, 1 eleventh grader, and 1 twelfth grader). Nine of the students were white and one was African-American. Our urban sample included 9 students; 2 boys (a ninth grader and a twelfth grader) and seven girls (1 ninth grader, 2 tenth graders, 2 eleventh graders, and 2 twelfth graders). Of the 2 boys, 1 was Haitian and the other Puerto Rican; of the 7 girls, 3 were African-American, 2 were Puerto Rican, 1 was Haitian, and 1 was white.

The Interview

The interview is semi-structured, and designed to explore the extent, nature, and quality of the participants' thoughts and feelings about a range of personal, interpersonal, and behavioral phenomena. The interview process is guided by open-ended questions that lead into topical areas including substance use. Initial responses to interview questions (such as "How often do you drink?" "What is it that you like about drinking?" "Why don't you drink more than you do?") were probed by the interviewer to invite increasingly detailed and thoughtful reports of students' self-perspectives on their substance use or nonuse. These kinds of questions were asked for each substance (e.g., "Why do you think you haven't tried marijuana?" "Why do you smoke cigarettes?" etc.). The goal of the interview is to explore the meaning and attributions that the students assign to their behavior.

Procedure

(32)   Interviews were conducted by advanced doctoral students in counseling or developmental psychology. Participants were interviewed in one-on-one meetings held in private rooms at the respective school sites. We assured all participating students of full confidentiality.

(33)   Our interview analyses consisted of detailed readings of students' perspectives on substance use and their reasons for choosing to use or abstain from use. Typical of many qualitative approaches, our method involved a content analysis in which interview data were partitioned into content domains for the comparison of themes across individual cases (Strauss, 1987). Three trained readers independently read for common themes in students' descriptions of their substance use patterns. Themes were identified and compared within and across schools. Only those themes that were identified by all three readers *independently* were considered common themes in the interviews. The following results section describes the common themes detected from the interviews of the urban and suburban depressed sample by the three data analysts.

---

[9]From the total sample in each school, interviews were conducted with 90 students in the suburban school and 85 students in the urban school. These students were randomly selected from each school sample (only 2 or 3 students in each school refused to be interviewed). The 19 students whose interviews were used for this qualitative analysis were all the students whose CDI scores were in the top 10% in the sample, and who were randomly selected to be interviewed from the total sample.

Results

Differences in Substance Use

(34)   The interviews indicated that substance use was more pervasive among the depressed students in the suburban sample than among those in the inner-city sample. Seven of the 10 students in the suburban sample reported active substance use. Among the 7 current substance users, all reported smoking cigarettes, 6 reported drinking alcohol, 2 reported smoking marijuana, and 1 reported using harder drugs. In contrast to the students at the suburban school, only 3 of the 9 depressed inner-city teens reported active substance use. Of those 3, 2 claimed to smoke cigarettes and drink alcohol, and the third claimed only to drink alcohol. None of the depressed students in the inner-city sample reported current use of marijuana or experimentation (current or past) with drugs harder than marijuana.

Differences in Meaning

(35)   The readers independently identified three common differences across the two schools in the ways that these depressed youth spoke about substance use.

(36)   *Substance Use: Escape from Problems or Cause of Problems?* Five of the 10 depressed students at the suburban school spoke about cigarettes, alcohol, marijuana, and harder drugs as a way to "escape" problems or "relax," while only 1 out of 9 depressed students in the inner-city drew an association between substance use and "escaping" or "relaxing." Among most of the depressed urban youth (8 out of 9), substance use was described as a cause of stress, rather than as an escape from it. In contrast, in the suburban school, only 4 out of 10 depressed students mentioned problems that have resulted or could result from using substances. While both ways of describing substance use (an escape from problems and a source of problems or stress) were almost equally evident (5 vs. 4) in the suburban school, in the urban school, the view that substance use causes problems was clearly predominant among the depressed students.

> Qualitative data analysis consists of describing information and developing themes.

(37)   Included among students' responses from the suburban school is that of Millie, a tenth grader with a history of "off-again-on-again" cigarette and marijuana use, who reports resuming smoking cigarettes after a breakup with her boyfriend: "I got mad and started smoking [cigarettes] again [and] I was smoking weed all the time because I wanted to escape." Janice, a ninth grader at the same high school, smokes about eight cigarettes a day and claims that "something about it relaxes me—if I had to quit now I'd probably get real tense." She also views alcohol as a way to relax, even though "it makes you tired afterwards." Nicole, another ninth grader who smokes about a pack of cigarettes a day, says "I just like the way it makes me feel—it relaxes me sometimes." Drinking for Nicole is one way to "laugh a lot and forget about my problems." Alex, a junior at the suburban high school who has been heavily involved in drugs for many years, claims that while he does not necessarily use drugs to "run away," he views them as "a good way to get away." He also states that he uses LSD and other drugs "not *just* as an escape but because I like it."

(38)   In contrast, Roxie, a sophomore from the urban sample who occasionally drinks alcohol "but only a little bit," states that she sees no benefit to using, only costs:

> Qualitative data analysis consists of text analysis.

> Smoke, I think it smells. . . . Why, why should you risk the point of drinking, you know? I see it as pointless, I guess, to get drunk and have a hangover the next morning. . . . I don't see what's the point in doing those things. It'll mess your head up.

Glen, a freshman at the inner-city school, who occasionally drinks alcohol, says he does not want to drink more than he does because he sees the bad health effects drinking has had on his father. He also says he does not want to use marijuana because he watches his friends smoke and realizes that it leads only to problems. When asked by the interviewer why he stays away from marijuana, he says:

> Just, you cut school, people use it in school, my friends, before school starts and they all be dazed and they got a headache and stuff like that. I don't want to get that.

Vera, a sophomore at the inner-city school who occasionally smokes cigarettes and drinks "sips" of alcohol claims that she controls her use of these substances because she thinks using them often is "stupid" and pointless. She has decided to stop using marijuana because she had a bad experience with it and believes that using drugs just leads to trouble:

> Because to me I think that cigarettes are just like weed. Because I'm like, none of them. Cigarettes always gave me nothing. All weed gave me was that [a "bad trip" on marijuana]. You know, I could have died. . . . It was so scary. . . . So it's like dumb you know, why people do it. Now I think why do they do it? I mean they could die.

Mara, a senior, who does not use any substances, claims that she does not drink because:

> Sometimes when you get drunk you might react improperly, and then you might hit someone and hurt someone that you—that's close to you. So I don't want it to affect anyone.

With regard to drugs, she claims the following:

> Drugs can make people very, very, very—not unattractive, but they might look like someone who is sick and I don't want to look like someone—when people's on the diet and they never eat—they become skinny, skinny and you see bones only. . . . They look like that when they do drugs all the time and never stop.

Yolanda, a freshman in the urban school, claims that she does not use drugs because "I just hear too many people dying . . . of overdose . . . I don't want to be one of them."

(39) In short, substance use was depicted primarily as a cause of problems by the depressed students in the inner-city sample. In the depressed suburban sample, by contrast, substance use was described both as an escape and as a potential problem. It is important to note that the depressed students from each school who depicted substance use as a cause of problems included both substance users and nonusers.

(40) *Interpersonal Relationships and Substance Use.* Students from both the urban and suburban samples discussed the connection between substance use and relationships with family and friends. However, there were differences between the two samples in the way that relationships were reported to affect their substance use decisions. Six out of 10 of the depressed students from the suburban sample emphasized the fear of disappointing or angering someone important to them as a primary inhibitor of substance use, while only 1 out of 9 inner-city students mentioned these factors as reasons not to use. On the other hand, most of the depressed inner-city students (7 out of 9) cited examples of the negative impact drugs or alcohol has had on someone close to them and on people in the community, and stated that this influenced their decisions to abstain or use at low levels. Only 3 out of 10 depressed students from the suburban sample mentioned seeing the negative effects on others as a reason to abstain or modulate use.

(41)   Alisann, a senior at the suburban school, stopped using LSD and cocaine because of disapproval from friends. Gaby, a junior at the suburban school, has decided not to drink more than two bottles of beer at a time "because like my parents, they're trusting me tonight, and look what I'm doing, they'll never be able to trust me again and I wouldn't drink that much, you know." And Terence, a suburban freshman, told the interviewer how he could possibly lose friends if he used drugs, and "I don't think my mother would like it either."

(42)   Unlike these suburban teens, stories from the depressed, inner-city teens speak poignantly of the negative impact of substance use on people close to them. For example, Tara, a senior at the inner-city school, talks about earlier childhood memories of her mother's heavy use of marijuana and alcohol, recalling that "when she was high or drunk she was the meanest person in the world." Such memories, Tara says, make her want to prevent similar experiences for her own children:

> The reason why I don't do it [drugs], because my mother used to do it, and now because I got two kids. So I said I'm not even gonna—I mean, I don't want them to grow up the way I grew up. So I'm not even gonna do it.

(43)   Glen, an urban freshman, says he does not want to drink because he sees the effects on his alcoholic father:

> I don't want to be like him, I don't want to drink that much. Because I think sometimes he's going to pass away because of his liver—because he drinks too much.

In addition, he says he does not use marijuana or cocaine because he has watched his ex-best friend and his uncle become heavily involved in drugs and destroy their lives. Similarly, Elena, an urban junior, has decided not to drink anymore because she has seen the negative impact of alcohol on a boy whom she liked.

(44)   Relationships are mentioned among both the suburban and urban students as influencing their decision to abstain or modulate their use of substances. However, the specific effects of their relationships differed: At the suburban school, the majority of students cited a reluctance to disappoint others, whereas in the urban school, almost all of the teenagers stated that seeing the negative impact on others was one of their main reasons to modulate or abstain from use.

(45)   *Peer Pressure and Substance Use.* Six of the 10 depressed students in the suburban sample reported succumbing to peer pressure to use substances, while none of the depressed students in the urban sample reported being influenced by peer pressure to use or not to use substances. Five of these urban students explicitly stated that they have avoided peer pressure, while none of the depressed suburban students spoke about avoiding peer pressure.

(46)   A suburban sophomore, Millie, provided this telling account of peer pressure:

> I don't like drinking. I don't enjoy it, but everyone else was partying so what else is there to do. . . . I don't want to drink but I want to have a good time with everybody so I do.

Millie adds that when she is at a party drinking she is afraid that she would accept harder drugs if someone were to ask her. Blane, a suburban senior, says he has recently stopped drinking, and that doing so required his complete disassociation from all of his friends who drink. He said the pressure to drink when he was with them would have prevented his efforts toward abstinence. Terence, a suburban freshman, says that while he has not yet experienced pressure to use substances, he can imagine drinking to fit in at a party "but that hasn't happened yet." Alisann, a suburban senior, openly acknowledges that she began to smoke and drink because her friends were doing it. However, she said she eventually stopped because she switched friends and her current friends disapprove of her drinking and using drugs. MaryAnn, a suburban freshman, says that she has increased the number of cigarettes she smokes a day "not because of any reason—just because of the kids I've been hanging around with increased, so I've just increased and there's no reason why I have."

(47)   In contrast, Elena a junior at the inner-city school, stresses her independent stance with her friends:

> If my friends choose to do it, they do it. But they know me. They know me, I don't do it [use substances]. If I wanted to do it, I'd do it, but they have [no] control over me. . . . They know that I'll do what I want to do when I want to do it, and they can't tell me.

Mara, an inner-city senior, matter-of-factly states "I don't do drugs just because I don't want to do it." Glen, a freshman, claims that there is peer pressure to use marijuana but that he "just stays out of that." But, he adds, he feels pressure from his father to drink and he finds that kind of pressure harder to resist. Yolanda and Roxy, a freshman and sophomore, respectively, say that they are aware of peer pressure to use substances but that they have never felt it personally. Yolanda says the pressure has not affected her because nobody in her family or among her friends drinks or uses drugs. In sum, the suburban depressed students report being more influenced by peer pressure to use substances than their counterparts in the urban sample.

Summary and Discussion

(48)   This comparative study of urban and suburban high school students found between-school similarities in levels of reported depression, differences in levels of reported substance use, and most importantly, differences in the *relationships* among depression and substance use. In addition, our qualitative analyses provide possible explanations for the quantitative differences revealed in the relationships among depression and substance use across the two schools.

(49)

Quantitative interpretations compare results with predictions.

It is noteworthy, in our quantitative findings, that levels of depression were similar across the urban and suburban school samples. This finding stands in contrast to what one might expect given the relatively more stressful environment of the inner-city. It is possible that inner-city adolescents may develop psychological and emotional resilience in response to the extraordinary stresses of their social environment, resulting in levels of depression that do not exceed what might be expected in other populations of adolescents.

(50)   While there were no significant gender differences in the mean level of depression within each school, girls were overrepresented in the top 10% of depression scores in both schools, suggesting gender differences in the severity, if not the overall prevalence, of depression. The lack of significant gender differences in mean depression scores on the CDI is consistent with previous findings in other large scale studies (Doerfler *et al.,* 1988; Green, 1980; Kovacs, 1983; Weissman *et al.,* 1980). However, similar to our findings, studies that have looked beyond the mean scores on the depression scale have found, typically, that more girls score in the higher range of depression scores on the CDI than boys (McCauley *et al.,* 1988; Reinherz *et al.,* 1991; Worchel *et al.,* 1987).

(51)   Our failure to find grade differences in levels of depression within either school is consistent with previous findings on the relationship be-

tween age and depression among adolescents (Doerfler *et al.,* 1988; Green, 1980; Kovacs, 1983; Weissman *et al.,* 1980). The CDI has been administered to children and adolescents from varying backgrounds and has consistently revealed no significant relationship between the age of the respondent and the severity of self-rated depressive symptomatology (Doerfler *et al.,* 1988; Weissman *et al.,* (1980).

(52)   The suburban school students in our study reported higher levels of cigarette, alcohol, and harder drug use than the inner-city school students, while there were equal levels of reported marijuana use in both schools. These findings are similar to related research that has found a lower rate of reported drug use among African-American youth when compared with other ethnic groups such as European-Americans (Darling and Brown, 1992; McCord, 1990). When interpreting our findings, however, one must consider the drop-out rates of public education. The inner-city school, which is quite typical of urban public schools, has a drop-out rate approximately eight times higher than that of the suburban school (32% vs. 4% respectively). Our school-based study, therefore, excludes those adolescents who have left school, perhaps as a result of substance use problems or other high-risk behaviors. It is important to remember, however, that not only were there equal levels of reported marijuana use across the two schools, but the distribution of cigarette, marijuana, and alcohol use was normal in both schools. Therefore, the exclusion of many of the urban dropouts did not lead to the exclusion of urban alcohol and drug users.[10]

(53)   Levels of reported substance use differed by gender and by grade in the suburban school; in the urban school, alcohol use varied by grade, and marijuana use differed only by gender for the African-American youth. These findings are somewhat similar to those of other studies, which have found age and gender differences in levels of substance use among adolescents; younger adolescents and girls have reported less substance use than older adolescents and boys respectively (Andrews *et al.,* 1992). However, contrary to findings in previous studies, our data from the urban school indicate that younger adolescents were not less likely to use cigarettes, marijuana, or harder drugs than older adolescents, and with the exception of marijuana use among African-American youth, girls were not less likely to use substances than boys. The finding that African-American girls used significantly less marijuana than African-American boys is similar to the finding among Caucasian youth in the suburban school.

(54)   A possible explanation for this lack of grade differences in the level of substance use in the urban sample is that drugs may be more accessible to adolescents not yet in high school in the inner-city than they are for their peers in the suburbs. Therefore, urban adolescents who decide to experiment with substances may begin at an earlier age (e.g., seventh or eighth grade) than their peers in the suburbs. Thus, when the relationship between age and substance use is examined in a high school population, transitions from not using to experimentation, or from experimentation to regular or heavy substance use, are not as readily apparent among inner-city students as among suburban students. Another equally plausible explanation for the lack of grade differences in substance use in the urban

[10]This may not be the case for harder drug users. Since few students in the urban school reported using harder drugs, we believe the high dropout rate in the inner-city may have led to a very negatively skewed distribution of harder drug use in the urban school. Mensch and Kandel (1988) concluded, in their research on dropouts, that there is a strong positive association between heavy drug use and dropping out of school.

school is that the urban students who increase their use of substances during high school may be more likely to drop out than their peers in the suburban school. Therefore, the expected relationships among grade and substance use are not apparent in the urban sample because the older adolescents who may use more substances than the younger adolescents simply are not in school anymore.

(55)   Our findings indicated gender and school differences in the relationships among substance use and depression. In the suburban sample, gender differences were detected specifically in the relationships between depression and marijuana use, and between depression and harder drug use. The relationships between depression and these substances, respectively, was greater for suburban girls than for suburban boys. This finding replicates previous findings regarding the differences between white girls and boys in the relationships among depression and substance use (Paton and Kandel, 1978; Reinhertz *et al.*, 1991). If suburban girls are more likely to be socially stigmatized for using drugs, such as marijuana or harder drugs, than suburban boys (in middle class communities, at least, there may be more pressures for girls not to use drugs than boys), then perhaps the suburban girls who decide to engage in drug use (ignoring the social consequences) may be more likely to experience or be experiencing psychological difficulties (i.e., feeling depressed) than the suburban boys who engage in drug use. For suburban boys, drug use may be more commonly sanctioned and, therefore, suburban male substance users may be more psychologically or socially heterogeneous than their female counterparts (i.e., it may not only be the boys who are feeling depressed who choose to use drugs). Suburban boys may be also less likely to become depressed after using drugs because they may not be as socially stigmatized for using drugs as are suburban girls. Because of the possible social stigmatization for suburban girls who use drugs, those who decide to use drugs may be more likely to be on the "fringe" of their female peers. Those on the "fringe" may more likely be depressed or become depressed as a result of the social stigmatization of either using drugs or simply being on the "fringe."

(56)   There were no gender differences, however, in the urban school with respect to the relationships among depression and substance use. There were no relationships among depression and substance use. There were no relationships among depression and substance use for either the boys or the girls. Given these findings, it is difficult to explain the apparent absence of gender differences in these relationships. It appears that the phenomena of substance use and depression are different among the urban students from those among the suburban students. These phenomena for urban adolescents must be explored further before hypotheses can be made concerning the lack of gender differences between depression and each of the substances.

(57)   With regard to school differences, depression in the suburban school was positively correlated with the use of cigarettes, marijuana, and harder drugs, while in the urban school, depression was not correlated with the use of any substances. This finding lends support to Siegel and Ehrlich's (1989) and Paton and Kandel's (1978) contention that "adolescents from different ethnic [and] or socio-economic backgrounds may take drugs for different reasons" (Siegel and Ehrlich, 1989, p. 925). This finding also suggests that depression may be associated with different behaviors depending on the social context. Darling and Brown (1992) recently found that delinquency, including heavy drug use, and academic disengagement were related among adolescents in rural and suburban areas, but not in urban areas. They assert, along with Sutherland and Cressey (1978), that problem behaviors may cluster differently depending on the social context

in which the child lives. With respect to the current study, depression may simply be a different type of phenomenon for urban youth than for suburban youth.

(58)   However, it is important to remember that *both* schools revealed no significant correlations between alcohol use and depression (although the relationship was significant for suburban girls, there were no gender differences found in the interactional analyses). Given the prevalence and social acceptability of alcohol use among many high school students, one of the reasons for this finding may be that those students who do use alcohol to deal with their depression or become depressed after using alcohol may be outnumbered by those who use alcohol to have "fun" or "relax" with their peers in a socially acceptable way. This type of phenomenon could explain the nonsignificant correlation between depression and alcohol use in both schools.

(59)   The qualitative analyses described in this paper focused on one major finding of this study, namely, the differential relationship between depression and substance use across the suburban and inner-city school samples. Analyses of interview data from the most depressed students in each school elucidated possible reasons for this dissimilar relationship. First, the view that substance use is a vehicle for relaxation or "escape" may be a perspective unique to individuals living in relatively sheltered environments. Our interview data suggest that depressed children in the inner-city sample are markedly more in touch with the deleterious effects of substance use than are depressed students from the suburban school. The urban students commonly gave examples of the negative effects of drug and alcohol use on close family members or friends. The suburban depressed students rarely gave such responses; when they did speak about the negative aspects of substance use, these students primarily focused on their fears of disappointing others if they engaged in substance use. Since the urban students seem to be more acutely aware of the potential negative effects of substance use itself, perhaps these students may be less likely than the suburban students to use substances to cope with depression.

(60)   Varying perspectives on depression may further explain school differences in the relationships among depression and substance use. For example, the belief that depressed or painful feelings are "treatable" (e.g., through the use of substances) may be more common among people living in relative privilege than among people for whom depression associated with life's difficulties may seem as endemic as the difficulties themselves.

(61)   The aforementioned interpretations, however, assume depression to be a cause, rather than a consequence, of substance use. Given that our quantitative analyses highlight associations rather than directionality between the variables, no conclusions are being drawn about cause and effect between depression and substance use.[11] However, if substance use is causing depression rather than vice versa, perhaps the social stigmatization that suburban substance users may feel leads them to become increasingly depressed. Social stigmatization may occur for suburban boys who are *heavily* involved with substances as opposed to suburban girls for whom it may occur at all levels of involvement with substances. There were stories in the interviews among the nondepressed girls and some of the nondepressed boys that conveyed a sense of disgust at their peers, girls or boys, whom they thought were heavily involved in drugs.

---

[11]Given that our study assesses one point in time and does not include a control group, we were not able to determine causality among the variables.

(62)   Finally, depressed students in the inner-city who are reporting less susceptibility to peer pressure and reporting a perspective that substance use augurs trouble rather than relief may be describing aspects of a need to preserve a measure of personal security that the urban environment cannot consistently provide for them. A commitment to avoid drugs in the interest of maintaining personal safety may prevail especially in the face of depression or despair when life may feel particularly out of one's control. In contrast, children raised in the suburbs may feel a greater personal freedom to take certain risks when they are feeling depressed, or to consciously experience depression when they are using substances, believing that the fundamental securities of their environment will nonetheless remain intact.

(63)   Our qualitative study of depressed students' beliefs and attitudes about substance use suggests that depressed urban and suburban students may differ in their views about substance use. These different attitudes and beliefs may be centrally important to understanding why depression and substance use are differently related across schools. However, in future studies it would be important to examine beliefs and attitudes concerning substance use held by a broader population of students, including those reporting no, low, or moderate levels of depression. Such an examination could help determine whether the attitudes and beliefs revealed in our qualitative analyses are unique to depressed students (and somehow related to "being depressed") or whether these beliefs are typical of the larger student body in each school.

Qualitative interpretations situate findings within larger meanings.

Implications

(64)   Our finding concerning urban and suburban school differences in the relationship between substance use and depression has implications for future research, and potentially, for the goals of adolescent substance use treatment programs. First, subsequent research is needed to determine whether the apparent relationship between depression and substance use for suburban students, and the apparent absence of this relationship for urban students, is representative of the experiences of urban and suburban adolescents in other geographical areas. If, as suggested by our study and by previous research, the psychological correlates of substance use typically vary across urban and suburban populations of adolescents, than the effective treatment of adolescent substance use and abuse will necessarily rest upon a consideration and incorporation of these differences. Effective treatment for suburban adolescents, for example, should include a concurrent focus on the depression that may both motivate and ensue from substance use, particularly for adolescent girls. In addition, further research on the psychological correlates of urban adolescents' substance use is needed to enhance the efficacy of treatment programs for this population. Increasing evidence that the psychological diversity of adolescent substance users is informed by factors such as gender, ethnicity, and environmental context argues strongly for prevention and intervention efforts that are sensitive to the role of these differences in the etiology and psychological consequences of substance use.

Quantitative research reports use standard, fixed structures and evaluation criteria.

Qualitative research reports use flexible and emerging structures and evaluation criteria.

References

Andrews, J. A., Hops, H., Duncan, S. C., Tildesley, E., Ary, D., and Smolkowski, K. (1992, March). Long-term consequences of level of substance use in adolescence. Paper presented at the fourth biennial meetings of the Society for Research on Adolescence, Washington, DC.

Aneshensel, C. S., and Huba, G. J. (1983). Depression, alcohol use, and smoking over one year: A four wave longitudinal causal model. *J. Abnorm. Psychol.* 92: 134–150.

Blau, G., Gillespie, J., Felner, R. D., and Evans, E. G. (1988). Predisposition to drug use in rural adolescents: Preliminary relationships and methodological considerations. *J. Drug Educat.* 18: 13–22.

Braucht, G. N., Brakarsch, D., Follingstad, D., and Berry, K. L. (1973). Deviant drugs use in adolescence: A review of psychological correlates. *Psychol. Bull.* 79: 92–106.

Darling, N., and Brown, B. B. (1992, March) Patterning of academic performance and deviance among African-American and European-American youths in three communities. Paper presented at the biennial meetings of the Society for Research on Adolescence, Washington, DC.

Dembo, R., Burgos, W., Des Jarlais, D., and Schmeidler, J. (1979). Ethnicity and drug use among urban junior high school youths. *Intl. J. Addict.* 14: 557–568.

Doerfler, L., Felner, R., Rowlison, R., Raley, P., & Evans, E. (1988). Depression in children and adolescents: A comparative analysis of the utility and construct validity of two assessment measures. *J. Consult. Clin. Psychol.* 56: 769–772.

Donovan, J., Costa, F., and Jessor, R. (1985). *Health Questionnaire.* University of Colorado, Institute of Behavioral Science.

Finch, A. J., Saylor, C. F., and Edwards, (1985). Children's Depression Inventory: Sex and grade norms for normal children. *J. Consult. Clin. Psychol.* 53: 424–425.

Green, B. J. (1980). Depression in early adolescence: An exploratory investigation of its frequency, intensity, and correlates (Doctoral dissertation, Pennsylvania State University). *Dissert. Abst. Int.* 41: 3890B.

Hager, D. L., Verner, A. M., & Stewart, C. S. (1971). Patterns of adolescent drug use in middle America. *J. Counsel. Psychol.* 18: 292–297.

Harris, E. M. (1971). Measurement of alienation of college students: Marijuana users and nonusers. *J. School Health* 41: 130–133.

Kaminer, Y. (1991). The magnitude of concurrent psychiatric disorders in hospitalized substance abusing adolescents. *Child Psychiat. Human Develop.* 22: 89–95.

Kaplan, S. L., Nussbaum, M., Skomorowsky, P., Shenker, R., and Ramsey, P. (1980). Health habits and depression in adolescence. *J. Youth Adolesc.* 9: 299–304.

Kaplan, S. L., Landa, B., Weinhold, C., and Shenker, R. (1984). Adverse health behaviors and depressive symptomatology in adolescents. *J. Am. Acad. Child Psychiat.* 23: 595–601.

Kennedy, B., Konstantareas, M., and Homatidis, S. (1987). A behavior profile of polydrug abusers. *J. Youth Adolesc.* 16: 115–117.

Kovacs, M. (1980–1981). Rating scales to assess depression in school-aged children. *Acta Paedopsychiat.* 46: 305–315.

Kovacs, M. (1982). The Children's Depression Inventory: A self-rated depression scale for school-aged youngsters. Unpublished manuscript, University of Pittsburgh.

Kovacs, M. (1983). Definition and assessment of childhood depressions. In Ricks, D. F., and Dohrenwend, B. S. (eds.), *Origins of Psychopathology: Problems in Research and Public Policy.* Cambridge University Press, New York.

Kovacs, M. (1985). The Children's Depression Inventory. *Psychol. Bull.* 21: 995–998.

Mensch, B. S., and Kandel, D. B. (1988). Dropping out of high school and drug involvement. *Sociol. Educat.* 61: 95–113.

McCauley, E., Burke, P., Mitchell, J., and Moss, S. (1988). Cognitive attributes of depression in children and adolescents. *J. Consult. Clin. Psychol.* 56: 903–908.

McCord, J. (1990). Problems behaviors. In Feldman, S. S., and Elliot, G. R. (eds.), *At the Threshold: The Developing Adolescent.* Harvard University Press, Cambridge, MA.

Paton, S., and Kandel, D. B. (1978). Psychological factors and adolescent illicit drugs use: Ethnicity and sex differences. *Adolescence* 13: 187–199.

Paton, S., Kessler, R., and Kandel, D. (1977). Depressive mood and adolescent illicit drug use: A longitudinal analysis. *J. Genet. Psychol.* 131: 267–289.

Prendergast, T. J. (1974). Family characteristics associated with marijuana use among adolescents. *Int. J. Addict.* 12: 625–632.

Reinherz, H. Z., Frost, A. K., and Pakiz, B. (1991). Changing faces: Correlates of depressive symptoms in late adolescence. *Family Commun. Health* 14: 52–63.

Robins, L. N., & Przybeck, T. R. (1985). Age of onset of drug use as a factor in drug and other disorders. In Jones, C. L., and Battjes, R. J. (eds.), *Etiology of Drug Abuse: Implication for Prevention.* National Institute of Drug Abuse, Rockville, MD.

Saylor, C. F., Finch, A. J., Spirito, A., and Bennett, B. (1984). The Children's Depression Inventory: A systematic evaluation of psychometric properties. *J. Consult. Clin. Psychol.* 52: 955–967.

Shiffman, S., and Wills, T. A. (1985). *Coping and Substance Use.* Free Press, New York.

Siegel, R. A., and Ehrlich, A. (1989). A comparison of personality characteristics, family relationships, and drug-taking behavior in low and high socioeconomic status adolescents who are drug abusers. *Adolescence* 24: 925–936.

Simons, R. L., Whitbeck, L. B., Conger, R. D., and Melby, J. N. (1991). The effects of social skills, values, peers, and depression on adolescent substance use. *J. Early Adoles.* 11: 466–481.

Simons, R., Conger, R. D., and Whitbeck, L. B. (1988). A multistage social learning model of the influences of family and peers upon adolescent substance abuse. *J. Drug Issues* 18: 293–315.

Skager, R., and Firth, S. L. (1988). *Identifying High Risk Substance Users in Grades 9 and 11: A Report Based on the 1987/1988 California Substance Abuse Survey.* Crime Prevention Center, Office of the Attorney General, Sacramento, CA.

Strauss, A. (1987). *Qualitative Analysis for Social Scientists.* Cambridge University Press, New York.

Smart, R. G., and Fejer, D. (1969). Illicit drug users: Their social backgrounds, drug use and psychopathology. *J. Health Social. Behav.* 10: 297–308.

Sutherland, E. W., and Cressey, D. R. (1978). *Criminology* (10th ed.). Lippincott, Philadelphia, PA.

Way, N., Stauber, H., and Nakkula, M. (1990). Hopelessness, depression, and substance use in two divergent cultures. Paper presented at the Society for Research on Child Development in Seattle, WA.

Weissman, M. M., Orvaschel, H., and Padian, N. (1980). Children's symptom and social functioning self-report scales: Comparison of mothers' and children's reports. *J. Nervous and Mental Dis.* 168: 736–740.

Worchel, F., Nolan, B., and Wilson, V. (1987). New perspectives on child and adolescent depression. *J. School Psychol.* 25: 411–414.

Action Research Designs

Let's assume that Maria, our high school teacher, chooses to conduct action research for her school committee and graduate program. An action research study addressing a practical school issue would have both applied interest to her school violence committee as well as to her faculty advisor who sees the value of bridging academic research with application. Maria's research question might be: "How can I change the attitudes of students in my class to be more concerned about the potential for violence in schools?" To study this question, Maria might collect information from her students using procedures such as a brief survey (for quantitative data) and have them journal for a couple of months about their experiences with weapon possession in the high school (for qualitative data). Maria might share results of this data with her fellow teachers, Alis, John, and Jane, and obtain their reaction to her information. Based on this assessment as well as her own, Maria will devise a plan of action—to try some approaches to change student attitudes, such as role-playing typical student-to-student interactions about potentially violent incidents. Maria will then assess whether her research changes student attitudes, and share her information with the school committee and graduate program faculty.

As you can see with Maria's design, action research has an applied focus. Similar to mixed method research, action research uses data collection based on either quantitative or qualitative methods. However, it differs in that action research addresses a specific, practical issue and seeks to obtain solutions to a problem.

As a design, action research provides educators an opportunity to reflect on their own practices. Within the scope of a school, action research offers a means for staff development, for teachers' development as professionals, and for addressing schoolwide problems (Allen & Calhoun, 1998). In fact, the scope of action research provides a means for the teachers or educators in the schools to improve their practices (i.e., taking *action*) and to do so in disciplined inquiry (i.e., *research*). The following action research studies illustrate typical examples of this design.

▶ In her third year of teaching, Sue had no experience in the concepts of emergent literacy, such as allowing children to choose their own topics, engage in free journal writing, and experiment with invented spelling (Ceprano & Garan, 1998). As a result she engaged in an action research project. In this project she allowed

18 students in a graduate class to become pen pals with each of her first-grade students. During the semester, the 18 students wrote weekly letters to Sue's first-graders and the elementary students wrote back. As the student letters came back, the graduate students analyzed the letters for qualitative themes, such as voice and technical writing. The letters gave the graduate students an opportunity to reflect on the children's early writing development. Sue then modified her classroom instruction and implemented interclass pen pal writing between her first-graders and eighth-graders.

▶ A teacher studied his one-semester biochemistry course in a residential school for talented math and science students using a quantitative action research study (Dods, 1997). This instructor was curious about whether problem-based learning was superior to the traditional lecture format. As a result of the surveys, the teacher concluded that problem-based learning promotes in-depth understanding and that lectures enhance content coverage.

▶ Three full-time and two part-time faculty formed a research team in one university to conduct an action research study about the constraints facing part-time faculty (Watters, Christensen, Arcodia, Ryan, & Weeks, 1998). They sought to change the campus practices by collecting and analyzing data from a demographic survey, focus groups, and selective interviews. They then conducted a one-day workshop based on issues and concerns raised, and formed action groups to conduct ongoing research. As a result of the study, the campus administrators acknowledged, for the first time, the contribution of part-time faculty. The school also initiated structural change, and the part-time staff formed a professional association to dialogue with the university administration.

These studies illustrate how individual teachers, a school-university team, and university faculty can engage in action research. They also show how both quantitative and qualitative methods can help individuals and teams understand practical problems in education. Action research is a useful design to address specific classroom problems and to empower individuals to improve their work situations. In all of these projects, **action research** is systematic inquiry done by teachers (or other individuals in an educational setting) to gather information about—and subsequently improve—the ways their particular educational setting operates, how they teach, and how well their students learn (Mills, 2000). It aims to improve the practice of education by individuals studying issues or problems they face. Educators reflect about these problems, collect and analyze data, and implement changes based on their findings. In some cases, the research is aimed at solving a local, practical problem, such as a classroom issue for a teacher. In other situations, the researcher seeks to empower, transform, and emancipate individuals from situations that constrain their self-development and self-determination. This chapter explores the broad scope of action research as it is practiced in education today.

By the end of this chapter you should be able to:

▶ Identify major events in the historical development of action research.
▶ Describe the use of practical and participatory action research designs.
▶ Describe key characteristics of action research.
▶ Identify the steps in conducting an action research study.
▶ List the criteria for evaluating an action research report.

A BRIEF HISTORY OF ACTION RESEARCH

The development of action research may be conveniently presented as three distinct stages. The first stage consisted of the identification of a process for addressing societal issues. The second stage turned toward practice and the need to involve practitioners, such as teachers, in the solution to their own problems. The third and most recent phase represented the participatory, emancipatory, or community action research approach in which groups assumed responsibility for their own emancipation and change.

The social-psychologist Kurt Lewin coined the term "action research" in the 1930s (Mills, 2000). Lewin felt that social conditions in the 1940s—such as the shortage of meat, the need for aerial reconnaissance during World War II, and the improvement of inter-cultural group relations after the war—might be enhanced through the process of group discussions. These group processes consisted of four steps: planning, acting, observing, and reflecting. By focusing on group process and identifying phases of action, Lewin's approach presaged many of the modern ideas of action research: a process of steps, participation, the democratic impulse of involvement, and the contribution to social change (Kemmis, 1994). Spreading from the social sector to education, Lewin's ideas were adopted at the Horace-Mann-Lincoln Institute at Teachers College, Columbia University, and in England at the Tavistock Institute.

This spread of action research slowed during the mid- to late 1950s. The growing gulf between theory and practice, the emphasis on research development in regional educational laboratories, and the emphasis on experiments and systematic research all contributed to this decline. Then, in the 1970s, action research projects in Great Britain, the United States, and Australia reemerged. For example, the Fort Teaching project in England focused on teachers studying their own practices. The *Classroom Action Research Network* at the Cambridge Institute of Education in Great Britain addresses practical issues between teachers and students. Team-based inquiry between researchers and the schools emerged at Columbia University in the United States. The emancipation of individuals in education based on the German writings of Habermas became the focus of inquiry by the Australian Stephen Kemmis and his colleagues (Kemmis & McTaggart, 2000).

Having teachers study their own classroom problems and issues has emerged as an important direction for school renewal today. As shown in Figure 18.1, the movement toward action research has evolved from the "in-service" days of the 1970s, to the site-based plans for staff development during the 1980s, to the present emphasis on educators reflecting on their own practices (Schmuck, 1997). Reasons cited today for the importance of action research reinforce these trends. Action research:

- encourages change in the schools
- fosters a democratic (i.e., involvement of many individuals) approach to education
- empowers individuals through collaboration on projects
- positions teachers and other educators as learners who seek to narrow the gap between practice and their vision of education
- encourages educators to reflect on their practices
- promotes a process of testing new ideas (Mills, 2000)

Although action research has gained support in education, it is not without critics who are reluctant to view it as a legitimate form of inquiry (Stringer, 1999). Action research may be viewed as an informal process of research conducted by teachers and other educators who are not formal academic researchers. The practical aspect of action research also suggests an "applied" orientation to this form of inquiry—something viewed as less than scientific. Action researchers typically report results of their studies not to scholarly journals in education, but to on-line journals, Web sites, or local school groups. The methods are adapted and changed in response to the practitioners' objectives to understand a

FIGURE 18.1

Evolution of Action Research for Teachers and Schools

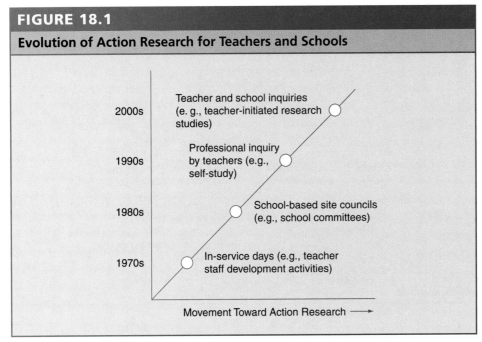

Source: Adapted from Schmuck, 1997.

practical problem. Hence, the design may not have the rigor and systematic approach found in other designs.

Despite these concerns, action research fulfills an important role for the teacher researcher and school-based teams formed to study local school issues. It also provides a design that encourages collaboration among school and community participants to help transform schools and educational practices.

TYPES OF ACTION RESEARCH DESIGNS

To see how these objectives are met, we need to explore the primary types of action research studies being used today. Unquestionably, action research means different things to different people, and some writers hold limited views as to what counts as action research (Watters, et al., 1998). A review of the major writers in education, however, shows that the two following basic research designs are typically discussed (Mills, 2000):

- practical action research
- participatory action research

As you read about these two forms of action research, the overview of their differences shown in Figure 18.2 will help distinguish between their major features.

Practical Action Research

Teachers seek to research problems in their own classrooms so that they can improve their students' learning and their own professional performance. Teams comprised of teachers, students, counselors, and administrators engage in action research to address common issues, such as escalating violence in school. In these illustrations, educators seek to enhance the practice of education through the systematic study of a local problem. This form of action research is called **practical action research** and its purpose is to research

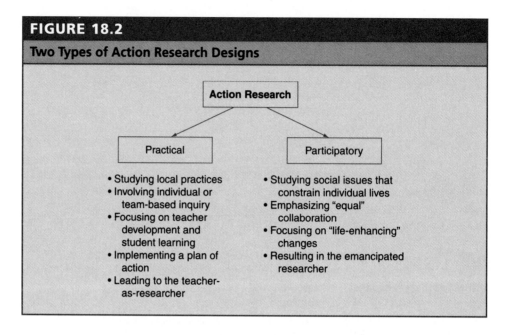

FIGURE 18.2

Two Types of Action Research Designs

a specific school situation with a view toward improving practice (Schmuck, 1997). Practical action research focuses on a small-scale research project, narrowly focused on a specific problem or issue, and undertaken by individual teachers or teams within a school or school district. Examples of practical action research studies are:

▶ An elementary teacher studies the disruptive behavior of a child in her classroom.
▶ A team composed of students, teachers, and parents studies the results of implementing a new math program in the junior high.
▶ A community college instructor studies his professional development using technology in teaching.
▶ A high school teacher collaborates with students to study the implementation of writing portfolios in a new writing program.

In all of these examples, action research seeks to improve specific, local issues. It calls for educators to involve teachers in research to study concerns in their own schools or classrooms and to implement site-based councils or committees in schools to enhance research as an integral part of daily classes and education. In this spirit, educators can test their own theories and explanations about learning, examine the effects of their practices on students, and explore the impact of approaches on parents, colleagues, and administrators within their schools.

A drawback of this approach is that while teachers seek to improve their classroom practices, they have little time to engage in their own research. Although teachers may be good at what they do and familiar with teaching kids in classes, they may need assistance in becoming researchers. To this end, they can participate in graduate classes, which will help them renew or develop the requisite skills for inquiry required in an action research project (e.g., Hughes, 1999; Kosnik, 1996).

To understand practical action research we need to review its major ideas or principles. As identified by Mills (2000), the principles below focus on assumptions about the role of teachers as learners, as reflective practitioners, and as individuals engaging in small-scale research projects.

▶ Teacher researchers have decision-making authority to study an educational practice as part of their own ongoing professional development.

▶ Teacher researchers are committed to continued professional development and school improvement, a core assumption for any teacher who decides to engage in action research.

▶ Teacher researchers want to reflect on their practices. This reflection is seen as a means for improving practices and it shows concern for improvement. This reflection can be conducted individually or in school-based teams composed of students, teachers, and administrators.

▶ Teacher researchers use a systematic approach for reflecting on their practices, meaning that they use identifiable procedures to study their own problems rather than using a random, anything-goes design.

▶ Teacher researchers will choose an area of focus, determine data collection techniques, analyze and interpret data, and develop action plans.

This final point refers to the process of research. The books about practical action research advance detailed steps that teachers and other educators might use to conduct a study. Mills (2000), for example, discusses several of these models, then advances his own and uses it as the framework for chapters in his book. He calls his model the "dialectic action research spiral." This model, shown in Figure 18.3, provides teachers with a four-step guide for their action research project. Mills emphasizes that it is a model for teachers to use to study themselves, not a process of conducting research *on* teachers. It is a "spiral" because it includes four stages where investigators cycle back and forth between data collection and a focus, and data collection and analysis and interpretation.

In this procedure, the teacher researcher identifies an area of focus. This process involves defining an area of focus, doing reconnaissance (self-reflection and description), reviewing the literature, and writing an action plan to guide the research. Then the teacher researcher collects data by gathering multiple sources of data (quantitative and qualitative) and by using a variety of inquiry tools, such as interviews, questionnaires, or attitude scales. Data collection also consists of attending to issues of validity, reliability, and ethics, such as provisions for informed consent. The action researcher follows this phase by analysis and interpretation. The process includes identifying themes; coding surveys, interviews, and questionnaires; asking key questions; doing an organizational review; engaging in concept mapping (i.e., visualizing the relationship of ideas); analyzing antecedents and consequences; and displaying findings. Interpretation involves extending the analysis by raising questions, connecting findings to personal experiences, seeking the advice of critical friends, and contextualizing the findings in literature and theory. In the final stage, the teacher researcher finally completes an action plan or chart. This chart includes a summary of findings, recommended

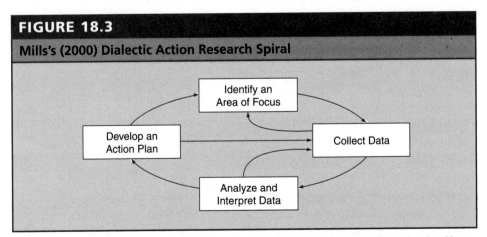

FIGURE 18.3

Mills's (2000) Dialectic Action Research Spiral

Identify an Area of Focus

Develop an Action Plan

Collect Data

Analyze and Interpret Data

Source: Action Research by Mills, © 2000. Reprinted by permission of Pearson Education, Inc. Upper Saddle River, NJ 07458.

actions, and the identification of individuals responsible for action and individuals who need to be consulted and informed. The chart also indicates who will monitor and collect the data, the time line to be used, and the resources needed to carry out the action.

Overall, this process emphasizes practical action research centered around studying a local problem, engaging in inquiry by an individual teacher (teacher-as-researcher) or a team, and focusing on teacher development. A review of an actual study can illustrate this practical approach to action research.

Hughes (1999) was a fourth-grade teacher in a small country-suburban K–8 district school. She begins by describing her class and the problem of not having in-class support for high-ability students in her room. The gifted students were pulled out of her classroom daily during math instruction in order to work on special science projects. In view of this, she wondered whether she was meeting the needs of these high-ability students and she initiated an action research study. Here were the steps she took:

1. She first reviewed the published literature on her issue (e.g., pull-out programs, inclusion of gifted in the classroom, and meeting the needs of the gifted).
2. In addition, she interviewed colleagues from her school and neighboring elementary schools for their perspectives.
3. From the literature review and her interviews, she identified four themes—school reform, enrichment versus acceleration, pull-out versus in-class, and new educational strategies—and developed a flowchart listing the factors that surfaced for each theme, such as:

school reform-movement ideas

equity for all—every child receives what he or she needs to grow and learn, and not every child receives the exact same instruction

excellence for all where every child is challenged to the limit of his or her abilities (p. 284)

4. Based on this information, she refined her original research questions and collected both quantitative and qualitative data through parent telephone interviews, student surveys, teacher conferences with students about their work portfolios, and classroom observations by six different teachers for each question. She placed this information in a chart so that her team members could help her analyze the data.
5. She enlisted the study-team members of six other elementary teachers from her building to help with the process of data analysis.
6. The team first skimmed the data to obtain a clear picture of it and then sorted all of the data under four themes about how to incorporate gifted children into the class (in-class flexible groups, differentiated instruction, enrichment, and acceleration).
7. These themes were turned into four major activities for the teacher to try in her classroom.
8. Next she put the findings into an "action plan," resulting in specific activities (e.g., continue to self-evaluate and find ways to incorporate differentiated instruction and assessment in the classroom).
9. She shared her findings with others, to "make a difference on a larger scale." (p. 295). This included sharing her study with other fourth-grade teachers, her principal, and a district committee.
10. The study ended with Hughes reflecting on future questions that she needed answered, such as, "Which is better, pull-out programs, in-class programs, or a combination?".

The ten steps above illustrate a good practical action research study in which a teacher collaborates to study a local problem, develops as a professional, uses a systematic approach to inquiry (e.g., gathering and analyzing data), and implements a plan of action.

Participatory Action Research

Participatory action research (PAR) has a long history in social inquiry involving communities, industries and corporations, and other organizations outside of education (e.g., see Whyte, 1991). Rather than a focus on individual teachers solving immediate classroom problems or schools addressing internal issues, participatory action research has a social and community orientation and an emphasis on research that contributes to emancipation or change in our society. Drawing on the work of the South American Paulo Freire, the German critical theorist Jurgen Habermas, and more recently Australians Stephen Kemmis and Ernest Stringer (Schmuck, 1997), this approach has emerged as an action-oriented, advocacy means of inquiry. Often PAR includes qualitative data collection, but it may also involve quantitative data collection.

Participatory action research is referred to by different, but compatible names, such as "community-based" inquiry (Stringer, 1999, p. 9), "collaborative action research" or "participatory research" (Kemmis & McTaggart, 2000, p. 567), or "critical" action research (Mills, 2000, p. 7). To acknowledge the collaborative nature of this type of inquiry, this chapter will use the term "participatory action research."

The purpose of **participatory action research** is to improve the quality of people's organization, community, and family lives (Stringer, 1999). Although espousing many of the ideas of teacher and school-based practical action research, it differs by incorporating an emancipatory aim of improving and empowering individuals and organizations in educational (and other) settings. Applied to education, there is a focus on improving and empowering individuals in schools, systems of education, and school communities. Participatory action research also has a distinct ideological foundation that shapes the direction of the process of inquiry in the type of issue that commands attention of the action researcher; in the procedures of research, especially data collection; and in the intent and outcomes of the inquiry.

For example, participatory action researchers study issues that relate to a need to address social problems that constrain and repress the lives of students and educators. For example, consider these issues that address social, economic, political, and class problems in our society that may be the focus of a PAR study:

- tests that label and stereotype students
- curricula that deny students enrollment in established fields of study
- texts that omit important historical persons or events of cultural and ethnic groups
- assessments that serve to confirm student failure rather than learning
- K–12 classroom interactions that silence or quiet the voices of certain students
- inequitable distribution of college faculty salaries that favor men over women

In addition to studying these sensitive issues, the participatory action researcher also engages in a process of research that promotes equalitarian and democratic aims. PAR researchers strive for an open, broad-based involvement of participants in their studies by collaborating in decisions as consensual partners and engaging participants as "equals" to ensure their well-being. For example, in their inquiries researchers emphasize the importance of establishing contacts, identifying stakeholder groups, identifying key people, negotiating the researcher's role, and building a preliminary picture of the field context of the study (Stringer, 1999). The social values of liberation and life-enhancing changes also are important, and action researchers seek to bring about a new vision for schools, community agencies, youth clubs, and ethnic groups within schools.

Kemmis and Wilkinson (1998) summarize six central features of participatory action research, listed below.

1. PAR is a social process where the researcher deliberately explores the relationship between the individual and other people. The object is to understand how

individuals are formed and re-formed through social interaction. Applied to education, participatory action researchers might explore teachers working together in teams.

2. This form of inquiry is participatory. This means that individuals conduct studies "on" themselves. During this process, people examine how their own understandings, skills, values, and present knowledge both frame and constrain their actions. Teachers, for example, would study themselves to gain a better understanding of their practices and how this knowledge shapes (and constrains) their work with students.

3. This form of research is practical and collaborative. It is collaborative because it is inquiry completed "with" others. It is practical because researchers typically explore acts of communication, the production of knowledge, and the structure of social organization with an intent to reduce irrational, unproductive, unjust, or unsatisfying interactions. Teachers, for example, might collaborate with other teachers to reduce the unproductive and unsatisfying levels of bureaucracy in a school that might inhibit classroom innovations.

4. PAR is emancipatory in that it helps unshackle people from the constraints of irrational and unjust structures that limit self-development and self-determination. The intent of a study, for example, might be to change the bureaucratic procedures for teachers in schools so that they can better facilitate student learning.

5. One intent of PAR research is to help individuals free themselves from constraints found in the media, in language, in work procedures, and in the relationships of power in educational settings. For instance, teachers may be constrained by a subservient role in the school district so that they do not feel empowered in their classrooms.

6. PAR is recursive (reflexive or dialectical) and focused on bringing about change in practices. This occurs through spirals of reflection and action. When teachers reflect on their roles in schools, they will try one action and then another, always returning to the central question of what they learned and accomplished as a result of their actions.

The action research process is best reflected in a spiral of looking, thinking, and action. This process, called the "interacting spiral" approach by Stringer (1999), is shown in Figure 18.4. This model contains three phases: look, think, and act. The spiral of this model

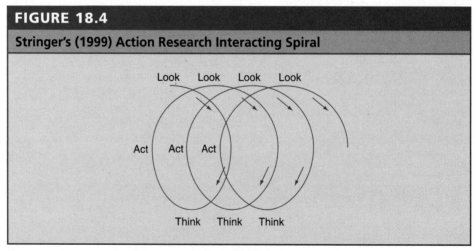

FIGURE 18.4

Stringer's (1999) Action Research Interacting Spiral

Source: Stringer, E. T. *Action Research*, p. 19, copyright © 1999 by Sage Publications. Reprinted by permission of Sage Publications.

conveys that action research is not neat, orderly, and linear, but is a process of repeating and revising procedures and interpretations.

Let's examine more closely the components of the action research process for looking, thinking, and acting. The detailed analysis of the three phases is shown in Figure 18.5. In this model, Stringer (1999) places emphasis on the importance of "looking" to build a picture in order to help stakeholders understand issues they are experiencing. The "look" phase consists of collecting data (e.g., through interviews, observation, and documents); recording and analyzing the information; and constructing and reporting to stakeholders about the issue. The "think" phase then moves into interpreting the issues in greater depth and identifying priorities for action. In the final phase, "act," practical solutions to the problems are identified. This involves devising a plan and setting direction, such as objectives, tasks, persons to carry out the objectives, and securing needed resources. It also means implementing the plan, encouraging people to carry it out, and evaluating it in terms of its effect and achievements.

Let's examine a participatory action research study to see this process at work. Stanulis and Jeffers (1995) studied the mentoring relationship between a fifth-grade classroom teacher (Lynn), her student teacher (Shawna), and a university coordinator (Randi). Called "critical action research" (p. 14), the authors described Lynn's mentoring of Shawna. Randi, as the Coordinator of Field Experiences and university mentor, worked with Lynn to compile data to assess her mentoring of the student teacher. They collected three sets of data listed below to explore this mentoring.

- Five videotaped conferences were recorded between the student teacher and the classroom teacher every other week during a 10-week period.
- Weekly personal journal entries of the classroom teacher and the student teacher were reviewed.
- Five interviews were conducted by the university coordinator with the classroom teacher and the student teacher using the method of individual stimulated recall, a procedure of viewing the videotapes and answering interview questions (e.g., "Was there a point in the conference that you chose not to say something?").

Based on this data, the university coordinator and the classroom teacher identified four themes: (1) the process in which the student teacher gained the students' respect, (2) how the student teacher learned about the children as a learning community (e.g., their family backgrounds, their interests), (3) the mentoring relationship between the student teacher and the classroom teacher, and (4) ideas learned from action research.

Consistent with participatory action research, the authors mentioned that the student teacher brought to the classroom issues of knowledge and authority. The mentoring teacher viewed authority, embedded within the structure of the student-teaching experience, as shifting and changing during the course of the experience. The mentoring began as a "springboard" where the teacher told and shared how to teach the children and shifted to a "sounding board," in which the mentor teacher served as someone to listen and help clarify the student's ideas. The semester ended with the student teacher and mentor teacher viewing each other as "colleagues" sharing ideas and, in this process, they loosened the constraints of teacher authority lodged within a student-teaching experience. The mentoring relationship changed or was transformed during this work together—a result consistent with participatory action research. Also, in the student teacher-teacher conferences, the opportunity to reflect on each individual's approach to teaching provided collaboration and reflection before action. Each individual, as well, learned about himself or herself and became sensitive to changes in the teacher-student relationship.

FIGURE 18.5

Detailed Steps in Stringer's (1999) Action Research Model

Look: Building the Picture	Think: Interpreting and Analyzing	Act: Resolving Problems
PURPOSE: To assist stakeholding groups to build a picture that leads to: Understanding — What and how events occur Clarity — A detailed picture of the context Insight — An extended understanding of the issue	**PURPOSE:** To use interpretive processes to extend and clarify people's understanding of the issue and identify priorities for action	**PURPOSE:** To formulate practical solutions to problems that have been the focus of research
PROCESS: **Gather information** Interviews — Key people from each stakeholding group Observation — Significant settings, events, and/or activities Review — Documents, records, and materials	**PROCESS:** **Extend participants' understanding:** **Frameworks for interpretation** Interpretive questions: Why, what, how, who, where, when Organizational review: vision, mission, structure, operation, problems Concept mapping: Issue, concepts/influences, links Problem analysis: Problem, antecedents, consequences	**PROCESS:** **Plan** Priorities: Arrange projected actions in order of importance Goals: State the broad actions required to resolve prioritized issues Objectives: List actions required to accomplish goal(s) Tasks: Stipulate the sequence of tasks required to accomplish each action Persons: Specify those who will carry out the tasks Time: Determine time frame within which each task will be completed Resources: Calculate materials, equipment, and funds required to complete tasks
Record information Notes — A written record of what people said and/or did Audiotapes — Audio record of interviews Videotapes — Video record of events, people, places, etc. Photographs — Photographs of events, people, places, etc.	**Group processes for interpreting issues** Meet with representatives of all stakeholding groups Set the agenda: Clarify the purpose of the meeting Review descriptive information: Identify key elements of experience Distill the information: Analyze by sorting elements into categories Extend understanding of issues: Enact interpretive activities described in a "Framework for Interpretation"	**Implement** Communicate: Inform people of each other's activities Nurture: Praise people's efforts Reflect: Assist participants in reflecting on problems and progress Assist: Actively assist people when difficulties hinder progress Model: Apply working principles in all activities Link: Connect people in a mutually supportive network
Analyze information Identify key elements — Identify significant items of information Formulate categories — Group similar items Formulate themes — Group similar categories	**Identify priorities for action** Formulate follow-up activities: Identify next steps; formulate working party	

FIGURE 18.5

Detailed Steps in Stringer's (1999) Action Research Model (continued)

Look: Building the Picture	Think: Interpreting and Analyzing	Act: Resolving Problems
Construct reports Using themes as headings, categories as subheadings, and key elements as content, construct an account for each stakeholding group that describes Research activities Who has done what, where, when, and why The situation/context Group members' descriptions The issue Group members' experiences and perspectives **Communicate** Inform people of research activities by distributing reports as Meeting minutes For meeting participants Bulletins For stakeholding groups Interim reports For key stakeholders	**Construct joint reports** **Working party:** Organize meeting of stakeholder representatives **Review materials:** Identify key elements from previous activities **Formulate structure of report:** Arrange in appropriate sequence of headings **Write report:** Write draft, obtain feedback, write final manuscript	**Evaluate** **Review** the plan **Assess** the effect of activities **Revise** the plan if needed **Prioritize** unresolved issues **Celebrate** achievements

Source: Stringer, E. T. *Action Research*, p. 134, copyright © 1999 by Sage Publications. Reprinted by permission of Sage Publications.

613

KEY CHARACTERISTICS OF ACTION RESEARCH

Despite differences between practical and participatory action research, both types of designs have common characteristics that are often found in action research. Understanding these characteristics will help you better design your own study or read, evaluate, and use an action research study published in the literature. These characteristics are:

- a focus on practical issues
- the study of the educator-researcher's own practices
- the collaboration between the researcher and the participants
- a dynamic process of spiraling back and forth among reflection, data collection, and action
- the development of a plan of action to respond to the practical issue
- the sharing of the research report with local school, community, and educational personnel

Studying Practical Issues

The aim of action research is to address an actual problem in an educational setting. Thus, action researchers study **practical** issues that will have immediate benefits for education. These issues may be a concern of a single teacher in a classroom or a problem involving many educators in a building. It may be a need for a school-community issue, an issue with a school policy or structure that constrains individual freedom and action, or a concern of individuals in towns and cities. Research is not undertaken to advance knowledge for knowledge's sake, but for an immediate, applied goal.

Examining the Educator-Researcher's Practices

When action researchers engage in a study, they are interested in examining their own practices rather than studying someone else's practices. In this sense, action researchers engage in **participatory** or self-reflective research in which they turn the lens on their educational classroom, school, or practices. As they study their own situation, they reflect on what they have learned—a form of self-development—as well as what they can do to improve their educational practices. Action researchers deliberately experiment with their own practices, monitor the actions and circumstances in which they occur, and then retrospectively reconstruct an interpretation of the action as a basis for future action. In this reflection, action researchers weigh different solutions to their problems and learn from testing ideas. Action research has been called "a spiral of self-reflection" (Kemmis, 1994, p. 46).

Collaborating with Others

Action researchers **collaborate with others,** often involving coparticipants in the research. These coparticipants may be "inside" individuals within a school or "outside" personnel, such as university researchers or professional association groups. This does not mean that outsiders should co-opt practitioners by gathering data that serve only their needs. So that this co-opting will not occur, outsiders need to negotiate their entry to a site with participants and be sensitive to the involvement of participants in the project (Stringer, 1999). It involves establishing acceptable and cooperative relationships, communicating in a manner that is sincere and appropriate, and including all individuals, groups, and issues. As shown in Figure 18.6, many individuals and groups may participate in an action research project. Individuals may review results of findings with the researcher, help collect data, or

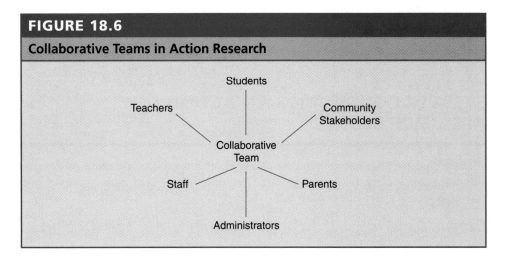

FIGURE 18.6

Collaborative Teams in Action Research

assist in the presentation of the final report. Many aspects of the research process are open to collaboration in an action research project. During this collaboration, roles may vary and be negotiated, but the concept of interacting is central to understanding one's practices.

Using a Dynamic Process

Action researchers engage in a **dynamic process** involving iterations of activities, such as a "spiral" of activities. The key idea is that the researcher "spirals" back and forth between reflection about a problem, data collection, and action. A school-based team, for example, may try several actions after reflecting on the "best" time for high school classes to begin. Reflecting, collecting data, trying a solution, and "spiraling" back to reflection are all part of the process of action research. The process does not follow a linear pattern or a causal sequence from problem to action.

Developing a Plan of Action

The next step is to identify a **plan of action.** At some point in the process, the action researcher formulates an action plan in response to the problem. This "plan" may be simply presenting the data to important stakeholders, establishing a pilot program, starting several competing programs, or implementing an ongoing research agenda to explore new practices (Stringer, 1999). It may be a formal written plan or an informal discussion about how to proceed, and it may engage a few individuals (e.g., students in a classroom) or involve an entire community (e.g., in a participatory research study).

Sharing Reports

Unlike traditional research that investigators report in journal and book publications, action researchers report their research to educators that can immediately use the results. Action researchers often **share reports** with local school, community, and educational personnel. Although action research can be shared in published journals, the inquirer is more interested in sharing the information locally with individuals who can promote change or enact plans within their classroom or building. Action researchers share results with teachers, the building principal, school district personnel, and with parent associations (e.g., Hughes, 1999). In addition, on-line journals (both with and without standards for inclusion), Web sites, and listservs (on-line computer discussion groups typically "hosted" by a university computer system) provide opportunities for action researchers to publicize their studies (see Mills, 2000). Innovative forums also exist for "performance" texts where the researchers perform what they have learned through action research (see Denzin, 1997). These performances might be a play, a poem, a reading of text, slides, or music.

STEPS IN CONDUCTING AN ACTION RESEARCH STUDY

In the steps that follow keep in mind that action research is a dynamic, flexible process and that no blueprint exists for how to proceed. However, several steps in the process can illustrate a general approach for your use.

Step 1. Determine If Action Research Is the Best Design to Use

Action research is an applied form of inquiry and it is useful in many situations. You might use it to address a problem, typically one in your work situation or community. It requires that you have the time to collect and analyze data and to experiment with different options for solving the problem. To help with the process of reflection, you ideally need collaborators with whom to share findings and who can potentially serve as co-researchers on the project. It also requires a broad understanding of the many types of data collection—both quantitative and qualitative—to gather information in order to devise a plan of action.

Step 2. Identify a Problem to Study

The most important factor in action research is that a problem needs to be solved. This may be one that you face in your own practice or in your community (see Kemmis & Wilkinson, 1998). Through reflection, the educator considers the problem that needs to be studied. You might write down the problem or phrase it as a question to be answered.

The research problem is only one place that you might begin your study. In addition to starting with a problem that needs to be solved, many points of entry exist for beginning a study (Schmuck, 1997). Action researchers may begin with collecting data, evaluating existing information, or even planning an action to try. Figure 18.7 shows these multiple entry points to start an action research study. Viewing action research as a "spiral" of activities with multiple entry points expands our possibilities.

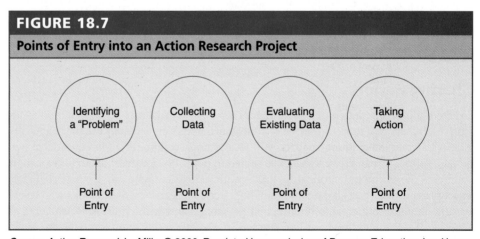

FIGURE 18.7

Points of Entry into an Action Research Project

Source: Action Research by Mills, © 2000. Reprinted by permission of Pearson Education, Inc. Upper Saddle River, NJ 07458

Step 3. Locate Resources to Help Address the Problem

Explore several resources to help study the problem. Literature and existing data may help you formulate a plan of action. You may need to review the literature and determine what others have learned about solving the issue. Asking colleagues for advice helps initiate a study. Teaming with university personnel or knowledgeable people in the community provides a resource base for an action research project. Individuals who have conducted action research projects can also help you during your research study.

Step 4. Identify Information You Will Need

Plan a strategy for gathering data. This means that you need to decide who can provide data, how many people will be studied, your access to individuals, and the rapport and support you can expect to obtain from them. Perhaps you may need to file a proposal for data collection with the institutional review board if you plan to use the research for your graduate research project.

Another consideration is what type of data you need to collect. Your choices are to collect quantitative or qualitative data or both. It is helpful to understand the possibilities that exist for both forms of data. Mills (2000), for example, has organized quantitative and qualitative sources, as shown in Figure 18.8, into three dimensions:

- ▶ *experiencing*—observing and taking fieldnotes
- ▶ *enquiring*—asking people for information
- ▶ *examining*—using and making records

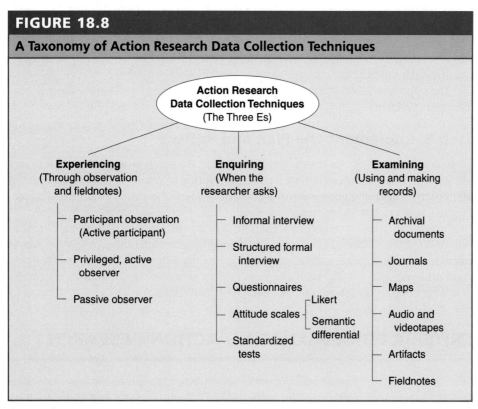

FIGURE 18.8

A Taxonomy of Action Research Data Collection Techniques

Action Research Data Collection Techniques (The Three Es)

Experiencing (Through observation and fieldnotes)
- Participant observation (Active participant)
- Privileged, active observer
- Passive observer

Enquiring (When the researcher asks)
- Informal interview
- Structured formal interview
- Questionnaires
- Attitude scales — Likert / Semantic differential
- Standardized tests

Examining (Using and making records)
- Archival documents
- Journals
- Maps
- Audio and videotapes
- Artifacts
- Fieldnotes

Source: Mills, 2000.

The choice of data sources depends on the questions, time and resources, the availability of individuals, and sources of information. As a general rule, the more sources used and the more triangulation among them (Sagor, 2000), the more you will be able to understand the problem and develop viable action plans. It is probably wise to limit data collection in your first action research study so that you have a manageable amount of information to analyze. For example, as noted in Chapter 9 on "Transcribing Data," qualitative interviews involve labor-intensive work.

Step 5. Implement the Data Collection

Implementing data collection will take time, especially if you gather multiple sources of information. In addition, your participants may have limited time to complete instruments or engage in interviews. Keeping an accurate record of the information collected, organizing it into data files for numeric or theme analysis, and examining the quality of the information are important data collection steps.

Step 6. Analyze the Data

You may decide to analyze the data yourself or enlist the help of other educators or data analysts. You might show your results to others to find out how they would interpret the findings. In most situations, descriptive statistics as discussed in Chapter 8 will suffice for your analysis, although you may want to compare some group data or relate several variables. The major idea is to keep the data analysis manageable so that you can identify useful information in formulating a plan of action.

Step 7. Develop a Plan for Action

A plan may be an informal statement about a new educational practice to be implemented. It might be a plan to reflect on alternative approaches to addressing the problem, or to share what you have learned with others, such as other teachers, individuals in district offices, or other schools and communities. This plan might be written formally or developed as a general outline. It can be collaboratively developed with other educators or initiated by yourself. The important point is that you now have a strategy for trying out some ideas to help solve your problem.

Step 8. Implement the Plan and Reflect

In many action research projects, you will implement your plan of action to see if it makes a difference. This involves trying out a potential solution to your problem and monitoring whether it has impact. To determine this difference, you might consult your original objectives or the research question that you sought to answer in the action research project.

You will also need to reflect on what you have learned from implementing your plan and sharing it with others. You may need to share it broadly with school colleagues, school committees, university researchers, or policy makers. In some cases, an adequate solution is not achieved, and you will need to try out another idea and see if it makes a difference. In this way, one action research project often leads to another.

CRITERIA FOR EVALUATING ACTION RESEARCH

To evaluate an action research study, consider using the following criteria to assess its quality. Criteria below are designed to be applicable to both practical and participatory action research (e.g., see Mills, 2000; Kemmis & Wilkinson, 1998):

❱ Does the project clearly address a problem or issue in practice that needs to be solved?

❱ Did the action researcher collect sufficient data to help address the problem?

❱ Did the action researcher collaborate with others during the study? Was there respect for all collaborators?

❱ Did the plan of action advanced by the researcher build logically from the data?

❱ Is there evidence that the plan of action contributed to the researcher's reflection as a professional?

❱ Has the research enhanced the lives of participants by empowering them, changing them, or providing them with new understandings?

❱ Did the action research actually lead to a change or did a solution to a problem make a difference?

❱ Was the action research reported to audiences who might use the information?

APPLYING WHAT YOU HAVE LEARNED: AN ACTION RESEARCH STUDY

To apply ideas in this chapter, read through the action research study on page 625, noting the marginal annotations that identify the characteristics of action research and the characteristics of quantitative and qualitative research introduced in Chapter 2 on "Distinguishing Between Quantitative and Qualitative Research."

Dicker, M. (1990). Using action research to navigate an unfamiliar teaching assignment. *Theory into practice, XXIX,* 203–208.

The Dicker (1990) study is practical action research that focuses on the problem of how Dicker, a teacher with a background in teaching drama and mathematics, taught a new course on communications in a secondary school. In this project, Dicker reflects on her own knowledge base, applies teaching approaches that worked for her in mathematics and drama, readjusts after a loss of focus, and returns at the end of the semester to her drama-based teaching style. Throughout this process, Dicker collects and uses qualitative data from her own reflective journal, student journals, comments from a former teacher, and tape recordings of lessons.

This study represents a reflective teacher who sought to improve learning for students by trying out different practices. As a practical action research study, it signifies the elements of teacher development, the improvement of student learning, and the collaborative research. In this classroom project, we see the major elements of action research. It focuses on a practical classroom problem (teaching a new course without the requisite skills). The teacher reflects on her experiences and participates with another former teacher of English. Throughout the study, a dynamic process unfolds with this teacher trying out an idea, making adjustments, and exploring another idea. A series of mini-plans ensues as this author shares her personal frustrations and successes in teaching an unfamiliar subject in a high school.

The Research Problem and Qualitative Approach to Research

Problem—Paragraphs 01 and 04

Qualitative Approach—throughout the article

At the beginning of the study, Dicker shares her anger about being assigned a communications course after teaching mathematics and drama at her high school for several years (Paragraph 01). She also reflects (Paragraph 04) on how teachers often face the problem of limited resources after being assigned new courses outside their teaching area. It is not difficult to identify the research problem in this study—Dicker's teaching dilemma—and how it is consistent with action research.

Dicker's approach is to use qualitative research and she displays this approach with the following characteristics:

- ▶ *exploring a process*—The problem requires the author to understand and explore her own experiences in the process of teaching a new course (Paragraphs 01 and 04).
- ▶ *minimal use of literature*—The literature does not shape the questions asked in this study. Rather, the questions evolve out of the author's personal reflection. The literature, when presented (Paragraph 05), describes the research procedure of action research, but it does not reflect on the topic (i.e., teaching a new course) presented in this study. In fact, this article shows minimal use of literature in a study based on the personal experiences of the author-researcher.
- ▶ *a focus on a single phenomenon*—In Paragraph 04, Dicker states that the purpose of her study is to understand her own questions (e.g., "How do teachers cope in such situations?"). The object of the study, then, was for Dicker to understand her own questions related to how to teach outside her area.
- ▶ *collecting text data from a small number of people*—Dicker relies on collecting data from a small number of individuals, including her personal reflections in journal entries (text data) as the most important source of information (Paragraphs 06–10).
- ▶ *analysis of text*—She performs an informal analysis of data from her own journals, the student journals, conversations with a friend, and tape recordings. Her analysis, as shown by a continuous return to reflections from her journal (e.g., Paragraphs 17 and 20) informs the strategy that she will try next as she adjusts to the class.
- ▶ *analysis by description*—Dicker's data analysis reflects analyzing her information to build a description. This process emerges (as is consistent with qualitative research) and consists of trying out practices from drama and mathematics (Paragraph 11), reflecting on this practice, adopting a new practice using a textbook (Paragraph 21), and then returning to the drama teaching style (Paragraph 27).
- ▶ *interpretation based on the larger, more abstract meaning*—At the end of the article (Paragraph 38), Dicker interprets the larger meaning of her experience: knowledge of various teaching styles, a willingness to try them out, a continual monitoring process, and learning along with students.
- ▶ *reporting research flexibly and reflexively*—The qualitative writing style is personal, informal, and in a storytelling form. The presence of the author is apparent throughout the study.

Use of the Literature

Paragraph 05

The only literature found in this personal, reflective study is when Dicker reviews studies about action research in order to inform the reader about this type of design.

The Purpose Statement and Research Questions

Paragraph 04

This study does not contain a specific purpose statement. Instead, the author relies on research questions to carry the major intent of the study. A purpose statement might have strengthened the direction of the project and focused the reader's attention on the teacher's emerging understanding. For example, the purpose might have been described as "a practical action research study to reflect and make adjustments on my own teaching of an unfamiliar course at one high school in Canada." The action researcher is also the participant in his or her own study, and this author seeks to answer her own questions using her personal reflections (Paragraph 06).

Types of Procedures of Data Collection

Paragraphs 06–10

The data collection is described well and we learn that the author used four sources of data in this project: her own journals (the major source), student journals, comments from a former teacher, and tape recordings. With the inclusion of the students and a former teacher, we see the use of co-participants in the project (e.g., Paragraphs 07 and 09).

Types of Procedures of Data Analysis and Interpretation

Analysis—not specifically mentioned

Interpretation—Paragraphs 36–39

The author does not formally mention her data analysis—how she analyzed the tape recordings or the student journals. From quotes in this article, however, we see that she used her own journal entries to reflect on specific changes or ideas that would inform her practice. From a close reading of the study, we must conclude that her analysis is informal and addresses her specific classroom problem (changing from mathematics and drama teaching to only the drama teaching style). This exhibits an iterative, dynamic process found in action research (e.g., see Paragraph 27).

The author's interpretive insights are clearly articulated in the final paragraphs of the study. We find that she reflects on her years as a teacher to draw conclusions about the importance of action research and her professional development. In the final paragraph (Paragraph 39), she discusses how she took action research to the final step of sharing her results with the principal and expressing a desire not to teach the course again.

The Overall Writing Structure

The reporting structure was informal—a storytelling approach to qualitative research. We learn much about the author-researcher as she reflected on her progress in teaching the new course and how she plans and monitors changes (e.g., Paragraph 38). Without knowing the elements of action research, a reader might dismiss this study as "less-than-scientific," but the researcher includes all major elements of an action research project and illustrates the practical form of inquiry that full-time teachers might conduct in order to understand pressing problems in their classrooms.

KEY IDEAS IN THE CHAPTER

The purpose of action research is to improve the practice of education with researchers studying their own problems or issues in a school or educational setting. Educators engage in reflection about these problems, collect and analyze data, and implement changes or a plan of action based on their findings. In some cases, the research is aimed at solving a local, practical problem, such as a classroom issue for a teacher. In other situations, the research seeks ideological aims, such as to empower, transform, and emancipate individuals.

Action research developed in the 1930s with citizen group processes. After a short period of time, it resurfaced in the 1970s with projects in Great Britain, the United States, and Australia. These projects focused on teachers studying their own practices, educators working with schools, and researchers helping individuals emancipate themselves from social issues in educational settings. Today, action research has grown in importance as a means for enhancing school renewal, promoting teacher development, and testing new ideas.

Action research is best viewed as an informal process of research where educators engage in a study of their own practices. This inquiry may be undertaken by individual teachers, teams within a school or district, or by school-community inquiry groups. Two types of action research designs are frequently discussed in the literature. The first design, practical action research, is an approach that involves educators examining a school situation with a view toward improving practice. Rather than a focus on individual teachers solving immediate classroom problems or schools addressing internal issues, a second design, participatory action research, has a social and community orientation, and places emphasis on research that contributes to emancipation or change in our society. The participatory action research approach seeks to improve the quality of people's organizations, community, and family lives. It espouses an objective of improving and empowering individuals and organizations in educational settings. Both the practical and the participatory forms of action research have basic principles and models for conducting research.

A basic process of inquiry is used in action research, regardless of design. The teacher or educator becomes the researcher. As the researcher, the practitioner becomes self-reflective about the process. Action researchers often engage others collaboratively in the process as co-participants and enact a dynamic model of inquiry involving iterations of activities—a cycling back and forth between identifying a problem, trying a solution, reflecting on learnings, and trying new solutions. During this process, they use a plan of action to guide the use of a new practice. This plan is based on what was learned about the research problem and it is shared with others, such as in informal reports to colleagues, school officials, school boards, and community members.

Useful Information for Producers of Research

▸ Design an action research project that matches your time and resources.
▸ Recognize that the process of conducting an action research study is like a spiral with phases that repeat, such as "looking," "thinking," and "acting," as in the Stringer (1999) model.
▸ Remember that in action research, you will be the participant in your own research project. You are not studying someone else; instead, you are examining your own practices.
▸ It is useful to collaborate with others in action research. Consider university personnel, other colleagues, or individuals familiar with action research. They may have insight or be able to draw conclusions that you cannot.
▸ Collect data and analyze it so that it will be understandable to the applied audience for action research studies in your school, district, or other educational unit.
▸ Consider the full array of data collection types for your action research, such as quantitative and qualitative data.
▸ Decide on the point of entry into your study that best fits your present understanding of the problem. This point may be at several phases in a research project.
▸ Construct a plan of action that you can realistically carry out in your school or educational setting.

USEFUL INFORMATION FOR CONSUMERS OF RESEARCH

▶ Recognize the differences between practical action research and participatory action research. The former has an intent of addressing a practical problem in education while the latter has a social or community orientation and emphasizes emancipation or change in our society.

▶ Action researchers study their own situation and attempt to develop solutions to practical (or community) problems. When you review a study, identify the intent of the researcher and look for the study that addresses some issue in which the researcher is involved.

▶ Action research studies are applied and the results should be action-oriented and easy to understand.

▶ Evaluate whether the action research study made a difference or changed the situation presented in the research problem.

ADDITIONAL RESOURCES YOU MIGHT EXAMINE

A number of useful books can help expand your understanding of action research:

Geoffrey Mills (2000) has authored an excellent guide for the teacher-researcher who seeks to engage in action research. Mills provides a good discussion of both practical and critical action research perspectives and reviews the primary process models available for conducting this form of inquiry. His discussion about on-line electronic journals, Web sites, and listservs to connect with other action researchers is a unique, timely contribution. See:

Mills, G. E. (2000). *Action research: A guide for the teacher researcher.* Upper Saddle River, NJ: Merrill.

Sagor (2000) has authored a "practical" action research guide to help teachers become action researchers. This guide provides a useful, readable approach to practical action research with a focus on teachers collaborating with other teachers. Published by the Association for Supervision and Curriculum Development, this guide takes the reader through the many aspects of action research. Examine:

Sagor, R. (2000). *Guiding school improvement with action research.* Alexandria, VA: Association for Supervision and Curriculum Development.

Another book on practical action research by Schmuck (1997) is for teachers, curriculum specialists, counselors, psychologists, school administrators, parents, and students who want to form groups and conduct action research studies. This book contains many exercises, step-by-step guides, and useful visuals to help you understand action research. A book on practical action research is by Calhoun (1994) from the Association for Supervision and Curriculum Development. It focuses on inquiry for educators to assist in our renewal of American schools. See:

Schmuck, R. A. (1997). *Practical action research for change.* Arlington Heights, IL: IRI/SkyLight Training and Publishing.

Calhoun, E. F. (1994). *How to use action research in the self-renewing school.* Alexandria, VA: Association for the Supervision and Curriculum Development.

Turning to participatory action research, Stringer's (1999) book provides an excellent guide to the principles of community-based action research (e.g., relationships, communication, participation, and inclusion) as well as how to negotiate entry to a research site. An entire chapter addresses writing formal reports, theses, and dissertations—an invaluable guide to students who plan to undertake their own action research studies within a critical, emancipatory, and participatory framework. Examine:

Stringer, E. T. (1999). *Action research* (2nd ed.). Thousand Oaks, CA: Sage.

Another participatory perspective is available in the works by Kemmis (e.g., Kemmis & McTaggart, 1988). Kemmis, along with Atweh and Weeks (Atweh, Kemmis, & Weeks, 1998), have edited a book of readings about participatory action research in education. This book offers numerous examples of action research projects based on projects included in the Participatory Action Research for the Advancement of Practice in Education and Teaching (PARAPET) at the Queensland University of Technology in Australia. Especially valuable in this volume is the chapter by Kemmis and Wilkinson (1998) that advances the central features of participatory action research and its interface with the study of practice in education. See:

Kemmis, S., & McTaggart, R. (1988). *The action research planner.* Geelong, Victoria, Australia: Deakin University Press.

Kemmis, S., & Wilkinson, M. (1998). Participatory action research and the study of practice. In B. Atweh, S. Kemmis, and P. Weeks (Eds.) *Action research in practice: Partnerships for social justice in education.* (pp. 21–36). London and New York: Routledge.

Qualitative Characteristics	# Using Action Research to Navigate an Unfamiliar Teaching Assignment	**Action Research Characteristics**

Mary Dicker

Mary Dicker

(01) It was the last week of June, just before the summer holidays, that I learned about the change in my teaching assignment for the following year. I was teaching five mathematics courses and two drama courses in a secondary school in Burns Lake, British Columbia. Proud of my achievement in both of these areas, I assumed that this situation would continue the following year. A casual check of the next year's timetable in the principal's office, however, stopped me in my tracks. My 11th-grade drama course (Acting 11), had been cut from the schedule and in its place I had been assigned an 11th-grade English course, Communications 11. I was both angry and apprehensive—angry that my hard won victory establishing drama in our school program was so short lived and apprehensive that the course I was being assigned was in an area in which I had no professional expertise or experience.

Action researchers study practical issues.

(02) Communications 11 was a new course developed by the ministry of education to replace an 11th-grade English course called Minimum Essentials, a course intended for students with weak English skills. The new course, aimed at the same audience, was to be implemented for the first time the following year. I was given the assignment despite the fact that I had no formal training or expertise in the teaching of English.

(03) My anxiety increased when I learned that the only materials available from the ministry prior to September were a thin curriculum guide summarizing the learning outcomes expected in reading, writing, listening, and speaking and two writing textbooks, one of which was a reference communications handbook. It was expected that teachers would rely largely on their own knowledge of and training in the subject. The difficulties of my situations were compounded by the fact that there were not enough textbooks for each student in the class. I expressed my feelings on the matter to the administration and was assured that, although I was not qualified to teach English as such, my general professional skills combined with a knowledge base in drama would enable me to teach the new course.

(04) Many teachers have been placed in similar predicaments, being faced with new courses outside their teaching area and limited resource materials with which to teach them. How do teachers cope in such a situation? How do they utilize their own knowledge and organize their teaching so that the learning situation becomes a viable one for their students in spite of the circumstances? Assuming the role of teacher researcher, I decided to undertake an action research project to answer these questions.

A qualitative problem requires exploration and understanding.

The qualitative purpose statement and research questions seek participants' experiences.

(05) Action research is a form of self-reflective inquiry that can be utilized by teachers in order to improve the rationality and justice of (a) their own practices, (b) their understanding of these practices, and (c) the situations in which these practices are carried out (Carr & Kemmis, 1983, p. 152). It seemed an appropriate choice of inquiry for my situation. Therefore, applying the four components of the action research cycle, planning, acting, monitoring, and reflecting (Kemmis & McTaggart, 1982, p. 7), I examined the knowledge I used in teaching Communications 11 and how I used this knowledge.[1]

Qualitative researchers take a reflexive and biased approach.

Examining My Knowledge

(06)

Qualitative data collection involves gathering text or image data.

The examination of my knowledge base took place over approximately 3 months from the first day of classes in September to the beginning of December. Following the recommendations of Kemmis and McTaggart (1982), the major data collection device was my own reflective journal or diary, written each evening following a class period. The journal had two purposes: to shed a focused light on the previous lesson and to clarify plans for the following lesson. It was in fact a record of my thinking, revealing my practical knowledge and the particular way it was held and used. A further reflection was written each weekend in order to extend and deepen the reflections on the week's work and to develop a sufficiently thick description for the study.

Action researchers study their own practices.

(07)

Qualitative data collection involves studying a small number of individuals or sites.

As a second source of data, students wrote journals during the last 10 minutes of each class or for homework. Not only did this deepen the students' thinking about their work but it provided me with a different perspective on the events that were happening in the class. Anticipating that students might need some assistance in writing the journal, I posed several questions for them to answer.[2] Using the daily journal as a basis, the students wrote a longer reflection for homework every 2 weeks. Again they were asked to respond to specific questions.[3]

(08)

The students' journal writing was not only educationally valid as an assignment that encouraged writing skills as they reflected on their experiences in the class and organized their thoughts, but it also provided a basis for my future planning. The knowledge gained from my reading and reflection on the student journals became an integral part of my own journal as I commented on student writings.

(09)

A third source of data for the study of my practical knowledge use was a former teacher of English who took the role of "critical friend." In this role she read my journal and asked questions that helped me reveal the thinking that was not always fully expressed in the journal. This critical friend was an important part of the study. As I developed insights during the progress of the study, the validity of these interpretations were checked by this independent critic.

Action researchers often collaborate with co-participants.

(10)

Qualitative data analysis consists of text analysis.

A final monitoring technique was the tape recording of the first and final lessons of the period under study and occasional other discussions, brainstorming lessons, and oral work. Not only did the tapes capture the "teacher-in-action" but, like the student journals, they also provided a student perspective. The tape recordings were a valuable check on the accuracy of my interpretations as I analyzed my journal.[4]

My Teaching Styles

(11)

The journal analysis and other monitoring devices made it clear that I had used two major teaching styles while teaching the course. As teachers gain experience in the art of teaching they inevitably develop a style reflecting a basic philosophy about how a particular subject should be taught. My two different teaching styles reflect my philosophy in each of my teaching areas, mathematics and drama. I regard mathematics as a formal and logical subject that requires a formal, ordered approach. Although students can work together to achieve understanding, the test of student mastery is their ability to solve problems individually. In my view, the British Columbia mathematics curriculum is process oriented,[5] with a correct answer for each problem. The underlying question is, "Which process has to be used in order to get the correct result?" Even if one can take several routes to solve the problem, the student is still looking for the "right" answer.

(12)

In order to achieve individual mastery of mathematical processes, I use a traditional, teacher-directed approach. I follow the curriculum by ad-

Qualitative data analysis consists of describing information and developing themes.

hering to the textbook and supplementing this with worksheets. The students sit in rows facing the chalkboard. I explain, the students learn, and I check their understanding with questions, quizzes, and tests. The premise in my math teaching is that I know the correct processes and the correct answers. My job is to show the student these processes so they can find the correct answers. In addition to my own evaluation of student progress, the benchmark of my success in covering the prescribed courses is the evaluation tests the ministry gives at the end of grade 10 and the provincial exam at the end of grade 12.

(13)   My view of educational drama, on the other hand, is that it should encourage students' creative thinking by inviting them to solve problems through the drama mode. Student learning is a group process rather than an individual one. In my drama classroom, I encourage students to share ideas and possible solutions, for the problems are open ended with no one "correct" answer. The "solution" is usually the consensus of the group. Even this solution is not always the final one, but is changed and modified as circumstances require.

(14)   I also encourage students to make their own improvements to the work in progress. For the initial brainstorming sessions we are usually seated in a circle to allow all ideas to be considered equally. As the work progresses I question the students to make them think a little deeper about their work. It is a probing rather than a deliberate attempt to get at a "right" answer. Presentation is not my primary goal, although the work is frequently presented to an audience. Of most concern is the development of the work and the learning inherent in this development. The personal growth of each student is not easily evaluated. Their input is necessary to judge this, in addition to my own observations.

(15)   Thus, in my two different teaching areas, I have two different teaching styles. These teaching styles reflect not only the nature of the subjects being taught but my philosophy of how each one should be taught. Both styles were used in implementing Communications 11 but I was not aware of this while I was teaching. It was not until I had reflected on and analyzed my data that I realized that I possessed two teaching styles and that they both had had a strong impact on the progress of the course. The following description of what took place in my classroom is the result of my reflection on and analysis of the data collected. It reveals the knowledge I used when teaching Communications 11 and how I used this knowledge.

Knowledge from Drama

(16)   In teaching Communications 11 I was forced to examine what strategies I had for coping with my situation. From the outset I had felt that the only way I could cope with teaching this course was by using my background knowledge in drama. If I could interpret "communication" in its broadest sense, I could teach a quasi-acting course by disguising it as Communications 11. In this way I could combat two problems. I would have an acting class and would also be on familiar ground even though the subject area itself was unfamiliar.

(17)   As the work progressed I discovered I had chosen an approach that not only could be adapted to the course but that also allowed the course to be adapted to it. As in my drama courses, I wanted the students to be actively involved in their own learning in the course. I wanted to explore communication *with* the students instead of trying to instruct them directly. Note the journal entry made in preparation for the first lesson:

> I want to find out what students think Communications 11 means. *Discussion*—round the table—different format might help the students to

think differently—they're weak students—I want to encourage their ideas and let them see I *listen* to *them*.

(18)   I was able to start the course by using a previous drama lesson plan. I observed in my journal, "Today's lesson was almost identical to the first lesson in Acting 11 last year. I changed 'teenage interests and problems' to 'communication' but method the same." The ability to adapt materials and ideas from other sources is an integral part of the art of teaching. I had embarked on my quasi-acting course with a familiar strategy that I knew would be successful.

(19)   The first idea that was contributed by the students and which could be used in developing the course was a list of the different ways people communicate. They developed the list through their own discussion. I wrote in my journal,

> I didn't make nearly enough of their lists which had good ideas—I want to make up for this by using the lists next lesson somehow. . . . Interesting to see that the students are coming up with the wider view of "communication"—more along my conception.

Using the lists was important not only for the ideas. It was a way of demonstrating my acceptance and approval of students' suggestions. What they had to offer was worthwhile, and I wanted them to know that I thought so. We expanded the lists the next day and used the dramatic technique of "tableaux" (frozen action pictures created by students) to depict the means of communication contained in the lists. Their view of communication was even broader than mine, including such areas as sign language, Braille, Morse code, and even smoke signals. I felt my concept for the course had been justified, and I believe the "meeting of minds" enhanced students' confidence and developed rapport.

(20)   By continually being aware of and recording the general reactions of the students, I think I became more sensitive to their needs. I was ready to make adjustments if I thought them necessary. By reading the "pulse" of the class I was brought closer to them and this, in a subtle way, helped in further establishing the rapport. A few lessons later I commented,

> A nice atmosphere—relaxed. I felt this lesson was an important one. I was able to talk to all the students individually or in small groups. There was an atmosphere similar to my drama class last year. I was very pleased to be able to praise their work.

The use of my knowledge from drama appeared to be working well, and as I confidently developed lessons around themes taken from the initial communications lists, I inevitably pushed the drama mode further. As time went on, however, a change occurred in my teaching style. I slipped out of the drama mode and into the formality of my mathematics style of teaching. It was at this time that my knowledge of class control stood me in good stead.

A Loss of Focus

(21)   Twice it happened that my teaching lost focus and direction and seemed to flounder, but my control of the class did not. I was able to continue teaching and I doubt if the students were aware of the change. In both instances the loss of focus came after active periods of group work using drama techniques. There was a need for a change of pace, a need to "settle down" for a while. It seemed to me that this was probably a good time to start using the textbook. The favorable impression I had formed about the text is recorded in my journal.

> I've been looking at the text, *Writing Sense* [Potter, 1981]. I like the way it's written and presented—pictures, activities, common-sense down-to-earth style. Emphasis seems to be on writing flow rather than grammar. The first four chap-

ters contain ideas I have emphasized with the students—honesty in writing—reading aloud to improve writing.

(22) Philosophically it seemed the perfect book for me to use. It also appeared to be suitable for use by students weak in English as the chapters were short and easy to read. What I did not realize at the time was that each short chapter is on a different topic with no real link between chapters. This deficiency may not create difficulties for a qualified English specialist, but for someone in my position it created an unforeseen problem that I will say more about later.

(23) I had the feeling that I ought to use the text at some point in the course so that I could say I was following the curriculum. My instincts seemed justified when I was told that I was to be evaluated for my teaching report. This knowledge prompted me to write in my journal, "I'm wondering if I have enough marks for the class at the present time—I think I'll have to make specific parts of my lessons markable. The type of work I've been doing is difficult to mark." Not only was the text the prescribed one for the course but it also had exercises in it that were markable.

(24) I used the text two lessons in a row to encourage a feeling of continuity. The actual lessons themselves, however, were not linked as each chapter was on a different topic. My reflection for the lessons shows that the students were not enthusiastic.

> The reading was fine but they did not really apply themselves to the questions—a few of the girls did. The reporting back was not successful—students didn't listen so I eventually abandoned this and got them down to write. . . . I did not have them read aloud as I had planned because of the previous lack of concentration. Instead I had them proof-read each other's work to themselves.

The desks went back in rows as this seemed the appropriate arrangement for students who had to concentrate on individual writing assignments. I think perhaps this was one of the subtle ways in which I was influenced by the textbook. The formality of using the text demanded the formality that I used in math class.

(25) Because each lesson was on a different topic, it meant I was planning one lesson at a time. I wrote, "I'm beginning to feel the need for a little longer planning—one day at a time is difficult." As I limped from lesson to lesson a feeling of desperation began to creep into my journal.

> I am now beginning to get a "swamped" feeling. I am not having enough time to plan and organize because of the work in other classes. I have marking to do all the time. I also feel I am losing my efficiency which is compounding the problem. I am needing help from colleagues. I think I have passed the "going it alone" stage. What are they actually *learning* at the moment—I am beginning to wonder. . . . I am not sure what to do about the books they are reading—do I have them write a report?—or does that kill the enjoyment of the book? Could they communicate the ideas in the book another way? Should I give a deadline by which the book should be read? Better ask my colleagues these questions.

(26) By turning to the textbook I inadvertently moved into a series of short, teacher-directed lessons more like math teaching than drama teaching. This teacher-directed style worked well in math, where I was knowledgeable; in Communications 11, it took me into an area where my knowledge of the subject was at its weakest. I lost my original focus and although my experience as a teacher enabled me to continue teaching without a loss of control or rapport, I was not pleased with the work I was doing.

Back to a Drama Teaching Mode

(27) Toward the end of October a resource book for the course appeared in my box in the office. I found that it contained some philosophical ideas that

supported my approach to the course. It emphasized the value of student based literature content and the importance of finding situations in which students want to learn and can find success. Reading the resource book prepared the ground for the development of a new focus and a return to my drama teaching style.

Action researchers engage in an iterative, dynamic process.

(28)   I noticed in the section on short stories a story about nuclear war. Initially I asked the department head for advice on reading the story. He suggested I read it aloud, with the students following in their own books. In my journal I commented, "I thought this would be too similar to them listening to the record, but the fact that they are reading along silently will be sufficiently different." The unfamiliarity of the subject was prompting me to assume I always had to be doing a new activity or slightly varying the activity. Yet I often repeated activities when teaching in my own subject areas.

(29)   The reading of the story aloud was not only a natural progression from the silent reading I was doing with the students each lesson but also encouraged me to abandon desks in rows and place them in a circle again. I began to feel the pull of my drama background again and this was evidenced in the first lesson on the new topic of nuclear war. Having read the story to them, we did an activity used by drama teachers called "hot-seat." Several students volunteered to be characters from the story and, in role ourselves, we all asked them questions. This was quite successful and a positive end to the lesson. I was back in my drama mode with a focus that lasted nearly 3 weeks.

(30)   Unfortunately, at the end of the 3 weeks, as I again sensed the need to vary the pace, I repeated my previous mistake of using the textbook. By the third lesson I was caught in the one-lesson-at-a-time trap and had returned to the traditional teaching style of my math classes, which included arranging the desks in rows. When I tried to conduct a discussion on phobias without changing the desks, my journal records,

> The discussion tended to be "patchy." Groups would take part but often the others didn't really listen—I had to do my "policeman act."

Again I felt the need to control students' behavior, using body language, direct looks, and spoken admonitions. I was aware that part of the trouble was because of the struggle to think of what to do each lesson. I talked to my husband and he suggested that I follow the example of the head of the English department and give them a project that would last 2 weeks (survival tactics!).

(31)   Even though I had done several longer units and knew this was the answer, I needed this reminder. Teaching an unfamiliar subject seems to make a person react in a similar way to being in unfamiliar situations—thinking is thrown off balance and one can miss the obvious. A project had the advantage that, once the parameters had been established, the students would work for several lessons without the teacher having to prepare new lessons. Each lesson would be spent helping the students develop their ideas in the project. I had done many a project with eighth-grade drama students.

(32)   Teachers frequently utilize the year's calendar when planning their work. Seasons and specific dates become a meaningful focus for a variety of educational activities. As it was less than 3 weeks to the Christmas holidays I decided to devise a project on the Christmas theme that applied specifically to the course. I felt some intellectual satisfaction in arriving at an idea that would tie together the work done in the term. In groups of about four, the students would make presentations on the theme of Christmas utilizing all the means of communication used in their term's work. In my journal I described how I started the project:

We then sat in the circle again and I started the discussion on Christmas—why we have it, themes associated with it etc. We then established a list of the forms of communication used so far. They made the major suggestions in both parts of the discussion with some minor prompting from me. . . . They then split up into their groups and started to discuss the project. They seemed interested and enthusiastic.

All the elements I had hoped for at the beginning of the course and had partially lost at two stages during the term combined to make this project a satisfying one for both me and the class. The students were making a positive contribution of their own ideas. They were involved in their own learning and making their own decisions in a relaxed atmosphere under my guidance, not my direction.

(33) A few new developments also occurred during the project. The students started to search out suitable poetry to be part of their presentation—an area we had not explored as yet in the course. Kathy,[6] who had refused to speak in front of the class during the oral presentation on music because of her shyness, read aloud with Wilma during their presentation. One group read a poem as a radio play and Don learned his part by heart. Another group unified all means of communications into an effective dramatic presentation.

(34) The written components also showed that students had thought about their work. Wilma, Sonja, and Kathy based their writing on a dictionary exercise we had done. They thought of a long list of words associated with Christmas and gave definitions for each. Ron's group researched Christmas customs in other countries. The satisfaction I had as a teacher was in seeing how much the class had progressed as a whole, and how individuals had demonstrated a personal growth.

(35) Knowing that one has taught and the students have learned is essential for any teacher, but it is particularly important for teachers working in a subject area outside their specialty. I did not have teaching knowledge of specific English skills. However, I do believe my own knowledge of how to teach contributed to students' ability to communicate and think clearly.

Conclusions

(36) Teaching Communications 11 was a professional development activity that contained as much learning for me as for the students. By reflecting on my teaching decisions through action research, I was able to cope with teaching a course in a subject area that was unfamiliar. Teaching a new course outside one's own area forces teachers to examine the strategies that are available to them. My reflection made me aware that I was using the two teaching styles with which I was already familiar, and that one of these styles was more appropriate for this circumstance than the other.

(37) My 15 years experience as a teacher has given me practical knowledge that has been constructed through time by the actions taken (Connelly & Elbaz, 1982, p. 117). An important element in my practical knowledge was the ability to maintain a disciplined learning environment. While this knowledge gave me confidence in my ability in dealing with students, it was not sufficient. During the time I was using my more traditional teaching style, the monitoring techniques of action research enabled me to see that while the situation was under control, it was not the learning atmosphere I wanted to create.

Qualitative interpretations situate findings within larger meanings.

(38) As Fullan (1982) has stated, one dimension of educational change is the possible use of new teaching approaches. For teachers faced with assignments outside their areas, the need for a new approach, or at least a modification, is highly probable. In order to cope with unfamiliar assignments

teachers require not only knowledge of various teaching styles but a willingness to try them out. Action research provides the opportunity of trying out a new approach while monitoring what is occurring. Through the use of journals, tape recordings, and discussions with other educators, I was able to become a learner along with my students. Action research created the possibility for perpetual, self-generated, professional development.

Action researchers implement an action plan in response to their research.

(39)   I learned a lot from Communications 11, but I did not want my professional development to continue through this course for another year. My goal was to reinstate Acting 11 on the timetable and work to improve it. So I tackled the principal early in spring and elicited a firm commitment on the matter. While I do not want to repeat the experience of teaching a course for which I am unprepared, the experience of coping with new subject matter materials using action research techniques has probably made me a better teacher.

Action researchers share results of their studies with other practitioners.

Qualitative research reports use flexible and emerging structures and evaluation criteria.

Notes

1. This article is based on a longer study undertaken as part of a M.Ed. degree in curriculum studies at the University of Victoria, British Columbia, 1986–87.

2. Examples of questions posed:
- How did *you* practice communication today?
- Did you feel your communication was successful? Why or why not?
- How well did your group work together?
- What were your thoughts when you showed your work to the class?

3. Examples of questions posed:
- What do you feel you have learned so far in this course?
- Which activities have you enjoyed the most, and why?
- Which activities have you not enjoyed, and why?
- What other activities do you think we should do?

4. See Kemmis & McTaggart (1982, pp. 39–42) for a full list of techniques to use as possible monitoring devices.

5. Since the writing of the original M.Ed. study on which this article is based, a new math curriculum has been implemented in British Columbia which is less process oriented. Considerable emphasis is now placed on the development of problem-solving skills.

6. The student names used here are not their real names.

References

Carr, W., & Kemmis, S. (1983). *Becoming critical: Knowing through action research.* Geelong, Victoria, Australia: Deakin University.

Connelly, F. M., & Elbaz, F. (1982). Conceptual bases for curriculum thought: A teacher's perspective. In A. W. Foshey (Ed.), *Considered action for curriculum improvement* (pp. 95–119). Alexandria, VA: Association for Supervision and Curriculum Development.

Fullan, M. (1982). *The meaning of educational change.* Toronto: Ontario Institute for Studies in Education.

Kemmis, S., & McTaggart, R. (1982). *The action research planner* (2nd ed.). Geelong, Victoria, Australia: Deakin University.

Potter, R. (1981). *Writing sense.* Toronto: Globe/Modern Curriculum Press.

Appendix A

Determining Size Using Sample Size Tables

In the process of collecting data, researchers need to determine the number of participants for their studies. Several options are available. They can make an educated guess as to how many people are needed, such as 10% of the population. They can ask as many people to participate as possible within the resources and time that both researchers and participants can provide. They can select a number that satisfies different types of statistical procedures, such as the need for approximately 30 scores for each variable in a correlational analysis.

A more rigorous approach than any of these is to systematically identify the number of participants based on sample size tables available in published texts. To understand these tables, you need to understand the fundamentals of the formulas used. Two formulas will be explained here, the sampling error formula and the power analysis formula.

This discussion about the two formulas builds on earlier comments about the importance of systematically calculating sample size using formulas in quantitative research. This importance was introduced in Chapter 6 on "Sample Size" and reinforced in Chapter 11 on experimental and quasi-experimental designs under "Step 4. Identify Study Participants." It was also mentioned in Chapter 12 on correlational designs, although sample size is often dictated by the required size for making assumptions about normality of the distribution of scores (see Chapter 12 discussion about size in correlation studies in "Step 2. Identify Individuals to Study"). However, a sampling error formula may be used when the intent of the correlational study is to generalize from a sample to a population. Using a formula was also encouraged again in Chapter 13 on survey designs in "Step 3. Identify the Population, the Sampling Frame, and the Sample." Here we will explore the calculations involved in the sample size formulas and present tables that simplify the process of making the calculations.

SAMPLING ERROR FORMULA

A sampling error formula is often used in survey or correlational research (see Fink & Kosekoff, 1985; Fowler, 1988) when investigators seek to generalize results from a sample to a population. A **sampling error formula** is a calculation for determining size of a sample based on the chance (or proportion) that the sample will be evenly divided on a question, sampling error, and a confidence interval.

The formula is based on the proportion of the sample that will have the desired characteristic that you are trying to estimate. For example, when parents are polled to determine whether they would vote "yes" or "no" on a school bond issue, there is a 50–50 chance that they will vote "yes." Selecting a proportion of 50/50 means that the population will be evenly split, and this proportion yields the largest size for your sample.

633

The sampling error formula is also based on stating the amount of sampling error you are willing to tolerate. Recall that sampling error (stated as a percent, such as from 4% of the time) is the difference between your sample mean and the true population mean. This error results because samples are randomly selected from population and may not represent the true characteristics of the population (see Chapter 6 on "Specifying the Population and Sample"). Finally, the formula also includes identifying a confidence interval, such as a 95% confidence interval. Recall that a confidence interval indicates the upper and lower values that are likely to contain the actual population mean (see Chapter 8 on "Interpreting the Results in Terms of Statistical and Practical Significance").

Understanding these three factors helps you interpret a sample size formula table, such as Table A.1 by Fowler (1988, p. 42).

The first row in this table shows the percentage of the sample with the desired characteristic, ranging from 5/95 (small chance) to 50/50 (equally split chance). To maximally divide the sample, researchers typically select 50/50 as the proportion of the sample with the characteristic they are trying to estimate. In terms of the confidence interval, this table only reports a 95% confidence interval (default), which means that 95 out of 100 times the sample mean will fall within the upper and lower limits, or range, of the population mean. This is a rigorous standard to use. In the columns under the "percentage of sample with characteristic," we see values, such as 17, 14, 12, under the 50/50 column. These values are the amount of sampling error we are willing to tolerate. Typically, researchers set a small error that they are willing to tolerate, such as 4% or 6%. This means that only 4% or 6% of the time the sample mean will differ from the true population mean. Finally, on the left column we see the sample size recommendation that you would use as a guide to the minimum sample size for the sample in your study.

TABLE A.1

Fowler's (1988, p. 42) Sample Size Table: Confidence Ranges for Variability Due to Sampling*

Sample Size	Percentage of Sample with Characteristic				
	5/95	10/90	20/80	30/70	50/50
35	7	10	14	15	17
50	6	8	11	13	14
75	5	7	9	11	12
100	4	6	8	9	10
200	3	4	6	6	7
300	3	3	5	5	6
500	2	3	4	4	4
1000	1	2	3	3	3
1500	1	2	2	2	2

Note: Chances are 95 in 100 that the real population figure lies in the range defined by +/− number indicated in table, given percentage of sample reporting characteristics and number of sample cases on which the percentage is based.

*This table describes variability due to sampling. Errors due to nonresponse or reporting errors are not reflected in this table. In addition, this table assumes simple random sample. Estimates may be subject to more variability than this table indicates due to the sample design or the influence of interviewers on the answers they obtained; stratification might reduce the sampling errors below those indicated here.

Source: Fowler, F. J. *Survey Research Methods*, p. 42. copyright © 1988 by Sage Publications, Reprinted by permission of Sage Publications.

Let's apply information from this table to a study to see how it works. Assume that you need to determine the size of your sample in a study of Native American students in a school district. You seek to survey students in high schools in a large metropolitan district to determine if students plan to enroll in advanced placement courses ("yes" they plan to enroll, "no" they do not plan to enroll). The procedure needs to be as rigorous as possible, so you decide to use Fowler's (1998) table to calculate the sample size for your study.

A given in Fowler's table is that you will use a rigorous confidence interval standard—a 95% confidence interval (95 out of 100 times your sample value will fall within the range of the population mean). You assume that students have a 50–50 chance of participating in these courses. Based on this information, you select the column 50/50. Further, you want a low error rate—a small percentage of the time your sample mean will differ from the population mean. You select an error of 4% (4 out of 100 times).

To identify the appropriate sample size you need in your study, you look at the last column (50/50), go down the column to "4" (4%), and then look across the row and find that the ideal sample size is 500 Native American students. This number, based on the sample size formula, will ensure that 95 out of 100 times (95% confidence interval) your sample mean will have an equal chance (50/50 split) of differentiating among the students 96% of the time (or an error of 4%).

POWER ANALYSIS FORMULA

In many experiments, the size of the overall number of participants (and participants per group) is dictated by practical issues related to the number of volunteers who enroll for the study or the individuals who are available to the researcher. Researchers can also use statistics to analyze the data, and these statistics call for minimum numbers of participants for each group when group comparisons are made.

A rigorous, systematic approach is to use a power analysis. A **power analysis** is a means of identifying appropriate sample size for group comparisons by taking into consideration the level of statistical significance (alpha), the amount of power desired in a study, and the effect size. By determining these three factors, you can look up the adequate size for each comparison group in an experiment and use tables available in published texts (e.g., Lipsey, 1990). The process works this way as shown in Table A.2:

▶ First identify the statistical level of significance to use in testing your group comparison hypothesis, typically set at $p = .05$ or $p = .01$. See Chapter 8 on "Setting the Level of Significance, or Alpha Level."

▶ Next identify the power needed to reject the hypothesis when it is false, typically set at .80. See Chapter 8, and Table 8.7 on types of outcomes of hypothesis testing.

▶ Determine the effect size, which is the expected differences in the means between the control and experimental groups expressed in standard deviation units. This effect size is often based on expectations drawn from past research and is typically set at .5 for much educational research (Murphy & Myors, 1998). See Chapter 8 on "Interpreting the Results in Terms of Statistical and Practical Significance."

▶ Go to a table for calculating the size of the sample given these parameters, and identify the size of each group in the experiment. This size becomes the number of participants you need for each group in your sample. The approximate sample size per experimental group with an alpha set at .05 is given in Table A.2 (Lipsey, 1990, p. 137).

Let's take an example to apply the power formula and Lipsey's table. Assume that elementary education children identified as gifted in a school district are assigned to one of two groups. One group receives an enrichment program (the experimental group), and the

TABLE A.2

Lipsey's (1990, p. 137) Sample Size Table: Approximate Sample Size per Experimental Group Needed to Attain Various Criterion Levels of Power for a Range of Effect Sizes at Alpha = .05

Effect size	Power Criterion		
	.80	.90	.95
.10	1570	2100	2600
.20	395	525	650
.30	175	235	290
.40	100	130	165
.50	65	85	105
.60	45	60	75
.70	35	45	55
.80	25	35	45
.90	20	30	35
1.00	20	25	30

Source: Lipsey, M. W. *Design Sensitivity: Statistical Power For Experimental Research,* p. 137, copyright © 1990 by Sage Publications. Reprinted by permission of Sage Publications.

other group receives traditional instruction (the control group). At the end of the semester both groups are tested for creativity. How many gifted students are needed for both the experimental and control groups? We might use the number of students available and equally assign them to groups. Although such an experiment could be made, we want a sufficient number of students in our groups so that we can be confident in our hypothesis test of no differences between the control and experimental groups.

In other words, we need an experiment with sufficient size to have power (see Table 8.7 on possible outcomes in hypothesis testing). We turn to Lipsey's (1990) power analysis table for assistance in determining the appropriate sample size for our experimental and control groups. This table will indicate the size needed given a confidence level, the amount of power desired, and the effect size. Examining Lipsey's table, we find that the significance level for the table is set at an alpha = .05.

We use a rigorous standard for power, such as .80 (80% of the time we will reject the null when it is false), and select the column ".80." Then we look at the column for effect size and choose ".50" as to the standard for differences in the means (in standard deviation units) that we will expect between the two groups. Using this information, and going down the column of .80 to the row .50, we find that 65 students are needed for each of our two groups, the experimental and control groups, in our study of gifted children.

Appendix B

Strategies for Defending a Research Proposal

In doctoral programs and in many master's programs, students are required to complete a formal research study as part of their requirements for graduation. This requirement is included in programs so students can demonstrate their knowledge and application of research. As a first step in preparing the formal research study, a student developes a proposal or plan for the study. The proposal is distributed to the student's faculty. Then, a short time later, the student presents the proposal to the faculty in a meeting called a "proposal defense." The intent of this meeting is for faculty to have a chance to react and provide constructive comments about the study before the student begins the project. It also serves to provide an opportunity for the student to carefully review the entire project, practice giving an oral presentation of research, and improve the study based on faculty feedback.

The proposal defense meeting varies in length. A typical meeting might last about one hour. During this meeting, the student presents an overview of the study and faculty asks questions that arose when they read the proposal. Some defense meetings are open to all faculty and students while others are closed to all participants except for the student's faculty committee. To best prepare for this meeting and to leave with productive ideas, several strategies are identified that students might use before, during, and after the meeting.

Prior to the Meeting

- Look over the composition of your committee. Do you have individuals who can assist you in all phases of your research? Can you substitute faculty on your committee to obtain needed faculty resources at this point in your program? An ideal committee consists of a statistician or research methodologist who can help with the technical aspects of a study, an editor who can help you shape your writing, a content specialist who knows the literature about your topic, and a supporter who can give positive feedback throughout the process.
- Talk with your advisor about the degree of formality required during the meeting. A formal meeting consists of a brief, organized presentation by the student followed by faculty questions. It may also include a slide presentation to present the proposal for the research study. An informal meeting may be a discussion or conversation about your proposed project without the use of a slide presentation or an organized, formal presentation.
- If possible, attend proposal defenses held by other students so that you can gain some experience with the procedures of this meeting.
- Visit with your faculty committee members before the meeting to gauge their feedback. They will likely have suggestions for improving the study before the defense meeting.

- Consider how you will build rapport with your faculty committee prior to the meeting and during your program. Rapport might be established informally through social interaction or formally through collaboration on projects or by serving as a teacher's assistant.
- Discuss with your advisor her or his role during the meeting. Advisors assume different roles, such as advocate, supporter, arbitrator, and adversary. The better you understand his or her role, the better you can anticipate how your advisor will respond during a defense meeting.
- Anticipate questions that faculty will ask during a proposal meeting. Sample questions during a meeting of a *quantitative* proposal might be:

Research design questions:
- Is the problem trivial?
- What is the research question being addressed?
- Is the theory a good predictor to use?
- Is the study internally valid?

Data collection and analysis questions:
- Are the methods detailed?
- Is the best data collection approach used?
- Was the most appropriate statistic chosen?
- Are the constructs valid?
- Do items on the instrument need refinement?
- Was a good instrument chosen to use in the study?

- Sample questions during a meeting of a *qualitative* study will likely range from research design to the legitimacy of the design as compared with quantitative research.

Design questions:
- Why did you choose a qualitative study (instead of a quantitative study)?
- What is the type of design you are using? (e.g., ethnography, grounded theory)
- Is the study valid?

Quantitative-type questions that require knowledge about *qualitative* research:
- How can you generalize from this study?
- Are your variables measurable and valid?
- Do you plan to use theory in this study?
- Why did you conduct a brief literature review?

Legitimacy questions:
- Are there journals that will publish this type of research?
- Is this type of research rigorous enough?
- Will your involvement in the study influence the findings?

During the Meeting
- Keep your presentation brief—15 minutes or less.
- Be open, negotiable, and responsive to faculty questions.
- Restate questions in your own words to indicate that you have correctly heard them.
- Be willing to admit that you have not considered the question being raised.
- Have your advisor intercede if the questions become unfair or unrelated to your topic.
- Listen for the constructive suggestions for improving your project. Keep notes of these suggestions or have your advisor take notes for you so that later there will not be any question about changes needed.

After the Meeting

▶ Review the events of the meeting with your advisor.

▶ Note suggestions that need to be made to improve or change your study. Negotiate with your advisor about what committee suggestions need to be implemented and what suggestions need to be revisited with members of the committee.

▶ Visit with faculty on your committee, if needed, to clarify their suggestions for improvement.

▶ Talk with your advisor about the next step in the process—what chapters you should begin to write and when.

Glossary

A/B designs are single-subject studies in experimental research that consist of observing and measuring behavior during a trial period (*A*), administering an intervention, and observing and measuring the behavior after the intervention (*B*).

Abstracts are summaries of the major aspects of a study or article, conveyed in a concise way (for this purpose, often no more than 350 words), and inclusive of specific components that describe the study.

Action research designs are systematic procedures used by teachers (or other individuals in an educational setting) to gather quantitative and/or qualitative data about—and subsequently improve—the ways their particular setting operates, how they teach, and how well their students learn (Mills, 2000).

Adding to knowledge means that educators undertake research in order for it to contribute to existing information about issues.

Adding voices of individuals to knowledge indicates that educators present perspectives of individuals who have not been heard or whose views have been minimized in society.

Addressing gaps in knowledge means that educators study an area of research because the inquiry will help fill a void in existing information.

Alternate forms and test-retest reliability is an approach to reliability in which the researcher administers the test twice and also uses an alternate form of the test from the first administration to the second.

Alternative forms reliability involves using two instruments, both measuring the same variables and relating (or correlating) the scores for the same group of individuals to the two instruments.

Alternative treatment designs are single-subject studies in experimental research in which the researcher examines the relative effects of two or more interventions and determines which intervention is the more effective treatment on the outcome.

Analyzing and interpreting the data indicates that researchers analyze the data, represent it in tables, figures, and pictures, and explain it for answers to research questions and statements asked in the research.

Attitudinal measures seek to assess affect or feelings toward educational topics (e.g., assessing positive or negative attitudes toward giving students a choice of school to attend).

Audience consists of individuals who will read and potentially use information provided in a research study. These audiences will vary depending on the nature of the study, but several often considered by educators include researchers, practitioners, policy makers, and individuals participating in the studies.

Audio-visual materials consist of images or sounds that are collected by the qualitative researcher to help understand the central phenomenon under study. Photographs, videotapes, digital images, paintings and pictures, and physical traces of images (e.g., foot-steps in the snow) are all sources of information for qualitative inquiry.

Autobiography is a narrative account written and recorded by the individual who is the subject of the study.

Axial coding is when the grounded theorist selects one open coding category, positions it at the center of the process being explored (as the core phenomenon), and then relates other categories to it.

Behavior in ethnography is an action taken by an individual in a cultural setting.

Belief in ethnography is how an individual thinks about or perceives things in a cultural setting.

Beta weights are coefficients indicating the magnitude of prediction for a variable after removing the effects of all other predictors.

Between-group designs are those in which the researcher compares results between different groups in terms of outcome scores.

Biography is a form of narrative study in which the researcher writes and records the experiences of another person's life.

Blocking variable is a variable in an experiment that the researcher controls before the experiment starts by dividing (or "blocking") the participants into subgroups (or categories) and analyzing the impact of each subgroup on the outcome.

Case study is a variation of an ethnography in that the researcher provides an in-depth exploration of a bounded system (e.g., an activity, an event, a process, or an individual) based on extensive data collection (Creswell, 1998).

Categorical score is a value of a variable assigned by the researcher into a small number of groups or categories. This type of score is also called a "discrete" or "nominal" score, and it is illustrated by groups of students, such as males and females.

Categories in grounded theory designs are themes of basic information identified in the data by the researcher and used to understand a process.

Central phenomenon is an issue or process explored in qualitative research.

Central question is the overarching question being asked in a qualitative study. It is the attempt by the researcher to ask the most general question that can be addressed in a study.

Changing observational role is one where researchers adapt their role to the situation, such as entering a site and observing as a nonparticipant and then later becoming a participant.

Children's stories in educational research are narrative studies in which children in classrooms are asked to present orally, or in writing, their own stories about their learnings.

Choosing a quantitative or qualitative approach means selecting either quantitative or qualitative research to use, and employing it as a framework for planning, conducting, and evaluating a project.

Chronology in narrative designs means that the researcher analyzes and writes about the individual's life using a time sequence or chronology of events.

Cleaning the data is the process of visually inspecting the data for scores (or values) that are outside the accepted range of scores.

Closed-ended questions in surveys consist of questions posed by the researcher in which the participant responds to preset response options.

Closed-ended responses are options to questions that specify the choices open to the participant.

Codes are labels used to describe a segment of text or an image.

Coding paradigm is a diagram that portrays the interrelationship of causal conditions, strategies, contextual and intervening conditions, and consequences in grounded theory research.

Coding process is a qualitative research process in which the researcher makes sense out of text data, divides it into text or image segments, labels the segments, examines codes for overlap and redundancy, and collapses these codes into themes.

Coefficient alpha is a measure of the internal consistency of items on an instrument when the items are scored as continuous variables (e.g., strongly agree to strongly disagree).

Coefficient of determination assesses the proportion of variability in one variable that can be determined or explained by a second variable.

Cohort studies are longitudinal survey designs in which a researcher identifies a subpopulation based on some specific characteristic, and studies that subpopulation over time.

Collaborate with others is often central to action research, and it involves actively participating with others in research. These co-participants may be "inside" individuals in a school or "outside" personnel, such as university researchers or professional association groups.

Collaboration in narrative research means that the inquirer actively involves the participant in the inquiry as it unfolds. This collaboration may include many steps in the research process, from formulating the central phenomena to be examined, to the types of field texts that will yield helpful information, to the final written "restoried" rendition of the individual's experiences by the researcher.

Collecting data means identifying and selecting individuals for a study, obtaining their permission to be studied, and gathering information by administering instruments through asking people questions or observing their behaviors.

Comparison group is the group in an experiment that receives an alternative treatment (e.g., a variation of the new procedure or activity) rather than nothing at all so that they can benefit during an experiment.

Comparison question addresses how two or more groups differ in terms of one or more outcome variables. A comparison question is typically used in an experiment, and the researcher provides some intervention to one group and withholds it from the second group.

Compensatory equalization is a potential threat to internal validity when only the experimental group receives a treatment and an inequality exists that may affect the experiment.

Compensatory rivalry is a potential threat to internal validity when rivalry develops between the groups because the control group feels that it is the "underdog."

Computer-analysis of qualitative data means that researchers use a qualitative computer program to facilitate the process of storing, analyzing, and making sense of the data.

Conference papers are research reports presented to an audience at a state, regional, national, or international conference typically sponsored by professional associations (e.g., American Educational Research Association, American Association of Teacher Educators).

Conference proposals are short summaries of a study, typically about three pages, that reviewers use to determine whether research studies should be presented at conferences.

Confidence intervals or interval estimates are the range of upper and lower sample statistical values that are consistent with observed data and are likely to contain the actual population mean.

Confirming and disconfirming sampling is a purposeful strategy used during a qualitative study to follow up on specific cases to test out or explore further specific findings.

Confounding variables (sometimes called spurious variables) are attributes or characteristics that the researcher cannot directly measure because their effects cannot be easily separated from other variables, even though they may influence the relationship between the independent and the dependent variable.

Constant comparison is an inductive (from specific to broad) data analysis procedure in grounded theory research of generating and connecting categories by comparing incidents in the data to other incidents, incidents to categories, and categories to other categories.

Construct is an attribute or characteristic expressed in an abstract, general way; whereas, a variable is an attribute or characteristic stated in a specific, applied way.

Construct validity is a determination of the significance, meaning, purpose, and use of scores from an instrument.

Content validity is the extent to which the questions on the instrument and the scores from these questions are representative of all the possible questions that could be asked about the content or skills.

Context in ethnography is the setting, situation, or environment that surrounds the cultural-sharing group being studied.

Continuous score is value of a variable assigned by the researcher to a point along a continuum of scores, from low to high values. This type of score is also called an "interval," "rating" or "scaled" score. The most typical example of a continuous score would be age (i.e., from 25 years old to 65 years old) or height (i.e., from 5 feet to 6 feet).

Contrary evidence is information that does not support or confirm the themes and provides contradictory evidence for a theme.

Control means that the researcher attempts to study all factors that might help explain the relationship between an independent and dependent variable.

Control group is the group in an experiment that does not receive the treatment.

Control variable is a variable that the researcher does not want to measure directly, but is important to consider and "neutralize" because it potentially influences the dependent variable. Typically, control variables are personal, demographic attributes or characteristics.

Convenience sampling is a quantitative sampling procedure in which the researcher selects participants because they are willing and available to be studied.

Core category in grounded theory research is the central category around which the theory is written.

Correlation is defined as a statistical test to determine the tendency or pattern for two variables (or more) or two sets of data to vary consistently.

Correlation matrix is a visual display of the correlation coefficients for all variables in a study.

Correlational research designs are quantitative designs in which investigators use a correlation statistical technique to describe and measure the degree of association (or relationship) between two or more variables or sets of scores.

Covariates are variables that the researcher controls for using statistics and that relate to the dependent variable, but do not relate to the independent variable.

Co-vary means that a score can be predicted on one variable with knowledge about the individual's score on another variable.

Criterion-related validity is whether the scores from an instrument are a good predictor of some outcome (or criterion) they are expected to predict.

Criterion variable is the outcome variable being predicted in correlational research.

Critical ethnographies are a type of ethnographic research in which the author has an interest in advocating for the emancipation of groups marginalized in our society (Thomas, 1993).

Critical region is the area on the normal curve for low probability values if the null hypothesis is true.

Critical sampling is a qualitative purposeful sampling strategy in which the researcher selects an exceptionally vivid case for learning about the phenomenon.

Cross-sectional survey design is a design in which the researcher collects data at one point in time.

Cultural theme in ethnography is a general position, declared or implied, that is opened, approved, or promoted in a society or group (Spradley, 1980).

Culture is "everything having to do with human behavior and belief" (LeCompte, Priessle, & Tesch, 1993, p. 5). It can include language, rituals, economic and political structures, life stages, interactions, and communication styles.

Culture-sharing group in ethnography is two or more individuals that have shared behaviors, beliefs, and language.

Curve of dramatic action shows that the action in a story rises to a climatic peak or turning point and then falls to resolution, or denouement.

Curvilinear distribution is a U-shaped distribution in scores on a graph.

Data analysis in ethnography consists of distilling how things work and naming the essential features in themes in the cultural setting.

Data recording protocols are forms designed and used by qualitative researchers to record information during observations and interviews.

Deficiencies in the evidence means that the past literature or practical experiences of the researchers do not adequately address the research problem. In the "Statement of the Problem" the researcher summarizes the ways the literature or experiences are deficient.

Degree of association means the association between two variables or sets of scores with a correlation coefficient of -1.00 to $+1.00$, with .00 indicating no linear association at all.

Dependent variable is an attribute or characteristic that is influenced by the independent variable. Dependent variables are dependent or influenced by independent variables.

Describing and developing themes from the data in qualitative research consists of answering the major research questions and developing an in-depth understanding of the central phenomenon.

Description in ethnography is a detailed rendering of individuals and scenes to depict what is going on in the culture-sharing group.

Description in qualitative research is a detailed rendering of people, places, or events in a setting.

Descriptive fieldnotes record a description of the events, activities, and people (e.g., what happened).

Descriptive question identifies participants' responses to a single variable or question in quantitative research.

Descriptive statistics present information that help a researcher describe responses to each question in a database as well as determine overall trends and the distribution of the data.

Diffusion of treatments is a potential threat to internal validity when the experimental and control groups can communicate with each other, and the control group may learn from the experimental group information about the treatment.

Dimensionalized properties are when the grounded theory researcher views the property on a continuum and locates, in the data, examples representing extremes on this continuum.

Directional alternative hypothesis predicts a certain direction for the relationship between the independent variable and the dependent variable. This prediction is typically based on prior research conducted by the investigator or reported by others in the literature.

Discriminant sampling in grounded theory is when the researcher poses questions that relate the categories, and then returns to the data and looks for evidence, incidents, and events in order to develop a theory.

Dissertation or thesis proposal are plans for a research report, initiated and developed prior to the actual conduct of research.

Dissertations and theses are the doctoral and masters' research reports prepared by students for faculty and graduate committees.

Documents consist of public and private records that qualitative researchers can obtain about a site or participants in a study, such as newspapers, minutes of meetings, personal journals, or diaries.

Dynamic process in action research involves iterations of activities, such as a "spiral" of activities. The key idea is that the researcher "spirals" back and forth between reflection about a problem and data collection and action.

Educational topic is the broad subject matter area that a researcher wishes to address in a study.

Effect size is a means for identifying the strength of the conclusions about group differences or about the relationship among variables in a quantitative study. The calculation of this coefficient differs for statistical tests (e.g., R^2, eta^2, omega^2, Phi, Cohen's D) (American Psychological Asssociation, 1994).

Electronic questionnaire is a survey instrument for collecting data that is available on the computer.

E-mail interviews consist of collecting open-ended data through interviews from individuals using the technology of Web sites or the Internet.

Emerging design in grounded theory research is the process in which the researcher collects data, immediately analyzes it rather than waiting until all data are collected, and then bases the decision about what data to collect next on this analysis. The image of a "zig-zag" helps understand this procedure.

Emerging process indicates that the intent or purpose of a qualitative study and the questions asked by the researcher may change during the process of inquiry based on feedback or participants' views.

Emic data is information supplied by participants in a study. It often refers to first-order concepts, such as local language, concepts, and ways of expression used by members in a cultural-sharing group (Schwandt, 1997).

Encoding is the intentional use, by an author, of specific terms to convey ideas, such as using research terms.

End-of-text references are references listed at the end of a research report.

Equating groups means that the researcher randomly assigns individuals to groups equally and equally distributes any variability of individuals between or among the groups or conditions in the experiment.

Equivalent time series design is an experimental design in which the investigator alternates a treatment with a posttest measure. The data analysis then consists of comparing posttest measures or plotting them in order to discern patterns, over time, in the data.

Essays are discussions about a topic where the author develops a thought and elaborates on it through points or themes.

Ethnographic designs are qualitative procedures for describing, analyzing, and interpreting a cultural group's shared patterns of behavior, beliefs, and language that develop over time.

Etic data is information representing the ethnographer's interpretation of the participant's perspective. Etic typically refers to second-order concepts, such as the language used by the social scientist or educator to refer to the same phenomena mentioned by the participants (Schwandt, 1997).

Evaluating research involves making an assessment of the quality of a study using standards advanced by individuals in education.

Expanding knowledge suggests that educators study an area of research to extend it to new ideas or practices.

Experiences in narrative research are both personal—what the individual experiences—as well as social—the individual interacting with others (Clandinin & Connelly, 2000).

Experimental group is a group in an experiment that receives the treatment (e.g., the activity or procedure) that the researcher would like to test.

Experimental or quasi-experiment designs (also called an "intervention" or a "group comparison study") are procedures in quantitative research in which the investigator determines the impact of an intervention on an outcome for participants in a study.

Experimental treatment is when the researcher physically intervenes to alter the conditions experienced by the experimental unit.

Experimental unit of analysis is the smallest unit treated by the researcher during an experiment.

Explanatory mixed method design (also called a two-phase model, Creswell, 1994) consists of first, collecting quantitative data, and then collecting qualitative data to help explain or elaborate on the quantitative results.

Explanatory research design is a type of correlational research in which the researcher is interested in the extent to which two variables (or more) co-vary, where variance or change in one variable is reflected in variance or change in the other.

Exploratory mixed method design consists of first, gathering qualitative data to explore a phenomenon, and then collecting quantitative data to test relationships found in the qualitative data.

External audit in qualitative research is when a researcher hires or obtains the services of an individual outside the study to review many aspects of the research. This auditor reviews the project and writes or communicates an evaluation of the study.

Extraneous factors are any influences in the selection of participants, procedures, statistics, or design likely to affect the outcome and provide an alternative explanation for the results than what was expected.

Extreme case sampling is a form of purposeful sampling in which the researcher studies an outlier case or one that displays extreme characteristics.

Factorial designs represent a modification of the between-group design in which the researcher studies two or more categorical, independent variables, each examined at two or more levels (Vogt, 1999).

Factual or personal documents consist of numeric data in public records of individuals. This data can include grade reports, school attendance records, student demographic data, and census information.

Fieldnotes are text (or words) recorded by the researcher during an observation in a qualitative study.

Fieldwork in ethnography means that the researcher gathers data in the setting where the participants are located and where their shared patterns can be studied.

Figures are summaries of quantitative information presented as a chart, graph, or picture that shows relations among scores or variables.

Focus group interviews are the processes of collecting data through interviews with a group of people (typically 4–6) in which the researcher asks a small number of general questions and elicits responses from all individuals in the group.

Focus group interviews in survey research involve the researcher locating or developing a survey instrument, convening a small group of people—typically a group of 4–6 people—who can answer the questions on the instrument, and recording their comments to the instrument.

Future research directions are suggestions made by the researcher about additional studies that need to be conducted based on the results of the present research.

Gatekeepers are individuals who have an official or unofficial role at the site, provide entrance to a site, help researchers locate people, and assist in the identification of places to study.

Grounded theory designs are systematic, qualitative procedures that researchers use to generate a theory that explains, at a broad conceptual level, a process, action, or interaction about a substantive topic.

Group comparison is an analytic process in experiments of obtaining scores for individuals or groups on the dependent variable and making comparisons of their means and variance both within the group and between the groups.

Hand-analysis of qualitative data means that researchers read the data and mark it by hand and divide the data into parts. Traditionally, hand-analyzing text data involves using color-coding to mark parts of the text or by cutting and pasting text sentences onto cards.

History is a potential threat to internal validity in an experiment in which time passes between the beginning of the experiment and the end, and events may occur during which time that affect the outcome of the experiment.

Homogeneous samples are individuals in an experiment who vary little in their personal characteristics.

Homogeneous sampling is a purposeful sampling strategy in which the researcher samples individuals or sites based on membership in a subgroup with defining characteristics.

Hypotheses are declarative statements in quantitative research in which the investigator makes a prediction or a conjecture about the outcomes of a relationship.

Hypothesis testing is a procedure for making decisions about results by comparing an observed value with a population value to determine if no difference or relationship exists between the values.

Identifying a research problem consists of specifying an issue to study, developing a justification for studying it, and suggesting the importance of the study for select audiences that will read the report.

Implications in a study are those suggestions for the importance of the study for different audiences. They elaborate on the significance for audiences presented initially in the statement of the problem.

In vivo codes are labels for categories (or themes) that are phrased in the exact words of participants, rather than in the words of the researcher or in social science or educational terms.

Independent variable is an attribute or characteristic that influences or affects an outcome or dependent variable.

Inferential statistics enable a researcher to draw conclusions, inferences, or generalizations from a sample to a population of participants.

Informed consent form is a statement that participants sign before they participate in research. This form includes language that will guarantee them certain rights. When they sign the form, they agree to be involved in the study and acknowledge that their rights are protected.

Inputting the data means that the researcher transfers the data from the responses on instruments to a computer file for analysis.

Institutional review board is a committee of faculty who reviews and approves research so that the rights of humans are protected.

Intrinsic case is a type of qualitative case study in which the researcher studies the case itself because it is of exceptional interest.

Instrumental case is a type of qualitative case study in which the researcher studies a particular issue and finds one or more cases that illuminates the issue.

Instrumentation is a potential threat to validity in an experiment when the instrument changes during a pretest and a posttest.

Instruments are tools for measuring, observing, or documenting quantitative data. Researchers identify these instruments before they collect data, and they may include a test, a questionnaire, a tally sheet, a log, an observational checklist, an inventory, or an assessment instrument.

Interaction effects exist when the influence on one independent variable depends on (or covaries with) the other independent variable in an experiment.

Interaction of history and treatment is a threat to external validity in an experiment that arises when the researcher tries to generalize findings to past and future situations.

Interaction of selection and treatment is a threat to external validity in an experiment that involves the inability to generalize beyond the groups in the experiment, such as to other racial, social, geographical, age, gender or personality groups.

Interaction of setting and treatment is a threat to external validity in an experiment that arises from the inability to generalize from one setting where the experiment occurred to another setting.

Interactions with selection may pose a potential threat to internal validity in an experiment. Threats may interact with selection of participants, such as individuals selected may mature at different rates (e.g., 16-year-old boys and girls may mature at different rates during the study), historical events may interact with selection because individuals in different groups come from different settings, or the selection of participants may also influence the instrument scores, especially when different groups score at different mean positions on a test whose intervals are not equal.

Interconnecting themes means that the researcher connects the themes to display a chronology or sequence of events, such as when qualitative researchers generate a theoretical and conceptual model or report stories of individuals.

Internally consistent means that scores from an instrument are reliable and accurate if they are consistent across the items on the instrument.

Interpretation in ethnography consists of the process in which the researcher draws inferences and forms conclusions about what was learned.

Interpretation in qualitative research means that the researcher steps back and forms some larger meaning about the phenomenon based on personal views and/or comparisons with past studies.

Inter-rater reliability means that two or more individuals observe an individual's behavior, record scores, and then the scores of the observers are compared to determine whether they are similar.

Interrupted time series design consists of experimental procedures for studying one group, obtaining multiple pretest measures, administering an intervention (or interrupting the activities), and then measuring outcomes (or posttests) several times.

Interval or rating scales provide "continuous" response options to questions that have presumably equal distances between options.

Intervening variable is an attribute or characteristic that "stands between" the independent and dependent variables and exercises an influence on the dependent variable apart from the independent variable. Intervening variables transmit (or mediate) the effects of the independent variable on the dependent variable.

Interventions (or manipulations) in an experiment are ways a researcher physically intervenes with one or more conditions so that individuals experience something different in the experimental conditions than those in the control conditions.

Interview protocol is a form designed by the researcher that contains instructions for the process of the interview, the questions to be asked, and space to take notes on responses from the interviewee.

Interview surveys are forms on which the researcher records answers supplied by the participant in the study. The researcher asks a question from an interview guide, listens for answers or observes behavior, and records responses on the survey.

Interviewing in qualitative research is the process where researchers ask one or more participants in a study general, open-ended questions and record their answers.

Issue subquestions are questions that narrow the focus of the central question into specific topics the researcher seeks to learn from participants in a qualitative study.

Journal articles are polished, shorter research reports that have been sent to an editor of a journal, accepted for inclusion, and published in a volume of the journal.

Justifying a research problem means that the researcher presents reasons for the importance of studying the issue or concern.

Kuder-Richardson split half test (KR20, KR21) is a formula for calculating reliability of scores when items on an instrument are (a) scored as right or wrong as categorical scores, (b) the responses are not influenced by speed, and (c) the items measure a common factor.

Kurtosis distribution is a distribution of scores that pile up at the middle or spread out to the sides.

Language in ethnography is how an individual talks to others in a cultural setting.

Latent variable causal modeling (also called structural equation modeling) uses a procedure similar to path analysis but which yields more valid and reliable measures of the variables being analyzed. For each variable in the path (called latent variables), the researcher obtains multiple measures of the variables (called manifest variables), and the manifest variables are the only ones actually measured by the researcher.

Layering the analysis (also called first and second order abstractions) in qualitative research means representing the data using interconnected levels of themes.

Levels in an experiment are categories of a treatment variable.

Levels of headings in a scholarly study and literature review provide logical subdivisions of the text.

Life history is a narrative study of an individual's entire life experiences.

Limitations are potential weaknesses or problems in quantitative research that are identified by the researcher. In quantitative research, these weaknesses are enumerated one by one, and they often relate to inadequate measures of variables, loss or lack of participants, small sample sizes, errors in measurement, and other factors typically related to data collection and analysis.

Linking devices in writing are words or phrases that tie together sections of a research report.

Literature map is a figure or drawing that displays the research literature (e.g., studies, essays, books, chapters, and summaries) on a topic.

Literature review is a written summary of articles, books, and other documents that describe the past and current state of knowledge about a topic.

Longitudinal survey design is a design in which the researcher collects data about trends with the same population, changes in a cohort group or subpopulation, or changes in a panel group of the same individuals over time.

Mailed questionnaires are forms of data collection in survey research where the investigator mails a questionnaire to members of the sample.

Main effects are the influence of each independent variable (e.g., type of instruction or extent of depression) on the outcome (e.g., the dependent variable, rate of smoking) in an experiment.

Matching is the process of identifying one or more personal characteristics that influence the outcome and assigning individuals to the experimental and control groups equally matched on that characteristic.

Maturation is a potential threat to internal validity in an experiment in which individuals develop or change during the experiment (i.e., become older, wiser, stronger, and more experienced). These changes may affect their scores between the pretest and the posttest.

Maximal variation sampling is a purposeful sampling strategy in which the researcher samples cases or individuals that differ on some characteristic.

Measured variable is an independent variable that is measured or observed by the researcher and consists of a range of continuous or categorical scores for variables.

Measurement means that the researcher records information from individuals by: asking them to answer questions on an instrument (e.g., a student completes questions on a survey asking about self-esteem) or by observing an individual and recording scores on an instrument (e.g., a researcher watches a student playing basketball).

Measures of central tendency are summary numbers that represents a single value in a distribution of scores (Vogt, 1999).

Measures of relative standing are statistics that describe one score relative to a group of scores. Two frequently used statistics are the z-score and the percentile rank.

Measures of variability indicate the spread of the scores in a distribution. Variance, standard deviation, and range all indicate the amount of variability in a distribution of scores.

Member checking is a qualitative process during which the researcher asks one or more participants in the study to check the accuracy of the account.

Memos are notes the researcher writes throughout the research process to elaborate on ideas about the data and the coded categories.

Meta-analysis is a type of research report in which the author integrates the findings of many (primary source) research studies.

Missing data is information that is not supplied by participants to specific questions or items. This information may be lost, individuals may skip questions, participants may be absent when observational data is collected, or persons may actually refuse to complete a sensitive question.

Mixed method designs are procedures for collecting both quantitative and qualitative data in a single study, and for analyzing and reporting this data based on a priority and sequence of the information.

Modifying an instrument means locating an existing instrument, obtaining permission to change it, and making changes in it to fit the participants.

Mortality is a potential threat to internal validity in an experiment when individuals drop out during the experiment for any number of reasons (e.g., time, interest, money, friends, or parents who do not want them to participate).

Multiple baseline designs are single-subject studies in experimental research consisting of procedures in which the participant receives an experimental treatment at a different time (hence, multiple baselines exist) so that treatment diffusion will not occur among participants.

Multiple perspectives in qualitative research means that evidence for a theme is based on several viewpoints from different individuals and sources of data.

Multiple regression (or multiple correlation) is a statistical procedure for examining the combined relationship of multiple independent variables on a single dependent variable.

Multistage cluster sampling is a quantitative sampling procedure in which the researcher chooses a sample in two or more stages because the populations cannot be easily identified or they are extremely large.

Narrative discussion is a written passage in a qualitative study in which authors summarize, in detail, the findings from their data analysis.

Narrative hooks are the first sentences in a research report that draw readers into a study, cause readers to pay attention, elicit a response, such as emotional or attitudinal, from readers, and encourage readers to continue to read on.

Narrative research designs are qualitative procedures in which researchers describe the lives of individuals, collect and tell stories about these individuals' lives, and write narratives about their experiences (Connelly & Clandinin, 1990).

Negative correlations (indicated by a "−" correlation coefficient) are when the points move in the opposite direction—when X increases, Y decreases and when X decreases, Y increases.

Negative linear relationship results when low scores (or high scores) on one variable relate to high scores (or low scores) on the other variable.

Negotiated data consists of information that the participant and the researcher agree to use in a study.

Net or difference scores are scores in a quantitative study in which the researcher develops a score that represents a difference or change for each individual.

Nominal (or categorical) scales provide response options where participants check one or more categories that describe their traits, attributes, or characteristics.

Non-directional alternative hypothesis predicts a difference between groups on the dependent variable but does not indicate the direction of this prediction (e.g., positive or negative).

Non-parametric (or distribution free) **statistics** are statistical tests that only make the assumption of the independent observations of scores for each individual in the study.

Non-participant observer is an observational role adopted by researchers where they visit a site and record notes without becoming involved in the activities of the participants.

Nonprobability sampling is a quantitative sampling procedure in which the researcher chooses participants because they are available, convenient, and represent some characteristic the investigator seeks to study.

Normal distribution or normal probability curve is a distribution of scores by participants that can be represented by a graph that approximates a bell-shaped curve.

Null hypotheses make predictions that there will be no statistically significant difference between the independent variable and the dependent variable.

Observation is the process of gathering firsthand information by observing people and places at a research site.

Observational protocol is a form designed by the researcher, before data collection, that is used for taking fieldnotes during an observation.

Observations of behavior consist of selecting an instrument to record a behavior, observing individuals for that behavior, and checking points on a scale that reflect the behavior (e.g., behavioral checklists).

One-on-one interviewing in survey research consists of investigators conducting an interview with an individual in the sample and recording responses to questions.

One-on-one interviews are the data collection processes in which the researcher asks questions to and records answers from only one participant in the study at a time.

One-tailed tests of significance are when the region for rejection of the null hypothesis is placed only at one end of the distribution.

Open coding is the process used by the grounded theorist to form initial categories of information about the phenomenon being studied.

Open-ended questions in surveys consist of questions posed by the researcher in which the participant provides her or his own responses to questions.

Open-ended responses to a question allow the participant to create the options for responding.

Operational definitions are the specification of how variables will be defined and measured (or assessed) in a study.

Opportunistic sampling is purposeful sampling undertaken after the research begins in order to take advantage of unfolding events.

Ordinal scales or ranking scales are response options where participants rank order from best, or most important, to worst, or least important, some trait, attribute, or characteristic.

Outcomes (or "responses," "criteria," or "posttests") are the dependent variables in an experiment that are the presumed effect of the treatment variables. They are also the effects predicted in a hypothesis in the cause-and-effect equation.

Panel studies are longitudinal survey designs in which a researcher examines the same people over time.

Parametric statistics are statistical tests based on the premise that the population from which samples are obtained follows a normal distribution and the parameters of interest to the researcher are the population mean and standard deviation.

Participant observer is an observational role adopted by researchers where they take part in activities in the setting they observe.

Participatory in action research means that the researchers are self-reflective and study their own classrooms, schools, or practices.

Participatory action research is a design in action research aimed at improving the quality of people's organization, community, and family lives (Stringer, 1999). Although espousing many of the ideas of teacher and school-based practical action research, it differs by incorporating an emancipatory aim of improving and empowering individuals and organizations in educational (and other) settings.

Path analysis is a statistical procedure for testing a theory about a causal sequence of three or more variables on an outcome variable.

Pearson product-moment correlation coefficient is called the bi-variate correlation, the zero-order correlation, or simply the Pearson r, and it is indicated with an "r" for its notation. The statistic is calculated for two variables (r_{xy}) by multiplying the z scores on X and Y for each case and then dividing by the number of cases minus 1 (e.g., see the detailed steps in Voelker and Asher, 1995).

Performance measures assess an individual's ability to perform on an achievement test, an intelligence test, an aptitude test, an interest inventory, or on a personality assessment inventory.

Personal experience story is a narrative study of an individual's personal experience found in single or multiple episodes, private situations, or communal folklore (Denzin, 1989).

Phi-coefficient is the correlation statistic used to determine the degree and direction of association when *both* variables being related are dichotomous measures.

Physical structure of a study is the underlying organization of topics that form a structure for a research report.

Pilot test of a questionnaire or interview survey is a procedure in which a researcher makes changes in an instrument based on feedback from a small number of individuals who complete and evaluate the instrument.

Plan of action in action research is where the researcher formulates an action plan in response to a problem. This plan may be presenting the data to important stakeholders, establishing a pilot program, starting several competing programs, or implementing an ongoing research agenda to explore new practices (Stringer, 1999).

Point-biserial correlation is the correlation statistic used when one variable is measured as an interval or ratio scale, and the other has two different values (a dichotomous scale).

Population is a group of individuals that comprise the same characteristics. For example, all teachers would make up the population of teachers, and all high school administrators in a school district would make up the population of administrators.

Positive correlations (indicated by a "+" correlation coefficient) are when the points move in the same direction—when X increases, so also does Y increase, or alternatively, if X decreases, so also does Y decrease.

Positive linear relationship means that low (or high) scores on one variable relate to low (or high) scores on a second variable.

Posttest in an experiment measures some attribute or characteristic that is assessed for participants after a treatment.

Power in quantitative hypothesis testing is the probability of correctly rejecting a false null hypothesis.

Power analysis is a means of identifying appropriate sample size for group comparisons by taking into consideration the level of statistical significance (alpha), the amount of power desired in a study, and the effect size.

Practical action research is a design in action research in which educators study a specific school situation with a view toward improving practice (Schmuck, 1997). This form of action research focuses on a small-scale research project, narrowly focused on a specific problem or issue, and undertaken by individual teachers or teams within a school or school district.

Practical issues are often the focus of action research. These issues are concerns or problems that teachers or other school officials have in their educational setting.

Practical research problems are those that arise from the setting and activities of educators.

Prediction research design is a type of correlational research in which the researcher identifies variables that will positively predict an outcome or criterion.

Predictor variable is the variable the researcher uses to make a forecast about an outcome in correlational research.

Preliminary exploratory analysis in qualitative research consists of obtaining a general sense of the data, memoing ideas, thinking about the organization of the data, and considering whether more data are needed.

Preparing and organizing data for analysis in quantitative research consists of assembling all data, transforming it into numeric scores, creating a data file for computer or hand tabulation, and selecting a computer program to use in performing statistical tests on the data.

Presentation of results in quantitative research is where the investigator presents detailed information about the specific results of the descriptive and inferential statistical analyses.

Pretest in an experiment measures some attribute or characteristic that is assessed for participants before they receive a treatment.

Primary source literature is literature reported by the individual or individuals who actually conducted the research or who originated the ideas.

Probability sampling is a quantitative sampling procedure in which the researcher selects individuals from the population so that each person has an equal probability of being selected from the population.

Probable causation means that researchers attempt to establish a likely cause-and-effect relationship between variables, rather than *prove* the relationship.

Probes are subquestions under each question that the researcher asks to elicit more information. These probes vary from exploring the content in more depth (elaborating) to asking the interviewee to explain their answer in more detail (clarifying).

Procedural subquestions indicate the steps in analyzing the data to be used in a qualitative study. This form of writing subquestions is less frequently used than issue questions.

Process in grounded theory research is a sequence of actions and interactions among people and events pertaining to a topic (Strauss & Corbin, 1998).

Process of research consists of a series of five steps used by researchers when they conduct a study. They are identifying a research problem, reviewing the literature, specifying a purpose and research questions or hypotheses, collecting data, analyzing and interpreting the data, and reporting and evaluating research.

Properties are subcategories in grounded theory of open codes that serve to provide more detail about each category.

Purpose of the research consists of identifying the major intent or objective for a study and narrowing it into specific research questions or hypotheses.

Purpose statement is a declarative statement that advances the overall direction or focus for the study. Researchers describe the purpose in one or more succinctly formed sentences. It is used both in quantitative and qualitative research and it is typically found in the introduction or beginning section of research.

Purpose statement in qualitative research indicates the need to explore or understand the central phenomenon with specific individuals at a certain research site.

Purposeful sampling is a qualitative sampling procedure in which researchers intentionally select individuals and sites to learn or understand the central phenomenon.

Purposes of a proposal are to help an investigator think through all aspects of the study and anticipate problems.

P-values are the probability (p) that a result could have been produced by chance if the null hypothesis were really true.

Qualitative computer programs are programs that store and organize qualitative data (i.e., text, such as transcribed interviews or typed fieldnotes) and facilitate the process of analyzing data.

Qualitative research is an inquiry approach useful for exploring and understanding a central phenomenon. To learn about this phenomenon, the inquirer asks participants broad, general questions, collects the detailed views of participants in the form of words or images, and analyzes the information for description and themes. From this data, the researcher interprets the meaning of the information, drawing on personal reflections and past research. The final structure of the final report is flexible, and it displays the researcher's biases and thoughts.

Qualitative research questions are open-ended general questions that the researcher would like answered during the study.

Qualitative scientific structure of a research report includes detailed procedures of inquiry, and follows a traditional form for reporting research to include the introduction, the procedures, the findings, and a discussion.

Qualitative storytelling structure is a flexible approach to writing a qualitative report. The meaning of the study unfolds through descriptions, an author's reflection on the meaning of the data, a larger understanding of the phenomenon, and a return to the author's stance on the topic.

Quantitative purpose statement identifies the variables, their relationship, and the participants and site for research.

Quantitative research is an inquiry approach useful for describing trends and explaining the relationship among variables found in the literature. To conduct this inquiry, the investigator specifies narrow questions, locates or develops instruments to gather data to answer the questions, and analyzes numbers from the instruments using statistics. From results of these analyses, the researcher interprets the data using prior predictions and research studies. The final report, presented in a standard format, displays researcher objectivity and lack of bias.

Quasi-experiments are experimental situations in which the researcher assigns, but not randomly assigns, participants to groups because the experimenter cannot artificially create groups for the experiment.

Questionnaires are forms used in a survey design that participants in a study complete and return to the researcher. Participants mark choices to questions and supply basic personal or demographic information about themselves.

Random assignment is the process of assigning individuals at random to groups or to different conditions of a group in an experiment. It is a characteristic of a true experiment in research.

Ratio or true zero is a response scale in which participants check a response option with a true zero and equal distances between units.

Realist ethnography is a type of ethnographic design in which the researcher provides an objective account of the situation, typically written in the third-person point of view, reporting objectively on the information learned from participants at a field site.

Reflective fieldnotes record personal thoughts that researchers have that relate to their insights, hunches, or broad ideas or themes that emerge during an observation.

Reflexivity in ethnography means that the researcher is aware of and openly discusses his or her role in a study in a way that honors and respects the site and the people being studied.

Reflexivity in qualitative research means that the researchers reflect on their own biases, values, and assumptions and actively write them into their research.

Regression is a potential threat to internal validity in an experiment in which the researchers select individuals for a group based on extreme scores, and, because they will naturally do better (or worse) on a posttest than the pretest regardless of the treatment, they will threaten the validity of the outcomes.

Regression line in correlation research is a line of "best fit" for all of the points of scores on a graph. This line comes the closest to all of the points on the plot and it is calculated by drawing a line that minimizes the squared distance of the points from the line.

Regression tables show the overall amount of variance explained in a dependent variable by all independent variables, called R^2 (R-squared).

Relationship questions seek to answer the degree and magnitude of the relationship between two or more variables. These questions often relate different types of variables in a study, such as independent variables to independent variables or dependent variables to control variables.

Reliability means that individual scores from an instrument should be nearly the same or stable on repeated administrations of the instrument and that they should be free from sources of measurement error and consistent.

Repeated measures design is an experimental design in which all participants in a single group participate in all experimental treatments. Each group becomes its own control. The researcher compares a group's performance under one experimental treatment with another experimental treatment.

Replicating knowledge means that educators test old results with new participants or at new research sites.

Reporting research involves deciding on audiences, structuring the report in a format acceptable to these audiences, and then writing the report in a manner that is sensitive to all readers.

Research is a cyclical process of steps that typically begins with identifying a research problem or issue of study. It then involves reviewing the literature, specifying a purpose for the study, collecting and analyzing data, and forming an interpretation of the information. This process culminates in a report, disseminated to audiences, that is evaluated and used in the educational community.

Research designs are procedures for collecting, analyzing, and reporting research in quantitative and qualitative research.

Research objective is a statement of intent for the study that specifies specific goals that the investigator plans to achieve in a study.

Research problems are the educational issues or concerns studied by researchers.

Research questions are interrogative statements that narrow the purpose statement to specific questions that researchers seek to answer in their studies.

Research report is a study that reports an investigation or exploration of a problem, identifies questions to be addressed, and includes data collected, analyzed, and interpreted by the researcher.

Resentful demoralization is a potential threat to internal validity when a control group is used and individuals in this group feel resentful and demoralized because they perceive that they receive a less desirable treatment than other groups.

Response bias occurs in survey research when the responses do not accurately reflect the views of the sample and the population.

Response return rate is the percentage of questionnaires that are returned from the participants to the researcher.

Restorying is the process in which the researcher gathers stories, analyzes them for key elements of the story (e.g., time, place, plot, and scene), and then rewrites the story to place it in a chronological sequence.

Reviewing the literature means locating summaries, books, journals, and indexed publications on a topic, selectively choosing which literature is relevant, and then writing a report that summarizes that literature.

Sample is a subgroup of the target population that the researcher plans to study for the purpose of making generalizations about the target population.

Sample size formulas provide formulas, based on several parameters, that can be used to calculate the size of the sample.

Sampling error is the difference between the sample estimate and the true population score.

Sampling error formula is a calculation for determining the size of a sample based on the chance (or proportion) that the sample will be evenly divided on a question, sampling error, and a confidence interval.

Saturation in qualitative research is a state in which the researcher makes the subjective determination that new data will not provide any new information or insights for the developing categories.

Scales of measurement are response options to questions that measure (or observe) variables in nominal, ordinal, or interval/ratio units.

Scatterplot (or scatter diagram) is a pictorial image of two sets of scores for participants on a graph.

Scoring means that the researcher assigns a numeric score (or value) to each response category for each question on the instruments used to collect data.

Secondary source literature summarizes primary sources and it does not represent material published by the original researchers or the creators of the idea.

Selection is a potential threat to internal validity in an experiment where "people factors" may introduce threats that influence the outcome, such as selecting individuals who are brighter, more receptive to a treatment, or more familiar with a treatment.

Selective coding is the process in which the grounded theorist writes a theory based on the interrelationship of the categories in the axial coding model.

Semiclosed-ended questions in a survey consist of questions that include both closed-ended and open-ended questions.

Semistructured interviews are interviews in which the researcher asks some questions that are closed-ended and some that are open-ended.

Sequence in mixed method designs means that the researcher collects data using concurrent or sequential procedures.

Setting in narrative research may be friends, family, workplace, home, social organization, or school—the place in which a story physically occurs.

Shared pattern in ethnography is a common social interaction that stabilizes, as tacit, rules and expectations of the group (Spindler & Spindler, 1992).

Sharing reports in action research means that the inquirer shares the action research study locally with individuals who can promote change or enact plans within their classroom or building. Action researchers share results with teachers, the building principal, school district personnel, and parent associations (e.g., Hughes, 1999).

Significance level (or alpha) is a probability level that reflects the maximum risk you are willing to take that any observed differences are due to chance. It is called the "alpha level" and is typically set at .01 (1 out of 100 times the sample statistic fall will be due to chance) or .05 (5 out of 100 times it will be due to chance).

Simple random sampling is a quantitative sampling procedure in which the researcher selects participants (or units, such as schools) for the sample so that any sample of size N has an equal probability of being selected from the population. The intent of simple random sampling is to choose units to be sampled that will be representative of the population.

Single-item scores are an individual score to each question for each participant in your study.

Single-subject research (also called *N*=1 research, behavior analysis, or within-subjects research) involves the study of single individuals, their observation over a baseline period, and the administration of an intervention. This is followed by another observation after the intervention to determine if the treatment affects the outcome.

Skewed distribution is a distribution of scores when they tend to pile up toward one end of the scale and they taper off slowly at the other end (Gravetter & Wallnau, 2000).

Snowball quantitative sampling is a sampling procedure in which the researcher asks participants to identify other participants to become members of the sample.

Snowball sampling is a form of qualitative purposeful sampling that typically proceeds after a study begins in which the researcher asks participants to recommend individuals to study.

Spearman-Brown formula is a formula for calculating the reliability of scores using all questions on an instrument. Since the split half test relies on information from only half of the test, a modification in this procedure is to use this formula to estimate full-length test reliability.

Spearman rho (r_s) is the correlation statistic used for non-linear data when the data are measured on ordinal scales (rank order scales).

Statement of the Problem is a section in a research report that contains the topic for the study, the research problem within this topic, a justification for the problem based on past research and practice, deficiencies or shortcomings of past research or practical knowledge, and the importance of addressing the problem for diverse audiences.

Statistical significance is when the observed values (e.g., before and after a treatment in an experiment, the difference between mean scores for two or more groups or the relationship between two variables) provide a statistical value (p-value) that exceeds the predetermined alpha level set by the researcher.

Statistical tests are procedures for calculating the actual statistic (e.g., t-statistic, F-statistic) in quantitative research.

Statistics are the numbers derived from formulas to measure aspects of a set of data.

Story in narrative research is a first-person oral telling or retelling of events related to the personal or social experiences of an individual. Often these stories have a beginning, a middle, and an end.

Stratified sampling is a quantitative sampling procedure in which researchers stratify the population on some specific characteristic (e.g., gender) and then sample, using simple random sampling, from each stratum of the population.

Structured interviews are interviews in which the researcher asks questions with close-ended response options for the participant.

Study-based research problems emanate from a need to extend knowledge or resolve conflicting views in published studies.

Study-by-study review of the literature is a detailed summary of each study grouped under a broad theme.

Subquestions in qualitative research refine the central question into subtopics or indicate the processes to be used in research. These subquestions contain the same elements as in central questions (e.g., open-ended, emerging, neutral in language, and are few in number), but they provide greater specificity to the questions in the study. They are of two types: issue and procedural subquestions.

Summaries in research are statements that review the major conclusions to each of the research questions or hypotheses.

Summaries in the literature provide overviews of the literature and research on timely issues in education.

Summed scores are scores of an individual added over several questions that measure the same variable.

Survey designs are procedures in quantitative research in which investigators administer a survey or questionnaire to a sample or to the entire population of people in order to describe the attitudes, opinions, behaviors, or characteristics of the population.

Systematic design in grounded theory emphasizes the use of data analysis steps of open, axial, and selective coding, and the development of a logic paradigm or a visual picture of the theory generated.

Systematic sampling is a quantitative sampling procedure in which the researcher chooses every "*n*th" individual or site in the population until the desired sample size is achieved.

Tables are summaries of quantitative data organized into rows and columns.

Target population (or sometimes called the sampling frame) is a group of individuals with some common defining characteristic that the researcher can identify with a list or set of names.

Teacher's stories are narrative research, personal accounts by teachers of their own personal classroom experiences.

Telephone interview survey are interviews in which the researcher records comments by participants to questions on instruments over the telephone.

Telephone interviews are the processes of gathering data using the telephone and asking a small number of general questions.

Testing is a potential threat to validity in an experiment when participants become familiar with the outcome measures and remember responses for later testing.

Test-retest reliability examines the extent to which scores from one sample are stable over time from one test administration to another.

Text segments are sentences or paragraphs that all relate to a single code in qualitative research.

Thematic review of the literature includes a theme and supporting literature found by the researcher to document the theme.

Themes in qualitative research are similar codes aggregated together to form a major idea in the database.

Theoretical lens in narrative research is a guiding perspective or ideology that provides a structure for advocating for groups or individuals and writing the report.

Theoretical propositions in grounded theory research are statements indicating the relationship among categories, such as in the systematic approach to axial coding that include causal conditions, the core category or phenomenon, the context, intervening conditions, strategies, and consequences.

Theoretical sampling in grounded theory means that the researcher chooses forms of data collection that will yield text and images useful in generating a theory.

Theory in grounded theory research is an abstract explanation or understanding of a process about a substantive topic "grounded" in the data. The theory is "middle-range" (Charmaz, 2000), drawn from multiple individuals or data sources, that provide an explanation for a substantive topic.

Theory in quantitative research explains and predicts the relationship between independent and dependent variables. They are called the outcome, effect, criterion, or consequence variables.

Theory or concept sampling is a purposeful sampling strategy in which individuals or sites are sampled because they can help the researcher generate or discover a theory or specific concept within the theory.

Threats to validity means statistical and design issues may threaten the experiment so that the conclusions reached from data may provide a false reading about probable causality—the relationship between the treatment and the outcome.

Threats to construct validity are problems that threaten drawing correct inferences because of the measures used in the experiment for the treatment (independent variable) and the outcome (dependent variable).

Threats to external validity are problems in experiments that threaten drawing correct inferences from the sample data to persons, settings, and past and future situations.

Threats to internal validity are potential problems that threaten drawing correct inferences that arise because of the experimental procedures or the experiences of participants.

Threats to statistical conclusion validity represent potential problems that threaten drawing correct inferences because of statistical procedures.

Time series is an experimental design consisting of studying one group, over time, with multiple pretest and posttest measures or observations made by the researcher.

Transcription is the process of converting audiotape recordings or fieldnotes into text data.

Treatment variable is an independent variable that the researcher manipulates to determine the effect it will have on an outcome. It is always a categorically scored variable measuring two or more groups or levels.

Trend studies are longitudinal survey designs that involve identifying a population and examining changes within that population over time.

Triangulation is the process of corroborating evidence from different individuals (e.g., a principal and a student), types of data (e.g., observational fieldnotes and interviews), or methods of data collection (e.g., documents and interviews) in descriptions and themes in qualitative research.

Triangulation mixed method design consists of simultaneously collecting both quantitative and qualitative data, merging the data, and using the results to best understand a research problem.

True experiments are experimental situations in which the researcher randomly assigns participants to different conditions (or levels) of the experimental variable.

Two-tailed tests of significance are when the critical region for rejection of the null hypothesis is divided into two areas at the ends of the sampling distribution (Vogt, 1999).

Type I error occurs when the null hypothesis is rejected by the researcher when it is actually true. The probability of this error rate is "alpha."

Type II error occurs when the researcher fails to reject the null hypothesis when an effect actually occurs in the population. The probability of this error rate is called "beta."

Typical sampling is a form of purposeful sampling in which the researcher studies a person or site that is "typical" to those unfamiliar with the situation.

Uncorrelated relationship of scores means that the scores in the distribution are independent of each other.

Unit of analysis refers to the unit (e.g., individual, family, school, school district) the researcher uses to gather the data.

Unstructured interviews are interviews in which the researcher asks open-ended questions that permit the participant to create response possibilities.

Validating findings in qualitative research means that the researcher determines the accuracy or credibility of the findings through strategies such as member checking or triangulation.

Validity means that researchers can draw meaningful and justifiable inferences from scores about a sample or population.

Values are scores assigned to response options for questions.

Variable is a characteristic or attribute of an individual or an organization that can be (1) measured or observed by the researcher and that (2) varies among individuals or organizations studied.

Variance means that scores will assume different values depending on the type of variable being measured.

Visualization in mixed method research consists of a figure or drawing displaying the procedures of a study.

Wave analysis is a survey research procedure to check for response bias in which investigators group returns by intervals (e.g., by week) and check to see if the answers to a few select questions change from the first week to the final week in a study.

Weight or **priority** in mixed method designs means that the researcher places more emphasis on one type of data than another in the research and the written report.

Within-group designs are those in which the researcher studies a *single group* and provides the new idea or approach to this single group at some point in time during the experiment.

Within-group experimental design is an experiment design in which the researcher studies only one group of individuals, such as time series or repeated measure designs.

Within individual design is an experimental design in which the researcher studies single individuals, such as single-subject designs.

Within-text references are references cited in a brief format within the body of the text to provide credit to authors.

References

Abel, M., & Sewell, J. (1999). Stress and burnout in rural and urban secondary school teachers. *Journal of Educational Research, 92,* 287–293.

Abelson, R. P. (1995). *Statistics as principled argument.* Hillsdale, NJ: Lawrence Erlbaum Associates.

Agar, M. H. (1980). *The professional stranger: An informal introduction to ethnography.* San Diego, CA: Academic Press.

Alkin, M. C. (Ed.). (1992). *Encyclopedia of educational research* (6th ed.). New York: Macmillan.

Allen, L., & Calhoun, E. F. (1998). Schoolwide action research: Findings from six years of study. *Phi Delta Kappan, 79*(9), 706–710.

American Educational Research Association (1999). American Educational Research Association 2000 Annual Meeting call for proposals. *Educational Research, 28,* 33.

American Educational Research Association, American Psychological Association, National Council on Measurement in Education (1999). *Standards for educational and psychological testing.* Washington, DC: American Educational Research Association.

American Psychological Association (1994). *Publication manual of the American Psychological Association* (4th ed.). Washington, DC: American Psychological Association.

American Psychological Association. (1927–). *Psychological abstracts.* Washington, DC: American Psychological Association.

American Psychological Association. (1992). Ethical principles of psychologists and code of conduct. *American Psychologist, 47*(2), 1597–1611.

American Psychological Association. (1994). *Publication manual of the American Psychological Association* (4th ed.). Washington D.C.: American Psychological Association.

Anderson, E. S., & Keith, T. Z. (1997). A longitudinal test of a model of academic success for at-risk high school students. *Journal of Educational Research, 90,* 259–266.

Angrosino, M. V. (1989). *Documents of interaction: Biography, autobiography, and life history in social science perspective.* Gainesville, FL: University of Florida Press.

Annual review of psychology. (1950–). Stanford, CA: Annual Reviews.

Asmussen, K. J., & Creswell, J. W. (1995). Campus response to a student gunman. *Journal of Higher Education, 66,* 575–591.

Atweh, B., Kemmis, S., & Weeks, P. (1998). *Action research in practice: Partnerships for social justice in education.* London and New York: Routledge.

Auh, M. (1997). Prediction of musical creativity in composition among selected variables for upper elementary students. *Bulletin of the Council for Research in Music Education, 123,* 1–8.

Babbie, E. (1990). *Survey research methods.* Belmont, CA: Wadsworth.

Babbie, E. (1998). *The practice of social research* (8th ed.). Belmont, CA: Wadsworth.

Babchuk, W. A. (1996). *Glaser or Strauss?: Grounded theory and adult education.* Paper presented at the Midwest Research-to-Practice Conference in Adult, Continuing and Community Education, University of Nebraska–Lincoln.

Babchuk, W. A. (1997). *The rediscovery of grounded theory: Strategies for qualitative research in adult education.* Unpublished doctoral dissertation, University of Nebraska–Lincoln.

Baker, R. W., & Siryk, B. (1989). *Student adaptation to college questionnaire (SACQ).* Los Angeles: Western Psychological Services.

Banks, J. A., & Banks, C. A. (1995). *Handbook of research on multicultural education.* New York: Macmillan.

Barth, J. (1999). Incremental perturbation: How to know whether you've got a plot or not. In J. Checkoway (Ed.), *Creating fiction,* 126–134. Cincinnati, OH: Story.

Barzun, J., & Graff, H. G. (1985). *The modern researcher* (4th ed.). New York: Harcourt Brace & World.

Baszanger, I. (1997). Deciphering chronic pain. In A. Strauss & J. Corbin (Eds.), *Grounded theory in practice* (pp. 1–34). Thousand Oaks, CA: Sage.

Batsche, C., Hernandez, M., & Montenegro, M. C. (1999). Community needs assessment with Hispanic, Spanish-monolingual residents. *Evaluation and Program Planning, 22,* 13–20.

Bauermeister, M. L. (1998). *The child of the mist: Enculturation in a New Zealand Kohanga Reo.* Unpublished doctoral dissertation, University of Nebraska–Lincoln.

Bausell, R. B. (1994). *Conducting meaningful experiments.* Thousand Oaks, CA: Sage.

Bazeley, P. (2000). *Mixed methods data analysis using NUD*IST/Nvivo with table based software and/or a statistics program.* Paper presented at the American Educational Research Association Annual Meeting, New Orleans, LA.

Becker, P. H. (1993). Common pitfalls in published grounded theory research. *Qualitative Health Research, 3,* 254–260.

Benson, J., & Clark, F. (1983). A guide for instrument development and validation. *The American Journal of Occupational Therapy, 36,* 790–801.

Bickman, L., & Rog, D. J. (2000). (Eds.). *Handbook of applied social research methods.* Thousand Oaks, CA: Sage.

Billington, R. (1994). Effects of collaborative test taking on retention in eight third-grade mathematics classes. *The Elementary School Journal, 95,* 23–31.

Blustein, D. L., Phillips, S. D., Jobin-David, K., Finkelberg, S. L., & Roarke, A. E. (1997). A theory-building investigation of the school-to-work transition. *The Counseling Psychologist, 25,* 364–402.

Bogdan, R. C., & Biklen, S. K. (1982; 1998). *Qualitative research for education: An introduction to theory and methods.* (1st, 3rd ed.). Boston, MA: Allyn & Bacon.

Boruch, R. F. (1998). Randomized controlled experiments for evaluation and planning. In L. Bickman & D. J. Rog (Eds.), *Handbook of applied social research methods* (pp. 161–191). Thousand Oaks, CA: Sage.

Bracht, G. H., & Glass, G. V. (1968). The external validity of experiments. *American Educational Research Journal, 4,* 73–81.

Brewer, J., & Hunter, A. (1989). *Multimethod research: A synthesis of styles.* Newbury Park, CA: Sage.

Brickhouse, N., & Bodner, G. M. (1992). The beginning science teacher: Classroom narratives of convictions and constraints. *Journal of Research in Science Teaching, 29,* 471–485.

Brown, M. L. (1993). *Ethnic minority students' process of community building on a predominantly white campus.* Unpublished doctoral dissertation, University of Nebraska–Lincoln.

Brown, R. (1998). *Theory about the process of community-building in distance learning courses.* Unpublished dissertation proposal, the University of Nebraska at Lincoln.

Brown, S. P., Parham, T. A., & Yonker, R. (1996). Influence of a cross-cultural training course on racial identity attitudes of white women and men: Preliminary perspectives. *Journal of Counseling & Development, 74*(5), 510–516.

Bruner, E. M. (1993). Introduction: The ethnographic self and the personal self. In P. Benson (Ed.), Anthropology and literature (pp. 1–26). Urbana: University of Illinois Press.

Bryman, A. (1988). *Quantity and quality in social science research.* London and New York: Routledge.

Budnitz, J. (2000). Flush. In M. Cunningham, P. Houston, and G. Saunders (Eds.), *Prize stories 2000.* New York: Random House.

Burrell, G., & Morgan, G. (1979). *Sociological paradigms and organisational analysis: Elements of the sociology of corporate life*. London: Heinemann.

Calhoun, E. F. (1994). *How to use action research in the self-renewing school*. Alexandria, VA: Association for the Supervision and Curriculum Development.

Cameron, C. A., & Lee, K. (1997). Bridging the gap between home and school with voice-mail technology. *Journal of Educational Research, 90*(3), 182–190.

Campbell, D. T., & Fiske, D. W. (1959). Convergent and discriminant validation by the multitrait-multimethod matrix. *Psychological Bulletin, 56*, 81–105.

Campbell, D. T., & Stanley, J. C. (1963). Experimental and quasi-experimental designs for research. In N. L. Gage (Ed.) *Handbook on research in teaching* (pp. 1–80). Chicago: Rand-McNally.

Campbell, W. G., & Ballou, S. V. (1977). *Form and style: Theses, reports, and term papers* (5th ed.). Boston: Houghton Mifflin.

Caracelli, V. J., & Greene, J. C. (1993). Data analysis strategies for mixed-method evaluation designs. *Educational Evaluation and Policy Analysis, 15*(2), 195–207.

Carspecken, P. F. (1995). *Critical ethnography in educational research: A theoretical and practical guide*. London: Routledge.

Carspecken, P. F., & Apple, M. (1992). Critical qualitative research: Theory, methodology, and practice. In M. D. LeCompte, W. L. Millroy, & J. Preissle (Eds.), *The handbook of qualitative research in education* (pp. 507–553). San Diego, CA: Academic Press.

Carter, K. (1993). The place of a story in the study of teaching and teacher education. *Educational Researcher, 22*(1), 5–12, 18.

Casey, K. (1995, 1996). The new narrative research in education. *Review of Research in Education, 21*, 211–253.

Ceprano, M. A., & Garan, E. M. (1998). Emerging voices in a university pen-pal project: Layers of discovery in action research. *Reading Research and Instruction, 38*(1), 31–56.

Charmaz, K. (1990). "Discovering" chronic illness: Using grounded theory. *Social Science Medicine, 30*, 1161–1172.

Charmaz, K. (1994). Identity dilemmas of chronically ill men. *The Sociological Quarterly, 35*, 269–288.

Charmaz, K. (2000). Grounded theory: Objectivist and constructivist methods. In N. K. Denzin and Y. S. Lincoln (Eds.), *Handbook of qualitative research* (2nd ed., pp. 509–535). Thousand Oaks, CA: Sage.

Clandinin, D. J., & Connelly, F. M. (2000). *Narrative inquiry: Experience and story in qualitative research*. San Francisco, CA: Jossey-Bass.

Clifford, J., & Marcus, G. E. (Eds.). (1986). *Writing culture*. Berkeley: University of California Press.

Cocklin, B. (1996). Applying qualitative research to adult education: Reflections upon analytic processes. *Studies in the Education of Adults, 28*, 88–116.

Cohen, J. (1977). *Statistical power analysis for the behavioral sciences* (Rev. ed.). New York: Academic Press.

Cohen, L., & Manion, L. (1994). *Research methods in education* (4th ed.). London and New York: Routledge.

Congressional Information Service. (1973–). *American statistics index*. Washington, DC: Congressional Information Service.

Connelly, F. M., & Clandinin, D. J. (1988). *Teachers as curriculum planners: Narratives of experience*. New York: Teachers College Press, Columbia University.

Connelly, F. M., & Clandinin, D. J. (1990). Stories of experience and narrative inquiry. *Educational Researcher, 19*(5), 2–14.

Connelly, F. M., & Clandinin, D. J. (1999). *Shaping a professional identity*. New York and London: Teachers College Press, Columbia University.

Connelly, F. M., Dukacz, A. S., & Quinlan, F. (1980). *Curriculum planning for the classroom*. Toronto, Canada: OISE Press.

Cook, T. D., & Campbell, D. T. (1979). *Quasi-experimentation: Design and analysis issues for field settings*. Boston, MA: Houghton Mifflin.

Cooper, H. (1984). *The integrated research review: A systematic approach*. Beverly Hills, CA: Sage.

Cooper, H. M., & Lindsay, J. J. (1998). Research synthesis and meta-analysis. In L. Bickman and D. J. Rog (Eds.), *Handbook of applied social research methods*, 315–337. Thousand Oaks, CA: Sage.

Cooper, J. O, Heron, T. E., & Heward, W. L. (1987). *Applied behavior analysis*. Columbus, OH: Merrill.

Cortazzi, M. (1993). *Narrative analysis*. London: The Falmer Press.

Courtney, S., Jha, L. R., & Babchuk, W. A. (1994). Like school?: A grounded theory of life in an ABE/GED classroom. *Adult Basic Education, 4*, 172–195.

Cowles, M. (1989). *Statistics in psychology: A historical perspective*. Hillsdale, NJ: Lawrence Erlbaum Associates.

Creswell, J. W. (1994). *Research design: Qualitative and quantitative approaches*. Thousand Oaks, CA: Sage.

Creswell, J. W. (1998). *Qualitative inquiry and research design: Choosing among five traditions*. Thousand Oaks, CA: Sage.

Creswell, J. W. (1999). Mixed-method research: Introduction and application. In G. J. Cizek (Ed.), *Handbook of educational policy* (pp. 455–472). San Diego: Academic Press.

Creswell, J. W., & Brown, M. L. (1992). How chairpersons enhance faculty research: A grounded theory study. *The Review of Higher Education, 16*(1), 41–62.

Creswell, J. W., & Miller, D. M. (2000). Determining validity in qualitative inquiry. *Theory into Practice XXXIX*(3), 124–130.

Creswell, J. W., Goodchild, L. F., & Turner, P. (1996). Integrated qualitative and quantitative research: Epistemology, history, and designs. In J. Smart (Ed.), *Higher education: Handbook of theory and research* (Vol. XI) (pp. 455–471). New York: Agathon Press.

Creswell, J. W., Tashakkori, A., Jensen, K., & Shapley, K. (in press). Teaching mixed methods research: Practice, dilemmas and challenges. In A. Tashakkori and C. Teddlie (Eds.), *Handbook of mixed method in the behavioral and social sciences*. Thousand Oaks, CA: Sage.

Creswell, J. W., Wheeler, D. W., Seagren, A. T., Egly, N. J., & Beyer, K. D. (1990). *The academic chairperson's handbook*. Lincoln and London: The University of Nebraska Press.

Csikszentmihalyi, M., Rathunde, K., Whalen, S., & Wong, M. (1993). *Talented teenagers: The roots of success and failure*. New York: Cambridge University Press.

Dahmus, S., Bernardin, H. J., & Bernardin, K. (1992). Test review: Student adaptation to college questionnaire. *Measurement and evaluation in counseling and development, 25*, 139–142.

Datta, L. (1994). Paradigm wars: A basis for peaceful coexistence and beyond. In C. S. Reichardt and S. F. Rallis (Eds.), *The qualitative-quantitative debate: New perspectives* (pp. 53–70). New Directions for Program Evaluation, No 61. San Francisco: Jossey-Bass.

Davis, T. C., Arnold, C., Nandy, I., Bocchini, J. A., Gottlief, A., George, R., & Berkel, H. (1997). Tobacco use among male high school athletes. *Journal of Adolescent Health, 21*, 97–101.

De Landsheere, G. (1988). History of educational research. In J. P. Keeves (Ed.), *Educational research, methodology, and measurement: An international handbook*. Oxford, Pergamon Press.

Degh, L. (1995). *Narratives in society: A performer-centered study of narration*. Helsinki, Norway: Suomalainen Tiedeakatemia, Academia Scientiarum Fennica.

Delgado, R., & Stefancic, J. (Eds.). (1997). *Critical white studies: Looking behind the mirror*. Philadelphia, PA: Temple University Press.

Denzin, N. (1989). *Interpretative biography*. Newbury Park, CA: Sage.

Denzin, N. K. (1997). *Interpretive ethnography: Ethnographic practices for the 21st century*. Thousand Oaks, CA: Sage.

Denzin, N. K., & Lincoln, Y. S. (1994). Introduction: Entering the field of qualitative research. In N. K. Denzin and Y. S. Lincoln (Eds.), *Handbook of qualitative research*. Thousand Oaks, CA: Sage.

Denzin, N. K., & Lincoln, Y. S. (Eds.). (2000). *Handbook of qualitative research*. (2nd ed.). Thousand Oaks, CA: Sage.

Dey, E. L., & Hurtado, S. (1996). Faculty attitudes toward regulating speech on college campuses. *The Review of Higher Education, 20*, 15–32.

Dey, I. (1993). *Qualitative data analysis: A user-friendly guide for social scientists*. London: Routledge.

Dicker, M. (1990). Using action research to navigate an unfamiliar teaching assignment. *Theory into practice, XXIX*, 203–208.

Dods, R. F. (1997). An action research study of the effectiveness of problem-based learning in promoting the acquisition and retention of knowledge. *Journal for the Education of the Gifted, 20*(4), 423–437.

Educational Resources Information Center (U.S.). (1966–). *Resources in education*. Washington, DC: Author.

Educational Resources Information Center (U.S.). (1967–). *Thesaurus of ERIC descriptors*. New York: Macmillan Information.

Educational Resources Information Center (U.S.). (1969–). *Current index to journals in education*. New York: Macmillan.

Educational Resources Information Center (U.S.). (1986). *ERIC (CD-ROM version)*. Washington, DC: Author.

Educational Resources Information Center (U.S.). (1991). *ERIC directory of education-related information centers*. Washington, DC: Author.

Ehrlich, E., Flexner, S. B., Carruth, G., & Hawkins, J. M. (1980). *Oxford American Dictionary*. New York and Oxford: Oxford University Press.

Elbaz-Luwisch, F. (1997). Narrative research: Political issues and implications. *Teaching and Teacher Education, 13*(1), 75–83.

Emerson, R. M., Fretz, R. I., & Shaw, L. L. (1995). *Writing ethnographic fieldnotes*. Chicago: University of Chicago Press.

Epper, R. M. (1997). Coordination and competition in postsecondary distance education. *Journal of Higher Education, 68*(5), 551–587.

Errante, A. (2000). But sometimes you're not part of the story: Oral histories and ways of remembering and telling. *Educational Researcher, 29*, 16–27.

Ethical standards of the American Educational Research Association. (1992). *Educational Researcher, 21*(7), 23–26.

Feen-Calligan, H. (1999). Enlightenment in chemical dependency treatment programs: A grounded theory. In C. A. Malchiodi (Ed.), *Medical art therapy with adults* (pp. 147–161). London: Jessica Kingsley Publishers.

Ferguson, C. D., & Bunge, C. A. (1997, May). The shape of services to come: Values-based reference service for the largely digital library. *College and Research Libraries, 58*(3), 252–265.

Fetterman, D. M. (1998). *Ethnography: Step by step* (2nd ed.). Thousand Oaks, CA: Sage.

Finders, M. J. (1996). Queens and teen zines: Early adolescent females reading their way toward adulthood. *Anthropology and Education Quarterly, 27*, 71–89.

Fink, A. (1995). *The survey handbook*. Thousand Oaks, CA: Sage.

Fink, A., & Kosecoff, J. (1985). *How to conduct surveys: A step-by-step guide*. Newbury Park, CA: Sage.

Firestone, W. A. (1987). Meaning in method: The rhetoric of quantitative and qualitative research. *Educational Researcher, 16*(7), 16–21.

Fisher, R. A. (1935). *The design of experiments*. London: Oliver & Boyd.

Fisher, R. A. (1936). *Statistical methods for research workers*. London: Oliver and Boyd.

Fluehr-Lobban, C. (1991). *Ethics and the profession of anthropology*. Philadelphia: University of Pennsylvania Press.

Fowler, F. J. (1988). *Survey research methods*. Newbury Park, CA: Sage.

Fowler, F. J. (1988). *Survey research methods* (2nd ed.). Newbury Park, CA: Sage.

Fraenkel, J. R., & Wallen, N. E. (2000). *How to design and evaluate research in education* (4th ed.). Boston: McGraw-Hill.

Frontman, K. C., & Kunkel, M. A. (1994). A grounded theory of counselors' construal of success in the initial session. *Journal of Counseling Psychology, 41*, 492–499.

Gall, M. D., Borg, W. R., & Gall, J. P. (1996). *Educational research: An introduction*. White Plains, NY: Longman.

Gall, M. D., Borg, W. R., & Gall, J. P. (1996). *Educational research* (6th ed.). White Plains, NY: Longman.

Gallik, J. D. (1999). Do they read for pleasure? Recreational reading habits of college students. *Journal of Adolescent and Adult Literacy, 42*, 480–488.

Garland, M. (1993). Ethnography penetrates the "I didn't have time" rationale to elucidate higher order reasons for distance education withdrawal. *Research in Distance Education, 5*, 6–10.

George, D., & Mallery, P. (2001). *SPSS for Windows: Step by step. A simple guide and reference 10.0 update*. Boston: Allyn & Bacon.

Gettinger, M. (1993). Effects of error correction on third graders' spelling. *Journal of Educational Research, 87*, 39–45.

Glaser, B. G. (1978). *Theoretical sensitivity*. Mill Valley, CA: Sociology Press.

Glaser, B. G. (1992). *Basics of grounded theory analysis*. Mill Valley, CA: Sociology Press.

Glaser, B., & Strauss, A. (1967). *The discovery of grounded theory*. Chicago: Aldine.

Glesne, C., & Peshkin, A. (1992). *Becoming qualitative researchers: An introduction*. White Plains, NY: Longman.

Goldberg, N. (2000). *Thunder and lightning: Cracking open the writer's craft*. New York: Bantam Books.

Goodman, J., & Adler, S. (1985). Becoming an elementary social studies teacher: A study of perspectives. *Theory and Research in Social Education, 15*, 1–20.

Gravetter, F. J., & Wallnau, L. B. (2000). *Statistics for the behavioral science* (5th ed.). Belmont, CA: Wadsworth/Thomson Learning.

Greene, J. C., & Caracelli, V. J. (Eds.). (1997). *Advances in mixed-method evaluation: The challenges and benefits of integrating diverse paradigms*. New Directions for Evaluation, no. 74. San Francisco: Jossey-Bass.

Greene, J. C., Caracelli, V. J., & Graham, W. F. (1989). Toward a conceptual framework for mixed-method evaluation designs. *Educational Evaluation and Policy Analysis, 11*(3), 255–274.

Guba, E. G. (1978). *Toward a methodology of naturalistic inquiry in educational evaluation*. Monograph 8. Los Angeles, CA: UCLA Center for the Study of Evaluation.

Guba, E. G., & Lincoln, Y. S. (1988). Do inquiry paradigms imply inquiry methodologies? In D. M. Fetterman (Ed.), *Qualitative approaches to evaluation in education*. New York: Praeger.

Gudmundsdottir, S. (1997). Introduction to the theme issue of "narrative perspectives on teaching and teacher education." *Teaching and Teacher Education, 13*(1), 1–3.

Hall, B. W., Ward, A. W., & Comer, C. B. (1988). Published educational research: An empirical study of its quality. *Journal of Educational Research, 81*, 182–189.

Hammersley, M., & Atkinson, P. (1995). *Ethnography: Principles in practice* (2nd ed.). New York: Routledge.

Harry, B., Day, M., & Quist, F. (1998). "He can't really play": An ethnographic study of sibling acceptance and interaction. *JASH, 23*(4), 289–299.

Hill, B., Vaughn, C., & Harrison, S. B. (1995). Living and working in two worlds: Case studies of five American Indian women teachers. *The Clearing House,* September–October, 42–48.

Hinkelmann, K., & Kempthorne, O. (1994). *Design and Analysis of Experiments*. New York: Wiley.

Hittleman, D. R., & Simon, A. J. (1997). *Interpreting educational research: An introduction for consumer of research*. Upper Saddle River, NJ: Merrill.

Holland, T. P., Chait, R. P., & Taylor, B. E. (1989). Board effectiveness: Identifying and measuring trustee competencies. *Research in Higher Education, 30*, 435–453.

Houston, W. R., Haberman, M., & Sikula, J. P. (1990). *Handbook of research on teacher education*. New York: Macmillan.

Houtz, L. (1995). Instructional strategy change and the attitude and achievement of seventh- and eighth-grade science students. *Journal of Research in Science Teaching, 32*(6), 629–648.

Hovater, S. E. (2000). *Preparing culturally responsive teachers through preservice teaching programs*. Unpublished manuscript, University of Nebraska at Lincoln.

Howe, K. R., & Dougherty, K. C. (1993). Ethics, institutional review boards, and the changing face of educational research. *Educational Researcher, 22*, 16–21.

Huber, J. (1999). Listening to children on the landscape. In F. M. Connelly and D. J. Clandinin (Eds.), *Shaping a professional identity: Stories of educational practice* (pp. 9–19). New York and London: Teachers College Press, Columbia University.

Huber, J., & Whelan, K. (1999). A marginal story as a place of possibility: Negotiating self on the professional knowledge landscape. *Teaching and Teacher Education, 15*, 381–396.

Huberty, C. J. (1993). Historical origins of statistical testing practices: The treatment of Fisher versus Neyman-Pearson views in textbooks. *Journal of Experimental Education, 61*, 317–333.

Hubley, A. M., & Zumbo, B. D. (1996). A dialectic on validity: Where we have been and where we are going. *The Journal of General Psychology, 123*, 207–215.

Hughes, L. (1999). Action research and practical inquiry: How can I meet the needs of the high-ability student within my regular educational classroom? *Journal for the Education of the Gifted, 22*, 282–297.

Husen, T., & Postlethwaite, T. N. (Eds.). (1994). *The International Encyclopedia of Education* (2nd ed.). Tarrytown, New York: Elsevier Science Ltd.

Impara, J. C., & Plake, B. S. (Eds.). (1999). *The thirteenth mental measurements yearbook*. University of Nebraska at Lincoln: Buros Institute of Mental Measurements.

Institute for Scientific Information. (1969–). *Social sciences citation index*. Philadelphia: Author.

Institute for Scientific Information. (1989–). *Social sciences citation index (compact disc ed.)*. Philadelphia: Author.

Jeffries, R. B. (1993). To go or not to go: Rural African-American students' perspective about their education. *Journal of Negro Education, 62*(4), 427–432.

Jick, T. D. (1979). Mixing qualitative and quantitative methods: Triangulation in action. *Administrative Science Quarterly, 24*, 602–611.

Johnson, B., & Christensen, L. (2000). *Educational research: Quantitative and qualitative approaches*. Boston: Allyn and Bacon.

Jones, J. (1999). *The process of structuring a community-based curriculum in a rural school setting: A grounded theory study*. An unpublished doctoral dissertation, University of Nebraska at Lincoln, Lincoln, NE.

Josselson, R., & Lieblich, A. (Eds.). (1993). *The narrative study of lives* (Vol. 1). Thousand Oaks, CA: Sage.

Jungnickel, P. W. (1993). *Workplace correlates and scholarly performance of pharmacy clinical faculty.* Unpublished doctoral dissertation, University of Nebraska–Lincoln.

Keeves, J. P. (Ed.). (1988). *Educational research, methodology, and measurement: An international handbook.* Oxford: Pergamon.

Kelchtermans, G. (1993). Getting the story, understanding the lives: From career stories to teachers' professional development. *Teaching and Teacher Education, 9,* 443–456.

Kellogg, J. M. (1997). A study of the effectiveness of self-monitoring as a learning strategy for increasing on-task behavior. Unpublished masters thesis. Western Illinois University, Macomb, Illinois.

Kemmis, S. (1994). Action research. In T. Husen & T. N. Postlethwaite (Eds.), *International encyclopedia of education* (2nd ed., pp. 42–49). Oxford and New York: Pergamon and Elsevier Science.

Kemmis, S., & McTaggart, R. (1988). *The action research planner.* Geelong, Victoria, Australia: Deakin University Press.

Kemmis, S., & McTaggart, R. (2000). Participatory action research. In N. K. Denzin and Y. S. Lincoln (Eds.), *Handbook of qualitative research* (2nd ed.), 567–605. Thousand Oaks, CA: Sage.

Kemmis, S., & Wilkinson, M. (1998). Participatory action research and the study of practice. In B. Atweh, S. Kemmis, & P. Weeks (Eds.) *Action research in practice: Partnerships for social justice in education* (pp. 21–36). London and New York: Routledge.

Keppel, G. (1991). *Design and analysis: A researcher's handbook.* Englewood Cliffs, NJ: Prentice-Hall.

Kerlinger, F. N. (1964). *Foundations of behavioral research.* New York: Holt, Rinehart and Winston.

Kerlinger, F. N. (1972). *Behavioral research: A conceptual approach.* New York: Holt, Rinehart and Winston.

Kester, V. M. (1994). Factors that affect African-American students' bonding to middle school. *The Elementary School Journal, 95*(1), 63–73.

Ketner, C. S., Smith, K. E., & Parnell, M. K. (1997). Relationship between teacher theoretical orientation to reading and endorsement of developmentally appropriate practice. *Journal of Educational Research, 90,* 212–220.

Keyes, M. W., Hanley-Maxwell, C., & Capper, C. A. (1999). "Spirituality? It's the core of my leadership": Empowering leadership in an inclusive elementary school. *Educational Administration Quarterly, 35,* 203–237.

Kiger, D. M., & Johnson, J. A. (1997). Marketing the perceptions of a community college's postsecondary enrollment options program. *Community College Journal of Research and Practice, 21,* 687–693.

Klassen, C., & Burnaby, B. (1993). Those who know: Views on literacy among adult immigrants in Canada. *TESOL Quarterly, 27,* 377–397.

Kline, R. B. (1998). *Principles and practice of structural equation modeling.* New York: Guilford Press.

Knapp, S. (1995). *Reframing paradox: A grounded theory of career development in HRD.* Unpublished doctoral dissertation, University of Nebraska–Lincoln.

Kos, R. (1991). Persistence of reading disabilities: The voices of four middle school students. *American Educational Research Journal, 28*(4), 875–895.

Kosnik, C. (1996). *The effects of action research on a teacher education community.* Paper presented at the American Educational Research Association Conference, New York, NY.

Kramer, J. J., & Conoley, J. C. (Eds.). (1992). *The Eleventh Mental Measurements Yearbook.* University of Nebraska at Lincoln: Buros Institute of Mental Measurements.

Krueger, R. A. (1994). *Focus groups: A practical guide for applied research* (2nd ed.). Thousand Oaks, CA: Sage.

Larson, B. W. (1997). Social studies teachers' conceptions of discussion: A grounded theory study. *Theory and Research in Social Education, 25,* 114–146.

Lather, P. (1991). *Getting smart: Feminist research and pedagogy with/in the postmodern.* New York and London: Routledge.

Laursen, B., Coy, K. C., & Collins, W. A. (1998). Reconsidering changes in parent-child conflict across adolescence. *Child Development, 69*(3), 817–832.

Lawrence-Lightfoot, S., & Davis, J. H. (1997). *The art and science of portraiture.* San Francisco: Jossey-Bass.

LeCompte, M. D., & Schensul, J. J. (1999). *Designing and conducting ethnographic research,* Ethnographer's Toolkit, Number 1. Walnut Creek, CA: AltaMira.

LeCompte, M. D., Millroy, W. L., & Preissle, J. (1992) *The handbook of qualitative research in education.* San Diego, CA: Academic Press, Inc.

LeCompte, M. D., Preissle, J., & Tesch, R. (1993). *Ethnography and qualitative design in educational research* (2nd ed.). San Diego, CA: Academic Press.

Leedy, P. D., & Ormrod, J. E. (2001). *Practical research: Planning and design.* (7th ed.). Upper Saddle River, NJ: Prentice-Hall.

LeTendre, G. K. (1999). Community-building activities in Japanese schools: Alternative paradigms of the democratic school. *Comparative Education Review, 43,* 283–310.

Libutti, P. O., & Blandy, S. G. (1995). *Teaching information retrieval and evaluation skills to education students and practitioners: A casebook of applications.* Chicago: Association of College and Research Libraries.

Lieblich, A., Tuval-Mashiach, R., & Zilber, T. (1998). *Narrative research: Reading, analysis, and interpretation.* Thousand Oaks, CA: Sage.

Lincoln, Y. S. (1995). Emerging criteria for quality in qualitative and interpretive research. *Qualitative Inquiry, 1,* 275–289.

Lincoln, Y. S., & Guba, E. G. (1985). *Naturalistic inquiry.* Newbury Park, CA: Sage.

Lipsey, M. W. (1990). *Design sensitivity: Statistical power for experimental research.* Newbury Park, CA: Sage.

Lipsey, M. W. (1998). Design sensitivity: Statistical power for applied experimental research. In L. Bickman & D. J. Rog (Eds.), *Handbook of applied social research methods* (pp. 39–68). Thousand Oaks, CA: Sage.

Locke, L. F., Spirduso, W. W., & Silverman, S. J. (1999). *Proposals that work: A guide for planning dissertations and grant proposals* (4th ed.). Thousand Oaks, CA: Sage.

Lofland, J., & Lofland, L. H. (1995). *Analyzing social settings: A guide to qualitative observation and analysis* (3rd ed.). Belmont, CA: Wadsworth.

Lomax, R. G., West, M. M., Harmon, M. C., Viator, K. A., & Madaus, G. F. (1995). The impact of mandated standardized testing on minority students. *Journal of Negro Education, 64,* 171–185.

Maggio, R. (1991). *The bias-free word finder: A dictionary of nondiscriminatory language.* Boston: Beacon Press.

Malloy, H. L., & McMurray, P. (1996). Conflict strategies and resolutions: Peer conflict in an integrated early childhood classroom. *Early Childhood Research Quarterly, 11,* 185–206.

Marshall, C., & Rossman, G. B. (1989, 1995). *Designing qualitative research* (1st, 2nd ed.). Newbury Park, CA: Sage.

Marshall, C., & Rossman, G. B. (1999). *Designing qualitative research* (3rd ed.). Thousand Oaks, CA: Sage.

Martens, M. L. (1992). Inhibitors to implementing a problem-solving approach to teaching elementary science: Case study of a teacher in change. *School Science and Mathematics, 92,* 150–156.

Mastera, G. (1996). *The process of revising general education curricula in three private baccalaureate colleges: A grounded theory study.* Unpublished doctoral dissertation, University of Nebraska–Lincoln.

Maxwell, J. (1996). *Qualitative research design: An interactive approach.* Thousand Oaks, CA: Sage.

McAllister, G., & Irvine, J. J. (2000). Cross cultural competency and multicultural teacher education. *Review of Educational Research, 70*(1), 3–24.

McCall, W. A. (1925). *How to experiment in education.* New York: Macmillan.

McCarthey, S. J. (1994). Opportunities and risks of writing from personal experience. *Language Arts, 71,* 182–191.

McCaslin, M. L. (1993). *The nature of leadership within rural communities: A grounded theory.* Unpublished dissertation, University of Nebraska–Lincoln.

McEwan, H., & Egan, K. (1995). *Narrative in teaching, learning, and research.* New York: Teachers College Press, Columbia University.

Mead, M. (1928). *Coming of age in Samoa: A psychological study of primitive youth for Western civilization.* New York: Morrow.

Merriam, S. B. (1998). *Qualitative research and case study applications in education.* San Francisco: Jossey-Bass.

Messick, S. (1980). Test validity and the ethics of assessment. *American Psychologist, 35,* 1012–1027.

Metzner, B. (1989). Perceived quality of academic advising: The effect on freshman attrition. *American Educational Research Journal, 26*(3), 422–442.

Meyer, R. C. (1996). *Stories from the heart.* Mahwah, NJ: Lawrence Erlbaum and Associates.

Miles, M. B., & Huberman, A. M. (1984, 1994). *Qualitative data analysis: A sourcebook for new methods.* (1st, 2nd ed.). Thousand Oaks, CA: Sage.

Miller, D. L. (1992). *The experiences of a first-year college president: An ethnography.* Unpublished doctoral dissertation, University of Nebraska-Lincoln.

Miller, D. L., Creswell, J. W., & Olander, L. S. (1998). Writing and retelling multiple ethnographic tales of a soup kitchen for the homeless. *Qualitative Inquiry, 4,* 469–491.

Mills, G. E. (2000). *Action research: A guide for the teacher researcher.* Upper Saddle River, NJ: Merrill.

Morgan, D. L. (1998). Practical strategies for combining qualitative and quantitative methods: Applications to health research. *Qualitative Health Research, 3,* 362–376.

Morrison, T. G., Jacobs, J. S., & Swinyard, W. R. (1999). Do teachers who read personally use recommended literacy practices in their classrooms? *Reading Research and Instruction, 38,* 81–100.

Morrow, S. L., & Smith, M. L. (1995). Constructions of survival and coping by women who have survived childhood sexual abuse. *Journal of Counseling Psychology, 42,* 24–33.

Morse, J. M. (1991). Approaches to qualitative-quantitative methodological triangulation. *Nursing Research, 40,* 120–123.

Murphy, K. R., & Myors, B. (1998). *Statistical power analysis: A simple and general model for traditional and modern hypothesis tests.* Mahwah, NJ: Lawrence Erlbaum Associates.

Murphy, L. L., Impara, J. C., & Plake, B. S. (Eds.). (1999). *Tests in Print V.* University of Nebraska at Lincoln: Buros Institute of Mental Measurements.

Nath, L. R., Ross, S., Smith, L. (1995/1996). A case study of implementing a cooperative learning program in an inner-city school. *The Journal of Experimental Education, 64,* 117–136.

National Center for Educational Statistics. (1997). *Digest of educational statistics 1997.* Washington, DC: U.S. Department of Education, Office of Educational Research and Improvement.

Neff, J. M. (1998). From a distance: Teaching writing on interactive television. *Research in the Teaching of English, 33,* 146–157.

Nelson, L. W. (1990). Code-switching in the oral life narratives of African-American women: Challenges to linguistic hegemony. *Journal of Education, 172*(3), 142–155.

Nesbary, D. K. (2000). *Survey research and the World Wide Web.* Boston: Allyn and Bacon.

Neuman, S. G., & McCormick, S. (Eds.). (1995). Single-subject experimental research: Applications for literacy. Newark, DE: International Reading Association.

Neuman, W. L. (2000). *Social research methods: Qualitative and quantitative approaches* (4th ed.). Boston: Allyn and Bacon.

O'Brien, N. P., & Fabiano, E. (Eds.). (1990). *Core list of books and journals in education.* Phoenix, AZ: Oryn.

Ollerenshaw, J. A. (1998). A study of the impact of a supplemental storytelling (oral narrative) strategy on fourth grade students' understanding of the physics of sound. Unpublished doctoral dissertation, University of Iowa, Iowa City.

Ollerenshaw, J. A., & Creswell, J. W. (2000). *Data analysis in narrative research: A comparison of two "restorying" approaches.* Paper presented at the Annual American Educational Research Association, New Orleans, LA.

Orona, C. J. (1997). Temporality and identity loss due to Alzheimer's disease. In A. Strauss & J. Corbin (Eds.), *Grounded theory in practice* (pp. 171–196). Thousand Oaks, CA: Sage.

Padula, M. A., & Miller, D. L. (1999). Understanding graduate women's reentry experiences. *Psychology of Women Quarterly, 23,* 327–343.

Pajak, E. F., & Blas,, J. J. (1984). Teachers in bars: From professional to personal self. *Sociology of Education, 57,* 164–173.

Patton, M. Q. (1990). *Qualitative evaluation and research methods* (2nd ed.). Newbury Park, CA: Sage.

Pedhazur, E. J. (1997). *Multiple regression in behavioral research: Explanation and prediction* (3rd ed.). Ft. Worth, TX: Harcourt Brace College Publishers.

Perrine, R. M., Lisle, J., & Tucker, D. L. (1996). Effects of a syllabus offer of help, student age, and class size on college students' willingness to seek support from faculty. *Journal of Experimental Education, 64*(1), 41–52.

Personal Narratives Group. (1989). *Interpreting women's lives.* Bloomington, IN: Indiana University Press.

Plano Clark, V. L., Creswell, J. W., Miller, D. L., Harter, L. M., Mickelson, W. T., McEntarffer, R., & McVea, K. (2001). Exploring the student and adult perceptions of teen smoking in four midwestern high schools. Unpublished manuscript, University of Nebraska-Lincoln.

Poling, A., & Grosset, D. (1986). Basic research designs in applied behavior analysis. In A. Poling & R. Fuque (Eds.), *Research methods in applied behavior analysis: Issues and advances.* New York: Plenum.

Ponec, D. L. (1994). *African-American females: A theory of educational aspiration.* Unpublished doctoral dissertation, University of Nebraska–Lincoln.

Preissle, J. (1996). *Jude's juicy journals: Periodicals friendly to qualitative research.* Athens, GA: College of Education, University of Georgia.

Punch, K. F. (1998). *Introduction to social research: Quantitative and qualitative approaches.* London: Sage.

Reichardt, C. S., & Cook, T. D. (1979). Beyond qualitative versus quantitative methods. In T. D Cook and C. S. Reichardt (Eds.), *Qualitative and quantitative methods in evaluation research* (pp. 7–32). Beverly Hills, CA: Sage.

Reichardt, C. S., & Mark, M. M. (1998). Quasi-experimentation. In L. Bickman & D. J. Rog (Eds.), *Handbook of applied social research methods* (pp. 193–228). Thousand Oaks, CA: Sage.

Reichardt, C. S., & Rallis, S. E. (1994). *The qualitative-quantitative debate: New perspectives* (pp. 5–11). New Directions for Program Evaluation, Number 61. San Francisco: Jossey-Bass.

Reid, R., Hertzog, M., & Snyder, M. (1996). Educating every teacher, every year: The public schools and parents of children with ADHD. *Seminars in Speech and Language, 17,* 73–90.

Review of Educational Research. (1931–). Washington, DC: American Educational Research Association.

Rhoads, R. A. (1995). Whales tales, dog piles, and beer goggles: An ethnographic case study of fraternity life. *Anthropology and Education Quarterly, 26,* 306–323.

Rhoads, R. A. (1997). Implications of the growing visibility of gay and bisexual male students on campus. *NASPA Journal, 34,* 275–286.

Richardson, L. (2000). Writing: A method of inquiry. In N. K. Denzin & Y. S. Lincoln (Eds.), *Handbook of qualitative research* (2nd ed.). Thousand Oaks, CA: Sage.

Richie, B. S., Fassinger, R. E., Linn, S. G., & Johnson, J. (1997). Persistence, connection, and passion: A qualitative study of the career development of highly achieving African American-Black and White women. *Journal of Counseling Psychology, 44,* 143–148.

Riessman, C. K. (1993). *Narrative analysis.* Newbury Park, CA: Sage.

Robrecht, L. C. (1995). Grounded theory: Evolving methods. *Qualitative Health Research, 5,* 169–177.

Rosenau, P. M. (1992). *Post-modernism and the social sciences: Insights, inroads, and intrusions.* Princeton, NJ: Princeton University Press.

Rossman, G. B., & Wilson, B. L. (1985). Number and words: Combining quantitative and qualitative methods in a single large-scale evaluation study. *Evaluation Review, 9*(5), 627–643.

Royal, M. A., & Rossi, R. J. (1999). Predictors of within-school differences in teachers' sense of community. *The Journal of Educational Research, 92*(5), 259–265.

Rudestam, K. E., & Newton, R. R. (1992). *Surviving your dissertation.* Newbury Park, CA: Sage.

Rudner, L. M. (1993). Test evaluation. [On-line]. Available at: www.ericae.net.

Russek, B. E., & Weinberg, S. L. (1993). Mixed methods in a study of implementation of technology-based materials in the elementary classroom. *Evaluation and Program Planning, 16,* 131–142.

Rust, F. O. (1999). Professional conversations: New teachers explore teaching through conversation, story, and narrative. *Teaching and Teacher Education, 16,* 367–380.

Sagor, R. (2000). *Guiding school improvement with action research.* Alexandria, VA: Association for Supervision and Curriculum Development.

Salant, P., & Dillman, D. A. (1994). *How to conduct your own survey.* New York: John Wiley & Sons.

Salkind, N. J. (2000). *Statistics for people who (think they) hate statistics.* Thousand Oaks, CA: Sage.

Schelske, M., & Deno, S. (1994). The effects of content-specific seminars on student teachers' effectiveness. *Action in Teacher Education, 16*(1), 20–28.

Schmuck, R. A. (1997). *Practical action research for change.* Arlington Heights, IL: IRI/SkyLight Training and Publishing.

Schwandt, T. A. (1997). *Qualitative inquiry: A dictionary of terms.* Thousand Oaks, CA: Sage.

Schwandt, T. A., & Halpern, E. S. (1988). *Linking auditing and metaevaluation: Enhancing quality in applied research.* Newbury Park, CA: Sage.

Shapiro, E. S., & Lentz, F. E. (1991). Vocational-technical programs: Follow-up of students with learning disabilities. *Exceptional Children, 58,* 47–59.

Sieber, S. (1973). Integration of fieldwork and survey methods. *AJS, 78,* 1335–1359.

SilverPlatter Information, Inc. (1974/86–). *Sociofile.* Wellesley Hills, MA: SilverPlatter Information Services.

SilverPlatter Information, Inc. (1986). *PsycLIT*. Wellesley Hills, MA: SilverPlatter Information Services.

Sleeter, C. (1996). *Multicultural education as social activism*. Albany, N. Y.: State University of New York Press.

Smetana, J. G., & Asquith, P. (1994). Adolescents' and parents' conceptions of parental authority and personal autonomy. *Child Development, 65,* 1147–1162.

Smith, J. K. (1983). Quantitative versus qualitative research: An attempt to clarify the issue. *Educational Research (March)*, 6–13.

Smith, M. L., & Glass, G. V. (1977). Meta-analysis of psychotherapy outcome studies. *American Psychologist, 32,* 752–760.

Society for Research in Child Development. (1945–). *Child development abstracts and bibliography*. Washington, DC: Committee on Child Development, National Research Council.

Sociological abstracts. (1953–). San Diego, CA: Author.

Spindler, G., & Spindler, L. (1992). Cultural process and ethnography: An anthropological perspective. In M. D. LeCompte, W. L. Millroy, & J. Preissle (Eds.), *The handbook of qualitative research in education* (pp. 53–92). San Diego, CA: Academic Press.

Spradley, J. P. (1980). *Participant observation*. New York: Holt, Rinehart and Winston.

Spradley, J. P. (1980). *The ethnographic interview*. Ft. Worth, TX: Harcourt Brace Jovanovich College Publishers.

Stake, R. E. (1995). *The art of case study research*. Thousand Oaks, CA: Sage.

Stake, R. E. (2000). Case studies. In N. K. Denzin and Y. S. Lincoln (Eds.). *Handbook of qualitative research* (2nd ed.), (pp. 435–454). Thousand Oaks, CA: Sage.

Stanulis, R. N., & Jeffers, L. (1995). Action research as a way of learning about teaching in a mentor/student teacher relationship. *Action in Teacher Education, XVI*(4), 14–24.

Steckler, A., McLeroy, K. R., Goodman, R. M., Bird, S. T., & McCormick, L. (1992). Toward integrating qualitative and quantitative methods: An introduction. *Health Education Quarterly, 19*(1), 1–8.

Strauss, A. (1987). *Qualitative analysis for social scientists*. New York: Cambridge University Press.

Strauss, A., & Corbin, J. (1990). *Basics of qualitative research: Grounded theory procedures and techniques*. Newbury Park, CA: Sage.

Strauss, A., & Corbin, J. (1998). *Basics of qualitative research: Techniques and procedures for developing grounded theory* (2nd ed.). Thousand Oaks, CA: Sage.

Stringer, E. T. (1999). *Action research* (2nd ed.). Thousand Oaks, CA: Sage.

Subject guide to books in print. (1957–). New York: R. R. Bowker.

Tashakkori, A., & Teddlie, C. (1998). *Mixed methodology: Combining qualitative and quantitative approaches*. Thousand Oaks, CA: Sage.

Tashakkori, A., & Teddlie, C. (in press). *Handbook of mixed methods in the social and behavioral sciences*. Thousand Oaks, CA: Sage.

Tesch, R. (1990). *Qualitative research: Analysis types and software tools*. Bristol, PA: The Falmer Press.

The Spencer Foundation. (1999). *Annual report*. Chicago: The Spencer Foundation.

Theberge, N. (1997). "It's part of the game": Physicality and the production of gender in women's hockey. *Gender & Society, 11*(1), 69–87.

Thomas, J. (1993). *Doing critical ethnography*. Newbury Park, CA: Sage.

Thomas, W. I., & Znaniecki, F. (1927). *The Polish peasant in Europe and America*. New York: Knopf.

Thompson, B. (1996). AERA editorial policies regarding statistical significance testing: Three suggested reforms. *Educational Research, 25,* 26–30.

Thorndike, R. M. (1997). *Measurement and evaluation in psychology and education* (6th ed.). New York: Macmillan.

Thorndike, R. M. (1994). Correlational procedures in data analysis. In T. Husen and T. N. Postlethwaite (Eds.), *International encyclopedia of education* (2nd ed.) (pp. 1107–1117). Oxford and New York: Pergamon and Elsevier Science.

Tierney, W. (1997). *Academic outlaws: Queer theory and cultural studies in the academy*. Thousand Oaks, CA: Sage.

Tierney, W. G. (1993). *Building communities of difference: Higher education in the twenty-first century*. Westport, CT: Bergin & Garvey.

Ting, S. R. (2000). Predicting Asian-Americans' academic performance in the first year of college: An approach combining SAT scores and noncognitive variables. *Journal of College Student Development, 41,* 442–449.

Travers, R. M. W. (1992). History of educational research. In M. C. Alkin, *Encyclopedia of educational research* (6th ed.), 384–389. New York: Macmillan.

Tuckman, B. W. (1999). *Conducting educational research* (5th ed.). Ft. Worth, TX: Harcourt Brace College Publishers.

Turabian, K. L. (1973). *A manual for writers of term papers, theses, and dissertations* (4th ed.). Chicago: University of Chicago Press.

Unger, H. G. (1996). *Encyclopedia of American education*. New York: Facts on File, Inc.

University Council for Educational Administration. (1966–). *Educational administration abstracts*. Columbus, OH: Author.

University Microfilms International. (1938–1965/66). *Dissertation abstracts*. Ann Arbor, MI: Author.

University Microfilms International. (1987–). *Dissertation abstracts on disc (computer file)*. Ann Arbor, MI: Author.

University of Chicago Press (1993). *The Chicago manual of style* (14th ed.). Chicago: University of Chicago Press.

University of Nebraska at Lincoln (January, 1997). *Institutional review board guidelines for the protection of human subjects in research studies*. Lincoln, NE: University of Nebraska at Lincoln.

Valois, R. F., & McKewon, R. E. (1998). Frequency and correlates of fighting and carrying weapons among public school adolescents. *American Journal of Health Behavior, 22,* 8–17.

Van Maanen, J. (1988). *Tales of the field: On writing ethnography*. Chicago: University of Chicago Press.

VanHorn-Grassmeyer, K. (1998). *Enhancing practice: New professional in student affairs*. Unpublished doctoral dissertation. University of Nebraska at Lincoln.

Viadero, D. (1999). What is (and isn't) research? *Education Week, XVIII*(41), 33, 34–36.

Vockell, E. L., & Asher, J. W. (1995). *Educational research* (2nd ed.). Englewood Cliffs, NJ: Prentice-Hall.

Vogt, W. P. (1999). *Dictionary of statistics and methodology: A nontechnical guide for the social sciences* (2nd ed.). Thousand Oaks, CA: Sage.

Vooijs, M. W., & van der Voort, T. H. A. (1993). Learning about television violence: The impact of a critical viewing curriculum on children's attitudinal judgments of crime series. *Journal of Research and Development in Education, 26*(3), 133–142.

Walker, J. C., & Evers, C. W. (1998). The epistemological unit of educational research. In J. P. Keeves (Ed.), *Educational research, methodology, and measurement: An international handbook*. New York: Pergamon Press.

Wang, J., & Staver, J. R. (1997). An empirical study of gender differences in Chinese students' science achievement. *Journal of Educational Research, 90,* 252–255.

Ward, P. (1999). Chapter 3: Design of the Saber-Tooth Project. *Journal of Teaching in Physical Education, 18,* 403–416.

Ward, P., Barrett, T. M., Evans, S. A., Doutis, P., Nguyen, P. T., & Johnson, M. K. (1999). Chapter 5: Curriculum effects in eighth-grade lacrosse. *Journal of Teaching in Physical Education, 18,* 428–443.

Watters, J. J., Christensen, C., Arcodia, C., Ryan, Y., & Weeks, P. (1998). Occasional visits to the kingdom. In B. Atweh, S. Kemmis, & P. Weeks, *Action research in practice: Partnerships for social justice in education* (pp. 250–279). London and New York: Routledge.

Way, N., Stauber, H., Nakkula, M. J., & London, P. (1994). Depression and substance use in two divergent high school cultures: A qualitative and quantitative analysis. *Journal of Youth and Adolescence, 23*(3), 331–357.

Weitzman, E. A., & Miles, M. B. (1995). *Computer programs for qualitative data analysis*. Thousand Oaks, CA: Sage.

Whyte, W. F. (Ed.). (1991). *Participatory action research*. Newbury Park, CA: Sage.

Wilkinson, L., and the Task Force on Statistical Inference (1999). Statistical methods in psychology journals. *American Psychologist, 54*(8), 594–604.

Williams, F. (1992). *Reasoning with statistics: How to read quantitative research* (4th ed.). Ft. Worth: Harcourt Brace Jovanovich College Publishers.

Wilson, H. W. (1929/32–). *Education index*. New York: H. W. Wilson Company.

Winthrop, R. H. (1991). *Dictionary of concepts in cultural anthropology*. Westport, CT: Greenwood.

Wolcott, H. F. (1974). The elementary school principal: Notes from a field study. In G. Spindler (Ed.), *Education and cultural process: Toward an anthropology of education* (pp. 176–204). New York: Holt, Rinehart and Winston.

Wolcott, H. F. (1983). Adequate schools and inadequate education: The life history of a sneaky kid. *Anthropology and Education Quarterly, 14,* 3–32.

Wolcott, H. F. (1992). *Writing up qualitative research.* Newbury Park, CA: Sage.

Wolcott, H. F. (1994). *Transforming qualitative data: Description, analysis, and interpretation.* Thousand Oaks, CA: Sage.

Wolcott, H. F. (1995). *The art of fieldwork.* Walnut Creek, CA: AltaMira.

Wolcott, H. F. (1999). *Ethnography: A way of seeing.* Walnut Creek, CA: AltaMira.

Wright, D. B. (1997). *Understanding statistics: An introduction for the social sciences.* London: Sage.

Zeichner, K. (1999). The new scholarship in teacher education. *Educational Researcher, 28*(9), 4–15.

Ziller, R. C. (1990). *Photographing the self: Methods for observing personal orientation.* Newbury Park, CA: Sage.

Author Index

Subject Index

A/B design, 340, 341
Abstract series, 95
Abstracts
    of essays or opinions, 115
    examples of, 114, 115
    explanation of, 113
    of qualitative studies, 113–115
    of quantitative studies, 113, 114
Accessibility relevance, 109
Action research
    characteristics of, 614–616
    elements of, 619–621
    evaluation of, 618–619
    example of, 625–632
    explanation of, 61, 603
    historical background of, 604–605
    participatory, 606, 609–613
    practical, 605–608
    resources on, 623–624
    steps in, 616–618
    studies using, 602–603
    useful information on, 622–623
Advocacy practices, 49
Alpha level, 242
Alternating treatment designs, 341, 343
Alternative forms and test-retest
        reliability, 181, 182
Alternative forms of reliability, 181–182
Alternative hypothesis, 143–145, 241
American Anthropological Association,
        217
American Educational Research
        Association (AERA), 49
    "Call for Proposals," 293–294
    journals of, 93, 95
American Psychological Association
        (APA)
    nondiscriminatory language use,
        guidelines of, 99, 101
    Psychological Abstracts, 99, 101
    Publications Manual, 116, 250, 251
        (*See also* APA style)
Analysis, 492–493
Analysis of variance test, 252
Annual Report 1999 (Spencer
        Foundation), 47, 50
APA style
    for end-of-text references, 116
    for headings, 117–118

for nondiscriminatory language use,
        301
    for within-text references, 116–117
ATLAS.ti, 262
Attitudinal measures, 173–175
Audience
    explanation of, 12–13, 78
    identified in problem statements, 78
    writing standards for specific,
        288–289
Audio-visual materials, 210–211
Axial coding, 441, 444

Background questions, 405
Bar charts, 251
Behavior, 490
Behavioral observations
    example of, 175–177
    explanation of, 174, 175
Belief, 490
Beta weight, 376–377
Between-group designs
    explanation of, 317, 329
    quasi-experiments and, 333–336
    true experiments and, 332–333
    types of, 332
Biographies, 523
Bivariate correlation, 374, 375
Blocking variables, 321–322

"Campus Response to a Student
        Gunman" (Asmussen &
        Creswell)
    data analysis for, 257, 270–274
    data collection for, 191
    purpose statement and research
        questions in, 125
    as qualitative study, 43–44, 52–58,
        62
    reprint of, 30–40
    research problem in, 67, 72, 75, 76
    writing strategies in, 285, 287
Case studies, 484–486, 496–498
Categorical scores, 130
Causation, probable, 139
Census study, 402
Central phenomenon, 146–147
Central questions, 150–152
Charts, 251

Chi-square analysis, 247
The Chicago Manual of Style (University
        of Chicago Press), 116
*Child Development Abstracts and
        Bibliography* (Society for Research
        in Child Development), 95
Chronology, 527
Cleaning the data, 228–229
Closed-end questions, 406
Closed-end responses, 204
Co-vary, 370
Coding
    axial, 441, 444
    to build description, 269–271
    to develop themes, 271–273
    open, 441, 444
    sample of, 267, 268
    selective, 444
    in systematic design, 441–444
Coding paradigm, 444
Coding process, 266–267
Coefficient alpha, 182
Coefficient of determination, 371–372
Cohort studies, 399–400
Collaboration, 531, 614–615
Collective case study, 485
Comparison group, 317
Comparison questions, 142
Comparison table, 277
Computer-analysis of qualitative data,
        261
Computer software
    qualitative data analysis using,
        261–265
    quantitative data analysis using,
        225–226
Concept sampling, 195–196
Conference papers, 292–293
Conference proposals, 293–294
Confidence intervals, 248, 249
Confirming and disconfirming
        sampling, 197
Confounding variables, 136
Constant comparison, 451
Construct validity, 324, 327
Constructivism, 49
Constructs, 130
Context, 494
Continuous scores, 130